REMBRANDT
A GENIUS AND HIS IMPACT

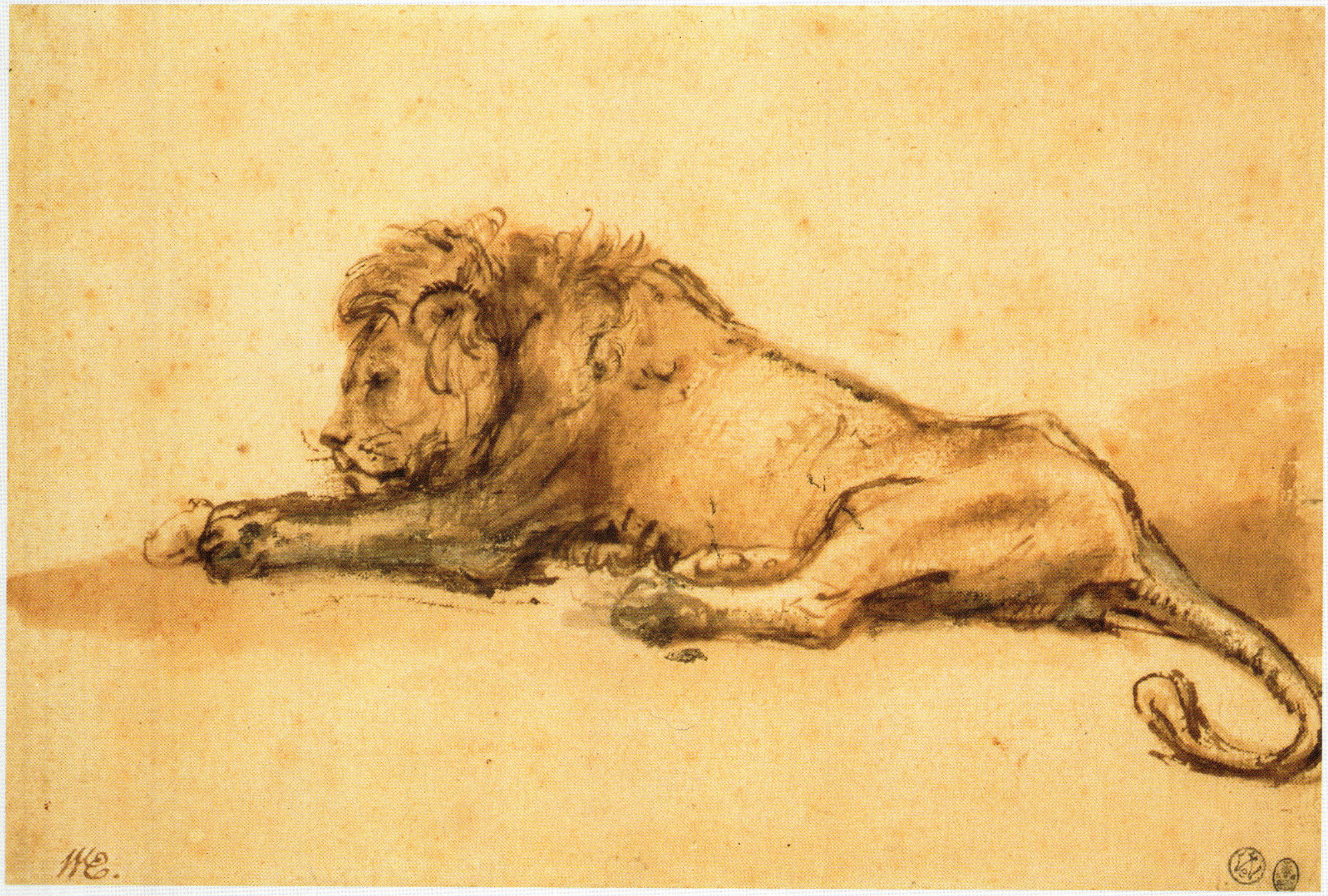

REMBRANDT
A GENIUS AND HIS IMPACT

Albert Blankert

with contributions by:

Marleen Blokhuis
Ben Broos
Jeroen Giltaij
Volker Manuth
Timothy Potts
William W. Robinson
Peter C. Sutton
Jaap van der Veen
Ernst van de Wetering
Christopher White
Irena Zdanowicz

NATIONAL GALLERY OF VICTORIA, MELBOURNE
ART EXHIBITIONS AUSTRALIA LIMITED, SYDNEY
WAANDERS PUBLISHERS, ZWOLLE

EXHIBITION DATES:
National Gallery of Victoria, Melbourne:
1 October – 7 December 1997
National Gallery of Australia, Canberra:
17 December 1997 – 15 February 1998

Exhibition organized by the National Gallery of Victoria and Art Exhibitions Australia Limited
Curator: Albert Blankert
Exhibition Co-ordinator (Australia): Timothy Potts

Published in 1997 by the National Gallery of Victoria, 180 St Kilda Road, Melbourne, 3004; and by Art Exhibitions Australia Limited, 98 Cumberland Street, The Rocks, Sydney, 2000.

National Library of Australia Cataloguing-in-Publication data:

Rembrandt: a genius and his impact.

Bibliography.
ISBN 0 7241 0196.

1. Rembrandt Harmenszoon van Rijn, 1606–1669.
2. Rembrandt Harmenszoon van Rijn, 1606–1669 – Influence – Exhibitions.
3. Rembrandt Harmenszoon van Rijn, 1606–1669 – Exhibitions.
4. Rembrandt Harmenszoon van Rijn, 1606–1669 – Criticism and interpretation.
5. Art, Dutch – Exhibitions.
6. Art, Modern – 17th–18th centuries – Netherlands – Exhibitions. I. National Gallery of Victoria. II. Title.

759.992

ISBN 90 400 9981 2 (hardback edition)
NUGI 921/911

DESIGN:
Roelof Koebrugge BNO

TRANSLATOR:
Yvette Rosenberg

EDITING:
Edited and proofread for the National Gallery of Victoria, Melbourne

WORDPROCESSOR:
Judy Shelverton

PRINTING:
Waanders Printers, Zwolle, The Netherlands

CONTRIBUTORS TO THE CATALOGUE:
Albert Blankert (AB)
Marleen Blokhuis (MB)
Ben Broos (BB)
Jeroen Giltaij
Volker Manuth (VM)
Timothy Potts
William W. Robinson (WWR)
Peter C. Sutton (PCS)
Jaap van der Veen
Ernst van de Wetering
Christopher White
Irena Zdanowicz (IZ)

COVER:
Rembrandt
Self-Portrait at the Age of 34 1640 (detail)
Canvas
The Trustees of the National Gallery, London
(cat. no. 13)

FRONTISPIECE:
Rembrandt
Recumbent Lion c.1650
Pen and ink and brush
14.0 x 20.3 cm
Museum Boijmans Van Beuningen, Rotterdam
(cat. no. 87)

BACK COVER:
Rembrandt
Two Old Men Disputing 1628
Panel
72.4 x 59.7 cm
National Gallery of Victoria, Melbourne; Felton Bequest 1934
(cat. no. 3)

Contents

International Advisory Committee

Prof. Dr Henning Bock, former Director, Gemäldegalerie, Berlin

Dr Christopher Brown, Chief Curator, The National Gallery, London

Drs Erik Hinterding, University of Utrecht

Dr Jan Kelch, Director, Gemäldegalerie, Berlin

Prof. Ronald de Leeuw, Director, Rijksmuseum, Amsterdam

Dr Simon Levie, former Director, Rijksmuseum, Amsterdam

Neil MacGregor, Director, The National Gallery, London

Prof. Dr Henk van Os, former Director, Rijksmuseum, Amsterdam

Drs Peter Schatborn, Keeper of Prints and Drawings, Rijksmuseum, Amsterdam

Prof. Dr Ernst van de Wetering, Head of the Rembrandt Research Project

Prof. Christopher White, CVO, FBA, Director, Ashmolean Museum, Oxford

Foreword by the Prime Minister of The Netherlands

Around the year 1600, scores of Dutchmen, fired by the spirit of commerce and a lively sense of curiosity, left their native country, the relatively new republic in the delta region of the Rhine, Maas and Scheldt rivers, to sail the oceans and explore the most remote corners of the world. Where Africa, India and the Indonesian archipelago were concerned, they were following in the wake of other voyagers, notably the Portuguese. In 1606, the year Rembrandt was born in Leiden, Willem Jansz reached the Australian mainland with the *Duyfken*. Dirck Hartog reached Australian shores in 1616, and was the first Westerner to leave a mark of his presence there. This same mercantile spirit led to the founding of the Dutch East Indies Company, a classic example of a centrally managed, tightly organized trading company with a monopoly protected by the state.

Another seventeenth-century development was the growth of a new tradition of painting in the Netherlands, in which artists were encouraged to explore the limits of their own capabilities and to specialize in a particular type of work. Grandiose schemes had little place in this tradition, which was one of individual artists working not for a sovereign, a public authority or another powerful client, but for the free market, for the general public, a public ranging from simple folk to the wealthiest ranks of the bourgeoisie. In the main, it was no longer the client who determined the subject but the artists themselves, who selected the themes that were best suited to their talents. The surrounding landscape was a popular choice, as were scenes from everyday life and still-life paintings with their play of light.

Within this large, gifted community of artists, Rembrandt stands out particularly. While others were perfecting their rendering of rich apparel or, for instance, a polder scene, Rembrandt explored ways of conveying human emotion. His portraits and other paintings – many focusing on biblical or mythological tales – in which he laid bare the inner life of his human subjects in a way equalled by none, make him one of the greatest artists the world has known. Greatly interested in everything he saw, Rembrandt also set down the landscape, and the little events that took place in his own surroundings, in numerous etchings and drawings.

The spirit of commerce that impelled the Dutch explorers of the seventeenth century forged a bond between the Netherlands and Australia. This exhibition of works by Rembrandt, one of the greatest – if not the greatest of all – painters of the seventeenth century, and by his pupils and followers, gives our traditional ties a cultural dimension.

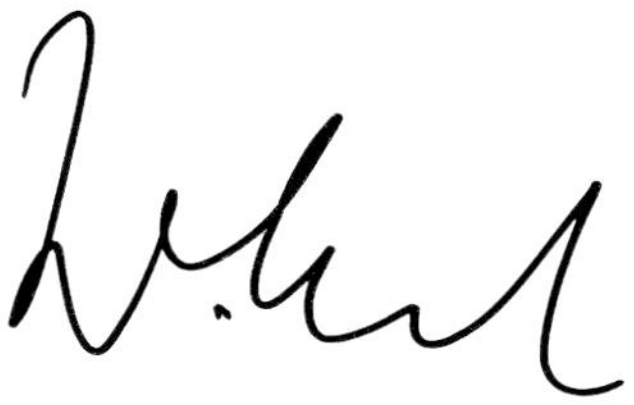

Wim Kok
Prime Minister of The Netherlands

Foreword by the Prime Minister of Australia

Dutch master painter Rembrandt needs hardly any introduction, such is the worldwide recognition of his immense contribution and influence in the art world at large.

The title and composition of this major exhibition aptly convey Rembrandt's masterly technique, style and influence. Twenty-eight original paintings by the master are included, which are representative of his career, covering all major themes in which he worked. To illustrate Rembrandt's inspiration and profound impact on the art world, forty works by his pupils and followers are also included in the exhibition.

Perhaps less well known is Rembrandt's reputation in drawing and etching, and a number of major works on paper are being exhibited, thus providing a balanced appreciation of the extent of his artistic talent.

Australians are indeed fortunate in having a unique opportunity to witness such a prestigious international art exhibition visiting these shores. For its part the Commonwealth, through Art Indemnity Australia, is pleased to assist in making that opportunity possible for the enjoyment of the Australian public.

We are indebted to all those associated with the exhibition, particularly to the museums and private lenders who have loaned works, to Shell Australia and Singapore Airlines as the major sponsors, and to other sponsors for their generous assistance in making this exhibition possible. On behalf of the government, I commend their continuing support of the arts in Australia for the benefit of the general community.

I encourage all Australians to visit this magnificent display of the work of one of the world's acknowledged great artists and to enjoy the breadth of his immense vision and impact. I extend best wishes for the success of *Rembrandt: A Genius and His Impact* on its Australian tour.

John Howard
Prime Minister of Australia

Sponsor's Foreword

Shell Presents Rembrandt: A Genius and His Impact marks Shell's second major sponsorship of the visual arts in Australia and we are delighted to be involved with the most significant exhibition of Rembrandt paintings ever to come to the southern hemisphere.

Whilst, as a company, we are conscious of our heritage through Royal Dutch Petroleum, our enthusiasm for the exhibition goes beyond that. Rembrandt, like all great artists, belongs to the world. In becoming the exhibition's major sponsor, our goal is to make the works of this great master accessible to a wide audience.

On behalf of the other sponsors, Singapore Airlines, Channel 7, Triple M, Ansett Australia, and Hotel Sofitel Melbourne and Novotel Melbourne on Collins, I would like to thank Art Exhibitions Australia Limited, the National Gallery of Victoria and the National Gallery of Australia for enabling us to join them as partners in such an exceptional enterprise.

It is our wish that as many people as possible take the opportunity to visit and enjoy the exhibition – one of a magnitude not often seen in this country, or indeed in the world at large.

J. Roland Williams
Chairman and Chief Executive
Shell Australia Limited

Foreword by the Chairman of Art Exhibitions Australia Limited

This exhibition traces the work and influence of Rembrandt Harmensz van Rijn, an extraordinary master in the history of western art. Initiated and funded by Art Exhibitions Australia, it represents a new benchmark in Australian international cultural management. The most recent memorable projects staged by Art Exhibitions Australia have included historical surveys of *Renoir*, *Matisse* and *Van Gogh*. The public success of these exhibitions has helped pave the way for *Rembrandt: A Genius and His Impact.*

We are particularly proud to be the manager of the major arts event documented in this catalogue and, through our associated body, the Australian International Cultural Foundation Limited, to be a major sponsor of the symposium of international Rembrandt scholars that is to be held in conjunction with this exhibition.

International exhibitions have become extraordinarily complex, involving skills in negotiation, administration and logistics. Satisfying the demands that priceless objects make at every stage in their movement and display is now virtually a science. Even so, it is not too fanciful to imagine that Rembrandt himself might have understood the mechanics of a major exhibition. As well as being a painter, he oversaw a busy workshop, trained apprentices, generated custom and monitored the nuts and bolts of studio production on a considerable scale. The seventeenth-century equivalent of today's complex project management would not have been unfamiliar to him.

At AEA, our efforts in that direction have been greatly facilitated by Art Indemnity Australia, an Australian Government program through the Department of Communications and the Arts, for the indemnification of cultural material exhibited in this country. The Government has recently doubled the upper limit of coverage under this program, and the increase has enabled all the works in this exhibition to be covered by the indemnity.

The vision of Professor Ronald de Leeuw, Director, Rijksmuseum, and Dr Albert Blankert, guest curator, has paved the way for the project to happen. Ronald de Leeuw proposed a Rembrandt exhibition for Australia following the success of our *Van Gogh* exhibition, and identified Dr Blankert for the crucial role of guest curator. With the support of Dr Timothy Potts, Director of the National Gallery of Victoria and Australian curator, Dr Blankert crafted a unified visual experience out of a compelling series of individual images. Heading an international team of contributing art historians and scholars, both curators have ensured that the significance of *Rembrandt* extends beyond any narrowly academic context to achieve the widest possible response within Australia.

Shell Australia Limited as the major sponsor has joined us in presenting the exhibition in Australia. Its generous continuing support for the visual arts is warmly acknowledged. It is fitting that Singapore Airlines is the official international carrier of the exhibition and a very major sponsor. They are joined as national sponsors by Channel 7 and Triple M, providing significant media support nation-wide. Ansett Australia has assisted with internal travel arrangements, and Hotel Sofitel Melbourne and Novotel Melbourne on Collins join the list of national sponsors by providing considerable support. Art Exhibitions Australia is very grateful to all the national sponsors for their extraordinary generosity. Without them, *Rembrandt: A Genius and His Impact* would remain in the realm of a great but unrealized idea.

We are also greatly indebted to the many public and private collections which have lent so generously to this exhibition. The exhibition represents a geographical as well as an art historical precedent. It is fascinating to reflect that, when Rembrandt painted these pictures, his countrymen had barely made their first, tentative investigations of the outlines of *terra australis.* Now, with every continental contour in the world complete, Art Exhibitions Australia is proud to join with the National Gallery of Victoria and the National Gallery of Australia in bringing to Australian audiences *Rembrandt: A Genius and His Impact.*

Michael Darling
Chairman
Art Exhibitions Australia Limited

Directors' Foreword

Rembrandt: A Genius and His Impact brings to Australia the first exhibition of one of the towering figures of art history. It has two aims: first, to present the master of the Golden Age of Dutch art through works of the highest quality in all aspects of his oeuvre – painting, drawing and etching; and second, to document the pervasive and enduring impact which this extraordinary teacher had on his pupils and followers.

Rembrandt occupies a very singular place in the history of western art. His contribution to the history of European painting, drawing and etching is so important, well known and admired that there is nowhere in the western cultural orbit, and very few areas outside it, where an exhibition of his work would not represent a major cultural event. His popular image as the archetypal artistic genius has ensured him a special relationship with the art-loving public, one that has been further enhanced in recent years by the uniquely didactic state of Rembrandt studies. There are today many active programs of research by scholars the world over (spearheaded in the last thirty years by the Rembrandt Research Project) on the critical problem of attribution – precisely which of the hundreds of paintings attributed to Rembrandt over the past three centuries are by him and which by his pupils and followers? This has involved a greatly intensified focus on the work of these pupils, many of whom are extraordinary talents in their own right. Rembrandt's drawings too have come under renewed scrutiny, with an eye to the similarly problematic question of their attribution.

The rapid pace and broadening scope of this research means that each exhibition presents a slightly different Rembrandt, and each such occasion makes a contribution to the advance of scholarship, for which the rare opportunity to see paintings side by side is invaluable.

The organization of this exhibition has represented a challenging and exciting three years for the National Gallery of Victoria, in collaboration with our partners Art Exhibitions Australia Limited and second venue, the National Gallery of Australia. It has been a pleasure throughout to work with Robert Edwards and his team at AEA.

The International Advisory Committee listed elsewhere is an indication of the extraordinary support and assistance we have had from sister institutions around the world. To all of these we extend our sincere thanks. It would be remiss not to acknowledge especially Ronald de Leeuw and Henk van Os, current and former Directors of the Rijksmuseum, Amsterdam, and Neil MacGregor, Director of the National Gallery, London, for the critical support and co-operation they have provided from the initial conception of this project through to its fruition.

We are grateful too to the scholars from Europe, the United States of America and Australia, all prominent experts in this field, who have found time among their many other commitments to contribute to this catalogue and in some cases also to select the works for inclusion: Peter Schatborn for the drawings and Christopher White for the etchings. The paintings have been selected by the exhibition's curator, Albert Blankert, whose originality of mind and preparedness to ask bold questions are largely responsible for what we hope will be the lasting contribution this exhibition makes to the better understanding of Rembrandt and his times.

It has been our intention from the inception of the exhibition that it benefit not only its Australian audience but also the international art community, and to this end a symposium has been organized in Melbourne at which many of the leading experts from around the world will speak on Rembrandt and his pupils. This has kindly been convened by Christopher White, Director of the Ashmolean Museum, Oxford, and Christopher Brown, Chief Curator, National Gallery, London, to whom we likewise express our gratitude.

Rembrandt is the most ambitious and most costly exhibition ever to have come to Australia. It is then more than usually appropriate to acknowledge and applaud the enlightened generosity of the principal sponsor of the exhibition, Shell Australia, as well as the other supporting sponsors, Singapore Airlines, Channel 7, Triple M Radio Station, Ansett Australia, Hotel Sofitel Melbourne and Novotel Melbourne on Collins, the RACV, The Herald and Weekly Times, and Tourism Victoria.

For the National Gallery of Victoria, *Rembrandt*'s coming to Australia represents the consummation of a long history of admiring, collecting and studying his work, crowned by Melbourne's acquisition of two highly significant paintings, as well as a fine selection of his etchings and two sheets of drawings. It is a great privilege to have the treasures from so many major collections around the world join Australia's Rembrandts for this exhibition in Melbourne and Canberra. Our final and most heartfelt thanks therefore go to the many generous public and private lenders who have made this splendid exhibition possible.

Timothy Potts
Director
National Gallery of Victoria

Brian Kennedy
Director
National Gallery of Australia

Lenders to the Exhibition

Amsterdam, Amsterdam Historical Museum (cat. nos 78, 84)

Amsterdam, Museum het Rembrandthuis (cat. nos 85, 102A, 102B)

Amsterdam, Netherlands Institute for Cultural Heritage (cat. nos 41, 56, 65, 70)

Amsterdam, Rijksmuseum (cat. nos 5, 11, 36, 83, 86, 88, 98, 99, 118, 120)

Baltimore, The Baltimore Museum of Art (cat. no. 18)

Berlin, Staatliche Museen zu Berlin, Gemäldegalerie (cat. no. 16)

Berlin, Staatliche Museen zu Berlin, Kupferstichkabinett (cat. nos 73, 77, 92)

Birmingham, The Barber Institute of Fine Arts, The University of Birmingham (cat. no. 79)

Boston, Museum of Fine Arts (cat. no. 71)

Brighton, Art Gallery & Museums (cat. no. 37)

Budapest, Szépmüvészeti Múzeum (cat. nos 38, 67, 68)

Cambridge, Fitzwilliam Museum (cat. nos 104, 114, 115A, 121)

Dordrecht, Dordrechts Museum (cat. nos 45, 49, 61, 65)

Dresden, Gemäldegalerie (cat. nos 44, 54)

Dublin, National Gallery of Ireland (cat. no. 63)

Edinburgh, National Galleries of Scotland (cat. no. 14)

England, The Trustees of the Cowdray Estate (cat. no. 28)

Fort Worth, Kimbell Art Museum (cat. no. 25)

Glasgow, Glasgow Museums (cat. no. 15)

Göteborg, Göteborg Museum of Art (cat. no. 24)

Groningen, Groninger Museum voor Stad en Lande (cat. nos 76, 91)

The Hague, Schilderijengalerij Prins Willem V (cat. no. 56)

The Hague, Royal Cabinet of Paintings, Mauritshuis (cat. no. 10)

The Hague, Museum Bredius (cat. nos 31, 89, 94)

Hamburg, Kunsthalle (cat. no. 2)

Helsinki, Sinebrychoff Museum (cat. no. 20)

Kansas City, Missouri, The Nelson-Atkins Museum of Art (cat. no. 26)

Kingston, Ontario, Agnes Etherington Art Centre, Queen's University (cat. no. 42)

Leiden, Stedelijk Museum de Lakenhal (cat. no. 33)

Leipzig, Museum der bildenden Künste (cat. no. 34)

Le Mans, Musées du Mans (cat. no. 48)

London, The British Museum (cat. nos 74, 81, 93, 100, 117B)

London, Dulwich Picture Gallery (cat. no. 8)

London, The National Gallery (cat. nos 13, 23, 57)

London, Victoria and Albert Museum (cat. nos 30, 117A)

Los Angeles, Armand Hammer Museum of Art and Cultural Center (cat. no. 12)

Melbourne, National Gallery of Victoria (cat. nos 3, 27, 52, 69, 75, 80, 103, 106, 107, 108, 109, 110A, 111, 112, 113, 115B, 116)

Milwaukee, Milwaukee Art Museum (cat. nos 50, 51)

Montreal, Montreal Museum of Fine Arts (cat. nos 59, 66)

New York, Newhouse Galleries, Inc. (cat. no. 39)

Oxford, The Ashmolean Museum (cat. nos 82, 96, 101, 105, 122)

Paris, Musée du Louvre (cat. nos 22, 47, 72)

Philadelphia, Philadelphia Museum of Art (cat. no. 29)

Rotterdam, Museum Boijmans Van Beuningen (cat. nos 32, 43, 60, 87, 90)

San Diego, Timken Museum of Art (cat. no. 17)

Springfield, Massachusetts, Museum of Fine Arts (cat. no. 46)

Stockholm, Nationalmuseum (cat. nos 7, 95, 97)

USA, Drs Isabel and Alfred Bader (cat. nos 4, 35, 55)

Utrecht, Museum Catharijneconvent (cat. nos 41, 53, 70)

Vienna, Gemäldegalerie der Akademie der bildenden Künste (cat. nos 58, 62)

Washington DC, National Gallery of Art (cat. nos 19, 119)

and private collections in Europe and the United States (cat. nos 1, 6, 9, 21, 40, 64, 110B)

Acknowledgements

Dr Albert Blankert wishes to make the following acknowledgements to those who have assisted with his work on this exhibition and catalogue.

Dr Robert Edwards, Chief Executive and Director of Art Exhibitions Australia Limited, Sydney, is acknowledged for his tireless and dedicated work in making this exhibition and catalogue possible.

Particular acknowledgement is made of the contribution of Drs Rudi E. O. Ekkart, Director, and his staff, at the Netherlands Institute for Art History (RKD), The Hague, and of Drs Peter Schatborn, Keeper of Prints and Drawings at the Rijksmuseum, Amsterdam, for his help in all matters regarding the drawings.

Acknowledgement is also made to the following:

Sir Jack Baer, London; Laurie Benson, Melbourne; Dr Marten Jan Bok, Utrecht; Prof. Dr Josua Bruyn, Amsterdam; Dr Görel Cavalli-Björkman, Stockholm; Heidi Chin, New York; Drs Henri Defoer, Utrecht; Henk Diele, Zwolle; Drs Bas Dudok van Heel, Amsterdam; Drs Frits Duparc, The Hague; Dr Ildikó Ember, Budapest; Richard L. Feigen, New York; Dr Jan Piet Filedt Kok, Amsterdam; Jacques Foucart, Paris; Drs Michiel Franken, Amsterdam; Burton Fredericksen, Santa Monica, California; Drs Jub de Groot, Dordrecht; Dr Herwig Guratzsch, Leipzig; Prof. Dr Egbert Haverkamp Begemann, New York; Dr Harald Hendrix, Utrecht; Sarah Herring, London; Wim Huyskens, Monnickendam; Drs Guido Jansen, Amsterdam; Prof. Eddy de Jongh, Utrecht; Dr Raymond Keaveney, Dublin; Dr Jan Kelch, Berlin; Dr T. Ketelsen, Hamburg; Drs Wouter Kloek, Amsterdam; Yoriko Kobayashi-Sato, Kawasaki; Drs Gerbrand Kotting, The Hague; Dr Helmut R. Leppien, Hamburg; Dr Walter Liedtke, New York; Julia Lloyd Williams, Edinburgh; Dianne Loxton, London; Drs Ger Luijten, Amsterdam; Prof. Dr Harald Marx, Dresden; Prof. Dr Bert Meijer, Florence; Dr Cornelia Moiso-Diekamp, Turin; Dr Otto Naumann, New York; Dr Uta Neidhardt, Dresden; Robert Noortman, Maastricht; Alice L. Roessingh, The Hague; Yvette Rosenberg, Amsterdam; Dana Rowan, Melbourne; Dr George Shackleford, Boston; Gary Schwartz, Maarssen; Prof. Seymour Slive, Cambridge, Mass.; Dr J. E. A. L. Struick, Utrecht †; Carol Togneri, Santa Monica, California; Dr Renate Trnek, Vienna; University of Utrecht, Department of Art History; F. L. T. Verdonk, Utrecht; Els Verhaak, Amsterdam; Dr John Walsh, Malibu; Willem L. van de Watering, The Hague; Dr Arthur K. Wheelock, Jr., Washington DC; Drs Hans van de Willige, Zwolle; Drs Marieke de Winkel, Amsterdam.

Dr Albert Blankert also thanks the staff members of AEA, Sydney, especially Carol Henry and Michael Jones, for their invaluable assistance. Dr Robert Edwards would also like to acknowledge Carol Henry, Kylie Dennis, Michael Jones, Tara Ebes, Lorraine Wright and Sarah Warn for management expertise provided by Art Exhibitions Australia.

Laurie Benson, Tracey Judd, Dr Jacqueline Strecker and Jason Smith provided curatorial assistance to Dr Timothy Potts during the organization of this exhibition.

Drs Jaap van der Veen's contribution to the catalogue was written with the support of the Netherlands Organization for Scientific Research (NWO) and forms part of the studies conducted by the Rembrandt Research Project, Amsterdam. Dr Volker Manuth wishes to acknowledge Axel Rügen, Kingston, Ontario.

'Holland to New Holland': Rembrandt in Australia

TIMOTHY POTTS

In 1933, when the National Gallery of Victoria bought its first Rembrandt painting (or so the experts thought), *The Times* of London celebrated the event in an editorial entitled 'Holland to New Holland'. The painting was a late 'self-portrait' (fig. 1), in whose 'arrogant and melancholy' expression *The Times*'s art critic saw 'a man refusing to sink under misfortune' – an allusion to Rembrandt's bankruptcy and other personal tragedies. 'And to Rembrandt', *The Times* continues, 'the strangest thing ... would surely be that [the portrait] should be bought, at a price that would have paid his debts a hundred times over, for a great public picture gallery in a huge city on the other side of the world, where there was not a house nor a white man for nearly two hundred years after the picture was painted'. The irony is justified, so *The Times* goes on, by the beacon Rembrandt's image would bear to this remote outpost of Commonwealth, then nearing its centenary of foundation: 'hanging in the National Gallery of Victoria, it may carry its timely message of courage and determination, and rouse a proper pride in a community which has so swiftly become able and worthy to possess a masterpiece'.[1]

The unselfconscious – and probably unintended – patronage of these sentiments is of a piece with the in-joke of the headline: a passing compliment by one great colonial power to another. But today it serves also to remind us of the crucial role the Dutch played in the early 'discovery' of Australia by Europeans. Indeed, Rembrandt's life neatly spans the precise period when his countrymen became the first Europeans to set foot on the vast landmass they would dub 'New Holland': the *terra australis* or Great South Land which geographers had for centuries posited to balance – quite literally – the northern continents of Europe and Asia. Early in 1606, a few months before Rembrandt's birth, Willem Jansz sailed south from New Guinea and soon after made landfall at Cape York Peninsula, setting the first verifiable European footstep on Australian soil. Others soon followed: Dirck Hartog in the north-west in 1616, Frederik de Houtman in the south-west in 1619, and Abel Tasman along the north and south coasts in the 1640s.

By the time of Rembrandt's death in 1669, Dutch interest in what was turning out to seem an unrelentingly inhospitable territory had waned. It was the British who, a century later, resolved to persevere. The rest, for any Australian schoolchild, is more familiar history.

Rembrandt in Australia

The first retrospective exhibition of Rembrandt's paintings was held at the Stedelijk Museum in Amsterdam and opened in September 1898, on the occasion of the inauguration of Queen Wilhelmina. The current exhibition thus marks a convenient book-end to the first century of the public display and celebration of Rembrandt's achievement. Three works in the Australian exhibition were also included in the Amsterdam show,[2] a not insignificant link in view of the six to eight hundred paintings then generally thought to be by the master. The Stedelijk exhibition was not only the first for Rembrandt but also the first of its scale for any old master artist in Holland, reflecting both the high esteem in which he was held and his unique status as the embodiment of Dutchness – perfect to celebrate a new queen's inauguration.

And yet Rembrandt had at this point become largely foreign property. At the time of the Stedelijk exhibition, only about fourteen of his paintings were left in Dutch collections (a situation that is rightly much changed today): the vast majority of works had to be borrowed from other European countries. That there are twice that number of autograph Rembrandts in the current exhibition is therefore of some historical interest: the scope of Rembrandt's painted work that visitors to Melbourne and Canberra will experience is one which a century ago was denied even to the Dutch in their own country.

Rembrandt: A Genius and His Impact sets out to present a rounded view of the great master of the Golden Age and his seminal influence on the art of his time. It also takes a fresh look, as any survey today must, at the complex and volatile question of what to attribute to Rembrandt vis-à-vis his pupils and on what grounds, this being the pivot upon which recent interpretation and assessment of his achievement turns. The master himself is represented by paintings, drawings and etchings, many of which rank with the finest he produced. Works by the best of his many pupils have been selected to show the decisive influence which Rembrandt had on them and also, in some cases, to illustrate the path away from the master's 'dark painting' to a smoother, more colourful, Italianate style which many of them later took. One of the most positive outcomes of the recent reassessment of Rembrandt's oeuvre has been the realization that his pupils, at their best, can be every bit as good as their master. Indeed, it is this that has supported for so long the veritable industry that is Rembrandt connoisseurship.

The most major survey of Rembrandt's work by the current generation of scholars was that mounted in Berlin, Amsterdam and London in 1991–92. One-third of the Rembrandt paintings currently in Australia were also in that exhibition. A number of new insights gained six years ago can now be drawn upon but already the understanding of certain works has moved on. Other paintings and drawings are here juxtaposed for the first time. Events of this kind are a powerful reminder that it is only by seeing works side by side that the subtle nuances of style, technique and palette can properly be compared. Previous exhibitions have led to a number of reattributions and it may be that Rembrandt leaves Australia a little leaner or more expansive than he arrived.

The scholars who have contributed to this catalogue bring to the task a variety of perspectives and viewpoints, reflecting the highly didactic state of the subject. The exhibition curator, Albert Blankert, has published widely on seventeenth-century Dutch art and offers here, as in his previous work, many new and challenging ideas on Rembrandt's painted oeuvre. Other authors provide overviews of other areas and aspects of

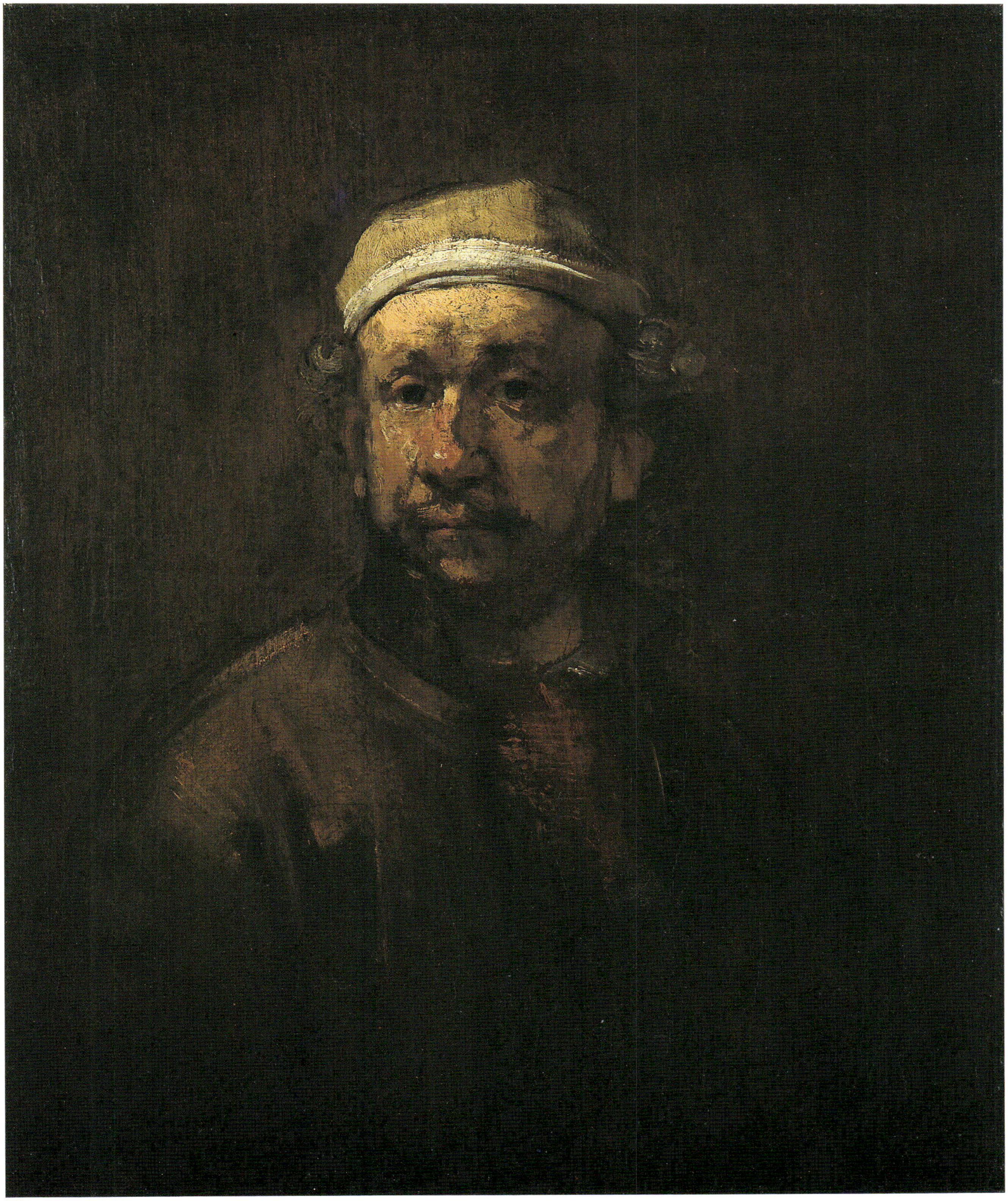

FIG. I
Manner of Rembrandt
Portrait of Rembrandt
Canvas
76.5 x 61.6 cm
National Gallery of Victoria, Melbourne;
Felton Bequest 1933

Rembrandt's work and that of his principal pupils. All have written extensively on these topics before but focus here particularly on fresh evidence and new approaches. The Rembrandt presented here is one that in a sense did not exist, and could not have existed, a decade ago.

Few areas of art history have been the subject of such extensive collaborative investigation or have benefited so much from direct scholarly exchange as Rembrandt. An exhibition of this kind is therefore an important opportunity to bring scholars and paintings face to face. A symposium has been organized in Melbourne during the course of the exhibition at which more than a dozen of the foremost international scholars of Rembrandt and his pupils will present the results of recent research. The proceedings of this event, convened jointly by Christopher White and Christopher Brown, will be published separately.

Beyond hype and hagiography: In search of the 'real' Rembrandt

Rembrandt occupies a singular place in the popular artistic consciousness. One of the very few artists whose name is common currency – at least within occidental cultures – across all educational, social and other divides, Rembrandt is that uncommon 'artist's artist' who is also a postcard best-seller. To blockbuster audiences the world over, his name is synonymous with artistic genius, his work the paradigmatic 'masterpiece'. Thanks to his compulsion for self-portraiture (more than one self-image has survived for every year of his forty-year career, and there were doubtless many more), his face is probably the best known of any artist in history, rivalled only by his later compatriot van Gogh. And this celebrity is nothing new: the first catalogue raisonné in art history was that created in 1751 for Rembrandt's etchings.

The popular conception of Rembrandt as the quintessential artistic genius took root in the romanticizing hothouse of the nineteenth century and has as much to do with his life as with his work; or, more accurately, the one has subtly but unmistakably influenced the other. As more has become known about Rembrandt the man, and as society's own conception of the 'ideal artist' has changed, so too has each generation's image of him been transfigured.

It is true that Rembrandt's life was often traumatic and at times tragic, and this goes a long way to explaining why the Romantics saw in him the archetypal tortured artistic genius, and projected onto these circumstances the psychic underpinnings of his art. Born of fairly humble origins – the son of a miller – Rembrandt established a reputation as one of the great talents of his generation at a precociously young age. Art training started young (Rembrandt was apprenticed to his first teacher at thirteen) and his early recognition was not unique for a gifted artist. Even this, however, does not prepare us for the hyperbole of his most famous fan, the Secretary to the Prince of Orange, Constantijn Huygens, who described the 23-year-old Rembrandt's work as

> on a par with whatever beauty has been created throughout the ages ... I maintain that no-one, be he Protogenes, Apelles or Parrhasius, ever conceived or – were they to return to earth – ever could conceive what has been gathered in a single human figure [of Judas repentant (p. 23, fig. 2)] and expressed in its totality by a beardless boy, a Dutchman, a miller's son. I say this in pure amazement. Rembrandt, I salute you!

At twenty-seven Rembrandt married into a well-connected family and his future was looking bright. Within eight years, however, he had suffered the tragic loss of three children, each within weeks of birth, and of his wife Saskia two years after the last. Rembrandt then began an affair with the nanny of his only surviving child, a son, a liaison destined to bring opprobrium on all concerned. The affair ended messily and expensively for Rembrandt, who had meanwhile transferred his affections to another, Hendrickje Stoffels. Though they did not marry, Hendrickje became Rembrandt's de facto wife and companion for fifteen years. Such an unsanctified relationship was a scandal in Calvinist Holland, and when in 1654 Hendrickje fell pregnant she was duly summoned before the Church council and charged with having 'given herself over to harlotry with Rembrandt the painter'.

Fate remained unkind to Rembrandt, who outlived Hendrickje by six years and his beloved only son Titus by one, both falling victim to plague. Rembrandt had earlier been forced to sell Saskia's grave in the Oude Kerk and had in the end to rely on the savings of his young daughter by Hendrickje to survive. He was buried in 1669 in a rented Westerkerk grave beside Titus and Hendrickje.

Comfortable if not wealthy throughout most of his life, Rembrandt's great weakness was great art. He amassed a large collection of Italian, Flemish, German and Dutch prints, drawings and sketches as well as assorted antiquities and curiosities of natural history. Art was also his principal investment, not land and property like most businessmen. It proved his financial undoing. Caught up in a general economic downturn, burdened with a mortgage he could not afford, and with his teaching and commissions in decline, Rembrandt in 1656 was forced into voluntary bankruptcy. All his possessions, including his own paintings and his large art collection, were sold at auction in 1657 and 1658. While the inventory of these sales has proved a boon to art historians, the auction yielded far less than Rembrandt had paid for his treasures, a result that must have grieved his Dutch soul as merchant and art lover in equal measure.

The popular image of Rembrandt today – still essentially the nineteenth-century Romantic conception of the tragic artistic genius – contrasts dramatically with that which professional art historians have gleaned from the surviving documents. It is not so much the difference between one 'real' Rembrandt and another, but between one clear if idealized Rembrandt and a myriad of others – an elusive, shifting, often contradictory Rembrandt who refuses ever quite to crystallize. In a subject whose bread and butter today is reassessment, 'deconstruction' and contextualization, the study of Rembrandt stands out for its perennial interpretive gyrations. Rembrandt the man, his life and his art have come to form an inseparable interpretive matrix, and each successive generation of scholars has found sufficient purchase on one dimension or other to shift the centre of gravity of the whole in some new direction. It is also an academic minefield into which those of us who are not specialists venture at our peril.

Rembrandt turned upside-down

In 1708, the artist and writer Roger de Piles published his *Cours de peinture par principes* (The Principles of Painting), in which he included a 'Comparison of Painters', an analytical table which scores the fifty-seven 'best-known painters' of history by four criteria: composition, drawing, colour and expression. Like contestants at an artistic Olympics, de Piles awarded points from zero to eighteen (no perfect twenties were given) to each artist against each criterion. Raphael and Rubens were joint winners with totals of sixty-five. Nine other artists come before Rembrandt, who scores a total of fifty (the Carracci and Domenichino equal second; Le Brun third; van Dyck fourth; Correggio, Poussin and Vanni equal fifth; Guercino sixth; Titian seventh). Rembrandt's highest score (seventeen) was for colour and his lowest (six) for drawing (i.e., the use of line in painting, *not* his drawings, which were already highly regarded).

It is easy today to ridicule de Piles's calculus of artistry as fatuous and wrongheaded – a bean-counting vivisection of creative wholes which cannot be reduced to any quantification of their 'parts'. But misguided though his purpose may now seem to us, the categories into which de Piles analysed the artist's craft were those in which artists themselves thought of, and taught, their trade in the guilds, academies and studios. Though many may have disputed de Piles's scores, few at the time would have denied that such analysis had meaning (and indeed the relative importance of two of these categories – colour and drawing – was hotly debated in the *Académie* between the so-called *rubénistes* and *poussinistes* respectively).

De Piles's table is also interesting as a gauge of the relatively inferior status to which Rembrandt had fallen in the decades immediately after his death. In 1641 he had been 'one of the most renowned painters of our time' (Orlers), and late in life 'the miracle of our age' (Bucelinus, on whom see the contribution by van de Wetering below). By the end of his career, while still famous and highly respected, Rembrandt was regarded as 'old-fashioned' compared to the smooth, classicizing Italianate style then in vogue. And now, forty years later, though singled out by de Piles as the sole seventeenth-century Dutch painter in the pantheon of fifty-seven, Rembrandt does not rank with the great Italian and French masters – principally because he lacks an understanding of classical types and so is unable to 'improve' upon the raw veracity of nature.

In time, however, this great failing was to become his great genius. What the classicists abhorred in Rembrandt the nineteenth-century Romantics applauded: his eschewal of the traditional canon of subjects and treatments; his very Dutch love of the quotidian and ephemeral (his 'caprices' as they were often called) above the grand and ideal; and especially the transfixingly psychological dimension of his portraits, which seemed to penetrate the heart and soul of his subjects (above all Rembrandt himself in his self-portraits) as few artists ever had. At times this view took on a political aspect, seeing in the artistic heretic the cultural equivalent of the free-spirited Protestant republican.

This reification of Rembrandt the painter of raw nature and inner soul went hand in hand with an increasing focus on Rembrandt the individual genius. Both were fuelled by nineteenth-century archival research which brought to light new details of Rembrandt's traumatic, licentious and often tragic life. The raw impasto and loose 'impressionist' brushstroke of his late technique; his sombre 'melancholy' palette; his penchant for exotic eastern costume – these and other aspects of his style came to be seen as physical manifestations of the heretical artist cutting through the overlay of culture and erudition to the real nature (both inner and outer) of his subjects – melding verism and idealism, visual and spiritual actuality, the Platonic form and its instantiation. The 'tame' environment of other Dutch seventeenth-century art reinforced the Romantics' case: Rembrandt the 'impressionist' revolutionary worked a stone's throw from practitioners of that most meticulous of all schools, the Dutch flower painters. The conceptual gulf separating Rembrandt and de Heem is indeed every bit as wide as that between the French impressionists and their Salon contemporaries.

Intimately connected with this phenomenon has been the reassessment of the checklist of Rembrandt's oeuvre. Around the time of the Stedelijk exhibition in 1898, anywhere from 595 (Hofstede de Groot) to 800 paintings were attributed to Rembrandt's hand, though only the lower number had any credence. By 1921 (Valentiner) this had grown through new 'discoveries' to well over 700; then shrunk back through more critical vetting to 630 by 1935 (Bredius); and to 420 by 1968 (Gerson). Current estimates put it somewhere around 300, though one recent study (Tümpel 1993) has it at 234. Such radical trimming of an artist's corpus does not just truncate his output: it affects fundamental aspects of the appreciation of his style and achievement – especially when, as with Rembrandt, some of the deattributed works are among his previously core masterpieces: Berlin's *Man in the Golden Helmet* and (less definitively) New York's *Polish Rider*. A consequence of the past century's shrinkage has therefore been to metamorphose Rembrandt the artistic construct into a new form. The Rembrandt to which scholars today assign a painting is, in a certain sense, not the same Rembrandt to which that painting was assigned a century ago. This means that the disparaging question of how anyone could ever have thought *that* painting a 'real Rembrandt' is grossly unfair. No stylistic attribution is any better than its stylistic touchstones. The corpus is everything.

It was the appreciation of this fact that underlay the most radical revolution in Rembrandt studies to date, that witnessed in recent years through the activities of the Rembrandt Research Project, a Dutch Government–funded examination of the entire corpus of reputedly autograph paintings. For the first time, stylistic judgements have been grounded in an exhaustive visual scrutiny of all the works, supplemented by a barrage of scientific analyses of pigment, ground, support and technique. Established in 1968, the Rembrandt Research Project has so far published its views on Rembrandt's corpus up to 1642, the year of his famous *Night Watch* (p. 26, fig. 7). A largely new team under the direction of Ernst van de Wetering is currently working on the remaining, and often more difficult, works.

The Rembrandt Research Project represents a uniquely thorough-going attempt to wrestle with a uniquely intractable problem of attribution. Its results have already transformed Rembrandt studies, as much by the more objective tenor and scientific underpinnings of its arguments as by its results. Perhaps predictably, the central question of how and what to attribute to Rembrandt has proved to be more complex than ever. Rembrandt's pupils have emerged from the shadows to play a more meaningful part in his studio practice (as discussed below by Blankert in 'The Impact of a Genius'). Detecting the hand of the master cannot now be divorced from detecting the hands of his many pupils and followers. Indeed, the greatest measure of the revolution in Rembrandt studies is that not only the answers but also the questions have now changed: no longer 'Is it or isn't it a Rembrandt?' but 'How much (or in what ways) a Rembrandt?' Black and white have given way to shades of grey: fully autograph works; paintings on which both Rembrandt and his pupils worked; pupils' copies of autograph works (including self-portraits!); paintings made by pupils under Rembrandt's close supervision; paintings made in his studio but conceived and executed by the pupil alone. To make things worse, it was forbidden by guild regulation (at least in Utrecht) for pupils in a studio to place any signature on their works other than their master's. Strange, even unethical, as this may seem to us today it had a certain logic: the master was expected to place his stamp very firmly on his pupils' style and they in turn placed his stamp (i.e. signature) on their work.

The evidence adduced by the Rembrandt Research Project brings a level of visual scrutiny and a scientific dimension to the analysis of Rembrandt's work that has transformed the basis of informed opinion. Analyses of paints, canvases and panels (now datable by dendrochronology), as well as radiographic imaging of underpainting, pentimenti and brush technique, have yielded a wealth of new evidence that provides the first radically new basis of assessment since the seventeenth century. Likewise for the works on paper (outside the Rembrandt Research Project's purview), attributions during this century have increasingly looked to the inscriptions, signatures, collectors' marks, paper types and watermarks to complement judgements of style and quality.

This is not to say that connoisseurship no longer comes into play. Indeed, in many cases the scientific evidence is to a greater or lesser degree inconclusive, and stylistic judgements remain the final (so far) arbiter. But it is now a connoisseurship that latches onto descriptive rather than evaluative terms, that is specific and concrete rather than general and metaphysical, that seeks to be objective and falsifiable rather than subjective and incontrovertible. Today's Rembrandt connoisseur must regularly forsake his copy of Sandrart or Hoogstraten for the laboratory.

The 'real' Rembrandt has not weathered these storms unscathed. The more evidence that has come to light on Rembrandt and his studio practice, the more complex and intangible the character at centre stage has become. The picture we have of Rembrandt today, while more defensible and richer in many points of detail, is infinitely more nuanced, changeable and intangible than before. As Boomgaard and Scheller concluded in 1991, 'amid all this clarity, confusion flourishes as never before ... every painting presents us with a different Rembrandt'.[3]

The uniquely didactic and revisionist state of Rembrandt studies has important consequences. When works that have been so central to the conception of an artist's achievement are stripped from him, not only is the arithmetic of his corpus affected but aspects of his place in art history may change. Equally important is the flipside of the reattributions away from Rembrandt – the implication that these paintings were made by his now much less famous pupils and that the question of what is and is not a Rembrandt is thus not (or not just) a matter of quality. A painting of the very highest quality in the style of Rembrandt, made in the age of Rembrandt, need not have been painted *by* Rembrandt.

Not surprisingly, there have been sporadic neo-Romantic backlashes in some quarters, perhaps best epitomized by the delightfully forthrightly named 'Save Rembrandt from the Experts Society'. Fortunately, he needs not so much to be 'saved' as to be understood for the more complex and interesting character that he is turning out to be.

Collecting Rembrandt in Australia

The *'Self-Portrait'* which arrived in Melbourne with such fanfare in 1933 was not the first work of the master to reach New Holland. Just as, two centuries earlier, the spread of Rembrandt's works across Europe had been spearheaded by collectors of his etchings, so too it was these less spectacular but equally exceptional works which were first acquired by the National Gallery of Victoria.

A first group of eleven etchings (including cat. nos 103, 106, 110A, 111 and 113) was bought by Melbourne in 1891 from the sale of the English collector and artist Francis Seymour Haden.[4] These, and prints of other artists purchased at the Seymour Haden sale, were the first original European old master works acquired by the Gallery, which had hitherto concentrated on casts of antiquities and other reproductions of famous masterpieces, as well as 'modern' Australian and European artists. Another group of fifty-three etchings was acquired in 1933 (the same year as the *'Self-Portrait'*) from the collection of Lionel Lindsay, like Seymour Haden a great admirer of Rembrandt. A firm basis having now been laid, further purchases over the next half-century saw the collection grow to some 125 works representing all of Rembrandt's primary subject areas and nearly all of his major works. These etchings are on display in Melbourne in a pendant exhibition.

The etchings were joined by two sheets of Rembrandt drawings in 1936 (cat. nos 75, 80), though this relatively late start was never followed up and remains the weakest area of the Gallery's coverage of Rembrandt. A factor in this neglect was the still somewhat negative regard for Rembrandt's drafting skills, deriving from the academicians' criticism back to de Piles. In this the past half-century has seen a sea change.

If the etchings first signalled Melbourne's serious intentions towards Rembrandt it was the three paintings acquired between 1933 and 1951 that consummated the engagement. The Gallery had been intent on acquiring major masterpieces for some time, with Rembrandt at the top of the list, and had in the Felton Bequest one of the few public sources of funding which could oblige. Along with two works by Vermeer and a Frans Hals investigated by the Felton adviser Frank Rinder in the 1920s was a masterful Rembrandt of *'Titus' at His Writing Desk*, now in Rotterdam (fig. 2). But the then owner decided in the end not to sell. So too did the great Rembrandt scholar Abraham Bredius when approached (through a dealer with the propitious name of van Diemen) about his *Bust of Christ* (cat. no. 31), now in The Hague but belatedly making a trip to its would-be adoptive home. Thus the first great Rembrandts Melbourne tried to acquire got away.

Then in 1933 came the *'Self-Portrait'*. Already before the painting left London there were rumblings about whether it was 'right'. These soon grew into a small torrent of scepticism after the work arrived (on the same ship as Tiepolo's *Banquet of Cleopatra*) and was put on display in Melbourne. The press had a field day, the *Herald* calling the painting 'hideous', while the *Sun* reported a sally from the north in the headline 'New Rembrandt Doubted. "Gallery Diddled Again", Says N.S.W. Director. "Poor Thing Indeed"'. Arthur Streeton's enthusiastic reception of the portrait as 'an unmistakable work of the master, fine in form and modelling, and broadly and vigorously painted' was very much the exception.[5]

The doubts about the work were indeed well founded and did not go away. Expert opinion increasingly relegated the painting to a follower of Rembrandt and thus it was duly reattributed in 1984 after a visit by the Rembrandt Research Project. It is now assigned to the hand of an imitator of the late seventeenth or early eighteenth century.

Despite the controversy over the *'Self-Portrait'*, it was only a year later that the Felton Bequest agreed to purchase another Rembrandt for the Melbourne Gallery, *Two Old Men Disputing* (or *The Two Philosophers*, as it was then generally known) of 1628 (cat. no. 3). The diametrically opposing views taken on this early and less 'typical' Rembrandt by the Gallery's Director, Bernard Hall, and the principal Felton adviser illustrate vividly the susceptibility of expert opinion, no less than public taste, to personal preference and fashion. Fortunately, Hall's heartfelt exhortation in a letter from London to 'trust me now or never' was eventually followed and the Gallery acquired what is now regarded among the greatest of Rembrandt's first mature masterpieces. The 'taste' issue was not dispelled however. As late as 1951, even as subtle and perspicacious a judge as Daryl Lindsay, then Director of the National Gallery of Victoria, advocated selling the work to help finance the last of the three painting purchases, dismissing the earlier work as a 'doubtful picture, and at best a poor example of Rembrandt's early period ... [which] can be classed as a student's picture'.

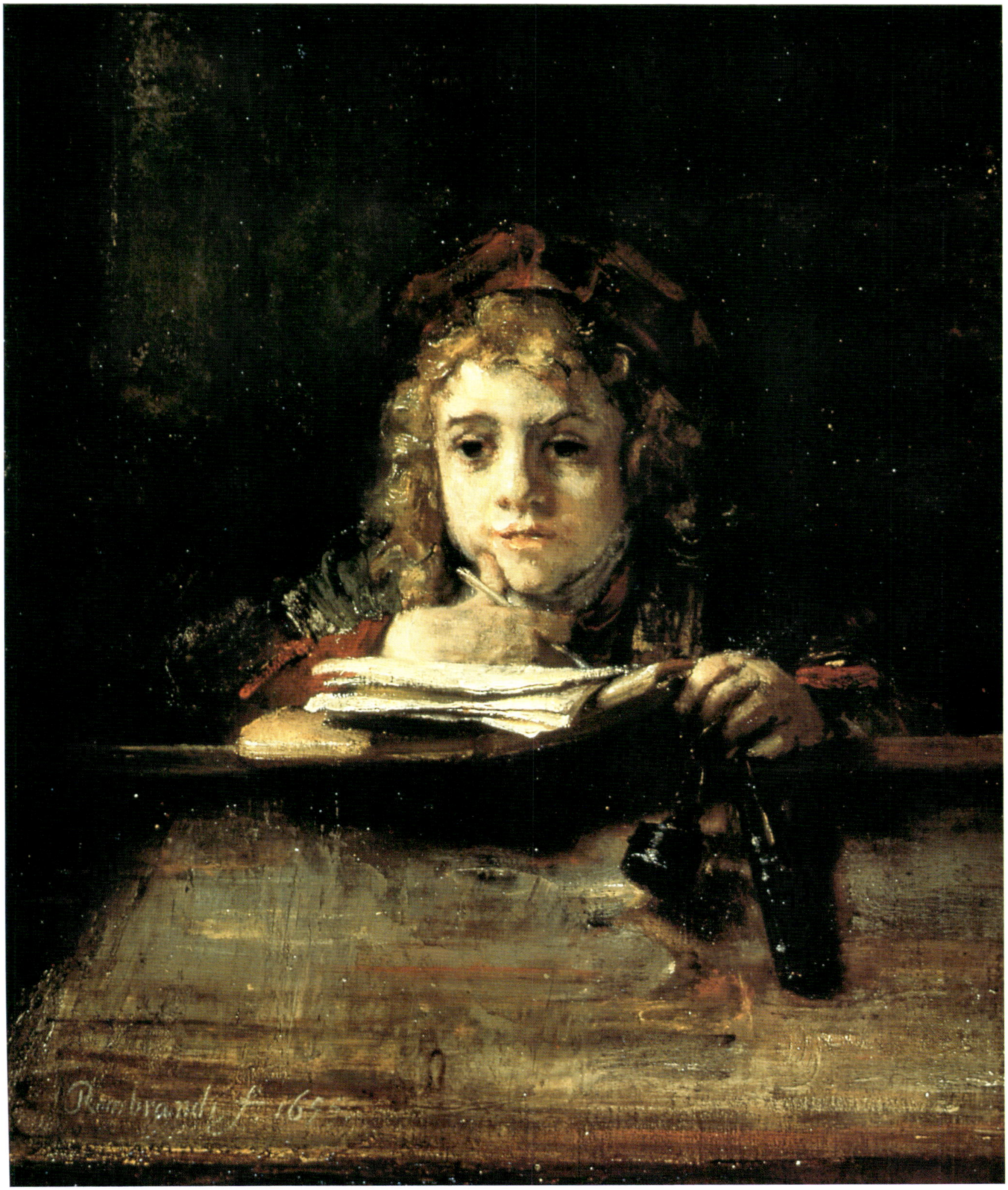

FIG. 2
Rembrandt
'Titus' at His Writing Desk
Signed and dated 1655
Canvas
77.0 x 63.0 cm
Museum Boijmans Van Beuningen, Rotterdam

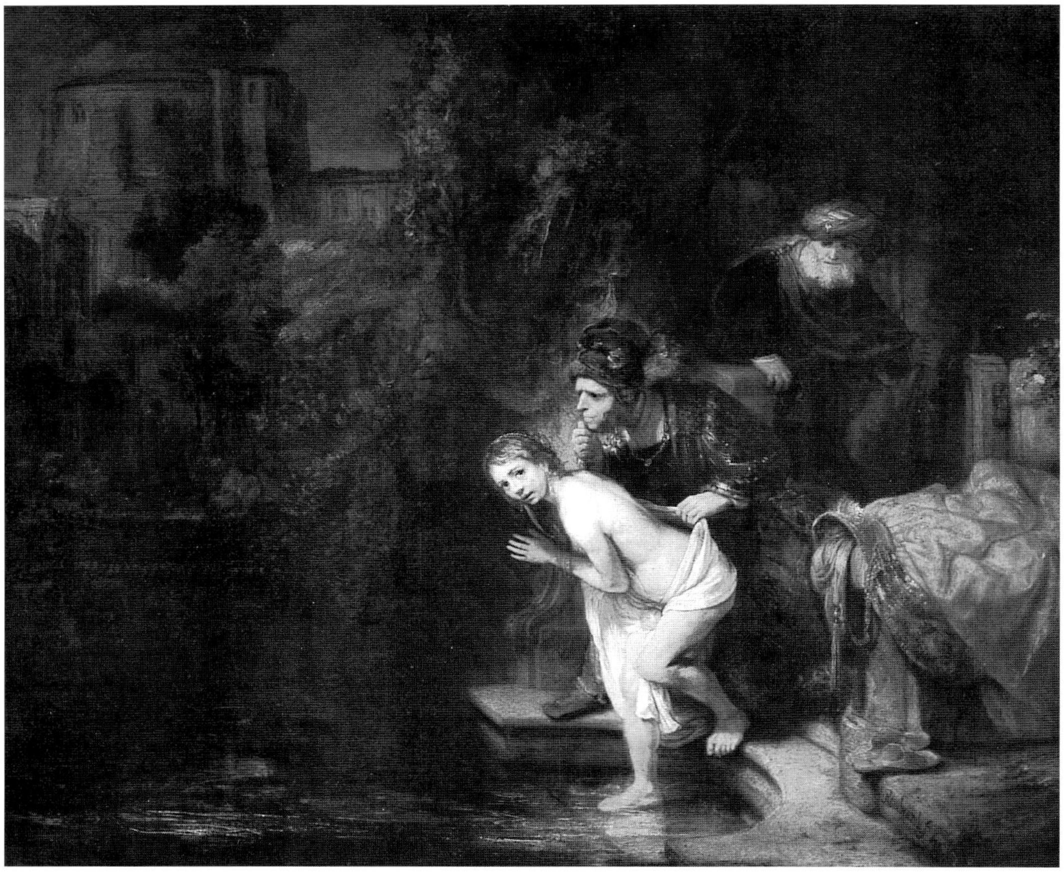

FIG. 3
Rembrandt
Susanna and the Elders
Signed and dated 1647
Panel
76.6 x 92.8 cm
Staatliche Museen zu Berlin, Gemäldegalerie

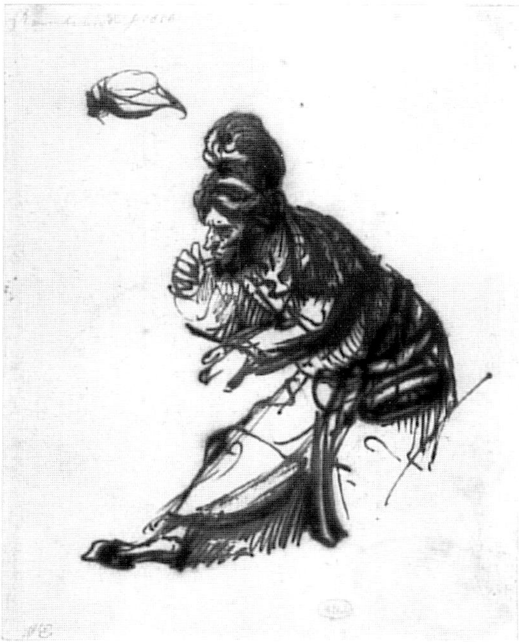

FIG. 4
Rembrandt
An Elder c.1638
Pen and ink on tinted paper
17.3 x 13.5 cm
National Gallery of Victoria, Melbourne;
Felton Bequest 1936
(our cat. no. 80)

The third and last acquisition, *Portrait of a White-Haired Man* of 1667 (cat. no. 27), occasioned neither controversy nor even significant comment. One of Rembrandt's last two dated portraits, however, it has come to be regarded as one of his finest late works and thereby found a place in the great 1991–92 exhibition. Here in Australia, it is paired for the first time with the very last dated portrait, from the collection of Lord Cowdray (cat. no. 28).

The Melbourne Rembrandt acquisitions remain to this day one of the most successful exercises in judicious collecting in Australia's history. Of no other old master artist of the very first rank can it be said that this country possesses representative and, in some cases, outstanding examples of his work in all media of his oeuvre: two major paintings, two sheets of drawings, and a fine selection of etchings.

The occasional sidelights thrown on works in this exhibition by other areas of the Melbourne collection are happy reminders of its impressive range and depth. The Berlin *Susanna and the Elders* (fig. 3), a later version of cat. no. 10, contains the lecherous elder for which Melbourne's drawing (fig. 4) is a preparatory sketch. The figure of Susanna herself seems to be based loosely on the Roman Capitoline Venus *(Venus pudica)* of which, likewise, a version is in Melbourne (fig. 5). The Jacques de Gheyn III of cat. no. 8 was the original owner of Melbourne's *Two Old Men Disputing* (cat. no. 3).

Rembrandt and the cultural paradigm

It has often been remarked that the cultural *leitmotifs* of Holland are overwhelmingly visual rather than literary or intellectual. As one nineteenth-century observer remarked, 'What other people has written

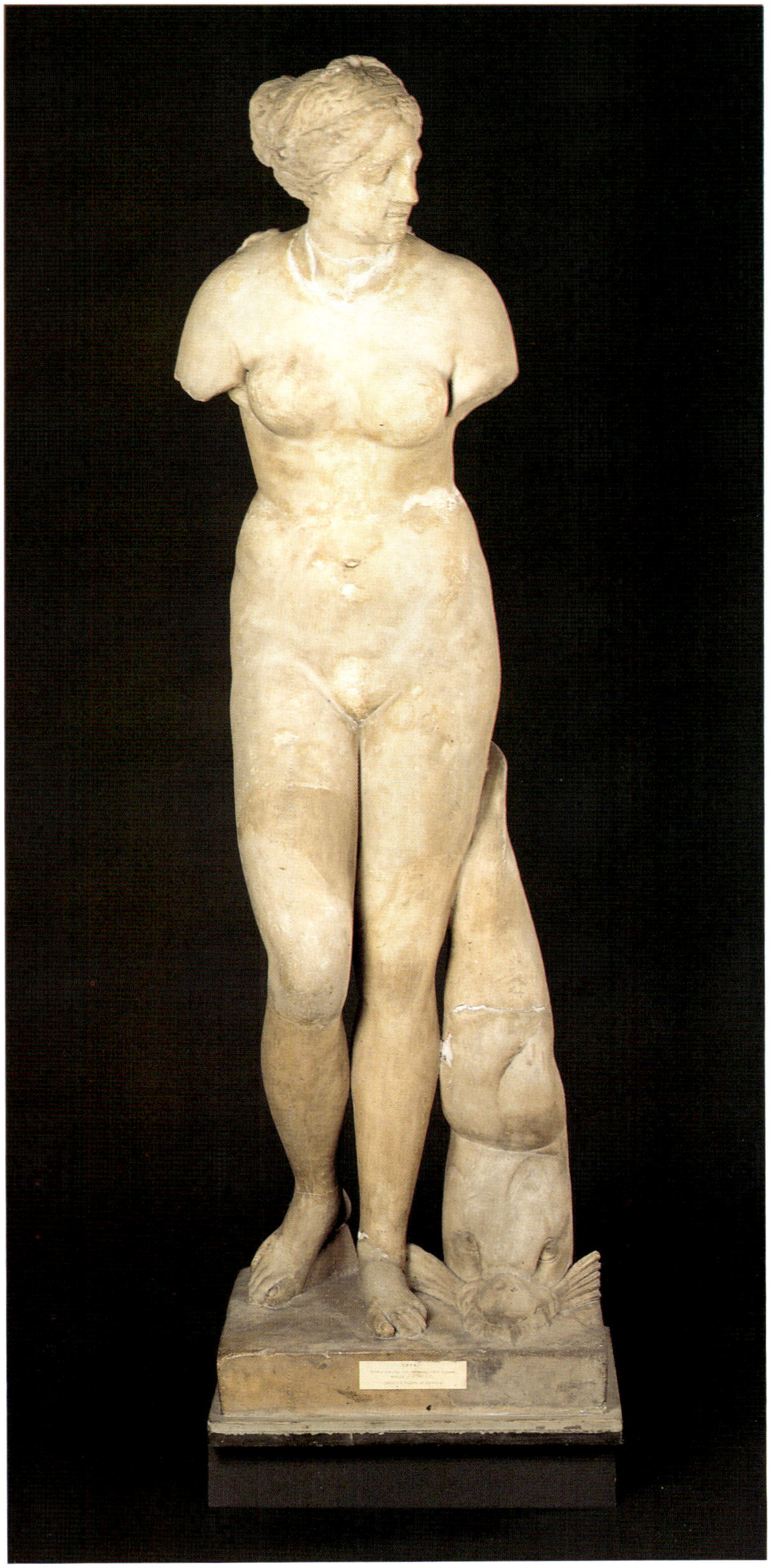

FIG. 5
Roman (copy after Greek original)
Version of Capitoline Venus (Venus pudica)
Marble
National Gallery of Victoria, Melbourne;
Felton Bequest 1929

its history in its art?'[6] The heroes of Dutch culture, and indeed of Dutch life and achievement in general, are predominantly artists, and none more pervasively so than Rembrandt.

Indeed, there could be no more compelling illustration of the power of art to permeate a people's sense of national identity than Rembrandt, who during the nineteenth century became the defining presence of Dutch culture. To an extent unmatched even by Rubens in Belgium or Dürer in Germany, he became the one person who encapsulated the Dutch self-image of Dutchness. That the Dutch national museum of art, the Rijksmuseum, was built around a particular Rembrandt painting (the *Night Watch*) is no historical accident and neatly symbolizes the focal point that Rembrandt had by then (1885) come to occupy at the heart of Dutch culture. In parallel with this, Rembrandt's flouting of contemporary artistic and social mores, and the soul-gazing inner life of his late portraits, made him the paradigm of the Romantics' intuitive hero, the transcultural free spirit whose luminous humanity transcends time and place. In an alchemy of apparent opposites he thus became both the quintessence of Dutchness and the fountainhead of universal artistic genius.

The broad cultural and nationalistic resonance which Rembrandt and his art acquired for the Netherlands has a timely relevance to Australia. As we approach the centenary of Federation, Australian cultural identity is assuming both a higher profile and a sharper polemical edge. The reflective question of 'what and who we are' is taking on an explicit and more urgent tone that has culture historians and sociologists casting around for more tangible manifestations of self-image. Increasingly, these self-images are visual as well as literary, historical or intellectual. The pictorial icons of the Australian way of life, and of the landscape in which it has been played out, are now just as likely to be invoked as touchstones of 'Australianness' as is a classic novel, historical event or bush ballad. What it is to be an Australian today, whether of indigenous or non-indigenous descent, is explained more by a way of life – increasingly *ways* of life – than by a defining historical event, a constitution or a particular colonial baggage.

As the repositories of our visual icons, major public art galleries have an important role to play in this dialogue – and it is increasingly a dialogue rather than a piece of reasoning that comes to an agreed end point. Both as historical memory banks and as arenas of continuing debate, art galleries can help us to define aspects of our cultural orientation which, while keenly felt, often remain poorly articulated. They can help us to do, in other words, what Rembrandt in a much more specific way did for the nineteenth-century Dutch, and to provide, as he has continued to provide, a point of reference against which subsequent cultural growth and change may be measured.

1 *The Times*, 19 September 1933, p. 13.
2 *The Apostle Peter Kneeling* (cat. no. 6), *The Departure of the Shunamite Woman* (cat. no. 30) and *Man in Armour* (cat. no. 15).
3 Boomgaard & Scheller 1991–92, p. 121.
4 For a full account of the collecting of Rembrandt by the National Gallery of Victoria, see J. Gregory, in Gregory & Zdanowicz 1988, pp. 8–18.
5 *Argus*, 10 November 1933, p. 10.
6 Bürger 1858–60, vol. 1, p. 323.

On the Life of Rembrandt van Rijn 1606–1669

MARLEEN BLOKHUIS

The first biographer to write about Rembrandt described him as 'one of the most celebrated painters of our age'. These were the words of the Leiden burgomaster and chronicler Jan Jansz Orlers, written in 1641.[1] Since that time, Rembrandt's reputation has lost none of its lustre. Over the past three and a half centuries, admirers as well as critics have written reams about his work, his person and his private life.[2]

Orlers's biography is still one of the principal sources of information about the first few decades of Rembrandt's life. Shortly after the artist's death several new commentaries appeared, covering his life and work not only in these early years, but also in the period after 1641.[3] The first author to comment specifically on his person and lifestyle was the Italian artists' biographer Filippo Baldinucci, who in 1686 described Rembrandt as an 'umorista di prima classe, e tutti disprezzava'. By this he would have meant that Rembrandt was a most capricious man who did not care at all what people might think or say of him.[4] The most comprehensive of Rembrandt's early biographers was Arnold Houbraken. The image that emerges from his account of 1718 is one of a determined and acquisitive, yet extravagant, man who sought the company of people beneath his station. This view is consistent with the so-called classicist doctrine embraced by Houbraken and other early writers, who saw Rembrandt as a renegade in his art as well as in his private life, and criticized his lack of discernment in both.

This image of Rembrandt as a non-conformist was to persist for over a century. Not until the middle of the nineteenth century, when he acquired the stature of a folk hero in the Netherlands, did a different picture emerge. To mark the unveiling of the Rembrandt statue in Amsterdam in 1852, the city archivist P. Scheltema produced a treatise on Rembrandt's 'life and accomplishments', which included previously unpublished archive material.[5] Scheltema was delighted to find 'satisfactory evidence' to exonerate Rembrandt from charges of 'moral turpitude', 'greed' and 'extravagance'.[6] One of the aims of his work was obviously to restore Rembrandt's good name.

Scheltema thus set the tone for later publications containing archive material. In the late nineteenth century Abraham Bredius and Nicolaas de Roever published various documents concerning Rembrandt's life and work, accompanied by glowing commentaries testifying to their respect for the artist as a man.[7] In 1906 Cornelis Hofstede de Groot published *Die Urkunden über Rembrandt (1575–1721)*, a compilation of all the archive records and accounts of early writers on Rembrandt that were known in 1906. Embroidering on Scheltema, Bredius and de Roever, the monograph by the critic and artist Jan Veth (1906) – one of the first to make use of Hofstede de Groot's book – portrays Rembrandt as an artist with a deep commitment to his work, indifferent to gain or prestige:

> Not one of the endless deeds he signed betrays a man who sought advantage. If anything, he gave away what he had. And throughout he remained steadfastly devoted to that [i.e. art] which he cherished more dearly than the world.[8]

Many of the documents that have come to light since 1906 were found by the Amsterdam archivists Isa van Eeghen and Sebastian Dudok van Heel. Others discovered additional material relating to Geertje Dircx (see below).[9] In 1979, these new findings, together with fresh interpretations of the documents that had surfaced earlier, were published in *The Rembrandt Documents*, an expanded version of *Die Urkunden*.[10] It seems unlikely that there is much more material still to be found.

In contrast to the situation in the nineteenth century, it is no longer taboo to admit that even an artist of Rembrandt's stature might have had a less pleasant side to his nature. Hints to this effect by his earliest biographers are now being looked at more closely. In 1984, for instance, Gary Schwartz expressed the relatively extreme view that 'Rembrandt had an unpleasant disposition and an unreliable nature'.[11]

It seems that much the same sources of information can give rise to quite different views of Rembrandt's personality. However, the purpose of this article is to present the facts of his life and career, not to create yet another interpretation of this kind.

Rembrandt Harmensz van Rijn was born in the Weddesteeg in Leiden on 15 July 1606.[12] His father, Harmen Gerritsz van Rijn (*c.*1568–1630), was a miller, as his forefathers had been for three generations, and his mother, Cornelia (Neeltgen) Willemsdr. van Zuytbroeck (1568–1640), was the daughter of a baker: the family belonged to the well-to-do bourgeoisie. The couple are believed to have had ten children, a number of whom died young. Rembrandt was the ninth. His six surviving siblings learned a trade, but Rembrandt attended the Latin School, where he received a sound education in the classical languages and in the Bible. Although his studies qualified him to attend university, the young Rembrandt, according to Orlers, was 'by nature ... moved toward the art of painting and drawing',[13] and was less interested in an academic career. He did in fact register at Leiden University on 20 May 1620, but appears not to have actually studied there.[14] Around this time he was apprenticed to Jacob Isaacsz van Swanenburgh (1571–1638), a figure painter in Leiden whose oeuvre consists mainly of scenes of hell, densely populated with small figures. Orlers reports that 'art lovers were most amazed' at Rembrandt's progress under Swanenburgh, for it was clear that he had the makings of an 'exceptional painter'.[15]

After leaving Swanenburgh's studio three years later, Rembrandt spent a period of six months, presumably around the mid-1620s, studying with Pieter Lastman (1583–1633) in Amsterdam. Lastman had visited Italy and was renowned for his history paintings. He would presumably have had a varied collection of work by Dutch and other artists, which Rembrandt would have seen at his studio in St Anthonisbreestraat. According to Houbraken's account, Rembrandt subsequently spent some time at the workshop of the landscape and history painter Jacob Pynas (*c.*1585–after 1648), whose work bears a close resemblance to Lastman's.[16]

In 1625, after returning to Leiden, Rembrandt produced *The Stoning of Stephen*, his first dated painting and the first to bear his mark (fig. 1).[17]

Jan Lievens (1607–1674), who had studied under Lastman in 1617, was also working in Leiden at the time. Rembrandt and Lievens are commonly thought to have shared a studio between 1625 and 1630, a conclusion based mainly on the fact that the same models can be recognized in their paintings from this period and that the two artists worked in a similar style. Although there is no hard evidence to confirm that they shared a studio, Rembrandt and Lievens would certainly have been acquainted with one another and familiar with each other's work. Rembrandt also took on his first pupils in Leiden, and probably started etching at around the same time.

In 1628 or 1629, both Lievens and Rembrandt received a visit from Constantijn Huygens (1596–1687), secretary to the stadholder, Prince Frederik Hendrik.[18] Moved by what he saw, Huygens wrote an accolade to the two 'beardless youths', which was published in 1897 and has been frequently quoted ever since.[19] He was deeply impressed by Rembrandt's ability to convey feeling. The *Judas* in particular inspired a torrent of praise (fig. 2).[20] Both Rembrandt and Lievens, Huygens wrote, were so immersed in their work – he mentions mainly history pieces – that he feared for their health. His only disappointment was that neither of them saw the point of visiting Italy to study the works of Raphael, Michelangelo and other great masters. Defying a time-honoured practice, they argued that they were unable to spare the time and that there was sufficient Italian art to be seen in the countries north of the Alps.

From Orlers we learn that Rembrandt moved to Amsterdam in about 1630, attracted by the increasing number of commissions he was receiving for portraits and other work.[21] In documents of 1632, 1634 and 1635 Rembrandt gave his address as that of Hendrick Uylenburgh of St Anthonisbreestraat in Amsterdam,[22] into whose house he is generally assumed to have moved in 1630 or 1631. However, it was recently suggested that he may have stayed with Uylenburgh on several occasions, but kept his Leiden studio until 1633.[23] Uylenburgh (1587–1661) was an

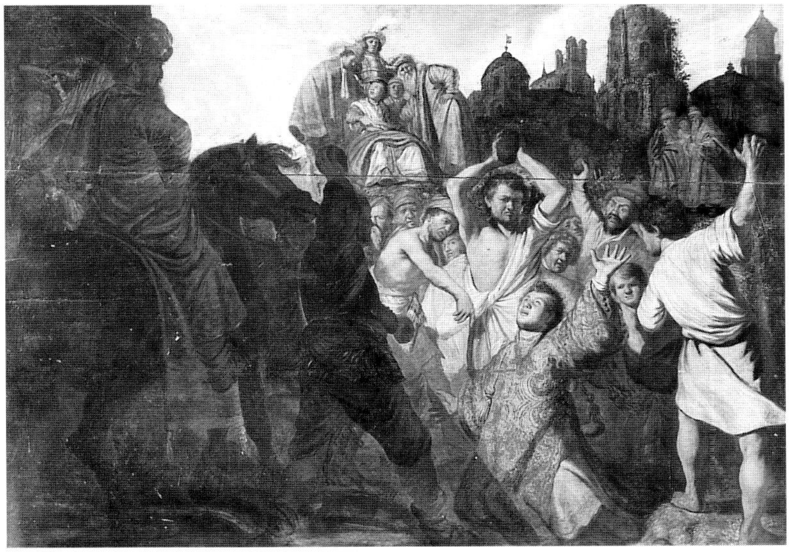

FIG. 1
Rembrandt
The Stoning of Stephen
Signed and dated 1625
Panel
89.5 x 123.6 cm
Musée des Beaux-Arts de Lyon, Lyon

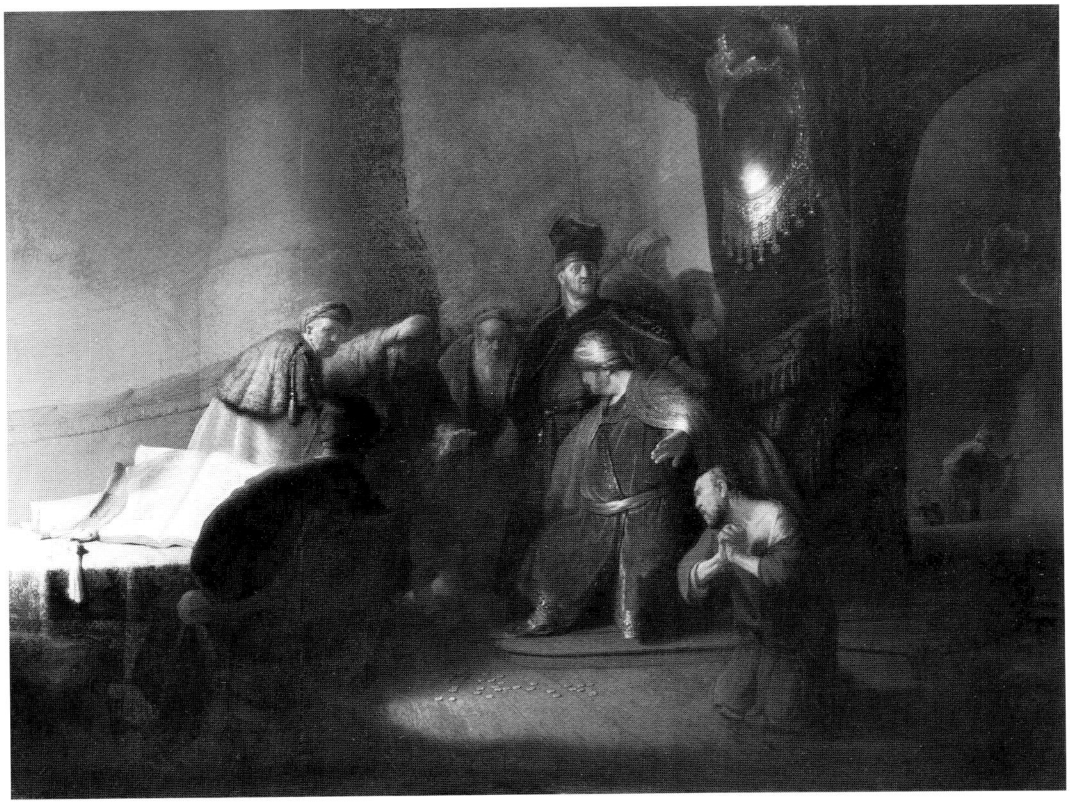

FIG. 2
Rembrandt
Judas Repentant, Returning the Pieces of Silver
Signed and dated 1629
Panel
79.0 x 102.3 cm
Private collection, England

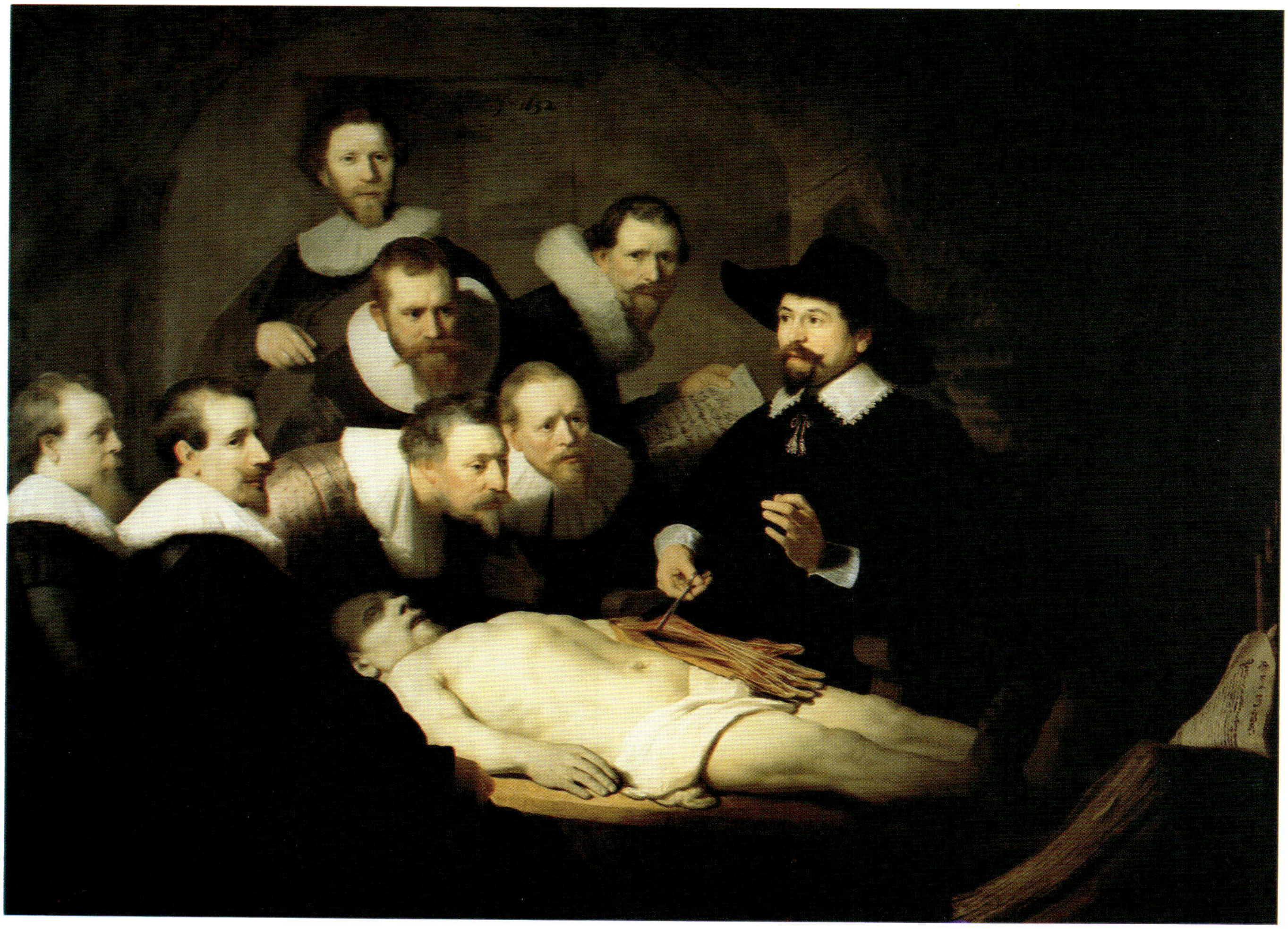

FIG. 3
Rembrandt
The Anatomy Lesson of Nicolaes Tulp
Signed and dated 1632
Canvas
169.5 x 216.5 cm
Mauritshuis, The Hague
Photograph: © Mauritshuis, The Hague, inv. no. 146

art dealer, who also had painters in his employ. It is not clear what position Rembrandt occupied in his enterprise, but he may have been responsible for supervising assistants, who presumably made copies of paintings, including of Rembrandt's own *tronies*.[24]

In the early 1630s, Rembrandt himself produced numerous portraits to order. Most of his commissions came from prosperous merchants, many of whom he may have met through Uylenburgh.[25] He received his first order for a group portrait from the Amsterdam chamber of the Surgeons' Guild, for whom he executed the *Anatomy Lesson of Nicolaes Tulp* (fig. 3).[26] The stadholder's court in The Hague also made use of Rembrandt's services, probably on Constantijn Huygens's recommendation. In 1632, for instance, Rembrandt painted a portrait of Princess Amalia van Solms, wife of Prince Frederik Hendrik (fig. 4).[27] The picture is listed in the stadholder's inventory of 17 February 1632, together with three history pieces, also by Rembrandt.[28] In 1632/33 he painted a *Crucifixion* and a *Descent from the Cross* for the stadholder.[29] His patron was evidently pleased with the work, as he promptly ordered an *Ascension*, an *Entombment* and a *Resurrection* in the same format.[30] However, it took three years for the first of these paintings to arrive and no fewer than six for the other two.[31]

It would be interesting to know whether Rembrandt, whose oeuvre includes so many biblical scenes, had any religious affiliation himself.[32] Baldinucci, the only early author to touch on the subject, reports in 1686 that Rembrandt was a member of the Mennonite Church, a Protestant movement to which the Catholic Baldinucci would have been violently opposed. None of the extant documents, however, provide any clues.[33]

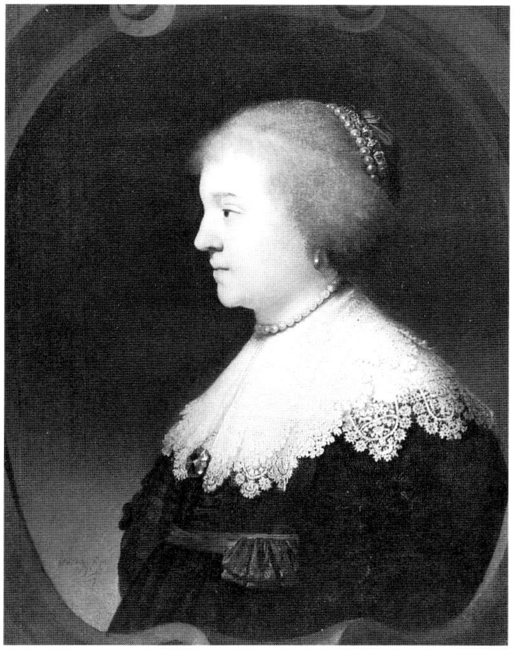

FIG. 4
Rembrandt
Portrait of Princess Amalia van Solms
Signed and dated 1632
Canvas
68.5 x 55.5 cm
Musée Jacquemart-André, Paris
(see also fig. 21a)

In June 1633 Rembrandt was betrothed to Saskia van Uylenburgh (1612–1642), the daughter of a former burgomaster of Leeuwarden and an orphan from the age of twelve (fig. 5).[34] Saskia was the niece of Hendrick Uylenburgh, and belonged to the Reformed branch of the family. Rembrandt and Saskia were married in Friesland in 1634.[35] They took lodgings in Uylenburgh's house until the following year, when they moved to a rented home of their own in Nieuwe Doelenstraat.

From 1635 Rembrandt is known to have collected art. Collecting was an interest he pursued for the rest of his life – regardless of the state of his finances. He attended auctions and public sales, where he bought prints, drawings, paintings and marble sculptures.[36] Though he subsequently sold some of these works, he would certainly have used the prints for study purposes. In addition to art he collected shells and other natural objects, as well as miscellaneous curiosa. His classicist biographers, disapproving of his choices in this as in so many other areas, describe his studio as a room crammed with old weapons, fabrics and 'frayed collars' (rafelkragen),[37] the items he evidently called his 'antiques'.[38] Many of his contemporaries, however, spoke with great admiration of his 'encyclopaedic collection'.[39]

In 1637 Rembrandt and Saskia moved from the Nieuwe Doelenstraat to another rented home, this time to 'de Suyckerbackerij' ('the Sugar Bakery') on Binnen Amstel. In January 1639, however, Rembrandt signed the deed of sale for a prestigious mansion in St Anthonisbreestraat (fig. 6).[40] In the same month he finally delivered the *Entombment* and *Resurrection* that the stadholder Prince Frederik Hendrik had ordered in 1633. The consignment was accompanied by a request that payment be made as promptly as possible, from which it seems that Rembrandt needed the money for the deposit of 1,200 guilders on his house.[41] He and Saskia moved into their new home in May 1639. Rembrandt

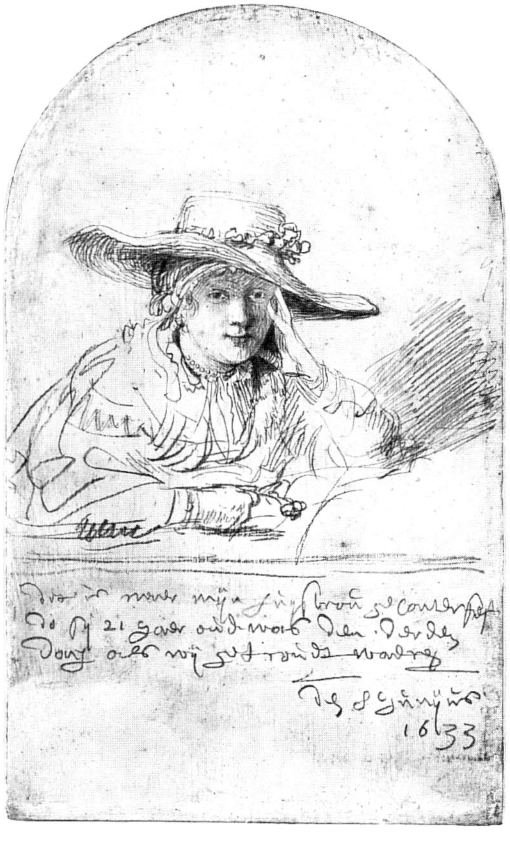

FIG. 5
Rembrandt
Portrait of Saskia
Dated 1633
Silverpoint on vellum
18.5 x 10.7 cm
Staatliche Museen zu Berlin, Kupferstichkabinett
(see also p. 328, fig. 10)

converted the attic into a workplace for the numerous pupils he was now teaching, erecting screens to create separate spaces for them.[42]

In 1642 Rembrandt completed his group portrait of *The Company of Captain Frans Banning Cocq*, better known as *The Night Watch*, which has long been his most famous work (fig. 7).[43] It was displayed in the newly built Calivermen's Hall, together with portraits of the other five companies of the Amsterdam civic guard. Considered in this context, Rembrandt's work stands out as a relatively unconventional piece, and as a far less formal portrait than those by his fellow artists (Joachim von Sandrart, Govaert Flinck, Nicolaes Eliasz (called Pickenoy), Jacob Adriaensz Backer and Bartholomeus van der Helst).

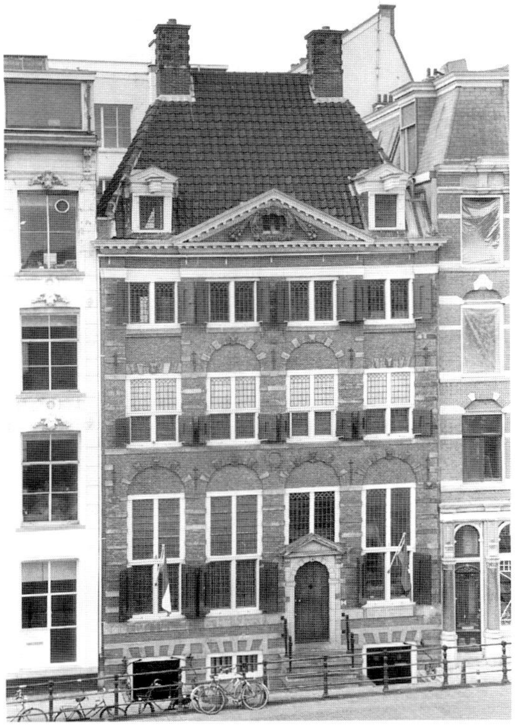

FIG. 6
The Rembrandthuis, at what is today Jodenbreestraat 6, opened as a museum in 1911. Photograph: Museum het Rembrandthuis, Amsterdam

FIG. 7
Rembrandt
The Company of Captain Frans Banning Cocq
(*The Night Watch*)
Signed and dated 1642
Canvas
363.0 x 437.0 cm
Rijksmuseum, Amsterdam

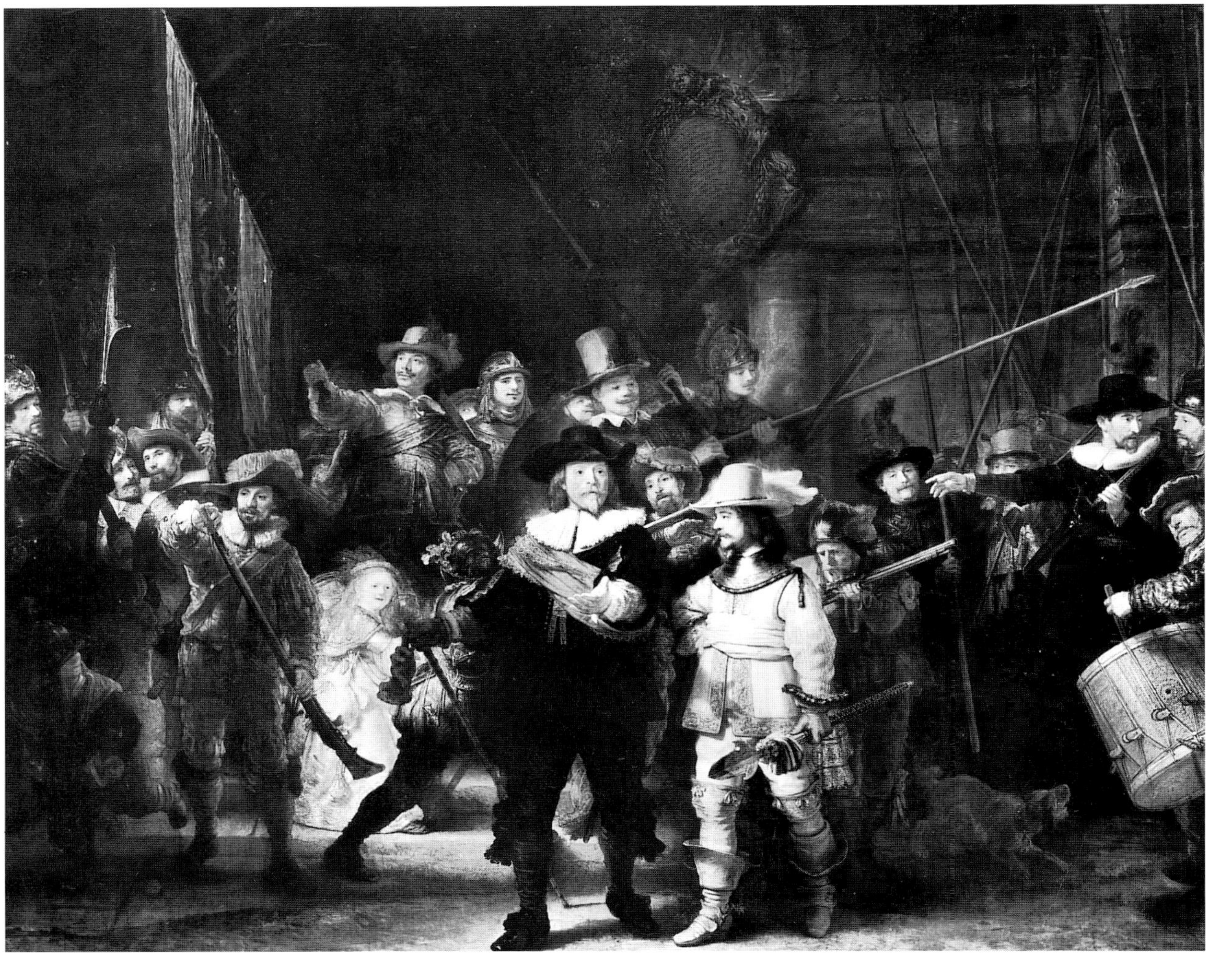

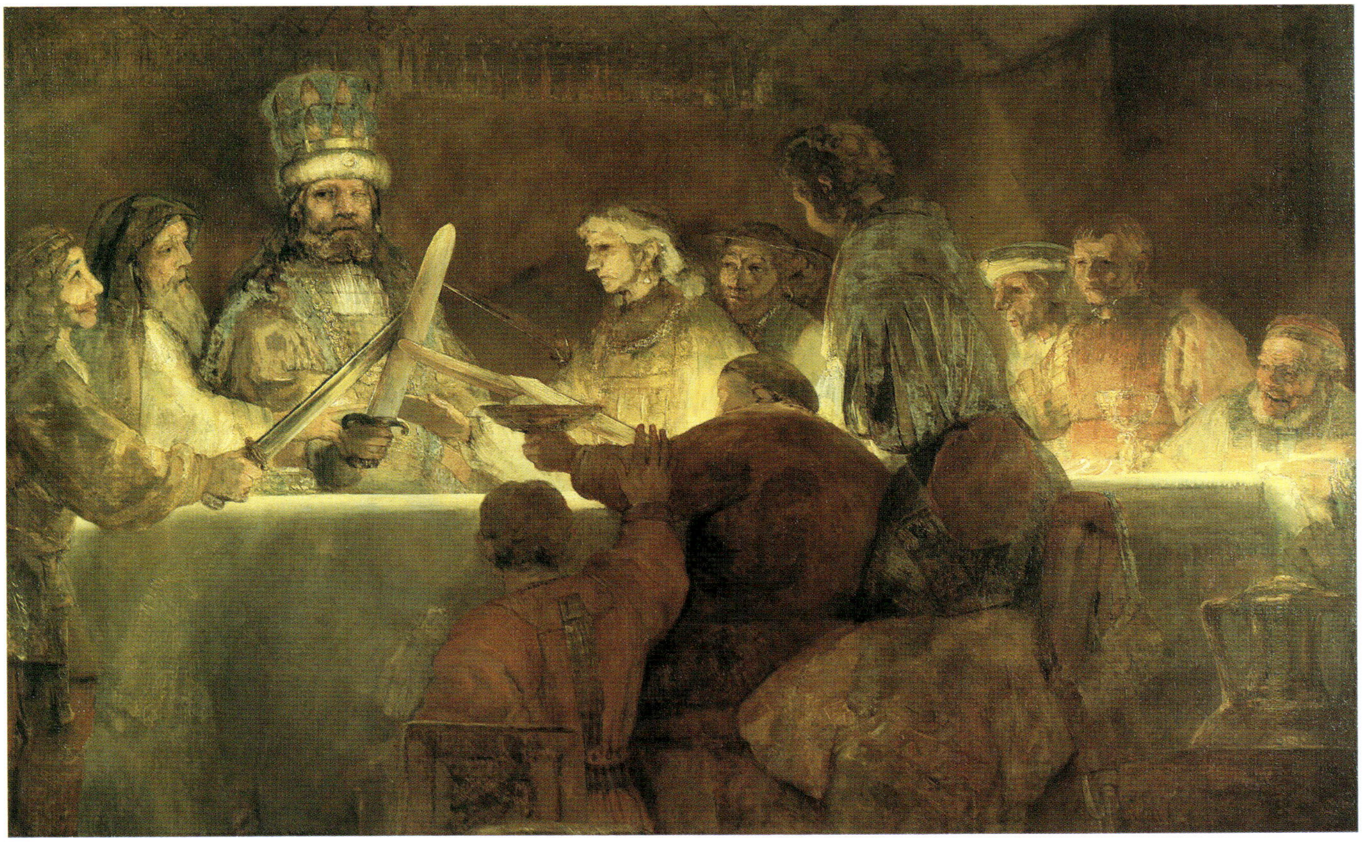

FIG. 9
Rembrandt
The Conspiracy of the Batavians under Claudius Civilis in the Schakerbos
Canvas (fragment)
196.0 x 309.0 cm
Nationalmuseum, Stockholm
Photograph: Nationalmuseum, SKM, Stockholm

FIG. 8
Rembrandt
Aristotle Contemplating the Bust of Homer
Signed and dated 1653
Canvas
143.5 x 136.5 cm
The Metropolitan Museum of Art, New York

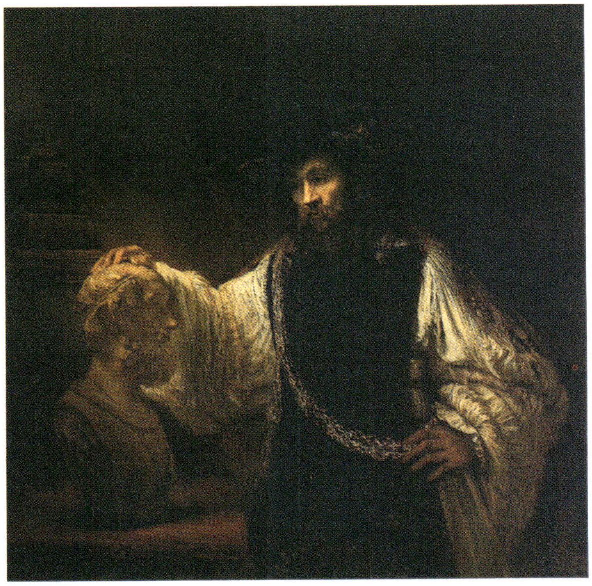

A son, Titus, was born in September 1641, while Rembrandt was still working on this commission.[44] Saskia had previously given birth to three other children, none of whom had survived for more than three months.[45] She herself died on 14 June 1642, when Titus was barely nine months old. The child was entrusted to the care of Geertje Dircx (1600/15–1656?),[46] the widow of a ship's trumpeter from Edam, who moved into Rembrandt's home.

Geertje is believed to be the 'peasant girl from Raarep or Ransdorp in Waterland', whom Houbraken describes as 'rather small but well-proportioned and plump', and whom he mentions as Rembrandt's wife.[47] The couple appear to have had an affair in the 1640s, but were never officially married. In 1648 Geertje drew up a will naming Titus as her beneficiary. He was to receive all her jewellery and property, with the exception of clothing and household linen.[48]

Geertje left Rembrandt's home for unknown reasons in June 1649, after committing him to a contract whereby she was to receive 160 guilders on the spot and 60 guilders a year thereafter. She in turn undertook to make no further claims and not to change the provisions of her will.[49] Yet three months later she lodged a petition against Rembrandt at the Chamber of Matrimonial Affairs at the Amsterdam Town Hall. Rembrandt received three summonses before finally appearing in court to answer Geertje's charges. Geertje alleged that he had 'slept with her on several occasions' and had promised to marry her. Rembrandt, however, denied having made any promise and refused to admit to her other accusation, arguing that 'the plaintiff herself [had] raised this point' and should be required to produce evidence in support of her claim.[50] He was nevertheless ordered to pay 'maintenance' of 200 guilders a year, while Geertje was to leave all her possessions, including a diamond ring (a gift from Rembrandt?), 'in free and unencumbered condition' at her death.[51]

After all this, the matter still was not settled. Following a statement made by her neighbours in July 1650, Geertje was committed to the Spinhuis in Gouda, a remand centre for women. She may perhaps have violated the terms of the agreement and sold her jewellery at a pawn-shop.[52] Six years later, witnesses testified that Rembrandt had not only paid the costs of her transport to Gouda, but that in 1655 he had also sought her parents' consent to have her detained for a further eleven years.[53] Moreover, he was said to have threatened Geertje's friend Trijn Jacobs of Edam, who tried to intervene on Geertje's behalf in 1655.[54] Despite Rembrandt's efforts to obstruct her, Trijn Jacobs managed to secure her friend's release from the Spinhuis on 31 May that year, almost five years after her detention.[55]

Since this affair first came to light through the discovery of several documents in the nineteenth century, authors have generally sought to cover up Rembrandt's role or to justify his behaviour. Geertje Dircx, for instance, was said to be 'mentally unstable'.[56] Only in 1965 were all the relevant documents published in full.[57]

By the time Geertje Dircx left Rembrandt's home in 1649, Hendrickje Stoffels (1626–1663), also known as Hendrickje Jeghers, had already entered Rembrandt's service.[58] In June 1654, when she was found to be carrying his child, she was ordered to appear before the consistory of the Reformed Church, of which she was evidently a member. She did so only after receiving four summonses,[59] and was 'punished severely, ordered to penitence and banned from the communion table'[60] for 'committing fornication with the painter Rembrandt'.[61] The child she was carrying was christened Cornelia on 30 October.[62] Documents refer to Hendrickje as Rembrandt's 'wife' (huysvrouw), as though the couple were married.[63] The fact that they were not officially husband and wife was probably due to a clause in Saskia's will, which provided that Titus was to inherit her share of the property she had held jointly with Rembrandt if the artist ever remarried.[64] By now Rembrandt's financial predicament was such that, if he had indeed remarried, he would not have been able to pay the sum (approximately 20,000 guilders) that Titus would have been entitled to receive.

In 1653 Rembrandt still owed money on the mortgage on his house, towards which he had made no payments since 1649. Anxious to conclude the transaction once and for all, the vendor asked Rembrandt to settle the outstanding sum of 7,000 guilders plus the interest due.[65] Rembrandt was forced to scrape the money together by borrowing wherever he could, thereby accumulating further liabilities. In order to obtain cash he organized a four-week sale of his possessions at the Keizerskroon tavern in December 1655,[66] but failed to raise enough to cover his debts. In July 1656 he applied to the Supreme Court in The Hague for a *cessio bonorum*.[67] This meant that he relinquished his property and effects in order for them to be distributed among his creditors, but it also afforded him the court's protection against further claims by those same creditors. The Bankruptcy Chamber compiled an inventory of all his paintings, furniture and household effects, which were then, together with his house, sold at auction between 1656 and 1659.[68]

Rembrandt himself attributed his misfortune to 'losses suffered in business and damage and losses [caused] by the sea'.[69] In fact it seems he was probably inclined to spend more than he earned, and he may also have made some risky investments.[70] In the end he was incurring new debts simply to settle old ones. Moreover, the economy in general went into recession in the 1650s. In Amsterdam, for instance, an unprecedented 104 bankruptcies were registered in 1656 alone.[71]

Dudok van Heel recently suggested that, by the standards of the day, Rembrandt's conduct of his affairs in this instance may not have been entirely honourable. He made no effort to negotiate acceptable terms with his creditors, but confronted them with his bankruptcy as a *fait accompli*. Moreover, he made an unsuccessful attempt to salvage the title to his house by conveying it to Titus before declaring himself insolvent.[72]

Rembrandt, Hendrickje, Titus and Cornelia must have left the house in St Anthonisbreestraat at the beginning of 1658. They moved to a considerably humbler dwelling on Rozengracht in the Jordaan, a neighbourhood which had recently gained a large population of artists. In 1660, Hendrickje and Titus, who was now sixteen years old, formed a partnership and started a new art business together. A contract was drawn up whereby Rembrandt was to 'live with them, receive free board, and be exempt from housekeeping expenses and rent', in return for which he was to assist them by every means possible.[73] His official status as being in the employ of Hendrickje and Titus protected him from further claims from any still unsatisfied creditors.

In spite of his reduced circumstances, Rembrandt continued to receive prestigious commissions throughout the 1650s and 1660s. One example was his painting of *Aristotle Contemplating the Bust of Homer*, a work he made on request in 1653 for the Sicilian nobleman and collector Don Antonio Ruffo (fig. 8).[74] He received a fee of 500 guilders and orders for two more pictures (see commentary to cat. no. 15). In 1656 he made a second group portrait for the Amsterdam Surgeons' Guild, *The Anatomy Lesson of Joan Deyman* (the only surviving fragment of which is now at the Amsterdam Historical Museum).[75] In 1661 he was invited to contribute to the decoration of the new Amsterdam Town Hall in Dam Square. His former pupil Govaert Flinck had initially been commissioned to produce fourteen paintings of scenes of the Batavian rebellion against the Romans in AD 69, to decorate the galleries of this monumental building. However, as Flinck died shortly after completing his design sketches for the project, the work was divided among Jacob Jordaens, Jan Lievens and Rembrandt. Rembrandt was to paint the *Conspiracy of Claudius Civilis* in one of the lunettes in the galleries. It appears from a description of 1662 that this immense canvas (545 x 545 cm) was hanging in the Town Hall at the time.[76] However, the picture had vanished by the autumn of that year, and it seems that Rembrandt was never paid for his work.[77] His pupil Jurriaen Ovens was awarded the commission to work up Flinck's original sketch. It would appear that Rembrandt had failed to complete his task to satisfaction, although the reasons for the dissatisfaction with his picture are unknown.[78] A remaining fragment of the work is now at the Nationalmuseum in Stockholm (fig. 9).[79] Another important commission Rembrandt received was the painting he made for the syndics of the Drapers' Guild in 1662. It was to be his last portrait of regents (fig. 10).[80] Notwithstanding these and various other commissions, however, including some for portraits, Rembrandt was beleaguered by financial problems for the rest of his life.

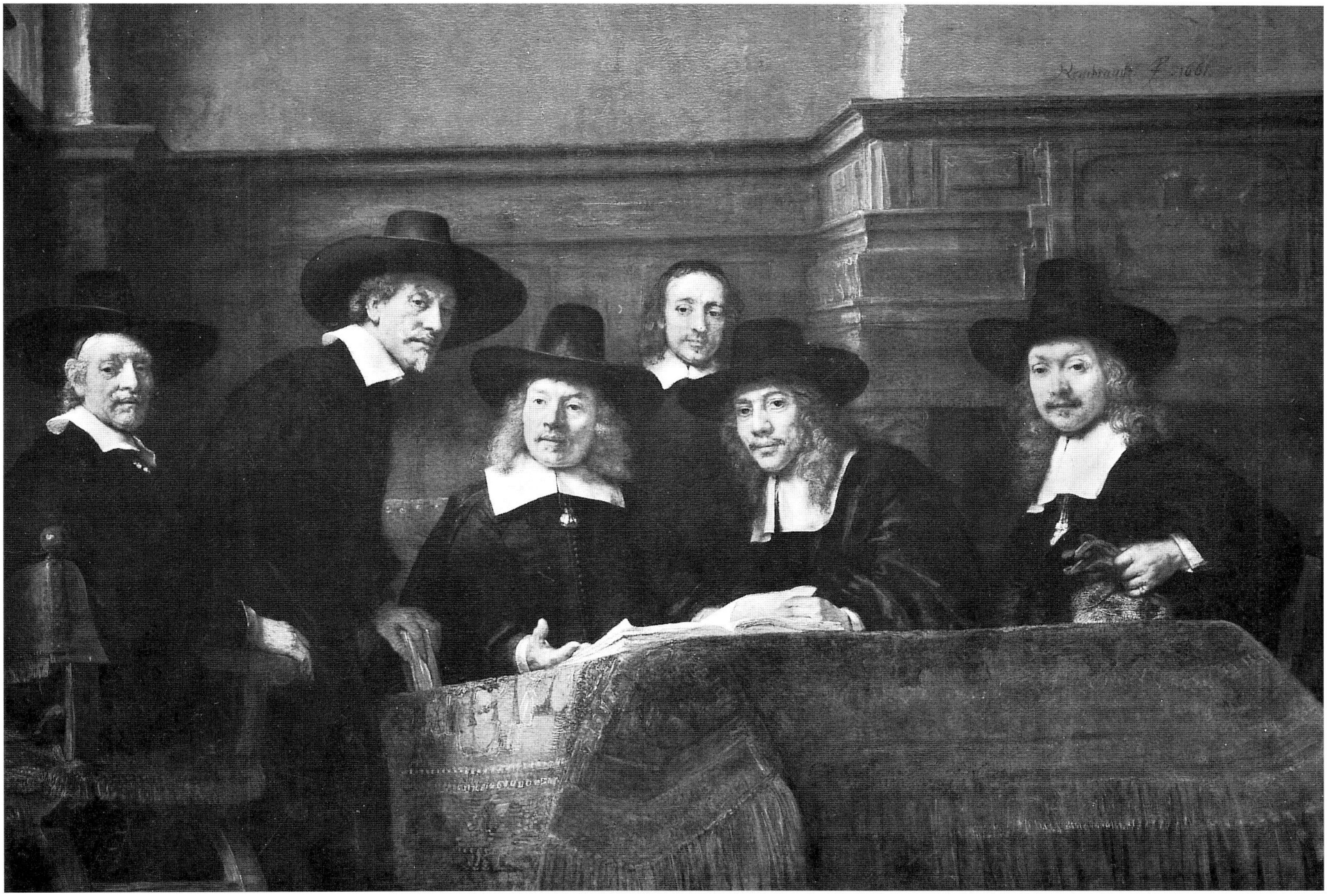

FIG. 10
Rembrandt
The Syndics
Signed and dated 1662
Canvas
191.5 x 279.0 cm
Rijksmuseum, Amsterdam

After Hendrickje's death during a plague epidemic in 1663, the now adult Titus continued to run the art business on his own. He himself died five years later, only six months after his marriage and six months before the birth of his daughter Titia.[81] Rembrandt survived his son for less than a year. He died on 4 October 1669 and was buried in the Westerkerk on 8 October 1669.[82] By then he was known as an artist of stature throughout Europe.[83]

1 Strauss & Van der Meulen 1979, p. 217, no. 1641/8 (Orlers 1641, p. 375).

2 On the appreciation of Rembrandt over the years, see Slive 1953; see also (more recently) Boomgaard & Scheller 1991–92.

3 Hofstede de Groot 1906a, nos 329 (Sandrart 1675), 338–343 (Van Hoogstraten 1678), 352 (Pels 1681), 358 (Félibien 1684), 360 (Baldinucci 1686), 381 (Piles 1699), 395 (Lairesse 1707), 407 (Houbraken 1718–21, vol. I, 1718).

4 Hofstede de Groot 1906a, p. 422, no. 360 (Baldinucci 1686). Baldinucci obtained his information from Bernard Keil, who had been apprenticed to Rembrandt for eight years in the 1640s. The *Vocabolario degli Accademici della Crusca* (Venice, 1612) gives as a definition for 'umorista': 'E ad huomo fantastico, ed incostante, il che gli e' cagionato dagli umori stemperati, e predominanti, diciamo Umorista'; see also Tommaseo & Bellini 1865–79, vol. IV, 1879, p. 1661. More or less in line with this, Baldinucci's words have been variously taken to mean 'unconventional and morose', 'temperamental', and even 'melancholy, unpleasant and cantankerous' (by, respectively, Kolloff 1854, p. 420, and Six 1925, p. 232; Goldscheider 1960, p. 23; and Gherardini 1878, p. 203). The author is indebted to Dr H. Hendrix, University of Utrecht.

5 Scheltema 1853.

6 Scheltema 1853, pp. 16–17: 'If one thing has emerged from this study that fills me with pleasure, it is the discovery once and for all that these scurrilous rumours are deceitful fabrications'.

7 See also Vosmaer 1877, ch. XLI ('L'Homme').

8 Veth 1906, p. 128.

9 See, for example, Gonnet 1920; Vis 1965, pp. 125–31, 138–9.

10 Strauss & Van der Meulen 1979. Unlike Hofstede de Groot 1906a, however, this publication does not include documents from after 1669, the year of Rembrandt's death. Though now a standard work, the book contains numerous inaccuracies; see, for example, Broos 1981–82.

11 Schwartz 1984, p. 363.

12 Orlers 1641, p. 375.
13 Orlers 1641, p. 375.
14 Strauss & Van der Meulen 1979, p. 51, no. 1620/1. Rembrandt may have registered well in advance, as many people did in Leiden (Dudok van Heel 1991–92c, p. 53). Alternatively, he or his parents may have been interested in the non-academic benefits of being enrolled as a student at Leiden University, benefits that included exemption from service in the civic militia and an entitlement to untaxed beer and wine (Schwartz 1984, p. 21).
15 Orlers 1641, p. 375.
16 Houbraken 1718–21, vol. I, 1718, p. 254. In fact, Houbraken is more likely to have meant Jacob's brother Jan Pynas; see Bauch 1960, p. 122.
17 Bredius / Gerson 1969, no. 531A; *Corpus*, vol. I, 1982, no. A1.
18 This visit is widely believed to have taken place during Huygens's documented trip to Leiden in or before November 1628 (Worp 1911–17, vol. I, letter 412; Schneider / Ekkart 1973, p. 310). Huygens, however (see below), refers to Rembrandt's *Judas* which is dated 1629 (Worp 1897; Huygens / Kan 1946, p. 79).
19 Worp 1897; Huygens / Kan 1946, pp. 77–83.
20 Bredius / Gerson 1969, no. 539A; *Corpus*, vol. I, 1982, pp. 193–4, no. A15.
21 Orlers 1641, p. 375; see also Houbraken 1718–21, vol. I, 1718, p. 256.
22 Strauss & Van der Meulen 1979, pp. 87, 107, 116, nos 1632/2 (Rembrandt said that he 'ten huijse aldaer logeerde'), 1634/2 (Rembrandt said to be living 'op de Brestraet'), 1635/1 ('Rembrant van Rijn tot Hendrick Uylenburch').
23 Dudok van Heel 1991–92c, p. 54. Hinterding 1996, p. 25, endorsed this suggestion: 'the watermarks on the prints by Rembrandt and van Vliet seem to correspond to the very year with this version of events'.
24 Broos 1981–82, p. 252, suggested this. On the hypothesis that Rembrandt occupied a supervisory role in Uylenburgh's 'Accademia', see also Van de Wetering 1986, pp. 56–60.
25 Broos 1981–82, p. 252; Van de Wetering 1986, p. 58.
26 Bredius / Gerson 1969, no. 403; *Corpus*, vol. II, 1986, no. A51.
27 Bredius / Gerson 1969, no. 99; *Corpus*, vol. II, 1986, no. A61.
28 Strauss & Van der Meulen 1979, pp. 87–9, no. 1632/3. The history pieces in question are probably the *Proserpine* and *Minerva* at the Gemäldegalerie in Berlin (Bredius / Gerson 1969, nos 463, 466; *Corpus*, vol. I, 1982, nos A39, A38), and the *Simeon in the Temple* at the Mauritshuis in The Hague (Bredius / Gerson 1969, no. 543; *Corpus*, vol. I, 1982, no. A34), or possibly the *Simeon Speaking to Mary in the Temple* in Hamburg (our cat. no. 2).
29 Alte Pinakothek, Munich (Bredius / Gerson 1969, nos 548, 550; *Corpus*, vol. II, 1986, nos A69, A65). See Strauss & Van der Meulen 1979, p. 129, no. 1636/1.
30 Alte Pinakothek, Munich (Bredius / Gerson 1969, nos 557, 560, 561; *Corpus*, vol. III, 1989, nos A118, A126, A127).
31 Strauss & Van der Meulen 1979, pp. 129–33, 161–75, nos 1636/1, 1636/2, 1639/2–1639/7.
32 See, for example, Wijnman 1959, pp. 7–8.
33 Baldinucci obtained most of his information from the Danish painter Bernard Keil, who apparently worked with Rembrandt in the 1640s and subsequently spent a few years with Uylenburgh. Baldinucci may have drawn this conclusion himself, prompted by the fact that Hendrick Uylenburgh and some of Rembrandt's portrait clients were members of the Mennonite community (Baldinucci 1686, pp. 78–9).
34 Benesch 1973, vol. II, no. 427.
35 Strauss & Van der Meulen 1979, p. 110, no. 1634/5. The wedding was held in Sint Annaparochie, the village in which Saskia's sister Hiskia lived with her husband, Gerrit van Loo, Saskia's guardian since 1628 (Broos 1981–82, pp. 253–4).
36 Strauss & Van der Meulen 1979, esp. pp. 349–88, 583–4, nos 1656/12, 1669/3. The inventory of Rembrandt's effects, drawn up at the time of his bankruptcy in 1656, was first published in Smith 1829–42, vol. VII, 1836, pp. xli–liv.
37 Hofstede de Groot 1906a, no. 352 (Pels 1681); see also Baldinucci 1686, pp. 79–80.
38 Hofstede de Groot 1906a, no. 381, para. 3 (Piles 1699); Dezallier d'Argenville 1745–52, vol. II, 1745, p. 25.
39 For example, Sandrart 1675: 'deswegen er auch von vielen sehr hoch geschätzet und gepriesen worden' (Hofstede de Groot 1906a, p. 394, no. 329); see also Scheller 1969.
40 Strauss & Van der Meulen 1979, p. 159, no. 1639/1.
41 Strauss & Van der Meulen 1979, pp. 161–75, nos 1639/2–1639/7.
42 Strauss & Van der Meulen 1979, p. 412, no. 1658/3; cf. Houbraken 1718–21, vol. I, 1718, pp. 256–7.
43 Bredius / Gerson 1969, no. 410; *Corpus*, vol. III, 1989, no. A146.
44 Strauss & Van der Meulen 1979, p. 209, no. 1641/4.
45 Strauss & Van der Meulen 1979, pp. 124, 135, 155, 189, nos 1635/6, 1636/3, 1638/8, 1638/9, 1640/5, 1640/6.
46 Vis 1965, p. 53, estimates Geertje's date of birth as between 1610 and 1615; Dudok van Heel 1991–92c, p. 57, suggests a date between 1600 and 1610.
47 Houbraken 1718–21, vol. I, 1718, p. 272. See also Wijnman 1964, p. 151; Vis 1965, pp. 58–9; Blankert 1973, p. 39, note 46.
48 Strauss & Van der Meulen 1979, pp. 260–2, no. 1648/2.
49 Strauss & Van der Meulen 1979, p. 269, no. 1649/4.
50 Strauss & Van der Meulen 1979, pp. 267, 274–6, nos 1649/3, 1649/8, 1649/9.
51 Strauss & Van der Meulen 1979, pp. 270–3, no. 1649/6. The idea that the ring had been Saskia's has become a topos in biographies on Rembrandt, but I have found no evidence to this effect.
52 Strauss & Van der Meulen 1979, pp. 390–1, no. 1656/17.
53 Strauss & Van der Meulen 1979, pp. 339–42, nos 1656/4, 1656/5.
54 Strauss & Van der Meulen 1979, pp. 340–2, no. 1656/5.
55 Strauss & Van der Meulen 1979, p. 327, no. 1655/2.
56 Bredius & De Roever 1890, p. 175.
57 Vis 1965, pp. 67–72. Wijnman 1964 presents the first interpretation of this affair that does not attempt to spare Rembrandt.
58 Strauss & Van der Meulen 1979, p. 269, no. 1649/4.
59 Strauss & Van der Meulen 1979, pp. 318, 320, nos 1654/11, 1654/12, 1654/14, 1654/15.
60 Strauss & Van der Meulen 1979, p. 320, no. 1654/15.
61 Strauss & Van der Meulen 1979, p. 318, no. 1654/11.
62 Strauss & Van der Meulen 1979, p. 321, no. 1654/18.
63 Strauss & Van der Meulen 1979, pp. 491–2, no. 1661/12. Rembrandt openly acknowledged paternity at Cornelia's christening (Strauss & Van der Meulen 1979, p. 321, no. 1654/18).
64 Rembrandt had an inventory of his property drawn up five years after Saskia's death, in 1647. Vis 1965, pp. 60–1, suggests he may have done so in connection with his intention to marry Hendrickje, a prospect that even then was not feasible, if only for financial reasons. Vis further speculates that Geertje Dircx's jealousy in these circumstances may ultimately have precipitated her departure.
65 Strauss & Van der Meulen 1979, pp. 295–6, no. 1653/2.
66 Strauss & Van der Meulen 1979, pp. 331–3, no. 1655/7.
67 Strauss & Van der Meulen, pp. 345–7, no. 1656/10.
68 Strauss & Van der Meulen, pp. 349–88, 390, 402, 410–13, 419–22, 425–6, 429, 431–2, 435–6, nos 1656/12, 1656/15, 1657/7, 1658/5, –10, –12, –15, –16, –19, –21, –29, –30, –31, 1659/3.
69 Strauss & Van der Meulen 1979, p. 345, no. 1656/10: 'verliesen geleden in de negotie alsmede schaden ende verliesen bij der zee'. What Rembrandt meant by 'losses [caused] by the sea' is unclear; for a theory on this, see Dudok van Heel 1991–92c, p. 60.
70 Van Deursen 1991–92, p. 49; Broos 1981–82, p. 259. According to Smith, Rembrandt was said in his day to have been persuaded by Menasseh ben Israel and Ephraim Bonus to invest money in alchemy experiments. Smith believes that Rembrandt's bankruptcy was most likely due to 'indiscreet conduct in the management of his affairs' (Smith 1829–42, vol. VII, 1836, p. xxvii).
71 Strauss & Van der Meulen 1979, p. 389.
72 Dudok van Heel 1991–92c, p. 61; Strauss & Van der Meulen 1979, p. 342, no. 1656/6.
73 Strauss & Van der Meulen 1979, p. 463, no. 1660/20.
74 Bredius / Gerson 1969, no. 478.
75 Bredius / Gerson 1969, no. 414.
76 Fokkens 1662, p. 159; see Strauss & Van der Meulen 1979, pp. 499–502, 516–19, nos 1662/6, 1662/15.
77 Strauss & Van der Meulen 1979, pp. 499–502, no. 1662/6.

78 Blankert 1975a, p. 27, suggests that Rembrandt's design included 'too much bare, non-functional space' and provides references to other literature concerning possible reasons for the dissatisfaction with the picture.

79 Bredius / Gerson 1969, no. 482.

80 Bredius / Gerson 1969, no. 415.

81 Strauss & Van der Meulen 1979, pp. 575, 579–80, 583, nos 1668/2, 1668/8, 1669/1.

82 Strauss & Van der Meulen 1979, pp. 585, 589–90, nos 1669/4, 1669/6.

83 See the essay by Ernst van de Wetering in the present catalogue.

Looking at Rembrandt, Past and Present

ALBERT BLANKERT

I Rembrandt's 'ignoble selection'

This exhibition, *Rembrandt: A Genius and His Impact*, traces each stage of Rembrandt's development as a painter. The *Bust of a Man in a Gorget and Cap*, made in *c.*1626–27 when he was approximately twenty years old, is rendered in the lively mix of colours that characterizes his earliest works (cat. no. 1). He subsequently committed himself definitively to yellows and browns as a binding element in his compositions, employing them mostly against a dark background. These are the colours we still regard as 'Rembrandtesque'. Rembrandt first used them in finely executed paintings such as the *Two Old Men Disputing* of 1628 (cat. no. 3). After that he occasionally worked in broad brushstrokes that were visible on the painted surface – as, for instance, in the *Bearded Old Man* of *c.*1630 (cat. no. 4) – while in other paintings, such as the *Self-Portrait at the Age of 34* of 1640 (cat. no. 13), he continued to work in a highly detailed manner. The Rembrandt of later years, now painting primarily with broad brushstrokes, begins to emerge in the *Young Woman in Bed* from the latter half of the 1640s, although the ornament in the woman's hair is still executed with great finesse (cat. no. 14). The Rembrandt who applied thick paint with a wide, loaded brush and palette knife comes to the fore in the *Man in Armour* of 1655 (cat. no. 15). This piece was followed by typically late works, in which the artist applied the paint with a degree of freedom that was used and appreciated again only after 1860. In the exhibition, the evolution of Rembrandt's style and technique culminates in the *Portrait of an Elderly Man* of 1667 (cat. no. 28). This corpulent figure is a heavy and impressive presence, although these qualities, and the figure itself, are in fact merely suggested by patches of paint.

Rembrandt's ambition

It seems as though Rembrandt spent forty years exploring all the possibilities of paint, as is discussed in more detail in the catalogue entries on the individual paintings. His reasons for these investigations will always be the subject of debate. This introduction deals first with what appears to have been one of the master's most important guiding principles. The two sections that follow look at the way in which his contemporaries and later generations have viewed his work.

From the *Schilder-Boeck* (Painter's Book) of 1604 by the older Netherlandish painter and writer Karel van Mander, Rembrandt would have learned that the great Italian painter Titian had initially worked in a 'neat' manner and only later had begun to work 'with bold brushstrokes and dabbed patches' in pictures that were meant to be viewed from a distance. Ernst van de Wetering astutely argues that the passage in question from van Mander may have inspired Rembrandt to work in a refined manner at first and to adopt a broader style later. Indeed van Mander, echoing the words of Titian's Italian biographer, Giorgio Vasari, urges painters to employ a polished manner at an early age. A bold manner, he adds, is more difficult and is thus more suitable for when the artist has gained experience.[1]

The notion that Rembrandt, in this respect at least, may have been inspired by the example of the great Titian is not as far-fetched as it might seem. There is indeed evidence that Rembrandt aspired to measure himself against the greatest artists of earlier times. In opting for history painting, for example, he was choosing to work in what was considered, as we shall see, the most prestigious genre of all. Furthermore, he sought inspiration for his compositions from Michelangelo, Titian, Raphael, Leonardo, and other by then canonical masters of more than a century earlier.[2] The prevailing idea was that an artist with ambition did well to follow the example of these great sixteenth-century Italians. Rembrandt's compatriot of a generation earlier, the Flemish painter Peter Paul Rubens,

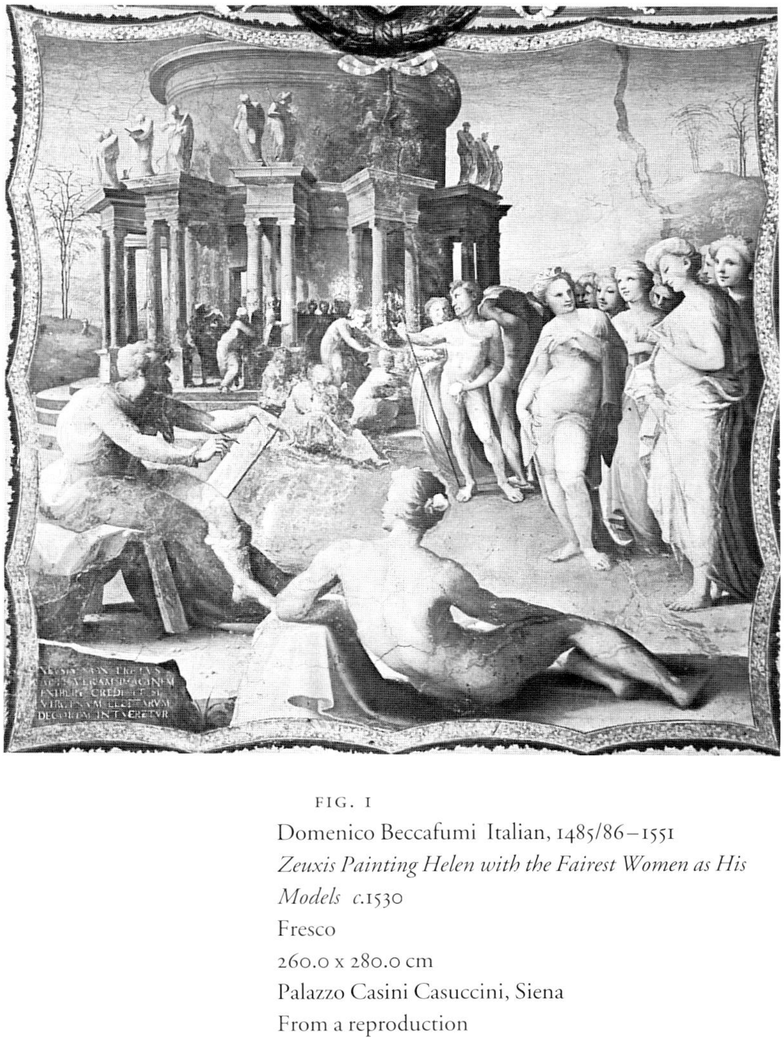

FIG. 1
Domenico Beccafumi Italian, 1485/86–1551
Zeuxis Painting Helen with the Fairest Women as His Models c.1530
Fresco
260.0 x 280.0 cm
Palazzo Casini Casuccini, Siena
From a reproduction

had done the same and with great success. In Rembrandt's youth, Rubens was renowned throughout Europe.

The Hague poet and diplomat Constantijn Huygens waxed lyrical about Rubens's 'divine talent'. At around the same time, when Rubens was well over fifty, Huygens discovered the genius of the young Rembrandt, who was then twenty-three years old. Huygens considered it 'lunacy of a kind' when Rembrandt and his fellow artist Jan Lievens told him they had no intention of travelling to Italy. With their talent, Huygens believed, they could surpass Raphael and Michelangelo, but to do so they would need to have seen the work of the great Italians at first hand. The reason offered by the youthful artists for their not visiting Italy was that they had ample opportunity to see Italian paintings closer to home, in countries north of the Alps.[3] It was indeed true that major examples of Italian art sometimes came onto the market in Holland (see commentary to cat. no. 13 and figs 13b, 13c). Apart from this, however, as far as the canonical Italians were concerned, Rembrandt had to make do with prints, and over his lifetime he acquired a huge collection of them. But prints could not convey a true impression of Michelangelo's Sistine Chapel, nor of Raphael's Stanze. It is impossible to imagine that Rubens's work as we know it could have existed without his actually having seen the original models.

Rembrandt's borrowings from the Italian masters are always obviously at second hand, and it should be emphasized here that he was apparently less interested in their works than were others. Though Rembrandt sought to achieve the stature of the luminaries, he did not share Rubens's desire to become a kind of 'Italian of the North'. What Rembrandt aspired to do was to adhere strictly to nature. He sought to achieve 'the maximum and most natural movement'. This is the only comment he is known to have made about his own art.[4] The classical, Italian ideal that Rubens pursued likewise required the artist to be true to life, but to select the noblest and most beautiful, and to depict nothing else. The artist pursuing this ideal could even transcend nature.

The story invoked in art literature since the Renaissance to illustrate this idea was that of the legendary Greek artist Zeuxis, who painted Helen, the most beautiful woman in the world. To capture her beauty, Zeuxis chose the fairest women in the city and proceeded to select the best features of each. Hence, through a process of 'noble selection', he created an idealized, preternaturally beautiful Helen.[5] Of the many tales that were known about Zeuxis, this is the only one to have been illustrated since the Renaissance (fig. 1).

Caravaggio, Ter Brugghen, and Rembrandt's naturalism

One Italian, in Rembrandt's day far more modern than Raphael or Titian, adamantly refrained from adopting the philosophy of 'noble selection'. Michelangelo da Caravaggio (1573–1610) painted, so it was said, purely from life. Karel van Mander was the first to publish his views on this approach. It was excellent, van Mander felt, to portray reality as did Caravaggio, providing one had the sense 'to discern and select that which is the most beautiful'.[6] Caravaggio was subsequently criticized in Italy for failing to do so. He came under attack, for instance, for choosing 'a dirty strumpet' to model for the figure of Mary in his *Death of the Virgin*.[7]

Caravaggio had followers in the Netherlands who were even less heedful of van Mander's advice to 'select that which is the most beautiful'. In the northern Netherlands, Caravaggism reached its height in the 1620s, with Utrecht as its centre. At the time, it set the tone for young artists working in the figure piece genre. Among them were the fledgling painters Rembrandt and Jan Lievens in Leiden. The Caravaggist influence is clear in Lievens's *Young Man Tuning a Violin* of *c.*1623, a picture strongly reminiscent of works by painters of the Utrecht School (cat. no. 33). In Rembrandt's case, it was the palette he chose a few years later – a palette we have now come to regard as 'Rembrandtesque' – that was inspired by the dramatic chiaroscuro of the Utrecht Caravaggisti. No less important, however, it seems to me, is the very specific lesson Rembrandt learned from these artists: that the best Italian art of recent

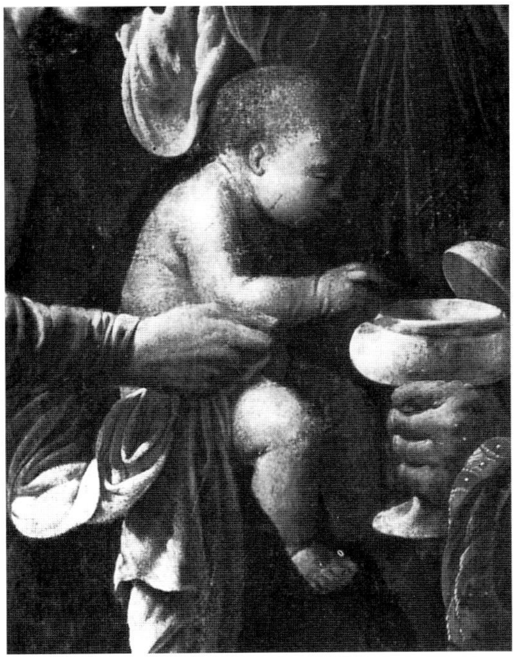

FIG. 2a
Hendrick ter Brugghen
The Adoration of the Kings 1619
(detail showing overpainting)

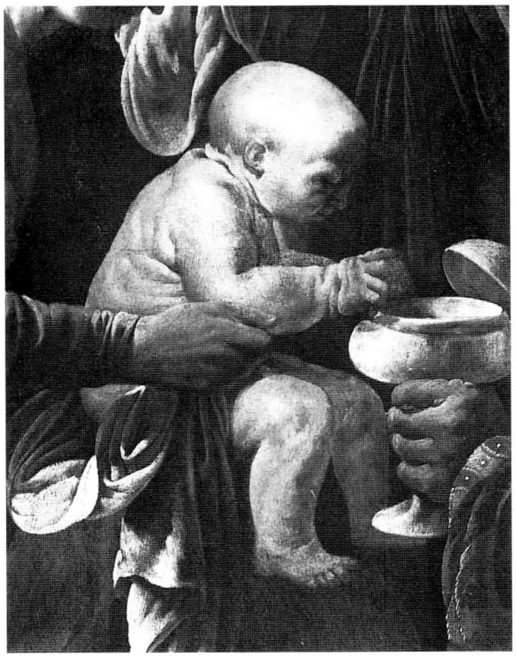

FIG. 2b
Hendrick ter Brugghen
The Adoration of the Kings
(detail showing area seen in fig. 2a, after restoration)

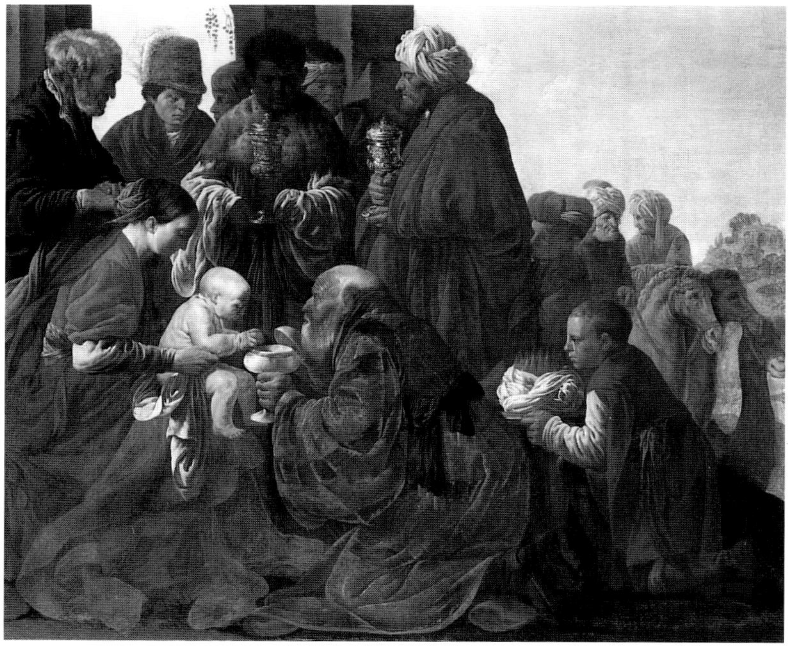

FIG. 2C
Hendrick ter Brugghen 1588–1629
The Adoration of the Kings
Signed and dated 1619
Canvas
134.0 x 160.0 cm
Rijksmuseum, Amsterdam
(the complete painting after restoration)

times could serve as an example of artists successfully depicting reality *without* having to make a 'noble selection'.

In 1619 the Utrecht Caravaggist Hendrick ter Brugghen painted an *Adoration of the Kings*, which the Rijksmuseum in Amsterdam bought in 1970 (fig. 2c). At the time, the Infant Christ appeared as a charming, Raphael-like putto (fig. 2a). When the canvas was cleaned, however, this figure was found to be painted over an entirely different child – arguably the ugliest Christ Child ever portrayed in a painting (fig. 2b).[8]

A similar anti-aesthetic naturalism can be seen in Rembrandt's *Ganymede Abducted by Jupiter* of 1635 (fig. 3). Here Rembrandt was seeking to achieve the 'maximum and most natural movement'. He wanted a true-to-life child, kicking, screaming and even urinating, out of sheer fear and anger. What one does *not* imagine from Rembrandt's painting is that Jupiter abducted Ganymede because he was 'inflamed with love' for him. The odious child seems an unlikely object for such passion. This 'ignoble selection' becomes even more obvious when the figure of Ganymede is compared with a celebrated version by one of Rembrandt's great Italian predecessors, Correggio (fig. 4). Rembrandt seems to have known Correggio's composition, presumably from a print. But the main difference between the two versions is that Correggio's Ganymede is a suitably attractive young man. That Rembrandt's Jupiter could be inflamed with passion for Ganymede is as paradoxical as the grotesque infant in ter Brugghen's *Adoration of the Kings* being a representation of God incarnate (fig. 2b). The anti-classical trend in seventeenth-century Dutch 'naturalism' is nowhere so explicit as in ter Brugghen and Rembrandt. They could not have been unaware of this fact, nor could it have escaped the attention of their contemporaries.

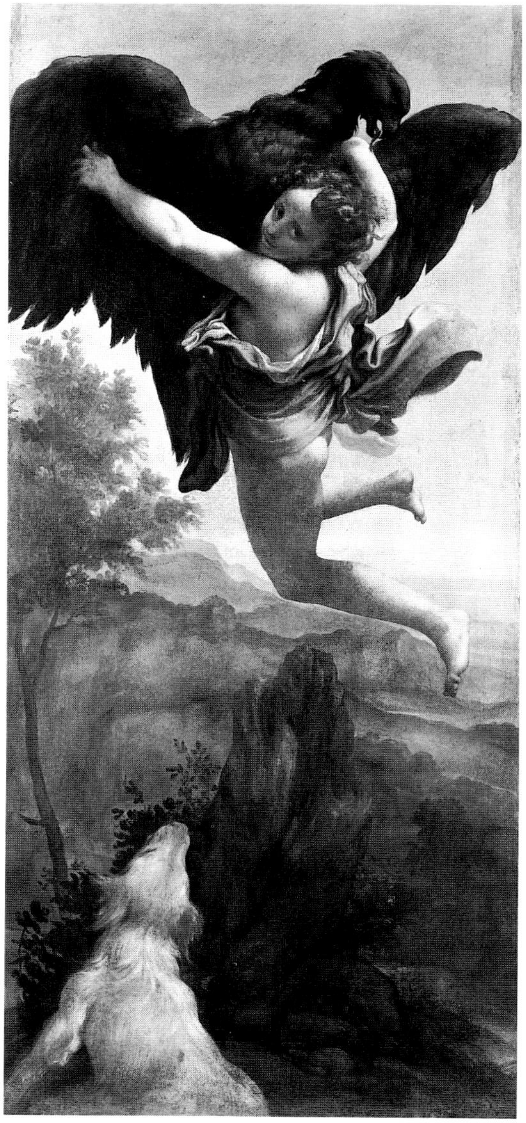

FIG. 4
Correggio Italian, *c.*1489–1534
*Ganymede Abducted by Jupiter c.*1531
Canvas
163.0 x 71.0 cm
Kunsthistorisches Museum, Vienna

In the present exhibition this naturalistic tendency in Rembrandt's work is evident in his *Susanna* (cat. no. 10). Susanna, who appears nude in the painting, was a woman of extraordinary beauty. In later centuries, in various places and at various times, Rembrandt's nude Susanna was in fact scorned for her 'ugliness'. It is difficult to imagine that tastes were so radically different in Rembrandt's day, but there is no contemporary evidence from which a conclusion can be drawn either way. The painting of a *Young Woman in Bed* has been interpreted in a variety of ways, but it is generally thought to have erotic implications (cat. no. 14) – in which case it is all the more difficult to understand why the woman has such coarse, rough-looking hands. Rembrandt's saint and apostle *Matthew* is portrayed as a labourer, unaccustomed, one would imagine, to holding the pen (cat. no. 22). A Rembrandt drawing of *Venus and Mars in Vulcan's Net* similarly de-idealizes its subject, which in this case was

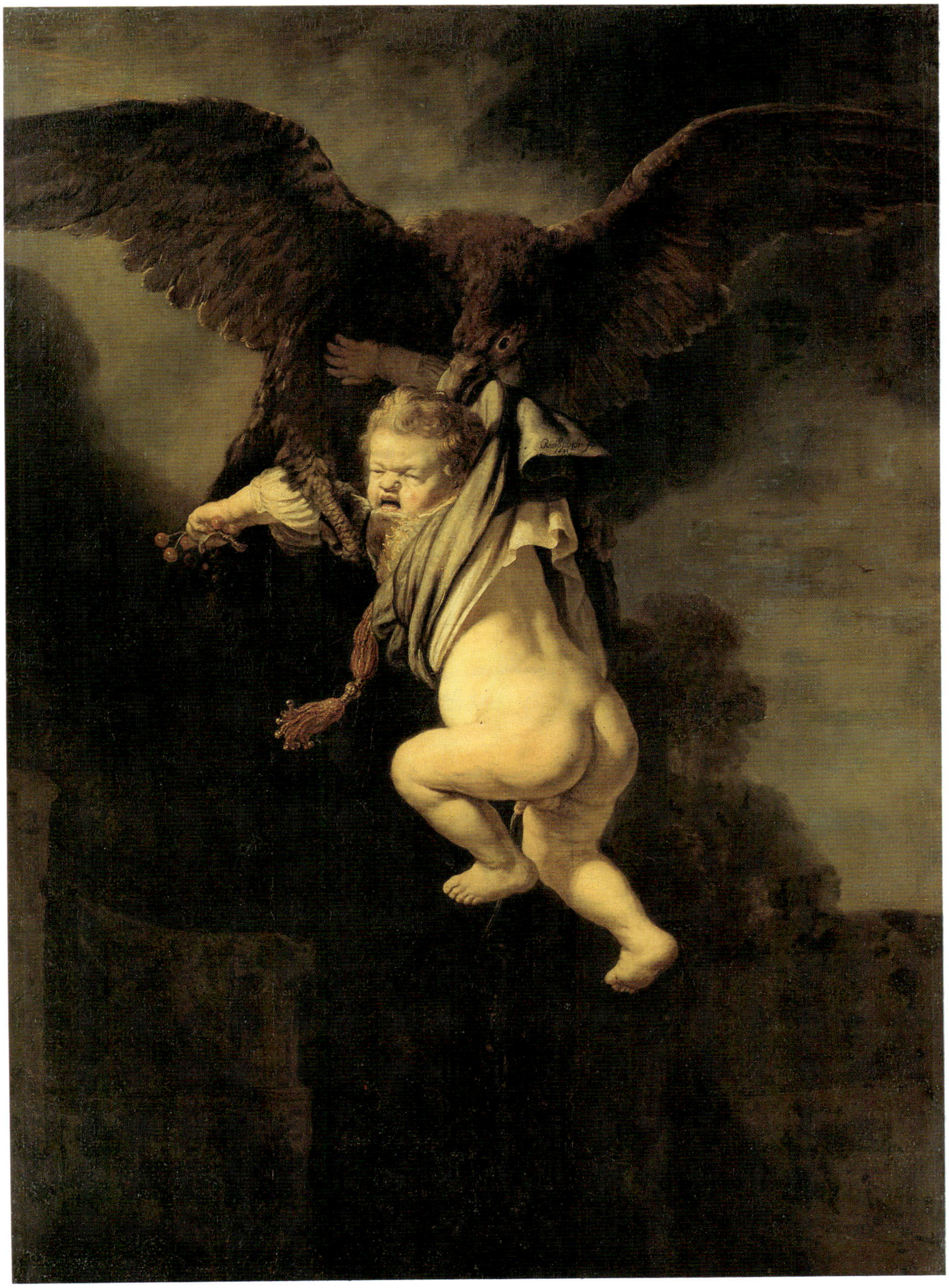

FIG. 3
Rembrandt
Ganymede Abducted by Jupiter
Signed and dated 1635
Canvas
177.0 x 130.0 cm
Staatliche Kunstsammlungen Dresden, Gemäldegalerie
Alte Meister

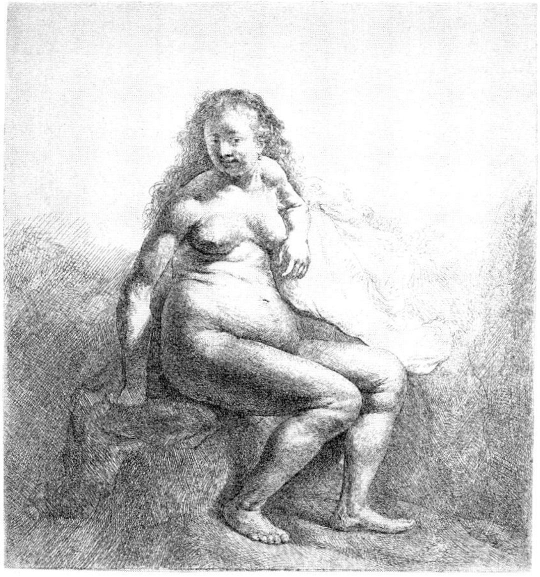

FIG. 5
Rembrandt
Naked Woman Seated on a Mound c.1631
Etching
17.7 x 16.0 cm
Rijksprentenkabinet, Rijksmuseum, Amsterdam
(our cat. no. 99)

probably taken from a print after Raphael (see cat. no. 78 and fig. 78a).

The catalogue entry on the etching of a *Naked Woman Seated on a Mound* of *c.*1631 (cat. no. 99) (fig. 5) cites the Dutch critic Andries Pels who, in 1681, twelve years after Rembrandt's death, commented on the artist's nudes:

> He [Rembrandt] chose no Greek Venus as his model
> But rather a washerwoman or a treader of peat from the barn
> And called this whim 'imitation of nature'
> Everything else was idle ornament. Flabby breasts
> Ill-shaped hands, nay, the traces of the lacings of the corsets on the stomach, of the garters on the legs
> Must be visible.

This is the earliest known criticism of Rembrandt's 'ignoble selection'.

Current opinion tends to the view that Rembrandt's nudes do in fact reflect the ideal of beauty in his own time (see commentary to cat. no. 10). However, this seems highly questionable. The engraver Wenceslaus Hollar made a copy after the *Naked Woman Seated on a Mound* directly after the etching was published (fig. 6). The fact that he did so reflects his admiration for Rembrandt, and particularly for his rendering of the woman's attitude and expression. Yet in my view Hollar also tried to 'correct' Rembrandt's work by making his own nude more attractive. He stylized the forms and modelled them more smoothly. The figure in Hollar's copy has a sleeker, tauter and less wrinkled abdomen, and her shins and calves are smoother. Younger and in better health than Rembrandt's figure, she reflects Hollar's attempt to improve on the original by making a more 'noble selection'.

Rembrandt's etching of *Adam and Eve Eating the Apple,* of 1638 (B.28), seems to accord with the dictum that 'the best painters are those who achieve the closest approximation of life' (fig. 7). This was the view expressed by a Dutch poet when Rembrandt was still a young man.[9] A century later, in 1713, another painter advised artists to fashion Adam and Eve 'after the most perfect beauty' – they were, after all, created in God's image. One should neither 'gape at nor copy the misshapen Adam and Eve portrayed in Rembrant van Rijn's print' (fig. 7).[10] In what was meant to be a descriptive catalogue of Rembrandt's etchings, Adam Bartsch in 1797 apparently felt compelled to air a similar view with regard to the print of Adam and Eve: 'As Rembrandt was completely unable to render nudes, this print is quite incorrect, and the heads are most unpleasant'.[11] Even the author of a recent newspaper article describes Adam's body as that of 'an old man'.[12] If this is how Rembrandt's figures have been perceived over three centuries, it seems highly improbable that they were judged any differently in the artist's own day.

Rembrandt was alone among the foremost Netherlandish masters of his day in portraying the 'ignoble' theme of a couple copulating, the subject of two etchings (B. 186, 187).[13] Equally unconventional are his etchings of a man and a woman urinating, with their genitals fully exposed (B. 190, 191). Far less explicit but nonetheless comparable is the famous painting of *A Woman Bathing* (fig. 8). The woman in this work has been taken for Susanna, Bathsheba, Diana and, recently, the nymph Callisto.[14] However, in 1988 van der Waals observed that a woman lifting her shift in this manner is a representation of a '*Mulier impudica*', a familiar image of immodesty at the time, inspired by a print after an antique sculpture.[15] The woman in Rembrandt's painting gazes at her reflection in the water, apparently pleased with what she sees.

Dürer and Rembrandt

It is interesting that Rembrandt's print of Adam and Eve (fig. 7) was inspired by an engraving by Albrecht Dürer (fig. 9).[16] One need only

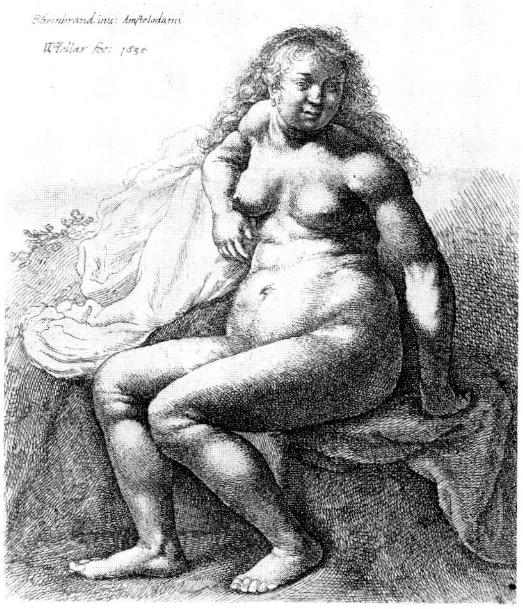

FIG. 6
Wenceslaus Hollar (Bohemian, 1607–1677), after Rembrandt
Naked Woman Seated on a Mound
Inscribed *Rheinbrand inv. Amstelodami / WHollar fec 1635*
Etching
8.6 x 6.9 cm
Museum Boijmans Van Beuningen, Rotterdam

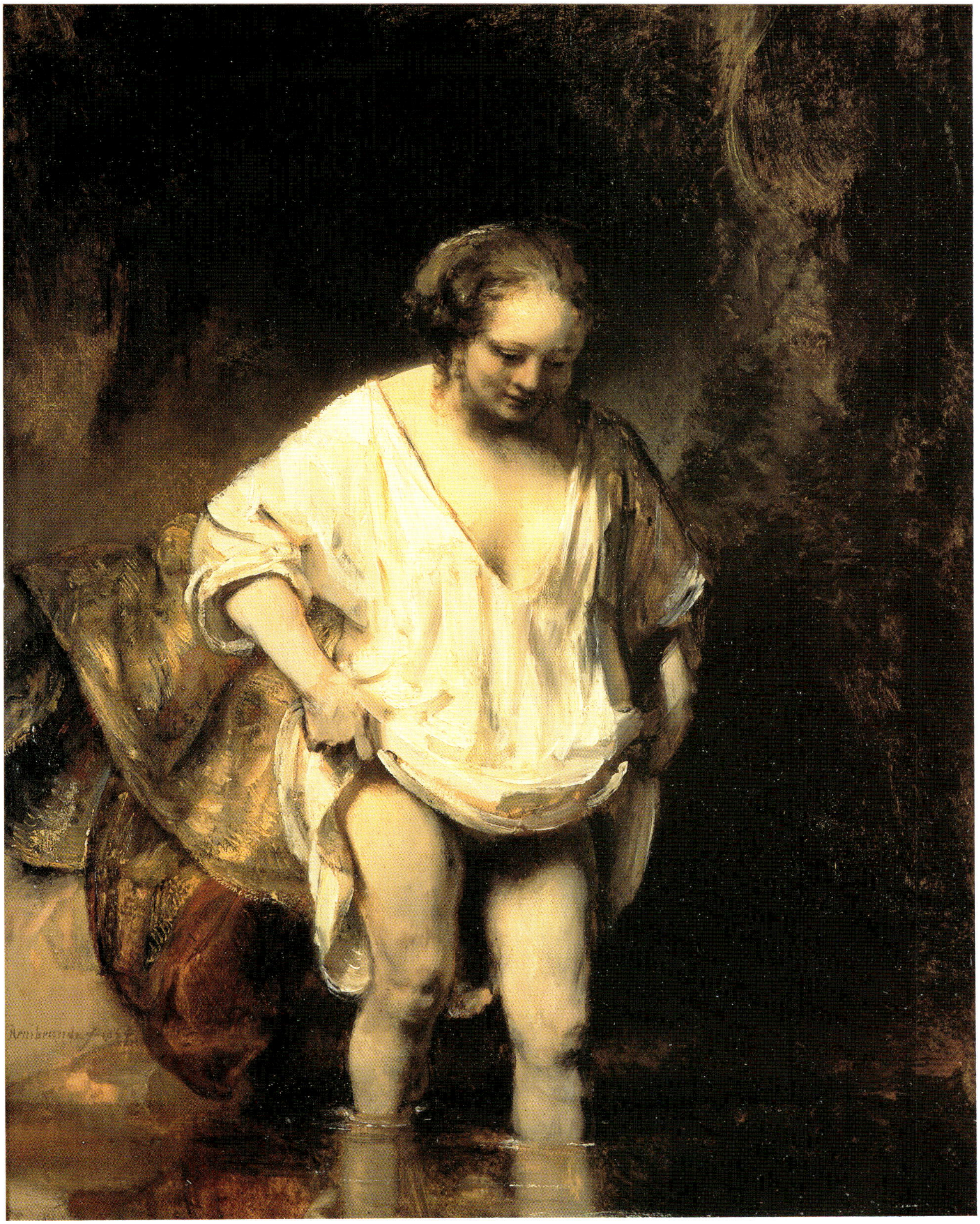

FIG. 8
Rembrandt
A Woman Bathing
Signed and dated 1654
Panel
61.8 x 47.0 cm
The Trustees of the National Gallery, London

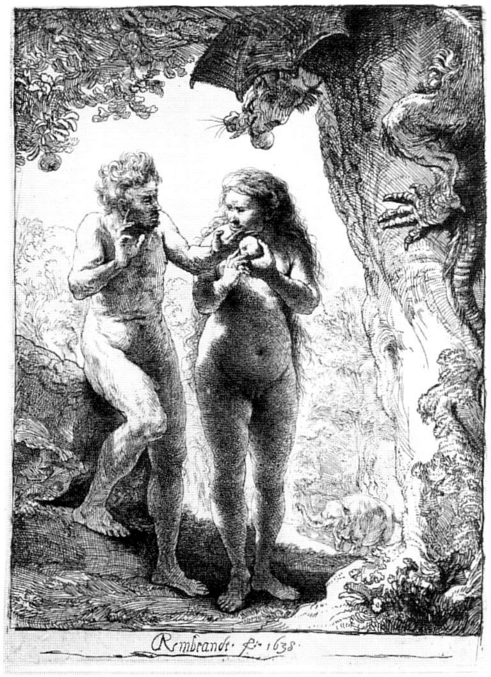

FIG. 7
Rembrandt
Adam and Eve Eating the Apple
Etching
16.2 x 11.6 cm
Rijksprentenkabinet, Rijksmuseum, Amsterdam

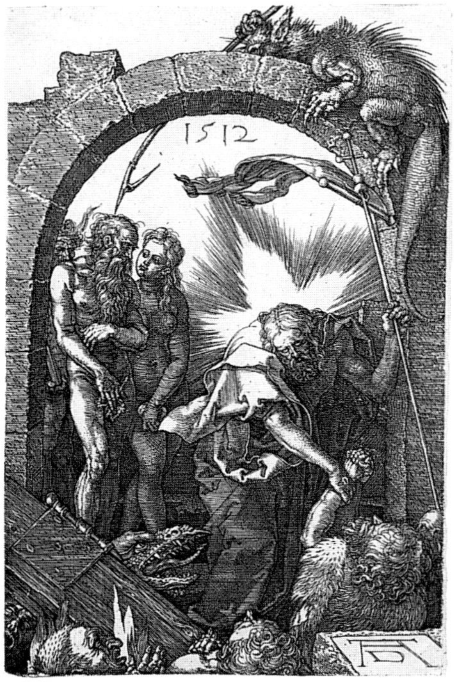

FIG. 9
Albrecht Dürer German, 1471–1528
Christ in Purgatory
Monogrammed and dated 1512
Engraving
11.7 x 7.5 cm
From a reproduction

look at the dragon-like demon at the upper right, which appears in the same attitude in both works. Dürer's influence has been detected in a further fifty or more paintings, etchings and drawings by Rembrandt.[17] At an auction held in 1638, Rembrandt bought no fewer than eight sets of Dürer's series of twenty woodcuts of the *Life of the Virgin*.[18] He was obviously a profound admirer of Dürer's work and turned to it as a source of inspiration.

In 1604 Karel van Mander had written of Dürer: 'He applied himself to the imitation of life in all he did, but without carefully seeking or selecting the most beautiful of the beautiful'.[19] This remark recalls his earlier comment on Caravaggio's naturalism – namely that one must 'discern and select that which is the most beautiful' – but with respect to Dürer van Mander is much more critical. Both Dürer and Caravaggio apparently favoured a form of naturalism that van Mander, who was oriented towards Renaissance Italy, found incompatible with true beauty. The Italian Vasari had been even more precise in his assessment of Dürer. He was unstinting in his praise, but nevertheless added that Dürer was 'compelled to draw his own pupils when he did nudes. These formed bad models, like most Germans, though they appear fine men enough when clothed'.[20]

Rembrandt loved Dürer's work, but would have been aware that it was criticized for showing the world as it was, without reflecting a process of 'noble selection'. We can probably assume that Rembrandt himself not only rejected this criticism, but was in fact inspired by it to follow a course similar to Dürer's. The great northern master of earlier times – Vasari was under the impression that Dürer lived in Antwerp – had already paved the way.

'The laughing painter': Rembrandt and Zeuxis

The ideas set out above cannot be proven, but we may assume that contemporary critics objected to Rembrandt's 'ignoble selection', or at least were doing so by the end of his life. The artist's *Laughing Self-Portrait* in Cologne, the last self-portrait he made, gives a hint that this was so. On the left in this painting are traces of an indistinct figure, often thought to be an antique bust (fig. 10). The motif of a laughing painter glancing at us over his shoulder appears in few other extant works. Among those known to us, however, is a painting by Rembrandt's pupil Arent de Gelder. And there, in exactly the same place as the 'bust' in the Rembrandt, is the figure of an elderly woman being painted by the artist (fig. 11). All in all, de Gelder's painting bears a distinct resemblance to that by his teacher Rembrandt,[21] and when it became known that in 1761 Rembrandt's *Laughing Self-Portrait* had been described as 'Rembrandt painting an old woman' it was clear that the subject of the work had probably once been the same as Arent de Gelder's.[22]

With regard to the identification of the subject in the *Laughing Self-Portrait*, it can now be added that the picture was described as 'Rembrandt painting an old woman' on at least six occasions between 1758 and 1808.[23] Hence the 'bust', now indistinct, was once clearly recognizable as an elderly woman – probably, like the figure in de Gelder's painting, a woman sitting for her portrait. To accommodate this figure, Rembrandt's painting was presumably larger at first. Visitors to the present exhibition can compare this case with that of de Gelder's *Homer*, a painting likewise based on a composition by Rembrandt, only a fragment of which survives today (see cat. nos 70 and 97, and fig. 97b).

As we shall see, a laughing painter portraying an elderly woman, such as the figure both Rembrandt and de Gelder depicted, can be none other than the legendary Greek Zeuxis, famed for his composite of the most beautiful features of the most beautiful women, the paradigm of 'noble selection'. By the end of Rembrandt's life, Dutch art theorists were newly

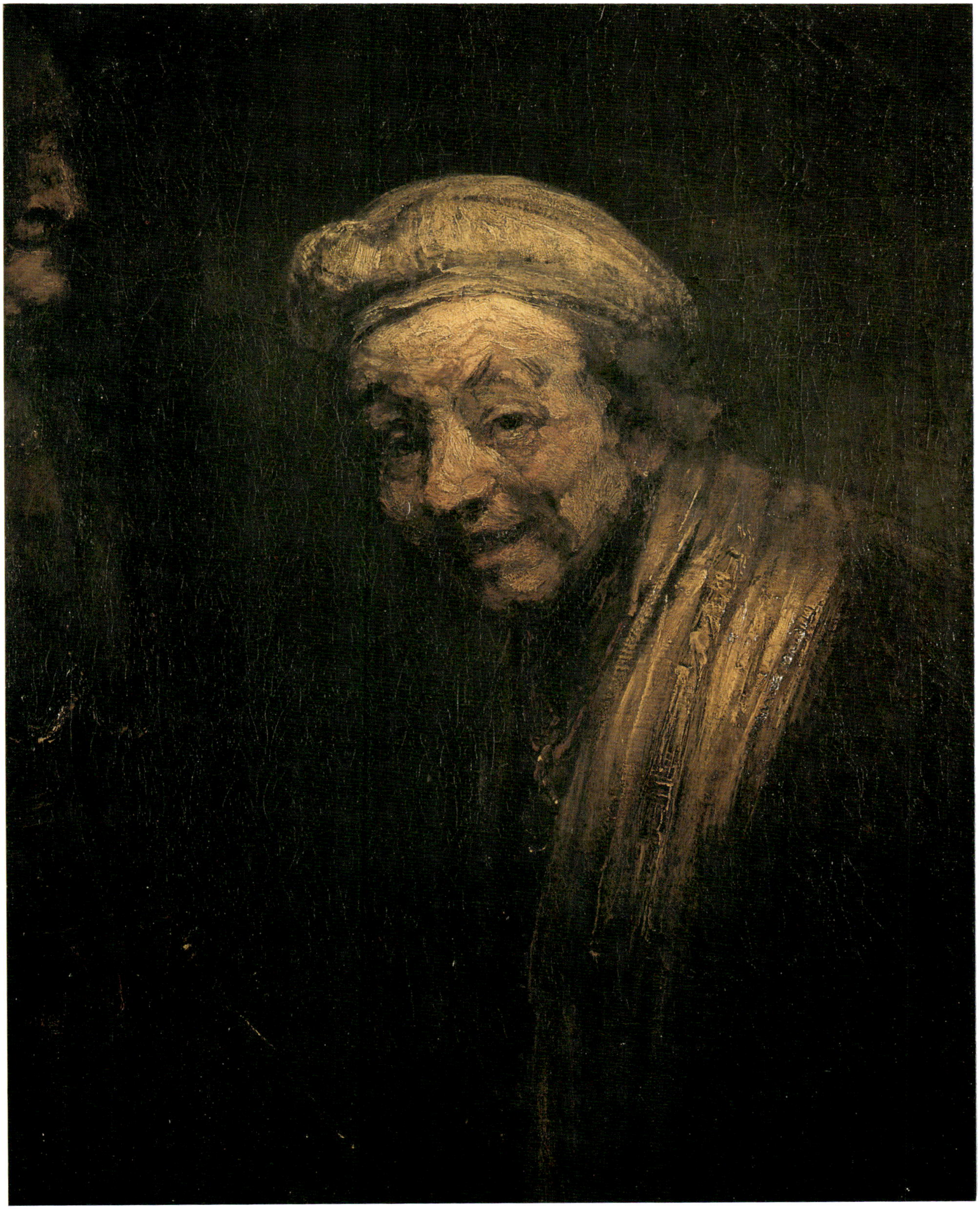

FIG. 10
Rembrandt
Self-Portrait as the Laughing Zeuxis
Canvas
82.5 x 65.0 cm
Wallraf-Richartz-Museum, Cologne
Photograph: Rheinisches Bildarchiv, Cologne

and emphatically postulating that artists should select the most beautiful the world had to offer. They must have had Zeuxis in mind. Their views were expressed in what is now called the 'classicist' critique. Andries Pels's criticism of Rembrandt's female nudes, with 'traces of the lacings of the corsets on the stomach, of the garters on the legs', was one expression of that classicism.[24] The painter Samuel van Hoogstraten had expressed similar views in 1678, in other words even before Pels, but his comment has gone unnoticed. Advising young painters on choosing their female models, he urged them to 'ensure that [the models'] knees have not been ruined by garters ... that their shins and calves are not pinched out of shape. This is a condition to which women are prone. See that the abdomen and limbs have not been disfigured by the tightness of their clothing'. Interestingly enough, Hoogstraten's exhortation is followed directly by the story of 'the great painter' who 'picked the fairest daughters of the city' to use in his composite portrait of the beautiful Helen.[25] Hoogstraten does not mention Rembrandt by name in his implied critique of the naturalist approach. Elsewhere in his book, however, he again urges painters to choose beautiful models, adding: 'Looking at my old Academy drawings, I regret that we were taught so little about such matters in our youth, for it is no more trouble to copy a graceful figure than an ugly one'.[26] This was without any doubt a criticism of Rembrandt, to whom Hoogstraten had once been apprenticed. The now classicist Hoogstraten, reflecting on his time at the master's 'Academy', was protesting about the lack of comely models there.[27]

It must have been criticism of this kind that prompted Rembrandt – and later his most faithful follower, de Gelder – to portray themselves as the Zeuxis of a completely different tale, one that had never been illustrated before. Zeuxis, now grown old, was painting a wrinkled old

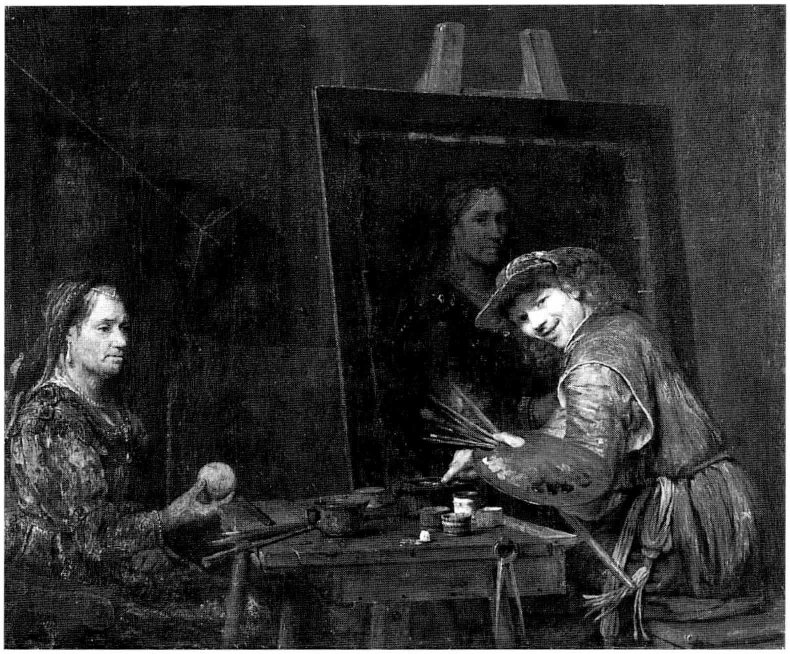

FIG. 11
Arent de Gelder
Self-Portrait as the Laughing Zeuxis Painting an Old Woman
Signed and dated 1685
Canvas
142.0 x 169.0 cm
Städelsches Kunstinstitut, Frankfurt

woman when, overcome by mirth, he laughed so much that he choked and died. This story from antiquity was far less well known than that of Zeuxis as a younger man, although it is related by both Karel van Mander and Hoogstraten, who happened to be Arent de Gelder's first teacher. This obscure tale must have held such appeal for Rembrandt, and in his footsteps de Gelder, that they decided to illustrate it. The laughing artist portraying an old woman, as depicted by both of these history painters, can be none other than the Zeuxis of that story (figs 10, 11). It is hardly possible to imagine a more striking contrast to the Zeuxis of the 'noble selection'. But was this later incarnation of the laughing Zeuxis, who immortalizes beauty faded and lost forever (thereby functioning as a critical comment on all followers of the Zeuxis of the 'noble selection) sarcastic, or merely ironic? Whatever one's interpretation, the *Laughing Self-Portrait* is the first reaction we know of to the charge that Rembrandt painted ugly women, and it came from Rembrandt himself.

That the *Laughing Self-Portrait* would once have been recognized as a depiction of Zeuxis is apparent from the *Epigrams upon ... Paintings* published by J. Elsum in London in 1700, a book not previously cited in this context. Elsum stands out for being one of the first to praise the 'coarse rugged way of painting' that characterizes Rembrandt's late work. His book also contains an ode to Rembrandt's *Aristotle*[28] and he knew other paintings in Amsterdam as well.[29] Epigram no. 4 is a tribute to Zeuxis's portrait of Helen ('A Beauty never parallel'd by Nature. / The sev'ral Graces that lie scatter'd there, / Are all collected and united here'), and epigram no. 5 to a painting of 'An old Woman's Head, by the same Zeuxis ... what Charm is there in a shrivel'd Face? / Look with an *Artist's* eye and you will see / The Work exceeding fanciful and free, / You'l see a pleasant, but a fatal Head, / Such as with transport struck its Author dead'.[30] It thus seems that Elsum was interweaving the two Zeuxis stories in much the same ways as Rembrandt and de Gelder appear to have done in their paintings (figs 10, 11).

'Expressive naturalism'

The idea that Rembrandt depicted an 'ugly version' of life needs extra attention in 1997. We who live in the wake of twentieth-century expressionism, with its distortions of reality, have not always appreciated the eloquence of extreme naturalism in the art of earlier times. However, it is important to know that this was the most striking aspect of Rembrandt's art for many generations. Influential nineteenth-century writers, such as John Ruskin and Jacob Burckhardt, were violently opposed to Rembrandt's work for this very reason.[31] Today, accustomed as we are to expressionism, it is precisely the 'expressive naturalism' of expressionism's most illustrious forerunner that tends to be overlooked. Rembrandt, I believe, followed in Dürer's footsteps out of conviction. In his quest to achieve the 'maximum and most natural movement', he paid little heed to the Italian principle of 'noble selection'. His pupil Samuel van Hoogstraten quoted Dürer himself in this connection: 'Abandon your false illusion of creating something better than God [has created], for your efforts will be in vain'.[32] In other words, God's creation is best represented as it is – it needs no improvement. By embracing this principle, Rembrandt consciously opted to follow a northern tradition, as he did in his choice of subject matter (see below). He remained faithful to this ideal throughout his life, in his early, most detailed, style as well as in the broad technique of his late period. It is a hallmark of his person and of his work.

Two questions

How to view Rembrandt in relation to the principle of 'noble selection' – an issue that has been the subject of heated debate for centuries – has

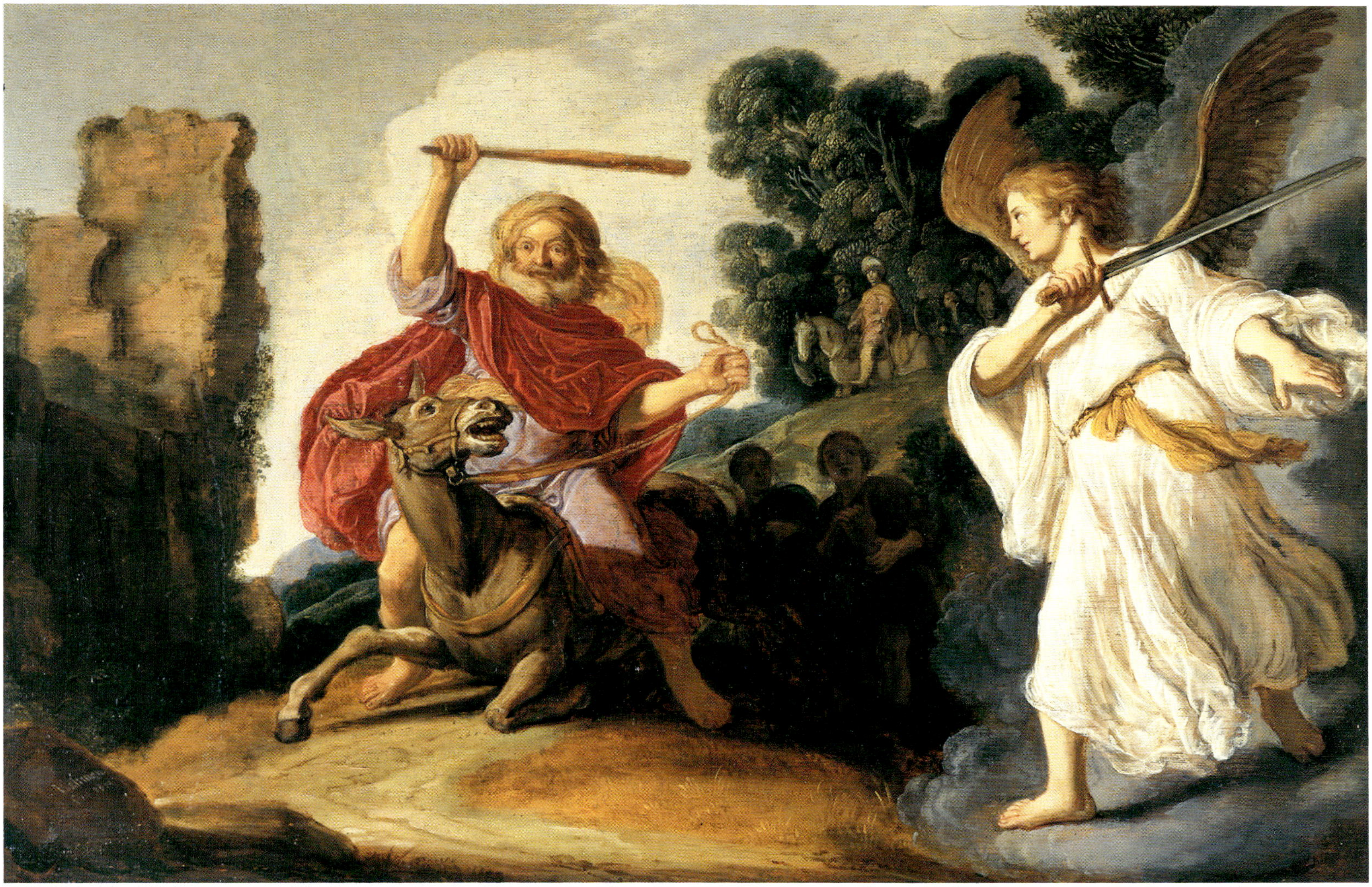

now been superseded by other preoccupations. The controversies surrounding Rembrandt today have merged into a cacophony of different views. Whereas Vermeer scholars conduct orderly meetings and keep minutes, which are available for public perusal, the Rembrandt forum is more like a stadium filled with a tumultuous crowd. There does not even exist a properly organized, up-to-date Rembrandt bibliography – with the result that anyone wishing to air a point of view is hard put to establish whether or not it has been presented before. Two questions in particular seem to rise above the general tumult. The first is: What in fact are the subjects of so many of the paintings? And the second: Are they really Rembrandts? These questions and various answers to them are discussed in the following pages and in the catalogue entries.

Some voices in the hubbub attract more attention than others, undoubtedly sometimes by chance. Among the names that occur fairly frequently in the following pages and elsewhere in the catalogue are those of the English art dealer John Smith and of the Dutch art historians Cornelis Hofstede de Groot, Abraham Bredius, Horst Gerson and Christian Tümpel (the latter two, as it happens, born in Germany). The eighteenth-century Hague painters Gerard Hoet and Pieter Terwesten, and the German museum director Wilhelm Bode, are likewise mentioned more than once in this introduction. Reference is also made to the first and second teams of the Rembrandt Research Project, authors of the as yet incomplete *Corpus of Rembrandt Paintings*. To many, these names will be unfamiliar, hence they are introduced here.

FIG. 12
Pieter Lastman 1583–1633
Balaam and the Ass
Signed and dated 1622
Panel
40.3 x 60.6 cm
Richard L. Feigen & Co., New York

II Rembrandt's themes and their interpretations

History pieces, portraits, tronies *and works on paper*
Rembrandt and his work aside, Dutch seventeenth-century painting in general is considered unique, as subjects that had rarely been painted before this time were now depicted by a great many outstanding specialists: groups of figures in contemporary costume (peasants as well as prosperous burghers), still lifes, landscapes, marine paintings, and city views. Holland's seventeenth-century masters were the first to develop and perfect these new subjects, which they produced in vast numbers. For the first time in history, artists took their contemporary culture and environment as the principal themes of their paintings. Fine examples of work from the Dutch School of this period can be seen in museums all over the world. The National Gallery of Victoria, for instance, has a *Wedding Party* by Jan Steen, a *Flower-piece* by Rachel Ruysch and a *Landscape with Cattle* by Aelbert Cuyp.[33]

Rembrandt's paintings are not of these contemporary subjects. In Amsterdam he studied under the artist Pieter Lastman (1583–1633), who was renowned in his day as a painter of biblical and mythological scenes. The six months Rembrandt spent at Lastman's studio, shortly before 1625, were to have a decisive influence on his choice of themes. The field he chose was traditional 'history painting', a genre that in Dutch art theory was rated above all others. To depict correctly an episode or character from a biblical, historical or mythological narrative, an artist had to be an expert at rendering the human figure. The history painter also had to represent the landscapes and interiors in which his figures were set, and all the appropriate still-life features. Moreover, he could not simply represent what he saw before him, but had to draw on his imagination to visualize the figures or scenes he wished to depict. Hence, a good history piece was the highest goal to which a painter could aspire.[34]

This was the ideal Lastman pursued and the ideal Rembrandt embraced for the rest of his life. In 1622 Lastman painted the Old Testament account of *Balaam and the Ass* (fig. 12). Rembrandt's version of the same subject, executed four years later, was inspired directly by Lastman's. Even at this early stage, Rembrandt sought greater intensity in his treatment of the theme. His figures, huddled more closely together and towering one above the other, form a concentration of energy (fig. 13). Though his style was to change dramatically, Rembrandt's aim throughout his career was to make history pieces with the greatest possible degree of expressiveness (cat. nos 2, 10, 16, 22). Lastman's influence remained a constant feature of his work, as can be seen, for instance, in the *Susanna* of 1636 (cat. no. 10). Rembrandt also required his own pupils to study Lastman, whose influence can still be discerned, generations later, in the work of Gerbrand van den Eeckhout (cat. no. 53).

Rembrandt did not paint portraits in his early Leiden period. In Amsterdam, however, he emerged as a 'society' portraitist in the 1630s, with some of the city's most distinguished personalities among his clientele (figs 12a, 18a). Portraiture was another traditional branch of painting; in the Netherlands, Jan van Eyck (*c.*1390–1441) had already produced lifelike portraits. Seventeenth-century art theorists rated portraiture lower than history painting, for the portraitist had simply to render what he saw. In Karel van Mander's view, the genre represented a 'side alley in art', one taken by painters who were 'lured by the prospect of gain or were seeking to earn a livelihood'.[35] At the same time, however, there was a huge market for portraits, and discerning clients demanded the highest standards. In their eyes, of course, a good likeness of themselves or of those dear to them ranked more highly than any other subject in art.

Rembrandt also made '*tronies*', works that fall somewhere between history paintings and portraits. *Tronie* (literally 'face') was the term used in the seventeenth century to designate an anonymous figure in an exotic or fantastic costume. Many of these figures were highly expressive (cat. nos 1, 4, 9, 14, 25).[36] Unlike portraits, which were intended only for the client and his family, *tronies* were made for the open market. Sometimes they may even have been reminiscent of paintings of earlier times. Artists and connoisseurs of Rembrandt's day displayed an intense interest in, and paid high prices for, pictures they attributed to Dürer, Lucas van Leyden and Hans Holbein.[37] These artists' subjects were often as intriguingly puzzling to seventeenth-century audiences as that of Rembrandt's *tronie* of a *Scholar in His Studio* still is for us today (fig. 14). We may reckon with the possibility that Rembrandt intended this ambiguity.

Apart from the occasional landscape (cat. no. 11), the subjects of Rembrandt's paintings were largely traditional. He appears to have confined himself to the themes favoured by famous northern artists of earlier generations. His etchings, however, explore a far wider range of subjects (cat. nos 99–122). The same was true of Lucas van Leyden (*c.*1494–1533), Rembrandt's fellow townsman of a century earlier, whose paintings cover a narrower range of subjects than do his prints. Like van Leyden before him, Rembrandt gained a reputation for his prints that, even in his own day, extended as far as Italy.

Yet only in his drawings did Rembrandt truly spread his wings to observe the world in all its manifold forms. He produced brilliant drawings of every conceivable subject – including scenes and figures from everyday life. Exhibiting his work without including the drawings would be like showing only the facade of a house. Hence twenty-six of his best sheets have been selected for the present exhibition (cat. nos 73–98). Rembrandt himself regarded and probably used these drawings as study material, although a market for them quickly developed (for the etchings and drawings, see the essays in this catalogue by Christopher White and Ben Broos).

Interpretations

While the subjects of Rembrandt's paintings were traditional, the manner in which he depicted those subjects has always captivated those who see the works. The proof of this, or perhaps its corollary, is that often so much more is read into them than is actually there. Rembrandt's paintings apparently give the impression that there is a great deal to be seen, and that the observer needs both to see it and to give it a name. It is as though the viewer experiences a powerful need to label, to categorize, to define.

The way in which this need is expressed differs from one generation to the next: what is seen in Rembrandt's works has changed with the passage of time. Johannes van Vliet, Rembrandt's own engraver in his early period, inscribed the name of the Prince of Transylvania, George Rácóczy I, on a number of impressions from the edition of a print after one of the master's fantasy *tronies*.[38] Between 1630 and 1650, French engravers copied other *tronies* from prints by Rembrandt, adding captions that identified them as Mohammed, the laughing philosopher Democritus, the weeping philosopher Heraclitus, Philo of Alexandria, Faust, Merlin and Plato.[39] The engravers themselves knew that Rembrandt had not supplied these titles, and that they sprang purely from their own imaginations. I assume that their public was aware of this as well.

In 1836, John Smith, the first to compile a catalogue of Rembrandt's painted oeuvre, described many works as portraits of famous seventeenth-century men from different parts of Europe. Examples were the theologian Jansenius, founder of the 'heretical' Jansenist movement in the Catholic Church; Prince Rupert, the naval commander of Charles II of England; the admirals de Ruyter and Tromp, commanders of the Dutch fleets in the great naval battles against the English; the philologist Lipsius; and Louis XIV's distinguished officer Maréchal Turenne.[40] Smith took many of these identifications from older descriptions, but it is unclear how reliable he himself believed them to be. None are given credence today.

Abraham Bredius: Rembrandt's oeuvre reordered

A century after Smith, the eminent Dutch art historian Abraham Bredius (1855–1946) published his fully illustrated Rembrandt catalogue (fig. 15).[41] Bredius thought the sitters in Rembrandt's paintings less likely to be celebrities than people from the artist's immediate environment. The 'Portraits' section of his catalogue contains reproductions of seventy paintings, identified respectively as Rembrandt's mother, Neeltgen Willemsdr. van Zuytbroeck; his father, Harmen Gerritsz van Rijn; his sister Liesbeth van Rijn; his wife Saskia van Uylenburgh; his mistress

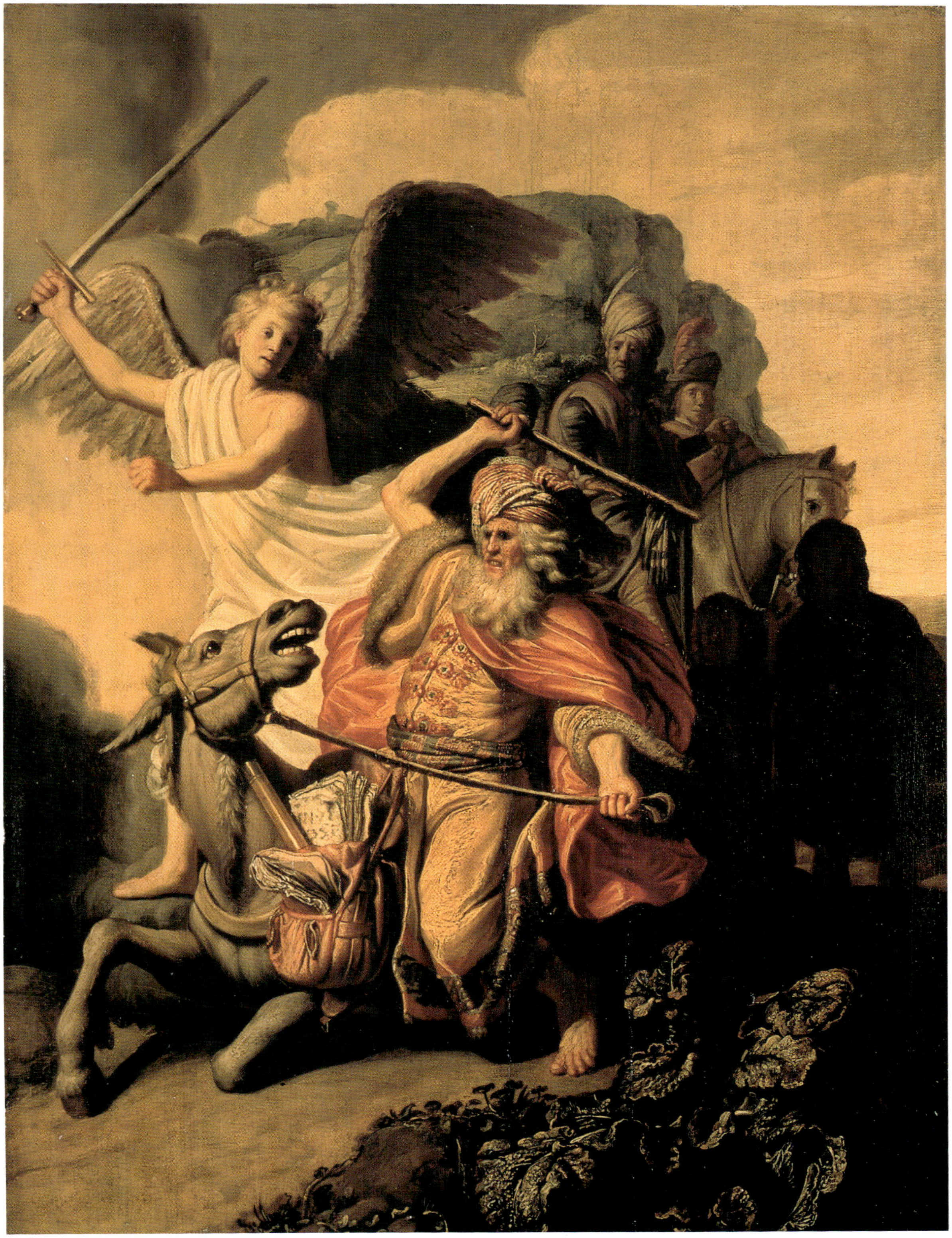

FIG. 13
Rembrandt
Balaam and the Ass
Signed and dated 1626
Panel
65.0 x 47.0 cm
Musée Cognacq-Jay, Paris
© Photothèque des Musées de la Ville de Paris

FIG. 14
Rembrandt
A Scholar in His Studio
Signed and dated 1634
Canvas
141.0 x 135.0 cm
Národní Galerie, Prague

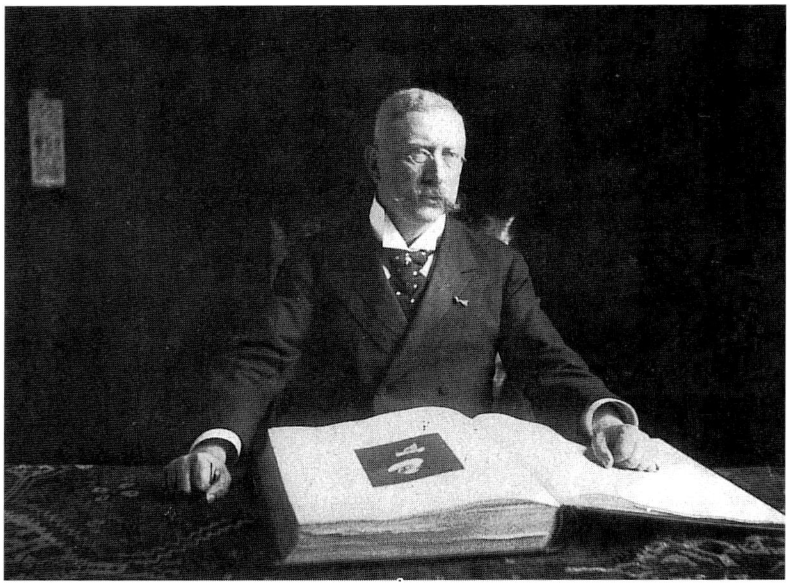

FIG. 15
Abraham Bredius, *c.*1935, around the time his Rembrandt catalogue was published.
From a reproduction

Hendrickje Stoffels; his son Titus; and his brother Adriaen van Rijn. (None are identified as Geertje Dircx, the woman with whom Rembrandt is believed to have had an affair after Saskia's death and before his liaison with Hendrickje.)

Bredius presented the material in his catalogue in a most unusual sequence.[42] Catalogues of this kind had always opened with an artist's biblical scenes, in the sequence in which the stories occur in the Scriptures; these were then followed by other religious subjects and, subsequently, by mythological and allegorical themes. Next were genre scenes, portraits, landscapes and finally still lifes. This order corresponded to the conventional hierarchy of the genres. Smith's oeuvre catalogue of 1836 and Hofstede de Groot's of 1915[43] were organized along these lines. Bredius, however, defied convention and placed the works with mythological and allegorical themes at the end of the book, and the religious works last of all. His catalogue opens with Rembrandt's self-portraits, a total of sixty-one works.[44] They are followed by the seventy portrayals of members of the artist's family and then by the remaining 'portraits', a miscellany of elegant men and women in seventeenth-century costume – works that were indeed commissioned portraits – indiscriminately combined with figures in the most fantastic apparel, the works that are now called *tronies* (for example, our cat. no. 1). Bredius apparently took for one of Rembrandt's contemporaries or fellow townsmen any figure he failed to recognize as a member of the artist's inner circle.

Bredius's system of classification has had a lasting impact on the way Rembrandt is viewed: Horst Gerson's authoritative 1969 catalogue of the paintings is a reworking of Bredius's book, with the material presented in the same sequence.[45] The only change Gerson made with respect to Bredius's presentation of the paintings was to add quotation marks to many of the names of so-called members of Rembrandt's family.

Bredius's arrangement of his catalogue may be seen to reflect the thinking of his own time: steeped in nineteenth-century individualism, it has also had a profound impact in terms of the enduring image of Rembrandt as an artist who focused his energies on portrayals of himself and the people around him. Moreover, Bredius's approach epitomizes the artistic ideal of the nineteenth-century realist painters and critics, and that of the Impressionists who succeeded them. This ideal was consistent with the prevailing image of seventeenth-century Dutch painting, as outlined above and as first propagated by E.T. Thoré-Bürger, the French critic who rediscovered and championed Johannes Vermeer and Frans Hals. In 1858 Thoré-Bürger wrote that seventeenth-century Dutch painting was 'no longer a mystical art shrouding ancient superstitions, no longer a mythological art resurrecting old symbols ... no longer an art of popes and kings, of gods and heroes', but the representation of 'living life'. It was 'a kind of photography of their glorious seventeenth century, people and objects, feelings and habits – the deeds and gestures of an entire nation'.[46] According to this line of reasoning, Dutch history painting in Rembrandt's time was merely a regrettable mistake.[47] Bredius's decision to place Rembrandt's biblical scenes at the end of his catalogue was taking Thoré-Bürger's views to the extreme. By Thoré-Bürger's own count, Rembrandt's paintings included only a handful of biblical subjects, and he saw them as 'little more than a pretext to portray ... humankind of his own time and of all times'.[48] The idea of Rembrandt's work as 'a kind of photography' is presumably what prompted Bredius to introduce a comprehensive 'family album' at the beginning of his catalogue of the master's oeuvre. In this he could include the names of various members of Rembrandt's family culled from the archives in the nineteenth century. Bredius was eighty years old when his book appeared in 1935, and his views are typical of the previous century.

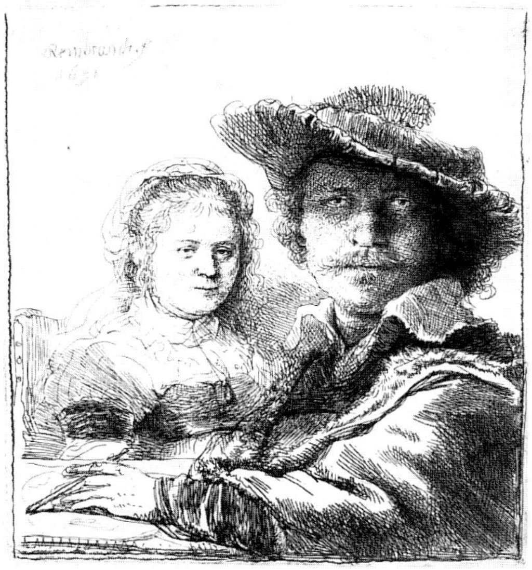

FIG. 16
Rembrandt
Self-Portrait with Saskia
Signed and dated 1636
Etching
10.4 x 9.5 cm
Rijksprentenkabinet, Rijksmuseum, Amsterdam

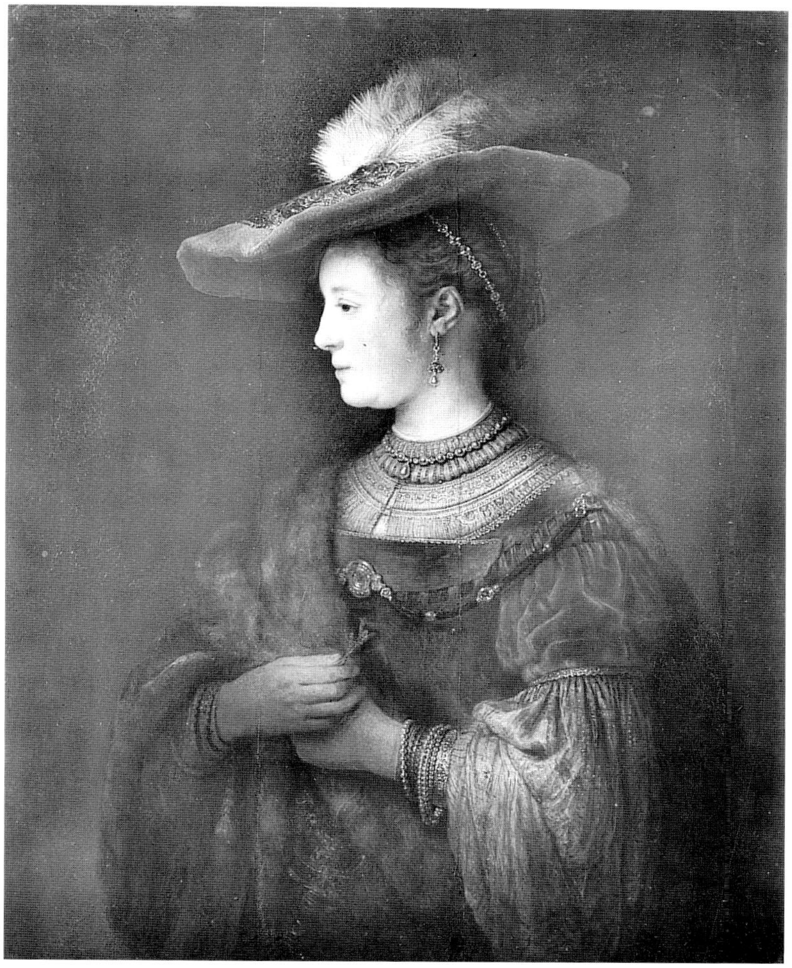

FIG. 17
Rembrandt
Saskia van Uylenburgh in Rich Apparel c.1634–42
Panel
99.5 x 78.8 cm
Gemäldegalerie, Kassel

Rembrandt's 'family album'

The 'family album' was not entirely a product of Bredius's imagination. Rembrandt has an extraordinary gift for drawing the observer into aspects of his personal life. His oeuvre, more than that of any other artist, includes a very large number of self-portraits. In one of his etchings, he portrayed himself drawing with a young woman at a table behind him (B.19) (fig. 16). Unlike paintings, etchings were intended for a relatively large public, yet here Rembrandt openly shows himself with his partner. Referring to this etching in 1718, Houbraken described Rembrandt's 'wife' (huisvrouw) as 'a peasant girl from Raarep', a description that could allude only to Geertje Dircx.[49] Houbraken was apparently oblivious to the fact that Rembrandt had shared his home with more than one woman. However, the compilation of the 'family album' coincided – not by chance – with the rise of archival research in the nineteenth century. Only at this stage were documents found which disclosed that the name of Rembrandt's partner in 1636 – the year of the etching – was Saskia van Uylenburgh and that she lived from 1612 to 1642.

Other documents revealed that there was a demand for paintings of Saskia even during Rembrandt's lifetime. In 1658 Rembrandt supplied a painting of his 'huijsvrouwe' in settlement of a debt. His creditor was the patrician poet Jan Six, from whose collection the painting's later fate can be traced, providing almost conclusive evidence that the picture in question was the *Saskia in Rich Apparel* now in Kassel, a work dating from between 1634 and 1642 (fig. 17).[50] There is also the famous drawing in Berlin, on which Rembrandt inscribed the words 'my wife' (mijn huijsvrou) (p. 328, fig. 10). Hence three portrayals of Saskia are known that were intended as such, and that were seen as such in Rembrandt's own day. Though she has sometimes been recognized in other pictures as well, I would seldom presume to judge whether or not a person portrayed in one picture is the same as that in another.

Representations of people thought to be other members of Rembrandt's household and family circle were also soon in circulation. The 1679 inventory of the estate of the print dealer Clement de Jonghe (1624/25–1677), who himself appears in an etched portrait by Rembrandt (B.272), includes seventy-four copperplates for Rembrandt's etchings, with titles. Among them are 'Rembrandt's mother' (no. 10), 'Rembrandt's father' (no. 53), a 'portrait of Titus' (or 'Titus making a portrait' – here the Dutch text is ambiguous) (no. 58), and 'Rembrandt's concubine' (no. 47). De Jonghe probably bought the plates directly from Rembrandt.[51] The titles in his inventory may therefore have been provided by Rembrandt himself, or possibly by Titus, since Houbraken names him as the person who sold his father's etchings.[52] However, it is not possible to identify any of the four plates referred to here with any of the etchings known today. All one can do is guess as to which works they might be.[53] All things considered, de Jonghe's inventory provides no clue that would enable us to add any extra portraits to the 'family album'.

Apart from Clement de Jonghe's list, there are no known early documents to indicate that Rembrandt's mother posed for him, although the idea that she did so gained currency in the eighteenth century. In

1836 Smith described seven paintings as 'the mother of the artist'.[54] He thus counted almost as many 'portrayals' of her as the nine Bredius reproduced in 1935, one of which was an *Old Woman Reading* (fig. 18).

References to a painting of 'Rembrandt's father' occur as early as 1644 and 1680,[55] and there is also a drawing that bears the inscription *Harman. Gerrits. van de Rhijn.*[56] The words are written in a seventeenth-century hand, but not that of Rembrandt. The names of Rembrandt's parents had been published in 1641 in Jan Jansz Orlers's *Beschrijvinge der Stadt Leyden* (Description of the City of Leiden).[57] The idea that the *Old Man Asleep, Seated by the Fire*, for instance, is a portrayal of the artist's father is a modern fiction (fig. 19).[58]

Sifting through the 'portraits of Titus', we find that in October 1669 the estate of Titus's widow, Magdalena van Loo, included a 'portrait of the deceased husband [Titus] leaning on a railing', but the painter's name is not mentioned.[59] The text has been taken, without justification, to refer to a Rembrandt.[60] Some seventy years later, in 1738, a painting of a helmeted warrior wearing a coat of mail and holding a shield was auctioned as 'Rembrandt's son' (see commentary to cat. no. 15), and in 1770 an engraving was made after a *tronie* described as a portrait of Titus by Rembrandt (fig. 20). This print is most unlikely to have been based on a painting by Rembrandt, however, and the title is likewise apocryphal. This was the only 'Titus' that Smith mentioned in 1836. Nevertheless, in 1915 Hofstede de Groot counted a total of ten 'portraits of Titus', all based purely on recent speculation.[61] In the present exhibition, cat. no. 18 and the angel in cat. no. 22 both belong to this category.

The only early reference to a portrayal of Rembrandt's 'concubine' was that relating to the unidentifiable etching in Clement de Jonghe's inventory of 1679. Such a person was not mentioned again until 1781, when a print after the painting of a *Young Woman in Bed* (cat. no. 14) appeared, with the title 'Rembrandt's Mistress' (fig. 14d). Only many decades later were archive documents published concerning Hendrickje Stoffels, resurrecting her for the first time. The result was that eight paintings have been identified as representations of her since the publication of Hofstede de Groot's catalogue of 1915.

There are no early references at all to portraits of Rembrandt's brother Adriaen or of his sister Liesbeth, who were first 'recognized' in a few *tronies* and portraits at the end of the nineteenth century, after their names had emerged from the archives.[62] Even as late as 1966, the model for our cat. no. 1 was presented as a new candidate for Adriaen van Rijn.[63]

All in all, however, despite the various 'identifications' suggested over the centuries, the only people with a rightful claim to a place in the 'family album' are Rembrandt himself and Saskia.[64] All Bredius's additions were based on then recent speculation.

Herauslösung

In the intervening years a change has taken place which now seems to represent the opposite extreme. The identification of Maréchal Turenne in a Rembrandt is a thing of the past, and the naming of sitters as

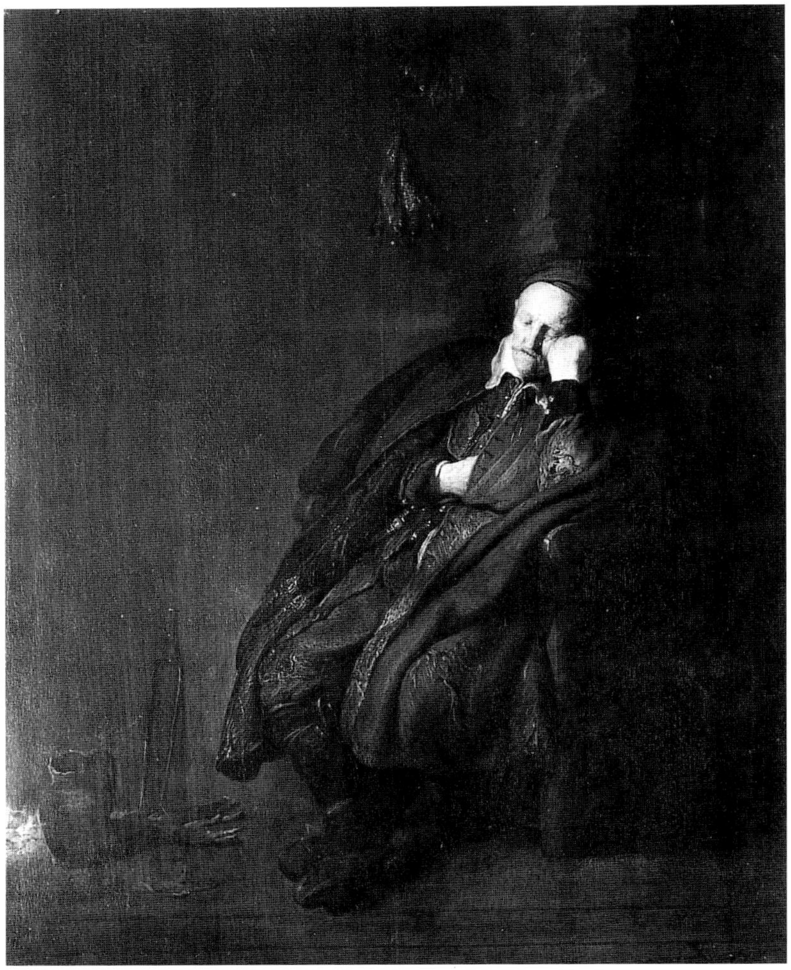

FIG. 19
Rembrandt
Old Man Asleep, Seated by the Fire
Signed and dated [16]29
Panel
51.9 x 40.8 cm
Galleria Sabauda, Turin

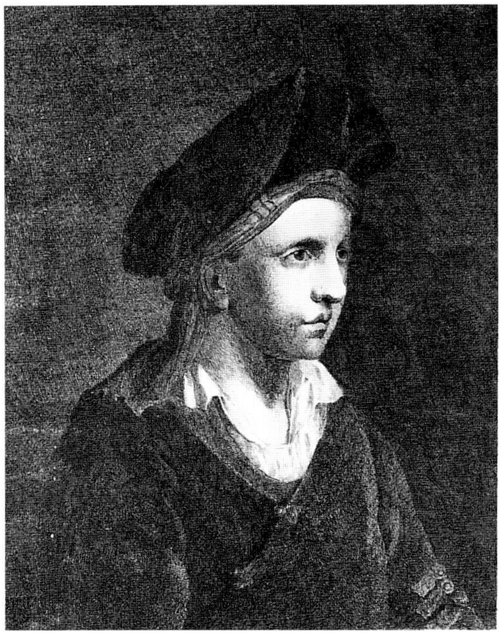

FIG. 20
August Ludwig Stein (German, 1732–1814), 'after Rembrandt'
'Rembrandt's Son Titus'
Inscribed *Titus Rembrands Sohn*
Dated 1770
Etching
Photograph: RKD

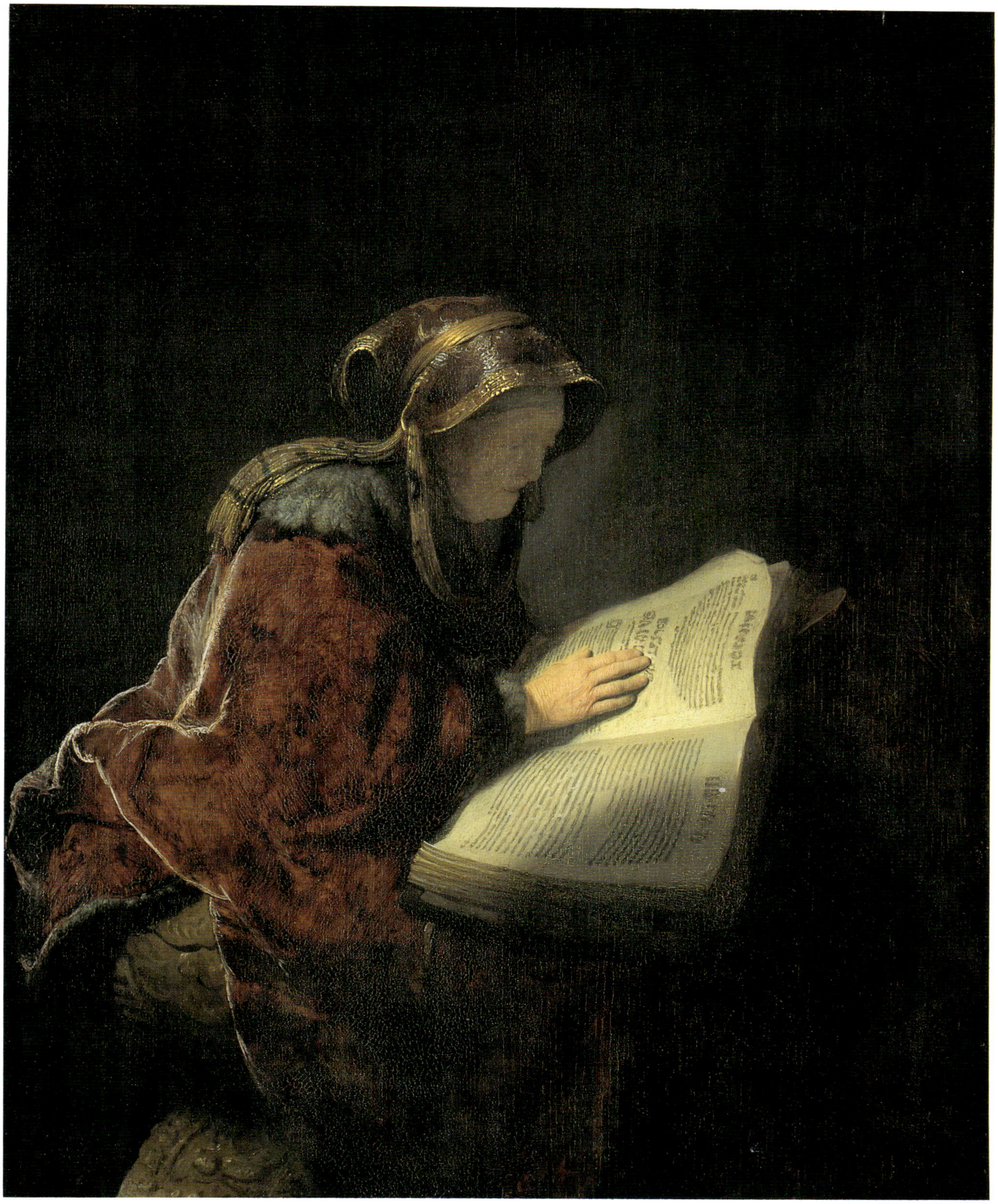

FIG. 18
Rembrandt
Old Woman Reading
Monogrammed and dated 1631
Panel
59.8 x 47.7 cm
Rijksmuseum, Amsterdam

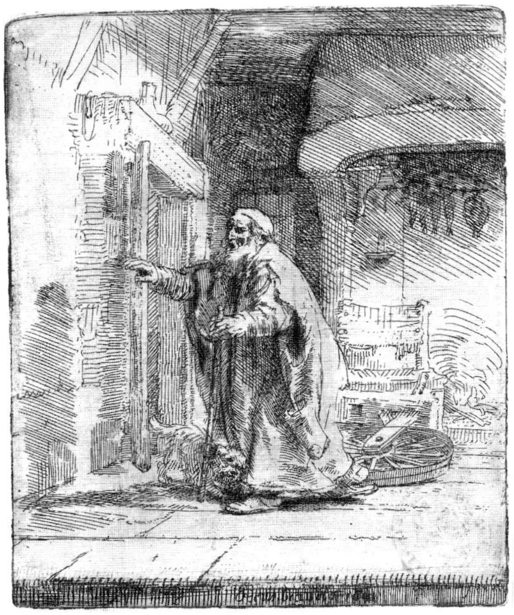

FIG. 21
Rembrandt
The Blind Tobit
Signed and dated 1651
Etching
16.1 x 12.9 cm
Rijksprentenkabinet, Rijksmuseum, Amsterdam

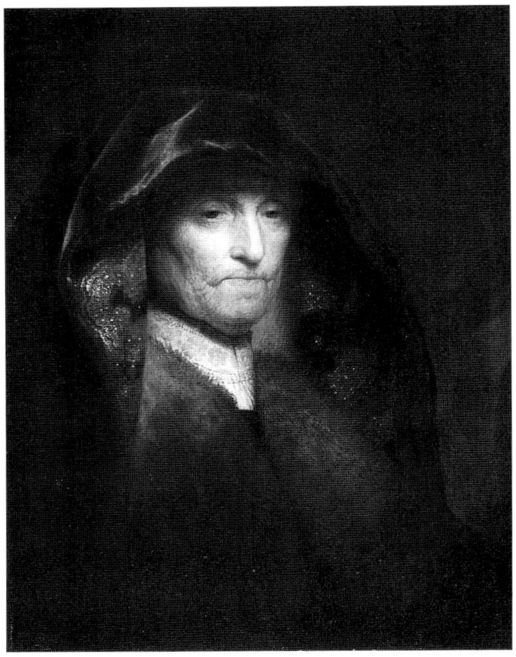

FIG. 22
Rembrandt(?)
Bust of an Old Woman
Panel
61.0 x 47.4 cm
The Royal Collection © Her Majesty the Queen

Rembrandt's brother Adriaen or sister Liesbeth is no longer treated seriously either. Nor are Rembrandt's biblical scenes any longer relegated to last in line. On the contrary, biblical themes are now being seen where they were never seen before. In this respect Professor Christian Tümpel of Nijmegen has strongly influenced the way Rembrandt is viewed today.

In 1968 Tümpel published the first of a series of impressively substantiated studies demonstrating that Rembrandt's religious scenes were inspired by sixteenth-century prints and book illustrations to a far greater extent than had hitherto been assumed.[65] He was able to show, for instance, that cat. no. 30 is the *Departure of the Shunamite Woman* and not the 'Banishment of Hagar' it had always been thought to represent. In addition, Tümpel emphasized that Rembrandt sometimes singled out one particular character to illustrate a story. For example, the solitary man in the etching reproduced here as fig. 21 (B.42) is the blind Tobit, stumbling to the door to welcome the son who will restore his sight. Although the Apocrypha explicitly mention that Tobit's wife, Anna, was present at the time, she is not depicted in the etching (Tobit 11:10). Tümpel presents a convincing case for his view that this concentration on a main character is a way of 'heightening the contrast between the psychological content of a scene and its traditional representation, or of bringing its distinctive qualities into sharper focus'.[66] This is indeed true of the Tobit etching.

In this case, the isolating of a character, or the *Herauslösung* to use Tümpel's term, has never sown confusion, for the print in question has never been interpreted as anything other than a portrayal of the blind Tobit. Tümpel, however, applies his principle more widely and regards a number of figures in Rembrandt's paintings – figures that previously had a different designation, or none at all – as 'isolated' biblical characters. He argues at length, for instance, that the *Old Woman Reading* in fig. 18 was the New Testament prophetess Anna.[67] His views on her identity were accepted in the Rembrandt *Corpus* and other publications.[68] However, this interpretation was recently shown to be unsubstantiated. A print by Johannes van Vliet, made after the picture while it was still being painted, bears no inscription, and in 1668 the print was referred to simply as 'a woman reading'.[69] According to the Bible (Luke 2:37), the prophetess Anna 'departed not from the temple ... night and day'. The Temple can be seen in the print of *Anna* that Tümpel cites by way of comparison, but there is no sign of it in Rembrandt's painting. Over the years the old woman reading has been cast in different roles. She was formerly held to be Rembrandt's mother, but this identification was rejected in the *Corpus*.[70]

The painting is definitely not a portrait, if only because the face is entirely in shadow. Moreover, the woman's clothing is fairytale-like. The work is executed in Rembrandt's early, finely detailed technique, and the open pages of the book can be seen quite clearly, though the writing on them is illegible.[71] The picture is highly evocative: the figure does in fact recall a prophetess or sibyl, but Rembrandt has chosen not to provide any explicit clues.[72]

The *Bust of an Old Woman* in the British royal collection has likewise been read in various ways at different stages of its history (fig. 22). At the beginning of the eighteenth century the picture was thought to represent the Countess of Desmond, a woman renowned for her longevity. From the end of the century the *Old Woman* was taken to be Rembrandt's mother, while Tümpel again (initially) saw a prophetess Anna, before also subscribing to the identification with the artist's mother.[73] Christopher White commented, however, that the oldest description of the work, from the 1630s, refers simply to 'an old woeman with a great scarfe uppon her heade with a peaked falling band'.[74] It may be added that another version of this piece was described in 1641 as an 'old *tronie* with violet velvet lined with gold cloth on the head' (see commentary to cat. no. 8). Once again, we have a composition that had no title in Rembrandt's time but was later given a variety of interpretations.

The same is true of the *Two Old Men Disputing* in Melbourne which, in line with another of Tümpel's hypotheses – but without good reason – came to be seen as the apostles Peter and Paul (cat. no. 3). Here, too, Rembrandt hints at such ideas – as well as at some quite different ones! – but without being in any way specific. Another comparable case is that of the *Young Woman in Bed*, which Tümpel interprets, even less plausibly, as an illustration of the apocryphal episode of Sarah awaiting her bridegroom Tobias (see commentary to cat. no. 14).

A '*herausgelöste*' blind, stumbling Tobit is readily recognized, even if his wife is not depicted with him (fig. 21). But in the *Old Woman Reading*, the *Bust of an Old Woman* and the *Young Woman in Bed* any single interpretation must contend with the fact that the figures could just as well be fragments (or building blocks) of a different structure altogether. The very fact that they cannot be moulded to fit any one particular narrative makes them all the more evocative.

Tümpel's theory of the 'isolated' figure had an enormous impact. Others tried to apply it to the painting referred to earlier as the '*Mulier impudica*', variously identifying the subject as Bathsheba, Susanna, Diana and Callisto (fig. 8). In trying to impose these interpretations upon the picture, they read into it ideas of their own invention. Even so, their titles were meant more seriously than the 'Mohammed' or 'Merlin' captions that engravers in Rembrandt's day added to their prints after his works. As a 'building block' the *Woman Bathing* can, though with considerable difficulty, be made to fit the stories of all four women equally well – from which I would conclude that Rembrandt himself did not intend his bather to represent any one of the four.

The concept of *Herauslösung* aside, Rembrandt scholars often feel the urge to give a painting one, specific title. The authors of the *Corpus*, for example, conclude quite rightly with respect to the *Scholar in His Studio* (fig. 14) that the painting 'offers little help in identifying its subject', yet they nonetheless seriously consider the possibility that Rembrandt might have intended the scholar to represent the astrologer Paracelsus (1493–1541).[75] A similar phenomenon occurs in the master's etchings. The print that is best known by the fanciful title *The Great Jewish Bride* has also been interpreted as Esther, as Minerva or as a sibyl (see commentary to cat. no. 101).

These changing interpretations over the years show just how evocative Rembrandt's art can be. They also highlight a remarkable paradox: whereas Rembrandt apparently often sought to achieve a timeless quality in his paintings, observers have always tried to pin his subjects down to a single time, place and person.

III The boundaries of Rembrandt's oeuvre

Headline news

Identifying exactly which works constitute Rembrandt's oeuvre is another controversial area. Today, the question as to whether or not a painting is a blue-chip Rembrandt is of interest to more than merely a handful of connoisseurs. For over a century, the re-designation of a so-called Rembrandt so that it becomes a work by someone else has been headline news. In 1890, for instance, 'newspapers throughout Europe and even America carried daily reports on the bitter controversy' as to whether the 'Rembrandt du Pecq', *Abraham and the Angels*, was a Rembrandt or an Arent de Gelder.[76] In the event, the picture has been at the Museum Boijmans Van Beuningen in Rotterdam since 1916 – securely ascribed to de Gelder.[77] There was a similar outcry in 1911, when Abraham Bredius took the Rijksmuseum *Portrait of Elisabeth Bas* away from the famous and cherished Rembrandt and gave it to Ferdinand Bol (fig. 23).[78] Another tremor shook the world when Josua Bruyn hinted in an article published in a Dutch art historical journal in 1984 that Willem Drost may have been the author of the *Polish Rider* (fig. 24).[79] More excitement followed in 1985, when the Berlin Museum transferred the attribution of its *Man in the Golden Helmet* from Rembrandt to an artist in his immediate circle (fig. 25).[80] Interestingly enough, no attempt was made in this last case to 'fill the vacuum' and attribute the work to a particular artist.

Before 1800

It is interesting that we know of hardly any instances of attributions to Rembrandt giving rise to controversy in the more distant past – though this is by no means to say that buyers and owners in Rembrandt's own day were indifferent as to whether a painting was the work of a distinguished artist or of someone else. In the seventeenth century, protracted battles were fought in Holland to establish whether paintings from abroad, particularly from Italy, were indeed the work of the master credited with their execution, or whether they were copies – or even just 'rubbish'. Specialists were summoned to give expert opinions, with painters being considered the best qualified to do so. Both Rembrandt and Vermeer were appointed as expert witnesses in cases of this kind.[81]

As far as Rembrandt is concerned, autograph paintings as well as copies are mentioned in contemporary documents. Copies were made because it was not yet possible to produce other kinds of faithful reproductions. Seldom was there any dispute as to whether a painting was a Rembrandt or a copy, let alone a studio piece or the work of a

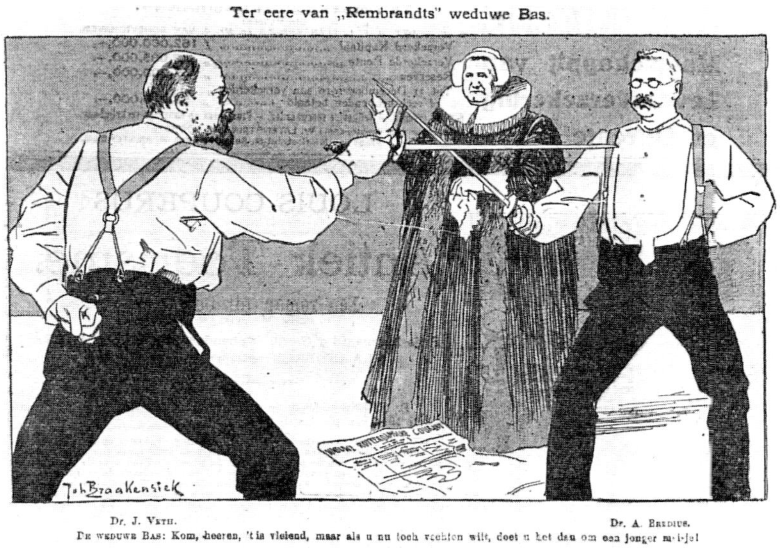

FIG. 23
J. Braakensiek's cartoon of Dr J. Veth (left) and Dr A. Bredius (right) with *Elisabeth Bas* between them. The caption reads: 'In honour of "Rembrandt's" widow Bas'. She says: 'Come gentlemen! It's flattering, but if you really want to fight, then fight over a younger woman!' (from *De Amsterdammer*, no. 1795, 19 November 1911, p. 11).

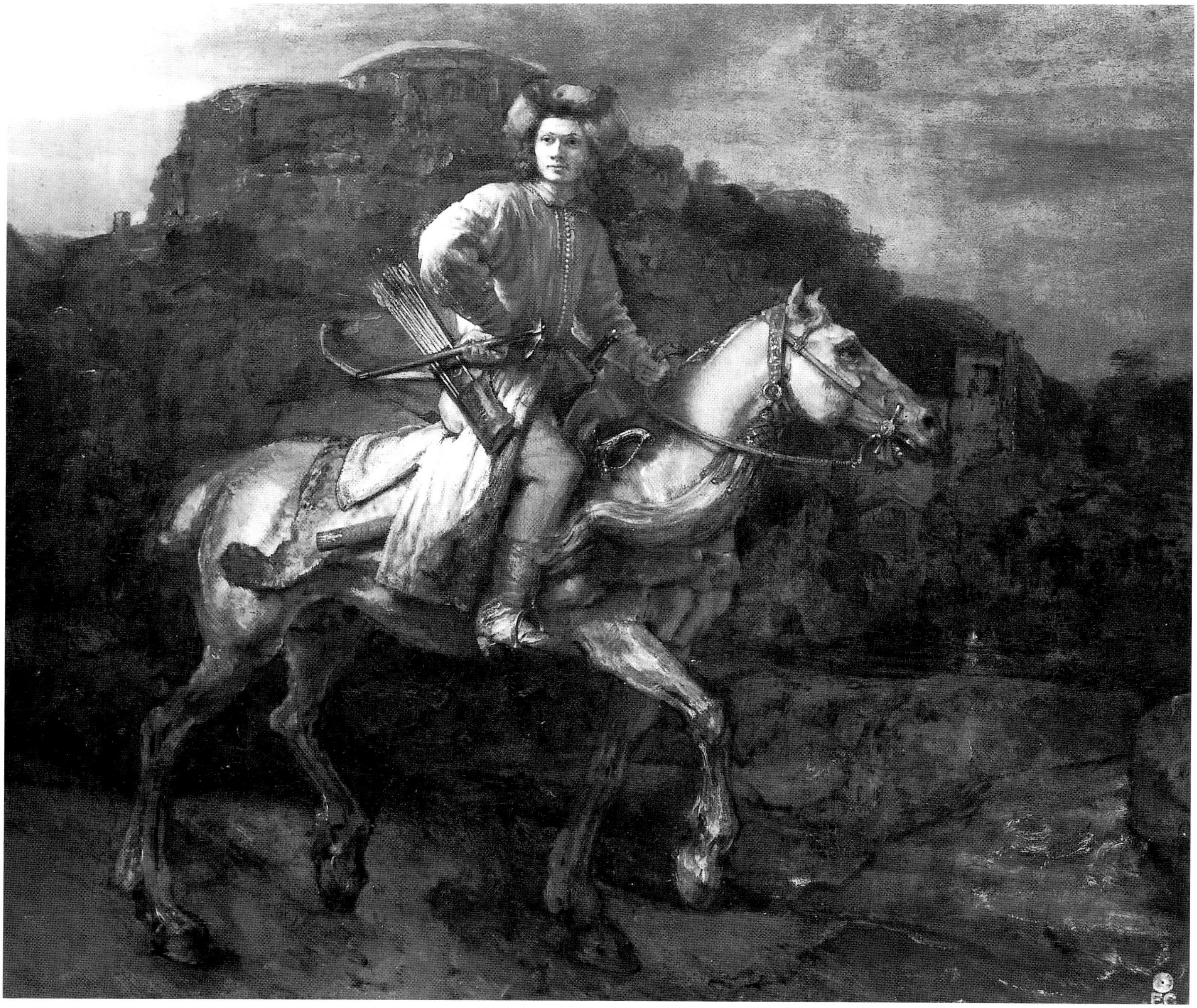

FIG. 24
Rembrandt? (attribution unquestioned 1897–1984)
The Polish Rider
Signed
Canvas
116.8 x 134.0 cm
The Frick Collection, New York
Copyright The Frick Collection, New York

pupil: it seems that in most cases people whose views are recorded knew for certain, either at first hand or from others, whether a painting was a Rembrandt or not. Only once was the word 'autograph' (principael) in a manuscript sales catalogue deleted, by a different hand, and replaced with the words 'after Rembrandt' (nae Rembrandt).[82] And only in one instance, likewise in Rembrandt's lifetime, did someone in a moment of uncertainty record the words 'by or after Rembrandt'.[83] In the 1630s, however, there were a few instances of uncertainty as to whether a work was by Rembrandt or Jan Lievens.[84] Some of the two artists' early works are indeed very similar and still cause confusion today (see commentaries to cat. nos 2, 8). In Rembrandt's own inventory of 1656, six of the pieces

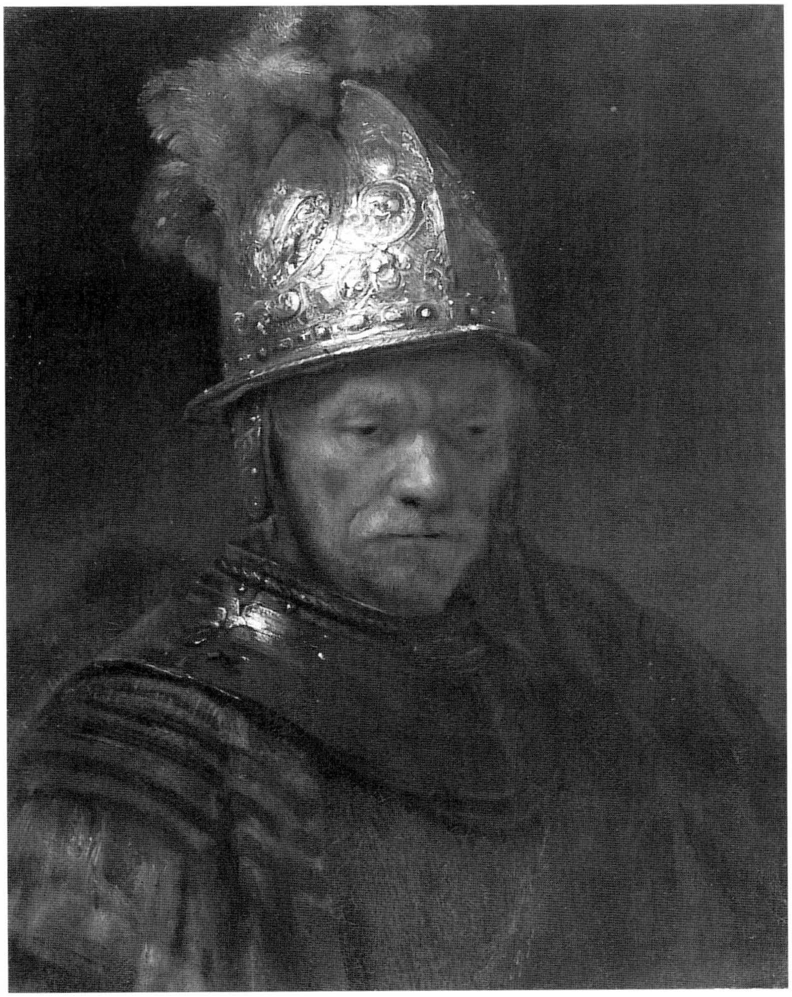

FIG. 25
Rembrandt? (attribution rarely questioned 1891–*c.*1985)
The Man in the Golden Helmet
Canvas
67.5 x 50.7 cm
Staatliche Museen zu Berlin, Gemäldegalerie

listed are said to have been 'retouched by Rembrandt', rather than being entirely by his own hand.

Before 1700 only two works are recorded as being in 'the manner of Rembrandt', and two as the work of 'a pupil of Rembrandt's'. All four were characterized thus only after the master's death.[85]

Although countless paintings said to be Rembrandts were auctioned in the eighteenth century, rarely was there any uncertainty about their authenticity. Specialized brokers were responsible for attributions at reputable auctions and also for compiling the auction catalogues. In 1752 Gerard Hoet (d. 1760) of The Hague published two large volumes containing the texts of (mainly Dutch) sale catalogues, and the individual prices fetched by the paintings in them. His fellow townsman Pieter Terwesten (1714–1798) continued the project and produced an even larger sequel in 1770.[86] Both Hoet and Terwesten were painters themselves and members of prominent families of artists.

A total of 246 paintings in their books are listed as Rembrandts, with prices ranging from a few guilders to several thousand. In the case of the works that sold for low prices, it may be that the bidders mistrusted the attribution, although, like today, other factors would undoubtedly have played a role. Prices were – as they still are – affected by the size of a piece, its condition, the appeal of its subject matter, and its style, which in Rembrandt's case was certainly variable.

Hoet and Terwesten also include three copies after works by Rembrandt, one of which fetched as much as fifty-nine guilders in 1738.[87] Six paintings in the sale catalogues are described as 'in Rembrandt's style'. Auctioneers were obviously able to recognize the artist's style, but in these cases could not tell whether or not the works in question were autograph. Buyers were evidently unimpressed by them, however, as their prices ranged from six guilders to no more than twenty-five guilders.[88] The same is true of the one 'School of Rembrandt' painting listed in 1763, which fetched the meagre sum of seventeen guilders.[89] The auctioneers expressed doubts on at least three further occasions, in one instance appending the designation 'believed to be by Rembrandt'; the piece nevertheless brought forty guilders.[90] The two others, described as 'by or in the manner of Rembrandt', sold for substantially lower amounts.[91]

All told, problems regarding the pictures' authenticity were few and far between. Works by Rembrandt's best pupils, such as those brought together for the present exhibition, were sold under the maker's name.[92]

In this context the Leiden burgomaster Johan Aegidiusz van der Marck (1707–1772) was a man ahead of his time. He was a passionate art collector, and the sale catalogues he owned have survived. When a painting depicting Isaac Blessing Jacob was sold as a Rembrandt, van der Marck crossed out Rembrandt's name in the catalogue and replaced it with 'Flink'. He apparently considered the work below Rembrandt's standard, and recognized in it the style of the master's pupil Govaert Flinck. It has since transpired that van der Marck was quite correct. The subject matter and size of the picture in question indicate that it must have been the Flinck in the present exhibition (cat. no. 41) (or perhaps the artist's similar version of the same subject (fig. 41a)). During a later restoration, apparently, Flinck's (overpainted?) signature was revealed. To the best of my knowledge, van der Marck was therefore the first

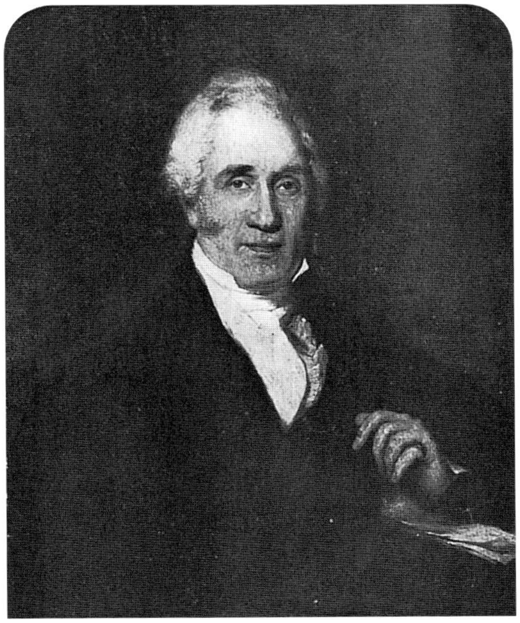

FIG. 26
Portrait of John Smith (from *The Connoisseur*, vol. V, 1903).

– followed by Abraham Bredius and Josua Bruyn – to distinguish the hand of a particular pupil in a work accredited to Rembrandt.[93] His attribution has now been upheld for almost 240 years.

After 1800: John Smith

The English art dealer John Smith (1781–1855) was the first to publish complete catalogues raisonnés of the oeuvres of a number of Dutch masters, including Rembrandt in 1836 (fig. 26). Older Dutch and French sale catalogues were a rich source of information for Smith, who commended 'the talents of their writers, as well for their perspicuity and intelligence' as for the 'correctness and veracity with which [the catalogues] are generally written'. As Smith notes in the introduction to his catalogue as a whole, his work was the result of 'the observation of many years collecting, in France, Holland, Germany and England'. His volumes contain paintings 'from all the public and private collections in those countries'.[94]

In the foreword to the volume cataloguing Rembrandt's works, Smith points out that several paintings are included and described solely because of prints then in circulation. Though he concedes that this approach could be misleading, he did not believe he could justify rejecting paintings he had seen only in the form of prints made after them by other artists.[95] In this respect, Horst Gerson, who followed in Smith's footsteps many years later, adopted a similar approach. Gerson's *Rembrandt: The Complete Edition of the Paintings*, published in 1969, likewise pronounces on the authenticity of only those paintings the author had seen in person. The only comment, for instance, on the *Portrait of Rembrandt* in Melbourne is: 'I know the painting only from photographs, which do not give a favourable impression' (p. 15, fig. 1).[96]

Unlike Smith, we now consider it justifiable to reject as inauthentic paintings that are known as 'Rembrandts' only on the basis of old prints (figs 20, 3b). During the eighteenth century, in Germany and England in particular, engravings were made of numerous pictures, and most implausibly inscribed with the name Rembrandt.[97] It is also now thought that compositions were spuriously engraved as Rembrandts even in the artist's own time.[98]

Modern research

Since John Smith's time, rail and air travel have enabled scholars to view large numbers of paintings in a short space of time. Even more important, perhaps, was the advent of photography, which made it possible to compare truly reliable images of paintings. The tireless Dutch scholar Cornelis Hofstede de Groot (1863–1930) (fig. 27) assembled a collection of approximately 100,000 photographs and reproductions of the complete range of seventeenth-century Dutch painting, and expanded Smith's compilation of excerpts from auction catalogues. Hofstede de Groot's collection now forms the core of the famous Rijksbureau voor Kunsthistorische Documentatie (Netherlands Institute for Art History) in The Hague. Even today, the catalogue raisonné Hofstede de Groot published in 1915, with the subtitle 'based on the work of John Smith', is the starting point for all serious research on Rembrandt's paintings.[99]

With these resources available from the end of the nineteenth century, it also became possible to distinguish with greater certainty between the paintings of Rembrandt's pupils and followers. These studies culminated in the six-volume *Gemälde der Rembrandt-Schüler*, published by the distinguished German scholar Werner Sumowski between 1983 and 1995.

Archival research, first undertaken in the nineteenth century, has yielded a wealth of biographical and other data on Rembrandt and his pupils. Many seventeenth-century estate inventories – one of the richest sources of information – contain concise but adequate descriptions of paintings, among them the *Two Old Men Disputing* now in Melbourne (cat. no. 3).

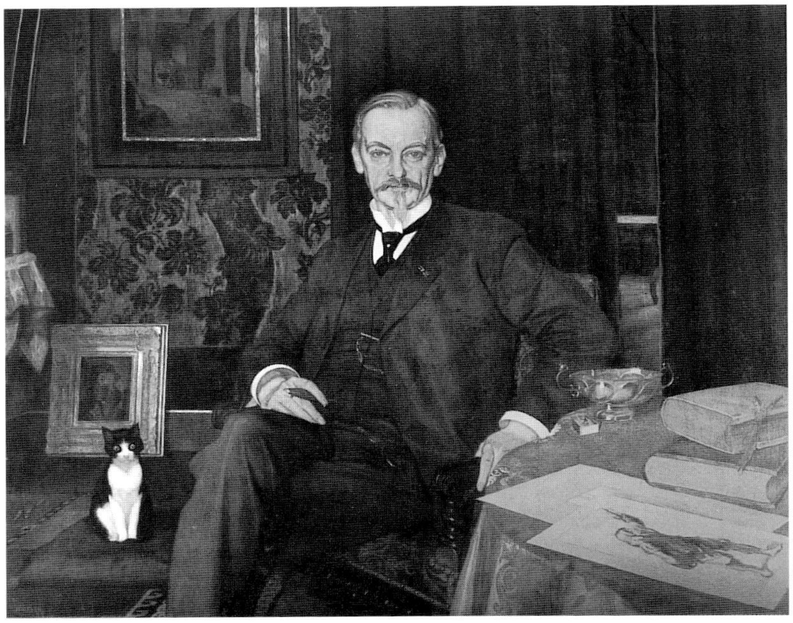

FIG. 27
Henk Meyer
Portrait of Cornelis Hofstede de Groot
Signed and dated 1923
Canvas
112.5 x 140.5 cm
Groninger Museum, Groningen
Photograph: John Stoel

In the late nineteenth century, moreover, the press developed into a mass medium, and famous painters became household names. Any dispute over a picture by an admired artist was likely to incite a public outcry. It was also around this time that eminent scholars first became embroiled in sordid arguments, some of them fought out in the courts and in the press, over the authenticity of certain 'Rembrandts'. The professional literature on Rembrandt has sometimes also been coloured by a similar lack of restraint. In 1910, for instance, the German scholar Alfred von Wurzbach launched a savage tirade against the 'Rembrandt-Doktoren', notably Hofstede de Groot, concluding: 'He moves with the speed of an automobile and, wherever he goes, leaves an unpleasant smell behind'. This remark was published not in a newspaper but in a manual that is still widely used today.[100]

Dissension of this kind is apparently an inevitable part of the ongoing debate that art history has become. What the art dealer John Smith once studied in his spare time is now the object of a life's work for professional art historians who, since the end of the nineteenth century, have occupied their own university chairs. The study of paintings is no longer the informal debate among an in-crowd of art lovers and connoisseurs that it seems to have been in Rembrandt's day, and even in the time of Hoet and Terwesten.

A devoted public

Today Rembrandt occupies a special place in people's hearts. In 1906, the distinguished Berlin museum director Wilhelm Bode (1845–1929) recalled the words the French painter Eugène Delacroix had written in his journal almost sixty years earlier: 'Perhaps the world will discover that Rembrandt is a far greater painter than Raphael'. Delacroix added apologetically: 'I write these blasphemous words – enough to raise the hackles of any schoolmaster – without actually taking sides in the matter'.[101] According to Bode, Delacroix had been right, for Rembrandt 'comes closer to our modern view of art [*Kunstanschauung*] than either Raphael or Michelangelo'.[102] Though more than ninety years have passed since Bode wrote these words, they are no less apposite today. In Bode's day, his own Kaiser-Friedrich-Museum in Berlin boasted the richest collection of Rembrandts in the world.

Works by the old master who so closely approached 'our modern *Kunstanschauung*' were increasingly sought after towards the end of the nineteenth century. There was a huge demand for Rembrandts, particularly among American collectors and the newly established museums in the United States. There may be a connection between this demand and the tremendous increase in the number of 'Rembrandts' in circulation.

In 1883 Bode counted 377 paintings, and in 1885 Eugène Dutuit in France arrived at a total of 452.[103] Between 1897 and 1905, Bode and Hofstede de Groot published eight lavish volumes containing what they regarded as Rembrandt's complete autograph oeuvre. The first fully illustrated study of its kind, the catalogue included reproductions of 595 paintings in all.[104] In 1908, the German Wilhelm R. Valentiner (1880–1958), assistant to Hofstede de Groot and subsequently to Bode, moved to the United States. In the same year he published his *Rembrandt* in a more popular series called 'Klassiker der Kunst', which included a further seventeen pictures.[105] The aforementioned von Wurzbach was sceptical about these spiralling numbers: 'It's a wonder that there are only 600 of these "Rembrandts" and not 6000'.[106] Nevertheless, in 1921 Valentiner compiled a supplement listing a further 120 'rediscovered' paintings by Rembrandt (*Wiedergefundene Gemälde*) that had meanwhile come to light. Although no more than a dozen of these works are still accepted today, some of them, such as the early *David Presenting the Head of Goliath to Saul* (fig. 4c) and the late *Apostle Bartholomew* (cat. no. 17), are among the highlights of Rembrandt's oeuvre.[107] The majority of the 'rediscovered' paintings that are still retained in Rembrandt's oeuvre were pictures that Hofstede de Groot had discussed in his standard work of 1915. In Hofstede de Groot's catalogue, as in that of his predecessor John Smith, the total number of Rembrandts can hardly be counted, because both authors include large numbers of pictures that may in fact be identical with other of the works they list.

Never before had Rembrandt's oeuvre been so large – nor the supply of paintings so seemingly endless. Valentiner came under attack, mainly from Bredius, whose own version of Rembrandt's oeuvre, compiled in 1935, itself came to a total of 630. This number included the *Polish Rider*, which Bredius had discovered in a castle in Poland (fig. 24).

In 1969, when Gerson, who had assisted in the compilation of Bredius's catalogue of 1935, published his new edition of the book, he added a few paintings of which Bredius had not been aware. But it transpires that Gerson, in his brief commentaries on each of the paintings, in fact rejected a third of those which Bredius had included as autograph: Gerson kept only 420 Rembrandts. By this time, new – and lasting – attributions to Rembrandt were rare. Gerson found no more than one new Rembrandt – the earliest painting of all – a work that had been languishing in the storeroom of the Lyon Museum (p. 23, fig. 1).[108]

The Rembrandt Research Project

All of the scholars discussed to date worked on their own, and were therefore solely responsible for deciding whether or not a picture was autograph. In 1968 their task was taken over by the Rembrandt Research Project, a team of five Dutch scholars, four of whom were born around 1925. Though they shared responsibility for their work, it is common knowledge that Josua Bruyn was the *primus inter pares*. The team's objective, to be met by serious discussion and by the careful division of tasks, was to produce a more reliable, and more fully documented, definition of Rembrandt's oeuvre.[109]

The first volume of their *Corpus of Rembrandt Paintings*, published in 1982, had a profound impact. The team had taken full advantage of new research techniques. Dendrochronology, for instance, enabled them to establish by scientific means whether the tree from which a given panel had been cut was indeed felled before the presumed date of the painting: if the tree was felled after Rembrandt's death, then obviously the painting could not be by the master's hand. Dendrochronology also made it possible to show that some of the paintings studied by the team had been executed on panels cut from one and the same tree.[110] Similarly, volumes II and III of the *Corpus* were able to report that the canvas used for some of the paintings came from the same rolls of linen.[111] Moreover, by comparing X-ray photographs of many different paintings, the team was able to conclude whether or not the X-ray image of any given piece revealed characteristics that were 'typical' of Rembrandt. All of these factors were taken into account as the team considered whether to maintain or overturn the individual attributions.

Volume I of the *Corpus*, which covers Rembrandt's earliest period, from 1625 to 1631, the years he was still working entirely on his own in Leiden, was generally received with awe and admiration. Volumes II and III, however, which appeared in 1986 and 1989, additionally aroused irritation and even dismay. They concern the period 1631 to 1642, when Rembrandt was living and working in Amsterdam. These were the years in which he rose to fame and took on numerous pupils and, presumably, assistants. An important question is whether these others had a hand in Rembrandt's paintings or whether he still produced all of his work completely on his own. The team concluded that he indeed continued to execute fully autograph paintings, but that in addition his workshop produced work of their own, while adhering entirely to the master's style. Exactly what the division of labour was under Rembrandt's roof was not made clear, but the *Corpus* did attribute many traditionally accepted Rembrandts to his studio.

Surprisingly, the *Corpus* accepted no more than about half the paintings Gerson had listed as autograph Rembrandts. Nevertheless, Gerson's book by implication remained the canon, as the majority of paintings whose authenticity he had doubted were not even discussed in volumes II and III of the *Corpus* (one exception being the *Man Holding His Hat* (cat. no. 12)).

Despite the new scientific techniques available to the Rembrandt Research Project, paintings were ultimately accepted in or rejected from the *Corpus* on the grounds of their quality. In the second and third volumes, more than in the first, certain paintings executed on panels from the same tree, or on canvases from the same roll, were accepted – while others were rejected – on the basis of perceived differences in quality. At the end of the day, time-honoured connoisseurship prevailed as the decisive factor.

The subjective element became clearer still when Ernst van de Wetering (b. 1938), the youngest member of the team, insisted on having his own view on record in certain cases, in each instance in support of a painting rejected by the rest of the team. Volume I of the *Corpus*, for example, in which the *Bearded Old Man* is ascribed to an artist 'from Rembrandt's immediate circle', includes a note to the effect that van de Wetering considered the work to be autograph (cat. no. 4).[112]

Despite this dissension within the group, it still came as a surprise when the four older members of the team published a letter in the *Burlington Magazine* in 1993 announcing that the remainder of the *Corpus* was to be completed by van de Wetering. In particular, they wrote, van de Wetering's wish to abandon the 'rigorous classification' of paintings as Rembrandts, non-Rembrandts and inconclusive attributions 'failed to generate the enthusiasm necessary for a concerted change of course'.[113] Since that time, work on the Rembrandt *Corpus* has been continued by van de Wetering and his six younger assistants, who form the second Rembrandt Research team. Their aim now, according to van de Wetering, is 'to project all the arguments for and against attribution to Rembrandt without the need to force individual paintings into the straitjacket of a simple "yes" or "no"'.[114]

Recent studies

The debates among the members of the first Rembrandt Research Project team may have encouraged others to express more freely their own views on the authenticity of supposed Rembrandts. In a fascinating book on Rembrandt published in 1984 – the first to reproduce in colour the works regarded by the author as belonging to Rembrandt's oeuvre – Gary Schwartz still adhered almost entirely to the selection made by Gerson and to that in the then recently published first volume of the *Corpus*. Yet in his *Rembrandt* of 1986 Christian Tümpel expressed reservations about many other paintings than those queried by the *Corpus*, and again completely revised his opinion about many of them in a new edition of the book, which appeared in 1993.[115] Leonard Slatkes, in his 1992 oeuvre catalogue of Rembrandt's paintings, likewise expressed his own firmly held views on the attributions.[116] More recently, Walter Liedtke and Hubert von Sonnenburg, curator and conservator respectively at the Metropolitan Museum of Art in New York, have done outstanding work in their examination of the forty or more 'Rembrandts' acquired by this august institution since 1889. The majority, which had been presented as gifts, were still displayed with labels carrying the museum's original title and attribution, out of respect for the generous donors and their families. Liedtke and von Sonnenburg accepted only half of these pictures as Rembrandts, and even then held different opinions about some of them. Each was subsequently given the opportunity to compile his own 'corpus' of Rembrandts at the Metropolitan Museum in the two-volume *Rembrandt / Not Rembrandt* catalogue of 1995–96.[117] Neither of the authors appears to have been greatly influenced by the opinions, whether published or unpublished, of the two Rembrandt Research Project teams.

Consensus

Readers not previously aware of the complexities involved in determining which works constitute Rembrandt's authentic oeuvre are likely to think this an impossible task. However, as regards the general outlines of Rembrandt's oeuvre, the opinions of the authors mentioned above are more closely aligned than one might expect. By and large, the works listed as Rembrandts in early inventories and auction catalogues have remained unchallenged, although a few of the early attributions have indeed been revised, mainly as a result of research conducted after about 1890, when art history was evolving into a professional discipline. At that stage a number of paintings were definitively transferred from Rembrandt to explicitly named pupils. (One example is cat. no. 46 in the present catalogue, which was taken from Rembrandt in 1899 and given to Ferdinand Bol.) There is now a general consensus regarding Rembrandt's output, although a great many 'Rembrandts' have come to be regarded as studio work since the publication of Gerson's book in 1969, and even more since the Rembrandt Research Project reported its findings between 1982 and 1989.

Some of the pictures added to Rembrandt's oeuvre around 1900 were 'comets' that suddenly flared up, only to vanish again. Other new stars shone brightly for a while – their lifespan often depending on the authority of particular connoisseurs. Two new Rembrandts that continued to sparkle for some time, and whose proposed removal from the oeuvre caused considerable upheaval, were the *Polish Rider* and the *Man in the Golden Helmet* referred to above (figs 24, 25). The *Man in the Golden Helmet*, which was relatively unknown until Wilhelm Bode acquired it for the Berlin Museum in 1897, had subsequently become an icon, for the German public in particular. In the same year, Bredius had jubilantly announced his discovery of the *Polish Rider*,[118] a canvas that the American magnate Henry Clay Frick added to his collection of masterpieces in 1910.

Most of the paintings recently removed from Rembrandt's oeuvre are now attributed to his studio. In no recent publication have I found persuasive attributions of such works to any one particular pupil, as occurred with Flinck's *Isaac Blessing Jacob* (cat. no. 41) for example, with the de Gelder in Rotterdam, and with the Bol in Springfield, Massachusetts (cat. no. 46).[119] The attribution of the *Polish Rider* to Willem Drost is shaky by comparison.

All told, the outlines of the map of Rembrandt's painted oeuvre are clear, but there is unlikely ever to be absolute consensus about the exact boundaries of the territories within it. It may one day be forgotten that many of the works whose authorship has been queried were ever rejected from Rembrandt's oeuvre. After all, the 'scientific evidence' produced around 1890 to support the view that most of the great Shakespearian dramas were written by assistants is now merely a historical curiosity. The plays are still read and produced with undiminished pleasure.[120] And the same could well happen to some (many?) of today's orphaned Rembrandts.

It is a common illusion that right and wrong in such matters can be demonstrated by producing sounder arguments or by finding the right method. Recognizing the author of a work of art is not a matter of applying a formula. It is knowledge that simply comes to a connoisseur of the painter, in the same way that one recognizes one's mother or neighbour, regardless of light conditions, viewpoint, clothing or facial expression. Issues surrounding recognition of the artist's hand may be discussed with others who share a similar interest, just as two brothers might confer about whether the woman in the distance is in fact their mother. John Smith knew it was impossible 'to lay down the rules that will enable every one to acquire the knowledge necessary to constitute a connoisseur'.[121] Talent and enduring commitment are the means by which one can try to hone a little more finely one's ability to recognize, and by which one may ultimately discover more than simply a painting or a face. In Rembrandt's case such efforts are fraught with extra difficulties, as others sought to be exactly like him, while he dedicated himself to teaching them how. Added to this is the steadily increasing distance in time, so that for every scrap of information we gain another is lost.

Transferring the attribution of a once unchallenged masterpiece by Rembrandt to a pupil or to the master's studio amounts to little more than fine-tuning a conclusion. De Gelder, Bol and Drost (cat. nos 69–72, 44–48, 63) were talented pupils who learned to follow Rembrandt's style with impeccable skill. If *Elisabeth Bas* is indeed a Bol and the *Polish Rider* a Drost, then their makers, under Rembrandt's influence, managed to transcend themselves. Their achievement may be compared to what a gifted musician working under a truly great conductor can accomplish, or an actor under the guidance of an outstanding director.[122] The paintings at issue may in fact be the fruits of a similar partnership, with the pupil, inspired by the master to surpass the limits of his talent, producing work of the most excellent quality. In this sense, a reattribution is merely a shift in emphasis.

Similar shifts have occurred fairly recently, with regard to the *Finding of Moses*, for instance, the *Departure of the Shunamite Woman*, and the *Man with a Red Cap* (cat. nos 29, 30, 32). Regarded as genuine Rembrandts for more than two hundred years, they are now often thought more likely to be studio pieces. This is no cause for turmoil and sensationalism, but it is certainly fascinating to ponder the questions surrounding these reattributions and to try to fathom the reasons for such changes. It is our hope that all who visit the present exhibition and read this catalogue will have the opportunity to do so.

1 Van de Wetering 1991–92a, p. 21.

2 Broos 1977. The pioneering classic on this topic is Van Rijckevorsel 1932.

3 Huygens / Kan 1946, p. 82.

4 Strauss & Van der Meulen 1979, p. 161, no. 1639/2 (Rembrandt letter, 12 January 1639) (with a discussion of the various connotations of these words).

5 Lee 1967, p. 11.

6 Van Mander 1604, fol. 191.

7 Mancini 1956–57, vol. I, p. 120: 'qualque meretrice sozza' (text from *c.*1620). The painting is now in the Louvre, Paris.

8 Van Thiel 1971.

9 Brederode 1622, p. 8.

10 A. Houbraken (under the *nom de plume* Philaléthes), *Verzameling van uitgelezene keurstoffen*, cited in Roscam Abbing 1994, p. 19: 'zich niet vergapen, veel min navolgen zoo een mismaakte afbeelding van Adam en Eva als onder de prentkonst van Rembrant van Rijn gevonden word'. Houbraken wrote about Rembrandt's female nudes in general in his more widely known *Groote schouburgh*: 'They are, as the proverb says, *too depressing* even to think about, for most of these apparitions are repulsive' (Houbraken 1718–21, vol. I, 1718, pp. 261–2).

11 Bartsch 1797, no. 28: 'Comme Rembrandt ne s'entendoit point à travailler le nud, ce morceau est assez incorrect, et les têtes sont tout à fait désagréables'. Gersaint's 1751 description of the print includes critical remarks along much the same lines (Gersaint 1751, no. 29).

12 Kielich 1997.

13 For B.186, *Le Lit français*, see E. de Jongh, in Amsterdam 1997, cat. no. 57.

14 C. Brown, in MacLaren / Brown 1991, vol. 1, pp. 332–3, no. 54. Callisto is proposed in Leja 1996.

15 Van der Waals 1988, p. 64, fig. 65 (the print after the sculpture), p. 67, note 113. For another reproduction of the print after the sculpture, see J. Kelch, in Berlin / Amsterdam / London 1991–92a, p. 248, fig. 40b. Rembrandt's version of the antique sculpture is more modest, as the figure in the *Woman Bathing* lifts little more than the hem of her shift.

16 First observed by Van Rijckevorsel 1932, p. 35.

17 Broos 1977, p. 132.

18 Strauss & Van der Meulen 1979, p. 150, no. 1638/2.

19 Van Mander 1604, fol. 208; Van Mander / Miedema 1994–96, vol. I, pp. 90–1.

20 Vasari 1906, vol. V, p. 400; Vasari 1963, vol. III, p. 70.

21 The similarities between the two works were observed in Blankert 1967, p. 108, no. 62.

22 Blankert 1973, pp. 32–9 (with references to literature relevant to much of the following section of the present introduction). The same theme must also be the subject of the *Laughing Self-Portrait* by Giacomo Francesco Cipper, called Todeschini (active 1707–1736), a work sold in New York in 1988 (New York (Sotheby's), 14 January 1988 [afternoon sale], lot 161, repr.). In this work, the artist, palette in hand, points at the head of an old woman he is depicting on the canvas on his easel. This reference was kindly provided by Josua Bruyn, Amsterdam. The story of the laughing Zeuxis depicting an old woman (see below) is also reported by the Dutch painter and writer J.C. Weyerman (Weyerman 1729–69, vol. I, 1729, p. 44).

23 See commentary to our cat. no. 28: the references in question occur in the catalogue of the Schaub sale of 1758, in Dodsley (1761), in the *English Connoisseur* (1766), in the *Ambulator* (1774, 1792), and in Brayley (1808).

24 Some time earlier, in 1675, the German painter Joachim von Sandrart, who had lived in Amsterdam, had criticized Rembrandt for defying 'our rules of art, of anatomy, human proportions and perspective, [and for] arguing against the use of antique sculptures, against Raphael's draughtsmanship and the systematic training of young artists, and against the Academies, so vital to our profession, asserting that one should rely only upon nature and observe no other rules' (Sandrart 1675, p. 202).

25 Van Hoogstraten 1678, pp. 64–5: 'Ziet toe, of de knien door de kouseband niet bedorven zijn ... of de scheenen en kuiten niet met kneepen, door 't binden, vervalst zijn. 't Vrouwvolk is dit veel onderhavich; zie toe of buik en lendenen door 't parssen der kleederen niet miswassen zijn'. The reference is to Zeuxis, although he is not actually named.

26 Van Hoogstraten 1678, pp. 284, 294.

27 Roscam Abbing 1994, p. 20, made this observation and also drew a connection between the two passages in Hoogstraten. For an earlier comment on Hoogstraten's text, see Emmens 1979, p. 220.

28 Slive 1953, pp. 147, 148. The picture referred to is probably that at the Metropolitan Museum of Art, New York (p. 27, fig. 8).

29 Elsum 1700, epigram no. 32: 'Appemantus at Dinner on a Turnip, at the Stadthouse at Amsterdam' (a reference to Govaert Flinck's painting *Consul Marcus Curius Dentatus Prefers Eating His Turnips to the Presents of the Samnites* of 1656, at the Royal Palace (formerly the Town Hall), Amsterdam (see p. 206, fig. 7).

30 Elsum 1700, epigram nos 4, 5 (no. 5 carries the footnote: 'Zeuxis upon a view of it died with laughing').

31 Van Os 1991.

32 Van Hoogstraten 1678, p. 48. Hoogstraten had in mind Dürer's *Die Lehre von menschlicher Proportion* (Treatise on Human Proportions) (first edition, Nuremberg, 1528); see *Schriftlicher Nachlass*, vol. III, p. 295.

33 For these works and others, see Hoff 1995.

34 For the importance of the history piece in Holland, see A. Blankert, in Washington / Detroit / Amsterdam 1980–81a, pp. 15–32.

35 Van Mander 1604, fol. 28r; Van Mander / Miedema 1994–96, vol. I, p. 382 (cf. Miedema 1973, vol. II, pp. 345–6). See A. Blankert, in Washington / Detroit / Amsterdam 1980–81a, pp. 16–18 (with references to other early authors).

36 The seventeenth-century term *tronie* was first introduced into the art historical literature, for the classification of Rembrandt's oeuvre into history pieces, portraits and *tronies*, in Blankert 1976, pp. 27–31; see also Blankert 1982, pp. 26–8.

37 Volker Manuth is preparing a study on the high esteem in which Holbein and Dürer were held in the seventeenth century.

38 C. Schuckman & M. Royalton-Kisch, in Amsterdam 1996, cat. no. 5.

39 Slive 1953, p. 32; Bruyn 1982, p. 40.

40 Smith 1829–42, vol. VII, 1836, nos 297, 243, 247, 477, 349, 323. From 1761, our cat. no. 28 was also long believed to represent 'Admiral Tromp' (see commentary to catalogue entry).

41 Bredius 1935; Bredius 1937.

42 This is briefly outlined in Blankert & Van Velzen 1986–87, pp. 9–11.

43 Hofstede de Groot 1907–28, vol. VI, 1915 (in German). The English edition of the following year, Hofstede de Groot 1908–27, vol. VI, 1916, is the edition generally cited in the present catalogue.

44 Gersaint and Bartsch had done the same, before Bredius: their catalogues of Rembrandt's etchings, published in 1751 and 1797 respectively, presented the works in the conventional sequence, but with Rembrandt's etched self-portraits at the beginning (B.1–27). See Gersaint 1751; Bartsch 1797.

45 Gerson began his career working on the annotations in the 1935 edition of Bredius's catalogue.
46 Bürger 1858–60, vol. 1, pp. 322–4.
47 A. Blankert, in Washington / Detroit / Amsterdam 1980–81a, pp. 15–16.
48 Bürger 1858–60, vol. 1, pp. 322–4.
49 Houbraken 1718–21, vol. I, 1718, p. 272. Geertje had many connections with Raarep, or Ransdorp, a village north of Amsterdam.
50 Strauss & Van der Meulen 1979, p. 422, no. 1658/18. For the portrait of Saskia, see *Corpus*, vol. II, 1986, no. A85; Schnackenburg 1996, vol. I, p. 231, no. GK 236. In 1647, portraits of Rembrandt and his wife were accepted as collateral in a business transaction; in 1648 what were possibly the same pieces were mentioned in a will (Strauss & Van der Meulen 1979, pp. 254, 262, nos 1647/1, 1648/7).
51 De Jonghe's inventory appears in Hofstede de Groot 1906a, pp. 406–10, no. 346. De Hoop Scheffer and Boon studied the document again and found that Hofstede de Groot had misinterpreted important parts of it (De Hoop Scheffer & Boon 1971).
52 Houbraken 1718–21, vol. I, 1718, p. 213. A document of 1665 confirms Titus's involvement in selling his father's prints (Strauss & Van der Meulen 1979, pp. 541, 543, no. 1665/6). Sandrart was the first to mention in print that Rembrandt had a son. Sandrart describes this son as an artist but does not give his name (Sandrart 1675, p. 202).
53 De Hoop Scheffer & Boon 1971, pp. 6, 10, 12, 14–16; De Hoop Scheffer 1972.
54 Smith 1829–42, vol. VII, 1836, nos 490–492, 517, 540, 542, 592. For eighteenth-century references to portraits of Rembrandt's mother, see Hofstede de Groot 1908–27, vol. VI, 1916, pp. 327–8, nos 688, 689, 689b, 689e. The index cards at the RKD mention ten references from before 1800.
55 Strauss & Van der Meulen 1979, p. 240, no. 1644/1 (1644, in Leiden); Hofstede de Groot 1906a, no. 350 (1680, in the collection of the painter Jan van de Cappelle).
56 Ashmolean Museum, Oxford (Benesch 1973, vol. I, no. 56).
57 Strauss & Van der Meulen 1979, p. 216, no. 1641/8.
58 Hofstede de Groot 1908–27, vol. VI, 1916, p. 173, no. 293, for instance, recognizes in this figure the features of Rembrandt's father.
59 Hofstede de Groot 1906a, no. 310: 'een counterfeytsel van des overleden man daar hij over de leuning legt'.
60 Hofstede de Groot 1908–27, vol. VI, 1916, p. 335, no. 709a.
61 Hofstede de Groot 1908–27, vol. VI, 1916, pp. 333–6, nos 702–710. For Smith's earlier reference to our fig. 20, see Smith 1829–42, vol. VII, 1836, p. 96, no. 251.
62 In 1915 Hofstede de Groot listed a dozen portraits of Liesbeth (Hofstede de Groot 1907–28, vol. VI, 1915, nos 691–701). Some twenty-five years before this, Bode had suggested that Rembrandt's brother Adriaen was the model in various paintings (Bode 1891). Hofstede de Groot 1908–27, vol. VI, 1916, p. 161, no. 261, dismissed this idea.
63 Bauch 1966, p. 8, no. 109.
64 In 1953 a study similar to the present one was carried out by Münz, who likewise sought to distinguish between the genuine and supposed portrayals of Rembrandt's parents and siblings (Münz 1953). He did so on the basis of a few so-called portraits of the parents, thereby relying on the old reading of Clement de Jonghe's inventory, a reading amended in 1971 (see above). Cf. *Corpus*, vol. I, 1982, pp. 204 (on the 'father'), 273 (on the 'mother'); vol. II, 1986, p. 437 (on Saskia, but without reference to the etching (our fig. 16)).
65 Tümpel 1969 (based on Tümpel's Hamburg dissertation of 1968).
66 Tümpel 1969, pp. 160–2: 'Um den psychologischen Gehalt einer Szene gegenüber den traditioneller Darstellung zu intensivieren oder das Besondere ... gesteigert zu Anschauung zu bringen'.
67 Tümpel 1969, pp. 179–80.
68 Hofstede de Groot 1908–27, vol. VI, 1916, p. 184, no. 316, refers to 'A Woman Reading [formerly called The Prophetess Anna]', and Bredius 1935, no. 69, describes the picture as 'Old Woman Reading (Rembrandt's mother as the prophetess Anna)'. In the *Corpus* the interpretation 'Anna' (Hannah in German) is erroneously attributed to Tümpel (*Corpus*, vol. I, 1982, p. 355, no. A37), who in fact argued an existing case, discussing the tradition of this identification.
69 C. Schuckman & M. Royalton-Kisch, in Amsterdam 1996, cat. no. 4.
70 *Corpus*, vol. I, 1982, p. 355, no. A37.
71 This is not to say that the words are in Hebrew, as Tümpel suggests (Tümpel 1969, p. 179, note 143).
72 Cf. *Corpus*, vol. I, 1982, p. 356, no. A37, on the idea of the painting's possibly being a depiction of a prophetess or sibyl.
73 Tümpel 1986, no. A54 (where he also attributes the picture to Jan Lievens). For the earlier interpretations of the picture, see commentary to our cat. no. 8.
74 White 1982, p. 101, no. 158.
75 *Corpus*, vol. II, 1986, pp. 517–18, no. A95. Although this picture could be the Rembrandt described in 1678 as a portrayal of Paracelsus, the interpretation says little of Rembrandt's own intention.
76 Michel 1893, p. 495.
77 J. Giltaij & G. Jansen, in Rotterdam 1988, pp. 41–3, cat. no. 9.
78 For a detailed account, see P. van Thiel, in Berlin / Amsterdam / London 1991–92c, cat. no. 63.
79 Bruyn 1984, p. 158. On the response to the reattribution of the *Polish Rider*, see Bailey 1990; Bailey 1994.
80 Kelch 1986.
81 Rembrandt was one of the experts who were at loggerheads over the authenticity of a landscape attributed to Paul Bril, an Antwerp artist working in Rome (Bredius 1889; see also Duverger 1965). Vermeer dismissed as 'rags' a collection that other prominent artists regarded as works by Titian, Raphael and others (Blankert 1978a, p. 148).
82 Van de Wetering 1986, p. 49 (with a reproduction of the document).
83 Strauss & Van der Meulen 1979, p. 456, no. 1660/5.
84 *Corpus*, vol. II, 1986, p. 839; see also commentary to our cat. no. 2 and p. 113, on our fig. 8h.
85 For details and references, see Blankert 1992–93, p. 59. However, the numbers cited there, which were provided by the Getty Provenance Index, need to be corrected (Burton Fredericksen, letter to the author, 26 March 1997). For a reference to these corrected numbers, to be published in greater detail at a later date, see the essay by Jaap van der Veen in the present catalogue. For the pieces 'van een discipel', see also Bruyn 1989, p. 26.
86 Hoet 1752; Hoet / Terwesten 1770.
87 Hoet 1752, vol. I, p. 564, no. 83. No. 87 in the same auction, 'a female *tronie* by Rembrandt' (Een vrouwe tronie door Rembrandt) fetched only seventeen guilders. The other two copies were in sales in 1701 (Hoet 1752, vol. I, p. 64, no. 36) and 1763 (Hoet / Terwesten 1770, p. 337, ex-catalogue).
88 The pieces in question were auctioned in the period 1748–67 (Hoet 1752, vol. II, p. 231, no. 90, p. 307, no. 164; Hoet / Terwesten 1770, p. 221, no. 119, p. 443, nos 143, 144; p. 601, no. 74).
89 Hoet / Terwesten 1770, p. 355.
90 Hoet 1752, vol. II, p. 285, no. 64 (1750).
91 Hoet / Terwesten 1770, p. 403, no. 115, 30 guilders (1765); Hoet / Terwesten 1770, p. 686, no. 10, 10 guilders (1768).
92 The situation with respect to the pupils whose works appear in the present exhibition (cat. nos 33–72) is that they are well represented in the early sale catalogues, except for the following. Jan Victors is not mentioned in Hoet or Terwesten: his work apparently attracted little interest at the time. Nor were many works sold by Samuel van Hoogstraten or Nicolaes Maes; only volume III (Hoet / Terwesten 1770) mentions two paintings by each of them. It also seems that no distinction was made between Barend and Carel Fabritius. Works by Willem Drost were as rare as they are today (four references in Hoet 1752, vol. I).
93 For van der Marck, see Blankert 1992–93, pp. 52–3.
94 Smith 1829–42, vol. I, 1829, p. xxi.
95 Smith 1829–42, vol. VI, 1836, p. v.
96 H. Gerson, in Bredius / Gerson 1969, p. 551, no. 56.
97 For the prints made in England, see the reproductions in New Haven 1983.
98 Bruyn 1982, pp. 35–59.
99 See note 43 above.
100 Von Wurzbach 1906–11, vol. III, 1911, p. 134: 'Er bewegt sich mit der Schnelligkeit eines Automobils und wo immer er vorüber kommt hinterlässt er einen üblen Geruch'.
101 Delacroix / Joubin 1950, vol. I, p. 439 (entry for 6 June 1851).

102 Bode 1907, p. 3.
103 Bode 1883, pp. 555–610; Dutuit 1885, pp. iii–iv, 59–65.
104 Bode & Hofstede de Groot 1897–1905.
105 Valentiner 1908.
106 Von Wurzbach 1906–11, vol. II, 1910, p. 389: 'Man kann nur staunen dass die Zahl der vermeintlichen Rembrandtbilder nur 600 und nicht 6000 beträgt'.
107 For *David Presenting the Head of Goliath to Saul*, see Hofstede de Groot 1908–27, vol. VI, 1916, p. 41, no. 34; Valentiner 1921, no. 1. For the *Apostle Bartholomew*, see Valentiner 1921, no. 82.
108 *The Stoning of Stephen*, Musée des Beaux-Arts, Lyon (Bredius / Gerson 1969, no. 531A; *Corpus*, vol. I, 1982, no. A1).
109 For the best discussion of the first Rembrandt Research Team, see Bailey 1990; Bailey 1994.
110 See the table in *Corpus*, vol. III, 1989, pp. 783–7.
111 See the table in *Corpus*, vol. II, 1986, pp. 26–9.
112 For such views held by van de Wetering alone, see *Corpus*, vol. I, 1982, pp. 235, 580, 601, nos A22, C22, C26; vol. II, 1986, pp. 587, 766, nos B8, C70; vol. III, 1989, p. 655, no. C103.
113 Bruyn et al. 1993.
114 Van de Wetering 1993, p. 765.
115 Tümpel 1986; Tümpel 1993. See also White 1994.
116 Slatkes 1992 (published in Italian only).
117 New York 1995–96.
118 For details of Bredius's discovery, see Broos 1991.
119 However, some interesting suggestions have been made, such as that the *Good Samaritan* in the Wallace Collection in London might be by Flinck (*Corpus*, vol. II, 1986, p. 614, no. C48).
120 Blankert 1992–93, p. 68 (with references to earlier literature).
121 Smith 1829–42, vol. I, 1829, p. xx.
122 This is Gombrich's analogy in respect of Raphael and his studio (Gombrich 1984, p. 173).

The Miracle of Our Age: Rembrandt through the Eyes of His Contemporaries

ERNST VAN DE WETERING

Introduction

Every once in a while a historical document concerning Rembrandt comes to light. A recent find rather surprisingly highlights the great admiration Rembrandt enjoyed both at home and abroad during his own lifetime. For anyone believing that Rembrandt died in obscurity – and there are still many who do – the contents of this document may come as quite a surprise.

The passage in question consists of only a few words in a document entitled 'The Names of the Most Distinguished European Painters', found among the papers left by the learned German clergyman and art lover Gabriel Bucelinus (1599–1681) (fig. 1). The document contains a long list of painters' names Bucelinus compiled in 1664,[1] five years before Rembrandt's death (fig. 2).

Among these 'distinguished' artists are many painters still renowned today, such as Leonardo da Vinci and Titian from the fifteenth and sixteenth centuries, and Rubens and Poussin from the seventeenth century, but there are also some who have fallen into obscurity, and who presumably lived near Bucelinus. All these names, 166 in all, are listed in seemingly endless succession.[2] In one case only, that of Rembrandt – spelt phonetically as *Rimprant* – does the author comment on the artist's merits. The Latin words *nostrae aetatis miraculum* (the miracle of our age) are inscribed in the same hand, Bucelinus's, after Rembrandt's name (fig. 3).

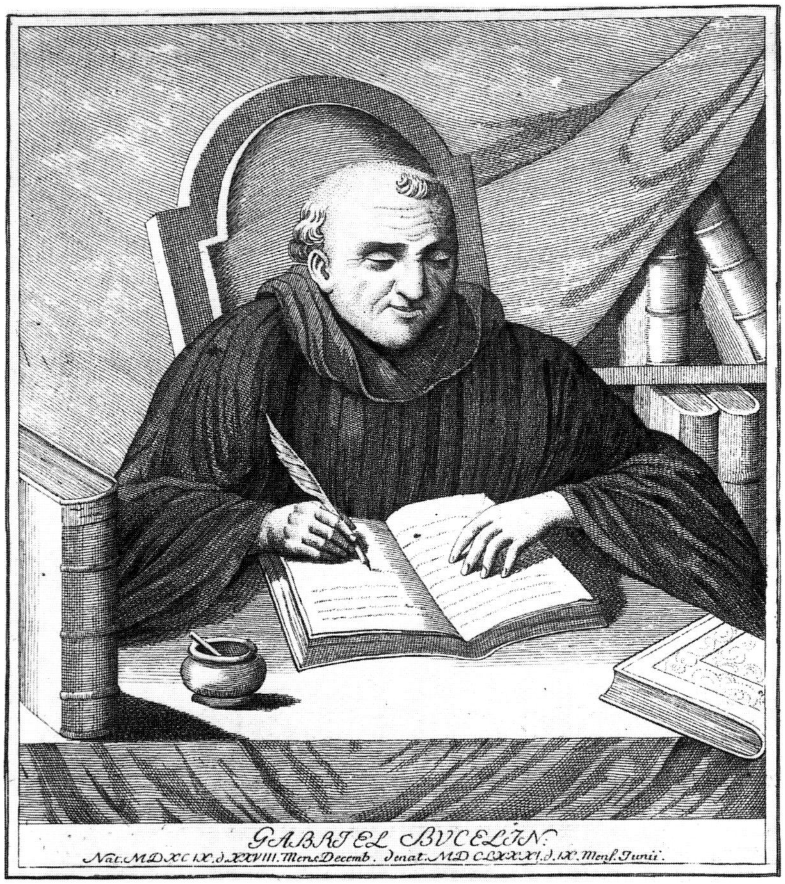

FIG. 1
Portrait of Gabriel Bucelinus (from Stump 1976).

Not only is it surprising that Rembrandt was singled out for this exalted commendation; no less intriguing is the question of how a clergyman from the south of Germany came to bestow such lavish praise on a Dutch painter living a journey of several weeks to the north.

The Dutch art historian Robert Schillemans, who found the document, published two articles on his discovery.[3] In neither of them, however, does he explore in depth the implications of Bucelinus's tribute in terms of the appreciation of Rembrandt in the seventeenth century. Since the publication of Schillemans's articles this tribute has been invoked as a stirring conclusion to many a speech or lecture on Rembrandt, but as far as can be determined the significance of the newly discovered text with respect to the way in which Rembrandt was received in the seventeenth century has not been probed. This present essay is an attempt to examine this question.

After considering the implications of a list like Bucelinus's in a wider context, an attempt will be made to reconstruct some of the criteria that may have inspired Bucelinus to single out Rembrandt for such exuberant praise. Those who look at Rembrandt's work today will then be in a position to view some of his accomplishments through the eyes of his contemporaries. This approach may also provide a clearer understanding of aspects of the art of painting that may have been of particular importance to Rembrandt.

The art lover and the artist

This is by no means the first study of the appreciation accorded to Rembrandt by his contemporaries. The sources on Rembrandt compiled by Hofstede de Groot and published in 1906 provided an impression of the way Rembrandt was regarded both in his own day and two generations later.[4] But only in 1953 were all the texts from the period between 1628 and 1730 that contained comments on Rembrandt as an artist compiled and annotated – in Seymour Slive's *Rembrandt and His Critics.*[5] Jan Emmens's *Rembrandt en de regels van de kunst* (Rembrandt and the Rules of Art) (1964) placed the range of views expressed in these comments in a wider art-theoretical framework.[6] Even at that stage, it was clear from both these works that the notion that Rembrandt ended his career in obscurity was a myth. The idea that a further contribution

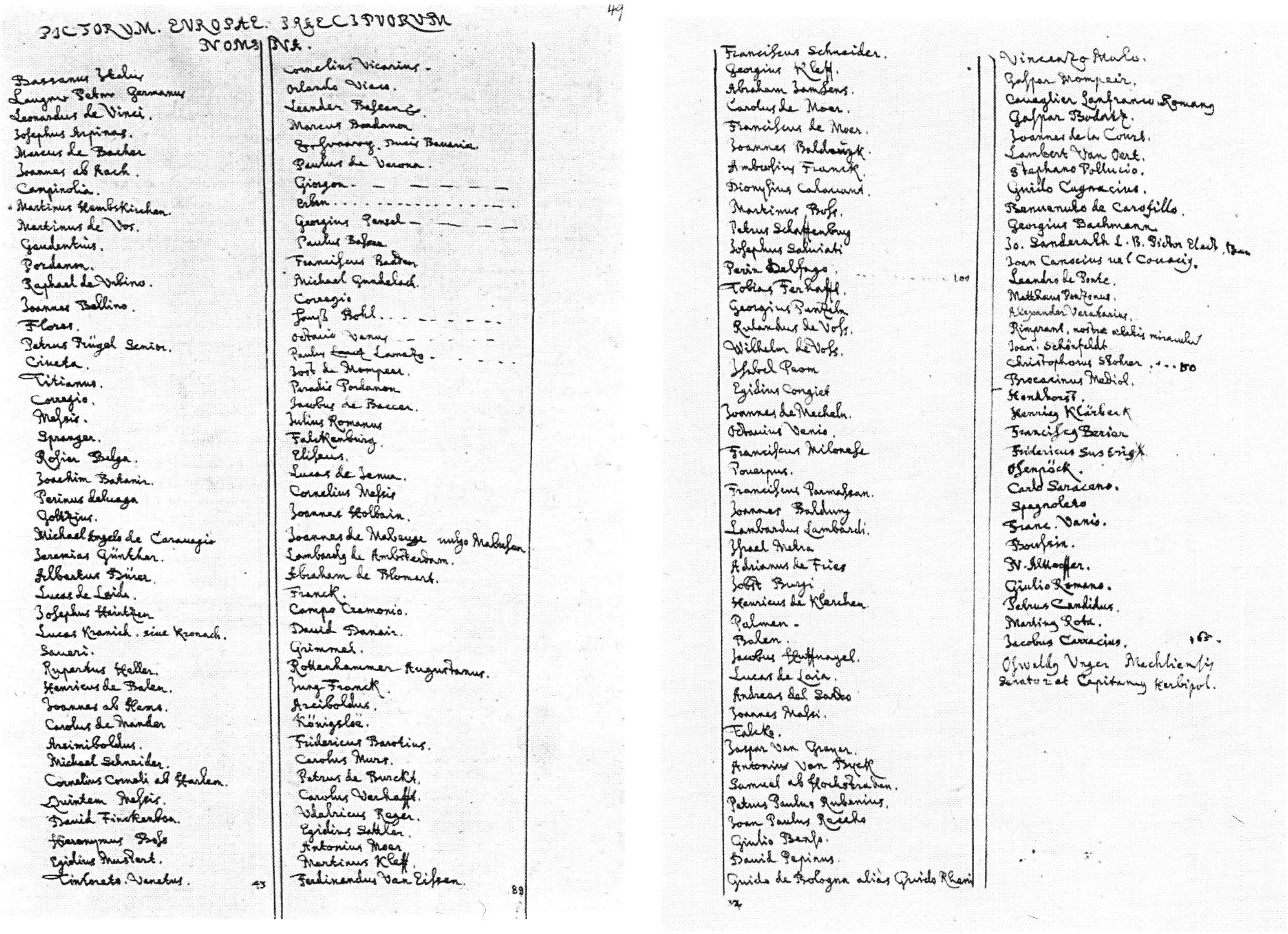

PICTORUM EUROPAE PRAECIPUORUM NOMINA.

Bassanus Italus
Langus Sabaudiensis Germanus
Leonardus de Vinci.
Josephus Arpinas.
Marcus le Backer
Joannes ab Aach.
Campinolia.
Martinus Hemskirchen.
Martinus de Vos.
Gaudentius.
Pordenon.
Raphael de Urbino.
Joannes Bellino.
Flores.
Petrus Brügel Senior.
Cineta.
Titianus.
Corregio.
Malsis.
Spranger.
Rosien Belga.
Joachim Bakanir.
Perinus de Vaga.
Goltzius.
Michael Angelo de Caravagio
Jeremias Günther.
Albertus Dürer.
Lucas de Leide.
Josephus Heintzen
Lucas Kranich. sive Kranach.
Saueri.
Rupertus Haller.
Henricus de Balen.
Joannes ab Haus.
Carolus de Mander
Arcimboldus.
Michael Schneider.
Cornelius Corneli ab Harlem.
Quintem Malsis.
David Finckenbon.
Hieronymus Bosse
Egidius Mustert.
Tintoretto Venetus. 43

Cornelius Vicarius.
Orlando Vicco.
Leander Bassano.
Marcus Bodanon
Paulus de Verona.
Giorgon.
Erben
Georgius Pencel
Paulus Bassano
Franciscus Badten
Michael Grabelach.
Corregio
Horst Bohl.
Paulus Lameto
Joost de Momper.
Paradis Pordanon
Jacobus de Bassan.
Julius Romanus
Falckenburg.
Eliseus.
Lucas de Jenua.
Cornelius Malsis
Joannes Holbain.
Joannes de Mabuse vulgo Mabusen
Lambardy de Amsterdam.
Abraham de Blomert.
Franck.
Campo Cremonio.
David Danair.
Grimmer.
Rothenhammer Augustanus.
Jung-Franck.
Arcimboldus.
Königsloe.
Fridericus Barolius.
Carolus Murs.
Petrus de Burckt.
Carolus Verhaff.
Udalricus Rager.
Egidius Sattler.
Antonius Moer
Martinus Klaff.
Ferdinandus Van Eissen. 89

Franciscus Schneider.
Georgius Klaff.
Abraham Bomberg.
Carolus de Moer.
Franciscus de Moer.
Joannes Balduinck.
Ambrosius Franck.
Dionysius Calvaert.
Martinus Bos.
Petrus Schaffenburg
Josephus Salviati
Perin del Vaga. 100
Tobias Ferhaght.
Georgius Pentz
Rulandus de Vos.
Wilhelm de Vos.
Ysbrand Paom
Egidius Congiet
Joannes de Mecheln.
Octavius Vanis.
Franciscus Milonese
Pouerpus.
Franciscus Parmesan.
Joannes Baldung
Lambardus Lambardi.
Ysrael Mehn
Adrianus de Fries
Jobst Brugi
Henricus de Klerchen
Palmen.
Balen.
Jacobus Hoffnagel.
Lucas de Leiden.
Andreas del Sarto
Joannes Malsi.
Falcke.
Jasper Van Grayer.
Antonius Van Dyck
Samuel ab Hochstraden.
Petrus Paulus Rubenius.
Joan Paulus Rasello
Giulio Bensi.
David Peyinus.
Guido de Bologna alias Guido Rheni

Vincenzo Malo.
Gaspar Momper.
Cavaglier Lanfranco Romano
Gaspar Bodart.
Joannes de la Court.
Lambert Van Oert.
Stephano Pollucio.
Guido Cagnacius.
Benvenuto de Carofillo.
Georgius Bachmann
Jo. Sanderath L. B. Pictor Elect. Bav.
Joan Carscius vel Coracij.
Leandro de Ponte.
Matthaus Perigrus.
Alexander Veronensis.
Rimprant, nostrae aetatis miraculum
Joan. Schönfeldt
Christophorus Storer ... 150
Brocarinus Medici.
Honthorst.
Henricus Klirbeck
Franciscus Berier
Fridericus Sustris
Ofenpöck.
Carlo Saraceno.
Spagnoleto
Giane Vanis.
Boulsin.
N. Altmoffer.
Giulio Romano.
Petrus Candidus.
Martinus Rota.
Jacobus Carracius. 165.
Oswaldt Unger Mechlienses
Senator et Capitaneus Kerlispol.

FIG. 2
Bucelinus's complete list (from the *Hoogsteder-Naumann Mercury*, no. 6, 1987).

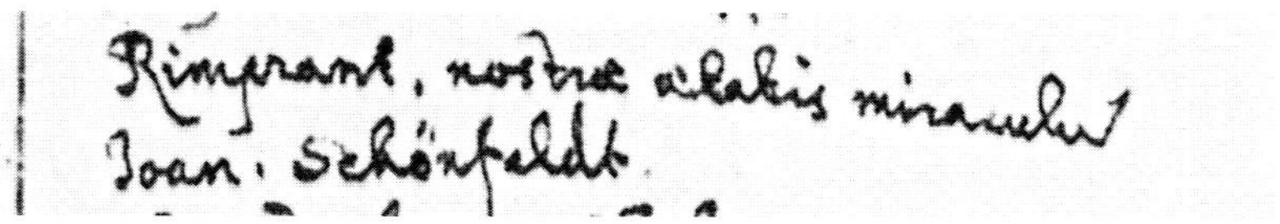

Rimprant, nostrae aetatis miraculum
Joan. Schönfeldt

FIG. 3
Detail of fig. 2 showing the passage concerning Rembrandt.

might be added to the work of Slive and Emmens stems from the fact that a more precise knowledge of Rembrandt's oeuvre has sharpened our understanding of his artistic goals and pictorial means[7] and that the seventeenth-century documents can be re-examined in the light of this enhanced understanding.

One question to consider is what actually prompted Bucelinus to compile his register of artists. Addressing this question involves the complex problem of the place that painting occupied in the culture of the seventeenth century. It also allows for the possibility of a new perspective on the image that an artist like Rembrandt might well have had of himself.

Bucelinus was an art lover, as can be assumed from the fact that he owned a collection of paintings[8] and that he produced his list of artists. Being an art lover at this time was not simply a matter of pursuing a hobby, of enjoying paintings that had actually been made for a different purpose. A certain class of cultivated Europeans took pride in being interested in and knowledgeable about the arts, particularly the art of painting. For some of these persons it was even a social imperative.[9] The same phenomenon had occurred in earlier periods of history – in classical Rome, for instance, but also in ancient China. These situations were marked by a type of symbiosis between art lovers and artists. In certain ways the two groups depended on each other and enhanced each other's prestige.

From the sixteenth century, an interest in art was one of the many intellectual pursuits and skills considered part of the standard repertoire of the upper class. The social élite was expected to be at least reasonably well-informed about art, particularly painting. *Il libro del cortegiano*

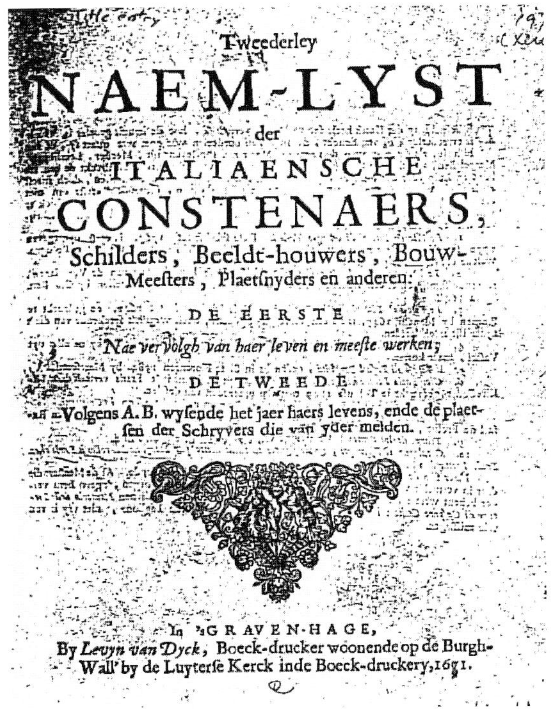

Tweederley
NAEM-LYST
der
ITALIAENSCHE
CONSTENAERS,
Schilders, Beeldt-houwers, Bouw-
Meesters, Plaetsnyders en anderen:
DE EERSTE
Nae vervolgh van haer leven en meeste werken;
DE TWEEDE
Volgens A. B. wysende het jaer haers levens, ende de plaetsen der Schryvers die van yder melden.
In 's GRAVEN-HAGE,
By Levyn van Dyck, Boeck-drucker woonende op de Burgh-Wall by de Luyterse Kerck inde Boeck-druckery, 1671.

FIG. 4
Front page of a printed list with the names of Italian artists, 1671. Wadsworth Atheneum, Hartford.

(The Courtier), written by Baldassare Castiglione (1475–1529) in 1528, described the traits constituting 'good breeding', which the courtier, as representative of the leisured class, was required to cultivate.[10] This text, which has had a tremendous influence on Western culture, is structured as a series of conversations about the wide range of subjects with which a courtier was supposed to be *au fait*. Among discussions about the use of arms, horses, music and rhetoric, to list a few examples, there is one about painting. From this particular discourse it transpires that the importance attached to art stemmed largely from the value it was accorded in classical writings on the subject.

This obligatory interest in art obviously had far-reaching consequences for sixteenth-century painters and their successors in subsequent generations, though for many the effects were slow to filter through. A large contingent of craftsmen continued to meet the demand for images of all kinds, while a minority of painters – among them Rembrandt – must have considered themselves 'artists' in a way that comes close to our modern conception of this term.[11]

It was *de rigueur* for the art lover to have a certain knowledge of painting. And that knowledge – apart from being found in manuals written especially for art lovers[12] – was best acquired from artists themselves. As Pierre Le Brun, one of the authors of a handbook for art lovers, wrote in 1635:

> Therefore, to know how to discourse on this noble profession, you must have frequented the studio and disputed with the masters, have seen the magic effects of the pencil, and the unerring judgement with which the details are worked out.[13]

A number of art lovers, heeding these instructions, became connoisseurs (even in the seventeenth century there was a distinction between the two).[14]

An art lover was also expected to know about the painters of the past and present, to possess some knowledge of the history of painting. The simplest way to record that information was in the form of a list of painters' names. Some of these lists, including Bucelinus's, have survived, but a great many more have undoubtedly been lost.

Bucelinus's list constitutes an inventory of past and present artists he must have heard of or read about, and whom, as the title of the list suggests, he regarded as 'the most distinguished European painters'. A few were people he knew personally; two of these – the painters and writers on art Samuel van Hoogstraten and Joachim von Sandrart – will be discussed at some length in this essay. Another surviving list is that of the Amsterdam physician and art lover Jan Sysmus. Sysmus kept a special notebook on art containing an alphabetical register of *huidendaegse* (contemporary) Dutch painters, many of whose names are followed by a brief description of the subjects in which they specialized. Rembrandt's name does not appear in this register. He was no longer alive when Sysmus assembled his notes (1669–78) and therefore no longer qualified as 'contemporary'.[15] That 'lists' of this kind, as postulated here, represented a specific form of seventeenth-century expertise, is borne out by the existence of a book printed in The Hague in 1671 entitled *Tweederley naam-lyst de Italiaansche constenaers, schilders, beeldt-houwers, bouw-meesters, plaetsnyders, en anderen* (Twofold List of the Names of Italian Artists, Painters, Master Builders, Engravers and Others). One of these lists was arranged by date of birth, the other alphabetically (fig. 4).[16] Constantijn Huygens the Younger compiled a list of Italian painters as well. And we know that the lawyer Johannes de Witt Stevenszoon collected a great many notes on painters in the period between about 1600 and 1627.[17]

There were early texts of this kind in which the young Rembrandt was listed and characterized. For several decades the Utrecht lawyer Arnold van Buchel, a friend and colleague of Johannes de Witt, made notes on artists and works of art that came to his attention. These notes, collected under the title *Res pictoriae* (On Painting), concerned 'predominantly Dutch paintings and works of art'. Van Buchel was the first art lover to record Rembrandt's existence in writing. The artist he described as 'a miller's son from Leiden' was, he wrote, 'esteemed highly, though prematurely'. Rembrandt was twenty-one years old at the time and had only recently established himself as an independent painter.[18]

Constantijn Huygens the Elder, the Dutch *uomo universalis* (literally, 'universal man'), and secretary to three consecutive stadholders, devoted a disproportionately large segment of the autobiography of his youth to information about painters he knew.[19] In the opening lines of that segment he proudly announced that he had formed 'close friendships' with a number of painters, adding *'I always like to seek out the friendship of famous people'*.[20] He visited Rembrandt in his studio and wrote a detailed analysis of the artist, who was twenty-two or twenty-three at the time.[21]

The painter and the concept of fame

The symbiotic relationship of artist and art lover is beginning to reveal its detail, fame being a main ingredient. It was fame that enabled the painter – a guild member trained in the workshop of another guild member, and thus in social terms no more than a craftsman – to win the admiration of intellectuals, wealthy merchants, noblemen and even princes. In Italy this transformation of the painter from craftsman into worthy companion of the higher classes had been well underway since the sixteenth century.

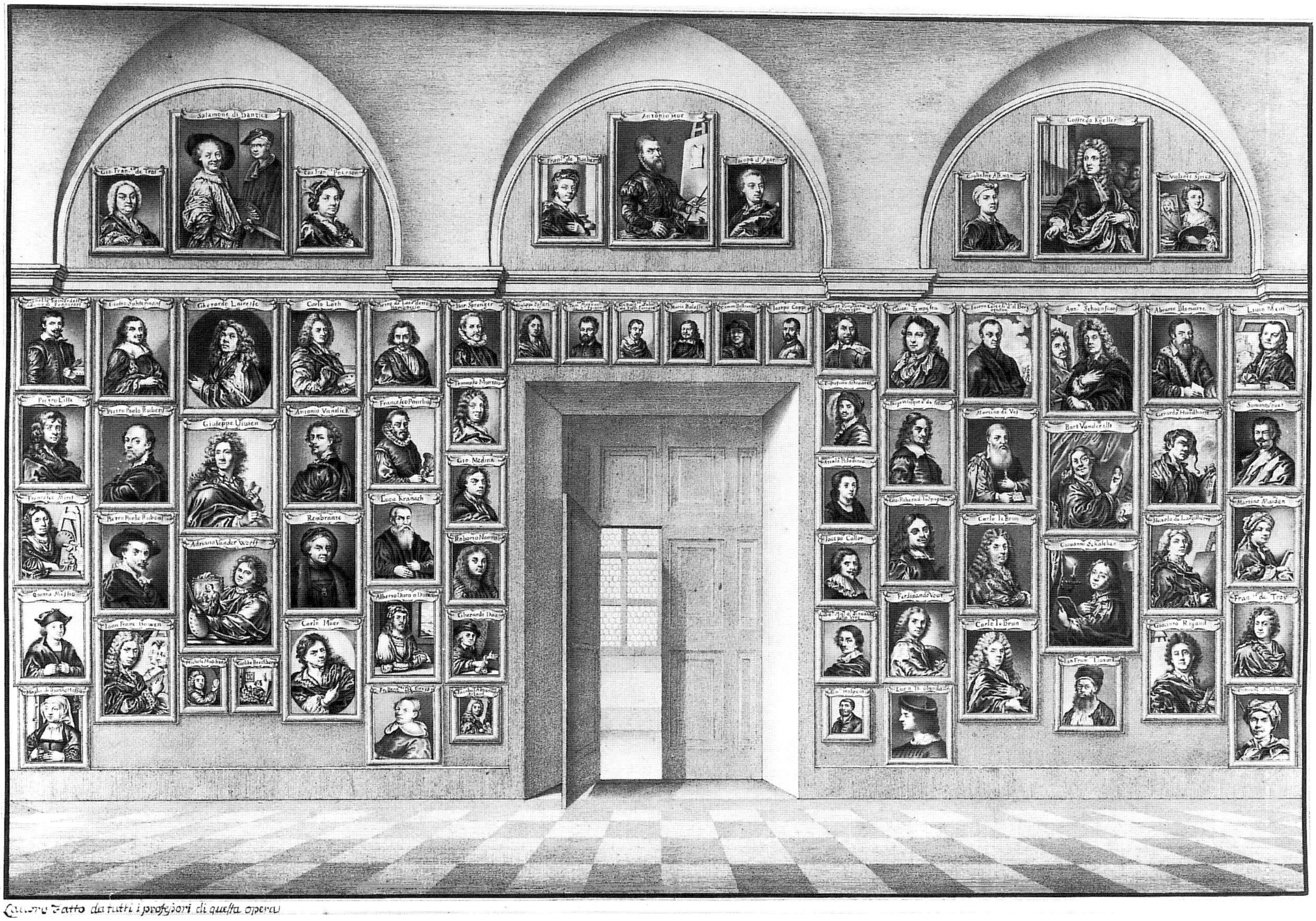

FIG. 5
The Galleria degli Autoritratti, Florence. Rembrandt's self-portrait of 1669 is in the fourth row from the left. Photograph: Bildarchiv der Österreichischen Nationalbibliothek, Vienna.

The *Lives*, by Giorgio Vasari (1511–1574), published in 1550 and expanded and reprinted in 1568, comprises of a comprehensive list of names, not unlike the one Bucelinus was to compile later. Vasari, however, included details about the lives and work of the artists, for the enlightenment of his patron, Cosimo I de' Medici (1519–1574).[22]

While Vasari enriched his list with details about these artists, the purpose of this list could also be illuminated in another way. For example, Cosimo III (1642–1723) and his successors created a gallery of self-portraits of the artists considered worthy of inclusion on his list. This gallery still exists in Florence today (fig. 5).[23]

North of the Alps, particularly in Antwerp – the wealthiest city in Europe in the sixteenth century – this love of art developed into a craze. A small painting by the Antwerp artist Hendrick van Steenwijk the Elder seems to make fun of this phenomenon (fig. 6). In this work we see a group of elegant men crowding at the open door of an artist's studio, to which they are admitted by *Fama* with her trumpet. They have evidently been attracted by the prominently placed personification of the art of painting and, in the second place, by sculpture (the background figure appears to be that of an engraver).

The vogue spread further north. The Dutch Vasari, Karel van Mander (1548–1606), trained as a painter in the southern Netherlands, and fled to Holland (like so many others) in the face of the Spanish occupation. In 1604 he published his *Schilder-Boeck* of 'the lives of eminent painters, past and present', and thereby enhanced these painters' fame. A few decades later, the Amsterdammer Pieter Codde portrayed art lovers in a painter's studio. The picture shows the artist with three fashionable young men who conscientiously examine his work (fig. 7). The scene could almost be a visualization of Constantijn Huygens's visit to Rembrandt's studio around that time, possibly in the company of his brother Maurits and their friend Jacques de Gheyn III (see cat. no. 8). Young as he was, Rembrandt was already one of those painters whose names Huygens was eagerly adding to his list of distinguished artists.

Rembrandt's name undoubtedly appeared on many more listings of noteworthy artists than those constructed by van Buchel, Huygens and Bucelinus. Many of these lists perhaps existed only in the minds of art lovers. Not until 1718 was the first printed 'list' of seventeenth-century

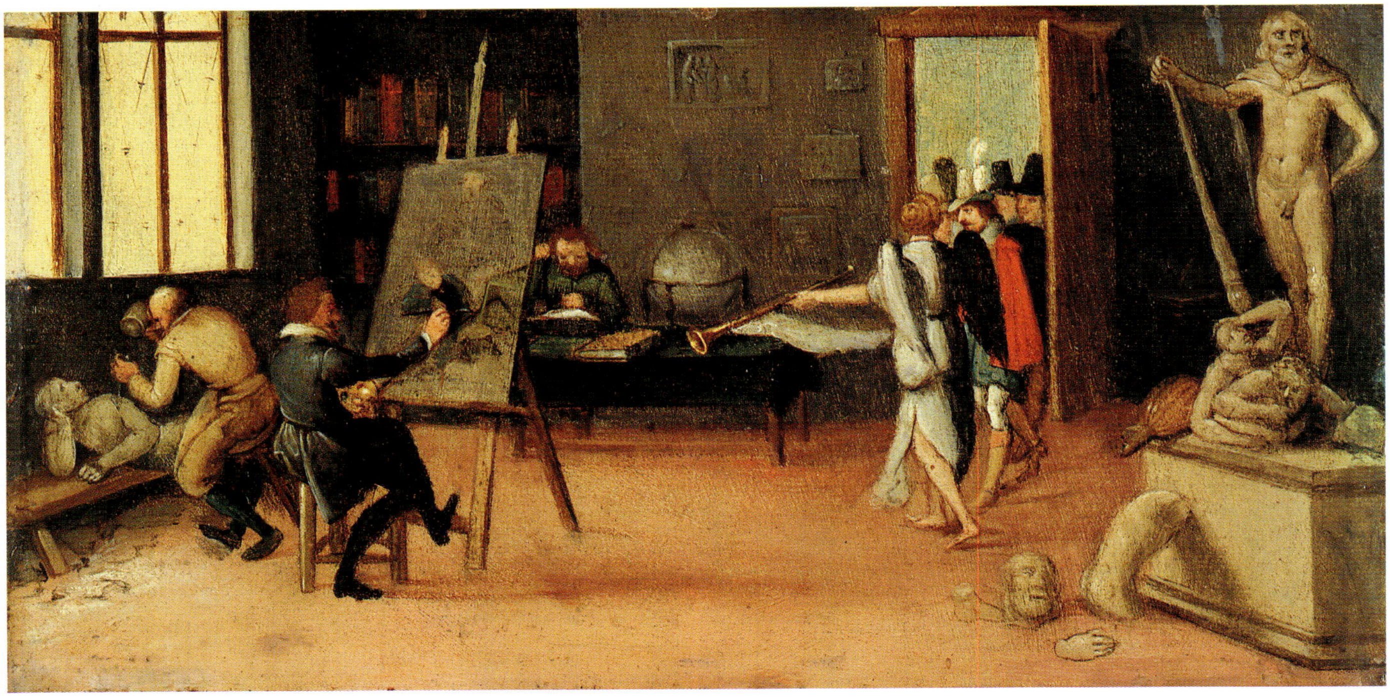

FIG. 6
Hendrick van Steenwijk the Elder 1550–1603
Art Lovers Welcomed by Fama c.1590
Copper
9.5 x 18.5 cm
J. O. Leegenhoek Collection, Paris

Dutch painters published, by the Dutch painter Arnold Houbraken (1660–1719).[24] This work contains biographies of or brief references to more than five hundred seventeenth-century Dutch painters. Rembrandt occupies a prominent place: Houbraken presents a detailed biography[25] and frequently cites Rembrandt as the teacher of other painters.

Rembrandt's fame soon spread abroad. When the Englishman Peter Mundy was making notes during his visit to the Netherlands in 1640, 'Rimbrantt' was the only Dutch painter who came to mind. Mundy's note, made two years before Rembrandt completed the *Night Watch* (p. 26, fig. 7), highlights the importance attached to painting in Holland at the time and shows what it must have meant to be regarded as the most outstanding representative of that art, especially in the eyes of a foreigner:

> As for the art off Painting and the affection off the people to Pictures, I thincke none other goe beeyond them, there having bin in this Country Many excellent Men in thatt Faculty, some att Presentt, as Rimbrantt, etts, All [Dutch people] in general striving to adorne their houses, especially the outer or street roome, with costly peeces.[26]

Towards the end of Rembrandt's life, a few years after Bucelinus had accorded him prominence in his now famous list, the painter received a visit from a traveller who likewise considered him one of the great attractions of the Netherlands. Cosimo III de' Medici of Florence, whose gallery of self-portraits (mentioned above) added a visual dimension to his list of famous artists, journeyed through the Netherlands in 1667.[27] In line with Castiglione's canon for the well-bred courtier of 150 years earlier, it was expected that Cosimo too would possess a knowledge of painting. In the course of his visit – ostensibly incognito, but with a large, conspicuous entourage – Cosimo called on several artists, including Frans van Mieris, Gerrit Dou and Willem van de Velde. The journal kept on his behalf by members of his retinue records that Cosimo spent the morning of 29 December 1667 viewing 'pictures by various masters, among them ... the famous painter Reinbrent'.[28] Cosimo appears to have paid Rembrandt another visit in 1669, no more than a few months before Rembrandt's death. It was on this occasion, presumably, that Cosimo bought one of the master's last self-portraits, and one of the first – perhaps the very first – of his self-portraits of famous artists (see fig. 5).[29]

The myth of Rembrandt's decline

This brief account could be augmented with far more information of this kind, which Slive has already dealt with in detail. The aim here has been to place this information against the background of the phenomenon of the seventeenth-century art lover and his need for a 'canon' of artists whom he considered worth knowing, by name at least, but ideally also in person. At the same time it is meant to demonstrate that from an early stage in Rembrandt's career, and right up to the time of his death, his name attracted the attention of art lovers both in Holland and abroad, not only as a painter but probably even more as an etcher. Slive presented evidence to show that during Rembrandt's lifetime the Dutch seventeenth-century reader or listener was expected to know immediately who was meant when Rembrandt's name occurred in a poem or play.[30] Such a person is famous.

Fame is a remarkable phenomenon. It sustains itself because those who perpetuate it have a vested interest in its survival. For it is that very fame which gives them the status of insiders, especially if they are acquainted with the famous person. Like Huygens, who 'always like[d] to seek out the friendship of famous people', many others must have derived satisfaction from knowing Rembrandt or simply having seen him, or from owning a work of his or merely having seen one.

Where, then, is the source of the persistent myth that Rembrandt was no longer appreciated by the end of his life? Scholars have examined this myth for the past fifty years to try to establish how it originated. It appears to have stemmed from three factors, which will be outlined below, and the arguments relating to them then refuted.

Firstly, an intrinsic aspect of the nineteenth-century cult of genius was that genius is by definition unrecognized.[31] A painter was only a genius if he braved untrodden paths. This model of misunderstood genius occurs time and again in the literature on Rembrandt and stems directly from Romanticism. This first aspect of the myth has centred upon the *Night Watch* in particular. As Slive has demonstrated, however, no historical source suggests (as the myth would have us believe) that Rembrandt's painting failed to gain acceptance.[32] The presumed relationship between genius and lack of recognition should be seen as a nineteenth-century fabrication.

The second factor on which the myth is based is Rembrandt's insolvency in 1656.[33] The documents regarding these circumstances, which came to light in 1833, gave rise to the notion that Rembrandt went bankrupt because there was no longer a demand for his work. From there it was only a short step to the Romantic myth of unrecognized genius. Later, other reasons were sought to explain Rembrandt's insolvency: it was attributed to financial mismanagement, his passion for collecting, his extravagant social aspirations and so forth. To be sure, Rembrandt's management of his financial affairs was not entirely judicious. But a new and more convincing explanation for his bankruptcy was recently proposed. Marten Jan Bok's socioeconomic study of seventeenth-century painting shows that Rembrandt's bankruptcy occurred when not only numerous other artists but also businesses in other fields were in financial difficulty.[34] It transpires that this wave of insolvencies coincided with the first Anglo-Dutch War (1652–54),[35] when a blockade of the Dutch coast dealt a severe blow to the country's trade with the East. Bok produces convincing evidence to show that it was precisely the manufacturers of luxury goods – and Rembrandt's expensive paintings can certainly be included in this category – who suffered most as a result. Hence insolvency as an indicator of Rembrandt's so-called lack of recognition can likewise be dismissed as fallacious.

The third factor underlying the 'underrated genius' myth is less easy to unmask. It concerns the criticism of Rembrandt's art expressed by his contemporaries. This is the aspect that Slive and Emmens concentrated upon. On the face of it, a significant number of seventeenth-century writings portrayed Rembrandt in an unfavourable light. He was said to be a heretic,[36] a fool,[37] an artist who painted with dung.[38] It is therefore hardly surprising that Schmidt-Degener (1881–1941) and other like-minded authors protested in defence of their idol. But there is little point in trying to discredit the authors who published these denigrations, all of which appeared in the 1670s or later. The way Slive and Emmens have analysed the problem makes far better sense. They examined the situation in the light of the ascendancy of classicism, which marked a radical change in taste, in the last two decades of Rembrandt's life. Joachim von Sandrart (1606–1688) – one of the painters Bucelinus knew personally[39] and with whom he must undoubtedly have talked about Rembrandt – was judging Rembrandt by the new ideology when he wrote the following in 1675:

> Adhering to the practice he had adopted, he was prepared to challenge our rules of art, of anatomy, human proportions and perspective, arguing against the use of antique sculptures, against Raphael's draughtsmanship and the systematic training of young artists, and against the Academies, so vital to our profession, asserting that one should rely only upon nature and observe no other rules.[40]

But the classicist ideology had not been embraced between 1637 and 1645, the period in which Sandrart must have been in contact with Rembrandt. Hence Sandrart's criticism of Rembrandt was retrospective. As Slive has shown, much of the criticism of Rembrandt was simply a projection of new rules on art onto a period – Rembrandt's active period – in which, apart from the last decade of his life, those rules did not yet apply. The conclusion Emmens drew on the basis of these insights is quite the opposite of the idea that Rembrandt's art was rejected:

> The criticism levelled against Rembrandt by the writers of the 1670s makes it clear that he was still the towering figure of an older, and now old-fashioned generation of Dutch painters. That is why the blows of the classicistic attack, which could have been just as well delivered to any other painter of his generation, all fell on his head.[41]

Bucelinus's recently uncovered description of Rembrandt as 'the miracle of our age' confirms Emmens's conclusion.

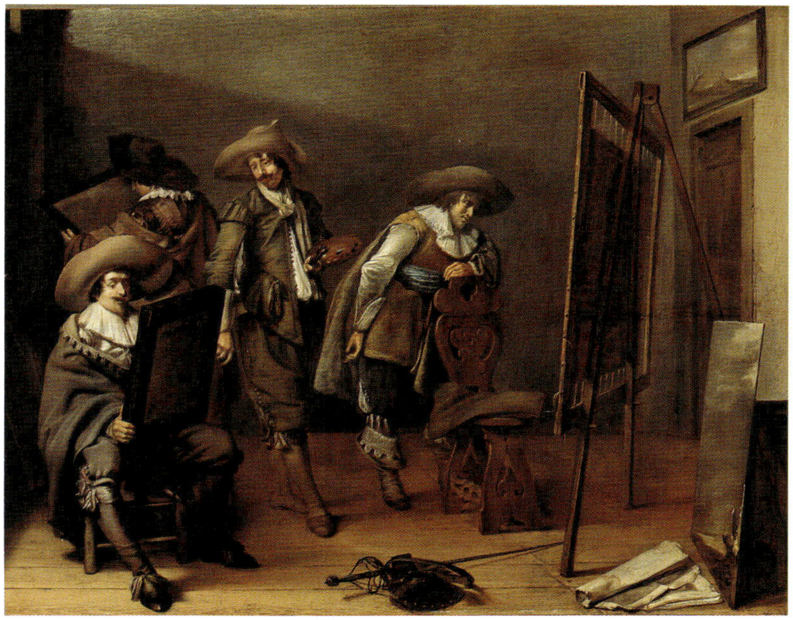

FIG. 7
Pieter Codde
Art Lovers Visiting a Painter's Studio c.1630
Panel
38.3 x 49.3 cm
Staatsgalerie Stuttgart

The perspectives of two contemporaries upon Rembrandt

Two writers of the 1670s, Samuel van Hoogstraten (1627–1678) (fig. 8) and the aforementioned Joachim von Sandrart (fig. 9), who were normally regarded as critics of Rembrandt, personally witnessed the latter's activity, and it is highly likely that they prompted Bucelinus's

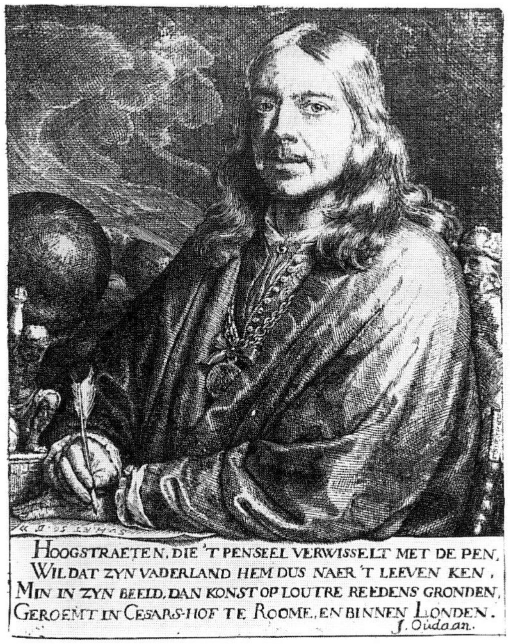

FIG. 8
J. Oudaan, after Samuel van Hoogstraten
Self-Portrait at the Age of Fifty
Etching
From Samuel van Hoogstraten's *De Inleyding tot de hooge schoole der schilderkonst*, 1678
(for Hoogstraten's self-portrait, see p. 291)

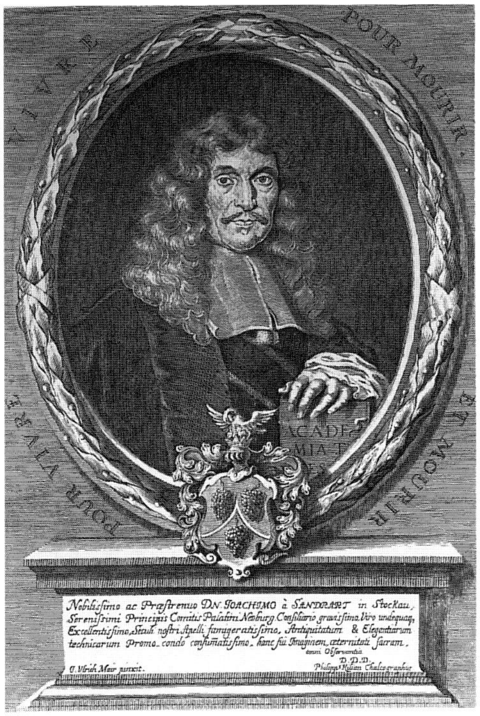

FIG. 9
Philipp Kilian (German, 1628–1693), after Johan Ulrich Mayr
Portrait of Joachim von Sandrart
Frontispiece to Joachim von Sandrart's *Academie der Bau-, Bild-, und Mahlerey-Künste*, 1675

praise of Rembrandt. If this is true, we might be able to discover what inspired this praise.

Samuel van Hoogstraten studied under Rembrandt between *c.*1643 and 1645 and, after establishing himself as an independent master, pursued a fairly successful career and gained a reputation abroad. In September 1653 and May 1654, he came into contact with Bucelinus, for whom he and Nicolaes Roosendael (*c.*1635–1686) painted an altarpiece of the *Vision of St Benedict*.[42] Bucelinus and Hoogstraten therefore knew one another and would certainly have talked about painting and inevitably about Rembrandt.

Interestingly enough, it was Samuel van Hoogstraten who shed light on a significant aspect of the relationship between artists and art lovers in general. Although the art lover, given his interest, was thought capable of holding a reasonably informed discussion on painting, Hoogstraten's book *De Inleyding tot de hooge schoole der schilderkonst* (Introduction to Higher Education on Painting), published in 1678 and intended for these art lovers, indicates that art lovers cannot discern the subtleties and merits of works of art, let alone understand them.[43] Hoogstraten outlines the objective of his book in the preface and, after enlarging upon the art lover's blindness to the true quality of paintings, writes:

> Not that my *Introduction* [which refers to the book as a whole] will open the eyes of art lovers such that they themselves will be able to judge art: far from it. But they will be able to understand what it is that one should judge in our work, so that with the help of an experienced painter they will be able to discern the strengths and weaknesses that every work contains.[44]

Hoogstraten was not alone in believing that only artists could see the subtleties in paintings. Albrecht Dürer (1471–1528) had already written: 'The art of painting cannot be properly judged except by those who are themselves good painters. In truth, to others it remains as hidden as a foreign language to you'.[45]

In 1670 the Dutch writer Goeree who, though not a painter himself, was an extremely committed theoretician in the fields of drawing and painting, likewise stated: 'The merits of even the best pictures are sometimes so well hidden, so skilfully blended and merged into the whole that the most discerning of masters will grasp them only after lengthy scrutiny'.[46]

We can thus assume that art lovers – and therefore Bucelinus himself – must have been all too aware of their apparent limitations when it came to understanding painting. Their acquaintance with Rembrandt must have made Samuel van Hoogstraten and Joachim von Sandrart important authorities in Bucelinus's eyes. Their classicist-tinged criticism of Rembrandt, written some twenty years after their conversations with Bucelinus, was mixed with extravagant praise. This praise may reflect their earlier opinions on Rembrandt. And it is these earlier views that may have prompted Bucelinus's accolade. This, it seems, is a hypothesis worth defending.

It is highly significant that the two painters praised Rembrandt for largely the same reasons, which could be a pointer to precisely those aspects of Rembrandt's qualities as a painter that inspired Bucelinus to describe him as the miracle of his age.

Both these artist-writers particularly praised the qualities of Rembrandt's work relating to his treatment of colour, and the consequences of his use of colour for other elements of his paintings – precisely the type of purely pictorial means of painting which it was believed only painters would recognize and fully appreciate. The way a non-painter perceives a picture is undoubtedly influenced by these effects, but only *the most*

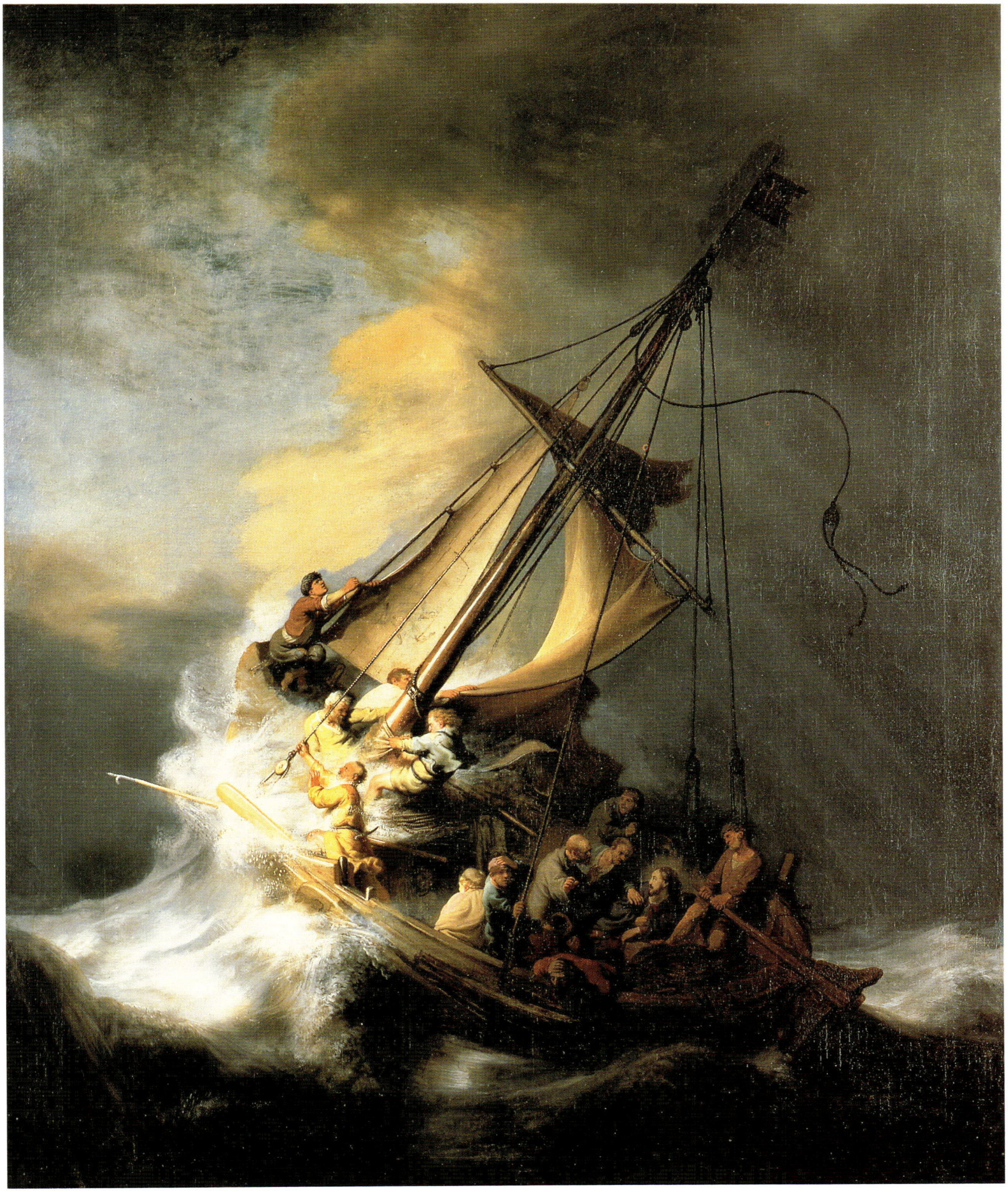

FIG. 10
Rembrandt
Christ in the Storm on the Sea of Galilee
Signed and dated 1633
Canvas
160.0 x 127.0 cm
Isabella Stewart Gardner Museum, Boston
(stolen 1990)

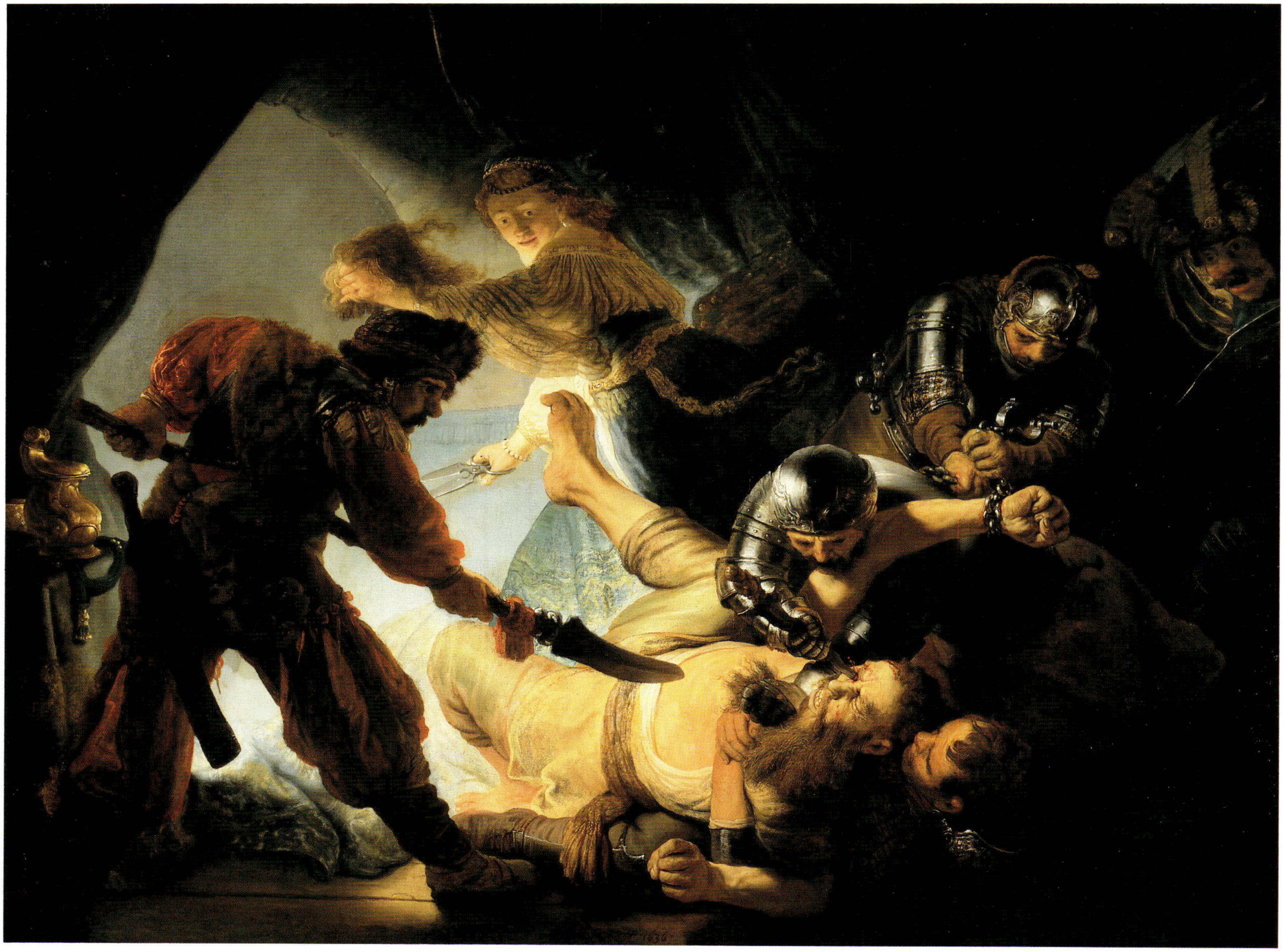

FIG. 11
Rembrandt
The Blinding of Samson
Signed and dated 1636
Canvas
205.0 x 272.0 cm
Städelsches Kunstinstitut, Frankfurt
Photograph: Artothek Spezialarchiv für Gemäldefotografie

discerning of masters, to quote Goeree again, would be in a position to identify them.

Both Hoogstraten and Sandrart enthuse about Rembrandt's treatment of *colour*. To the present-day reader, conditioned by developments in art over the past century, the concept of 'colour' evokes different associations from those that a seventeenth-century insider would have had. Today, the factors that first come to mind are the substitution of colour for tone (as by the Fauves), the expressive potential of colour (as explored by the Expressionists), and the boldness of colour combinations (as in certain types of abstract or decorative or applied art); for us, colour has become first and foremost an autonomous visual means. Hoogstraten and Sandrart, on the other hand, were referring to entirely different aspects of the manner in which colour is used. Their admiration centred mainly on the way Rembrandt shaded his colours in subtle tones and skilfully grouped them according to their gradations to achieve compositional unity, while retaining control of light and shadow, the suggestion of space, and other illusionistic aspects (figs 10, 11, 12).

In the passage below, Hoogstraten emphasizes the importance of grouping 'related' *(bevriende)* either pale or dark colours to achieve a convincing overall light effect. From the following passages we also learn that this manner of arranging colour had primarily spatial and compositional consequences. In his chapter on 'the arrangement of shadow and light', Hoogstraten remarks that a picture becomes like a chessboard if there is too much variation of light and dark, and adds (here addressing himself explicitly to the painter):

> I would therefore advise you not to go to extremes in alternating light and shadow, but to blend them carefully in groups. Have your strongest lights in a harmonious combination with weaker lights: I assure you they will

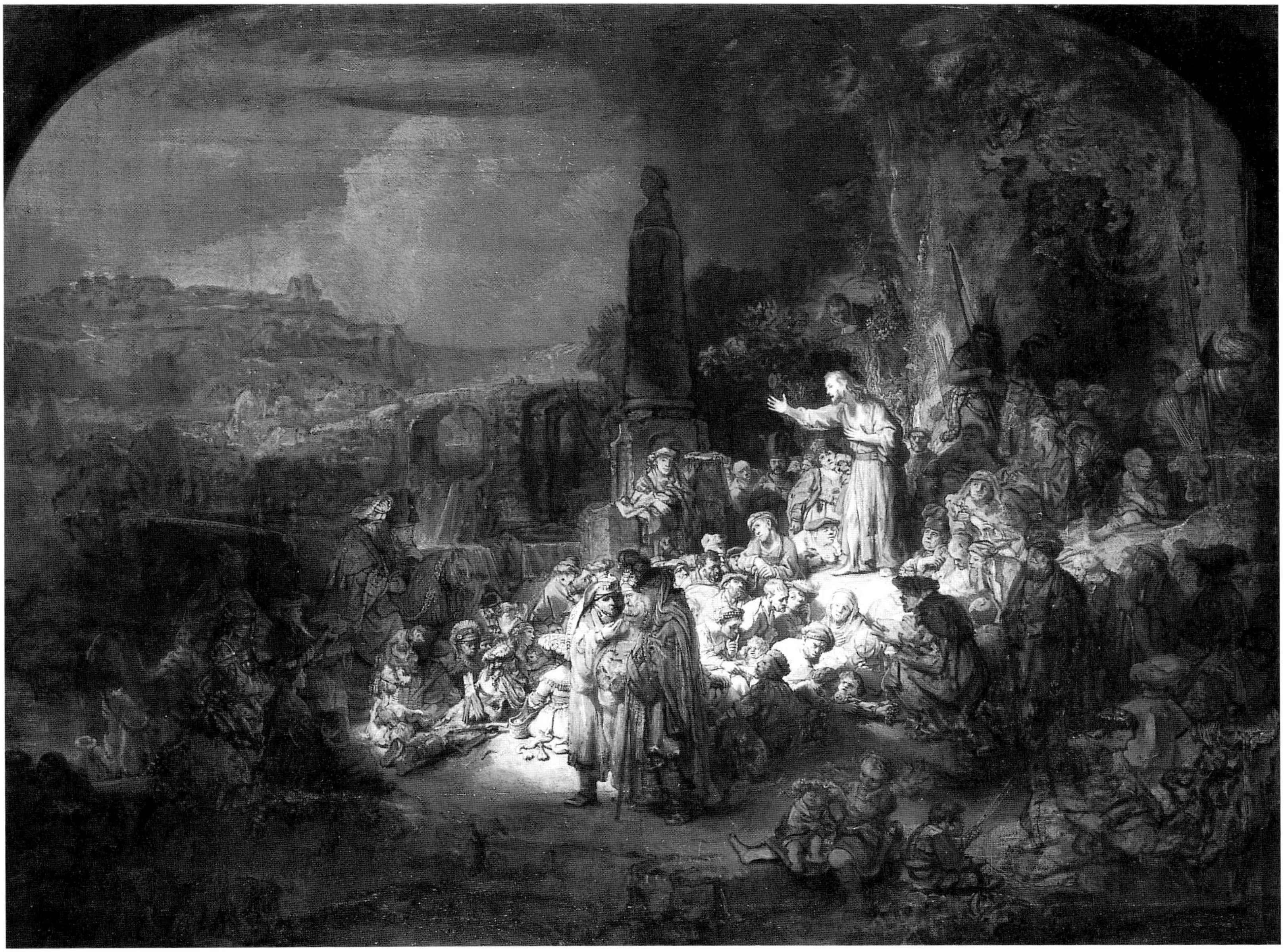

FIG. 12
Rembrandt
John the Baptist Preaching
Canvas on panel
62.0 x 80.0 cm
Staatliche Museen zu Berlin, Gemäldegalerie

stand out all the more beautifully. Surround the deepest of your dark areas with somewhat lighter tones so that they cause the strength of the light to contrast more forcefully. *Rembrandt* took this as far as possible and was perfect at combining related tones and colours.[47]

That Hoogstraten cites Rembrandt as an example in this connection can be seen as the highest praise. The same is true of certain passages in Sandrart's book on painting:

For the rest, it is my deep conviction, however much you may contradict me, that all harsh, bright, strong and 'high' colours should be avoided and rejected, as they cause complete discord in a painting unless their crudeness is relieved and toned down or prudently matched with other agreeable and related colours.

Sandrart adds at this point that Dutch artists in particular:

raised this art to the highest degree, mixing and breaking the colours and reducing their crudeness until they had matched everything to nature itself in their paintings. This gradual diminishing of colours can be seen [for instance] in a large altarpiece or other painting that requires many colours; little by little, in suitable degree, they fade, and independent of the colour chosen [for a figure], according to the rules of perspective, the colour is put in a sequence [of intensity] from one figure to the next, so that everything receives its own place: in Dutch we call this Hauding. This practice, though vital, is rarely understood. And in this we must learn from ... the industrious and in this regard most knowledgeable Rembrand [*sic*]: who, as we learn from his biography [elsewhere in Sandrart's book], worked miracles.[48]

As Taylor has shown, the concept of *Hauding* (in most Dutch sources spelt *houding*) as Sandrart defines it here – that is, choosing colours so that colour has a function in suggesting spatiality – was a big issue in the second half of the seventeenth century.[49] Achieving the right *houding* took a great deal of pictorial intelligence. Considering Sandrart's criticism of Rembrandt in other respects, and, in retrospect, the fact that he singles Rembrandt out as the worker of 'miracles' in this facet of the art of painting, this praise, like Hoogstraten's praise of Rembrandt's use of 'related' colours, is of extraordinary significance.

In another passage of his book, Hoogstraten again confirms that it was specifically Rembrandt who was regarded as an outstanding artist in this respect, because he was able to achieve such a degree of unity (*eenwezigheid*) and spatiality (*sprong*) in his paintings (he cites the *Night Watch* as an example) that 'all the other pieces [in the large hall of the Doelen, including, incidentally, a picture by Sandrart] hang there like playing cards'.[50]

Once we are able to grasp the importance of this specific quality of Rembrandt's paintings, it becomes clear that we are looking at one of the crucial developments in seventeenth-century thinking about painting. It is also apparent from the passages quoted above that pictorial questions were contemplated with considerable sophistication in this century.

We discover too that Rembrandt, who was described as 'extremely knowledgeable' (*hoch vernünftig*) in this respect, could indeed only be properly understood by insiders. From Hoogstraten's book it becomes clear that painters considered themselves the ultimate authorities in these matters. The discussion of the subtleties in the use of colour in relation to composition and the suggestion of space appears to have been a theme for painters among themselves. The fact that the art lover Bucelinus must have been introduced to Rembrandt's merits by two of what he calls the 'most distinguished European painters' – who, moreover, had known Rembrandt personally – may well have prompted his exceptionally lavish praise of the master.

1 Schillemans 1987; Schillemans 1991.
2 Three of the 163 artists named on the list have two entries (Schillemans 1987, p. 30).
3 Schillemans 1987; Schillemans 1991.
4 Hofstede de Groot 1906a.
5 Slive 1953.
6 Emmens 1964.
7 I refer here to the Rembrandt *Corpus*, vols I–III, 1982–89. See also Van de Wetering 1991–92a; Van de Wetering 1997.
8 Lindner 1909, pp. 101–4.
9 See, for instance, Gibson-Wood 1982; Schnapper 1994.
10 Castiglione 1528.
11 Van de Wetering 1995, pp. 219–39, 390–1.
12 Texts written for art lovers, such as Giulio Mancini's *Considerazioni sulla pittura* (*c.*1621); Abraham Bosse's *Sentimens sur la distinction des diverses manières de peinture, dessein & graveure, & des originaux d'avec leurs copies* (1649), and Roger de Piles's *Conversations sur la connoissance de la peinture* (1667), are discussed in Gibson-Wood 1982.
13 Le Brun 1849.
14 Gibson-Wood 1982, pp. 45–6; Van de Wetering 1995a, pp. 264–70.
15 Bredius 1890; Bredius 1894; Bredius 1895. Bredius did not publish Sysmus's notebook in its entirety. Although Rembrandt does not appear in Sysmus's list, he is mentioned elsewhere in the notebook. Jaap van der Veen, who has viewed the notebook, kindly informs me that Rembrandt (together with Rubens and Raphael) is described in it as an important painter of religious pictures. Also, annotations in the book show that Sysmus knew the year of Rembrandt's death.
16 Egbert Haverkamp Begemann was kind enough to draw my attention to this source, of which a copy is preserved in the Wadsworth Atheneum, Hartford.
17 Sterk 1974.
18 Hoogewerff & Van Regteren Altena 1928, pp. 66–7; Strauss & Van der Meulen 1979, p. 61, no. 1628/1.
19 Huygens / Heesakkers 1987. Huygens's manuscript (in Latin), now in the Royal Library in The Hague, was written between May 1629 and April 1631. I have used the most recent Dutch translation.
20 Huygens / Heesakkers 1987, p. 74 (my italics): 'in zeer nauwe vriendschap verbonden ... ik ben altijd gaarne uit op vriendschap met beroemdheden'.
21 Huygens / Heesakkers 1987, pp. 84–7. An English translation of this passage is in Strauss & Van der Meulen 1979, p. 71, no. 1630/5.
22 Vasari 1550.
23 Langedijk 1992.
24 Houbraken 1718–21.
25 Houbraken 1718–21, vol. I, 1718, pp. 254–73.
26 Strauss & Van der Meulen 1979, p. 202, no. 1640/16.
27 Hoogewerff 1919.
28 Hoogewerff 1919, pp. 66–7.
29 The Rembrandt literature makes no mention of the fact that Cosimo may have visited Rembrandt in 1669 as well. See *Corpus*, vol. IV (forthcoming) (in the catalogue texts concerning the two late self-portraits in the Uffizi).
30 Slive 1953, pp. 44–5.
31 Roh 1948.
32 Slive 1953, pp. 4–7.
33 For a brief account of what is currently known about Rembrandt's insolvency – in fact a *cessio bonorum* – see Dudok van Heel 1991–92a, esp. pp. 60–1.
34 Bok 1994.
35 The four Anglo-Dutch Wars fought between 1652 and 1784 were predominantly consequences of trade and colonial conflicts.
36 Pels 1681, pp. 35–7; Slive 1953, pp. 102–3.
37 Van Hoogstraten 1678, p. 183.
38 Lairesse 1707, Book V, p. 324.
39 Lindner 1909, p. 102; Stump 1976, pp. 62, 67; Schillemans 1987, pp. 30, 35 (no. 143).
40 Sandrart 1675, Part II, Book III, p. 326.
41 Emmens 1968, p. 274 (English summary).
42 Roscam Abbing 1993, pp. 45–6, 48–9, 89; Schillemans 1987, pp. 25–6.
43 Van de Wetering 1995a.
44 Van Hoogstraten 1678 ('Aen den Lezer', unpaginated).
45 *Schriftlicher Nachlass*, vol. II, p. 109.
46 Goeree 1670, p. 84.
47 Van Hoogstraten 1678, pp. 305–6.
48 Sandrart 1675, Part I, Book III, p. 85. Sandrart describes both Pieter van Laer and Rembrandt as excelling in *Hauding*.
49 Taylor 1992.
50 Van Hoogstraten 1678, p. 176.

Faces from Life: *Tronies* and Portraits in Rembrandt's Painted Oeuvre

JAAP VAN DER VEEN

Introduction

Rembrandt portrayed the human figure throughout his career. For more than forty years he painted, etched and drew people in representations of various kinds. His main ambition was to produce history pieces, to portray human figures in biblical, allegorical and historical scenes. In addition, he made self-portraits, and painted heads and portraits of ordinary people, in some cases from a model. Just what it is that defines and differentiates these *tronies* and portraits, the types of people they were painted for, and the roles they played in Rembrandt's overall art production, constitutes the subject matter of this essay.

The art theorists of the time considered portrait painting inferior to history painting. Portraitists were expected first and foremost to produce a faithful rendering of reality. They were not at liberty to portray their subjects as they pleased, but were obliged to respect the wishes of clients. For the ambitious artist seeking social equality with the patrician class, honour and gain were legitimate aspirations.[1] Honour was most clearly won by depicting historical scenes. However, although honour was unquestionably the higher goal in the sixteenth and seventeenth centuries, gain certainly carried no negative connotations. Naturally, artists made money from the sale of their work, an arrangement considered perfectly respectable. So portraiture was an important component of the painter's trade. Many artists depended on it to meet basic needs. Indeed, portraiture was often viewed as an unfortunate necessity.

Although art theorists were critical of painters who abandoned history painting for the more lucrative field of portraiture, they could have found no fault with Rembrandt in this respect. Rembrandt was above all a history painter. Yet he also painted a substantial number of portraits. This, as we shall see, was an intermittent rather than a regular activity. No portrait commissions are known from his Leiden period, even though in those years, and before (while still an apprentice), he studied the human face and practised rendering it. A number of small works in which his own features are recognizable date from that period (fig. 1). Other heads he portrayed are what were known in the seventeenth century as *tronies*, the majority of which were probably executed from life. His drawn, etched and painted self-portraits may be seen as studies of facial expressions. In some he has captured a gay or serious expression, in others he looks startled or pensive. Yet from all of them it is clear that he examined himself intently in a mirror.

We know from a contemporary that Rembrandt left Leiden in 1631 because he received portrait commissions in Amsterdam. Rembrandt demanded – and received – substantial fees for his work, and the city's well-to-do burghers appreciated his efforts, often asking him to 'make portraits or other pieces'.[2] He did in fact produce numerous portraits in his early years in Amsterdam (fig. 2). And, as most of his sitters posed in his studio (fig. 3), they had an opportunity to see what he had in stock. Often, they left with other works as well as the portrait.[3]

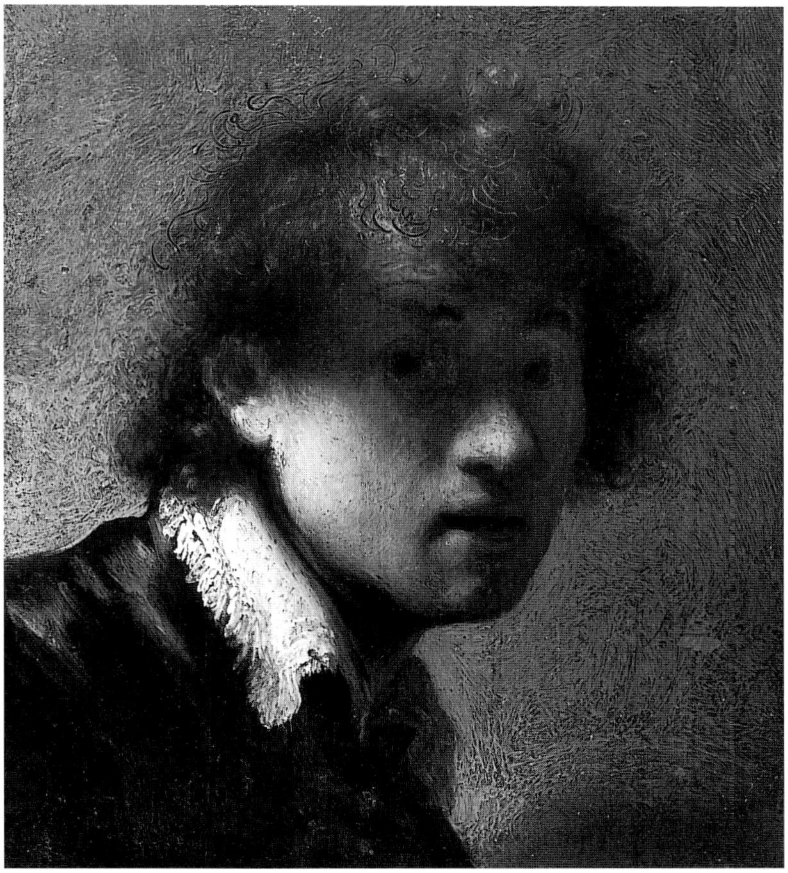

FIG. 1
Rembrandt
Self-Portrait
Monogrammed and dated 1629
Panel
15.5 x 12.7 cm
Alte Pinakothek, Munich

In order to arrive at a picture of who actually bought and owned Rembrandt's work, we need to examine in some depth the backgrounds and social environments of the people he portrayed. There is also the matter of *tronies* as compared to portraits. Rembrandt's *tronies*, though often painted from models, are not necessarily the same as his portraits. In what respects did they differ from formal portraits, and how large was the output of these from Rembrandt's studio? These questions are the subject of the first section. The second section is devoted to the portraits, and will show that Rembrandt's output of painted portraits was sporadic. Is there an explanation for this?

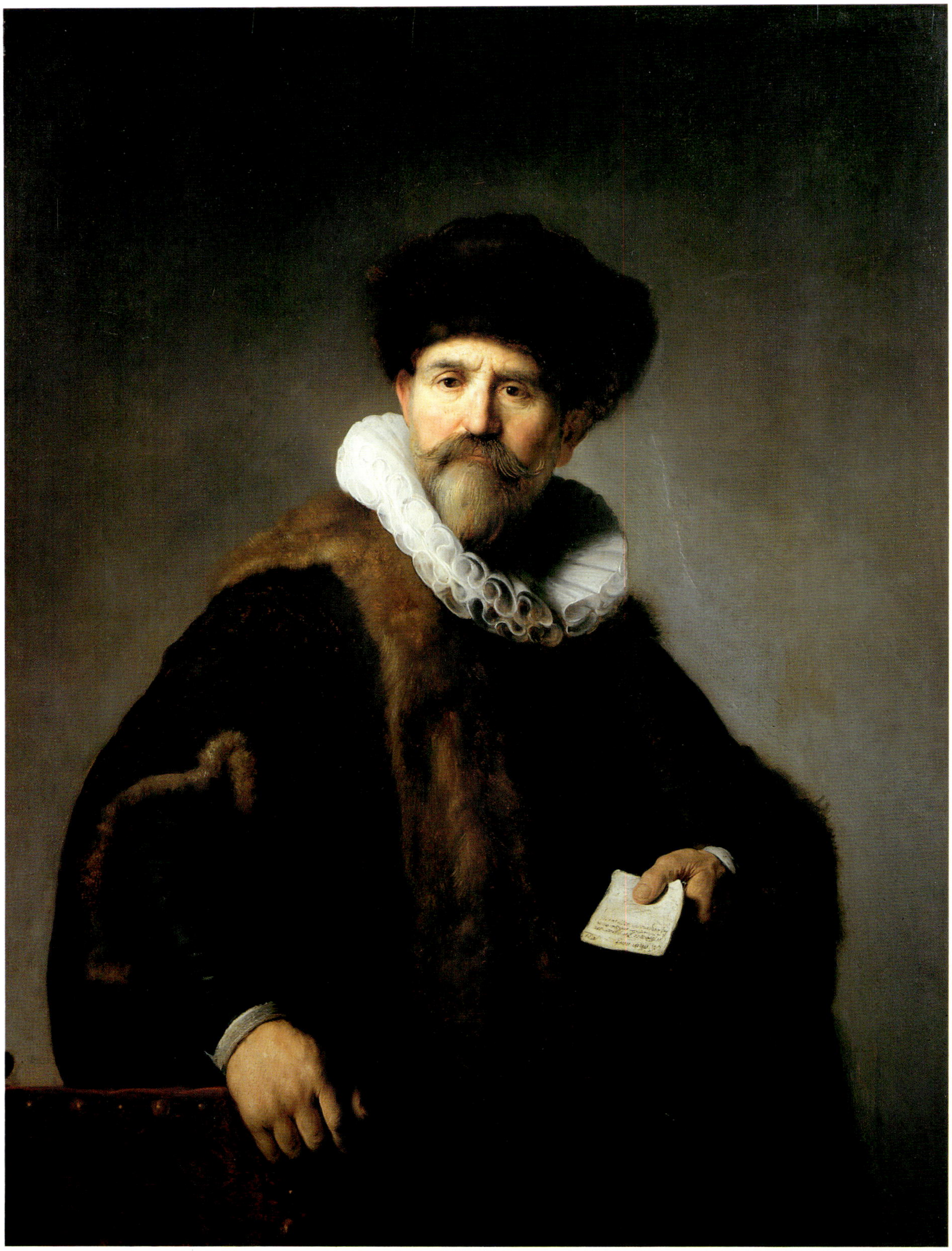

FIG. 2
Rembrandt
Portrait of Nicolaes Ruts
Monogrammed and dated 1631
Panel
116.0 x 87.0 cm
The Frick Collection, New York

Tronies

In the seventeenth century the term *tronie* signified a painting of a head, and more specifically a face, or aspect of a face, but *tronies* were not primarily intended to represent particular individuals.[4] While the *tronie* might be executed from a model, it was not intended to be an exact likeness of that person. There are several indications that *tronies* were in fact often painted from models (fig. 4). For instance, the autobiographical notes left by Constantijn Huygens mention that Jan Lievens's painting of a Turkish prince was based on a Dutch model (fig. 5).[5] Another fundamental difference is that *tronies* were often made for sale on the open market, whereas portraits were not. Inventories drawn up in the seventeenth century show that *tronies* found ready buyers.

Paintings of heads and half-length figures that were not made as portraits or devotional pictures first appeared in the Netherlands in the sixteenth century. Frans Floris's assistants used *tronies* painted by the master himself as examples for the large, multi-figure history paintings that they were mainly responsible for executing.[6] These *tronies* were made as studio material and were not intended for the market. Peter Paul Rubens's and Jacob Jordaens's assistants also worked from models of this kind. The *tronies* in Rembrandt's workshop had a different function, for these were produced for sale. Painting *tronies* constituted an important part of his pupils' work. They either copied those made by the master or worked directly from life. It may well have been a method allowing them to practise certain aspects of painting, such as rendering light and shadow or working with broad brushstrokes. In some *tronies* the lighting has been arranged so as to cast shadows over the face. Rembrandt's pupils must frequently have used themselves as models, but it would be going too far to assume that every *tronie* of a young man in a plumed beret is a self-portrait.

Tronies may have been prized for their exotic, 'picturesque' qualities. The subjects are frequently shown in unusual attire – a turban, plumed cap or gold necklace (fig. 6). Inventories often characterize *tronies* as 'foreign' or 'Turkish', or describe the subjects as figures in 'foreign robes' or other seemingly strange apparel. The word 'antique' is commonly used, in the sense of not contemporary, although the precise meaning of this term is sometimes unclear. Pictures of young people wearing costly jewellery and plumed berets are sometimes thought to have *vanitas* connotations, while those of old women reading or at prayer have been interpreted as allusions to pious old age.[7] The paintings may well have evoked these associations for their original buyers and owners, but their appeal probably stemmed just as much from their 'exotic' subjects and their artistic execution.

Heads and *tronie*-like self-portraits (fig. 7) were painted in large numbers for the market, generally fetching at most ten or twelve guilders each. Approximately 130 paintings are listed in Rembrandt's inventory of 1656, more than half of which works were made in his studio. A total of 10 are described as '*tronies* by Rembrandt', and 2 are explicitly said to have been rendered 'from life'.[8] The fact that such works were executed in Rembrandt's workshop is apparent from those that are still extant, and can also be deduced from references to them in contemporary sources.[9] From about 1630 to 1700 a total of 315 references were recorded concerning paintings by or after Rembrandt, at least 95 of which were *tronies*. Thirty-one paintings 'by', or 'after' Rembrandt (in Rembrandt's style), including 15 *tronies*, are listed for the period 1628–40; 28 works, including 9 *tronies*, for 1641–50; 67, including 18 *tronies*, for 1651–60; and 49, including 12 *tronies*, for 1661–70. The figures for the last three decades of the seventeenth century are 77, 43 and 20, incorporating 23, 12 and 6 *tronies* respectively. Some of the unspecified *conterfeytsels* (portraits) may also have been *tronies*, while the subjects of 21 paintings are not mentioned. The documents show that many *tronies* were the work of pupils. Approximately twenty-five per cent of them were

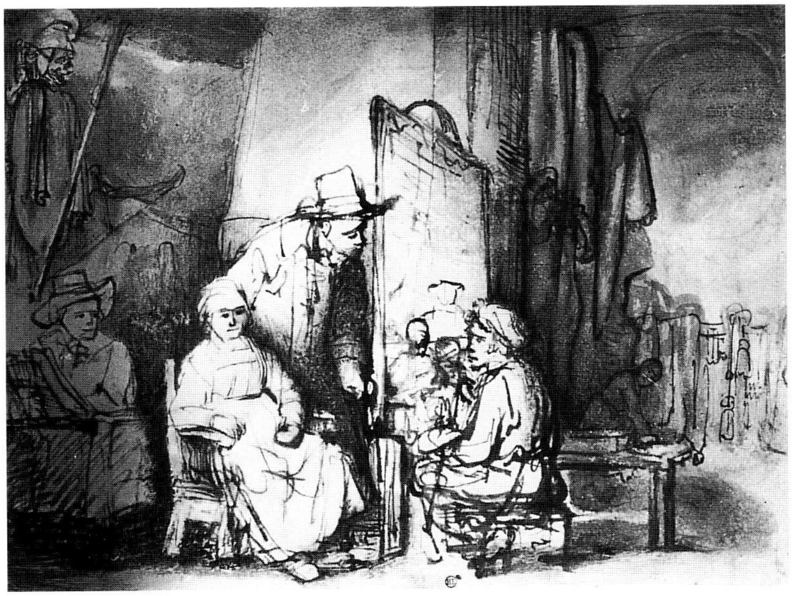

FIG. 3
Samuel van Hoogstraten?
Young Artist Portraying a Man and a Woman, the Man Inspecting the Result c.1640–45
Pen and ink and brush
17.5 x 23.4 cm
Musée du Louvre, Département des Arts Graphiques, Paris

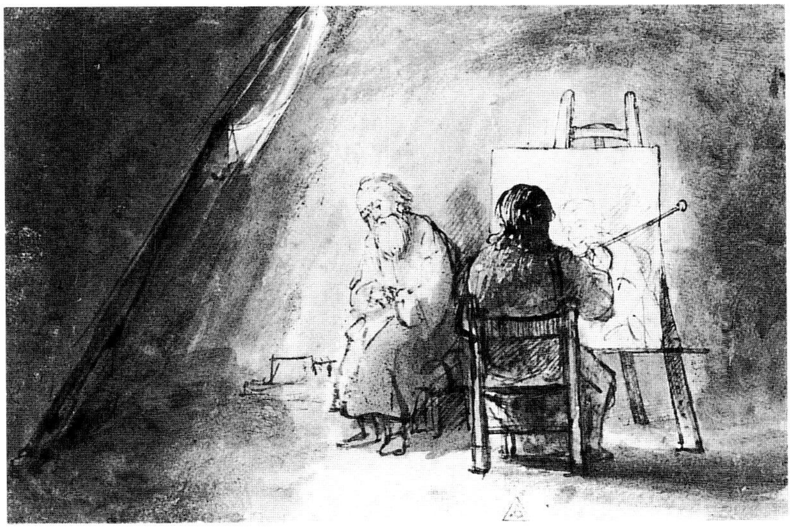

FIG. 4
Pupil of Rembrandt
Artist Painting an Old Man
Pen and ink and brush
9.1 x 13.9 cm
Collection Frits Lugt, Institut Néerlandais, Paris

identified as copies, virtually all in sources from before 1660.

The many references to 'Rembrandts' should not automatically be assumed to concern autograph work by the master. The inventories were simply intended to give an impression of what the valuers who made them saw, and their knowledge of art was usually quite limited. As the *tronies* were generally valued at no more than a few guilders, they cannot have been works by Rembrandt. The fact that art dealers and collectors were sometimes aware that what they were dealing with were the works of pupils emerges from two interesting but little-known sources published in the 1650s. A Paris inventory of 1653 lists 'deux têtes de vieillards, manière de Rembrandt' (two heads of old men, in the manner of Rembrandt);[10] and among the possessions of a Leiden bookseller a few years later were two 'old antique *tronies*' by a pupil of Rembrandt's,[11] each valued at eight guilders. We know that Rembrandt's pupils were required to produce *tronies* as a routine part of their training, as they frequently appear in inventories of his former apprentices. Several *tronies* are mentioned among the more than fifty paintings listed in the 1649 estate of Leendert van Beijeren, who had studied under Rembrandt around 1630.[12] Furthermore, an examination of the inventory of his father's estate, drawn up eleven years earlier, suggests that van Beijeren had copied Rembrandt's *tronies* during his apprenticeship. Four of these works formed part of the estate.[13] It is therefore clear that many *tronies* were copies of the master's work. This is confirmed by the fact that in quite a number of cases more than one version of a *tronie* is known, versions made by different artists.

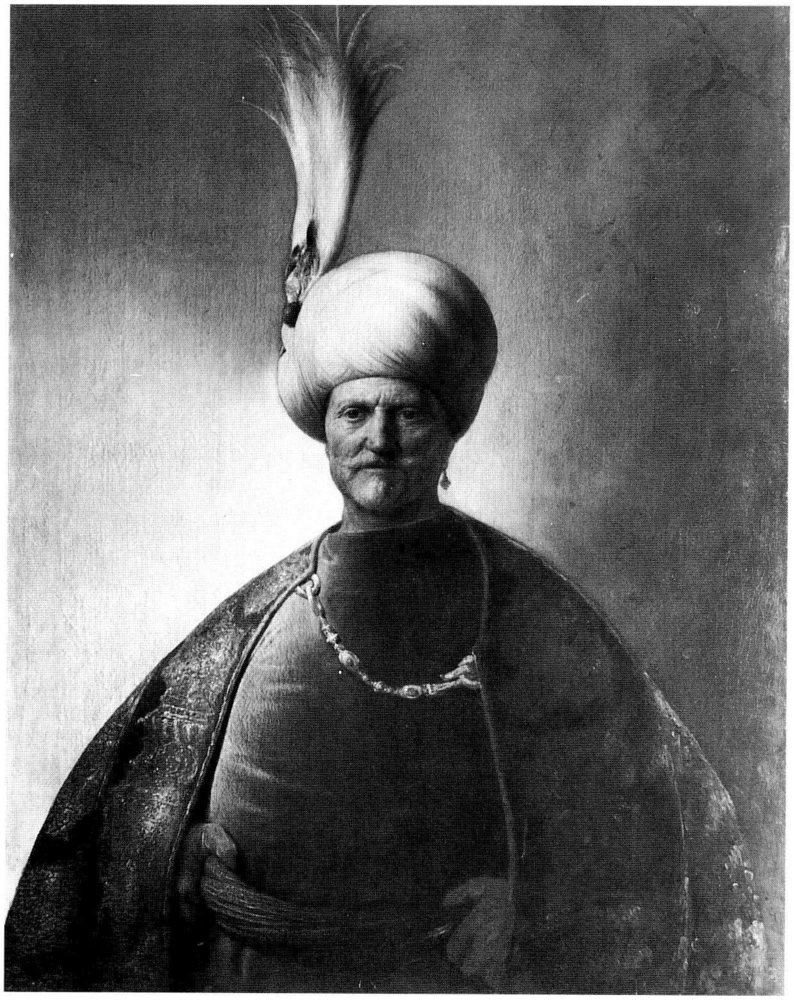

FIG. 5
Jan Lievens
Man in Oriental Costume c.1628
Monogrammed
Canvas
135.0 x 100.5 cm
Sanssouci, Gemäldegalerie, Potsdam

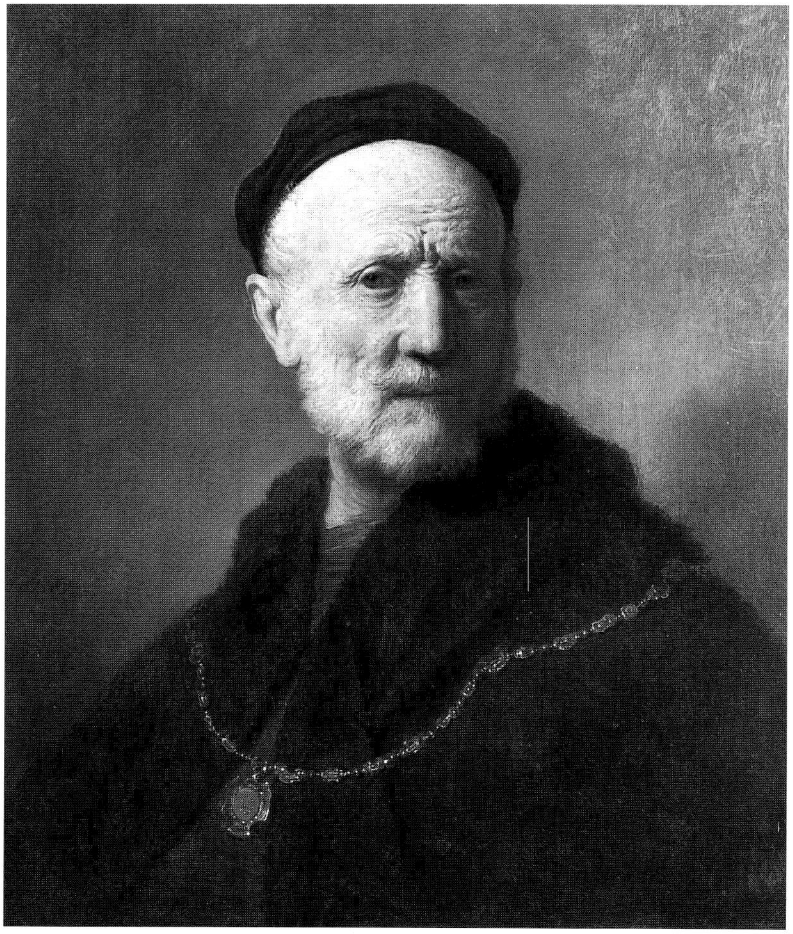

FIG. 6
Rembrandt
Bust of an Old Man with Cap and Gold Chain
Monogrammed and dated (added later?) 1631
Panel
59.5 x 51.2 cm
Private collection

Similar examples have been found in the inventory of Carel Fabritius's wife, compiled after her death in April 1643. This document is of particular interest because it was drawn up during or shortly after Fabritius's apprenticeship with Rembrandt, and thus gives an impression of Fabritius's output at that time. Besides four unspecified works, the list contains fourteen paintings, of which half were *tronies*: 'a *tronie* of a soldier', 'a *tronie* of an old woman', 'a roughly painted *tronie*', another 'roughly painted *tronie*', 'an antique *tronie*', 'a *tronie* of an old man, antique' and 'a shadow *tronie*'.[14] We can assume that most if not all of these *tronies* were painted by Fabritius, who worked at Rembrandt's studio between September 1641 and the spring of 1643.

Although it is possible that Rembrandt painted his *tronies* from imagination, he is far more likely to have worked from models. As is already indicated, he painted his own image in the mirror from the moment he completed his apprenticeship. The same faces can be recognized in a number of *tronies*, suggesting that much of the work from his studio must have been executed from models. A few documents show that Rembrandt's family and friends occasionally modelled for him. A representation of a certain elderly woman appears so frequently in his Leiden work that she is often taken to be his mother. Although this possibility cannot be ruled out, it should be remembered that the same woman also appears in paintings by Jan Lievens (cat. no. 35), Gerrit Dou and other artists. In any event, the elderly man who served as a model for Rembrandt's *tronies* during the same period, and who consequently was long thought to be his father, actually bore no resemblance to Rembrandt's father whatsoever.[15] It would therefore seem that other models posed for the youthful artists. Hendrick Uylenburgh's wife is believed to have posed for them in Amsterdam.[16]

There is one, largely untapped, source of information about the models who posed for Rembrandt that seems reliable. From the biography of the painter Adriaen van der Werff, written with his authorization by his son-in-law around 1720, we learn that van der Werff was often unable to find suitable models and that this was why the apostles depicted in one of his history pieces were not 'as lively and natural' as Rembrandt's. For Rembrandt, the author continues, lived at a time when 'men generally wore beards', and he 'turned the picturesque *tronies* in the Joode Breetstraet [where he lived] to good advantage'.[17]

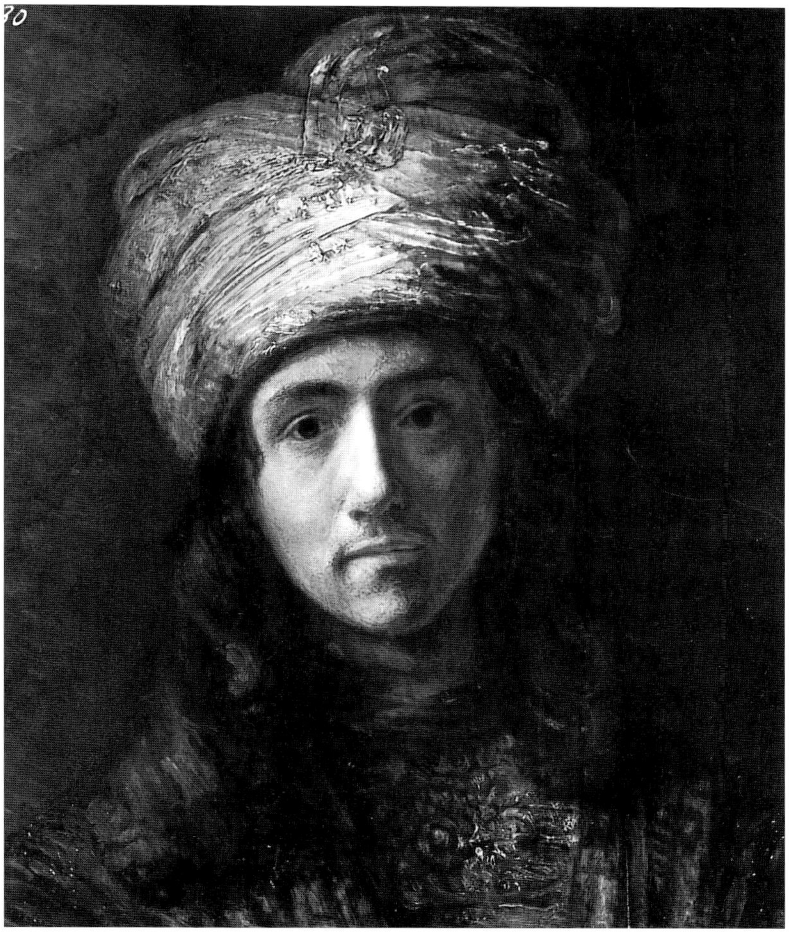

FIG. 7
Unknown artist
Young Man in a Turban
Panel
57.5 x 47.3 cm
The Art Institute of Chicago

Portraits

Practically all seventeenth-century Dutch sources refer to an individual portrait or a likeness of a particular individual as a *conterfeytsel* (likeness or exact imitation) or *portraict* (from the French *portrait*).[18] The word *effigie* may also sometimes occur, usually designating engraved or sculpted portraits.[19] As noted, art theorists tended to be disparaging about portrait painting: the portraitist was merely required to produce a faithful representation of his model. The term *portrayal (conterfeytsel)* meant either a painting or a literal copy, and was employed for townscapes or buildings as well as for people. For instance, in late 1538 or early 1539 the Amsterdam painter Cornelis Anthonisz received payment for having *gecontrefaict* the town. This painted and minutely detailed aerial view of the city was still referred to in 1608 as a *conterfeytsel* of Amsterdam.[20]

One of the principal requirements of a portrait was that it should resemble the subject. The artist's task was to render the sitter's features as faithfully as possible, although he was permitted – and indeed expected – to produce a flattering result. This is not to say that the artist sought to capture his model at a single moment in time. In the early modern period at least, a portrait was a carefully orchestrated form of 'self-representation',[21] aiming at realism while tending towards idealization, irrespective of the sitter's instructions.

It is also important to remember that although theorists may have deprecated the painting of portraits, the seventeenth-century burgher took a totally different view. Portraits were often bequeathed by will, and heirs were occasionally enjoined to take special care of them. The testators wished to ensure that their often costly portraits were preserved for later generations.[22]

From the information we have, it seems that commissioning a portrait in the seventeenth century was a relatively expensive venture. The price paid by the sitter should not be confused with the figures cited by the assessors who estimated the value of people's estates. Portraits, in particular, which were not readily marketable commodities, were valued by these assessors at far less than the price for which they had originally been bought.[23] Some artists charged between 10 and 20 guilders for a portrait, whereas others, with a more established reputation, received 60 to 100 guilders, depending on the format and on the particular wishes of the sitter. Finally, a small, select group of artists, whose number included Bartholomeus van der Helst and Rembrandt, were able to command substantially more.[24]

As noted, there are no portraits at all among the upwards of 40 paintings from Rembrandt's Leiden period.[25] This situation changed dramatically after his move to Amsterdam, where he proceeded to paint numerous portraits. Of the 60 or more paintings accepted as autograph from the period between 1631 and 1634, more than half are portraits (figs 8, 9). In 1635 this production of portraits came to an abrupt end. It seems that after this time Rembrandt accepted commissions for portraits only in exceptional cases. There was a slight upturn around 1640, but after the completion of the *Night Watch* (p. 26, fig. 7) in 1642 his turnout of portraits was again minimal. Indeed, his entire output during the 1640s shows a marked decline. The only portrait from those years is the

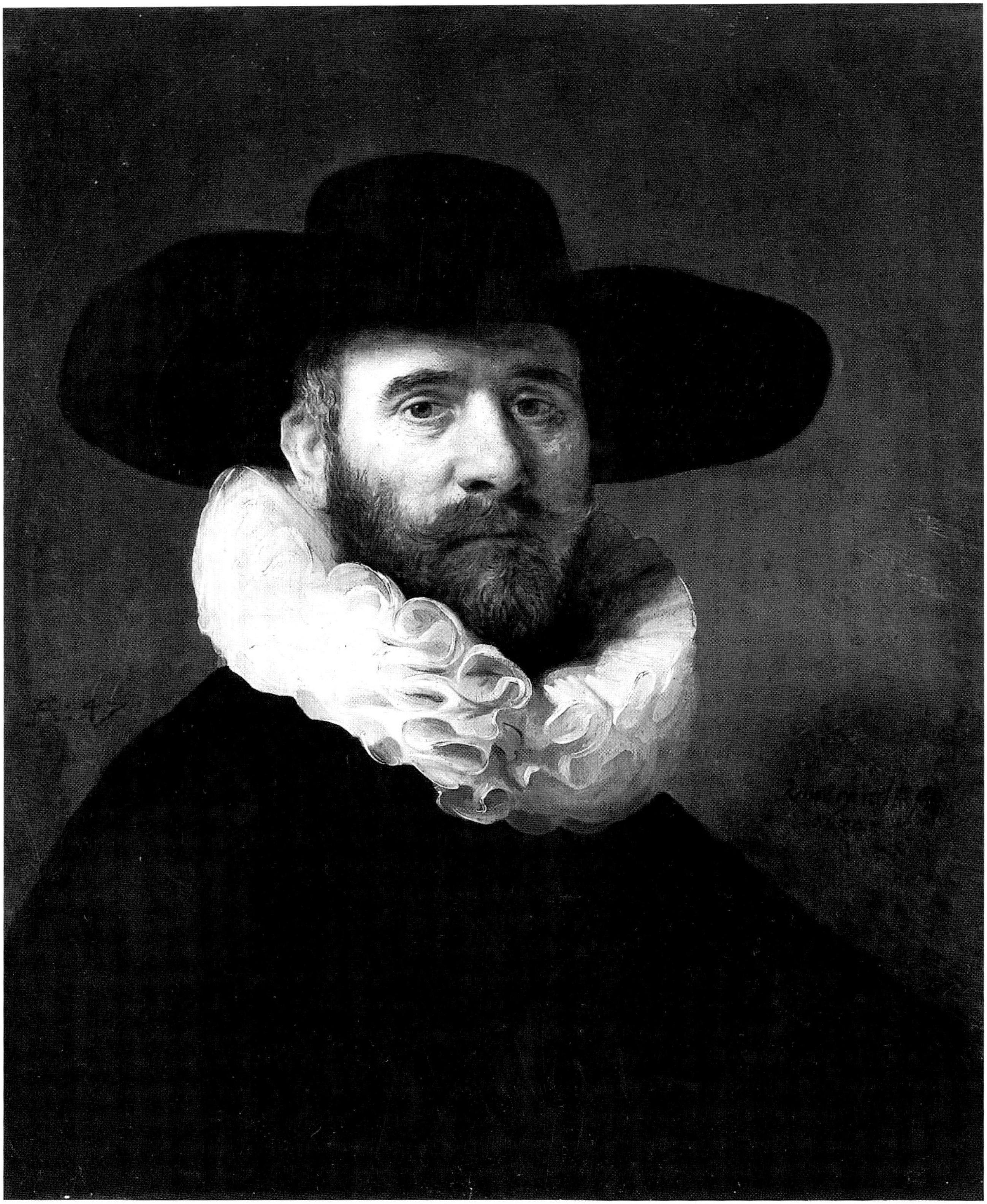

FIG. 8
Rembrandt
Portrait of Dirck Jansz Pesser
Signed and dated (added later?) 1634
Panel
68.9 x 53.2 cm
Los Angeles County Museum of Art

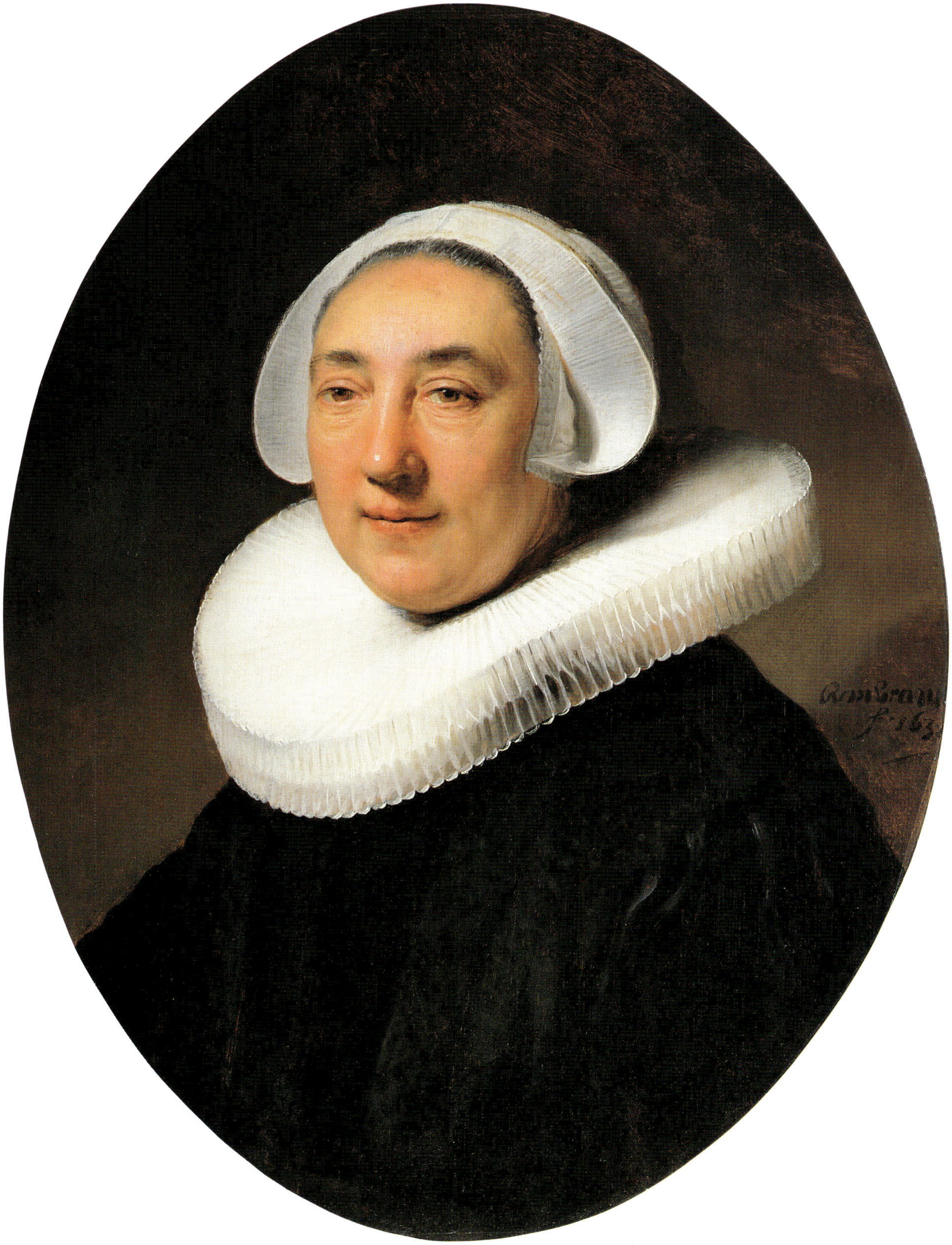

FIG. 9
Rembrandt
Portrait of Haesje Jacobsdr. van Cleyburg
Signed and dated 163[4]
Panel
68.6 x 53.4 cm
Rijksmuseum, Amsterdam

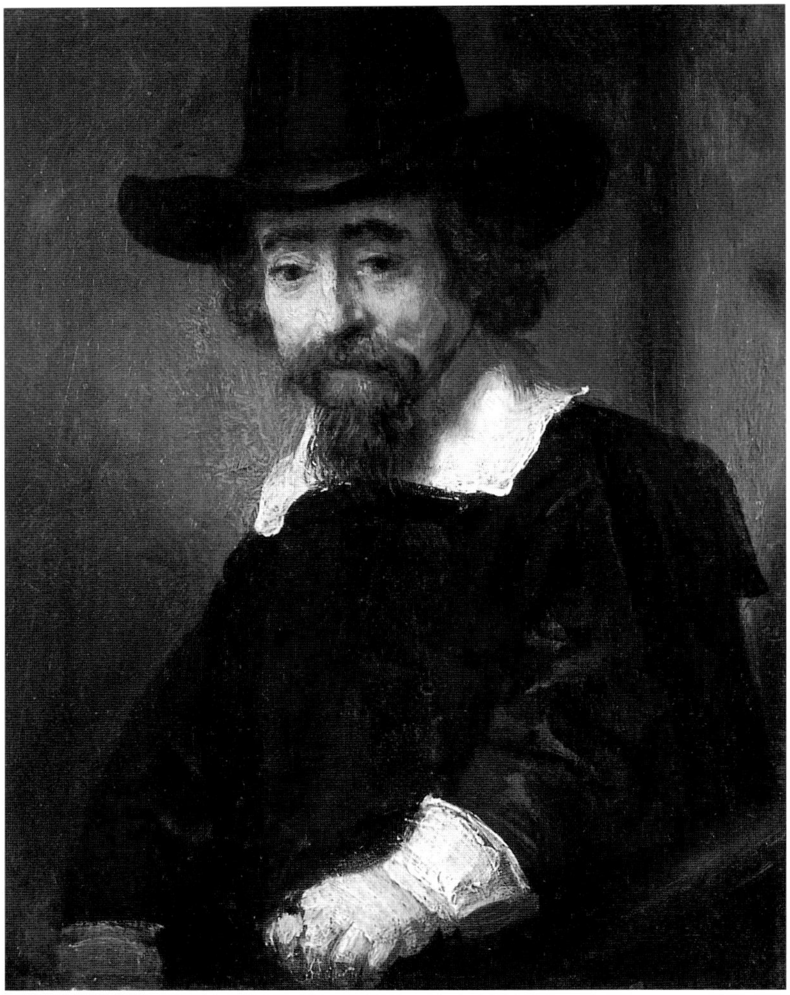

FIG. 10
Rembrandt
Portrait of Ephraïm Bueno c.1647
Panel
19.5 x 15.7 cm
Rijksmuseum, Amsterdam

oil sketch of Ephraïm Bueno (fig. 10),[26] probably a painted study for the etching (cat. no. 109). Rembrandt started painting portraits again in the mid-1650s. An interesting fact is that he received – and *accepted* – many commissions for single portraits at times when he was already working on prestigious group portraits: first in 1632, at the time of *The Anatomy Lesson of Nicolaes Tulp* (p. 25, fig. 3), then in 1656 during his work on the *Night Watch* (p. 26, fig. 7) and *The Anatomy Lesson of Joan Deyman*, and again in 1662, when he was painting *The Syndics* (p. 29, fig. 10).[27]

The same can be said of Rembrandt's etched portraits, for they too were not executed at regular intervals throughout his career, but were concentrated into a few periods. Most of the approximately 20 etched portraits date from 1633 to 1641, 1646 to 1647, and 1655 to 1658. The subjects of 18 of these works have been identified with reasonable certainty, while the identification that has been made of another is quite feasible.[28]

Is there an explanation for the rather intermittent nature of Rembrandt's portrait production? Could it be that he was initially in demand but, for a combination of reasons, considerably less popular later? Some factors might have been excessive fees, slow delivery, lengthy sittings, or client dissatisfaction with the results. Or could the explanation be that Rembrandt accepted commissions only when he was in need of money? It is also possible that he actually disliked painting portraits, as we know to have been the case with other painters. The low status attaching to portraiture may also have played a role. Though we cannot be certain about the operation of all these factors, the explosive output of portraits by Rembrandt and his assistants, at the beginning of the Amsterdam period at least, can be attributed to financial considerations. This financial aspect merits closer examination.

In the first half of the 1630s, a period when Rembrandt painted numerous portraits, he had lodgings in the home of the Amsterdam art dealer Hendrick Uylenburgh. Presumably he worked for Uylenburgh, but precisely what he did is unknown. They may have had an arrangement whereby Rembrandt produced paintings and prints while Uylenburgh procured commissions and managed the studio's output.[29] When Rembrandt set up on his own, it was probably Govaert Flinck who succeeded him at Uylenburgh's, where he likewise produced a large number of portraits. Sandrart remarked that not only had Flinck adopted Rembrandt's style but that his likenesses were considered superior to Rembrandt's.[30]

By about 1640 Rembrandt's reputation was established. An Englishman visiting the Dutch Republic in that year remarked on the excellence of its painters, but his journal mentions only Rembrandt by name.[31] Precisely because of this reputation, Rembrandt could probably now afford to accept fewer portrait commissions and devote more time to painting history pieces. Like Govaert Flinck and Adriaen van der Werff, Rembrandt had conceivably developed an aversion to portraiture,[32] and his earlier return to painting portraits in 1639 may be attributable to the fact that he signed the deed of purchase for his house in St Anthonisbreestraat in January of that year, the contract specified the terms of payment, and Rembrandt was short of cash. The same incentive to produce portraits may have reappeared in the 1650s, when he again found himself in serious financial difficulties.[33]

Once he had his own studio and his reputation was established, did Rembrandt ask too much for commissions? His fees were certainly high, about 200 guilders for a half-length portrait and up to 500 guilders for a double or a full-length portrait. Around 1642 a group of experts decided that Amsterdam's burgomaster, Andries de Graeff, was to pay Rembrandt 500 guilders for a portrait he had painted for him.[34] Rembrandt received the same amount for a double portrait of Abraham Wilmerdoncx and his wife.[35] In 1660 Adriaen Banck sold Rembrandt's portrait of him for the handsome sum of 150 guilders, but he himself had presumably paid Rembrandt more. In fact, many of Amsterdam's regents and wealthy merchants were prepared to part with substantial sums for their portraits. Bartholomeus van der Helst, for instance, who charged even more than Rembrandt, was never wanting for clients.

As Houbraken suggests, the answer could be that Rembrandt was slow to complete a work, but complaints on this score were made about other artists as well. The celebrated portraitist Michiel van Mierevelt sometimes kept clients waiting for long periods, yet the constant stream of commissions he received suggests that his popularity did not suffer. Rembrandt's work was also in demand, and – in the words of Houbraken, who was not referring to portrait commissions alone – he had to be cajoled and promised remuneration before he would accept a commission. It is not inconceivable that Rembrandt's approach to his work in the 1640s deterred prospective clients. In 1686 the Italian Filippo Baldinucci wrote that Rembrandt's reputation would have enabled him to paint far more portraits, but, when word got round that posing took two to three months, many prospective clients changed their minds. Baldinucci attributes the problem to Rembrandt's portrait technique. Rembrandt would apply a layer of paint and then wait for it to dry before proceeding with the following stage. In some cases he repeated this procedure several times, applying layer upon layer. According to Baldinucci, Rembrandt worked hard, but had difficulty completing a picture.[36]

It is important to understand that this description relates to the 1640s. Baldinucci's informant was Bernard Keil, a former pupil of Rembrandt. Baldinucci informs us that Keil worked with Rembrandt for eight years, which seems an extremely long time. It is true that Rembrandt painted few, if any, portraits during that period. Few people would have enjoyed posing for long stretches of time, and what this could actually entail was related by a daughter of the abovementioned Andries de Graeff, who reported that he had sat for Govaert Flinck fifty times while Flinck was executing his portrait.[37] One wonders whether Rembrandt's sitters were really required to endure such lengthy sessions. It seems more likely that Baldinucci meant to imply that the master's work tempo was slow and that his sitters had to keep returning.

Finally, the decline of Rembrandt's portrait production might in some part be attributable to the fact that his sitters were sometimes dissatisfied with the outcome. Two sources indicate that he was not always entirely successful in 'capturing' his subject's likeness. Constantijn Huygens, for instance, was mildly critical of the portrait of Jacques de Gheyn III (cat. no. 8), which in his opinion bore no resemblance to his friend.[38] The second source of information on this point merits more attention because it sheds interesting light on other aspects of Rembrandt's portraiture. It concerns a dispute between Rembrandt and the Portuguese merchant Diego d'Andrade over a portrait of a young woman. We know of the affair because d'Andrade instituted legal proceedings against Rembrandt.[39] He informed the artist that he had paid him 75 guilders in advance and would pay the balance when the picture was finished. He contended, however, that the work was 'far from a likeness of the person or the face of the aforesaid young woman'. Before the sitter's imminent departure for Hamburg, Rembrandt was asked to make such corrections to the portrait as were needed to achieve 'a proper resemblance': if he refused, he was to return the advance payment. Rembrandt's reply was unequivocal. He would not complete the work until he had received the full amount owing, whereupon he would request the authorities of the Guild of St Luke to judge whether it was a good likeness of the subject. Should they conclude it not to be so, he would be prepared to make alterations to the portrait, and if after that d'Andrade was still not satisfied he would put the painting up for sale at public auction. The portrait can no longer be identified, and it is unknown whether or not Rembrandt altered it.[40]

Rembrandt's attitude in this dispute is remarkable. His reply, as recorded verbatim by the notary, was arrogant. And he was obviously not willing to heed his client's wishes.[41] Altercations about a portrait's likeness were not unusual at that time. What is surprising in this affair is that Rembrandt considered putting the picture up for auction – clearly expecting to find a buyer. It implies that his works were sought after not just for what they depicted but also on the strength of his being the artist.

The d'Andrade affair is also interesting because it occurred in the 1650s, a period in which little is known about Rembrandt's clients. The serious financial difficulties in which he found himself around this time culminated in a *cessio bonorum*, which involved the transfer of his property. It might be thought that he received no important portrait commissions, but the d'Andrade affair disproves this. Although the woman's name is not mentioned in the legal document, she could have been a relative of d'Andrade's by the name of Beatriz Nunes Henriques, who married Manuel Teixeira de Sampayo (in Hamburg!) in 1654.[42] The portrait may have been intended to commemorate her betrothal, or perhaps Diego d'Andrade, in whose house Beatriz may have lived, wanted the picture as a memento. Whatever the circumstances, the fact is that Rembrandt received a portrait commission from a member of one of the wealthiest and most influential Portuguese-Jewish families in Amsterdam.

Archive records yield a considerable number of names of people whose portraits were painted by Rembrandt. These names help us understand further the types of people he painted and the circumstances in which he painted them. There are also the extant portraits, some of which have been identified quite definitely. First of all, Rembrandt painted people from his own environment, his immediate surroundings.[43] Houbraken reports that in his later years he associated mainly with other artists and with 'ordinary people'.[44] One of these 'ordinary people' was the poet Jeremias de Decker, whose portrait Rembrandt painted not for the

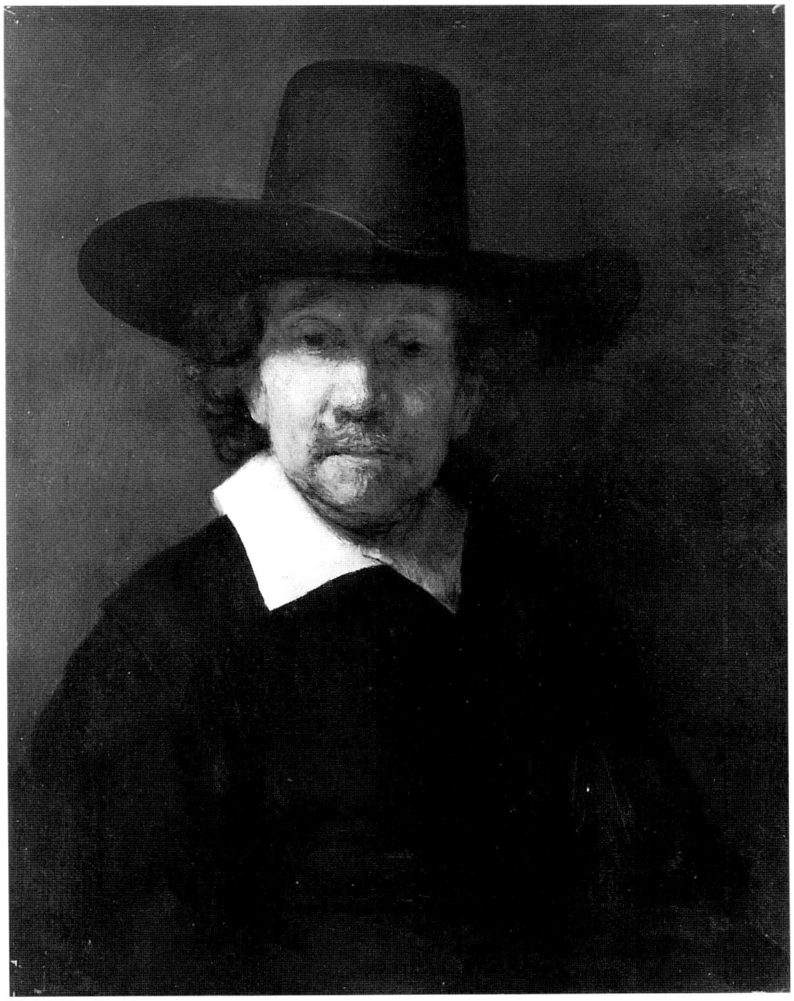

FIG. 11
Rembrandt
Portrait of Jeremias de Decker
Signed and dated 1666
Panel
71.0 x 56.0 cm
Hermitage, St Petersburg

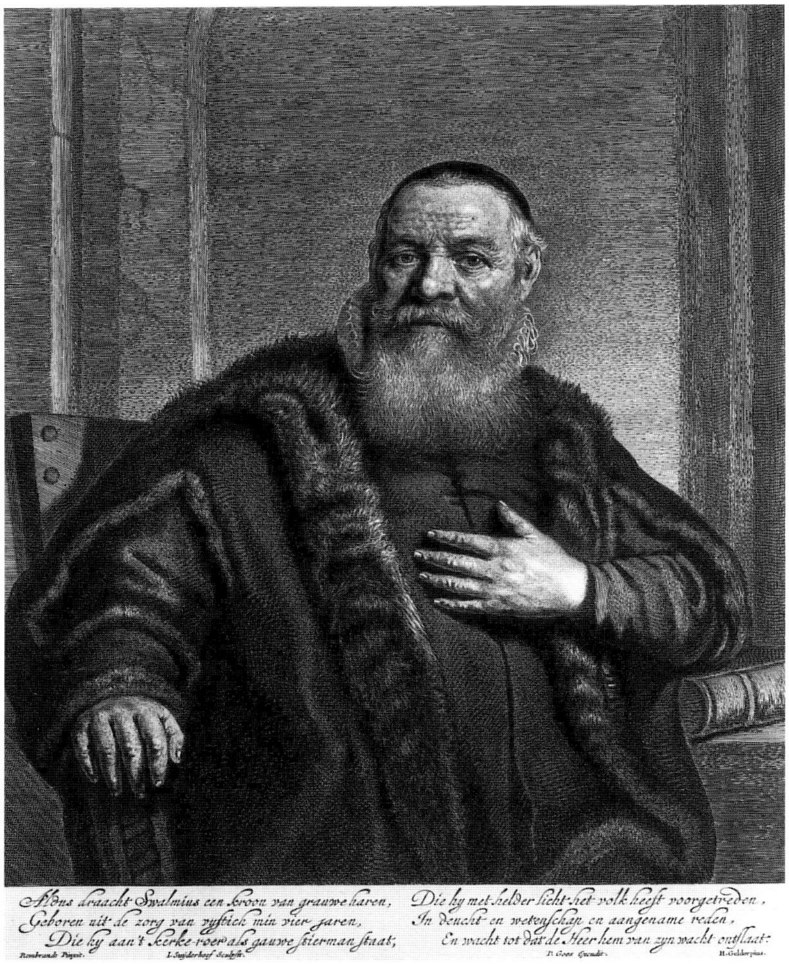

FIG. 12
Jonas Suyderhoef (*c.*1613–1686), after Rembrandt
Portrait of Eleazar Swalmius
Inscribed *Rembrandt Pinxit, I. Suijderhoef Sculpsit. P. Goos Excudit*
Engraving
32.8 x 25.7 cm
Rijksprentenkabinet, Rijksmuseum, Amsterdam

money, but purely as a favour (fig. 11).[45] For the rest, his clients came from the highest echelons of society – not surprisingly, perhaps, in view of the prices they paid. They included prosperous merchants, theologians, scholars and artists, as well as some of the city's administrators. They came from different religious backgrounds, although some denominations were better represented than others: the majority were members of the Reformed Church, but there were also Roman Catholics, Jews and Mennonites. Wealthy art lovers such as Jan Six and the painter-manufacturer Jan van de Cappelle ordered their portraits from Rembrandt, as did the prodigiously wealthy Jacob Trip and his wife Margaretha de Geer (see cat. no. 23 and fig. 23a). Hence it is clear that Rembrandt received important commissions in the 1650s and 1660s.

Finally, there were those with whom he had a professional relationship, like the book- and printseller Pieter de la Tombe. De la Tombe was an art lover who seems to have been a longstanding friend of Rembrandt's, for his will, dated 1671, refers to two portraits of himself painted 'in his youth and in his old age by Rembrandt van Rijn'.[46] Rembrandt may have painted the first portrait of de la Tombe, who was born in 1593, in the 1630s, and the second thirty years later. None of the extant portraits have been identified as that of Pieter de la Tombe. A second such example is Lodewijck van Ludick, a merchant who was also active in the art trade and who knew Rembrandt well. In 1662 he asked Rembrandt to keep a promise 'made to and accepted by Van Ludick on a certain occasion to paint a portrait'.[47] This picture has likewise remained unidentified, as there is no way of knowing what de la Tombe and van Ludick looked like.

In other cases there can be no doubt that certain portraits referred to in documents no longer exist. A well-documented portrait that has almost certainly been lost is that of the Amsterdam Reformed clergyman Eleazar Swalmius. We know what the painting looked like from a print after the work (fig. 12). Research on Swalmius and his descendants has revealed that besides Swalmius, Rembrandt must also have painted his wife, Eva Ruardus, as well as a daughter and her husband.[48] In 1655 Swalmius's widow stipulated that after her death the portraits of herself, her husband and a deceased daughter were to be kept for her grandson. She repeated these instructions two years later, on this occasion stating explicitly that the third portrait was that of her daughter Helena. The three works did indeed pass to the grandson, who in 1672 specified in his will that he bequeathed to his wife all his household effects with the exception of 'three portraits by Rembrandt'. These were undoubtedly the portraits of his grandparents and his aunt. In 1641 Helena Swalmius had married the Amsterdam merchant Adriaen Banck, whose portrait, as noted above, was known to have been painted by Rembrandt. In 1660 Banck parted with the portrait to settle a debt.[49]

When precisely were these portraits painted? Perhaps in years when Rembrandt painted very few portraits, years about which our knowledge is scant. On the basis of the print of Swalmius (fig. 12), a date in the mid-1630s seems likely. The portrait of his wife was presumably painted at about the same time. Rembrandt could have produced these pictures just before leaving Uylenburgh's studio, or shortly afterwards, when he had set up for himself. The portrait of Helena Swalmius could date from the same time, or possibly from 1641, the year of her marriage. The fact that Eva Ruardus had the disposal of this portrait of her daughter in 1655 indicates that it did not belong to Adriaen Banck. If his portrait was executed as a companion piece to that of his wife, it could likewise date to 1641. It could equally well date from 1647, the year in which Banck bought *Susanna and the Elders*[50] from Rembrandt for 500 guilders (p. 20, fig. 3).[51] If that is indeed the case, then Rembrandt's production of portraits was greater than has generally been assumed.

These portraits were passed on by inheritance and possibly sold in the eighteenth century, as happened with other portraits by important artists. It is tempting to try to trace the successive heirs, but caution is called for in the case of a well-known churchman like Swalmius. Two portraits of the married couple Swalmius–Ruardus were offered for sale in an auction in The Hague in 1743. They were described in the catalogue as works by Rembrandt, but they could very well have been copies. Portraits of prominent clergymen were sought after in the seventeenth century, and there must have been both engraved and painted versions in circulation. One example concerning Swalmius is documented. An Amsterdam inventory of 1656 refers to 'a portrait' of Eleazar Swalmius that was 'not quite finished'.[52] This could not be the autograph portrait by Rembrandt, as that version had presumably been completed. The portrait listed in the inventory must have been copied from an engraved or painted portrait for someone who evidently wanted a memento of Swalmius.

Though one should always be wary of the attributions to Rembrandt in documents, those concerning the portraits of Swalmius and his son-in-law seem to be perfectly reliable. But what about the portraits of his wife and daughter? The first mention of these two works as being autograph Rembrandts appears in a later will. They were to be given to a grandson, whom we can expect to have been reliably informed about the identities of the subjects and of the artist. Rembrandt's name was obviously important, because it is specially mentioned in the grandson's will. Nevertheless, it is possible that the daughter's portrait, for instance, was executed in Rembrandt's workshop, but not by the master himself.

Looking once again at Rembrandt's oeuvre as a whole, we find that his production of portraits was sporadic. His increased output in the first half of the 1630s came to an abrupt end once he had established himself as an independent master. Another peak around 1640 was followed by a relatively quiet period, in which he painted no more than the occasional portrait. Only from the 1650s on did he produce portraits more frequently. Was there a decline in demand, or had Rembrandt himself become more selective in taking on clients? There is much to be said for the latter case. After 1635 he could afford to pursue his main ambition, which was to be a history painter. His return to the lucrative genre of portraiture in later years was probably a matter of financial necessity. Notwithstanding the high fees he charged, the time he took to produce and finish his paintings, and his apparent lack of tact in dealing with clients who were dissatisfied with his prices or work, Rembrandt remained one of the most sought-after portraitists of his day.[53]

1 Scheller 1969.

2 Strauss & Van der Meulen 1979, p. 217, no. 1641/8: 'veeltijden versocht ... conterfeytselen ofte ander stucken ... te maecken'.

3 Bruyn 1986 cites several examples.

4 See the main entry in WNT, vol. 17, cols 3209–3221; De Pauw-de Veen 1969, pp. 190–3. Bauch 1960, pp. 168–81, posits that Rembrandt's character heads were finished, marketable works of art. For the application of the term *tronie* to such pieces by Rembrandt and his pupils, see Blankert 1976, p. 28; Blankert 1982, pp. 26–8, 57–9; cf. Blankert 1992–93, pp. 50–1. In regard to Rembrandt himself, see Bruyn 1982, pp. 40–51; Bruyn 1986, pp. 93–4; Bruyn 1989, pp. 22–6. See also Sumowski, *Gemälde*, vol. I, 1983, p. 16, note 68; Tümpel 1986, pp. 187–97. I have also made use of the following studies: De Vries 1989, Schwartz 1989, Kobayashi-Sato 1994.

5 Sumowski, *Gemälde*, vol. III, 1987, p. 1795, no. 1236; for Huygens's observation, see Huygens / Heesakkers 1987, p. 88.

6 Müller Hofstede 1968.

7 Van de Wetering 1986, pp. 22–6; *Corpus*, vol. I, 1982, pp. 272–5, no. A27; Bruyn 1987.

8 Strauss & Van der Meulen 1979, pp. 351–9, no. 1656/12 (nos 23, 24, 45 (2x), 48, 66, 90 (2x), 103, 105).

9 The figures cited here are based on references in inventories (though not that of Rembrandt's possessions), and on entries in ledgers concerning the transport of movable goods and purchases (Hofstede de Groot 1906a; Strauss & Van der Meulen 1979, with later additions and unpublished material).

10 Wildenstein 1957, pp. 219–22, esp. p. 221.

11 GAL, notary J. Dou, Notarial Archive 617, deed 59, dated 21 March 1657 (published in *Oud Holland*, vol. 53, 1936, p. 186).

12 GAA, notary J. Quirijnen Spithoff, Notarial Archive 1750, pp. 399–405, dated 10 October 1649 (excerpts published in Bredius 1915–22, vol. I, pp. 252–3, and *Oud-Holland*, vol. 5, 1887, pp. 238–9).

13 GAA, notary L. Lamberti, Notarial Archive 569, pp. 355–63, dated 7 May 1638 (excerpts published in *Oud-Holland*, vol. 5, 1887, pp. 236–7). In addition to some sixty paintings, including a portrait (self-portrait?) of Leendert van Beijeren and an 'antique *tronie* with a plume' (first described as a 'Polish *tronie*!), the inventory lists a further '107 small paintings, rondels and square, without frames, small and large'. Could this mean that the timber merchant also dealt in art? The four copies after Rembrandt listed in the estate are not mentioned in the inventory of his son Leendert. Had they been sold?

14 'Een krijgsmanstroony', 'een oude vrouwtronie', 'een ruwe aengesmeerde troony', 'een aengesmeerde troony', 'een antyckse troony', 'een oud manstrony, attyck' and 'een schaduwe trony' (GAA, notary D. de l'Hommel, Notarial Archive 1628, dated 24 April 1643; Brown 1981, pp. 17–21, 49–50, doc. 6). No description is given of Fabritius's clothing and painter's equipment. The document drawn up for the settlement of the estate refers to eleven paintings (the paintings in the inventory?) to be sold on behalf of his daughter, and to four portraits (Brown 1981, p. 148, doc. 8).

15 A signed drawing by Rembrandt bears an inscription, presumably by his hand, identifying the subject as Harmen Gerritsz van Rijn (Benesch 56) (Berlin / Amsterdam / London 1991–92c, p. 52, fig. 64). The following entry in a Leiden inventory provides evidence that Rembrandt painted his father on at least one occasion: 'Een out mans tronie, sijnde 't conterfeytsel van de vader van Mr. Rembrant' (A *tronie* of an old man, being a portrait of Rembrandt's father) (Strauss & Van der Meulen 1979, p. 240, no. 1644/1).

16 As appears from 'een cleine oostersche vrouwentroni, het conterfeisel van H. Ulenburgh[s] huysvrouwe, nae Rembrant' (a small *tronie* of an oriental woman, the portrait of H. Uylenburgh's wife, after Rembrandt), which was in the shop of the painter and art dealer Lambert Jacobsz (*c.*1598–1636) in Leeuwarden (Straat 1928, p. 73, no. 20; Strauss & Van der Meulen 1979, p. 144, no. 1637/4).

17 'men nog al veel gewent was baarden te draagen ... de schilderagtige tronien op de Joode Breetstraet ... wel ... tot zijn voordeel te verkiesen' (Gaehtgens 1987, p. 438). The information about Rembrandt may have come from Cornelis Brouwer, a former Rembrandt pupil who later joined the ranks of Rotterdam's well-to-do merchants and abandoned painting as a profession. As a young man, van der Werff had been Brouwer's protégé, and the two had frequently discussed *de konst* (art) (Gaehtgens 1987, pp. 48 (note 55), 76, 434). The biography seems perfectly reliable. Adriaen van der Werff made numerous corrections to the manuscript.

18 See WNT and De Pauw-de Veen 1969, pp. 193–202. Less common terms are *ymaige beeltenis* and *afbeeltsel*, all having the meaning of 'image'. De Jongh 1986, De Jongh 1991, and Campbell 1990 are indispensable sources in the study of portraits.

19 A source from 1665 refers to Rembrandt's son Titus as the subject of a 'seecker effigie gesneden bij eenen Holsteyn' (an effigy carved by Holsteyn) (Strauss & Van der Meulen 1979, p. 541, no. 1665/6). Yet the reference in a will to 'twee efigien van den constrijcken schilder Rembrandt met sijn vrouw' (two effigies of the accomplished painter Rembrandt and his wife) (Strauss & Van der Meulen 1979, p. 262, no. 1648/7) seems to mean painted portraits. An interesting example appears in a Leiden inventory of 1656 which lists painted 'contrefaitsels', 'effigien in prent' and 'geprente effigie op sattijn' of the deceased. The 'geschilderde effigie Joannis Calvini' was probably executed after a print (Lunsingh Scheurleer, Fock & Van Dissel 1986–92, vol. 6a, pp. 270–2).

20 Blankert 1975–79, pp. 9–10, no. 8 (with sources); Van Biema 1906, esp. p. 113 (citing a reference from 1609 to 'zeeckere contrefeytsels' of the Amsterdam Beurs, possibly a perspective drawing of the courtyard).

21 Scholten 1995, pp. 5–6.

22 See, for example, Van der Stighelen 1991.

23 A revealing example is the inventory of Govert Looten and Anna Rutgers, in which the portraits of his father and both her parents were valued collectively at the paltry sum of thirty guilders (GAA, notary J. van Loosdrecht, Notarial Archive 2002, pp. 296–315, dated 4 and 21 November 1678; GAA, arch. no. 5072, inv. no. 384, fols 153–64, dated 2/3 January 1679). Shortly afterwards they were valued by two painters at 99 guilders and 6 stuivers (ibid., fols 169v–172, dated 17 and 25 February 1679). For these portraits, the first of which was painted by Rembrandt (Los Angeles County Museum of Art; *Corpus*, vol. II, 1986, no. A52), and the others by Jurriaen Ovens, the fees paid to the artists would have been several times that amount.

24 The scale of commissions received by van der Helst is shown by the following. In 1665 two Haarlem painters agreed that his portrait of a married couple with a child and a greyhound would normally be valued at 300 guilders, 'maer ten respecte van de meester sijn naem en reputatie hebben 't selve op vierhondert gulden getaxeert' (but taking account of the master's name and reputation have valued the same at four hundred guilders) (Bredius 1915–22, vol. VII,

p. 301). In 1650 the Utrecht art lover Willem Vincent, Baron van Wyttenhorst (1613–1674), paid van der Helst 165 guilders each for portraits of himself and his wife, despite the fact, as he remarked drily, that the artist had 'wel ses weeken in ons huys gelogeert' (spent six weeks in our house)! In 1656, Rijckloff Volckertsz van Goens (1619–1682) paid van der Helst 1,400 guilders for a portrait of his family with a servant (Leupe 1856, pp. 28–48, esp. p. 48). Around the same time, Govaert Flinck painted portraits for van Goens at 200 guilders each.

25 Based on the *Corpus* and on Tümpel 1986. Obviously, this relates to the works which, by chance or not, have survived, and, at least in a number of cases, to disputed attributions.

26 Bredius / Gerson 1969, no. 252.

27 Mauritshuis, The Hague (*Corpus*, vol. II, 1986, no. A51); Rijksmuseum, Amsterdam (*Corpus*, vol. III, 1989, no. A146; and Bredius / Gerson 1969, nos 414, 415).

28 Ekkart 1986–87 provides a good overview of Rembrandt's etched portraits. We have an idea of the price of these works from a document concerning a 1655 transaction. This document states that Rembrandt was to be paid 400 guilders for an etched portrait of the same quality as the etching of Jan Six (B.285; our fig. 28b) (Strauss & Van der Meulen 1979, p. 333, no. 1655/8).

29 Van de Wetering 1986, pp. 56–60.

30 Sandrart 1675, p. 194: Flinck 'folgte in der Manier viel seinem Lehrmeister [Rembrandt], wurde aber in Gleichheit und Annehmlichkeit der Contrafäten glüchlicher geschätzt. Er hielte sich lange Jahre auf bey dem berühmten Kunsthändler Ulenburg, dem er viel ausbündige herrliche Contrafäten von eigner Hand hinterlassen'.

31 Strauss & Van der Meulen 1979, p. 202, no. 1640/16. Rembrandt's output at that time is discussed at length in Dickey 1994.

32 Houbraken, who was well informed about Flinck, writes that his 'spirit sought greater enterprises' (geest geneigt [was] tot grooter ondernemingen) and that he 'later refused those who wanted him to paint portraits' (de genen die hem pourtretten wilden laten schilderen naderhand af[wees]) (Houbraken 1718–21, vol. II, 1719, pp. 23–4). Van der Werff is said to have developed 'a strong dislike of painting portraits' (een groote tegenzin om contrefytsels te maaken) (Gaehtgens 1987, p. 438).

33 Dudok van Heel 1991–92c, pp. 56, 60–1.

34 Strauss & Van der Meulen 1979, p. 451, no. 1659/21. Hendrick Uylenburgh states that around 1642 he and other reputable persons had valued the portrait. Apparently Rembrandt and the burgomaster were not in agreement on the price. It is not clear from the wording of Uylenburgh's deposition whether the portrait was of Andries de Graeff himself. That de Graeff was portrayed by Rembrandt emerges from a later inventory listing a portrait of him by Rembrandt, valued at 120 guilders. The *Corpus*, vol. III, 1989, pp. 302–3, no. A129, disproves the identification of Andries de Graeff as the subject of the *Portrait of a Man, Standing* at the Staatliche Kunstsammlungen Kassel, but the recent identification of Cornelis Witsen as the subject of this work is not universally accepted either (P. van Thiel, in Berlin / Amsterdam / London 1991–92c, cat. no. 29).

35 Strauss & Van der Meulen 1979, p. 448, no. 1659/18. The double portrait appears to be lost.

36 Hofstede de Groot 1906a, no. 360, esp. p. 422; Slive 1953, pp. 104–15. Tümpel 1986, p. 209, notes that Rembrandt wanted to devote himself entirely to history painting and that his domestic situation was partly responsible for the crisis in the 1640s; he was not finished as a portraitist (pp. 235–6). Gerrit Dou is also said to have held prolonged sittings, working so slowly that he stopped receiving commissions (Sandrart 1675, pp. 195–6). For Rembrandt's technique, see Van de Wetering 1991–92c.

37 Huygens 1876–88, vol. 2, p. 289 (kindly drawn to my attention by Marieke de Winkel). This may be the portrait described by Von Moltke 1965, p. 107, no. 205 (canvas, 45 x 37 cm; present whereabouts unknown). Willem Vincent was full of praise for the portraits of himself and his wife painted by Bartholomeus van der Helst (see note 24 above), but nevertheless felt constrained to add that the artist had 'spent a long time on them' (daer langen tijt in versleeten).

38 This is the interpretation of Huygens's epigrams given by P. van Thiel, in Berlin / Amsterdam / London 1991–92c, cat. no. 12.

39 GAA, notary A. Lock, Notarial Archive 2196, p. 191, dated 23 February 1654 (Strauss & Van der Meulen 1979, pp. 310–11, no. 1654/4). For the correct reading by Bredius, see Bredius 1899a, p. 3.

40 In 1675 the art dealer Gerrit Uylenburgh owned 'an *unfinished* female portrait by Rembrandt' (een *begonne* vrouwe conterfeytsel van Rembrant) and 'a Jewish woman by Rembrandt' (een jodin van Rembrant) (Bredius 1915–22, vol. V, pp. 1668–9). The latter picture was valued in that year at 150 guilders (Dudok van Heel 1982, p. 85). If d'Andrade's advance payment to Rembrandt was one half of the full price, that would be consistent with this valuation.

41 Houbraken 1718–21, vol. I, 1718, pp. 254–74, characterizes Rembrandt as an extremely stubborn man unwilling to make concessions. As we have seen, Rembrandt did not shrink from a dispute (about the price only?) with the powerful Andries de Graeff.

42 Manuel Teixeira de Sampayo was the son of Diego Teixeira de Sampayo (1581–1665), and his second wife was Anna d'Andrade (1610–1693); see *Nederland's Adelsboek*, vol. 45, 1952, pp. 308–20. This Anna may have been the sister of Diego d'Andrade, or perhaps of his namesake Diego (Samuel) Rodrigues d'Andrade (1608–1660). For information on the family, see Kellenbenz 1958, pp. 163–6, 167, 170, 385–96, 482–5.

43 Of the portraits of his family, one of his wife Saskia and another of Titus's mother-in-law are documented. Geertje Dircx (1600/15–1656?), Titus's nurse and Rembrandt's mistress, disposed of a portrait of herself in a will dated 1648 (Strauss & Van der Meulen 1979, pp. 260–1, no. 1648/2); it was presumably painted by Rembrandt.

44 'Gemeene luiden' (Houbraken 1718–21, vol. I, 1718, p. 272). Rembrandt was on friendly terms with fellow artists like Roelant Roghman (1627–1692) and Christiaen Dusart (1618–1682/83).

45 'Maer louterlijck uyt gunst' (Strauss & Van der Meulen 1979, p. 572, no. 1667/11); Bredius / Gerson 1969, no. 320. The brothers Abraham and Daniel Fransz had the same social background as de Decker. Abraham, a struggling apothecary, was a great lover of art on paper; Daniel was a surgeon.

46 'zoo in zijn jonge als oude dagen door Rembrandt van Rijn' (GAA, notary J. Quirijnen Spithoff, Notarial Archive 1772, dated 21 February 1671); Van Eeghen 1956.

47 'een conterfijtsel aen Van Ludick in seeckere occasie toegezeyt ende aengenomen te maecken' (Strauss & Van der Meulen 1979, p. 499, no. 1662/6). The commentary suggests this was a portrait of van Ludick; this is possible but is not explicitly stated.

48 The author intends to publish an article on the new material outlined here. The portrait of a man at the Koninklijk Museum voor Schone Kunsten in Antwerp, which is not by Rembrandt (Bredius 1935, no. 213 (as Rembrandt); H. Gerson, in Bredius / Gerson 1969, p. 565, no. 213 (as Flinck?)), is not Eleazar Swalmius, but very probably his brother Hendricus; cf. *Corpus*, vol. III, 1989, p. 689, fig. 5. Grimm 1991, pp. 112–13, likewise concludes that the Antwerp portrait is of Hendricus Swalmius and cannot be attributed to Rembrandt.

49 Described as 'a piece by ditto [Rembrandt] being my portrait' (Een stuck van ditto [Rembrandt] zijnde mijn Conterfeijtsel) (Strauss & Van der Meulen 1979, p. 459, no. 1660/13 (erroneously citing the value of the portrait as 50 guilders; in fact it was 150 guilders)). The property was handed over to his brother-in-law, so it is likely that the portrait remained in Banck's possession.

50 Bredius / Gerson 1969, no. 516.

51 Strauss & Van der Meulen 1979, p. 446, no. 1659/17.

52 'een conterfeytsel ... niet ten vollen opgemaeckt' (GAA, notary J. Hellerus, Notarial Archive 2481, pp. 400–15, dated 29 February–1–2 March 1656).

53 I am most grateful to Michiel Franken for his comments during the preparation of this essay.

CATALOGUE OF WORKS IN THE EXHIBITION

I

Bust of a Man in a Gorget and Cap
c.1626–27

Panel
40.0 x 29.4 cm
Private collection

PROVENANCE: Private collection, Brussels, by 1930; H. Baron Thyssen-Bornemisza Collection, Lugano-Castagnola, from 1930; J. H. van Stratum, Geneva, 1973; sale, London (Christie's), 29 March 1974, lot 54, repr.

LITERATURE: Bauch 1966, no. 109; Bredius / Gerson 1969, no. 132; *Corpus*, vol. I, 1982, pp. 124–8, no. A8; Schwartz 1984, p. 62; Tümpel 1986, no. 126; P. ten Doesschate-Chu, in Basel 1987, p. 210, cat. no. 79.

A soldierly figure fixes us with a critical gaze from under his striking slashed beret. One of his eyes is in the light, the other in the shadow that the beret casts over the right half of his face. This gives him a slightly comical expression. The diagonal of the shadow falling on the white wall behind him can be drawn through his illuminated eye. The hilt and scabbard of the sword[1] he holds under his right arm are parallel to the shadow line on the wall. At an angle to these two diagonals we see a series of adjacent, roughly parallel, bands: the blue seam of the red cloak in front, set off against the brown sleeve above it; the metal gorget; and the bonnet with a whitish-yellow plume, whose upper surface is brightly lit.

The piece displays the variety of colour typical of Rembrandt's earliest works, from 1625–26. Two of them show a similar figure wearing a metal gorget and slashed beret (*Historical Scene*[2] and *Christ Driving the Money-Changers from the Temple* (fig. 1a)).[3] The slightly later *Bust* is the first work in which Rembrandt concentrated on a single figure, and he has achieved a more compactly arranged composition than in his earlier multi-figure pieces. The *Bust* is also his first study of the fall of light on a white wall. Shortly afterwards he masterfully elaborated that motif in the *Apostle Paul* in Stuttgart and the *Simeon Speaking to Mary* in Hamburg (see fig. 2a and cat. no. 2). At the top right of the *Apostle Paul* the plaster on the wall has crumbled in places, exposing the brick underneath. In the present work we see only cracks in the plaster (at left) and (lower down) the shapes of bricks through the plaster. A copyist evidently thought this handling was insufficiently Rembrandtesque or picturesque: in his copy he showed a place in the wall where the plaster has come loose and the bare brick can be seen (fig. 1b).[4]

The whitish-yellow of the plastered wall in

FIG. 1a
Rembrandt
Christ Driving the Money-Changers from the Temple (detail)
Monogrammed and dated 1626
Panel
Pushkin Museum, Moscow

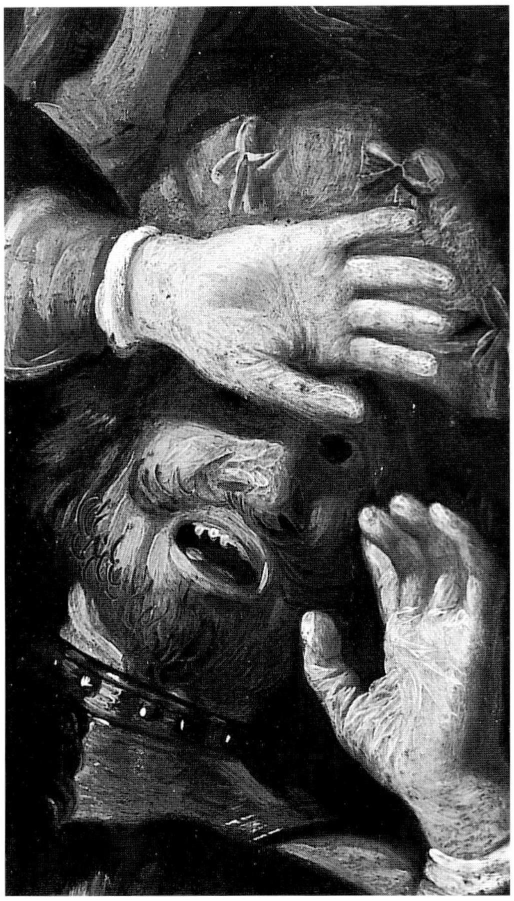

FIG. 1b
Unknown artist, after Rembrandt
Bust of a Man in a Gorget and Cap
Panel
39.5 x 33.0 cm
Present whereabouts unknown
Photograph: RKD

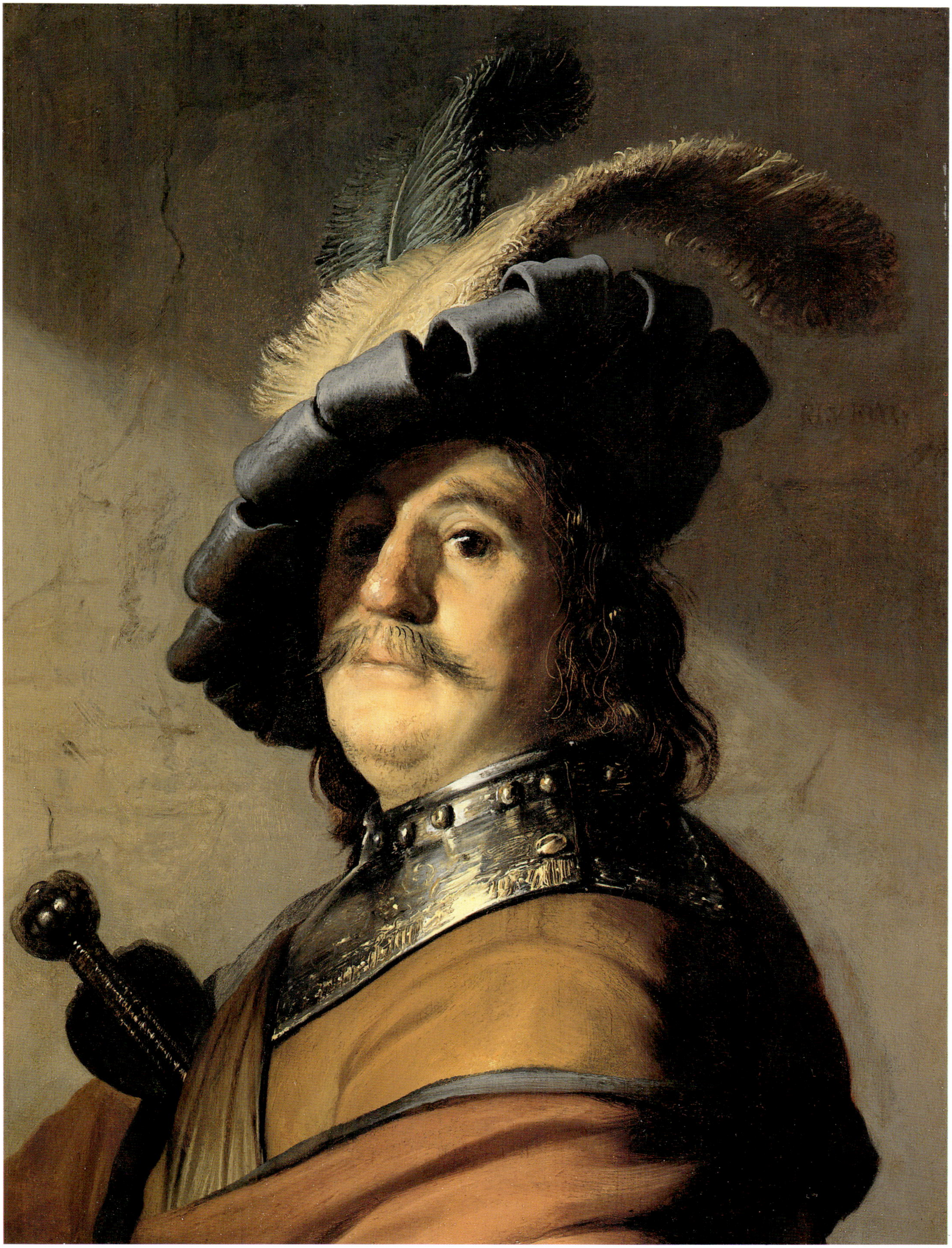

Rembrandt's *Bust* is skilfully repeated twice, in the rendering of entirely different substances: in the hard metal of the gorget, the reflections on which are painted in boldly broad brushstrokes, and in the soft texture of the feather. The piece must have been made around *c.*1626–27, when Rembrandt was approximately twenty years old.[5]

To some extent the figure's expression and pose seem to anticipate the *Self-Portrait at the Age of 34* of 1640 (cat. no. 13). In 1966 Bauch speculated that the model in the *Bust* may have been Rembrandt's brother Adriaen.[6] The *Bust*, however, is definitely not a portrait, but Rembrandt's first preserved *tronie*. *Tronies* were busts, or half-length figures, in bizarre, exotic or antique costumes, and were made for the open market. Pictures of this kind gave painters an opportunity to practise and also to demonstrate their skill at capturing different expressions and moods. For the rest of his life Rembrandt continued to concentrate on the motif of a single *tronie*, charged with expression.

For this *Bust* he must have drawn inspiration from early-sixteenth-century prints or drawings of the mercenary soldiers known as *Landsknechts* (lansquenets). The costume and characterization of the figure seen here recall these works, of which Rembrandt himself owned examples in 1656.[7] A figure such as the one in the *Bust* occurs in a drawing of *c.*1529–30 by Hans Holbein the Younger (fig. 1c).[8] Rembrandt knew drawings by Holbein, as he made free copies after them.[9]

An X-ray photograph shows that the *Bust* was painted over a head of an old man.[10] On other occasions too during this period Rembrandt is known to have painted over a picture that he evidently considered unsatisfactory.[11]

AB/MB

1 *Corpus*, vol. I, 1982, p. 126, no. A8. J. P. Puype, head conservator of the War Museum in Delft, has confirmed that this object must be the coquille of a sabre (letter, 18 February 1997); see also Puype 1981, figs 7–10, 185–194.

2 Stedelijk Museum de Lakenhal, Leiden (Bredius / Gerson 1969, no. 460; *Corpus*, vol. I, 1982, no. A6).

3 Bredius / Gerson 1969, no. 532; *Corpus*, vol. I, 1982, no. A4.

4 *Corpus*, vol. I, 1982, p. 128, refers to the copy without mentioning this departure from the original; see also *Connoisseur*, vol. CXXXIII, no. 536, March 1954, p. 120, and colour cover.

5 *Corpus*, vol. I, 1982, p. 126, no. A8.

6 Bauch 1966, no. 109.

7 P. ten Doesschate-Chu, in Basel 1987, p. 210 (with a reference to Strauss & Van der Meulen 1979, no. 1656/12). Bauch 1966, no. 109, refers to the *Bust* as 'Der Landsknecht'.

8 Schmid 1945, fig. 41.

9 Haverkamp-Begemann 1988, pp. 120–1, cat. no. 32.

10 *Corpus*, vol. I, 1982, p. 125, fig. 2.

11 For example, *Corpus*, vol. I, 1982, no. A9, *David Presenting the Head of Goliath to Saul* in Basel (our fig. 4c), which is painted on top of a (half-finished?) picture of a head.

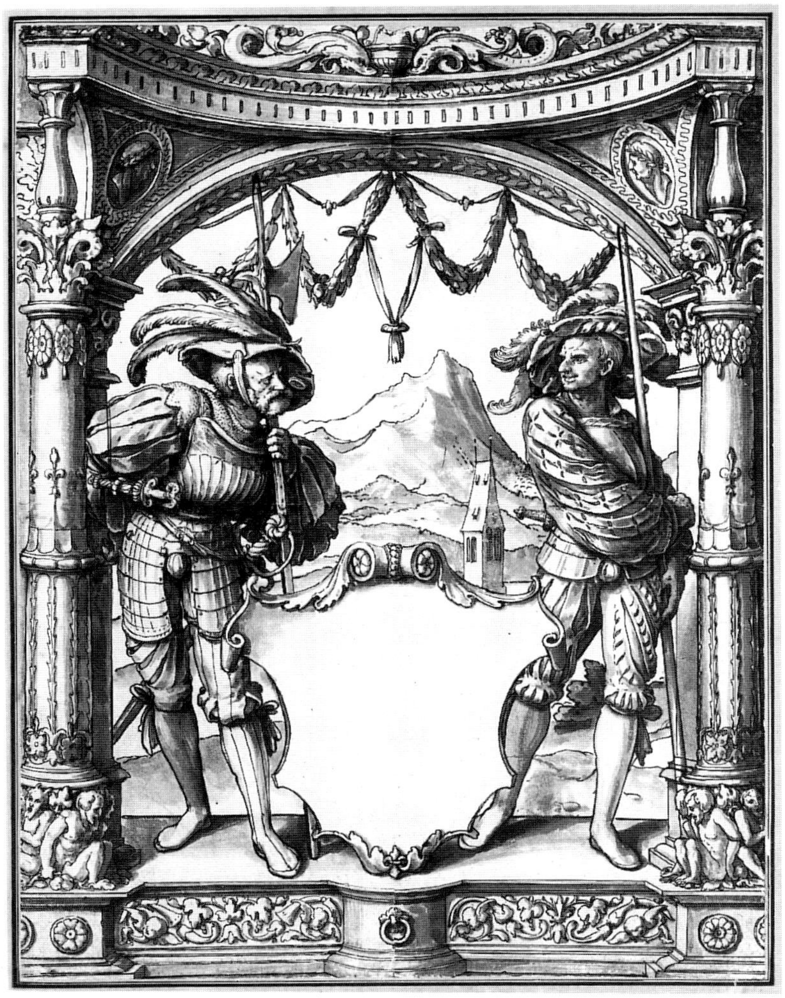

FIG. 1C
Hans Holbein the Younger German, 1497/98–1543
Two Lansquenets (design for a window) *c.*1529–30
Pen and ink and brush
43.8 x 32.3 cm
Öffentliche Kunstsammlung Basel, Kupferstichkabinett
Photograph: Öffentliche Kunstsammlung Basel, Martin Bühler

2

Simeon Speaking to Mary in the Temple
*c.*1627–28

Signed lower right *Rembrandt. f.* (probably a later addition)
Panel
55.4 x 43.7 cm
Hamburger Kunsthalle

PROVENANCE: Possibly the picture described as follows in 1632 and said to be at the stadholder's quarters in The Hague: 'A painting in which Simeon, being in the temple, has Christ in his arms, by Rembrandt or Jan Lievens' (see commentary below); possibly sale, Marinus de Jeude, The Hague, 18 April 1735, with description, for 41 guilders; Comte de Lassé; sale, Comte de la Guiche, Paris, 4–7 March 1771, lot 21; sale, Vassal de St Hubert, Paris, 17–21 January 1774, lot 23, for 1,500 frs to Le Brun for the Comte du Barry; sale, Comte Jean du Barry, 21 November 1774, lot 27, for 1,110 frs; with dealer J. B. P. Lebrun, 1776; sale, Everard George van Tindinghorste, Amsterdam, 26 March 1777, lot 55, for 3,000 guilders; gallery in the Ducal Castle at Sagan; Fürst zu Hohenzollern-Hechningen, Loewenberg i.S.; E. F. Weber, Hamburg, sale, Berlin, 20 February 1912, lot 212, to C. Sedelmeyer, Paris; acquired in 1912.

LITERATURE: Hofstede de Groot 1908–27, vol. VI, 1916, pp. 66–7, no. 81; Bredius / Gerson 1969, no. 535; Keller 1979, p. 97; *Corpus*, vol. I, 1982, no. A12; Schwartz 1984, p. 47; Tümpel 1986, no. 39; Warnke 1986; Haverkamp-Begemann 1993.

Rembrandt emerged as a great artist at the age of twenty-one or twenty-two, as can be seen from his masterpieces *The Apostle Paul in Prison* of 1627 and *Two Old Men Disputing* of 1628 (see fig. 2a and cat. no. 3). He presumably executed this equally impressive painting of *Simeon Speaking to Mary in the Temple* in the interval between the two, in *c.*1627–28.[1] The background consists of an illuminated plastered wall, similar to that in the *Man in a Gorget and Cap* of 1626/27 (cat. no. 1). It also resembles the wall in the *Apostle Paul in Prison* of 1627, although here we see a barred window beside this wall, which admits light into the cell. In *Simeon Speaking to Mary,* Rembrandt focused entirely on the figures and again omitted the window. He suggests it, however, by depicting the shadow of the bars on the lightest section of the wall. In this respect he created what is to the best of my knowledge a new and unusual effect in painting. A precedent and possibly the source from which he drew his inspiration was Dürer's engraving of *Jerome in His Study* of 1514, which includes a reflection of bars and bottle-glass windows (fig. 2b, B.60).[2]

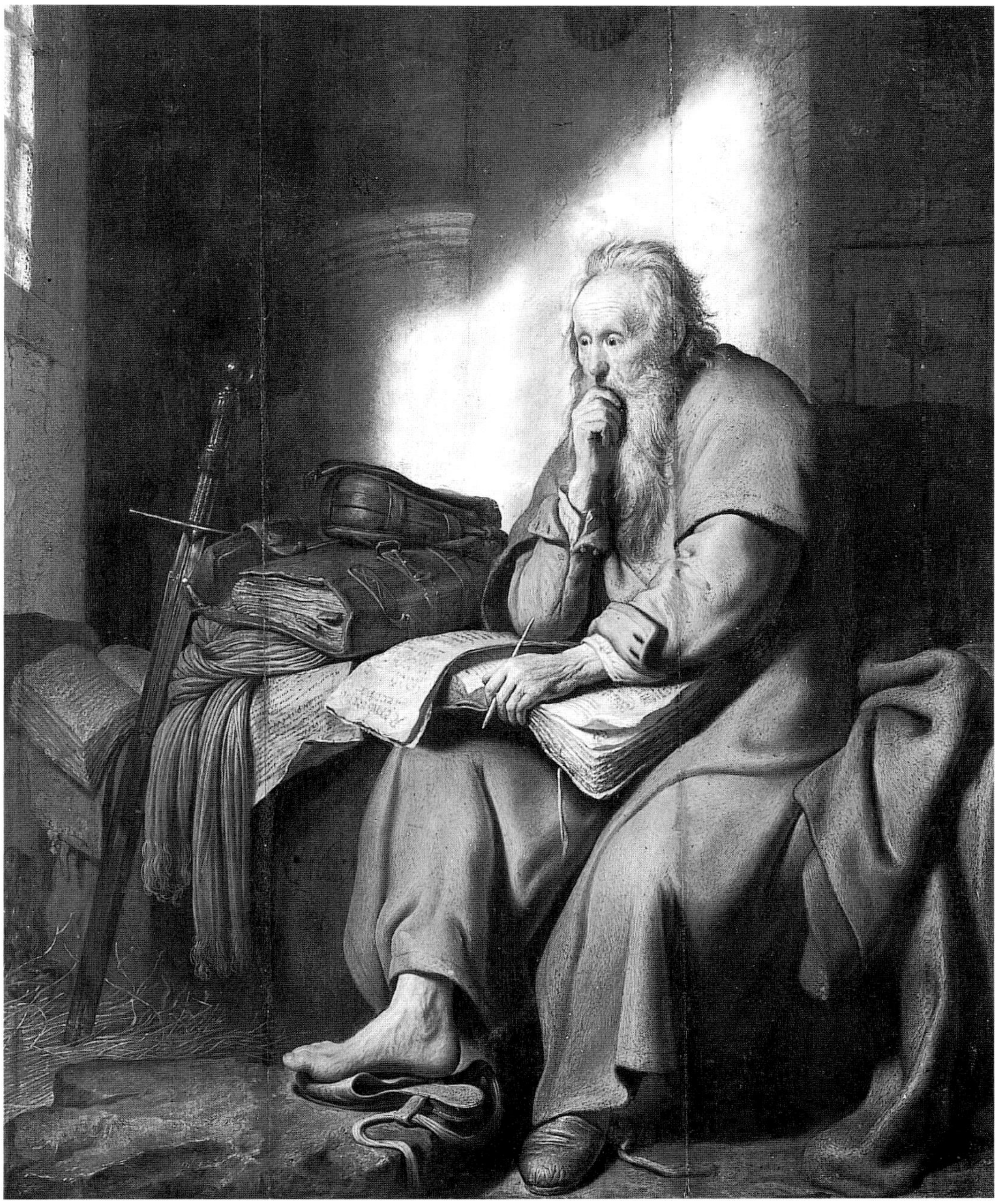

FIG. 2a
Rembrandt
The Apostle Paul in Prison
Monogrammed and dated 1627
Panel
72.8 x 60.2 cm
Staatsgalerie Stuttgart

FIG. 2b
Albrecht Dürer German, 1471–1528
St Jerome in His Study 1514 (detail)
Engraving
From a reproduction

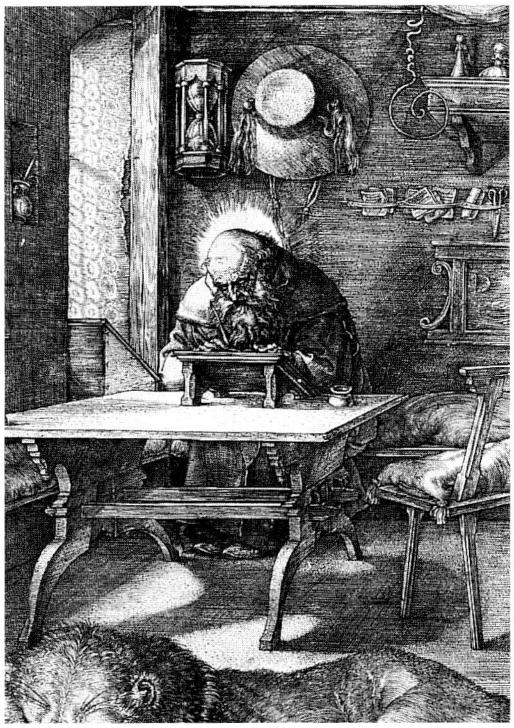

FIG. 2c
Albrecht Dürer
Presentation in the Temple
Monogrammed
Woodcut
29.3 x 20.9 cm
From a reproduction

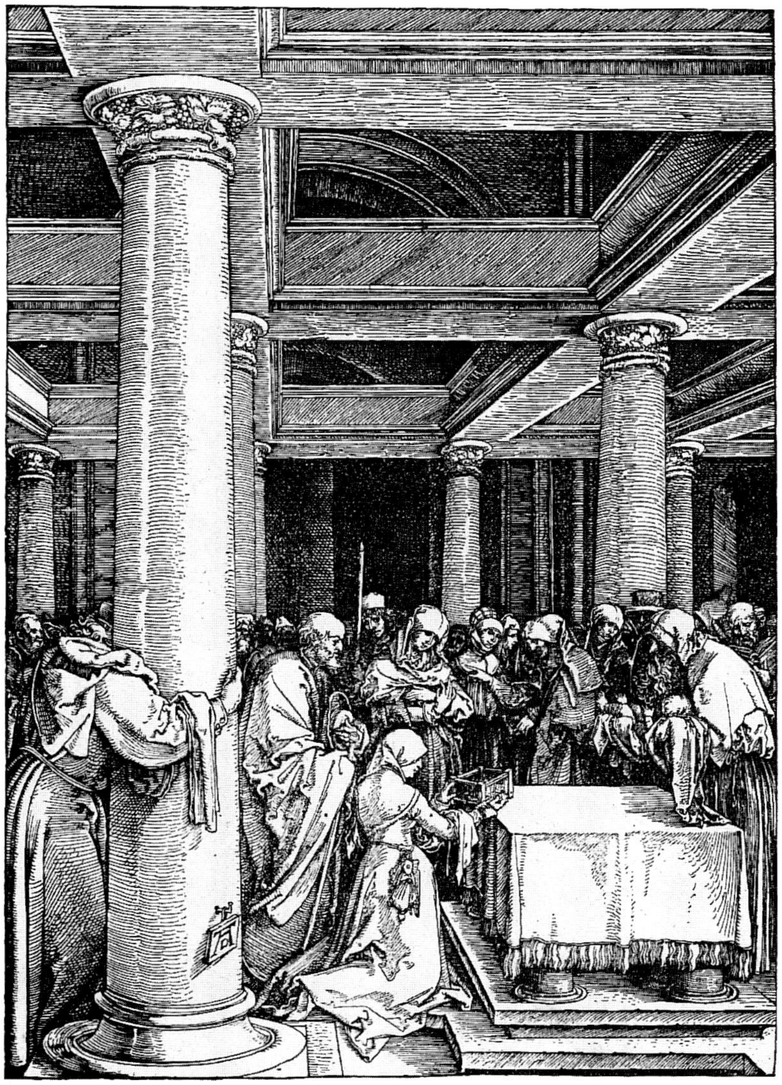

The bars in *Simeon Speaking to Mary* are not those of a prison, as in the *Apostle Paul in Prison* (fig. 2a), nor are they the bars of a monk's cell, such as in Dürer's print (fig. 2b). The space is more evocative of the interior of a Protestant church with whitewashed walls. The massive pillar and its base resemble those of a late Gothic Netherlandish church. The scene is set in a small room or side chapel. As prescribed by Mosaic law, Joseph and Mary have brought the infant Jesus to the Temple to present him to the Lord, a rite that required the sacrifice of two doves.[3] Simeon has also appeared at the Temple, at the bidding of the Holy Ghost. It has been revealed to him that he will not die before seeing Christ. Recognizing the child as the Saviour, Simeon gathers him in his arms and gives praise to God.

This is the moment Rembrandt originally intended to portray. An X-ray photograph shows that Simeon's face was initially turned towards heaven.[4] In the end, however, Rembrandt illustrated the following episode, in which Simeon blesses the young family and turns his attention to Mary: 'Behold, this child is set for the fall and rising again of many in Israel; and for a sign which shall be spoken against; Yea, a sword shall pierce through thy own soul also, that the thoughts of many hearts may be revealed'. Simeon's gesture and gaze are clearly directed to the Virgin, hence the present title of the painting. Mary kneels beside Joseph with her hands folded and appears to be regarding Simeon with astonishment. 'And Joseph and his mother marvelled at those things which were spoken of him.'

Also present is Anna, a prophetess of 'about four score and four years', who likewise recognizes Christ as the Redeemer. Rembrandt has portrayed her behind the group, gazing down at Jesus, her arms raised in awe. The aureola around the child's head identifies him for us quite clearly as a supernatural being. Simeon is viewed from the side, so that the child on his lap is foreshortened and his head and halo are therefore relatively large. The infant is most brightly illuminated, but light also emanates from his form. This, perhaps, illustrates Simeon's words: 'A light to lighten the Gentiles, and the glory of thy people Israel'. The effect is strengthened by the contrast with Joseph, who is rendered as a dark figure seen from the back. He recalls the man nearest the viewer, likewise at the left, in *Two Old Men Disputing*, which Rembrandt executed a short time later (cat. no. 3). The chiaroscuro is further heightened by the gloom on the right. All that can be seen distinctly is a candelabra suspended from the pillar and part of the panelled wall beneath it.[5]

In art from the late Middle Ages onwards, Simeon was identified with the high priest of the

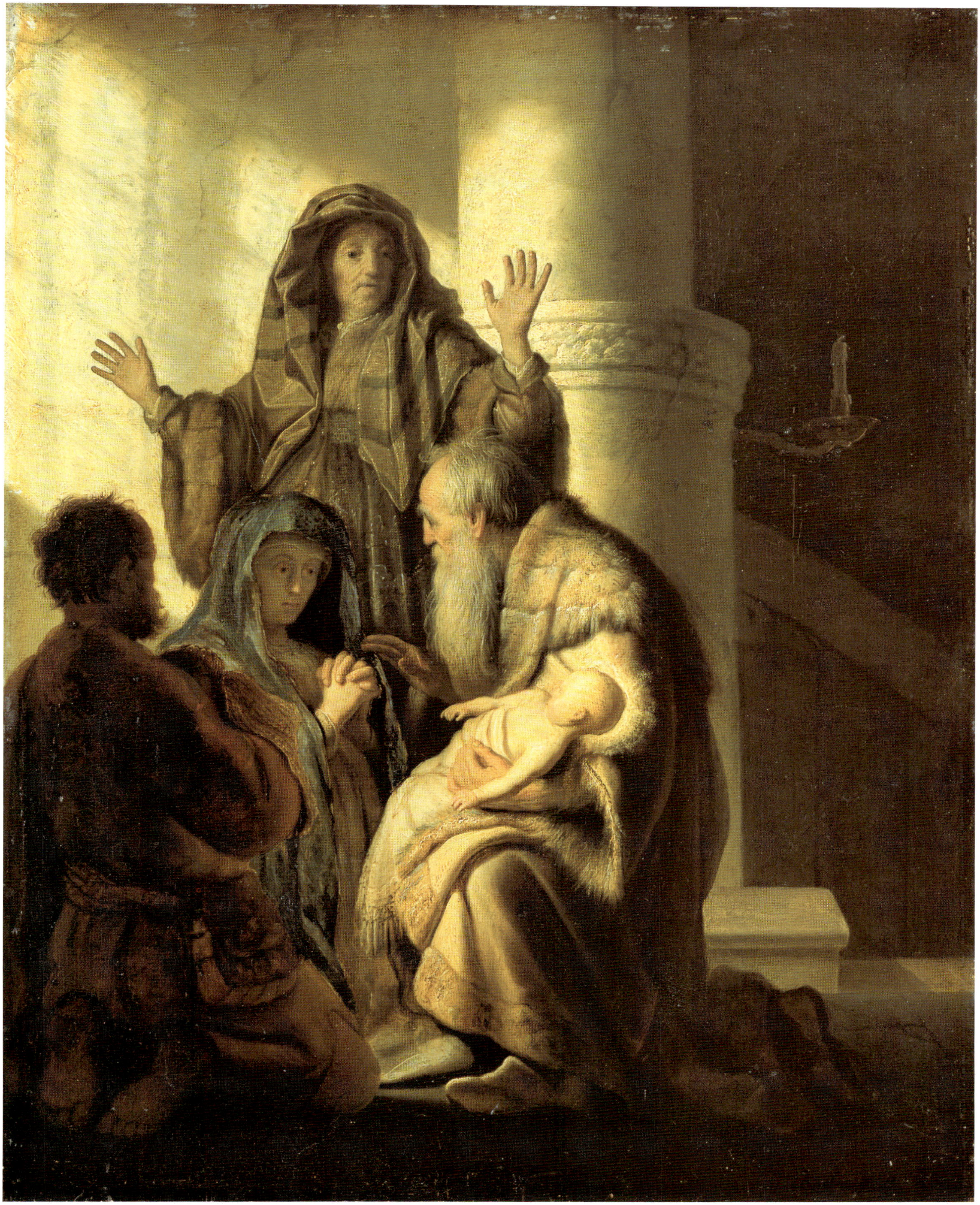

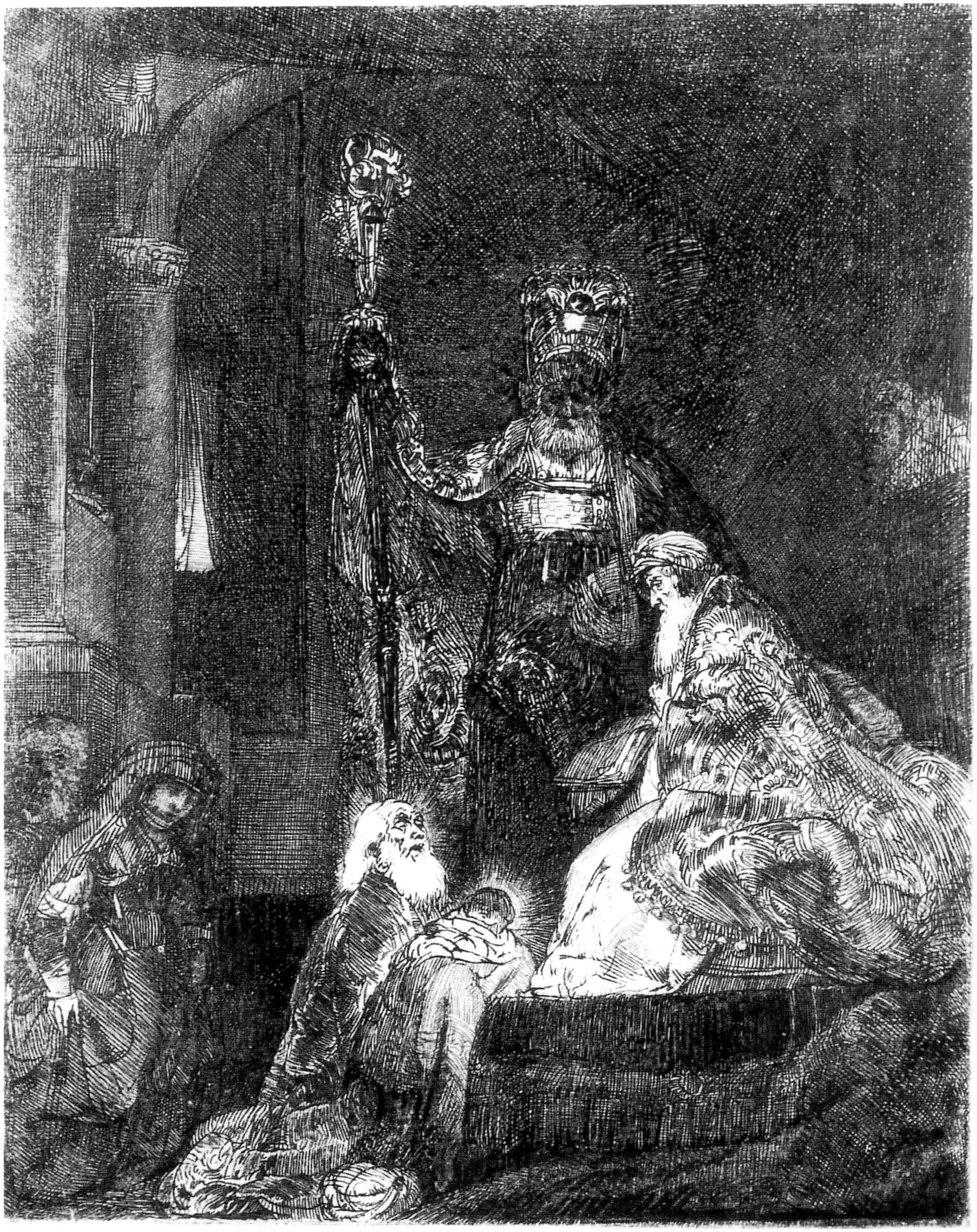

FIG. 2d
Rembrandt
Presentation in the Temple, in the dark manner
Etching
21.0 x 16.2 cm
From a reproduction

Temple who receives the sacrifice from Joseph and Mary during the Presentation in the Temple[6] or the Purification. A woodcut by Dürer, for instance, shows Simeon holding the Christ Child above the altar, on which Mary is placing a cage containing the pair of sacrificial doves (fig. 2c, B.88, before 1506). The Dürer scene appears to be a service for a full congregation, with worshippers in attendance around the altar. According to one interpretation, Rembrandt's omission of 'priest, altar and rite' represents an 'elimination' of the 'official church' in favour of 'spontaneous worship' in a secluded corner of the synagogue.[7] In any event, the theme of this early masterwork is an intimate gathering away from the public eye, rather than the ritual traditionally depicted.

The subject appealed to Rembrandt all his life. He returned to it in two paintings, three etchings and many drawings, some of which include curious onlookers and, further away, other visitors to the synagogue not particularly interested in the special event.[8] Simeon taking the child in his arms is always the central figure.[9]

Rembrandt gave the theme an entirely new and highly original interpretation in his late etching 'in the dark manner' (fig. 2d), which has been variously dated between *c.*1654 and the early 1660s (B.50). It is the only version that also shows the ritual of the *Presentation*. Here he has portrayed Simeon handing the child to the priest before whom he is kneeling, with Joseph and Mary behind him. The priest is seated on a platform high above them, overshadowed by the towering, forbidding figure of the high priest, who holds a large, elaborately wrought staff. It has often been suggested that Rembrandt sought to achieve bravura in the early part of his career and that his work from that period is 'extrovert' (*veruiterlijkt*). In his late work, by contrast, he is said to have concentrated on exploring man's inner life and presenting it in a more 'introverted' (*verinnerlijkte*) form.[10] However, the opposite seems to be the case if we compare an early painting (cat. no. 2) with the late etching (fig. 2d).

The early *Simeon Speaking to Mary in the Temple* (cat. no. 2) has often been taken for the picture mentioned as being at the palace of the stadholder Prince Frederik Hendrik in The Hague in 1632 (see Provenance), although this view is not unanimous.[11] At the time, Frederik Hendrik's painting was said to be 'by Rembrandt or Jan Lievens'. Even then, no more than a few years after the picture was made, there was apparently some confusion as to which of the two young masters had painted it.[12]

AB

1 *Corpus*, vol. I, 1982, nos A11, 12, 13.
2 I am indebted to Bert Krauwinkel of Bodegraven for this suggestion.
3 Luke 2:22–38. The doves cannot be seen, but they may originally have been on the floor between Joseph and Simeon (suggested by Dr T. Ketelsen, Hamburg, Kunsthalle).
4 According to the *Corpus*, vol. I, 1982, p. 153; the X-ray is illustrated in fig. 2, p. 151.
5 There was probably little more to be seen in the past, judging by W. Weisbrod's detailed reproduction print of 1775 (*Corpus*, vol. I, 1982, p. 155, fig. 5). The conclusion reached in the *Corpus* is that Mary's head and her blue cloak were repainted between 1760 and 1775 and that they had previously been paler (*Corpus*, vol. I, 1982, pp. 152, 156). It is also suggested here that the painting may have been cropped, although the possibility is considered remote, in my view correctly (*Corpus*, vol. I, 1982, p. 155).
6 This was the title formerly given to our cat. no. 2. Tümpel observed that etchings and drawings by Rembrandt also long thought to represent the Presentation in the Temple (see below) were actually illustrations of *Simeon Giving Praise to God* (Tümpel 1970, cat. nos 48–51, notably cat. no. 48). In 1979, Keller referred to our cat. no. 2 as *Simeon Giving Praise to God* (Keller 1979, p. 97), a designation Tümpel was to use subsequently (Tümpel 1986, no. 39). In fact the painting records the *subsequent* episode, where Simeon, having given thanks to God, turns to address Mary. This is reflected by the title under which the painting appears in the present catalogue.
7 Keller 1979, p. 97; Warnke 1986, p. 38.
8 In the etching (B.51) of 1630; the painting at the Mauritshuis, The Hague, of 1631 (Bredius / Gerson 1969, no. 543); the etching (B.49) of *c.*1639.
9 Haverkamp-Begemann 1993.
10 For a critical discussion of this view, see Emmens 1979, pp. 12–18.
11 Strauss & Van der Meulen 1979, pp. 87–9, no. 1632/3. This identification was accepted until doubts were expressed in the *Corpus*, vol. I, 1982, p. 157. The reasoning put forward in the *Corpus* is contradicted by Warnke 1986, pp. 34–7.
12 The literature contains no reference to the fact that a copy after our cat. no. 2 was auctioned as a Lievens in 1920; sale, Vienna, 26 March 1920, lot 90. This was before the archive document concerning the reference of 1632 was published (for this document, see Strauss & Van der Meulen 1979, pp. 87–8, no. 1632/3).

3
Two Old Men Disputing

Monogrammed and dated lower left *R.L. 1628* (date no longer visible)
Panel
72.4 x 59.7 cm
National Gallery of Victoria, Melbourne; Felton Bequest 1934

PROVENANCE: Jacques de Gheyn III (1596–1641); bequeathed by de Gheyn to his relative Johannes Wtenbogaert (1608–1680), Amsterdam, in 1641 [see below]; Bartolomeo (Bortolo) Bernardi, Venice, by 1740; (probably) sale, J. A. Sichterman, Groningen, 20 August 1764, lot 292; with dealer D. A. Hoogendijk & Co, Amsterdam, 1934; Felton Bequest 1934.

LITERATURE: (Possibly) Houbraken 1718–21, vol. I, 1718, p. 255; Smith 1829–42, vol. VII, 1836, nos 29, 169; Van Gelder 1935, p. 66; Van Gils 1936, p. 115; MacLaren 1960, p. 339; Bredius / Gerson 1969, no. 423; Tümpel 1969, pp. 182–7; *Corpus*, vol. I, 1982, pp. 159–68, no. A13; Van Regteren Altena 1983, vol. I, p. 154; Schwartz 1984, p. 93; Tümpel 1986, no. 38; J. Gregory, in Gregory & Zdanowicz 1988, pp. 21–43; Hoff 1995, pp. 229–32.

Two elderly bearded men are sitting in a room. It is dark except for a single shaft of bright light, coming from the left and falling between the two figures. The room looks like a study. A globe can be seen high up in the shadow in the background. On the table on the right are a pen and inkpot, and there is also a small wooden writing desk, on which we see a few books and papers. The candle behind the two men has been extinguished. Several large tomes and a leather valise are on the floor in front of the table, half in the full glare of the light and half in deep shadow. The man seen frontally is talking to his companion and looking at him with a penetrating gaze. He is indicating a passage in the open book, which the other man holds firmly on his lap, with both hands. Other passages have also attracted the men's attention, as the second man's fingers are inserted in the book to mark two other sections (Rembrandt employed the same motif – of fingers used as bookmarks – in a later etched portrait of the clergyman *Johannes Sylvius* (fig. 23d)). It is therefore clear that the men are studying and not simply reading.

The scene matches a beautifully concise description in the will drawn up in 1641 by Jacques de Gheyn III, who is portrayed in cat. no. 8. The will refers to a 'painting done by Rembrandt wherein two little old men are seated and disputing, one with a large book on his lap, while sunlight comes in'.[1] The use of the diminutive 'little old men' (*mannekens*) means that the figures are portrayed far smaller than lifesize. The only detail to which no allusion is made, in what must be the earliest description of the picture, is that the 'little old men' are wearing loose, 'antique' robes. They are not Rembrandt's contemporaries, but figures from days gone by. Engaging in discourse while poring over passages in books is a universal and timeless activity. Rembrandt has not specified who is disputing, or when.

But the present picture has such a strong narrative effect that later viewers could not refrain from identifying it as a representation of a specific episode. In 1743, Pietro Monaco (1707–1772) made a print after the work.[2] According to the inscription on this engraving, it depicts the prophet Elisha foretelling an attempt on his life by the king. The caption to the print includes a quotation from the Bible: 'Elisha sat in his house, and the elders sat with him' (2 Kings 6:32). However, the Bible makes no reference to books or to a deliberation of any kind. Cat. no. 3 also corresponds to the Rembrandt interpreted in 1764 as 'two portraits, whereof the one represents Peter, and the other, one of the evangelists'[3] (for Tümpel's far later, similar reading, see below). John Smith was an exception in that he assigned

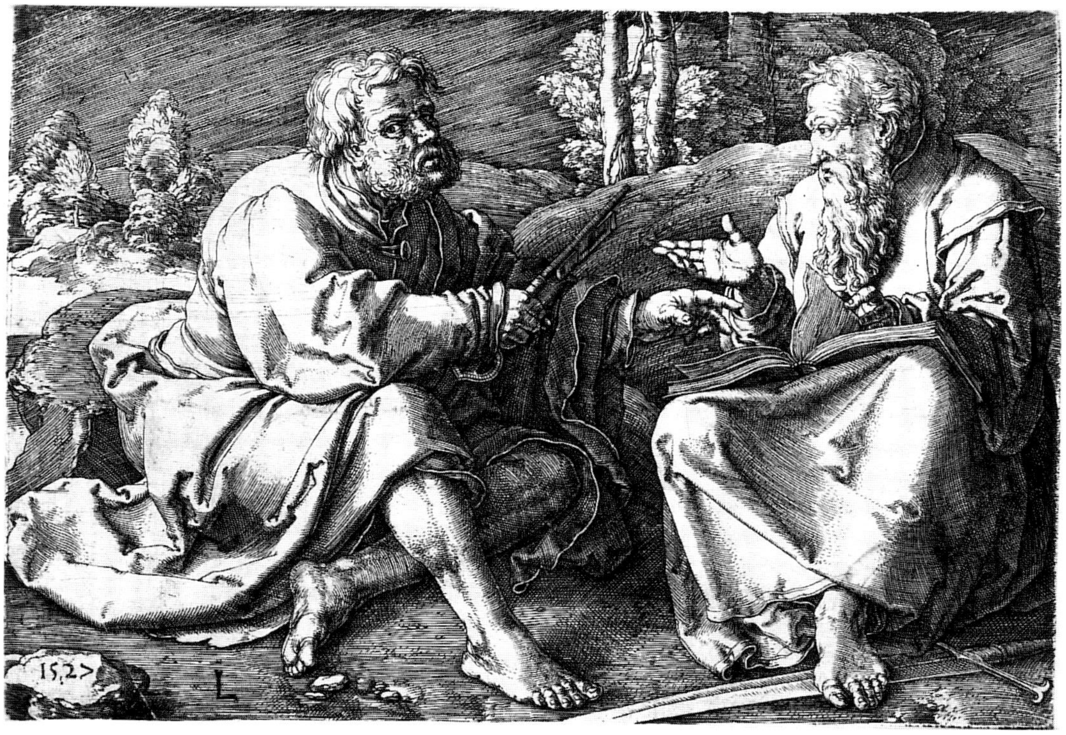

FIG. 3a
Lucas van Leyden *c.*1494–1533
Peter and Paul Seated in a Landscape
Monogrammed and dated 1527
Engraving
10.0 x 14.4 cm
Rijksprentenkabinet, Rijksmuseum, Amsterdam

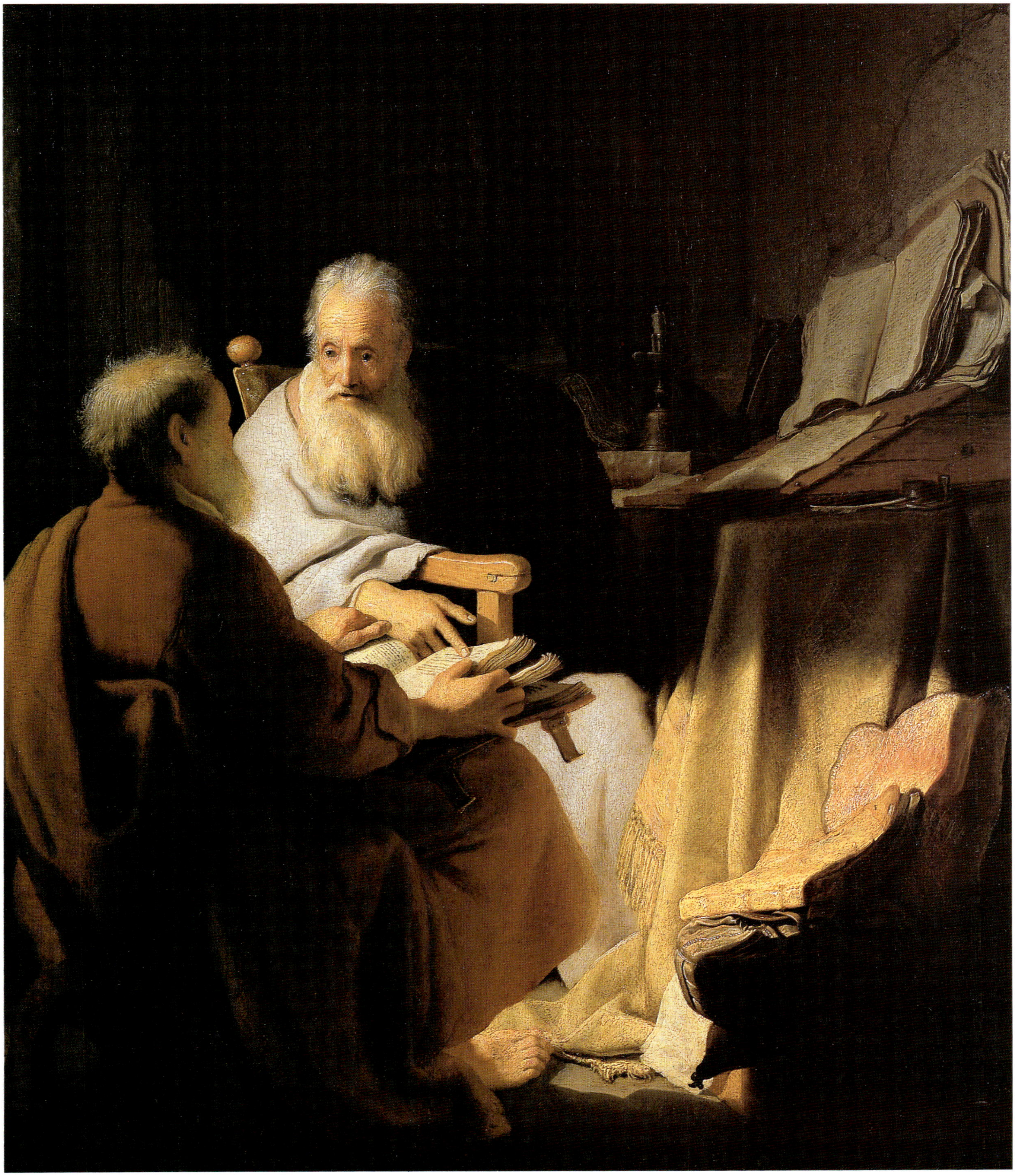

no identities to the figures. In 1836 he described the piece as: 'The theologians ... Their expression and gestures denote them to be discussing some abstruse subject'.[4] In 1934, when the painting itself was rediscovered, the two men were seen simply as philosophers, but it was later suggested that they might be Hippocrates and Democritus,[5] or perhaps Democritus and Heraclitus.[6] These pairs, however, are always portrayed quite differently.[7]

The men were also said to represent apostles.[8] Tümpel's theory, stated in 1969, that they were portrayals of the apostles Peter and Paul has received widespread support.[9] Tümpel referred to an engraving of 1527, by Rembrandt's fellow townsman Lucas van Leyden, as a possible precursor. This print shows Peter and Paul in conversation against a landscape background (fig. 3a). Peter is indicating a passage in the book in Paul's lap, exactly as does the man in the present painting. This similarity might suggest that Rembrandt was inspired by the print, but is not to say that he meant to depict the same theme. Seventeenth-century Caravaggist paintings of Peter and Paul conversing have more recently been related to Rembrandt's picture.[10] The fundamental difference, however, is that Rembrandt's 'little men' are not shown with attributes. In Lucas's print, Peter is portrayed with his key in his hand, and Paul with his foot on the sword that was used to behead him. In the Caravaggist paintings of Peter and Paul referred to above, Peter at least can be recognized by his key. Moreover, when Rembrandt himself wanted to portray Peter, he showed him with his key (two examples are cat. nos 6 and 7, which are likewise early works). If he had intended the present painting to represent Peter and Paul, or either one of them, he would have included at least one attribute, or else would have depicted the figures in such a way that there could be no mistake about their identity.[11]

The authors of the Rembrandt *Corpus* were aware that the earliest description of this picture says no more than that it shows two 'old men [who are] seated and disputing', without any reference to a narrative. Yet the authors of the *Corpus* nevertheless concluded, following Tümpel, that the figures probably represent Peter and Paul. This was not mentioned in de Gheyn's will, they reasoned, because 'a factual description was looked on as the best way of formally identifying de Gheyn's possessions'. In support of their argument they observed that the same will

The collection of Jacques de Gheyn III in 1641

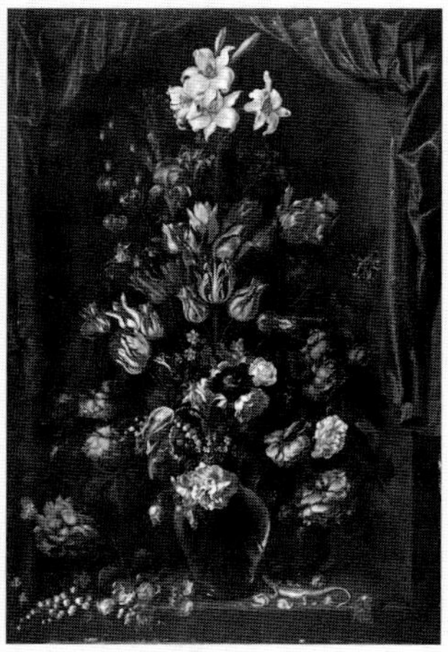

Jacques de Gheyn II (see fig. 8e)

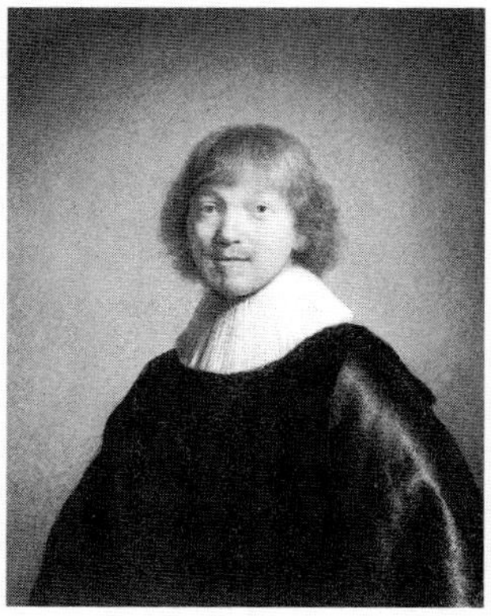

Rembrandt (cat. no. 8)

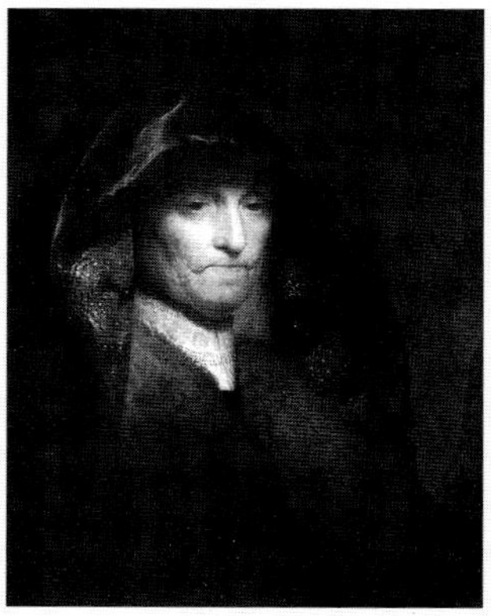

Rembrandt(?) (see fig. 8h)

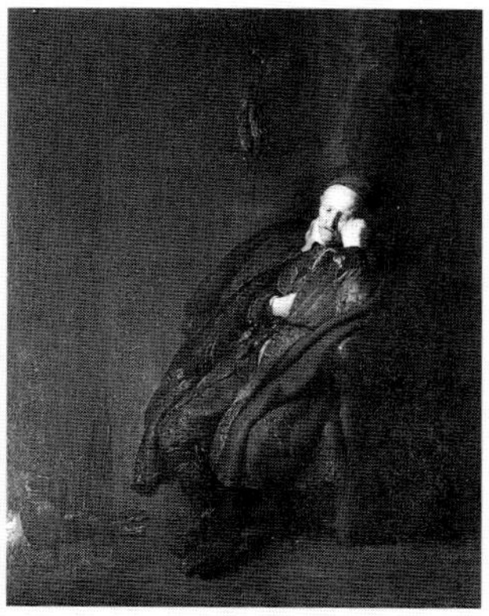

Rembrandt (see p. 46, fig. 19)

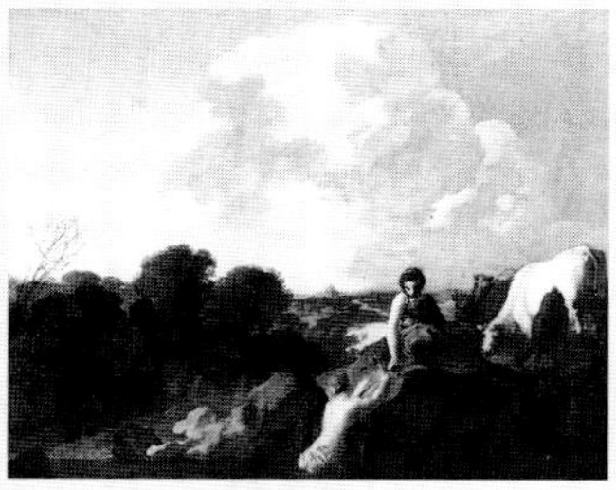

Mozes van Wtenbrouck (see fig. 8g)

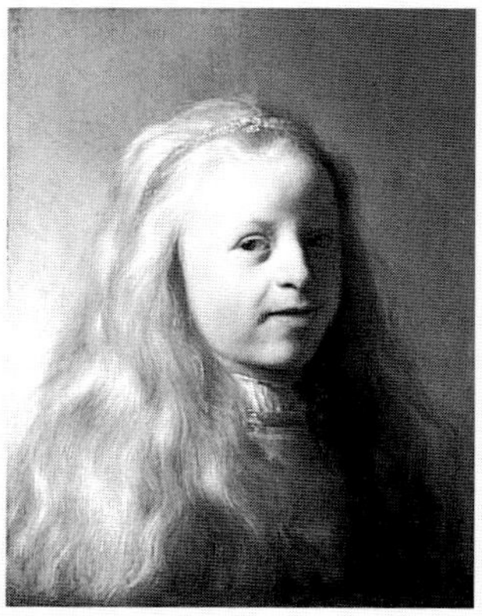

Jan Lievens (cat. no. 34)

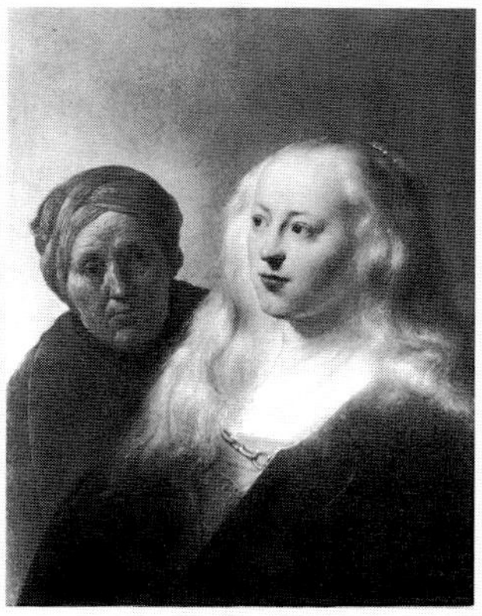

Jan Lievens (see fig. 34a)

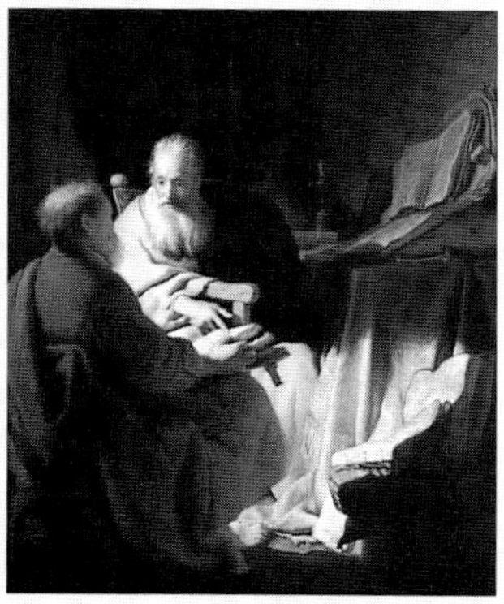

Rembrandt (cat. no. 3)

describes an extant painting by Jan Lievens as the '*tronige* of a beautiful damsel with an old woman beside her'. They believed this to be a Lievens 'that certainly represents Vertumnus and Pomona', a mythological tale.[12] The Lievens in question indeed matches the description in de Gheyn's will (fig. 34a). On closer inspection, however, we find that Lievens no more intended his characters to represent Vertumnus and Pomona than Rembrandt meant his *Two Old Men Disputing* to be Peter and Paul.[13]

De Gheyn's will also mentions another painting by Rembrandt, which is described as 'a little old man asleep seated by a fire, with his hand in his bosom'. This work, too, has survived (p. 46, fig. 19). The interesting point is that the titles proposed for this picture – 'Tobit' and 'Allegory of Sloth' – are equally unconvincing.[14] All things considered, de Gheyn appears to have had a special liking for paintings by Rembrandt and Lievens of the kind we would now call 'genre pieces'. A second Lievens in de Gheyn's will, 'a *tronigen* of a smiling young girl', would belong in the same category (cat. no. 34).

The many interpretations of the *Two Old Men Disputing*, with all their incongruities and contradictions, bear witness to Rembrandt's skill at suggesting that there is a story – while leaving it to the viewer to imagine it. The painting's first owner, Jacques de Gheyn III, made no attempt to pin the work down to a single interpretation. He was personally acquainted with Rembrandt and had his portrait painted by him in 1632 (cat. no. 8). De Gheyn would also have known exactly what Rembrandt meant the picture to represent, and this he expressed in his will as 'two little old men are seated and disputing'. Rembrandt left it for us to decide whether the two men are prophets, apostles, Church Fathers, philosophers, sages or merely scholars.

A painting that has been completely forgotten also showed 'two old men disputing' in a study filled with books and, in this case, two globes. As far as subject matter is concerned, it is a variant of the painting in Melbourne. It was engraved as a Rembrandt by the Antwerp printmaker Lambert Antoine Claessens (1763–1834), who also worked in Amsterdam and Paris (fig. 3b). In 1836, Smith described the painting from the Claessens print.[15] Hofstede de Groot quoted Smith's description and listed the painting as 'lost'.[16] As far as we know, it has never re-emerged, and the print has been ignored. Judging from the print, we may assert that the painting was probably not an autograph Rembrandt. It appears to have been an intelligent variant of the painting now in Melbourne, and made by a (Leiden?) follower of

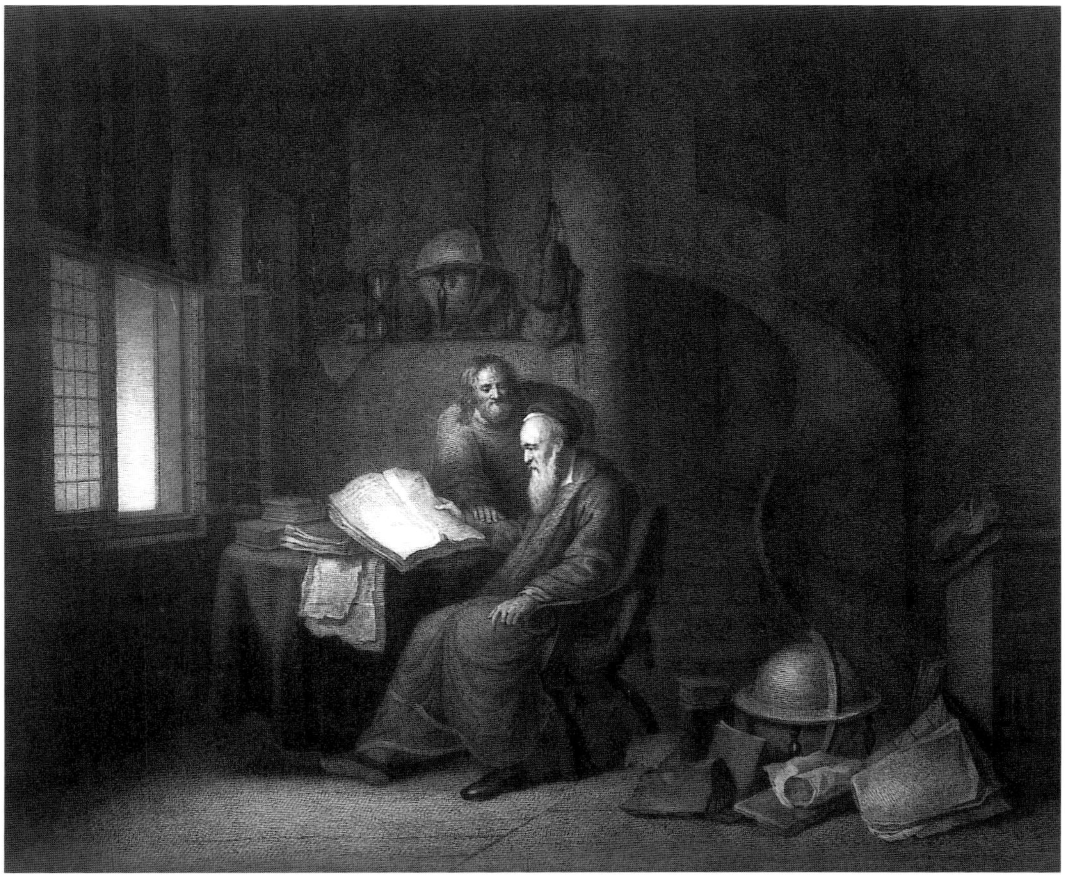

FIG. 3b
Lambert Antoine Claessens Netherlandish, 1763–1834
Two Men in a Study
Inscribed *Rembrandt pinx. PHILOSOPHE EN MÉDITATION. L. A. Claessens sculp*
Engraving
25.5 x 31.5 cm
Rijksprentenkabinet, Rijksmuseum, Amsterdam

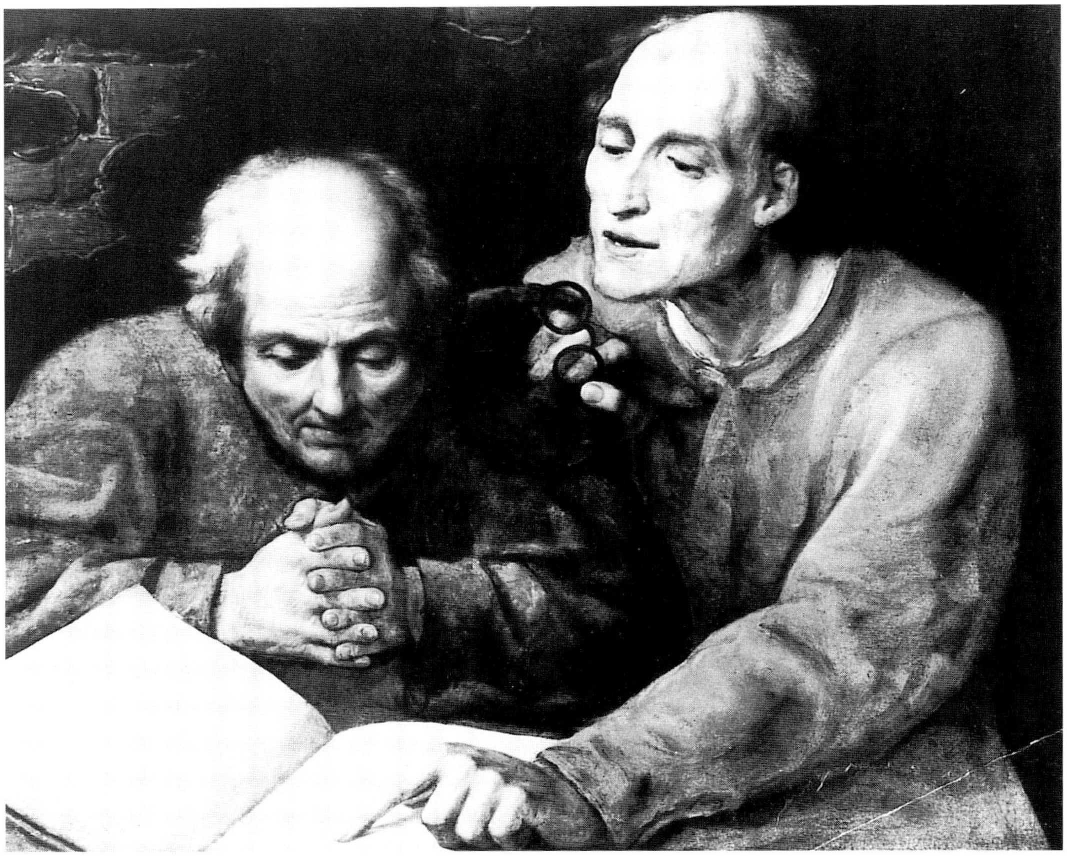

FIG. 3c
Jan Massys Flemish, *c.*1509–1573
Two Men with a Book
Panel
53.5 x 63.5 cm
Private collection, The Netherlands

FIG. 3d
Jacques de Gheyn II 1565–1629
Two Men with a Book
Inscribed on verso *de Gheyn*
Chalk and pen and ink
12.9 x 16.3 cm
Staatliche Museen zu Berlin, Kupferstichkabinett

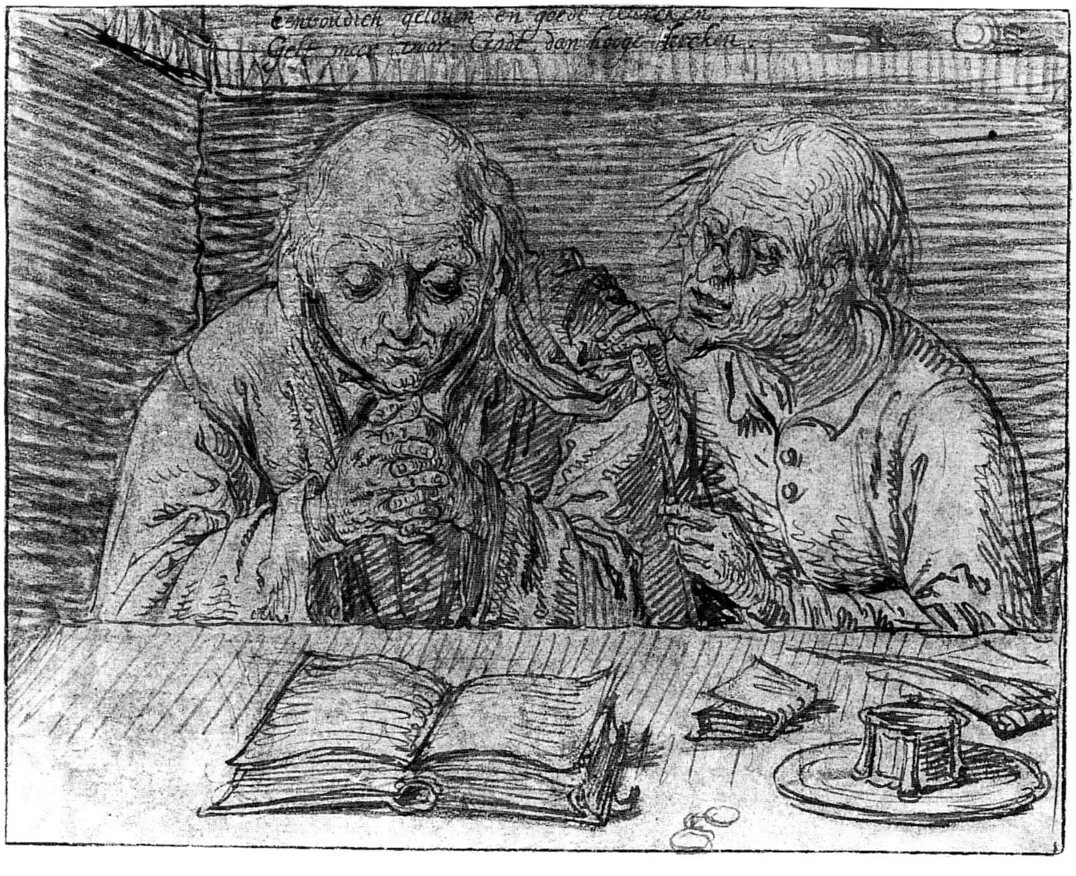

Rembrandt's in about 1645. The painter presumably interpreted the figures as learned men or philosophers, for the print contains no religious connotation. The same applies to a better known depiction of the subject, a work that in our century was attributed (likewise too optimistically) to Rembrandt.[17]

It should be pointed out that Rembrandt's painting of 1628 followed in a tradition. Other artists before Rembrandt had portrayed anonymous men pondering over the contents of solemn-looking books. An example is a picture by the Antwerp painter Jan Massys (fig. 3c), which is probably a copy after a lost painting of *c.*1526 by his father Quinten Massys (1465–1530).[18] In Jan's picture we see a man with his hands clasped, poring over a book on a table before him, while his companion points to a passage with his finger, as in Rembrandt's picture. An interesting point is that Jacques de Gheyn III's father, the outstanding draughtsman Jacques de Gheyn II, made a drawing after the composition by Jan or Quinten Massys, in which the figures, like those in fig. 3c, are seated in a narrow room, with two books, one open and one closed, on a table in front of them (fig. 3d).[19] De Gheyn's drawing does not include the motif of pointing at a passage in the book, but we see an inkwell, as in the Rembrandt.

Rembrandt may well have been familiar with one or more of these earlier versions of the theme, through de Gheyn II or III.[20]

As far as we know, authors on Rembrandt have not commented on van Regteren Altena's interesting proposal that the present painting was the piece Arnold Houbraken told a story about in 1718.[21] Houbraken tells of the young Rembrandt receiving a visit from an 'art lover' who 'drew his attention to a gentleman in The Hague to whom he might show and offer for sale a certain piece he had made'.[22] Rembrandt made the journey to The Hague on foot and sold the picture for one hundred guilders. If the picture in question is *Two Old Men Disputing*, the person who bought it would have been de Gheyn III. The hundred-guilder fee represented a fortune to the young artist, and his return journey held new adventures in store.

The motif of two figures disputing over an open book, with one figure pointing with his index finger to a passage in the book, recurs in the present exhibition in Gerbrand van den Eeckhout's *The Twelve-Year-Old Christ Disputing with the Doctors* of *c.*1670–72 (cat. no. 56). We may well see in van den Eeckhout's painting a late echo of the present work. Drawings by Rembrandt that relate directly to cat. no. 3 are cat. no. 73 and fig. 73a.

AB

1 Strauss & Van der Meulen 1979, p. 205, no. 1641/1: 'Item noch een schilderije van Rembrand gedaen, daer twee oude mannekens sitten ende disputeren, den eenen heeft een groot bouck op sijn schoot, daer comt een sonnelicht in'. For the unabridged text of the will, see Van Regteren Altena 1936, pp. 128–32.

2 *Corpus*, vol. I, 1982, p. 166, fig. 7.

3 *Corpus*, vol. I, 1982, p. 168.

4 Smith 1829–42, vol. VII, 1836, no. 169, bases his description on Monaco's print, exclusive of the inscription, which he cites elsewhere (no. 29). Smith's references to the Melbourne picture have not previously been noted in the modern literature on the piece.

5 Van Gils 1936, p. 115.

6 Benesch 1973, vol. I, p. 5, no. 7.

7 Blankert 1967.

8 MacLaren 1960, p. 339. Van Gelder 1935, p. 66, had previously interpreted the book over which the two are poring as 'the Book of Books'.

9 Tümpel 1969, pp. 182–7. J. Gregory, in Gregory & Zdanowicz 1988, pp. 32–8, later considered the discourse between these two 'apostles' in the light of the theological controversies that were current in Rembrandt's own times.

10 *Corpus*, vol. I, 1982, p. 166, figs 8, 9 (paintings by anonymous Caravaggisti).

11 There has been no confusion about the *Four Evangelists* in Jacob Jordaens's painting from the same period, *c.*1625–30, in the Louvre in Paris. Even without attributes, their identity is unmistakable (Tümpel 1969, p. 186). (In the *Apostles Peter and Paul* by Guido Reni (our fig. 5b), Peter is shown with keys.)

12 *Corpus*, vol. I, 1982, p. 165. The Lievens is described in de Gheyn's will as 'een fraye vrouwe tronige mit een out wijff daerbij'(Van Regteren Altena 1936, p. 129).

13 Sumowski, *Gemälde*, vol. III, 1987, p. 1779, no. 1188, observes that the idea of this picture's depicting Venus and Pomona 'should be rejected, because all attributes associated with this theme are missing'.

14 *Corpus*, vol. I, 1982, pp. 205–6, no. A17.

15 Smith 1829–42, vol. VII, 1836, p. 64, no. 146.

16 Hofstede de Groot 1908–27, vol. VI, 1916, p. 196, no. 340.

17 Private collection, Germany (Bredius / Gerson 1969, no. 424; *Corpus*, vol. I, 1982, pp. 524–8, no. C 13, as 'an imitation of Rembrandt's early work').

18 Buijnsters-Smets 1995, p. 159, no. 6.

19 The book and the room are not additions by Jacques de Gheyn II himself, as van Regteren Altena suggests (Van Regteren Altena 1983, vol. II, p. 158, no. 1047). The room was different in the versions he knew of the Jan Massys composition, which works show neither the book nor the room.

20 In some versions of the Jan Massys painting, one of the figures has a crucifix, making him look like a pious Catholic. De Gheyn also interpreted as a Christian theme the Massys picture he knew, as he added the following inscription to the drawing he made after it: 'God values simple faith and good works above tall churches' (*Eenvoudich geloven en goede wercken / Gelt meer voor Godt, dan hooghe Kercken*) (Van Regteren Altena 1983, vol. II, p. 158, no. 1047). This is not to say, however, that Rembrandt – whether or not he knew the Massys or the de Gheyn composition – intended the men in his picture to represent devout Christians: he did not include Christian attributes.

21 Van Regteren Altena 1983, vol. I, p. 154.

22 Houbraken 1718–21, vol. I, 1718, p. 255: 'eindelijk aanwyzing deden aan een Heer in Den Haag, ten einde hy zeker stukje 't geen hy toen gemaakt had aan den zelven zoude vertoonen en aanbieden'.

4

Bearded Old Man Wearing a Cap

*c.*1630

Monogrammed upper right *RHL*
Panel
24.3 x 20.3 cm
Drs Isabel and Alfred Bader

PROVENANCE: Prince Gonzaga, Vicenza; with Van Diemen Gallery, Amsterdam, 1931; D. Bingham, New York; with Ch. E. Duits Gallery, London; S. J. van den Bergh, Wassenaar; sale, London (Christie's), 30 March 1979, lot 127, repr.

LITERATURE: Bredius 1937, no. 633; Bauch 1960, p. 261, note 130; Bauch 1966, no. 343; Gerson 1968, p. 195, no. 29; Bredius / Gerson 1969, no. 633; Bruyn 1982, pp. 43–5; *Corpus*, vol. I, 1982, pp. 576–80, no. C22; Schatborn 1986, p. 59; Tümpel 1986, no. 128*; Haverkamp Begemann 1995, cat. no. 13 (with further literature); C. Schuckman & M. Royalton-Kisch, in Amsterdam 1996, cat. no. 10b (with further literature).

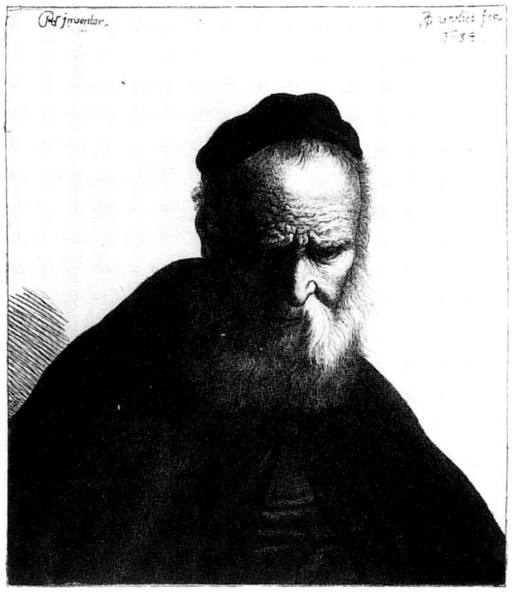

FIG. 4a
Johannes Gillesz van Vliet *c.*1605–1668
Bearded Old Man in a Cap
Inscribed *RHL* (in monogram) *jnventor. JG* (in monogram) *v. vliet fec. 1634*
Etching and burin
21.3 x 17.8 cm
Museum het Rembrandthuis, Amsterdam

This picture shows no more than the man's head and shoulders, yet it is obvious that he is seated. His head is slightly bowed, so that we see the whole of his high forehead, which catches most of the light. The paint in this part of the face ranges from pure white to dark brown and is applied in broad, impastoed strokes. Yet the brushstrokes nevertheless capture every wrinkle and fold, including the deep grooves above the bridge of the nose, between the dark, bristly eyebrows. A few eyebrow hairs have come loose of the rest; Rembrandt picks them out and renders them lighter in colour by means of spiky scratches in the paint, through which the light ground can be seen. The man is knitting his brows and seems to be peering at something. His prominent nose is also rendered in a sketchy but evocative style. Two white flecks above his right nostril denote the reflection of light above his skin, while a small patch of rosy paint is suggestive of the flesh itself.

Rembrandt has given most of his attention to the face, which is the most expressive part of the figure and which he therefore made the most brightly lit. The face is framed and accentuated by the man's downy beard and by the tufts of grey hair straying from under his cap. Here, however, Rembrandt has avoided any conspicuous details like the stark hairs protruding from the eyebrows. Similarly, only a few, sketchy folds can be seen in the man's black cap and clothing: not even a button draws our attention away from his face. The background suggests that he is sitting in a room, but it is impossible to distinguish a wall. Our gaze therefore remains fixed on the old, timeworn countenance.

The painting bears Rembrandt's monogram, and a man of this type can be seen in several of the artist's works from the period around 1630. The figure was presumably based on a single Leiden model – the question of whether he was Rembrandt's father has been a subject of debate. Many have recognized this same old man in the pictures of *Jeremiah* and the *Apostle Peter Kneeling* (cat. nos 5, 6).[1]

In 1634 the Leiden engraver Johannes Gillesz van Vliet made a reverse-image etching of the present picture, as a work by Rembrandt (fig. 4a). The design of the print, which is almost the same size as the painting, is primitive and crude by comparison. Indeed, none of van Vliet's prints after Rembrandt and other masters quite match up to the standard of their examples. In all other respects, however, the etching is a faithful rendering of the painting.

In spite of the existence of this print, doubts have been cast on the authenticity of the painting. Initially hinted at by Bauch in 1960 and 1966,[2] the question was subsequently examined at length in the Rembrandt *Corpus* in 1982.[3] The picture was relegated to category 'C', the 'Paintings Rembrandt's authorship of which cannot be accepted', mainly on the grounds that '[e]xcessive attention to rendering the appearance of old, wrinkled skin has led to a configuration of dabs and strokes of paint that do not really come together to form an integrated whole' and because 'the manner of painting exhibits a coarseness in the modelling and a lack of cohesion in the background that one cannot accept as possible with Rembrandt'.[4] The authenticity of the signature was also called into question. The team, which usually presented a unanimous conclusion, reported that 'the majority of the authors believe that opinion to be correct' – namely, that the work was not authentic. For once, however, 'one of the authors [Ernst van de Wetering] does not rule out the possibility of [the piece] being an autograph work by Rembrandt'. Van de Wetering remarked in defence of his view that 'the coarseness of [the picture's] execution should not be entirely excluded from our conception of Rembrandt's manner of painting'.[5] Since 1982, several other scholars have argued emphatically that the piece is indeed autograph.[6]

The majority of the *Corpus* authors accepted that van Vliet's print of 1634 was indeed made after the present painting and not after another version.[7] They believed the painting had been made by an artist from 'Rembrandt's immediate circle', and that van Vliet had erroneously put Rembrandt's name on his print. This would be a feasible proposition if van Vliet and Rembrandt had worked independently of one another.[8] In 1996, however, the results of a study regarding the watermarks on van Vliet's prints and Rembrandt's etchings were published; this study suggests, with a degree of probability bordering on certainty, that the two artists shared a studio in Leiden in 1631–32. An otherwise unique watermark found in many of van Vliet's sheets from the period between 1631 and 1634 can also be seen in works by Rembrandt, but only in a few impressions and proofs of his etchings from 1633 and 1635. Scholars had previously speculated, on stylistic grounds, that van Vliet had co-operated in making these sheets. Now there was evidence that the proofs were actually produced in van Vliet's studio. So we see that even after 1632 Rembrandt and van Vliet worked together from time to time. Moreover, the same unique watermark has now also been found in impressions of van Vliet's etching of 1634 (fig. 4a).[9] Given that the two artists were working in such close partnership in 1634, it would be beyond the bounds of plausibility to assume that van Vliet would, or even could, have been mistaken in naming

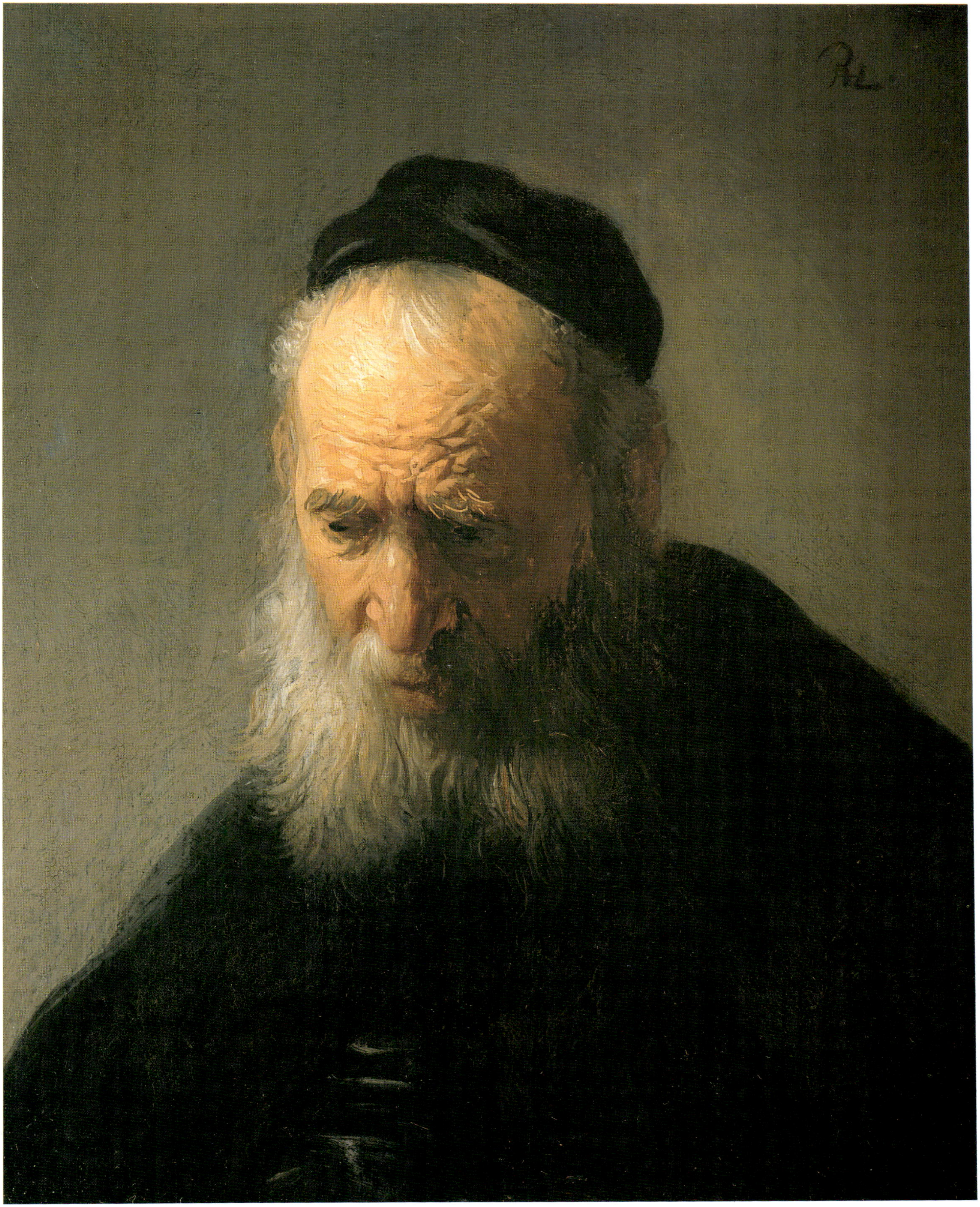

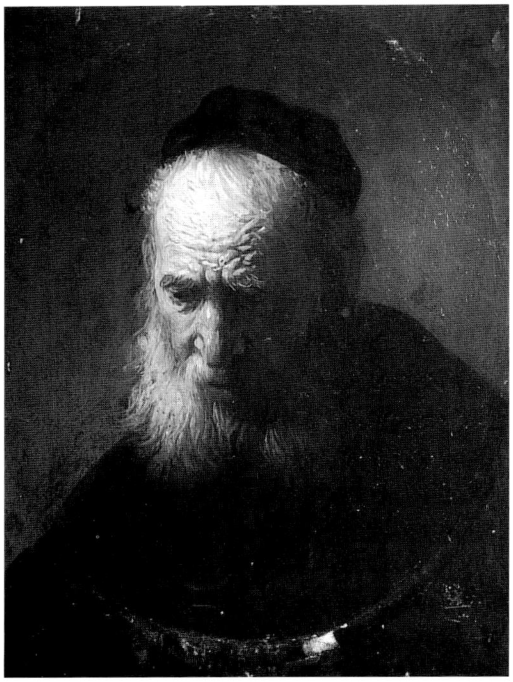

FIG. 4b
Cat. no. 4 (earlier condition)
Photograph: RKD, from the estate of Dr H. Schneider

Rembrandt as the inventor on his etching.

The *Corpus* also observes that there is a 'striking lack of homogeneity in the paint layer' in the present picture.[10] This may be explained by the fact that the painting was once in an oval frame, which covered all four corners of the area around the figure. This frame left distinct marks in the paint layer, as can be seen in the old photograph published here (fig. 4b). The marks were later removed during restoration, but this operation would also have left traces in the paint layer.

Hence the picture is without any doubt an early work by Rembrandt. The so-called 'coarseness' of modelling may indeed be unusual in Rembrandt's early oeuvre, but this is not the only example of this kind of handling. *David Presenting the Head of Goliath to Saul* of 1627, for instance, is rendered in a no less sketchy technique (fig. 4c).[11] The brilliant and evocative *Bearded Old Man* is held to have been made about three years later, *c.*1630. The present exhibition will enable us to compare it with Rembrandt's *Bust of an Old Man* of 1633, which is rendered in a similarly broad and vigorous technique (cat. no. 9).

AB

1 Haverkamp Begemann 1995, cat. no. 13.
2 Bauch 1960, p. 261, note 130; Bauch 1966, no. 343.
3 *Corpus*, vol. I, 1982, pp. 576–80, no. C22.
4 *Corpus*, vol. I, 1982, p. 579, no. C22.
5 *Corpus*, vol. I, 1982, p. 580, no. C22.
6 Schatborn 1986, p. 59; Haverkamp Begemann 1995; C. Schuckman and M. Royalton-Kisch, in Amsterdam 1996, cat. no. 10b (with a note to the effect that Ben Broos also agreed). Tümpel 1986, no. 128*, included the work but marked it with an asterisk to indicate that he was not entirely certain.
7 Bauch 1960, p. 261, note 130, and Bauch 1966, no. 343, seem to imply that the print may indeed have been based on a different version.
8 Bruyn 1982, p. 45, implicitly draws this conclusion with respect to van Vliet's prints after Rembrandt.
9 Hinterding 1996, pp. 24, 34–5, watermark no. 12, with the monogram *4 HP*, figs 3a, 3b. Schatborn 1986, p. 59, had earlier considered it highly probable that Rembrandt and van Vliet had continued to work together after 1631.
10 *Corpus*, vol. I, 1982, p. 578, no. C22.
11 *Corpus*, vol. I, 1982, pp.129–36, no. A9.

FIG. 4c
Rembrandt
David Presenting the Head of Goliath to Saul
Signed and dated 1627
Panel
27.2 x 39.6 cm
Öffentliche Kunstsammlung Basel, Kunstmuseum
Bequest Max Geldner 1958
Photograph: Öffentliche Kunstsammlung Basel, Martin Bühler

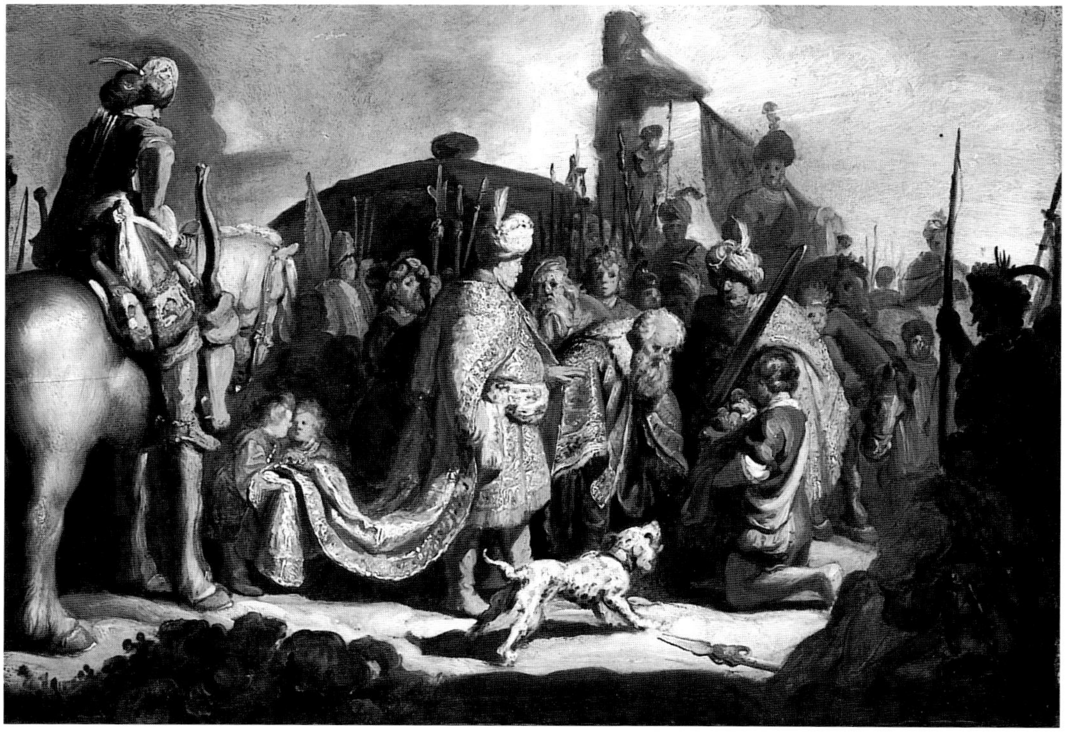

5
Jeremiah Lamenting the Destruction of Jerusalem

Monogrammed and dated on stone ledge at centre *RHL 1630*
Panel
58.3 x 46.6 cm
Rijksmuseum, Amsterdam

PROVENANCE: (This picture or a copy [see Blankert 1992–93, p. 53]) Sale, Margaretha Helena Graafland, widow of Jacob Alewijn, Amsterdam, 10 June 1767, lot 13; (possibly) César collection, presumably Berlin, 1768; Count Sergei Stroganoff, St Petersburg, later Paris [1800 cat., no. 51]; H. Rasch, Stockholm; acquired in 1939.

LITERATURE: Bode & Hofstede de Groot 1897–1905, vol. I, 1897, no. 39; Hofstede de Groot 1908–27, vol. VI, 1916, pp. 49–50, no. 49; Réau 1955–59, vol. II, pt 1, 1956, p. 371; Landsberger 1962, p. 109; Van Gelder 1963, p. 15a; Gerson 1968, p. 489, no. 24; Bredius / Gerson 1969, no. 604; Bruyn 1970–71, pp. 32–4; *Corpus*, vol. I, 1982, pp. 276–84, no. A28; Schwartz 1984, p. 101; Tümpel 1984, p. 185; *Corpus*, vol. II, 1986, p. 839; Tümpel 1986, no. 6; Budick 1988; *Corpus*, vol. III, 1989, p. 773 (reference to a drawn copy); P. van Thiel, in Berlin / Amsterdam / London 1991–92a, pp. 144–7, cat. no. 8; Blankert 1992–93, p. 53; Perlove 1995.

An old man sits at the foot of a massive column in an enclosed area that must be a vault yet evokes a grotto. An assortment of objects – an oriental carpet, costly metal vessels, a scarf, a bag and a bottle – can be seen on a large stone ledge beside him.[1] Supporting his head with his left arm, the man leans on a weighty tome inscribed with the word *BiBeL*. The inscription runs across the fore-edge of the book, and thus is most unusual and is probably a later addition.[2] In iconographic terms, the man's attitude expresses melancholy or sorrow.[3] The figure itself is brightly lit, whereas the surrounding space is mainly in shadow. Through an opening on the left we see buildings in flames, and various figures. One covers his eyes with his hands (in dismay?). Others (soldiers?) appear to be preparing to invade the city. It seems to be the fate of the city that preoccupies the man, who has a worried expression on his face.

In 1897 Bode identified the figure as the prophet Jeremiah. He had previously been taken for the biblical Lot (with Sodom ablaze), for Virgil's Anchises at the destruction of Troy, for an anonymous philosopher, or simply for a figure in a *vanitas* picture.[4] However, the painting does not correspond to any known episode relating to Lot or Anchises, nor to depictions of them. The identification with Jeremiah has also been called into question,[5] but at present it is generally accepted.

The Old Testament Book of Jeremiah tells how the prophet spoke the words of the Lord, warning the people of Judah to return to the God they had forsaken. But his prophecies were ignored and he was made to witness the downfall of the nation, the tragic fall of Jerusalem, and the start of the Babylonian exile in 586 BC.[6] Instead of selecting a particular episode from Jeremiah's life, it seems that Rembrandt has depicted a compilation of motifs associated with the destruction of Jerusalem. Harking back to a medieval tradition, sixteenth-century Bible illustrations showed a similar Jeremiah seated outside the city, mourning. At his side in these prints is the Book of Lamentations, of which he himself was the author (fig. 5a). The prints may have inspired Rembrandt's painting.[7] As in the prints, the large domed building on the left is the Temple of Jerusalem, and the book, perhaps, Jeremiah's own Lamentations.[8]

The precious objects on the ledge are usually regarded as the treasures of the Temple, treasures which, according to the apocryphal Book of Maccabees, Jeremiah managed to save.[9] They were recently interpreted as the gifts Jeremiah received from Nebuzaradan, the Babylonian captain of the guard.[10] In the modern literature, the man who seems to be fleeing the burning city, covering his eyes with his hands, is taken to be King Zedekiah

Jeremias beclaghinghe.

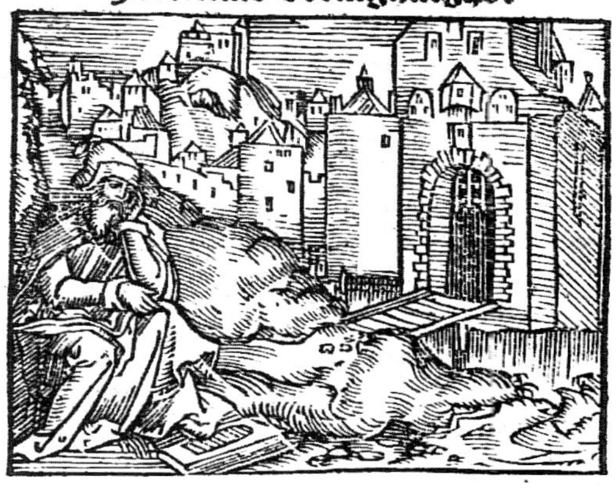

¶ Hoe Jeremias beclaechde ende beweende die verwoestinghe der stadt van Jerusalem/ en des tempels verwoestinghe. En hoe hi noch meer menschen tot medelijden beweghet. Ende hoe hi kende die rechtuaerdicheyt Gods. En onder zijn lijden/dat lijden Christi propheteerde.

FIG. 5a
Lamentations of Jeremiah
Frontispiece to *Den Bibel ...*, Antwerp (Willem Vorsterman), 1532, fol. 101ro
From a reproduction

of Judah, who was blinded at the command of the Babylonian king Nebuchadnezzar.[11] The small winged figure with a burning torch, hovering over the city, has not yet been satisfactorily linked to a specific biblical text.[12]

Some of the details thus remain enigmatic. But it is unlikely that Rembrandt would have brought them all together purely from his imagination and without the figure of the man representing a particular individual. Nor is the artist likely to have expected the observer (whether his own contemporary or someone from a later generation) to identify this principal figure immediately. It seems to have been Rembrandt's intention – though this is rarely true in his work – to present us with a puzzle. He does not allow us to see immediately that the picture indeed represents Jeremiah. This kind of refusal to reveal meaning too readily was a device in contemporary Dutch poetry, and one that was employed by Rembrandt's ardent admirer Constantijn Huygens. Huygens's fellow poet Jacob Cats, who himself sought to achieve in his work a 'pleasing obscurity' (aengename duysterheyt), attempted to counter the objections to Huygens's poetry, which is far more abstruse than his own: 'Consider, worthy friend, that none at court serves from an open dish'.[13]

For its theme and composition, the present work may best be compared to a drawing by Jacob Pynas from the same period, *c.*1631 (fig. 5b).[14] Without Pynas's inscription stating that his drawing represents the prophet Micaiah seeing the fulfilment of his prediction that King Ahab would be killed in battle, no one would guess that it illustrates an event described in the Book of Kings (1:22).

The *Jeremiah* is of modest proportions, yet it makes a monumental impression. Rembrandt has managed more successfully than in his earlier work to integrate a variety of disparate elements in a harmonious composition. The diagonal formed by Jeremiah's body and heightened by the distribution of dark and light has been compared with similar compositional elements in works from the Italian Baroque. Rembrandt may have been inspired by a figure such as the Peter in Guido Reni's *The Apostles Peter and Paul* (fig. 5c). Rembrandt's teacher Pieter Lastman may have drawn his attention to Italian compositions of this kind.[15] The diagonal line of Jeremiah's body is extended by the edge of the fringe on the carpet on which he rests his foot. It continues above his head as well, in the outlines of the column and plinth. This principal diagonal is repeated on the left, in the boundary between light and dark on the wall, and in the right foreground, in the contours of the carpet and still life.

AB/MB

1 Budick 1988, pp. 261–2, sees the scarf as a girdle, which he takes to be a reference to Jeremiah 13:1–11. He associates the bottle with the 'potter's vessel' in Jeremiah 19.

2 *Corpus*, vol. I, 1982, p. 280, no. A28. Budick 1988, p. 262, advances bold speculations about the book.

3 Klibansky, Panofsky & Saxl 1964, passim.

4 *Corpus*, vol. I, 1982, pp. 282–4.

5 Van Gelder 1963, p. 15a; Gerson 1968, p. 489, no. 24.

6 2 Kings 25; 2 Chronicles 36:11ff.

7 Bruyn 1970–71, p. 32, note 8; *Corpus*, vol. I, 1982, p. 282. For another such illustration to the Book of Lamentations, from an Antwerp Bible of 1556, see Perlove 1995, fig. 4.

8 For Rembrandt and the pictorial tradition of the Temple in Jerusalem, see Wischnitzer 1957.

9 Landsberger 1962, p. 109.

10 These gifts are mentioned in Flavius Josephus's *History of the Jewish War*, which C. Tümpel assumes Rembrandt would have consulted (Tümpel 1984, p. 185ff). In the context of a highly speculative theory as to how the present work would have related to the theological disputes current in Holland at the time it was made, Perlove rightly observed that in this instance Rembrandt would not have needed Flavius Josephus; the Bible too (Jeremiah 40:1–6) gives an account of these gifts (Perlove 1995, pp. 162–3).

11 For instance, *Corpus*, vol. I, 1982, p. 282, no. A28; P. van Thiel, in Berlin / Amsterdam / London 1991–92a, p. 146, cat. no. 8. Budick 1988, p. 261, suggests that the figure might be Pashur, the son of Immer the priest (Jeremiah 20:1–6), or Rachel weeping for her children (Jeremiah 31:15), or Jeremiah himself.

12 Réau 1955–59, vol. II, 1956, p. 371, sees this figure as a demon setting fire to the city. Both Budick and Perlove argue that it is an angel rather than a demon (Budick 1988; Perlove 1995).

13 Schwartz 1984, p. 95: 'So denckt, o weerde vrient, / dat niemand in het hoff met open schotels dient'. For Cats's 'aengename duysterheyt', see Amsterdam 1976, p. 20.

14 For this drawing, see Schatborn 1997, p. 14.

15 Bruyn 1970–71, pp. 32–4. Van Rijckevorsel 1932, p. 80, first related the Reni picture to Rembrandt's works of *c.*1630.

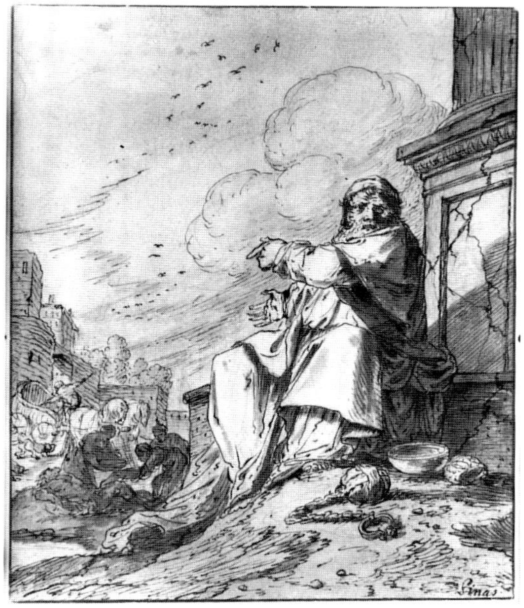

FIG. 5b
Jacob Pynas *c.*1587–1656
The Prophet Micaiah at the City Walls of Samaria *c.*1631
Pen and ink and brush, with chalk
20.7 x 17.0 cm
Royal Museum of Fine Arts, Brussels, De Grez Collection

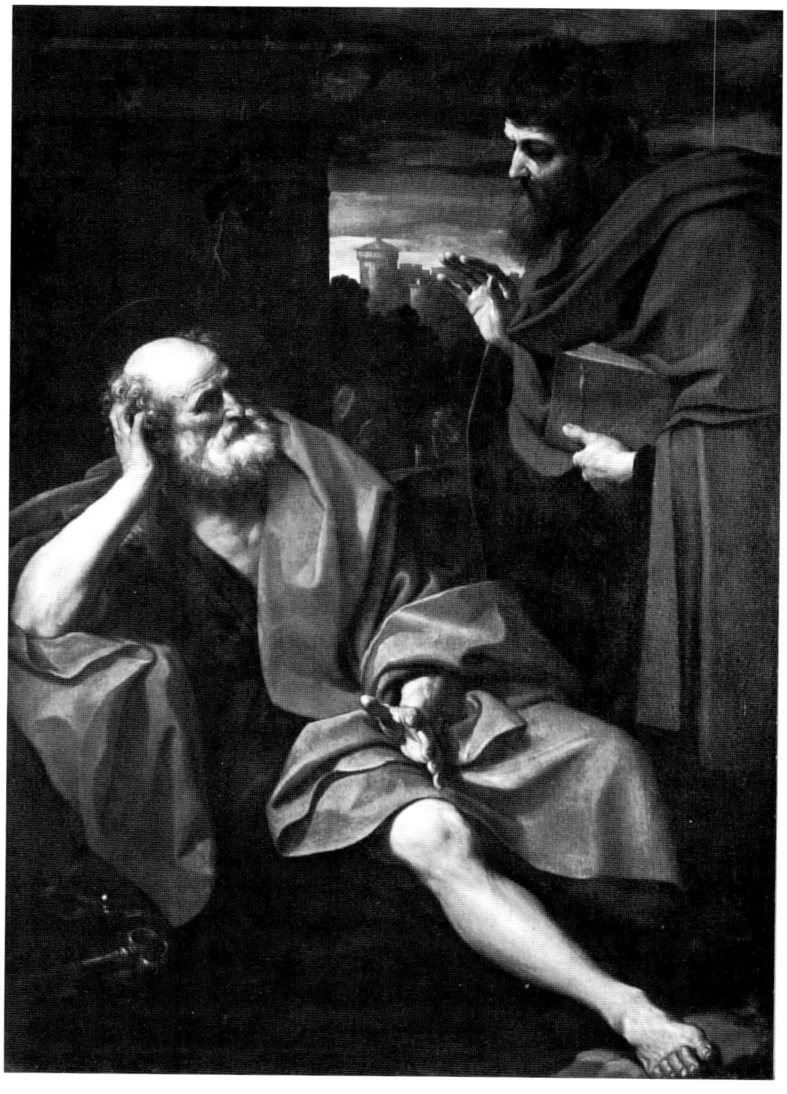

FIG. 5c
Guido Reni Italian, 1575–1642
The Apostles Peter and Paul
Canvas
197.0 x 140.0 cm
Pinacoteca di Brera, Milan

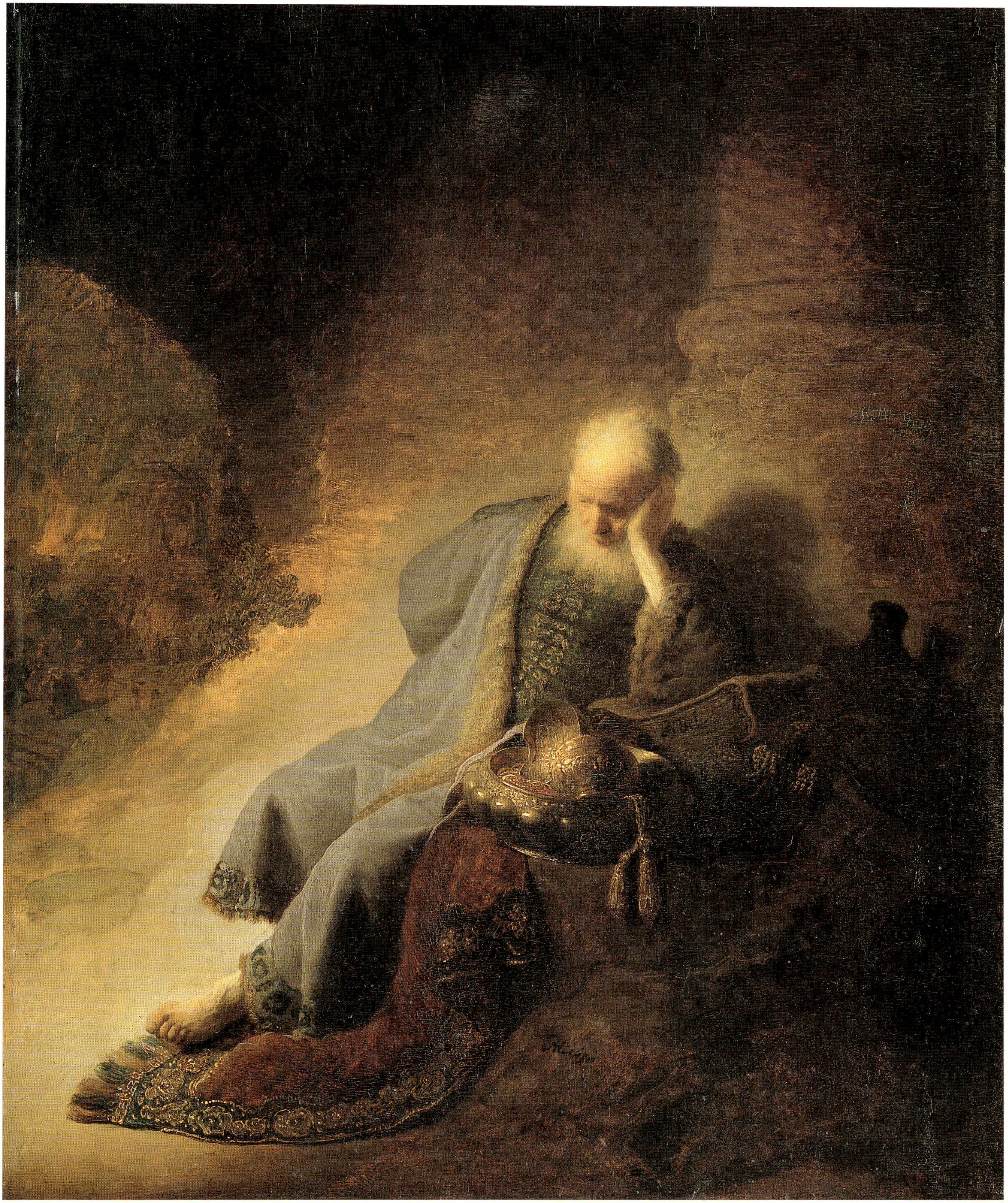

6
The Apostle Peter Kneeling

Monogrammed and dated lower right *RHL. 1631*
Panel
59.0 x 47.8 cm
Private collection, USA

PROVENANCE: (Possibly) Sale, Pieter Habet, Amsterdam, 11 April 1764, lot 1; sale, Comte de Choiseul-Praslin, Paris, 18–25 February 1793, lot 42; Prince de Rubempré de Mérode, Westerloo, Belgium; sale, New York (Christie's), 31 May 1990, lot 149.

LITERATURE: Vosmaer 1877, p. 489; Hofstede de Groot 1908–27, vol. VI, 1916, p. 95, no. 122; Gerson 1968, p. 190, no. 25; Bredius / Gerson 1969, no. 607; *Corpus*, vol. I, 1982, pp. 346–50, no. A36; Schwartz 1984, p. 99; Tümpel 1986, no. K2; London 1988–89, p. 52; Haverkamp-Begemann 1990.

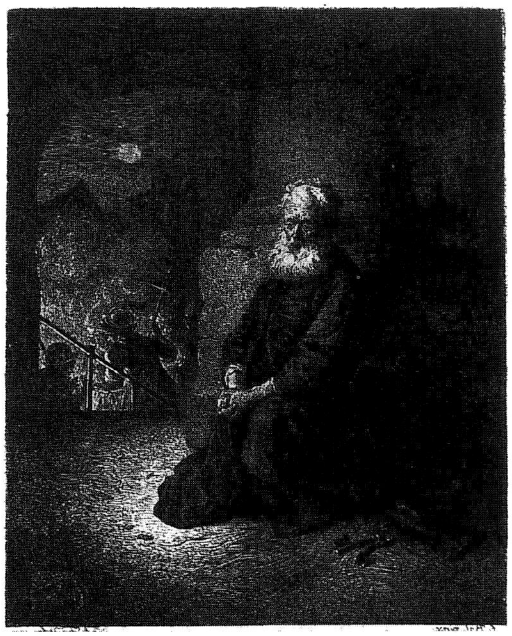

FIG. 6a
Georg Friedrich Schmidt (German, 1712–1775), after Rembrandt or a copyist
The Apostle Peter Kneeling
Inscribed *f: Bol. pinx: – G. f. Schmidt, fec: 1770. / du Cabinet de Monsieur C^{ller} Trible*
Etching (reproduced in reverse)

A frail old man with a wizened face and white beard is bent down on one knee. His other leg is extended and he rests his clasped hands on it. His expression is anxious, or perhaps sorrowful. The space around him is dimly lit, and all we see is stone. The lower part of a large pillar, with its octagonal base, can be seen behind him. The man's cloak lies beside him, and at his feet is a little bundle of straw, in front of which are two conspicuously placed keys identifying him as Peter (compare the key in *The Apostle Peter Standing* (cat. no. 7)).

This painting has been interpreted in two different ways. One theory is that it is a portrayal of Peter in prison.[1] According to this interpretation he is shown in his cell, with straw for his humble bedding.[2] However, this reading does not tally with the biblical account, nor is it in line with any pictorial tradition. Peter was bound in chains during his confinement in prison, but there are none to be seen in the Rembrandt. Peter was also guarded by soldiers, and while he slept an angel awakened him and broke the chains (cf. Hendrick ter Brugghen's *Peter's Release from Prison* (fig. 7a)), delivering him from captivity. These details are normally depicted in representations of Peter's imprisonment, but are not included in the present work. Moreover, the Bible does not describe the imprisonment as an ordeal (Acts 12:4–7). Peter was the leader of the apostles at the time of his captivity, long after Christ's Ascension, and it would have been unfitting for a man of his stature to feel distressed at being in prison.

The second interpretation of the picture is more plausible. Earlier in the biblical narrative, Peter, having denied Christ three times, was repentant at the end of his master's life.[3] He had promised to follow Christ even into prison and to death, but Christ had said: 'I tell thee, Peter, the cock shall not crow this day, before that thou shalt thrice deny that thou knowest me' (Luke 22:34). However, when Christ was taken captive that same evening, Peter sat down with the soldiers at their fire. A serving-maid recognized him and said that he had been with Jesus, whereupon Peter denied this three times. Upon the third denial, 'immediately, while he yet spake, the cock crew ... And Peter remembered the word of the Lord ... [a]nd went out and wept bitterly' (Luke 22:54–62).[4] Peter's clasped hands and sorrowful expression in the present painting convey the remorse he would have felt as a result of this episode.

Most depictions of the repentant Peter show him wringing his hands in grief, just as Rembrandt has portrayed him here. The evangelists say that Peter 'went out', and artists have therefore generally rendered the scene by showing him outdoors in a landscape, usually with a crowing cock. Often included is the company to whom Peter had denied knowing his master – the guards and the serving-maid at the fire. Rembrandt's decision not to include these details[5] was seen as an omission: an old copy of the picture includes an additional scene at the left, where we see soldiers around a fire in a moonlit landscape;[6] an etching of 1770, after this or a related copy, shows the cock as well (fig. 6a).[7] The copyist/s evidently interpreted the Rembrandt as a portrayal of 'Peter Repentant' and therefore felt that there were elements that they could not leave out.

The representation of Peter in a landscape, together with the soldiers and the cock, is part of the conventional pictorial imagery associated with the scene, but is not entirely consistent with the text of the seventeenth-century authorized version of the Dutch Bible, which says that Peter betrayed Christ when he, the soldiers and the serving-maid were 'in the midst of the hall [*zaal*]' (Luke 22:55).[8] (Most other Dutch translations, both earlier and later, translate the Greek *aule* as *hof* (a court or garden) and thus read 'in the court/garden'.) There, indoors, Peter heard the cock crow. The fact that he 'went out' to weep and mourn in solitude means that he left the hall, but this is not necessarily to say that he went outdoors. It is quite possible that we see Peter here in a porch or entrance hall – this would correspond to the translation in the Authorized King James Version, which indeed says that Peter 'went out into the porch' (Mark 14:68). The space in the painting recalls the interior in which Rembrandt depicted the slightly earlier episode of *Judas Repentant, Returning the Pieces of Silver* (p. 23, fig. 2).[9]

Rembrandt has sought to convey the full force of Peter's isolation. The bare stone walls around him heighten this sense of solitude. What little light there is falls only on Peter's face and hands. An X-ray photograph shows that his left foot was originally exposed, having the effect of drawing attention away from the face and hands (fig. 6b).[10] Rembrandt apparently had second thoughts, and covered the bare foot with the robe. Before he introduced this change, however, his studio had made a copy of the picture, in which work Peter's foot can still be seen (fig. 6c).[11]

In terms of dating, style and format, as well as the characterization and placing of the figure, the *Peter* is generally thought to be closely related to the *Jeremiah* dated 1630 (cat. no. 5).[12] The *Peter* is believed to have been made slightly later, in 1630–31, and dated by Rembrandt in the latter year.[13] The present exhibition enables us for the first time to compare the two pictures side by

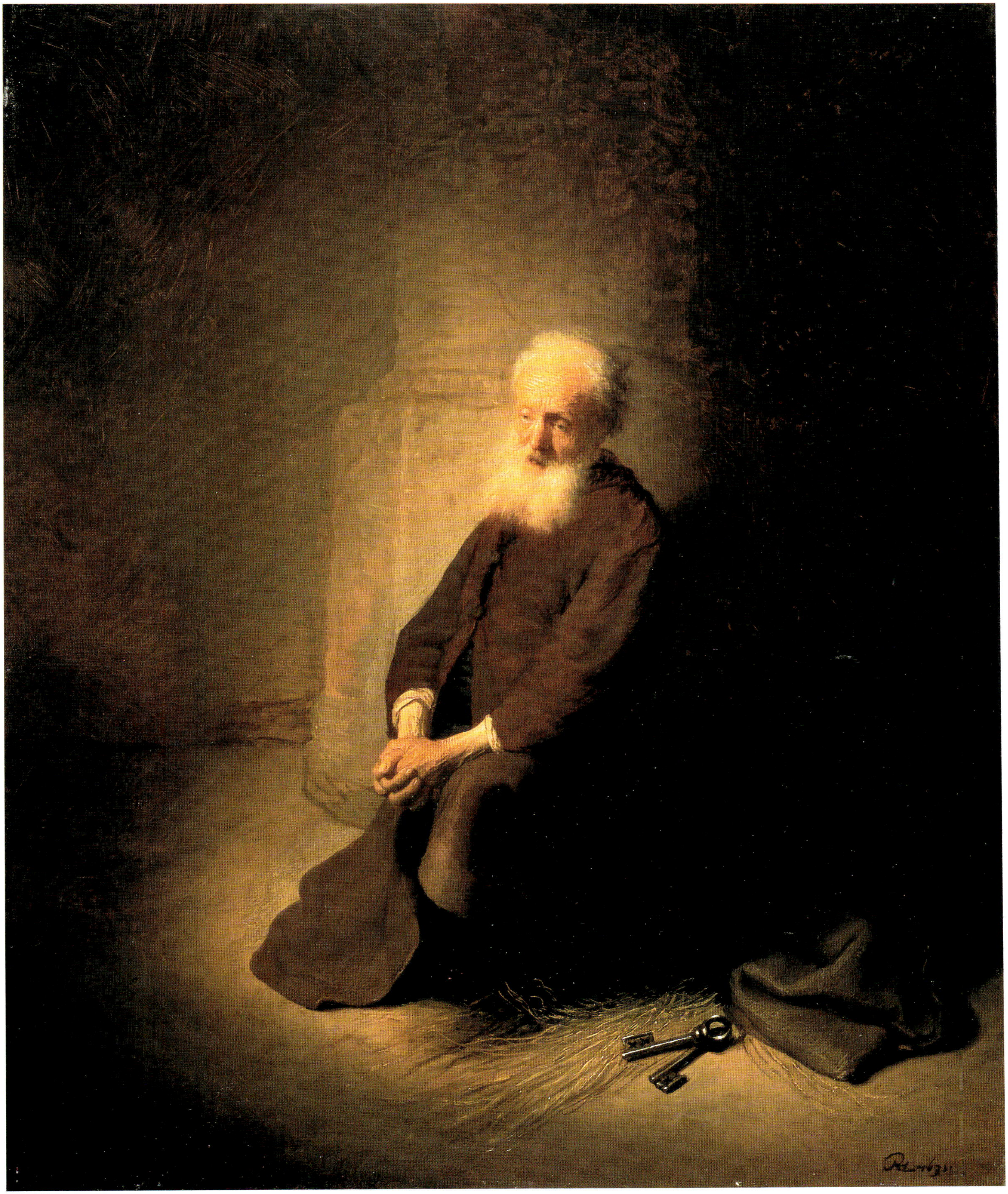

side. The model for the *Peter* is thought to be the same man seen in a number of Rembrandt's early paintings, drawings and etchings. He has also been identified as the man in the *Jeremiah* and the man facing the viewer in *Two Old Men Disputing* (cat. nos 5, 3).[14] This, too, is something we will be able to judge for ourselves at the exhibition. The model was an elderly man in 1631 and this is how we see Peter in the painting – with deep lines etched into his face and hands. Although Peter is generally portrayed as a mature figure, in other representations he tends to be shown as a man in his prime, younger than the old man we see here (cf. the younger-looking man depicted in cat. no. 7).

AB/MB

1 *Corpus*, vol. I, 1982, pp. 346–50, no. A36, describes the picture as 'S. Peter in Prison', as Vosmaer had done in 1877 (Vosmaer 1877, p. 489).

2 Hofstede de Groot 1908–27, vol. VI, 1916, p. 95, no. 122: 'a bundle of straw for his bed'.

3 Haverkamp-Begemann 1990 presented a compelling argument in support of this interpretation. An early scholar to refer to the picture as *St Peter Repentant* was Hofstede de Groot (Hofstede de Groot 1908–27, vol. VI, 1916, p. 95, no. 122).

4 Cf. Matthew 26:75; Mark 14:66–72.

5 Tümpel 1986, p. 419, no. K2, regards cat. no. 6 as a combination of two biblical themes: 'Rembrandt has combined two images – Paul in prison and Peter as the repentant sinner – traditional pictorial motifs which do not in fact belong together, in a single composition'. Tümpel believes that the piece is a copy.

6 For a reproduction of the copy, formerly in the Lanckoronski Collection, Vienna, see *Corpus*, vol. I, 1982, p. 350, fig. 5.

7 Hofstede de Groot 1908–27, vol. VI, 1916, p. 95, no. 122, was the first to discuss the Lanckoronski copy (given to Ferdinand Bol in 1770) and the etching. On two occasions, in 1764 and 1793 (see Provenance) – in the same period as the print was made – the Rembrandt painting was sold as Peter 'in prison' (*Corpus*, vol. I, 1982, p. 350). There are five further copies after our cat. no. 6 (*Corpus*, vol. I, pp. 349–50).

8 The relevant passages in the authorized seventeenth-century Dutch translation of the Bible (*Statenvertaling*) read as follows: Matthew 26:69: 'without in the hall', Mark 14:66: 'beneath in the hall'. The *Statenvertaling* was published in 1637, after cat. no. 6 was painted. It merits further study to establish to what extent its renderings of the biblical texts were current before this.

9 Private collection, England (Bredius / Gerson 1969, no. 539A; *Corpus*, vol. I, 1982, no. A15).

10 Haverkamp-Begemann 1990, p. 16, fig. 2, offers this interpretation and adds that Peter's robe was originally wider and that Rembrandt narrowed it to enhance the diagonal effect. As a result of the artist's adjustments, Peter looks frailer than he did at first.

11 Haverkamp-Begemann 1990, p. 15, fig. 1.

12 Gerson 1968, p. 190, suggests that both pieces, possibly the *Anastasius*, of the same size, at the Nationalmuseum Stockholm (Bredius / Gerson 1969, no. 430), and the *Old Woman Reading* (the so-called *Prophetess Hannah*) in Amsterdam (p. 47, fig. 18) 'may have belonged to a still larger series of religious figures'.

13 *Corpus*, vol. I, 1982, p. 348, no. A36.

14 *Corpus*, vol. I, 1982, pp. 149, 348; Haverkamp-Begemann 1990, pp. 18–21. Haverkamp-Begemann also mentions works by Lievens featuring a man he believes to be the same model.

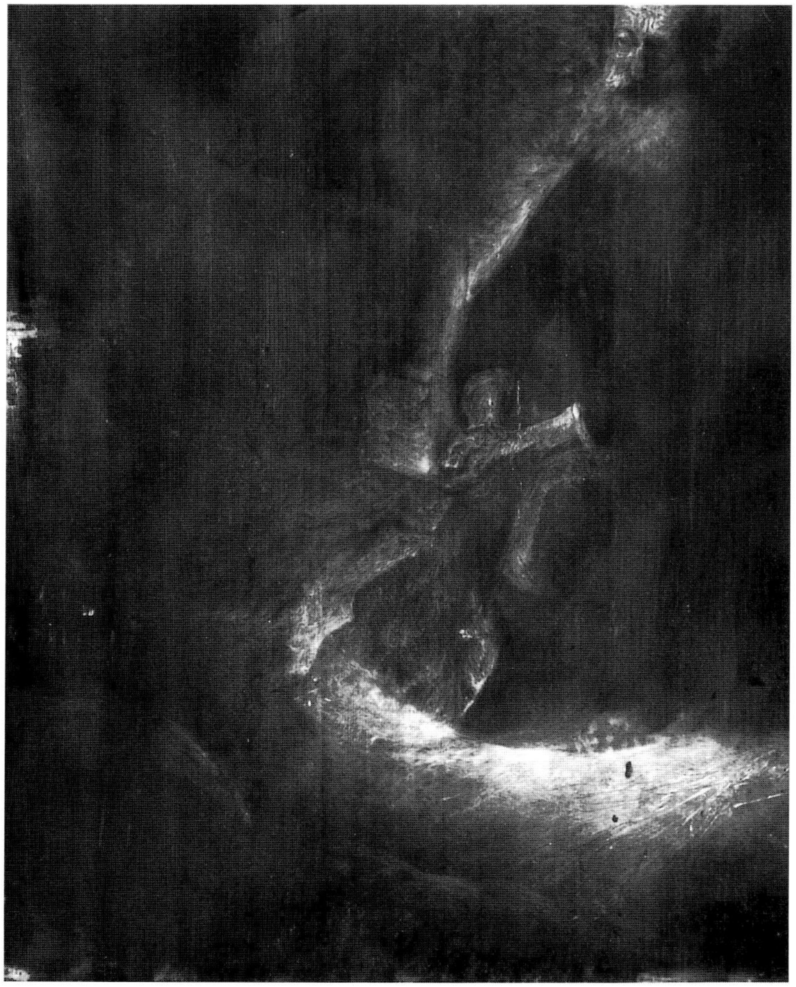

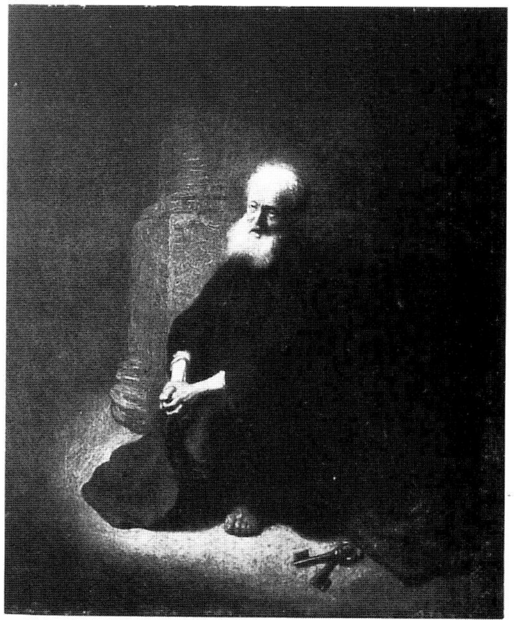

FIG. 6c
Studio of Rembrandt
The Apostle Peter Kneeling
Panel
59.0 x 50.0 cm
Formerly Comtesse de la Béraudière collection; present whereabouts unknown

FIG. 6b
X-ray photograph of *The Apostle Peter Kneeling*
From Haverkamp-Begemann 1990

7
The Apostle Peter Standing

Signed and dated in grey in right background *RHL* (in monogram) *[van] Ry[n] / 1632.* (barely discernible)
Canvas
81.3 x 66.2 cm
Nationalmuseum, Stockholm

PROVENANCE: Traditionally said to have been purchased by Carel Carelsz van Cracau(w) (or Cracou) (agent of the Admiralty of Holland at Helsingoer and Resident (envoy) of the States-General to the Danish Court) in Amsterdam, 1646; M. Durell; T. Carlheim-Gyllensköld, Stockholm (as Jusepe de Ribera); purchased 1881 (as by unknown Italian artist).

LITERATURE: Hofstede de Groot 1908–27, vol. VI, 1916, pp. 125–6, no. 181; Bredius / Gerson 1969, no. 609; *Corpus*, vol. II, 1986, pp. 138–44, no. A46; G. Cavalli-Björkman, in Stockholm 1992–93, pp. 190–1, cat. no. 54.

An almost lifesize bearded old man appears to be scrutinizing us. The large key he holds to his breast identifies him as the apostle Peter. This attribute derives from a passage in Matthew in which Christ addresses Peter, saying: 'I will give you the keys of the kingdom of heaven' (Matthew 16:19a). Throughout the century preceding the execution of this painting, people had been debating whether Christ had meant to designate Peter as his successor in Rome, as the Catholics believed, or whether, as the Protestants countered, he had intended nothing of the sort.[1] In the visual arts, however, whether Catholic or not, a key or keys had remained Peter's conventional attribute (see also cat. no. 6).

Rembrandt has portrayed Peter in a purple-tinged brown robe against a dark background. His right hand, with which he holds a staff, is enveloped in shadow. The figure gives the impression of having glanced up while walking past us. His left hand and one side of his wizened face are illuminated and therefore draw all our attention. A weak light directly to the right of the figure creates an illusion of space around him.

Both the pronounced chiaroscuro and this particular type of elderly, bearded man are strongly reminiscent of the style of Caravaggio. But nothing comparable can be found among the works of Rembrandt's fellow painters in Utrecht, which had emerged as the centre of Dutch Caravaggism. The Utrecht masters tended to take Caravaggio's bold, naturalistic effects to even further extremes. The great Utrecht Caravaggist Hendrick ter Brugghen portrayed the main figure in *Peter's Release from Prison* (1624) with the grotesque, bulbous nose of a dipsomaniac vagrant (fig. 7a). Later in the 1630s, Rembrandt occasionally drew inspiration from ter Brugghen's radically naturalistic approach, as in the *Ganymede* (p. 35, fig. 3). But his *Peter* from Stockholm seeks to achieve a more dignified, classical effect. The picture recalls Italian and Spanish masters who were truer than were artists such as ter Brugghen to the classicist principles that always continued to be important in Caravaggio's own work. Rembrandt would have seen paintings from Italy and other countries that found their way onto the market in Amsterdam. A *Peter* bearing the inscription *J. de Ribera* and now attributed to the Spaniard Antonio del Castillo is reproduced here (fig. 7b). Though this work is unlikely to have influenced (or been influenced by) Rembrandt's *Peter*, both pictures nevertheless show distinct similarities in type and pose. It is therefore not so outrageous that Rembrandt's *Peter* was once thought to be a Ribera, or that the Nationalmuseum in Stockholm acquired it as the work of an anonymous Italian master (see Provenance).

Rembrandt's majestic Peter, swathed in a toga with wide, flowing folds, also recalls work that Jacob Backer (1608–1651) was producing in Amsterdam around the same time. Backer was long regarded as a pupil of Rembrandt's. I have challenged this premise, if only on the grounds that it is no more than a late-nineteenth-century idea. Moreover, from about 1630 on, Backer created a unique classicizing style, which was to influence many other artists.[2] Backer himself was greatly inspired by his real teacher, Lambert Jacobsz, who developed a classicizing style with a

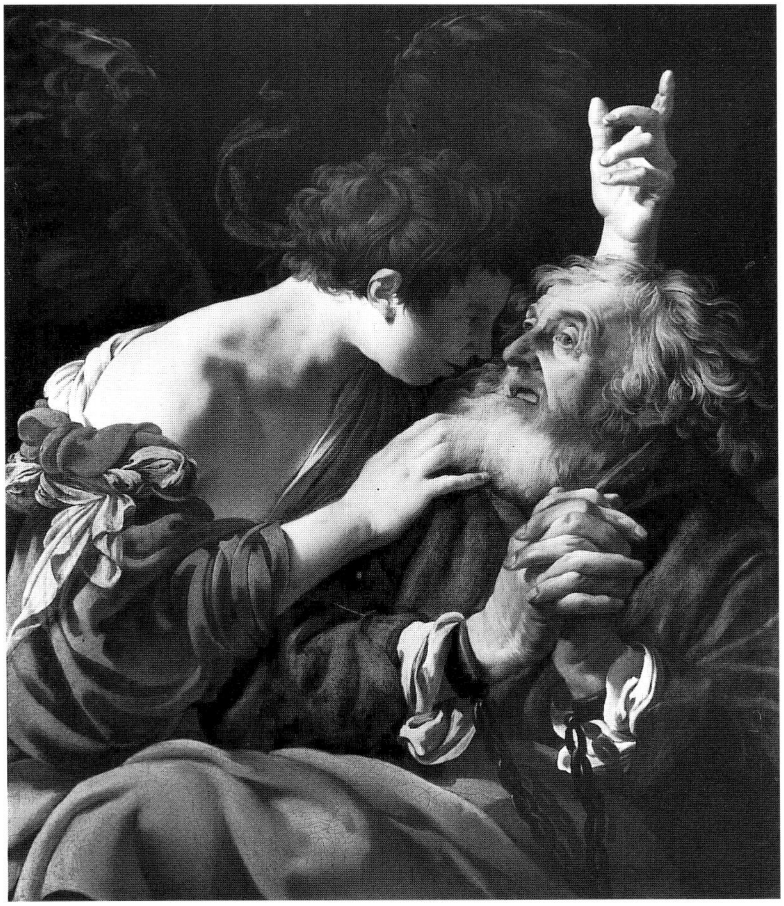

FIG. 7a
Hendrick ter Brugghen 1588–1629
Peter's Release from Prison
Signed and dated [16]24
Canvas
105.0 x 85.0 cm
Mauritshuis, The Hague
Photograph: © Mauritshuis, The Hague, inv. no. 966

strong Caravaggist tinge even earlier, probably during a stay in Rome.[3] Jacobsz eventually settled in Leeuwarden, Friesland, where he painted his impressive *Apostle Paul* in 1629 (fig. 7c). Leeuwarden was far away from Amsterdam, but we know that Jacobsz was in close contact with the Amsterdam art dealer Hendrick Uylenburgh, whose house Rembrandt was living in when he painted the *Apostle Peter Standing*. A few years later, Uylenburgh was in debt to Jacobsz, who at that time owned a Rembrandt and various copies after him, one of the latter being a *tronie* of 'an oriental woman, being the portrait of H. Uylenburgh's wife'. A picture by Backer belonging to Jacobsz was on loan to Uylenburgh's shop.[4]

It would seem that Rembrandt's *Apostle Peter Standing* of 1632 is an instance of the artist following the example of both Backer and Jacobsz and creating the same type of classical, distinguished, southern European figure as the *Apostle Andrew*, which either Backer or Jacobsz had presumably made a short time earlier (fig. 7d).[5] The present picture's outlines are smoother and its chiaroscuro less dramatic than in Jacobsz's earlier *Apostle Paul* (fig. 7c). In this respect the *Apostle Peter Standing*, which Rembrandt tackled with restraint, more resembles the *Apostle Andrew*. Rembrandt has here avoided the expressive bravura and much of the chiaroscuro of his own *Man in Oriental Costume* from the same year, 1632.[6] His treatment of the paint in both works is nevertheless related.

AB/MB

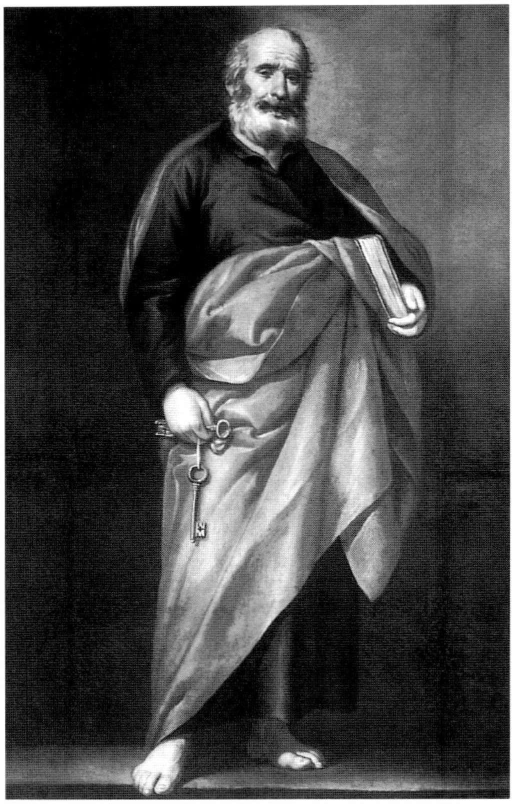

FIG. 7b
Antonio del Castillo Spanish, *c.*1603–1667
Peter
Canvas
175.8 x 109.5 cm
Sale, London (Christie's), 29 October 1993; present whereabouts unknown
From a reproduction

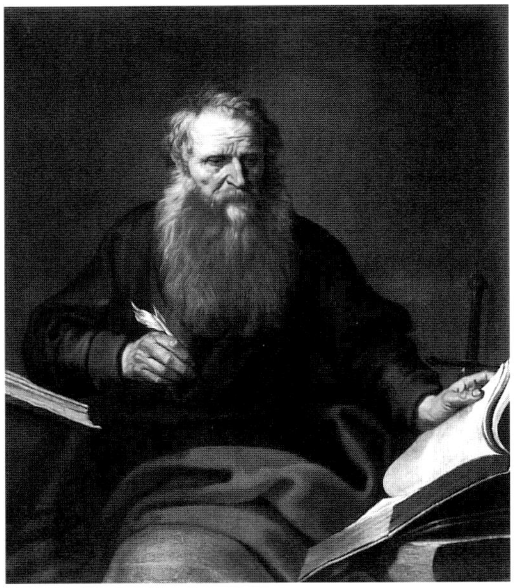

FIG. 7c
Lambert Jacobsz *c.*1592–1637
The Apostle Paul
Signed and dated 1629
Canvas
114.0 x 101.0 cm
Fries Museum, Leeuwarden

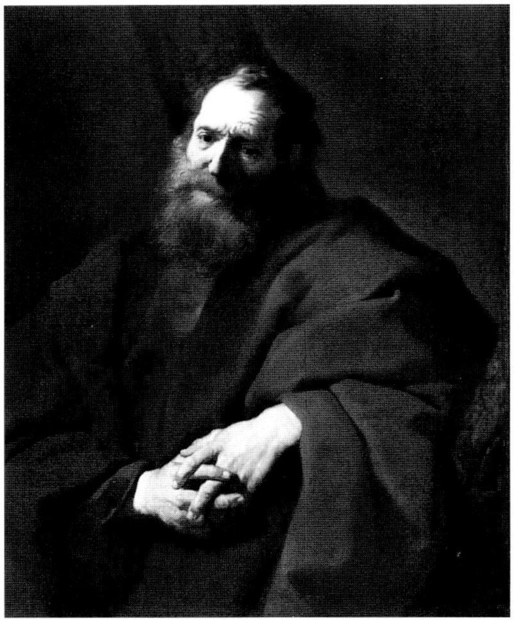

FIG. 7d
Jacob Backer or Lambert Jacobsz
The Apostle Andrew
Canvas
99.0 x 80.2 cm
York City Art Gallery, York

1 Mâle 1932, p. 49ff.
2 A. Blankert, in Washington / Detroit / Amsterdam 1980–81a, pp. 185, 206; Blankert 1982, p. 37.
3 For Jacobsz's probable stay in Rome, see Straat 1928, pp. 56–7.
4 These facts are known from the inventory drawn up after Jacobsz's death in 1637 (published in Straat 1928, pp. 67, 72–4, 76).
5 Sumowski, *Gemälde*, vol. I, 1983, p. 195, no. 16, attributed the *Apostle Andrew* to Backer and dated it *c.*1630. Bruyn 1996, pp. 167–8, writes that the *Andrew* is more likely a Backer-like work by Jacobsz. It may be added here that as early as 1637 doubt existed as to whether a certain picture was by Backer or by his teacher Jacobsz (Straat 1928, p. 71).
6 Metropolitan Museum of Art, New York (Bredius / Gerson 1969, no. 169; *Corpus*, vol. II, 1986, no. A48). The differences between the present piece and that in New York may be what induced Gerson to consider *The Apostle Peter Standing* a copy (H. Gerson, in Bredius / Gerson 1969, p. 613, no. 609). His doubt about the authenticity of the piece, a unique viewpoint on this picture in modern times, was followed by Schwartz in 1984 and by Tümpel in 1986. *Corpus*, vol. II, 1986, p. 142, no. A46, convincingly refutes Gerson's opinion.

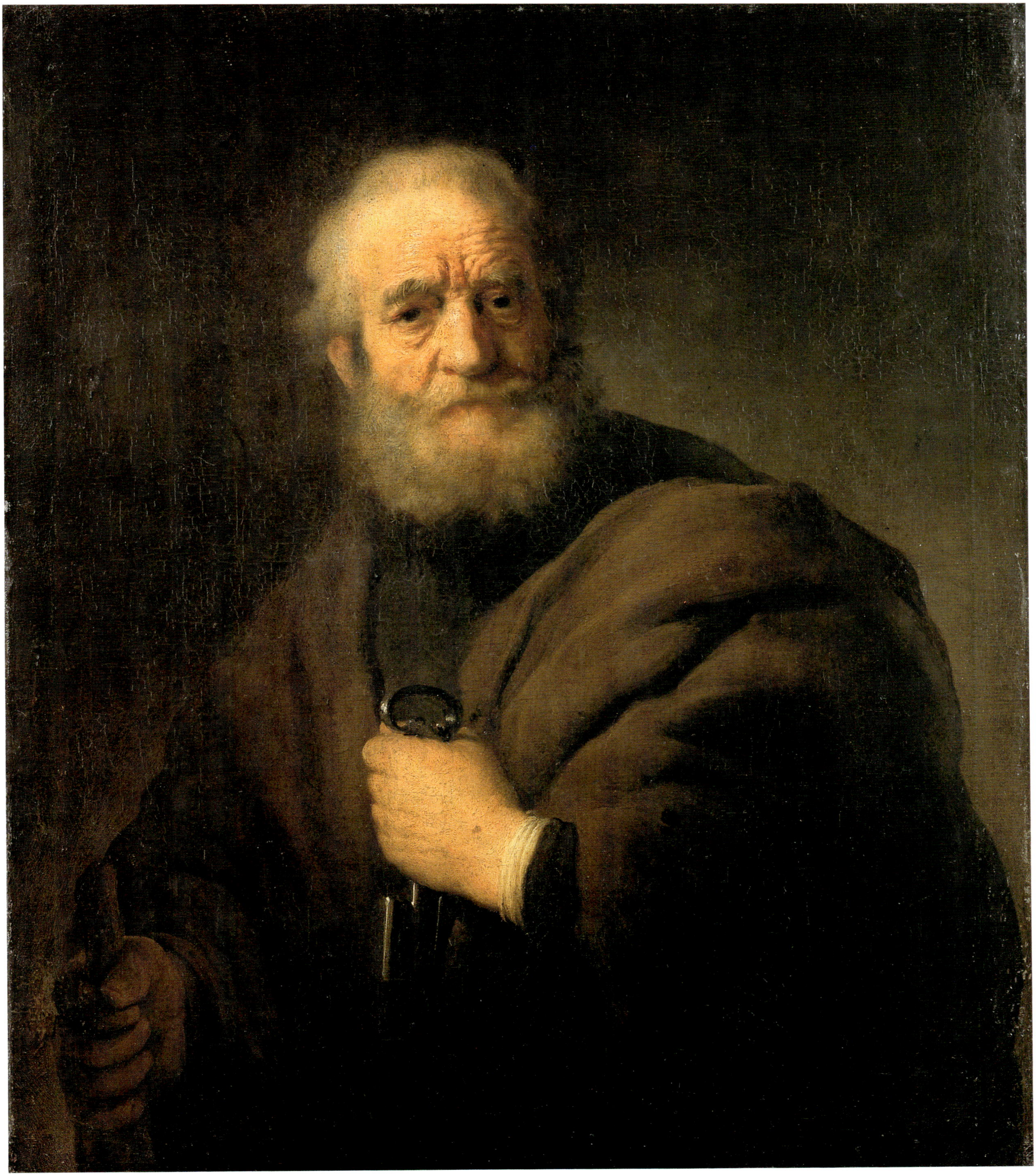

8
Portrait of Jacques de Gheyn III

Signed and dated upper left *RH* (in monogram) *van Ryn / 1632*
Inscribed on back of panel (partly effaced) *JACOBVS GEINIUS IVN*[R] */ H[...]NI IPSIVS / EFFIGIE[M] / EXTREMVM MVNVS MORIENTIS / R / [...] MO.IE.STE. UN.HABET ISTA SECUNDUM HEU* (last passage also read as: *MORIENTE.NUNC.HABET ISTA SECUNDUM HEU)*
Panel
29.9 x 24.9 cm
By permission of the Trustees of Dulwich Picture Gallery, London

PROVENANCE: Bequeathed by the sitter, Jacques de Gheyn III (1596–1641), to Maurits Huygens (1595–1642), Secretary of the Council of States in The Hague. Together with *Portrait of Maurits Huygens*: sale, Allard Rudolph van Waay, Utrecht, 27 February 1764, lot 123, and sale, Aubert, Paris, 2ff March 1786, lot 17. Cat. no. 8 alone: (conceivably) Desenfans private sale, London, 8ff June 1786, lot 264; (conceivably) sale, Pieter Cornelis Baron van Leyden (Amsterdam), Paris, [5 July, postponed to] 10 September [actually held 5 November] 1804, first suppl. no. 152; Noel Joseph Desenfans (Douai 1745 – London 1807); bequeathed by Desenfans to his friend Sir Francis Bourgeois in 1807; Sir Francis Bourgeois, RA, London (1756–1811); bequeathed by him to Dulwich College in 1811.

LITERATURE: Hofstede de Groot 1908–27, vol. VI, 1916, p. 350, no. 745; Bredius / Gerson 1969, no. 162; Schwartz 1984, pp. 91–7; *Corpus*, vol. II, 1986, pp. 219–24, no. A56; Tümpel 1986, no. 194; P. van Thiel, in Berlin / Amsterdam / London 1991–92a, pp. 152–5, cat. no. 12.

Rembrandt started painting portraits only after he had moved to Amsterdam. Nine pictures of august gentlemen, all of them lifesize, are known from 1631–32, his first years in Amsterdam (p. 70, fig. 2).[1] Compared to these imposing figures, this portrait of 1632, with the head no more than eight centimetres high, looks like a miniature. Rembrandt was clearly seeking to achieve a less ostentatious, more intimate, effect. The picture is executed with such delicacy and care that in the sale catalogue of 1786 it was even likened to the manner of Gerrit Dou.[2] The finesse of the piece's execution does not in the least diminish the penetrating effect of the face, which seems to be surveying us with lively interest. The light is concentrated on the head and on the intense white of the collar with the face poised above it. The model's fine, golden-blond hair frames his face like a halo of light. The restoration of the picture directly prior to this exhibition enhances the effect. Our colour reproduction is the first to show this painting in its new condition.

An old Latin inscription on the back of the picture is still faintly legible. It tells us that the portrait is of Jacques de Gheyn junior, that he bequeathed it to 'H...ni', and that the piece thereby acquired a *secundum*, or pendant. The inscription was published only in 1950, but it confirmed what had previously been assumed. The painting is a portrait of the painter and draughtsman Jacques de Gheyn III (1596–1641), the son and pupil of the far better known artist Jacques de Gheyn II (1565–1629). The father's work, and his drawings in particular, may have had a decisive influence on Rembrandt.[3] The de Gheyns, father and son, spent most of their lives in The Hague, where they were neighbours and close friends of the Huygens family. Both were wealthy and distinguished families.[4]

Famous as a poet, writer, musician, courtier and artist, Constantijn Huygens (1596–1687), who was the same age as de Gheyn III, wrote about the de Gheyns with affection and admiration in his autobiography of *c.*1629–30. But he was also critical. The young de Gheyn, Huygens wrote, had great talent and skill, but 'I cannot conceal my vexation that through sheer indifference this beginning has yielded so little, and that a man born among the Dutch to grace his fatherland for all times has buried his talent and dozed into an unproductive and reprehensible sloth'. The reason, Huygens thought, might be that de Gheyn III was a man of considerable means.[5] The fact that he was neither very active nor energetic is all too clear from his small extant oeuvre.[6] But the beautiful pieces it contains confirm Huygens's words regarding de Gheyn III's talent and skill. Some of de Gheyn III's prints (fig. 8a) are thought to have influenced early paintings by Rembrandt.[7]

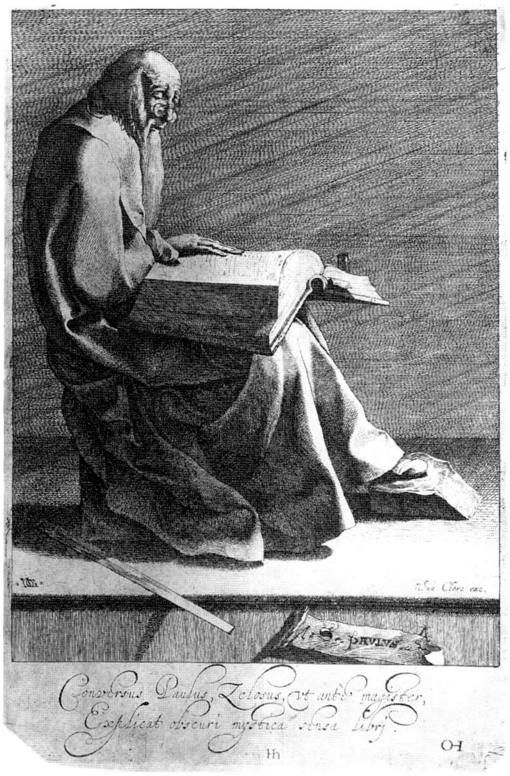

FIG. 8a
Jacques de Gheyn III 1596–1641
The Apostle Paul
Etching
25.7 x 19.0 cm
Rijksprentenkabinet, Rijksmuseum, Amsterdam

De Gheyn III moved from The Hague to Utrecht in 1634, when he became canon of the Protestant – formerly Catholic – Mariakerk, with responsibility for the church's property. This was a highly lucrative position, which only the nobility or members of otherwise prominent families were entitled to procure.[8] De Gheyn had an extra advantage in that his family was originally from Utrecht.

De Gheyn dictated his will in Utrecht on 3 June 1641, a day or two before his death. At the time he was 'physically ill and confined to bed, but quite evidently in control of his mind, memory and five senses'.[9] He gave a concise but accurate description of his paintings. They were with other possessions that he kept 'in both [his] present lodgings and in the room above the chapterhouse of the Mariakerk, here in Utrecht'.[10] According to the will, de Gheyn III's 'lodgings' were on the St Maartensdam in Utrecht, where his landlord was a Mr Gerrit van Helsdingen. Other documents refer to van Helsdingen as an 'innkeeper' and give his address as Oudmunstertrans. As Oudmunstertrans (the present-day

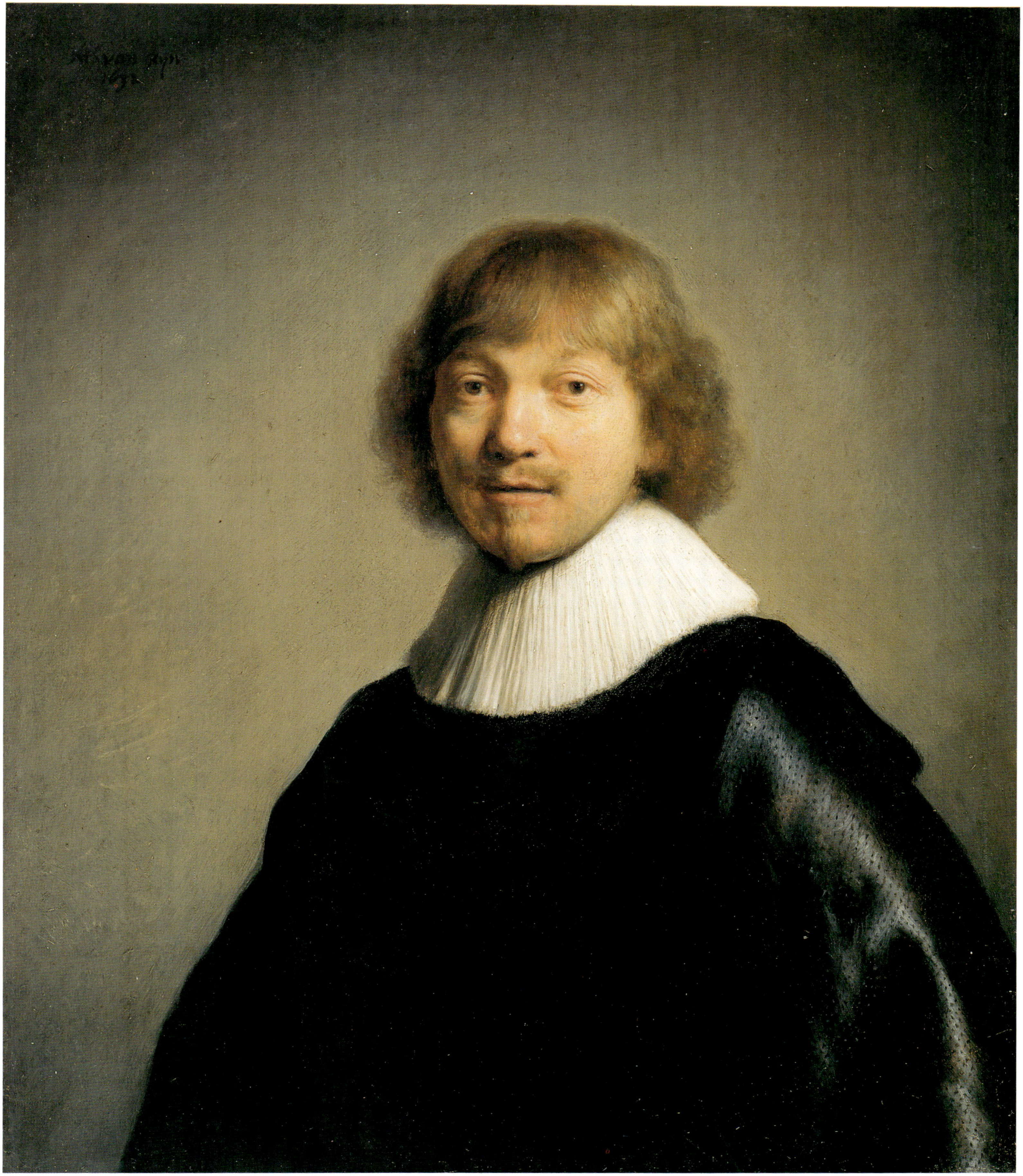

Trans) intersects the Maartensdam (now known as the Pausdam), de Gheyn's home must have been on the corner of these two streets (fig. 8b).[11]

De Gheyn apparently also kept some of his works of art in the 'room above the chapterhouse of the Mariakerk'. Although the church and its annexes were demolished around 1800, the late Dr J. E. A. L. Struick, former municipal archivist in Utrecht, managed to identify the 'room above the chapterhouse' in a drawing by Pieter Saenredam of the Mariakerk seen from the east. The drawing dates from 1636, when de Gheyn was canon of the church (fig. 8c).[12] De Gheyn's 'room' there was evidently an attic of sorts, safe within the precinct of the church. Saenredam later made a painting after his drawing. It is clearer in the painting that the extension to the church had a gable, which would have allowed for a window, and, in the wall below the gutter, the tops of two windows seem to be visible. This means there would have been light for de Gheyn's paintings on the upper floor (fig. 8d).

Figs 8b, 8c and 8d show precisely where the owner of these pictures kept this important collection: part was in his lodgings and part (temporarily?) in what would now be called a secure storeroom. De Gheyn curated his paintings as meticulously as collectors and museums were to do later. In more recent times, as we shall see, his task has been taken over by museums in Melbourne, Turin, Dulwich and Leipzig.

De Gheyn III's will first refers to a large flowerpiece, painted by de Gheyn's father (fig. 8e),[13] and after that to Rembrandt's *Two Old Men Disputing*, now in Melbourne (cat. no. 3). The document also enables us to reconstruct more of the collection. The *Two Old Men Disputing* is mentioned together with 'a little old man asleep seated by a fire, with his hand in his bosom, also made by Rembrandt'.[14] This picture is now in Turin (p. 46, fig. 19). The next two items in the will can be identified as works by Jan Lievens – *A Young Woman and an Old Woman* (fig. 34a) and a *Smiling Girl with Long Blond Hair* now in Leipzig (cat. no. 34). These are followed by a peasant fair by Adriaen Brouwer and a few sixteenth-century paintings.

De Gheyn, who was unmarried, left all these pictures to his relative Johannes Wtenbogaert (1608–1680), who was twelve years his junior and a receiver of taxes in Amsterdam. Wtenbogaert is now known mainly because of the etching in which Rembrandt portrayed him in 1639 (B.281) (fig. 8f).[15] A relative of his, François Wtenbogaert, inherited a Carel de Hooch landscape from de Gheyn, with figures painted by Cornelis van Poelenburch (pictures by C. de Hooch with figures by Poelenburch occasionally appeared in

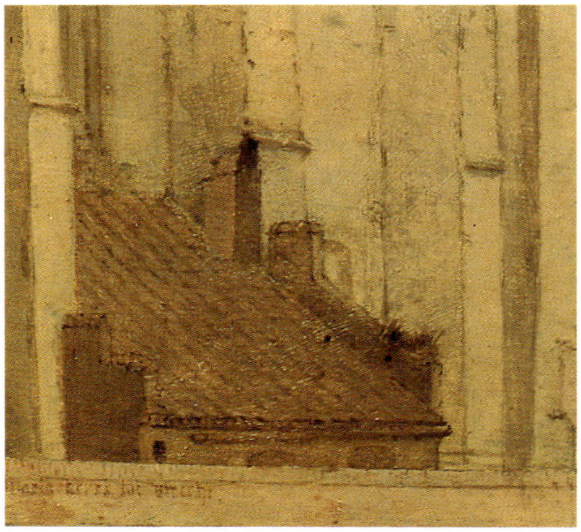

FIG. 8d
Pieter Saenredam 1597–1665
Former Church of St Marie, Utrecht. Exterior Viewed from the Choir Along the North Wall (detail)
Dated 10 November 1659
Panel
Mauritshuis, The Hague
This is the 'chapterhouse' with the 'room above' in which Jacques de Gheyn III stored some of his paintings. Saenredam based his picture on a drawing he had made from the same vantage point in 1636, when de Gheyn III was still living in Utrecht (fig. 8c). The medieval Mariakerk was later demolished.
Photograph: © Mauritshuis, The Hague, inv. no. 974

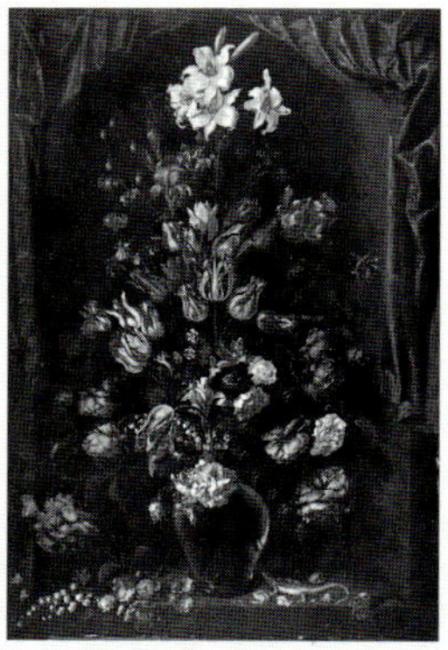

Jacques de Gheyn II (see fig. 8e)

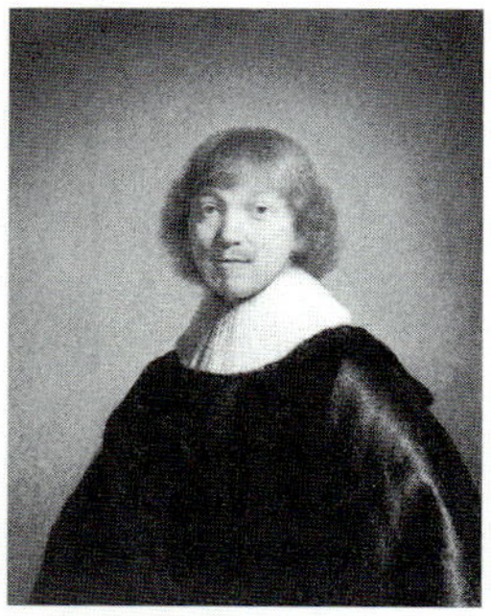

Rembrandt (cat. no. 8)

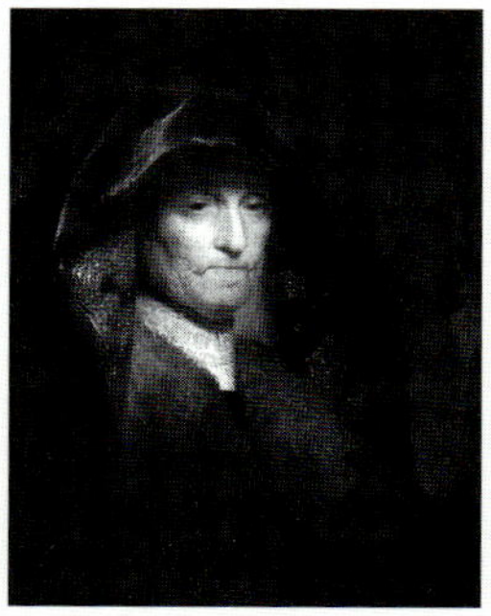

Rembrandt(?) (see fig. 8h)

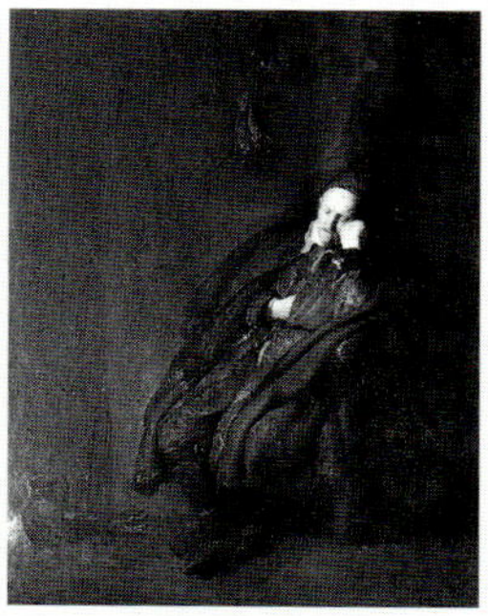

Rembrandt (see p. 46, fig. 19)

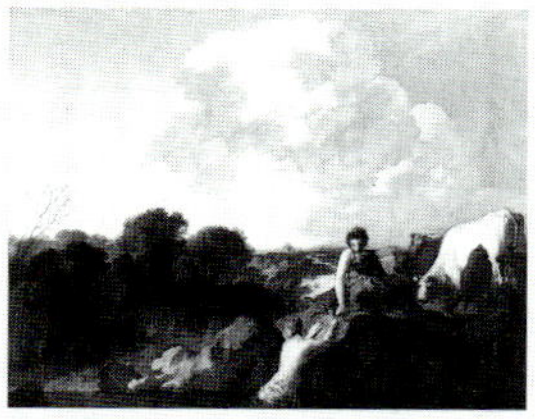

Mozes van Wtenbrouck (see fig. 8g)

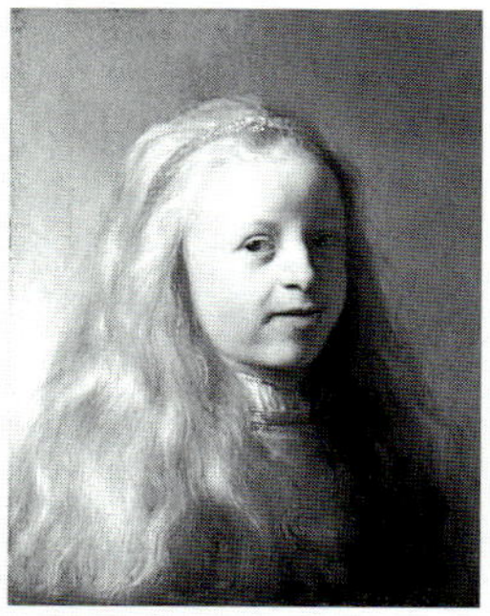

Jan Lievens (cat. no. 34)

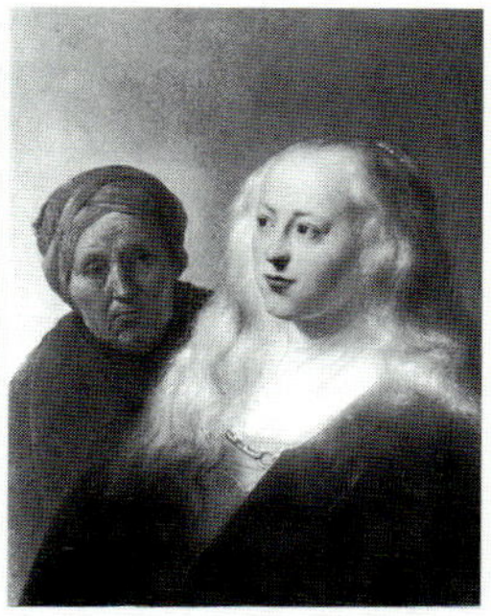

Jan Lievens (see fig. 34a)

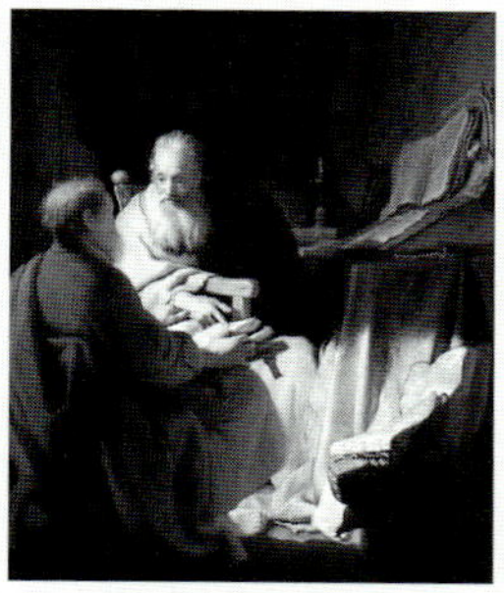

Rembrandt (cat. no. 3)

The collection of
Jacques de Gheyn III in 1641

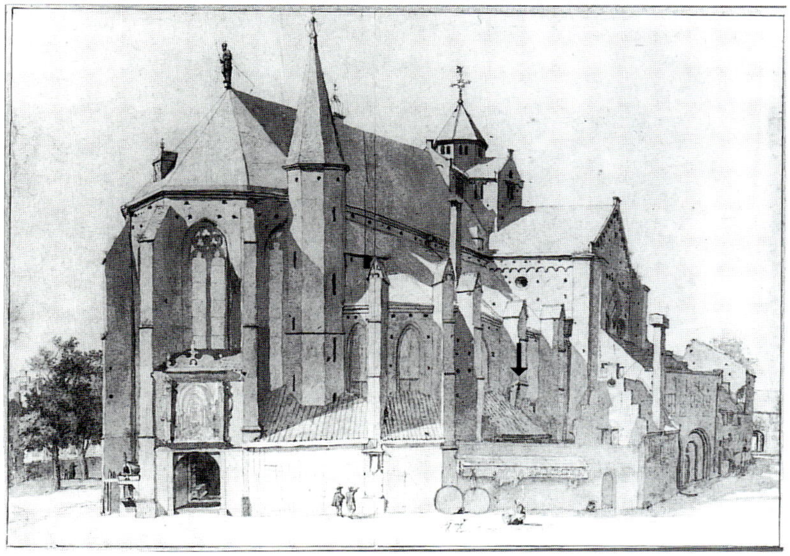

FIG. 8c
Pieter Saenredam 1597–1665
Exterior of the Mariakerk, Utrecht, from the Choir Along the North Wall
Signed and dated 12 July 1636
Pen and ink and watercolour
35.2 x 48.7 cm
Gemeentelijke Archiefdienst, Utrecht
Saenredam used this drawing as the basis for the painting of which fig. 8d is a detail.

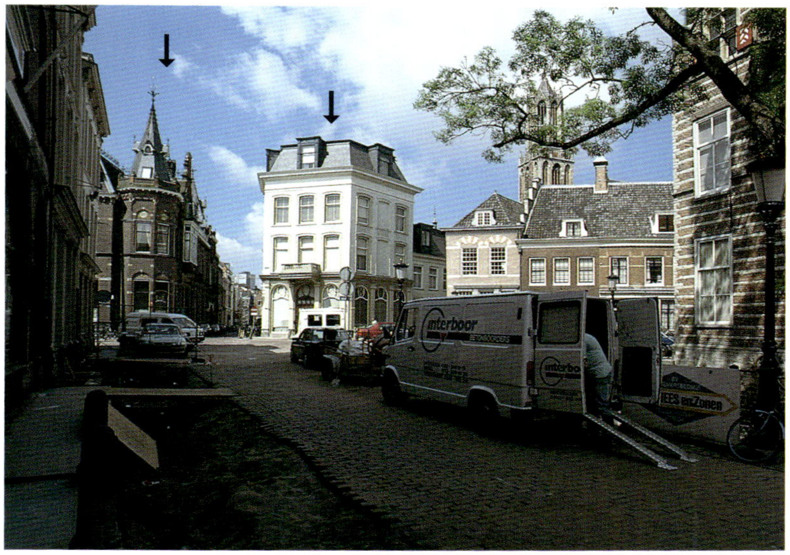

FIG. 8b
The Pausdam in Utrecht today (June 1997, during roadworks). Jacques de Gheyn lived in and kept his paintings at one of the two locations marked with an arrow. The present nineteenth-century buildings are far larger than those that stood here in de Gheyn's time. The surroundings, however, have remained largely the same. Photograph: F. L. T. Verdonk, Utrecht University.

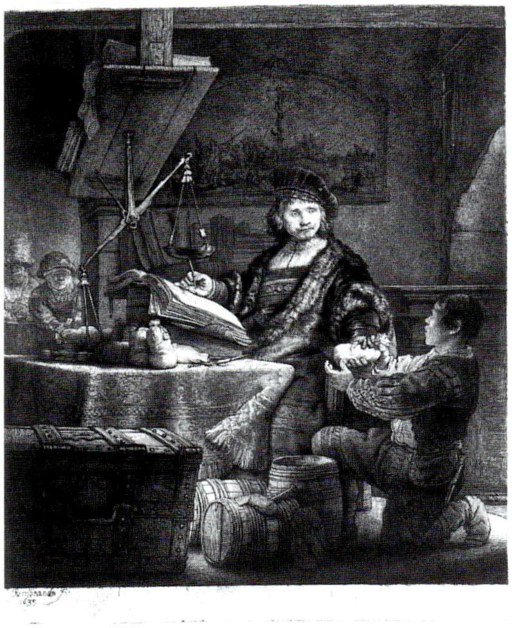

FIG. 8f
Rembrandt
Johannes Wtenbogaert, 'The Goldweigher'
Signed and dated 1639
Etching and drypoint
25.0 x 20.4 cm
Rijksprentenkabinet, Rijksmuseum, Amsterdam

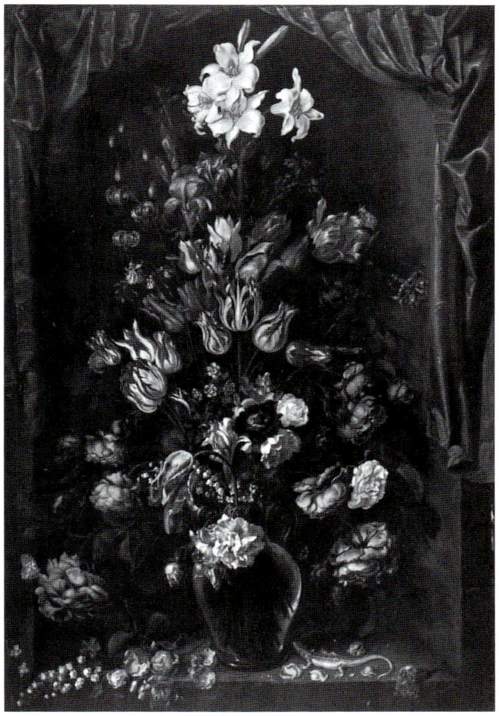

FIG. 8e
Jacques de Gheyn II 1565–1629
Large Flowerpiece
Signed and dated 1615
Panel
109.0 x 74.0 cm
Present whereabouts unknown
Photograph: RKD

FIG. 8g
Mozes van Wtenbrouck
Shepherdess and Nymph
Panel
23.0 x 27.0 cm
Kunstmuseum, Düsseldorf

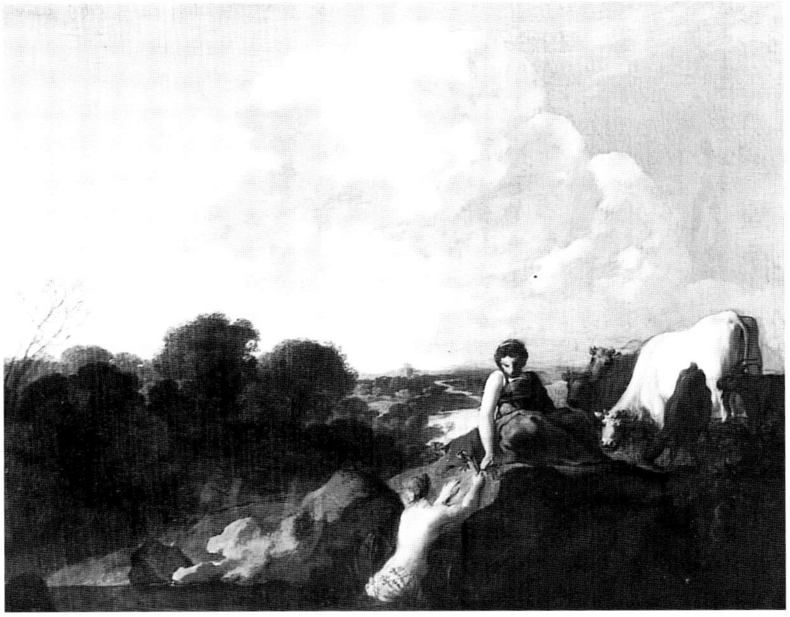

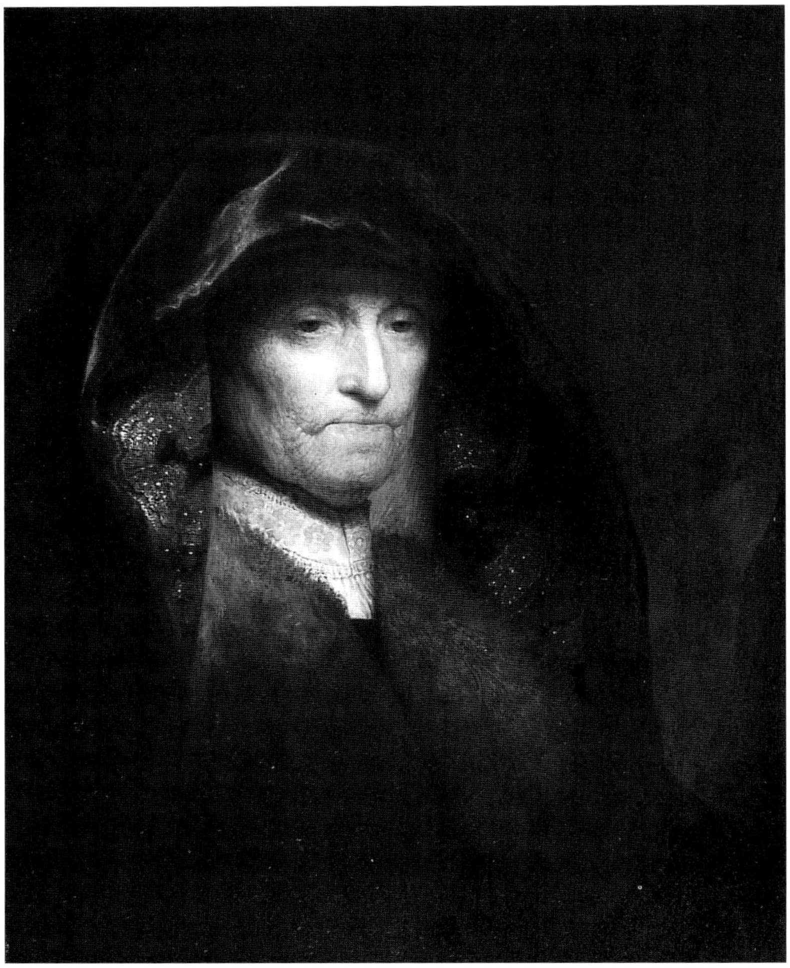

FIG. 8h
Rembrandt(?)
Bust of an Old Woman
Panel
61.0 x 47.4 cm
The Royal Collection © Her Majesty the Queen

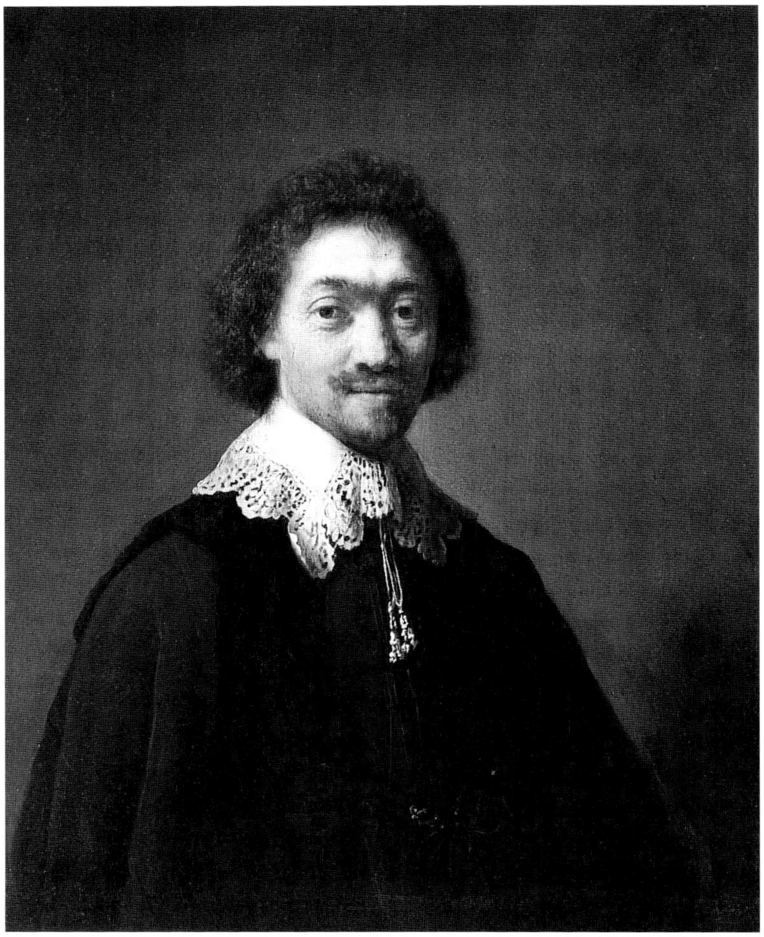

FIG. 8i
Rembrandt
Portrait of Maurits Huygens
Signed and dated 1632
Panel
31.1 x 24.5 cm
Hamburger Kunsthalle, Hamburg
Copyright Elke Walford, Hamburg

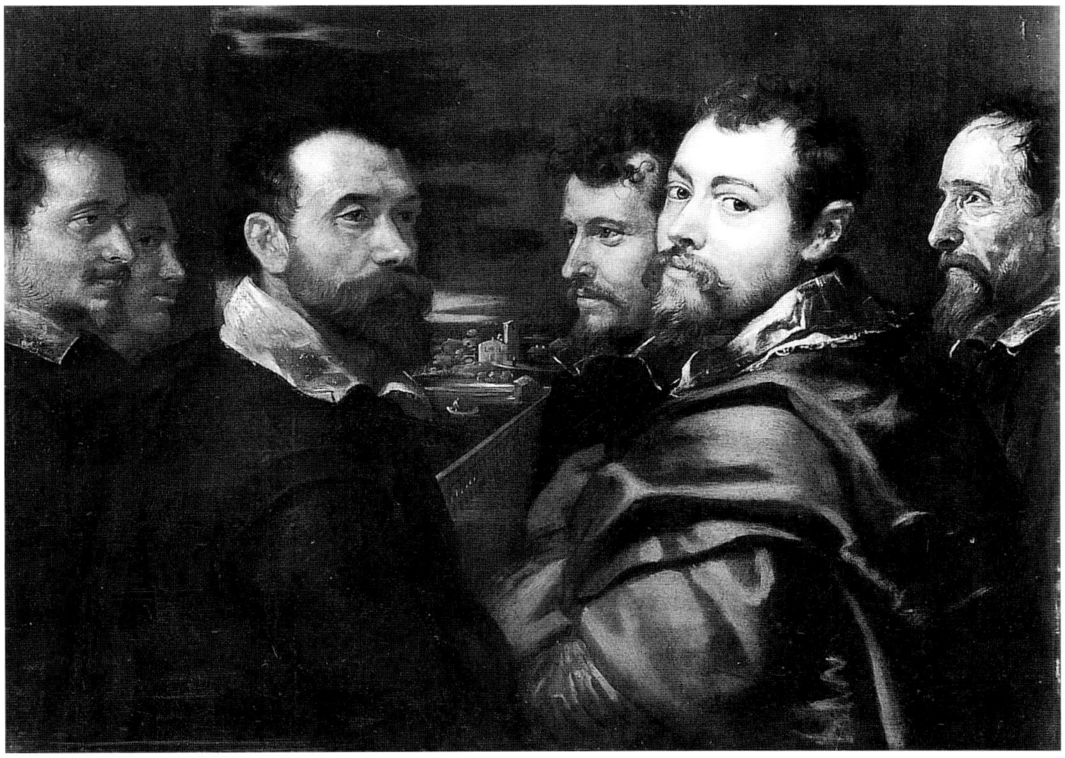

FIG. 8j
Peter Paul Rubens Flemish, 1577–1640
Self-Portrait with Five Friends
Canvas
77.5 x 161.0 cm
Wallraf-Richartz-Museum, Cologne
Photograph: Rheinisches Bildarchiv, Cologne

inventories and other documents, but none are known today).[16] François also received two landscapes of the same size by Mozes van Wtenbrouck; fig. 8g may have been one of them.[17] Like de Gheyn III, François (1606–1661) was a canon in Utrecht, in his case of the St Pieterskerk. Also a receiver of taxes in Utrecht, he held a similarly lucrative position to Johannes Wtenbogaert's in Amsterdam.[18]

De Gheyn III's will also made the following provision: 'to Mr Maurits Huygens, Secretary of the Council of States in The Hague, his, the testator's, own portrait, painted by Rembrand'.[19] The painting in question must be our cat. no. 8. After it, but in the same sentence, the will disposes to the same Maurits Huygens 'a painting of an old *tronie*, with violet velvet lined with gold cloth on the head, as large as life, in a frame'.[20] The authors of the Rembrandt *Corpus* observed that this description, including the colours, corresponds perfectly to a painting in the collection of Queen Elizabeth II (fig. 8h). They initially assumed the piece to be a Rembrandt dating from *c.*1630–31 or slightly later,[21] but finally concluded that it should rather be attributed to Lievens.[22] The piece is described as early as *c.*1639 as a Rembrandt in the English royal collection. So according to the Rembrandt team's most recent view the attribution must have been incorrect even at that early stage. The fact that the piece was already in England *c.*1639 proves in any event that it could not be the painting in de Gheyn's will of 1641. His must have been another, very similar, version.[23]

In addition to these two pieces, Maurits Huygens received three landscapes by Cornelis Vroom and a storm at sea by Jan Porcellis. It is interesting to note that in 1656 Rembrandt himself owned six paintings by Porcellis.[24]

Maurits Huygens (1595–1642), the 'H...ni' referred to in the inscription on the back of cat. no. 8, was Constantijn's one-year-older brother. In 1624 Maurits was appointed to a senior government position, succeeding his father Christiaan Huygens as Secretary of the Council of States. The pendant (*secundum*) to the present work is the *Portrait of Maurits Huygens*, which is now in Hamburg (fig. 8i).[25] The Hamburg painting is the same size, is also dated 1632, and its subject is rendered on the same scale and against a similar background. That the sitter is indeed Maurits Huygens is confirmed on this piece, too, by an old inscription on the back.

We can deduce from the two pendants that Maurits Huygens and de Gheyn III must have been close friends. Companion portraits of men are rare.[26] It may have been after hearing about the *Self-Portrait with Five Friends* that Peter Paul Rubens made in Mantua in 1602 (fig. 8j), or about his *Portrait of the Humanist Justus Lipsius with Three Pupils,* of *c.*1611–12 (Galleria Pitti, Florence), that Huygens and de Gheyn were inspired to have the pair of portraits made.[27] Maurits's brother Constantijn was an ardent admirer of both Rubens and Lipsius.[28]

The two portraits by Rembrandt were hanging in The Hague, possibly together, until 1654. De Gheyn took his own portrait with him when he moved to Utrecht, but took steps to ensure that it would be reunited with the picture of Maurits Huygens (the *secundum*) after his death. The paintings remained together until the auction of 1786 (see Provenance). They were recently said not to be 'true' pendants at all, as the light in the pictures enters from different sides, but this view is hardly plausible.[29]

In January and February 1633, the year after the portraits were made, Constantijn Huygens wrote eight Latin epigrams in couplets on de Gheyn's portrait (not on that of his own brother Maurits). In one of these epigrams he mentions Rembrandt's name, so there is no doubt that they refer to cat. no. 8: 'Rembrantis est manus ista Gheinij vultus / Mirare, lector, et iste Gheinius non est' (This is the hand of Rembrandt, the face of de Gheyn / Look in wonder, reader, it also is not de Gheyn). Each of the eight poems gives a different twist to the same theme: the portrait does not resemble de Gheyn. In modern times it has been suggested that Huygens was expressing the neoplatonic idea that an image of a person is not the person as such.[30] It has also been thought that the verses were written out of spite towards

Rembrandt,[31] though this is highly improbable. Some years later, in 1644, when Constantijn Huygens published the verses as *Joci* (jokes) in his anthology *Momenta desultoria*, he had the discretion to omit one poem only – and that was precisely the poem in which Rembrandt is named. Huygens must honestly have believed that Rembrandt's portrait did not resemble de Gheyn.[32] Rembrandt received more than one complaint to this effect about his portraits. In 1654, a Portuguese merchant insisted that the artist change a commissioned portrait of 'a certain young lady' (seeckere jonge dochter), which in the merchant's view did not 'look remotely like her' (op verre nae niet en gelijckt) (see p. 77). Rembrandt refused to alter the picture.[33]

In considering Constantijn Huygens's criticism of cat. no. 8, we should not forget that he was the first (*c*.1629–30) to write lengthy paeans to the work of the then 23-year-old Rembrandt and the 22-year-old Lievens. Huygens's friend, and neighbour in the Hague, Jacques de Gheyn III also held Rembrandt in high esteem: the two Rembrandts owned by de Gheyn III in addition to the companion portraits date from 1628 and 1629 (see cat. no. 3 and p. 46, fig. 19), and de Gheyn may have bought them shortly after they were made. Maurits Huygens shared his brother Constantijn's and de Gheyn's admiration for Rembrandt, for he would not otherwise have had the artist portray him together with de Gheyn.

On 3 April 1635 the Utrecht lawyer and art connoisseur Arnold van Buchel made an interesting note in his journal, saying that he had visited de Gheyn in Utrecht, where he saw his shell collection, the flowerpiece by de Gheyn II (fig. 8e) and some of his works on paper, as well as a variety of other objects – all of which are mentioned in de Gheyn III's will of 1641. In addition, van Buchel studied a variety of prints. Finally, he 'also saw [at de Gheyn's] paintings by Rembrandt of Leiden and Jan Lievens'.[34] Brief as it is, this is the oldest attestation to the superior collection of paintings discussed here, and this is what makes it so interesting. Van Buchel apparently considered only the paintings by Rembrandt and Lievens worth mentioning, apart from work by the father of his host, and the prints that caught his eye. For he says nothing about the works by Porcellis, Vroom, C. de Hooch and Poelenburch, or van Wtenbrouck, that appear in de Gheyn's will.

AB/MB

1 *Nicolaes Ruts*, 1631, Frick Collection, New York (p. 70, fig. 2); *A Man Sitting*, 1631, Hermitage, St Petersburg; *A Man Seated*, 1631–32, Kunsthistorisches Museum, Vienna; *Portrait of Marten Looten*, 1632, Los Angeles County Museum of Art; *Joris de Caullery*, 1632, M. H. de Young Memorial Museum, San Francisco; *A Man Trimming His Quill*, 1632, Gemäldegalerie, Kassel; *The Artist as a Burgher*, Glasgow Art Gallery; *A 40-Year-Old Man*, Metropolitan Museum of Art, New York; *A Young Man*, formerly on the art market (*Corpus*, vol. II, 1986, nos A43, A44, A45, A52, A53, A54, A58, A59, A60).

2 With the portrait of Maurits Huygens (see below), the present picture was described as in a 'manière moins libre que celle de différens ouvrages connus de Rembrandt, nous fait juger qu'ils ont été peints dans sa jeunesse, & pendant qu'il suivoit l'Ecole de Gerardow' (*Corpus*, vol. II, 1986, p. 224).

3 Van Regteren Altena 1983, vol. I, p. 155; Judson 1973.

4 Van Regteren Altena 1983, vol. I, p. 132.

5 Huygens / Kan 1946, p. 71.

6 Van Regteren Altena 1983, vol. II, pp. 162–77.

7 Rembrandt's two versions of the *Apostle Paul*, at the Staatsgalerie Stuttgart (fig. 2a) and the Germanisches Nationalmuseum, Nuremberg (*Corpus*, vol. I, 1982, nos A11, A26), are said to have been influenced by de Gheyn III's etching of *Paul* (our fig. 8a) and/or by his *Philosopher Chilo* (*Corpus*, vol. I, pp. 148, 270). Schwartz 1984, fig. 85, reproduces the *Philosopher Chilo*, with further interesting suggestions.

8 Van Regteren Altena 1983, vol. I, p. 160.

9 Van Regteren Altena 1936, p. 128: 'zieckelick van lichaem te bedde leggende, edoch sijn verstant, memorie ende vijff sinnen wel machtich sijnde, als claerlick bleecke'. For de Gheyn's death, see Van Regteren Altena 1983, vol. I, p. 164.

10 Van Regteren Altena 1936, p. 129: 'soe in zijn, comparants, jegenwoordich logement wesende als op die camer boven het capittelhuys vande kercke van Ste Marien alhier binnen Utrecht'.

11 Van Regteren Altena 1936, p. 101. Van Helsdingen was described in a property transfer register as an 'innkeeper' (GAU, Municipal Archives II, 3243, Property Transfer Register, pp. 203–4). He was living on Oudmunstertrans at the time of his marriage on 20 April 1637 (GAU, DTB 96, Reformed Church Marriages, p. 89). According to other documents, he moved to the Janskerkhof after his marriage. However, he presumably kept the house where de Gheyn had his lodgings, and this would explain why de Gheyn's will refers to him as being 'at the home of Mr Gerrit van Helsdingen'. We are grateful to Dr M. J. Bok of Utrecht for this information.

12 Dr J. E. A. L. Struick, Utrecht, letter and documentation, 11 March 1997. Dr Struick died suddenly on 1 May 1997.

13 Van Regteren Altena 1983, vol. II, p. 21, no. 41, assumes the work reproduced here to be the flower painting in question.

14 Van Regteren Altena 1936, p. 129: 'Noch een out slapent manneken bij een vuyr sittende, sijn hant inden bosem hebbende mede van Rembrand gemaeckt'. For the Turin painting, see *Corpus*, vol. I, 1982, pp. 202–7, no. A17.

15 For Wtenbogaert, see Schwartz 1984, passim.

16 P. van den Brink, in Utrecht / Frankfurt / Luxembourg 1993–94, p. 188 and note 12.

17 In Weisner's oeuvre catalogue of Wtenbrouck's work, fig. 8g and a *Shepherd and Shepherdess*, both in Düsseldorf, are the only surviving companion pieces by this outstanding landscape painter from The Hague (Weisner 1964, p. 221, nos 20, 21, figs 14, 15).

18 For François Wtenbogaert, see genealogy in Rogge 1868, vol. I, fold-out sheet and p. 293, note 36.

19 Van Regteren Altena 1936, p. 129: 'aenden Heere Maurits Huygens, secretaris vanden Raedt van Staten inden Hage, sijn, comparants, eygen conterfeytsel bij Rembrand geschildert'.

20 Van Regteren Altena 1936, p. 129: 'ende een schilderije van een oude tronigne, die violet fluweel mit goude laecken gevoedert op het hooft heeft, wesende soe groot als het leven mit een lijst daerom'. Van Regteren Altena 1983, vol. I, p. 154, assumed this to be a Rembrandt as well.

21 *Corpus*, vol. I, 1982, pp. 315–21, no. A32.

22 *Corpus*, vol. II, 1986, p. 839.

23 For the piece belonging to Her Majesty Queen Elizabeth II, and this question, see also White 1982, pp. 101–3, no. 158. White points out that the various titles by which the painting was later known – 'Portrait of the Countess of Desmond' (given in the time of Queen Anne), 'Rembrandt's Mother' (held since Horace Walpole) and 'The Prophetess Anna' (proposed by C. Tümpel in 1968) – do not correspond to the earliest description of *c*.1639. At that time the painting was simply described as 'an old woeman with a great scarfe uppon her heade with a peaked falling band'. Tümpel subsequently revised his opinion, as he later referred to the piece as *Rembrandt's Mother as a Historical Figure* and attributed it to Jan Lievens (Tümpel 1986, no. A54). For this painting, see also Schwartz 1984, pp. 65–6.

24 Strauss & Van der Meulen 1979, pp. 353, 355, 357, no. 1656/12.

25 *Corpus*, vol. II, 1986, no. A57.

26 Schwartz 1984, p. 96, suggests precedents.

27 Suggested orally by R. E. O. Ekkart, The Hague.

28 For Constantijn Huygens's admiration for Rubens, see Huygens / Kan 1946, pp. 73–4. According to an entry in his journal, Monconys had seen 'tous les livres & papiers de Lipse' (i.e. Lipsius) at Huygens's home in 1663 (Monconys 1667, p. 150).

29 The idea was advanced in *Corpus*, vol. II, 1986, pp. 222, 228, and by P. van Thiel, in Berlin / Amsterdam / London 1991–92a, p. 152, cat. nos 11, 12. However, the sitters in the two portraits are turned three-quarters to face one another, as in other counterpart portraits. The two pictures also correspond in terms of format, etc.

30 Tümpel 1986, pp. 133, 381, note 120. Cf. Slive 1953, pp. 19–20.

31 Schwartz 1984, p. 96.

32 P. van Thiel, in Berlin / Amsterdam / London 1991–92a, p. 153, cat. nos 11, 12; cf. De Jongh 1986, p. 21.

33 Strauss & Van der Meulen 1979, pp. 310–11, no. 1654/4. De Jongh 1986, p. 20, had earlier quoted the merchant's complaint, in this connection.

34 Strauss & Van der Meulen 1979, p. 117, no. 1635/3.

9
Bust of an Old Man
(grisaille)

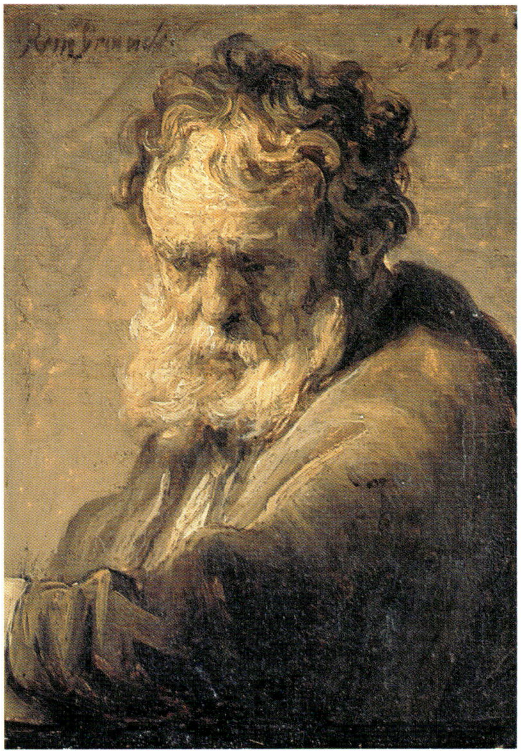

Signed and dated along upper margin
Rembrandt. 1633.
Paper pasted on panel
10.8 x 7.0 cm
Private collection, London

PROVENANCE: (Possibly) Mrs van Sonsbeeck before 1751; sale, Fr. Szarvady, Paris, 21 February 1874, lot 39; V. Boric, Paris, 1881; sale (anonymous), Paris, 1900, where bought by F. Kleinberger, Paris, from whom acquired by Baron Emile Janssen, Brussels; his sale, Amsterdam (Frederik Muller), 26 April 1927, lot 94, to dealer M. Knoedler & Co., New York, for 32,000 florins; Andrew Mellon, Washington DC, by 1935; Paul Mellon, Washington DC; Arthur Armory Houghton, Jr, Queenstown, Maryland, by 1955; Richard L. Feigen & Co., from whom acquired by Saul P. Steinberg, 1986; his sale, New York (Sotheby's), 30 January 1997, lot 39.

LITERATURE: Hofstede de Groot 1908–27, vol. VI, 1916, p. 206, no. 369; Bredius 1937, no. 183; Bredius / Gerson 1969, no. 136; *Corpus*, vol. II, 1986, pp. 351–4, no. A74; Tümpel 1986, no. 134; Adams 1988, p. 103, no. 38; Slatkes 1992, no. 213; sale cat., Sotheby's, New York, 30 January 1997, lot 39 (with earlier literature).

The size of a playing card, this painting is the smallest known by Rembrandt. Though it has little colour, being in shades ranging from dark brown through yellowish-brown to white, it is nevertheless a finished painting.[1] With broad brushstrokes and pronounced chiaroscuro, Rembrandt has conjured up the image of an old, bearded man sitting opposite us, peering at something and frowning. One arm is extended, and perhaps rests on the arm of a chair. The man's tousled hair and unkempt beard add extra liveliness to this tiny painting.

Rembrandt apparently delighted in this type of character study of elderly, bearded men. In 1630 and 1631, shortly before executing this painting of 1633, he made four etchings of the subject, all roughly the same size as the painting. These etchings, as well as the painting, are reproduced at actual size in the present catalogue (figs 9a–9d). Etching B.260 in particular has been linked to the painting (fig. 9c).[2] In one etching the hair and beard are relatively neat (fig. 9a), in another as wild as the sea (fig. 9d). In the painting they are somewhat tousled. In all cases the figure leans slightly forward, so that the forehead is large in relation to the rest of the face. The figure in the larger *Bearded Old Man* of *c.*1630 is portrayed in a similar fashion, although his hair is a less prominent feature (cat. no. 4).

As Rembrandt made several grisailles as designs for etchings, it has been suggested that cat. no. 9, which is also a grisaille, was likewise meant as a modello for an etching.[3] The piece has also been compared with a half-length drawing of an old man that Rembrandt made for an *album amicorum* in 1634. It was suggested that the painting 'may have had a comparable purpose, and this could explain the prominent signature and date'.[4] An *album amicorum* is a book that is stored with the leaves closed. An oil painting has relief and is therefore not suited to being kept in this way.

Rembrandt based this painting (cat. no. 9) and the corresponding etchings (figs 9a–9d) on the chalk drawings after a live model – an elderly man seated on a folding chair – that he executed around the same time (fig. 9e, *c.*1630–31).[5] In this case the figure is portrayed full-length. The drawing is accordingly larger than the painting and the etchings. The sheet is also reproduced here at actual size, allowing the proportions to be compared. In the painting (cat. no. 9) and the etchings (figs 9a–9d) Rembrandt condensed the drawing 'from life' to no more than the figure's head, arm, and either one or both shoulders. He did the same in the late 1640s with his drawings 'from life' of a *Woman in Bed* (see fig. 14a and cat. no. 82), reducing the figure to a single, well-considered principal motif in his painting of a *Young Woman in Bed* (cat. no. 14).

AB

1 *Corpus*, vol. II, 1986, p. 353, dismisses Gerson's idea that it might be a fragment (cf. H. Gerson, in Bredius / Gerson 1969, p. 563, no. 183).

2 Notably a print with additional drawing possibly by Rembrandt himself, in the Rijksprentenkabinet in Amsterdam (our fig. 9c); see *Corpus*, vol. II, 1986, p. 353, fig. 3. I am grateful to Iris Holthuizen for collecting the other illustrations.

3 Suggested, but also dismissed, in *Corpus*, vol. II, 1986, p. 353; see also Slatkes 1992, no. 213.

4 *Corpus*, vol. II, 1986, p. 353. For the *album amicorum*, see Strauss & Van der Meulen 1979, p. 111, no. 1634/6.

5 For these chalk drawings, see Benesch 1973, vol. I, no. 20, fig. 20, monogrammed and dated 1631 (for this drawing, see also P. Schatborn, in Berlin / Amsterdam / London 1991–92d, cat. no. 2); Benesch 1973, vol. I, no. 40, fig. 49, monogrammed and dated 1631, Teylers Museum, Haarlem; Benesch 1973, vol. I, no. 41, fig. 50 (fig. 9e in the present catalogue).

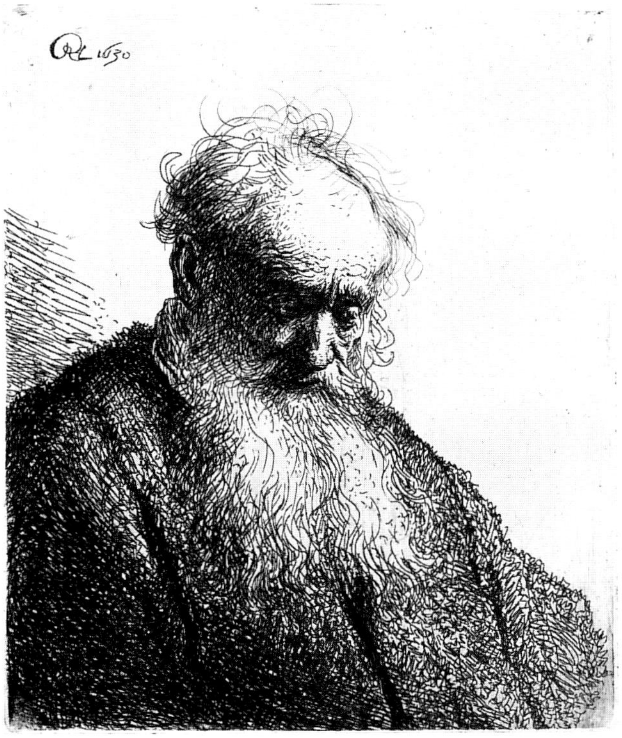

FIG. 9a
Rembrandt
Old Man with Flowing Beard
Monogrammed and dated 1630
Etching B.309
9.8 x 8.1 cm
Rijksprentenkabinet, Rijksmuseum, Amsterdam

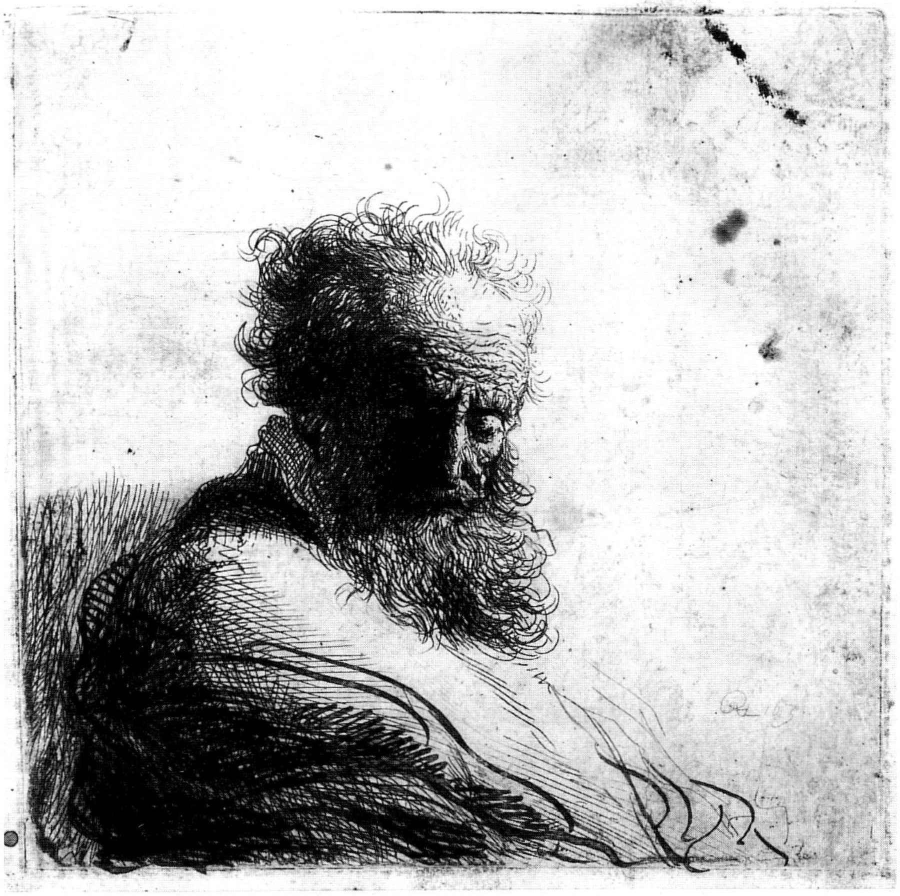

FIG. 9c
Rembrandt
Bust of an Old Bearded Man
Monogrammed and dated 1631
Etching B.260, with corrections (by Rembrandt?) in pen and ink
11.9 x 11.7 cm
Rijksprentenkabinet, Rijksmuseum, Amsterdam

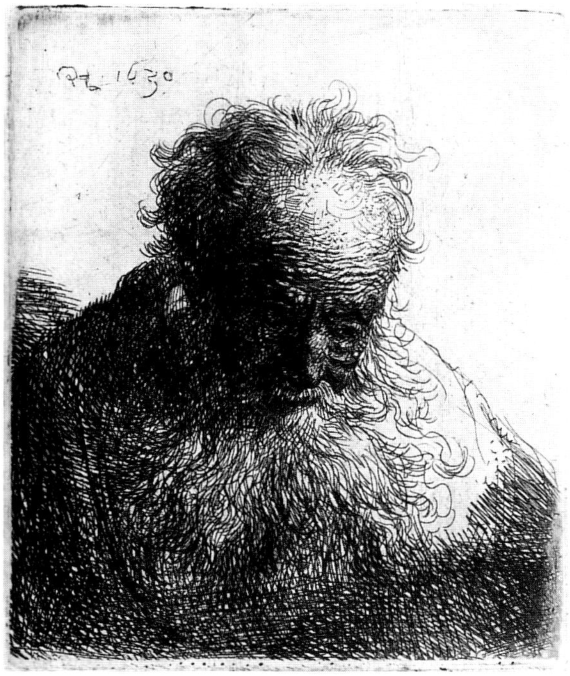

FIG. 9b
Rembrandt
Bust of an Old Man with a Flowing Beard
Monogrammed and dated 1630
Etching B.325
9.1 x 7.6 cm
Rijksprentenkabinet, Rijksmuseum, Amsterdam

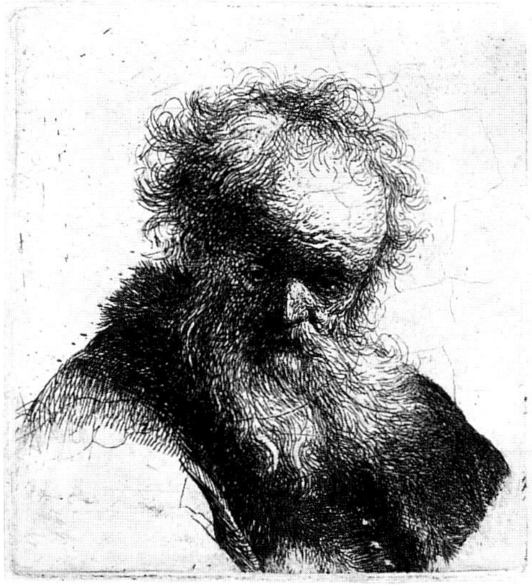

FIG. 9d
Rembrandt
Bust of an Old Man with Flowing Beard
*c.*1630
Etching B.291
7.1 x 6.4 cm
Rijksprentenkabinet, Rijksmuseum, Amsterdam

Cat. no. 9 and figs 9a–9e are reproduced at actual size.

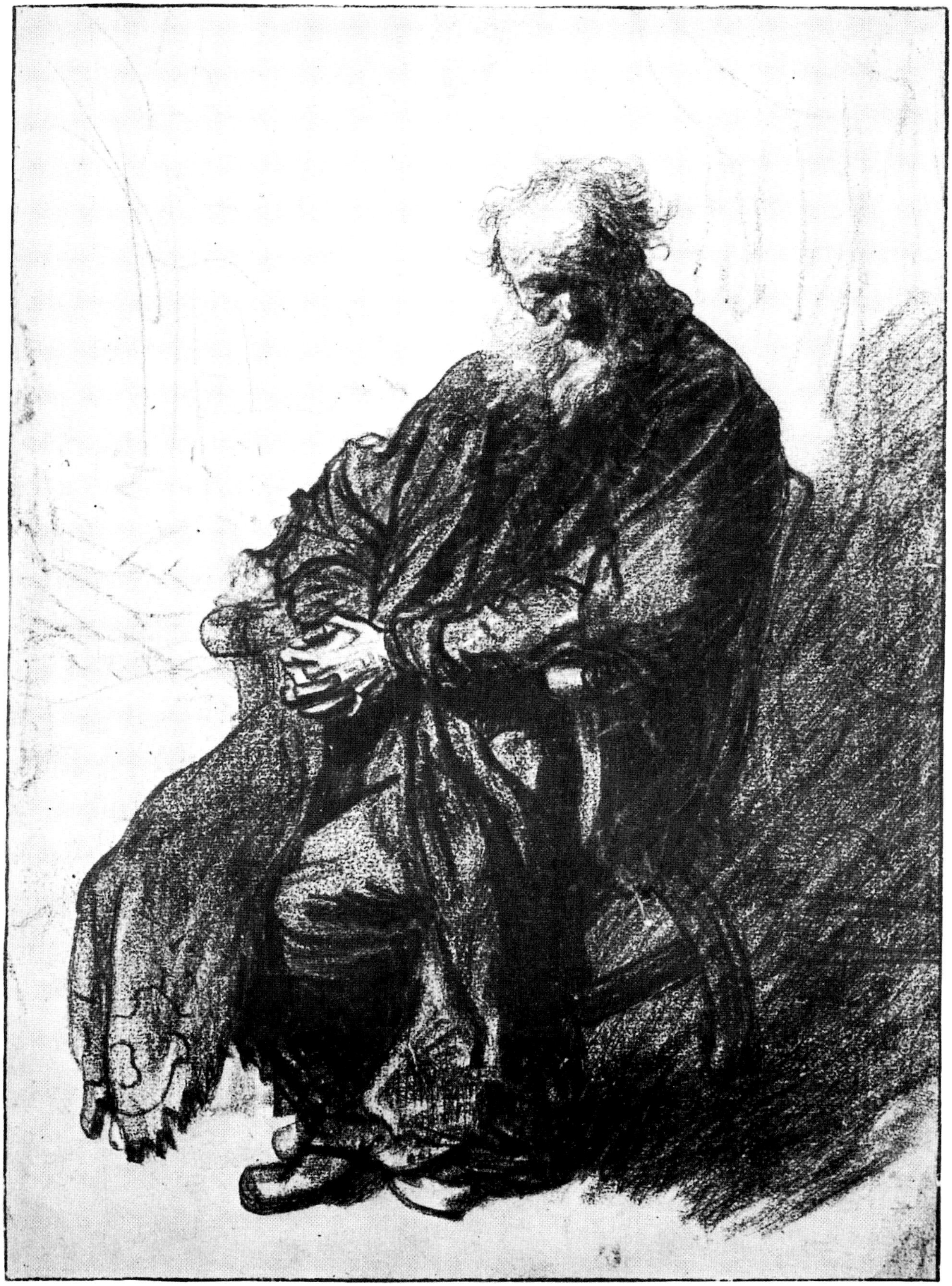

FIG. 9e
Rembrandt
Old Man with Clasped Hands, Seated in an Armchair
Chalk
22.6 x 15.7 cm
Staatliche Museen zu Berlin, Kupferstichkabinett

10

Susanna

Signed and dated lower right *Rembr[ant] f 163[6]*
Panel
47.4 x 38.6 cm (a strip measuring 4 cm has been added to the right-hand side)
Royal Cabinet of Paintings, Mauritshuis, The Hague

PROVENANCE: Sale, P. J. Snijers, Antwerp, from 23 May 1758, to Fierens for 157 guilders; sale, Govert van Slingeland, The Hague, 18 May 1768, lot 12 (as 'Bathsheba Bathing'), to Collection of the Stadholder William V (sold before 1 March); Louvre, Paris, 1795–1815; Koninklijk Kabinet van Schilderijen Galerij Willem V, The Hague, 1815; Koninklijk Kabinet van Schilderijen Mauritshuis, The Hague.

LITERATURE: Reynolds 1801, vol. II, pp. 344–5; Vosmaer 1877, p. 163; Hofstede de Groot 1908–27, vol. VI, 1916, pp. 53–4, no. 57; Bredius / Gerson 1969, no. 505; De Vries, Tóth-Ubbens & Froentjes 1978, pp. 121–31; Schwartz 1984, p. 173; Tümpel 1986, no. 14; J. Gregory, in Gregory & Zdanowicz 1988, pp. 52–3; *Corpus*, vol. III, 1989, pp. 196–201, no. A117; P. van Thiel, in Berlin / Amsterdam / London 1991–92a, pp. 196–9, cat. no. 25; Broos 1993, no. 32; Sluijter 1993a.

This picture illustrates an episode from the apocryphal part of the Book of Daniel (Daniel 13:1–64). The 'very fair' Susanna, who was married to the 'great rich' Joacim, goes to wash 'in the garden: for it was hot'. She has sent her maids to close the doors to the garden (in the background we see her palatial home and the walls enclosing the garden). Believing herself alone, Susanna has undressed and has laid her clothing down behind her. Her toiletries are on a pedestal at her side. To her left is a staircase leading down to the bathing pool. But now she suddenly leans forward, covering her breasts with her left arm, and clutches the hem of her white gown to her lap. She looks out at us in fear and dismay.

Rembrandt has recorded the moment at which Susanna hears the two men who have hidden in the bushes behind her. We catch a glimpse of one man's face but see no more than a fragment of his accomplice's plumed turban. These are the two elders and magistrates whose 'lust was inflamed' towards Susanna. They have hatched a plot to confront and forcibly seduce her by threatening to accuse her of adultery. Knowing she will be condemned to death, the chaste Susanna will nevertheless choose to die innocent, refusing to yield to her pursuers. It is only the intervention of the prophet Daniel that eventually saves her from execution.

The episode of Susanna Bathing was represented by artists from early Christian times on. After the Renaissance, artists chose to portray Susanna naked, and the theme gained immense popularity. Countless works have been proposed as Rembrandt's example and reference point, from antique sculptures (fig. 77b) to contemporary paintings and prints. The most similar, in terms of Susanna's pose and entourage, is a painting of 1614 by Rembrandt's teacher Pieter Lastman (fig. 10a). It becomes even more likely that this work inspired Rembrandt when we find that he had made a drawing of it (cat. no. 77) a short time before his painting. However, Susanna looking at the observer while leaning forward to conceal her nakedness was probably based on a print after Rubens (fig. 10b).[1]

Lastman shows the elders approaching Susanna and addressing her with words and gestures. In the print after Rubens we see them tearing her clothes from her body. Rembrandt alone shows the two men still in hiding, almost invisible to the viewer.[2] It has been suggested that Susanna's gaze turned towards us is imploring our help,[3] yet also that we too indulge in the same voyeuristic pleasure as the two villains in the bush.[4]

Some of Rembrandt's Dutch contemporaries were offended and outraged by erotic subjects of this kind in paintings. The depiction of Susanna bathing was singled out by a Dutch poet as a target of righteous wrath, and as a 'cancer on morality and a venom for the eyes'. Rubens, on the other hand, referred in a letter to a picture of Susanna as 'una galanteria'. The reply from the elderly gentleman to whom this letter was addressed was that he had every confidence that Rubens's painting would 'prove beautiful enough to enamour even old men'.[5] Hence the subject obviously aroused different responses in Rembrandt's day, though the erotic aspect never failed to attract attention.

The English painter Joshua Reynolds commented on the picture in 1781: 'It appears very extraordinary that Rembrandt should have taken so much pains, and have made at last so very ugly and ill-favoured a figure'.[6] The director of the Mauritshuis expressed a similar view in 1826–30: 'One searches in vain in this Susanna for the attractions with which other painters have usually endowed her; the figure is very vulgar, and even were it not Rembrandt's work, one would say it is badly drawn'.[7] Not until 1877 was a word spoken in her defence: 'No, this woman is not

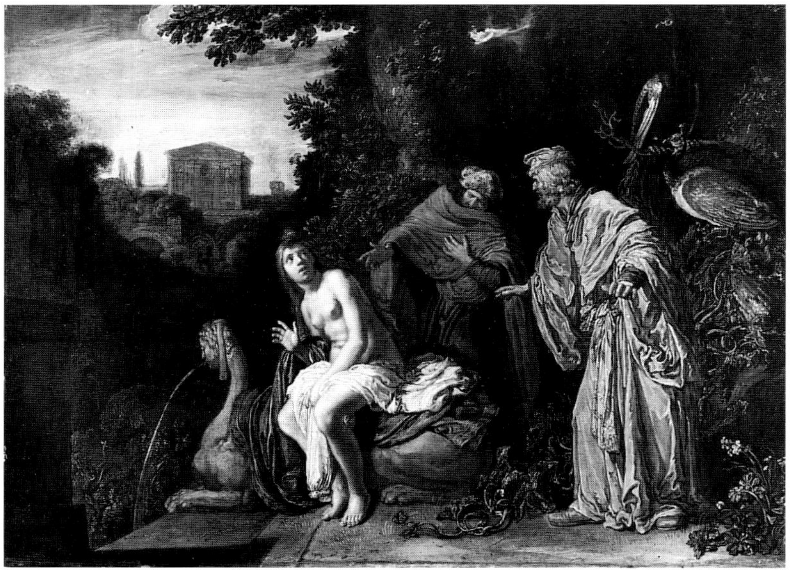

FIG. 10a
Pieter Lastman 1583–1633
Susanna and the Elders
Signed and dated 1614
Panel
42.0 x 58.0 cm
Staatliche Museen zu Berlin, Gemäldegalerie

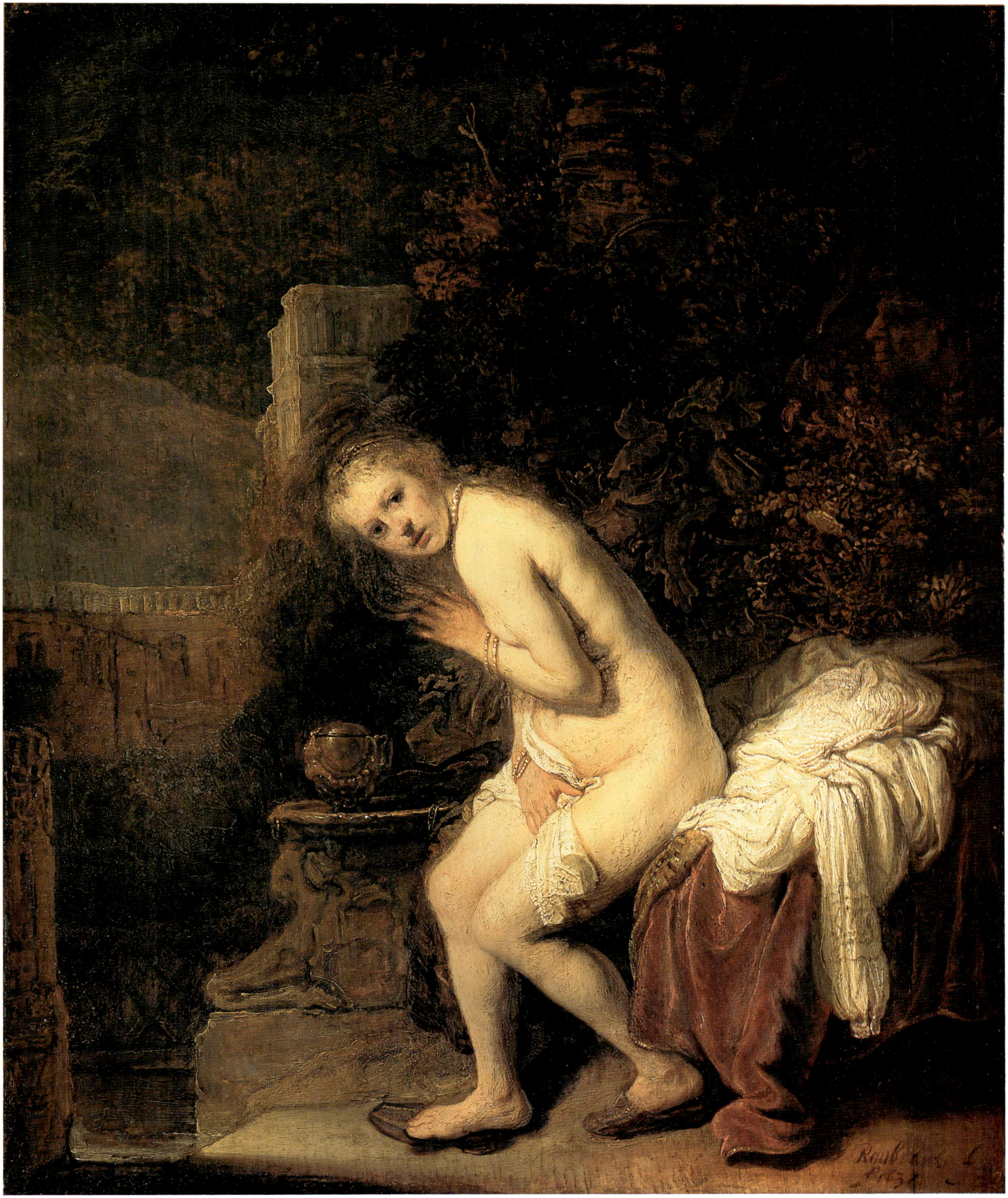

ugly', Vosmaer wrote, and yet even this is qualified: 'only a few minor changes would make her quite comely'.[8] In our own times it has been argued that Rembrandt's nudes from this period would have embodied the contemporary ideal of beauty.[9] But as early as 1681 Andries Pels spoke of Rembrandt's women in disparaging terms: 'When he [Rembrandt] painted a nude woman / He chose no Greek Venus as his model / But rather a washerwoman or a treader of peat from a barn ... / ... Flabby breasts / Ill shaped hands ... ' etc.[10] It would therefore be surprising if Rembrandt's nudes, much-criticized from (before?) 1681 to at least 1877, were indeed considered beautiful in their day.

Rembrandt was seeking to achieve the 'maximum and most natural movement'[11] and/or 'innate emotion', rather than physical beauty. This emerges from his representation of *Ganymede*, which dates from around the same time (1635) (fig. 10c).[12] Ganymede's ravishing beauty caused Jupiter to transform himself into an eagle and carry him away. Rembrandt, however, turned Ganymede into an odious child – wriggling, squealing and urinating. We can assume that his Susanna, too, was meant above all to be real. For Rembrandt's later version on the theme of Susanna and the Elders, see commentary to cat. no. 77 and p. 20, fig. 3.

AB/MB

1 Observed by J. Gregory, in Gregory & Zdanowicz 1988, p. 52; see also P. van Thiel, in Berlin / Amsterdam / London 1991–92a, pp. 198–9, cat. no. 25 (after a suggestion by Jan Kelch).

2 Sluijter 1993a, p. 42. On these grounds the Mauritshuis interpreted the picture for some time as 'Bathsheba Bathing'. The mansion in the background was taken to be the palace from which David saw her (De Vries, Tóth-Ubbens & Froentjes 1978, p. 126). The piece was also listed as 'Une Batseba ... ' in the auction of 18 May 1768 (see Provenance).

3 P. van Thiel, in Berlin / Amsterdam / London 1991–92a, p. 199, cat. no. 25.

4 Sluijter 1993a, esp. p. 41.

5 Sluijter 1993a, p. 38 (citing the poet Raphael Camphuyzen, Rubens, and Sir Dudley Carlton).

6 Reynolds 1801, vol. II, pp. 344–5.

7 Steengracht van Oost-Capelle 1826–30, no. 27 (previously cited by De Vries, Tóth-Ubbens & Froentjes 1978, p. 126).

8 Vosmaer 1877, p. 163: 'Non, cette femme n'est pas laide, il ne faudrait que de très-légers changements pour la rendre jolie'.

9 Hollander 1975, pp. 108, 160; Reznicek 1977, pp. 91–9.

10 Slive 1953, p. 102 (original Dutch text on p. 210).

11 Strauss & Van der Meulen 1979, p. 161, no. 1639/2: 'meeste ende die naetuereelste beweechgelickheijt' (Rembrandt letter, 12 January 1639).

12 *Corpus*, vol. III, 1989, no. A113.

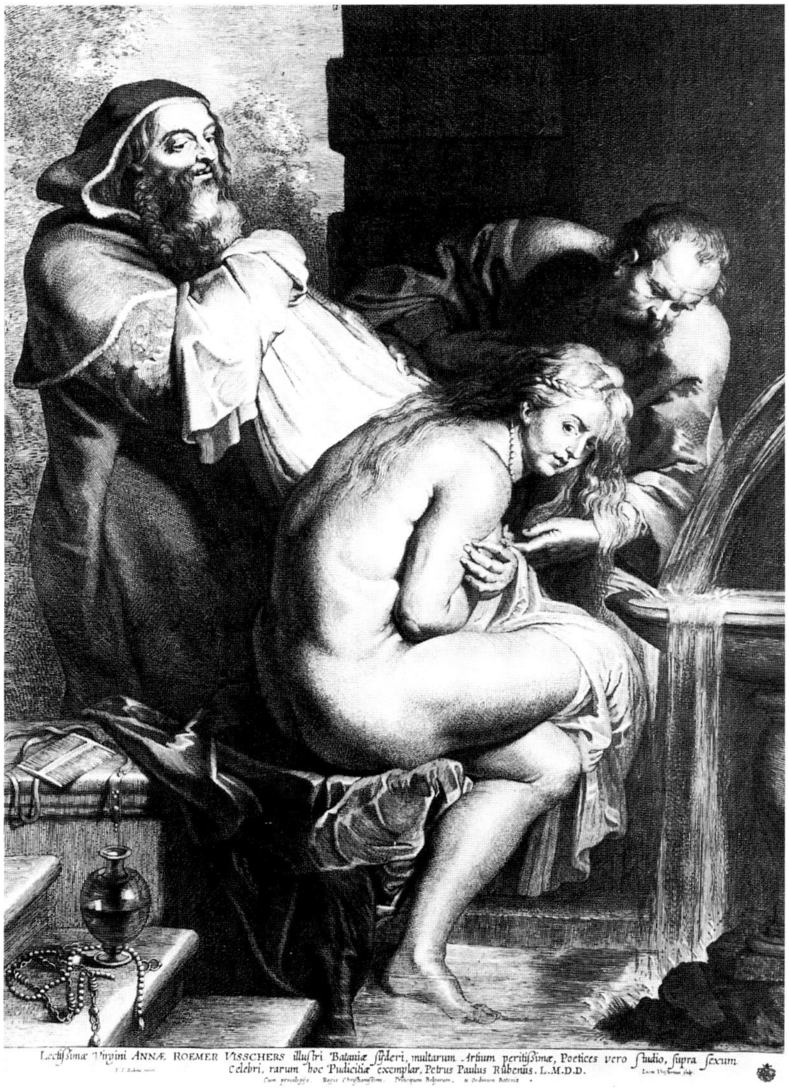

FIG. 10b
Lucas Vorsterman (1595–1675), after Peter Paul Rubens
Susanna and the Elders 1620(?)
Engraving
38.7 x 28.0 cm
Rijksprentenkabinet, Rijksmuseum, Amsterdam

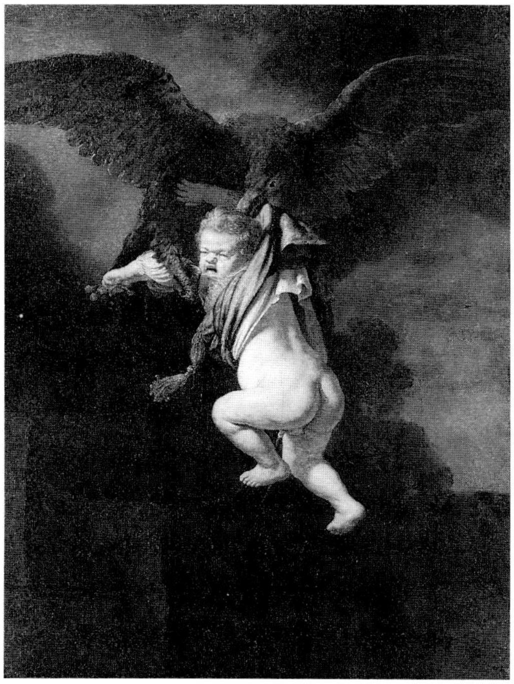

FIG. 10c
Rembrandt
Ganymede Abducted by Jupiter
Signed and dated 1635
Canvas
177.0 x 130.0 cm
Staatliche Kunstsammlungen Dresden, Gemäldegalerie Alte Meister
(for colour reproduction, see p. 35, fig. 3)

11

Landscape with a Stone Bridge

*c.*1638–40

Panel
29.5 x 42.3 cm
Rijksmuseum, Amsterdam

PROVENANCE: Sale, Lapeyrière, Paris, from 14 April 1817, lot 46, to Huybens for 1505 frs; James Gray, Versailles, 1863; Marquess of Landsdowne, Bowood, 1883; sale, James Reiss, London (Christie's), 12 May 1900, lot 63; purchased by the Rijksmuseum with support from Dr A. Bredius and the Rembrandt Association.

LITERATURE: Michel 1893, p. 314; Hofstede de Groot 1908–27, vol. VI, 1916, p. 429, no. 939; Van de Waal 1958; Stechow 1966, p. 58; Bredius / Gerson 1969, no. 440; Schwartz 1984, p. 249; Tümpel 1986, no. 260; J. Bruyn, in Amsterdam / Boston / Philadelphia 1987–88, pp. 97–8; C. J. de Bruyn Kops, in Amsterdam / Boston / Philadelphia 1987–88, pp. 426–32, cat. no. 76; *Corpus*, vol. III, 1989, pp. 357–61, no. A136; Schneider 1990, no. 1; P. van Thiel, in Berlin / Amsterdam / London 1991–92a, pp. 214–17, cat. no. 31.

The foreground in this painting is dominated by a river or canal. Two men are standing in a small boat, propelling the vessel with bargepoles. The wooden landing that juts out from the bank was probably used for mooring. A path runs alongside the water, and a house can be seen in a cluster of trees on the left. A signboard hanging from the wall shows this building to be a hostelry. An open wagon stopping at the door is presumably bringing guests. Across the water are cows in a meadow. A road runs from left to right, and over the bridge, in the middle ground. A second boat can be seen directly through the arch of the bridge. The crew are holding up a bargepole as if preparing to push the boat under the bridge. A few figures straggle along the road. One of them is a man driving a cow ahead of him. Trees stretch into the distance behind the road, completely obscuring our view of the horizon. In the centre we see a farmhouse and haystack among the trees. The spire of a church tower is visible above the trees in the distance on the right.

The picture shows a typical Dutch polder landscape of the kind many artists portrayed with convincing realism from the beginning of the seventeenth century. It has been plausibly suggested that Rembrandt's example and reference point for the picture was an etching of 1616 by Jan van de Velde (fig. 11a).[1] Van de Velde's composition is essentially the same, except that in it the water is frozen. The boats have therefore been drawn onto the bank, and most of the figures are on the ice.

But Rembrandt wanted something more than a typical Dutch landscape. He dramatized the motif to extraordinary effect. It looks as if dusk has settled on the water, the path running beside it, the meadow, and the right-hand section of the road behind it. A huge, dark cloud looms overhead, covering almost a third of the sky on the right.[2] The rest of the sky is a far more natural blue, with white clouds. The tallest trees and the fence directly beneath them are bathed in a radiant light. The effect is spectacular rather than true to life. The smaller trees, with the farmhouse nestling among them, are even more sharply illuminated. Nor is this realistic, as the lower area would receive less light and even be shadowed by the taller trees. It looks as if all these bright parts of the scene have been caught in a flash of lightning. The details here are both starker, in terms of light/dark contrasts, and more refined in their modelling, than in the rest of the picture. The same light also catches the edge of the bridge and the stretch of road to the left of it, and touches the bowed figure of a man with a staff over his shoulder who is heading towards the bridge.

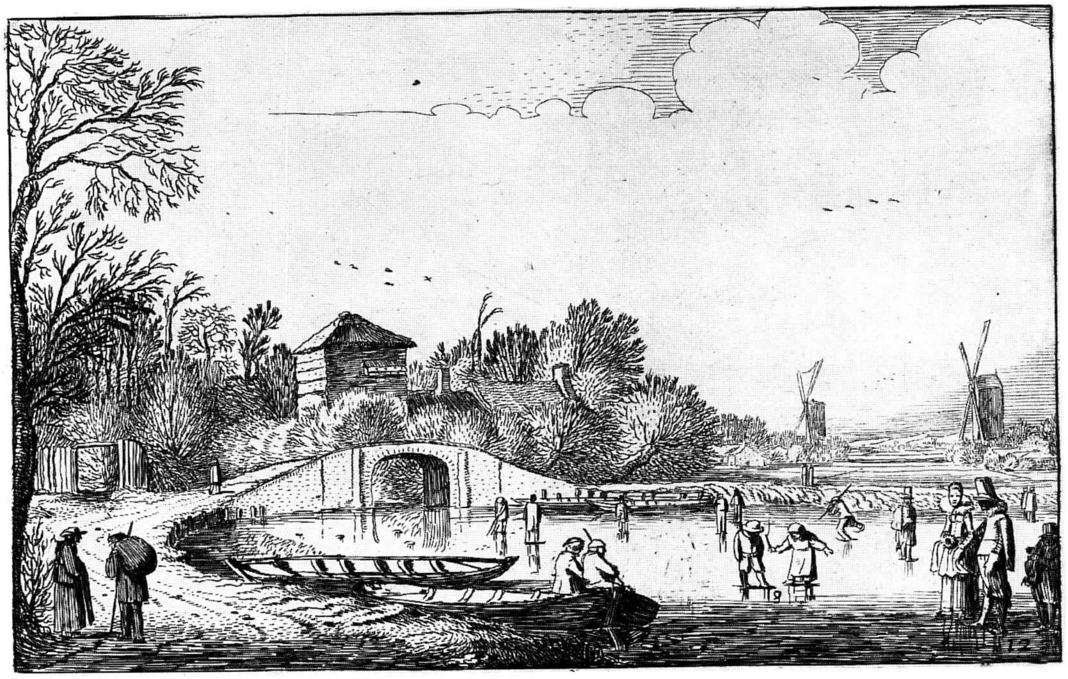

FIG. 11a
Jan van de Velde 1593–1641
Skating on the Ice 1616
Etching
12.0 x 18.8 cm
Rijksprentenkabinet, Rijksmuseum, Amsterdam

Rembrandt painted no more than a few landscapes, the majority of them representing imaginary countryside with desolate mountains and wide views into the distance (fig. 11b),[3] though he made many drawings and etchings of Holland's familiar polder landscapes (cat. nos 83, 90, 91, 105, 107, 113). He developed an interest in rendering landscapes relatively late in his career, shortly before 1640. The *Landscape with a Stone Bridge* dates from this period. Dendrochronological examination of the panel has established that it would not have been ready to be used for painting before 1638.

De Bruyn Kops suggested in 1987 that in the *Landscape with a Stone Bridge*, an ordinary Dutch landscape with extraordinarily dramatic lighting, Rembrandt 'as an ambitious history painter was seeking to capture the intrinsic mood or atmosphere of a landscape even in a simple rural scene'.[4] In 1893 Emile Michel mused in rather more visionary terms: 'One senses the painter's reluctance to free himself from the visions that obsess him and from the reality that holds him captive'.[5] In other writers, the picture has evoked religious associations. The Dutch art historian H. van de Waal reflected in 1958 that 'Rembrandt's entirely unexotic world [radiates] the light of an unfathomable miracle'.[6] In 1966 Stechow remarked on 'a chiaroscuro that lends to the simple motif the mysterious air of his biblical works of the same period'.[7] Alluding to Moses's vision of the burning bush, described in Exodus 3:1–10, another author wrote of the picture in the following terms: 'An ordinary scene is ... transformed for the visionary Rembrandt into this burning bramble bush'.[8] Bruyn in 1987 saw the entire picture as a Christian metaphor, interpreting the man with the staff over his shoulder as the protagonist. He is not headed for the inn – an allusion to sin – but for the bridge, which symbolizes Christ. He will then pass the fence, an emblem of death, and proceed to the church, his salvation.[9] Slive's response to this way of looking at such paintings is not hard to understand: 'To maintain that the principal intent of the [Dutch] landscapists was to paint visual sermons ... strains credulity to the breaking point'.[10]

AB

1 C. J. de Bruyn Kops, in Amsterdam / Boston / Philadelphia 1987–88, p. 429, cat. no. 76.
2 In my view, the strokes showing traces of brush-hair that can be seen in the cloud were not supposed to be visible (they could already be seen in photographs taken before the painting was restored in 1985). This treatment differs too sharply from the delicate handling of the trees, besides which, it renders the shape of the cloud unclear. The cloud was probably always as dark as it is today, but defined with greater subtlety.
3 Bredius / Gerson 1969, no. 442; *Corpus*, vol. III, 1989, no. A125.
4 C. J. de Bruyn Kops, in Amsterdam / Boston / Philadelphia 1987–88, p. 427, cat. no. 76.
5 Michel 1893, p. 314.
6 Van de Waal 1958.
7 Stechow 1966, p. 58.
8 Eugénie de Keyser, printed text with colour illustration, in RKD files.The printing appears to date from *c.*1970. No further details concerning this publication could be found in the Rijksmuseum's documentation or elsewhere.
9 J. Bruyn, in Amsterdam / Boston / Philadelphia 1987–88, pp. 97–8. Cf. *Corpus*, vol. III, 1989, pp. 357–61, no. A136. For a more tentative position on the reading of paintings of Dutch landscapes as representations of 'the pilgrimage of life', see Raupp 1980, pp. 85–110, esp. pp. 94, 102, 104.
10 Slive 1988, p. 398.

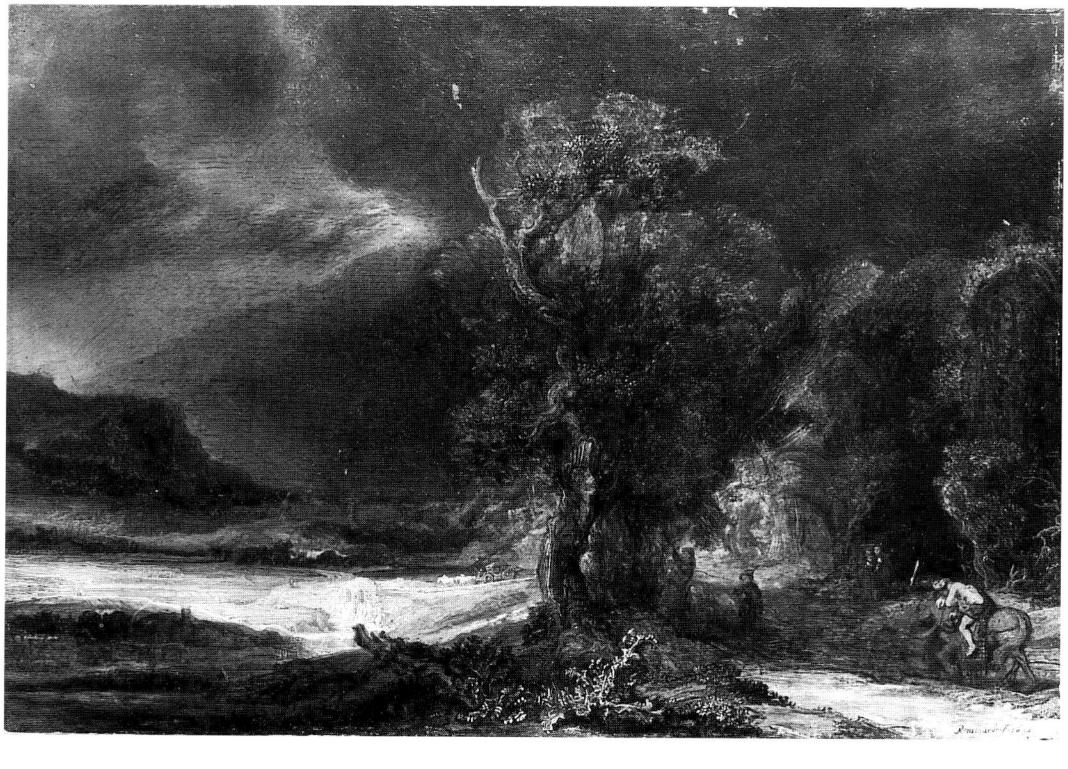

FIG. 11b
Rembrandt
Landscape with the Good Samaritan
Signed and dated 1638
Panel
46.5 x 66.0 cm
Czartoryski Museum, Cracow

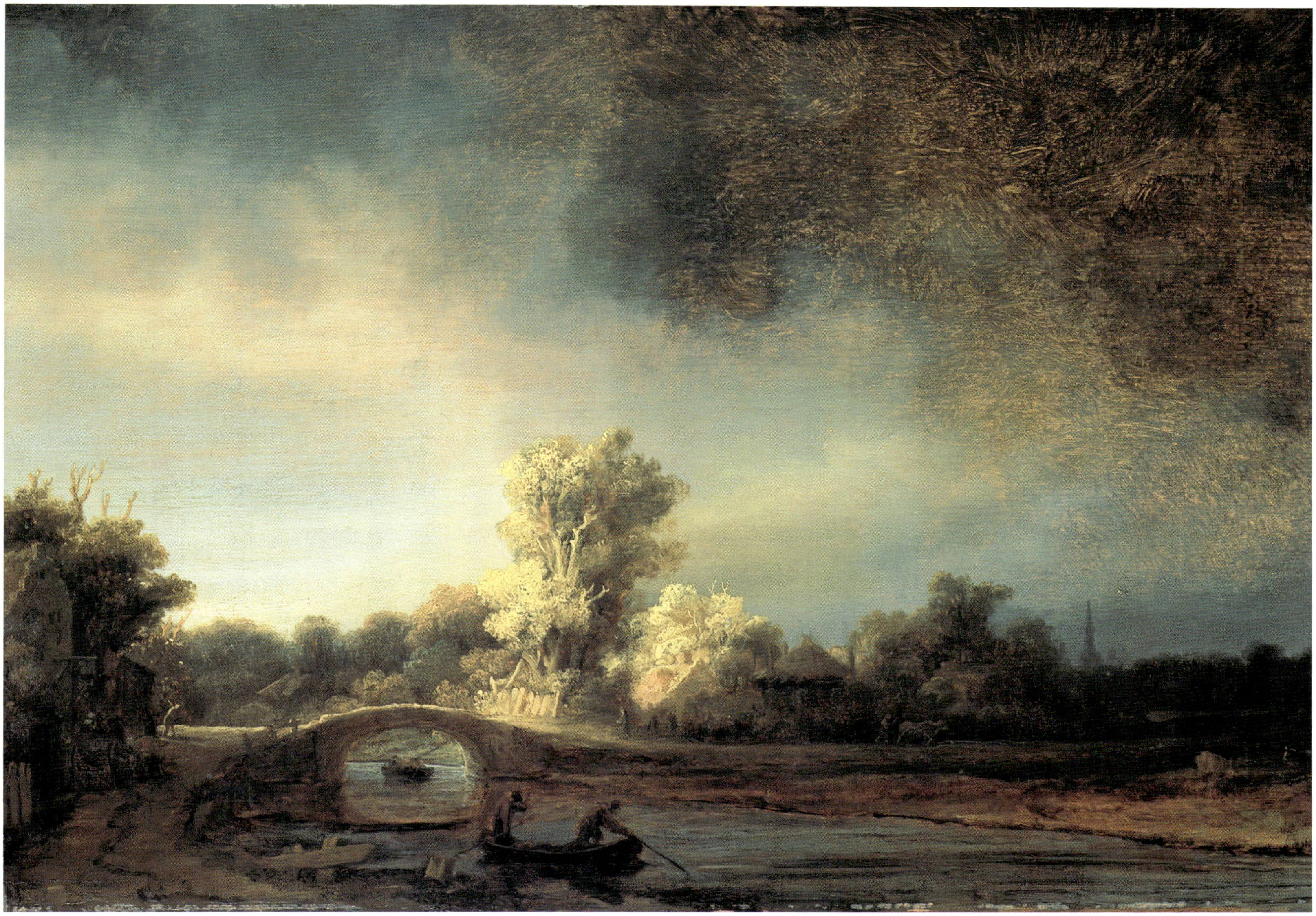

12

Portrait of a Man Holding His Hat
*c.*1639

Signed lower right *Rembrandt* (added later?)
Panel
81.4 x 71.4 cm
Armand Hammer Collection, UCLA, at the Armand Hammer Museum of Art and Cultural Center, Los Angeles, California, USA

PROVENANCE: Sale, Gabriel Huquier Sr, Paris, 1–23 July 1771, lot 1; sale, Watelet, Paris, 12 June 1786, lot 44, to 'Changran'; sale, Marquis de Chamgrand, Paris, 20–24 March 1787, lot 24, to Paillet; Collection of the Princes Gagarin, Moscow; sold by Prince Nicolas Gagarin; sale, Alfred W. Erickson (New York), New York, 15 November 1961, lot 14; J. William Middendorf II; on loan to the Metropolitan Museum of Art, New York, until 1979.

LITERATURE: Smith 1829–42, vol. VII, 1836, no. 263; Hofstede de Groot 1908–27, vol. VI, 1916, p. 353, no. 751; Valentiner 1908, p. 217; Bauch 1966, no. 379; Slive 1980, pp. 36–7, no. 12; *Corpus*, vol. III, 1989, pp. 305–11, no. A130.

A man whom one would judge to be in his forties stands turned to the right, looking down on us slightly from over his shoulder. He holds his hat in both hands in front of him. The light falling from the left shines brightly on most of his face, his white lace collar and his doublet and cloak. His costume is contemporary, but it is not the sober black in which most adult men and women of the time, including Rembrandt's clients, almost invariably had themselves portrayed. Instead he is wearing a striking outfit of 'light grey taffeta with a pinkish-purple lustre', trimmed with 'golden-yellow braiding along the hems and seams'.[1] At the left of the painting, a table is vaguely discernible. An X-ray photograph shows that it was initially planned for the right-hand side.

The piece was described as a Rembrandt by Smith in 1836, by Valentiner in 1908, by Hofstede de Groot in 1916 and by Bauch in 1966.[2] However, it was not included in Bredius's influential oeuvre catalogue of 1935 or in Gerson's edition of 1969, nor by Schwartz in 1984 or by Tümpel in 1986. Surprisingly, the portrait was restored to Rembrandt in volume III of the *Corpus* in 1989, whereas most works rejected by Gerson were not taken into consideration. The *Corpus* refers to the piece as a 'painting that despite a few unusual features is convincing as to its authenticity'.[3] An important discovery published in the *Corpus* is that the piece had been described at length as a Rembrandt in the sale catalogues of 1771, 1786 and 1787 (see Provenance). The commentary in the *Corpus* is convincing. The authors compare the shadows in the clothing, for instance, with those in the *Portrait of Marten Looten* of 1632 (Los Angeles County Museum), and many of the details with those in the *Portrait of a Young Woman (Maria Trip?)* in Amsterdam (fig. 12a).[4] They also examine the man's strikingly colourful sleeve in relation to Titian's *Portrait of 'Ariosto'*, which inspired Rembrandt's *Self-Portrait at the Age of 34* of 1640 (see cat. no. 13 and fig. 13a). Particularly compelling is the observation that a *Portrait of a Man* of 1641 by Rembrandt's pupil Govaert Flinck[5] was quite obviously influenced by cat. no. 12 (fig. 12b).

Hofstede de Groot, Valentiner and Bauch mention a signature and the date 1637 at the lower right. The authors of the *Corpus* found no date, and argue that the picture is more likely to have

FIG. 12a
Rembrandt
Portrait of a Young Woman (Maria Trip?)
Signed and dated 1639
Panel
107.0 x 82.0 cm
Rijksmuseum, Amsterdam; on loan from the Van Weede Family Foundation

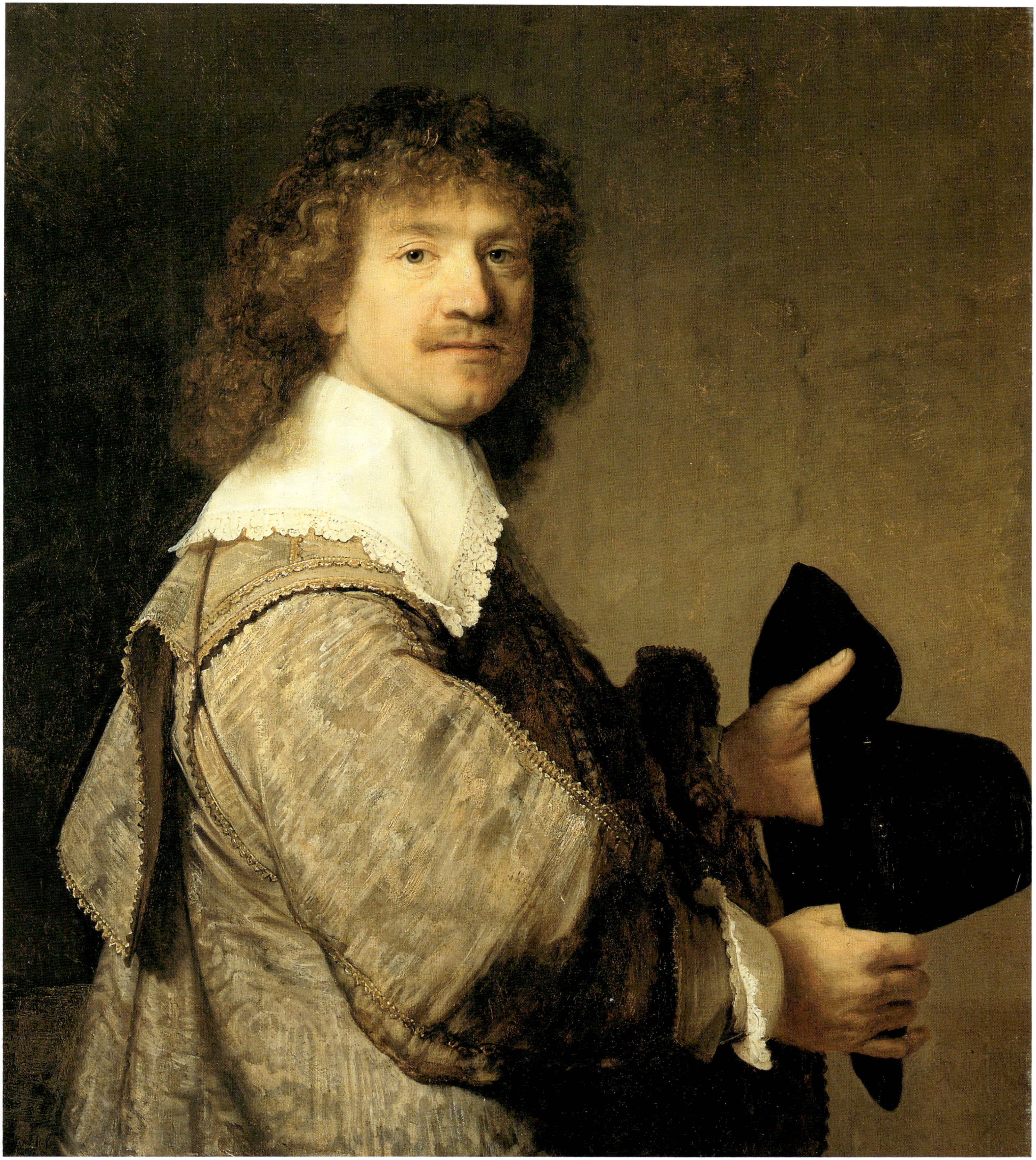

been made in 1639. They believe the signature was added later, possibly after a strip was sawn off the right-hand side of the panel, as is said to have been the case. They surmise that the piece bore an even closer resemblance to the Flinck (fig. 12b) before the purported removal of this strip.[6] In the Flinck we see a similar crack in the wall in the background. This is unusual. In most portraits of this kind a wall is suggested behind the sitter, but its texture is generally indistinct and its distance from the figure hard to gauge.

The sale catalogues of 1786 and 1787 interpreted the picture as a 'portrait d'un artiste', possibly because of the man's elegant and unusual costume. In 1908 Valentiner speculated that the subject may have been Prince Frederik Hendrik of Orange (1584–1647), stadholder of the United Provinces. A short time earlier, an archive document had been discovered in which was mentioned a portrait of Frederik Hendrik by Rembrandt.[7] However, this reference, which appears in the inventory of Frederik Hendrik's widow, Amalia van Solms, in 1667, concerns a portrait in profile and therefore cannot, if only for that reason, be the present work: 'A painting of His Highness Prince Frederik Hendrik of esteemed memory, in profile, done by Rembrandt'.[8] Moreover, the clerk probably made a mistake, since what was meant was a profile portrait of Frederik Hendrik by Gerrit van Honthorst. That picture had been in the palace since 1632, with a portrait of Amalia van Solms – which was indeed by Rembrandt – as a pendant (fig. 21a).[9] All things considered, there is no evidence to support the assumption that Rembrandt portrayed Frederik Hendrik, and even less to indicate that the present work is a representation of him, as the man in cat. no. 12 bears no resemblance to any portrait of the prince, who was around fifty-five years old at the time cat. no. 12 was executed.[10] In view of the costume, the authors of the *Corpus* concluded that the model was more likely to have been 'a (perhaps) foreign aristocrat' than a citizen of Amsterdam.

AB

1 *Corpus*, vol. III, 1989, p. 305, no. A130. Slive 1980, pp. 36–7, no. 12, describes the outfit as 'a grey moiré jacket'.
2 Smith 1829–42, vol. VII, 1836, no. 263; Valentiner 1908, p. 217; Hofstede de Groot 1908–27, vol. VI, 1916, p. 353, no. 751; Bauch 1966, no. 379.
3 *Corpus*, vol. III, 1989, p. 305, no. A130.
4 *Corpus*, vol. II, 1986, no. A52; vol. III, 1989, no. A131.
5 Sumowski, *Gemälde*, vol. II, 1985, p. 1038, no. 697.
6 *Corpus*, vol. III, 1989, p. 305, no. A130.
7 Valentiner 1908, p. 556, mentions E. W. Moes's discovery of the document; see also Strauss & Van der Meulen 1979, p. 570, no. 1667/7.
8 Strauss & Van der Meulen 1979, p. 570, no. 1667/7: 'Een schilderije van sijne Hoogheyt Prince Frederick Hendrick Ho. Lo. memorie in profijl, bij Rembrant gedaen'.
9 For the 1632 references to the van Honthorst and Rembrandt pictures, see Strauss & Van der Meulen 1979, pp. 87–8, no. 1632/3; see also the summary and references in Bredius / Gerson 1969, p. 555, no. 99.
10 See also Slive 1980.

FIG. 12b
Govaert Flinck
Portrait of a Man Holding His Hat
Signed and dated 1641
Panel
91.5 x 73.5 cm
Collection of the J. Paul Getty Museum, Los Angeles, California

13
Self-Portrait at the Age of 34

Signed and dated on sill lower right *Rembrandt f 1640* (beneath this an old inscription *Conterfeycel* [portrait])
Canvas (arched)
93.0 x 80.0 cm
The Trustees of the National Gallery, London

PROVENANCE: General Dupont, Paris (either Pierre Comte Dupont de l'Etang (1765–1840) or his elder brother Dupont-Chaumont (1759–1838), both of whom served under Napoleon); by descent to the Comte, Vicomte and Baron de Richemont; purchased from them (after an exhibition in Paris) in 1861.

LITERATURE: Hofstede de Groot 1908–27, vol. VI, 1916, p. 272, no. 550; Bredius / Gerson 1969, no. 34; De Jongh 1969; Brown 1980; Raupp 1984, pp. 168–81; Schwartz 1984, p. 215; Tümpel 1986, no. 168; London 1988–89, pp. 80–5, cat. no. 8; *Corpus*, vol. III, 1989, pp. 375–81, no. A139; Chapman 1990, pp. 69–78; MacLaren / Brown 1991, vol. 1, pp. 339–41, no. 672; P. van Thiel, in Berlin / Amsterdam / London 1991–92a, pp. 218–21, cat. no. 32.

Rembrandt seems to be regarding us with an air of self-assurance in this picture from 1640. Wearing an unusual costume of costly fabric, he is seen with his right arm resting on a balustrade. Diffuse light filters through the composition, diagonally illuminating both the face and the even background. The refined manner of painting and the subtle contrasts of light and shadow make this self-portrait one of the highlights of Rembrandt's work from the period around 1640.[1] The composition is a variation, in reverse, of his etched *Self-Portrait Leaning on a Stone Sill* of 1639 (B.21) (see cat. no. 103 and fig. 13a).

Although Rembrandt must have used a rectangular canvas, he probably left the upper corners unpainted and may have cut them away later; this would mean that the upper edge has been rounded right from the start, or was cut soon after the painting was made.[2] Later – it is uncertain when – a strip along the top was lost, and this had the effect of evening out the upper edge. X-ray photographs show further that Rembrandt changed his design while painting. The collar was originally flat rather than upright, and the fingers of the left hand were also on the balustrade. Ferdinand Bol used the piece at this stage as the example for a picture (fig. 45c).[3]

Since 1905, the present painting has been related to two seventeenth-century Italian portraits – Titian's *Portrait of an Unknown Man* (fig. 13b), which in Rembrandt's day was thought to be a portrait of the poet Ariosto, and Raphael's *Portrait of Baldassare Castiglione* (fig. 13c).[4] In April 1639 Rembrandt saw the Raphael at the auction of the Van Uffelen Collection in Amsterdam, where it was bought by Alphonso Lopez. Either during or after the sale, Rembrandt made a sketch after the painting (fig. 13d).[5] Between about 1637 and 1641, the Titian portrait (or a faithful copy) was also in Lopez's possession. A Portuguese-Jewish merchant, Lopez had previously bought work directly from Rembrandt, and from this we can assume that Rembrandt knew him and had seen his collection.

Motifs such as the figure leaning on the balustrade, the voluminous right sleeve, and the man's rather haughty expression were irrefutably inspired by the Titian. No one comparing the two pictures has commented, however, on the fact that the balustrade in the Titian is marble, whereas Rembrandt has obviously tried to capture the effect of wood. In the self-portrait etching of 1639 (fig. 13a), the balustrade appears to be made of stone or brick.

The relationship of the present painting to the Raphael and to Rembrandt's sketch after it is

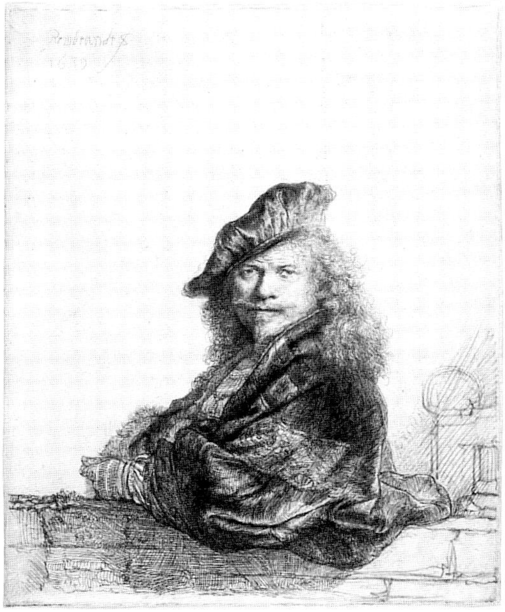

FIG. 13a
Rembrandt
Self-Portrait Leaning on a Stone Sill
Signed and dated 1639
Etching
20.5 x 16.4 cm
National Gallery of Victoria, Melbourne; purchased 1891
(our cat. no. 103)

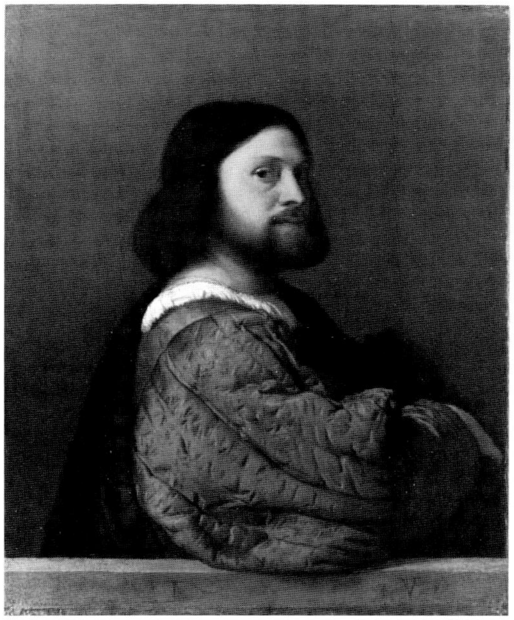

FIG. 13b
Titian Italian, *c.*1485/90–1576
Portrait of an Unknown Man ('Ariosto')
Canvas
81.0 x 66.0 cm
The Trustees of the National Gallery, London

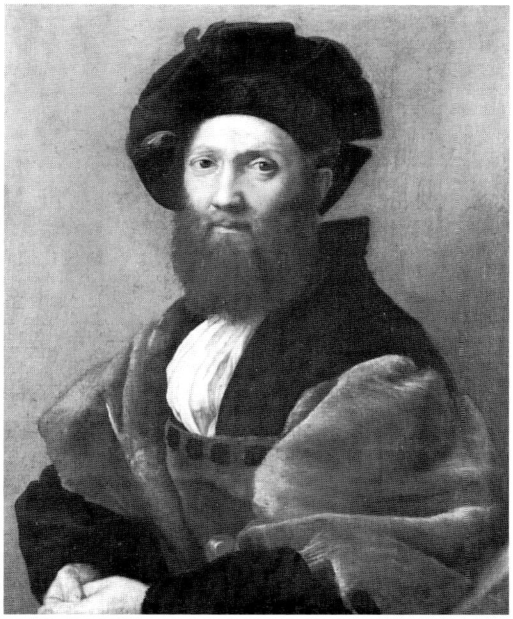

FIG. 13c
Raphael Italian, 1483–1520
Portrait of Baldassare Castiglione
Canvas
82.0 x 67.0 cm
Musée du Louvre, Paris

more indirect: the Raphael seems rather to have inspired the etching from the previous year. In all three Rembrandt versions, however, the beret is worn at a casual baroque angle, unlike the 'classically' symmetrical headgear in the Raphael.

It has been suggested that in this piece Rembrandt was aiming to surpass the highly esteemed Titian, in accordance with the principle of *aemulatio*, or 'superior' emulation. It has even been said that he may have been trying to rival not only Titian but also the supposed subject of his painting, the poet Ariosto.[6] Another idea is that by referring to the courtier Baldassare Castiglione, whom Raphael portrayed, Rembrandt was seeking to gain an aristocratic allure.[7] Be that as it may, given that Rembrandt did not slavishly follow Titian's example, but added an unmistakable touch of his own, the term *aemulatio* is certainly apposite here. The self-confident expression, and the fact that Rembrandt has portrayed himself in a smart, 'antique' sixteenth-century costume, seem to imply that he wanted to present himself as a distinguished and, in a sense, timeless figure. In this connection it should also be said that by signing with his first name only, a practice that was unusual in the Netherlands, Rembrandt was following the example of the great, acclaimed Renaissance masters from Italy.[8] He certainly had reason to be proud: by the time he painted cat. no. 13, another *Self-Portrait*, showing him 'in a ... furrd habbitt with a litle goulden chaine uppon both his Shouldrs',[9] had been in the superb collection of paintings belonging to Charles I of England for at least seven years, together with self-portraits by Rubens, van Dyck and famous Italian masters. Rembrandt's attitude in the present *Self-Portrait* can be recognized as the example for portraits by several of his pupils (see cat. nos 45, 46).

As far as we know, no one has commented on a striking difference between cat. no. 13 and the *Self-Portrait* etching of 1639. In the etching, Rembrandt's hair is far longer than in the painting, falling past the shoulders. In the canvas from 1640 it is cut just below the ear. Rembrandt had apparently shorn his long locks in the intervening period, possibly because of the 'hairy war' (*hairige oorlog*), which broke out around that time.

In 1640, church councils in Holland started complaining that members of their congregations, and even their clergymen, were committing a sin by following the new 'outlandish' vogue for long hair. The critics invoked the words of the apostle Paul: 'Doth not even nature itself teach you, that, if a man have long hair, it is a shame unto him?' (1 Corinthians 11:14). A struggle ensued, fought through dire sermons, pamphlets and scathing satire and culminating in a doctrinal dispute, family feuds, and even breaches of the peace. For the new fashion, which was later to become entrenched, also found avid support. So bitter was the controversy that a ruling had to be made in Dordrecht in 1645 that 'hayrige quaestiën' (disputes on hair) were no longer to be the subject of sermons.[10] We would be thinking along too rigid lines if we were automatically to assume that Rembrandt, an exponent of the liberal arts, would have been impervious to the arguments that were causing tempers to flare at the time. He may have been susceptible to the reasoning that the ancient Hollanders and Zeelanders had worn their hair short, rather than long as Absalom had done. In any event he had opted for short hair from the very start of the conflict.

AB/MB

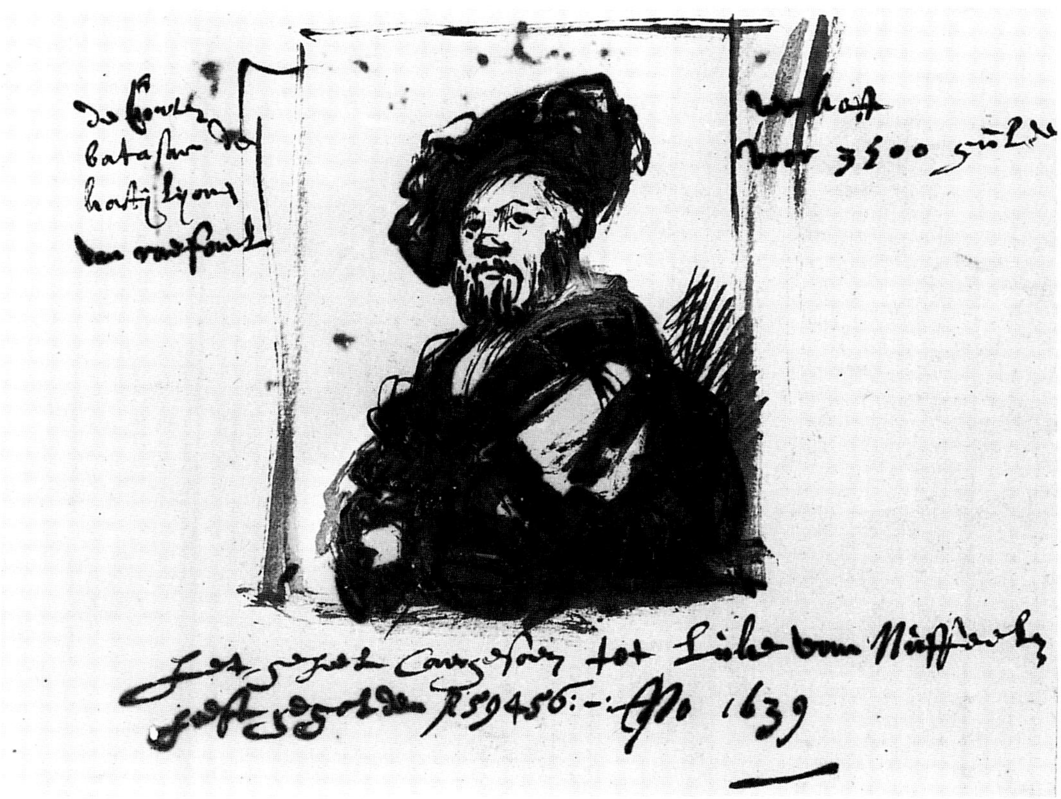

FIG. 13d
Rembrandt, after Raphael
Portrait of Baldassare Castiglione
Inscribed [in Dutch]: 'Duke Batasar de Kastijlyone by Raphael / sold for 3500 guilders ... in the year 1639'
Pen and ink
16.3 x 20.7 cm
Graphische Sammlung Albertina, Vienna

1 *Corpus*, vol. III, 1989, p. 379, no. A139; P. van Thiel, in Berlin / Amsterdam / London 1991–92a, p. 220, cat. no. 32.
2 *Corpus*, vol. III, 1989, p. 375, no. A139.
3 *Corpus*, vol. III, 1989, p. 380.
4 Broos 1977, p. 37.
5 Benesch 1973, vol. II, no. 451.
6 De Jongh 1969; Brown 1980, p. 4. Raupp 1984, pp. 168–81 (also on a seventeenth-century print after the Titian).
7 Brown 1980, p. 4; Tümpel 1986, p. 205. Cf. Chapman 1990, p. 49.
8 Blankert 1973, pp. 35–6.
9 Walker Art Gallery, Liverpool (Bredius / Gerson 1969, no. 12; *Corpus*, vol. I, 1982, pp. 322–30, no. A33); see also Chapman 1990, pp. 46–7.
10 Perk 1900, pp. 217–54.

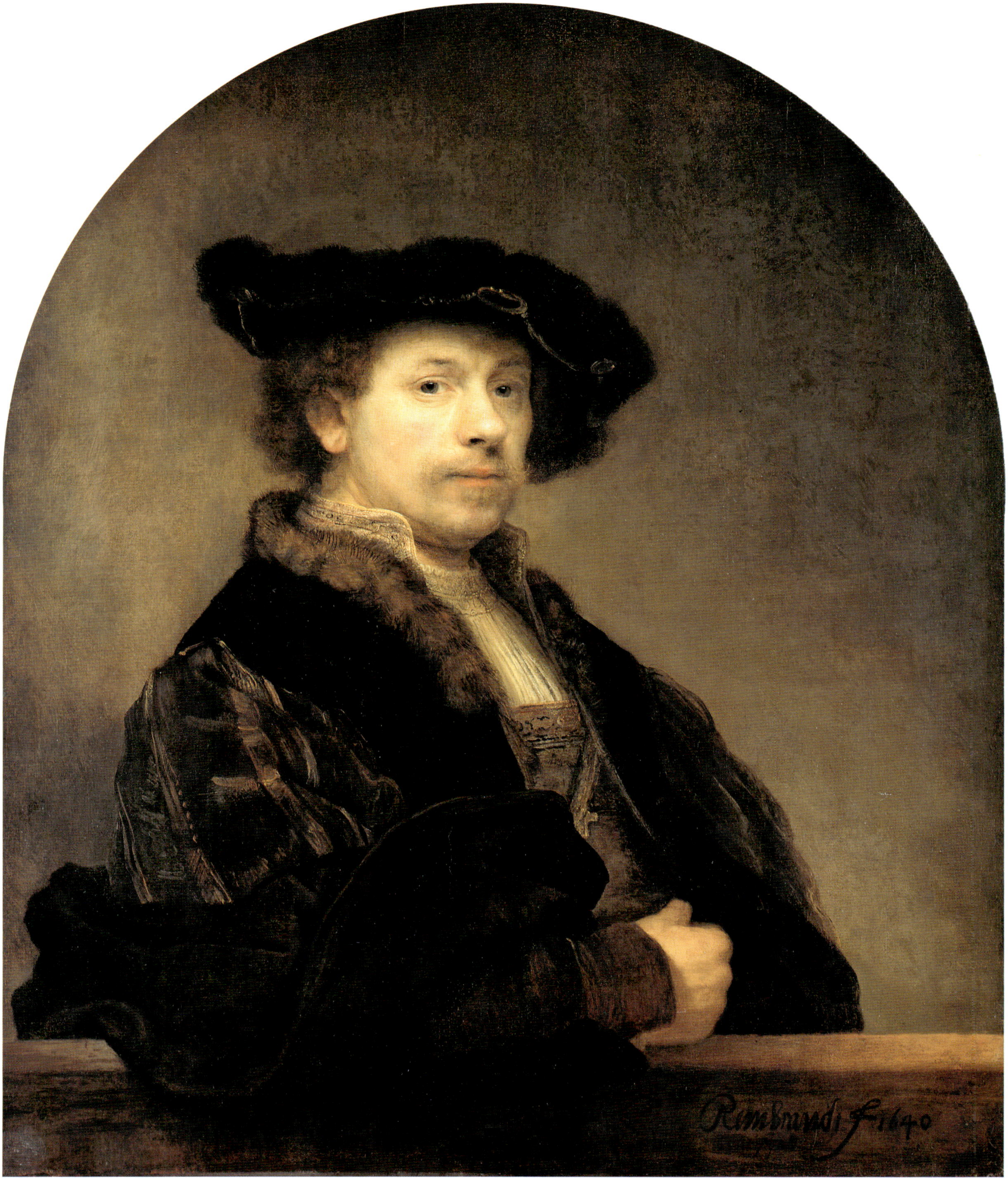
Rembrandt f 1640

14
Young Woman in Bed

Signed and dated lower left *Rembra[...] f. 164[.]*
Canvas (arched)
81.1 x 67.8 cm
National Galleries of Scotland, Edinburgh

PROVENANCE: (Possibly) Bartered for boat supplies in Amsterdam in 1647 [see commentary below]; [after Lloyd Williams 1992: not, as stated in previous literature, in sale, Prince de Carignan, Paris, 30 July 1742]; François Tronchin, Geneva, by 1757; given by Tronchin (in exchange) to Count Vitturi, Venice, by 1765; Thomas Moore Slade, by 1776; purchased from Slade by Viscount Maynard, *c.*1790; Sir Henry St John Mildmay, before 1836; purchased from his collection by Samson Wertheimer of Bond Street; his sale, London (Christie's), 19 March 1892, lot 706, bought in at £5250; C. J. Wertheimer; purchased from Wertheimer by the Rt Hon. William McEwan in 1892 for £5775; presented by him in the same year.

LITERATURE: Smith 1829–42, vol. VII, 1836, pp. 65–6, no. 151 (as dated 1650); Hofstede de Groot 1908–27, vol. VI, 1916, p. 179, no. 305 (as dated 1657); Bredius / Gerson 1969, no. 110 (as dated 164..: 'must date from the late 1640s'); Tümpel 1969, pp. 176–8; Schwartz 1984, p. 241; Tümpel 1986, no. 23; De Vries 1989, pp. 186–8; J. Kelch, in Berlin / Amsterdam / London 1991–92a, pp. 230–2, cat. no. 36 (as dated 164[.]); Lloyd Williams 1992, cat. no. 50; Slatkes 1992, no. 292.

A young woman in bed lifts herself up from her pillow. Her nightgown covers only half of her body. With her left arm she raises the bed-curtain and draws it aside. Something outside the bed, over to our right, has caught her attention. She regards it with great interest and, it seems, friendliness. Rembrandt made several drawings of a young woman in bed, seen from the waist up. An example in the present exhibition is the *Saskia in Bed* (cat. no. 82). There, too, the bed-curtain is visible. The motif of a sleeping woman appears in different forms on other sheets.[1] Other, related, drawings show the woman awake.[2] On a further sheet she is leaning on one elbow, as in the painting (fig. 14a).[3] The motif obviously fascinated Rembrandt. This is one explanation as to how he arrived at the idea for his unique painting.

A comparison between the drawings and the painting shows how differently Rembrandt worked in each of these media. The drawings are done from life. The model wears an ordinary seventeenth-century nightcap (the one in cat. no. 82 is similar to that in fig. 14a). In the painting, however, the woman wears a headdress consisting of two round, decorated bands, made of gold or gilt, with a similar metal plaited between them. The head-dress holds her swept-back hair in place, leaving only a few curls on her forehead. A chain studded with precious stones loops down from the headdress. This is not what Dutch women used to wear to bed, nor do they do so today.

The figures in the drawings 'from life' are in poses that suggest the subjects were caught unawares. In the painting of the *Young Woman in Bed*, however, the action has been carefully orchestrated, and concentrated on the arrested gaze of the woman. Hence the bed-curtain does not hang idly to one side, as in the drawings cat. no. 82 and fig. 14a. Its purpose here is to emphasize the curiosity of the woman drawing it aside in order to look out from the pictorial space into that of the viewer. The motif recalls the *trompe l'oeil* effect in Rembrandt's *Holy Family* of 1646 in Kassel (fig. 14b).[4] In this picture, a curtain drawn aside has been painted in front of the Holy Family, while a frame has been painted around them. Real frames and curtains were used to protect paintings. Their painted equivalents in the *Holy Family* are situated outside the 'narrative' space of the composition, with the curtain thus being used in an even more complex and sophisticated way than in cat. no. 14.[5]

The convincing staging of the scene in the *Young Woman in Bed* prompted John Smith to comment as follows in 1836 in the first catalogue raisonné of Rembrandt's paintings: 'The figure is of the size of nature, and is so close a resemblance of nature, both in colour and expression, as to be almost illusion'.[6] Smith refers to the subject simply as a 'Young woman'. Not content with this, later authors – depending on the period to which they dated the picture – took the painting for a portrayal of Rembrandt's wife Saskia (1612–1642), Geertje Dircx, who is thought to have been his first mistress after Saskia's death, or Hendrickje Stoffels, his second (for the dating of the picture, see below).[7]

Identifying Rembrandt's subjects as members of his household has become less popular in

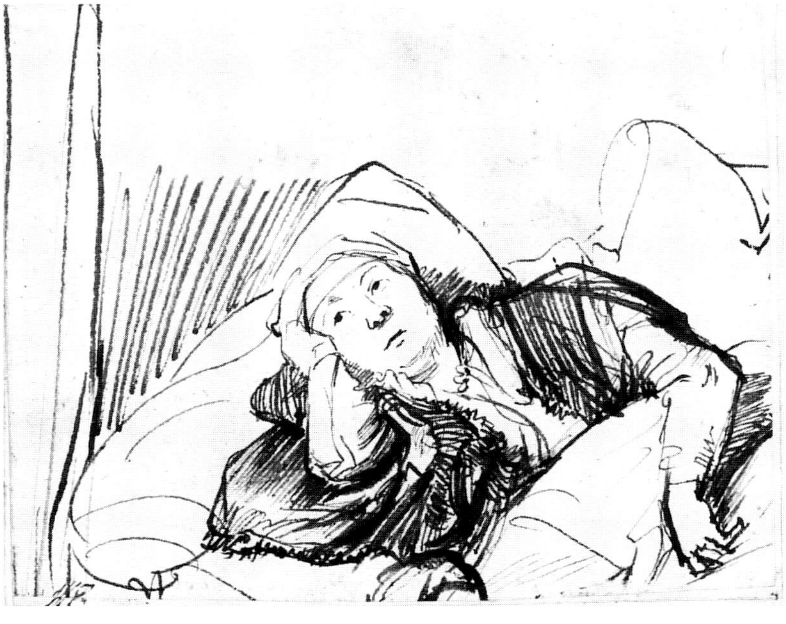

FIG. 14a
Rembrandt
Young Woman in Bed
Pen and bistre
8.4 x 10.4 cm
Copyright © The British Museum, London

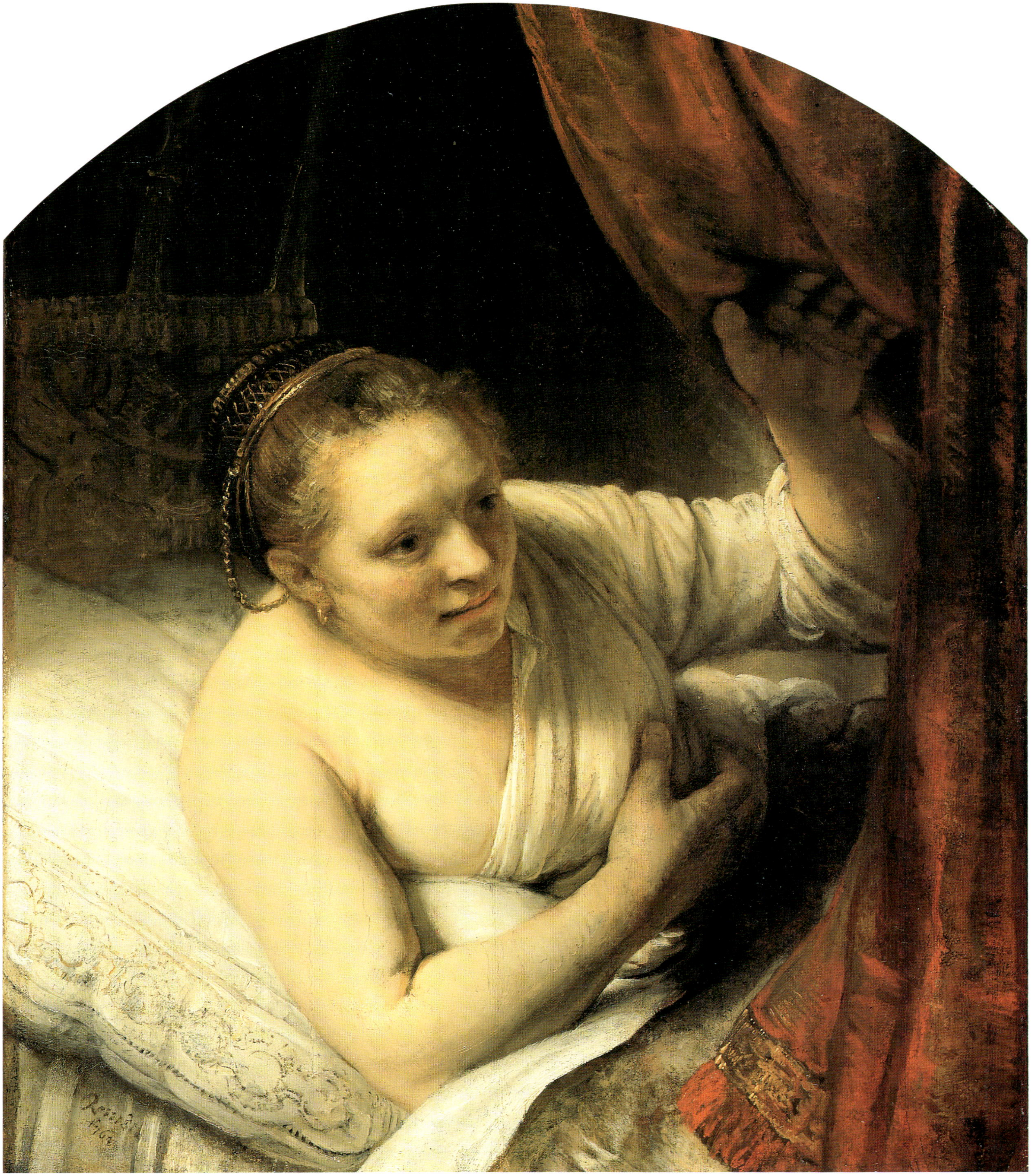

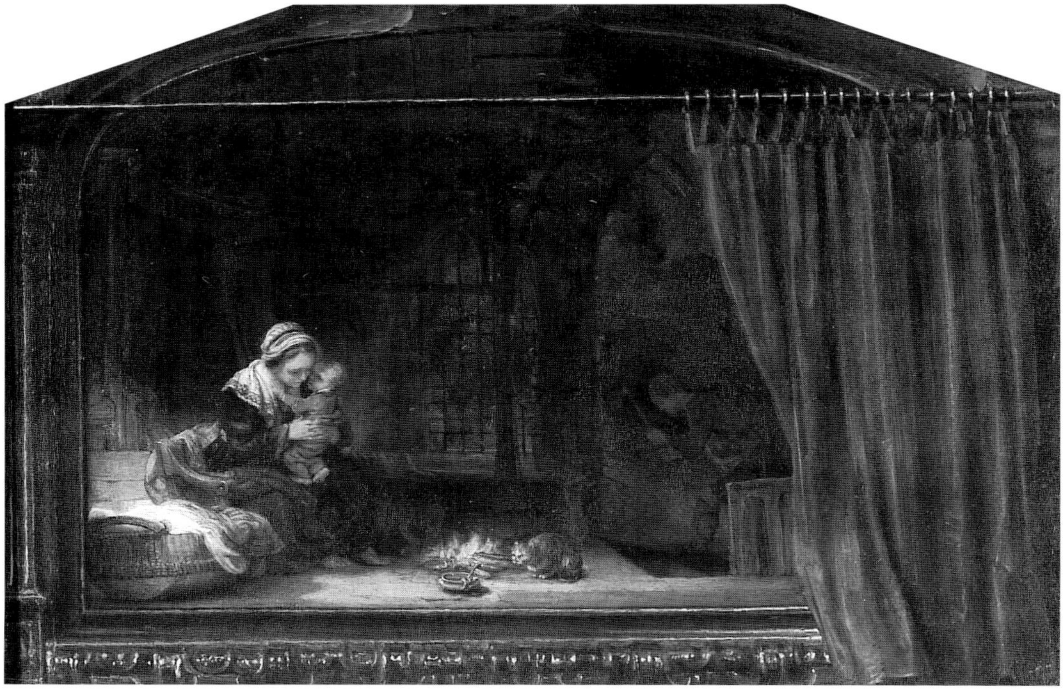

FIG. 14b
Rembrandt
The Holy Family with Painted Frame and Curtain
Signed and dated 1646
Panel
46.5 x 68.5 cm
Gemäldegalerie, Kassel

FIG. 14c
Pieter Lastman 1583–1633
The Wedding Night of Tobias and Sarah
Signed and dated 1611
Panel
41.0 x 58.0 cm
Juliana Cheney Edwards Collection
Courtesy, Museum of Fine Arts, Boston

recent times. People have started to discover biblical representations where they had not been seen before. Sumowski suggested that the present piece might represent Hagar Waiting for Abraham or Sarah Waiting for Tobias. The latter idea was developed by C. Tümpel in 1969, as an example of *Herauslösung*, or the isolation of a single figure from a narrative, and has since found lasting support.[8] Tümpel relates cat. no. 14 to a painting by Rembrandt's teacher Pieter Lastman, which shows Sarah raising herself up in her bed and surveying her room with interest (fig. 14c). Her bridegroom, Tobias, is placing the heart and liver of a miraculous fish on a sacrificial fire. The smoke is to dispel the evil spirit Asmodeus, whose jealousy caused him to kill Sarah's seven previous husbands on their wedding nights. We see Tobias's

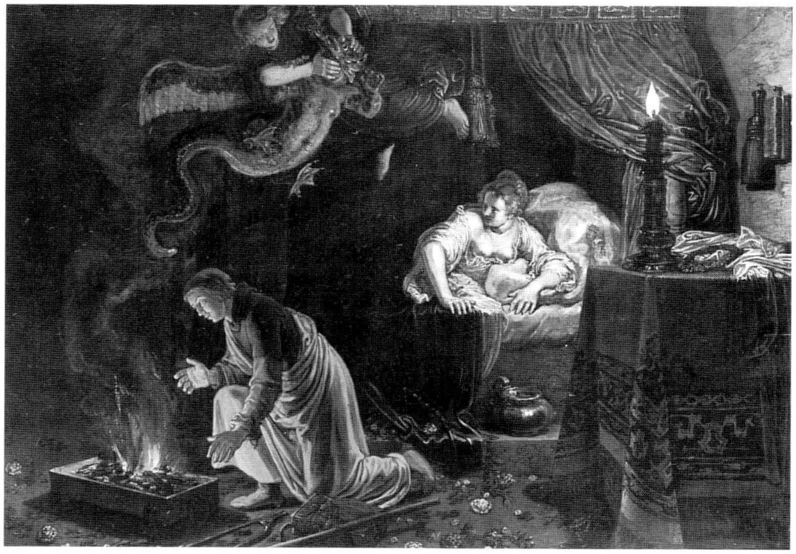

guardian angel, Raphael, sweeping down and binding Asmodeus, enabling Sarah to consummate her marriage with Tobias. Other Netherlandish artists have also depicted this graphic episode from the apocryphal Book of Tobit (8:3), but they show Tobias and Sarah later on, kneeling on the floor in prayer as they are joined together in matrimony.[9] Hence had Rembrandt meant his *Young Woman in Bed* to be Sarah, waiting for Tobias, he would have expected the observer to be familiar with Lastman's picture, in which Sarah is shown in bed.[10] In this case, however, Rembrandt's expectations of the viewer would have been quite unrealistic. The viewer would have had to remember one specific detail (Sarah) from the Lastman painting, and then imagine for himself everything else to be seen in that picture. The idea is consequently unacceptable.

To my knowledge, no one has remarked on the fact that Rembrandt's amiable-looking and expensively adorned young woman has exceptionally large, rough hands. With swollen fingers and reddish skin, they look like the hands of a labourer.[11] The erotic aura of the picture thus does not rely on the overall beauty of the model. The strongly realistic effect that emerges as a result may be compared with that in the *Susanna* and the *Ganymede* (see cat. no. 10 and p. 35, fig. 3).

It seems that on this occasion Rembrandt was predominantly interested in achieving just this effect. There is nothing to suggest that he intended to illustrate a particular event or story. Yet the picture does recall facts which only people in his immediate circle would have known, and which have only recently gained wider currency through documents. After Saskia's death in 1642, her son Titus's nurse Geertje Dircx (1600/15–1656?) – by her own account – became Rembrandt's mistress. Geertje was the widow of a ship's trumpeter and had previously served as a waitress and housekeeper. Rembrandt had given her gold and jewellery and a promise of marriage. The couple became embroiled in a serious dispute after Rembrandt's later companion, Hendrickje Stoffels, moved into his home. The conflict, which involved the return of the valuables, took place in 1648–49.[12] Today the present painting is very plausibly dated to these same late years of the 1640s.[13] It does not seem far-fetched to assume that when painting the resplendent woman with rough, labourer's hands, Rembrandt was at least thinking of Geertje Dircx.

At the same time, it is most unlikely that he intended the piece to represent nothing more than a scene from his personal domestic life. Prompted by the picture's former title, 'Hendrickje Stoffels in Bed', de Vries commented that 'Such a journalistic approach to the intimacies of the artist

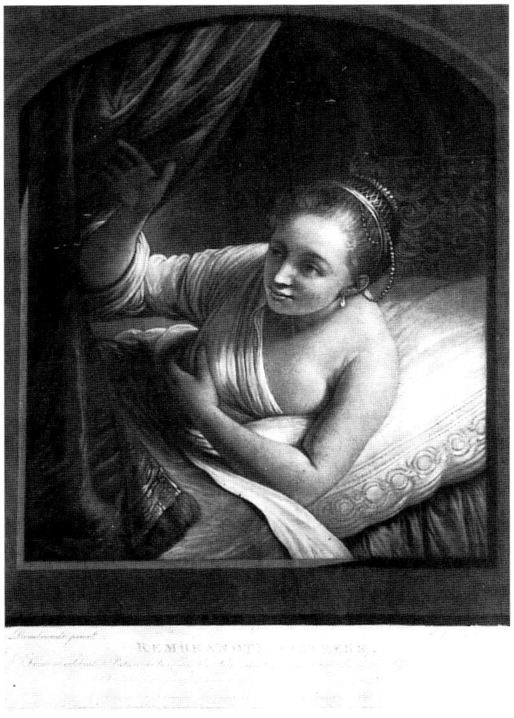

FIG. 14d
Richard Cooper (British, 1740–1814), after Rembrandt
Young Woman in Bed
Mezzotint
Inscribed *Rembrandt pinxt. R: Cooper delt. & sculpt. REMBRANDT'S MISTRESS. From a celebrated picture as large as the Life mentioned particularly in the Life of Rembrandt ... [1781].*
30.0 x 22.7 cm

and his nearest relatives is extremely exceptional, if not completely unthinkable, in the middle of the seventeenth century. Even in our time it could be considered as a sign of bad taste'.[14] Such an interpretation is, however, certainly 'thinkable' in the case of drawings such as fig. 14a and cat. no. 82, though far more difficult when it comes to this ambitious and carefully considered painting. The headdress the woman is wearing in bed would have looked neither normal nor contemporary in Rembrandt's day. It is nonetheless remarkable that even in 1781 the piece was engraved as 'Rembrandt's mistress' (fig. 14d).[15] Hence it is not only a modern 'journalistic approach' that prompts an interpretation of this kind.

Like Rembrandt's *Two Old Men Disputing* (cat. no. 3) and his 'philosophers' (p. 44, fig. 14), the picture must have been meant as an astonishingly natural depiction of a *type*, in this case a scantily clad young woman in bed. Erotic or other implications are left to the viewer's imagination. Rembrandt's inventory of 1656 includes a painting he made of 'A courtesan adorning herself'.[16] It is conceivable that the *Young Woman in Bed* could also be seen as a depiction of a 'courtesan', a traditional theme in Dutch visual art.[17] However, cat. no. 14 could be identical with, or very similar to, a Rembrandt that was bartered for boat supplies in 1647, on which occasion it was described as 'de minnemoer van Rembrant'.[18] This can be translated as 'Cupid's mother [i.e. Venus] by Rembrandt', but it could just as well mean 'Rembrandt's children's nurse'.[19] In the latter case we would have to imagine that the woman's gaze was turned towards a child.[20]

It is possible that Rembrandt intended neither to imply nor to preclude any of the possibilities mentioned above. His main object was probably to achieve the lifelike effect that John Smith still sensed many years later.

AB

1 Benesch 1973, vol. II, nos 281, 287–290, figs 336, 345–348.
2 Benesch 1973, vol. II, nos 282, 283, figs 338, 340.
3 Benesch 1973, vol. II, no. 286; Royalton-Kisch 1992, p. 69, cat. no. 19 (as *c.*1635).
4 Bredius / Gerson 1969, no. 572.
5 For the connotations of the curtain, see Schnackenburg 1996, vol. I, p. 242, no. GK 240.
6 Smith 1829–42, vol. VII, 1836, pp. 65–6, no. 151.
7 J. Kelch, in Berlin / Amsterdam / London 1991–92a, pp. 230–2, cat. no. 36.
8 Tümpel 1969, pp. 176–8. For interpretations of the picture as *Sarah Waiting for Tobias*, see Gerson 1968, p. 497, no. 227; Schwartz 1984, p. 240; J. Kelch, in Berlin / Amsterdam / London 1991–92a, p. 232, cat. no. 36 (with reservations); Slatkes 1992, p. 442.
9 Nicolaus Knüpfer (Centraal Museum, Utrecht); Jan Steen (Museum Bredius, The Hague; in 1996 the right-hand half of this picture was reunited with the left, previously on loan to the Centraal Museum in Utrecht). For these and other examples, see Blankert 1991, pp. 207–11, no. 155, figs 155A, 155B.
10 Only in Rembrandt's drawing of the same subject is Sarah also shown in bed (Metropolitan Museum of Art, New York) (Tümpel 1969, fig. 56; Benesch 1973, vol. III, no. 633, fig. 810).
11 The hands are similarly depicted in Jean-Etienne Liotard's 1757 portrait of François Tronchin (Cleveland Museum of Art). Tronchin was then the owner of the *Young Woman in Bed.* In his portrait, the present painting is shown on an easel beside him (Schwartz 1984, fig. 26; Berlin / Amsterdam / London 1991–92a, fig. 36a). The figure, and the hands in particular, are slimmer and more elegant in Richard Cooper's print after the Rembrandt (our fig. 14d).
12 For a summarized account, see Schwartz 1984, pp. 240–8; and Marleen Blokhuis's biography of Rembrandt in the present catalogue.
13 The dates 1650, 1657 (see Literature), and 1641 are no longer accepted. For a summary, see J. Kelch, in Berlin / Amsterdam / London 1991–92a, pp. 230–2, cat. no. 36.
14 De Vries 1989, p. 188. De Vries accepted the title *Sarah Waiting for Tobias,* but felt that with this subject 'the possibility of misinterpretation has increased. The first owner surely belonged to a circle of well-informed art lovers who knew how to "read" a painting like this'. The implication is that it took more than three hundred years, from the time of this hypothetical 'first owner', for a similar 'circle of well-informed art lovers' to emerge!
15 For this print, see J. Charrington & D. Alexander, in New Haven 1983, p. 124, cat. no. 39II. Three preparatory drawings for Cooper's print are in the National Galleries of Scotland, Edinburgh (photographs kindly sent by Julia Lloyd Williams of the National Galleries).
16 Strauss & Van der Meulen 1979, p. 353, no. 1656/12 (no. 39): 'Een Cortisana haer pallerende' (mistranslated as 'A "Courtesan Doing Her Hair"').
17 Compare, for instance, Jacob Backer's painting of a bare-breasted woman who smiles at the observer and holds up a coin, and who simultaneously represents the sense of touch (Museu Nacional de Arte Antiga, Lisbon) (Sumowski, *Gemälde,* vol. I, 1983, no. 25).
18 Bredius 1915–22, vol. II, pp. 640–1; Strauss & Van der Meulen 1979, p. 254, no. 1647/1.
19 WNT, vol. 9, 1913, col. 779.
20 If 'de minnemoer van Rembrant' is taken to mean 'Rembrandt's children's nurse' and is indeed a portrayal of Geertje Dircx – and assuming the picture bartered in 1647 is identical with the *Young Woman in Bed* – the object of Geertje's attention would be Titus. An additional problem is posed by the words 'van [by or of] Rembrant' in the barter document, which refers to several other paintings alternately as 'painted by Rembrandt' and 'Rembrandt's' (Strauss & Van der Meulen 1979, p. 254, no. 1647/1). The bartered goods included 'een contrefeytsel *van* Rembrant's vrouw' (a portrait *of* Rembrandt's wife) and 'een lantschap *van* Rembrant' (a landscape *by* Rembrandt).

15
Man in Armour

Signed and dated lower left *Rembrandt f / 1655*
Canvas
137.5 x 104.5 cm (strips have been added at each edge)
Glasgow Museums: Art Gallery and Museum, Kelvingrove

PROVENANCE: Sir Joshua Reynolds (1723–1792), London, *c.*1764; purchased from Reynolds by the Earl of Warwick in 1790; sale, [Warwick?], London (Christie's), 29 June 1833, lot 93, to Woodburn; John Graham-Gilbert, *c.*1860; presented by Mrs Graham-Gilbert in 1877.

LITERATURE: Hofstede de Groot 1908–27, vol. VI, 1916, p. 138, no. 208 (as 'Mars'); Miles 1961, vol. 1, pp. 109–12, no. 601 (with earlier literature); Bauch 1966, no. 280; Bredius / Gerson 1969, no. 480; Schwartz 1984, p. 303; Tümpel 1986, no. 109*; C. Brown, in Berlin / Amsterdam / London 1991–92a, pp. 258–61, cat. no. 43; Brown & Roy 1992; Tümpel 1993, p. 465 ('Must be considered authentic'); Giltaij 1997, pp. 49–54.

This imposing picture is a half-length figure of a warrior, seen in profile. He wears an elaborately wrought helmet, adorned at the front with a shape resembling the head of a bird. A heavy ornamented plate attached to the back of the helmet functions as a neck-guard. The sharply etched profile is visible as far as the eyes, which are hidden in the shadow of the helmet. An extremely large eardrop, either a huge pearl or a ball of silver, hangs from the man's ear. The figure wears an ornate cuirass, and a deftly folded scarf, over which he seems to have a medallion. His gauntleted right hand grips a massive lance, only part of which is visible. His left arm is concealed behind a gigantic round shield, which appears to be of metal and is itself partly covered by a dark red mantle falling from the shoulder.

Architectural elements are discernible on the left in the dark background. At the extreme left are pilasters, while the warrior's face and helmet stand out against a darker window aperture. The light in the picture falls on the helmet and breastplate, creating a dramatic contrast to the shadowed face of the figure, sunk so deep in thought. The way in which the warrior looms up, as it were, against a mysterious background makes a powerful impression on the viewer. And it is fascinating to see how Rembrandt managed to render his textures using such a limited palette. Black, white and a few touches of red suffice to depict the heavy metal of the helmet and breastplate, while a smudged dark red conveys the softness of the fabric.

X-rays show that Rembrandt had made earlier use of the canvas on which this picture is painted. Viewing the vertical picture in horizontal orientation revealed a seated figure wearing a veil.[1] Furthermore, one can see with the naked eye that the helmet originally covered more of the cheek, exposing far less of the face.

The earliest certain provenance for the painting is the collection of Sir Joshua Reynolds (1723–1792), the brilliant English portraitist, knighted in 1769, who owned a large collection of paintings and drawings, among them our cat. nos 17 and 32. In 1764, while the present work was still in Reynolds's possession, the Augsburg artist Johann Gottfried Haid made a mezzotint engraving of it which is now undeservedly forgotten (fig. 15a). It is clear from the caption under the print that Reynolds thought the warrior portrayed by Rembrandt was Achilles. Haid's is a perfect reproduction, although the facial expression is somewhat more animated in the print than in the painting.

The painting was formerly thought to have been in the sale of the collection of Count Fraula, held in Brussels on 21 July 1738. Because of the description in the sale catalogue, the present picture was taken to be a portrait of Rembrandt's son. But the measurements given in the catalogue – equivalent to 121.5 x 99 cm – do not correspond to those of our cat. no. 15. However, the dimensions recorded in 1738 are consistent with those of a comparable work measuring 118 x 91 cm (now at the Museu Calouste Gulbenkian in Lisbon (fig. 15b)). Cat. no. 15 was also formerly thought to have been one of the works in a sale in Amsterdam on 5 June 1765, at which was listed a Rembrandt painting, measuring 102.8 x 84.8 cm, of a helmeted warrior bearing a shield on the left arm. Given that this picture would be considerably smaller in size than the Glasgow work, together with the simple fact that the painting was in Reynolds's collection between 1764 (the date on the Haid print) and 1790 (see Provenance), it cannot be the work auctioned in 1765.

Another question is whether it is the painting commissioned from Rembrandt by the seventeenth-century collector Antonio Ruffo (1610/11–1678). According to a comprehensive series of articles on Ruffo's collection published in 1916 by a descendant, Vincenzo Ruffo,[2] this Sicilian nobleman commissioned a half-length figure from Rembrandt in about 1652. This work was entered in the Ruffo inventory in 1654 as 'Aristotle'. A commission for two more half-length figures followed in around 1660, the first being a portrayal of Alexander the Great, and the second, a depiction of Homer. Soon after the appearance of Vincenzo Ruffo's articles, Hoogewerff published suggestions concerning the identification of these paintings.[3] He equated the first with *Aristotle Contemplating the Bust of Homer*, 1653, now at the Metropolitan Museum of Art, New York (p. 27, fig. 8),[4] and the third with the *Homer Teaching His Pupils* fragment in the Mauritshuis, The Hague (fig. 97b). In Hoogewerff's view the second work, 'Alexander the Great', could be either the Glasgow painting or that formerly at the Hermitage, St Petersburg, and now at the Museu Calouste Gulbenkian (fig. 15b). Since the publication of Hoogewerff's article in 1917, these two alternatives have been constantly under discussion. One of the issues in question relates to Ruffo's complaint to Rembrandt that his 'Alexander the Great' was painted on four strips of canvas sewn together. This seemed to point to the Glasgow painting, to which strips have been attached on all four sides of the canvas (see below). In preparation for the major Rembrandt exhibition of 1991–92, the Glasgow picture underwent a restoration that

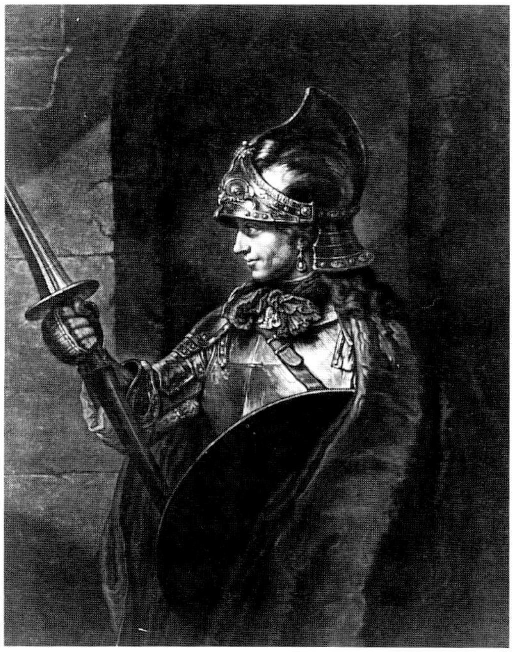

FIG. 15a
Johann Gottfried Haid (German, 1710–1776), after Rembrandt
Man in Armour
Mezzotint
Inscribed *Rembrandt pinx^t J. Boydell excudit, J. G. Haid fecit. ACHILLES. From the original picture by Rembrandt, in the Collection of Mr Reynolds. Published by J. BOYDELL Engraver in Cheapside, London, Novr 1764. No. 8.*
40.5 x 35.5 cm

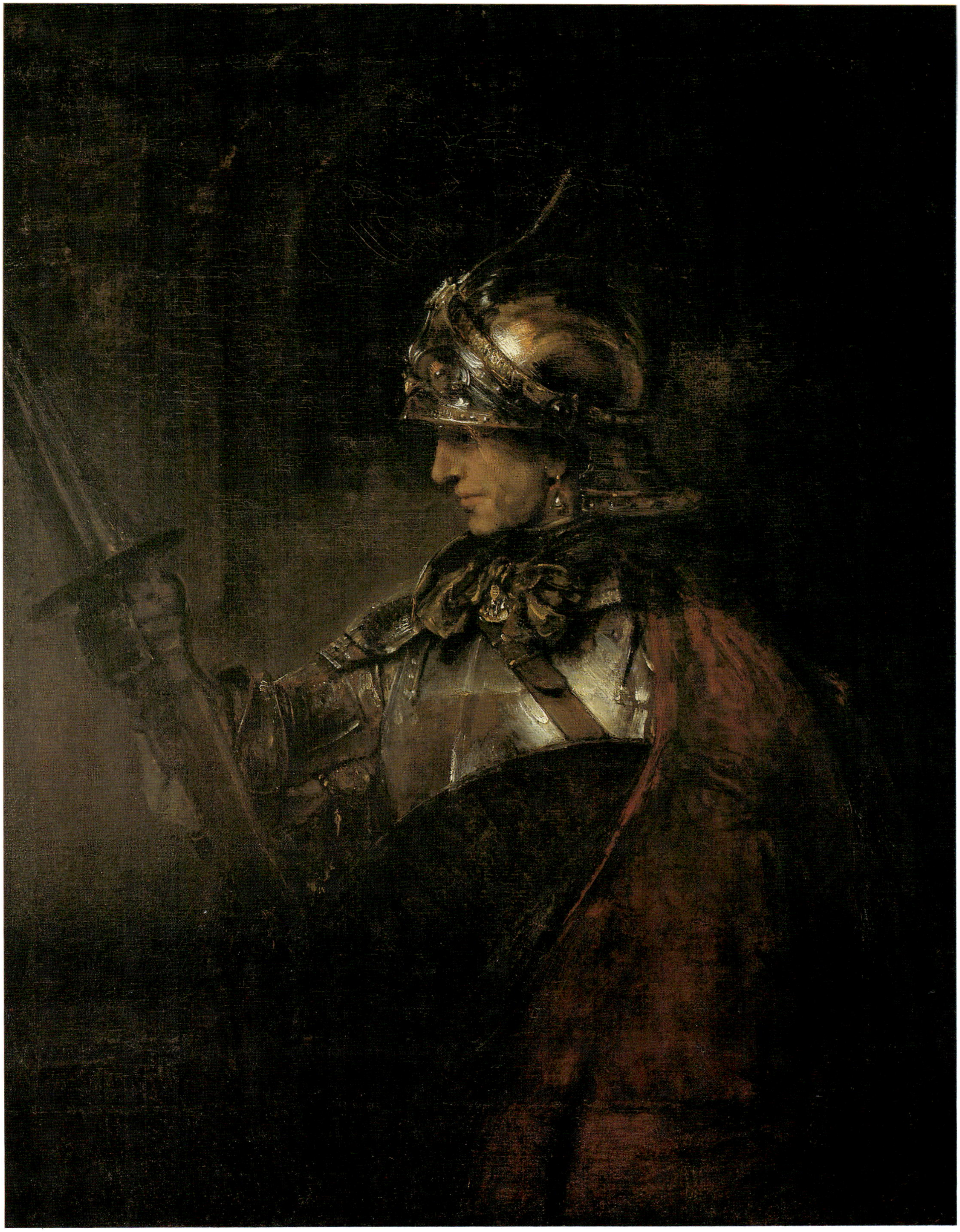

involved scientific research. The results of the research were published in 1992 by Brown and Roy, who state that cat. no. 15 is definitely the picture from the Ruffo Collection,[5] despite convincing arguments to the contrary presented by Miles, for instance, in the 1961 catalogue of the Glasgow collection.[6]

In a letter to Rembrandt, Ruffo mentioned that the picture he first received consisted of only a head, and that the artist had subsequently decided to convert it into a half-length figure. It is true that the Glasgow work has strips attached, measuring approximately 10 cm at the top, 4.5 cm at the left, 10 cm at the right, and 14 cm along the bottom.[7] They have not been used for any part of the representation, and are covered with paint of a smoother structure than that used in the central section. Brown and Roy argue that this paint could nevertheless date from the seventeenth century, and could have been applied by Rembrandt himself or under his supervision.[8] This seems unlikely. The authors also state that the measurements given in the Ruffo inventory, 8 by 6 *palmi* or approximately 200 x 150 cm, are not exact and are thus not an impediment to identification, particularly as, they believe, the picture may have been cropped.[9] However, it is clear from the identification of other paintings from the Ruffo Collection that the measurements in the inventory, while not exact to the last centimetre, are nonetheless reasonably consistent and nowhere deviate by as much as 60 cm and 45cm, as would be the case here. If the picture was cut, this must have occurred between 1739, the date of the last inventory of the Ruffo Collection,[10] which was unknown to earlier writers and in which the picture is listed, and 1764, the date of Haid's engraving (fig. 15a).

Moreover, the 'Alexander' listed in the inventory is described as seated. Curiously, Brown and Roy find it quite conceivable that the figure in the Glasgow picture could be seated, even though there is nothing to indicate a sitting position and it would seem to be almost physically impossible for a warrior sustaining the combined weight of an iron helmet, a cuirass, a shield and a massive lance to be sitting on a chair. The authors also suggest that the date on the painting, hitherto accepted as 1655, can equally well be read as 1659.[11] It would indeed be highly unlikely that a picture that arrived in Messina in 1661 would have been painted in 1655. A somewhat later date would obviously fit more readily into this theory. Be that as it may, the present writer formed the opinion back in 1989 that '5' was the most probable last digit, the conclusion also reached in 1983 through research conducted by the museum. Brown and Roy also argue that the picture in the Fraula sale of 1738 cannot be identified as that in Glasgow, while they say it is uncertain that the Ruffo Collection was still intact in 1739. This latter argument is refuted by the discovery that a complete inventory was drawn up, as noted earlier, in that year.

For the reasons outlined here, it must be assumed that the Glasgow painting is not the

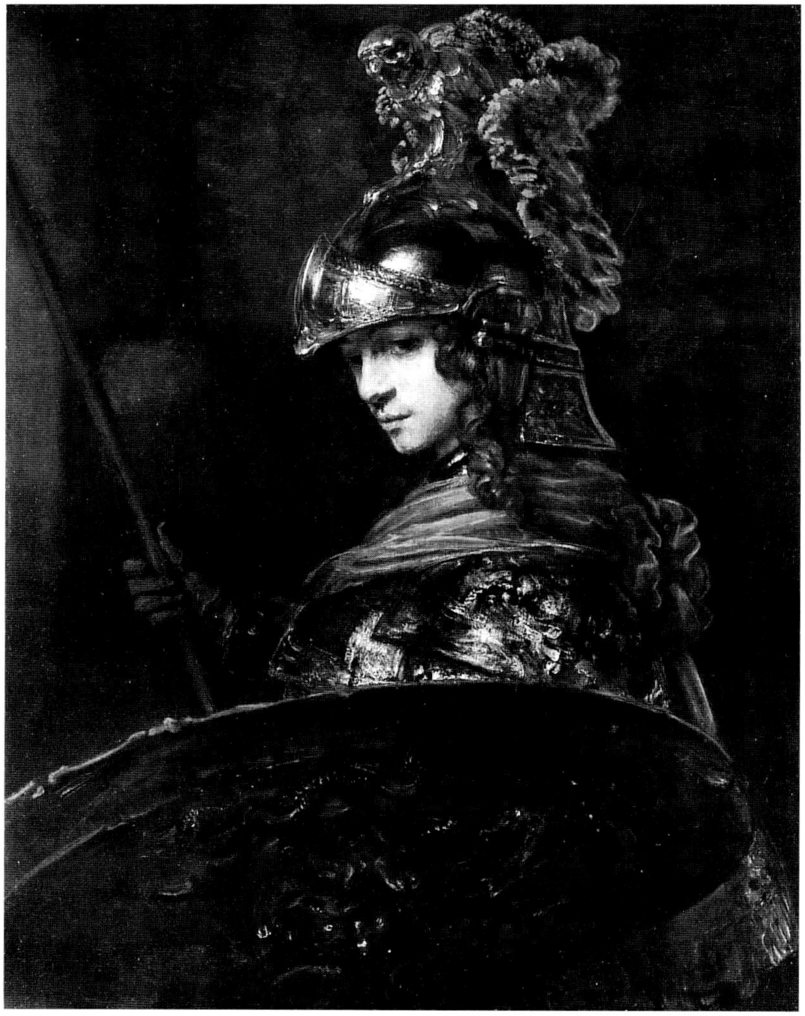

FIG. 15b
Rembrandt(?)
A Warrior
Canvas
118.0 x 91.0 cm
Museu Calouste Gulbenkian, Lisbon

work in the Ruffo Collection in 1739. Similarly, it cannot be identified with the picture in the Fraula sale of 1738, nor with that in the Amsterdam sale of 1765. It is in fact one of Rembrandt's fantasy warrior figures, variously thought in the past to represent Pallas Athena, St Michael, Achilles, Mars, Apollo, Erictheus or Bellona.[12] The figure portrayed here is presumably a man with the strength needed to support the weight of a helmet, a cuirass, a lance and a shield of large proportions. However, there would seem to be little point in seeking to attach a name to the figure. The earliest known title for the picture, 'Achilles', by which it was known when in the Reynolds collection, probably means no more than that at that time Achilles was a familiar hero of classical antiquity – not that this identification echoed an original title.

The Glasgow *Man in Armour* is part of a genre characteristic of the artist's work from an early stage onwards. This genre is typified by curiously attired martial figures with helmets, armour and weapons, such as the *Bellona*, dated 1633, at the Metropolitan Museum of Art, New York (fig. 15c).[13] The often magnificently wrought attributes of war held a special attraction for Rembrandt, and he used them in several self-portraits, like the *Self-Portrait with Helmet* of 1634 at the Gemäldegalerie, Kassel.[14] He himself owned several such objects, as appears from the inventory of his possessions drawn up in 1656: 'Two iron helmets, one Japanese helmet, one "carbatian" helmet, one iron suit of armour and a helmet, one wondrous figured iron shield of Quintijn the smith, one Turkish powder flask, one pellet bow [etc.]'.[15] With the aid of these antique or oriental attributes, Rembrandt created a mysterious, mythological world of his own. The *Man in Armour* is a fascinating example of this.

JEROEN GILTAIJ

1 For a large reproduction of the X-ray photograph, see Brown & Roy 1992, fig. 3.
2 Ruffo 1916, pp. 21–64, 95–128, 165–92, 237–56, 284–320, 369–88; Ruffo 1919, pp. 3–16.
3 Hoogewerff 1917.
4 Bredius / Gerson 1969, no. 478.
5 Brown & Roy 1992.
6 Miles 1961, vol. 1, pp. 109–12, no. 601.
7 For a drawing of the attached strips, see Brown & Roy 1992, fig. 2; see also the X-ray, fig. 3.
8 Brown & Roy 1992, pp. 295–6.
9 Brown & Roy 1992, p. 288.
10 For the 1739 inventory, see Giltaij 1997, pp. 103–4.
11 Brown & Roy 1992, p. 296.
12 Bauch 1966, p. 15, no. 280.
13 *Corpus*, vol. II, 1986, no. A70.
14 *Corpus*, vol. II, 1986, no. A97.
15 Strauss & Van der Meulen 1979, pp. 363–7, no. 1656/12: 'Twee Isere helmetten, Een Japanse hellemet, Een carbaetse helmet, Een isere rusting met een hellemet, Een raer gefigureert Iser schilt van Quintijn de Smith, Een turcxe kruijtfles, Een Cluijtbooch [etc.]'.

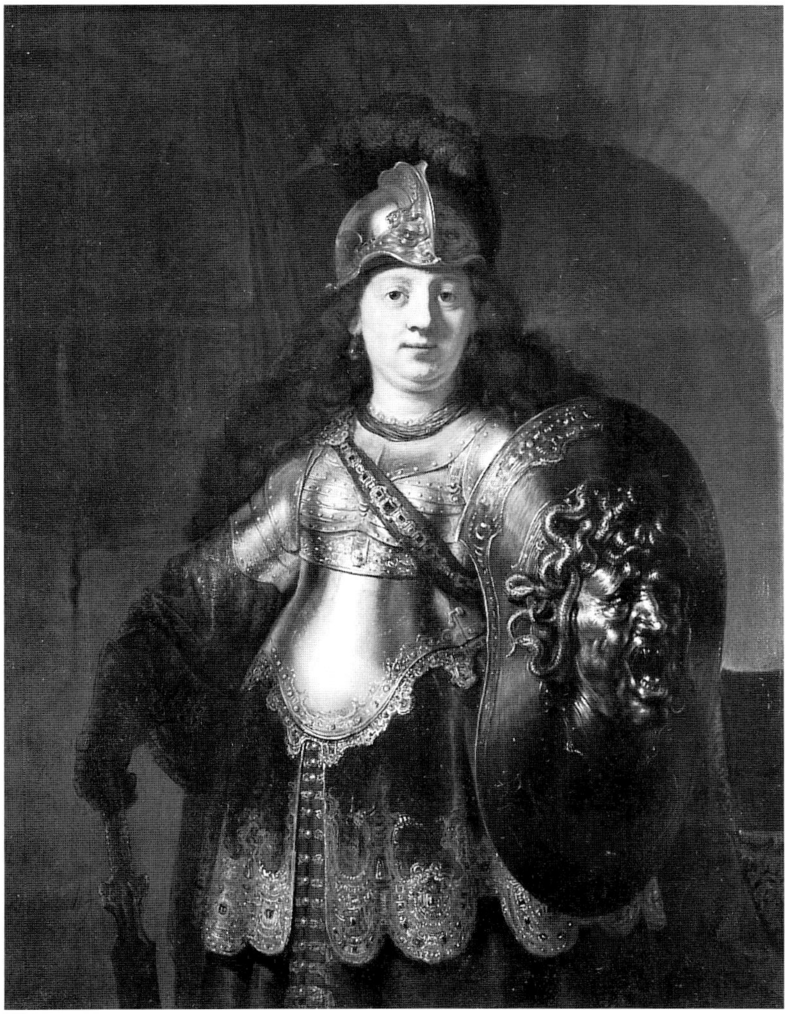

FIG. 15C
Rembrandt
Bellona
Signed and dated 1633
Canvas
127.0 x 97.0 cm
The Metropolitan Museum of Art, New York

16
Joseph Accused by Potiphar's Wife

Signed and dated lower right *Rembran[dt] f. 1655*
Canvas
113.5 x 90.0 cm (cropped slightly on all sides)
Staatliche Museen zu Berlin, Gemäldegalerie

PROVENANCE: Sale, Lord Willoughby, London, *c.*1820, to Hickman & Carpenter, sold to Sir Thomas Lawrence; his sale, London, 15 May 1830; Joseph Neeld, Grittleton House, 1836; Sir John Neeld; purchased from Sedelmeyer's, Paris, in 1883.

LITERATURE: Smith 1829–42, vol. VII, 1836, no. 20; Wustmann 1906; Hofstede de Groot 1908–27, vol. VI, 1916, p. 32, no. 17; Van Guldener 1947, esp. pp. 37–40; Bredius / Gerson 1969, no. 524; Albach 1972, p. 121; Kaufmann 1973; Schwartz 1984, p. 274; Tümpel 1986, no. 25; C. Tümpel, in Amsterdam / Jerusalem / Münster 1991–94, p. 200, cat. no. 24; Wheelock 1995, pp. 316–20.

Joseph, the favourite son of Jacob, was sold into slavery by his envious brothers (see cat. no. 92). He was taken to Egypt and bought by Potiphar, an officer of the Pharaoh and captain of his guard. Joseph found grace with his master, who appointed him overseer in his house and 'left all that he had in Joseph's hand'. And it came to pass that Potiphar's wife 'cast her eyes upon Joseph' and, finding him fair to behold, bade him 'Lie with me' (Genesis 39:1–20). Joseph refused, pleading loyalty to Potiphar, but the woman persisted. One day, when they found themselves alone in the house, she 'caught him by his garment, saying, Lie with me: and he left his garment in her hand, and fled, and got him out'. Thirsting for revenge, Potiphar's wife called her servants and said, 'See, [Potiphar] hath brought in an Hebrew unto us, to mock us; he came in unto me to lie with me, and I cried with a loud voice: And it came to pass, when he heard that I lifted up my voice and cried, that he left his garment with me, and fled, and got him out'.

Rembrandt's painting of 1655 shows the sequel to this episode. Potiphar has returned home and his wife repeats her story. She sits with her legs modestly crossed and rearranges her 'dishevelled' clothing with her left hand. She tramples Joseph's garment underfoot. Potiphar stands beside his wife, one hand on the armrest of her chair and the other on his hip. He is portrayed as an oriental and resembles the hero of a fairytale. His tunic and large turban, low-slung sabre and flat shoes were inspired by the Mogul miniatures that Rembrandt often copied in that period. Potiphar even has the relatively flat, stiff aspect – by Western European standards – of the figures from the Mogul sheets, a quality that also characterizes Rembrandt's copies of these miniatures (fig. 93a).

Potiphar listens to his wife's words, and has not yet formed a judgement. His wife points an accusing thumb at Joseph, who raises his left arm and lifts his eyes to the heavens with a look of despair. According to the biblical text, Joseph had fled and was not present to hear the charge against him. However, he does appear in this scene in *Joseph in Egypt*, a play published by the Dutch poet Joost van den Vondel in 1640 and frequently produced in Amsterdam ever since. Vondel's Potiphar asks his wife what has happened: 'Why is thy robe in disarray?' To which she brazenly replies: 'Behold that garment [Joseph's]. Thou hast brought the Hebrew, the slave, into the house and thus has he desired to defile thy bed and home'. Whereupon Joseph appears on the scene and pleads in his defence: 'The deed of which I am accused never entered my thoughts'.[1]

With this in mind, it has often been suggested that Rembrandt based his painting partly, if not primarily, on Vondel's play.[2] Nevertheless, a Joseph who is present to witness the accusations brought against him by Potiphar's wife and at

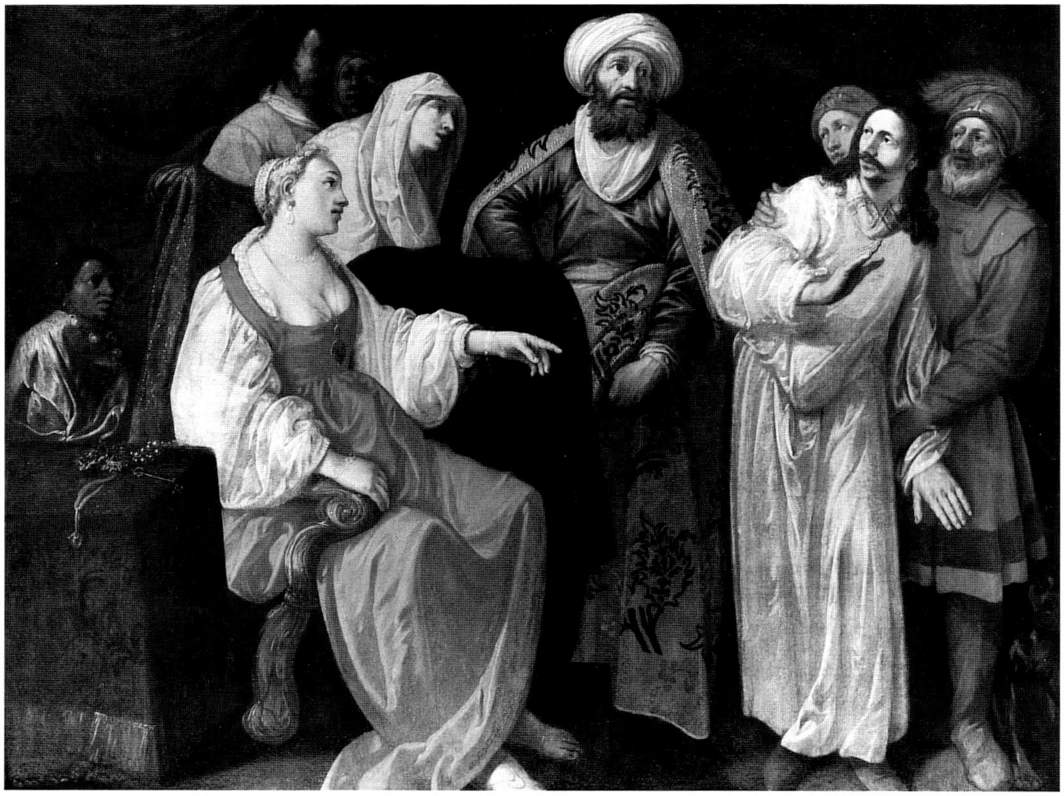

FIG. 16a
Jan Pynas *c.*1585–after 1650
Joseph Accused by Potiphar's Wife
Signed and dated 1629
Canvas
101.6 x 127.0 cm
Collection of Alfred Bader, Milwaukee

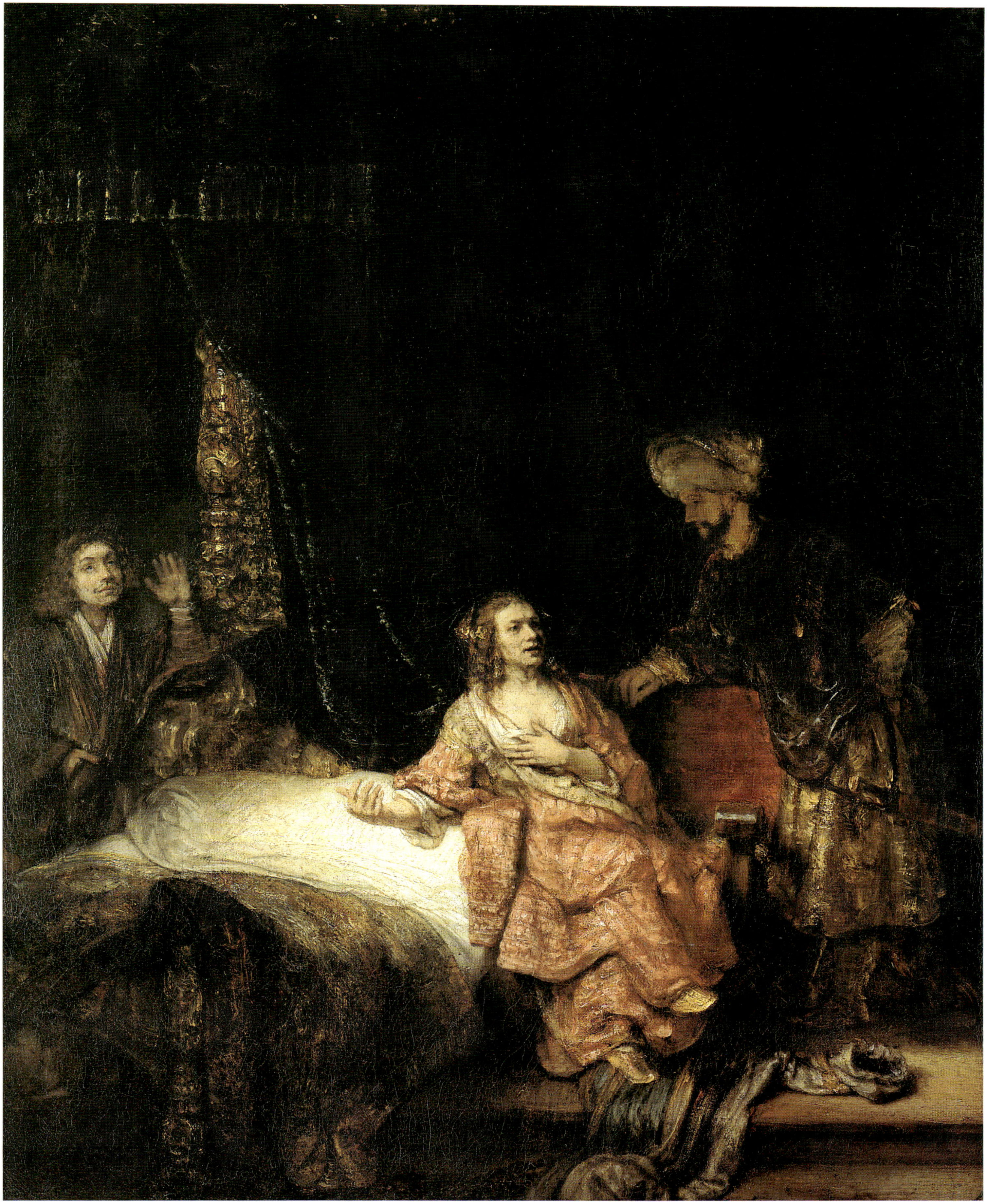

whom she points a finger can also be seen in a painting by Jan Pynas (*c.*1585–after 1650) of 1629 (fig. 16a).[3] Jan Pynas may have been one of Rembrandt's teachers.[4] The motif also appears in a picture that is listed, probably correctly, as an early Salomon Koninck (1609–1656) dating from soon after 1630 (fig. 16b).[5] Hence Rembrandt need not necessarily have taken the motif from Vondel.[6]

A striking feature of cat. no. 16 is the prominence accorded in the composition to the elaborate, gilt, canopied bed, which stands between Joseph and the woman, heightening the opulence and the oriental atmosphere of the scene. The bed is not mentioned in the biblical text. The story of Joseph is related in greater detail in *Of the Antiquities of the Jews* by the Jewish Roman historian Flavius Josephus (*c.*AD 37 – after AD 100), a work which, as Tümpel has shown, was often consulted by painters.[7] In 1656, the year after cat. no. 16 was made, Rembrandt is known to have been in possession of a luxury edition of Josephus's book.[8] According to Josephus's account, Potiphar's wife addresses her husband as follows: 'O husband ... mayst thou not live a day longer, if thou dost not punish the wicked slave, who has desired to defile thy bed'.[9] Tümpel speculates that this description may have inspired Rembrandt to highlight the motif of the bed.[10]

It is clear from the passage quoted above that Vondel took the words 'defile thy bed' straight from Josephus's text. The bed also looms large in Rembrandt's etching of 1634 illustrating the preceding episode of the story (fig. 16c, B.39). The etching shows with inescapable realism that it was Potiphar's wife herself who sought to 'defile' the bed. Potiphar, however, chose to give credence to his wife's account of the affair and consigned Joseph to the dungeon. The scene of his being taken captive is the subject of Pynas's painting (fig. 16a). A virtuous man and an influential interpreter of dreams, Joseph was later made viceroy of Egypt.

Joseph's adventures, which the twelfth sura of the Koran describes as 'the most beautiful of tales', have inspired painters for centuries. In Christian art they were often depicted as a series of episodes. In Dutch literature of the seventeenth century Joseph's purity as the antithesis of the lust of Potiphar's wife was the theme of countless poems and plays.[11] Rembrandt also produced drawings of *Joseph Accused by Potiphar's Wife,* Joseph himself is not shown.[12] One sheet bears a sketch of Potiphar as he appears in the painting, listening to his wife with one hand on his hip and the other on the armrest of her chair. Here too we see the canopied bed; a maidservant crouches on the left (fig. 16d).[13]

A second version of the composition of cat. no. 16 is at the National Gallery of Art in Washington (fig. 16e).[14] Though it was formerly regarded as a second autograph version, the general consensus since the 1960s is that it was executed by Rembrandt's studio.[15] The Washington picture is less sculptural, as is apparent even from reproductions (fig. 16e). The position and shape of the woman's legs are far less clearly defined. There is no step in the foreground, so that the illusion of depth is reduced.[16] Yet the painting in Washington is more than simply a copy. It incorporates several variations, apparently conceived in Rembrandt's workshop and possibly at his own instigation. Joseph's incriminating cloak, for instance, hangs

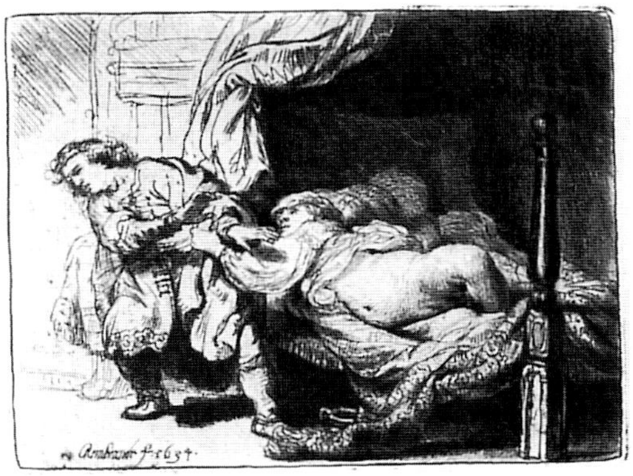

FIG. 16c
Rembrandt
Joseph and Potiphar's Wife
Signed and dated 1634
Etching
9.0 x 11.5 cm
From a reproduction

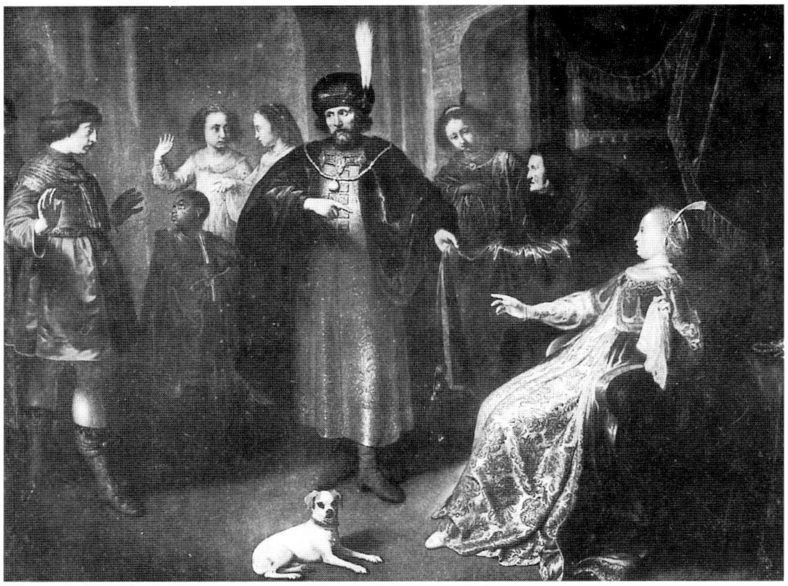

FIG. 16b
Salomon Koninck 1609–1656
Joseph Accused by Potiphar's Wife
Canvas
118.0 x 160.0 cm
Formerly Khanenko Collection, Kiev; present whereabouts unknown
From a reproduction at the RKD

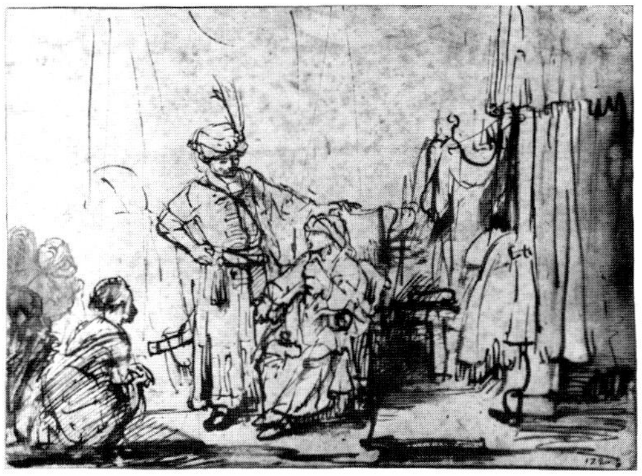

FIG. 16d
Rembrandt
Potiphar and His Wife
Pen and ink and brush
20.1 x 26.7 cm
Private collection
From a reproduction

conspicuously on the post at the foot of the bed. The woman points at the garment, this time with her index finger instead of her thumb. She is now also wearing a string of pearls and gold bracelets. Joseph no longer holds his hands out in despair: he bows his head in meek resignation and stands with his hands before him. A bunch of keys, alluding to his office of steward of the household, hangs like a badge of trust from his girdle. Neither the canopy nor the carved headboard is depicted in the painting.

The Washington picture shows how the workshop absorbed Rembrandt's impact and developed his ideas. A similar example, in this case from 1635, is the studio version of *Abraham's Sacrifice*, with a completely different angel from that in Rembrandt's original (see commentary to cat. no. 74).[17] Here, too, the change has far-reaching repercussions for the emphasis in the composition. These examples give a good impression of the way Rembrandt's studio explored a range of possibilities when deciding how best to portray a 'history'. Both versions of *Joseph Accused by Potiphar's Wife* are painted in glowing colours with lashings of red. The wide brushwork reflects Rembrandt's interest in Venetian art in the 1650s, and especially his admiration for the work of the mature Titian.

AB

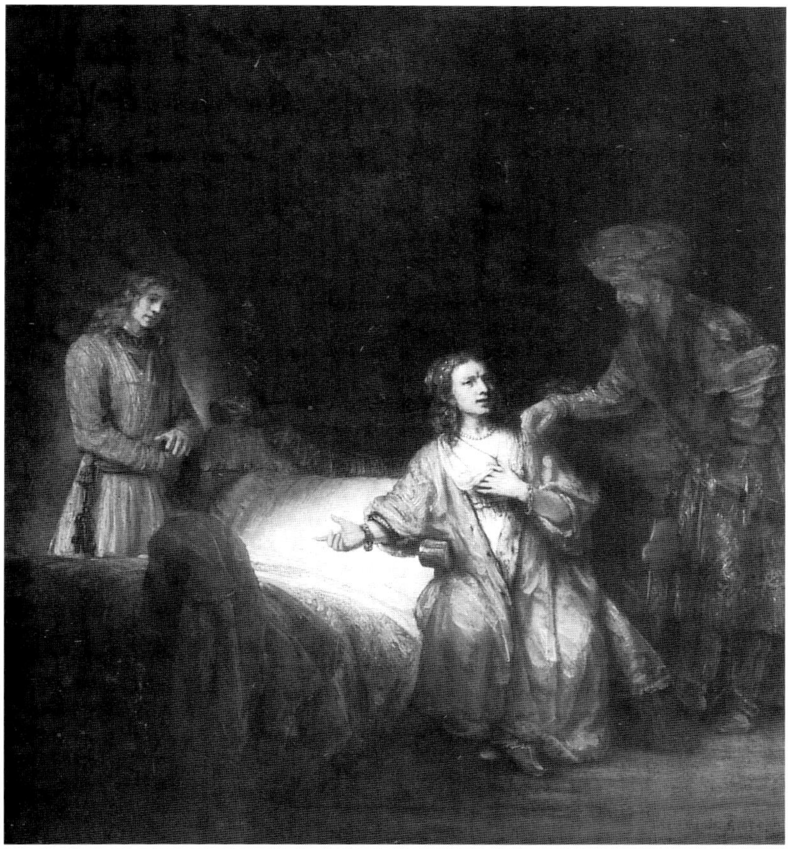

FIG. 16e
Studio of Rembrandt
Joseph Accused by Potiphar's Wife
Bearing a signature and the date 1655
Canvas
105.7 x 97.8 cm
National Gallery of Art, Washington DC

1 Van den Vondel 1640, lines 1304–1350: 'Hoe komt uw kleet aldus uit zijne ploy gesleurt?' 'bezie dat kleet. Ghy hebt my dien Hebreeuw, dien slaef in huis gebraght, Op dat uw bedde en huis al t'effens werd geschonden'. 'Wat leit men my te last het geen ick nimmer docht'.

2 First by Wustmann 1906, pp. 81–4; subsequently by Albach 1972, p. 121; Kaufmann 1973, p. 52; and Schwartz 1984, pp. 272, 274. Kaufmann also speculates that Rembrandt may have identified with Joseph because of the charges brought against him by Geertje Dircx and others.

3 Observed by Bauch 1960, pp. 126, 258, note 96.

4 See note 16 in M. Blokhuis, 'On the Life of Rembrandt van Rijn', in the present catalogue.

5 Sumowski, *Gemälde*, vol. III, 1987, no. 1077, formerly attributed to Ferdinand Bol. Van Guldener 1947, p. 122, suggests that it may have been inspired by Vondel's play, but the picture was probably made earlier. Sumowski published a later painting (present whereabouts unknown) of *Potiphar's Wife Accuses Joseph*, in which Joseph himself plays a prominent role, as a work by Johan van Neck (1635–1714) (Sumowski, *Gemälde*, vol. VI, 1995, no. 2392a, repr.).

6 In any event, Joseph appears in Vondel's play only after Potiphar expresses his rage, and there is also an elderly nurse in attendance.

7 Tümpel 1991–94, pp. 194–206, with references to earlier versions of this article.

8 Strauss & Van der Meulen 1979, p. 379, no. 1656/12 (no. 284).

9 *Of the Antiquities of the Jews*, Book 2, chap. 4, sect. 5, English trans. by W. Whiston, London, 1755, vol. I, pp. 82–3, cited in Wheelock 1995, p. 20, note 5.

10 Tümpel 1991–94, p. 200.

11 Eyffinger 1987, pp. 33–7.

12 For Joseph in work by Rembrandt and his circle in relation to seventeenth-century literature, see Van Guldener 1947. The drawings are reproduced in Benesch 1973, vol. III, nos 494, 623, figs 652, 799. The drawing in Benesch 1973, vol. V, no. 958, fig. 1239, which is said to be a study for the painting in Washington (fig. 16e), is a forgery (see Van Guldener 1947, p. 40; Rosenberg 1959, pp. 108–19).

13 Benesch 1973, vol. III, no. 623, fig. 799, as dating from *c.*1648–49. There are three sketches of a second figure beside the maidservant, two of which were subsequently concealed with white. Benesch identifies the figure as Joseph kneeling. Surprisingly, however, Potiphar and his wife pay no heed to him. The figure presumably represented, therefore, another servant.

14 Bredius / Gerson 1969, no. 523.

15 Wheelock 1995, no. 1937.1.79, pp. 314–21, esp. p. 317.

16 Wheelock 1995, p. 320, note 28, has observed that the step is in fact illogical, as it suggests that the head of the bed is raised but not the foot. Sandrart, as we know, criticized Rembrandt's indifference to the rules of 'Perspectiva' (Sandrart 1675, p. 202).

17 Rembrandt's version is in St Petersburg and the studio variant in Munich. Both are discussed in Bredius / Gerson 1969, no. 498, and in *Corpus*, vol. III, 1989, under no. A108.

17
The Apostle Bartholomew

Signed and dated centre left *Rembrandt f. 1657*
Canvas
122.7 x 99.7 cm
Timken Museum of Art, San Diego

PROVENANCE: [After White (1983), Broun (1987) and Liedtke (1996)] Sale, Jonathan Richardson, London, 3–4 March 1747, lot 49, to William Fauquier; sale, Dr Robert Bragge, London (Prestage), 9 February 1757, lot 48 (as 'a man with a knife'), to Joshua Reynolds (1723–1792) [with whom listed in 1769–70 ledger]; Anne-Adriaen-Pierre de Montmorency, Duc de Laval, from *c.*1790; by descent to his daughter, Princess Troubetzkoy; by descent to her daughter, Princess Davidoff; by descent to her grandson, Prince Wassili Davidoff, Kiev; [according to Hofstede de Groot (1916)] with Thos Agnew & Sons, London, and with Duveen Brothers, New York; Henry Goldman, New York; acquired by the Putnam Foundation in 1952.

LITERATURE: Hofstede de Groot 1908–27, vol. VI, 1916, p. 120, no. 169; Benesch 1956, p. 338; Rosenberg 1964, p. 118; Bauch 1966, no. 217; Bredius / Gerson 1969, no. 613; C. White, in New Haven 1983, p. 113; Schwartz 1984, p. 310; Tümpel 1986, no. 80; Broun 1987, pp. 52–4, no. 10; W. Liedtke, in Adelson et al. 1996, pp. 90–4, no. 16 (with earlier literature).

It seems as if Rembrandt's object in this picture was to demonstrate his ability to make efficient use of paint. He has achieved the greatest possible expression with the most economical means, knowing that our eye would automatically go first to the man's face. Of the various elements in the composition, only the face is clearly defined and, even then, only the side in the light. In this respect, this canvas from 1657 develops a principle that Rembrandt had already applied *c.*1630 in the *Bearded Old Man* in the Bader Collection (cat. no. 4). But here he has taken the idea several steps further. Only the triangle formed by the forehead, right cheek and bridge of the nose is illuminated: the triangular shape looms out of the dimness.

Rembrandt's modelling of this section suggests a man in the prime of his life whose attention has suddenly been distracted. He glances up as though he has seen or heard something unexpected. He is frowning and his gaze is fixed somewhere to the left of the viewer. The suggestion of vitality is heightened by the curls of the man's dark hair and beard, and his demeanour implies both energy and vigour. Supporting himself with his right arm, he seems to be about to rise from his seat. Sketchy folds in his robe and coat hint at the shape of his frame.

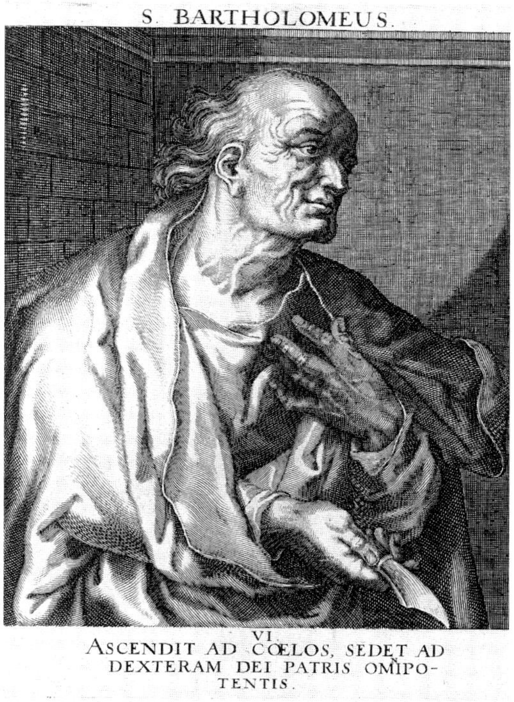

FIG. 17a
Peter Isselburg (German, *c.*1575–after 1630), after Gabriel Weyer, after Peter Paul Rubens
The Apostle Bartholomew
Engraving
23.2 x 19.9 cm
Herzog Anton Ulrich-Museum, Braunschweig
Photograph: B. P. Keiser

Light also falls on the man's cuff and right hand,[1] which Rembrandt has reduced to angular shapes in much the same way as Cézanne was to do centuries later. Another shape in this section is the knife. The man is holding it in the middle, between his thumb and index finger, so that we see the handle as well as the blade. He seems to be showing the knife though has no intention of using it. The wide-grooved blade is rendered in greyish-white. This white is not as bright as that of the cuff, but it is sufficiently so: the area behind the knife is the darkest part of the figure and the shapes in it are hardly distinguishable. The overall effect is that as soon as we have finished surveying the man's face our eye moves down to the knife, the standard attribute of Christ's apostle Bartholomew since medieval times.

The passage in Matthew 10:3 listing the twelve apostles mentions no more than Bartholomew's name. Legend has it that after Christ's Ascension Bartholomew converted heathens in India, Mesopotamia, Lycaonia and Armenia. He is said to have been flayed alive in Armenia and therefore has a knife as his attribute. He is often portrayed with his flayed skin as well, and sometimes with a book. He appears with only the knife in a picture by Rubens, who made a series of twelve apostles for the Duke of Lerma in 1603 (now Prado, Madrid). Rembrandt may have seen a print after Rubens's picture (fig. 17a).[2]

We know from cat. no. 17 that by 1657 Rembrandt had returned to representing apostles as lifesize half-length figures. As far as we know, he had not done so for twenty-five years, since painting the *Apostle Peter*, 1632, now in Stockholm (cat. no. 7). Rembrandt painted other apostles and evangelists after the *Bartholomew* of 1657, some of which works are dated 1661 (cat. nos 21, 22). They are a little smaller than this *Bartholomew*. However, a picture of *Paul Writing* in Washington DC,[3] though a little larger (131.5 x 104.4 cm), is roughly the same size as the *Bartholomew*. This is presumably why the two pictures were thought to have been made at the same time, possibly as part of a cycle.[4] Yet they are quite different in character. Moreover, the *Paul* was initially smaller and oval in format, and is now generally rejected as an autograph work.[5]

The motif of the apostle with the knife evidently captured the artist's imagination. A smaller bust figure of *Bartholomew* of *c.*1634 is known from several non-autograph versions. Gerson in 1969 considered the version at the Worcester Art Museum the best of these (fig. 17b).[6] Since then, this interesting composition has not been mentioned in the literature on Rembrandt.[7] Yet the piece in Worcester has its admirers.[8] The

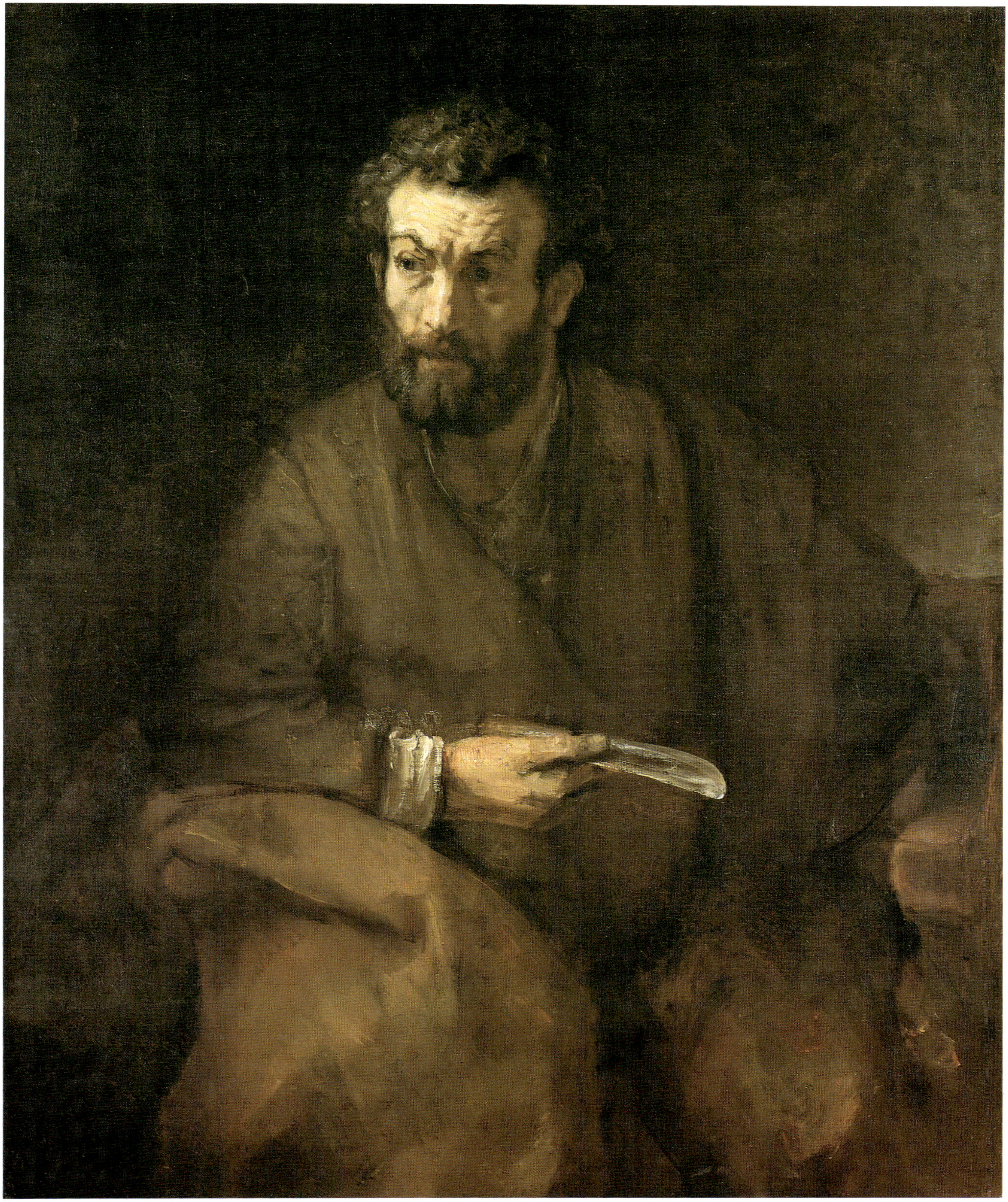

frowning apostle in the painting fixes us with an intense gaze, holding his knife at the ready as though we were threatening him. The overall design is repeated in the late *Bartholomew*, dated 1661, at the J. Paul Getty Museum in Malibu (fig. 17c).[9] Here, too, the figure has protruding ears, is viewed from the front, and looks out at the observer. In the Getty picture, the apostle looks more introverted and resigned, and presents an imposing, sprawling figure by comparison with the one in Worcester.

In Gerson's view, the Getty piece is 'handled with extraordinary vigour, and if it had not been engraved in the 18th century, one might have been induced to believe that a picture like this could only have been conceived and executed in the 19th century'.[10] Gerson's association of the picture with the nineteenth century may have been prompted to some extent by the apostle's short, 'modern' hairstyle. Interestingly enough, the early Bartholomew in Worcester also has short hair, although the cut is not so modern (fig. 17b). The Bartholomew in the Getty Museum painting has his fingers on his throat. It seems to me that Rembrandt may have wanted to hint at the apostle's premonition of his decapitation, which took place after he was flayed.[11] The man holds the knife to one side in his large right hand as if it were a potato-peeler.

The *Bartholomew* at the Getty Museum has been identified with a piece that is described in almost exactly the same terms in the catalogues of two auctions held in Amsterdam in 1764 and 1772: 'A bust of an old man with a beard holding a knife. A powerful painting on canvas by Rembrandt, 38 inches high and 25 wide [97 x 63 cm]'.[12] The measurements are indeed closest to those of the Getty Museum picture. But the fact that the subject is said to have 'a beard' calls cat. no. 17 to mind. The characterization 'old man' is equally appropriate – or inappropriate – in both cases. In fact, however, the picture in the Amsterdam sales must have been yet another depiction of Bartholomew, because (as discovered recently) the present piece was in the collection of Sir Joshua Reynolds between 1764 and 1772. He had bought it at auction in 1757 as 'a man with a knife'.[13]

What is clear from the descriptions in the various auction catalogues is that by 1757, 1764 and 1772 the subject was not recognized as Bartholomew. This is confirmed by a print after

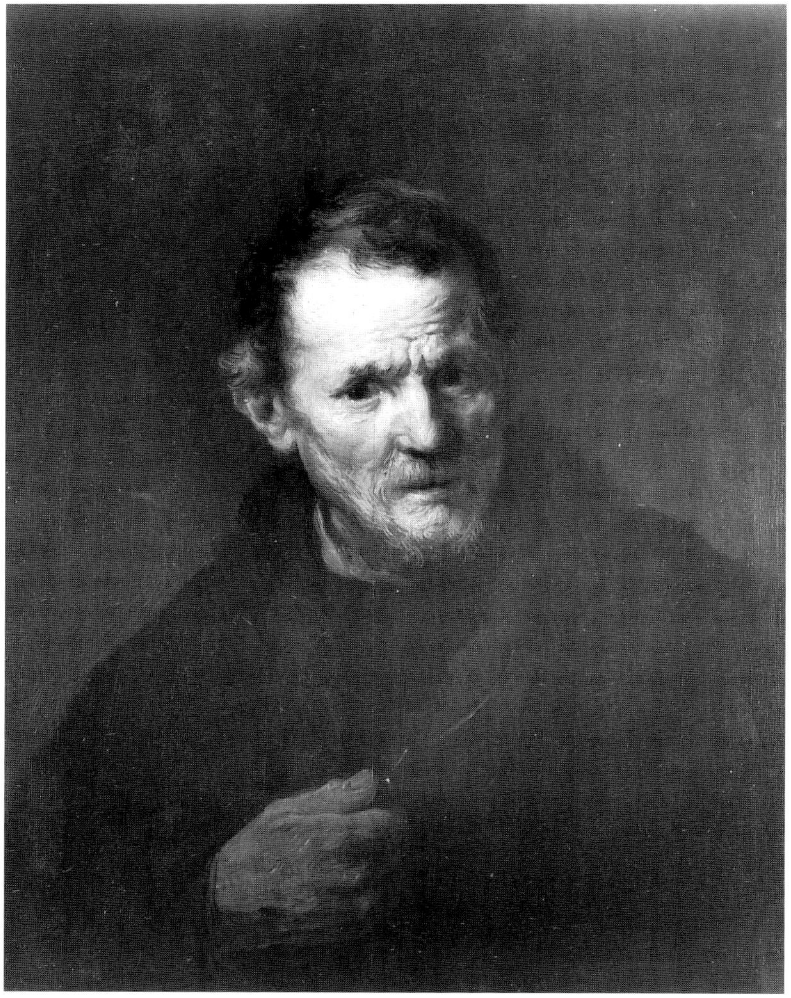

FIG. 17b
Attributed to Rembrandt
The Apostle Bartholomew
Signed
Panel
62.0 x 46.0 cm
Worcester Art Museum, Worcester, Massachusetts
Charlotte E. W. Buffington Fund

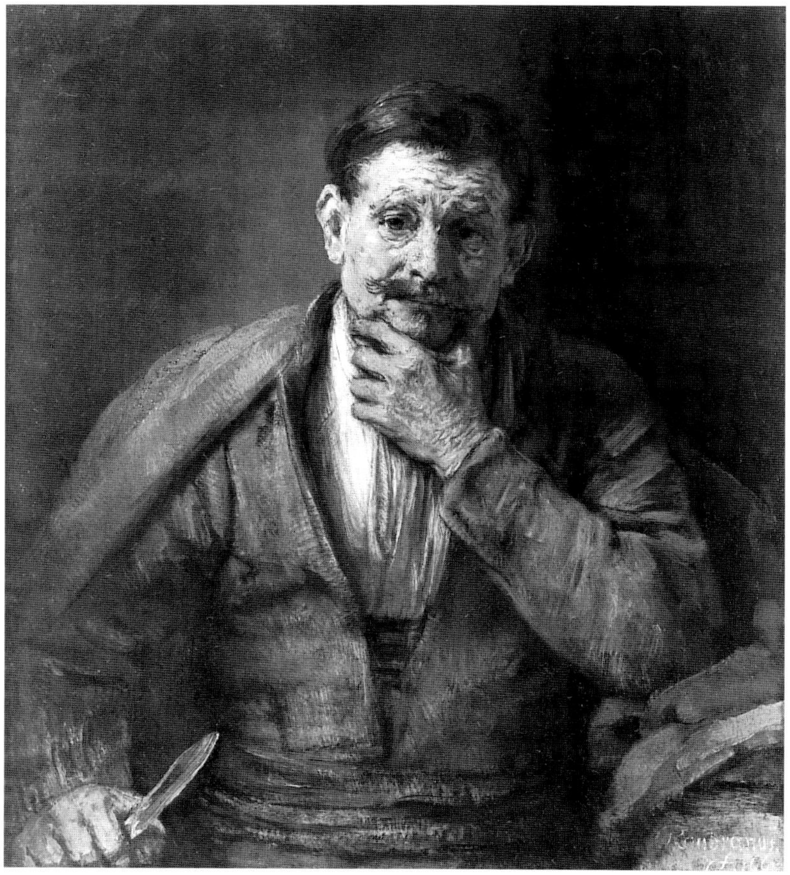

FIG. 17c
Rembrandt
The Apostle Bartholomew
Signed and dated 1661
Canvas
86.5 x 75.5 cm
Collection of the J. Paul Getty Museum, Los Angeles, California

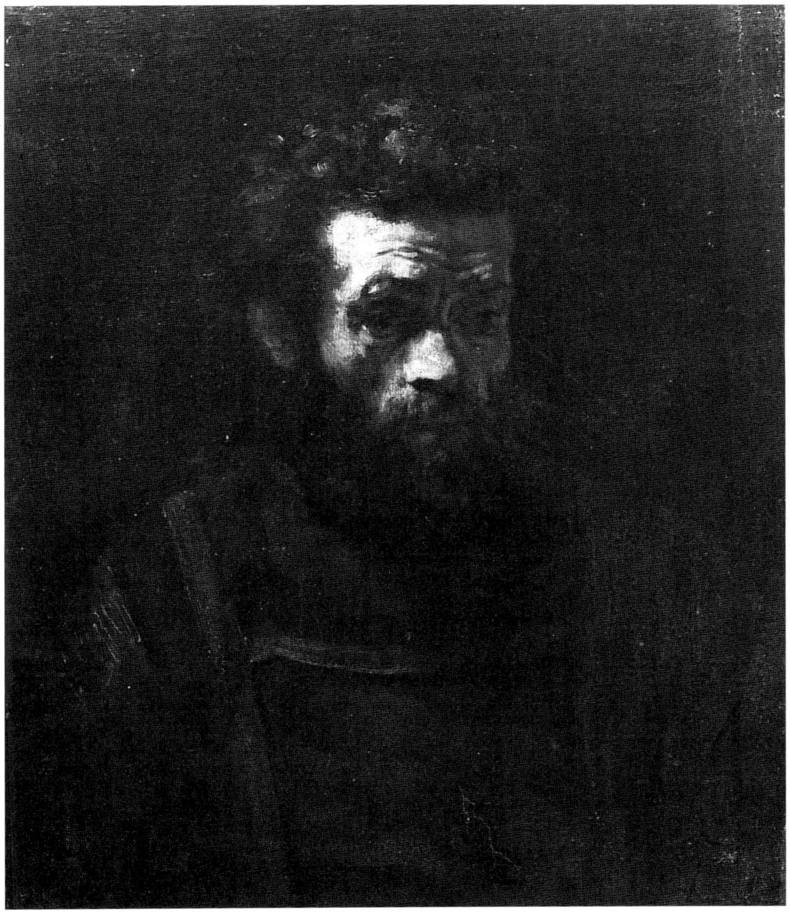

FIG. 17d
(Studio of) Rembrandt
Bust of a Bearded Man
Canvas
70.5 x 58.5 cm
Staatliche Museen zu Berlin, Gemäldegalerie

the Getty *Bartholomew*, by the engraver Charles Phillips (active 1766–1783). Phillips gave the piece a caption with the title 'The Assassin'.[14] The Getty picture was thought to represent 'Rembrandt's cook' in the time of John Smith, who in 1836 judged the figure to be 'about forty years of age'.[15] Reynolds, however, gave our cat. no. 17 the correct title, 'St. Bartholomew', when the piece was in his collection (see Provenance).

The knife is more conspicuous in the present painting than in that at the Getty Museum. In cat. no. 17 it appears to have met with disapproval, as at some stage before 1915 a book was painted on top to conceal it. The knife came to light only after the picture had been cleaned.[16]

The curly-haired man in cat. no. 17 has been recognized in other paintings as well, but they are no longer accepted as Rembrandts.[17] In my view, the subject of the *Bust of a Bearded Man* in Berlin (fig. 17d) bears the closest resemblance to the man in the present picture.[18] It has been suggested that the *Bust* may have been a preliminary study for the *Bartholomew*.[19] Ernst van de Wetering considers it likely, however, that the *Bust* was one of the many studies and copies that Rembrandt's studio evidently made when Rembrandt produced a piece like the *Bartholomew*.[20]

AB

1 Pentimenti can be seen above the cuff and wrist.
2 For the Rubens and prints after it, see Vlieghe 1972–73, vol. I, p. 43, no. 12.
3 National Gallery of Art, Washington DC (Bredius / Gerson 1969, no. 612).
4 Benesch 1956, p. 338.
5 Tümpel 1986, no. A16 (as Rembrandt Circle); Wheelock 1995, pp. 241–7, no. 1942.9.59(655) (as Rembrandt (and Workshop?)), with details concerning the picture's original, oval shape.
6 By choosing this version for reproduction (Bredius / Gerson 1969, no. 606A).
7 It is not mentioned in the *Corpus* or in Schwartz (1984) or in Tümpel (1986).
8 Sutton 1986, p. 327: 'without rival the greatest Dutch history painting in the [Worcester Art Museum] is Rembrandt's *Saint Bartholomew*'. On the basis of a transparency, I would conclude, however, that the piece is not autograph.
9 Bredius / Gerson 1969, no. 615.
10 H. Gerson, in Bredius / Gerson 1969, p. 613, no. 615.
11 According to the medieval *Legenda Aurea*, Bartholomew is said to have been crucified upside-down, flayed, and finally beheaded (Voragine, p. 483).
12 'Een oudt Man met een Baard, zynde een Borststuk, hebbende een Mes in de hand, zeer kragtig op doek geschildert, door Rembrandt, hoog 38, breet 25 duimen' (Sale cat., Prince Trivulzio sale, Amsterdam, 29 August 1764, lot 109; Hoet / Terwesten 1770, p. 393, no. 109; sale cat., Amsterdam, 30 November 1772, lot 137). The identification with the Getty picture has been current since 1916 (Hofstede de Groot 1908–27, vol. VI, 1916, p. 120, no. 168). Fredericksen 1972, pp. 88–9, no. 117, added the word 'perhaps' to the identification.
13 The provenance of cat. no. 17 before it went to Russ a was unknown until it was established by Broun, and reported by White, by Broun, and by Liedtke (C. White, in New Haven 1983, p. 113; Broun 1987, pp. 52–4, no. 10; W. Liedtke, in Adelson et al. 1996, pp. 90–4, no. 16).
14 C. White, in New Haven 1983, p. 139, cat. no. 130.
15 Smith 1829–42, vol. VII, 1836, no. 359.
16 Hofstede de Groot 1908–27, vol. VI, 1916, p. 120, no. 169.
17 Benesch 1956, p. 58, identified the same man in the following, now rejected, works: *David Playing the Harp for Saul*, Mauritshuis, The Hague; *The Adoration of the Kings*, Buckingham Palace, London; *Man Holding a Long Stick*, 1657, Louvre, Paris (Bredius / Gerson 1969, nos 526, 592, 286). Like Bode (see note 18, below), Benesch took the last-mentioned for a 'Russian pilgrim'.
18 Bredius / Gerson 1969, no. 284. Bode 1917 published this picture as a representation of a 'Russian pilgrim'.
19 Rosenberg 1964, p. 118.
20 Verbal communication.

18

Portrait of a Young Man Resting His Chin on His Hand
('Titus, the Artist's Son')

Canvas
Signed and dated halfway up arm of chair on right
Rembrandt f. 1660
81.5 x 78.5 cm
The Baltimore Museum of Art
The Mary Frick Jacobs Collection (BMA 1938.206)

PROVENANCE: Probably acquired by the 5th Duke of Rutland, Belvoir Castle, between 1820 and 1836 [Burton Fredericksen, The Getty Provenance Index, letter, 13 January 1997]; [according to Smith (1836)] at Belvoir Castle in 1836; with dealer Sir Joseph Duveen; [according to Hofstede de Groot (1916)], with dealer Krämer, Paris; with dealers Gimpel & Wildenstein, Paris; [according to NRC 1927] purchased from Gimpel & Wildenstein by James Stillman, Paris, and bequeathed by Stillman to his son, Charles Chauncey Stillman; on loan to Metropolitan Museum of Art, New York, 1921–26; sale, James Stillman, New York (American Art Gallery Bernet & Parke), 3 February 1927, lot 25; with Duveen Brothers, New York; Mrs Henry Burton Jacobs, Baltimore; acquired in 1938.

LITERATURE: Smith 1829–42, vol. VII, 1836, p. 133, no. 379; Waagen 1854, vol. III, p. 398; Dutuit 1885, p. 48; Michel 1893, p. 432; Bredius 1899; Bode & Hofstede de Groot 1897–1905, vol. VI, 1901, no. 446; Hofstede de Groot 1908–27, vol. VI, 1916, pp. 334–5, no. 707; NRC 1927; Rosenberg 1948, pp. 57, 220, note 22; Bredius / Gerson 1969, no. 124; Silberfeld 1972; Sutton 1986, p. 5; Giltaij 1988, no. 180, note 2; Slatkes 1992, no. 304.

This piece has been unanimously accepted as a first-rate autograph Rembrandt ever since John Smith wrote the first catalogue raisonné of Rembrandt's paintings in 1836. In 1927, for example, the present work was the highlight of an auction in New York, where it fetched $US250,000. Even the Dutch newspaper the *Nieuwe Rotterdamsche Courant* (NRC) published several columns reporting the event.[1] The tide turned in 1969, when Gerson placed a question mark beside his reference to the signature, thereby implying that he was doubtful about its authenticity. He also observed that 'the picture [was] heavily restored, partly over-painted and partly very thin', and concluded that 'a definitive judgement about its original quality and character is impossible'.[2] The painting has not been included in the Rembrandt canon since. It does not appear in the books by Schwartz (1984) or Tümpel (1986), both of which purport to present Rembrandt's complete oeuvre of paintings. The view expressed by Peter Sutton in 1986 thus reflects a *communis opinio*: 'If genuine – and the possibility seems remote ...'.[3] The only exception has been Slatkes, who in 1992 described the piece as 'possibly partly autograph'.[4]

The various opinions took no account of the painting's condition. The work had been examined in 1967 and restored by Kay Silberfeld, who published a detailed report in 1972. She had found a paint surface 'disfigured by the natural resin varnish which had become slightly yellowed and darkened and was extremely cloudy over the dark areas of the painting'. Gerson had evidently seen the piece in the same state. However, once most of the old varnish had been removed, 'the painting appeared free of any major areas of restoration'. This conclusion was substantiated by illustrations.[5]

The piece is without any doubt an outstanding, autograph late Rembrandt. It is a portrait, but without the least suggestion of a pose. A young man is shown slouching casually in a chair, at an angle to the back and right side of his seat. Resting his chin on his hand, he is in the attitude conventionally associated with contemplative melancholy.[6] The way Rembrandt has rendered this traditional motif, with the young man's thumb and index finger cupping his chin, makes the pose even more informal. Rembrandt was undecided about the exact position of the hand. A repentir, which can be seen through the paint on the right cheek, shows that the thumb was initially higher and on the chin itself. Now, with the thumb slightly lower, only the lower part of the chin is hidden from view. The man's gaze, and the hint of a smile about his lips, could be interpreted as contemplative, in accordance with the traditional reading of his pose, but they also give him an air of being exceptionally alert.

The background is dark, with only a little light coming from an unidentifiable source behind the man's hat and right shoulder (Rembrandt had used the same effect in his *Apostle Peter Standing* of 1632 (cat. no. 7)). Moreover, the man is dressed in a dark brown costume, the only strong accent being the deep red of the sleeve of the garment he wears underneath. Hence his face and hand stand out even more sharply against the surrounding darkness. There is extra light on them too – from a source as mysterious as that behind the figure. The light seems, then, to emanate from various 'sources', perhaps, for instance, from windows, one of which might be covered by a semi-transparent curtain; during the same period as this work was executed, Pieter de Hooch and Emanuel de Witte were experimenting with similar effects in paintings of interiors. This complex illumination casts specks of light on the man's face, giving it more life. Both eyes are in shadow, although a few flecks of light also shimmer on the eyelids. Similar flecks can be seen on the faces in other 'informal' portraits from Rembrandt's relatively late period. A good example is the Kassel portrait of *Nicolaes Bruyningh*, who is also slouching casually in his chair (fig. 18a).[7] The same effect can be seen in the *Young Man Singing ('Titus')* in Vienna (fig. 18b),[8] and in the face of the angel in cat. no. 22.

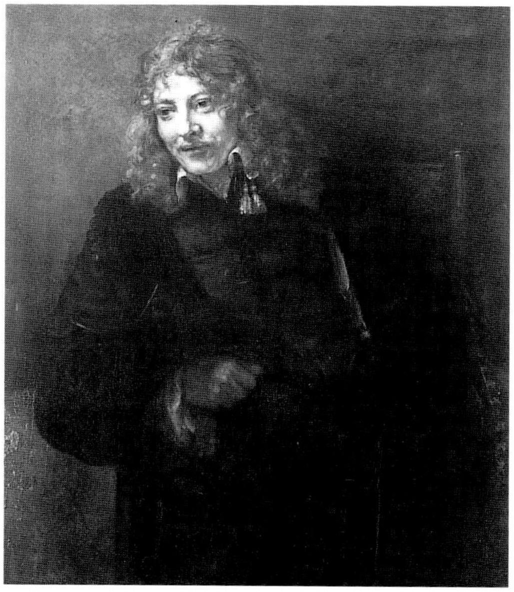

FIG. 18a
Rembrandt
Nicolaes Bruyningh
Signed and dated 1652
Canvas
107.0 x 91.5 cm
Gemäldegalerie, Kassel

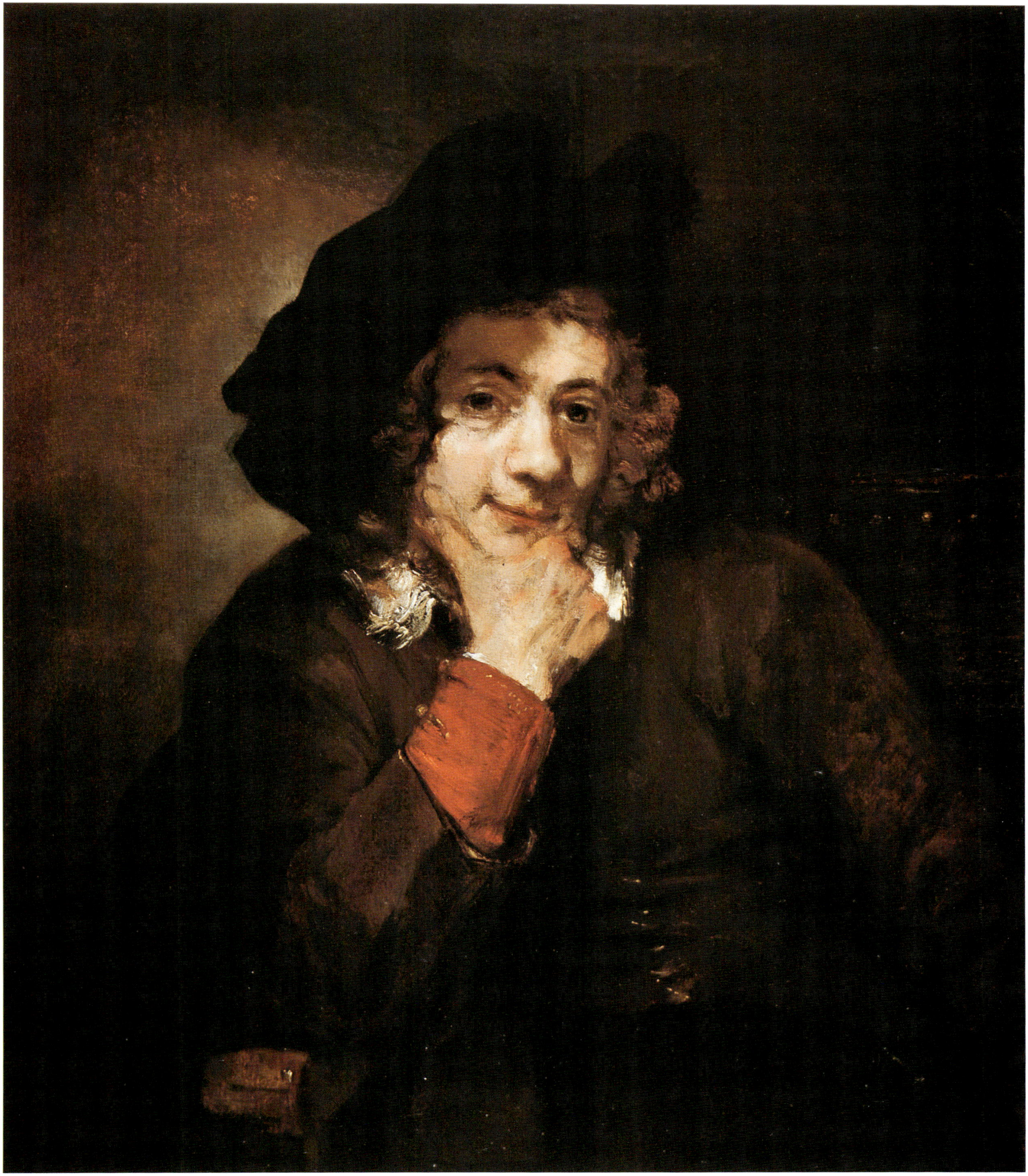

The present picture is rendered entirely in Rembrandt's broad, late technique – applied here with perfect precision. The irregular row of buttons down the front of the jacket suggests not only the bearing and shape of the man's body but also the exact position of the folds of the garment. Only the chestnut hair and white collar are painted with complete nonchalance, in extra-wide strokes. The form created by the even contours of the figure is interrupted by the outline of the man's head, with its irregularly shaped black beret. This beret lends another touch of informality to the painting.

Men in commissioned portraits from this period generally appear in more formal costumes. They mostly wear far larger collars, of white lace (cat. no. 27), and have larger hats, which they either wear or have beside them (cat. nos 19, 27). The beret was an artist's attribute (cf. Rembrandt's *Self-Portrait at the Age of 34* (cat. no. 13) and two Bols (cat. nos 45, 46)), just as it was at the beginning of the twentieth century. Cat. no. 18 may therefore be a portrayal of one of Rembrandt's fellow painters. The informality of the piece suggests, too, that it may have been made as a courtesy for a friend rather than as a paid commission. Rembrandt is known to have made a portrait of the poet Jeremias de Decker, for instance, who thanked him with a poem (p. 77, fig. 11).[9] The poem, entitled 'Token of Gratitude', explicitly mentions that when Rembrandt made Decker's portrait he 'did not even ask a fee. / He did it from the heart ... Inspired by love of art'.[10] However, it would not surprise me either if Rembrandt – whatever the identity of his sitter – made the Baltimore masterpiece for the market, or for an anonymous buyer with no connection to the model.

In the earliest known reference to the piece, John Smith in 1836 called it 'A portrait of a man'.[11] The same title appears in later publications.[12] But in 1899 Bredius wrote a review of the Royal Academy Winter Exhibition in London, where the painting was on display at the time. He says: 'Dr [Hofstede] de Groot believes – and rightly, in my opinion – that he recognizes in this young man the nineteen-year-old Titus'.[13] The work has appeared in the literature ever since as a portrait of Rembrandt's son Titus van Rijn (1641–1668). Smith had estimated what he saw as an anonymous model to be 'about thirty years of age'. In his oeuvre catalogue of 1916, Hofstede de Groot again described the piece as a portrait of Titus and, presumably reckoning on the basis of Titus's date of birth and the date of 1660 on the present picture, judged him to be 'about nineteen'.[14]

Although no documented portrait of Titus

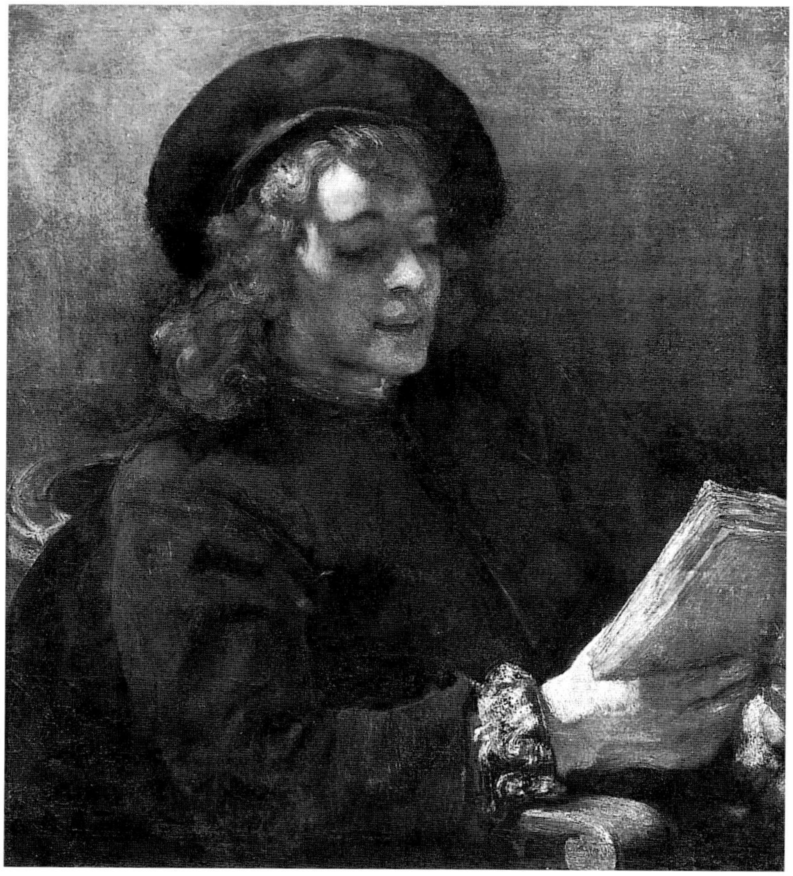

FIG. 18b
Rembrandt
Young Man Singing ('Titus')
Canvas
70.5 x 64.0 cm
Kunsthistorisches Museum, Vienna

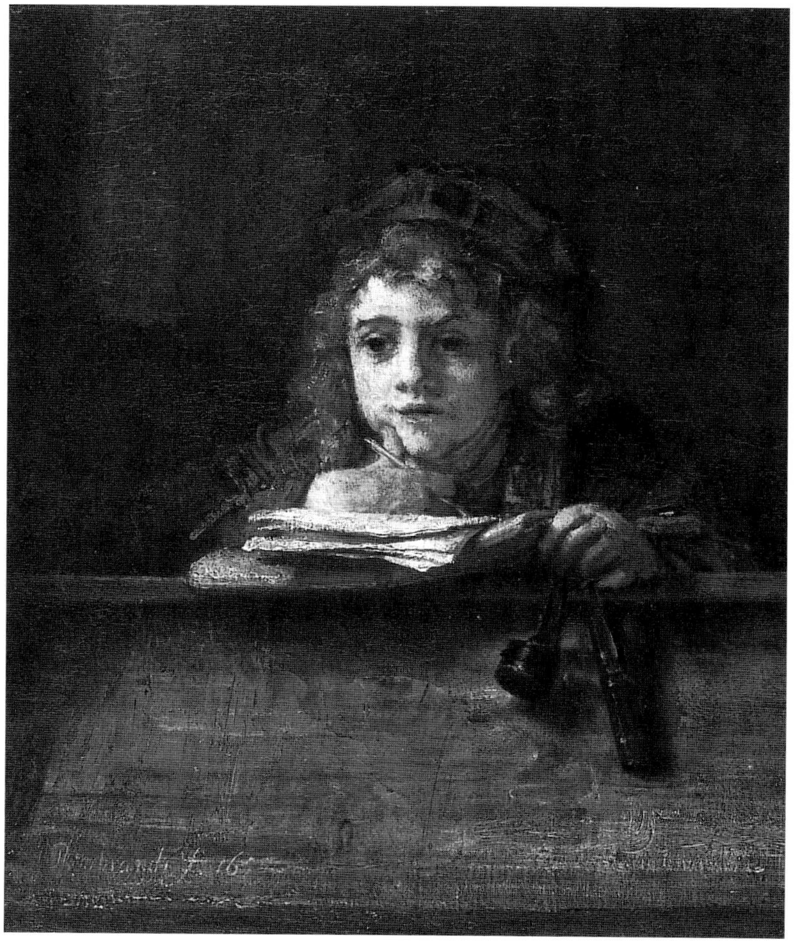

FIG. 18c
Rembrandt
'Titus' at His Writing Desk
Signed and dated 1655
Canvas
77.0 x 63.0 cm
Museum Boijmans Van Beuningen, Rotterdam
(for colour reproduction, see p. 19, fig. 2)

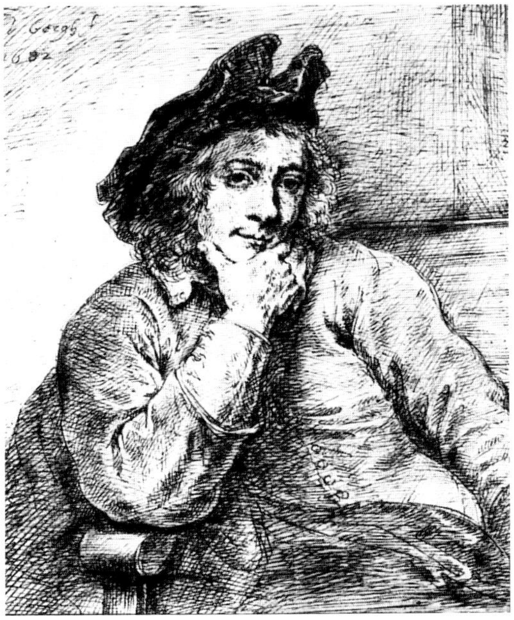

FIG. 18d
Matthys van den Bergh (1617–1687), after Rembrandt
Portrait of a Young Man Resting His Chin on His Hand
Signed and dated *V bergh f 1682*; and on verso *V bergh delineavit 1682*
Pen and ink
25.2 x 19.9 cm
Staatliche Museen zu Berlin, Kupferstichkabinett

exists (see p. 46), in modern times seven other Rembrandt paintings have likewise been called portraits of Titus, most of them being informal pictures of children.[15] The best-known is probably '*Titus' at His Writing Desk* of 1655, in Rotterdam (fig. 18c). In the Rotterdam piece, too, the model is wearing a beret and resting his chin on his hand. Fig. 18b is also said to represent Titus, as is the angel in cat. no. 22. Extant documents describe Titus as a painter, and he is known to have remained close to Rembrandt up to the end of his life. In my view, the man in cat. no. 18 is too old to represent Titus, who was not yet twenty years of age in 1660. The sitter may, however, have been another artist from Rembrandt's circle.

The outstanding quality of the picture was appreciated early on. In 1682 the painter and draughtsman Matthys van den Bergh made a meticulously faithful drawing after the piece (fig. 18d). Van den Bergh originally came from Ieperen, but worked in Leiden and Alkmaar. He specialized in accurate drawings after paintings by Peter Paul Rubens, Adriaen Brouwer, Frans Hals, Rembrandt and other still well-known masters. All his work shows the same fine, hatched technique as in fig. 18d. His sheets bear only his own signature and the year in which the drawing was made; the painters whose examples he copied are not named on the sheets.[16] These interesting documents have never been studied in depth.[17] The drawing after the present painting is one of seven such copies by van den Bergh in the Printroom in Berlin. These sheets originally came from different collections.[18] The date of 1682 on fig. 18d proves that the present painting had been made by that year. It is most unusual to find a late painting by Rembrandt firmly documented so early.

In 1916 Hofstede de Groot (as the first commentator to do so?) mentioned the existence of the drawing.[19] It was subsequently published in 1930 with exact details.[20] But the sheet was reproduced only in 1972, by Silberfeld.[21] In our century, the owners and/or restorers of the painting must have known about the drawing. In 1916 Hofstede de Groot described the canvas as 'rounded at top'.[22] At the time of the restoration in 1972, it was found that the upper left and right corners of the original canvas were missing. New corners as well as an extra strip had recently been added to restore the picture to the rectangular shape and format we see in van den Bergh's drawing. But Rembrandt experts after 1930 paid little attention to the drawing. It is mentioned only by Rosenberg, in a footnote, in 1948, and by Slatkes in 1992.[23]

Cat. no. 18 has been compared to a drawing of a seated young man that some attribute to Rembrandt and others to his German pupil Johan Ulrich Mayr. The similarities, however, are only superficial.[24]

AB

1 NRC 1927 (cutting in auction catalogue at RKD).
2 H. Gerson, in Bredius / Gerson 1969, p. 558, no. 124.
3 Sutton 1986, p. 5.
4 Slatkes 1992, no. 304.
5 Silberfeld 1972, esp. pp. 4–5, fig. 6 (with a study of previous restorations).
6 Klibansky, Panofsky & Saxl 1964, pp. 286, 288.
7 Bredius / Gerson 1969, no. 268.
8 Bredius / Gerson 1969, no. 122. The '*Titus*' in Vienna is most often interpreted as a man *reading*. This ignores Hofstede de Groot's highly plausible suggestion that it might be the '"Singer" by Rembrant' mentioned in a document of 1668 (Hofstede de Groot 1906, p. 296; see also Strauss & Van der Meulen 1979, p. 575, no. 1668/3 (no. 158)).
9 For the work at the Hermitage, St Petersburg, identified as the Decker portrait, see Bredius / Gerson 1969, no. 320. The portrait is a bust. The man is wearing a hat, but the piece is otherwise informal.
10 Schwartz 1984, p. 340: 'niet om wat loons daer uit te mogen spinnen, Maar louterlyk uit gunst ... uit liefde tot de kunst'. For the poem in English, see Schwartz 1985, p. 340.
11 Smith 1829–42, vol. VII, 1836, p. 133, no. 379.
12 Waagen 1854, vol. III, p. 398; Dutuit 1885, p. 48; Michel 1893, pp. 432, 555; London 1899, cat. no. 97.
13 Bredius 1899, p. 12: 'Dr. [Hofstede] de Groot meent, terecht geloof ik, in dezen jongeling den 19-jarigen Titus te herkennen'.
14 Hofstede de Groot 1908–27, vol. VI, 1916, pp. 334–5, no. 707.
15 Bredius / Gerson 1969, nos 119–123, 125, 126.
16 Jacques de Gheyn II also made drawn copies of paintings by other masters and signed them with his own name only (see our fig. 3d; and Van Regteren Altena 1983, vol. II, nos 1045, 1048, and others).
17 Photographs of van den Bergh drawings are at the RKD. The following have appeared in reproduction: *King David Playing the Harp* (after Rubens), *Deposition from the Cross* (after Anthony van Dyck), *Pastoral Scene* (after Hendrik Mommers) (Haverkamp Begemann & Logan 1970, nos 342–344, pls 232, 233, 231). A sketch in a private collection that is attributed to van den Bergh after the painting *Portrait of Eleazar Swalmius* (Koninklijk Museum voor Schone Kunsten, Antwerp), a picture until recently attributed to Rembrandt, was drawn by a different artist (Hanover / Wellesley / Providence / Storrs 1969, cat. no. 12, repr.).
18 Bock & Rosenberg 1930, vol. I, pp. 82–3.
19 Hofstede de Groot 1908–27, vol. VI, 1916, p. 335, no. 707 (without mentioning its whereabouts).
20 Bock & Rosenberg 1930, vol. I, no. 524 (drawing identified as from the Suermondt Collection, acquired in 1874).
21 Silberfeld 1972, fig. 3.
22 Hofstede de Groot 1908–27, vol. VI, 1916, p. 335, no. 707.
23 Rosenberg 1948, p. 220, note 22; Slatkes 1992, no. 304.
24 The drawing is at the Fondation Custodia, Paris; a copy is at the Museum Boijmans Van Beuningen, Rotterdam. In 1915 Schmidt-Degener suggested a link with our cat. no. 18 (Giltaij 1988, no. 180, note 2 (with reference and illustrations, including one of a print after a related lost painting by J. U. Mayr)).

19
Portrait of a Young Man at a Table

Signed centre right *Rembrandt 166[.]*
Canvas
109.9 x 89.5 cm
National Gallery of Art, Washington
Andrew W. Mellon Collection 1937.1.77

PROVENANCE: [After Broos (1991) and Wheelock (1995), uncertain up to 1837] Gustaf Adolf, Count of Sparre, *c.*1770, Göteborg and Kulla Gunnarstorp, after 1775–94; bequeathed by Gustaf Adolf to his wife Elisabeth, Countess of Sparre, née Ramel, in 1794; bequeathed to her grandson Gustaf Adolf Frederik, Count of Gardie, Kulla Gunnarstorp, in 1830; bequeathed to his father, Jacob, Count of Gardie, Kulla Gunnarstorp, in 1833; Carl, Count of Geer van Leufstra, Kulla Gunnarstorp, after 1837; by descent to his granddaughter Elisabeth, Countess Wachtmeister, Wanås, 1855; by family trust in the collection of the Wachtmeister family, Wanås, 1855–1926; purchased from Carl Wachtmeister, for $US410,000, by Duveen Brothers, 1926; Andrew Mellon Collection, Pittsburgh and Washington DC, 1926–37; presented by deed of 1934 to the A. W. Mellon Educational and Charitable Trust, Pittsburgh, 1937–41; acquired by the National Gallery of Art in 1941.

LITERATURE: Hofstede de Groot 1908–27, vol. VI, 1916, p. 366, no. 784; Bredius / Gerson 1969, no. 312; Schwartz 1984, p. 339; Tümpel 1986, no. 217; B. Broos, in The Hague / San Francisco 1990–91a, pp. 387–93, cat. no. 53 (with earlier literature); Wheelock 1995, pp. 265–70, no. 1937.1.77(77) (with earlier literature).

Relatively few portraits of a single figure are known from Rembrandt's late years. He appears to have received fewer orders for work of this kind than he did in the 1630s. A large proportion of the small portrait oeuvre he produced in his late period can be seen in the present exhibition (cat. nos 18, 23, 26–28). Most prospective clients presumably wanted to see themselves portrayed in bright colours and sharp detail rather than in the wide brushstrokes and sombre palette that Rembrandt favoured at the time. His pupil Govaert Flinck, who specialized in portraiture (cat. no. 43), initially imitated Rembrandt to such an extent that their work was almost indistinguishable. Later, when, as Houbraken recounts, 'the clear manner of painting again rose to prominence', Flinck made a determined effort to alter his style to suit the tastes of the day.[1] The elegant young man who posed for this portrait was evidently indifferent to the popular trend. Dressed in sombre clothing, he seems to loom out from the dark background. His collar and hands function as three angular, stylized patches of light, above which the sensitively modelled face looks out at us with a proud yet affable gaze. The man's face is framed by long brown curls. The tassels at his collar add two more brisk accents. The contours of his clothing are rendered in stark, stylized lines, which continue around his hat on the table on the right. His left hand rests on the table. Gerson described the picture as '[o]ne of the most beautiful of the late commissioned portraits'.[2]

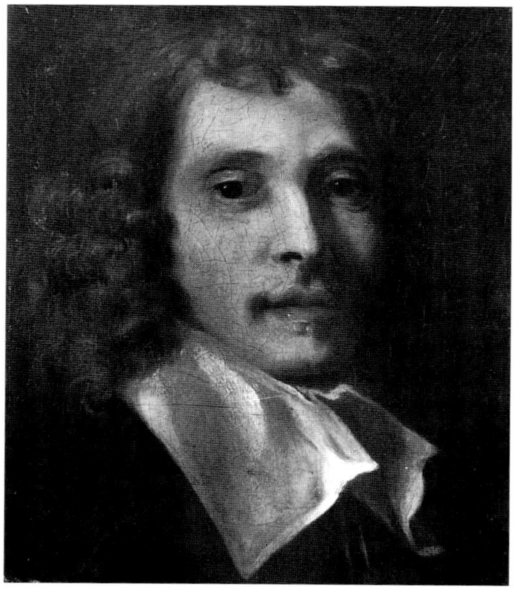

FIG. 19a
Unknown artist, after Rembrandt
A Young Man [copy after the head in cat. no. 19]
Canvas
40.5 x 34.5 cm
J. Mlodecki Collection, Warsaw, in 1935
Photograph: RKD

The surface of the paint layer is less lively and varied than that of the *Portrait of a White-Haired Man* from Melbourne, for instance (cat. no. 27). But then the *Portrait of a Young Man* is not in optimal condition. The paint layer has suffered and the varnish has turned yellow.[3] A copy after the man's head and collar shows more detail, which may originally have been visible in the painting itself (fig. 19a).[4] The picture would also have been less dark when it was first made, with the figure set off more distinctly against the background.

If we imagine a sharper contrast between the figure and the background, the *Portrait of a Young Man at a Table* would bear a close resemblance to Frans Hals's equally large *Portrait of a Standing Man*, which was made fifteen to twenty years earlier, *c.*1643–45 (fig. 19b).[5] The compositions are almost identical: Hals's subject is also seen with his right hand on his hip, with the palm half-turned towards the viewer, while the face, collar and hands form accents in the same parts of the picture. Rembrandt must have been familiar with examples of Hals's work. Rembrandt had already gained a strong reputation as a portraitist when in 1633 the Amsterdam commission for the monumental *Corporalship of Captain Reynier Reael* was given to the Haarlem painter (fig. 19c).[6] It was most unusual for a painting made up of numerous portraits to be ordered from an artist from out of town. The situation predictably created problems. Hals complained that he had agreed to make the militia piece in Haarlem. Instead, he found himself wasting his time travelling to and from Amsterdam and waiting at an inn for sitters who often failed to appear. In the event, the picture was completed only in 1637, by the Amsterdam painter Pieter Codde. What we learn from this incident is that Hals was favoured above any artist in Amsterdam, Rembrandt included. Not until 1642 did Rembrandt execute an equally prestigious commission, with his painting of the *Night Watch* (p. 26, fig. 7).

Over time, Hals's reputation in Amsterdam lost none of its lustre. In 1669 – the year of Rembrandt's death – an inventory listing 104 contemporary paintings belonging to the Amsterdam collector Laurens Douci was drawn up. Douci's superb collection consisted of landscapes, marines, genre paintings and history pieces. It also included two portraits of unnamed sitters; both were painted by Frans Hals.[7] The fact that these works were in Douci's art collection was quite unprecedented. Contemporary portraits were normally family heirlooms and were not

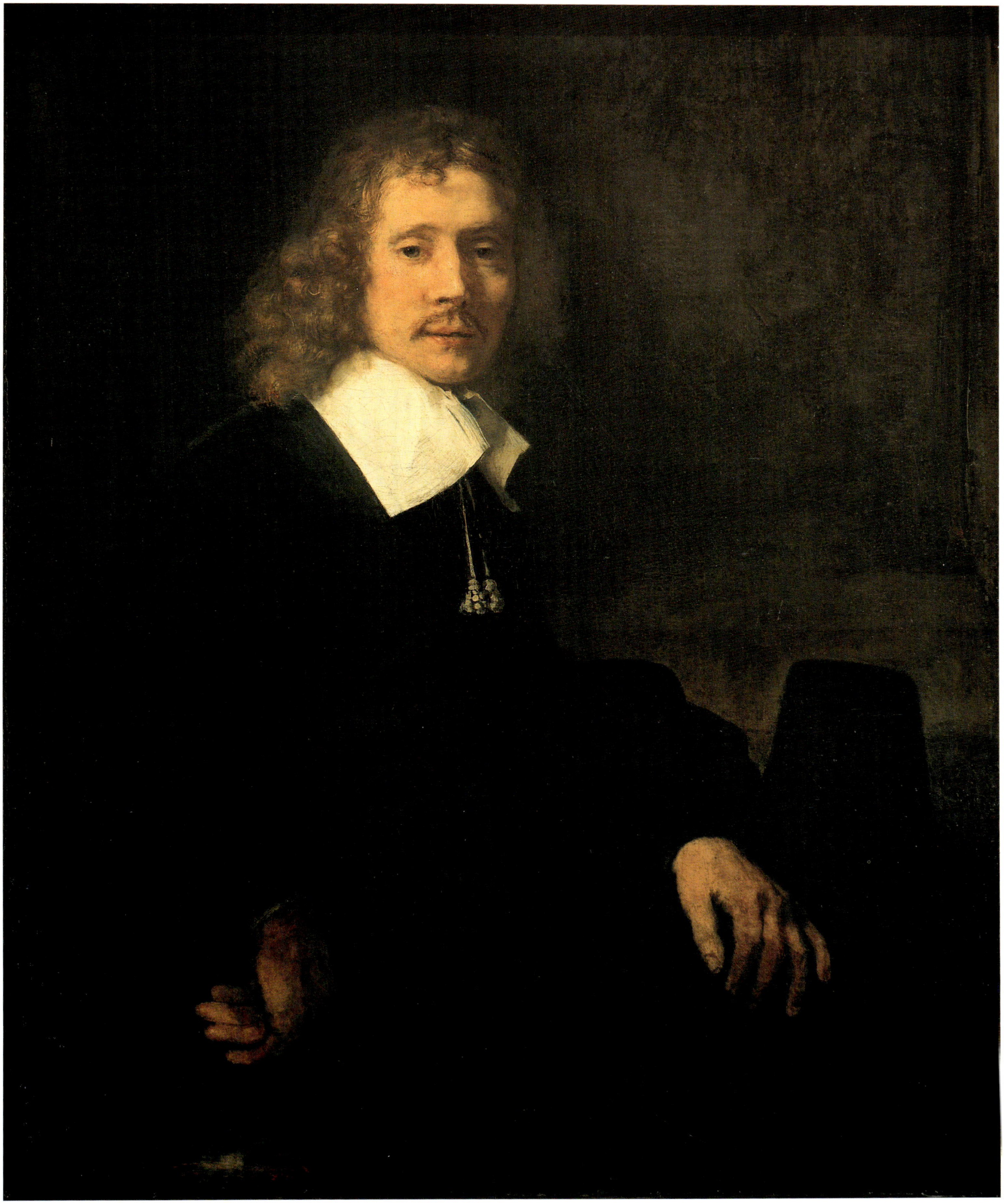

FIG. 19b
Frans Hals 1581/85–1666
Portrait of a Standing Man
Canvas
114.9 x 86.0 cm
National Galleries of Scotland, Edinburgh

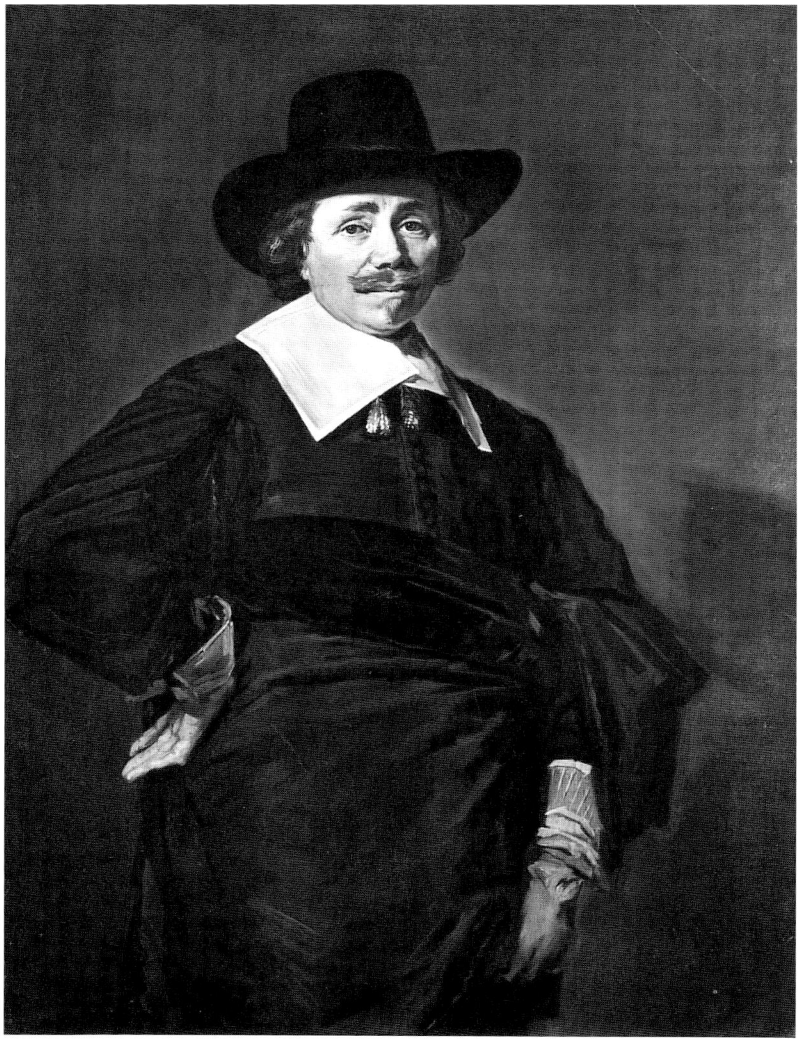

FIG. 19c
Frans Hals and Pieter Codde (1599–1678)
Corporalship of Captain Reynier Reael and Lieutenant Cornelis Michiels Blaeuw
Dated 1637
Canvas
209.0 x 429.0 cm
Rijksmuseum, Amsterdam

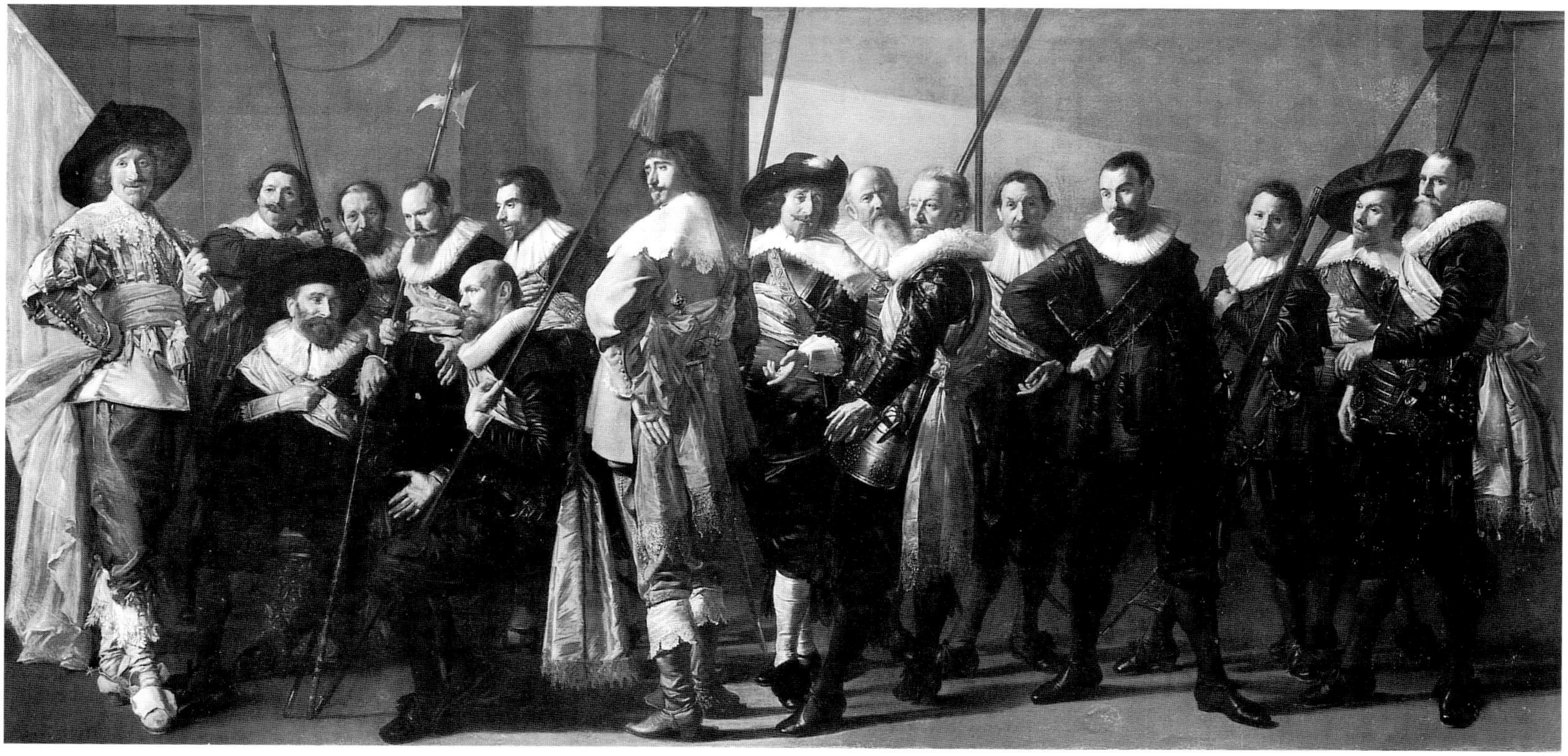

acquired by 'outsiders'. In this respect, Hals was an exception in his day – a fact that would not have escaped Rembrandt's attention.

The similarities between the Hals (fig. 19b) and the present picture may of course be purely coincidental. If so, we could conclude that, in spite of their originality, both masters employed stock types for their portraits. After all, other artists also portrayed subjects with their right hand on their hip and their palm turned towards the observer.[8] But no portrait comes to mind that resembles either the Rembrandt or the Hals as closely as the two resemble each other.

The darkened background of Rembrandt's *Young Man* might help to explain why descriptions of the picture refer to objects that cannot be seen and may never have been there at all. Some commentators refer to a signature on the right, others to one on the left. The date has been cited with conviction as 1662, but also as 1663. Today, all that is visible beside the signature – on the right – is 166[.], although the picture was probably made between *c.*1660 and 1663. In 1935 there was said to be a 'bluish black window curtain' in the background and to the right of it a 'vaguely indicated window opening with beveled sill'.[9] In 1995 Wheelock expressed the view that there might be a stretched canvas in the background. He compared the man's face with that of Rembrandt's successful pupil Govaert Flinck in an engraved portrait published in 1719, and concluded that Flinck may have been the sitter in cat. no. 19.[10] In this event the present portrait would date from 1660, shortly before Flinck's death at the age of forty-five. Hofstede de Groot in 1916 had judged the *Young Man* to be about thirty years old.[11] An earlier engraved portrait of Flinck is reproduced here so that readers can form their own opinion. This print was published soon after Flinck's death in 1660, with a eulogy by the poet Joost van den Vondel (fig. 19d).[12]

Ben Broos has discovered new information about the *Young Man*'s provenance, and we now know that the picture was in the collection of the Swede Count Carl de Geer van Leufstra, from 1837 to 1855. De Geer van Leufstra was descended from a family of Dutch manufacturers who had owned large factories in Sweden since the seventeenth century. It is thus conceivable that he inherited the picture from one of his relatives on the de Geer side of the family.[13] The man in the portrait could therefore have been a member of the Trip–De Geer family, one of whose members – Jacob Trip – was portrayed by Rembrandt in *c.*1661 (cat. no. 23). It is possible, for instance, that he was Jacob Louysz Trip (1630–1664) and that he ordered the picture to mark the occasion of his marriage a short time earlier.[14] In this case the painting would most probably have had a pendant, as Frans Hals's portrait (fig. 19b) still has to this day.[15] However, the question of the identity of the sitter in cat. no. 19 ultimately remains unresolved.

AB

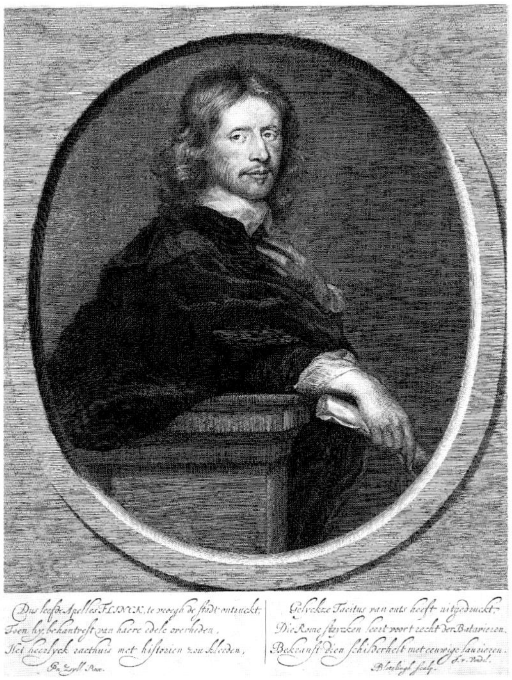

FIG. 19d
Abraham Blotelingh (1640–1690), after Cornelis van Dalen, after Gerard van Zijl
Portrait of Govaert Flinck
Engraving
From a reproduction at the RKD
(see also p. 234)

1 Houbraken 1718–21, vol. II, 1719, p. 20.
2 H. Gerson, in Bredius / Gerson 1969, p. 574, no. 312.
3 B. Broos, in The Hague / San Francisco 1990–91a, p. 388, cat. no. 53; Wheelock 1995, pp. 265–8. H. Gerson, in Bredius / Gerson 1969, p. 574, no. 312; and Wheelock 1995, p. 268, report damage in the hands of cat. no. 19.
4 Photograph at RKD. B. Broos, in The Hague / San Francisco 1990–91a, p. 388, describes the copy as an 'impressionistic variant'.
5 Slive 1970–74, vol. III, 1974, p. 80, no. 156, suggested this dating.
6 Slive 1970–74, vol. III, 1974, pp. 48–50, no. 80.
7 A. Blankert, in Washington / Detroit / Amsterdam 1980–81, p. 24; see also Bredius 1915–22, vol. II, p. 422ff.
8 Cf. De Jongh 1986, figs 4, 25a, 30a, 34, 37, 37a, 40, 59, 83a.
9 For references, see B. Broos, in The Hague / San Francisco 1990–91, p. 388, cat. no. 53.
10 Wheelock 1995, pp. 265–70, no. 1937.1.77(77). The engraving appears in Houbraken 1718–21, vol. II, 1719, pl. B1, opp. p. 18.
11 Hofstede de Groot 1908–27, vol. VI, 1916, p. 366, no. 784.
12 De Bruyn Kops 1965, pp. 20–9; Van Hall 1963, Flinck, no. 16. Cf. Welcker 1940, pp. 115–22, fig. 2 (the drawing by van Dalen that served as the example for our fig. 19d)
13 If this is the case, the names listed in the Provenance as possible owners before 1837 must be eliminated.
14 B. Broos, in The Hague / San Francisco 1990–91a, p. 392.
15 *Portrait of a Woman*, also in Edinburgh (Slive 1970–74, vol. III, 1974, no. 157).

20
Monk Reading

Signed and dated above shoulder at centre right
Rembrandt f 1661 (date presently not discernible)
Canvas
81.0 x 65.0 cm
Sinebrychoff Museum, Helsinki

PROVENANCE: [After Smith (1836)] Sale, Comte de Vence, Paris, 1750; Earl of Wemyss, Gosford House, Scotland [seen while in the collection by J. Smith at an exhibition in London in 1835], 1835–*c.*1915; Hjalmar Linder Collection, London; acquired in 1920.

LITERATURE: Collection catalogue, Comte de Vence, 1759, p. 24; collection catalogue, Comte de Vence, 1761, no. 47; Smith 1829–42, vol. VII, 1836, no. 132; Vosmaer 1877, p. 561; Michel 1893, p. 444; Bode & Hofstede de Groot 1897–1905, vol. VI, 1901, no. 483; Hofstede de Groot 1908–27, vol. VI, 1916, pp. 129–30, no. 190; Valentiner 1920, p. 221; Amsterdam / Rotterdam 1956, pp. 174–5, no. 85; Bauch 1966, no. 232; Bredius / Gerson 1969, no. 307; Schwartz 1984, p. 314; Tümpel 1986, no. 92; Slatkes 1992, no. 226.

This painting shows an elderly monk reading a sheet of paper, which he holds close to his eyes. He has folded it over to make it easier to manage, as we might do today with a newspaper. He supports the paper between the thumb, index finger and middle finger of his left hand. The small, yet wonderfully evocative, gesture recalls Rembrandt's drawings. The man's other arm rests on the side of his chair, and his right hand lies limp in his lap. This inertia heightens the impression that all the energy he has is devoted to the act of reading.

Rembrandt has taken the bold and unconventional step of using exclusively dark shades to model the monk's face and habit. The only bright accent in the painting is the ribbon of light along the folded edge of the paper. The surface the monk is reading, which is hidden from our view, also catches the light. This is suggested by the gleam at the base of the index finger of the left hand. The light must be entering the picture space, from a point outside it, through a very small chink. The monk has positioned himself in such a way that the tiny ray of light falls directly onto his paper.

Rembrandt made two other paintings of men in the same monk's habit. Both are likewise half-length figures. His *Franciscan Friar* at the National Gallery in London dates from 165(5?) (fig. 20a).[1] The more famous is the beautiful painting of 1660 at the Rijksmuseum in Amsterdam, a work that is said to represent Titus (fig. 20b).[2] In all of the modern literature the present work is said to be dated 1661 (today only the word *Rembrandt* is discernible). It is therefore probably the last in the series.[3] In all three pictures we see the same roughly stitched brown habit, and a cowl that appears to extend down to form a collar. The cowl seems to have been a separate garment that was drawn over the head and arranged over the shoulders. Rembrandt may have asked his model to pose in this costume for the *Franciscan Friar* and for the picture known as 'Titus in a Monk's Habit' (figs 20a, 20b). Both are portrait-like works. However, this is not true of cat. no. 20, the last version of the theme, if only because the face is entirely in shadow. This picture is the most interesting of the three for its invention, for here Rembrandt has combined the motif of the monk's habit with the image of a

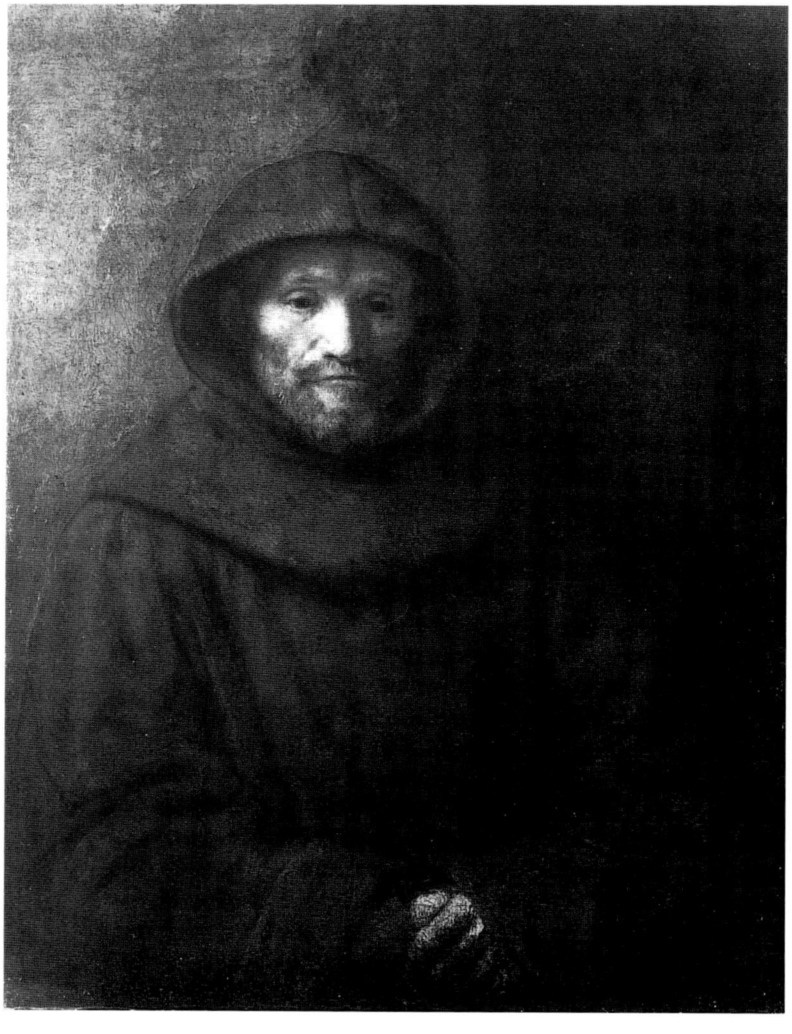

FIG. 20a
Rembrandt
Franciscan Friar
Signed and dated 165[5?]
Canvas
89.0 x 66.5 cm
The Trustees of the National Gallery, London

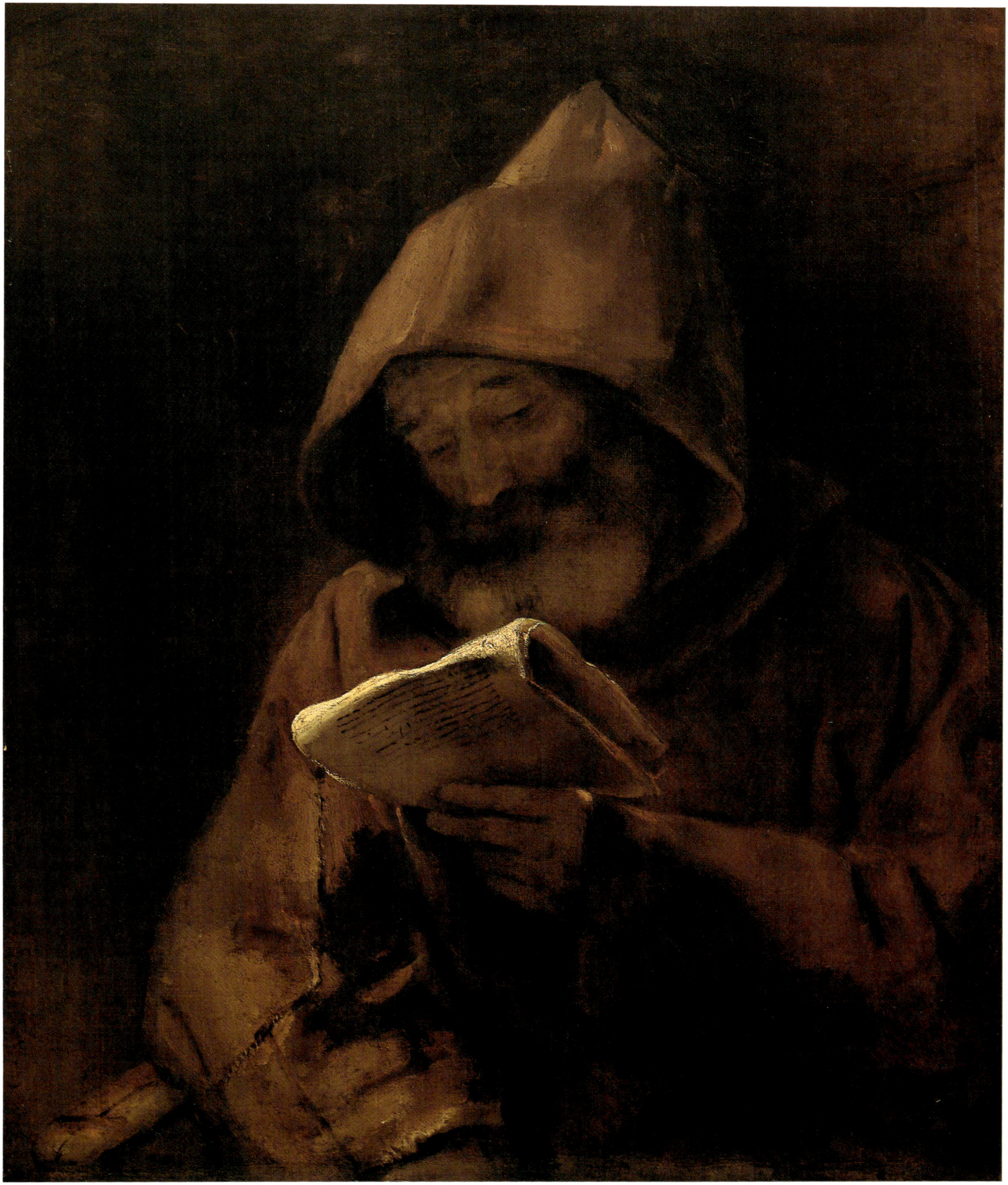

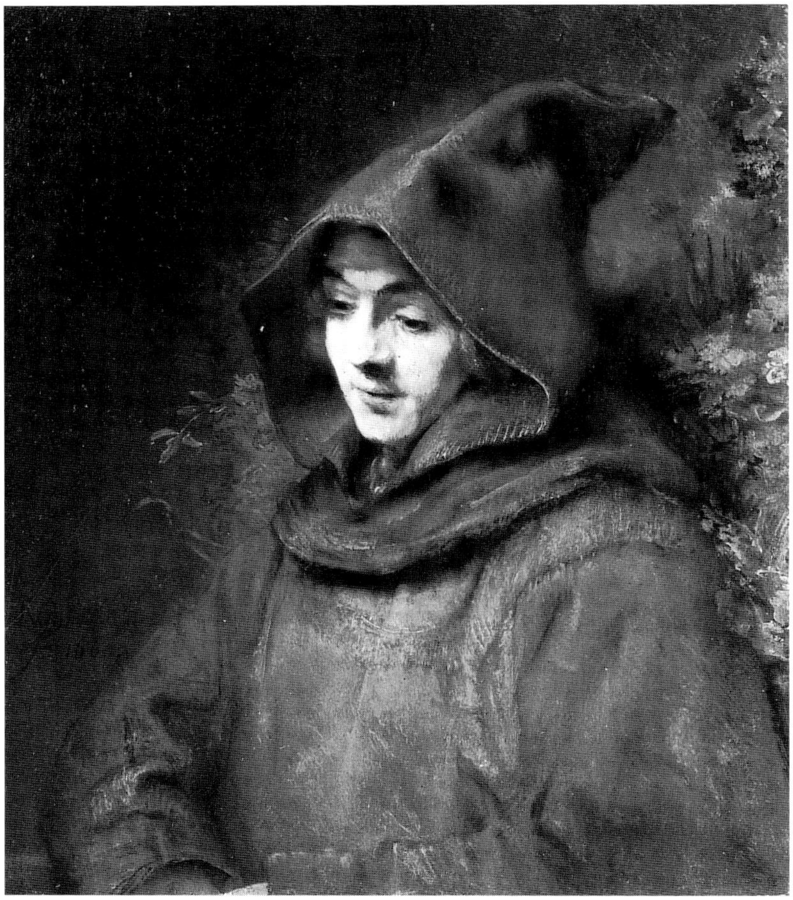

FIG. 20b
Rembrandt
A Young Capuchin Monk
Signed and dated 166[0]
Canvas
79.5 x 67.5 cm
Rijksmuseum, Amsterdam

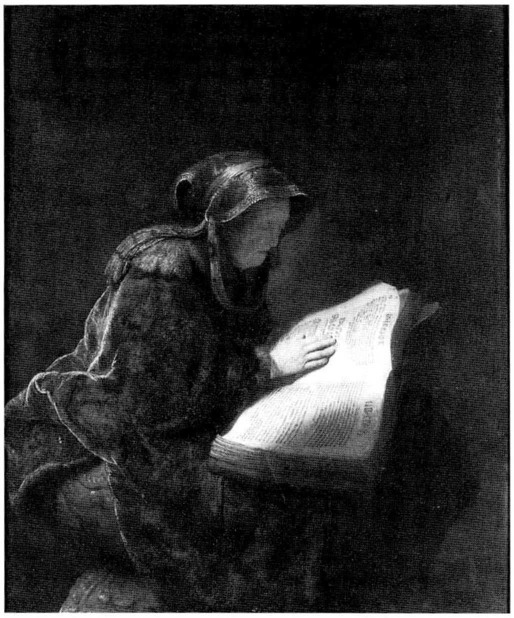

FIG. 20c
Rembrandt
Old Woman Reading
Monogrammed and dated 1631
Panel
59.8 x 47.7 cm
Rijksmuseum, Amsterdam
(for colour reproduction, see p. 47, fig. 18)

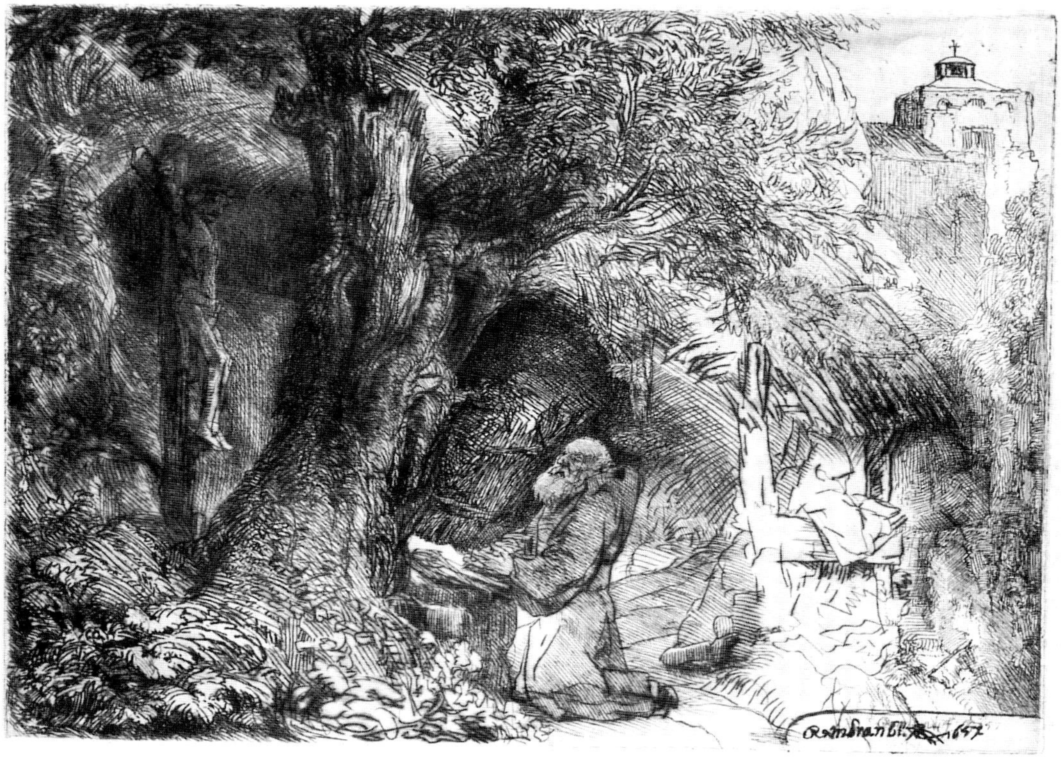

FIG. 20d
Rembrandt
Two Monks (the One on the Left St Francis or St Jerome?)
Signed and dated 1657
Etching
18.0 x 24.4 cm
Rijksprentenkabinet, Rijksmuseum, Amsterdam

person totally absorbed in reading. Cat. no. 20 appears to be a follow-up to an early masterpiece of 1631, the picture of an *Old Woman Reading* (fig. 20c).[4] Here again the subject's face is entirely in the shadow, and what little light there is falls mainly on the page she is reading, which in this case is turned towards us.

The *Franciscan Friar* is in poor condition (fig. 20a).[5] 'Titus in a Monk's Habit' is the best preserved of these three late paintings, and the man portrayed in it is the youngest (fig. 20b). The Helsinki painting (our cat. no. 20) was last shown together with other Rembrandts at the Rembrandt exhibition held in Amsterdam and Rotterdam in 1956. Some time later Gerson described its condition as follows: 'Its surface has suffered, but the original delicacy can still be appreciated. There are some pentimenti in the area of the left shoulder'.[6] In 1893 the present picture was still being described as 'd'une excellente conservation'.[7] Discussing the painting in 1986, Tümpel put a question mark behind Rembrandt's name,[8] but the work, which is known to have been in outstanding collections since 1750, is of too high a standard to warrant this doubt. On the other hand, certain irregularities in the modelling suggest that the piece is not in optimal condition.[9]

The picture is generally described as a representation of a monk.[10] In 1920, Valentiner attempted to reconstruct a series of apostles from Rembrandt's late oeuvre (see commentary to cat. no. 22) and concluded that the monks in cat. no. 20 and figs 20a and 20b may have 'belonged to a smaller series of individual figures of evangelists and holy men'.[11] The hypothesis received lukewarm support from Gerson.[12] Bauch in 1966 suggested that figs 20a and 20b and cat. no. 20 were representations of St Francis.[13] Tümpel in 1986 supported this view.[14] Both were apparently unaware that as early as 1759 the catalogue of the Comte de Vence's collection listed our cat. no. 20 as a 'St Francis', a title that was changed to 'Priest of the Franciscan Order' in the subsequent version of the catalogue in 1761.[15] Vosmaer too had given the present picture the title 'St François, ou moine franciscain' in 1877.[16] The brown habit and peaked cowl is indeed worn by friars of the Capuchin order, a branch of the Franciscans, and although the order as such was established only in 1528, Francis himself was portrayed in a 'Capuchin' habit long before that time.

Born in 1182, Francis died in 1226 at the age of forty-four. He is therefore always depicted as a relatively young man, or at least as a man in the prime of his life, and his attributes and/or the expression of his famous ecstasy make him unmistakably recognizable.[17] The figure in the present picture, whom Hofstede de Groot in 1916 estimated to be 'about fifty',[18] looks older rather than younger.[19] Tümpel, who himself observed that the monk looked old for a Francis, compared the painting with Rembrandt's etching of 1657 known as 'Francis Praying' (B.107) (fig. 20d), and concluded that the painting was also a portrayal of the saint.[20] The figure praying in the etching is likewise advanced in years. It is therefore interesting to note that the etching acquired the title 'St Francis' only in 1751, when the Frenchman Gersaint catalogued it under that name. Before that time – and on several occasions since – the etching had been described in Holland as a representation of St Jerome.[21] All things considered, it is difficult to establish whether the etching was meant to represent a particular saint or simply an anonymous monk with a companion. The image of Christ on the Cross, to which the figure on the left in the etching is turned in prayer, might recall Francis's receiving the stigmata in a vision of the Crucifixion.

Ultimately, however, as there are no attributes whatsoever in cat. no. 20 or figs 20a and 20b, it would be purely speculative to identify any of the figures in these pictures as other than 'a man wearing the habit of a Franciscan monk'. One saint whom Rembrandt did portray in a monk's habit on several occasions was the hermit Jerome, but in each case he can be recognized by the lion beside him (cat. no. 116).[22]

AB/MB

1 Bredius / Gerson 1969, no. 308; MacLaren / Brown 1991, vol. 1, p. 334, no. 166.

2 Bredius / Gerson 1969, no. 306.

3 The date on this painting has been cited as 1661 since 1901 (Bode & Hofstede de Groot 1897–1905, vol. VI, 1901, no. 483). Before that time it was generally read as 1660, the date cited in the Comte de Vence catalogues of 1759 and 1761 (see Provenance) (Smith 1829–42, vol. VII, 1836, no. 132; Vosmaer 1877, p. 561; Michel 1893, p. 444). Today no date is visible (information from Sinebrychoff Museum).

4 Bredius / Gerson 1969, no. 69; *Corpus*, vol. I, 1982, no. A37. For this picture and the subject of reading as portrayed in seventeenth-century Dutch art, see B. Werche, in Frankfurt 1993, cat. no. 69.

5 MacLaren / Brown 1991, vol. 1, p. 334, no. 166. Even in the nineteenth century, the picture was described as 'malheureusement un peu maltraitée par le temps' (Michel 1893, p. 444).

6 H. Gerson, in Bredius / Gerson 1969, p. 573, no. 308.

7 Michel 1893, p. 444.

8 Tümpel 1986, no. 92.

9 The painting was cleaned and varnished at the Rijksmuseum in Amsterdam in 1956. At the time, the paint layer was thought to be extremely thin (Dr A. van Schendel, letter to Sinebrychoff Museum, 29 January 1957).

10 Smith 1829–42, vol. VII, 1836, no. 132 (citing a description from 1750): 'a monk of the order of St Francis'; Michel 1893, p. 444: 'Jeune moine'; Hofstede de Groot 1908–27, vol. VI, 1916, p. 129, no. 190: 'A Capuchin Friar'.

11 Valentiner 1920, p. 221.

12 H. Gerson, in Bredius / Gerson 1969, p. 573, no. 307: 'This portrait [*sic*] may belong to the rather unspecific series of evangelists and holy men of the 1660s'.

13 Bauch 1966, nos 205, 227, 232.

14 Tümpel 1986, nos 91, 92, 93. Neither we nor others have been able to discern St Francis's stigmata, which Tümpel (no. 91) sees in the only partly visible hands of *A Young Capuchin Monk* (fig. 20b).

15 At the time, the piece had a pendant, which probably did not really belong to it, called 'Portrait of an Old Man'

16 Vosmaer 1877, p. 561.

17 Savelsberg 1992.

18 Hofstede de Groot 1908–27, vol. VI, 1916, p. 129, no. 190.

19 Michel 1893, p. 444, thought him to be approximately forty, and described his beard as blond.

20 Tümpel 1986, no. 92.

21 Hinterding 1993–94, p. 259, note 34. In 1735, etching B.107 was described as Jerome with the Cross ('de Hieronymus met het kruis') and in 1755 as St Jerome kneeling before a crucifix in a forest ('St. Hieronymus in een Boschagie, knielend voor een Kruissifix').

22 For the print by Johannes van Vliet after a lost painting of 1631, see *Corpus*, vol. I, 1982, p. 39, fig. 6. Etchings B.100–106, including our cat. no. 116 (B.104), also depict Jerome with a lion.

21
The Apostle James Major

Signed and dated lower right *Rembrandt f 1661*
Canvas
90.0 x 78.0 cm
Private collection, United States

PROVENANCE: [After Sutton (1992)] (?) Sale of the heirs of Caspar Netscher, A. Schouman et al., The Hague, 15 July 1749, lot 122 (as 'A Pilgrim Praying', without dimensions (Hofstede de Groot (1916), no. 194c)); collections of MacKenzies of Kintore; Sir J. Charles Robinson, CB, London; Consul Edmund Friedrich Weber, Hamburg [1872 cat., no. 213]; with Charles Sedelmeyer Gallery, Paris [1895 cat., no. 29, repr.]; Maurice Kann, Paris 1901; with Duveen Gallery, Paris; with Reinhardt Galleries, New York, 1913; John N. Willys, Toledo, Ohio; sale, Isabel van Wie Willys (formerly Mrs John N. Willys), New York (Parke-Bernet), 25 October 1945, lot 16, to Billy Rose for $US75,000; Billy Rose Collection, New York, 1950; Oscar B. Cintas (Ambassador to Cuba), New York; Mr and Mrs Stephen C. Clark, by 1955; on loan to Metropolitan Museum of Art, New York, 1958; on temporary loan to Israel Museum, Jerusalem.

LITERATURE: Hofstede de Groot 1908–27, vol. VI, 1916, p. 121, no. 170 [this picture possibly identical with Hofstede de Groot, no. 194c]; Benesch 1956, p. 346; Bauch 1966, no. 236; Bredius / Gerson 1969, no. 617; Schwartz 1984, p. 313; Tümpel 1986, no. 82; P. C. Sutton, in Boston 1992, pp. 198–9, cat. no. 121 (with earlier literature).

This painting was known as 'The Pilgrim' until Hofstede de Groot identified it as *The Apostle James* in 1915.[1] The Bible describes James as a fisherman. His relics are said to be in Santiago de Compostella on the western coast of Spain. After Rome, Compostella was the most important centre of pilgrimage in the Middle Ages. Pilgrims who had made the journey there returned with a shell badge – the scallop of James – fastened to their clothing. Surprisingly enough, artists tended to portray James in the guise of these medieval pilgrims. He is usually depicted wearing a pilgrim's cloak and hat, decorated with one or more shells, and he holds a staff. According to legend, Christ himself gave the staff to James. In the present picture we see a scallop shell on the man's shoulder. He has apparently used it to fasten his cape to his coat. A similar shell is attached to the pilgrim's hat in front of him. His staff is propped against the wall behind it.

The painting is dated 1661, as are several other works depicting apostles and evangelists.[2] The *James* and Rembrandt's other late apostles are all lifesize half-length figures. Yet within these parameters Rembrandt sought and found an astonishing diversity of types, compositions and light effects. This is particularly evident when we compare two paintings from San Diego and the Getty Museum, both of which works represent the apostle Bartholomew (see cat. no. 17 and fig. 17c).

The *Apostle James* reflects an entirely different approach, which merits closer examination. The figure is set to one side of the picture space, as occurs in paintings made with a pendant. Because of this, there is more space on the right, and this heightens the mood evoked by the apostle's clasped hands and closed eyes. Rembrandt portrayed him from the side and almost in profile, so the half-raised hands too could be seen in profile and there was no need to foreshorten them. In fact, with the light shining on them the hands are even larger than the face. The result is that this painting, more than any other figure piece, is like a portrait of two hands.

It is interesting that Rembrandt chose to portray the man directly from the side, as he rarely produced profile views of a single figure. Indeed, only one of his many single-figure portraits – the *Portrait of Princess Amalia van Solms* of 1632 – is in profile (fig. 21a).[3] This was one of the conditions attached to the commission: the painting had a companion piece, a profile portrait of Amalia's husband Prince Frederik

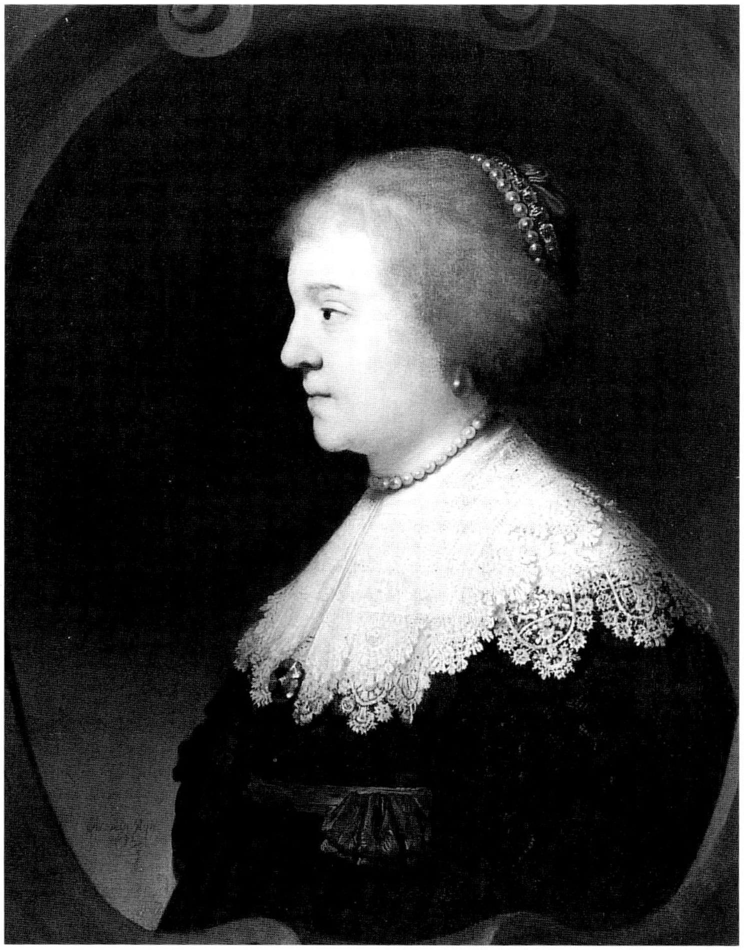

FIG. 21a
Rembrandt
Portrait of Princess Amalia van Solms
Signed and dated 1632
Canvas
68.5 x 55.5 cm
Musée Jacquemart-André, Paris

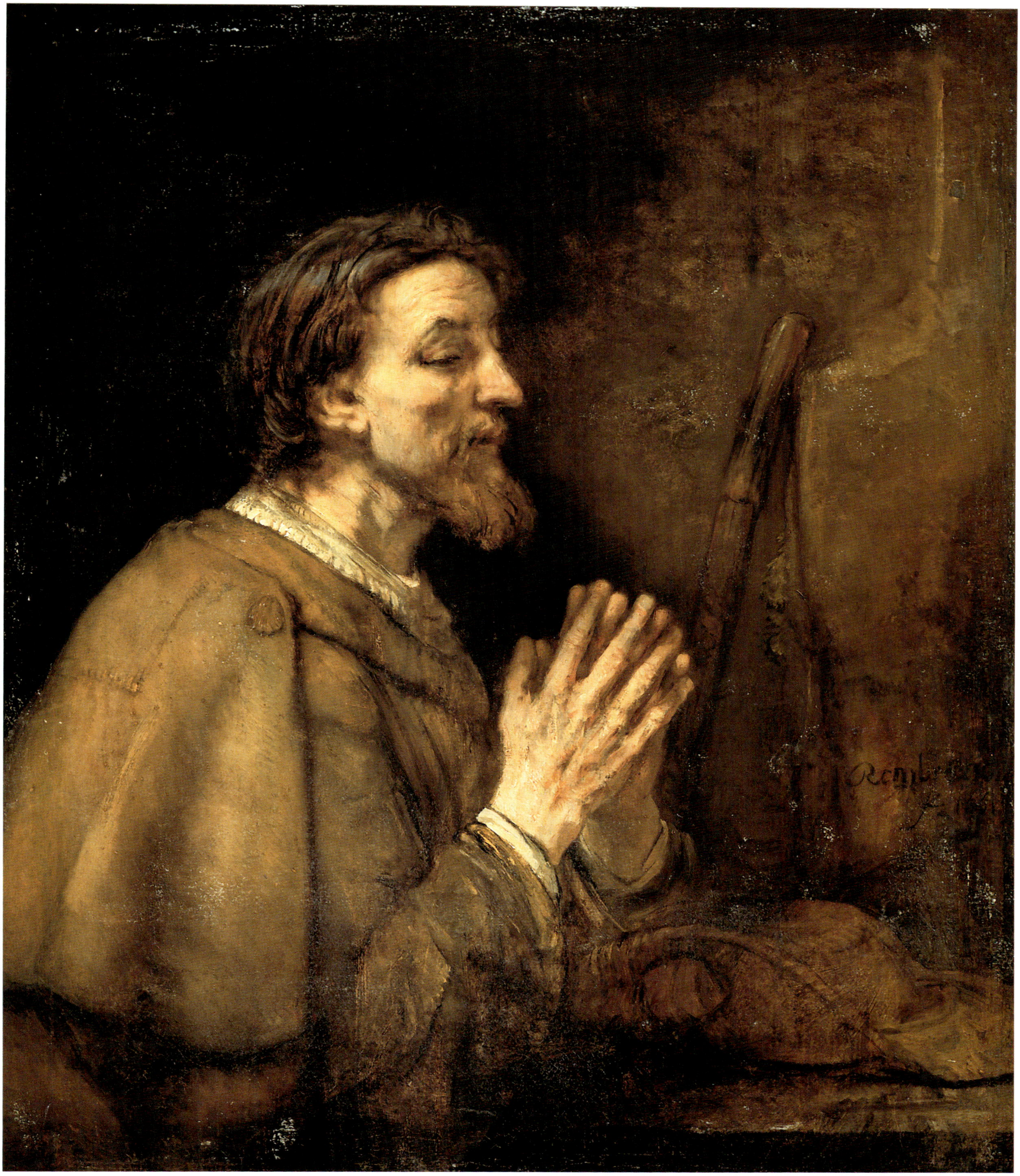

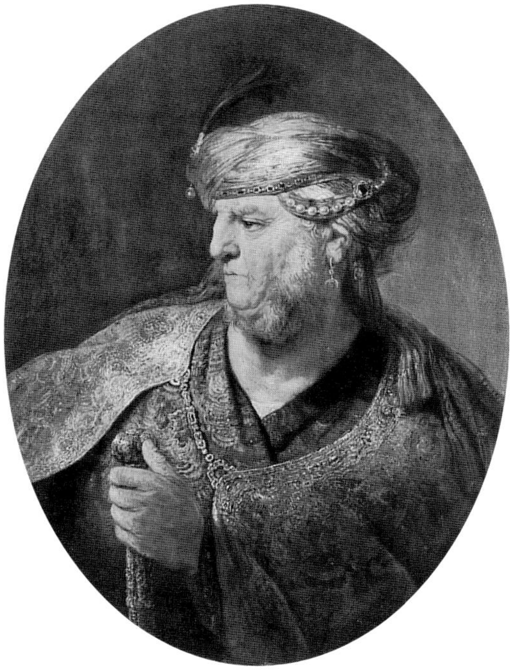

FIG. 21b
Rembrandt
Bust of a Man in Oriental Dress
Signed and dated 1633
Panel (oval)
85.8 x 63.8 cm
Alte Pinakothek, Munich

Hendrik by the painter Gerrit van Honthorst (see commentary to cat. no. 12). Rembrandt's *tronies*, which were made with no such constraints, include three profile views of women: the *Young Lady* of 1632 in Stockholm, *Saskia in Rich Apparel*, *c.*1634–42, in Kassel (p. 45, fig. 17), and the *Flora* of 1654–55 in New York.[4] For much of Rembrandt's career as a painter, his *Bust of a Man in Oriental Dress*, 1633, in Munich was his only profile *tronie* of a man (fig. 21b).[5] He occasionally rendered a profile in his multi-figure history pieces, to distinguish the main character. One example is his portrayal of the bewildered king surrounded by his guests in *Belshazzar's Feast* of *c.*1635 (fig. 21c).[6] Perhaps because of his use of figures in profile in this way, it has been suggested more than once that the *Bust of a Man in Oriental Dress* was a preliminary study for a multi-figure work.[7]

In Rembrandt's late period we suddenly find another male *tronie* in profile, in his picture of the *Man in Armour* of 1655 (cat. no. 15). In all the profile single-figure pieces mentioned above, the head is to one side of the centre of the composition, so that the distance between the face and the side of the picture frame is greater than that behind the head. Rembrandt apparently felt there should be 'breathing space' in front of the face. This device has been emphasized and exploited even further in the *James*, to add an extra dimension to the picture.

In the profile pictures referred to above, only the head is inclined to the left, while the torso is viewed either face-on or at an angle. Only *Amalia van Solms* (fig. 21a) and the *Young Lady* in Stockholm, both of 1632, are viewed completely from the side, like this *Apostle James* of 1661. In this case, unlike in that of the *Amalia van Solms*, it was Rembrandt himself who chose the profile position for his figure, the object being to emphasize the apostle's immersion in prayer as the main motif of the picture. To quote Benesch in 1956: 'he reminds us ... of a donor in a Gothic panel painting'.[8]

AB

1 Hofstede de Groot 1908–27, vol. VI, 1916, p. 121, no. 170.
2 *The Evangelist Matthew* (our cat. no. 22); *Self-Portrait as Paul*, Rijksmuseum, Amsterdam (Bredius / Gerson 1969, no. 59); *The Apostle Bartholomew*, J. Paul Getty Museum, Malibu (our fig. 17c); *Simon*, Kunsthaus, Zurich (Ruzicka Foundation) (first published by Münz 1948; Bredius / Gerson 1969, no. 616A). For these paintings, see also commentary to our cat. no. 32.
3 Bredius / Gerson 1969, no. 99; *Corpus*, vol. II, 1986, no. A61.
4 Nationalmuseum, Stockholm (Bredius / Gerson 1969, no. 85; *Corpus*, vol. II, 1986, no. A49); Gemäldegalerie, Kassel (Bredius / Gerson 1969, no. 101; *Corpus*, vol. II, 1986, no. A85; in the first draft Rembrandt apparently envisaged a less strictly profile view (*Corpus*, p. 430)); Metropolitan Museum of Art, New York (Bredius / Gerson 1969, no. 114).
5 Bredius / Gerson 1969, no. 178; *Corpus*, vol. II, 1986, no. A73.
6 Bredius / Gerson 1969, no. 497; *Corpus*, vol. III, 1989, no. A110. The profile figure of the protagonist Bathsheba in the painting of 1654 in the Louvre has a 'pendant' in the old maidservant at her feet (Bredius / Gerson 1969, no. 521).
7 For the adherents of this view, see *Corpus*, vol. II, 1986, pp. 348–9, no. A73.
8 Benesch 1956, p. 346.

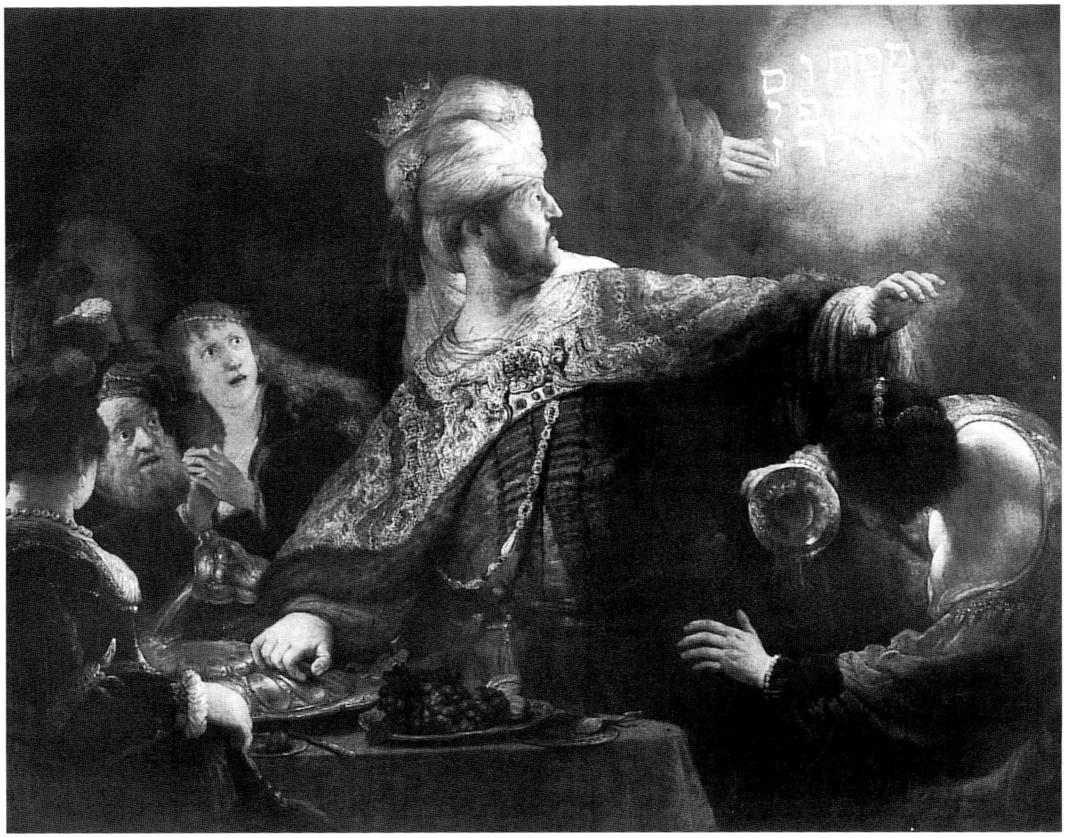

FIG. 21c
Rembrandt
Belshazzar's Feast
Signed and dated 163[?]
Canvas
167.0 x 209.0 cm
The Trustees of the National Gallery, London

22

The Evangelist Matthew

Signed and dated centre right *Rembrandt f. 1661*
Canvas
96.0 x 81.0 cm
Musée du Louvre, Département des Peintures, Paris
© Photo RMN

PROVENANCE: At the residence of the Comte d'Angiviller, Paris, possibly on loan from the royal collection; confiscated from there during the French Revolution, 4 July 1794.

LITERATURE: Lavallée 1804–15, vol. 8, 1812, p. 7 (with engraving); Hofstede de Groot 1908–27, vol. VI, 1916, p. 122, no. 173; Valentiner 1920; Benesch 1956, p. 343; Valentiner 1956, p. 400; Bauch 1966, no. 231; Bredius / Gerson 1969, no. 614; J. P. Cuzin, in Paris 1970–71, cat. no. 182 (with earlier literature); Brejon de Lavergnée, Foucart & Reynaud 1979, p. 110; Foucart 1982, pp. 83–8; Schwartz 1984, p. 311; Tümpel 1986, no. 88; C. Brown, in Berlin / Amsterdam / London 1991–92a, pp. 275–7, cat. no. 47; G. Cavalli-Björkman, in Stockholm 1992–93, pp. 208–9, cat. no. 61.

The Old Testament prophet Ezekiel saw a vision of fire in heaven and in its midst four winged creatures with the faces of a man, a lion, an ox and an eagle (Ezekiel 1:4–11). In Revelations, John describes the same four creatures around the throne of God (Revelations 4:6–8). In Christian art these creatures became the symbols of the four evangelists. Matthew is portrayed with an angel, Mark with a lion, Luke with an ox, and John with an eagle. The evangelists are also shown with the attributes of a pen and/or a book in which they inscribe their divinely inspired texts.

This painting is known as 'Matthew and the Angel', an interpretation prompted by the pictorial tradition. Only during the anti-clerical phase of the French Revolution was it described by the people who confiscated it (see Provenance) as 'no. 4, a painting by Rembrandt of an old man and a young man'.[1] In fact this was a more accurate description than 'Matthew and the Angel'. Cuzin observed in 1970 that the young figure should be described as a human rather than as a true angel. Indeed, the figure behind the man writing has no wings to identify him as an angel – the form above his head is completely indistinct. In about 1810 the engraver J. J. Oortman rendered this form in a manner that suggested a niche in the background (fig. 22a). By leaving out the wings, Rembrandt has humanized the angel

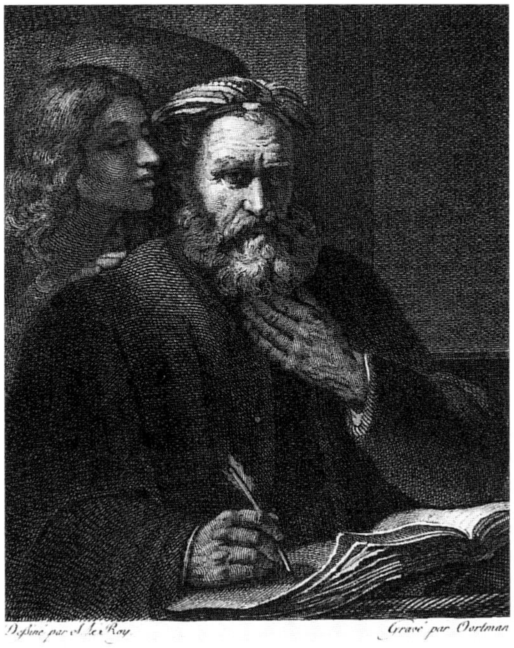

FIG. 22a
Joachim Jan Oortman (1777–1818), after Rembrandt
The Evangelist Matthew and the Angel c.1810
Engraving
From Lavallée 1804–15, vol. 8, 1812

without diminishing the mysterious undertones of the scene. A wingless angel can also be seen in Frans Hals's earlier *Evangelist Matthew* of c.1625 (fig. 22b).[2] The angel in the Hals has in fact been reduced to a small, inquisitive boy.

Matthew's large, rough, labourer's hands in the Rembrandt look even less like those of an intellectual than do those in the Hals. The apostle has paused from his arduous writing and gazes pensively before him. He strokes his beard with his left hand, as though trying to find a word or pondering how best to describe an event. He is not yet aware of the boy behind him, who gently brushes his shoulder. The boy leans closer to Matthew's ear to whisper words of divine inspiration.[3] He looms out of the shadows behind the apostle. The light falling on Matthew's face catches only the side of the boy's nose, his fingertips on Matthew's shoulder, and a few strands of his long, golden locks. During the period in which this picture was executed, Rembrandt applied these patches of light to his figures' faces to create an aura of mystery. One example is the *Portrait of a Young Man ('Titus, the Artist's Son')* from Baltimore (cat. no. 18).

Two authors have observed – apparently independently of one another – that Rembrandt's *Matthew* of 1661 displays distinct similarities to a painting of the same subject that his pupil Barend Fabritius had made five years earlier (cat. no. 59). Fabritius's *The Evangelist Matthew* of 1656 also shows a young angel – in this case with wings – laying his hand on the evangelist's shoulder and whispering into his ear. It is quite conceivable that Fabritius based his work on a preliminary sketch which is no longer recorded and which Rembrandt may have made, in or before 1656, for his painting of 1661.[4] It is possible too that Fabritius's painting inspired Rembrandt to paint his own.[5]

The boy in Rembrandt's *Matthew* can also be seen in other works from this period, executed in the same broad technique. He is easiest to recognize in the *Young Man Singing* in Vienna (fig. 18b). Here, as well, Rembrandt applied patches of light on the face. In this century many authors have taken the model in cat. no. 22 and in fig. 18b to be Rembrandt's son Titus (1641–1668), but this is pure conjecture (see p. 46).

Even more speculative, and more criticized, is Valentiner's suggestion, made in 1920, that the *Matthew* formed part of a series comprising the four evangelists, the twelve apostles, and Christ and the Virgin. He believes that these works 'may have been [commissioned] by a church'.[6] There are difficulties with Valentiner's hypothesis. None of the pictures that are supposed to represent the other three evangelists in the series

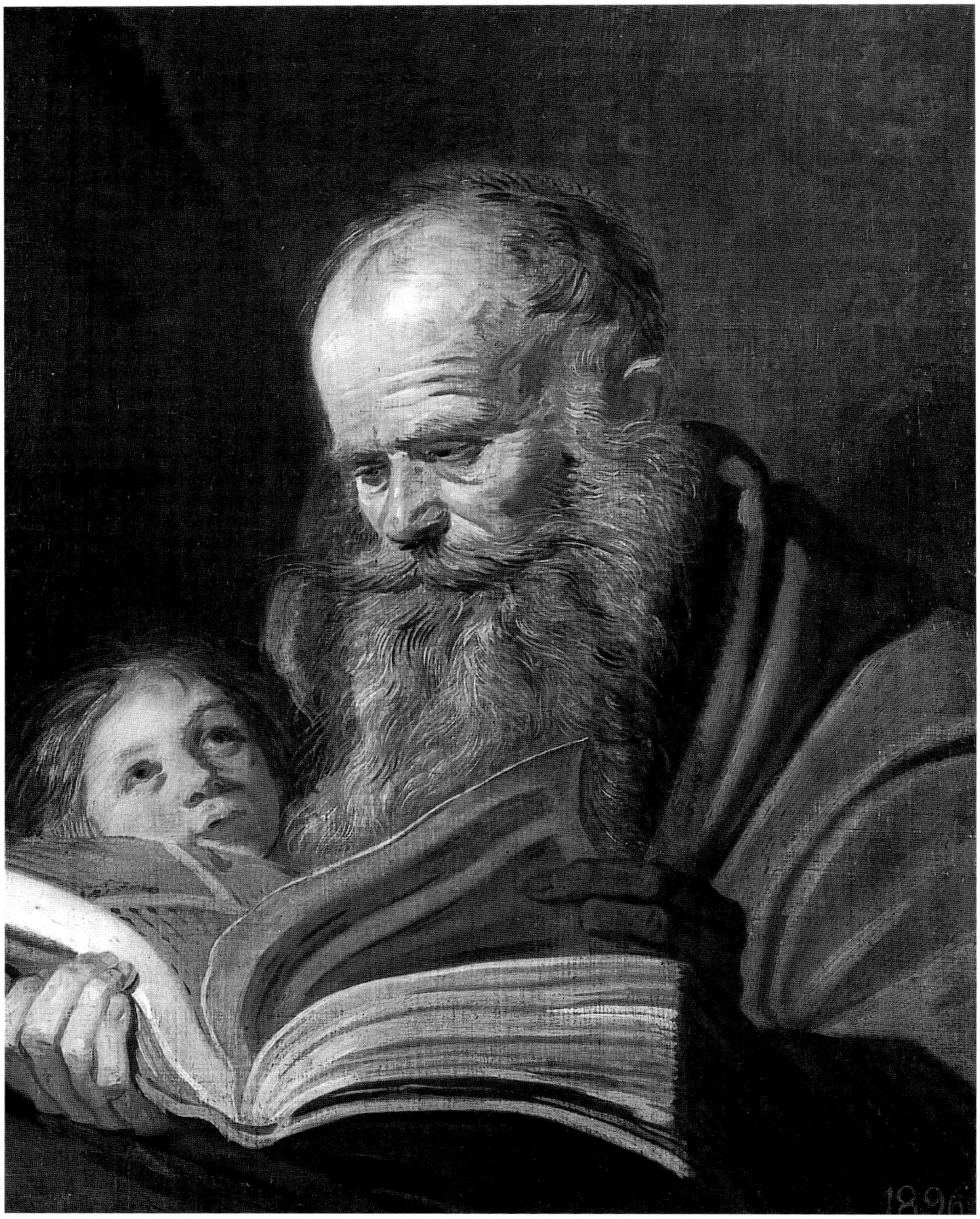

FIG. 22b
Frans Hals 1581/85–1666
The Evangelist Matthew
Canvas
70.2 x 55.0 cm
Museum of Western and Oriental Art, Odessa

include a lion, an ox or an eagle – as Valentiner himself observed – nor do they correspond in size. Moreover, the so-called 'John' and 'Mark' have been firmly rejected from Rembrandt's oeuvre, and recently the 'Luke' (cat. no. 32) was similarly rejected. Still accepted, however, is Valentiner's premise that Rembrandt presumably made the pieces in his 'series' to sell abroad. The fact is that none of them appear in early Dutch inventories, except for a 'small [!] painting of Paul' (stuckjen schilderij van Paulus) that occurs in a Delft inventory of 1667.[7]

A few oil sketches of a head, which bear a certain similarity to the *Matthew*, were long believed to be studies for the painting. They are now regarded as imitations or, at best, studio pieces.[8]

AB

1 J. P. Cuzin, in Paris 1970–71, cat. no. 182 (Provenance): 'No. 4, un tableau de Rembrandt représentant un vieillard et un jeune homme'. In two other documents from the period, the piece was referred to as 'un vieillard et une jeune femme' (copy received from J. Foucart, 1996). Around 1810 it was again called *Matthew and the Angel*, but with the comment that 'Quelques hommes, malicieux détracteurs de Rembrandt, ont dit et même écrit que cet inimitable peintre avait voulu représenter le Génie de Socrate inspirant à ce philosophe ses immortels écrits' (Some men, malicious detractors of Rembrandt, have said and have even written that this incomparable painter intended to depict Socrates's muse, inspiring that philosopher with his immortal writings) (Lavallée 1804–15, vol. 8, 1812, p. 7).

2 Slive 1970–74, vol. I, 1970, pp. 100–3; vol. II, 1970, no. 44. The *Matthew* by Hals, and its pendant, the *Evangelist Luke* (both in Odessa), are Hals's only paintings of religious subjects. Foucart 1982, p. 84, presents a *Matthew* by Artus Wolffort, in which the angel seems not to have wings (Prado, Madrid). The wingless 'angel' in a *Matthew* attributed to Abraham Bloemaert is a small boy who holds the book open for the evangelist and points inside it (sale cat., Christie's, London, 14 December 1990, lot 118, repr.; Roethlisberger 1993, vol. I, no. 706 (as not Bloemaert, 'either a genre scene or St Joseph')).

3 It is unlikely that Rembrandt intended the scene to merge with, or to evoke, the theme of the Calling of Matthew (Benesch 1956, p. 343, proposed this association). In that biblical episode, Matthew is called by Christ, not an angel, and, as a tax collector, is usually portrayed in this scene with his account books around him.

4 Suggested by Sumowski 1959, p. 290.

5 Suggested by Tümpel 1986, p. 400, no. 88.

6 Valentiner 1920. In 1956 Valentiner added to his theory by suggesting a 'hidden Mennonite church' (Valentiner 1956, p. 400). This is highly improbable in the Dutch seventeenth-century context.

7 Strauss & Van der Meulen 1979, p. 568, no. 1667/5 (inventory of the Delft clergyman Gerrit van Heusden).

8 Bredius 302–305. In Bredius / Gerson 1969, only Bredius 304 is considered autograph. See also Wheelock 1995, p. 333, no. 1942.9.58(654).

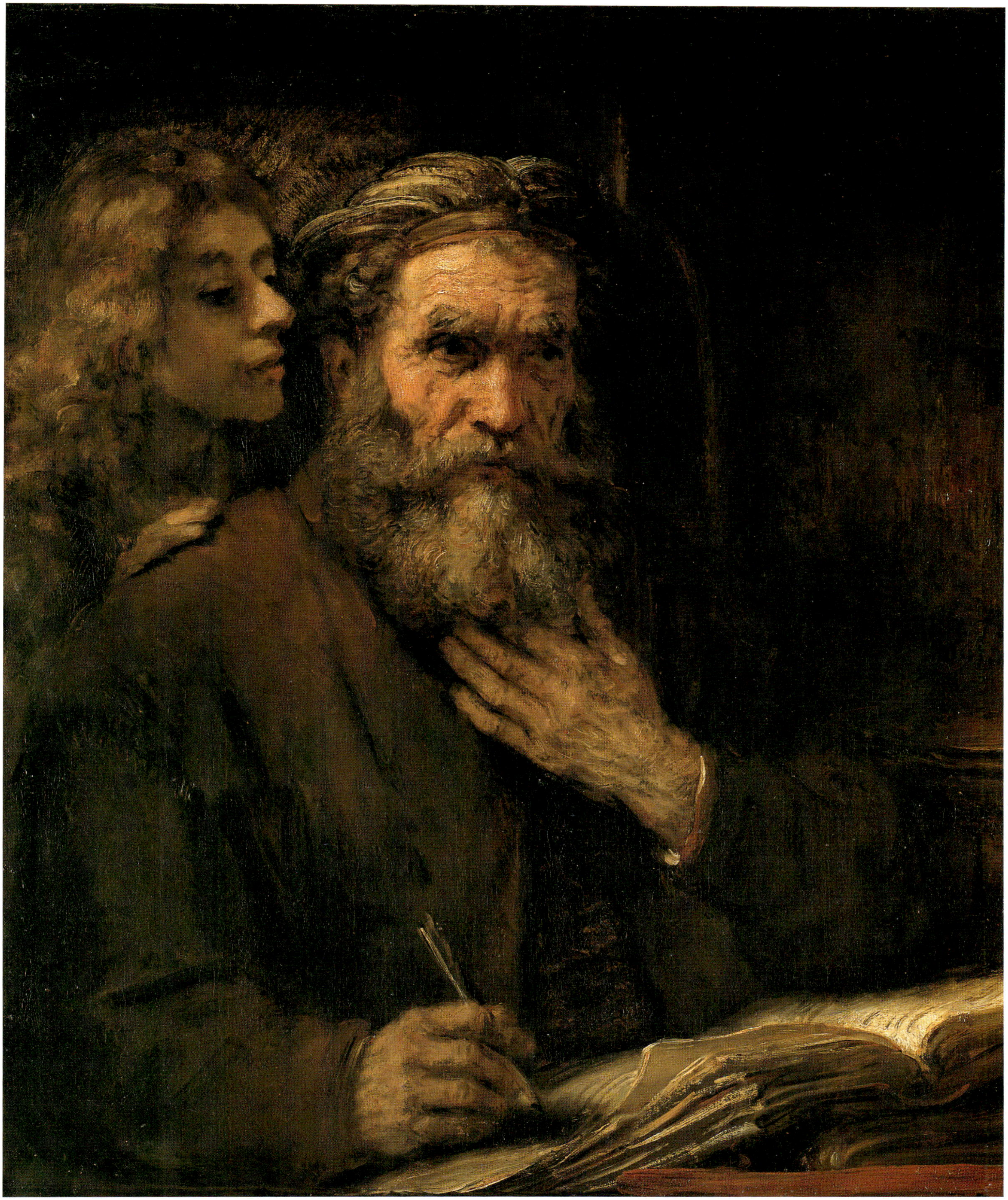

23
Portrait of Jacob Trip
*c.*1661

Signed a little above the level of the sitter's left hand, at right *Rembr* (interrupted by the present edge of the canvas)
Canvas
130.5 x 97.0 cm
The Trustees of the National Gallery, London

PROVENANCE: [After MacLaren / Brown (1991)] Lee family, 18th century; Sir William Fowle Middleton-Fowle, 2nd Baronet, 1837; Sir George Nathaniel Broke-Middleton, Baronet; Lady de Saumarez, 1887; purchased in 1899.

LITERATURE: Bode & Hofstede de Groot 1897–1905, vol. VII, 1902, no. 512; Hofstede de Groot 1908–27, vol. VI, 1916, p. 215, no. 393; Hofstede de Groot 1928; Gerson 1968, p. 132; Bredius / Gerson 1969, no. 314; Haak 1969, p. 297; Dudok van Heel 1979; Van Eeghen 1983; Schwartz 1984, p. 334; Tümpel 1986, no. 218; London 1988–89, pp. 120–5, cat. no. 16; MacLaren / Brown 1991, vol. 1, pp. 350–2, no. 1674; Baker & Henry 1995, p. 565, no. 1674; Dickey 1995, pp. 354–5.

This painting has a pendant representing an elderly woman (fig. 23a).[1] Doubts have occasionally been expressed as to whether the two works are indeed counterparts, since the woman is shown from the front, and the man inclines slightly towards her.[2] However, Rembrandt had made similar pendants in 1633 (fig. 27c), and again in 1641, of a woman portrayed face-on and a man half-turned towards her .[3] Hence Rembrandt's portrait of Margaretha de Geer is not his only departure from what Dickey in 1995 thought to be 'the time-honoured heraldic half-turn' towards the husband.[4]

The present picture was exhibited on its own in 1837 as 'A portrait supposed to be John Lutma, the Goldsmith' (a reference to the Amsterdam silversmith Johannes Lutma (1584–1669)).[5] The painting was shown in 1858 as 'a goldsmith of Antwerp'.[6] In the early 1900s, he was described as a 'burgomaster' and as a 'Jewish scholar'.[7] It was apparently hard to conceive of this resplendent figure simply as an anonymous gentleman. In 1928 Hofstede de Groot identified the model as the Dordrecht merchant Jacob Trip (1575–1661).[8] This identification has never been questioned. The companion piece was therefore a portrait of Trip's wife, Margaretha de Geer (1583–1672).[9] Hofstede de Groot based his identifications on the sitters' resemblance to Trip and his wife as portrayed by Jacob Gerritsz Cuyp, by his son Aelbert Cuyp (fig. 23b), and by Nicolaes Maes (cat. nos 67, 68).[10]

The Trip and de Geer families were partners in a hugely successful iron and arms business, operating on a scale that was unique in their time.[11] They owned mines, shipyards and fleets, many of them in Sweden. In 1660, two of Jacob Trip's sons, Hendrick and Louis, commissioned the construction of the Trippenhuis – a palatial home by Amsterdam standards – which was to house the Rijksmuseum collection from 1817 to 1885 (fig. 23c). The two chimneys surmounting the Trippenhuis are in the shape of cannon, signifying the products that the Trips manufactured. The

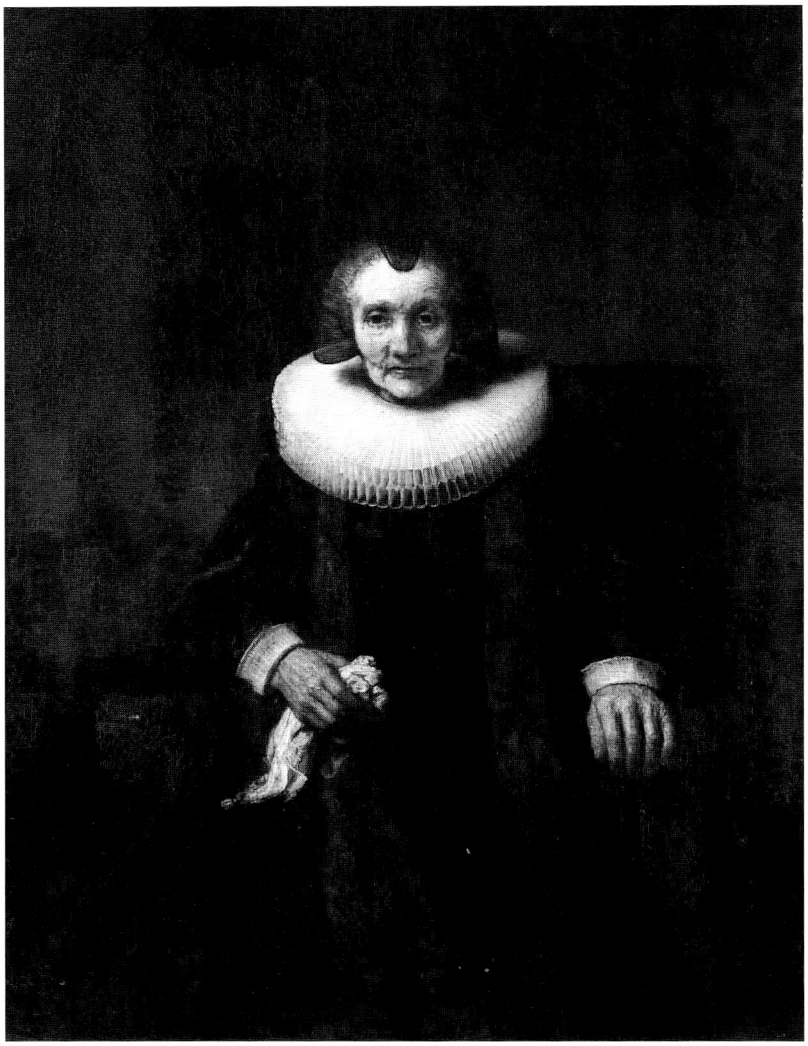

FIG. 23a
Rembrandt
Portrait of Margaretha de Geer, Wife of Jacob Trip c.1661
Canvas
130.5 x 97.5 cm
The Trustees of the National Gallery, London

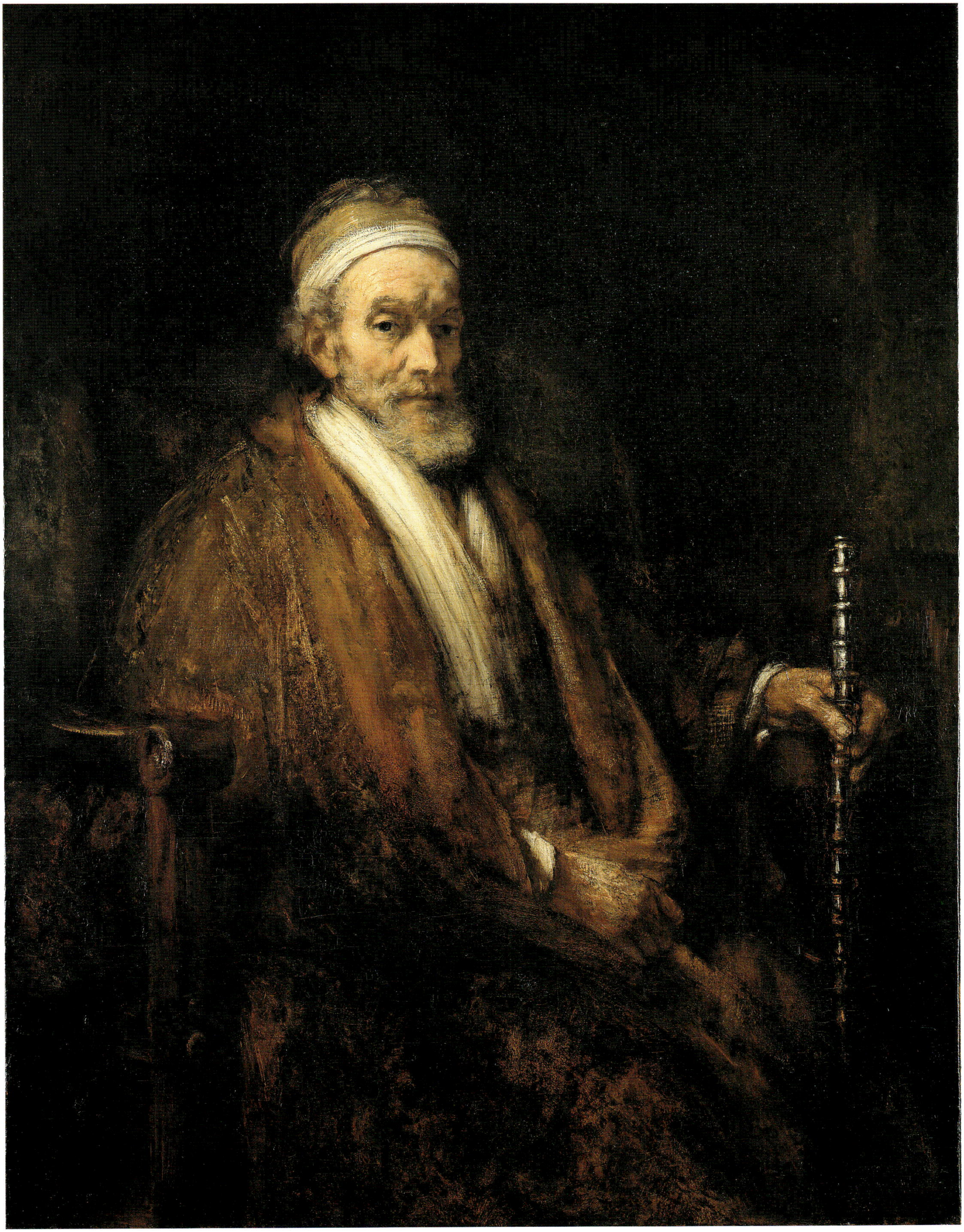

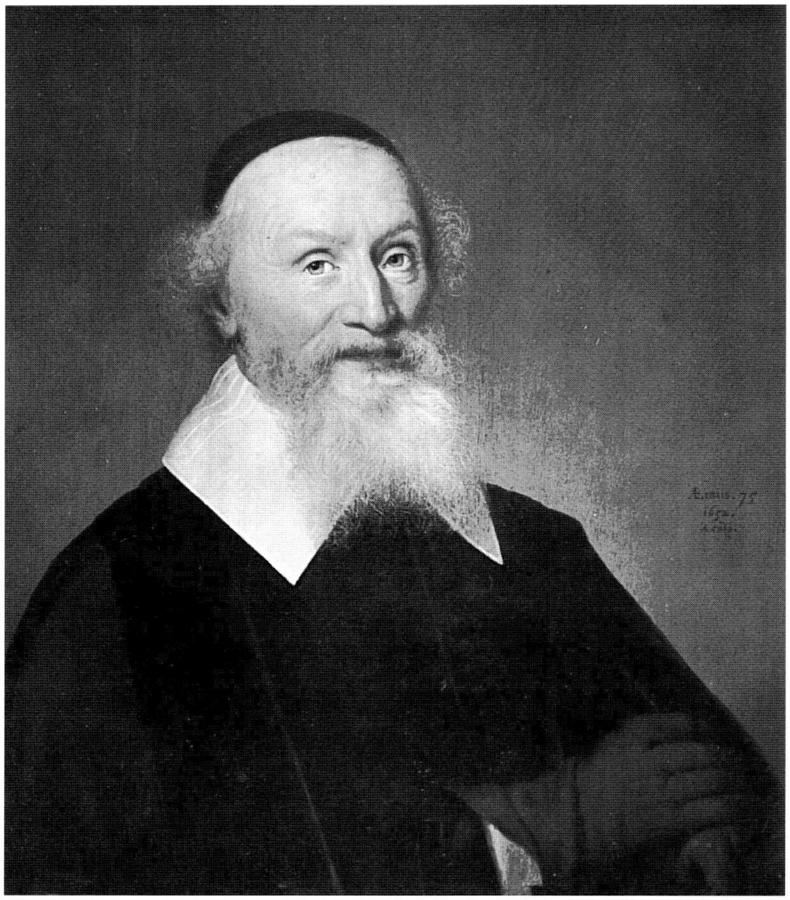

FIG. 23b
Aelbert Cuyp (1620–1691), after Jacob Gerritsz Cuyp (1594–*c.*1652)
Portrait of Jacob Trip
Signed and dated 1652
Panel
66.0 x 58.0 cm
Private collection
From a reproduction

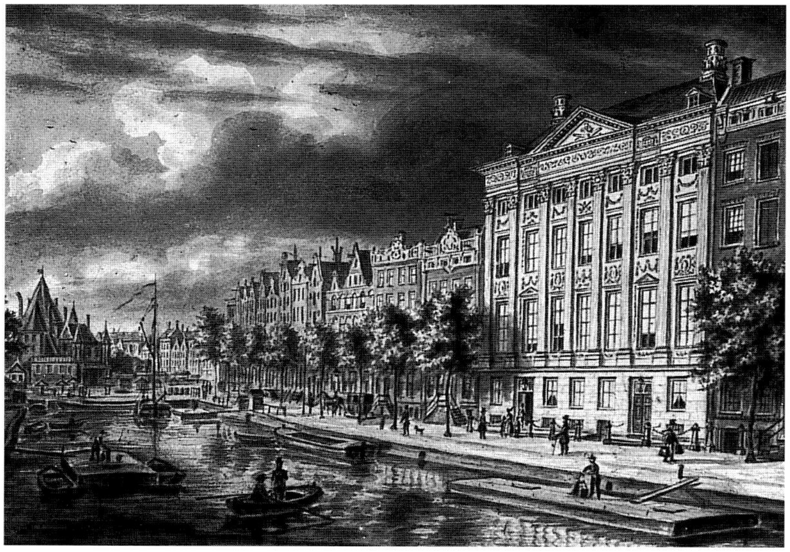

FIG. 23c
Augustus Wijnantz 1795–after 1848
The Trippenhuis on Kloveniersburgwal in about 1835, with the Weighing-House in the Background
Drawing
15.8 x 22.0 cm
Historisch-topografische Atlas van het Gemeentearchief van Amsterdam

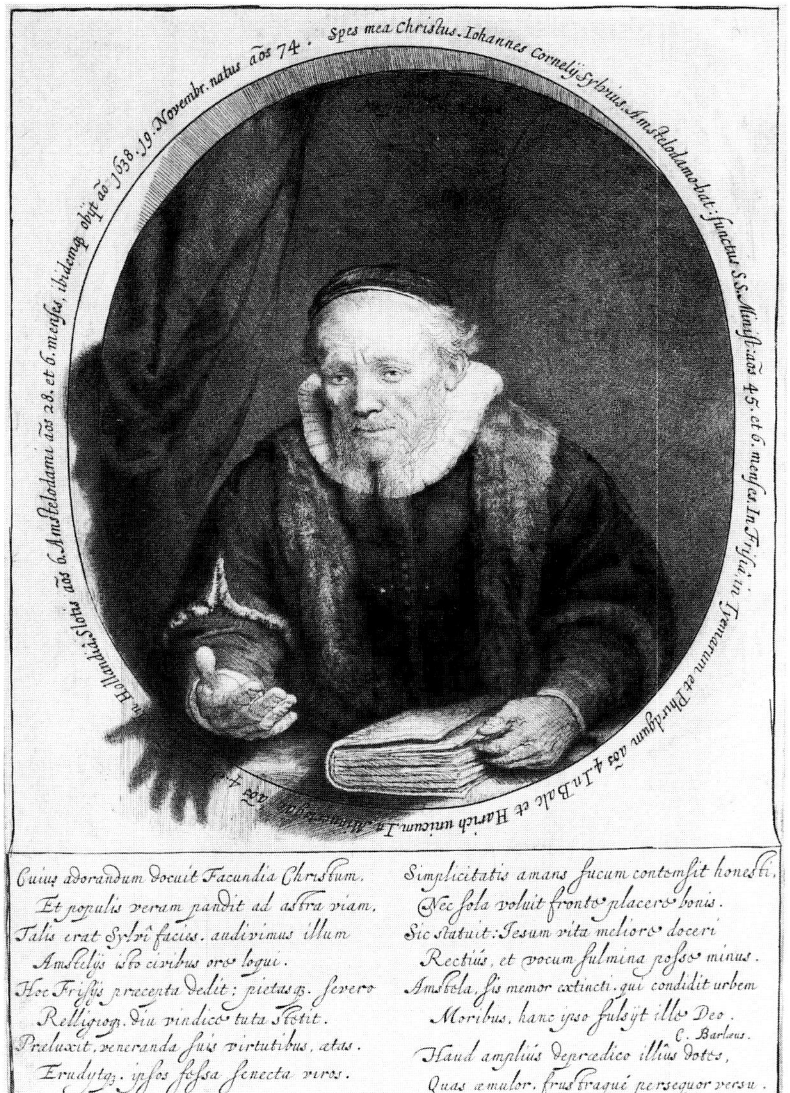

FIG. 23d
Rembrandt
Portrait of Johannes Sylvius
Signed and dated 1646
Etching
27.8 x 18.8 cm
Rijksprentenkabinet, Rijksmuseum, Amsterdam

two sons may also have ordered the portraits of their parents from Rembrandt in order to display them in their new home.[12]

In 1983, van Eeghen suggested that the painting of Jacob Trip, unlike that of Margaretha, may have been made only after his death in 1661. If this were the case, Rembrandt would have based his picture on an older portrait.[13] Others support this hypothesis. It has been invoked to explain the difference some perceive in the nature of the two pendants – 'his ... a hieratic image, hers an animated study'.[14] However, it remains questionable whether we can conclude, on the basis of the portrait alone, that it was made posthumously. If this were indeed to be true, we could assume that Rembrandt sought to represent Trip as he looked during his lifetime.[15] We see this approach in Rembrandt's etched portrait of the clergyman Johannes Sylvius (1564–1638). The etching was made in 1646, eight years after Sylvius's death, but the man looks alive and well (B.280) (fig. 23d).[16]

It has been observed on more than one occasion that the costume Trip is wearing makes him look more like a prophet than a distinguished Dutch merchant.[17] His tabard was associated throughout the seventeenth century with dignity, tradition and erudition.[18] It is therefore not surprising that the portrait was taken for that of a Jewish scholar. This picture, like several others by Rembrandt, seems almost a tribute to the dignity of age.

We can analyse this further by comparing the picture with a portrait of *c.*1659–60 by Nicolaes Maes (cat. no. 67), which, of all Trip's portraits, is the closest in date to that by Rembrandt. In Maes's version the face and hands take up much of the picture space, so that every detail of the man's features can be seen. On the basis of this portrait we would instantly recognize Trip, and would have no difficulty identifying his fur-trimmed tabard or the beautifully worked chair on which he sits.

Rembrandt's Trip, by comparison, has the appearance of a visionary figure, enthroned on his roughly sketched seat. In fact the chair and clothing seem rather too voluminous for the man's slight, wizened frame. The tabard is sketched with such bold, broad strokes that it could even be a toga. Trip's small, strictly oval face is firm and sculpted by contrast. He looks at us attentively – still very much alive – but seems to be absorbed in his own thoughts. He holds a sturdy cane to support himself.[19] The cane also adds a strong vertical accent at the right of the composition.

AB/MB

1 Bredius / Gerson 1969, no. 394.
2 Haak 1969, p. 297.
3 *Portrait of a Young Woman with a Fan* (frontal), Metropolitan Museum of Art, New York (our fig. 27c), and *A Man Rising from His Chair* (half-turned), Taft Museum, Cincinnati (both 1633) (Bredius / Gerson 1969, nos 341, 172; *Corpus*, vol. II, 1986, nos A79, A78); *Portrait of Agatha Bas* (frontal), Collection of Her Majesty Queen Elizabeth II, and *Portrait of Nicolaes van Bambeeck* (half-turned), Koninklijke Musea voor Schone Kunsten, Brussels (both 1641) (Bredius / Gerson 1969, nos 360, 218; *Corpus*, vol. III, 1989, nos A145, A144).
4 Dickey 1995, p. 354.
5 MacLaren / Brown 1991, vol. 1, p. 352, note 15.
6 MacLaren / Brown 1991, vol. 1, p. 352, note 16.
7 Inscribed on an undated photograph (from after 1909) of a copy after cat. no. 23, in the collection of J. H. A. Duynstee, Delft, in 1909 (photograph at RKD).
8 Hofstede de Groot 1928.
9 Hofstede de Groot had suggested this identification previously in 1902 and 1916 (Bode & Hofstede de Groot 1897–1905, vol. VII, 1902, nos 493, 512; Hofstede de Groot 1908–27, vol. VI, 1916, pp. 395–6, no. 857).
10 MacLaren / Brown 1991, vol. 1, p. 351, notes 4, 5 and 6, cite other portraits of Jacob Trip.
11 Klein 1965.
12 Dudok van Heel 1979, p. 22.
13 Van Eeghen 1983, p. 72.
14 London 1988–89, pp. 120–5, cat. no. 16. See also MacLaren / Brown 1991, vol. 1, p. 351, no. 1674; Baker & Henry 1995, p. 565, no. 1674; Dickey 1995, pp. 354–5, 366–7, note 104. Dickey suggests that the handkerchief may allude to Margaretha's mourning the death of Jacob. However, a handkerchief is a standard attribute in seventeenth-century portraits of women.
15 Letters are known from the same period concerning a commission to Jan Lievens for the portrayal of deceased parents-in-law. Lievens was asked to do the paintings for the very reason that he had known the deceased personally; he would therefore not have to rely solely on old portraits of his subjects, but could also draw on his 'imagination' (P. Leupe, 'De schilder Jan Lievensz en de portretten van de Bickers, 1663–1664', *De Nederlandsche Spectator*, 1874, reprinted in Blankert 1975–79, pp. 187–90).
16 Another work discussed in the context of posthumous portraits is the painted *'Portrait of Saskia'*, dated 1643 – the year after Saskia van Uylenburgh's death. However, this picture has not been regarded as autograph since 1969 (Bredius / Gerson 1969, no. 109).
17 For instance, Hofstede de Groot 1928, p. 262; Gerson 1968, p. 132.
18 De Winkel 1995.
19 Smith 1829–42, suppl. 1842, no. 6: 'a bamboo cane'. Bode & Hofstede de Groot 1897–1905, vol. VII, 1902, no. 512: 'hohem Rohrstock ... ein hohes Spanisches Rohr' (a long cane ... a long Spanish cane).

24

Man with a Falcon on His Wrist
*c.*1662–65

Canvas
98.5 x 79.0 cm
Göteborg Museum of Art

PROVENANCE: [After Fredlund (1992–93)] Lord Coventry, London; sale, George, Paris, 1853, 6,100 frs; sale, Gilkinet, Paris, 18 April 1863, lot 85, bought in at 10,000 frs; acquired in Paris by Erik Brodin, Stockholm, 1921; with Bukowski auction house; acquired from Bukowski (but not at one of its auctions) and presented to the Göteborg Museum by the director Gustaf Werner and private donors in 1921.

LITERATURE: Hofstede de Groot 1908–27, vol. VI, 1916, pp. 171–2, no. 287; Valentiner 1921, p. XXVII, no. 24, p. 97a; Benesch 1924–25; Gantner 1959; Gantner 1964, pp. 177–83; Gerson 1968, p. 428; Bredius / Gerson 1969, no. 319; Tümpel 1971, p. 20, note 2; Schwartz 1984, p. 314; Tümpel 1986, no. 93*; Slatkes 1992, no. 229; B. Fredlund, in Stockholm 1992–93, pp. 210–13, cat. no. 62 (with earlier literature).

This piece is generally dated to the 1660s. In these late years, Rembrandt frequently returned to the motif of a lifesize half-length figure in unusual costume. In this picture a bearded man is planted squarely before us and viewed face-on, as he looks straight past us into the distance. He is neither a monk nor an apostle, nor any other easily recognizable type. His black-rimmed red beret, rendered with irregular, wavy outlines, recalls the costumes in which Netherlanders from olden times were depicted by seventeenth-century artists, whose inspiration lay with 'old', that is fifteenth- and sixteenth-century, examples in the visual arts.[1] Not until the nineteenth century were artists able to render the distant past with any historical accuracy.

The Germanic Batavians who inhabited the present-day Netherlands in Roman times were sometimes portrayed in berets like the one shown here.[2] Rembrandt had to decide how best to render the ancestral Batavians when he came to paint his *Conspiracy of the Batavians under Claudius Civilis Against the Romans*, *c.*1661–62, an episode from 69 AD (fig. 24a).[3] Only a fragment has survived, but the picture originally measured approximately 550 x 550 cm, making it Rembrandt's largest painting – indeed it was substantially larger than the *Night Watch* (p. 26, fig. 7). While working on this huge commission, or shortly afterwards, Rembrandt painted the *Man with a Falcon*, whose costume is no less unusual than those of the conspiring Batavians.

Costume in seventeenth-century Dutch art cannot be used as a basis for distinguishing between different historical periods. But the cross on a ribbon around the neck of the *Man with a Falcon* points to a Christian – and therefore post-Batavian – era. Moreover, the plume-hooded falcon, perched on the man's wrist, identifies him as a falconer. Falconry dates only from the Middle Ages, and was the exclusive sport of the nobility. The cross, the falcon, the horse looming vaguely behind the figure, and the even sketchier servant to the left of the horse, all seem to be specific attributes.[4] The picture was definitely not made as an anonymous *tronie*, but as a portrayal of a particular character from the past.

Two suggestions have been made regarding the man's identity, both of which seem equally feasible.[5] The question therefore remains unresolved. Valentiner in 1948 thought the falconer might be the Dutch count Floris V (1254–1296). The tale of this medieval knight was widely known in Rembrandt's time. In a mixture of fact and fiction, it was promulgated in a popular song (fig. 24b), recounted in seventeenth-

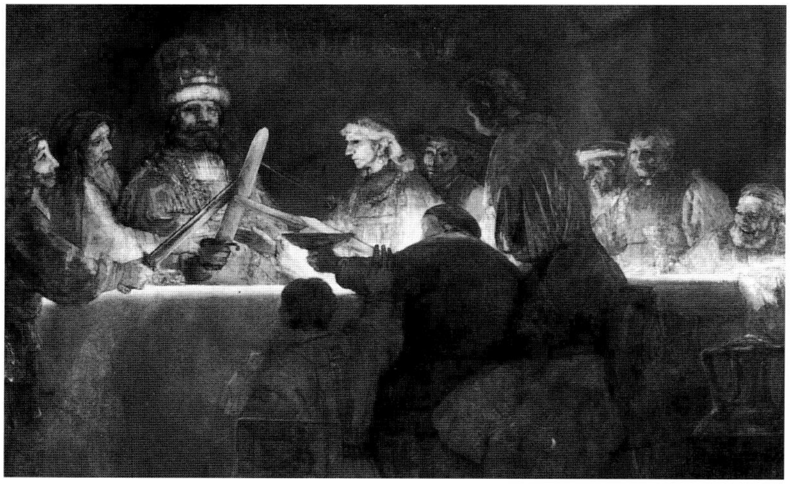

FIG. 24a
Rembrandt
The Conspiracy of the Batavians under Claudius Civilis Against the Romans *c.*1661–62
Canvas (fragment)
196.0 x 309.0 cm
Nationalmuseum, Stockholm
Photograph: Nationalmuseum, SKM, Stockholm
(for colour reproduction, see p. 27, fig. 9)

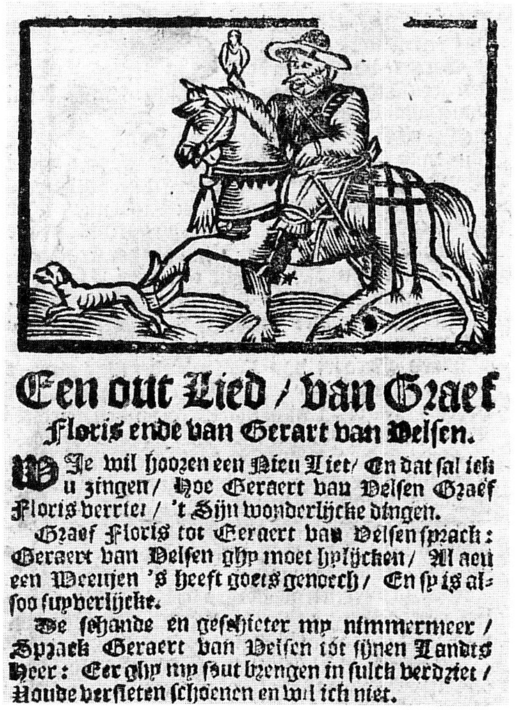

Een out Lied / van Graef
Floris ende van Geraert van Velsen.
Wie wil hooren een Nieu Liet/ En dat sal ick u zingen/ Hoe Geraert van Velsen Graef Floris verriet / 't Zijn wonderlijcke dingen.
Graef Floris tot Geraert van Velsen sprack: Geraert van Velsen ghy moet hylijcken/ Al aen een Weeutjen 's heeft goets genoech/ En sy is alsoo suyverlijcke.
De schande en geschiedet my nimmermeer / Sprack Geraert van Velsen tot sijnen Landts Heer: Eer ghy my sout brengen in sulck verdriet / Houde versleten schoenen en wil ick niet.

FIG. 24b
Song sheet, sold by 'Klein Jan', *c.*1650.
Atlas van Stolk, Rotterdam

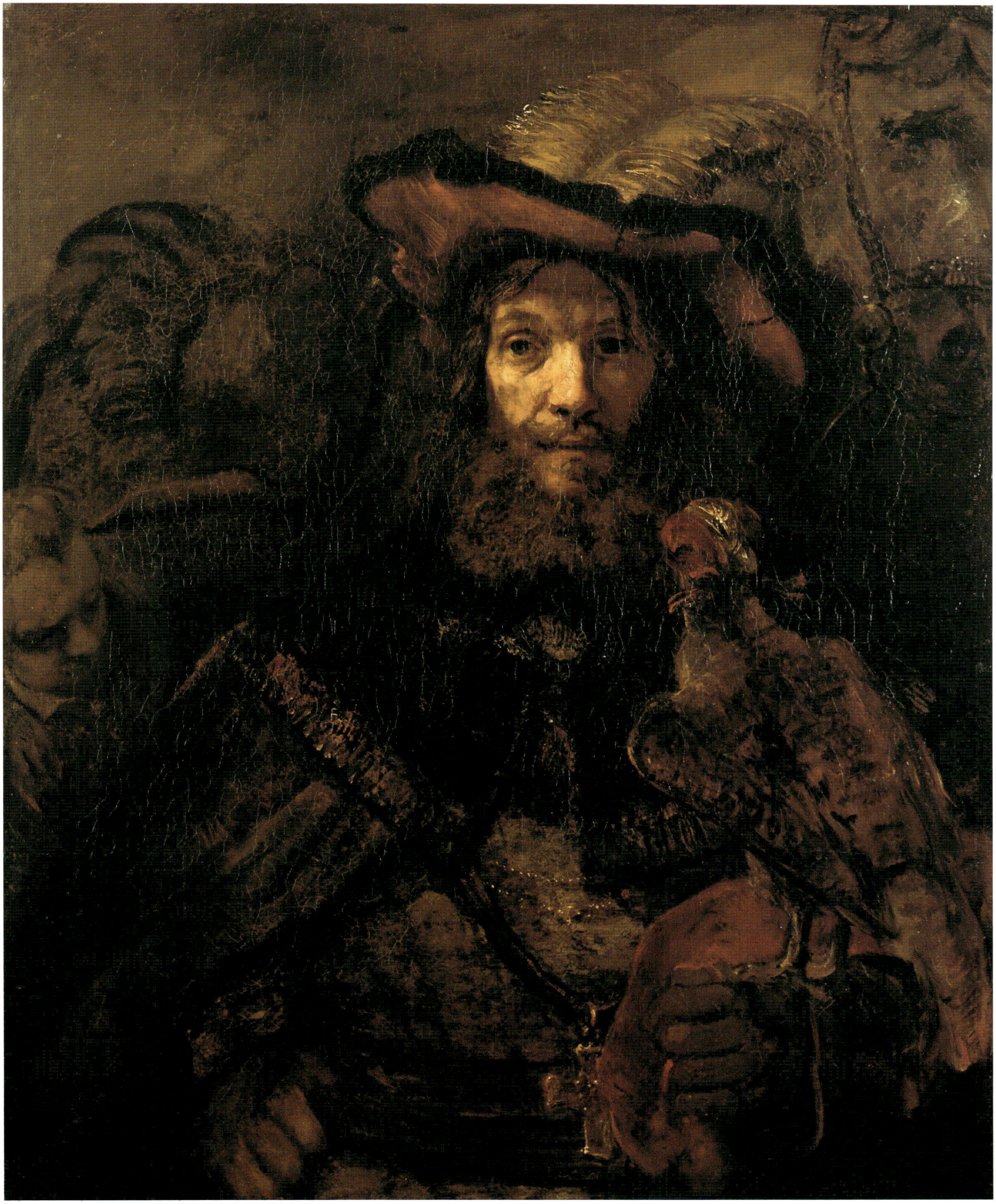

century city chronicles, and performed in the theatre. Floris was an ardent falconer, and was often portrayed with a falcon. While out hunting with his friends the noblemen Gerard van Velsen and Gijsbrecht van Amstel, he was captured and killed by his companions. According to Valentiner, the present picture shows Floris V about to mount his steed, pondering whether or not to trust Gijsbrecht van Amstel.[6] Floris's gaze is fixed on the men who are plotting to execute him, and about whom an old woman had warned him the previous day. This explanation inspired Gantner to propose, in 1959 and 1964, that the falconer's dramatic expression was based on that of the Christ in Leonardo da Vinci's *Last Supper*.[7] Rembrandt had seen prints of the painting, and he copied these in drawings (p. 327, fig. 8). Gantner maintains that Floris V is observing his betrayers as Christ did Judas, but this highly speculative hypothesis met with fierce criticism from Gerson in 1969.[8]

It should be said that in plays by the two great poets Pieter Cornelisz Hooft and Joost van den Vondel, Floris V is characterized as a tyrant who deserved his fate (*Geeraerdt van Velsen* (1612); *Gijsbreght van Aemstel* (1637)). In the plays, a parallel was drawn with the Dutch Revolt, when the provinces under King Philip II conspired against their legitimate ruler, who had likewise emerged as a despot.[9] Moreover, the murder of Floris V could be condoned as righteous revenge, for, according to the legend, Floris had brought Gerard van Velsen's brother to trial, had had him executed on trumped-up charges, and had subsequently raped Gerard's wife. Hence not all of Rembrandt's contemporaries saw Floris V as a heroic figure. When he is viewed in the light of his alleged atrocities, the comparison with Christ is all the more inappropriate.

A primitive woodcut shows that Floris V, like Rembrandt's falconer, could be portrayed with both a falcon and a horse. The woodcut, reproduced here for the first time in the context of identifying the subject of cat. no. 24 (fig. 24b), shows Floris V on horseback, with a falcon at his wrist. The print was made to illustrate 'An Old Song about Count Floris and Gerard van Velsen', referred to above.

The second suggestion with respect to the present picture's theme is that the *Man with a Falcon* represents St Bavo. Tümpel briefly reported in a footnote in 1971 that Hans Kaufmann had advanced this 'illuminating unpublished interpretation'.[10] No more was said until 1992, when Fredlund considered the hypothesis in an essay published in Swedish.[11] He drew attention to an engraving made in 1650 by Cornelis Visscher after Pieter Soutman, with an inscription identifying it as a depiction of St Bavo. The iconography in the engraving is closely related to that in the Rembrandt (fig. 24c). St Bavo is portrayed as a knight in a plumed 'medieval' beret, with a falcon on his wrist. He is dressed as a warrior and has a cross hanging from a chain around his neck. Also relevant in this connection is a portrayal of St Bavo dating from almost the same time as Rembrandt's painting: an etching by the Haarlem artist Leendert van der Cooghen, dated 1664 (fig. 24d).[12] Here, Bavo's helmet and armour give him a far more belligerent air, but he in fact also has a falcon with a plumed hood on his wrist.

Bavo is said to have been a wealthy Flemish nobleman who lived in the seventh century. He abandoned a life of dissipation in Ghent to become a penitent hermit. He is the name saint and patron of the St Baaf cathedral in Ghent, and the patron of the cathedral of the bishopric and

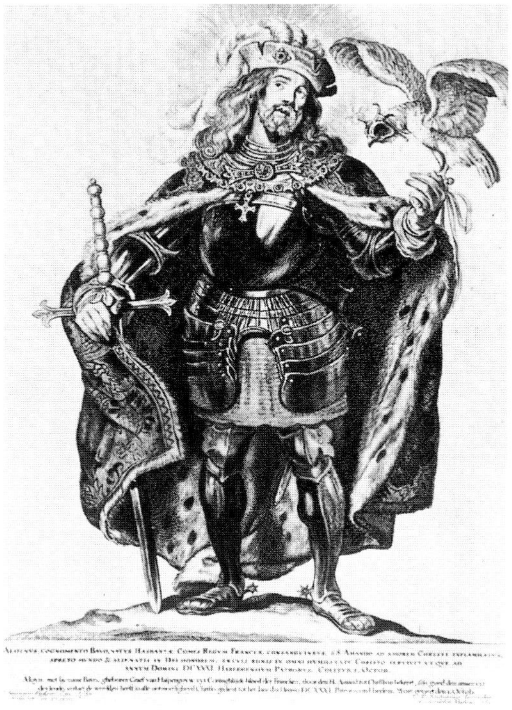

FIG. 24c
Cornelis Visscher (1629–1658),
after Pieter Soutman (1580–1657)
St Bavo
Dated 1650
Engraving
44.3 x 31.3 cm
Rijksprentenkabinet, Rijksmuseum, Amsterdam

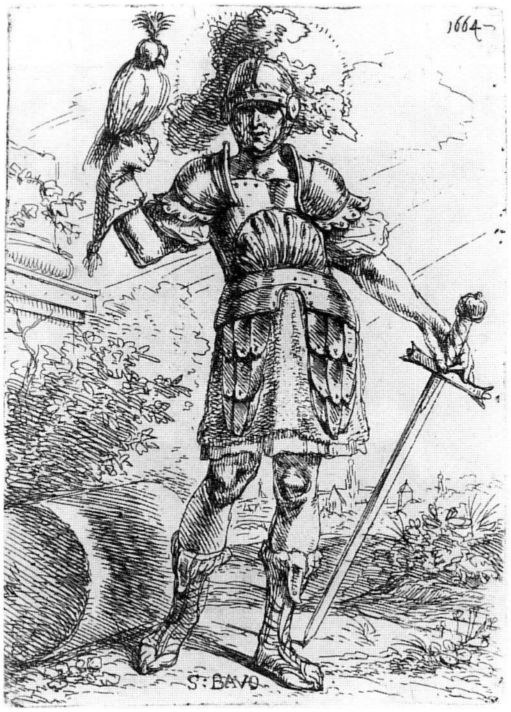

FIG. 24d
Leendert van der Cooghen 1630–1681
St Bavo
Dated 1664
Etching
18.9 x 13.2 cm
Museum Boijmans Van Beuningen,
Rotterdam

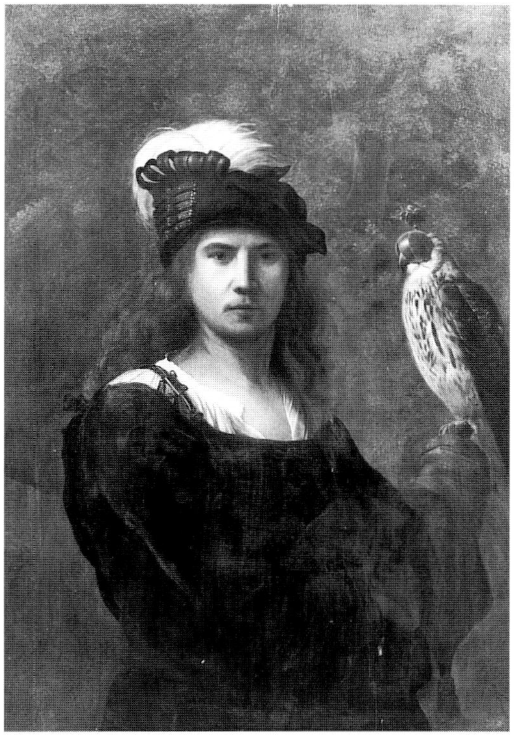

FIG. 24e
Circle of Rembrandt
Young Man in a Fancy Outfit Holding a Falcon
Panel
106.0 x 74.0 cm
Sale, Amsterdam (Christie's), 7 May 1997
Photograph: Christie's, Amsterdam

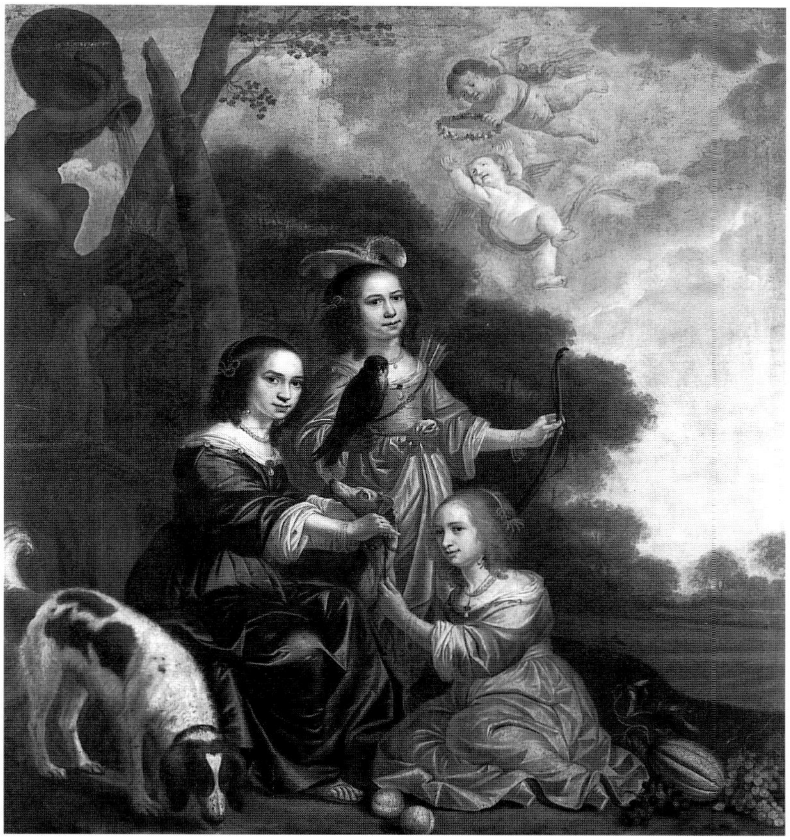

FIG. 24f
Attributed to Anthonie Palamedesz 1601–1673
Three Girls in a Landscape
Canvas
195.0 x 188.0 cm
Rijksmuseum, Amsterdam

city of Haarlem. Bavo is generally portrayed as the aristocratic warrior of the days before his conversion. The falcon seen in figs 24c and 24d symbolizes his standing as a man of high birth. It also recalls a legendary episode from his youth, when he was condemned to death for the theft of a falcon. Bavo is depicted in other guises as well, as, for instance, in the *Meeting Between St Bavo and St Amandus*, which Peter Paul Rubens made for the high altar of the St Baaf cathedral in Ghent.[13] The caption on the print reproduced as fig. 24c also emphasizes Bavo's role as the patron saint of Haarlem.

Fredlund argues that if the *Man with a Falcon* indeed represents St Bavo, Rembrandt meant to portray him at the moment of his conversion. His introverted, melancholy expression would denote his profound insight, and his remorse. Fredlund adds that Rembrandt's depiction is totally inconsistent with the prevailing Roman Catholic conventions for representing a saint.[14] One might comment that this observation applies just as well to Rembrandt's portrayals of the apostles *Bartholomew*, *James* and *Matthew*, from the same period (cat. nos 17, 21, 22). Although their attributes are those of the medieval Catholic tradition, they are otherwise unrecognizable as saints.

Fredlund also published an X-ray photograph of the present painting, from which we see that Rembrandt initially intended to portray the falconer with a large collar instead of a cape.[15] Fredlund also mentions other pictures by Rembrandt that he believes show the same man.[16] The most important of these is *Aristotle Contemplating the Bust of Homer*, 1653, in New York (p. 27, fig. 8).[17] It may be that Rembrandt used the same model (or type?) again and again, as he had done for example in his early Leiden period around 1630 (see commentary to cat. no. 6). Fredlund further refutes the previously held idea that the *Man with a Falcon* was first published by Valentiner in 1921.[18] The painting was known earlier, from nineteenth-century auctions referred to by Hofstede de Groot in 1915.[19]

Mr Wim Huyskens, an expert on falconry and its history, observes that neither the bird in Rembrandt's *Man with a Falcon* nor those in the prints by Visscher and van der Cooghen (figs 24c, 24d) can be identified as any of the species used in falconry. Moreover, from the falconer's point of view, the birds are perched in the wrong position and the hoods and laces are incorrect in all three pictures. The city-dwellers for whom these three artists worked were apparently undemanding when it came to accuracy with respect to these finer points, and therefore presumably knew little about falconry. Equally 'erroneous' from the point of view of falconry is the situation in the picture of a *Young Man in a Fancy Outfit Holding a Falcon*, which recently appeared on the art market and is of interest as a precursor to Rembrandt's painting (fig. 24e). Mr Huyskens points out that some seventeenth-century pictures of falconers are in fact correct, one example being the *Three*

Girls in a Landscape in Amsterdam, a work attributed to Anthonie Palamedesz (fig. 24f).[20]

Benesch observes that we find another falconry motif – otherwise unique in Rembrandt's oeuvre – in a quick sketch from the same late period, after 1660 (fig. 24g).[21] Here we see a gentleman escorting a lady on horseback with a falcon on her wrist. Benesch made no mention of the fact that Rembrandt's only other man with a cross hanging on his chest appears in the etching *Young Man at a Desk* (B.261) of 1641 (fig. 46b).

Even with its theme unidentified, the *Man with a Falcon* has never failed to impress. Much has been written about the expressive force that the painting projects. Suffice it here to quote from one early commentary, by Benesch, from 1924–25:

The picture shows a mature man whose features express wonderful spiritual depth. They have something of that Dostoevsky type we find in Rembrandt [*c*.1660]. They are features that have been formed in the span of a lifetime: they reflect heights and depths curiously combined, and are radiant not because of an aloofness from life, but because they are suffused with its very light. The face is imbued with an almost uncanny expressiveness. He bears the brightest light in the picture and thus brings it into the centre of the composition. All the work's emotional power is concentrated in the large, dark, impenetrably deep eyes, which exude a magical force. They are eyes that look out from under wide-open lids, that close for nothing, for their gaze penetrates all and rests at once tranquil and perplexed.[22]

AB/MB

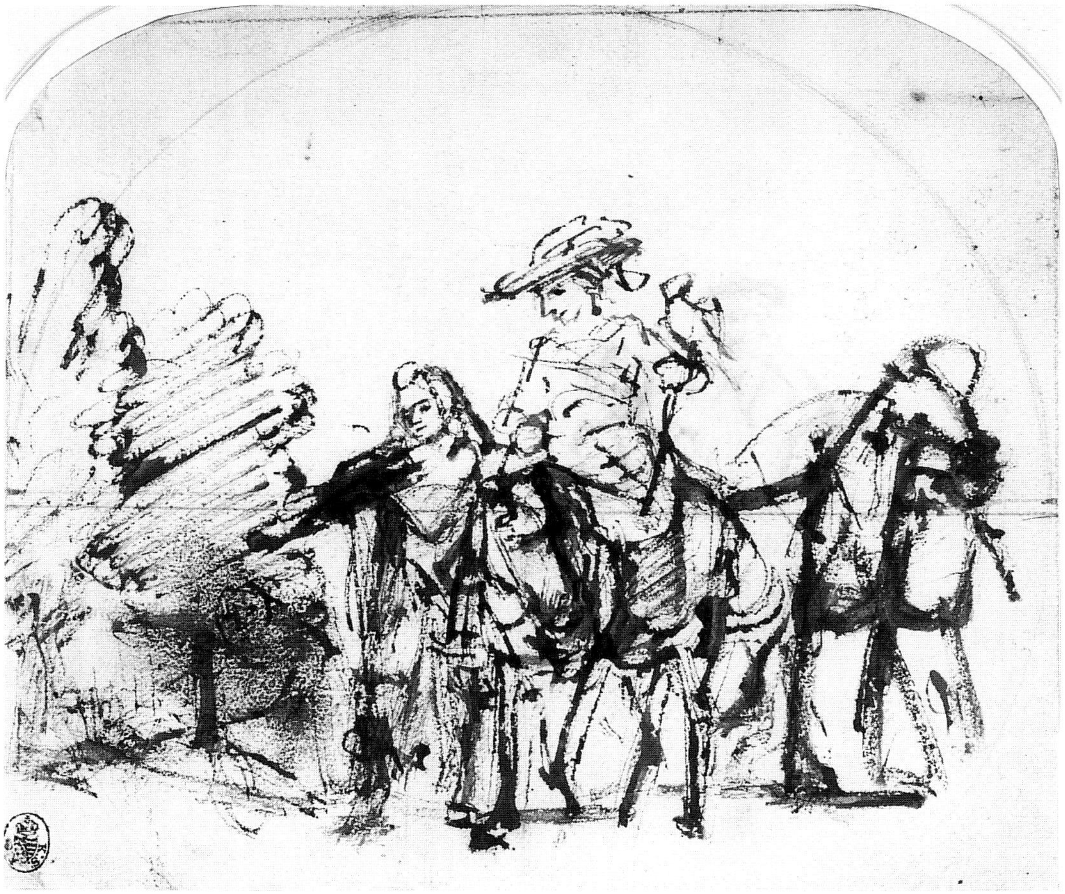

FIG. 24g
Rembrandt
A Lady Riding Out, Hawking
Pen and ink
21.4 x 24.5 cm
Staatliche Kunstsammlungen Dresden, Kupferstichkabinett

1 Van de Waal 1952, vol. I, p. 59ff.
2 For example, Van de Waal 1952, vol. II, fig. 83:2.
3 Bredius / Gerson 1969, no. 482.
4 The details in the background could only be seen after a restoration in about 1921 (Valentiner 1921, p. 97a). B. Fredlund, in Stockholm 1992–93, p. 210, cat. no. 62, suggests that part of the horse may have been cropped as the result of a relining or restoration of the canvas.
5 G. Schwartz, in Gerson 1968, p. 428, advances a far more speculative hypothesis, suggesting that the painting may have been commissioned by the Sicilian Antonio Ruffo (cf. commentary to our cat. no. 15) and that it might represent the Holy Roman Emperor Frederick II, the author of a book on falconry. Slatkes 1992, no. 229, speculates that the subject might be 'Aeneas Hunting', basing his theory on a comparison with the hunter holding a falcon in Ferdinand Bol's painting of that subject at Ranger's House, near London (Blankert 1982, no. 22, pl. 9).
6 Valentiner 1948, p. 128.
7 Gantner 1959; Gantner 1964, pp. 177–83.
8 H. Gerson, in Bredius / Gerson 1969, p. 574, no. 319.
9 Verkaik 1995, p. 212; the differences between Floris V as a historical and a legendary figure are also dealt with here. See also Van de Waal 1952, vol. I, p. 284; Hugenholtz 1977, p. 21.
10 Tümpel 1971, p. 20, note 2.
11 B. Fredlund, in Stockholm 1992–93, pp. 210–13, cat. no. 62. I am grateful to Ms J. G. Middelbeek-Oortgiesen for her translation from the Swedish.
12 *Illustrated Bartsch*, vol. 5 [formerly vol. 4], 1979, p. 153, no. 3 (132).
13 Van Brabant 1967. For the Rubens, see Vlieghe 1972–73, vol. I, no. 72, fig. 123.
14 B. Fredlund, in Stockholm 1992–93, pp. 212–13, cat. no. 62.
15 B. Fredlund, in Stockholm 1992–93, fig. 62a.
16 For this model, see MacLaren / Brown 1991, vol. 1, p. 335, no. 190, pl. 284 (with respect to *A Bearded Man in a Cap* at the National Gallery in London (Bredius / Gerson 1969, no. 283)).
17 Metropolitan Museum of Art, New York (Bredius / Gerson 1969, no. 478).
18 As stated *inter alia* by Gerson (H. Gerson, in Bredius / Gerson 1969, p. 574, no. 319).
19 Hofstede de Groot 1907–28, vol. VI, 1915, no. 287.
20 W. Huyskens, Monnickendam, letters, 2, 10 February and 28 April 1997. For the painting attributed to Palamedesz, see Huyskens 1992, p. 60; see also Van Thiel et al. 1976, p. 435, no. A861.
21 Benesch 1924–25. On the verso of the sheet is a study for a double portrait (Benesch 1973, vol. V, no. 1183, figs 1481, 1482).
22 Benesch 1924–25 (here translated from the German).

25
Bust of a Young Jew

Signed and dated upper right *Rembrandt f. 1663*
Canvas
65.8 x 57.5 cm
Kimbell Art Museum, Fort Worth, Texas

PROVENANCE: [According to Robb (1978)] (?) Despuig family, Palma de Mallorca, 18th century (said to have been presented to Cardinal Despuig by Pope Benedict XIV); Cotoner Collection, Palma de Mallorca, *c.*1880; sold in the 1890s; Rodolphe Kann, Paris, 1900–07; with Joseph Duveen Gallery, London and/or Paris; [according to Hofstede de Groot (1916)] with M. Knoedler & Co., London; Sir William C. van Horne, Montreal, 1909; Collection of the van Horne family; acquired in 1977.

LITERATURE: Valentiner 1908, p. 498; Hofstede de Groot 1908–27, vol. VI, 1916, p. 219, no. 407; Benesch 1956, pp. 350–1; Bredius / Gerson 1969, no. 300; Panofsky 1973, pp. 98–9; Robb 1978 (with earlier literature and reproductions of X-ray photographs); Tümpel 1986, no. 146; C. G. Cavalli-Björkman, in Stockholm 1992–93, p. 214, cat. no. 63 (with earlier literature).

The date on this painting was read as 1661 until a restoration in 1977 revealed it to be 1663.[1] The picture is dominated by the face of a young man – thought to be thirty years old[2] – who observes us with dark, penetrating eyes. The light shining on his forehead and on one side of his face forms a luminous triangle, which is similar to that in the *Bearded Old Man* of *c.*1630 and the *Apostle Bartholomew* of 1657 (cat. nos 4, 17). Here, as in both these earlier pictures, the unlit side of the man's face is in deep shadow from the eyebrow down. In this case, however, the eye, the eyelid and part of the cheek on the unlit side nevertheless catch a few rays of light. The white speck of light in the left eye causes it to stand out in sharper contrast than the other. The gradual transitions and stark contrasts in this painting are modelled with the greatest subtlety, and the full effect is immediately felt thanks to the excellent condition in which the painting has been preserved.[3]

The figure is viewed face-on and is set in the centre of the picture space, yet the effect is by no means rigidly symmetrical. This is because the head – from our point of view – is turned slightly to the right and inclined towards the observer. The middle of the face is also a little to the right of the central axis. The locks of hair falling onto the forehead from beneath the skullcap are in the right half of the painting. The background in this section, around the shadowed side of the face, is more brightly lit than the rest of the composition, with the darkness of the background to the left of the illuminated side of the face making it difficult to distinguish the outlines of the man's shoulder against the wall behind him. Rembrandt has deftly offset the seemingly strict symmetry of the composition in several different ways – despite the fact that extra emphasis has deliberately been placed on the central axis of the painting, for it coincides with the almost unnaturally straight shaft of light that marks the opening of the man's cloak.

The picture has been variously described in the literature as 'A Young Rabbi with a Black Cap',[4] 'A Young Jew'[5] and a 'Portrait of a Young Jew'.[6] It is highly unlikely to have been a commissioned portrait. Anyone who ordered a

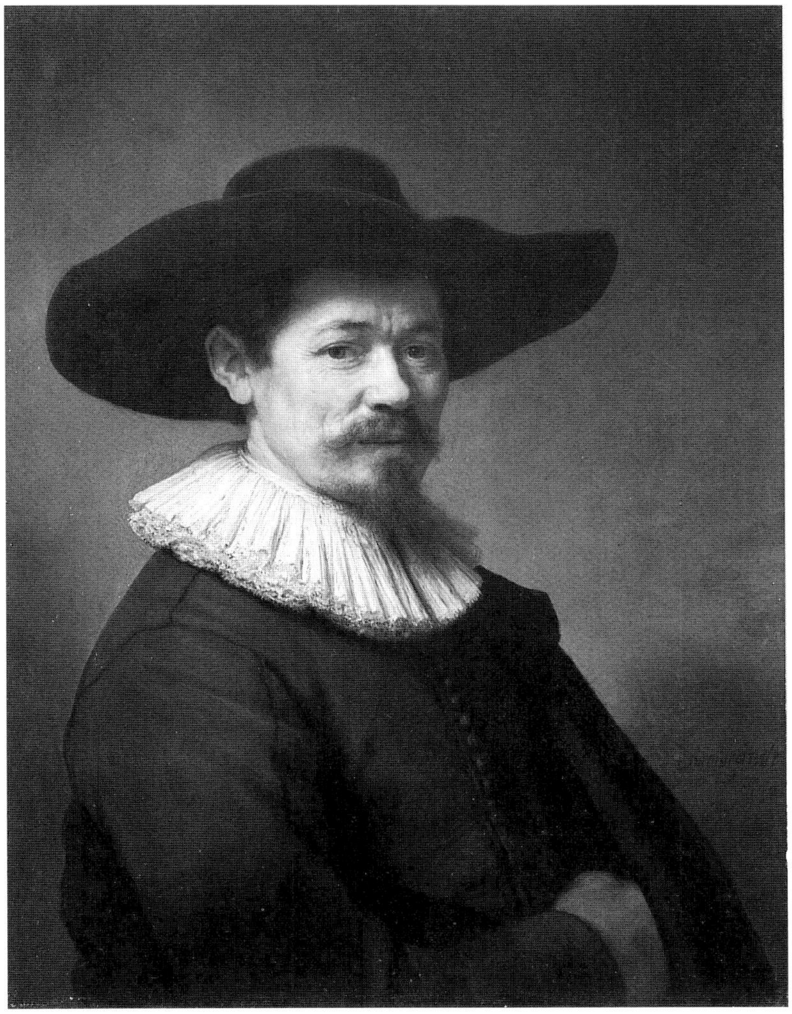

FIG. 25a
Rembrandt
Portrait of Herman Doomer
Signed and dated 1640
Panel
75.2 x 55.2 cm
The Metropolitan Museum of Art, New York

portrait in the seventeenth century would pose in the finest costume appropriate to his or her station in life. One need only look at the costly lace collars and hats worn by the gentlemen in cat. nos 8, 12, 19 and 27. Compared with them, in terms of social status, the frame- and cabinet-maker Herman Doomer was nothing more than a competent craftsman. In Rembrandt's portrait of him[7] he presents a less distinguished-looking figure than do the men referred to above, although several masterpieces of furniture were recently attributed to him (fig. 25a).[8] Doomer's simple doublet, which is fastened by a row of buttons, is not of the finest quality cloth. Yet even he wears a hat and a lace collar. By comparison, the man in the dark skullcap and plain, unadorned clothing in the present painting looks almost impoverished. In Rembrandt's time, no one without the means to cut a more prepossessing figure would have been able – or would perhaps even have wanted – to afford a portrait.

The Levantine features of the man in cat. no. 25 seem to support the assumption that he represents a Jew. From about 1600 on, the Dutch Republic, and Amsterdam in particular, attracted a large Jewish immigrant population. They regarded their adopted homeland as a 'new Jerusalem'. The most conspicuous among them were the Marrano Jews from Portugal, whose (nominal) conversion to Catholicism failed to protect them from continuing persecution in their own country. In 1638 they built the first Portuguese synagogue in Amsterdam.[9] The community included a large number of wealthy and distinguished merchants. A painting of the *Interior of the [later] Portuguese Synagogue in Amsterdam* by Emanuel de Witte (1617–1692) shows a prosperous community enjoying the freedom to practise their faith (fig. 25b).[10] Most members of the congregation are stylishly dressed, according to the taste in the Netherlands around 1680, the period in which de Witte made the painting. Many of those present, such as the two children on the right, also have the typically Jewish tallisim, or prayer shawls, draped over their hats. Rembrandt made four etched illustrations (B.36a–d) for a book by the famous decalingual Portuguese rabbi, Menasseh ben Israel, which appeared in 1655 (see fig. 44b). Doubts were recently expressed about the identity of the sitter in Rembrandt's etched 'portrait of Menasseh' (B.269) – we know what Menasseh looked like on the basis of his portrayal in a print of considerably inferior quality (fig. 25c).[11] It is certain, however, that Rembrandt portrayed the Portuguese-Jewish physician Ephraim Bonus in 1647 (cat. no. 109). The men in both B.269 and

FIG. 25b
Emanuel de Witte 1617–1692
Interior of the Portuguese Synagogue in Amsterdam
Canvas
110.0 x 98.0 cm
Rijksmuseum, Amsterdam

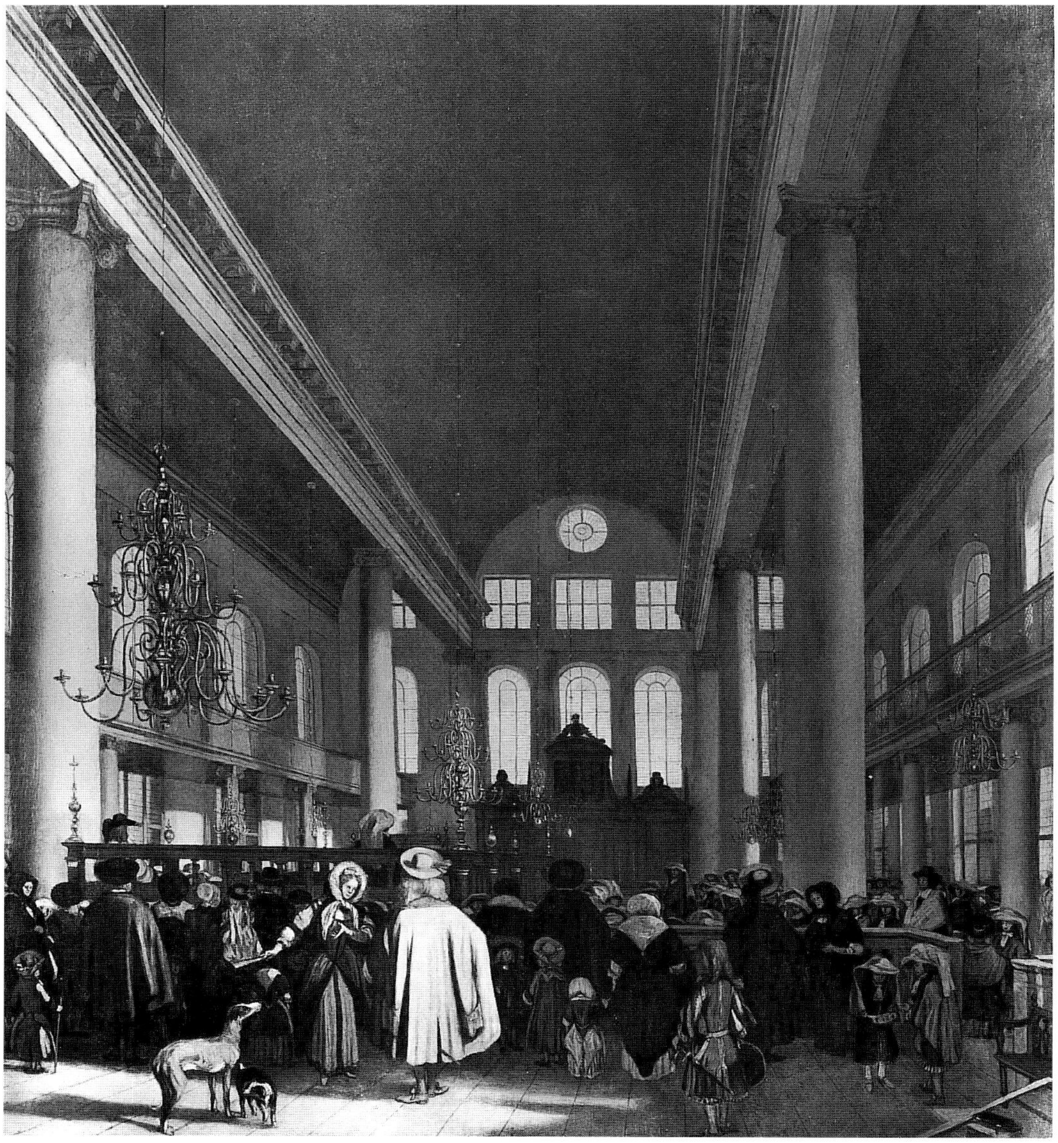

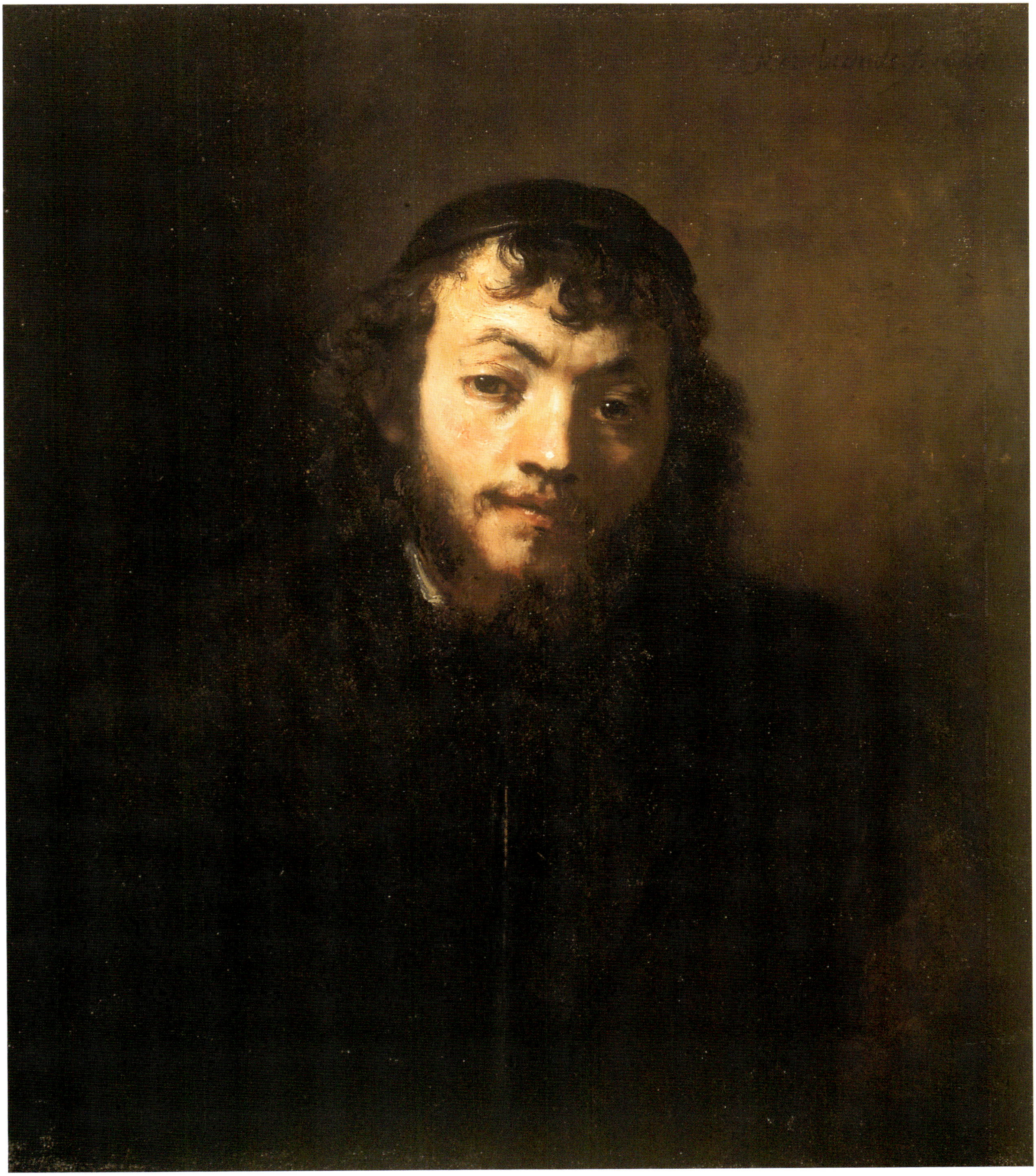

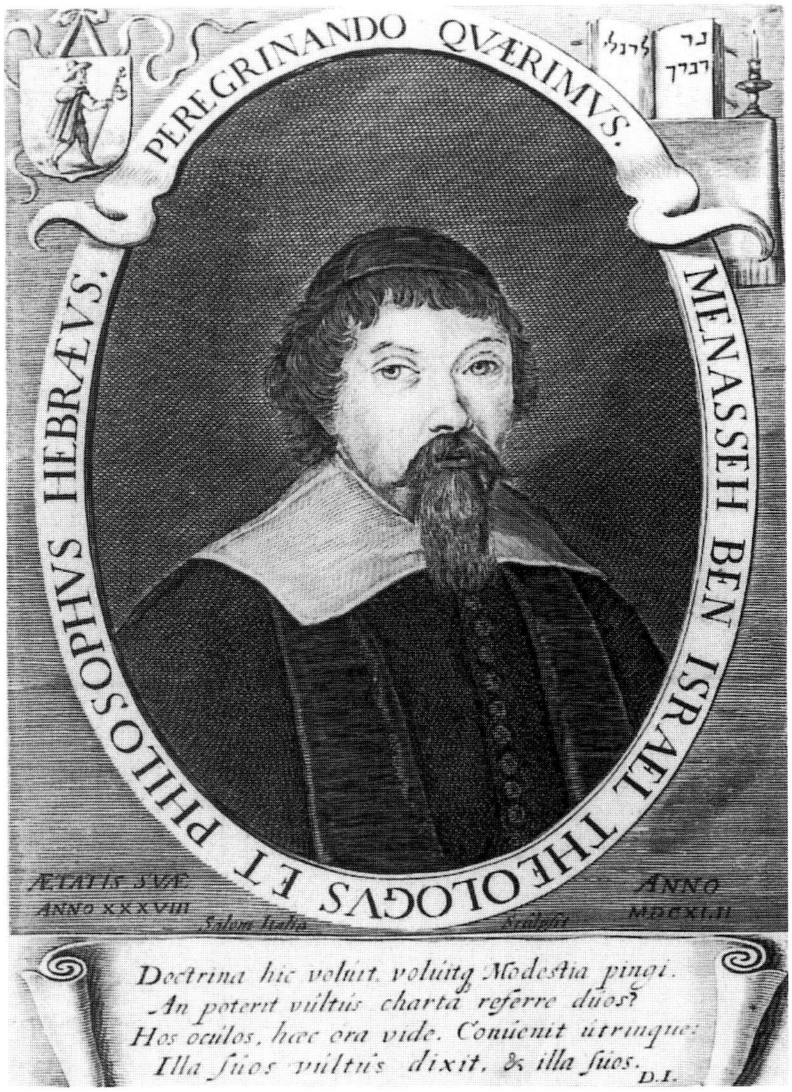

FIG. 25C
Salom Italia
Menasseh ben Israel
Inscribed and dated 1642
Engraving
19.2 x 13.0 cm
Private collection, The Netherlands
From a reproduction

cat. no. 109 are dressed in the contemporary Dutch fashion, and have flat collars. The great philosopher Spinoza came from the same background as Bonus and Menasseh.

Many German Jews also sought refuge in Amsterdam after the outbreak of the Thirty Years War in Germany (1610–48). They were followed by a wave of Polish Jews, who arrived after 1654. The immigrants from Germany and Poland were generally less prosperous than the Portuguese, and many of them earned a livelihood as street vendors. All three groups settled mainly in the vicinity of the St Anthonisbreestraat, outside the St Anthonispoort. This came to be known as the Jodenbreestraat. It is the street in which Rembrandt lived from 1639 to 1659, in the house that is now the Museum het Rembrandthuis (p. 26, fig. 6). Menasseh ben Israel lived nearby, and both the German and the Portuguese synagogues were around the corner (fig. 25b).

Since the early nineteenth century, when Rembrandt's association with the Jewish communities in Amsterdam became more widely known, many of his pictures have been interpreted as portrayals of Jews or rabbis. John Smith's 1836 catalogue of paintings by Rembrandt – the earliest work of its kind – lists twenty-eight pictures in a special section entitled 'Portraits of Jews and Rabbis'.[12] Valentiner's illustrated 1908 catalogue of Rembrandt's paintings describes nineteen pictures of unidentified men as 'Jews' or 'rabbis'.[13] These designations are now in themselves often considered dubious, and some of the works in question are no longer attributed to Rembrandt.[14]

The skullcap worn by the man in the present painting reinforced the idea that he was an orthodox Jew. Benesch, for instance, wrote in 1956: 'He wears the little cap of the orthodox Jew; perhaps he was a young scholar of the theological seminary'.[15] The designation 'rabbi' was the logical corollary. De Winkel, however, recently pointed out that the skullcap came into use as a specifically Jewish attribute only at the beginning of the twentieth century.[16] She explains: 'It is not so much the skullcap that distinguishes the man as a Jew as his Semitic features and the style in which he wears his hair and beard: a full beard of this type was not in fashion in the 17th century'.[17]

This painting can best be regarded as a *tronie*, or non-individualized head, of a Jew. There was evidently a demand for this type of work, as an inventory dating from 1681 lists 'A portrayal of a Polack jew', valued at four guilders. The piece in question therefore had a commercial value, even though the painter's name was not mentioned.[18] Cat. no. 25 must also have been intended to represent an impecunious 'Polack', rather than a distinguished member of the Portuguese community.

The painting recalls some of the heads of Christ that Rembrandt presumably painted slightly earlier, and probably likewise based on one or more young Jewish models (cf. cat. no. 31). It is possible that he made the present painting with the idea of using it for a Christ figure later. Benesch suggested in 1956 that this work served as Rembrandt's frame of reference for two late half-length paintings of Christ, one at the Metropolitan Museum of Art in New York and one at the Alte Pinakothek in Munich.[19] However, the Christ in the Metropolitan version[20] is blond, and the work itself is now attributed to a follower of Rembrandt.[21] As for the Munich painting,[22] which has been badly damaged over the years, any similarity, in my opinion, is extremely superficial. Most importantly, however, both half-length pictures of Christ are dated 1661. They were therefore made two years before the *Bust of a Young Jew*, which, as we have seen, Rembrandt is now known to have painted in 1663.

In 1920, the young Erwin Panofsky (1892–1968), later renowned as a founding father of iconology, delivered a lecture in which he argued that the figures Rembrandt created in his late works transcend both the individual and the universal, and that his representation of the human figure became increasingly metaphysical. Rembrandt chose mainly Jewish figures for these works, some of which are depictions of suffering or sorrow. In the *Bust of a Young Jew*, however, Panofsky asserts:

> This too is transcended: there is virtually nothing we can say about this human being, other than that he is a *human being*. These near expressionless features no longer betray anything of that which he as a real person may have experienced, or may still be experiencing, nor anything that we might expect from him were we able to meet him during his lifetime: the eyes seem neither joyful nor sad, nor describable by any psychological term at all; even words like 'pensive' or 'lost in thought' would not suffice: the expression in these eyes has no more empirical *meaning* than their gaze has an empirical *object*. Here we see expressed the timeless and unfathomable depth of a soul which, beyond the borders of the individual consciousness has been subsumed into a consciousness of all, now appearing only as a form of that ancient substance which metaphysics, depending on its standpoint, denotes as being or *divinity*. The late Rembrandt *gives the human being such depth* as to make it give up its individuality *in God*. Conversely, from this time he discovers *God in the human being itself*.[23]

AB

1 Robb 1978, pp. 44, 46, 47; the date 1663 was also mentioned in several sources in the nineteenth century.

2 Hofstede de Groot 1908–27, vol. VI, 1916, p. 219, no. 407; Robb 1978, p. 44.

3 Regarding the painting's condition, cf. Robb 1978, pp. 44, 46.

4 Hofstede de Groot 1908–27, vol. VI, 1916, p. 219, no. 407; Tümpel 1986 (Dutch edn), p. 322, caption to fig.

5 Bredius 1937, no. 300; Tümpel 1986, no. 146: 'A Young Jew with a Black Cap'.

6 Valentiner 1908, p. 458; Bredius / Gerson 1969, no. 300. The Kimbell Art Museum also uses this title.

7 Bredius / Gerson 1969, no. 217; *Corpus*, vol. III, 1989, pp. 382–9, no. A140; W. Liedtke, in New York 1995–96, vol. 2, pp. 58–61, cat. no. 8.

8 Baarsen 1996 made these attributions.

9 For the Jews in Amsterdam in the seventeenth century, see Brugmans 1930, vol. III, p. 175ff; Panofsky 1973; Van Voolen 1991–94.

10 Manke 1963, no. 206.

11 Dudok van Heel 1993, fig. 4.

12 Smith 1829–42, vol. VII, 1836, pp. 272–3. Among them, incidentally, are the Dutch Protestant clergyman Swalmius, and a poet with what was in the seventeenth century a typically Dutch name, Jeremias de Decker (see commentary to our cat. no. 18 and p. 77, fig. 11). Two paintings appear in Smith's book as 'The Jewish Bride' (p. 281, nos 493, 494); cf. our cat. no. 102.

13 Valentiner 1908, pp. 602–6. In a lecture delivered in 1920, Panofsky described many of the figures in Rembrandt's etchings, paintings and drawings as 'Jews' (published posthumously in Panofsky 1973).

14 Valentiner 1908, p. 188, described a painting at Hampton Court as 'A rabbi' by Rembrandt; H. Gerson, in Bredius / Gerson 1969, p. 565, no. 207, rejected the attribution to Rembrandt and called the picture 'A man in fanciful costume'. Christopher White agreed that it could not be a Rembrandt, but restored the title 'A Rabbi with a Cap' (White 1982 p. 111, cat. no. 167). A painting at the National Gallery in London, which was referred to as 'An old man's head' in 1798, and as 'A rabbi' from 1844 on, is now listed as *A Bearded Man in a Cap* (Bredius / Gerson 1969, no. 283; MacLaren / Brown 1991, vol. 1, p. 335, no. 190).

15 Benesch 1956, p. 351.

16 De Winkel 1995, p. 166, note 51 (with a reference to A. Rubens, *A History of Jewish Costume*, 2nd edn, London, 1973, esp. p. 11).

17 Letter, 19 December 1996.

18 'Een contrefijtsel van een Polacqse smous. 4' (notary G. Steeman, inventory dated 29 September 1681, NAA 2638). Cited in de Winkel letter of December 1996.

19 Benesch 1956, p. 351. Tümpel 1986, no. 146, sees no resemblance between these pictures.

20 Bredius / Gerson 1969, no. 629.

21 W. Liedtke, in New York 1995–96, vol. 2, p. 128, cat. no. 37 (as 'Follower of Rembrandt').

22 Bredius / Gerson 1969, no. 630.

23 Published posthumously in Panofsky 1973, p. 98 (here translated from the German).

26
Young Man in a Black Beret

Signed and dated lower left *Rembrandt f. 1666.*
Canvas
81.8 x 64.7 cm; since restoration 71.6 x 62.8 cm
The Nelson-Atkins Museum of Art, Kansas City, Missouri (Purchase: Nelson Trust) 31-75

PROVENANCE: Lord Leconfield, Petworth, 1883–1928; with Duveen Brothers, 1928–31; purchased from Duveen Brothers in 1931.

LITERATURE: Hofstede de Groot 1908–27, vol. VI, 1916, pp. 364–5, no. 780; Bauch 1966, no. 443; Bredius / Gerson 1969, no. 322; Schwartz 1984, p. 339; Tümpel 1986, no. 224.

Most of the half-length single figures from Rembrandt's late period are elderly people or at least people who are no longer young. These sitters inspired Rembrandt to work with rough-textured surfaces and angular lines and shapes, such as those we see in the *Apostle Bartholomew* and the *Apostle James* (cat. nos 17, 21). We need look only at the hands of the *Evangelist Matthew* or of the *White-Haired Man* (cat. nos 22, 27) to find forms of this kind. We see a similar approach in the Washington *Portrait of a Young Man*, which is rendered in abrupt, stylized shapes (cat. no. 19).

Rembrandt made the present beautiful picture of a far younger man in 1666, modifying his treatment of lines and paint in order to suit his subject. The engaging face, with its regular features, is modelled with fluid brushstrokes, while its graceful oval contour is punctuated by locks of hair rendered in calligraphic lines. The shape of the man's large, almond eyes is echoed in the curve of his beret. The figure is slightly off-centre in the picture space. Hofstede de Groot in 1916 suggested that the young man is standing.[1] He seems to be regarding us with good-natured interest. The beret may have been meant to identify him as a painter or aspiring artist (see also cat. nos 13, 18), or perhaps as a student or recent graduate.[2] Hofstede de Groot estimates him to be about sixteen years old.[3] It has also been suggested that he may have been Rembrandt's son Titus,[4] but Titus would have been twenty-five in 1666, the year in which the painting was made (for pictures thought to be portraits of Titus, see p. 46). Bauch's hypothesis that the sitter here was Rembrandt's pupil Samuel van Hoogstraten is even less plausible: the man in the picture bears no resemblance at all to Hoogstraten (see self-portrait reproduced with Hoogstraten biography, p. 291), who was in any event thirty-nine years of age in 1666.

The work was probably a commissioned portrait. Although Gerson suspected that the signature had been retouched, he described the painting as one of the 'genuine late official portraits of high quality'.[5] The technique recalls that of the *White-Haired Man*, which Rembrandt made a year later. The *White-Haired Man*, however, is entirely different, as it lacks the graceful elegance that Rembrandt was trying to achieve here. The profound earnestness of Rembrandt's late work has often been discussed. Yet this picture shows that he could strike a far lighter note, with just the same brilliance, in the last years of his life.

In May and June 1997, in advance of the present exhibition, the picture was cleaned and restored by Scott A. Heffley, Conservator of Paintings at the Nelson-Atkins Museum. The illustration on p. 179 shows the piece's previous condition, while in the exhibition it can be seen as it appears after restoration. The Museum has also allowed us to reproduce the picture in stripped condition, after cleaning and before restoration, with all retouchings removed (fig. 26a). Reproductions of paintings in stripped condition are generally found only in specialist conservation and museum periodicals. It might appear at first sight as though the paint layer has suffered considerably. However, the most important – that is, the most nuanced and modelled – parts of the picture (the beret, the face, the hair, the collar) are amazingly well preserved. Only in the young man's cloak does some modelling seem to have been lost. During the restoration, an old number '50', in the bottom right-hand corner, became visible to the naked eye. A strip at the top of the picture, a later addition,[6] has now been removed, while the original tacking edge at the bottom has been folded back out into the picture plane, increasing the painting's height by 1.8 cm. This edge is part of Rembrandt's painting, but had at some stage been folded over the stretcher. The marks of the nails used to attach the picture to its stretcher can be seen here. As usual after stripping, these bare and most damaged parts are made inconspicuous by retouching.

AB

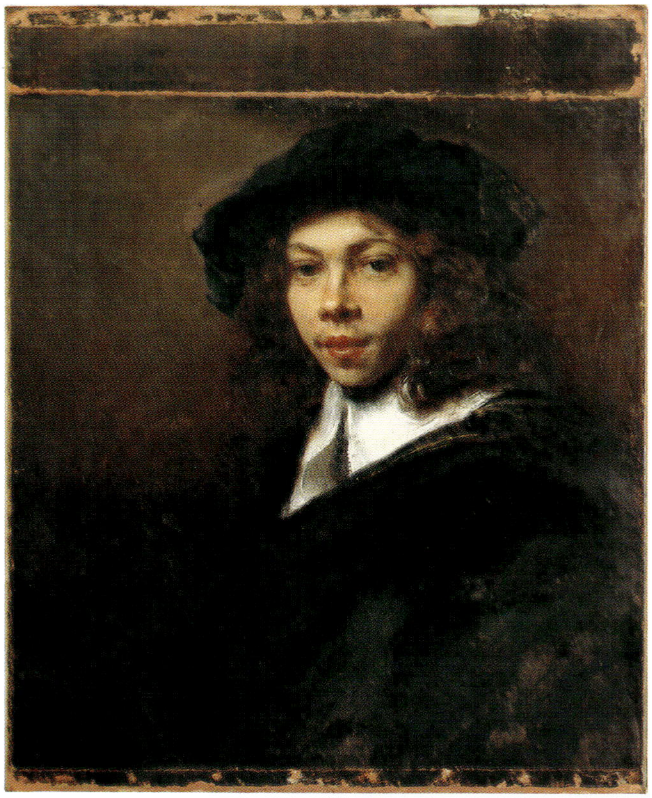

FIG. 26a
Cat. no. 26 in stripped condition, after cleaning, June 1997.

1 Hofstede de Groot 1908–27, vol. VI, 1916, p. 365, no. 780.
2 The possibility of its being a student's beret was suggested by Marieke de Winkel, who will write on berets in *Corpus*, vol. IV (forthcoming).
3 Hofstede de Groot 1908–27, vol. VI, 1916, p. 365, no. 780.
4 Reported by the Nelson-Atkins Museum.
5 H. Gerson, in Bredius / Gerson 1969, p. 575, no. 322.
6 It measured 8.5 cm on the left and 9.3 cm on the right.

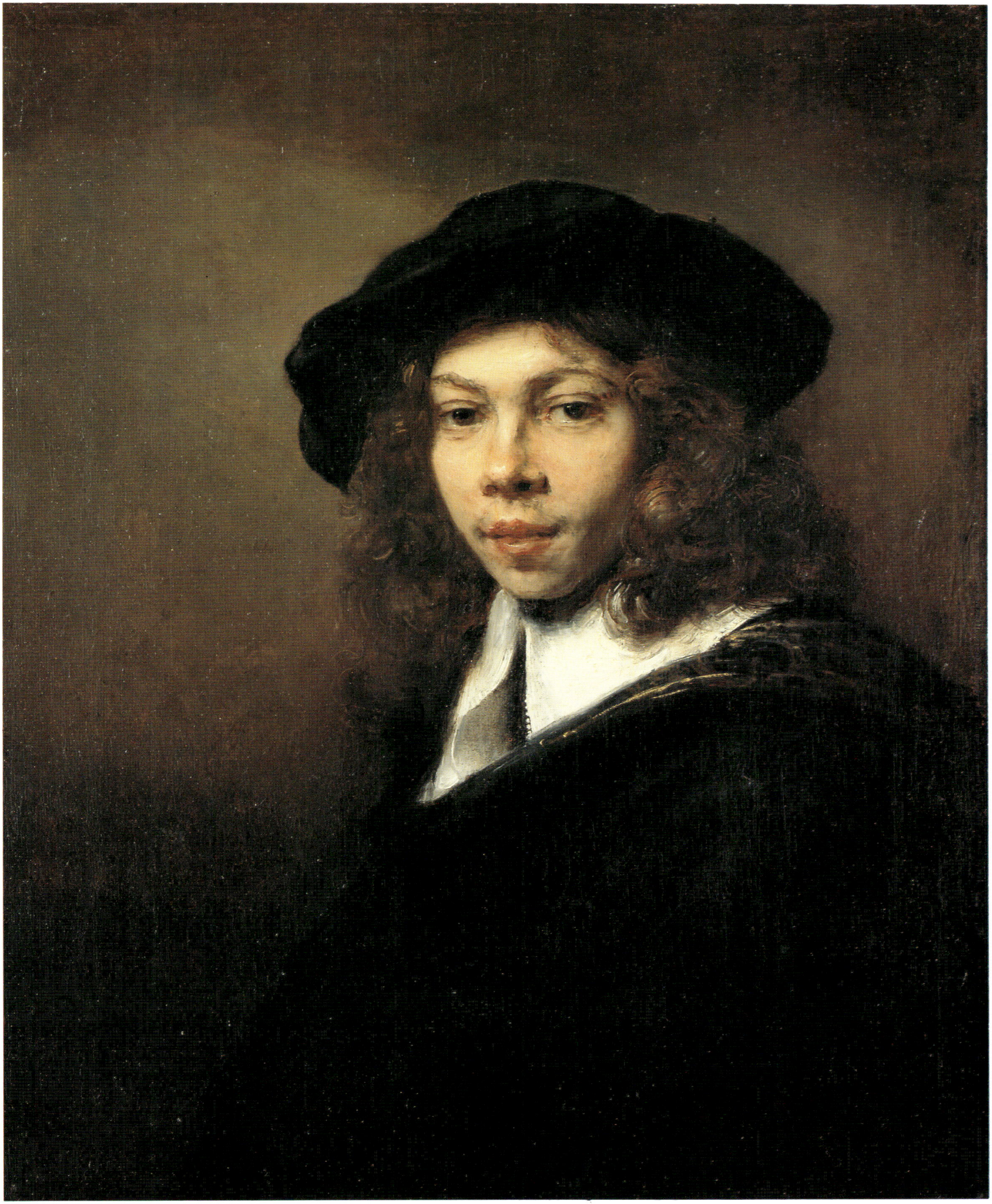

27
Portrait of a White-Haired Man

Signed and dated upper centre *Rembrandt f. 1667*
Canvas
108.9 x 92.7 cm
National Gallery of Victoria, Melbourne;
Felton Bequest 1951

PROVENANCE: [After Hoff (1995)] Sale, Vincent Donjeux, Paris, 29 April 1793, lot 148; Heneage Finch, 5th Earl of Aylesford, before 1836; Sir Alfred Beit, by 1899, and later; bequeathed by Sir Alfred Beit to his nephew, Sir Alfred Beit; with dealer C. Marshall Spink, London, 1951; Felton Bequest 1951.

LITERATURE: Hofstede de Groot 1908–27, vol. VI, 1916, p. 349, no. 743; Bredius / Gerson 1969, no. 323; Schwartz 1984, p. 344; Tümpel 1986, no. 226; J. Gregory, in Gregory & Zdanowicz 1988, pp. 58–76, 115; C. Brown, in Berlin / Amsterdam / London 1991–92a, pp. 288–9, cat. no. 50; Hoff 1995, pp. 232–4 (with earlier literature).

This and the comparable painting from the Cowdray Collection (cat. no. 28) are Rembrandt's last dated portraits.[1] Both were made in 1667. In the present picture, brown eyes survey us from a deftly modelled pink face. Rembrandt took grateful advantage of the sitter's luxuriant wavy hair, using it to form a baroque frame around the face. The hair is white with a few streaks of grey. The subject was formerly described as young and blond, as he indeed appears to be in old reproductions (fig. 27a). But a restoration carried out before 1951 revealed a far older, white-haired man.[2]

Rembrandt has painted the picture in his late, broad technique, but shows all the details distinctly. He has used the bounce of the man's curls to heighten the impression of vitality. A few stray wisps of hair stand out against the dark background above the crown of the head and to the left of the face, and a single lock curls onto the right cheek. After surveying the lively face and the hair, the viewer's eye comes to rest on the plain, snowy white collar, from which two tassels hang down. Beneath the collar, the man's clothing gathers into a large, even, dark surface. The brownish-black of the garments is so uniform that it is impossible to see from any reproduction made so far that the man is wearing a dark cloak over a coat. Nor can we see the hat tucked under his left arm.[3] We have already encountered a portrayal of a man holding a hat before him in Rembrandt's *Portrait of a Man Holding His Hat*, *c.*1639, from the Armand Hammer Collection (cat. no. 12). There the motif is much clearer, and indeed serves to suggest action. But it is barely discernible in the *White-Haired Man*, where the black of the hat is almost indistinguishable from that of the man's garments (fig. 27b).[4] A few evocative strokes behind and to the right of the figure trace the shape of a red curtain.

The man's right hand (the left hand from the observer's point of view) is on the armrest of a chair. It is further back than the left hand, which loosely cradles the hat and which, for reasons of perspective, is far larger. Rembrandt had used a similar effect in his *Portrait of a Young Woman with a Fan* of 1633 (fig. 27c).[5] There too the woman's left hand is larger than the right. Her left hand, which is extended before her and rests on the corner of the table, occupies the same position in the right foreground as does the left hand in the *White-Haired Man*. Rembrandt employed the same motif again in 1658, in his *Self-Portrait* in the Frick Collection in New York.[6] Here he himself is shown, holding a bamboo cane in his large left hand. He included the motif once again, though less conspicuously, in the *Portrait of Margaretha de Geer* of *c.*1661. In this painting, the woman's left hand grips the end of the armrest of her chair (fig. 23a).

The figures in all four of these pieces are seated squarely in front of us. Such a face-on scheme could easily have resulted in a strictly symmetrical and, from a spatial point of view, fairly flat, image. But Rembrandt was an artist of the Baroque, who tended to avoid symmetry, which he considered too stiff. We need only look at the baroque touch he added to his sketch after Raphael's consummately balanced *Portrait of Baldassare Castiglione*, by setting the man's cap at a jaunty angle (figs 13c, 13d). In the four frontal portraits under consideration here, bringing one of the model's hands into the foreground was clearly designed to break down the symmetry.

The difference in size between the left and right hands is most conspicuous in the *White-Haired Man*. In this picture the hands are also

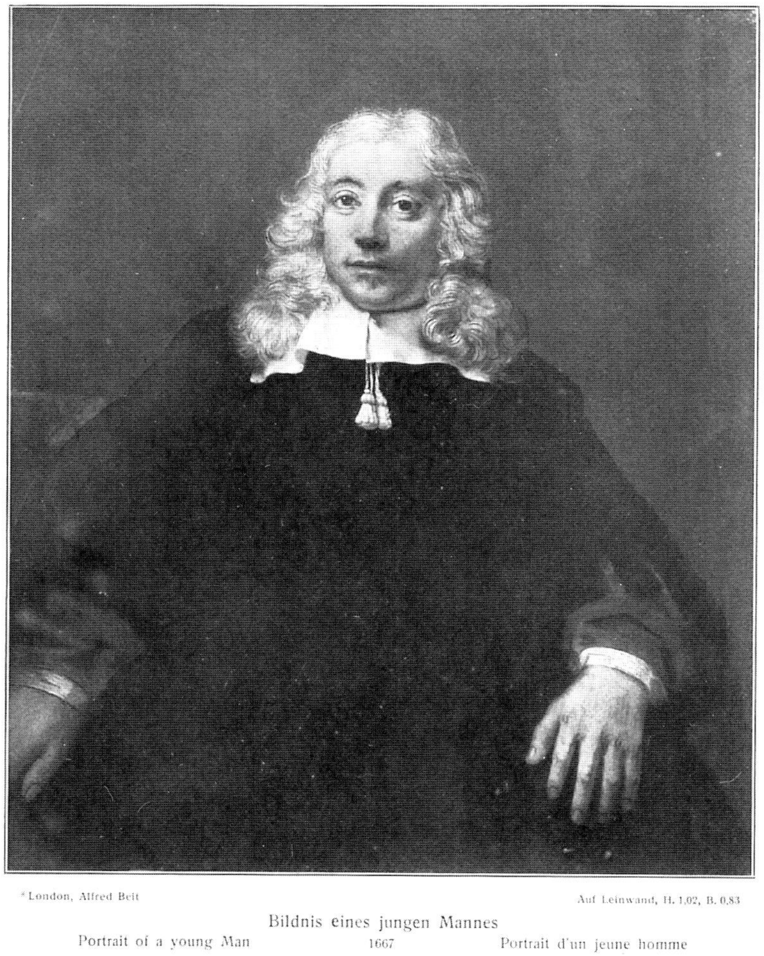

FIG. 27a
Cat. no. 27 (earlier condition)
From Valentiner 1908

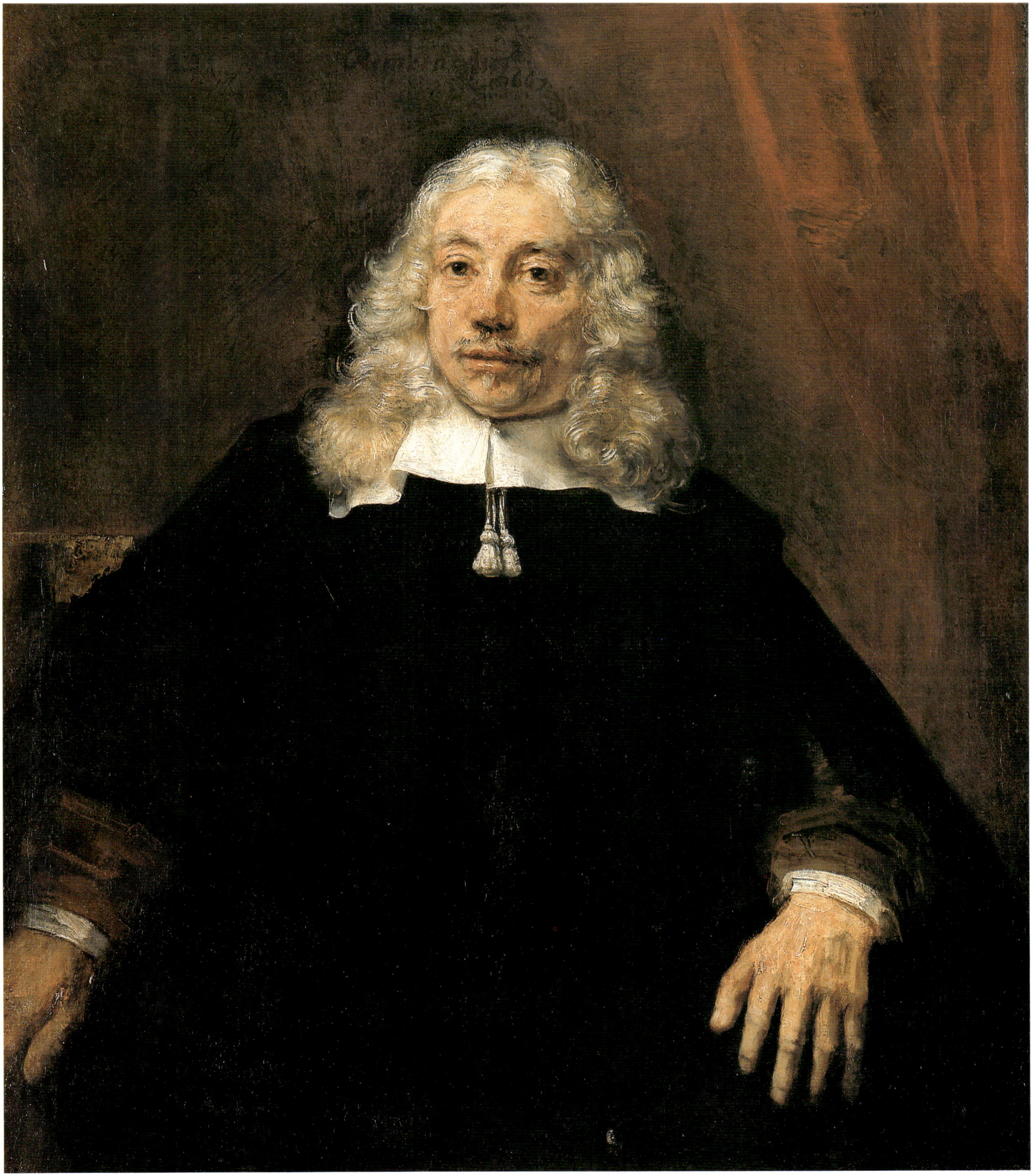

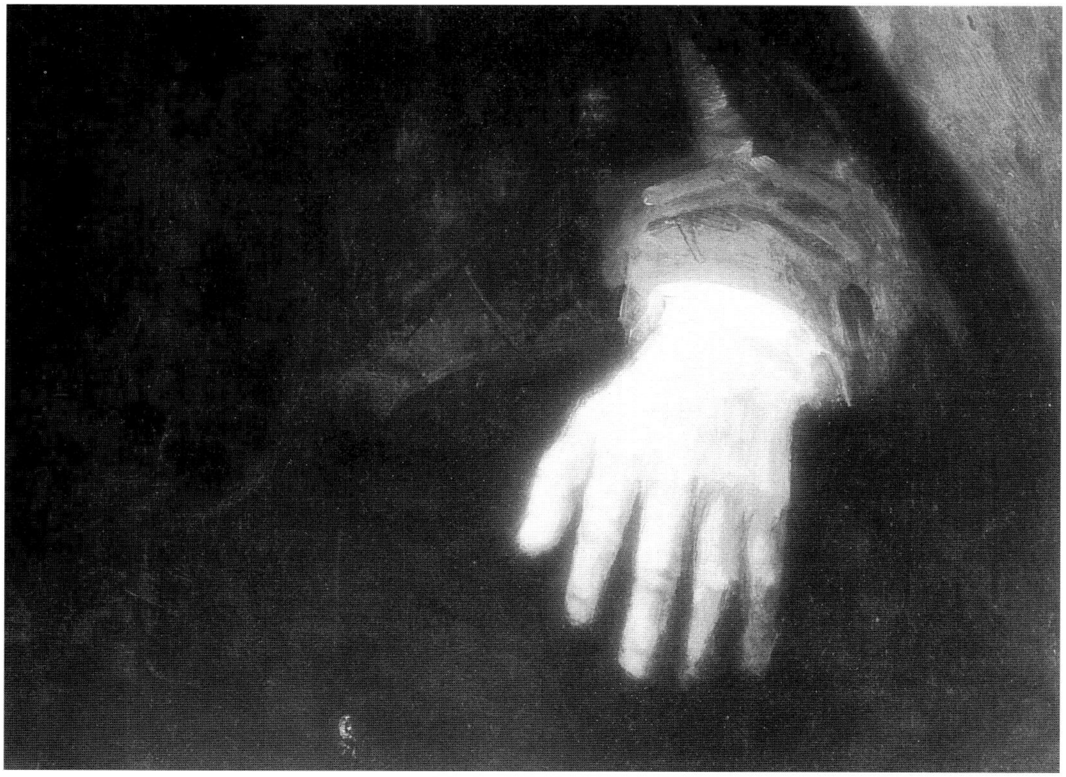

FIG. 27b
Infrared photograph of the area around the left hand in cat. no. 27. Photograph: National Gallery of Victoria, 1997.

painted in very different techniques. The hand nearer the viewer (the left hand) is modelled and almost palpable. It betrays the man's age as eloquently as does his face. The smaller, right hand is no more than a sketchy patch by comparison. In spite of the flat, unbroken surface of black presented by the man's clothing, this differential treatment of the hands creates a strong sense of space and volume. The symmetry of the frontal arrangement is broken, too, by the man's posture: he is leaning with most of his weight on his left arm. The left shoulder is lower than the right. Part of the back of the chair is visible beside the upper arm on the right, but nothing can be seen of the chair on the other side, as our view is obscured by the figure. The distribution of the sitter's weight is thus skilfully suggested, without the use of modelling.[7]

This picture shows that even in the last few years of his life Rembrandt sought and found even bolder applications for effects he had used far earlier in his career.

AB

1 Judging by the tacking edges that can be seen in an X-ray photograph of this work, the piece is intact and has not been cropped (photograph in the archives of the National Gallery of Victoria, Melbourne). Conclusion reached in consultation with M. Franken of the Rembrandt Research Project.

2 The piece was cleaned again in 1988 (Hoff 1995, p. 232). For the condition of the painting prior to 1988, see the reproductions in Gregory & Zdanowicz 1988, figs 31, 34, 40.

3 The hat is mentioned by C. Brown, in Berlin / Amsterdam / London 1991–92a, p. 288, cat. no. 50; Hoff 1995, p. 232.

4 Hofstede de Groot 1908–27, vol. VI, 1916, p. 349, no. 743, mentions the coat and cloak. He describes the figure as seated with both arms resting on the sides of the chair.

5 Bredius / Gerson 1969, no. 341; *Corpus*, vol. II, 1986, no. A79.

6 Bredius / Gerson 1969, no. 50.

7 I am grateful to Laurie Benson, who examined the picture in Melbourne for me.

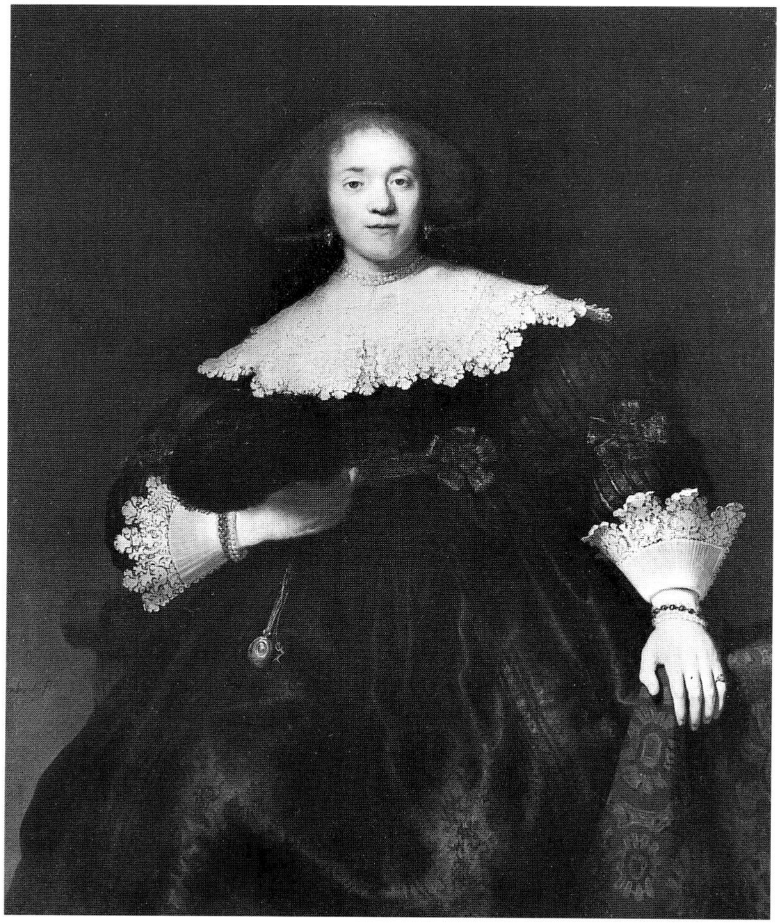

FIG. 27c
Rembrandt
Portrait of a Young Woman with a Fan
Signed and dated 1633
Canvas
125.7 x 101.0 cm
The Metropolitan Museum of Art, New York

28

Portrait of an Elderly Man

Signed and dated centre left *Rembrandt / f. 1667*
Canvas
81.0 x 67.0 cm
The Trustees of the Cowdray Estate, England

PROVENANCE: [After White (1983)] (?) Sale, Sir John Rawdon, 1744, lot 51, to dealer Bragge [see commentary below]; Sampson Gideon (1699–1762), Belvedere House, from 1761 [or earlier; see commentary below]; [after Hoff (1995), p. 198] bequeathed by Sampson Gideon, with Belvedere House, to his son, Sir Sampson Gideon (1745–1824), created Lord Eardley in 1789; same bequeathed by Sir Sampson Gideon to his son-in-law Lord Saye and Sele (1769–1844); same passed to Lord Eardley's second son-in-law, Sir Culling Eardley; same bequeathed by Sir Culling Eardley to his eldest daughter, Mrs Culling Hanbury [1876 RA exh. cat.]; [according to London 1938 (exh. cat.)] by descent to Col. F. E. Fremantle; [according to Dutuit (1885)] sold before 1885; with Thos. Agnew & Sons, London; purchased from Agnew's by Lord Cowdray in 1919.

LITERATURE: Dodsley 1761, vol. I, p. 272; Martyn 1766, p. 12; *Ambulator* 1774, p. 12; *Ambulator* 1792, p. 38; Brayley 1808, p. 546; London 1821, cat. no. 112; London 1845, cat. no. 78; Waagen 1854, suppl. 1857, p. 281; London 1876, cat. no. 255; Dutuit 1885, p. 58, no. 352; Von Wurzbach 1886, no. 173; Hofstede de Groot 1908–27, vol. VI, 1916, pp. 381–2, no. 829; Bredius 1921, p. 151; Valentiner 1921, p. 98; Hofstede de Groot 1922, p. 13; London 1938, pp. 66–7, cat. no. 128; Edinburgh 1950, cat. no. 35; London 1952–53, p. 40, cat. no. 175; Manchester 1957, cat. no. 105; Gerson 1968, pp. 130, 448, no. 409; Bredius / Gerson 1969, no. 323A; C. Brown, in London 1976, cat. no. 97; Schwartz 1984, p. 339; Tümpel 1986, no. 147*; Slatkes 1992, no. 179.

This portrait of 1667 is in many respects a variant of the *Portrait of a White-Haired Man* from the same year (cat. no. 27). The sitter is again portrayed from the front, seated in a chair. Here, too, his head, collar, hands and cuffs form brightly lit accents against all the black of his clothing, which is again very summarily modelled. Yet from other points of view the picture has been tackled quite differently.

The sitter in the present work is a corpulent figure. Rembrandt has conveyed even more powerfully a sense of the man's physical presence by cramping him into the area framed by the edges of the canvas. The figure's right hand is cut off at the edge of the picture. It is not surprising that Slatkes in 1992 assumed that all four sides of the painting might have been cropped.[1] However, an X-ray photograph shows the original tacking edges on all four sides of the canvas, confirming that the piece is intact.[2]

Rembrandt knew from the work of the Utrecht Caravaggisti that cramping a figure into the picture space has the effect of exaggerating the figure's physical presence. In some cases, the figures of the Utrecht masters are so narrowly confined that later owners failed to understand what the artists had sought to achieve – and added strips of canvas to the sides of their pictures on which to paint extra space for the figures.[3] To understand why, we need only look at the way the Caravaggist Hendrick ter Brugghen crammed six figures into his *Calling of Matthew* of 1621, packing them right up to the edges of the picture (fig. 28a). The principal figure, Christ, standing on the left in the shadows and pointing to Matthew, is severed by the edge of the picture. All we see of his head is part of the profile of his face.

Rembrandt likewise had no compunction about amputating half of the *Elderly Man*'s right hand. He brought the portly figure all the way to the front of the picture, with his arms close to his body and gripping the armrests of the chair (because the sitter's head is as close to the viewer as are the hands, the latter are relatively small). It is almost as though the man were seeking something to cling to, as though someone were trying to push him out of a window too small for his girth. All of this contributes to the intense energy that emanates from the picture.

Every detail in this painting is rendered with absolute accuracy but also with superior nonchalance. The man is wearing an elegant costume, but with casual ease. He wears his hat askew, and his white collar, unlike that of the man in cat. no. 27, is open. It is creased as a result, and this creates complex lines and an intricate play of light and shadow. All is suggested with perfect precision yet with a minimum of extra detail. Two white tassels hang down from the collar, trickling like melted candlewax. This type of open collar with tassels hanging down quite separately from one another was fashionable for young gentlemen around 1650, when the man in the picture would have been seventeen years younger. A similar, casually open collar is worn by Jan Six, for example, in the etched portrait Rembrandt made of him in 1647 (B.285) (fig. 28b).[4] Six was twenty-nine years old at the time.

Even more askew than the hat in the present work is that worn by the model in the *Portrait of a Man* painted by Frans Hals shortly before his death in 1666 (fig. 28c).[5] Both the Hals and Rembrandt's *Portrait of an Elderly Man* are painted in an

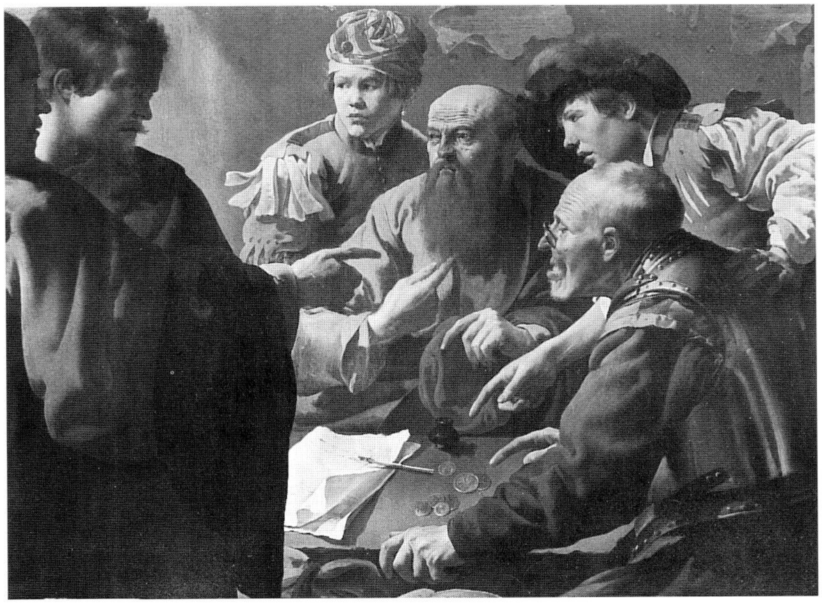

FIG. 28a
Hendrick ter Brugghen 1588–1629
The Calling of Matthew
Signed and dated 1621
Canvas
102.0 x 137.0 cm
Centraal Museum, Utrecht

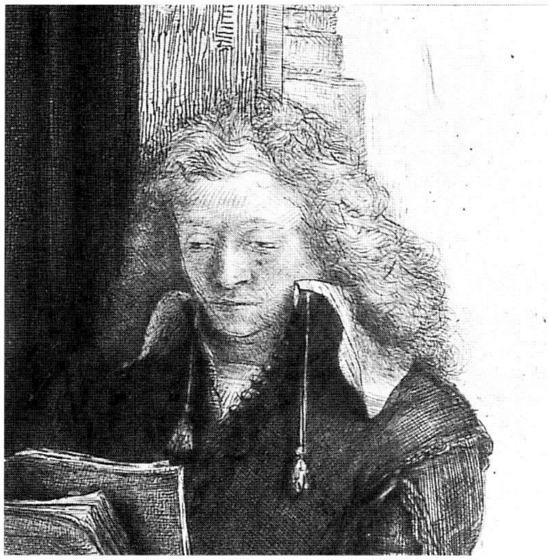

FIG. 28b
Rembrandt
Portrait of Jan Six (detail)
Etching
Rijksprentenkabinet, Rijksmuseum, Amsterdam

equally bold and broad manner. In this respect the two great masters were seeking to achieve similar effects in the same period. It is not surprising that the present work was long attributed to Hals (see below). Not until the later part of the nineteenth century did painters again experiment with effects of this kind. Both cat. no. 28 and Hals's *Portrait of a Man* therefore make an extraordinarily modern impression.

With this in mind it is easier to understand that Bredius wrote the following about the *Portrait of an Elderly Man* in 1921:

> I have examined the picture closely and consider it quite definitely a very skilful (Belgian?) forgery from the middle of the last century, like so many others I have seen. It was shown to me as 'van' Tromp by Frans Hals! The *Syndics* picture in particular must have served as the model.[6]

Even if Bredius had been correct in declaring the piece a forgery, his dating of it to around 1850 would have been decidedly too early. Manet turned to a similarly broad treatment only around 1860, though in the nineteenth-century context he was a pioneer in this field. Moreover, the sources that inspired him, including late work by Rembrandt and Frans Hals, were not rediscovered and reappraised by others until later in the century. To my mind, however, neither Manet nor any later nineteenth-century artist with a comparable technique ever managed to achieve the concentration of expression we find in cat. no. 28.

One should bear in mind here that Bredius could dismiss the piece as a forgery, but he had no grounds to date it any later than *c*.1856. For in the basic literature he had to hand he would soon have found that in 1857 the picture was listed, and described as a Rembrandt, by G. F. Waagen, who was reporting on his viewings of paintings in 1854 and 1856.[7] Hence the piece could not have been painted after that time.[8]

Bredius's bold assertion understandably met with dismay. Hofstede de Groot refuted his view:

> I see [the *Portrait of an Elderly Man*] as one of the finest creations from the last years of Rembrandt's life ... a picture with incredible expressiveness, a sight that remains unforgettable. It can even comfortably bear comparison with the heads in the *Syndics* [p. 29, fig. 10] ... it is ... sad that a man like Bredius should not immediately recognize such a picture as a masterpiece of the very first order.[9]

Gerson echoed this view almost half a century later: '[I]t has such an overwhelming power, character and directness of expression, that it matches perfectly the other commissioned portrait of 1667 [cat. no. 27]'.[10] Bredius's opinion nevertheless left seeds of doubt. Tümpel in 1986 assigned the present piece an asterisk, indicating that he was not 'entirely satisfied that the work [was] autograph'.[11]

The earlier provenance of the piece therefore becomes all the more important. As mentioned, Waagen in 1857 was the first to provide a description that can be used as the basis for a firm identification. He did so in his report of a visit to the collection of Sir Culling Eardley in Belvedere House, near Erith in Kent:

> Rembrandt.–1. Portrait of a man in a black dress, and in a black broad-brimmed hat and white collar, from which two strings depend. Signed and dated 1667. Of glowing colour, and, like most of his later pictures, of very broad treatment. The hands, especially the right, are only sketched.[12]

At the time, the piece was hanging only one picture away from Rembrandt's *Self-Portrait as*

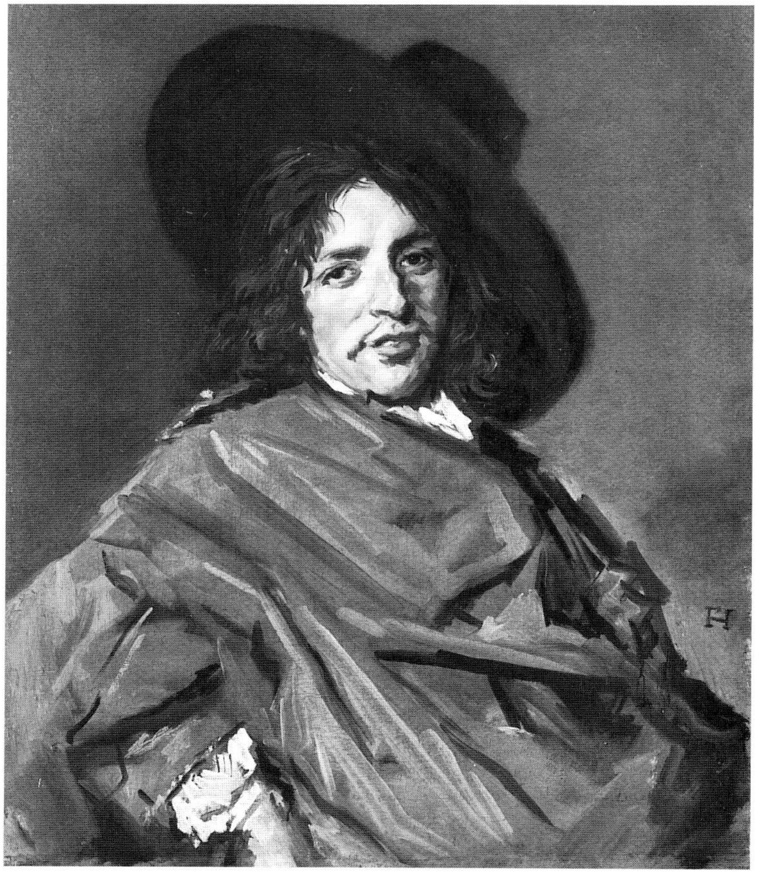

FIG. 28c
Frans Hals 1581/85–1666
Portrait of a Man
Monogrammed
Canvas
80.0 x 67.0 cm
Fitzwilliam Museum, Cambridge

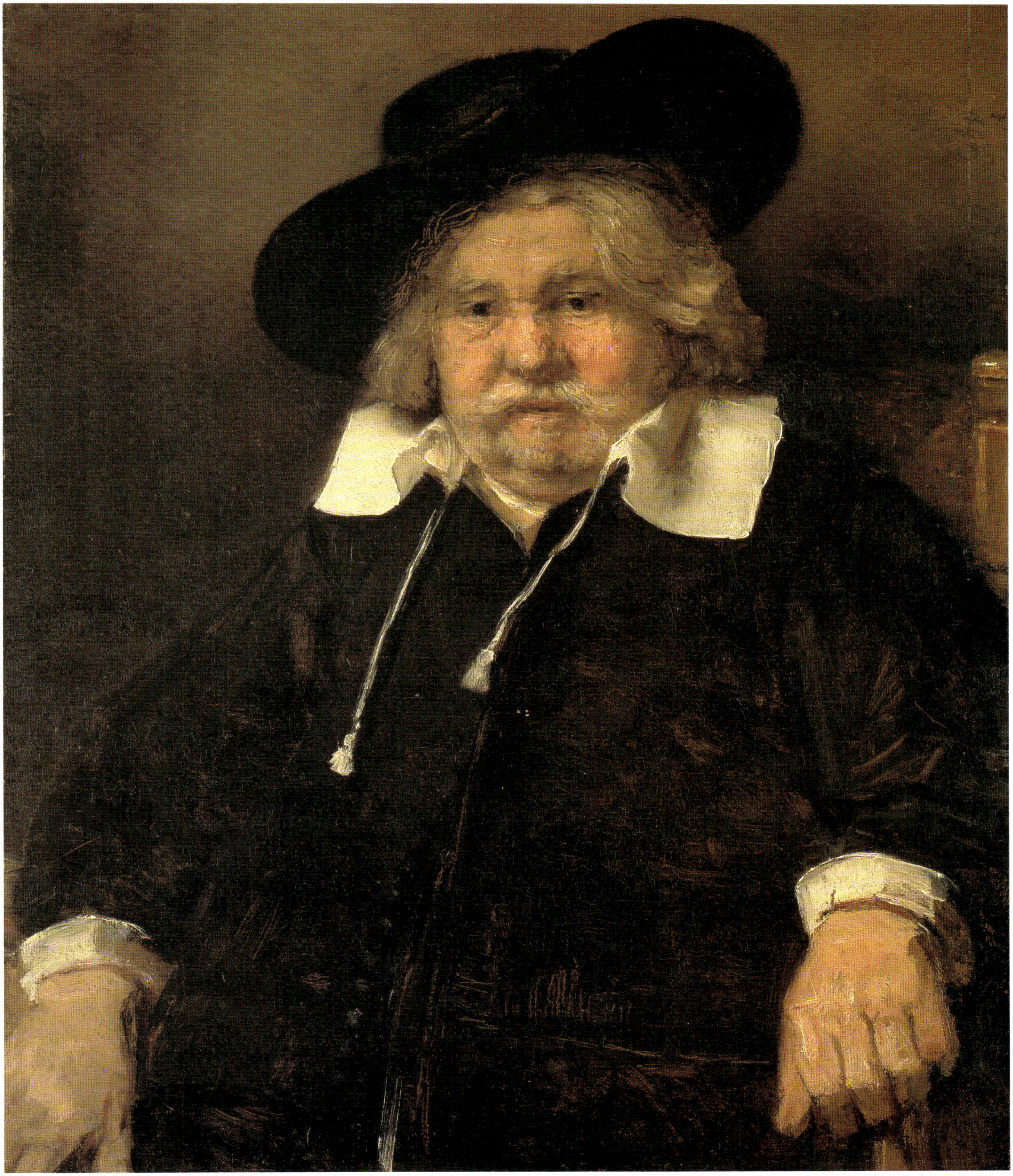

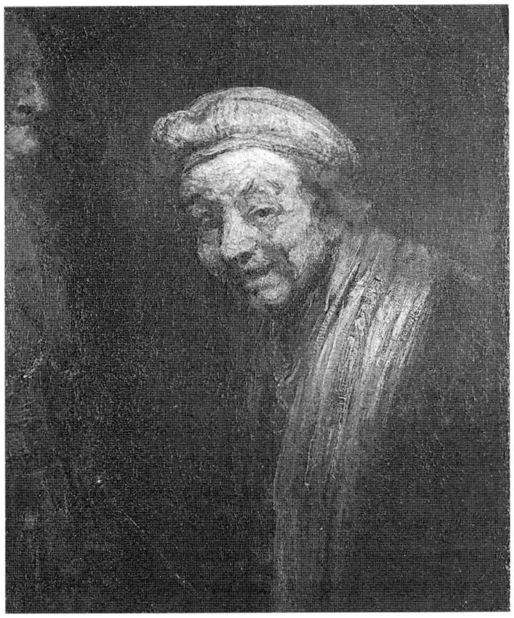

FIG. 28d
Rembrandt
Self-Portrait as the Laughing Zeuxis
Canvas
82.5 x 65.0 cm
Wallraf-Richartz-Museum, Cologne
(for colour reproduction, see p. 39, fig. 10)

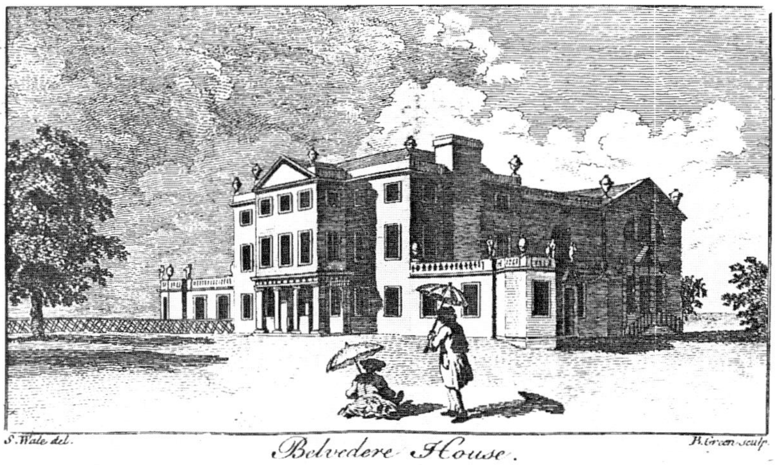

FIG. 28e
B. Green, after S. Wale
Belvedere House
From Dodsley 1761

FIG. 28f
Attributed to Rembrandt
Head of an Oriental with a Cap
Panel
66.5 x 51.5 cm
Present whereabouts unknown
Photograph: RKD

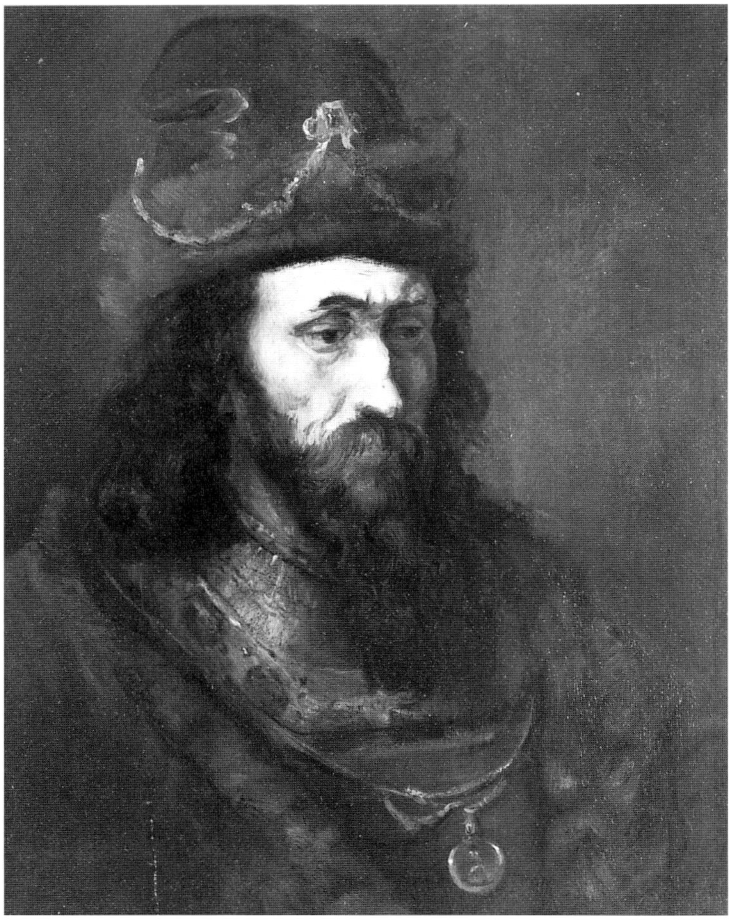

the Laughing Zeuxis, now in Cologne (fig. 28d). The catalogue of an exhibition at the Royal Academy, London, in 1938 provided some information on the earlier history of cat. no. 28.[13] Here in the present catalogue, for the first time, the provenance will be examined in more detail.

The collection Waagen saw in 1857 at Belvedere House, a mansion set in beautiful surroundings (fig. 28e), had been assembled by the financier Sampson Gideon (1699–1762). After Gideon's death, his collection passed by inheritance through several generations, remaining intact at Belvedere House until after 1857 (see Provenance).[14] The *Portrait of an Elderly Man* was in the collection for many years as a picture of 'Admiral van Trump' – either the Dutch Admiral Maarten Harpertsz Tromp (1598–1653) or his son Admiral Cornelis Tromp (1629–1691). In England both men enjoyed a formidable reputation as naval commanders in the Anglo-Dutch Wars.

At the auction of the Luke Schaub Collection in 1758, Sampson Gideon bought lot 40: 'Ditto Rembrandt, painting an old woman', in other words, Rembrandt's *Laughing Self-Portrait* (fig. 28d). It was in the sale together with 'its companion', lot 39: 'Rembrandt. Admiral Ruyter', leading to the assumption that Gideon bought both pieces as a pair: the latter piece has often been assumed to be identical with the *Portrait of an Elderly Man*, the painting later known as 'Admiral van Trump' in Gideon's collection.[15] Any confusion between 'Admiral van Trump' and 'Admiral Ruyter' seems fairly easy to explain: Michiel Adriaensz de Ruyter (1607–1676) was a Dutch admiral at the same time as the two Tromps. However, in fact the 'Admiral Ruyter' in the Schaub sale was not sold to Gideon, but to another bidder.[16] So Gideon must have acquired the *Portrait of an Elderly Man* on another occasion. His 'van Trump' may perhaps be identified with a painting sold some fourteen years earlier, in the Sir John Rawdon sale of 1744 (lot 51): 'Admiral Van Trump – Rembrandt'.[17]

The *Portrait of an Elderly Man* and the *Laughing Self-Portrait* are first described as objects of interest, in 'the long parlour' of Belvedere House, in R. & J. Dodsley's *London and Its Environs Described* (1761): 'Van Trump. Height 2 feet, 10 inches, Breadth 2 feet, 4 inches. Painted by Francis Hals' and 'Rembrandt painting an old woman. Height 2 feet, 10 inches, breadth 2 feet. Painted by himself'.[18] The measurements recorded are equivalent to 86 x 71 cm (the *Elderly Man* is now measured as 81 x 67 cm) and 86 x 61 cm (the *Laughing Self-Portrait* is now measured as 82.5 x 65 cm). Although it is surprising that Gideon and/or his advisers (and the previous owner?) should have taken the *Portrait of an Elderly Man* for a Frans ('Francis') Hals, the broad technique of the painting perhaps makes this understandable after all. The attribution to Hals was maintained for quite some time. The *English Connoisseur* of 1766 reported that 'Van Trump, Francis Hals' and 'Rembrandt painting an old woman' were 'in the lobby' of Belvedere House. In 1774, the *Ambulator* used the same wording with regard to both paintings, except that 'Van Trump' was corrected to read 'Van Tromp'. The two pictures appear with the same designation in the fourth edition of the *Ambulator* in 1792, and in Brayley's book of 1808.[19]

The *Portrait of an Elderly Man* was subsequently recognized as a Rembrandt rather than a Hals. The signature had apparently been discovered by the time the piece was listed in an exhibition catalogue in London in 1821 as 'Portrait. Rembrandt. [Loaned by] Lord Eardley'.[20] In a catalogue of 1845 the picture appears more specifically, as 'Van Tromp' by Rembrandt. It is described in exactly the same words in an 1856 manuscript catalogue of the collection at Belvedere House.[21] In 1876 the piece was loaned for exhibition, again as 'Rembrandt. Admiral Van Tromp', by another of Gideon's heirs.

The following may be added concerning Bredius's apparent mistake in this instance. A renowned art connoisseur, he was always suspicious that paintings brought for his judgement might be forgeries. In a personal letter he admitted: 'Unfortunately I also make a gaffe once in a while. Some forgers are extremely clever'. Only recently it emerged that his biggest blunder, his endorsement of the *Supper at Emmaus* by the forger Han van Meegeren (1889–1947) as a masterwork by Vermeer, had come in the wake of considerable hesitation, and that he had had misgivings about the whole matter. Bredius had previously validated another fake Vermeer, an error that probably came to his attention later.[22]

Bredius vacillated over attributions to Rembrandt as well. In 1924 he published a *Head of an Oriental with a Cap* as a newly discovered Rembrandt (fig. 28f).[23] But he did not include the piece in *The Paintings of Rembrandt*, which he published in 1935. Judging from a reproduction, one might suggest that the *Head of an Oriental* looks as if it were painted by an almost expressionistic impressionist who had cast an eye over Rembrandt's late work. Perhaps only the passage of time allows differences such as those between Rembrandt's late work and the innovations of nineteenth-century painting to be seen in their proper perspective.

In more recent times, the exceptional qualities of the *Portrait of an Elderly Man* were remarked on not only by Gerson but by Brown, who in 1976 described the piece as a 'vigorous portrait'.[24] In exhibition catalogues in London in 1938, in Edinburgh in 1950, and again in London in 1952–53, the work was still taken to be a portrait (albeit with some reservations) of Admiral Cornelis Tromp – the son. Brown in 1976 pointed out, however, that neither the firmly identified portraits of Tromp senior or Tromp junior, nor those of de Ruyter, bear any resemblance to this *Elderly Man*.

AB/MB

1 Slatkes 1992, no. 179.

2 Information from M. Franken of the Rembrandt Research Project, who also notes that the piece is painted on broadly woven, almost jute-like, canvas.

3 For instances of such enlargement, see Blankert 1986–87, p. 22.

4 Observed by Ms Marieke de Winkel of the Rembrandt Research Project. A similar collar can be seen in Bartholomeus van der Helst's *Portrait of Paulus Potter* of 1652, made when Potter was twenty-seven years old (Mauritshuis, The Hague).

5 Slive 1970–74, vol. III, 1974, p. 111, no. 218, observes that the jaunty angle of the hat in this piece was apparently considered inappropriate in later years, as it was painted over. For the vogue for wearing hats to one side, see Slive 1970–74, vol. I, 1970, p. 205.

6 Bredius 1921, p. 151: 'Das Bild habe ich genau untersucht und ich halte es ganz bestimmt für eine (belgische?) sehr geschickte Fälschung aus der Mitte des vorigen Jahrhunderts, wie ich deren so viele schon gesehen. Er wurde mir gezeigt als "van" Tromp von Frans Hals! Man hat besonders die *Staalmeesters* als Vorbild genommen'.

7 Waagen 1854, suppl. 1857, p. 281.

8 Bredius's statement appears in his review of Valentiner 1921, which refers to the description of the painting by Waagen in 1857, and to Hofstede de Groot (1916), no. 829, which also includes a reference to Waagen.

9 Hofstede de Groot 1922, p. 13 (here translated from the German).

10 H. Gerson, in Bredius / Gerson 1969, p. 575, no. 323A; see also Gerson 1968, p. 448, no. 409.

11 Tümpel 1986, p. 387, no. 147*.

12 Waagen 1854, suppl. 1857, p. 281.

13 London 1938, p. 67, cat. no. 128. For subsequent notes on the provenance, sometimes with slightly different details, see also Edinburgh 1950, cat. no. 35; London 1952–53, p. 40, cat. no. 175; Manchester 1957, cat. no. 105; Bredius / Gerson 1969, no. 323A; C. Brown, in London 1976, cat. no. 97.

14 Hoff 1995, pp. 7, 198–9, excellently documents the provenances of a Batoni and a Murillo, both from Belvedere House and now at the National Gallery of Victoria.

15 First proposed in Edinburgh 1950, cat. no. 35.

16 It was sold to a certain 'Steward', by some accounts, and to 'L. Anson' by others. It is most likely to have been the latter, as a later heir of George Admiral Lord Anson (1697–1762) – presumably the 'L. Anson' in question – owned a 'Rembrandt Admiral Ruyter', which was probably identical with no. 39 in the Schaub sale of 1758. This later heir was Thomas, Earl of Lichfield (1795–1854). His 'Rembrandt Admiral Ruyter' was sold at the Shugborough Hall auction on 10 August 1842, lot 49, to Nieuwenhuijs for £54.12 (Carol Togneri, The Getty Provenance Index, letter, 22 March 1997).

17 Suggested by C. White, in New Haven 1983, p. 103, cat. no. 42. Lot 51 was sold with lot 52: 'His wife, its comp ...] ditto [by Rembrandt]' (bought by art dealer Bragge, £141 15s for both). One must remember that in the eighteenth century arbitrary paintings were often hung together as 'pendants'.

18 Hoff 1995, p. 198, refers to a 1759 edition of Dodsley, *London and Its Environs Described*, but it is not in London libraries or reference works, nor is it known to the Getty Provenance Index in Santa Monica.

19 Brayley 1808, p. 546.

20 For the first reference to this mention of 1821, see London 1938, p. 67, cat. no. 128.

21 Data 1761–1856 obtained with the kind assistance of Sarah Herring and Dianne Loxton, both of London.

22 H. van Wijnen, in Kraaijpoel & Van Wijnen 1996, pp. 22, 77; Van der Meer Mohr 1996.

23 Bredius 1924, p. 159.

24 C. Brown, in London 1976, cat. no. 97.

29

Rembrandt?

The Finding of Moses

1640s

Formerly signed on wall at left
Canvas (oval)
48.3 x 60.3 cm
Philadelphia Museum of Art
The John G. Johnson Collection

PROVENANCE: Pierre Crozat (d. 1740); bequeathed by Crozat to his nephew, Louis-François Crozat, Marquis du Châtel; his sale, Paris, June 1751, lot 167 (dimensions given as 'haut de 2 pieds 8 pouces, large de 2 pieds 3 pouces'); Duc de Choiseul [whose wife was the daughter of Louis-François Crozat, and for whom it was engraved by Basan for the 'Choiseul Gallery', 1771, no. 41 ('22 pouces de large sur 18 pouces de haut', oval)]; his sale, Paris, 6 April 1772, lot 12, to Boileau, presumably acting as agent for Prince de Conti, for 2031 frs; sale, Prince de Conti, Paris, 8 April 1777, lot 284, to Langlier for 1400 frs; sale, Robert de Saint-Victor, Paris, 26 November 1822, lot 67, 2550 frs; Sir Robert Peel, Bart., Drayton Manor, 1836 [1845 cat., no. 32]; [according to Mireur] sold by Peel in 1845; (possibly) with dealer Kleinberger, Paris; acquired by John G. Johnson, Philadelphia, by 1906 [1914 and 1972 cats, no. 474].

LITERATURE: Smith 1829–42, vol. VII, 1836, no. 24; Bode & Hofstede de Groot 1897–1906, no. 195; W. R. Valentiner, in New York 1909, vol. I, pp. 86–7, cat. no. 86; Hofstede de Groot 1908–27, vol. VI, 1916, pp. 34–5, no. 23; Los Angeles 1947; Raleigh 1956, cat. no. 11; Jerusalem 1965, cat. no. 25; Bauch 1966, no. 12; Bredius / Gerson 1969, p. 598, no. 496; Sweeny 1972, pp. 69–70, no. 474; Yokohama / Fukuoka / Kyoto 1986–87, cat. no. 14.

Notwithstanding the fact that this canvas was substantially cut, from a rectangular shape to an oval, probably sometime between 1751 and 1771/72 (see Provenance; a 6.3 cm strip has also been added to the bottom), it resided during the later eighteenth century in three of the grandest and most selective aristocratic collections in France, namely those of Louis-François Crozat (Marquis du Châtel), the Duc de Choiseul, and the Prince de Conti. Later, in the nineteenth century, it was owned by Sir Robert Peel, many of whose Dutch paintings remain the pride of the National Gallery, London. Finally it was acquired by John G. Johnson (1841–1917), the lawyer whose vast and encyclopaedic collections are still preserved in his native Philadelphia and in their day inspired wealthier fellow collectors such as P. A. B. Widener to impassioned rivalry in the pursuit of works by the old masters. Thus the painting's extraordinary provenance attests to its appreciation by a sequence of discriminating connoisseurs.

In the Duc de Choiseul's sale catalogue of 1772, it was described in glowing terms: 'la lumière répandue sur les figures produit un grand effet, & quoiqu'elles soient nues & très-petites, la pâte de couleur en est admirable, & la touche des plus fines'.[1]

The picture was considered to be a Rembrandt until 1969. With its small-scale historical figures, theatrical lighting, and broad landscape setting featuring water in the foreground, the painting outwardly resembles several of Rembrandt's works from his first years in Amsterdam, notably the *Rape of Europa* dated 1632 and now at the J. Paul Getty Museum (Bredius 464) (fig. 29a), and another painting based on Ovid, *Diana, Actaeon and Callisto* (Bredius 472) (fig. 29b), in the collection of the Fürsten zu Salm-Salm, Anholt (compare also the *Rape of Proserpine* of *c.*1632, at the Staatliche Museen Preussischer Kulturbesitz, Berlin-Dahlem (Bredius 463)). Gerson first observed, in 1969, that the style of the Johnson Collection painting is not Rembrandt's.[2] We may

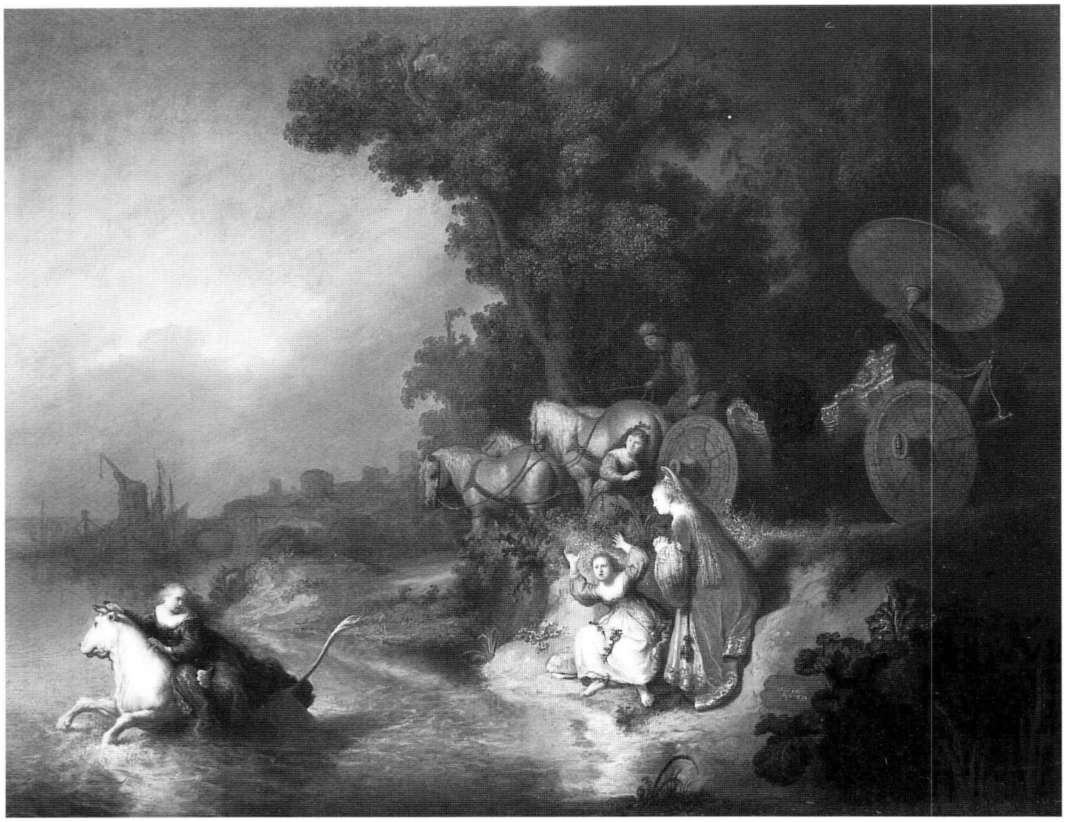

FIG. 29a
Rembrandt
Rape of Europa
Signed and dated 1632
Panel
61.0 x 77.5 cm
Collection of the J. Paul Getty Museum, Los Angeles, California

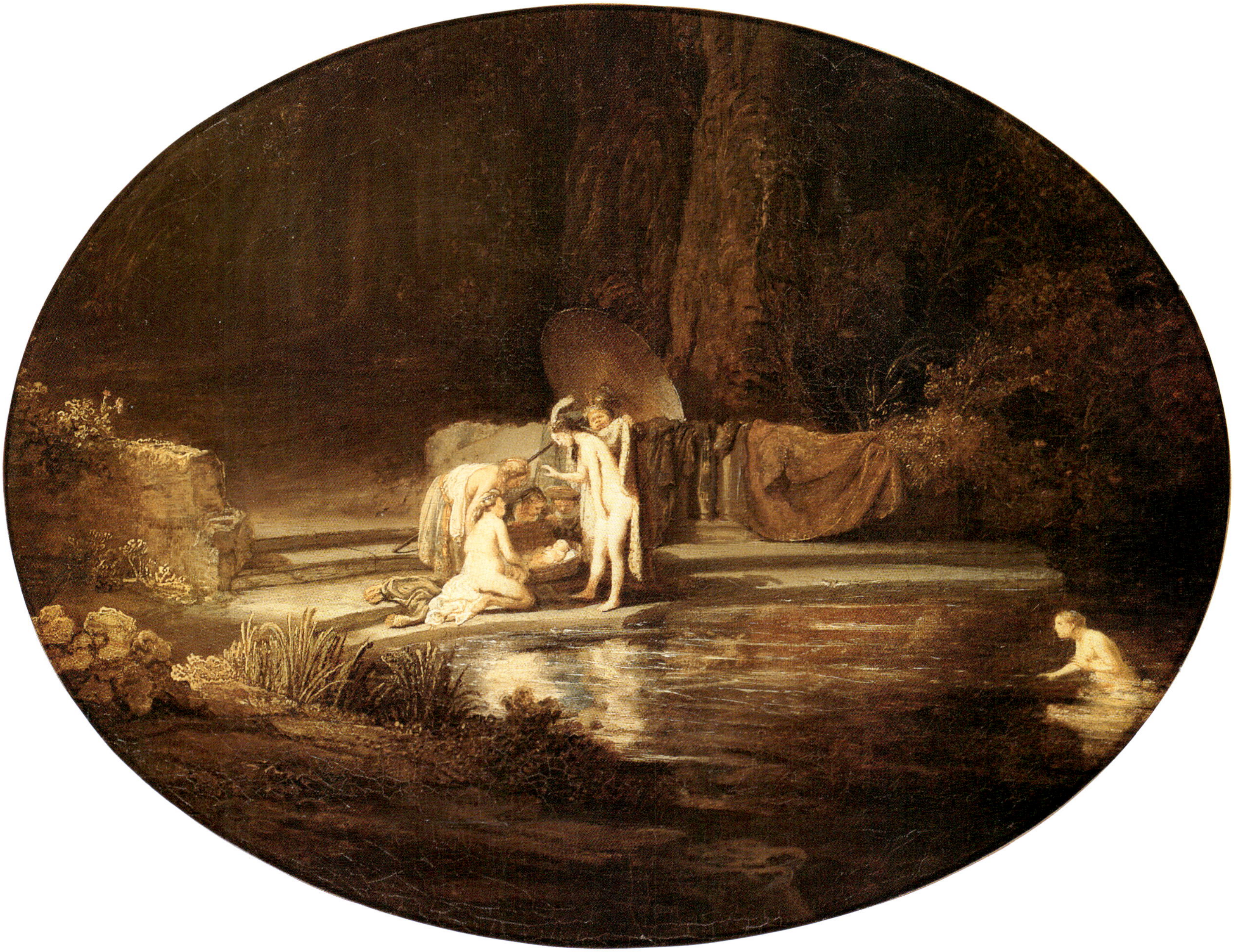

compare especially the drawing of the figures, the resolution of detail, and the palette in the *Europa*; the *Diana*, which is not as well preserved, is less reliable as a touchstone of comparison. As Hofstede de Groot pointed out, the remnants of the signature and the date 1656 [*sic*] are by a later hand.[3] Although clearly of the period, whether the painting dates as early as 1632–35 (the usual range of its dating) is questionable. A pen and bistre drawing alternatively assigned to Rembrandt or to Ferdinand Bol, in the Rijksprentenkabinet, Amsterdam, is sometimes wrongly assumed to be a preparatory drawing for the present work.[4]

In the biblical account of the Finding of Moses (Exodus 2:1–10), Pharaoh's daughter, following her father's order that all male children of the Hebrews be killed, went down to the Nile to bathe with her attendant. There she discovered the infant Moses floating in a small ark of rushes and pitch. Taking pity on the baby, she instructed that he be raised as her own child. Since the Middle Ages the subject had been regarded as prefiguring the Infant Christ's escape from the Massacre of the Innocents. The episode from the story of Moses most commonly depicted by seventeenth-century Dutch painters, the Finding of Moses was represented in a wide variety of settings, from a broad northern mountain valley (as in Nicolaes de Bruyn's engraving after Gillis van Coninxloo)[5] to the Italian campagna (as in the picture dated 1636 by Bartholomeus Breenbergh, at the National Gallery, London). In contrast to the present work is Haarlem artist Pieter de Grebber's version of this theme, dated 1634 (Gemäldegalerie, Dresden), with large-scale figures conceived in a classicizing manner that highlights the grace and elegance of the Pharaoh's daughter and her entourage – no such pretensions to monumentality for the party of skinny-dippers in the present painting. The depiction of Pharaoh's daughter naked (as opposed to her companions, as in Cornelis van Poelenburch's version at the Fitzwilliam Museum, Cambridge) is at this point something of an iconographic novelty, but was less so in Bol's later version, of *c.*1655, now in the Vredespaleis, The Hague.[6] However, Pharaoh's daughter's Moorish assistant, who hastens to drape her in ermine, like the exotic parasol beyond, is part of the standard property department of orientalism shared by Pieter Lastman, Rembrandt and their followers. Jacob de Wet,[7] Willem de Poorter and others in Rembrandt's circle would treat the Finding of Moses theme with similar small-scale figures and props.

PCS

1 Sale cat., Paris, June 1751, lot 67: 'The light cast over the figures produces a striking effect, & although they are nude & very small, the build-up of colour is admirable, and the touch is the very finest'.
2 H. Gerson, in Bredius / Gerson 1969, p. 598, no. 496.
3 Hofstede de Groot 1908–27, vol. VI, 1916, p. 34, no. 23.
4 Hofstede de Groot 1908–27, vol. VI, p. 34, no. 23; W. R. Valentiner, in New York 1909, pp. 86–7, cat. no. 86; Benesch 1973, no. 475, lists this drawing as only corrected by Rembrandt.
5 Franz 1969, p. 211, fig. 216.
6 Blankert 1982, pp. 93–4, no. 9, pl. 20; Sumowski, *Gemälde*, vol. I, 1983, no. 96. For a reconstruction of the original arrangement of the ensemble of which the Bol formed a part, see Blankert 1992.
7 For example, Sumowski, *Gemälde*, vol. VI, 1995, no. 2489.

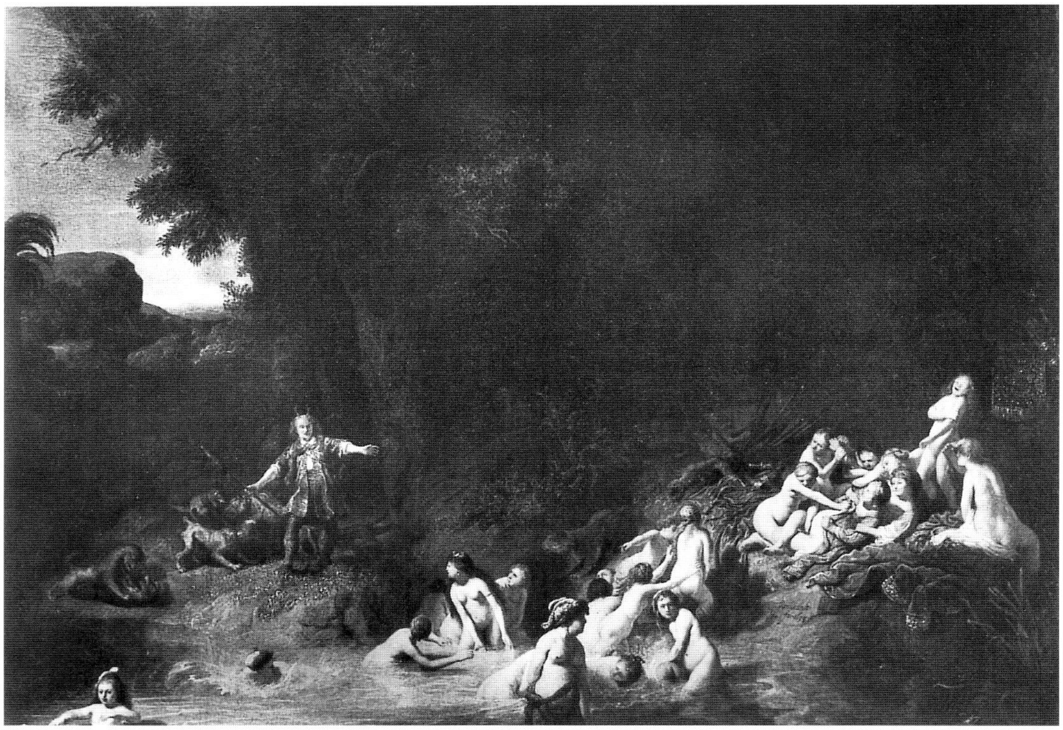

FIG. 29b
Rembrandt
Diana, Actaeon and Callisto
Signed and dated 163[4?]
Canvas
73.5 x 93.5 cm
Fürsten zu Salm-Salm, Anholt

30

Rembrandt?

The Departure of the Shunamite Woman

Signed and dated lower right *Rembrandt f. / 1640* (according to *Corpus*, vol. III, 1989, p. 544, the inscription is not by Rembrandt)
Panel
39.0 x 53.2 cm (a strip of wood measuring 3.5 cm later attached along the upper edge)
The Board of Trustees of the Victoria & Albert Museum, London

PROVENANCE: [after *Corpus*, vol. III, 1989, p. 549] Possibly in the estate of Nicolaes van Bambeeck Jr at the time of his death in Amsterdam in 1671, as 'an Abraham and Hagar, by a pupil of Rembrandt's'; possibly in the collection of Adriaen Bout, The Hague, who owned an 'Abraham and Hagar by Rembrandt' in 1734; possibly sale, Amsterdam, 15–16 April 1739, lot 85: 'The Banishment of Hagar and Ishmael, most accomplished, by Rembrandt van Rijn'; probably sold in Haarlem from the collection of Willem Fabricius of Almkerk on 19 August 1749, lot 12: 'Abraham Banishing Hagar, accomplished and powerful, by Rembrandt van Rijn', 36.4 x 53.3 cm; possibly sale, Blackwood, 1751, second day, lot 51, to Ellys; possibly sale, Rongent, 1758, second day, lot 58, to Brandenburgh; Bourchier Cleeve (1715–1760), Foots Cray Place [mentioned in 1761]; bequeathed by Cleeve to his daughter Elisabeth, who married Sir George Younge (1731–1812); sale, Sir George Younge, London (White), 24 March 1806, lot 32, to John Parke; his sale, London (Coxe), 8/9 May 1812, lot 29; sale, Woodburn, London, 1818 (bought in); sale, London (Christie's), 16 June 1821, lot 58; sale, J. Crespigny, London (Christie's), 23 April 1869, lot 31; Constantine Alexander Ionides, London, later Brighton (1885); bequeathed by him to the Victoria & Albert Museum in 1901.

LITERATURE: Smith 1829–42, vol. VII, 1836, no. 3; Hofstede de Groot 1899, p. 163; Hofstede de Groot 1908–27, vol. VI, 1916, p. 26, no. 5; Hamann 1936, pp. 515–16; Bauch 1966, no. 22; Bredius / Gerson 1969, no. 508; Tümpel 1969, pp. 118–24; Schwartz 1984, no. 239; Tümpel 1986, pp. 166–71, 390, no. 18 (as Rembrandt); *Corpus*, vol. III, 1989, pp. 542–50, no. C85; Tümpel 1993, p. 462 (as by studio or follower).

This painting has been known as 'The Banishment of Hagar', by Rembrandt, probably since 1749 or even earlier.[1] It was renamed *The Departure of the Shunamite Woman* in 1969, and the attribution to Rembrandt has been queried since 1989. A strip of wood measuring 3.5 cm has been attached to the upper edge of the original panel – since the sale of 1749 – and painted with a dark sky, which extends down to cover part of the picture itself. It was probably not originally a nocturnal scene.
A cowherd and his cattle can be vaguely discerned in the left background, and women, one of whom draws water from a well, can be seen far more clearly on the right. It is incongruous for these persons to be engaged in such activities at night. The painting may have been transformed into a nocturnal scene in the eighteenth century to make it more Rembrandtesque.[2]

The principal group in the foreground stands out quite prominently as a result. It is not surprising that the picture was for centuries interpreted as a depiction of the Banishment of Hagar (Genesis 21:8–14). The elderly man standing erect could be seen as the patriarch Abraham, who dismissed Hagar, the young mother of his first son, Ishmael, because of his wife Sarah's jealousy, and the boy beside the ass would be Ishmael. This story was illustrated on countless occasions. Rembrandt himself, and his pupils in particular, rendered it dozens of times.[3] Besides, the painting bears a close resemblance to Rembrandt's etching of the *Banishment of Hagar* of 1637 (fig. 30a, B.30), in which Abraham stands with his arms held out at his sides, like the man in cat. no. 30. In the etching, Hagar holds a handkerchief to her face to wipe away her tears,

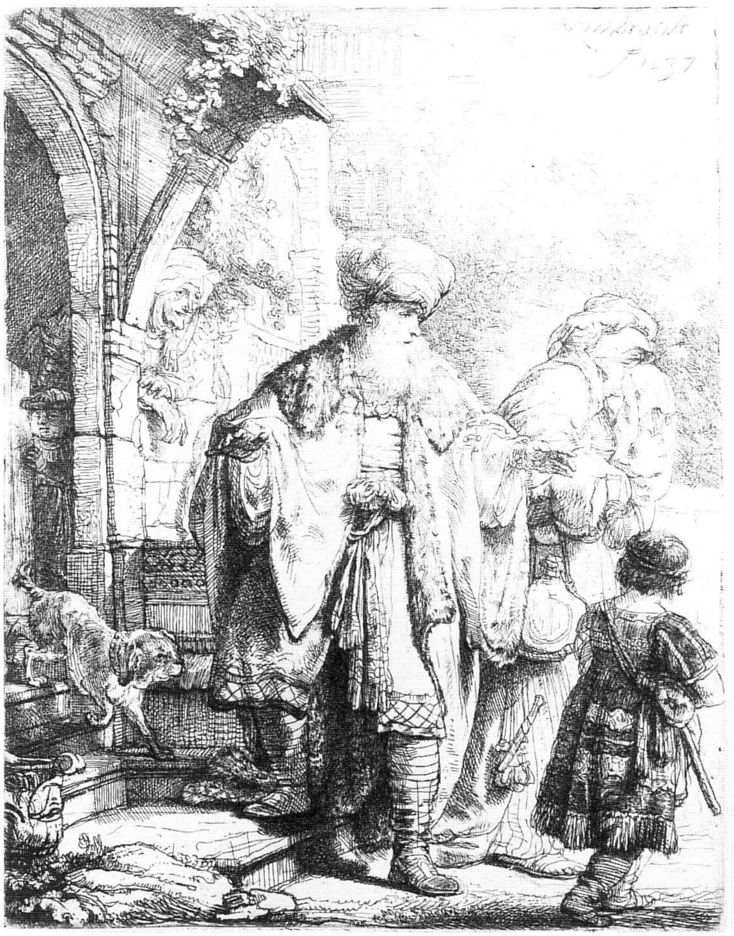

FIG. 30a
Rembrandt
The Banishment of Hagar
Signed and dated 1637
Etching
12.5 x 9.5 cm
Rijksprentenkabinet, Rijksmuseum, Amsterdam

as does the woman seated on the ass. Added to this, the Ishmael wearing a striped tunic in the etching strongly recalls the boy in the painting. The latter, moreover, carries a quiver, the attribute of Ishmael, who became an archer later in life (Genesis 21:20).

In 1899, however, it was observed that Hagar was always portrayed on foot at the time of her banishment and never seated on an ass (fig. 30a). This gave rise to the idea that Rembrandt may have started the picture as a Flight into Egypt, in which the Virgin is generally borne by an ass, but changed his mind and decided to depict the Banishment of Hagar.[4] A later suggestion was that Rembrandt had been inspired by Rubens's *Flight into Egypt*, now in Kassel, and that the ass derives from this source.[5]

According to the Bible, however, Abraham took 'a bottle of water, and gave it unto Hagar, putting it on her shoulder' (Genesis 21:14). Hence she had no ass to carry it. In 1969, Tümpel, moreover, argued that Rembrandt never departed from pictorial tradition to such a degree, and proposed a more convincing solution.[6] He observed that Rembrandt's teacher Pieter Lastman and the Amsterdam history painters of his generation, now known as the 'Pre-Rembrandtists', introduced new subjects in painting, many of which were relatively obscure episodes from the Old Testament. They sought inspiration from sixteenth-century prints of biblical themes and used them as examples for their own work. One of the stories first painted by the Pre-Rembrandtists was that of the prophet Elisha and the Shunamite woman (2 Kings 4:8–37). The Shunamite was a prominent woman who, to honour the prophet Elisha, gave him shelter in her own home. She herself had married an elderly man and expected to remain childless. As Elisha prophesied, however, she gave birth to a son. One day the boy took ill among the reapers in the field and died a short time later. After laying his body on the prophet's bed, his mother embarked on a journey to see the man of God, who had by then left her home and was on Mount Carmel. Moved by her pleas, he returned to her house and restored her son to life.

Lastman and other Pre-Rembrandtists, as well as Rembrandt's pupil Gerbrand van den Eeckhout, portrayed the Shunamite woman throwing herself at the prophet's feet on Mount Carmel.[7] In Lastman's painting of the episode we see Elisha's servant Gehazi in the background, brandishing a staff to drive the woman away. Elisha forbade him to do so (fig. 30b). Tümpel presents a plausible case for his view that Rembrandt's painting (cat. no. 30), as the only one of its kind, shows the preceding scene. After laying her son's body in the prophet's room, the Shunamite bade her husband send her a servant 'and one of the asses, that I may run to the man of God, and come again'. Ignorant of the fate that had befallen the boy, her husband asked why she wished to do so, for it was not the Sabbath. 'Then she saddled an ass, and said to her servant, Drive and go forward; slack not thy riding for me, except I bid thee' (2 Kings 4:22–24). Hence the ass is perfectly consistent with this story. The animal is in Lastman's picture as well (fig. 30b), which also shows the servant beside the Shunamite woman. In the present painting (cat. no. 30) the woman is mounted on the ass; she holds a handkerchief to her face to conceal her grief at the death of her child. Her aged husband waits to hear the reason for her departure, while the servant stands on the other side of the ass.

Tümpel substantiates his interpretation by identifying the sixteenth-century prints on which the painting was based. They form a series of six copperplate engravings by Hans Collaert (d.1620) after Maarten de Vos (1532–1603), executed in Antwerp in about 1579 and reprinted many times thereafter.[8] The prints illustrate the tale of the Shunamite and the prophet in six episodes. The motif of the woman holding a handkerchief to her eyes can be seen in the print reproduced in the present catalogue as fig. 30c. The painting (cat. no. 30) bears the closest resemblance to the following print, which must have been the example on which it was based (fig. 30d). Here we see the woman setting off on the ass and turning round to look at her husband. He stands to one side, holding a staff, just as he appears in the painting. In both cases the woman is elegantly dressed and seated on a high saddle. The servant holds the ass's bridle. In the print he is portrayed as an adult, as suggested by the word 'servant' in the Vulgate edition of the Bible, whereas in the painting he is merely a 'boy', in line with Luther's

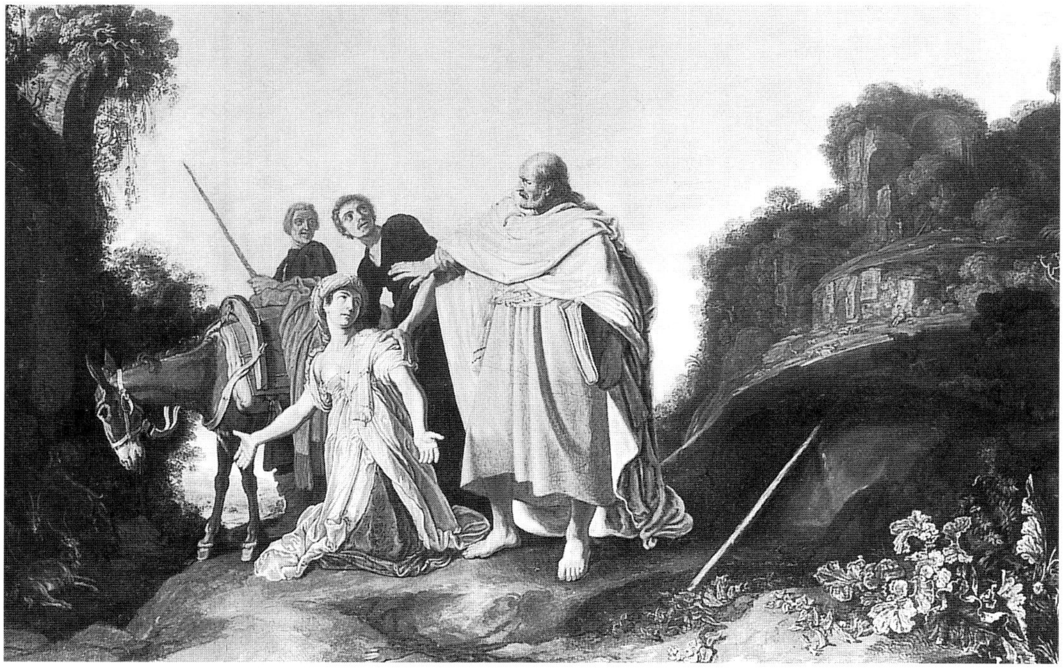

FIG. 30b
Pieter Lastman 1583–1633
The Shunamite Woman Pleads with the Prophet Elisha on Mount Carmel c.1616
Canvas
74.0 x 125.0 cm
Pushkin Museum, Moscow

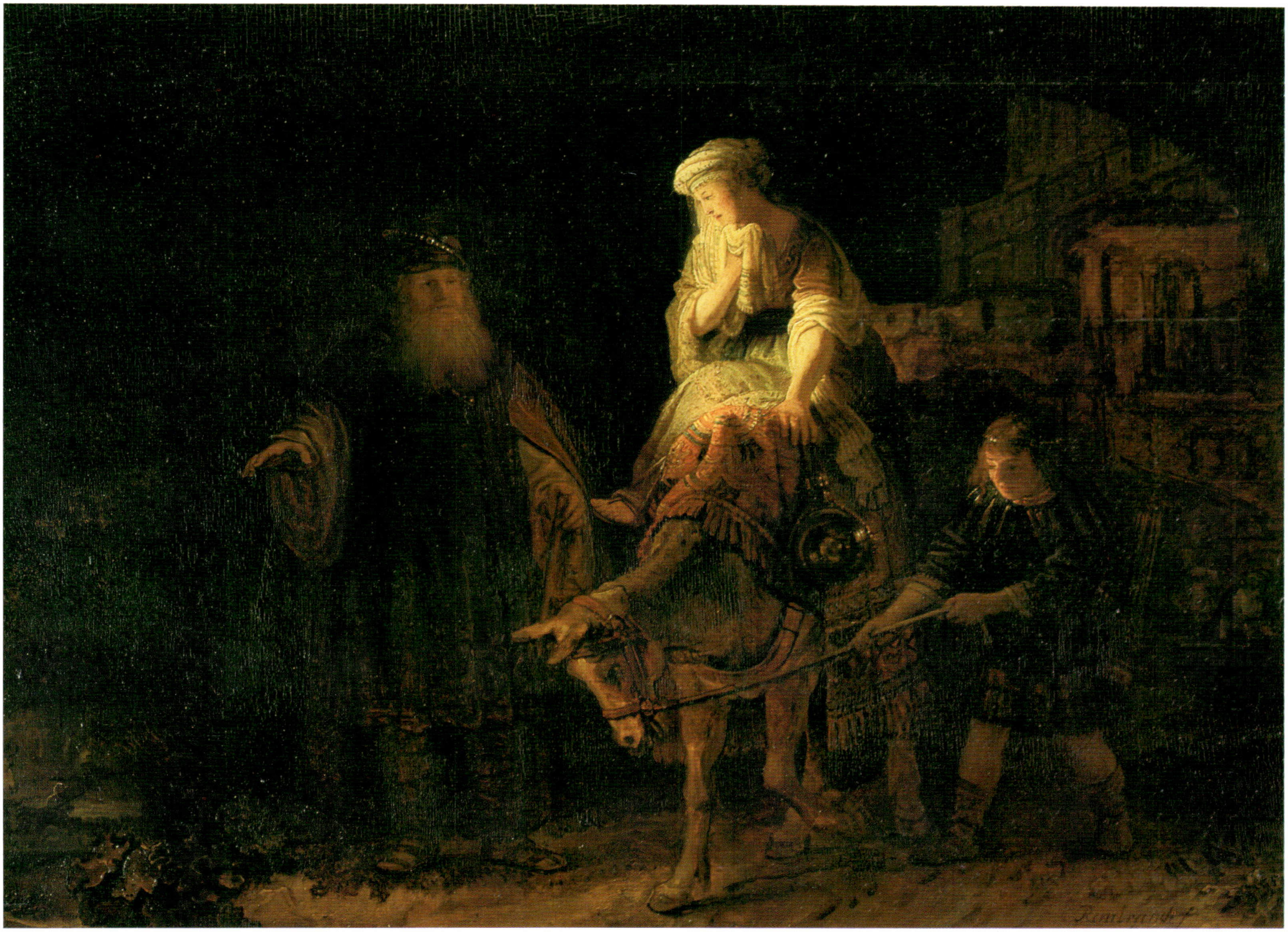

FIG. 30c
Hans Collaert (d. 1620), after Maarten de Vos
The Shunamite Woman Mourns the Death of Her Child Who Had Fallen Ill among the Reapers in the Field [left background] *and Lays His Body in Elisha's Bed* [right background]
Engraving
21.2 x 29.0 cm
From a reproduction

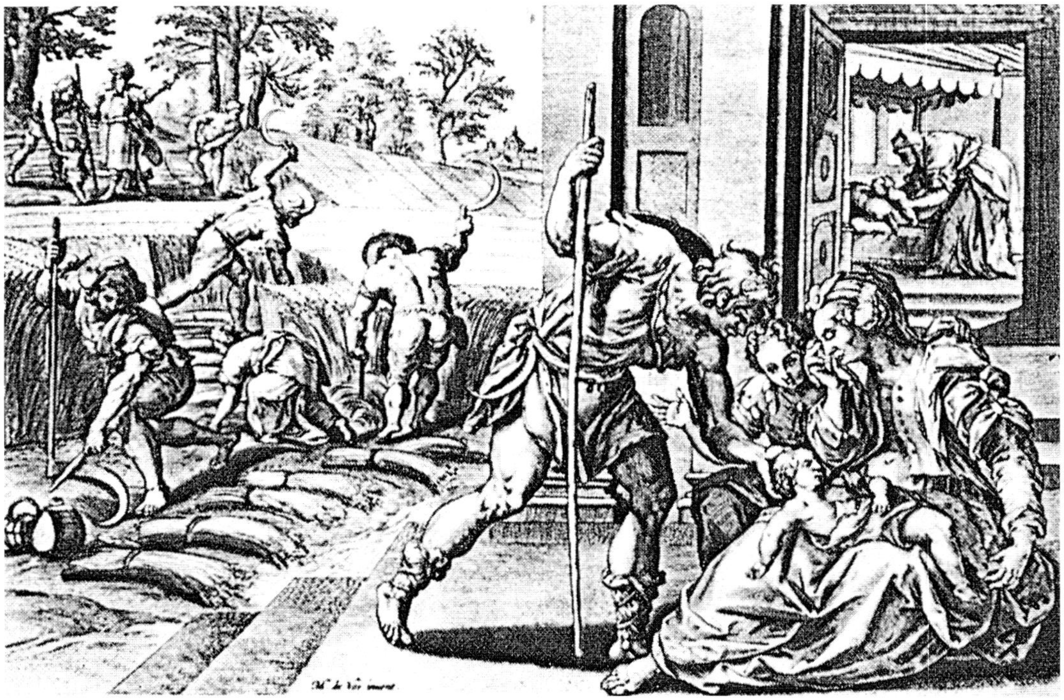

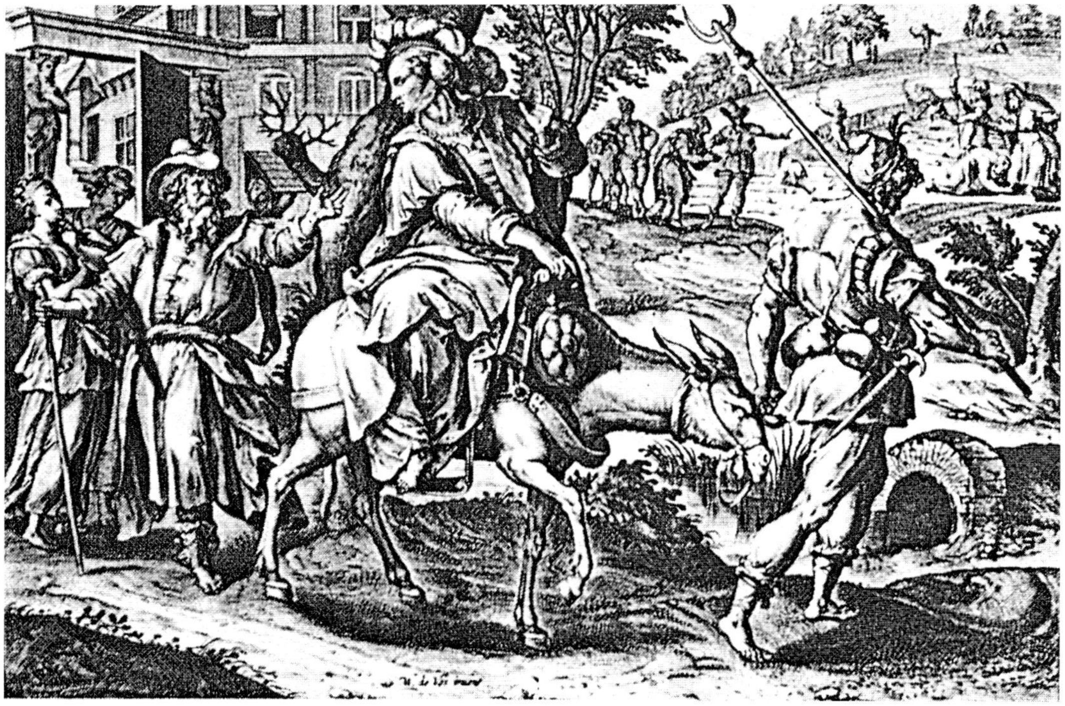

FIG. 30d
Hans Collaert, after Maarten de Vos
The Departure of the Shunamite Woman [Right background: The Shunamite Woman Falling at Elisha's Feet; Gehazi Standing Aside and Holding His Staff]
Engraving
21.2 x 29.0 cm
From a reproduction

translation and the rendering of the text in the Dutch *Statenbijbel.* Another detail that corresponds in both the painting and the print is the water jar attached to the front of the saddle.

The painting has always been regarded as a first-rate Rembrandt. Horst Gerson (1969), the most authoritative Rembrandt connoisseur of his generation, observed that 'the design and execution are of the utmost delicacy'.[9] However, the *Corpus* of 1989 was critical of the quality of many details in the picture. It says of the man, for instance, that the 'highlights are scattered in rather indeterminate fashion' and that his 'head and hands are poorly characterized'. It also faults the 'row of almost pedantically done catchlights on the chain running across his turban', while the illuminated parts of the woman's figure are said to be 'singularly lacking in articulation' and consequently of a 'somewhat syrupy appearance'.[10]

The gist of the commentary is that the piece is in many respects inferior to the *Visitation* (1640) in Detroit, a painting closely related to it in style and composition (fig. 30e).[11] In the context of Rembrandt's oeuvre, the *Visitation* is a work of exceptionally high quality and should therefore not be taken as the only standard. In any event, the fact that cat. no. 30 was probably formerly less dark than it is now suggests that it has not been preserved in perfect condition. There might be more to say about the work once it is viewed in the present exhibition, notably in relation to the

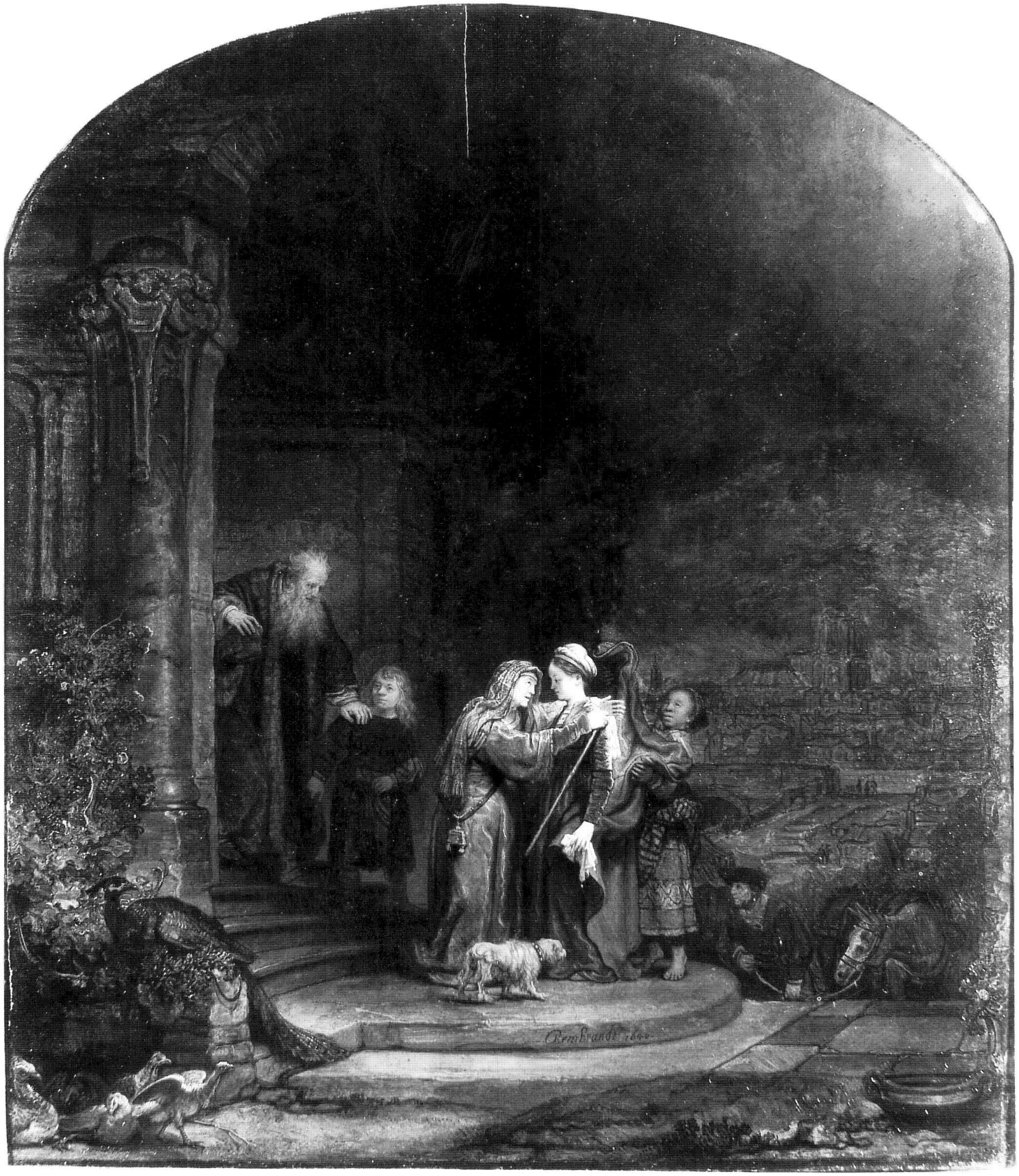

FIG. 30e
Rembrandt
The Visitation
Signed and dated 1640
Panel
56.6 x 47.8 cm
Detroit Institute of Arts
Photograph © 1997 The Detroit Institute of Arts,
Founders Society Purchase, Detroit

Susanna, which it resembles in both colour and technique (cat. no. 10). The *Corpus* lists cat. no. 30 as a studio piece and proposes an attribution to Ferdinand Bol,[12] suggesting that he inscribed the signature *Rembrandt f. / 1640* in Rembrandt's workshop, but that only the date is correct.

The *Corpus* makes no mention of the exceptional merits of the piece which, in the present author's view, are especially evident when the painting is compared with Collaert's print after de Vos, the example on which the picture was based (fig. 30d). The woman in the print could simply be setting off on a jaunt while her husband stands by to bid her farewell. The painting, however, has always been interpreted as representing a supremely poignant event, hence the association with the Banishment of Hagar.[13] In Collaert's print the servant escorting the woman walks ahead of her (fig. 30d). This motif has been completely transformed in the painting, where the youth is tugging at the ass's reins, thereby restraining the animal. The ass stubbornly thrusts its head forwards and raises its foreleg, as if protesting against this attempt to curb its movement. By thus holding the animal back, the servant affords the couple an opportunity to finish the conversation they were engaged in before the woman's sudden decision to depart. The man is still oblivious to his child's death, and his wife has no wish to tell him. She briefly lowers the handkerchief she holds before her grief-stricken face and insists that she must leave on her journey to the prophet. This dramatic, cardinal moment of confusion was singled out and illustrated with 'the most life-like emotion' (de meeste ende die naetuereelste beweechgelickheijt).[14] This is something Rembrandt could have done, but definitely not Bol. If the painting is not in fact a Rembrandt, it must have been executed by someone else after his concept or design.[15] The exhibition in Australia will provide an opportunity to judge whether Gerson or the authors of the *Corpus* were correct about the details. But nothing can detract from the painting's superior 'narrative quality', a hallmark of Rembrandt's work that goes unmentioned in the *Corpus*.[16]

The episode as such was unique and new in painting and therefore difficult to recognize. The servant, as we have seen, is virtually identical to the figure of Ishmael in Rembrandt's etching (fig. 30a) and carries Ishmael's attribute, the quiver of arrows. The painting's similarity to the etching must have been obvious right from the time it was made. It seems, therefore, as if the artist wanted the subject to be mistaken for a 'Banishment of Hagar'. This gave other viewers an opportunity to demonstrate their superior powers of observation. If this was the case, the painter succeeded remarkably well. It stands to reason that the servant would be armed to protect the woman, and therefore carries a quiver, yet it is incongruous that the youth cast in this role is still such a child.

AB

1 It was recently said to be identical with pieces referred to by the same title in 1671 and 1734 (see Provenance).

2 Tümpel 1986, p. 167; *Corpus*, vol. III, 1989, p. 544. The arched gateway at the upper right was probably part of the same overpainting.

3 Discussed at length in Hamann 1936.

4 Hofstede de Groot 1899, p. 163; Hofstede de Groot 1908–27, vol. VI, 1916, p. 26, no. 5.

5 See references in Broos 1977, p. 54; also suggested in Bauch 1966, no. 22.

6 Tümpel 1969, pp. 118–24, with reference to a publication by Tümpel from 1967.

7 See reproductions in Tümpel 1986, pp. 165–71, and Sumowski, *Gemälde*, vol. II, 1985, no. 440.

8 Hollstein, vol. IV, 1949, nos 5–8.

9 H. Gerson, in Bredius / Gerson 1969, p. 599, no. 508.

10 *Corpus*, vol. III, 1989, p. 546.

11 Bredius / Gerson 1969, no. 562; *Corpus*, vol. III, 1989, no. A138.

12 The author does not see the similarities listed in the *Corpus* (vol. III, 1989, pp. 546, 548) between this picture and others by or attributed to Bol.

13 Hagar's 'gesture and tears evince her grief at the compulsory separation' (Smith 1829–42, vol. VII, 1836, no. 3).

14 Strauss & Van der Meulen 1979, p. 161, no. 1639/2, regarding this statement by Rembrandt.

15 The author considers Bol unlikely to have been the executor of Rembrandt's design in this particular case.

16 The *Corpus* is criticized in this connection with respect to its rejection of other attributions, in Blankert 1992–93, p. 65.

31

Rembrandt?

Bust of Christ

*c.*1648–50

Panel
25.5 x 21.0 cm
Museum Bredius, The Hague

PROVENANCE: Previously unconvincingly identified with sale, M. (Lempereur), Paris, 24 May 1773, lot 61; acquired by Abraham Bredius in or shortly before 1912.

LITERATURE: Hofstede de Groot 1908–27, vol. VI, 1916, p. 117, no. 159; Slive 1965, pp. 411–12, no. 1; Bredius / Gerson 1969, no. 620; Schwartz 1984, p. 316; Blankert 1991, pp. 171–2, no. 135 (with earlier literature).

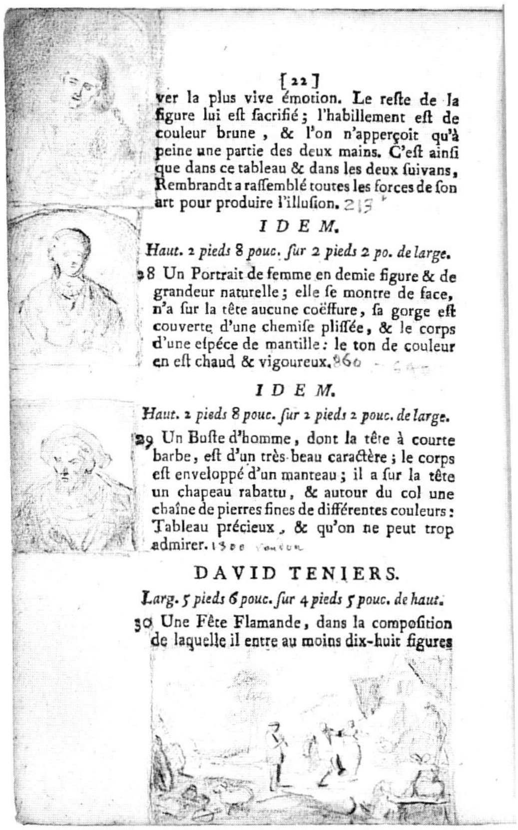
[22]
ver la plus vive émotion. Le reſte de la figure lui eſt ſacrifié; l'habillement eſt de couleur brune, & l'on n'apperçoit qu'à peine une partie des deux mains. C'eſt ainſi que dans ce tableau & dans les deux ſuivans, Rembrandt a raſſemblé toutes les forces de ſon art pour produire l'illuſion.

IDEM.

Haut. 2 pieds 8 pouc. ſur 2 pieds 2 po. de large.

28 Un Portrait de femme en demie figure & de grandeur naturelle; elle ſe montre de face, n'a ſur la tête aucune coëffure, ſa gorge eſt couverte d'une chemiſe pliſſée, & le corps d'une eſpéce de mantille: le ton de couleur en eſt chaud & vigoureux.

IDEM.

Haut. 2 pieds 8 pouc. ſur 2 pieds 2 pouc. de large.

29 Un Buſte d'homme, dont la tête à courte barbe, eſt d'un très beau caractère; le corps eſt enveloppé d'un manteau; il a ſur la tête un chapeau rabattu, & autour du col une chaîne de pierres fines de différentes couleurs: Tableau précieux, & qu'on ne peut trop admirer.

DAVID TENIERS.

Larg. 5 pieds 6 pouc. ſur 4 pieds 5 pouc. de haut.

30 Une Fête Flamande, dans la compoſition de laquelle il entre au moins dix-huit figures

FIG. 31a
Sketches by Gabriel de Saint-Aubin (1724–1780) in the catalogue for the sale of the Louis-Michel Vanloo Collection, 1772. At upper left, a *Christ* by Rembrandt auctioned on that occasion. This is probably the painting, now in different condition, in the John G. Johnson Collection at the Philadelphia Museum of Art.
Bibliothèque Nationale de France, Paris

Paintings such as this *Bust of Christ* can be traced all the way back to 1656, to Rembrandt's own home. At the end of July in that year, the inventory was drawn up for the sale of Rembrandt's property, a sale that was meant to save him from bankruptcy. The house was filled with works of art. Two painted *'tronies* of Christ by Rembrandt', nos 115 and 118, were in the 'back room or salon'.[1] A third *'tronie* of Christ', rendered 'from life' (see below), was listed as no. 326. The painter's name is not mentioned in the inventory, but the work was said to be in the 'small studio'.[2] The art collection left by the great marine painter Jan van de Cappelle (1626–1679) in 1680 also included a 'Christus trony' by Rembrandt.[3] Another 'picture of Christ by Rembrandt' appears in the 1708 inventory of the estate of the Haarlem peasant painter Cornelis Dusart.[4] Pictures of this kind are also referred to in a number of auctions in the course of the eighteenth century.[5] Gabriel Jacques de Saint-Aubin (1724–1780) drew a copy of one of these paintings in the margin of his catalogue of a Paris auction in 1772 (fig. 31a).[6]

Six extant heads of Christ were until recently unanimously accepted by twentieth-century connoisseurs as authentic Rembrandts (cat. no. 31, figs 31b, 31c).[7] These works are all roughly the same size and are dated by general consensus to *c.*1648–50. This conclusion was reached mainly on the basis of a comparison with the figure of Christ in Rembrandt's *Supper at Emmaus*, dated 1648, in the Louvre (fig. 31d).[8]

Over the years since the Rembrandt Research Project team made its first conclusions known in the early 1970s, the authenticity of a growing number of heads of Christ has been called into question. At present none of them are believed to be autograph. The painting in Berlin is considered the best, but even so is thought to be a studio piece (fig. 31b).[9]

This is a remarkable situation. A traditional consensus based on information that Rembrandt himself provided in 1656 – a consensus that was upheld by the most distinguished artists and auctioneers of the seventeenth and eighteenth centuries, and that survived the debate between modern connoisseurs – has come to an end. So far, no new facts or reasons have been advanced. As I understand it, the execution of the pictures is considered too superficial for them to be regarded as autograph. We should remember, however, that the literature consistently describes them as sketches.

The present *Bust of Christ* was rediscovered in about 1912 by the eminent art historian Abraham Bredius (1855–1946).[10] It is now in the museum that houses his private collection. Since it first appeared in the Rembrandt literature in 1912, the piece has received more admiration and attention than any of the heads of Christ mentioned above. It inspired feelings of almost religious awe in Holland and Germany in particular. F. Schmidt-Degener, director of the Museum Boymans in Rotterdam and subsequently of Amsterdam's Rijksmuseum, wrote the following in 1915: 'This small painting makes the very existence of the Nazarene plausible, and it is therefore one of the most precious monuments of Christian art'. What Rembrandt 'whispers to us are sermons on humanity and compassion'. A prominent critic referred to the piece as 'a spiritual event ... revealed', and concluded that Rembrandt must have 'seen the light'.[11]

In 1973, however, Professor J. Bruyn of the Rembrandt Research Project expressed the following view in a letter: 'At present we feel [the piece] cannot be accepted as authentic'. It is true that Christ looks out at us with a less lively and penetrating gaze than do the sitters in the Rembrandt portraits and *tronies* in the present exhibition. The picture has not been displayed alongside work by Rembrandt since its authenticity was called into question. In Australia we will be able to compare it with undisputed Rembrandts and possibly draw new conclusions. The opportunity to compare it with the *Bust of a Young Jew* from Fort Worth (cat. no. 25) should prove particularly interesting. Not only are the two works related in terms of design, but since

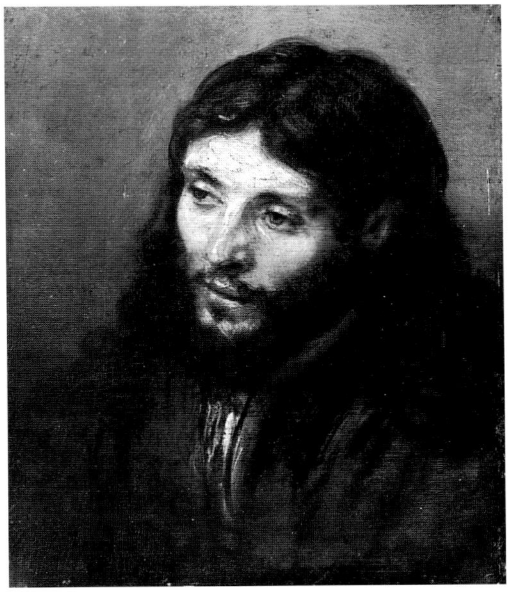

FIG. 31b
(Attributed to) Rembrandt
Head of Christ
Panel
25.0 x 20.0 cm
Staatliche Museen zu Berlin, Gemäldegalerie

about 1925 there has also been a general consensus that Rembrandt's model for this and other *tronies* of Christ was a young Jew. This would explain the curious description in Rembrandt's own inventory, which refers to a '*tronie* of Christ ... from life'.

Slive in 1965 argued that no artist before Rembrandt had based a representation of Christ on a Jewish model.[12] Referring to Rembrandt's heads of Christ, Schwartz cites a poem by the celebrated Jan Vos (1615–1667), on a Christ painted 'after a Jew' by Rembrandt's pupil Govaert Flinck.[13] The gist of the poem is that if Flinck's Christ could talk, he would, as a Jew, denounce Christ. What we learn from the poem, which was undoubtedly meant as a display of wit, is that at least one of Rembrandt's pupils also represented Christ as a Jew. However, not a single one of the heads of Christ until recently accepted as Rembrandts can reasonably be attributed to any of his pupils.

AB/MB

1 Strauss & Van der Meulen 1979, p. 361, no. 1656/12 (nos 115, 118): 'Een Cristi tronie van Rembrant'; 'Cristus tronie van Rembrant'.

2 Strauss & Van der Meulen 1979, p. 383, no. 1656/12 (no. 326): 'Een Cristus tronie nae 't leven'.

3 Hofstede de Groot 1906, no. 350; Bredius 1892, p. 33, no. 56.

4 'Christusbeelt van Rembrant' (Hofstede de Groot 1906a, no. 138; Bredius 1915–22, vol. I, p. 45).

5 Hofstede de Groot 1908–27, vol. VI, 1916, nos 159, 160, 161, 164e, 166, 167; see also Slive 1965. The following eighteenth-century auctions include heads or busts of Christ that can be added to those in Hofstede de Groot and Slive, on the basis of index cards at the RKD. Some of them are described in detail: sale, Willem Wis, Amsterdam, 12 May 1734, lot 173; sale, Brussels, 18 July 1740, lot 254; sale, Coypel, Paris, 27 March 1753, lot 34; sale, Lebrun, Paris, 20 December 1773, lots 14, 16; sale, John Stewart, London, 10 March 1783, lot 33; sale, Tronchin, Paris, 10 February 1785, lot 21bis; sale, London, 7 May 1792, lot 50.

6 Dacier 1911, pp. 18, 29; Slive 1965, p. 414, fig. 11.

7 Bredius / Gerson 1969, nos 620–626; Slive 1965. Gerson and Slive disagree only with regard to no. 626, at the Metropolitan Museum of Art in New York. Gerson considers the work to be autograph, whereas Slive makes no reference to it.

8 Bredius / Gerson 1969, no. 597.

9 Information from Professor Josua Bruyn and Professor Ernst van de Wetering.

10 The piece had hitherto been identified with that in the sale of M. (Lempereur), Paris, 24 May 1773, lot 61, where Christ was said to be portrayed with 'mains croisées' (hands crossed). This is not the case in cat. no. 31.

11 For these and other references and quotations, see Blankert 1991, p. 171, no. 135. The only critical comment is that by Gerson, on the condition of the piece: '[C]ondition ... not good, but the light parts of the face are well preserved' (H. Gerson, in Bredius / Gerson 1969, p. 614, no. 620).

12 Slive 1965.

13 Schwartz 1984, p. 284. The poem was published in 1662. Schwartz also refers to a commentary by Samuel van Hoogstraten – also a pupil of Rembrandt's (see our cat. nos 61, 62) – who explains how Christ should be portrayed (Van Hoogstraten 1678, p. 105).

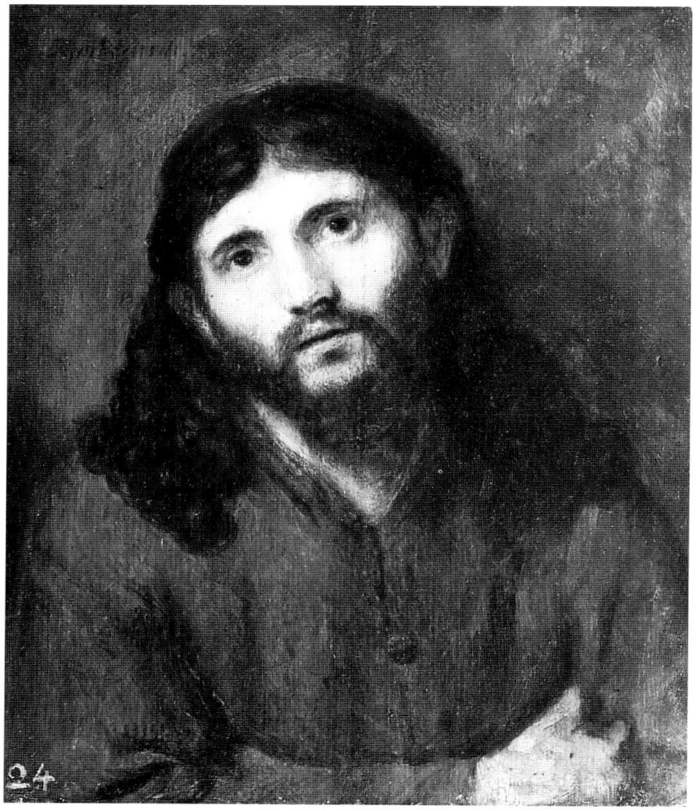

FIG. 31C
(Attributed to) Rembrandt
Bust of Christ
Signed (authentic?)
Panel
24.5 x 21.3 cm
Detroit Institute of Arts
Photograph © 1997 The Detroit Institute of Arts, Founders Society Purchase, Detroit

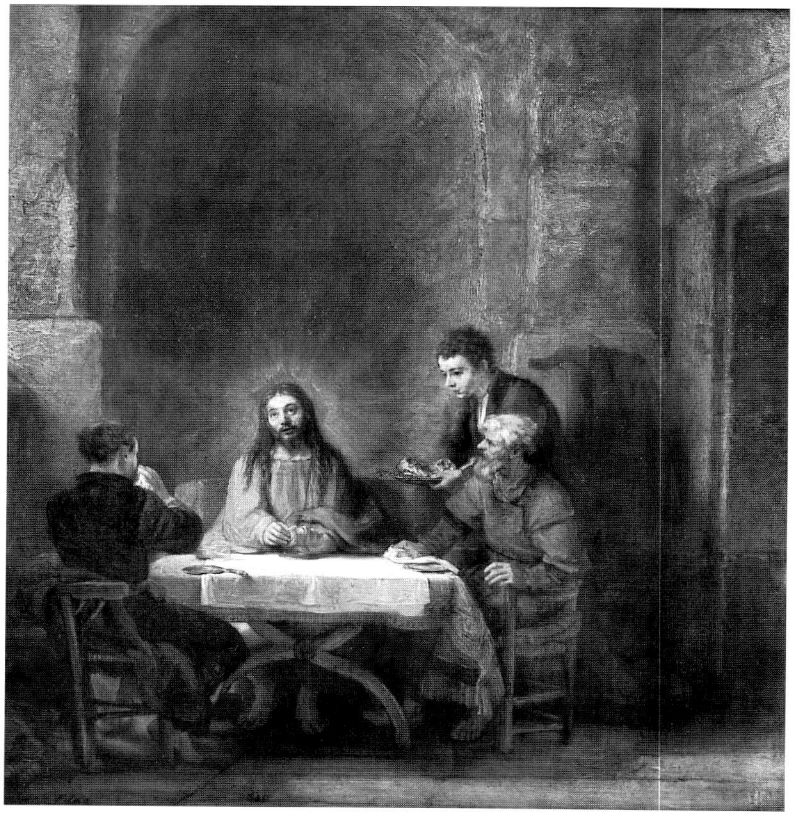

FIG. 31d
Rembrandt
Supper at Emmaus
Signed and dated 1648
Panel
68.0 x 65.0 cm
Musée du Louvre, Paris

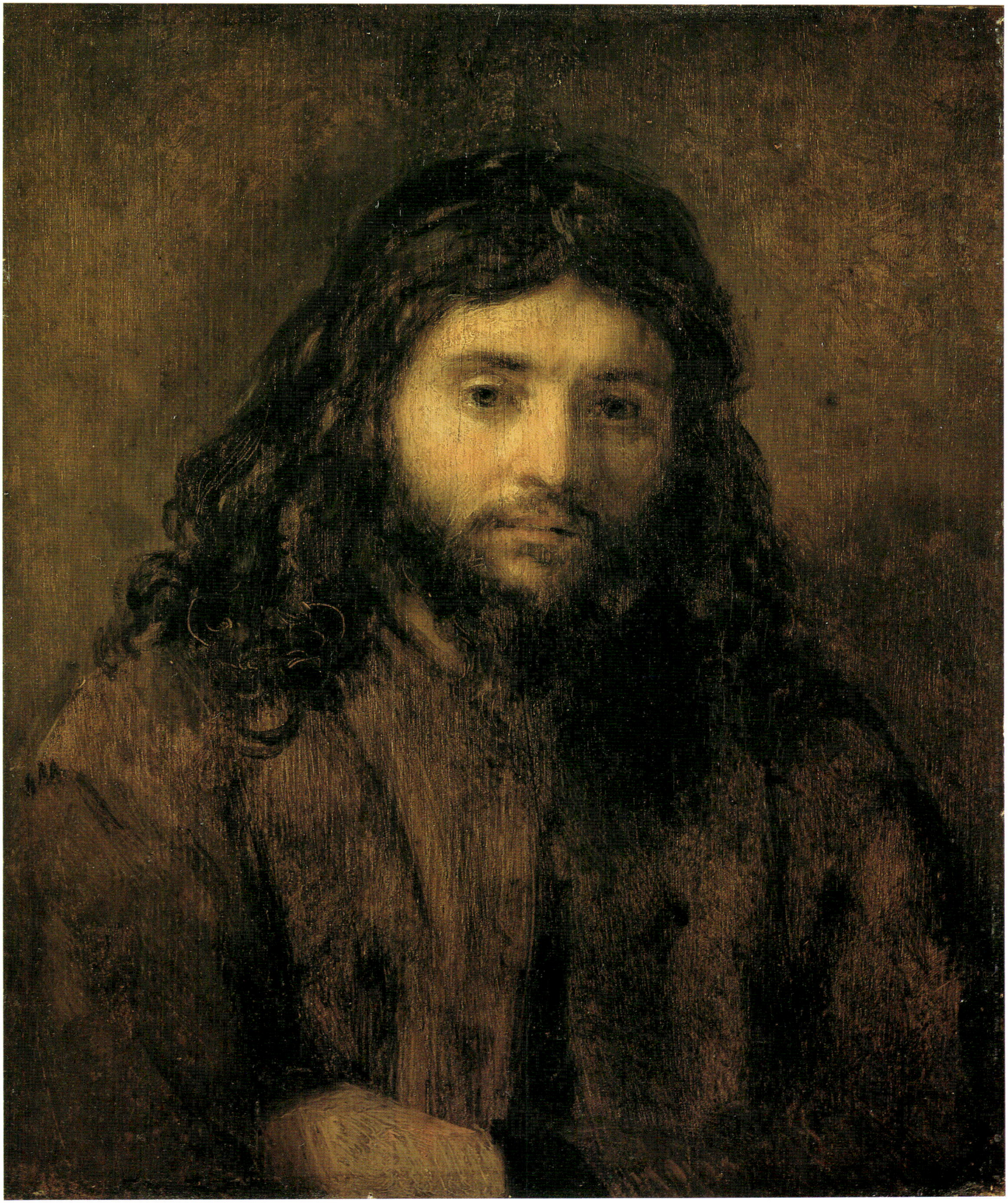

32
Rembrandt?
Man with a Red Cap
*c.*1660

Canvas
102.0 x 80.0 cm
Museum Boijmans Van Beuningen, Rotterdam

PROVENANCE: (Possibly) Sale, J. A. Sichterman, Groningen, 20 August 1764, lot 232; Sir Joshua Reynolds (1723–1792), by 1765; his sale, London (Christie's), 17 March 1795, lot 50, 50 gns; William Hardman, Manchester; his sale, Manchester (Winstanley and Sons), 19 October 1838, lot 52, 46 1/2 gns; sale, Thomas Green, London (Christie's), 20 March 1874, lot 93; sale, Mrs Owen Roe, London, 1889; with dealer Charles Sedelmeyer, Paris; P. C. Hanford, Chicago; with E. Fischof Gallery, New York; with Lord Duveen of Millbank, New York; with dealer D. Katz, Dieren; gift of the Vereniging Rembrandt and 100 Friends of the Museum in 1937.

LITERATURE: Smith 1829–42, vol. VII, 1836, no. 275, suppl. 1842, p. 195, no. 9; Bode & Hofstede de Groot 1897–1906, vol. VII, 1902, no. 526; Von Wurzbach 1906–11, vol. II, 1910, p. 410 (as attr. to C. Fabritius); Hofstede de Groot 1908–27, vol. VI, 1916, p. 127, no. 185; Valentiner 1920, pp. 219–22; Benesch 1935, p. 66; Bredius 1935, no. 618; Bredius / Gerson 1969, p. 613, no. 618; Schwartz 1985, p. 312; Tümpel 1986a, p. 338, no. 89; J. Giltaij & G. Jansen, in Rotterdam 1988, pp. 82–4, cat. no. 26 (with earlier literature).

This painting was always viewed as an autograph Rembrandt, until doubted by Jeroen Giltaij in 1988.[1] Although described by Smith (1836, 1842) simply as a portrait by Rembrandt of a gentleman, painted in a 'free and bravura manner', the subject was repeatedly identified in the nineteenth century as an accountant or clerk, no doubt because of his books, quill pen and robes, and the suggestion of a desk in the immediate foreground. Hofstede de Groot in 1916 first identified him as 'The Evangelist, also known as the Accountant',[2] an idea developed by W. R. Valentiner,[3] and still given credence by some authors today.[4]

In the mid-1650s and throughout the early 1660s, Rembrandt executed a considerable number of half-length figures in historical dress, some with identifying features or attributes, others unidentified. Notwithstanding the fact that these paintings date from different years (the largest group is dated 1661), differ in formats and dimensions, and surely were not all executed by Rembrandt himself, efforts have been made to reassemble a hypothetical series of Apostles and/or Evangelists.[5] Since Rubens had executed a series of twelve half-length apostles, as well as a figure of Christ, for the Duke of Lerma, and many other Baroque artists (including Guido Reni, Hendrick ter Brugghen, Frans Hals and Jan Lievens) had painted series of the Four Evangelists, there was ample precedent for such a project.

Benesch believed Rotterdam's painting depicted St John,[6] but Tümpel[7] agreed with Valentiner (1920)[8] that the figure was St Luke (although he has no ox), linking it with the so-called *Evangelist* or *Sybil* by a Rembrandt follower, at the Museum of Fine Arts, Boston (Bredius 619; identified by Tümpel as St John and by Valentiner as St Mark), and with the *Evangelist Matthew* in the Louvre, Paris (cat. no. 22). On the other hand, Gerson found the entire series notion 'rather unlikely' and others have expressed scepticism (cat. nos 17, 22).[9] Like some other works in the putative series, the present painting is no longer accepted by all as by Rembrandt. Wurzbach doubted it as long ago as 1910, suggesting an implausible reattribution to Carel Fabritius.[10] Tümpel assigned it to Rembrandt's workshop,[11] and a 1988 publication from the Museum Boijmans Van Beuningen reassigns it to the School of Rembrandt, noting 'anomalies in the rendering of the man's face' and weaknesses in the paint application and fall of light.[12] While the Rotterdam painting has not suffered as grievously as Boston's ruinous *Evangelist* mentioned above, Gerson was right to caution the viewer to consider condition in the painting's assessment; the paint film has been pressed in relining and is abraded, especially around the head and hands, and the tonal values and palette are out of balance and register. Some of the original form now lost is visible in William Humphrey's print executed after the painting, when in *c.*1765 it was in the collection of the English painter and art theorist Sir Joshua Reynolds (fig. 32a).[13]

PCS

FIG. 32a
William Humphrey British, 1740–1810
Man with a Red Cap [after cat. no. 32]
Signed and dated 1765
Mezzotint
35.3 x 25.3 cm
Museum Boijmans Van Beuningen, Rotterdam

1 J. Giltaij & G. Jansen, in Rotterdam 1988, p. 82, cat. no. 26.
2 Hofstede de Groot 1908–27, vol. VI, 1916, p. 127, no. 185.
3 Valentiner 1920, pp. 219–22; see also Valentiner 1956, p. 400.
4 For example, Tümpel 1986a, pp. 338–49, no. 89.
5 Bredius / Gerson 1969, nos 614, 615, 616, 616A, 617, 629, 397, 307, 59.
6 Benesch 1935, p. 66.
7 Tümpel 1968, no. 15; Tümpel 1986a, pp. 339, 400, no. 89.
8 Valentiner 1920, pp. 219–22.
9 H. Gerson, in Bredius / Gerson 1969, p. 613, under no. 614; see also J. Giltaij & G. Jansen, in Rotterdam 1988, p. 82, cat. no. 26.
10 Von Wurzbach 1906–11, vol. II, 1910, p. 410.
11 Tümpel 1986a, p. 339, no. 89.
12 J. Giltaij & G. Jansen, in Rotterdam 1988, cat. no. 26.
13 Rotterdam 1988, p. 82.

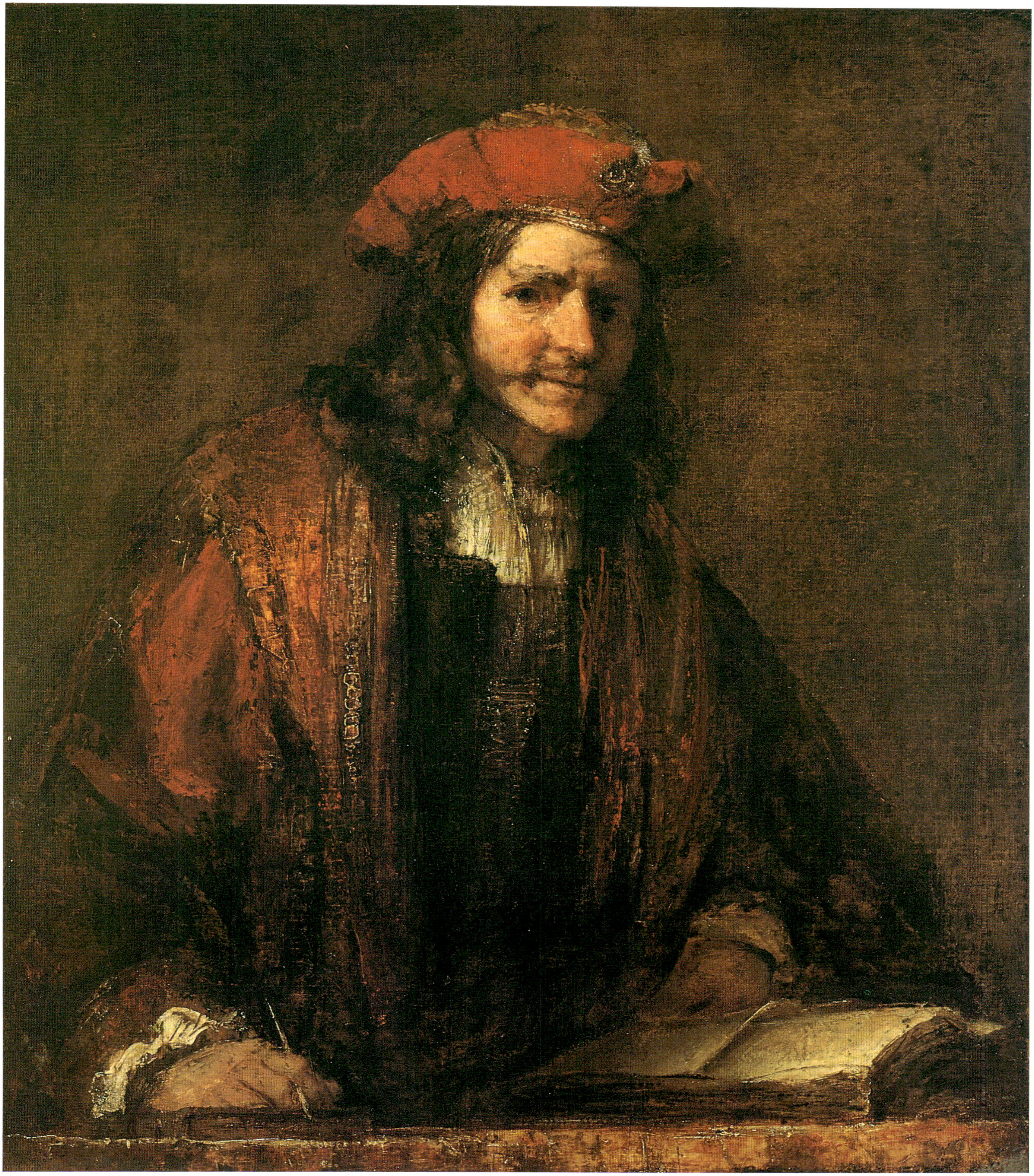

Rembrandt's Impact

ALBERT BLANKERT

Rembrandt occupies his very own place among the Dutch seventeenth-century painters of the human figure. Throughout the years he changed his technique, but his style remained personal and recognizable. For more than a century now a tendency has existed to see in this style a striving for the highest level of individual artistic self-expression. Recently, however, it has been posited that Rembrandt aimed at recognizability for the purpose of being as conspicuous as possible on the art market, almost in the sense of employing a trademark.[1] There is no evidence that either view explains Rembrandt's approach, or was shared by his contemporaries, yet it is certain that Rembrandt's 'manner' was recognized as such in his own time.

Even so, Rembrandt's manner cannot be said to be completely unique. In his Leiden period he and the slightly older Jan Lievens examined each other's work intensely, reacting and responding to each other to such a degree that their works of art show a close resemblance. For this reason, Lievens is represented in the present exhibition by paintings from those years (cat. nos 33–37).

Furthermore, Rembrandt had many pupils to whom he taught his 'manner', as well as followers who attempted to learn and assimilate it by themselves, for a long period subsequent to his death. One of these was the German painter Christian W. E. Dietrich, who, in the 1760s, attempted to make his *Adoration of the Shepherds* appear as much as possible like a Rembrandt (fig. 66a).[2]

It is often difficult to determine just who was a pupil and who was a follower of Rembrandt. In the course of the nineteenth century, an increasing number of seventeenth-century Dutch masters who applied the dramatic chiaroscuro effect were given the label 'pupil of Rembrandt'. John Smith, for instance, in his 1836 list of Rembrandt's pupils, included the Delft painter Leonart Bramer, even though he knew that Bramer (1596–1674) was considerably older than Rembrandt (in seventeenth-century Holland this would have meant a most exceptional circumstance in a master–pupil relationship).[3] In 1983, Ben Broos thoroughly sifted all these alleged pupils. He found that fifty-five featured in the art historical literature. He also discovered that fewer than half of these 'pupils' were documented in early sources.[4] In the present exhibition, Jan Victors and Barend Fabritius are our two examples from this dubious collection. We cannot be sure whether Victors and Fabritius were actually pupils of the master or whether they simply studied Rembrandt's work.

Nevertheless, the number of documented students remains large. Rembrandt was not only highly productive as an artist, but also very effective as a teacher, though there are no preserved works from some of the many pupils mentioned in the early written sources.[5] This is often seen as evidence that our knowledge in this area can only be fragmentary. It is regarded as incidental that many works by some pupils are known, while in the case of other pupils no works are known at all. Yet it should be borne in mind that Rembrandt could not have known beforehand whether a pupil he accepted had talent, let alone whether he would prove productive. More often than not, as is true today, neither quality would emerge. Naturally, Rembrandt was not some sort of power supply able to light up each and every lamp. In this respect, it has been observed that copies after *tronies* by Rembrandt are recorded fairly often in the inventories of the parents of the more obscure pupils. Presumably, these works were produced by these same pupils,[6] and it is interesting to ponder whether these students ever progressed any further. It may well have been the case that, outside their immediate families, nobody cared to preserve their works. This also applies to Rembrandt's own son, Titus, who was himself a painter, and by whom – although he only reached the age of twenty-seven and cannot be expected to have produced a large oeuvre – all we know are three paintings on simple themes that are mentioned as his work in Rembrandt's own inventory.[7]

In the present exhibition, works by only the most talented pupils – individuals who left an oeuvre of quality and importance – are included, and this essay is an attempt to place these works within a wider context. Thus it is important to note that even in his Leiden period it is clear that

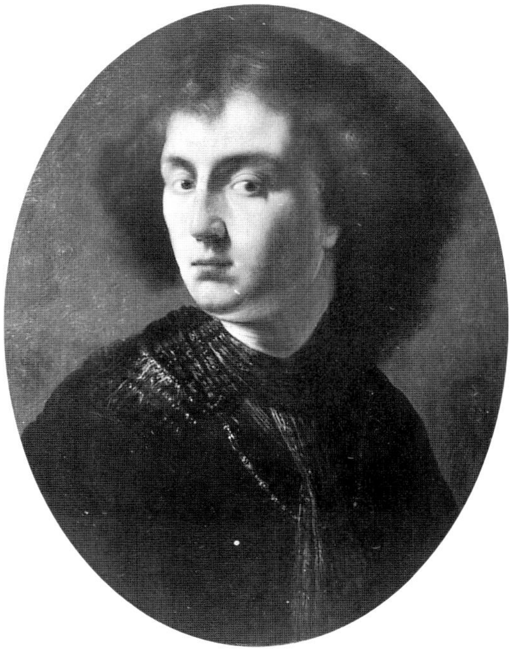

FIG. 1
Isack Jouderville 1612/13–*c.*1645–48
Tronie
Signed
Panel (oval)
48.0 x 36.0 cm
National Gallery of Ireland, Dublin

Rembrandt had talented as well as poorly endowed students. In Leiden, at the close of the 1620s, he took on the first two of his pupils that we know by name: Gerrit Dou and Isack Jouderville. Dou developed Rembrandt's refined technique of that period, as exemplified by *Two Old Men Disputing* (cat. no. 3), into his own speciality, and over a period of forty years achieved enormous success with his exquisite *feinmalerei* (cat. nos 38–40), with his work being much sought after today. In the case of Jouderville, one signed *tronie* by him has been preserved. This is in Rembrandt's style, though in a greatly simplified manner (fig. 1).[8] Ernst van de Wetering has assembled a group of other Rembrandtesque pieces that display similar shortcomings and has attributed these to Jouderville.[9] In these works it seems that Jouderville is still reaching beyond his own capacities, as though still leaning on Rembrandt. Three other signed paintings attest to this, as they are even more primitive, hardly rising above the amateur level.[10] Presumably, they originated later on, when Jouderville had to stand on his own two feet.

In Amsterdam, Rembrandt shared the home of the Mennonite Hendrick Uylenburgh (*c.*1587–1661), who a few years earlier had started out in business as an art dealer. Rembrandt married Uylenburgh's niece Saskia, but the relationship between the two men was also a professional one. In both 1631 and 1640, Rembrandt invested considerable sums of money in Uylenburgh's enterprise.[11] Many years later this business was described as Uylenburgh's 'academy', where he took in young painters and had them make copies 'no less for [their] learning from it than for his own profit'.[12] We also know from the inventory drawn up in 1637 of Uylenburgh's brother in faith, the Frisian painter and Mennonite preacher Lambert Jacobsz, that the latter possessed a Rembrandt and five copies after Rembrandt, including an oriental female *tronie* that was also a portrait of Uylenburgh's wife.[13]

From these intriguing facts it has been deduced that Rembrandt was the first artist-manager of Uylenburgh's business. It is assumed that he not only produced his own work in Uylenburgh's house, but also directed a studio, where pupils and assistants made marketable copies and works in his manner.[14]

In 1639 Rembrandt bought his own house, next to Uylenburgh's (p. 26, fig. 6). He apparently established a similar type of studio there. We learn about this from the account by the German painter Joachim von Sandrart, who lived in Amsterdam between 1637 and 1645 and enjoyed his own success there, primarily as a portrait painter.[15] In his book *Teutsche Akademie* (1675), Sandrart relates:

> Fortune meted him [Rembrandt] out considerable amounts of money, and filled his house in Amsterdam with well-nigh countless distinguished children [*fürnehme Kinder*] for instruction and teaching, each of whom paid him 100 guilders a year, quite apart from the profit he made from these pupils' paintings and prints, which also ran into a sum of 2,000 to 2,500 guilders, together with what he gained from works by his own hand.[16]

Sandrart's words might contain professional jealousy, yet he knew what he was talking about. The annual tuition fee of 100 guilders that he mentions was exactly the sum paid for Jouderville's apprenticeship under Rembrandt.[17]

It has often been thought that Sandrart, in using the term *fürnehme Kinder*, was referring to children from well-to-do families who, as part of a broad education, received drawing lessons; that is to say, that he was referring to amateurs. It has recently come to light, however, that Rembrandt's pupil Ferdinand Bol joined the master's studio when more than twenty years old, in the second half of the 1630s, after having established himself as a painter elsewhere. It is therefore likely that Bol did not come to Rembrandt to learn the trade, but rather Rembrandt's style. His being a fully fledged painter also enabled him to contribute to the production of the studio. That Rembrandt did sell studio works, as Sandrart says, is apparent from notes on such sales (including notes regarding a work by Bol) that he wrote on the back of one of his own drawings.[18] All of this allows the conclusion that fully fledged (or almost so) artists were at work in Rembrandt's studio, creating works in his manner and under his direction, having undoubtedly benefited from prior and expensive training.[19] It seems most probable, then, that Sandrart, in writing of *fürnehme Kinder* in Rembrandt's studio, had this type of person especially in mind.[20]

Subsequently, it has even been suggested that most of Rembrandt's new pupils were such 'graduates' or even 'postgraduates'.[21] Those in this category were therefore 'pre-selected' more than Jouderville was.[22] One such pre-selected pupil was Govaert Flinck. Flinck's Mennonite parents first apprenticed him to the preacher-painter Lambert Jacobsz in Friesland. This apprenticeship continued until, according to Houbraken, Flinck was able to 'fly on his own', which may have been around 1633. Houbraken states:

> As at that time, the manner of Rembrandt was generally praised, so that for pleasing the world everything had to be in that manner, [so] he [Flinck] followed the advice to learn with Rembrandt for a year. Thus he got used to and adapted to that treatment of colours and manner of painting, which in that short timespan he became so adept in imitating, that some of his works were viewed and sold as authentic works by Rembrandt.[23]

Houbraken relates a similar story about other students' work being taken for Rembrandts.[24]

There is therefore ample evidence available for us to attribute to these advanced studio pupils paintings that, after close study, appear to be below the standard of, or not sufficiently characteristic of, Rembrandt. Indeed, this is what in fact has happened to many paintings, for example the *Departure of the Shunamite Woman* (cat. no. 30). The piece used to be known as a Rembrandt, but in the Rembrandt *Corpus* it is now described as a studio piece, dating from 1640 and attributed to Ferdinand Bol. The present exhibition includes some typical, signed Bols, painted after Bol had re-established himself as an independent master in 1641. In the works of this latter period he is still greatly influenced by Rembrandt, yet at the same time shows himself to be an excellent painter in his own right, particularly adept at suggesting an elegiac atmosphere and marvellous in the handling of detail (cat. nos 44, 45).

My prediction is that, when seen next to these Bols in the exhibition, the *Departure of the Shunamite Woman* will not appear to be by the same hand. If it is neither a Bol, nor an authentic Rembrandt, but a studio piece, Rembrandt's own masterful inventiveness is still so pervasive in this work that it is quite likely that it will prove impossible to identify the hand that executed it. That Bol lacked this degree of inventiveness is apparent from his monumental *Rest on the Flight into Egypt* of 1644 (fig. 2). Here he assembled three lifesized full-length figures into an excellently balanced composition. Yet to achieve this he had to borrow the whole group (in reverse) from a tiny etching by Rembrandt – and, moreover, copied the figures of Mary and Child from Rembrandt's *Holy Family* (figs 3, 4).[25] As for the *Departure of the Shunamite Woman*, Bol certainly did not invent its composition (see commentary to cat. no. 30).

In Flinck's case, too, even the most Rembrandtesque works that he

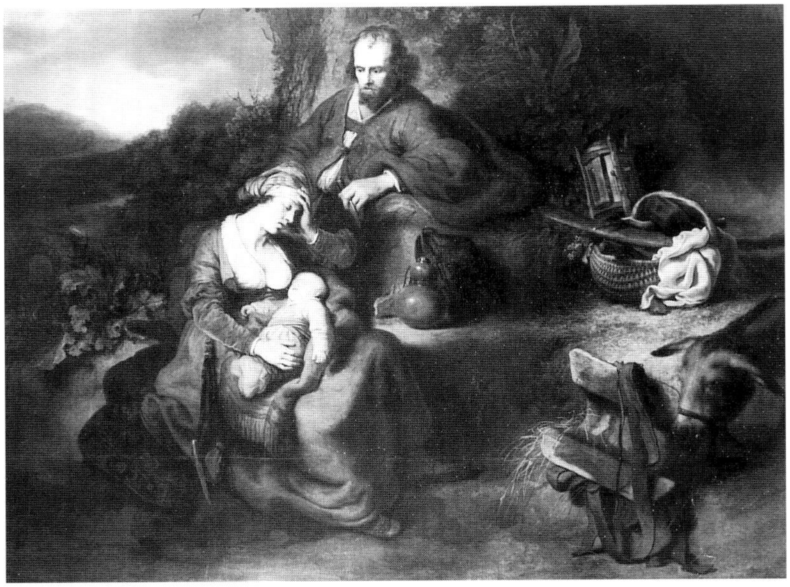

FIG. 2
Ferdinand Bol
The Rest on the Flight into Egypt
Signed and dated 1644
Canvas
203.0 x 261.0 cm
Staatliche Kunstsammlungen Dresden,
Gemäldegalerie Alte Meister

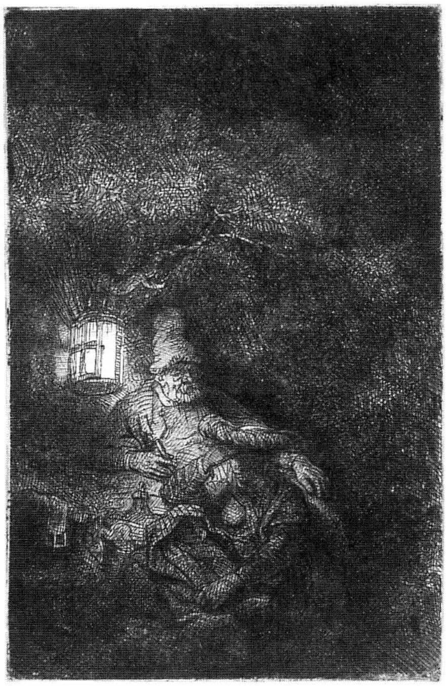

FIG. 3
Rembrandt
The Rest on the Flight into Egypt c.1644
Etching
9.2 x 5.9 cm
Rijksprentenkabinet, Rijksmuseum, Amsterdam
(actual size)

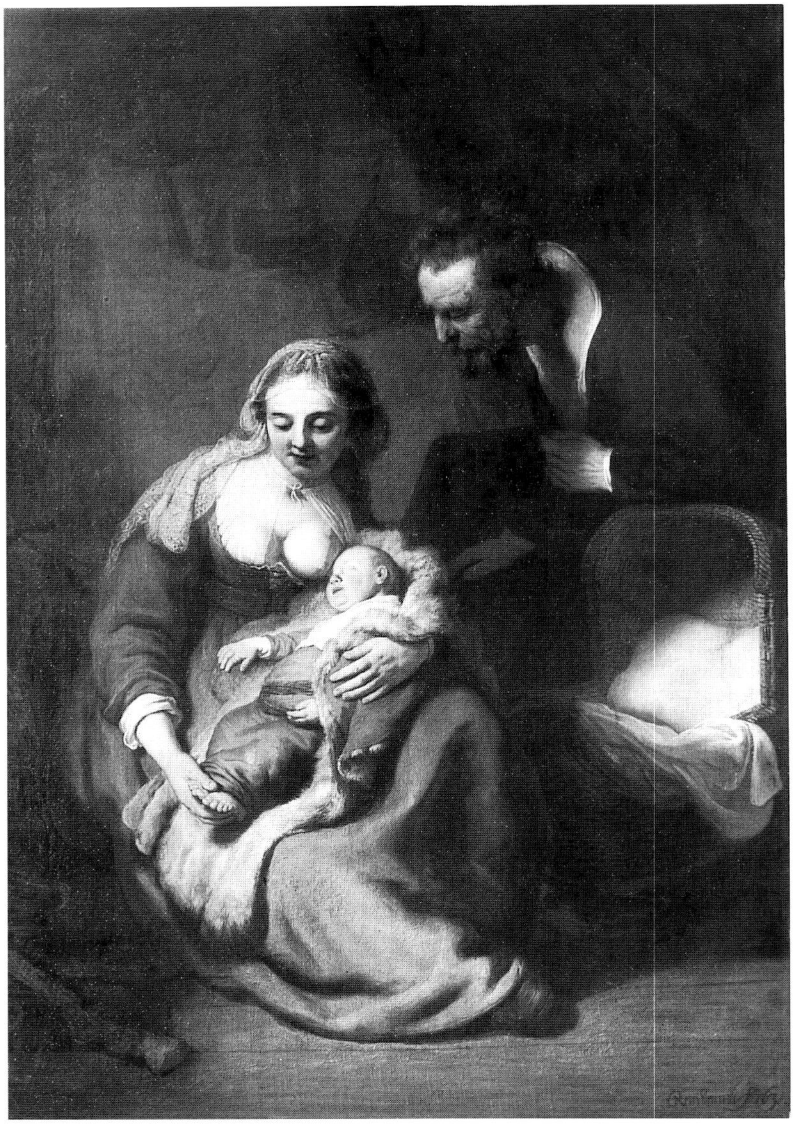

FIG. 4
Rembrandt
The Holy Family
Signed and dated 163[?]
Canvas
195.0 x 132.0 cm
Alte Pinakothek, Munich

signed himself clearly possess the characteristics of his personal style. They display decorative calligraphic outlines that also remained typical of his late works (fig. 7). Flinck's *Lamentation* of 1637 (fig. 5), his earliest signed and dated history painting, illustrates the point. (In that same year, Flinck was living with Hendrick Uylenburgh,[26] where he may well have succeeded Rembrandt as head of the studio in Uylenburgh's house.)[27] Such elegance is not in evidence in the work of Rembrandt himself, as can be clearly seen if a comparison is made with a Rembrandt of the same subject and from the same period (fig. 6).[28]

Totally different in character from the highly Rembrandtesque Flinck, from any work by Bol, or from that of any other pupil whose work has been identified, is the *Finding of Moses* in the present exhibition (cat. no. 29). This is another 'ex-Rembrandt', which is presently viewed as a studio piece, though not attributed to any particular pupil. In this work, four women display their surprise and interest in the baby they have found, each in a very different – but all in a most lively – manner. They simultaneously listen to their principal, Pharaoh's daughter, behind whom is a black servant, who places a mantle on her shoulders. A fifth woman has also become curious, and wades towards the others, carefully feeling for solid ground beneath her feet. In this work, too, the design must surely be Rembrandt's. The present exhibition may reveal how the execution of the *Finding of Moses* compares with that of the master. Rembrandt's stamp is so strongly present in this work that any other hand that may have executed it will undoubtedly be difficult to recognize.

It seems quite possible that for works like the *Departure of the Shunamite Woman* or the *Finding of Moses* Rembrandt provided the concept, while an assistant painted the piece under direct supervision – and in such close co-operation that the product could be viewed as an authentic work by Rembrandt, with the person who did in fact apply the paint remaining unknown. This idea of the concept being provided by Rembrandt and executed by an assistant has repeatedly been proposed. More often than not it has been dismissed, most recently in the *Corpus*.[29] Other, later works can also be considered as possible products of this process (cat. nos 31, 32). Too often and too easily, works from Rembrandt's school are labelled with the name of a particular student.[30] In the recent exhibition *Rembrandt: The Master and His Workshop*, of the many attempted new attributions to pupils, very few were convincing.[31] Barend Fabritius was one of those proposed as an author of ex-Rembrandts, works that he supposedly produced in Rembrandt's studio.[32] However, his stay with Rembrandt is, as already noted, no more than a hypothesis.

Following these problematic pieces (cat. nos 29–32), the exhibition presents works definitely produced by specific pupils or followers, nearly all of which form part of the kernel of these painters' oeuvres. To any person familiar with Rembrandt's school the authorship of these works is readily recognizable, as, for example, in the case of van den Eeckhout or de Gelder.

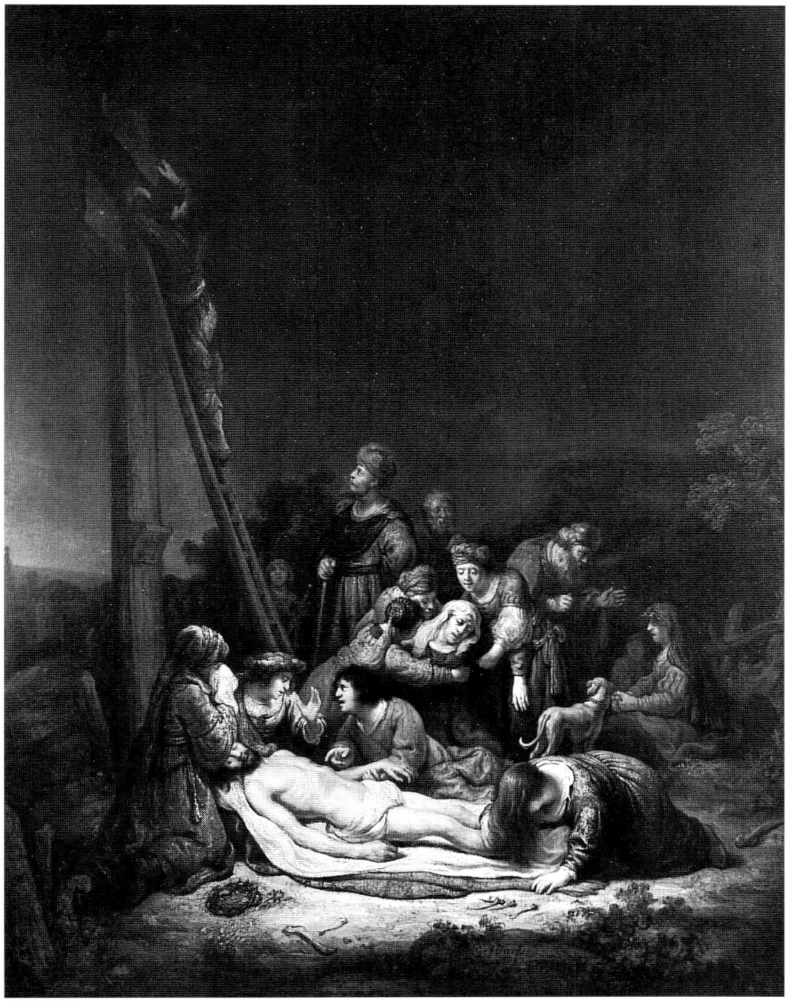

FIG. 5
Govaert Flinck
Lamentation of Christ
Signed and dated 1637
Canvas
89.5 x 71.5 cm
Present whereabouts unknown
Photograph: RKD

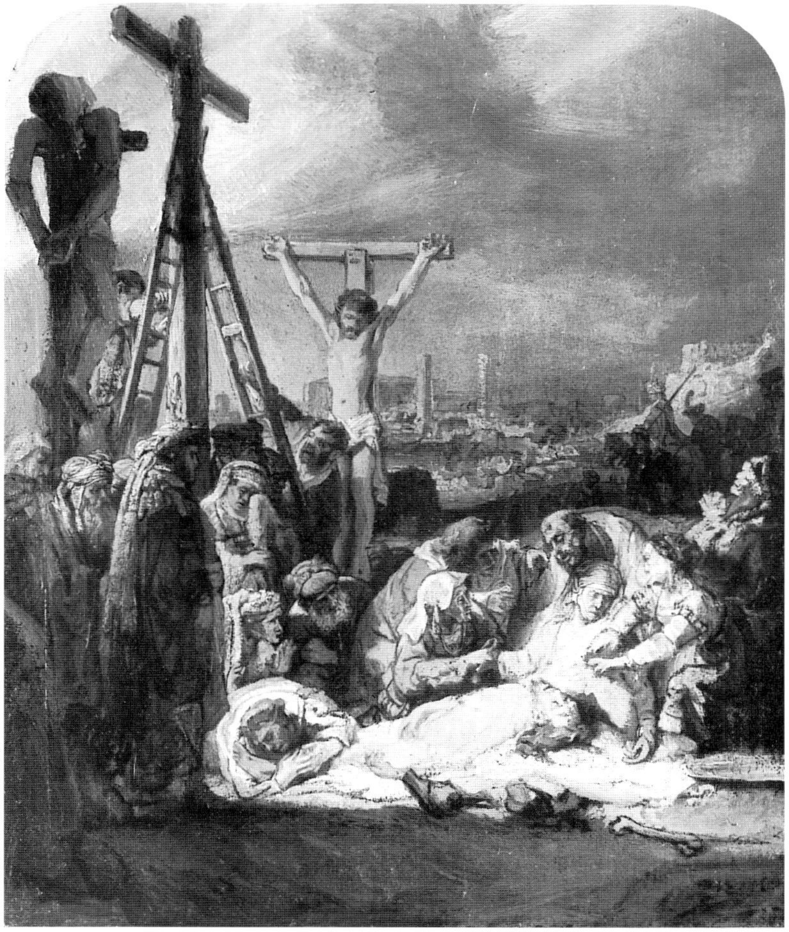

FIG. 6
Rembrandt
Lamentation
Canvas on panel
31.9 x 26.7 cm
The Trustees of the National Gallery, London

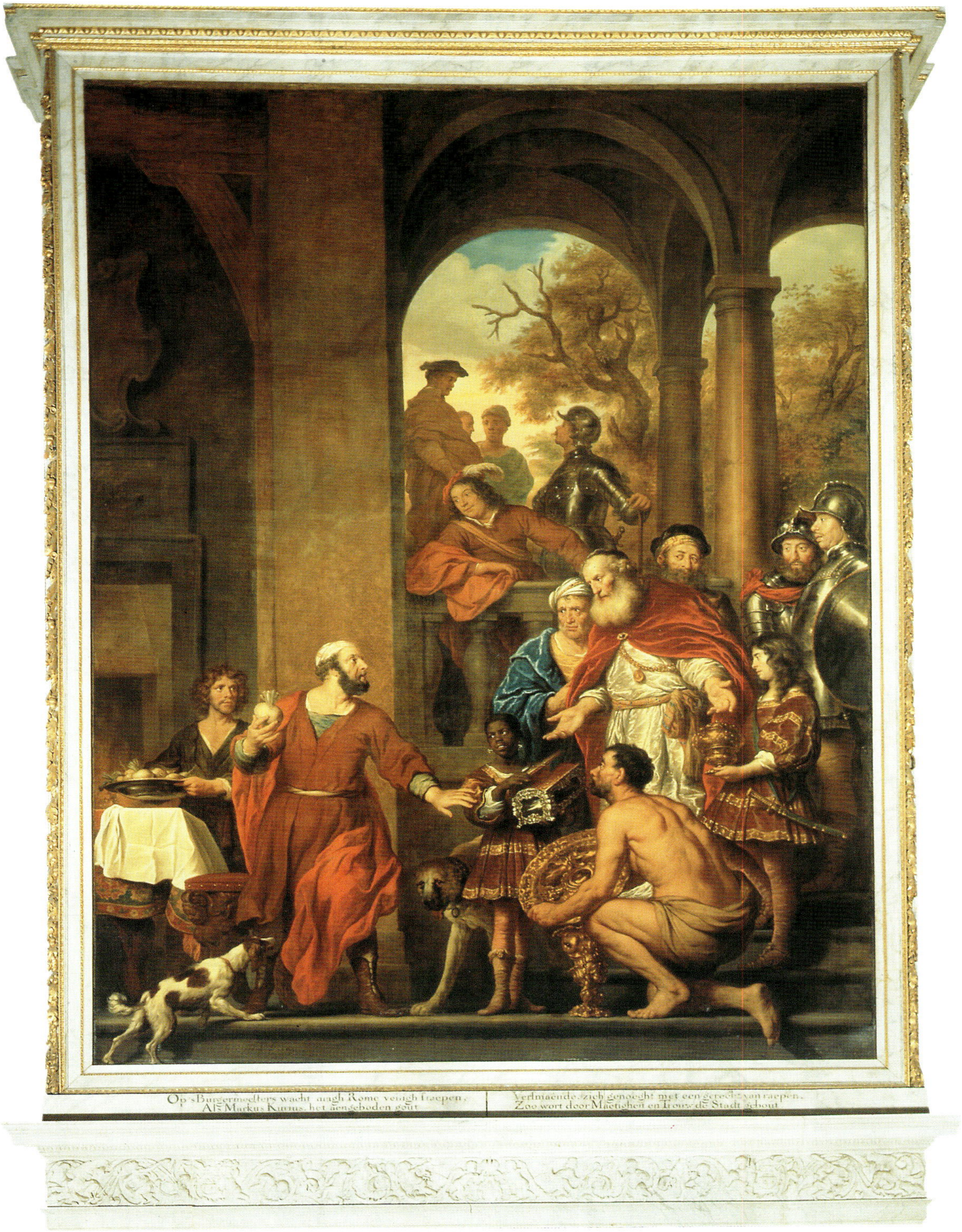

FIG. 7
Govaert Flinck
Consul Marcus Curius Dentatus Prefers Eating His Turnips to the Presents of the Samnites
Signed and dated 1656
Canvas
485.0 x 377.0 cm
Royal Palace, Amsterdam (formerly the Amsterdam Town Hall)
Stichting Koninklijk Paleis Amsterdam

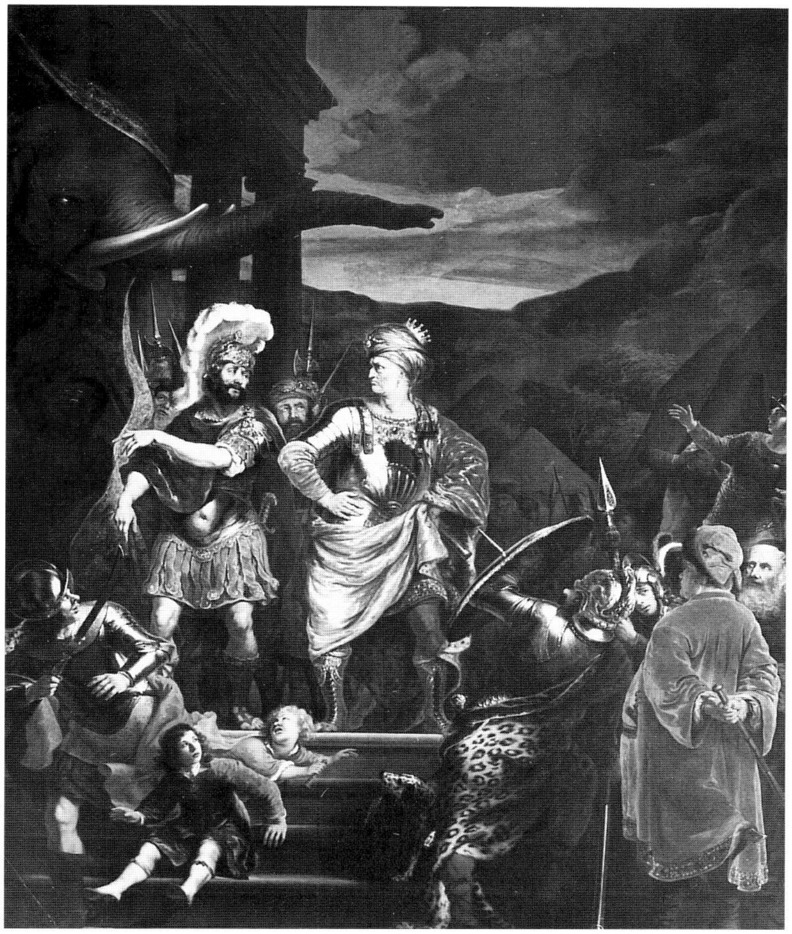

FIG. 8
Ferdinand Bol
Consul Fabritius Remains Unperturbed by the Trumpeting of the Elephant of King Pyrrhus
Signed and dated 1656
Canvas
485.0 x 350.0 cm
Royal Palace, Amsterdam (formerly the Amsterdam Town Hall)
Stichting Koninklijk Paleis Amsterdam

First and foremost the aim has been to assemble Rembrandtesque works by these pupils, so another phenomenon needs its own discussion here.

Houbraken wrote of Govaert Flinck, and of the much younger Samuel van Hoogstraten and Nicolaes Maes, that they first followed the style of their teacher Rembrandt but later abandoned it. For Flinck this would have involved a very great effort, but he felt it to be necessary when 'painting in the clear manner came back into fashion'.[33] Maes made this move primarily because he chose portraiture as his subject: 'He observed very well that the young ladies, especially, greatly prefer white to brown'.[34] The painter Jan de Baen (1633–1702), who was not a pupil of Rembrandt, was long undecided in his youth about whether to choose the manner of Anthony van Dyck or that of Rembrandt, as both were in high esteem at the time. He finally chose the manner of van Dyck because he decided it was 'of a more enduring nature'.[35]

In short, Rembrandt's manner went out of fashion, at least with Amsterdam's leading circles. This is confirmed by the later works of Flinck, Bol, Hoogstraten and Maes. Flinck was regarded in his later years, and from as far away as Italy, as the best master in Amsterdam.[36] He also received the most important commissions for the decoration of the vast new Amsterdam Town Hall. In his Town Hall chimney-piece, *Consul Marcus Curius Dentatus Prefers Eating His Turnips to the Presents of the Samnites*, 1656, bright and variegated colours replace his earlier Rembrandtesque chiaroscuro (fig. 7). From the top centre, figures flow downwards, via a stairway, until they occupy the full width of the foreground below. The effect, Flemish-Rubenesque, is also due to the 'correct antique' attire of the figures and to their dashing poses. According to various sources, Flinck learned a lot in this respect from a journey to Flanders and, especially, from a visit to Antwerp.[37]

The chimney-piece opposite in the same room is in the same style. This is Ferdinand Bol's *Consul Fabritius Remains Unperturbed by the Trumpeting of the Elephant of King Pyrrhus* (fig. 8). The preliminary studies for this piece reveal how much effort it took Bol to adapt to the new style. It appears that he must have been instructed to improve his composition. In his very first sketch, all the figures stand together in a line, an unsuitable arrangement for adequately filling the almost five-metre-high picture plane (fig. 9). In the final painting, Bol placed these figures one above the other, on a stairway as Flinck had done. In Bol's sketch the figures wear fantastic, Rembrandtesque costumes. In the painting they wear 'genuine' Roman armour and robes derived from Roman reliefs. And in the sketch both of the main figures stand stiffly, in a manner that contrasts with their swaying *contrapposto* poses in the painting. In the painting, calm deliberation is contrasted with the panic seen as members of the retinue, one of whom seeks cover behind his shield, flee from the elephant. Flinck's and Bol's new style in these paintings for the Amsterdam Town Hall might be called 'baroque-classicist'. These former pupils of Rembrandt became the leading masters of this style.

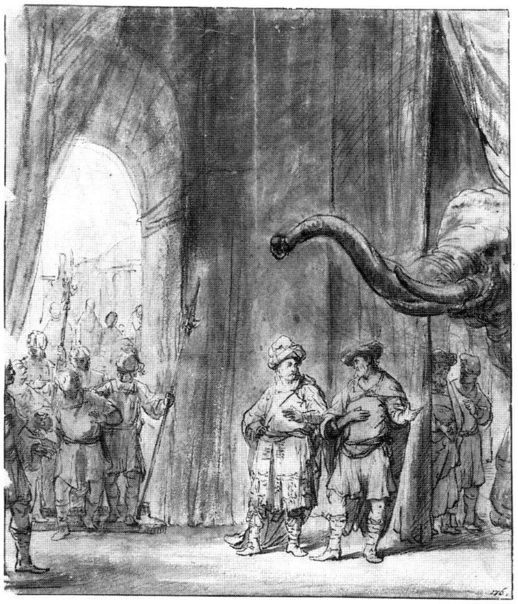

FIG. 9
Ferdinand Bol
Design for *Consul Fabritius* [fig. 8]
Pen and ink and brush
61.7 x 46.1 cm
Staatliche Graphische Sammlung, Munich

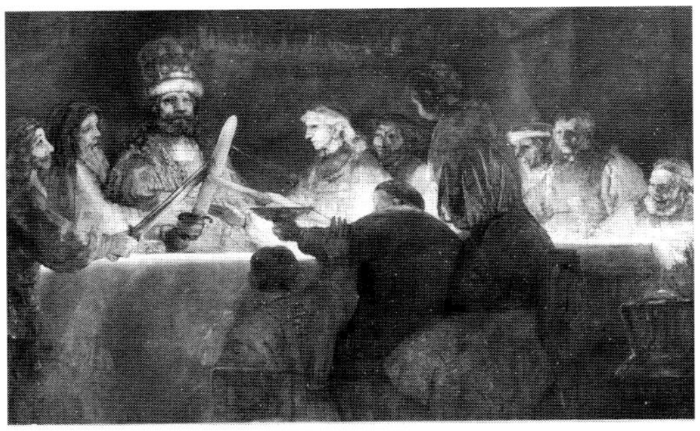

FIG. 10
Rembrandt
The Conspiracy of the Batavians under Claudius Civilis in the Schakerbos
Canvas (fragment)
196.0 x 309.0 cm
Nationalmuseum, Stockholm
Photograph: Nationalmuseum, SKM, Stockholm
(for colour reproduction, see p. 27, fig. 9)

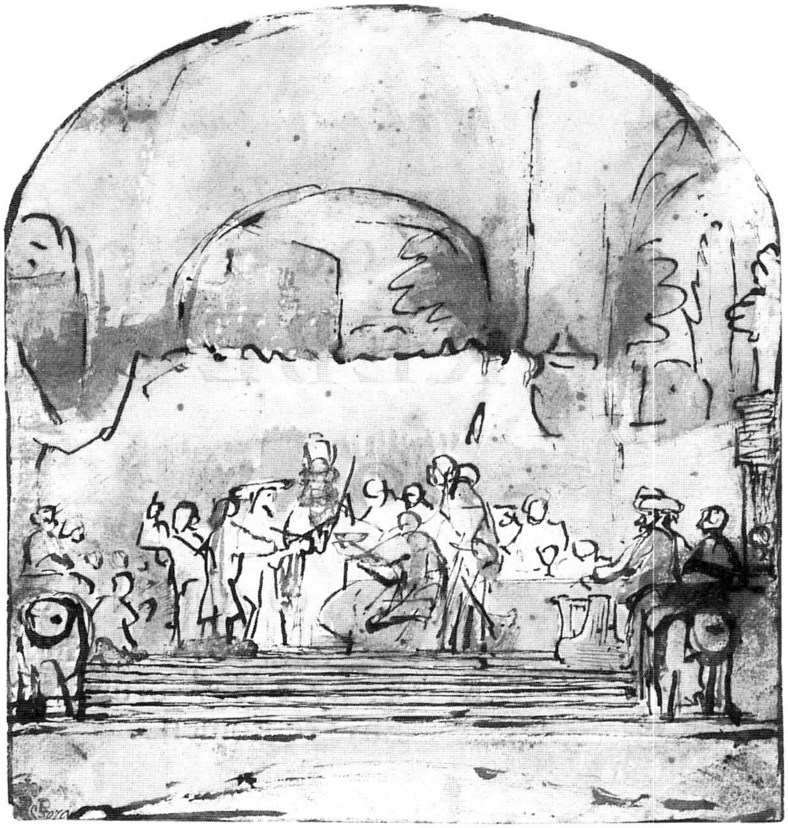

FIG. 11
Rembrandt
Sketch for *The Conspiracy of the Batavians* [fig. 10]
Pen and ink and brush
19.6 x 18.0 cm
Staatliche Graphische Sammlung, Munich

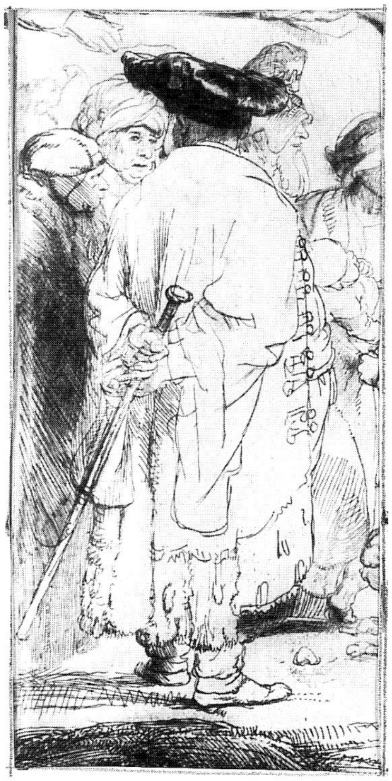

FIG. 12
Rembrandt
The Hundred Guilder Print finished *c.*1649 (detail)
Etching, drypoint and burin
National Gallery of Victoria, Melbourne; purchased 1891
(our cat. no. 111)

Rembrandt's own *Conspiracy of the Batavians under Claudius Civilis* was also produced for the new Town Hall, but was removed immediately after it had been installed. Only the fragmentary central section has been preserved (fig. 10), yet we know how the entire painting appeared, from Rembrandt's sketch for it (fig. 11). The removal of the painting becomes understandable when we realize that in most respects the piece more closely resembled Bol's first unsuitable sketch for his major Town Hall work than it did his finished painting *Fabritius and Pyrrhus*. Unlike Bol, Rembrandt did not conform to the demands of the 'baroque-classicist' style.[38] His figures fill only a small section of the picture plane, wear fancy costumes, and are not depicted in *contrapposto* poses.

In the Bol painting (fig. 8), however, we find one remnant of Rembrandt. The male figure on the right, who observes the turbulent events with his hands behind his back, clenching his cane, is taken from Rembrandt's *Hundred Guilder Print* (cat. no. 111). In that etching the comparable figure stands at the far left (fig. 12).

In this same period, the 1650s, the younger pupils – those who joined Rembrandt's studio after 1640 – remained far more outspokenly Rembrandtesque for some time. Examples are Willem Drost in his *Bearded Man in a Broad-Brimmed Hat*, *c.*1654, and Nicolaes Maes in his *Sacrifice of Isaac*, *c.*1653–54, and *Adoration of the Shepherds*, 1658 (cat. nos 63, 64, 66). Nonetheless, during the same period Maes began exploring a new area, in the form of genre pieces with contemporary

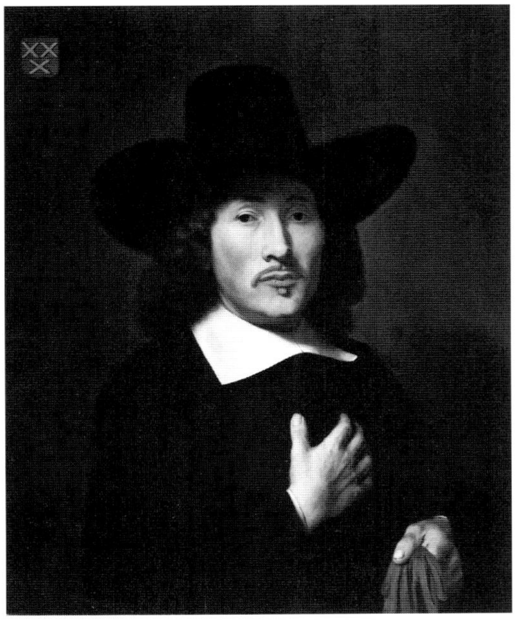

FIG. 13
Nicolaes Maes
Portrait of a Member of the van Zijdewint Family
Signed and dated 1656
Canvas
74.3 x 60.3 cm
Fine Arts Museums of San Francisco
Mildred Anna Williams Collection, 1942.5

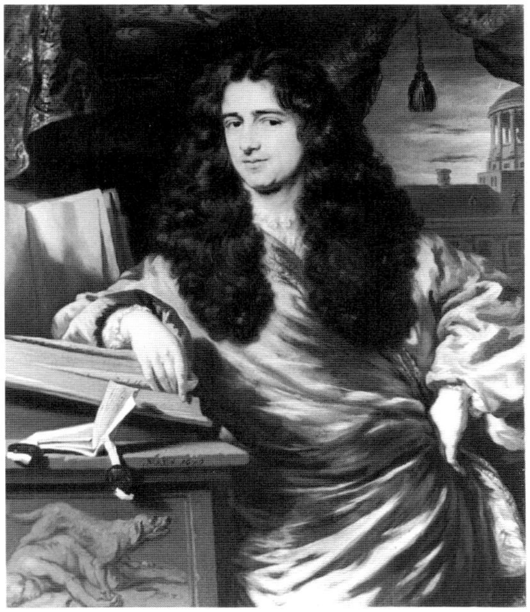

FIG. 14
Nicolaes Maes
Portrait of Cornelis Munter(?) with, in the Background, the New Amsterdam Town Hall
Signed and dated 1679
Canvas
56.0 x 47.5 cm
Amsterdam Historical Museum

figures in domestic environments, such as *Lovers, with a Young Woman Listening* (cat. no. 65). With Rembrandt, subject matter comparable to this can be found only in drawings (cat. nos 82, 95). As a portrait painter, Maes at that time was sober and prosaic. In 1656, the same year that Flinck and Bol executed their ambitious chimney-pieces for the Amsterdam Town Hall, Maes painted his *Portrait of a Member of the van Zijdewint Family*, which by comparison looks provincial (fig. 13). (Influences in this painting have been sourced to a particular art tradition in Dordrecht, Maes's city of origin, where he had by this time returned.)[39] Maes's subsequent portraits of *Jacob Trip* and his wife *Margaretha de Geer* are equally sober and straightforward in character (cat. nos 67, 68). It is most surprising that it was this same Maes, whose figures had always appeared a little wooden, who later emerged as the pre-eminent painter of the swaying and Flemish-style elegantly draped figures, in *contrapposto* poses, that appear in his later portraits (fig. 14).[40]

With Samuel van Hoogstraten, another pupil from Dordrecht, we see a comparable development. Hoogstraten began as a full-blooded Rembrandtist, as, for example, in the *Adoration of the Shepherds* (cat. no. 61). Later, he changed direction and created the *trompe l'oeil* type of still life seen in his *Still Life on a Cupboard Door*, 1655 (cat. no. 62). By arranging a small number of very shallow objects flatly, one on top of the other, within the pictorial space, he created an unprecedented illusion of reality. With this type of painting Hoogstraten began a tradition that was practised for centuries. It flowered, for instance, in American painting of the nineteenth century (fig. 15). Later, Hoogstraten, like Maes, specialized in genre scenes, but also made an occasional delicately painted classicist history painting (fig. 16).[41] It must have been when making such works that he most regretted that the models he had learned to draw from when

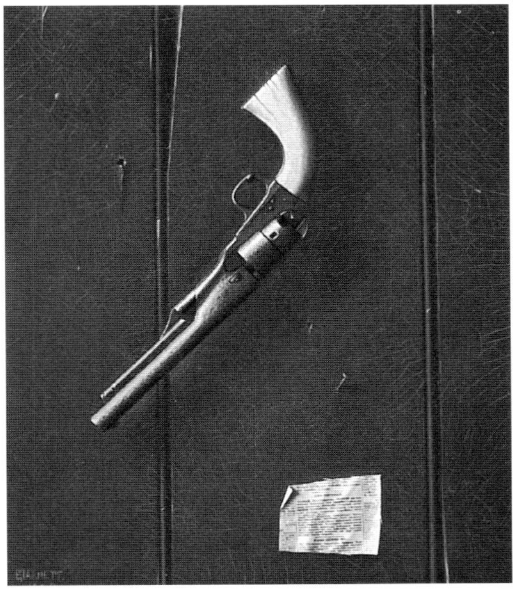

FIG. 15
W. H. Harnett American, 1848–1892
The Faithful Colt
Signed and dated 1890
Canvas
58.0 x 48.0 cm
Wadsworth Atheneum, Hartford
The Ella Gallup Sumner and Mary Catlin Sumner Collection Fund

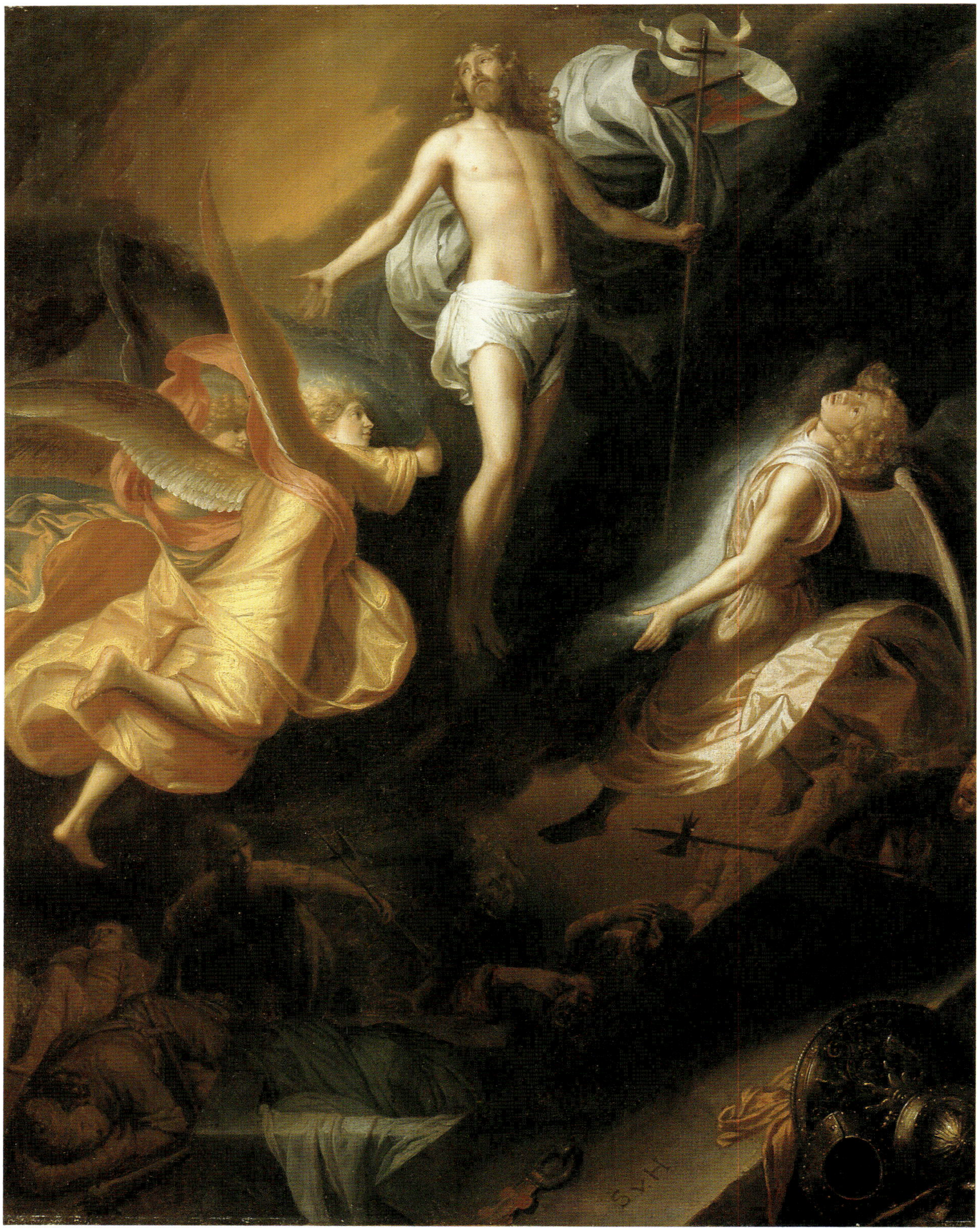

FIG. 16
Samuel van Hoogstraten
The Resurrection of Christ c.1670
Monogrammed
Canvas
78.7 x 63.2 cm
Sophia P. Morton Purchase Fund, 1969.110.
The Art Institute of Chicago

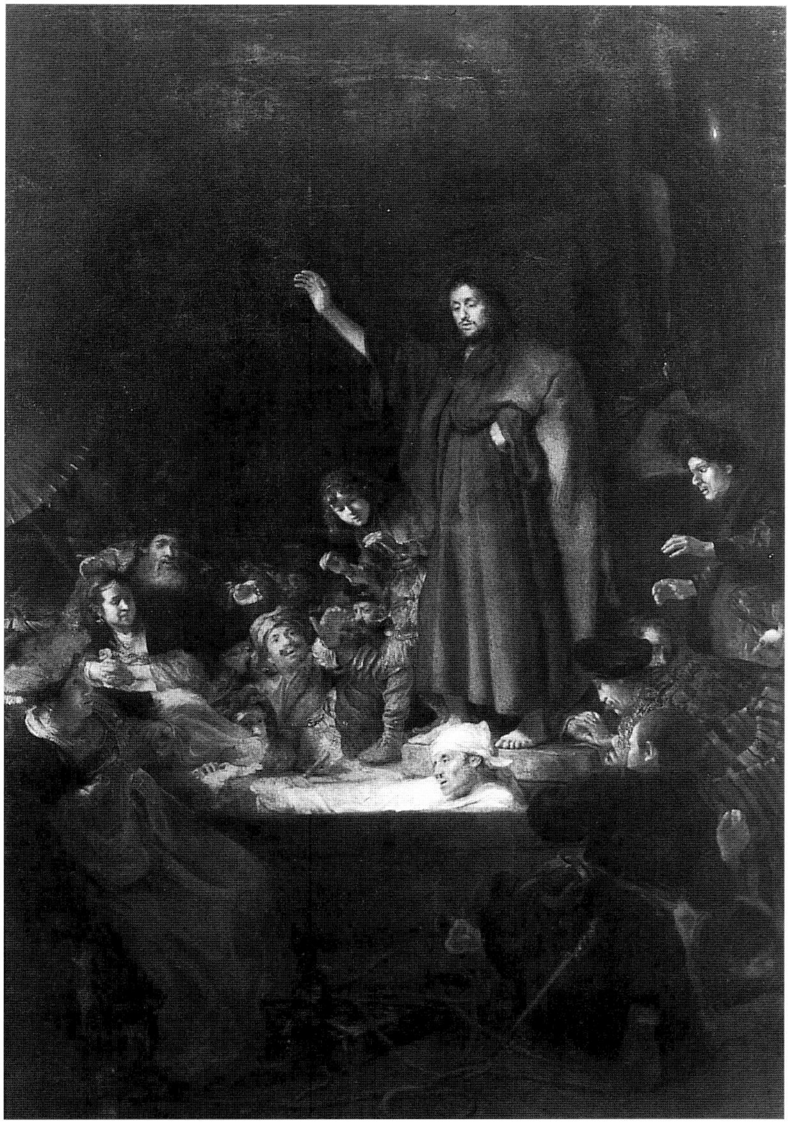

FIG. 17
Carel Fabritius
The Raising of Lazarus c.1642–43
Signed
Canvas
210.5 x 140.0 cm
Muzeum Narodowe, Warsaw

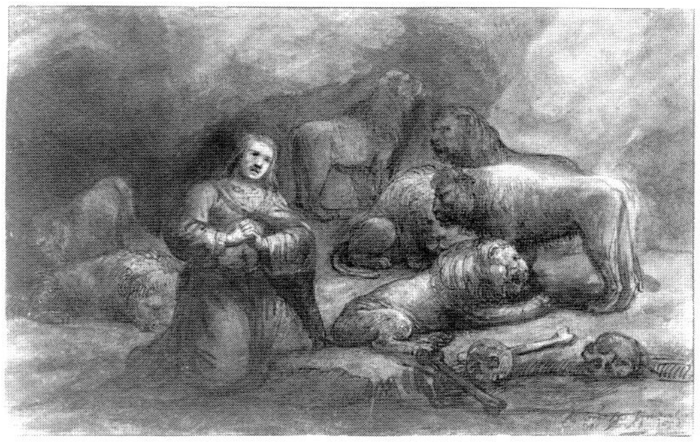

FIG. 18
Constantijn Daniël van Renesse 1626–1680
Daniel in the Lions' Den
Signed and dated 1652
Inscribed on verso [in Dutch]: 'C. A. Renesse, the first drawing shown to Rembrandt in the year 1649, on 1 October, it was the second time that I was at Rembrandt's'
Pen and ink and brush
20.6 x 32.0 cm
Museum Boijmans Van Beuningen, Rotterdam
(see also fig. 86b)

he was Rembrandt's apprentice had lacked in elegance (see p. 40).

A similar and comparable development can be discerned with Carel Fabritius, perhaps the greatest talent among all of Rembrandt's pupils, even though he died when only thirty-two years of age (only eight of his works have been preserved). Fabritius's early work *The Raising of Lazarus* is wholly Rembrandtesque (fig. 17), and can be compared to Jan Lievens's earlier treatment of the same theme (cat. no. 37). In the 1650s, Fabritius, like Hoogstraten, experimented with illusionistic effects, and also with the brightest representations of daylight (cat. no. 57). The work of his younger brother Barend Fabritius bears a resemblance (cat. no. 58) to that of Carel, but the charm of Barend's work lies mostly in its occasional and almost primitive naïveté (cat. nos 58, 59).

During the 1640s, Rembrandt's name still had such resonance that foreign students, too, came to his studio. Among these were Bernard Keil from Denmark and Jurriaen Ovens and Christoph Paudiss from Germany. Upon later returning to Germany, Paudiss practised an idiosyncratic Rembrandtism in the form of figure pieces, but was at his best in his small number of still lifes (see cat. no. 60 and fig. 60a).

Of the students of that generation, only Gerbrand van den Eeckhout remained faithful to Rembrandt's style during his entire painting life. Van den Eeckhout was an excellent teller of lively and colourful stories inspired by Rembrandt's etchings of the 1630s. He also worked irregularly with Rembrandt's chiaroscuro palette. Rembrandt's teacher Pieter Lastman was often a source of inspiration in van den Eeckhout's work (cat. no. 53). Lastman also had a significant influence upon Jan Victors. Victors's robust style approaches an amalgam of what he had observed in both Lastman and Rembrandt.

Rembrandt did in fact also teach amateurs. This is evident from the case of Constantijn van Renesse (1626–1680), a member of a prominent family and secretary of the town of Eindhoven. Van Renesse painted and drew as a hobby. On various sheets he proudly noted exactly when he had shown them to Rembrandt (fig. 18).[42] The clumsy angel upon which Rembrandt based his own visionary *Annunciation* is attributed to van Renesse, whose primitive attempt Rembrandt transformed into his own masterpiece (p. 325, fig. 5).

The large number of late paintings presently assumed to have been made in 'Rembrandt's studio' obliges us to suppose that in his later years, too, the master still had numerous assistants and pupils (cat. no. 32). It is difficult, however, to imagine that during his last eleven years, after the sale of his property, he still had a large studio running where these pieces could be produced. By this time he was living in modest housing in a lower-class neighbourhood, his production being officially directed by his mistress, the ex-servant Hendrickje Stoffels, and by his young son Titus. That this business had a large number of workers is hard to imagine under such circumstances, so just how these many late studio pieces originated is most puzzling.

Rembrandt found a late and faithful follower in Arent de Gelder, who became his pupil after an apprenticeship with Hoogstraten. De Gelder continued Rembrandt's late, broad style until well into the eighteenth century. He even extended its expressive effects and developed a very personal, often lyrical, palette (cat. nos 69–71).

In 1915 Hofstede de Groot described Rembrandt's teaching as the way in which he 'made his own ideas on art live on'.[43] Later, it became customary to maintain that Rembrandt aimed above all to have his students develop their own personalities.[44] This idea has recently met with the comment that his studio was organized in accordance with the traditional rules and goals associated with the guild of painters: the teaching of skills, and art production.[45] Nevertheless, the statements made and stories told about Rembrandt, and his studio, since his death prove very clearly – in fact prove incontrovertibly – that Rembrandt made a unique impression on those who came to work with him.[46] One of the most valuable outcomes of the present exhibition may well be tangible evidence that not only were many great talents profoundly inspired by Rembrandt, but that his openness to fostering the individual capabilities of these painters ultimately allowed each to find his own way.

1 Alpers 1988. The present chapter, 'Rembrandt's Impact', was translated into English by its author.

2 Cf. Gerson 1942, p. 305.

3 Smith 1829–42, vol. VII, 1836, p. 253.

4 Broos 1983, p. 44. Broos did not take Smith's list into account (Smith 1829–42, vol. VII, 1836, pp. 243–56). Werner Sumowski's monumental series *Gemälde der Rembrandt-Schüler* (Paintings by Rembrandt's Pupils) (1983–95) was already in production when Broos's article was published, even though most of the volumes appeared later. So Sumowski still includes many purely legendary pupils.

5 Among them are J. van Dorsten and J. van Glabbeeck.

6 Broos 1983, p. 41.

7 Strauss & Van der Meulen 1979, p. 381, no. 1656/12 (nos 298–300): three little dogs, a book, and a *tronie* of Mary. In 1656, Titus was only fifteen years old. Recently, Bruyn assembled a small group of paintings by a follower of Rembrandt's late style, which works he tentatively ascribed to Titus (Bruyn 1990). They are of too poor a quality to make it believable that Titus's work was in its day 'probably presented as work by the father', as Bruyn stated elsewhere (Bruyn 1991–92, p. 89, note 91). A few drawings are also attributed to Titus (Sumowski, *Drawings*, vol. 9, 1985, nos 2207–2209).

8 In 1899 Hofstede de Groot reported the discovery of its signature, adding that the owner of the piece immediately had a false Gerrit Dou 'signature' painted over it. Recently, Sumowski speculated that this Jouderville signature might be purely legendary (Sumowski, *Gemälde*, vol. II, 1985, p. 1436, no. 940). Following this, the picture was cleaned and the Jouderville signature proved to be still present (Potterton 1986, pp. 72–3, no. 433).

9 Van de Wetering 1983.

10 Sumowski, *Gemälde*, vol. II, 1985, nos 951, 953; vol. VI, 1995, no. 2332. Nonetheless, Jouderville received at least one commission for a portrait, and a few works by him occur in seventeenth-century Leiden inventories (Bredius 1915–22, vol. VI, p. 1963; Lunsingh Scheurleer, Fock & Van Dissel 1986–92, vol. IIIa, p. 337; vol. Va, p. 11). See also note 22 below.

11 Strauss & Van der Meulen 1979, pp. 75–6, 185–6, nos 1631/4, 1640/2.

12 Baldinucci 1681–1728, vol. IV, p. 511, writing on Rembrandt's pupil Bernard Keil (1624–1687), who from 1642 worked first at Rembrandt's and then at Uylenburgh's. Baldinucci communicated with Keil during the latter's stay in Italy.

13 Straat 1928, pp. 72–3. Uylenburgh also owed money to Jacobsz, and had a large painting (which belonged to Jacobsz), *The Tribute Money* by Jacob Backer, in his shop in Amsterdam (Straat 1928, pp. 67, 76).

14 Wijnman 1959, pp. 1–2; Broos 1981–82, p. 252; Van de Wetering 1986, pp. 57–60.

15 Klemm 1986, pp. 338–9.

16 Sandrart 1675, p. 203.

17 Bredius 1915–22, vol. VI, p. 1951.

18 The drawing is *Susanna and the Elders* (our cat. no. 77) (Benesch 1973, vol. II, no. 448). Rembrandt's notes on the back are transcribed in Hofstede de Groot 1906a, p. 39 (reproduced in Blankert 1982, fig. 3; Bruyn 1989, p. 14, fig. 2).

19 Blankert 1976, pp. 16–17; Blankert 1982, p. 19. Earlier, Haverkamp Begemann had written: 'Rembrandt also taught artists who had learned the basic principles of the craft elsewhere' (Haverkamp Begemann 1969, p. 25).

20 Van de Wetering 1986, p. 56; Blankert 1992–93, p. 42.

21 This proposition has been put most outspokenly by Bruyn (Bruyn 1991–92, p. 69).

22 The theory proposed in the *Corpus* that Jouderville would have executed important portrait commissions in Rembrandt's Amsterdam studio is not convincing (Bruyn 1989, pp. 31–4; cf. Blankert 1992–93, pp. 62–3).

23 Houbraken 1718–21, vol. II, 1719, p. 21.

24 Houbraken 1718–21, vol. II, 1719, p. 153 (on Jacob Levecq); vol. III, 1721, p. 80 (on Heyman Dullaert).

25 Blankert 1982, pp. 96–7, no. 16.

26 Bredius 1915–22, vol. I, p. 128. In the literature it is stated as a fact that Flinck was in Amsterdam from 1633 onwards, but I know of no proof of this.

27 Baldinucci 1681–1728, vol. VI, p. 484, says that in his youth Flinck worked with 'a certain merchant' and was allowed to make whatever he liked. This 'merchant' must have been Uylenburgh, because Sandrart says that Flinck stayed 'long years' at Uylenburgh's (Sandrart 1675, p. 194). Wijnman 1959, pp. 15, 16, suggests that Flinck was Rembrandt's successor at Uylenburgh's.

28 According to Sumowski, *Gemälde*, vol. II, 1985, p. 1019, no. 612, Flinck's *Lamentation* derives from Rembrandt's pictures of the *Deposition* at the Alte Pinakothek, Munich, and at the Hermitage, St Petersburg (Bredius / Gerson 1969, nos 550, 551). In the *Corpus,* Rembrandt's *Lamentation* at the National Gallery in London is cited more convincingly as Flinck's model (*Corpus*, vol. III, 1989, p. 97, no. A107).

29 This idea was formulated by W. Martin in 1921 and by E. Gombrich in 1970 (Blankert 1982, p. 19). It is dismissed by Bruyn (Bruyn 1989, pp. 13, 28–31). See also Blankert 1992–93, pp. 57–9, 63–7.

30 Blankert 1982, pp. 13–14; Blankert 1992–93, p. 51.

31 'The Rembrandt Re-Trial' [editorial], *Burlington Magazine*, vol. CXXXIV, no. 1070, May 1992, p. 285; Blankert 1993, p. 97, note 23.

32 V. Manuth, in Berlin / Amsterdam / London 1991–92c, pp. 376–9, cat. no. 80 (with earlier literature).

33 Houbraken 1718–21, vol. II, 1719, pp. 20 (Flinck), 155 (Hoogstraten).

34 Houbraken 1718–21, vol. II, 1719, p. 273.

35 Houbraken 1718–21, vol. II, 1719, p. 305.

36 Flinck had 'la fama del miglior pictore di Amsterdam' (Baldinucci 1681–1728, vol. VI, p. 484).

37 Baldinucci 1681–1728, vol. VI, p. 484; Houbraken 1718–21, vol. II, 1719, p. 22.

38 Blankert, 1975a, p. 27; Blankert 1982, pp. 42–8.

39 Sumowski, *Gemälde*, vol. III, 1987, p. 2026, no. 1388; Robinson 1993, pp. 101, 104.

40 Blankert 1975–79, p. 197, no. 257.

41 Sumowski, *Gemälde*, vol. II, 1985, p. 1293, no. 835; Roscam Abbing 1993, no. 42.

42 Sumowski, *Drawings*, vol. 9, 1985, nos 2145, 2151.

43 Hofstede de Groot 1915, p. 79.

44 Haverkamp Begemann 1969, p. 29; Sumowski, *Gemälde*.

45 Bruyn 1991–92, pp. 70–2.

46 Van Hoogstraten 1678, pp. 13, 212. See also the statements by Bernard Keil as mentioned by Baldinucci (Baldinucci 1686, p. 78ff) and the reports by Houbraken, collected by Hofstede de Groot (Hofstede de Groot 1906a, pp. 460–94).

Jan Lievens (1607–1674)

The son of an embroiderer from Ghent, Jan Lievens was born in Leiden in 1607. According to the Leiden chronicler Jan Jansz Orlers (1641), he was a pupil of Joris van Schooten in Leiden at the age of only eight and continued his precocious training with the renowned history painter Pieter Lastman in Amsterdam only two years later. After three years, he returned to his native Leiden as an independent master and in 1626–27 he painted a portrait of the stadholder's secretary, Constantijn Huygens (Musée de la Chartreuse, Douai; on loan to the Rijksmuseum, Amsterdam). Lievens was joined in Leiden by his only slightly younger colleague, Rembrandt, to whom at least initially he probably was a mentor. Their works of this period (see cat. nos 34–37) can be difficult to distinguish. Although there is no proof, it is assumed that the two shared a studio. Constantijn Huygens writes with admiration and insight about the two young artists' talents and differences (see commentary to cat. no. 36). The two painters parted ways when Rembrandt left for Amsterdam in 1631 and Lievens left for London the following year. While there he met Anthony van Dyck, who painted his portrait and influenced his style. However, Lievens soon departed for Antwerp, where he became a member of the St Luke's Guild in 1635 and married Susanna Colyns, a daughter of the sculptor Andries Colyns de Nole. Lievens prospered in Antwerp, remaining there for about ten years. On a visit to Leiden in 1639, he received from the Town Hall there a commission for a painting representing Scipio Africanus. The substantial payment for this work (1500 guilders and a gold medal), as well as the cost, both financial and political, of commissioning a painting that had to be transported from Antwerp to Leiden, attests to the international value placed on Lievens's art.

Lievens moved to Amsterdam by March 1644 and is recorded there until 1653. He was commissioned to paint two paintings for the Town Hall in Amsterdam and provided decorations for the Oranjezaal in the Huis ten Bosch in The Hague, where he lived from 1654 to 1658. He was one of the founders of Pictura, the painters' confraternity in The Hague. Among his commissions for important public decorations were two paintings produced in the 1660s for the Rijnlandhuis in Leiden. He was also active abroad, in Berlin and Cleves, and was permitted the title 'Painter to the Duke of Brandenburg'. Lievens's first wife died after the birth of their first son, Jan Andrea Lievens, who also became a painter. Lievens was married a second time, in 1648, to Cornelia de Bray. He died in Amsterdam on 4 June 1674.

Jan Lievens was a talented, productive and versatile painter who produced history paintings, genre scenes, portraits, landscapes and many drawings and prints. His earliest works are broadly painted large-scale allegories, history paintings and genre scenes, while he subsequently produced small-scale, tightly executed works in a style connected to the last years of Rembrandt's Leiden period. Following his exposure to van Dyck in England, Lievens's history paintings and portraits become more atmospheric, and the palette deeper and richer in that artist's manner. His late history and portrait painting style is international in flavour as befitted his personal experience, while his highly original landscapes acknowledge Peter Paul Rubens and Adriaen Brouwer.

LITERATURE: Orlers 1641, p. 375ff; Schneider 1932; Braunschweig 1979; Sumowski, *Gemälde*, vol. III, 1987, pp. 1764–1950.

PCS

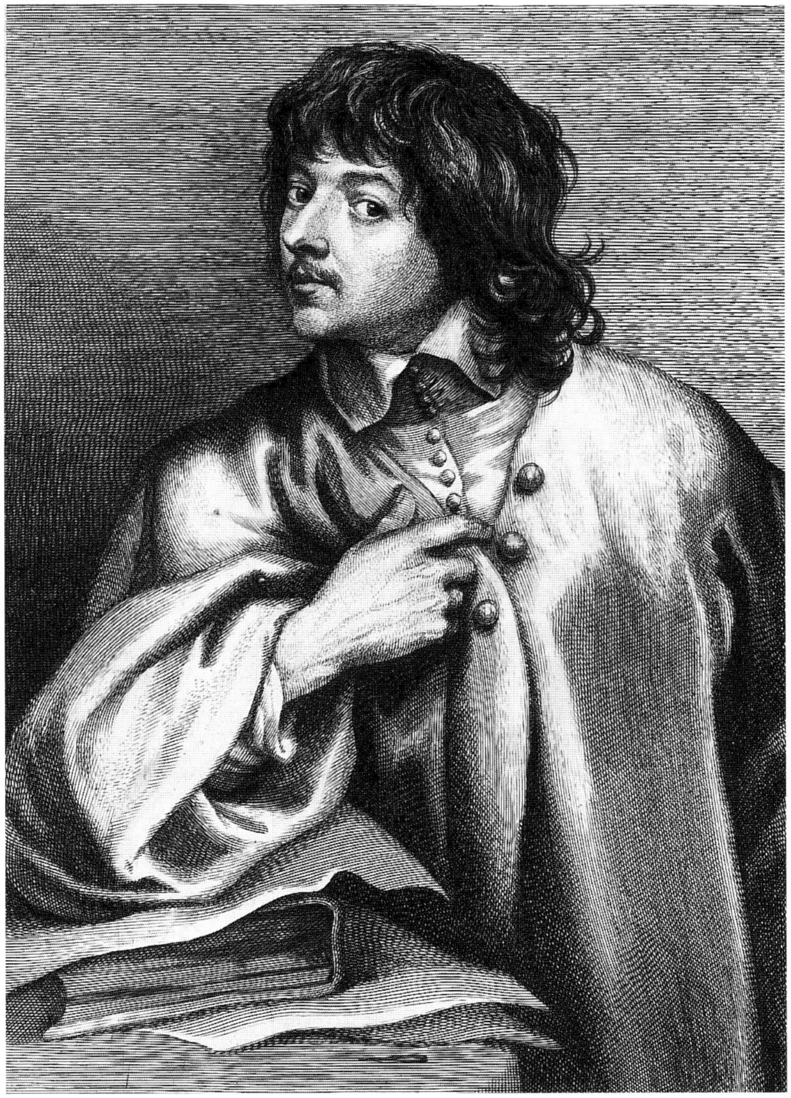

Lucas Vorsterman (1595–1675), after Anthony van Dyck
Portrait of Jan Lievens
Engraving
24.8 x 15.9 cm
Photograph: RKD

33

Jan Lievens

A Young Man Tuning a Violin

*c.*1623

Canvas
92.7 x 73.7 cm
Stedelijk Museum de Lakenhal, Leiden

PROVENANCE: Sale, London (Christie's), 7 July 1995, lot 58, repr.; with dealer R. Noortman, Maastricht/London; gift of the Foundation VSB-Fonds, Den Haag en Omstreken to the Museum in 1996.

Although neither signed nor dated, this unpublished painting is correctly regarded, on stylistic grounds, to be a very early work by Jan Lievens. Its broad painterly technique, colourful shrill palette, and subject matter all find parallels in Lievens's earliest paintings; we may compare, as examples, the treatment of the other half-length, lifesized figures in the artist's *Tric-Trac Players* (sale, London (Christie's), 8 July 1994, lot 86), *Pilate Washing His Hands* (Stedelijk Museum de Lakenhal, Leiden), *The Feast of Esther* (North Carolina Museum of Art, Raleigh) and the two signed paintings of allegorical figures blowing on coals (Muzeum Narodowe, Warsaw).[1] Indeed the same model seems to recur in some of these works.

Although none of Lievens's paintings bear dates earlier than 1627 (his *Vanitas Still Life*, dated that year (Hannema-De Stuers Fundatie, Kasteel het Nijenhuis, near Heino), also features sheet music, folios and a violin),[2] all of the paintings in the group referred to above are usually dated around 1625 or somewhat earlier.[3] According to the chronicler of Leiden, Jan Jansz Orlers, Lievens showed his talent early, and was apprenticed to the local painter Joris van Schooten when he was only eight years old. At the age of ten, he was sent to Amsterdam to the 'renowned P. Lastman', with whom he stayed for two years before embarking on his career as an independent master.[4] If one accepts this contemporary report of Lievens's accelerated development, notwithstanding its familiar topoi, as well as the usual dating of the young artist's stay with Lastman to *c.*1617–19, then it is quite possible that his earliest paintings were executed several years earlier than 1625. The daring, high-keyed colour scheme of the present painting may well acknowledge Lastman's recent influence.

However, the work's clearest debt is to the Utrecht Caravaggisti, specifically to almost exactly contemporary paintings of half-length musicians, in exotic striped costumes, by Gerrit van Honthorst (fig. 33a). Although there has been some inconclusive speculation about whether the vaguely pseudo-Burgundian costumes of the Caravaggisti's jolly toppers identify them as itinerant musicians or performers *(bravi)*, or merely as colourful tavern-dwellers, it is certain that the present figure's outfit is not conventional seventeenth-century Dutch street attire. It may also be significant that this thoughtful-looking musician tunes rather than plays his violin. Van Honthorst and other Caravaggisti repeatedly painted companion pieces of male and female musicians, usually in a hilarious state fortified by drink, and often with one or the other member of the couple tuning his or her instrument.[5] The time-honoured notion of the lover who tunes to the key of the beloved in the interest of harmony was certainly not lost on seventeenth-century poets, emblem designers or artists.[6] This is not to suggest that the present work ever had a companion, but only to call attention to a Caravaggesque pictorial tradition that may help to explain the peculiar concentration and ardour with which musicians in works by the Caravaggisti often attend to the tuning of their instruments (for example, Theodoor Rombouts's *Lute Player* in the John G. Johnson Collection at the Philadelphia Museum of Art).

PCS

1 Sumowski, *Gemälde*, vol. III, 1987, nos 1178, 1180, 1181, 1225, 1226.

2 Sumowski, *Gemälde*, vol. III, 1987, no. 1299.

3 The Rembrandt Research Project (*Corpus*, vol. I, 1982, p. 454) considers the Warsaw paintings to be Lievens's earliest, dating them *c.*1623.

4 Orlers 1641, p. 375.

5 See, as examples, van Honthorst's companion pieces at the Museum der bildenden Künste, Leipzig; the Hermitage, St Petersburg (signed and dated 1624), and the Picture Gallery, Lvov (signed and dated 1631) (Nicolson / Vertova 1989, pls 1245 & 1246, 1277 & 1278, 1302 & 1303).

6 For a discussion of the iconography, see Amsterdam 1976, pp. 106–7, cat. no. 21.

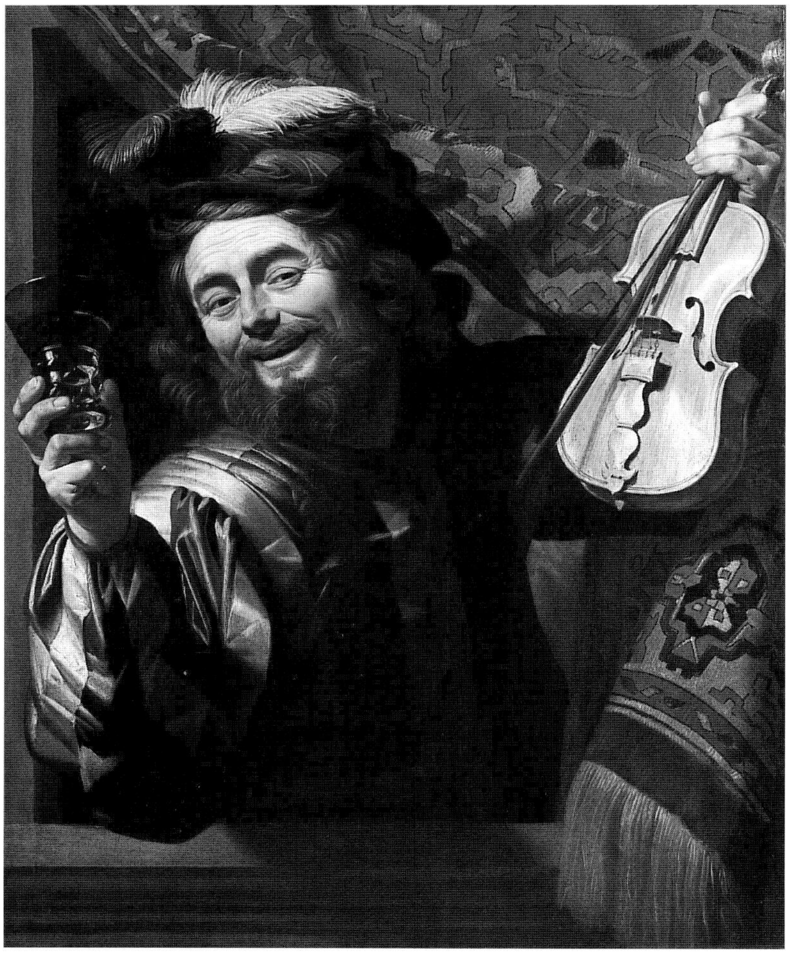

FIG. 33a
Gerrit van Honthorst 1590–1656
Violinist with a Glass
Signed and dated 1623
Canvas
108.0 x 89.0 cm
Rijksmuseum, Amsterdam

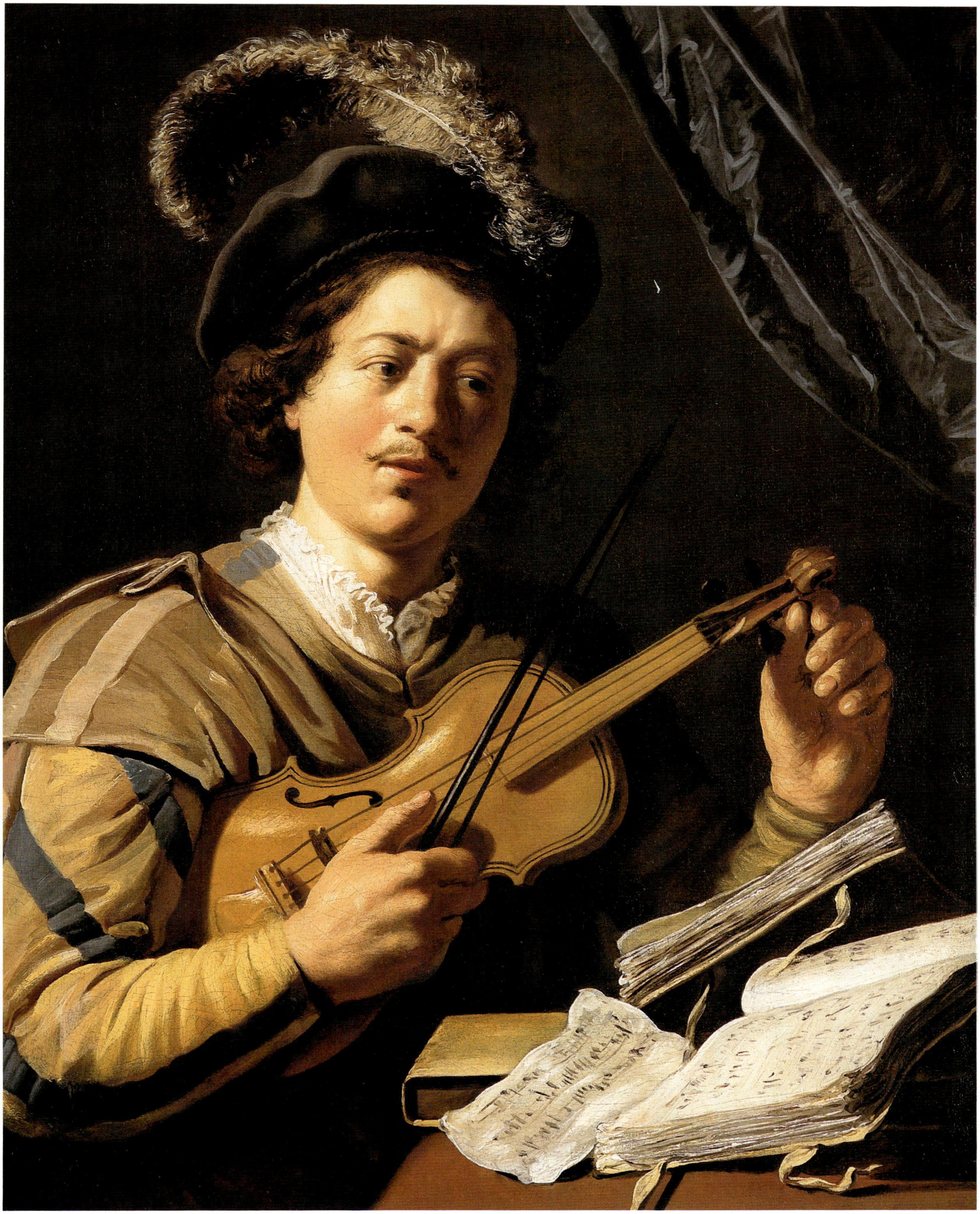

34

Jan Lievens

Smiling Girl with Long Blond Hair

*c.*1625–29

Panel
43.3 x 34.8 cm
Museum der bildenden Künste, Leipzig

PROVENANCE: Jacques de Gheyn III (1596–1641), probably initially in The Hague, *c.*1629, and in Utrecht by 1634; bequeathed by de Gheyn to his relative Johannes Wtenbogaert (1608–1680), Amsterdam, in 1641 [see commentary to cat. no. 8]; sale, Freiherr von Aretin, Munich, 1887, lot 59; Alfred Thieme, Leipzig; acquired by the Museum with the Thieme Collection in 1916.

LITERATURE: Bredius 1907, text to pl. 22; Schneider / Ekkart 1973, pp. 142, 332, no. 217; Sumowski, *Gemälde*, vol. III, 1987, p. 1805, no. 1275, with further literature.

This painting is almost certainly identical with a piece Jacques de Gheyn III (1596–1641) bequeathed to his relative Johannes Wtenbogaert in his will of 3 June 1641 (see commentary to cat. no. 8). It is mentioned in this document after Rembrandt's *Two Old Men Disputing* (cat. no. 3) and his *Old Man Asleep, Seated by the Fire* (p. 46, fig. 19), and is described as 'another *tronigen* of a smiling young girl, also painted by Jan Lievens'.[1] Sumowski dated the painting to *c.*1632–34.[2] However, de Gheyn had probably acquired the piece by *c.*1629, when he was still living in The Hague. Around that time, his friend Constantijn Huygens wrote an autobiography in which he mentions paintings by Lievens. It includes the following passage: 'at De Gheyn's, if I am not mistaken, a couple of heads of young people [*effigies ... iuvenilis*]'.[3] Translators have generally rendered the word *effigies* as 'portraits'.[4] From the context, however, it is clear that Huygens used the term to mean *tronies*, which are not portraits in the true sense: the noun *effigies* is used in the preceding sentence in Huygens's autobiography, where reference is made to an *effigies* by Lievens: 'Supposedly of a Turkish commander, rendered after the head of some Dutchman' (p. 72, fig. 5). The 'heads of young people' must therefore also have been fanciful heads of this kind, which were not made as portraits in the strict sense of the term. The *Smiling Girl* in Leipzig belongs to the same category. The profusion of long, flowing hair, the golden hairband and the little that can be seen of the girl's clothing distinguish the picture from portraits of children made on commission, where the subjects are generally shown in far more formal attire (cf. fig. 48a). As long ago as 1907, Bredius speculated that the present piece might be one of those referred to by Huygens, but in the later literature this mention of *effigies ... iuvenilis* by Lievens was disregarded altogether.

The blond tonality in this painting strongly recalls that in the *Head of an Old Woman* (cat. no.

The collection of Jacques de Gheyn III in 1641

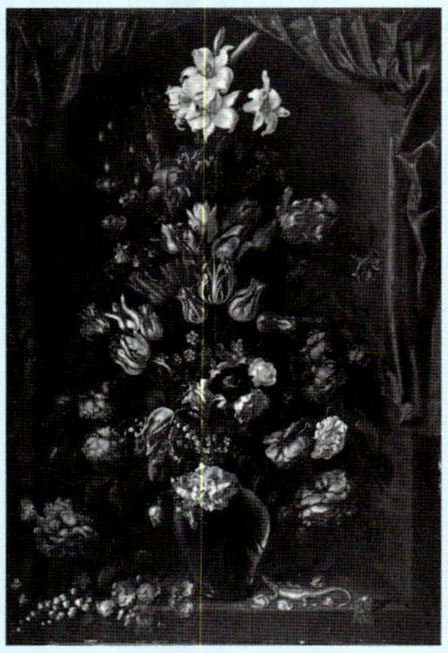

Jacques de Gheyn II (see fig. 8e)

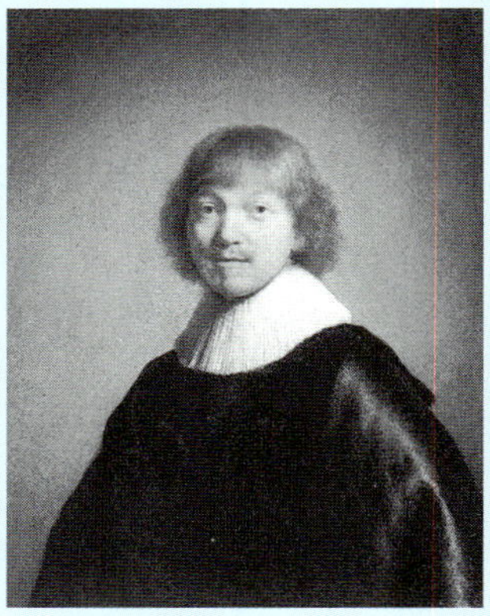

Rembrandt (cat. no. 8)

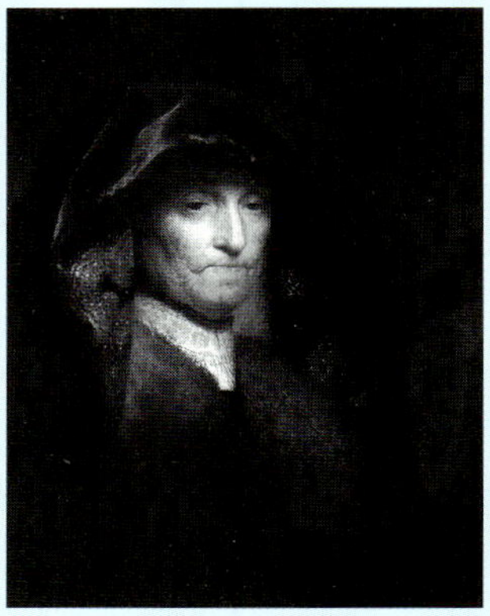

Rembrandt(?) (see fig. 8h)

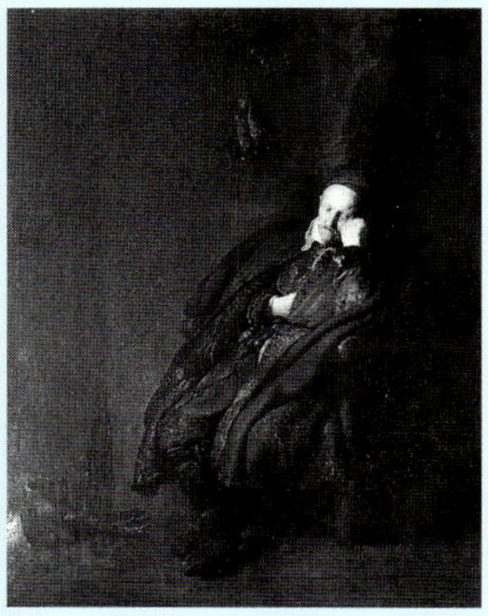

Rembrandt (see p. 46, fig. 19)

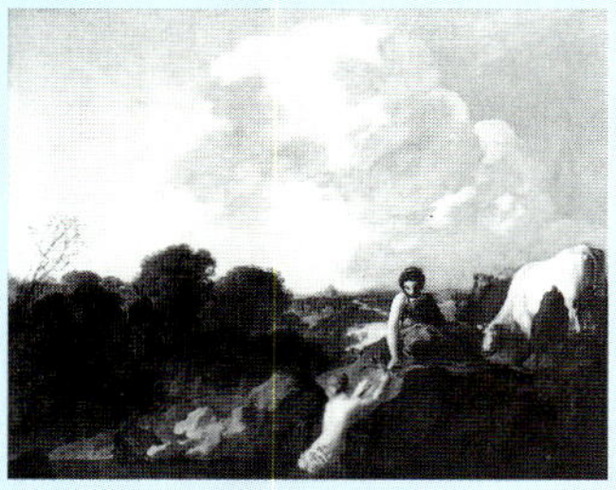

Mozes van Wtenbrouck (see fig. 8g)

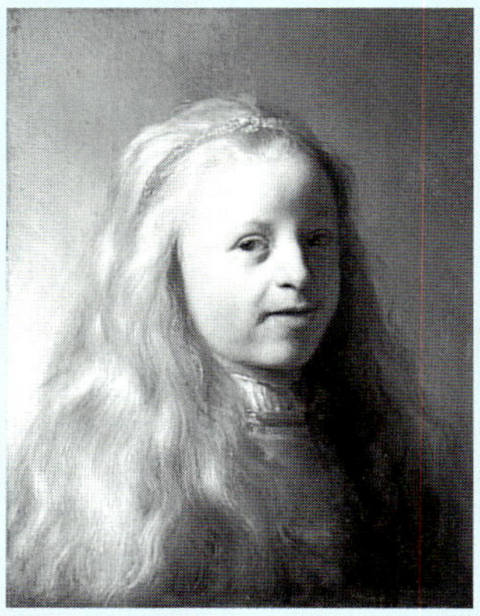

Jan Lievens (cat. no. 34)

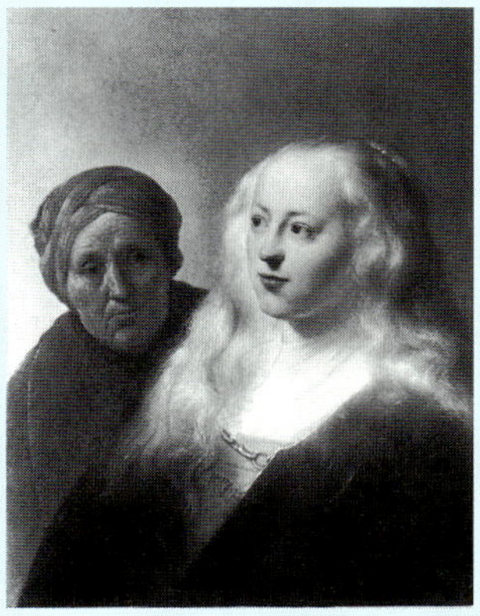

Jan Lievens (see fig. 34a)

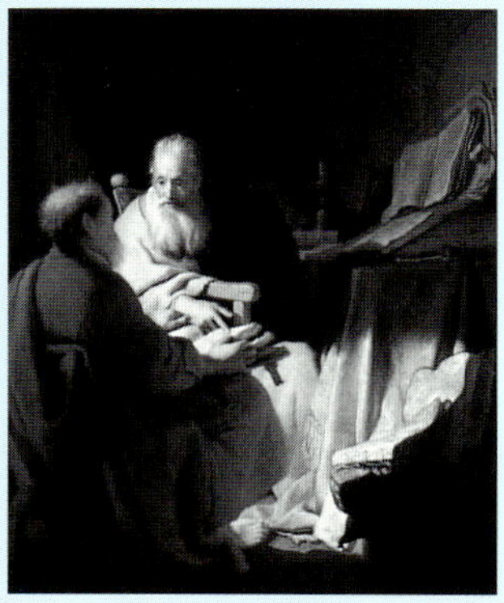

Rembrandt (cat. no. 3)

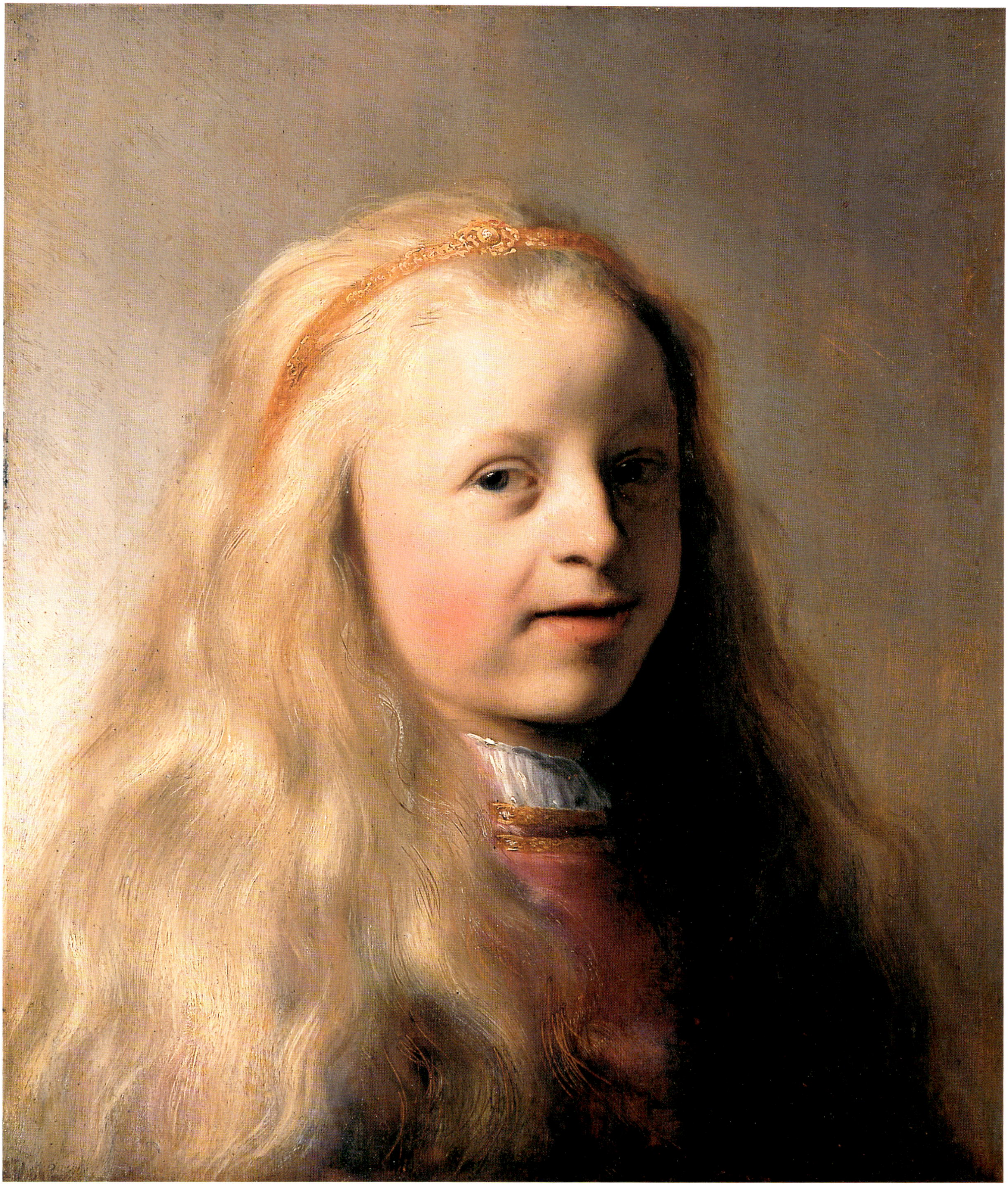

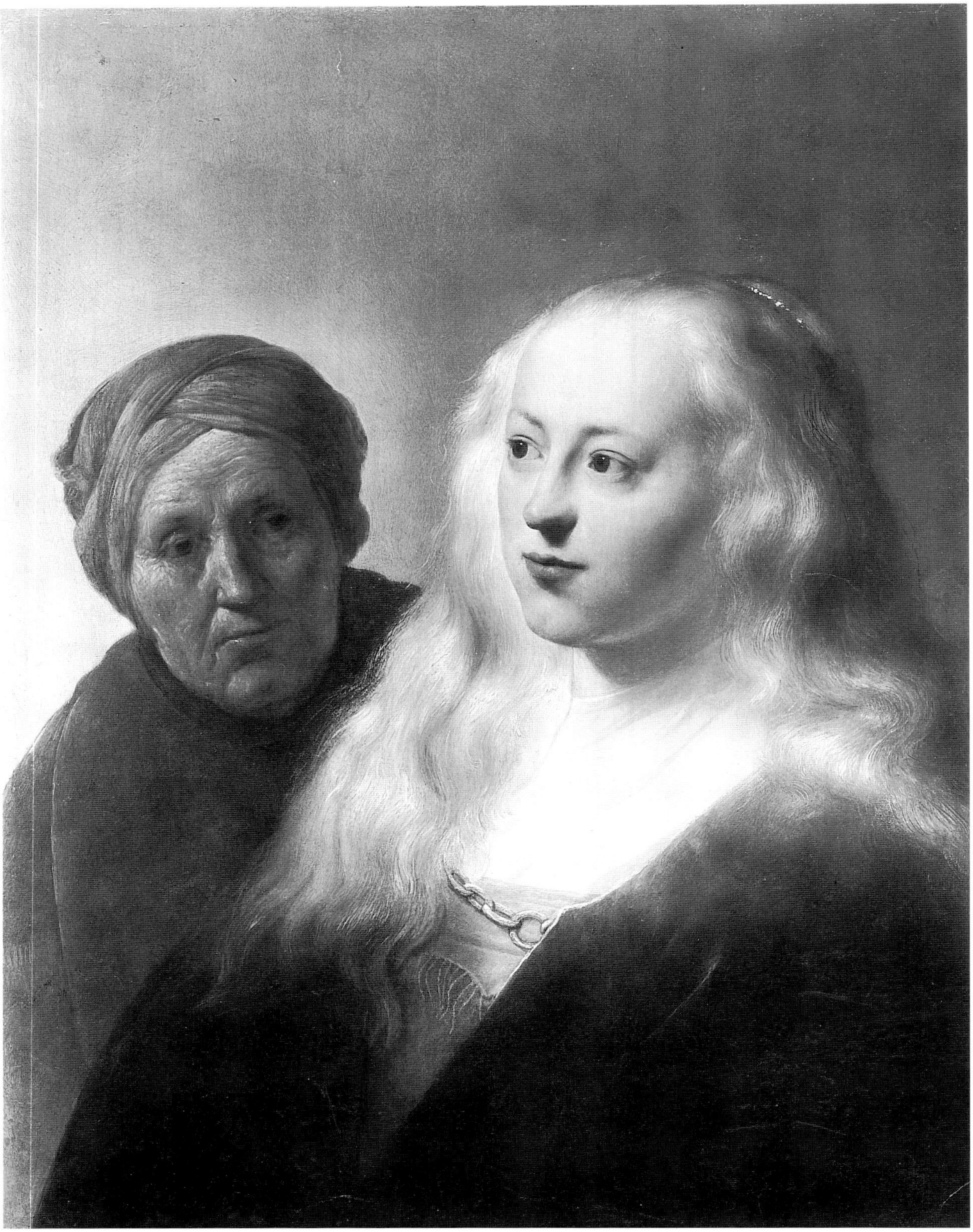

FIG. 34a
Jan Lievens
A Young Woman and an Old Woman
Monogrammed
Panel
66.0 x 53.0 cm
Formerly with dealers Hinrichsen & Lindpaintner, Berlin
Photograph: RKD

35). Moreover, the technique Lievens used to render the light reflecting off the girl's hairband is also very similar to that with which he suggested the golden sheen on the folds of the scarf in the *Head of an Old Woman*. Both pieces must have been made *c.*1625–29. Hence, if we accept that this work is one of the *effigies … iuvenilis* referred to in Huygens's autobiography, de Gheyn must have acquired the *Smiling Girl* soon after Lievens had made it.

If we juxtapose Lievens's *Smiling Girl* and *Head of an Old Woman*, we find that they are the same size and that the light falls from the left in both cases. The two pieces complement each other thematically: the freshness of youth in contrast to withered age. And the compositions are also compatible. We can thus assume the two paintings were meant as companion pieces. The present exhibition will reveal whether they indeed belong together.

Jacques de Gheyn III is known to have owned a work by Lievens that contrasted a young girl and an elderly woman. After his two Rembrandt paintings and immediately before the '*tronigen* of a smiling young girl', de Gheyn's will refers to 'another *tronige* of a beautiful damsel with an old woman beside her, painted by Jan Lievens'.[5] This was probably a painting that was last on the art market in Berlin in 1939 (fig. 34a).[6] I have made extensive enquiries to trace the picture's later whereabouts, but unfortunately to no avail. It seems to have been lost (during World War II?). The piece represented the striking contrast between blooming youth and weathered old age. Together, Lievens's *Smiling Girl* and *Head of an Old Woman* depict the same contrast. Perhaps not just the Leipzig picture and the picture formerly in Berlin, but also the *Head of an Old Woman*, were once in de Gheyn's collection.[7]

AB

1 Van Regteren Altena 1936, vol. I, p. 129: 'Noch een jonck lachent meyskens tronigen, oock van Jan Lievens geschildert'.
2 Sumowski, *Gemälde*, vol. III, 1987, p. 1805, no. 1275.
3 Worp 1897, p. 79: 'effigies … apud Gheynium iuvenilis, ni fallor, una atque altera'.
4 Huygens / Kan 1946, p. 81; Huygens / Heesakkers 1987, p. 88.
5 Van Regteren Altena 1936, vol. I, p. 129: 'Noch een fraye vrouwe tronige mit een out wijff daerbij, van Jan Lievens geschildert'.
6 See commentary to our cat. no. 3. Sumowski, *Gemälde*, vol. III, 1987, p. 1779, no. 1188, points out that there are no grounds for the piece's modern title, *Vertumnus and Pomona*.
7 In this case, de Gheyn disposed of the *Head of an Old Woman* after 1629, since it is not mentioned in the will of 1641.

35

Jan Lievens

Head of an Old Woman

*c.*1625–29

Monogrammed upper right (falsely) *RHL* (ligated)
Panel
43.5 x 35.0 cm
Drs Isabel and Alfred Bader

PROVENANCE: Sale, L. Merens, Amsterdam, 15 April 1778, lot 92 (as Rembrandt), to de Winter; sale, Cardinal Fesch, Rome, 17 March 1835, lot 193 (as Rembrandt); J. F. Winterbottom, East Woodhay, Newbury, Berkshire; his sale, London (Messrs Foster), 27 April 1870, lot 290 (as Rembrandt); Earl of Levin and Melville; with dealers Legatt Bros, London, 1956 (as Rembrandt); with dealers Oscar and Peter Johnson, London; with dealers K. and V. Waterman, Amsterdam; Gerald Guterman, Bedford, New York; his sale, New York (Sotheby's), 14 January 1988, lot 22, repr.

LITERATURE: Sumowski, *Gemälde*, vol. III, 1987, p. 1801, no. 1261; V. Manuth, in Braunschweig 1993–94, pp. 110–11, cat. no. 6.

The elderly woman in this scene reappears not only in other works by Jan Lievens (for example, Lady Exeter's painting at Burghley House and the painting at the Gemäldegalerie, Dresden, which may only be a copy after Lievens),[1] but also in paintings and graphic works by Rembrandt (for example, the paintings at the Residenzgalerie, Salzburg (Bredius 63); Windsor Castle (fig. 8h); and the Rijksmuseum, Amsterdam (Bredius 69) (p. 47, fig. 18))[2] and by his pupils, notably Gerrit Dou (for example, the pictures at the Rijksmuseum, Amsterdam; the Gemäldegalerie, Berlin;[3] and the Louvre, Paris[4]). Although there is no proof, the woman has traditionally been identified as Rembrandt's mother, Neeltgen Willemsdr. van Zuytbroeck (*c.*1568–1640). While the likeness of Rembrandt's father is known from an inscribed drawing in the Ashmolean Museum, Oxford (Benesch 56), there is no certain image of his mother. The earliest support for the long-standing traditional view that Rembrandt depicted her is the fact that one of the etching plates owned by Clement de Jonghe in 1679 – though it is not known which – was said to represent her (see pp. 45–6).[5] Closest to the present work is Rembrandt's etching of an old woman in profile of 1631 (B.348) (fig. 35a), entitled 'The Old Persian Woman' (*'de oude persiaanse vrou'*) in de Jonghe's inventory (no. 20). If one assumes that the model is in fact Rembrandt's mother, the inventory's anonymous title would simply acknowledge that the etching with the woman in exotic costume was a *tronie*, or depiction of an idealized figure type, evocative of history painting but extracted from any known narrative – historical, literary or allegorical.

With her expressive, deeply lined features, this old woman served as a model for biblical figures in several early history paintings by Rembrandt (for example, the widow Anna standing above Simeon in the Temple (Kunsthalle, Hamburg (cat. no. 2)), and Anna holding the kid with Tobit (Rijksmuseum, Amsterdam)).[6] She also appears as the figure of Job's wife in Lievens's *Job in Misery* of 1631 (National Gallery of Canada, Ottawa)[7] and in works by Rembrandt's anonymous followers (for example, *The Prophetess Anna* at the Kunsthistorisches Museum, Vienna).[8]
In the present work, the woman's colourful embroidered headdress, its transparent fabric rendered so brilliantly, surely evokes a historical personage, albeit unidentified. Like other Dutch history painters from this period, including the Haarlem artists Pieter de Grebber and Salomon de Bray, Lievens favoured bust-length profile images as anonymous character studies or *tronies*. And, like Rembrandt, he too repeatedly employed this format in his early etchings.

As Volker Manuth observed,[9] the stadholder's secretary, Constantijn Huygens, whose portrait by the artist is owned by the Musée de la Chartreuse, Douai,[10] commended the youthful Lievens on his skills as a portraitist. In his chronicle of Leiden, *Beschrijvinge der Stadt Leyden* (1641), Jan Jansz Orlers also remarked on Lievens's precocious interest in portraiture: 'In 1622 when he [Lievens] was 14 years old, he portrayed his mother so well and artfully that everyone was astonished'. Although this gift for achieving a persuasive likeness can no longer be tested against the sitters, Lievens's compellingly expressive head studies are surely an important factor in his achievement as a history painter.

Sumowski clarified the present work's provenance, which had been confused with that of another version of this image in the Braunschweig exhibition catalogue of 1979.[11] He also confirmed in the Guterman sale catalogue (Sotheby's, New York, 14 January 1988, lot 22) that he regards the present work as primary. H. Schneider mentions additional replicas or copies.[12]

PCS

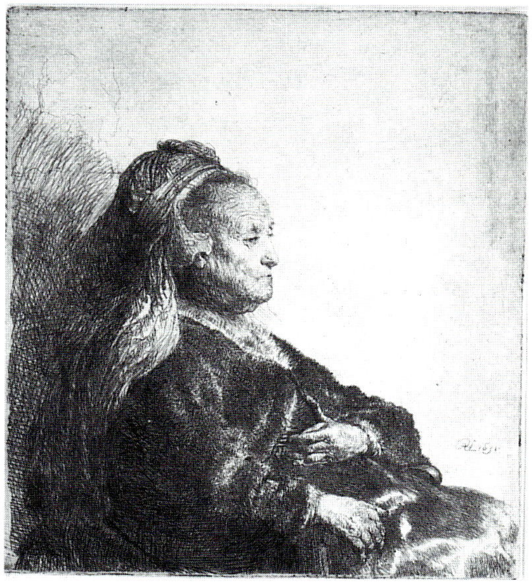

FIG. 35a
Rembrandt
'Rembrandt's Mother' (?)
Monogrammed and dated 1631
Etching
14.5 x 12.9 cm
Rijksprentenkabinet, Rijksmuseum, Amsterdam

1 Sumowski, *Gemälde*, vol. III, 1987, nos 1268, 1272.
2 *Corpus*, vol. I, 1982, nos A27, A32, A37.
3 Sumowski, *Gemälde*, vol. III, 1987, nos 245, 253.
4 Martin 1913, ill. no. 39R.
5 V. Manuth, in Braunschweig 1993–94, p. 110, cat. no. 18, discusses an unidentified etching described as 'Rembrandt's Mother'; see also De Hoop Scheffer & Boon 1971, p. 6, no. 10.
6 *Corpus*, vol. I, 1982, nos A12, A3.
7 Sumowski, *Gemälde*, vol. III, 1987, no. 1191.
8 *Corpus*, vol. III, 1989, no. C89.
9 V. Manuth, in Braunschweig 1979, cat. no. 30.
10 Baligand 1978–79, pp. 35–8, no. 30, repr.; Sumowski, *Gemälde*, vol. III, 1987, p. 1807, no. 1286.
11 Sumowski, *Gemälde*, vol. III, 1987, p. 1801, no. 1261 (cf. no. 1262).
12 Schneider 1932, p. 115, under no. 270.

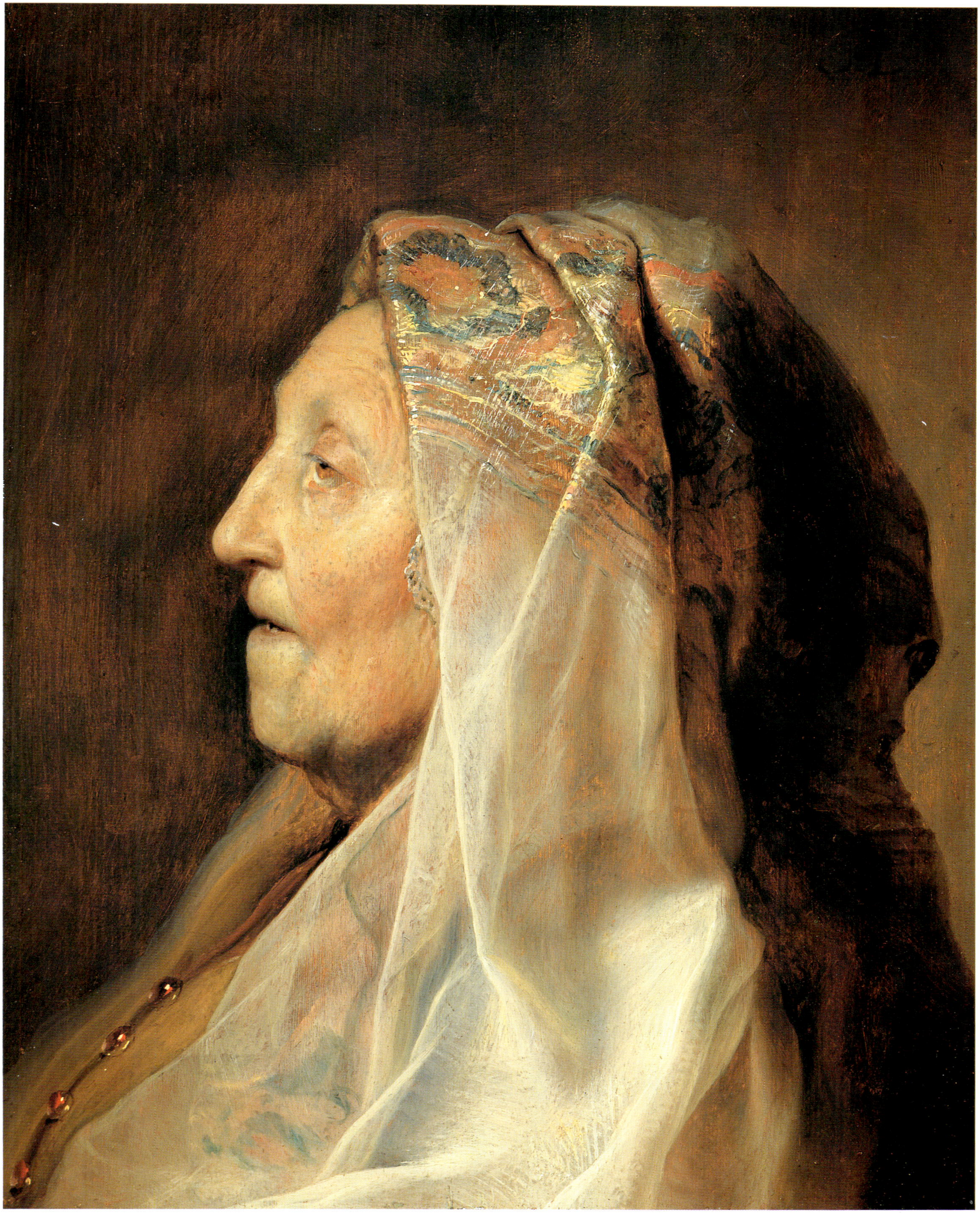

36

Jan Lievens

Samson and Delilah

*c.*1630

Signed upper left *IL*
Canvas
129.0 x 110.0 cm
Rijksmuseum, Amsterdam

PROVENANCE: Purchased from J. S. Hensé, Bradford, in 1895 (inv. no. A 1627).

LITERATURE: Schneider 1932; Tzeutschler Lurie 1969, p. 333; Kahr 1973, p. 240; Sumowski, *Gemälde*, vol. III, 1987, p. 1778, no. 1185; Leiden 1991–92, pp. 81, 108, fig. 60.

The invincible Samson was betrayed by his mistress, Delilah, when she cut off his locks while he slept in her lap, thus rendering him powerless so that she could hand him over to the Philistines, who blinded and imprisoned him. In this painting by Lievens, Samson slumbers as a determined Delilah gestures with a shears to a Philistine cohort, who seems to hold back in terror (Judges 16:19–21). The fact that Samson had tricked the conspirators three times previously about the source of his strength (Judges 16:4–16) surely justified their trepidation.

Lievens treated the same subject in a small panel in grisaille, now also preserved at the Rijksmuseum (fig. 36a).[1] This panel probably preceded the present work and more closely resembles in scale, conception, and its full-length composition Rembrandt's *Samson and Delilah* at the Gemäldegalerie, Berlin (Bredius 489) (fig. 36b). In his monograph on Lievens, H. Schneider[2] first noted that the contrast between the present work and Rembrandt's painting in Berlin seemed to illustrate the comments Constantijn Huygens, secretary to the stadholder, offered in his memoirs, where he compared the two young artists in their early Leiden period: Rembrandt, in Huygens's view, surpassed Lievens in the expressiveness of his small, carefully worked paintings, while the latter was superior in the grandeur of his invention and the boldness of his subjects and figures.[3]

The Amsterdam canvas employs a smoother technique, more monumental forms and a less shrill palette than Lievens's earlier history paintings, notably his *Feast of Esther* (North Carolina Museum of Art, Raleigh) and *Pilate Washing His Hands* (Stedelijk Museum de Lakenhal, Leiden).[4] These stylistic changes may signal Lievens's new receptiveness to Flemish art: A. Tzeutschler Lurie noted that a painting by Gerrit van Honthorst of *c.*1620 at the Cleveland Museum of Art, and the present work, both seem to acknowledge Peter Paul Rubens's famous *Samson and Delilah* painted in *c.*1609 for Nicolaes Rockox (National Gallery, London).[5] Van Honthorst and Lievens may have known Rubens's design through Jacob Matham's engraving, which reproduces the protagonists in the same sense as in their paintings. M. Kahr also purported to see the influence on the present work of a painting of 1619 assigned to Guercino (private collection, Bologna).[6]

In dating this painting, plausibly, to around 1630, Sumowski[7] connected it to Lievens's *Aristotle Instructing the Young Alexander*, which is monogrammed and dated 1631 (J. Paul Getty Museum, Malibu), and to the *Fortune-Teller* at the Gemäldegalerie, Berlin.[8]

PCS

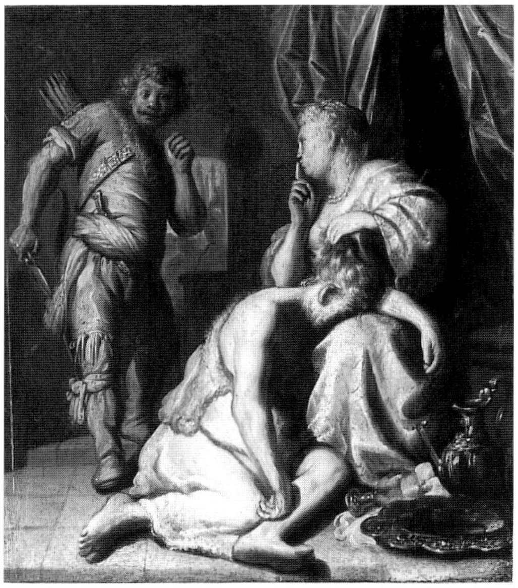

FIG. 36a
Jan Lievens
Samson and Delilah
Panel
27.5 x 23.7 cm
Rijksmuseum, Amsterdam

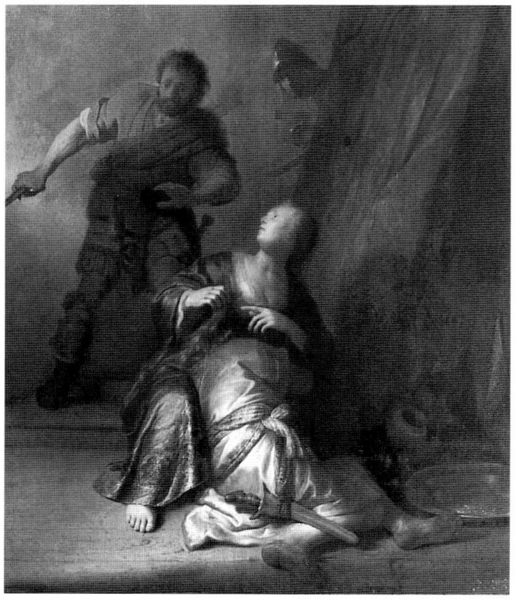

FIG. 36b
Rembrandt
Samson and Delilah
Monogrammed and dated 1628
Panel
61.3 x 50.1 cm
Staatliche Museen zu Berlin, Gemäldegalerie

1 Sumowski, *Gemälde*, vol. III, 1987, no. 1184.
2 Schneider 1932, p. 30.
3 Huygens's unfinished Latin manuscript was published only in the late nineteenth century. See Worp 1897; Huygens / Kan 1971, p. 79.
4 Sumowski, *Gemälde*, vol. III, 1987, nos 1181, 1180.
5 Tzeutschler Lurie 1969, p. 333.
6 Kahr 1973, p. 243, fig. 3.
7 Sumowski, *Gemälde*, vol. III, 1987, p. 1778, no. 1185.
8 Sumowski, *Gemälde*, vol. III, 1987, pp. 1778–9, nos 1186, 1187.

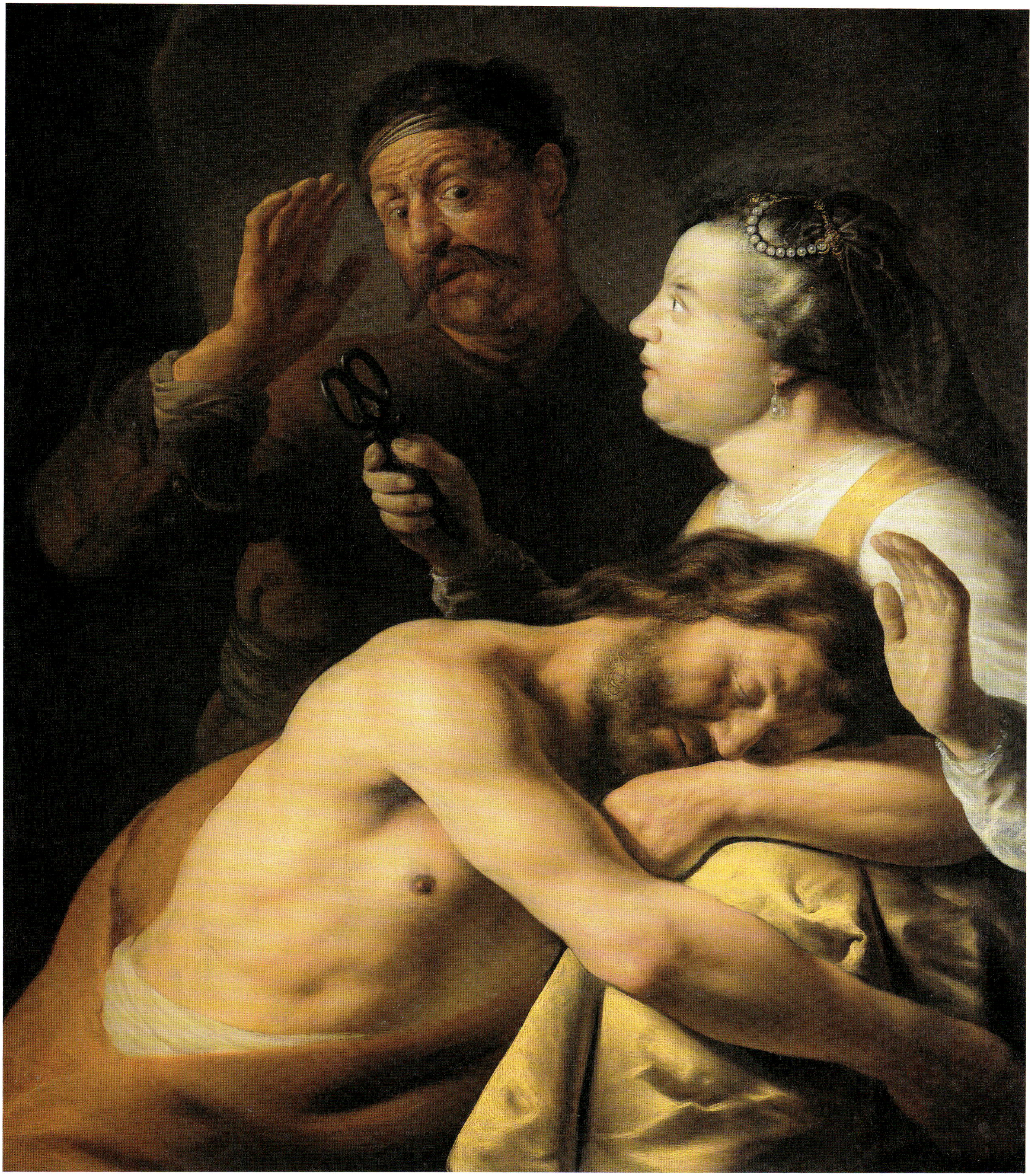

37

Jan Lievens
The Raising of Lazarus

Monogrammed and dated on parapet *IL / 1631*
Canvas
107.0 x 114.0 cm
Royal Pavilion, Art Gallery & Museums, Brighton

PROVENANCE: (Possibly) Rembrandt van Rijn [25 July 1656 inventory, no. 38: 'Een opweckinge Laseri van Jan Lievensz']; Jan Jacobs Hinlopen [where mentioned by the poet Jan Vos], 1662; sale, van Kretschmar, Amsterdam, 27 March 1757, lot 32, to Lintelo; sale, Amsterdam, 21 June 1774, lot 132, to Yver; sale, J. Knowles, London (Christie's), 15 April 1842, lot 113; J. Sidney North, London; Baroness North, London, 1871; sale, Sir George Buller, London (Christie's), 7 June 1884, lot 98; Henry Willett Foundation Bequest, Brighton, 1903.

LITERATURE: Sumowski, *Gemälde*, vol. III, 1987, pp. 1781–2, no. 1193 (with earlier literature); Royalton-Kisch 1991, p. 271; Los Angeles 1991–92, p. 14; Royalton-Kisch 1992, p. 62.

The scene depicts the Raising of Lazarus, brother of Mary and Martha, whose resuscitation was one of Christ's earliest and most dramatic miracles (John 11:41–44). Looking heavenward, Christ stands above the open grave with only the eerily pale arms of Lazarus visible, straining upward. The ample winding cloth arcs up to the right where the dumbstruck mourners are assembled. This remarkably theatrical image is a high point in the extensively discussed youthful dialogue between Lievens and Rembrandt. It is only one of at least five images that the two artists executed on this subject, perhaps partly in friendly competition. The year in which the present work was dated, 1631, was one of particularly close contact between Lievens and Rembrandt; for example, they both dated similarly conceived, dramatically lit paintings of Christ on the Cross in this year (Rembrandt's altarpiece in the parish church in Le Mas d'Agenais, Lot et Garonne,[1] and Lievens's painting at the Musée des Beaux-Arts, Nancy[2]).

Lievens's etching of the *Raising of Lazarus* (B.3) reproduces all the salient features of the present work's design, with minor changes, and supports the assumption that the painting has been cut down on all sides (fig. 37a).[3] X-rays of the Brighton picture also prove that it was begun on part of a canvas previously used for another composition; consequently we probably may assume that it was the artist's own initiative and not a commissioned work.

Most authors believe that Lievens based the present work on a design by Rembrandt and that it followed and was influenced by the latter's painting at the Los Angeles County Museum of Art (Bredius 538) (fig. 37b).[4] The tenebrous atmosphere, dramatic lighting and small-scale figures in the Brighton picture are more typical of Rembrandt than of Lievens in their shared late Leiden period. Through analysis of X-rays and other technical data, the Rembrandt Research Project concluded that the Los Angeles painting

FIG. 37a
Jan Lievens
The Raising of Lazarus
Etching
36.0 x 31.0 cm
Rijksprentenkabinet, Rijksmuseum, Amsterdam

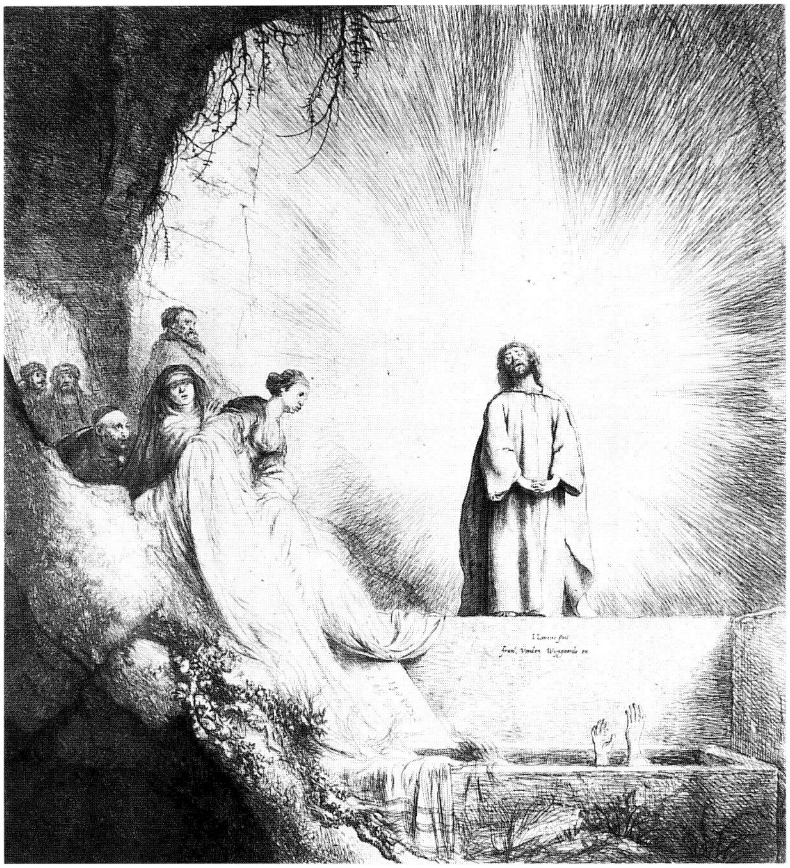

FIG. 37b
Rembrandt
The Raising of Lazarus
Panel
96.2 x 81.5 cm
Los Angeles County Museum of Art

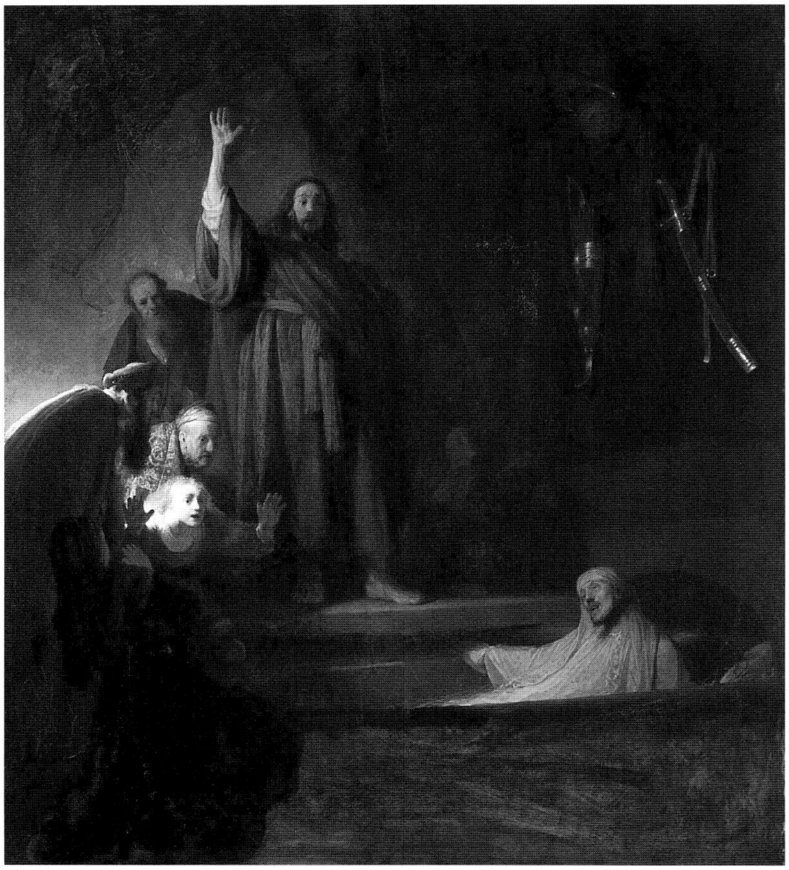

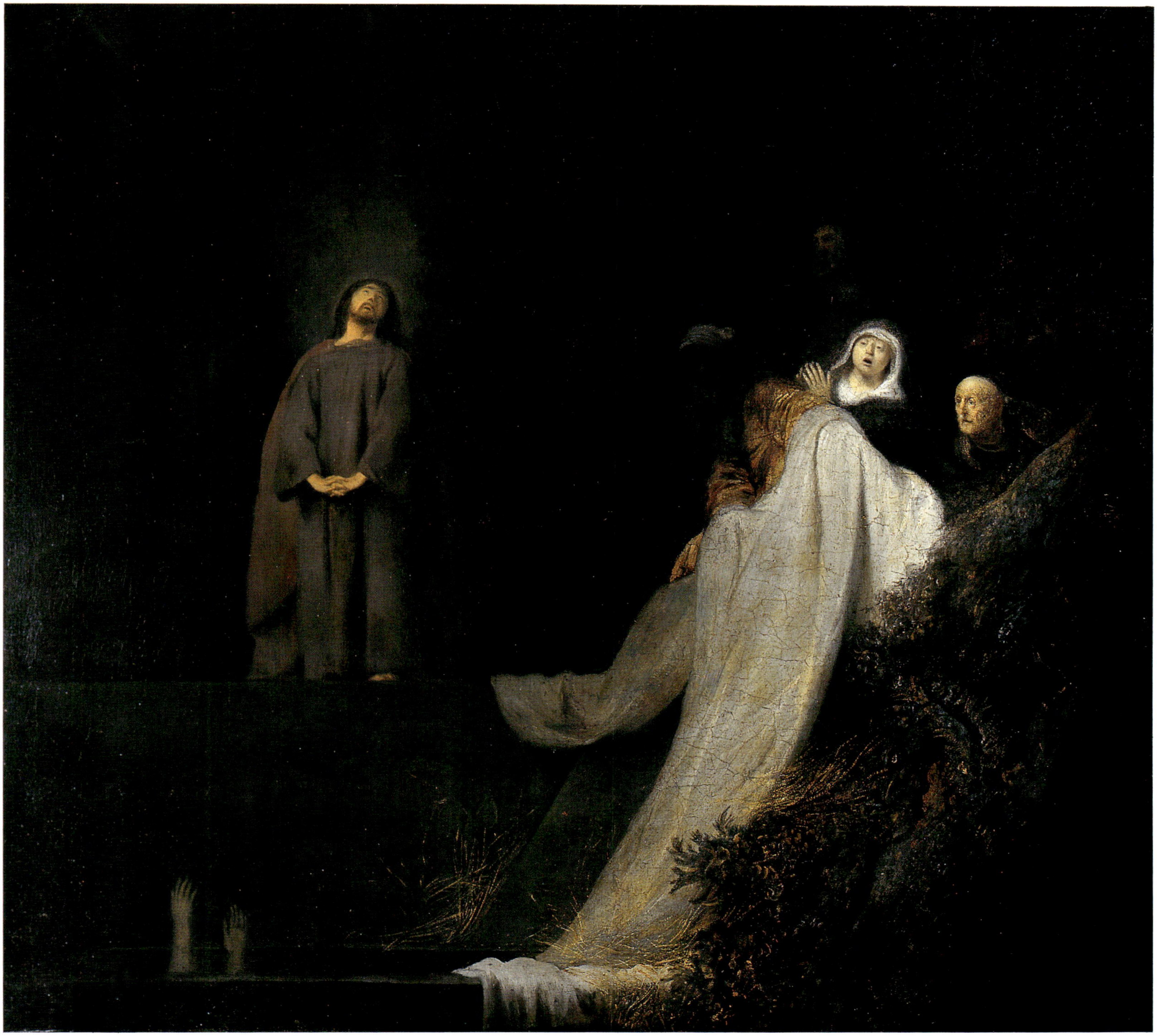

had a protracted birth and probably was altered extensively at least three times, but their proposed dating of *c.*1630–31 still suggests that it precedes the Lievens. Complicating the relationship of the two paintings is the date of 1630 on a drawing by Rembrandt in the British Museum, which began by paraphrasing Lievens's etching but was later altered to an *Entombment of Christ* (Benesch 17) (fig. 37c). The authors of the *Corpus* simply concluded that the date on the London drawing must be unreliable.[5] M. Royalton-Kisch also questioned the date,[6] pointing out that Rembrandt's drawing differs from the etching and seems to incorporate details of a print after Lievens's painting in Brighton, by Jacob Louijs and published by Pieter Soutman.[7] Royalton-Kisch concluded that the date on Rembrandt's drawing may refer not to the time of the work's execution but to the period of the composition's invention by Lievens. Relating the reworking of the drawing to Rembrandt's painted *Entombment* at the Alte Pinakothek, Munich (Bredius 560),[8] and the drawing's style to that of other sheets from the mid-1630s, Royalton-Kisch proposed a date of *c.*1635. Thus the traditional view that Rembrandt's drawing inspired Lievens's painting is now generally regarded as untenable. It also seems exceedingly unlikely that Lievens's etching preceded in date his painting of the subject.

The authors of the *Corpus* pointed out that Rembrandt's etching of the *Raising of Lazarus* (B.73)(cat. no. 100), though often dated *c.*1632, was probably executed earlier, since its design corresponds most closely to one of the initial phases in Rembrandt's development of his Los Angeles painting, a phase now visible only in X-rays.[9] However, the latter work in its final form most closely corresponds to the Brighton composition. In an independent composition, Rembrandt returned yet again to the subject in an etching of 1642 (B.72) (fig. 100a).[10]

In addition to Lievens's primary inspiration in his colleague Rembrandt's art, he may have been influenced by Italian art; F. Saxl pointed out that Christ's pose with hands clasped and celestial gaze recalls the pose of the Virgin in Guido Reni's *La Pietà dei Mendicanti* of 1613–16 (Pinacoteca Nazionale, Bologna), although the motif had probably already become emblematic of the attitude of spiritual infusion, at least in Bolognese art if not in Italian Baroque painting generally.[11] H. Guratzsch not only summarized the iconographic relationships of the various images of the Raising of Lazarus by Lievens and Rembrandt, noting that the former based his images on John 11:41 and the latter on John 11:43, but also addressed their relationship to earlier traditions of depicting this subject.[12] It is noteworthy, for example, that unlike in earlier representations of the theme neither the disciples nor Mary or Martha are clearly distinguishable in either the Lievens or the Rembrandt painting. It is unknown whether the two paintings of the Raising of Lazarus by Rembrandt and Lievens ('Een opweckinge Laseri van Jan Lievensz') that appeared in Rembrandt's inventory of 25 July 1656[13] were identical with either of the pictures here discussed, but it is significant that Rembrandt would have retained pictures of this theme.

PCS

FIG. 37C
Rembrandt
The Entombment of Christ over
The Raising of Lazarus *c.*1632
Dated 1630
Chalk
28.2 x 20.4 cm
Copyright © The British Museum, London

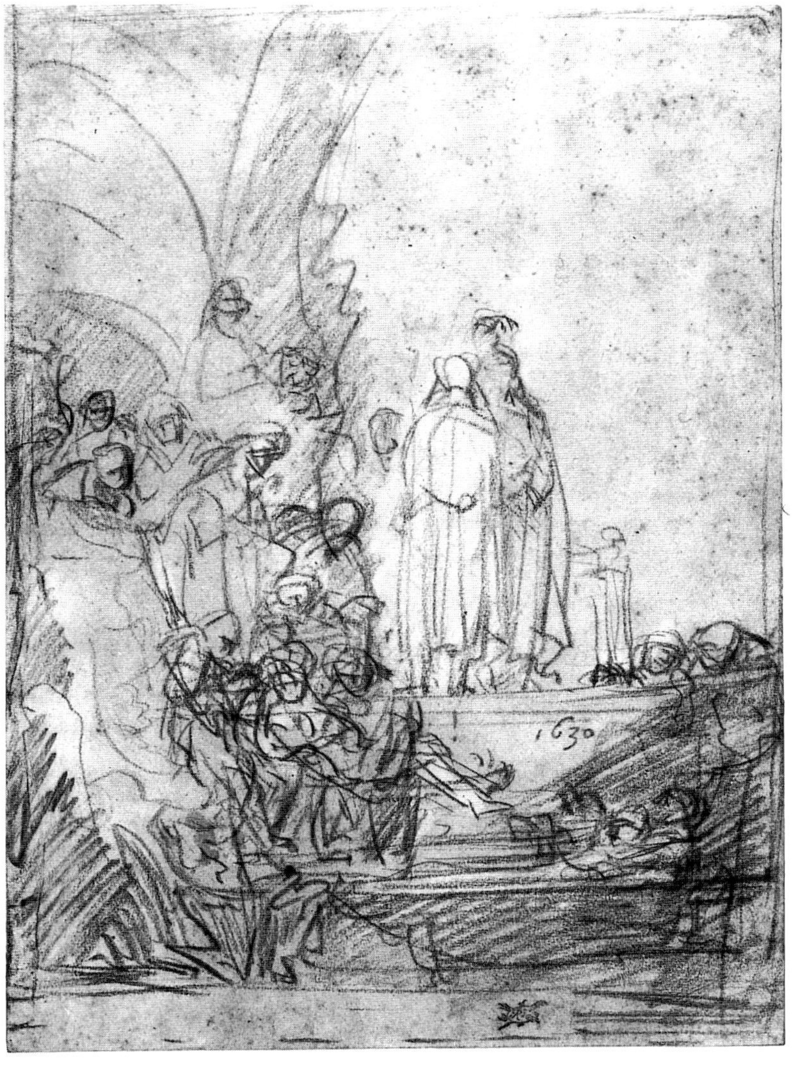

1 *Corpus*, vol. I, 1982, no. A35.
2 Sumowski, *Gemälde*, vol. III, 1987, no. 1245.
3 Hollstein 7.
4 *Corpus*, vol. I, 1982, no. A30.
5 *Corpus*, vol. I, 1982, p. 308.
6 Royalton-Kisch 1991, p. 271; Royalton-Kisch 1992, pp. 62–3, cat. no. 15.
7 Hollstein 1.
8 *Corpus*, vol. III, 1989, pp. 271–9, no. A126.
9 *Corpus*, vol. I, 1982, pp. 293–308, no. A30.
10 Hind 198.
11 Saxl 1923–24, p. 147.
12 Guratzsch 1975, p. 252f; Guratzsch 1976, p. 119ff.
13 Strauss & Van der Meulen 1979, p. 353, no. 1656/12 (no. 42).

Gerrit Dou (1613–1675)

Born in Leiden on 7 April 1613, Gerrit Dou was the son of a glassmaker and glass-engraver, Douwe Jansz de Vries van Arentsveld, who was sufficiently well-to-do to own three houses, which Gerrit would later inherit, on the Korte Rapenburg. According to the Leiden chronicler Jan Jansz Orlers, Gerrit's father enrolled him to be instructed as an engraver (on copper) with Bartholomeus Dolendo, who presumably trained him in drawing. Later he studied with the glass-engraver Pieter Couwenhorn. After a period of instruction in their father's atelier, Gerrit and his brother Jan registered with the Leiden Glassmakers' Guild. From 1625 to 1627, Gerrit was a member of the Guild. On 24 February 1628, he became a pupil of the 22-year-old Rembrandt and remained with the youthful master until the latter moved to Amsterdam in 1631. Subsequently Dou established himself as a master in his native Leiden and would remain there for his entire life. In 1640 and as late as 1657 he is recorded living at the Korte Oude Vest, no. 6, in Leiden. Dou probably had a role in the St Luke's Guild in Leiden, and was recorded in the documents of the Guild as having paid dues to the organization from 1644 to 1651, 1658–68 and 1673–74. In 1665, Johan de Bye, a local collector, organized an exhibition of twenty-seven of Dou's works in Leiden.

Many documents attest to the fame that Dou enjoyed and the high prices that he commanded, as well as the important patrons that pursued him. Houbraken claims that Dou worked slowly and fastidiously, and this may in part explain the demand. Among his noble patrons he counted King Charles II, Queen Christina of Sweden, and Archduke Leopold Wilhelm. In 1657, 1669 and 1674 he drafted wills in which he gave his four houses and his possessions to his family, and to his nephew and pupil, Dominicus van Tol.

Dou never married and throughout his life was attended by his niece. He was buried in the St Pieterskerk in Leiden in mid-February 1675. Documents prove that Matthijs Naiveu, Bartholomeus Maton and Gerrit Maes were his students, and we may be certain that Frans van Mieris, Pieter van Slingelandt and Dominicus van Tol were also his pupils. Houbraken's report that Carel de Moor and Godfried Schalcken also studied with Dou is probably reliable, and it seems likely that Adriaen van Gaesbeeck, Johan van Staveren and Abraham de Pape also spent time in his tutelage.

Gerrit Dou was a painter of unprecedentedly naturalistic, but also exceptionally fastidiously rendered, detailed images of historical, religious and allegorical subjects, portraits, genre scenes and still lifes. Inspired by the refined manner that Rembrandt conceived in Leiden in the late 1620s, Dou was the first to perfect what came to be known as the *fijnschilder* manner.

LITERATURE: Orlers 1641, pp. 377, 380; Van Hoogstraten 1678, pp. 163, 257, 262, 268; Houbraken 1718–21, vol. II, 1719, pp. 1–3; Martin 1901; Martin 1911; Martin 1913; Sumowski, *Gemälde*, vol. I, 1983, pp. 498–607; Leiden 1988, pp. 96–118; Amsterdam 1989, pp. 24–64; Baer 1990.

PCS

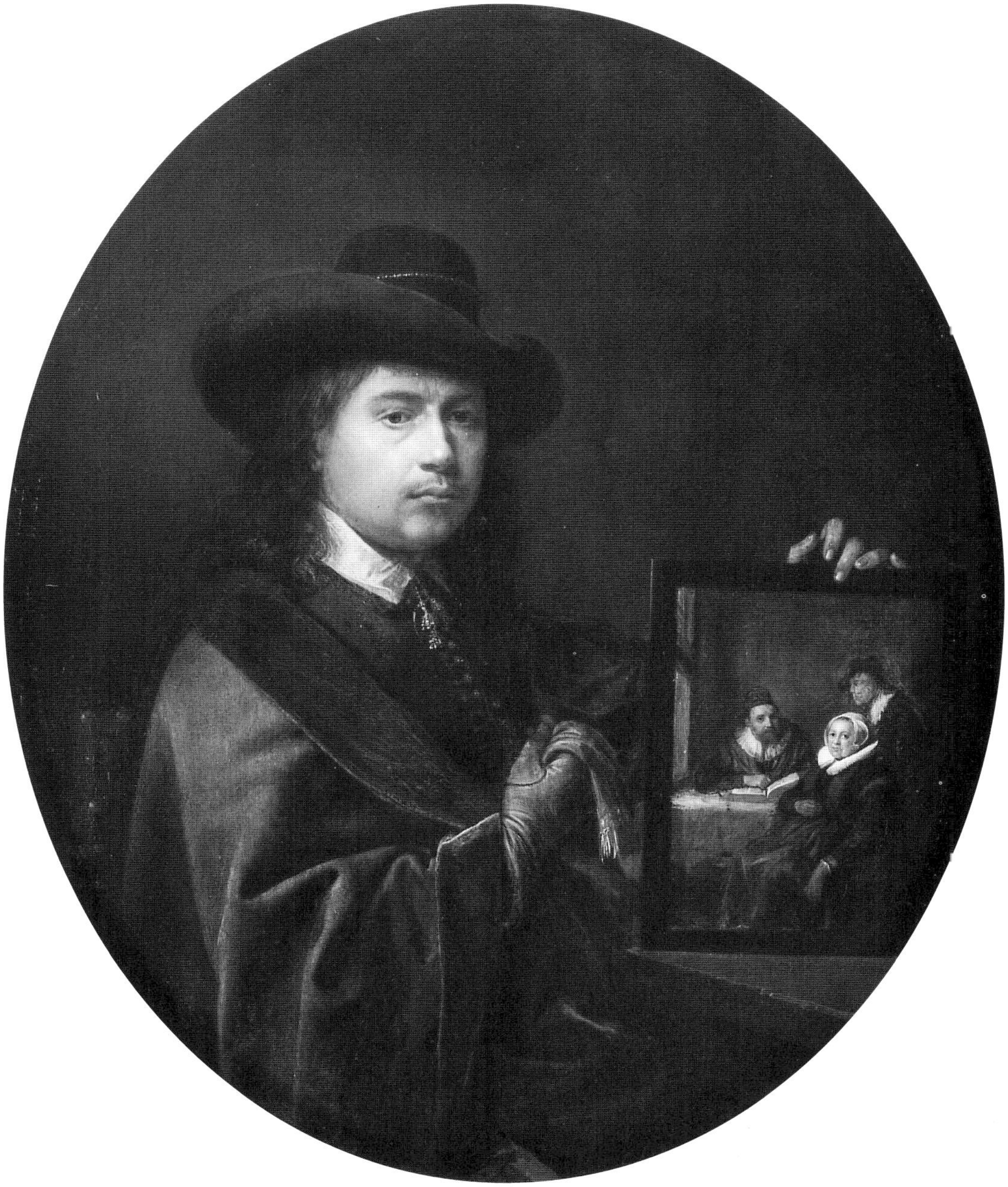

Gerrit Dou
Self-Portrait
Signed
Panel (oval)
27.0 x 23.0 cm
Herzog Anton Ulrich-Museum, Braunschweig
Photograph: B. P. Keiser

38

Gerrit Dou

Standing Soldier with an Arms Still Life

shortly after 1630

Panel
66.0 x 51.0 cm
Szépmüvészeti Múzeum, Budapest

PROVENANCE: Sale, T. Du Chatelard, Paris, 26 March 1900, lot 12; with dealer Charles Sedelmeyer, Paris; with dealer J. Goudstikker, Amsterdam; G. Hoschek von Mühlheim, Prague [1907 cat. (by W. Martin), no. 27]; Béda Surányi, Budapest; Dr Sigismund Jakabházy, Budapest; acquired from Dr Jakabházy in 1962.

LITERATURE: Martin 1913, p. 89 (repr. on left); Sumowski, *Gemälde*, vol. I, 1983, p. 530, no. 268; Sluijter 1993, pp. 40, 55.

Gerrit Dou was a gifted painter of still lifes as well as genre scenes, history paintings and portraits. His *fijnschilder* manner was especially well suited to the rendering of metalware, like the pile of glinting armour depicted here. Often helmets, shields, drums and other military supplies appear in the foregrounds of his paintings of artists' studios, outwardly functioning as studio props.[1] However, here the standing man armed with pike, sword and halberd is surrounded by a veritable armoury of seventeenth-century military equipment; in addition to his armour, there is a saddle, a banner, a musket with inlaid stock and a bandolier of charges, and at the right still heavier artillery – two cannons and several cannonballs.

W. Martin speculated that the man might be an officer of a Leiden militia company,[2] but Sumowski correctly rejected the notion that the painting is a portrait.[3] He argued instead that the soldier is a personification with attributes, concluding that the subject is an allegory of the Art of War and comparing the painting to an engraving by Johan Sadeler, after Stradanus, of *Arma*, dated 1597 (fig. 38a). In Dou's paintings of artists' studios, military supplies have been interpreted as symbols of the active life – to be contrasted with the cerebral life of the painter[4] – or as symbols of profane history as opposed to religious history painting.[5] Other authors have noted the cast-off armour's potential association with the lost power of Mars in allegories of Peace.[6] Later artists executed independent still lifes of armour and military supplies; examples are paintings by Willem de Poorter (Museum Boijmans Van Beuningen, Rotterdam; Herzog Anton Ulrich-Museum, Braunschweig)[7] and by Gerard van Steenwijck (formerly Butôt Collection),[8] which have been interpreted as allegories of the vanity of earthly power.[9]

PCS

1 Sumowski, *Gemälde*, vol. I, 1983, nos 261, 262, 267.
2 Martin 1913, p. 89.
3 Sumowski, *Gemälde*, vol. I, 1983, p. 530, no. 268.
4 O. Naumann, in Philadelphia / Berlin / London 1984, p. 182, cat. no. 31.
5 Raupp 1984, p. 349.
6 Leiden 1988, p. 117, cat. no. 17 (the *Artist's Studio* by Adriaen van Gaesbeeck, formerly attributed to Gerrit Dou).
7 Sumowski, *Gemälde*, vol. IV, 1990, nos 1653 (dated 1636), 1654.
8 Bol 1982, fig. 297.
9 For general discussion and reproductions, see Klemm 1980.

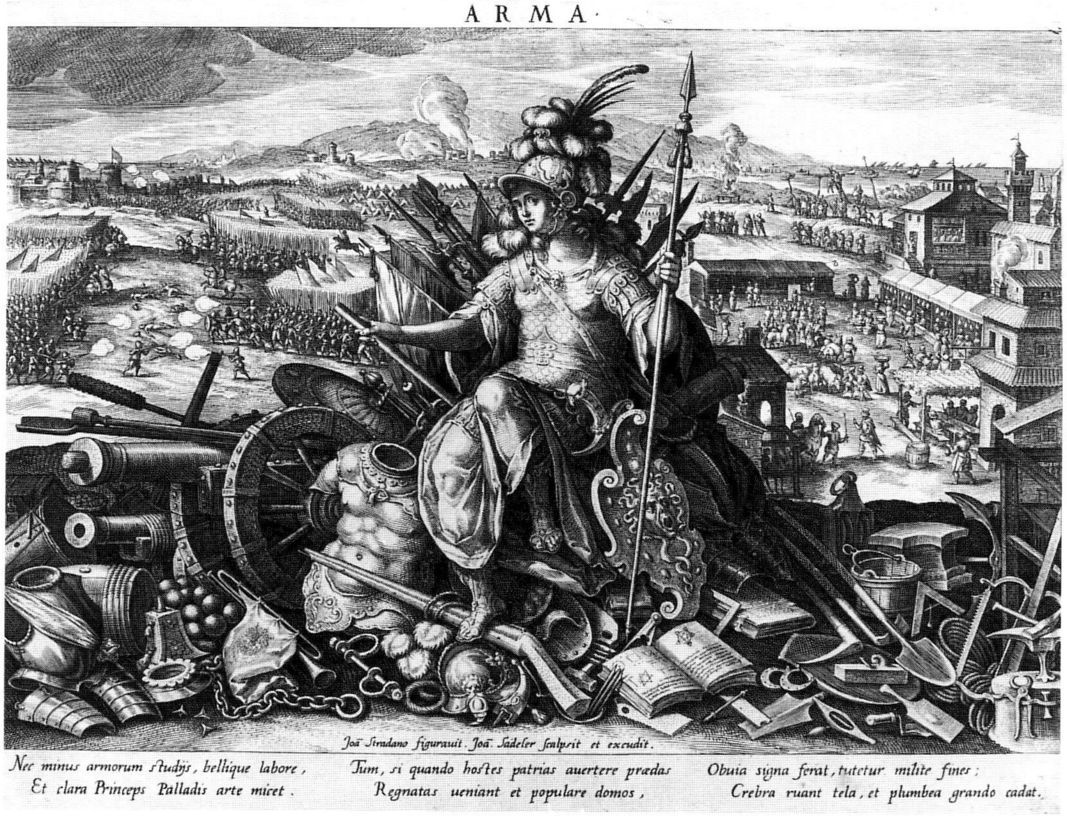

FIG. 38a
Johan Sadeler (1550–1600), after Stradanus
Arma
Dated 1597
Engraving
22.2 x 28.3 cm
Westfälisches Landesmuseum für Kunst und Kulturgeschichte, Münster

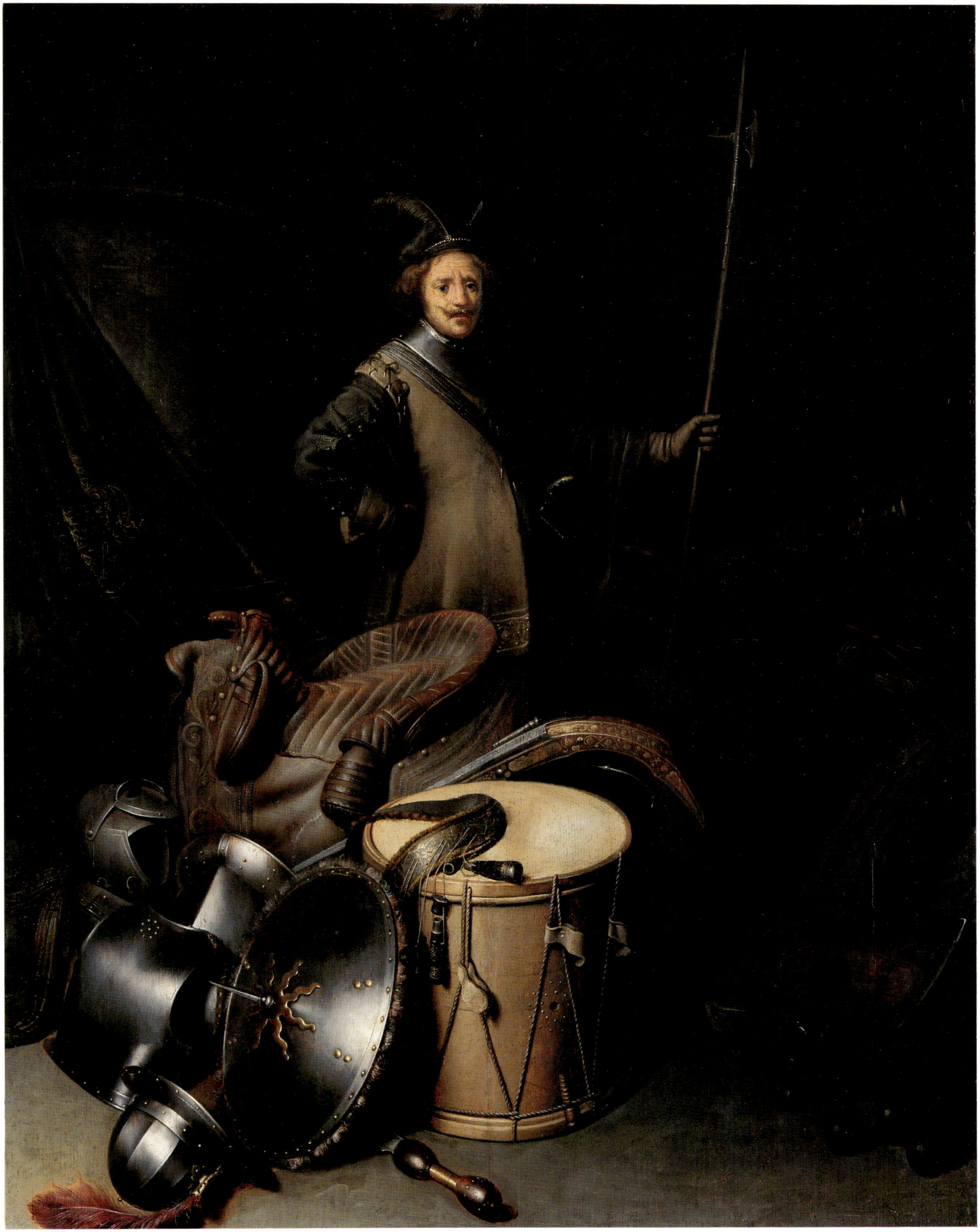

39

Gerrit Dou

Artist in His Studio

*c.*1630–32

Formerly signed on scroll of paper lower centre
Panel
59.0 x 43.5 cm
Newhouse Galleries, Inc., New York

PROVENANCE: With dealer Charles Sedelmeyer, Paris [1894 cat., no. 8, repr.]; John Wanamaker, Philadelphia; purchased from Wanamaker, New York, by G. F. Plympton, Hackensack, New Jersey; sale, New York (Sotheby's), 17 June 1982, lot 118, repr.; Frank Martelli, Bel Aire, California.

LITERATURE: Hofstede de Groot 1908–27, vol. I, 1908, pp. 443–4, no. 311; Martin 1911, p. 114; Martin 1913, pp. 12 (repr.), 180; Raupp 1984, pp. 276–7; Baer 1990, no. 6.

Gerrit Dou's early development is difficult to reconstruct because of an absence of dated works, but documents record that he became Rembrandt's pupil in Leiden in 1628 when he was only fifteen and that he opened his own atelier three or four years later. The present work has been assigned on stylistic grounds to the artist's early years under Rembrandt's tutelage: C. Hofstede de Groot stated simply that it was an 'early work'; W. Martin dated it to 'around 1628 to 1630'; and R. Baer adjusted this dating to '*c.*1630–32'.[1]

The subject of an artist in his studio was a well-established pictorial tradition by this time,[2] and had been addressed by Rembrandt himself in one of his small early Leiden period panels (Museum of Fine Arts, Boston) (Bredius 419).[3] While that work depicted the painter standing off from his easel in the sparsely furnished interior of his studio, the present work portrays the artist at closer quarters holding his palette and brushes, seated beside his easel and before a table with a still life of studio props – books, a lute, a skull; on the floor are a globe and a plaster cast (of a Roman emperor?), while on the back wall hangs a sword. H.-J. Raupp (1984) first suggested, and Baer (1990) allowed, that the source for this composition and its particular configuration of still-life objects might be Thomas de Keyser's *Portrait of the Artist David Bailly* of *c.*1627, in which David Bailly is usually assumed to have painted the still life (fig. 39a).[4] Together with Pieter Potter and the young Jan Davidsz de Heem, Bailly is generally regarded as one of the founders of the tradition of Leiden *vanitas* still-life painting, although his most famous painting of this type is dated 1651 (Stedelijk Museum de Lakenhal, Leiden).

While shared objects in the de Keyser and the Dou could certainly be associated with life's transience and *memento mori*, A. J. Adams argued that the former painting 'praises art's permanence in the face of transient nature, and its ability to elevate the [craftsman] to the status of a gentleman and humanist'.[5] Baer concluded that Dou's early painting conveyed a similar meaning,[6] noting that self-portraits with *vanitas* objects by later artists like Evert Collier include inscriptions with Seneca's motto 'Vita brevis, ars longa'.[7]

Among Dou's other images of artists in their studios, the painting of a young man at an easel, usually dated *c.*1630 (fig. 39b),[8] is probably the nearest in conception to the present work, but all of these other full-length images devote more attention to the interior space.[9] Notwithstanding the present work's focus on the artist and contrary to Hofstede de Groot's theory,[10] the sitter cannot be identified as Rembrandt, nor, as Martin supposed, as Dou himself.[11]

PCS

1 Hofstede de Groot 1908–27, vol. I, 1908, p. 444, no. 311; Martin 1913, ill. no. 12; Baer 1990, no. 6.
2 Raupp 1984.
3 *Corpus*, vol. I, 1982, no. A18.
4 Bruyn 1951, pp. 162–3; Popper-Voskuil 1973, p. 58; Adams 1985, vol. III, pp. 36–8, no. 14.
5 Adams 1985, vol. I, p. 151.
6 Baer 1990, no. 6.
7 See, for example, Collier's painting reproduced in Popper-Voskuil 1973, fig. 13.
8 Sumowski, *Gemälde*, vol. I, 1983, p. 528, no. 262.
9 Cf. Sumowski, *Gemälde*, vol. I, 1983, no. 267, and a painting at Sotheby's, London, in 1973 (sale, 21 March 1973, lot 10; see also Leiden 1976–77, p. 25, fig. e).
10 Hofstede de Groot 1908–27, vol. I, 1908, pp. 443–4, no. 311.
11 Martin 1913, ill. no. 12.

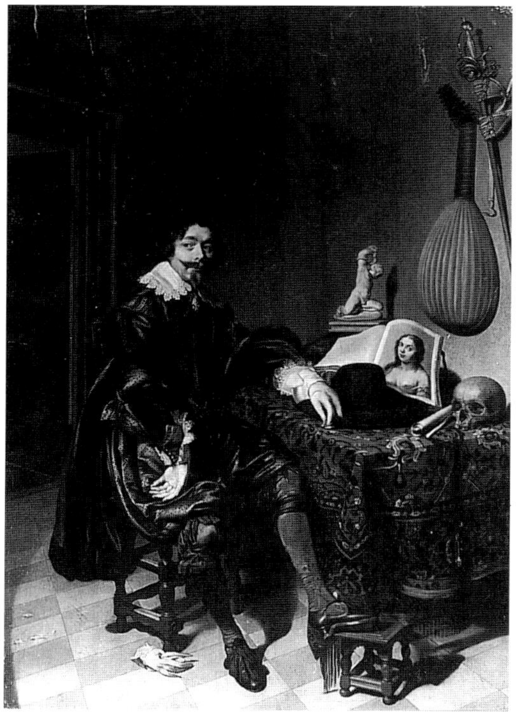

FIG. 39a
Thomas de Keyser 1596/97–1667 (and David Bailly?)
*Portrait of the Artist David Bailly c.*1627
Panel
73.5 x 50.5 cm (approx.)
Mme Edgar Stern, Paris, in 1951
Photograph: RKD

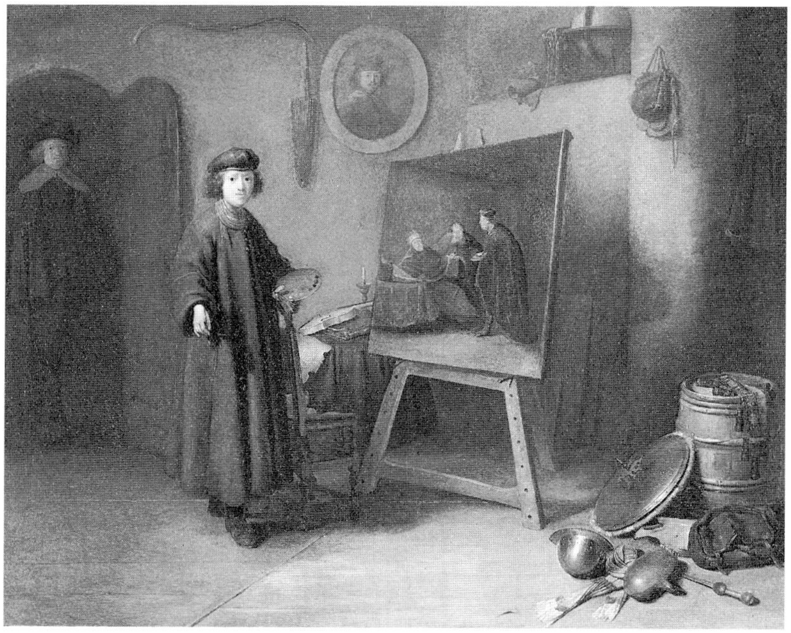

FIG. 39b
Gerrit Dou
Artist in His Studio
*c.*1630
Panel
53.0 x 64.5 cm
Private collection

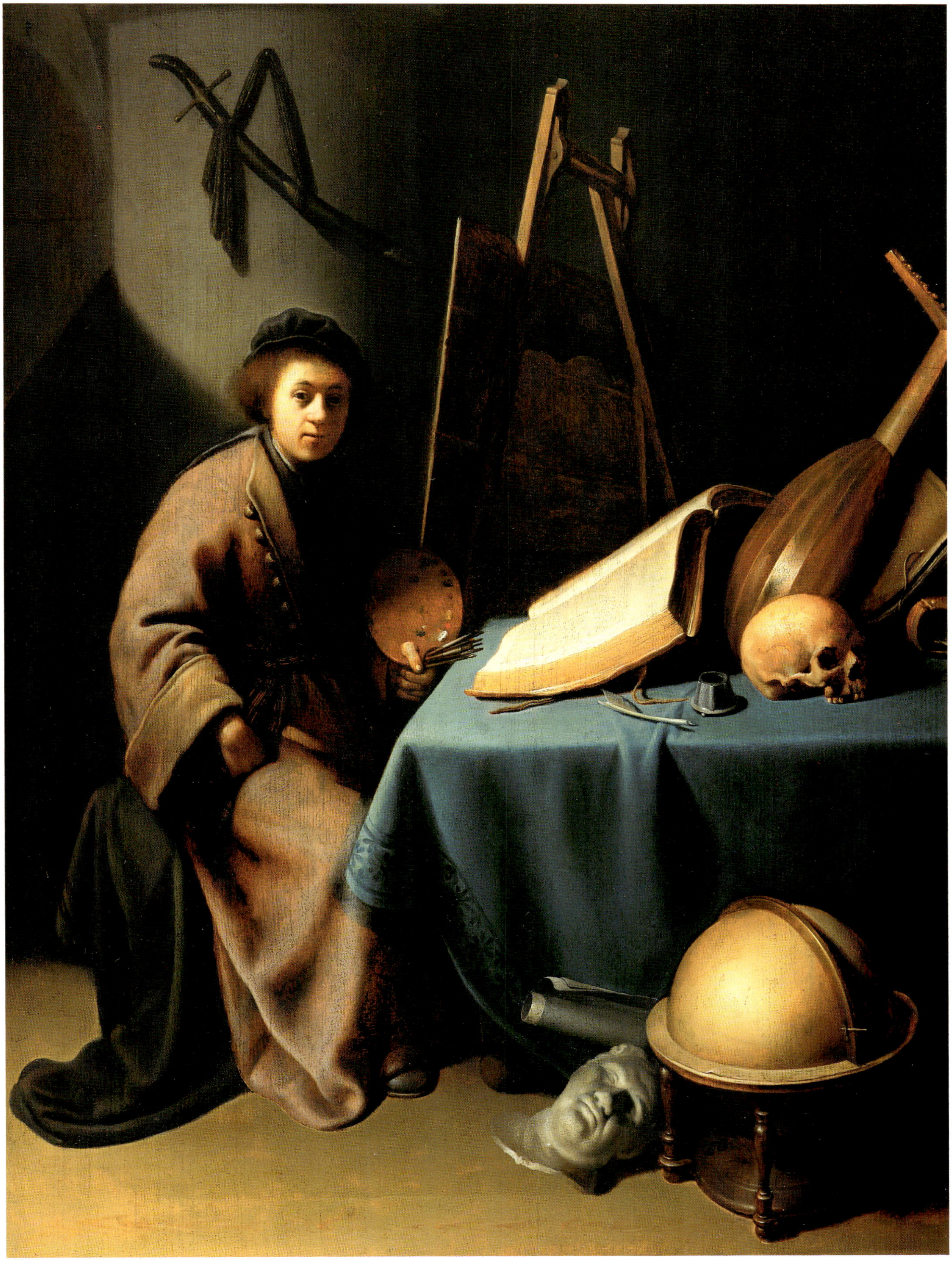

40
Gerrit Dou
Self-Portrait(?) in the Studio
*c.*1645–50

Signed upper left *GDou* (first two letters ligated)
Panel (arched)
12.4 x 8.3 cm
Private collection, Europe

PROVENANCE: (Possibly) Count Fraula, Brussels, and his sale, Brussels, 21 July 1738, lot 125, 105 fl.; Duque de Cadaval; sale, London (Christie's), 8 December 1995, lot 33A, repr.

Support for the identification of this small panel as the artist's portrait of himself from *c.*1645–50 is provided by a comparison with Dou's self-portrait, signed and dated 165[?], from the Czernin Collection, now preserved in Salzburg (fig. 40a).[1] Another small panel, it too depicts the artist half-length before a studio with easel, tall parasol and globe but he is now holding a palette and brushes as he leans out the casement of the arched masonry window of one of Dou's favoured 'niches'. A further revealing comparison is with Dou's oval-shaped self-portrait at the Herzog Anton Ulrich-Museum, Braunschweig (repr. with Dou biography), which depicts the artist half-length in a similar costume, hat and pose, again wearing one glove and holding the other, but supporting with his bare hand a small group portrait, no doubt an image of his parents and possibly his brother Jan.[2]

W. van de Watering (sale cat., Christie's, London, 8 December 1995, lot 33A) supports the identification of the present work as a self-portrait, but dates the painting *c.*1645 on the basis of the costume and age of the sitter.

The pose depicted in the present work and that in the Braunschweig painting, with the half-length sitter's amply draped arm drawn across his torso, probably derive from Rembrandt's famous *Self-Portrait at the Age of 34* of 1640 (cat. no. 13), which in turn was inspired by Titian and Raphael, and subsequently inspired many Dutch self-portraits as well as other portraits, including works by the Rembrandt followers Ferdinand Bol (cat. nos 45, 46), Govaert Flinck, Gerbrand van den Eeckhout (see self-portrait reproduced on p. 267), Arent de Gelder and Dou's pupil Frans van Mieris.[3] The studio props that appear in the background recur in other paintings by Dou of artists' studios, including the early work in this exhibition (cat. no. 39). The painting on the easel in the present work depicts the Rest on the Flight into Egypt and resembles several paintings of this subject by Leiden artists working in the circle of Dou and Rembrandt.[4]

The present painting may be the work that was in Count Fraula's collection in 1738;[5] the larger version of the composition that was in the E. Warneck collection in Paris in 1908 was probably only a copy.[6] When the present work was in the Duque de Cadaval's collection, it was paired and framed with a small portrait of a woman, by an entirely different hand.

PCS

1 Martin 1913, ill. no. 18; Blechinger 1980, p. 55 (inv. no. 536).
2 Martin 1913, ill. no. 18; R. Klessmann, in Braunschweig 1983, pp. 55–6, cat. no. 303; Sumowski, *Gemälde*, vol. I, 1983, no. 301.
3 C. Brown, in MacLaren / Brown 1991, vol. 1, pp. 339–41, no. 672; De Jongh 1969, pp. 49–67.
4 For example, *Corpus*, vol. I, 1982, no. C6.
5 Hofstede de Groot 1908–27, vol. I, 1908, p. 437, no. 279b (with incorrect Fraula sale lot number); Hoet 1752, no. 122 (with dimensions ('hoog 5 duym breet 3 duym en half') corresponding to those of the present work).
6 Hofstede de Groot 1908–27, vol. I, 1908, p. 443, no. 310 (as 'Portrait of Rembrandt(?)', panel, 61/2 x 5 in.); Martin 1913, ill. no. 21 (as by Dou, but the author notes (p. 180) that he found it 'impossible to certify its originality').

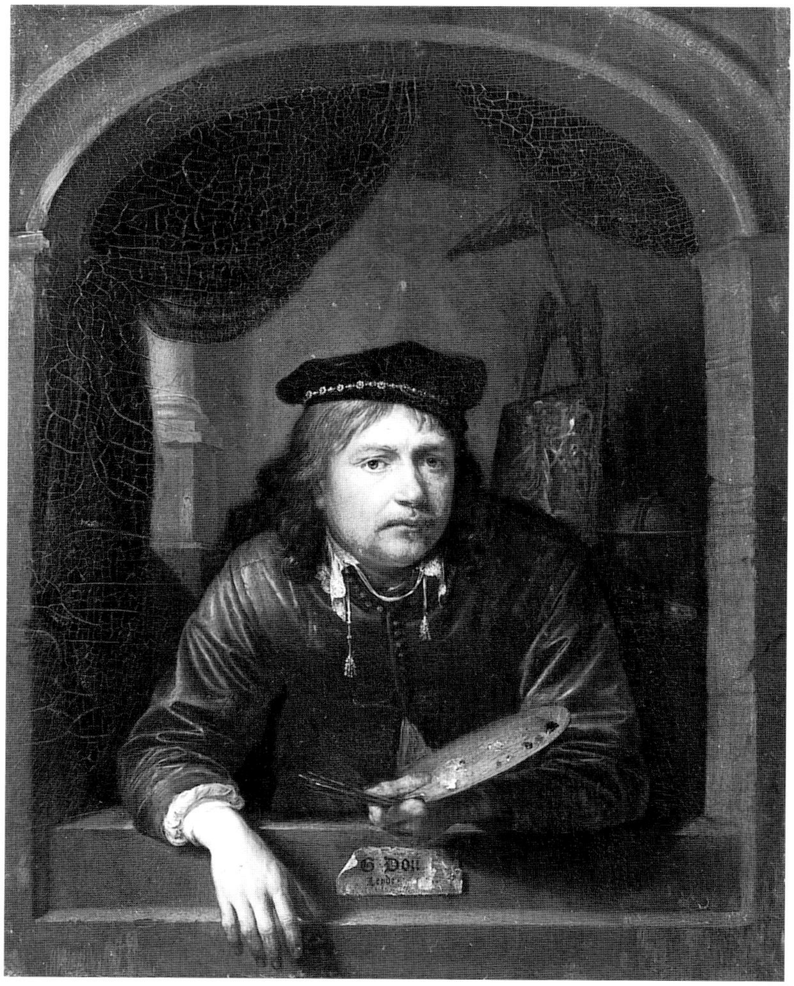

FIG. 40a
Gerrit Dou
Self-Portrait in a Window
Signed and dated 165[?]
Panel
23.0 x 17.0 cm
Residenzgalerie Salzburg

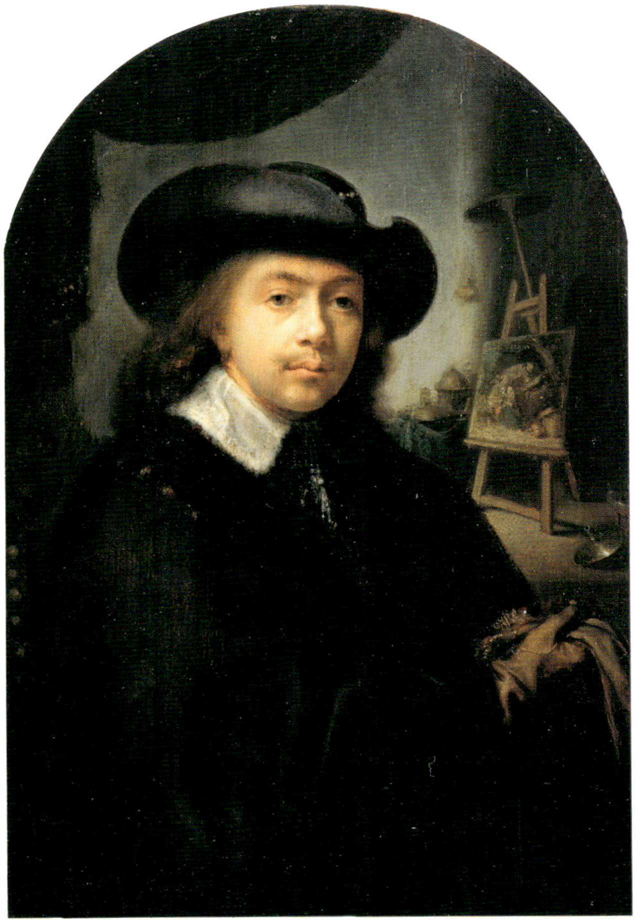

Govaert Flinck (1615–1660)

Born in Cleves on 25 January 1615, Govaert Flinck first studied with Lambert Jacobsz, who also trained Jacob Backer. As Houbraken reported, Flinck later travelled to Amsterdam to 'test his art' and there he studied with Rembrandt, entering the latter's studio in about 1633. In Amsterdam, Flinck lodged with the art dealer and in-law of Rembrandt, Hendrick Uylenburgh. Flinck signed and dated his first paintings in 1636, establishing himself as an independent master. Houbraken observed that his style remained close enough to that of Rembrandt that his works were often mistaken for the master's. According to Joachim von Sandrart (1675), Flinck's portraits were especially admired, though while they were in Rembrandt's manner they were 'judged to be more felicitous in their detail and in their pleasing quality of portrayal'.

By the 1640s Flinck was increasingly drawn to the art of the popular portraitist Bartholomeus van der Helst and to the styles and conventions of Flemish noble portraiture. Houbraken offers an account, albeit conventionalized, of Flinck's efforts to extricate himself from the tenebrous manner of Rembrandt and to accommodate the lighter hues of Italian painting. His conversion won him commissions from the Great Elector of Brandenburg, the Prince of Orange and Amalia van Solms, the stadholder's widow. He was also asked to produce commissions for the Town Hall of Amsterdam in 1656 and 1658, but died in that city in February 1660 before he could complete the decorations for the Grand Gallery. Subsequently the commission *The Conspiracy of the Batavians* (Nationalmuseum, Stockholm) (Bredius 482) (p. 27, fig. 9) was awarded to his teacher, Rembrandt.

Praised by leading poets such as Joost van den Vondel and Jan Vos, Flinck was one of the most successful artists of his day. His early portraits, *tronies*, history paintings, allegorical subjects, and landscapes initally owe a debt to Rembrandt but soon adopt a more international manner.

LITERATURE: Houbraken 1718–21, vol. II, 1719, pp. 18–21; Von Moltke 1965; Sumowski, *Drawings*, vol. 4, 1981, pp. 1883–2166; Sumowski, *Gemälde*, vol. II, 1985, pp. 998–1151.

PCS

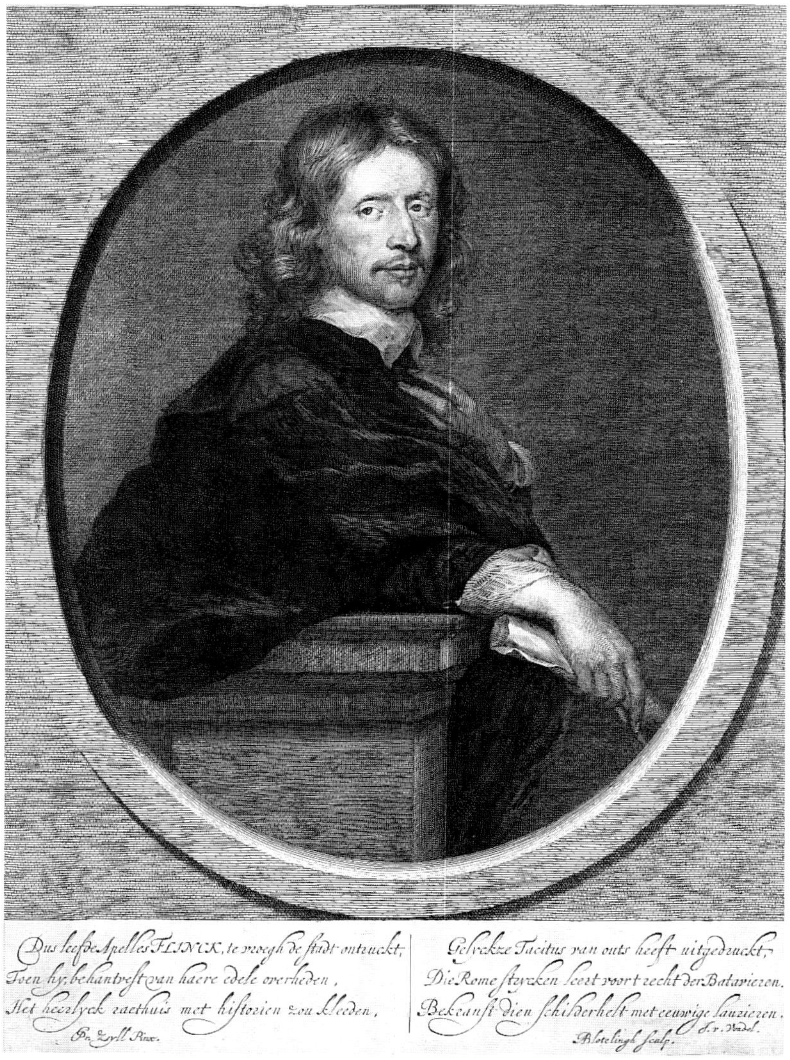

Abraham Blotelingh (1640–1690),
after Cornelis van Dalen,
after Gerard van Zijl
Portrait of Govaert Flinck
Engraving
From a reproduction at the RKD

41
Govaert Flinck
Isaac Blessing Jacob
*c.*1637

Signed on platter lower left *G. Flinck f.*
Canvas
124.0 x 151.0 cm
Collection Netherlands Institute for Cultural Heritage, Rijswijk, Amsterdam (on loan to the Museum Catharijneconvent, Utrecht)

PROVENANCE: (This picture or fig. 41a) Sale, Amsterdam, 17 April 1758 (as Rembrandt); sale, Six, Amsterdam, 25–26 October 1932, lot 500; with dealer Katz, The Hague. 1934; van Winter, Amsterdam; Dr H. W. J. Fockema, Arnhem; Rijksdienst Beeldende Kunst, The Hague (now Netherlands Institute for Cultural Heritage); on loan to Museum Catharijneconvent, Utrecht.

LITERATURE: Von Moltke 1965, p. 67, no. 9; Sumowski, *Gemälde*, vol. II, 1985, p. 1019, no. 613; N. van der Kamp, in Amsterdam / Jerusalem 1991–92, p. 222; Rijksdienst Beeldende Kunst 1992, p. 98, cat. no. 30; A. Blankert, in Stockholm 1992–93, p. 53.

The Old Testament subject of Isaac Blessing Jacob (Genesis 27:21–29) is a tale of subterfuge, deception and a stolen blessing. Earlier in the story (Genesis 25:29–34), Jacob had secretly purchased the birthright of his elder brother, Esau, for a mere bowl of porridge. Subsequently when their father, Isaac, was blind and near death, Jacob sought to secure that birthright with the old man's blessing. Preparing to bless his eldest, Isaac instructed Esau to bring him wild venison. Rebecca, Isaac's wife, overheard the exchange and conceived a plan to enable Jacob to take Esau's place. She hurriedly sent Jacob to slaughter two goat kids, which she prepared for her husband (note the meal of meat and wine in the left foreground of Flinck's painting), thereby confecting a substitute for the venison. Dressing Jacob in Esau's clothes she covered his hands and neck with the kids' skins to complete the deceit, since, as Jacob had observed (Genesis 27:11), 'Esau my brother is a hairy man, and I am a smooth man'. Then 'Jacob went near unto Isaac his father, and he felt him, and said, "The voice is Jacob's voice, but the hands are the hands of Esau" ... so he blessed him' (Genesis 27:22–23). In Flinck's painting, blind Isaac holds Jacob's gloved hand as his son leans in close, as if at the moment when 'Isaac said unto him, Come near now, and kiss me, my son. And he came near, and kissed him: and he smelled the smell of his raiment, and blessed him, and said, See, the smell of my son is as the smell of a field which the Lord hath blessed' (Genesis 27:26–27).

In both his painting in the Catharijneconvent and his similarly conceived but more colourful version of the same subject, dated 1638, at the Rijksmuseum (fig. 41a),[1] Flinck depicts the climax of the story, when the deception is virtually complete. Although not mentioned in the biblical account as actually present at the blessing, Rebecca is depicted at the bedside in both works, evidently to heighten the emotional anticipation. Here she looks out directly at the viewer, who would have shared her knowledge of the deceit.

Sumowski suggested and N. van der Kamp concurred that the present undated work probably preceded the more elaborate Rijksmuseum painting of 1638.[2] One of the two versions was auctioned in Amsterdam in 1758 as a Rembrandt. It was recognized as a Flinck by the Leiden collector Johan van der Marck, who crossed out Rembrandt's name and replaced it with 'Flink' in his copy of the sale catalogue.[3] No painting by Rembrandt himself of this subject is known, yet Sumowski believed that it was he who first conceived the bedside exchange, citing

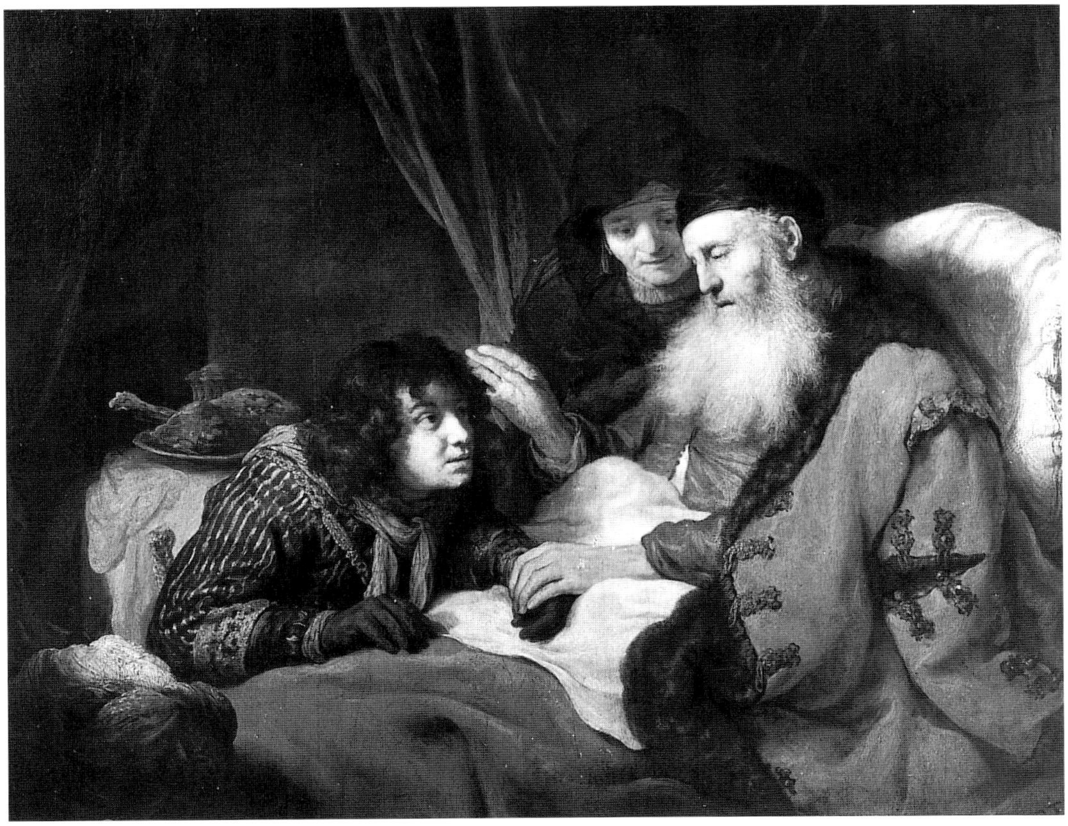

FIG. 41a
Govaert Flinck
Isaac Blessing Jacob
Signed and dated 1638
(signature and date no longer visible)
Canvas
117.0 x 141.0 cm
Rijksmuseum, Amsterdam

several wash drawings by the master, notably one formerly in the collection of Oskar Bondi, Vienna (Benesch 509).[4] J. W. von Moltke also raised the possibility of a lost painting by Rembrandt of this subject.[5]

The theme of Isaac Blessing Jacob was exceptionally popular with the artists in Rembrandt's circle and was treated repeatedly not only by Flinck but also by Gerbrand van den Eeckhout (for example, his painting dated 1642 at the Metropolitan Museum of Art, New York),[6] Gerrit Willemsz Horst (the picture dated 1638 at the Dulwich Picture Gallery; and that formerly at the Kaiser Friedrich Museum, Berlin)[7] and Jan Victors (Louvre, Paris; Art Gallery and Museums, Brighton; and location unknown).[8] As in the case of other history subjects that were unusually popular with Rembrandt's pupils, such as the Dismissal of Hagar, this dramatic theme may have been one that the master assigned as an exercise (as well as an enterprise) to his pupils and followers. The subject also had a topical appeal for theologians. Even before the birth of Jacob and Esau, it had been foretold to Rebecca that 'the elder shall serve the younger' (Genesis 25:23), and consequently the tale figured prominently in defences of Calvinist predestination. For the Church Fathers and the Middle Ages, Jacob was not the guilty party but the personification of the Christian Church succeeding over Esau, as representative of the Jews and the old dispensation. Calvin and the exegetes who provided the marginalia for the official *Statenbijbel* concurred in regarding Isaac's blessing of Jacob as a special fulfilment of divine promise with respect to the chosen ones.[9]

PCS

1 Sumowski, *Gemälde*, vol. II, 1985, no. 614.

2 Sumowski, *Gemälde*, vol. II, 1985, p. 1019, no. 613 (as *c.*1637); N. van der Kamp, in Amsterdam / Jerusalem 1991–92, p. 222.

3 A. Blankert, in Stockholm 1992–93, p. 53.

4 Sumowski's ideas were noted by von Moltke (Von Moltke 1965, p. 18); see also Sumowski, *Gemälde*, vol. III, 1985, p. 1019, no. 614. For the drawing, see Benesch 1973, vol. III, no. 509, fig. 669.

5 Von Moltke 1965, p. 18.

6 Sumowski, *Gemälde*, vol. II, 1985, no. 397.

7 Sumowski, *Gemälde*, vol. II, 1985, nos 908, 909.

8 Sumowski, *Gemälde*, vol. IV, 1990, nos 1746, 1782, 1769.

9 See especially N. van der Kamp, in Amsterdam / Jerusalem 1991–92, p. 37.

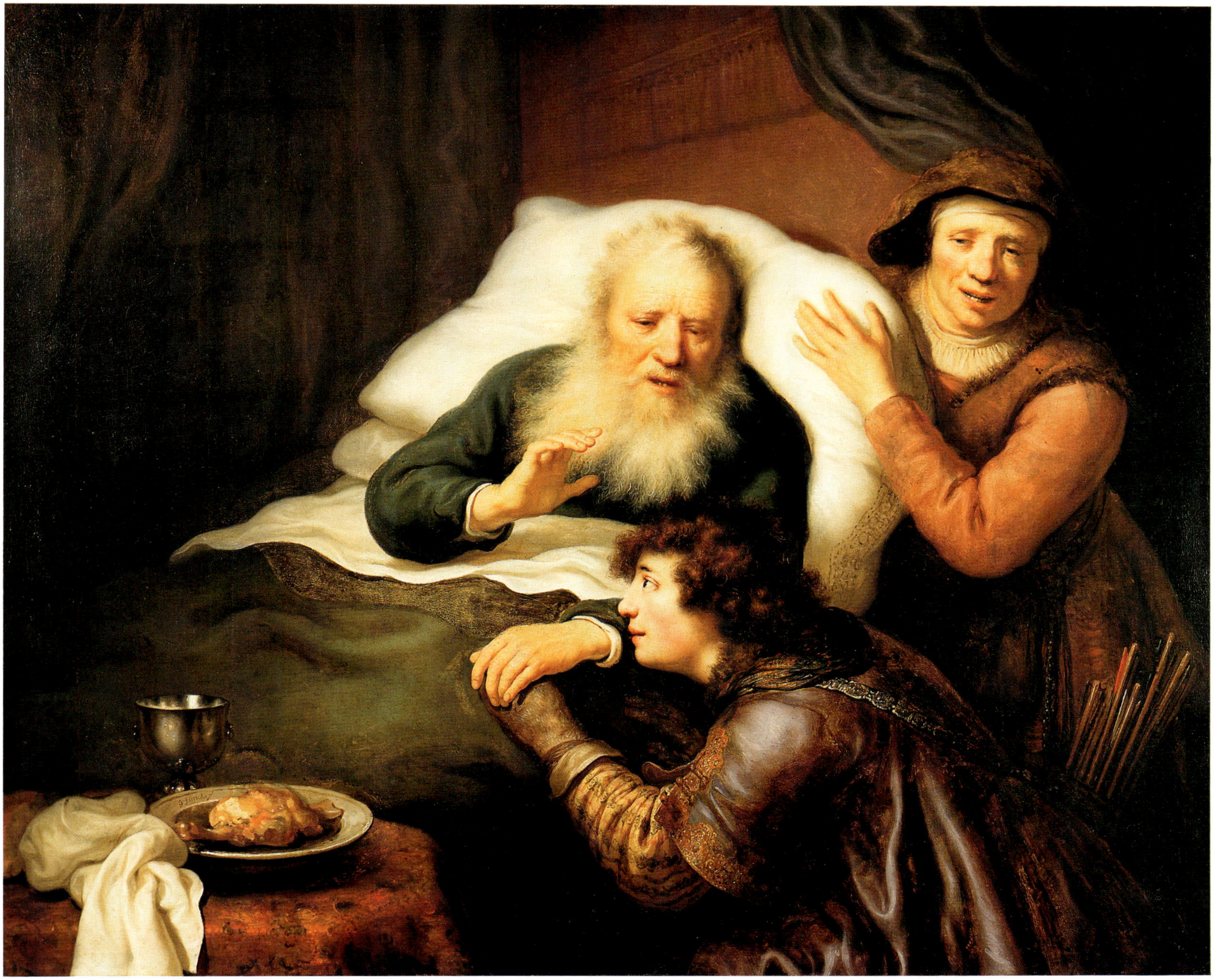

42

Govaert Flinck

Manoah's Sacrifice

Signed and dated lower centre *G. Flinck f. 1640*
Canvas
74.0 x 123.8 cm
Agnes Etherington Art Centre, Queen's University, Kingston, Canada
Gift of Drs Alfred and Isabel Bader, 1975

PROVENANCE: Dr van Hengel, Arnhem; with dealer D. Katz, Dieren; sale, Dr C. J. K. van Aalst, London (Sotheby's), 1 April 1960, lot 22, repr.; with dealer C. Marshall Spink, London [1963 cat., no. 4]; sale, London (Sotheby's), 10 July 1974, lot 50, repr.; Dr Alfred Bader, Milwaukee.

LITERATURE: Von Moltke 1965, pp. 19, 22, 69, no. 19; Sumowski, *Gemälde*, vol. II, 1985, p. 1020, no. 617; J. van Gent & G. M. C. Pastoor, in Amsterdam / Jerusalem 1991–92, p. 72.

Flinck entered Rembrandt's studio in about 1633 and probably remained there, as an assistant rather than as a pupil, until 1636, the year of his first dated paintings. By the latter date he had established himself as an independent master; however, he remained loyal and attuned to Rembrandt's style and subject matter (both large and small-scale history paintings, portraits, *tronies* and landscapes) long after achieving his independence. Indeed Houbraken affirms that Flinck's works were often mistaken for Rembrandt's. The present work attests to the master's ongoing influence not only in its tenebrist palette, dramatic conception of the theme, and strong contrasts of light and shade, but also in individual motifs. The arrangement of the three figures around the sacrificial altar recalls Rembrandt's animated pen drawing of the same subject of *c.*1639 in Berlin's Kupferstichkabinett (Benesch 180). In addition, as J. W. von Moltke observed,[1] the departing angel is based on that in Rembrandt's painting of 1637 of *The Angel Departing the Family of Tobias* (Bredius 503) (fig. 42a), which C. Hofstede de Groot long ago recognized as copied from Dirck Coornheert's woodcut after Maarten van Heemskerck's design of the theme, dated 1563.[2]

The subject of Manoah's Sacrifice had been treated by Rembrandt's teacher Pieter Lastman in at least two paintings (the version signed and dated 1624 in a private collection, Bolsward; and the work dated 1627 in a private collection, on loan to the Museum het Rembrandthuis, Amsterdam).[3] Some observers have speculated that the fact that Lastman's compositions were of such keen and ongoing interest to the pupils of Rembrandt may mean that the latter may have assigned his teacher's favoured themes to his students as exercises.

The Bible (Judges 13:19–21) recounts the story of a traveller who visited the house of Manoah, a Danite living in Zorah during the time of the Philistine occupation. Manoah made a sacrifice to honour the visitor, who had foretold that his host's barren wife would bear a son who would deliver Israel from the Philistines. As the fire ignited, the visitor revealed himself to be an angel of the Lord by ascending to heaven as Manoah and his wife recoiled in fear. Samson, the son who was born to the couple, became the military hero of Israel and subsequently was often regarded, even in the seventeenth century, as a prefiguration of Christ.

While several of Rembrandt's pupils and followers depicted the Sacrifice of Manoah as an internalized, spiritually charged moment (for example, the painting now attributed to Willem Drost at the Gemäldegalerie, Dresden), most delighted, as did Flinck, in the explosively terrifying moment of divine revelation. However, Flinck seems to have been the first Dutch history painter to conceive the subject in a horizontal format in a landscape with farmhouse, an interpretation that J. van Gent and G. M. C. Pastoor have suggested may acknowledge Flavius Josephus's claim (Book V, chap. 10) that Manoah's domicile was an estate outside the city.[4] The present work's composition later influenced, among others, Nicolaes Moeyaert.

A replica purported to be autograph is at the Musée des Beaux-Arts, Tours.[5]

PCS

1 Von Moltke 1965, p. 69, no. 19.
2 Hofstede de Groot 1894, p. 175.
3 Amsterdam 1991, pp. 120–1, 128–9, cat. nos 18, 21, reprs.
4 J. van Gent & G. M. C. Pastoor, in Amsterdam / Jerusalem 1991–92, p. 72.
5 Von Moltke 1965, p. 69, no. 20, repr.

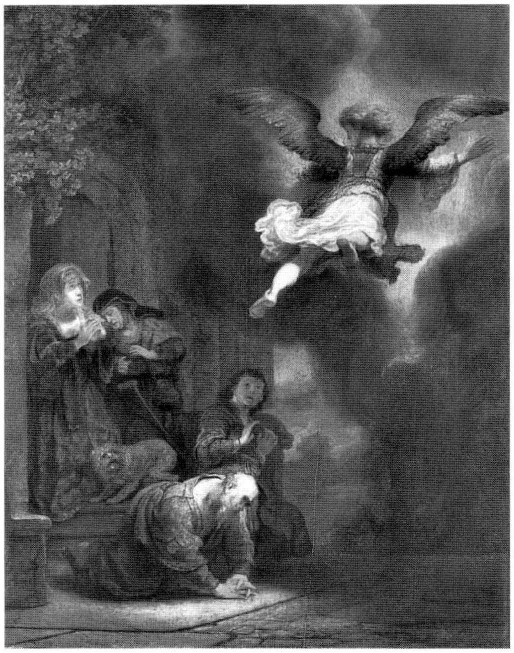

FIG. 42a
Rembrandt
The Angel Departing the Family of Tobias
Signed and dated 1637
Panel
66.0 x 52.0 cm
Musée du Louvre, Paris

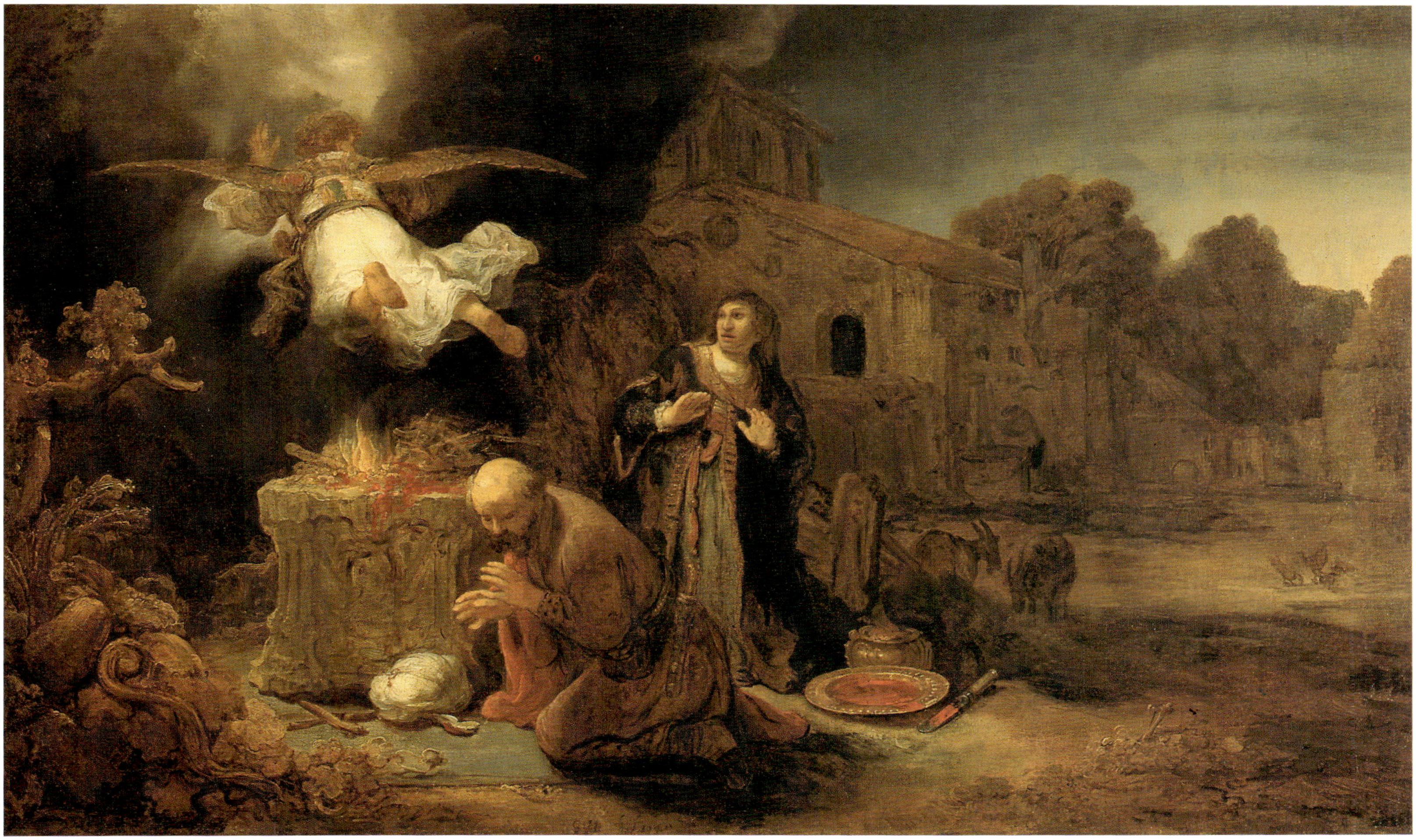

43

Govaert Flinck

Portrait of Dirck Graswinckel and Geertruyt van Loon in a Landscape

Signed and dated lower right *G. Flinck / 1646*
Canvas
107.5 x 91.0 cm
Museum Boijmans Van Beuningen, Rotterdam

PROVENANCE: (Possibly) Sale, Hendrik Reydon, Amsterdam (De Vries), 5–6 April 1827, lot 45, to Roos for 200 fl. (dimensions given as 115 x 85 cm, not 105 x 85 cm, as recorded in Von Moltke 1994, no. 472); acquired by the Boymans Museum for 500 fl. in 1854.

LITERATURE: Bürger 1858–60, vol. 2, pp. 176–9; Gudlaugsson 1948–49, p. 257, note 1; Von Moltke 1965, pp. 22–3, 164, no. 466 [this picture possibly identical with Von Moltke, no. 472]; G. Jansen, in Amsterdam / Groningen 1983, pp. 154–5, cat. no. 32; Sumowski, *Gemälde*, vol. II, 1985, p. 1040, no. 713; E. de Jongh, in Haarlem 1986, p. 155, cat. no. 28; J. Giltaij & G. Jansen, in Rotterdam 1988, pp. 38–40, cat. no. 8.

Although Govaert Flinck in his early years was one of his master's closest followers, Rembrandt painted only two or three double portraits and none (with the possible exception of the so-called *Jewish Bride* (Rijksmuseum, Amsterdam) (Bredius 416)) out-of-doors. The present painting is conceived instead in the Flemish marriage portrait tradition, which originated with Peter Paul Rubens's famous *Self-Portrait with Isabella Brandt in a Honeysuckle Bower* (fig. 43a) and was subsequently imported north in works like Frans Hals's *Married Couple in a Garden (Isaac Massa and Beatrix van der Laan)* (Frans Halsmuseum, Haarlem). J. W. von Moltke likened the present painting's style to Rembrandt's manner of 1630–35 when he was first in Amsterdam, but, as we have seen, the latter never attempted a double portrait out-of-doors.[1] S. J. Gudlaugsson first suggested, and von Moltke and Sumowski later concurred with his view, that the date of 1646 on the present work may have originally read '1640', which would be more compatible with the sitters' costumes and the painting's Rembrandtesque manner.[2] However, J. Giltaij and G. Jansen confirmed that the date of 1646 had not been altered and that it was probably reliable, allowing that it might have been added by Flinck himself after reworking the picture at a later date: X-rays reveal, among other changes, alterations to Graswinckel's hat.[3]

A member of a patrician family, Dirck Graswinckel (1600–1660) was a distinguished international jurist, statesman and author of legal and economic treatises as well as Latin poetry. He moved in elevated intellectual circles as a colleague of the legendary legal mind Hugo de Groot, and was a member of the literary *Muiderkring* as well as a friend of the stadholder's gifted secretary, Constantijn Huygens. He also served in high office as the Fiscal Advocate of the County Lands of Holland, and became the clerk to the Chambre Mipartie at Malines, where he

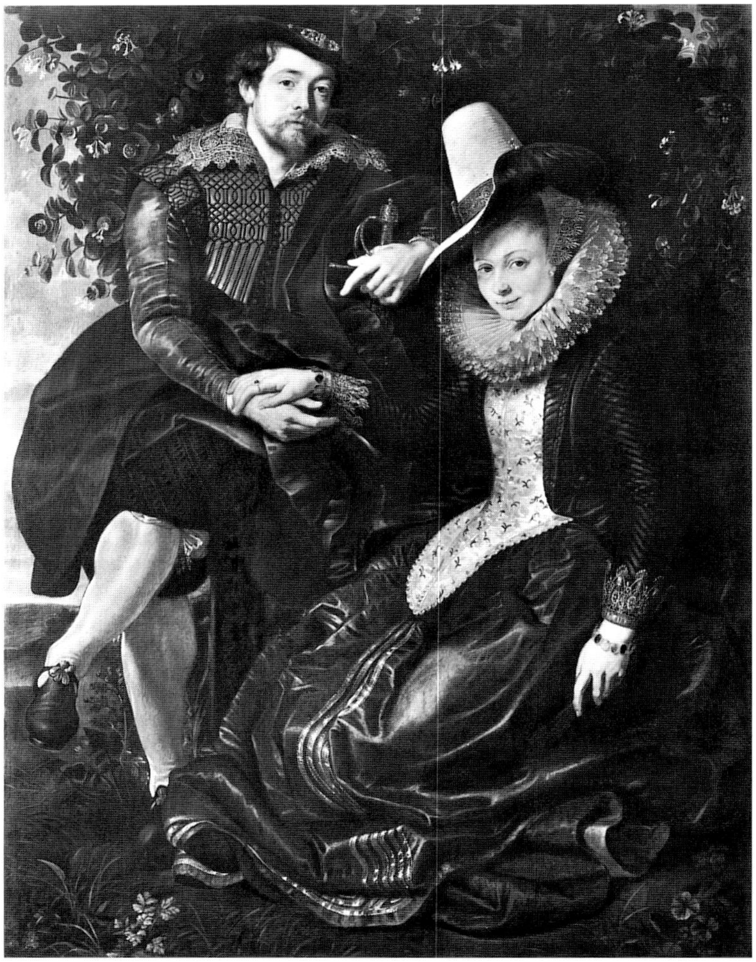

FIG. 43a
Peter Paul Rubens Flemish, 1577–1640
Self-Portrait with Isabella Brandt in a Honeysuckle Bower
Panel
178.0 x 136.0 cm
Alte Pinakothek, Munich

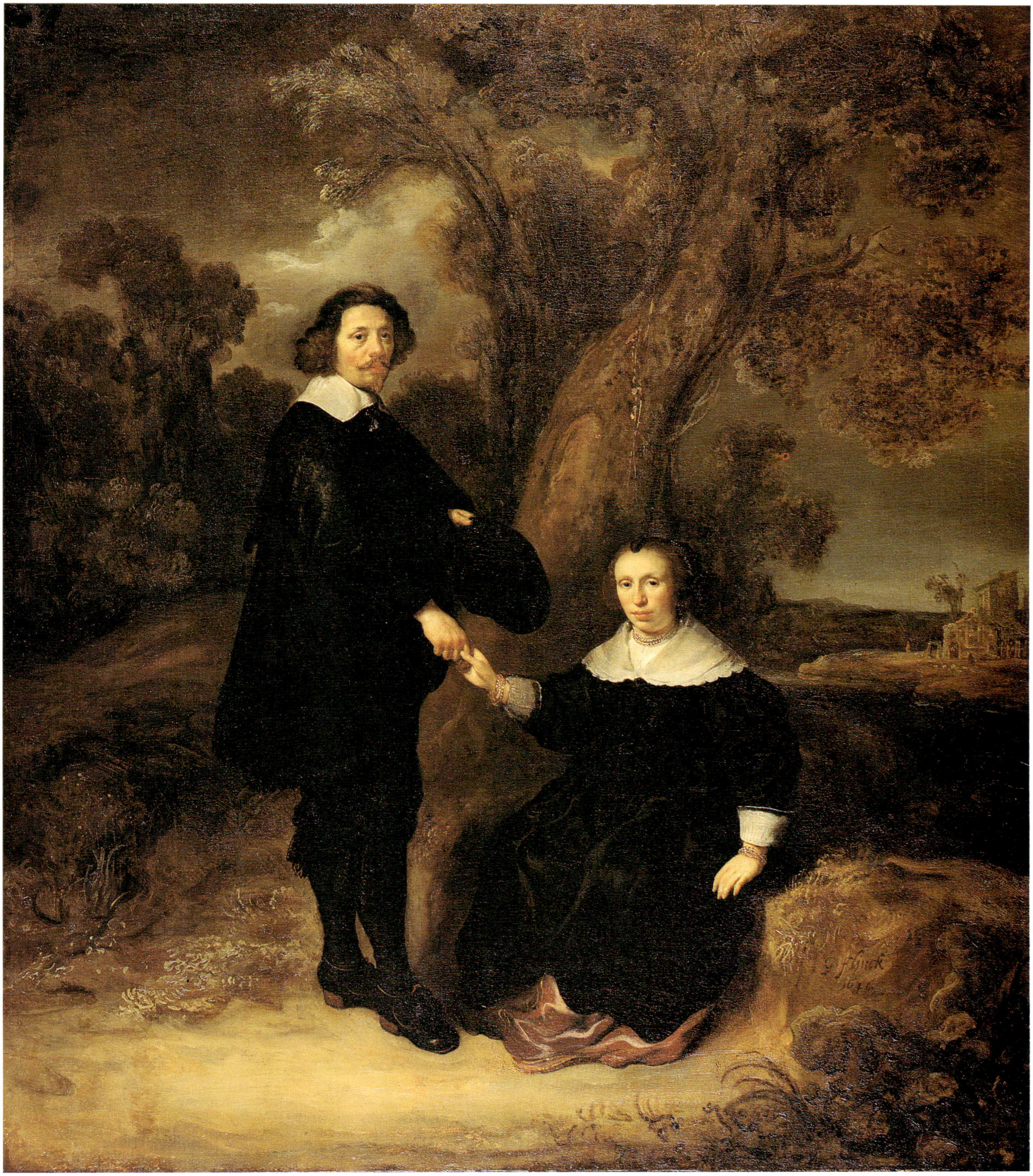

died. A conservative Calvinist, he believed that the sovereignty of the United Netherlands was divinely ordained. His marriage to Geertruyt van Loon in 1629 remained childless.[4]

As E. de Jongh demonstrated in extensive detail in his iconographic analysis, the eminently respectable Graswinckel was straining for the height of decorum in his marriage portrait.[5] The central motif is the couple's gesture of clasping each other's right hands. What the famous French nineteenth-century historian Théophile Thoré (W. Bürger) perceived merely as an affectionate gesture is a time-honoured symbol,[6] first recognized and analysed by E. Panofsky in his discussion of Jan van Eyck's *Arnolfini Portrait* (National Gallery, London).[7] Since antiquity, the *dextrarum iunctio*, or joining of right hands, had been the emblem of the sanctity of marriage and of concord between husband and wife. The motif recurs not only in seventeenth-century Dutch pictorial art but also in epithalamia, marriage medals, and wedding manuals, allegorical writings and emblem books.[8] Graswinckel probably would have appreciated the juridical implication of the *dextrarum iunctio*, which bound a couple legally until death. Undoubtedly it is also significant that he and his wife are seated before an oak tree, the traditional symbol of strength and steadfastness. Finally, holding one's hat was also a traditional gesture of respect and reverence, in this case presumably for the sanctity of marriage.

PCS

1 Von Moltke 1965, pp. 22–3.
2 Gudlaugsson 1948–49, p. 257; Von Moltke 1965, p. 164, no. 466; Sumowski, *Gemälde*, vol. II, 1985, p. 1040, no. 713.
3 J. Giltaij & G. Jansen, in Rotterdam 1988, p. 40, cat. no. 8.
4 For Graswinckel, see Knuttel 1914, pp. 489–90.
5 E. de Jongh, in Haarlem 1986, pp. 154–7, cat. no. 28.
6 Bürger 1858–60, vol. 2, p. 177.
7 Panofsky 1934, pp. 117–27.
8 E. de Jongh, in Haarlem 1986, figs 28a–c.

Detail of cat. no. 43

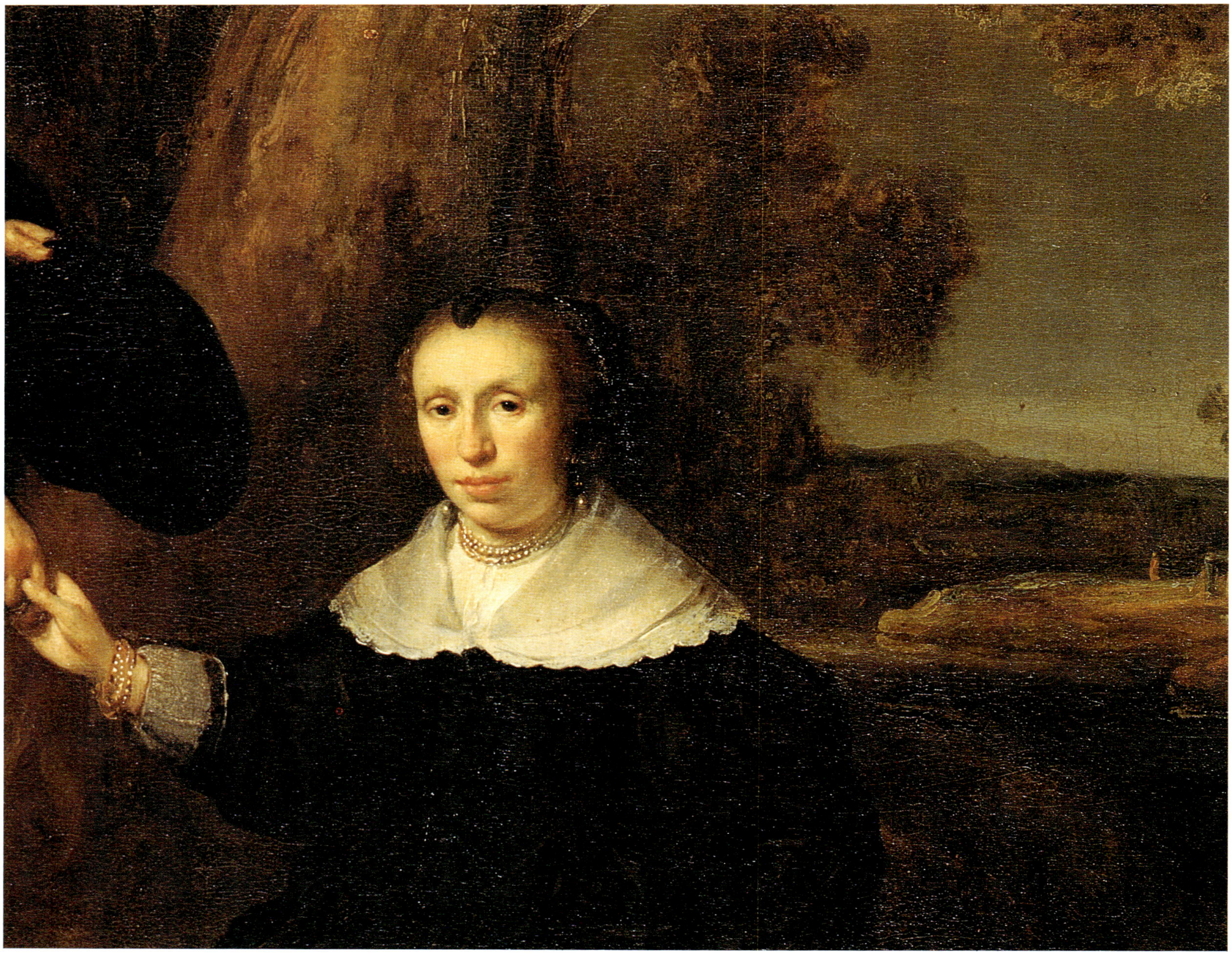

Ferdinand Bol (1616–1680)

Ferdinand Bol was born in Dordrecht in 1616, the son of a barber-surgeon. He died in Amsterdam in 1680. In 1635 he is documented as a painter in Dordrecht. An extant signed painting of *Vertumnus* (private collection) from this period recalls the work of the Dordrecht painter Jacob Gerritsz Cuyp (1594–1652). It was only after this time that Bol, as a qualified painter, came to Rembrandt's studio to learn his style and presumably to assist him. Around 1636 Rembrandt made a note about pupils whose works he had sold, one of whom was 'fardijnandus'. Dated works from the years 1641–69 show that during this period Bol was again established as an independent master, now in Amsterdam, where he was to remain for the rest of his life. Like Rembrandt, he confined himself almost exclusively to history pieces and portraits. At first his style was strongly Rembrandtesque, although the actions and expressions in his paintings are always more subdued than his teacher's. From about 1650, Bol turned to brighter colours, and figures in more elegant attitudes and more 'correct' antique costumes. On occasion he borrowed them literally from Peter Paul Rubens or from Anthony van Dyck. Yet he also continued to work in a more or less Rembrandtesque style. Bol was a great talent, but his strength lay in his beautiful rendering of detail rather than in his ability to convincingly portray figures in action.

Bol's social success as a painter was unique. In 1653 he married Elisabeth Dell, the daughter of one of the ruling families *(regenten)*. Bol received many prestigious commissions, in some cases through Elisabeth Dell's family. The best of his group portraits of regents are the *Governors of the Leper Asylum*, made in 1649 (Amsterdam Historical Museum), and the *Governors of the Wine Merchants' Guild* of 1659 (Alte Pinakothek, Munich). In 1656 he made a five-metre-high painting of *Fabritius and Pyrrhus* for the burgomasters' council room in Amsterdam's new Town Hall (now the Royal Palace) (p. 207, fig. 8). In this work, we see Fabritius refusing to be intimidated by the trumpeting of King Pyrrhus's elephant. Fabritius's valour was intended to inspire the burgomasters and encourage the public to see the same quality in their rulers. The studies for *Fabritius and Pyrrhus* show how much difficulty Bol had with large surfaces and how he gradually adapted his work to suit the wishes of his patrons (p. 207, fig. 9). His *Moses Descending from Mount Sinai with the Ten Commandments*, of *c.*1663, was specially made for the Magistrates' Courtroom. For the executive chamber of the new Admiralty building, Bol made overmantels of *Aeneas Awarding Prizes to His Captains and Sailors* and *Titus Marlius Torquatus Ordering the Decapitation of His Son for Disobedience in War*. These works were to remind the seafarers in the Admiralty's employ that their own superiors could be both generous and severe. Bol enjoyed the unusual distinction of receiving large orders of this kind from towns other than his own – his commissions include a militia piece in Gouda (now at the Municipal Museum), an overmantel for the Town Hall in Leiden, and opulent paintings for the grand salon of a residence in Utrecht.[1] In more modest works Bol often achieved a poetic tone, particularly in his portraits of children. Bol painted little, if anything, after his second marriage, to the wealthy Anna van Arckel, in 1669. He moved to a new home, one of the largest on the Keizersgracht, and was appointed to a board of regents – an honour conferred on no other Dutch painter of comparable origins. There is a marked contrast between Bol and his inspiring teacher Rembrandt, who had sold all his possessions in 1656–58 in an attempt to avoid bankruptcy.

Bol was always Rembrandt's best-known pupil. Even early on, many works that were not accepted as Rembrandts were attributed to Bol. On close examination, Bol's hand is clearly distinguishable. Of the almost five hundred works that were once ascribed to him, however, no more than about 190 can be endorsed. In his early period, Bol also made some sixteen etchings in Rembrandt's style.

1 For a reconstruction of the original arrangement of this ensemble, see Blankert 1992.

LITERATURE: Blankert 1976; Blankert 1982; Sumowski, *Gemälde*, vol. I, 1983, pp. 282–425; A. Blankert, in *Allgemeines Künstler-Lexikon*, vol. 12, 1996, pp. 358–60.
AB

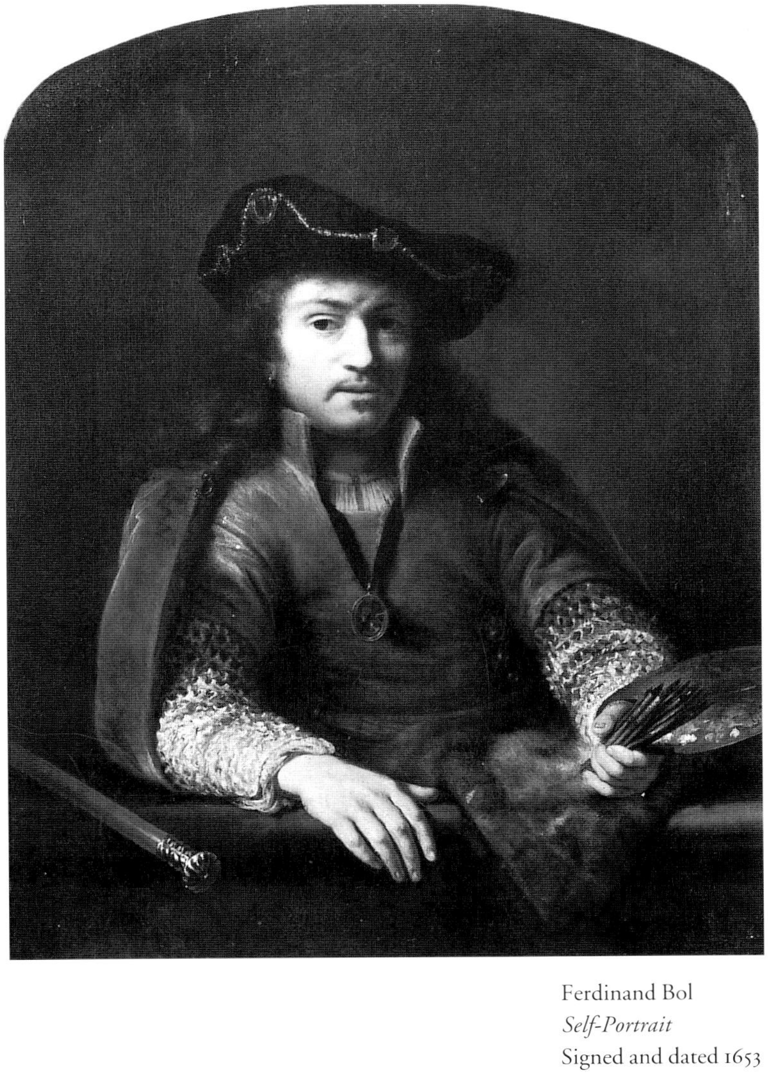

Ferdinand Bol
Self-Portrait
Signed and dated 1653
Canvas
105.0 x 82.5 cm
Private collection, London

44
Ferdinand Bol
Jacob's Dream
*c.*1642

Signed lower right *f Bol fecit*
Canvas
128.0 x 97.0 cm
Staatliche Kunstsammlungen Dresden, Gemäldegalerie Alte Meister

PROVENANCE: Probably sale, Amsterdam, 13 April 1695, lot 29: 'A sleeping Jacob, by Ferdinandus Boll', for 8 guilders; in Dresden from 1722 or earlier.

LITERATURE: Blankert 1982, pp. 29, 32, 48, 69, 91, no. 5 (with earlier literature); Sumowski, *Gemälde*, vol. I, 1983, p. 291, no. 80 (with earlier literature).

This masterpiece has perhaps been reproduced more often than any other as an example of the phenomenon of the 'school of Rembrandt'. Bol painted *Jacob's Dream* around 1642, shortly after establishing himself as an independent master for the second time. The dream motif is beautifully conveyed by the 'hovering' effect of the diffuse lighting. The elegant folds of the angel's robes are modelled with subtlety, yet the figure's anatomy and pose remain undefined. Though this may have been due to Bol's awkwardness, it nevertheless heightens the ethereal quality of this wraithlike apparition. Warm browns and yellows predominate, enlivened by a few hints of green in the angel's wings and in the tassel hanging from his back. The green is echoed in the ribbon around the neck of the graceful figure of Jacob, who lies asleep on a red-toned cloth. This painting, with its fairytale effect, is among the finest of Bol's works.

According to the biblical text, the young Jacob was sent on a long journey by his father Isaac. He was to visit Laban, a distant relative of his, and marry his daughter. En route, Jacob spent a night outdoors in Luz, where 'he took of the stones of that place, and put them for his pillows, and lay down in that place to sleep. And he dreamed, and behold a ladder set up on the earth, and the top of it reached to heaven: and behold the angels of God ascending and descending on it. And, behold, the Lord stood above it'. God made a pledge to Jacob: 'thy seed shall be as the dust of the earth' and 'I am with thee, and will keep thee' (Genesis 28:11–15).

From the early Christian era onwards, the scene had been illustrated literally, with angels on a ladder or staircase and God the Father at the top. The tradition of the ladder was maintained in seventeenth-century Dutch art as well (fig. 55a). Neither God himself, however, nor the ladder, is

FIG. 44a
Formerly attributed to Rembrandt, now to Ferdinand Bol
Jacob's Dream
Pen and ink
17.8 x 19.6 cm
Ecole des Beaux-Arts, Paris

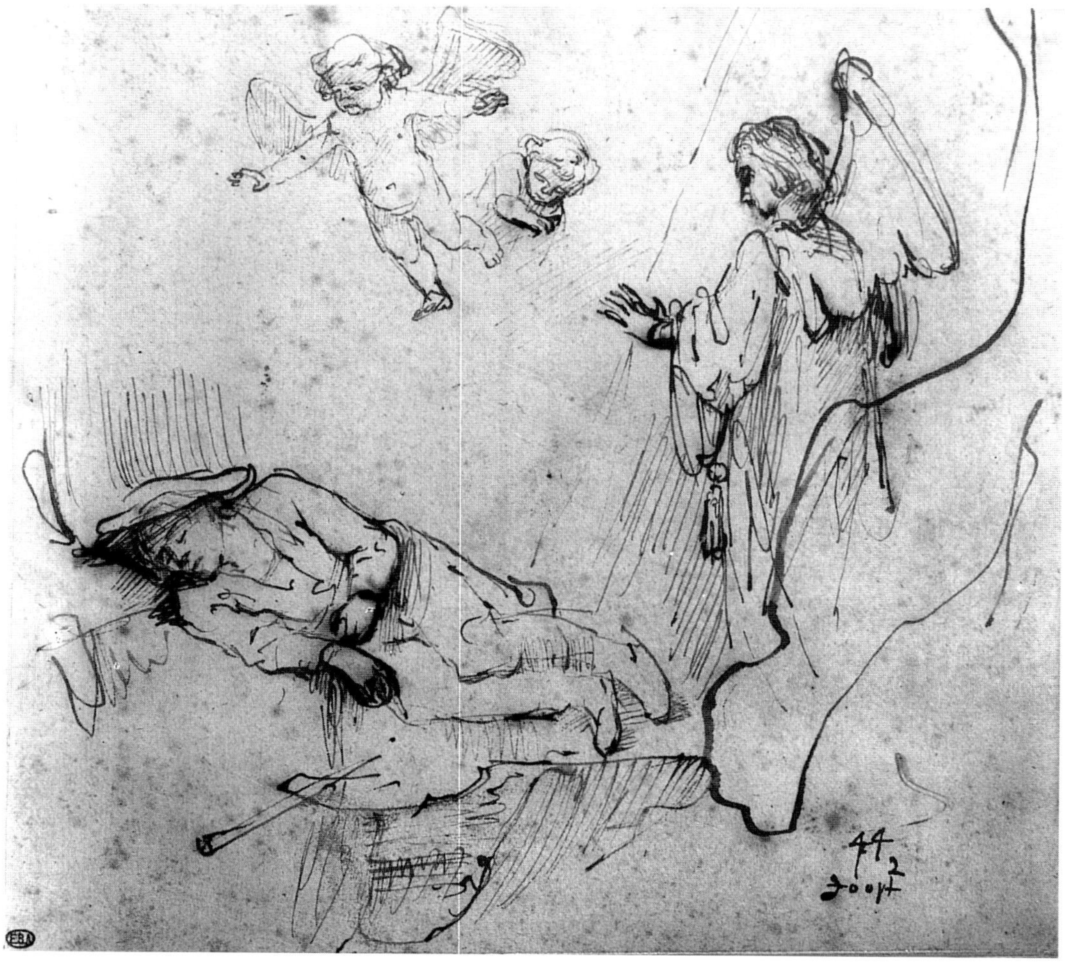

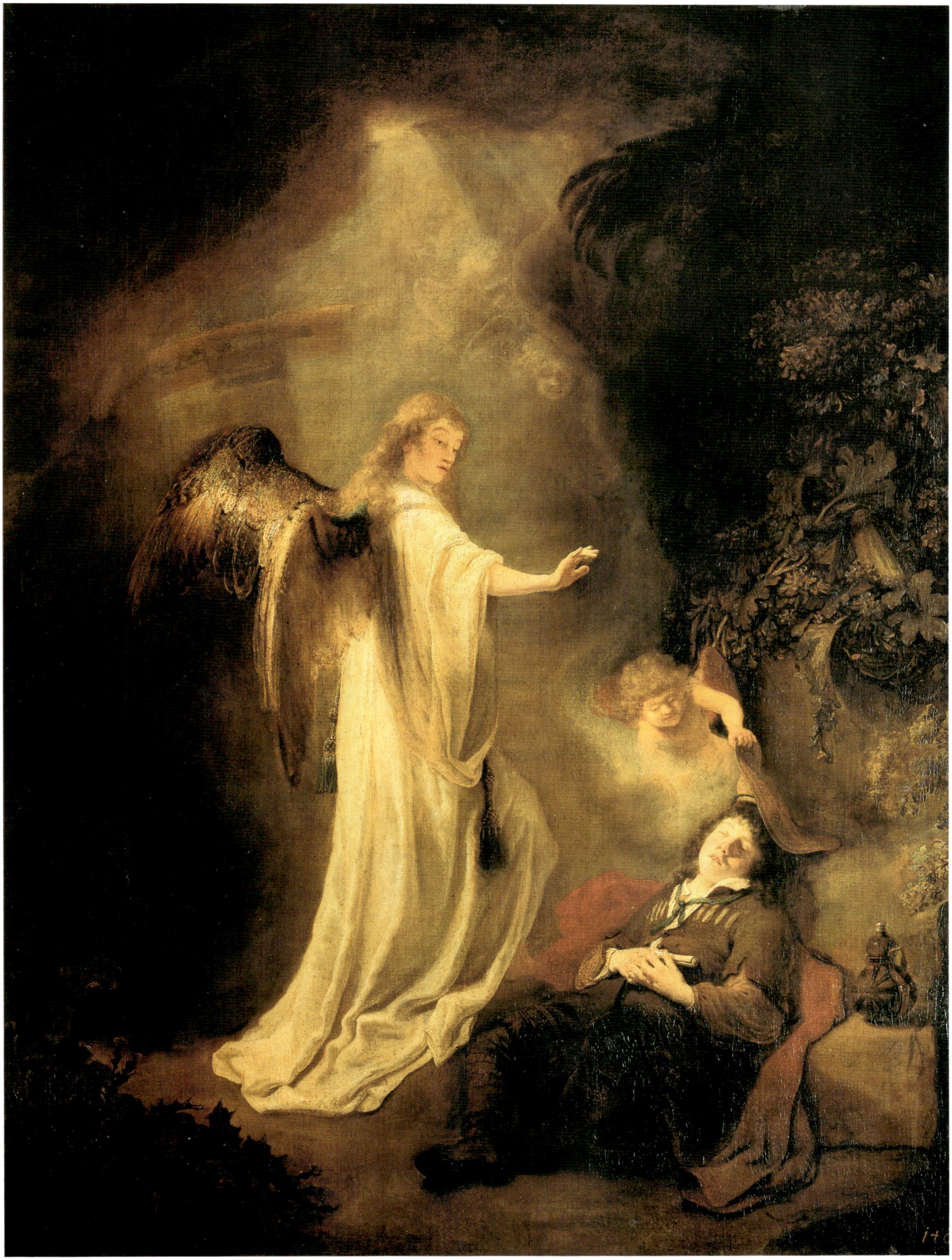

portrayed in works by Rembrandt or his school. God's place is taken by a single angel, here the main character beside Jacob. In most cases the angel's hand is raised protectively in an eloquent gesture. The ladder was evidently considered unnatural, for it was replaced by a shaft of light with cherubs in its gleam.[1] Bol's painting (cat. no. 44) and Gerbrand van den Eeckhout's rendering of *Jacob's Dream*, which likewise dates from 1642 (fig. 54a), are the earliest extant versions of this new image. Van den Eeckhout developed the type further in his later paintings of 1669 and 1672 (cat. nos 54, 55). The same pictorial type can be seen in drawings traditionally ascribed to Rembrandt, some of which are now attributed to Bol (fig. 44a).[2] It was probably Rembrandt who invented the type. In this event, he must presumably have made a (drawn?) version, which is no longer known, before Bol (cat. no. 44) and van den Eeckhout (fig. 54a) produced their paintings.

Interestingly enough, Rembrandt himself made an etching later, in 1655, showing the ladder with angels mounting and descending as described in the biblical text (fig. 44b, B.36). However, this was an illustration for Menasseh ben Israel's religious treatise, *Piedra gloriosa de le estatua de Nebuchadnesar*, and Menasseh presumably asked Rembrandt to illustrate the biblical text literally. In the etching Jacob himself lies asleep on the ladder, which creates a surreal effect.

In the Bol (cat. no. 44) the almost straight, horizontal shafts of light above the angel's left wing might be seen as an allusion to the ladder. A cherub lifts Jacob's hat, allowing the light and, with it, the vision of the dream, to reach him more easily. The scroll Jacob holds in his hand, another detail that occurs only in Bol's version of the theme, has never yet been mentioned. Bol probably intended it to be a letter of recommendation which he felt Jacob might need to present to his faraway uncle Laban. Or could it be intended as a map? Jacob's flask stands beside him at the right.

In later years Bol abandoned the Rembrandtesque manner that he employed most successfully in *Jacob's Dream*, and developed a far more colourful 'baroque-classicist' style, the finest example being his *Venus with Mars Asleep* of *c.*1660 (fig. 44c).[3] Yet even in this piece, which is so totally different in both style and subject matter, the principal motif is again a figure asleep on the ground with a towering white shape on the left and cherubs as attendant figures. Here, however, the sleeping figure represents Mars instead of Jacob, with the naked Venus beside him instead of the angel. The themes of *Jacob's Dream* and *Venus with Mars Asleep* involve only two main figures and hardly any action. Bol was apparently at his best in work of this kind.

AB

1 On this development, cf. Van de Kamp 1991–94, pp. 38–9.
2 Benesch 1973, vol. III, no. 555, fig. 727 (as Rembrandt) (our fig. 44a), attributed to Bol in Sumowski, *Drawings*, vol. I, 1979, no. 248; cf. Benesch 1973, vol. V, no. 996, fig. 1279, Copenhagen, *c.*1655–66. A drawing by Rembrandt from *c.*1636 shows only the *Sleeping Jacob* (Benesch 1973, vol. I, no. 125, fig. 147). Compare, too, the poor-quality studio drawing of *Jacob's Dream* in the British Museum in London (Benesch 1973, vol. VI, no. 1381, fig. 1695).
3 Blankert 1982, no. 33, pl. 45 and colour pl. opp. p. 50; Sumowski, *Gemälde*, vol. I, 1983, no. 105, with colour ill.

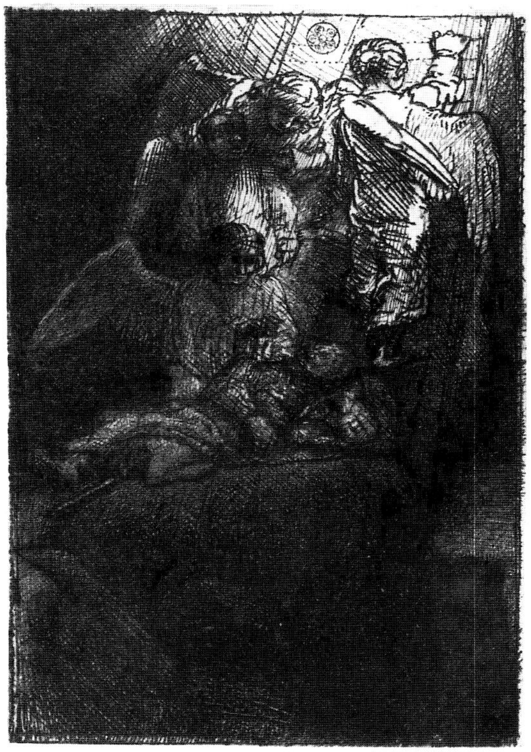

FIG. 44b
Rembrandt
Jacob's Dream
Signed and dated 1655
Etching
10.6 x 6.9 cm

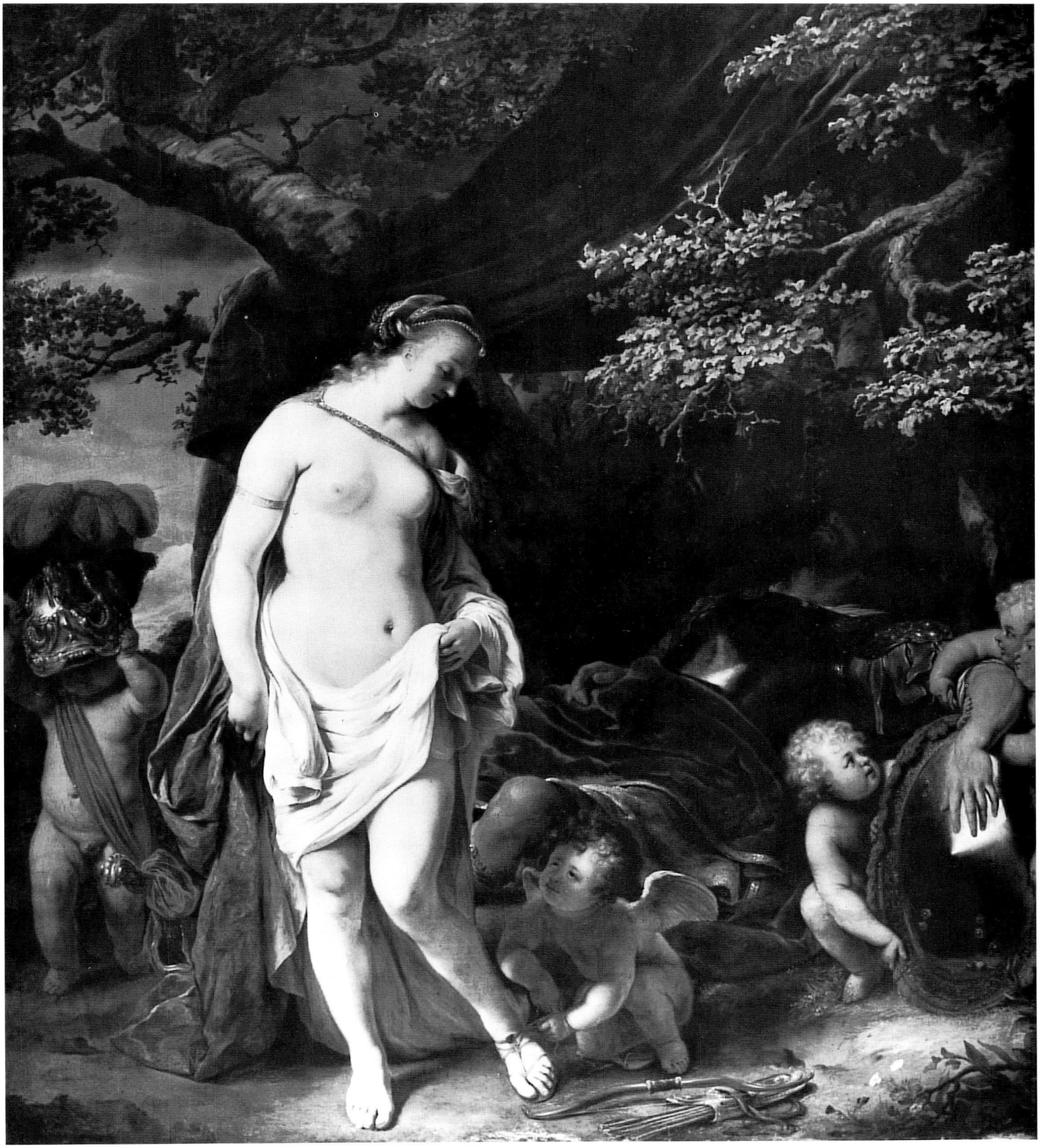

FIG. 44C
Ferdinand Bol
Venus with Mars Asleep
Canvas
228.0 x 200.0 cm
Herzog Anton Ulrich-Museum, Braunschweig

45
Ferdinand Bol
Self-Portrait

Signed and dated centre left beside shoulder
Bol [...] 1646
Canvas
90.0 x 72.0 cm
Dordrechts Museum, Dordrecht

PROVENANCE: Purchased from Colnaghi, London, in 1887.

LITERATURE: Verslag Dordrecht 1889, p. 3; Blankert 1982, pp. 58, 118, no. 60 (with earlier literature); Sumowski, *Gemälde*, vol. I, 1983, p. 305, no. 135 (with earlier literature).

This painting was cleaned especially for this exhibition. It is reproduced in fig. 45a in its condition before cleaning. The large reproduction on p. 249 is the first to show the work as it now appears. A large section of canvas on the right, which was formerly obscured by the frame and cannot be seen in older reproductions, can now be shown for the first time. The figure now appears smaller in relation to the picture space than was the case before.

Bol's earliest signed and dated pictures are from 1641. He had therefore been established as an independent painter for at least five years by the time he made this *Self-Portrait*, dated 1646. Yet the mood and colours are still completely Rembrandtesque. The face and collar are brightly lit in contrast to the greenish-grey background. The lace of the collar has a creamy delicacy, which has been enhanced by the cleaning. The beret and chain the artist is wearing, and his voluminously draped cloak, recall Rembrandt's *Self-Portrait at the Age of 34* of 1640 (cat. no. 13). Bol's picture is in fact a subdued variant of the Rembrandt. Bol's figures and poses are generally less exuberant than those of his teacher. But a year after the execution of the present work he followed Rembrandt's example more closely. In 1647 he made a *'Self-Portrait'*[1] that is an almost literal copy of Rembrandt's etched *Self-Portrait Leaning on a Stone Sill* of 1639, with the image in reverse (see fig. 45b and cat. no. 103). Bol, however, gave the figure a second hand, whereas only one can be seen in the etching.[2] He also made a second version of the 1647 painting, but gave the figure an entirely different face (fig. 45c).[3]

These and several other works by Bol are regarded as self-portraits, but since two of the faces are so different from one another the question obviously needs to be reviewed. This is why the title *'Self-Portrait'*, as used for figs 45b and 45c, is in quotation marks. In both cases Bol's intention was probably to portray 'a young artist' in general rather than to present his own image to the world. That said, the face in the engaging picture from Dordrecht looks much like that in a firmly identifiable self-portrait of Bol (repr. with Bol biography, p. 243).

A year after the Dordrecht painting was completed, another pupil of Rembrandt's, Gerbrand van den Eeckhout, made a drawing of a similar composition, which is a self-portrait (repr. with van den Eeckhout biography, p. 267).

AB

FIG. 45b
Ferdinand Bol
'Self-Portrait'
Signed and dated 1647
Canvas
101.0 x 88.0 cm
The Toledo Museum of Art, Toledo, Ohio

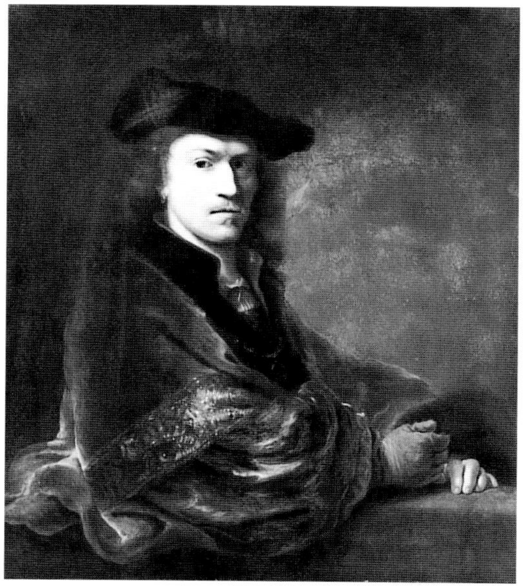

FIG. 45c
Ferdinand Bol
'Self-Portrait'
Canvas
93.0 x 83.5 cm
With dealer Gebr. Douwes Fine Art, Amsterdam, 1987
Photograph: RKD

1 Blankert 1982, no. 61.
2 As observed in the *Corpus*, Bol borrowed the second hand from an early phase of Rembrandt's painted *Self-Portrait at the Age of 34* (cat. no. 13); the hand can be seen in an X-ray photograph of Rembrandt's painting (*Corpus*, vol. III, 1989, pp. 380, 381, no. A139, fig. 2).
3 Blankert 1982, no. 62.

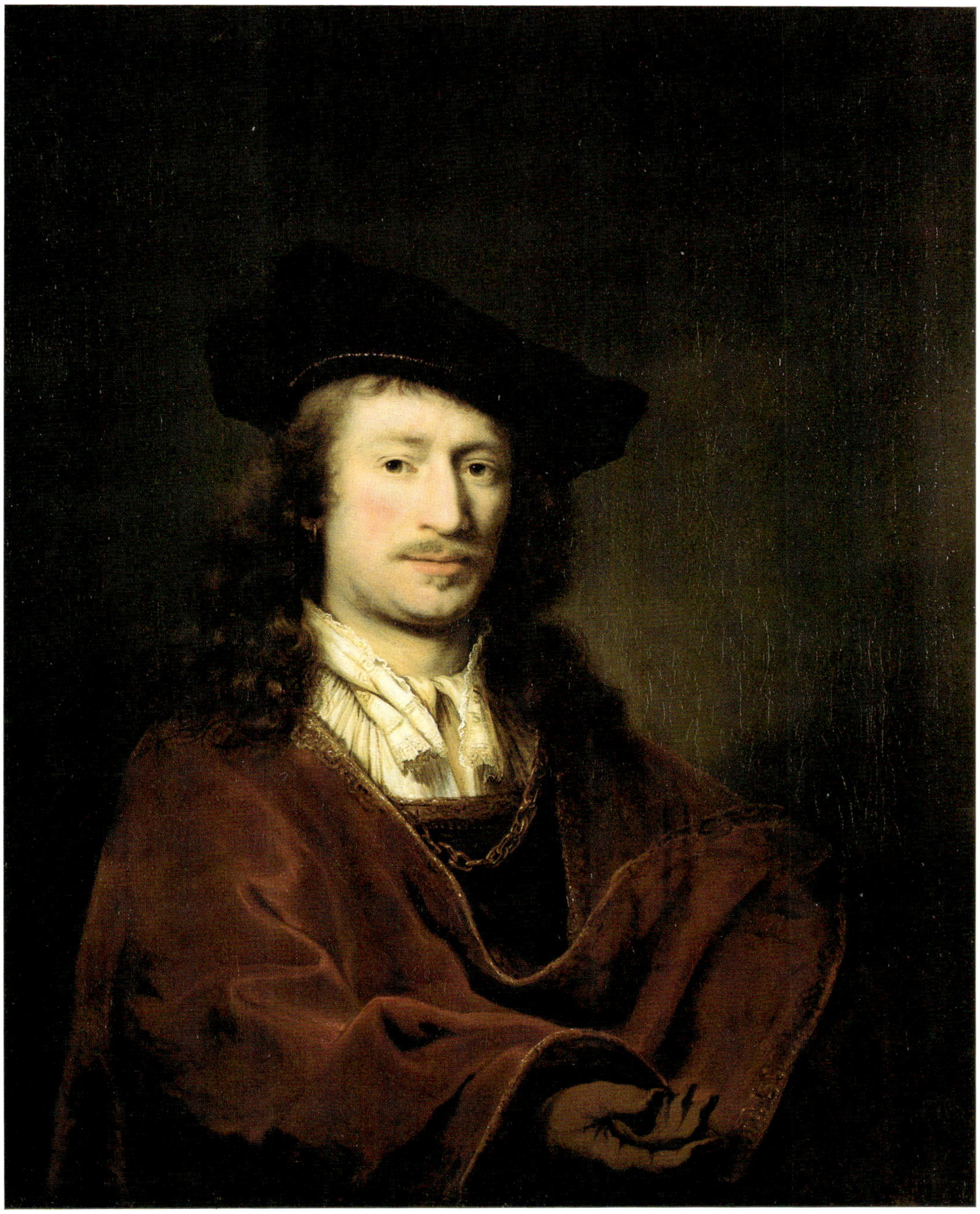

Cat. no. 45

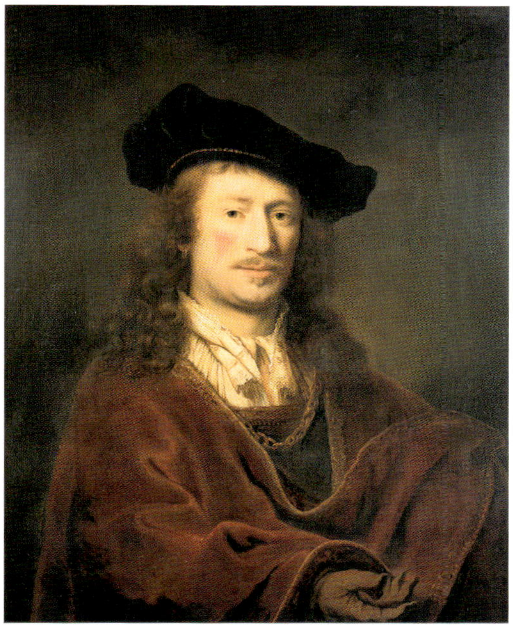

FIG. 45a
Cat. no. 45 in its previous condition

46
Ferdinand Bol
'Self-Portrait'
*c.*1648

Canvas
97.5 x 77.5 cm
Museum of Fine Arts, Springfield, Massachusetts
The James Philip Gray Collection

PROVENANCE: Duke of Newcastle, Clumber Park; sale, Earl of Lincoln, London (Christie's), 31 March 1939, lot 3, repr.; with Knoedler Gallery, New York.

LITERATURE: Smith 1829–42, vol. VII, 1836, no. 398 (as Rembrandt); Bredius 1911, p. 340; Blankert 1982, p. 119, no. 64 (with earlier literature); Sumowski, *Gemälde*, vol. I, 1983, p. 306, no. 138 (with earlier literature); Davies 1993, pp. 26–9, no. 2 (with earlier literature).

An arch seems to be vaguely discernible at the top of this picture (it was possibly intended only for the initial layout of the piece). The painting must originally have shown more of the balustrade at the bottom: the lower section of the painting has probably been trimmed.[1] Engraved as a Rembrandt in 1767, the piece held this attribution until the London Rembrandt exhibition of 1899, when 'all the connoisseurs' – as Bredius reports – recognized Bol's hand.[2] The Springfield picture is thus one of relatively few paintings that have been taken from Rembrandt and given – on convincing grounds – to a specific pupil. A comparison with cat. no. 45 and with figs 45b and 45c should suffice to demonstrate the validity of the attribution.

This piece must have been made slightly later than the abovementioned works, around 1648.[3] Even then, Bol's starting point was Rembrandt's etched and painted self-portraits of 1639 and 1640 (cat. nos 103, 13). A similar balustrade and curtain, likewise used to heighten the illusion of depth in the picture space, can be seen in a portrait dated 1644, made by Bol's fellow pupil in Rembrandt's studio, Gerbrand van den Eeckhout (fig. 46a).[4] A figure opening a curtain to 'reveal' the picture space can also be seen in Rembrandt's *Young Woman in Bed* (cat. no. 14), which is generally dated later than the Bol and the van den Eeckhout.

The beret and the golden chain of merit worn by the man in the present painting and in the one from Dordrecht (cat. no. 45) are the attributes of an artist. Here he has a cross of merit suspended from the chain. The same motif of a cross and chain can be seen in Rembrandt's etching of a *Young Man at a Desk* of 1641 (B.261) (fig. 46b). Maybe Rembrandt intended this figure to depict an artist drawing.[5] The rolled-up paper in the hand of Bol's young man is presumably a drawing or print.[6]

Dating from the same period, *c.*1648, or slightly later, is the *Young Man at a Window*, in which Bol used in a completely different way the motif of a young man at a window (fig. 46c). Both paintings were always referred to as 'self-portraits'.[7] From the differences between the faces in these two works and those in cat. no. 45 and figs 45b and 45c, it is clear that they are not portrayals of one and the same person. We might speculate that these paintings depict pupils with whom Bol had studied under Rembrandt, as well as Bol himself (cat. no. 45).

AB

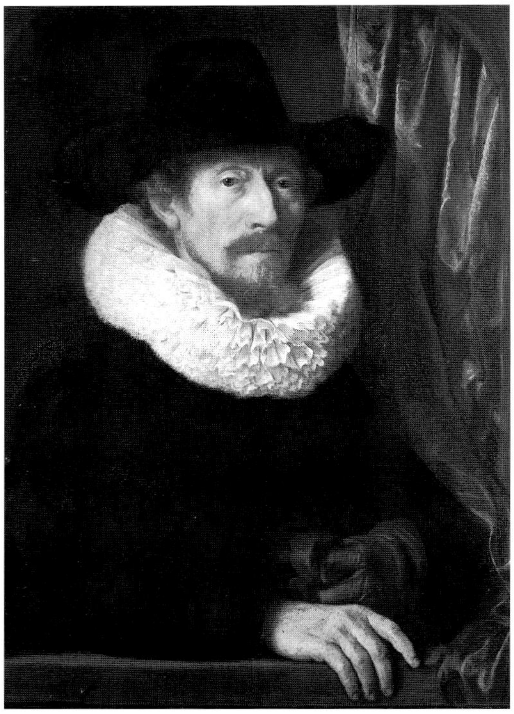

FIG. 46a
Gerbrand van den Eeckhout
The Goldsmith Jan Pietersz van den Eeckhout, Father of the Painter
Signed and dated 1644
Panel, 76.0 x 58.0 cm
Musée des Beaux-Arts, Grenoble
Photograph: Musée de Grenoble

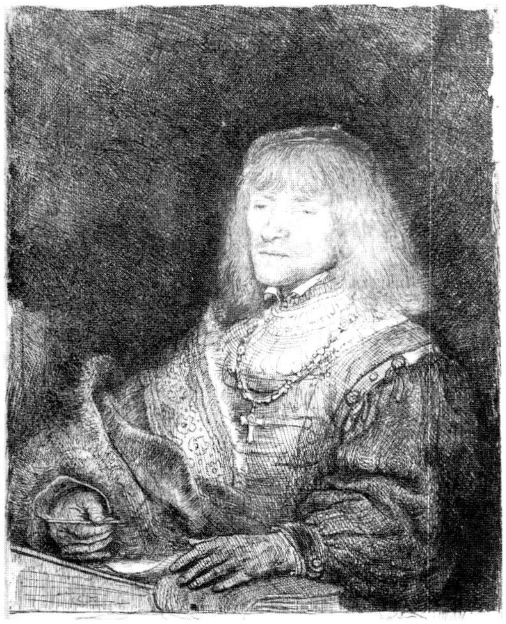

FIG. 46b
Rembrandt
Young Man at a Desk
Signed and dated 1641
Etching, 15.4 x 10.2 cm
Rijksprentenkabinet, Rijksmuseum, Amsterdam

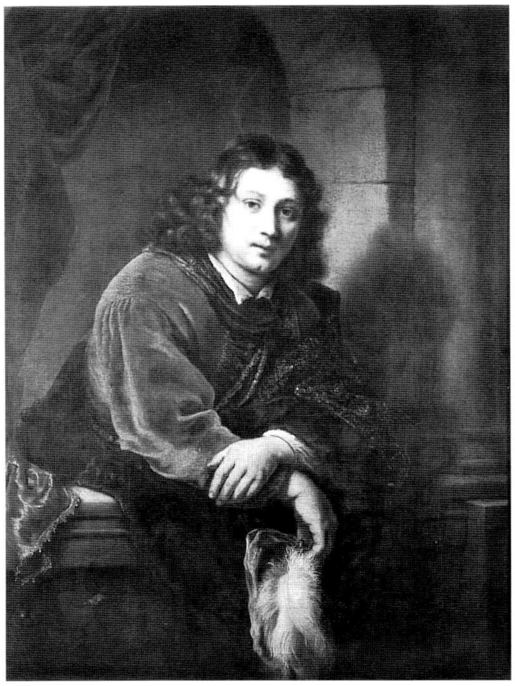

FIG. 46c
Ferdinand Bol
Young Man at a Window *c.*1648
Canvas, 143.5 x 99.0 cm
Private collection

1 Blankert 1982, p. 119, no. 64; Sumowski, *Gemälde*, vol. I, 1983, p. 306, no. 138.
2 Bredius 1911, p. 340.
3 Davies 1993, p. 26, no. 2, suggests 1647.
4 Sumowski, *Gemälde*, vol. II, 1985, no. 525.
5 The cross and chain in the etching certainly have a different function from those on the chest of Rembrandt's *Man with a Falcon on His Wrist* (our cat. no. 24).
6 Sumowski, *Gemälde*, vol. I, 1983, p. 306, no. 138, suggests a *Schriftrolle*, comparing it with a similar writing scroll held by the woman in Rembrandt's etching *The Great Jewish Bride*, of 1635 (cat. no. 101).
7 Blankert 1982, p. 131, no. 100.

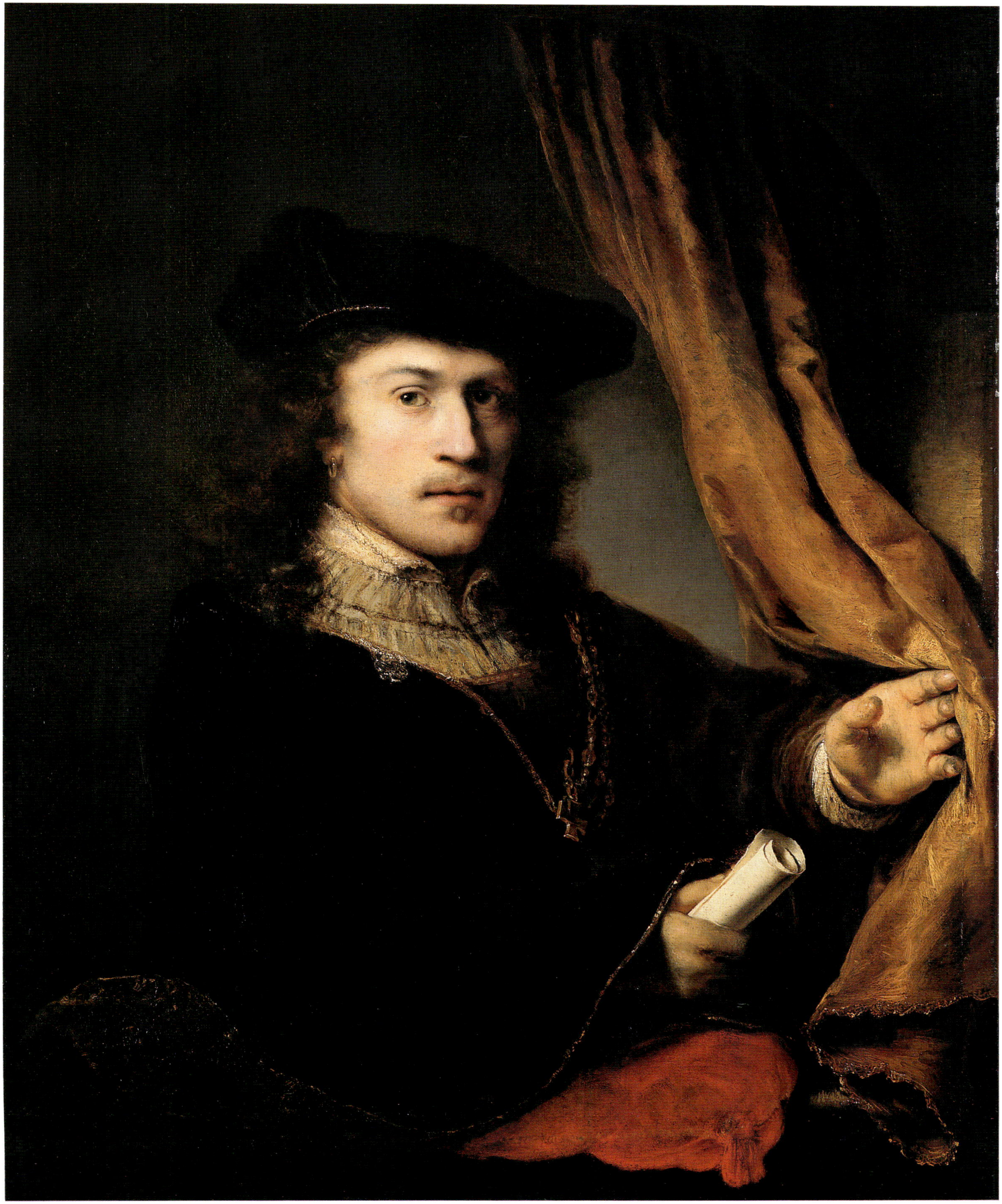

47
Ferdinand Bol
Couple on a Terrace

Signed and dated lower left *f Bol 1654*
Canvas
171.5 x 149.0 cm
Musée du Louvre, Département des Peintures, Paris
© Photo RMN

PROVENANCE: Probably forming a single painting together with cat. no. 48: Sale, G. Groeninx van Zoelen et al. (Rotterdam), 25 June 1800, no. 1, 11,000 guilders (211 x 211 cm [see commentary below]); sale, Rotterdam, 9 June 1828, no. 261 (220 x 210 cm [see commentary below]). Cat. no. 47 alone: Sale, Comte de Montbrison, Château de Saint-Roch; with F. Kleinberger Gallery, Paris; Baron de Schlichting, 1911; bequeathed by him to the Louvre in 1914.

LITERATURE: Blankert 1976, no. 173-1 (with earlier literature); Brejon de Lavergnée, Foucart & Reynaud 1979, p. 29; Blankert 1982, pp. 67, 154, no. 174-1 (with earlier literature); Sumowski, *Gemälde*, vol. I, 1983, p. 309, no. 152 (with earlier literature); De Jongh 1986, p. 90; Foucart 1988–89, pp. 38–41.

Ever since it was acquired by the Louvre in 1914, this picture has been exhibited, and often reproduced, as an intact example of Bol's art. However, an examination of Bol's works and their provenances led to the conclusion that it might be the picture described in identical terms in two Rotterdam sale catalogues, from 1800 and 1828 (see Provenance):

> This excellent Painting portrays a Country house with Steps and Balustrade, covered with a Carpet, where stands a Gentleman in dignified clothing, having in his left hand a Hat with Plumes and in his right a Lemon, beside him a Lady resting both arms on the Balustrade, and pointing her right hand at two children, which are portrayed in the foreground, on the right of the painting [seen from the figures' viewpoint], playing with a male Goat, on the left of the piece [also in the foreground] lie two Peacocks by a Sunflower, Thistle and other Plants; the background is a wooded view; the main Subjects are life-size, forcefully painted.[1]

Both catalogues mention the date 1654, which is also inscribed on the painting in the Louvre. All details in the descriptions correspond with those in the painting, except that the painting shows neither the children with the goat, nor the peacocks.

However, a canvas in Le Mans, which looks like a fragment, is a picture of two children with a goat (cat. no. 48). Both the painting in the Louvre and the one in Le Mans were in France by the nineteenth century. It seemed reasonable to conclude that they were the remaining fragments of the painting auctioned in 1800 and 1828. An attempt was made to confirm this, using the measurements given in the sales catalogues of 1800 (211 x 211 cm) and 1828 (220 x 210 cm) and those in the Louvre catalogues before 1979 (205 x 180 cm) and the catalogue of the Le Mans museum (109 x 68 cm). The combined measurements of the two surviving canvases were found to be larger than those of the picture auctioned in 1800 and 1828. This seemed to suggest that the paintings from Paris and Le Mans could still have been fragments of a larger version of the painting described in the auction catalogues, with the painting in the auctions being a smaller, now lost or hidden, version.[2]

However, it later transpired that the dimensions of the Louvre painting as cited in the museum's catalogues also included the frame. The correct measurements of the canvas, which appear only in the Louvre's more recent publications, are 171.5 x 149 cm.[3] This means that the Louvre and Le Mans paintings together in fact measure 149 + 68 cm (= 217 cm) in width, this dimension corresponding almost exactly to those given in 1800 and 1828 (211 and 210 cm). Hence there is every reason to suppose that the canvas in the nineteenth-century auctions has survived in the paintings from Paris and Le Mans. In Australia, where these works are being exhibited together for the first time, we will be able to judge whether they indeed belong together. The theory that they once formed part of the same picture gains further plausibility from very recent evidence that the signature and date on cat. no. 47 are in fact on a piece of canvas that has been cut out and pasted into place (fig. 47a).[4] In the original picture, the date and signature must have appeared close to the edge of the canvas, and were presumably replaced after being cut away.

Vertically, the Le Mans painting is 62.5 cm smaller than that in Paris, from which we can

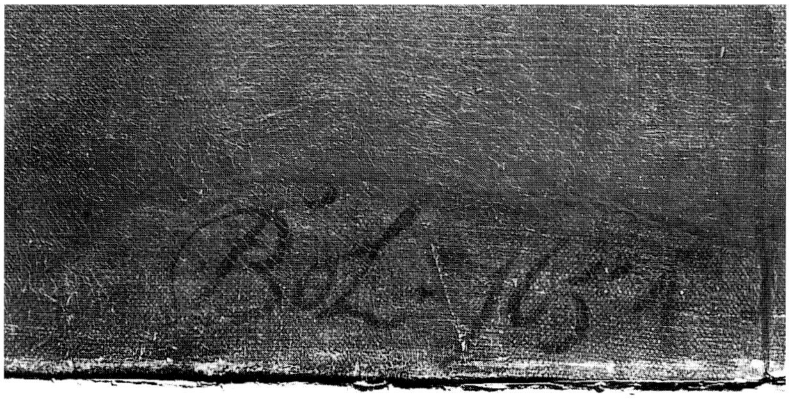

FIG. 47a
Signature and date on cat. no. 47, photographed in raking light (showing them to be on a separate piece of canvas). Photograph: Musée du Louvre, Paris, July 1997.

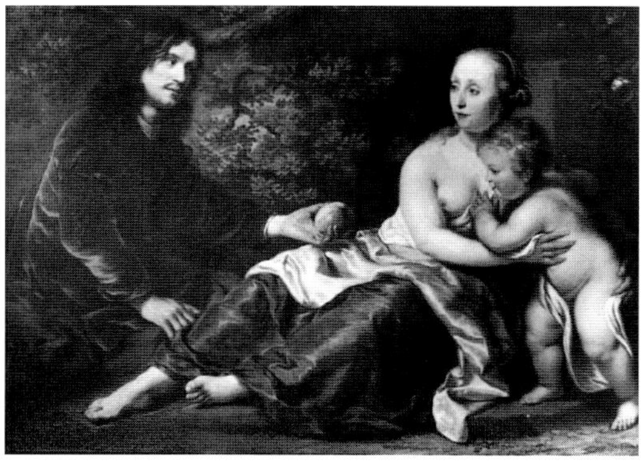

FIG. 47b
Ferdinand Bol
Married Couple with a Child in the Guise of Venus, Paris and Cupid
Signed and dated 1656
Canvas
116.0 x 157.0 cm
Dordrechts Museum, Dordrecht

conclude that a section of the former has been lost. This was presumably part of the 'wooded view', above the children. The Louvre painting, too, must have been forty to fifty centimetres taller than it is at present. The sunflower and carpet have been cropped, and according to the 1800 and 1828 catalogue descriptions there were once two peacocks in front of the sunflower. So the foreground must have been larger, which would have made for a better composition. The children in the Le Mans picture would therefore presumably also have had more ground under their feet.

The piece was probably cut after 1828 – like Rembrandt's *Night Watch* (Rijksmuseum, Amsterdam) (p. 26, fig. 7) in the eighteenth century – to fit on a wall or in a frame. In its original state it would certainly have had a monumental effect.

The thistles and sunflowers in the present work have been interpreted as symbols of the couple's conjugal love. Like the flower that turns its face to the sun, the faithful lover inclines towards his beloved.[5] The peacocks, which have now disappeared, are the attribute of Juno, the goddess of marriage, and were thus an allusion to matrimonial love.

Given its relatively late date of 1654, this piece by Bol is still surprisingly Rembrandtesque. Rembrandt's influence is evident in the fancy costumes and in the way in which the deep glowing red of the carpet hanging over the balustrade stands out against the background. Around the same time Bol was also making portraits in far lighter colours, with figures in what were meant to be classical robes (fig. 47b).[6] These differences may have been prompted by the wishes of his patrons. The present piece was formerly thought to represent Bol himself and his wife, but this cannot be the case.[7]

AB

1 The Dutch text is cited in Blankert 1976, no. 173-1. The description was translated from the Dutch by Ina Rike.
2 See reconstruction and arguments presented in Blankert 1976, no. 173-1; Blankert 1982, pp. 153–4, nos 174-1, 174-2, pl. 186.
3 The correct measurements were first given by Brejon de Lavergnée, Foucart & Reynaud 1979, p. 29, without indication that they were a correction. See the later, more detailed, discussion in Foucart 1988–89, pp. 38–41.
4 Information from M. Jacques Foucart, Musée du Louvre, 1997.
5 De Jongh 1986, p. 90.
6 Blankert 1982, no. 34.
7 For the reasons, see Blankert 1982, p. 154, no. 174-2.

48

Ferdinand Bol

Two Children Feeding a Goat

1654

Canvas
109.0 x 68.0 cm
Musée de Tessé, Le Mans, France
Cliché Musées du Mans, France

PROVENANCE: See Provenance for cat. no. 47. Acquired by the Musée du Mans in 1845.

LITERATURE: Blankert 1976, no. A174; Blankert 1982, p. 154, no. 174-2; Foucart 1988–89, p. 40.

This painting was probably once part of Bol's *Couple on a Terrace* (see commentary to cat. no. 47). It is hoped that the present exhibition will enable us to see whether this is indeed the case. If so, the children would be the offspring of the couple portrayed in cat. no. 47.

Viewed separately, this picture is certainly interesting in its own right, because of the charming characterization of the two naked children. The older and bigger child lays a protective arm on the shoulder of his or her sibling and gives him a chance to feed the goat. Bol was often at his best in portrayals of children. A portrait of an older boy, made two years earlier than cat. no. 47, and thus, presumably, than the present work, is reproduced here (fig. 48a).[1] We know from the inscription *Aetatis 8 sua* that the child in this work was eight years old at the time. He stands beside a table draped with an oriental carpet with a pattern similar to that in cat. no. 47.

AB

1 Blankert 1982, pp. 67, 142, no. 138; Sumowski, *Gemälde*, vol. I, 1983, no. 169.

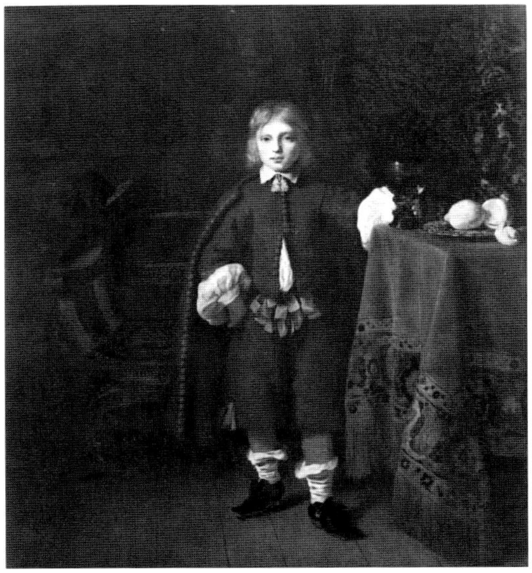

FIG. 48a
Ferdinand Bol
Eight-Year-Old Boy Holding a Glass of Wine
Signed and dated 1652
Canvas
175.0 x 150.0 cm
Castle Howard, Yorkshire

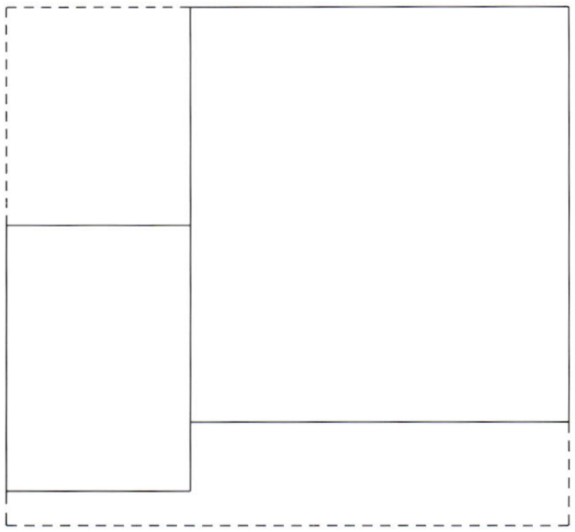

Proposed reconstruction of cat. nos 48 (left) and 47 (right)

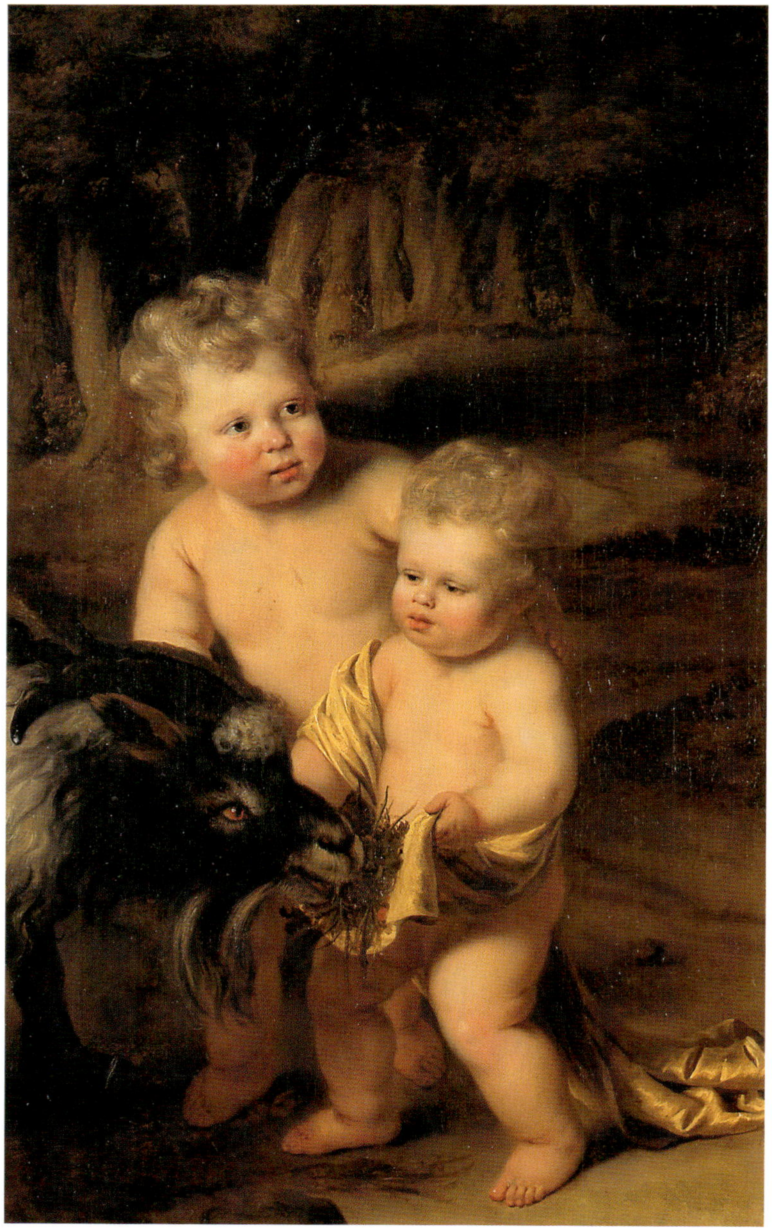

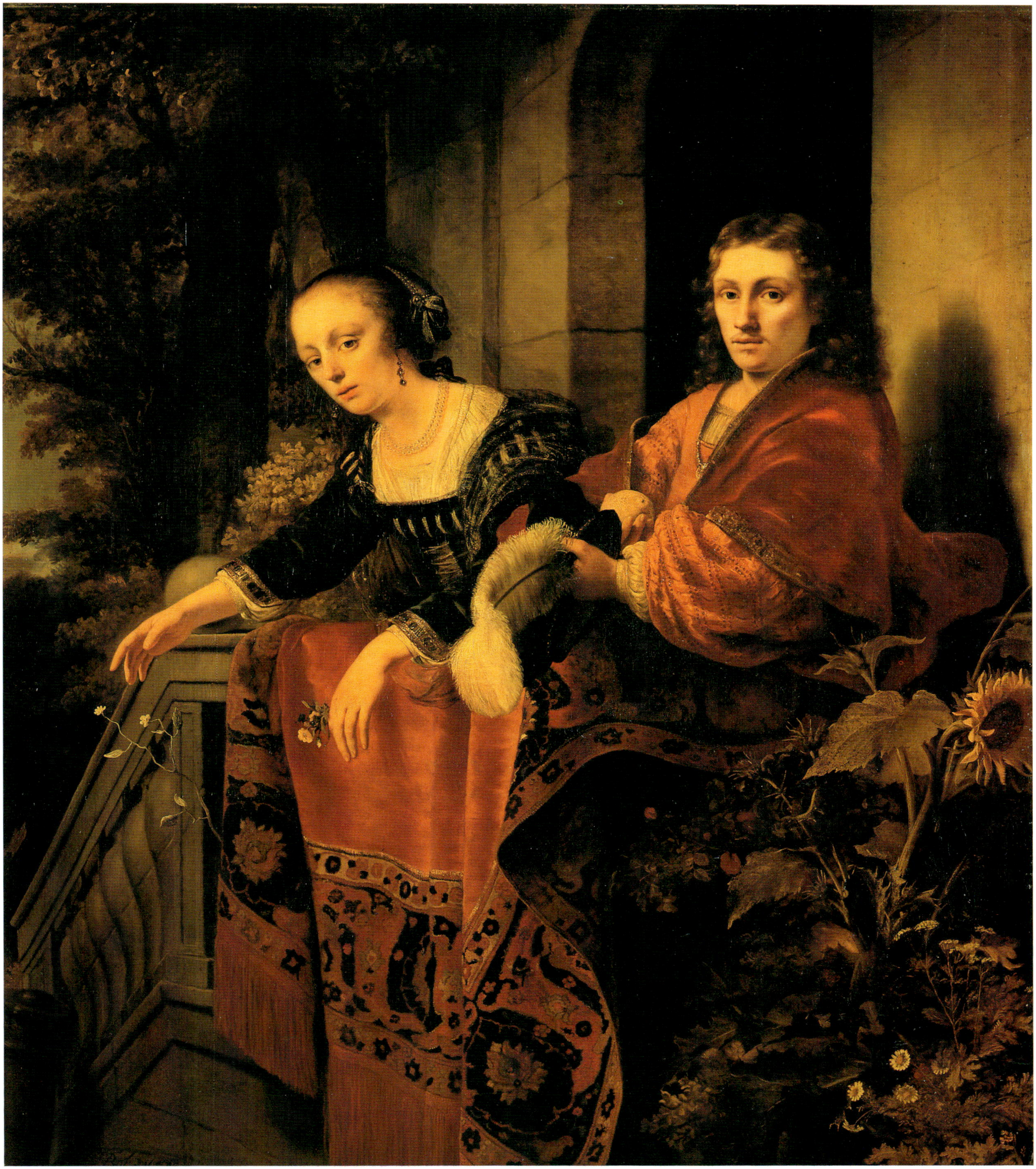

Jan Victors (1619 – *c.*1676 – 77)

The painter Jan Victors, born into a family of modest means, was baptized Hans in the Amsterdam Oude Kerk on 13 June 1619. His grandfather, who had left Antwerp for religious reasons, was a *stoelmaker* (chair-maker). Louis Victors, Jan's father, also started in this profession but in 1625 would become *bode op Dordrecht* (city messenger to Dordrecht) for the city of Amsterdam. He was betrothed in 1608 to Styntje Jaspers, the daughter of a town musician. The bird painter Jacobus Victors (1640 – 1705) is Jan's younger half-brother from his father's third marriage.

Documents concerning Jan's training have not survived. Consequently one can only speculate about the identity of his teacher. The iconography and style of Victors's early biblical history paintings indicate close contact with Rembrandt and Govaert Flinck. Therefore it seems probable that Victors trained in Rembrandt's workshop. The fact that his earliest dated painting is from 1640 (Hermitage, St Petersburg) suggests that his training may well have taken place during the second half of the 1630s.

In 1642, in Amsterdam, Jan married Jannetje Bellers, with whom he had at least nine children. The artist appears to have cultivated contacts with the orthodox Calvinists in Amsterdam. Towards the beginning of the 1660s he received a number of portrait commissions. He painted for example two group portraits (Amsterdam Historical Museum) of the female regents of the Amsterdam Diaconieweeshuis, an orphanage that had been established in 1657. In addition, he depicted subjects from classical antiquity and rural genre scenes. However, his success was not to last. Contemporary documents suggest that he was plagued by a perpetual shortage of money in his later years. In 1673 he joined the East India Company (VOC) after having stopped painting around 1670. As a so-called *ziekentrooster* he accompanied ships of the VOC, functioning as a nurse and lay preacher for the crew. Victors died abroad in 1676 or shortly thereafter.

Throughout his life Victors was evidently an orthodox Calvinist and was thus – as far as we know – an exception among the artists in the circle of Rembrandt. In his paintings he strictly adhered to the principles of the Decalogue and refrained from depicting God the Father in the shape of a human being. Accordingly he also avoided representing the figure of Christ and scenes taken from the New Testament.

The print reproduced here, an engraving by Theodor Matham (1605/06 – 1676) after a drawing by Jacob Backer (1608 – 1651), is a presumed portrait of Jan Victors.[1] The word *victor* appears in the motto in the print, and the attending Latin verses focus on a play of words involving the Latin for painter *(pictor)* and victor *(victor)*. The artist's surname derives from the latter. However, the coat of arms in the portrait has not yet been identified. The dress of the sitter suggests that the engraving must have been produced around 1645, with 1651, the year of Backer's death, as the *terminus ante quem*. In the mid-1640s Victors was only in his late twenties, though the man in the print looks rather older than this. For the time being, therefore, the identification with Victors remains doubtful.[2]

1 Hollstein, vol. I, 1949, p. 53, no. 6; vol. XI, 1955, p. 260, no. 146, repr. (both as Jan Victors). The print was first reproduced in Immerzeel 1855, vol. III, p. 191.

2 Kramm 1857 – 64, p. 1753, pointed out that the Latin verses give no clear indication of the sitter's identity. According to Kramm it is questionable whether the VICTOR in the motto refers to the first name or surname of the man portrayed. For a discussion of the identification, see also Miller 1985, vol. I, p. 33. Miller, following Kramm's not entirely convincing arguments, rejected the identification of the sitter in the print with the painter Jan Victors.

LITERATURE: Kramm 1857 – 64, p. 1753; Bredius 1915 – 22, vol. II, pp. 596 – 600; Miller 1985; Manuth 1987; Sumowski, *Gemälde*, vol. IV, 1990, pp. 2589 – 722; V. Manuth, in Berlin / Amsterdam / London 1991 – 92a, pp. 334 – 43; Miller 1992; Manuth 1993 – 94.

VM

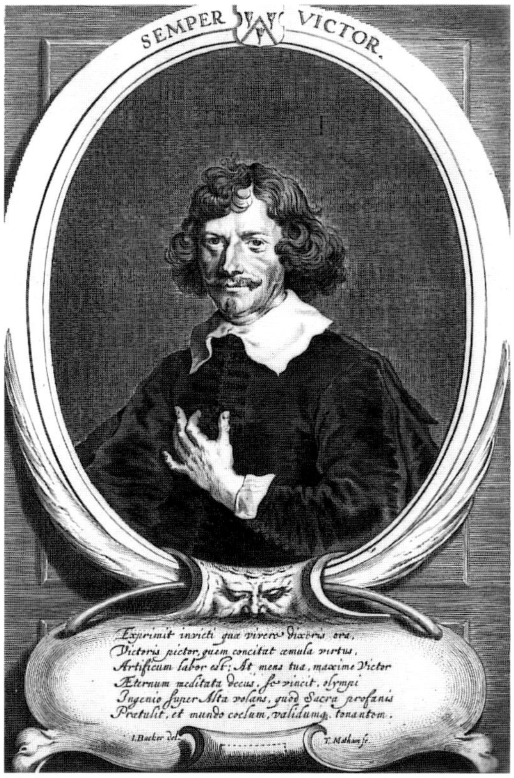

Theodor Matham (1605/06 – 1676),
after Jacob Backer
Presumed Portrait of Jan Victors c.1645 – 51
Engraving
26.0 x 16.7 cm
Rijksprentenkabinet, Rijksmuseum, Amsterdam

49
Jan Victors
Hannah, Mother of Samuel, Praying in the Temple

Signed and dated centre right *Jan. Victor fec / 1643*
Canvas
92.0 x 72.0 cm
Dordrechts Museum, Dordrecht

PROVENANCE: Dignus Cornelis Ketelaar, The Hague, 1794; Désiré van den Schriek, Louvain; her sale, Louvain (Le Roy), 8–11 April 1861, lot 136.

LITERATURE: G. Jansen, in Amsterdam / Groningen 1983, p. 222, cat. no. 65; Sumowski, *Gemälde*, vol. IV, 1990, p. 2611, no. 1786; Miller 1985, vol. I, pp. 53, 56, no. 71; Manuth 1987, p. 172, no. 48.

In the past this recently restored painting was considered to be a representation of the prophetess Anna (Luke 2:36–37). It was only in 1983 that Jansen identified the Old Testament subject correctly.[1] The painting in fact shows Hannah, the wife of Elkanah and future mother of Samuel, who is asking for a son in her prayer in the Temple (1 Samuel 1:9–13): 'And she was in bitterness of soul, and prayed unto the Lord, and wept sore ... O Lord of hosts, if thou wilt indeed look on the affliction of thine handmaid, and remember me, and ... give unto thine handmaid a man child, then I will give him unto the Lord all the days of his life' (1 Samuel 1:10–11). According to the Bible, Hannah only moved her lips as she beseeched the Lord – her voice was imperceptible. Therefore, the priest Eli who 'sat upon a seat by a post of the temple of the Lord' (1 Samuel 1:9) thought she was drunk.

Victors emphasizes the emotional content of the scene through the close-up view of Hannah, whom he shows as a kneeling half-figure filling almost the entire picture plane. He thereby approaches the pictorial type of the single historical figure. Hannah can be identified only because of the listening priest Eli in the background. The powerful lighting of her face marked by age and of her hands folded in prayer emphasizes the portrait-like quality of the image. The unforgiving realism with which Victors describes Hannah's physiognomy as a mirror of internal tensions suggests that this is a *portrait historié* – a portrait in which the sitter wears historical dress in order to identify himself or herself with a biblical or mythological figure, or with a figure taken from classical antiquity.

To the modern viewer the expression on Hannah's face may seem theatrical and exaggerated. However, the convincing representation of passions and emotions was one

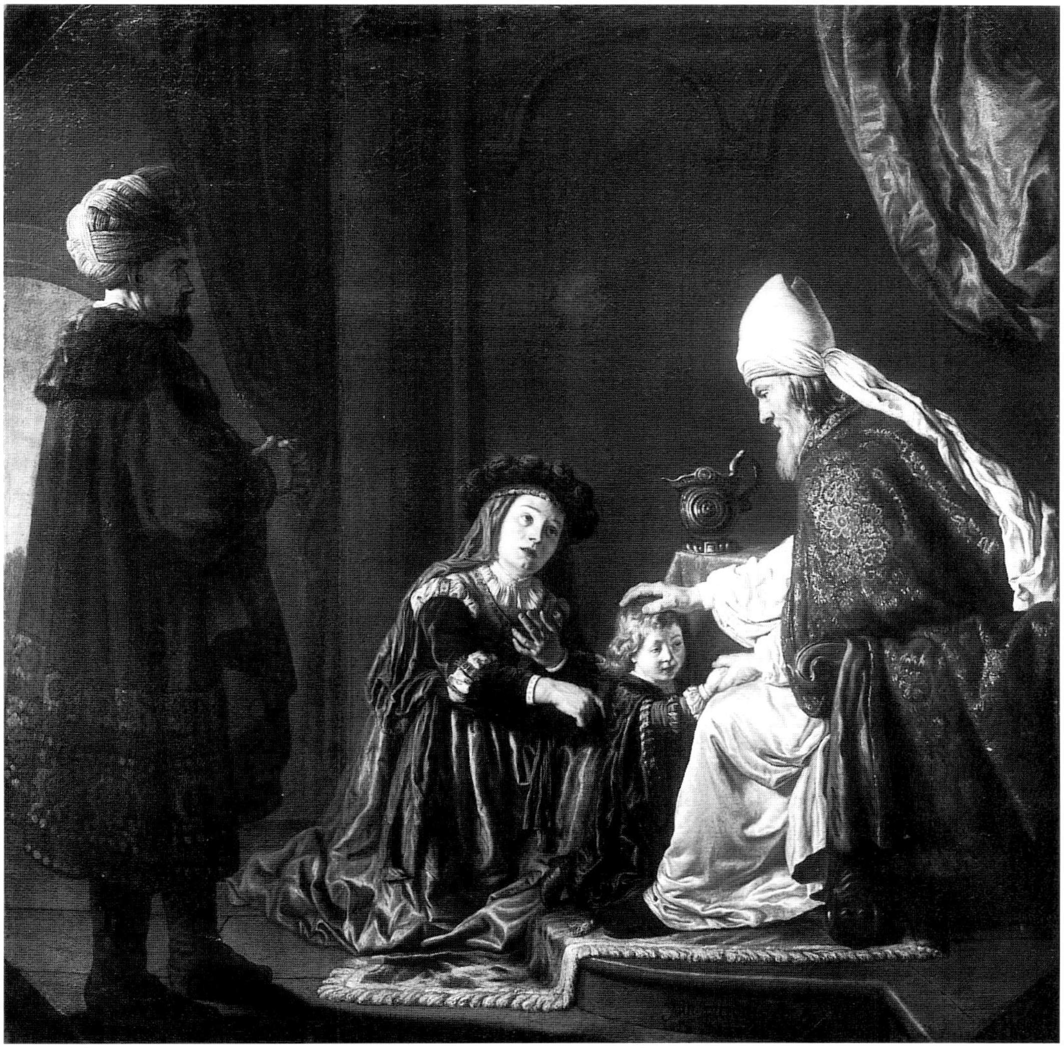

FIG. 49a
Jan Victors
The Infant Samuel Brought to Eli by Hannah and Elkanah
Signed and dated 1645
Canvas
139.0 x 137.5 cm
Staatliche Museen zu Berlin, Gemäldegalerie

of the chief concerns of history painters, not only in the seventeenth century. The Netherlandish painter and writer on art Karel van Mander (1548–1606) dedicated an entire chapter of his didactic poem for young painters *Den grondt der edel vry schilder-const* (The Foundation of the Noble Art of Painting), first published in 1604, to this problem. In his sixth chapter, 'Wtbeeldinghe der affecten, passien, begeerlijckheden en lijdens der menschen' (On Figuring Human Passions, Desires, and Sorrows), he discusses in detail the human physiognomy as an important vehicle for rendering negative and positive emotions. In this context he stresses explicitly that figures in history paintings must follow the rules of stage acting, whether comic or tragic (VI, 6). Van Mander advises young artists to pay particular attention to the position of the head, and to the eyebrows, mouth, facial creases and hands, in depicting disquiet and despair (VI, 44–45).[2] When considering Victors's Hannah in the context of van Mander's theories, one quickly realizes that there are remarkable parallels.

The scene the painter has chosen represents an Old Testament subject that is very rarely depicted in Dutch painting of the seventeenth century. In Rembrandt's circle it also occurs in two drawings attributed to Ferdinand Bol (E. Dahr Collection, Oslo; and present whereabouts unknown), both from the late 1630s or early 1640s.[3] But these works bear no direct connection to Victors's painting.

In 1645 Victors painted the *Infant Samuel Brought to Eli by Hannah and Elkanah* (1 Samuel 1:24–25) today at the Gemäldegalerie, Berlin (fig. 49a).[4] This subject, unlike the preceding episode in the Bible, has been repeatedly painted by other artists from Rembrandt's circle: Gerbrand van den Eeckhout (Ashmolean Museum, Oxford; Louvre, Paris)[5] and Lambert Doomer (Musée des Beaux-Arts, Orléans).[6]

Victors probably drew the inspiration for the subject of Hannah's prayer in the presence of the priest Eli from graphic sources of the sixteenth century. One can find the scene repeatedly represented in Bible illustrations, although in a more descriptive manner, without the concentration on Hannah's physiognomy. Here the woodcuts in Tobias Stimmer's *Neue künstliche Figuren Biblischer Historien*, published in Basle in 1576, and in Jost Amman's *Neuwe Biblische Figuren ...* of 1579 may serve as examples (fig. 49b).[7] Furthermore, in the course of the sixteenth century, images of Hannah entered print series of 'Celebrated Women of the Old Testament', which represent virtuous and pious women from the Bible. The most comprehensive series of twenty single figures, designed by Maarten de Vos (1532–1603), includes the praying Hannah before the Temple in the background.[8] The title page displays the motto 'But a woman that feareth the Lord, she shall be praised' (Proverbs 31:30). Jan Victors's expressive and passionately praying Hannah symbolizes strength of faith, and fear of God. If one accepts that this is a historicizing portrait, the motivation for its commission would undoubtedly have to be connected to the life circumstances and the faith of the hitherto unknown patron.

VM

1 G. Jansen, in Amsterdam / Groningen 1983, p. 222, no. 65.

2 For van Mander's instructions on how to depict human emotions, see also Miedema 1973, vol. I, pp. 157–82.

3 Sumowski, *Drawings*, vol. 1, 1979, nos 177[x], 247[x].

4 Sumowski, *Gemälde*, vol. IV, 1990, p. 2600, no. 1737.

5 Sumowski, *Gemälde*, vol. II, 1985, nos 433, 455.

6 Sumowski, *Gemälde*, vol. I, 1983, p. 466, no. 217.

7 For Tobias Stimmer (1539–1584) and Jost Amman (1539–1591) and their Bible illustrations, see P. Tanner, in Basel 1984, pp. 185–200.

8 Hollstein, vol. XLIV, 1996, p. 59, no. 234/I; vol. XLV, 1995, pl. 234/I.

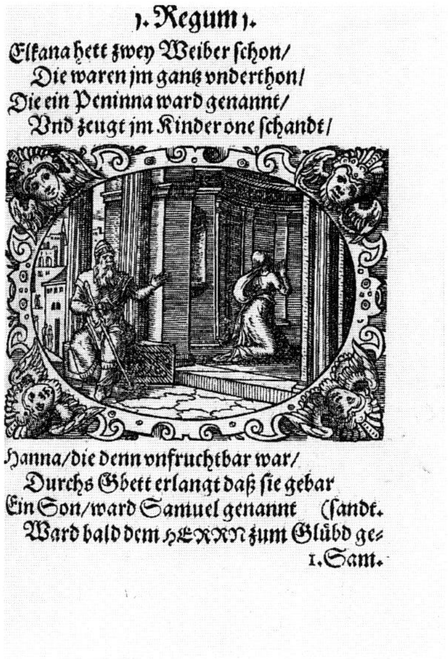
1. Regum 1.
Elkana hett zwey Weiber schon/
Die waren jm gantz vnderthon/
Die ein Peninna ward genannt/
Vnd zeugt jm Kinder one schandt/

Hanna/die denn vnfruchtbar war/
Durchs Gbett erlangt daß sie gebar
Ein Son/ward Samuel genannt (sandt.
Ward bald dem HERRN zum Glübd ge=
1. Sam.

FIG. 49b
Jost Amman Swiss, 1539–1591
Hannah at Prayer 1579
Woodcut
7.8 x 5.4 cm
Photograph: Collection of the author

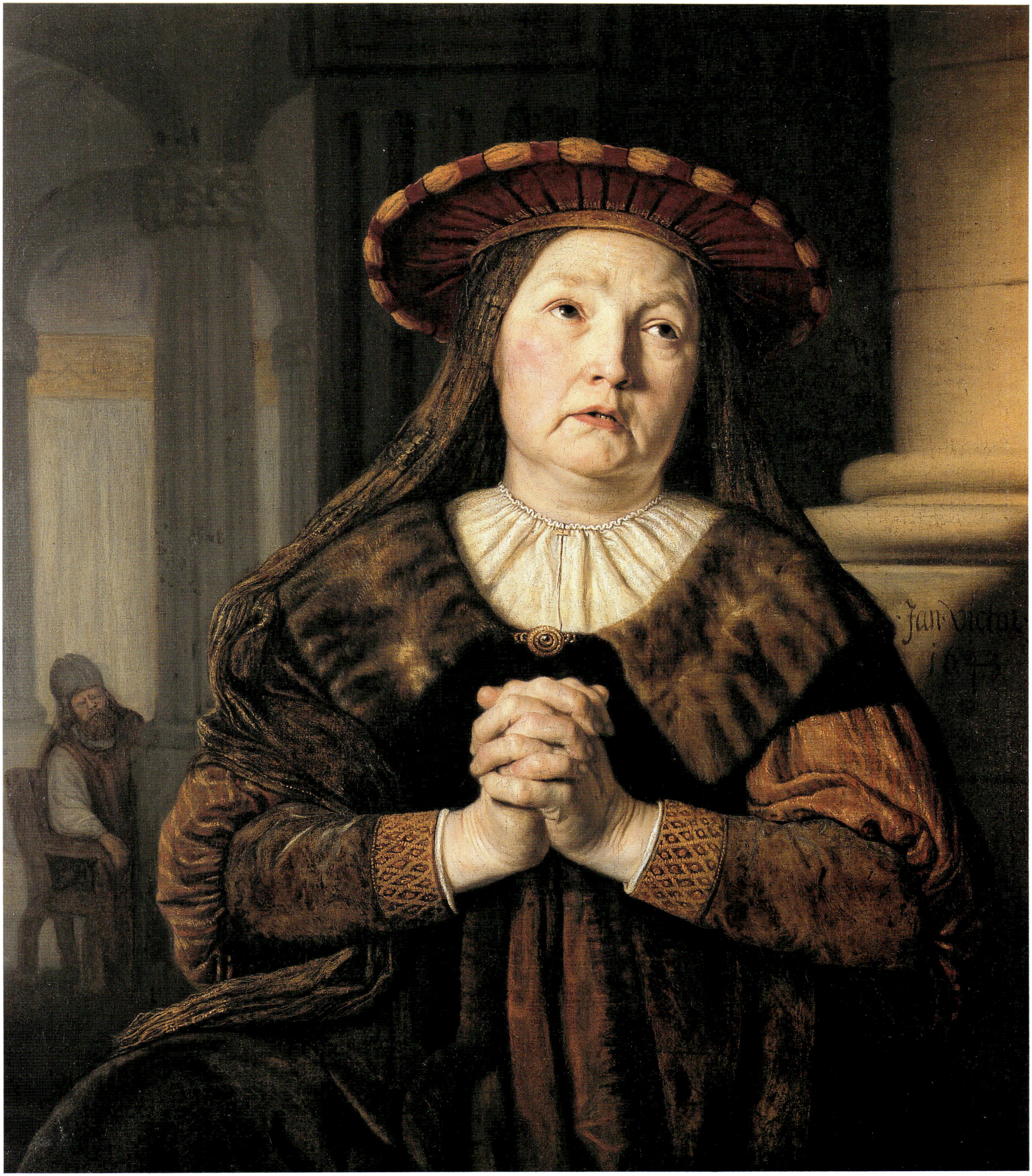

50
Jan Victors
Portrait of a Gentleman

Signed and dated below right centre
Johanes Victors fe / 1650
Canvas
97.0 x 81.0 cm
Milwaukee Art Museum
Gift of Mrs. William D. Vogel

51
Jan Victors
Portrait of a Lady

Signed and dated lower right
Johanes Victors fe / 1650
Canvas
97.0 x 81.0 cm
Milwaukee Art Museum
Gift of Mrs. William D. Vogel

PROVENANCE (cat. nos 50 and 51: Sale, Cologne, 11 October 1904 (as Jacob Backer); R. Langton Douglas, 1918; with dealer J. Goudstikker, The Hague, 1918 [1918 cat., nos 12, 24, reprs (as Bartholomeus van der Helst)]; with dealer K. Boothe, Detroit, 1950; private collection, New York, 1952; Mrs William D. Vogel.

LITERATURE (cat. nos 50 and 51: Sumowski, *Gemälde*, vol. IV, 1990, p. 2616, nos 1812, 1813; Miller 1985, vol. I, pp. 83, 281, nos 9, 10.

The impressive portraits of this solemn couple are among the finest works Jan Victors produced during his career. The as yet unidentified man and woman are depicted three-quarter length. Each is set against a rather undefined back wall on which the light, falling from the left, produces a soft, blurred shadow of the sitter's form.

The man wears at the neck a small band edged with white 'Dutch' lace and fastened with tasselled bandstrings. His cuffs are set off with white lace of the same dense pattern. The man's black cloak is draped around his body. He is holding brown gloves edged with black in his right hand.

His wife is wearing a round *halsneusdoek* (neckerchief) over a *neerstik* (partlet). These as well as her pair of cuffs are edged with white lace of the same pattern as the lace in the portrait of her husband. Her black gown is decorated with black silk bobbin-lace and has a stomacher of yellow damask. In her left hand she is holding the bunched-up skirt of her gown, under which is a skirt of a very dark aubergine colour, which is

FIG. 50/51a
Jan Victors
Portrait of a Gentleman
Signed and dated 1651
Canvas
79.5 x 72.5 cm
The Saul P. Steinberg Collection, New York

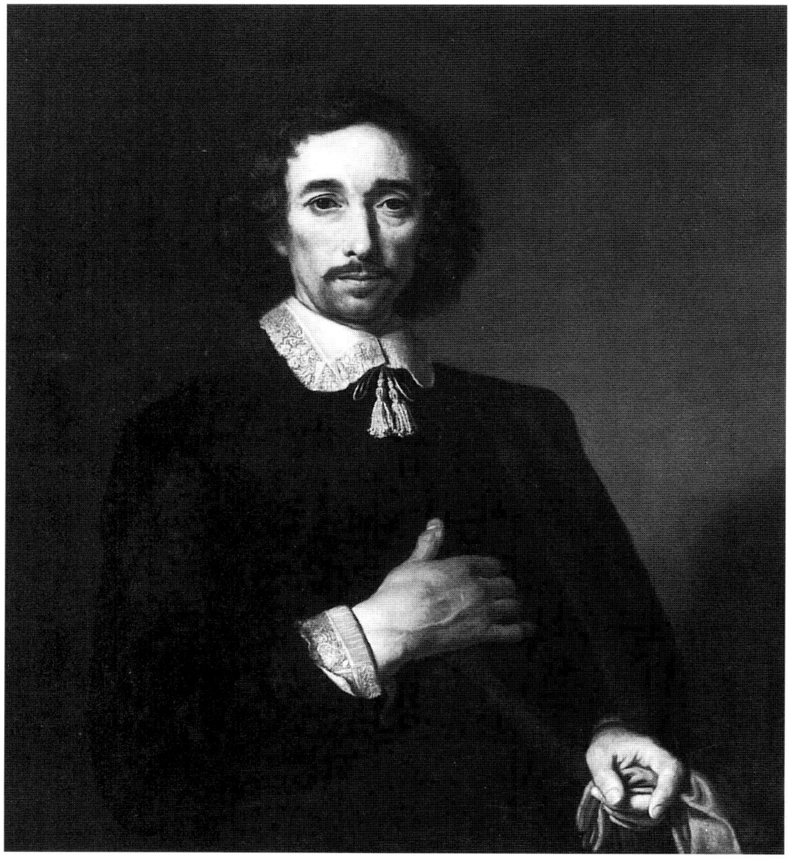

decorated at the front with four vertical passements. In her right hand, which is resting on the back of a chair, she is holding a small psalm book with a golden fastening. She wears small golden chains around her wrists and neck, and a garnet ring on the third finger of her left hand. On her chest a jewelled bow-knot brooch, the most characteristic jewel of the middle of the seventeenth century, can be seen. She is also wearing earrings with crescent moons and pearls, and in her hair a golden *haarnaalt* (bodkin).

Jan Victors's portraits are characterized by the strong physical presence of the sitters. Despite the use of rather conventional poses the artist manages to emphasize the sitters' human dignity and an unaffected naturalness.

Already fully developed by about 1640, the style of Victors's portraits remained almost unchanged until the end of his career. Towards the beginning of the 1650s, however, their expressiveness increased. Besides the pendants from Milwaukee, two portraits of 1651 of a married couple, works that are today in the collection of Saul Steinberg in New York, reflect this shift and the higher level of quality of this period (figs 50/51a, 50/51b).[1] Generally, Victors's models stand out clearly against the background and fill almost the entire picture plane, and this underscores their closeness to the viewer. The faces of the men always show richer contrasts in the colouring and illumination of the fleshtones than do those of the women, an aspect that is indeed in accordance with contemporary conventions for portraits of married couples. The main influence for Victors's approach was Rembrandt's portrait style of the 1630s.

VM

1 Sumowski, *Gemälde*, vol. IV, 1990, nos 1814, 1815.

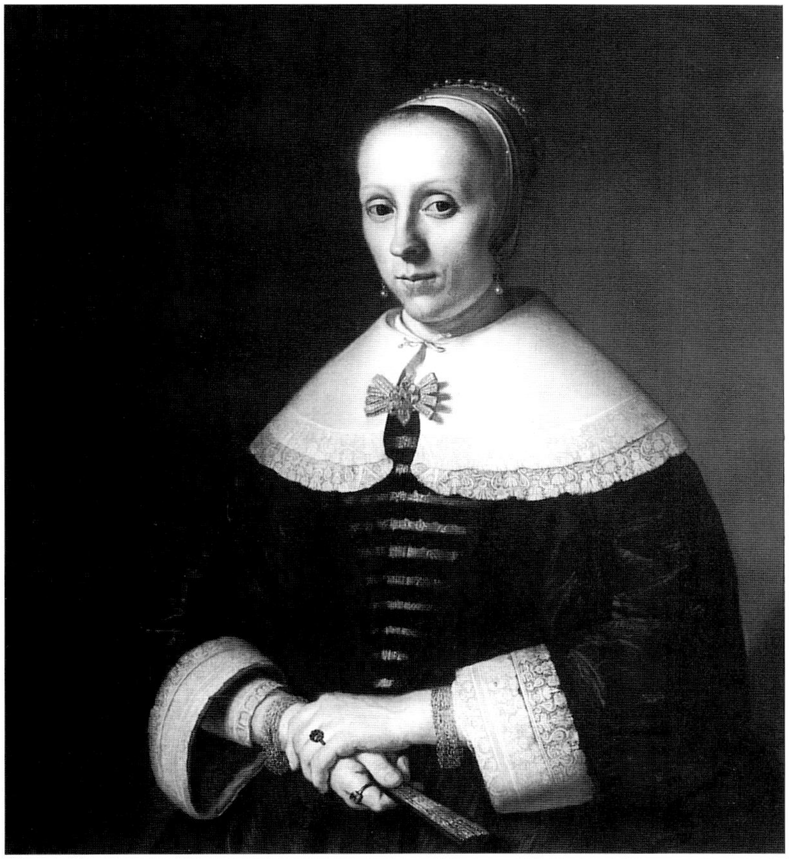

FIG. 50/51b
Jan Victors
Portrait of a Lady
Signed and dated 1651
Canvas
79.5 x 72.5 cm
The Saul P. Steinberg Collection, New York

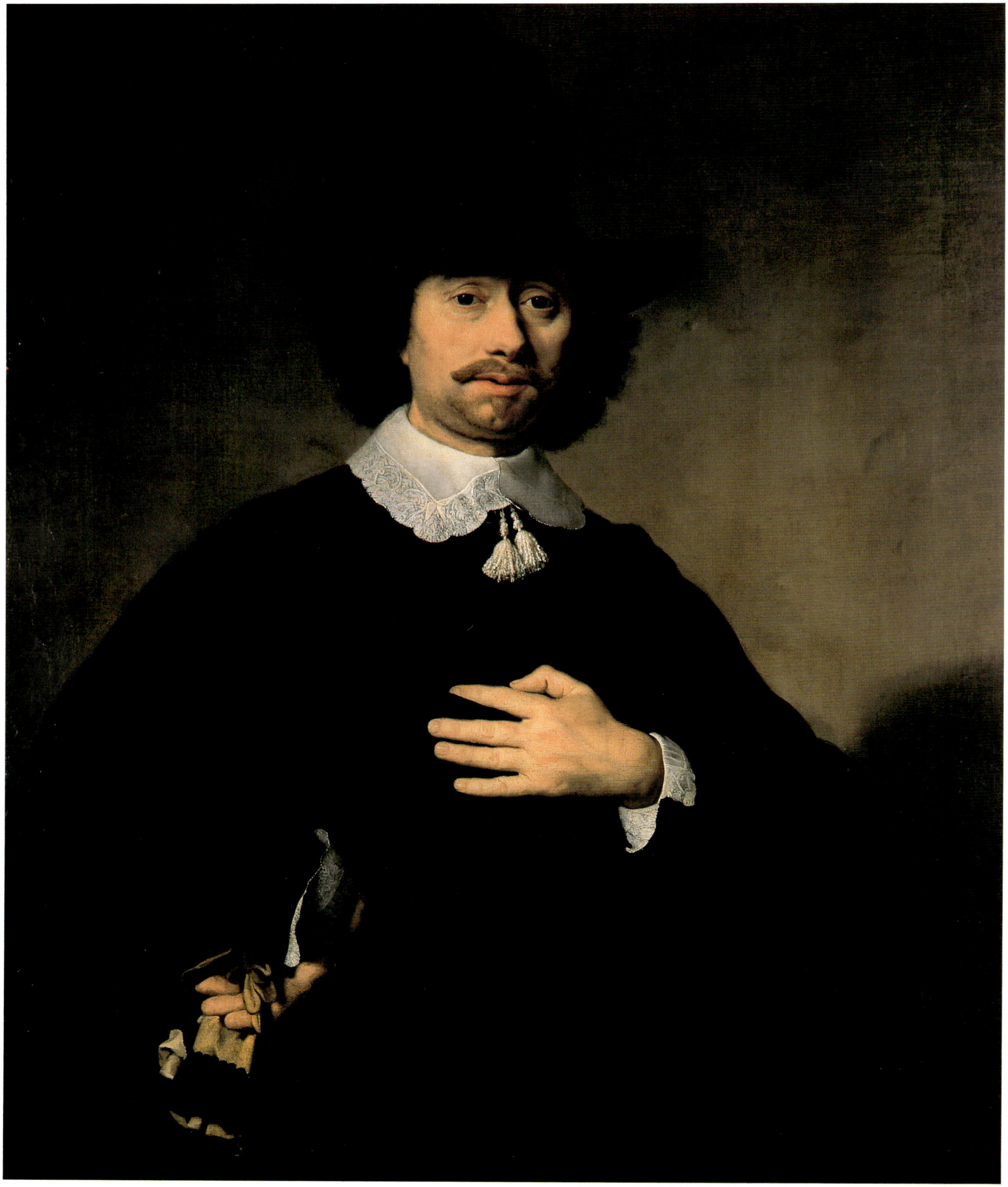

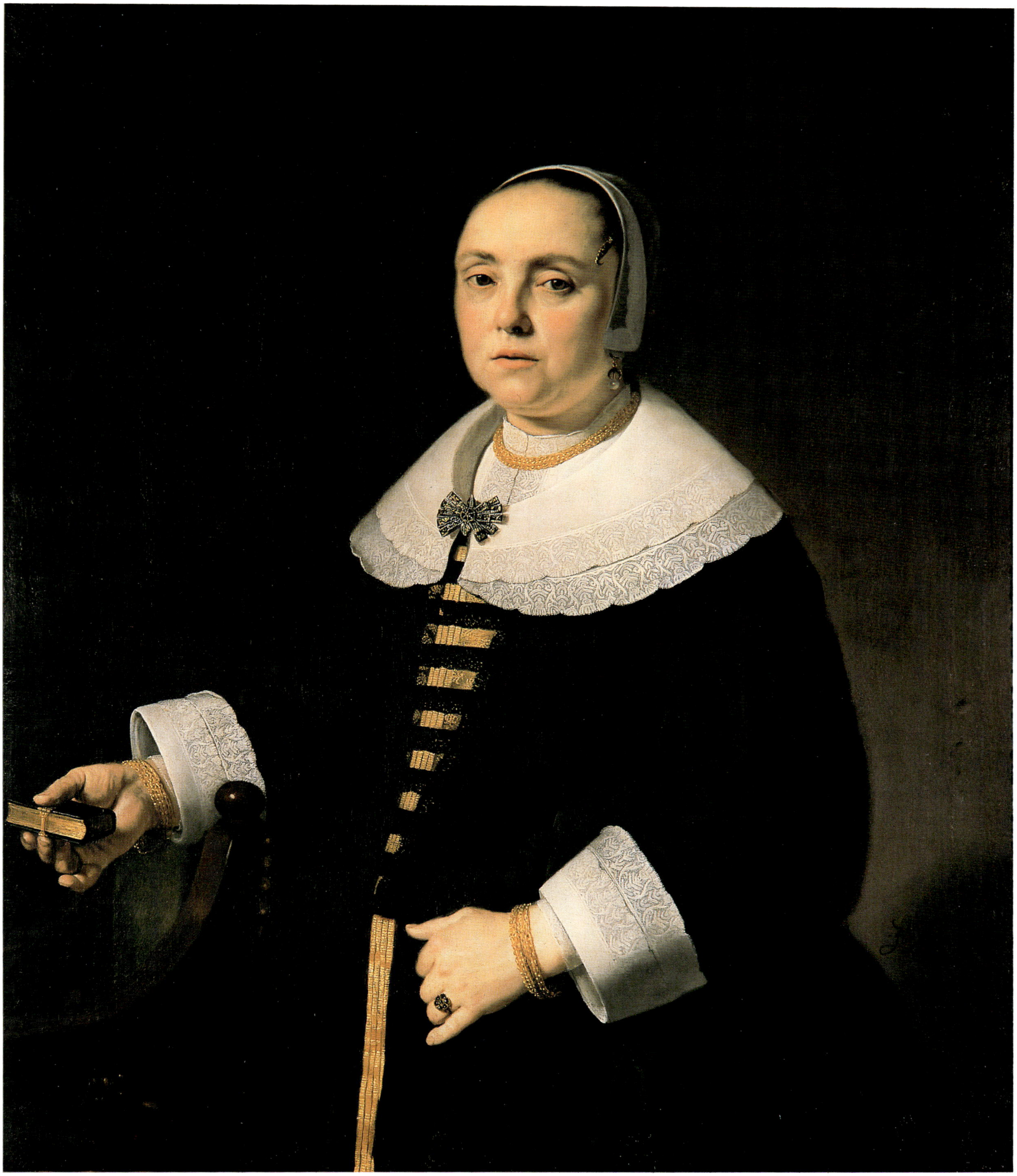

52

Formerly attributed to Jan Victors

Portrait of a Young Lady

*c.*1640

Canvas
126.0 x 104.0 cm
National Gallery of Victoria, Melbourne; purchased 1979

PROVENANCE: Sale, S.A.I. Princesse Mathilde Bonaparte (Princess de San Donato), Paris (G. Petit), 17–21 May 1904, lot 22, repr. (as Jan Fictoor), together with companion piece, *Portrait of a Gentleman*, to Agnew for 13,500 frs each; Mrs Robert Wallach, 'Hopefield', Warrenton, Virginia; Mr Cross Johnson; on loan to the Smithsonian Institution, Washington DC, *c.*1920–*c.*1940; Dr Rudolf Heinemann (Pinakos Inc.), New York; with M. Knoedler & Co., New York, 1945 [1945 cat. *Dutch Masters of the Seventeenth Century*, 5–24 February 1945, no. 19]; with Thos Agnew & Sons, London, 1976 [1976 cat. *Master Paintings*, 18 May – 18 June 1976, no. 6, repr.]; purchased from Agnew's by Norman V. Salter, Melbourne, 1976; acquired from Mrs Salter in 1979.

LITERATURE: Sumowski, *Gemälde*, vol. V, 1990, p. 3100, no. 2086 (as Govaert Flinck); Miller 1985, vol. I, p. 343, no. R19 (as 'reminiscent of Backer'); E. Devapriam, in Hoff 1995, p. 304 (as Jan Victors, *c.*1645).

This three-quarter-length portrait shows a young woman in elegant dress in front of a stone arch. She is wearing a white coif and a starched pleated ruff. Her black gown, whose square neckline is edged with a piece of white lace, has a slightly pointed bodice and is worn over a red skirt. The woman is holding a pair of gloves in her right hand and probably a watch in her left. On the table to the left one can see a preciously bound psalm book with metal clasps.

This picture was sold at auction in Paris in 1904 together with its male companion piece (fig. 52a).[1] Although the two paintings – the portraits of a married couple – bear no signatures, the auction catalogue listed them as works by Jan Victors. This is remarkable in so far as Victors was one of the lesser known artists of the Rembrandt circle at the beginning of this century. Moreover, the number of portraits by him which may lend themselves for comparison is small. Therefore it remains an enigma as to what may have led the authors of the 1904 auction catalogue to make their attribution to him. One possible source may have been Carel Vosmaer's monograph *Rembrandt, sa vie et ses oeuvres*, the second edition of which had appeared in The Hague in 1877. Vosmaer was the first author since Arnold Houbraken, in his *Groote schouburgh* of 1718–21, to provide a survey – although incomplete and riddled with mistakes – of pupils and masters from Rembrandt's immediate circle. His mentioning of Victors was one of the earliest positive accounts of the painter in art historical literature. Vosmaer, for the first time, regards him as one of the significant members of the Rembrandt circle of the 1630s.[2]

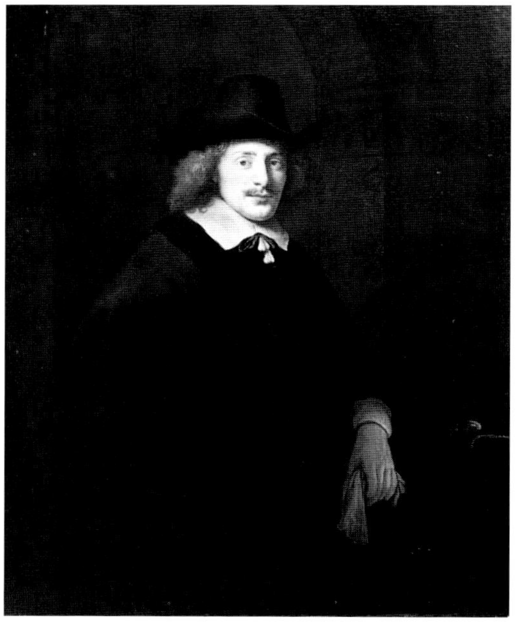

FIG. 52a
Jan Victors(?)
Portrait of a Gentleman
Canvas
125.7 x 104.0 cm
Sale, S. A. I. Princesse Mathilde Bonaparte, Paris (G. Petit), 17–21 May 1904; present whereabouts unknown
Photograph: RKD

A further explanation for the attribution to Jan Victors at the time of the Paris auction may lie with one of the artist's most important paintings, which had been in Paris since 1801. It is the *Young Woman at a Window*, signed and dated 1640, in the Louvre.[3] The illusionistically painted stone windowframe out of which the woman in this painting is leaning shows some obvious cracks in the masonry. This architectural detail suggests a certain similarity with the stone arches in the pendant portraits and this may have influenced the attribution to Victors. Nonetheless, Victors's authorship can no longer be supported.

In the context of the history of costume, the portrait should most likely be dated to around 1640, particularly because of the headdress and the shape of the ruff. Although this style was already somewhat out of fashion for a young woman of *c.*1640, it was not unusual in the more conservative circles of the time. The accomplished execution of the face and the quality of the rendering of the costume make it unlikely that the painting is the work of a beginner.

Victors's earliest dated portrait (Hermitage, St Petersburg), from 1640, clearly lacks some of the qualities of his later works.[4] Until the end of his career he remained faithful to a specific type of portrait. From the beginning, he showed his sitters as half- or three-quarter-length figures, usually rather close to the viewer (cat. nos 50, 51). This kind of close-up view reinforces the impression of the physical presence of the sitter, while the surrounding space and the diffuse background, which occasionally shows the sitter's shadow, are clearly subordinated. The emphasis is placed on the precisely observed and non-idealized physiognomies and hands of the sitters, this naturalism being further underscored by the subtle lighting. The fleshtones, depending on the age and sex of the sitter, are varied and lively. Accessories, such as gloves and books, are normally emphasized and are closely integrated with the figure. With respect to these characteristics, comparing the Melbourne portrait with authentic portraits by Jan Victors reveals more differences than similarities.

The use of architecture for the background of portraits had served since at least the sixteenth

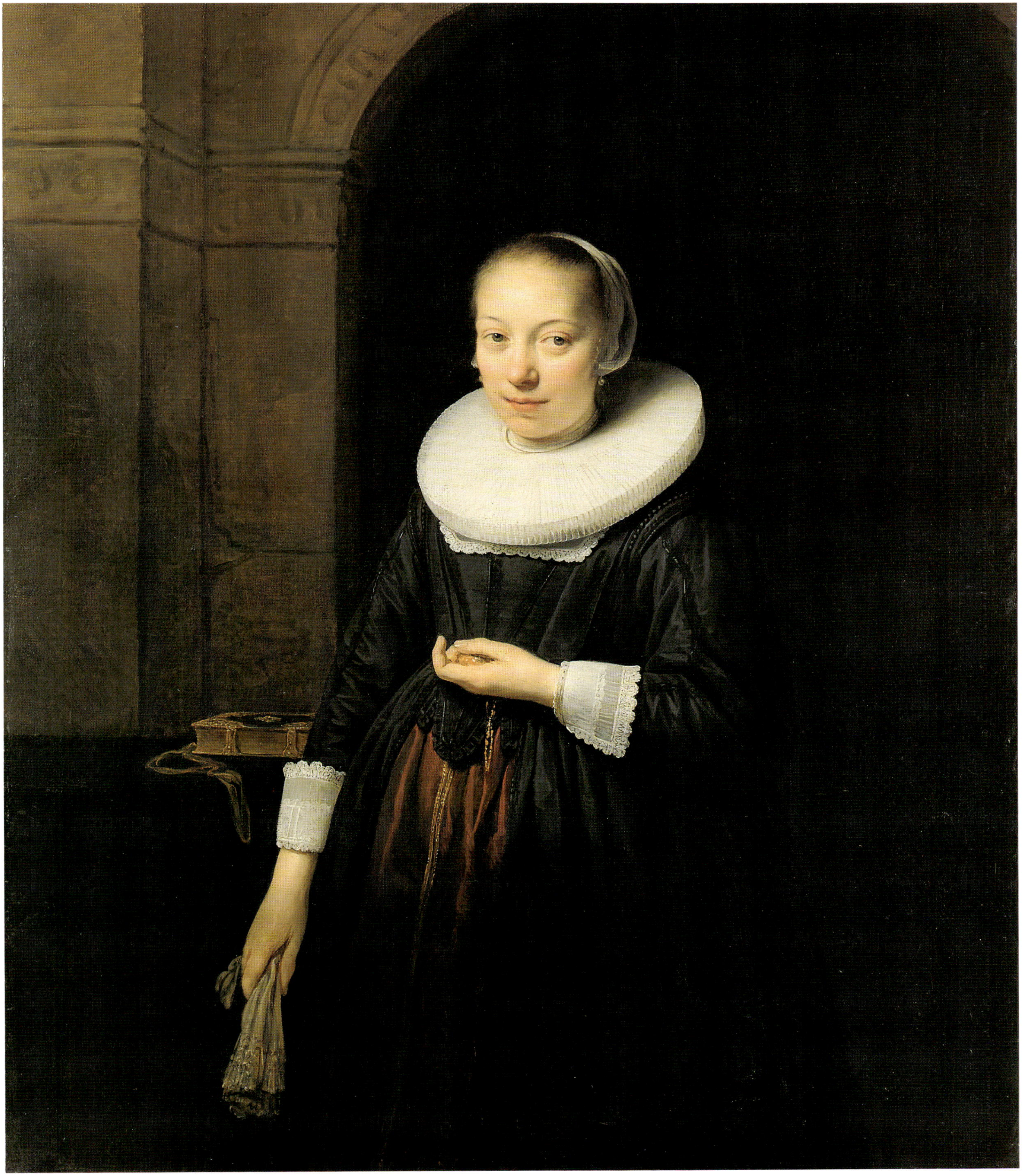

century as a means of ennobling the sitter and underlining his or her social status. Classical monumental architecture is thus predominantly found in portraits of monarchs and members of the European aristocracy, by artists like Titian, Bronzino, Antonis Mor, Rubens and Anthony van Dyck. In the northern Netherlands of the seventeenth century, artists adapted the format of the three-quarter- or full-length portrait before an architectural background to meet the growing desire for representation among their wealthy patrician patrons. In Amsterdam one increasingly finds this portrait type from the 1620s onwards, in individual and marriage portraits by artists such as Nicolaes Eliasz Pickenoy (1588–1650/56) and Thomas de Keyser (1596/97–1667).[5] Rembrandt too adopted this type into his repertoire after he had moved from Leiden to Amsterdam in 1631/32. The *Standing Man* at the Staatliche Kunstsammlungen, Kassel (Bredius 216), and the *Portrait of a Young Woman (Maria Trip?)* (Bredius 356) (fig. 52b), both executed in 1639, are fine and influential examples of the use of an architectural setting in Rembrandt's portraits around the time when the Melbourne picture must have been painted, by an artist probably from the master's circle.[6]

The rejection, in the most recent literature, of the attribution to Jan Victors is justified. However, connections to Jacob Backer (1608–1651), as suggested by Miller, cannot be accepted either. Independent of each other, van Regteren Altena and Sumowski considered an attribution to Govaert Flinck.[7] This suggestion deserves some attention. Similarities can be detected when we compare the Melbourne painting with a portrait by Flinck dated 1648 that was with a Hamburg auctioneer in 1983 (sale cat., Hauswedell & Nolte, Hamburg, 8 June 1983, lot 40, repr).[8] A connection to Flinck is further indicated by the portraits of a couple at the Milwaukee Art Museum, works that contain a comparable architectural background.[9]

In order to come to a more precise conclusion regarding the authorship of the Melbourne painting it would be most important to study its pendant, whose whereabouts have been unknown since 1918.[10] One can only hope that exhibiting the present portrait may provide the impetus for the rediscovery, and possibly the reunification, of the two pendants in the near future.

VM

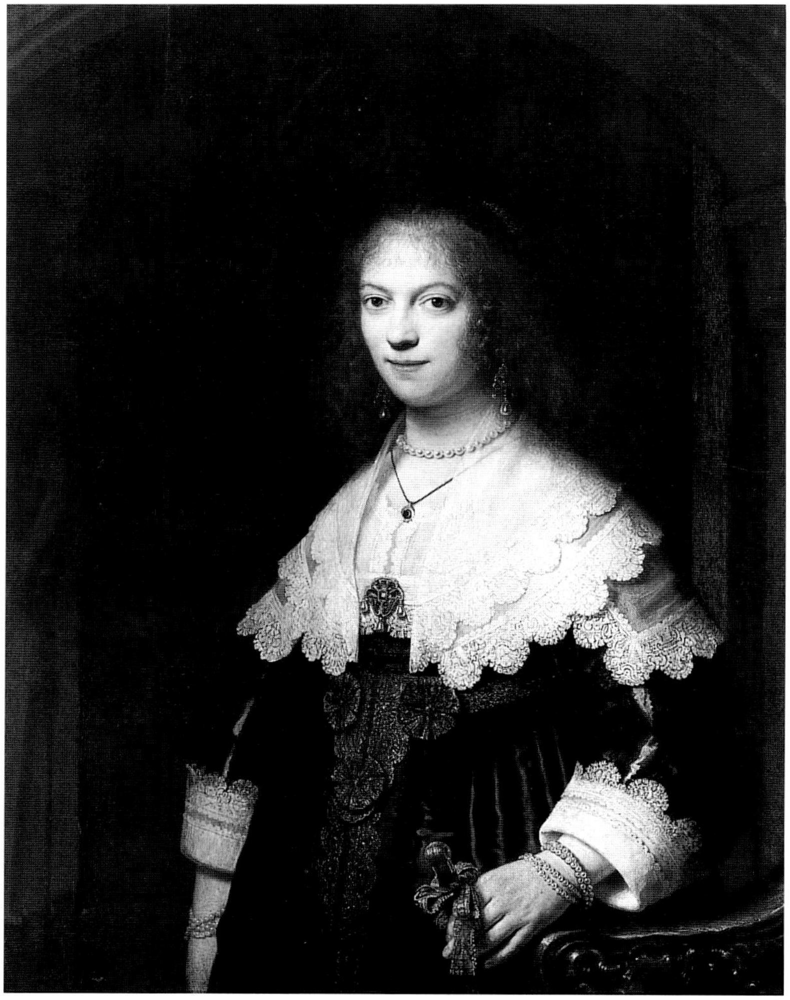

FIG. 52b
Rembrandt
Portrait of a Young Woman (Maria Trip?)
Signed and dated 1639
Panel
107.0 x 82.0 cm
Rijksmuseum, Amsterdam; on loan from the Van Weede Family Foundation

1 The companion pieces must have been separated between the Paris sale in 1904 and 1918 when the male portrait was sold in New York (sale, George A. Hearn, New York, 25 February – 4 March 1918, lot 416, repr. (as 'Portrait of a Gentleman'), to Henry Mack for US$1,500)).

2 Vosmaer 1877, p. 178. For the incomplete accounts of Jan Victors's life and the reception of his works in the art historical literature of the nineteenth century, cf. Miller 1985, vol. I, pp. 1–10.

3 Sumowski, *Gemälde*, vol. IV, 1990, p. 2610, no. 1785.

4 Sumowski, *Gemälde*, vol. IV, 1990, p. 2616, no. 1811.

5 For examples by Nicolaes Eliasz Pickenoy, see De Jongh 1986, pp. 137–40, cat. no. 23, repr.; for examples by Thomas de Keyser, see Adams 1985, esp. vol. IV, nos 33, 34, 37, 38, 48, 49, 50.

6 For Rembrandt's portraits, see *Corpus*, vol. III, 1989, nos A129, A131.

7 I. Q. van Regteren Altena's handwritten reference to Flinck as the author of the Melbourne portrait and of its companion piece (fig. 52a) can be found in a copy of the Paris auction catalogue of 1904 (sale cat., S. A. I. Princesse Mathilde Bonaparte sale, G. Petit, Paris, 17–21 May 1904) at the RKD; see also Sumowski, *Gemälde*, vol. V, 1990, p. 3100, no. 2086. On seeing the companion pieces, at some time between 1904 and 1918 when they were separated, Hofstede de Groot was reminded of Ferdinand Bol around 1640–45 (so-called HdG fiches, RKD, The Hague).

8 Von Moltke 1965, p. 163, no. 459, repr. For the similarities as mentioned by Sumowski, see Sumowski, *Gemälde*, vol. V, 1990, p. 3100, under no. 2086.

9 Von Moltke 1965, pp. 161–3, nos 456, 457, reprs.

10 See note 1 above.

Gerbrand van den Eeckhout (1621–1674)

Gerbrand van den Eeckhout was the son of the goldsmith Jan Pietersz van den Eeckhout and of Grietje Claesdr., the daughter of a shoemaker from Amsterdam. He was baptized Garbrant in the Reformed Oude Kerk in Amsterdam on 22 August 1621. His paternal ancestors had been *Doopsgezinden* (Mennonites). His grandfather Pieter Lodewijcksz had for religious reasons been forced to leave his native Brussels, and had become a citizen of Amsterdam in 1588.

Two years after the death of Gerbrand's mother, his father married Cornelia Willemsdr. Dedel from Delft, the daughter of a wealthy director of the East India Company (VOC). The ambitious father's second marriage elevated the family's social standing considerably and brought increased prosperity.

Houbraken reports that Gerbrand studied with Rembrandt. Although – as is so often the case – there are no extant archival documents regarding his training with Rembrandt, one may assume that he stayed in the master's workshop between *c.*1635 and 1640/41.

Gerbrand van den Eeckhout was one of Rembrandt's most versatile pupils. He painted subjects taken from the Bible, mythology, history and Roman antiquity. In addition, he produced landscapes, portraits, and genre scenes depicting musical companies as well as groups of soldiers engaged in leisure activities. His oeuvre also includes etchings, designs for metal objects, and ornamental engravings.

For the style and narrative mode of his history paintings, Gerbrand clearly drew inspiration from Rembrandt and occasionally also from Rembrandt's teacher Pieter Lastman (see commentaries to cat. nos 53, 55).

According to Houbraken, van den Eeckhout shared lifelong friendships with his teacher as well as with the landscape painter Roelant Roghman. After his brother Jan's death in 1669 Gerbrand, who remained a bachelor for his entire life, lived in the house of his sister-in-law on the elegant Herengracht. Upon his death on 26 September 1674 in Amsterdam, the proceeds from the sale of his artistic estate (which included drawings, prints and plaster casts) passed under the terms of his will to one of his nephews, who was also his godson and namesake.

LITERATURE: Houbraken 1719–21, vol. II, 1719, p. 100; Sumowski 1962; Roy 1972; Sumowski, *Gemälde*, vol. II, 1985, pp. 719–909; V. Manuth, in Berlin / Amsterdam / London 1991–92a, pp. 344–9.

VM

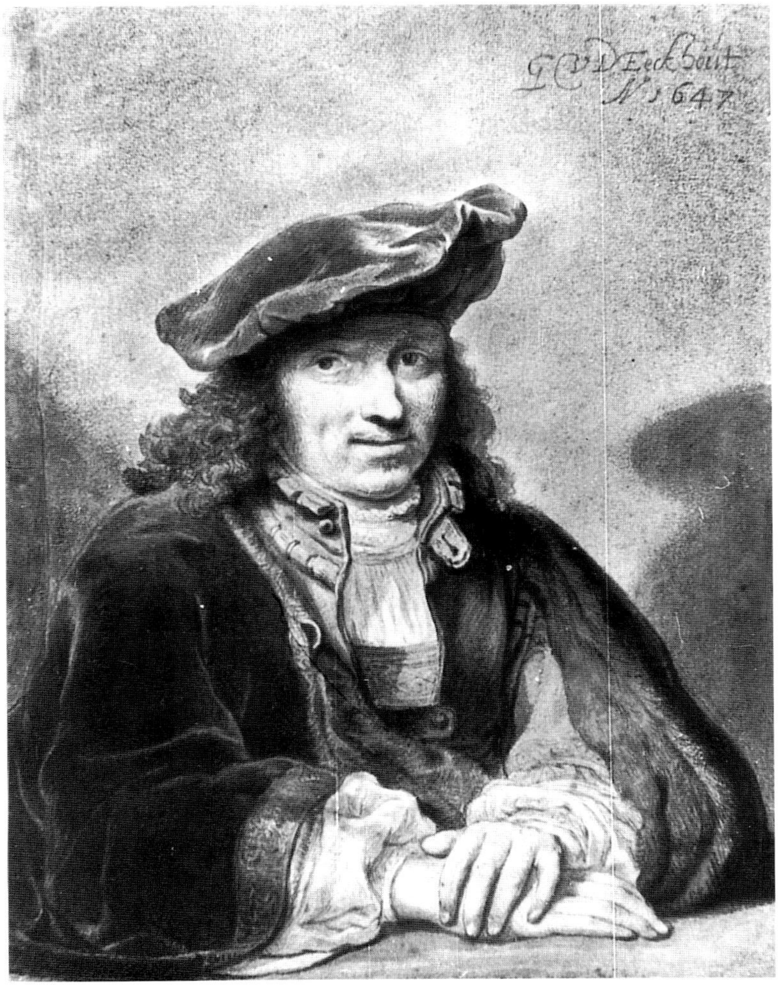

Gerbrand van den Eeckhout
Self-Portrait
Signed and dated 1647
Chalk and brush and ink
26.3 x 20.0 cm
Collection Frits Lugt, Institut Néerlandais, Paris

53

Gerbrand van den Eeckhout

Eliezer Presenting Gifts to Rebecca

Signed and dated lower left
G. V. Eeckhout. fe. / A° 1662
Canvas
77.0 x 107.5 cm
Museum Catharijneconvent, Utrecht

PROVENANCE: Private collection, the Netherlands, 1995; acquired in 1995.

LITERATURE: Dirkse & Kootte 1995.

In 1995 this painting by Gerbrand van den Eeckhout, a work unknown until then, came to the Catharijneconvent in Utrecht from a Dutch private collection. A history painting, reliably signed and dated 1662, it shows the encounter of Abraham's servant Eliezer and Isaac's future bride, Rebecca.

The picture belongs to the group of major works from the 1660s, a very productive decade for the artist during which Rembrandt's influence clearly decreases and makes way for a renewed attention to the work of Pieter Lastman (1583–1633). The close connection to the manner of Rembrandt's teacher becomes most apparent in the use of a stage-like platform, sloping towards the middle ground, as the space in which the figures are located. The proportions of the figures and the pronounced local colouring in the foreground, with its strong yellow, red and purple accents, are also reminiscent of Lastman. His *Expulsion of Hagar* of 1612 at the Hamburg Kunsthalle has been correctly suggested as a source of inspiration.[1] The background of van den Eeckhout's painting is clearly influenced by works by his colleague and friend the landscape painter Roelant Roghman (fig. 53a).

The events surrounding Eliezer's search for a bride for Isaac, as described in Genesis, chapter 24, occupied van den Eeckhout on several occasions, especially during the early 1660s.

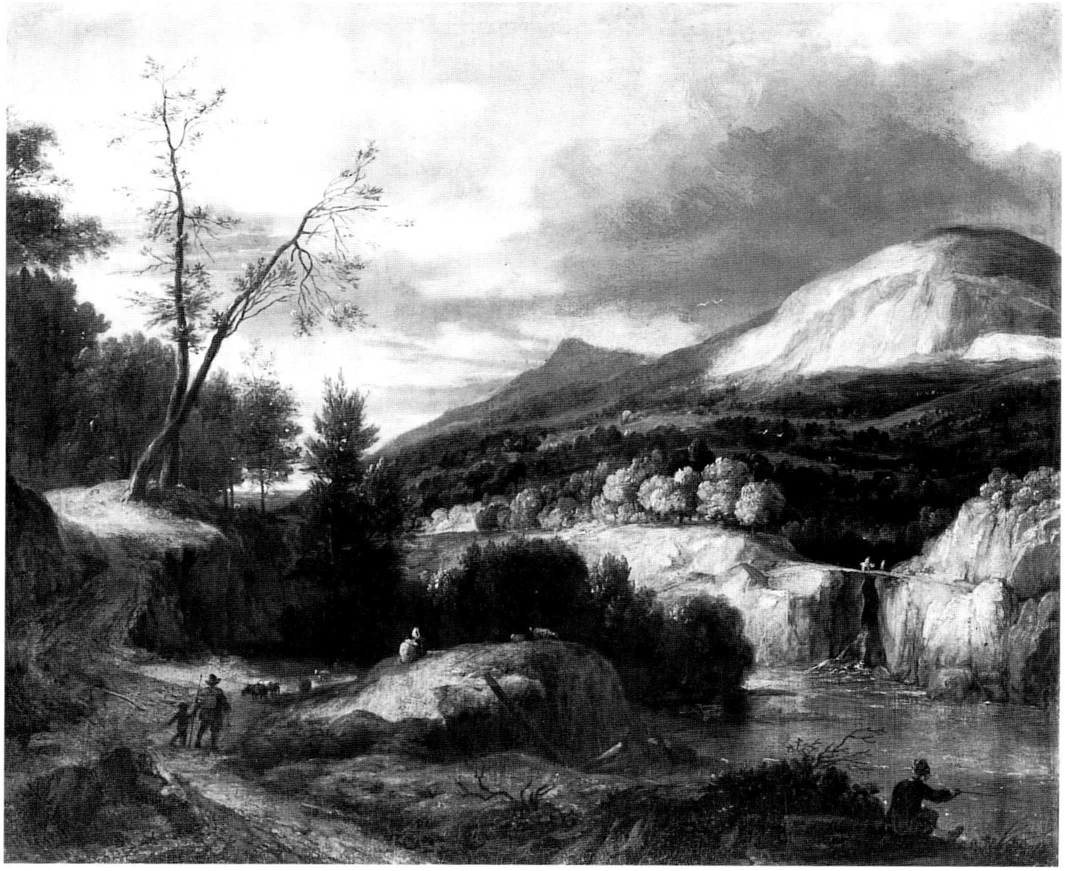

FIG. 53a
Roelant Roghman 1627–1692
Landscape with a Fisherman
Canvas
63.5 x 74.3 cm
The Trustees of the National Gallery, London

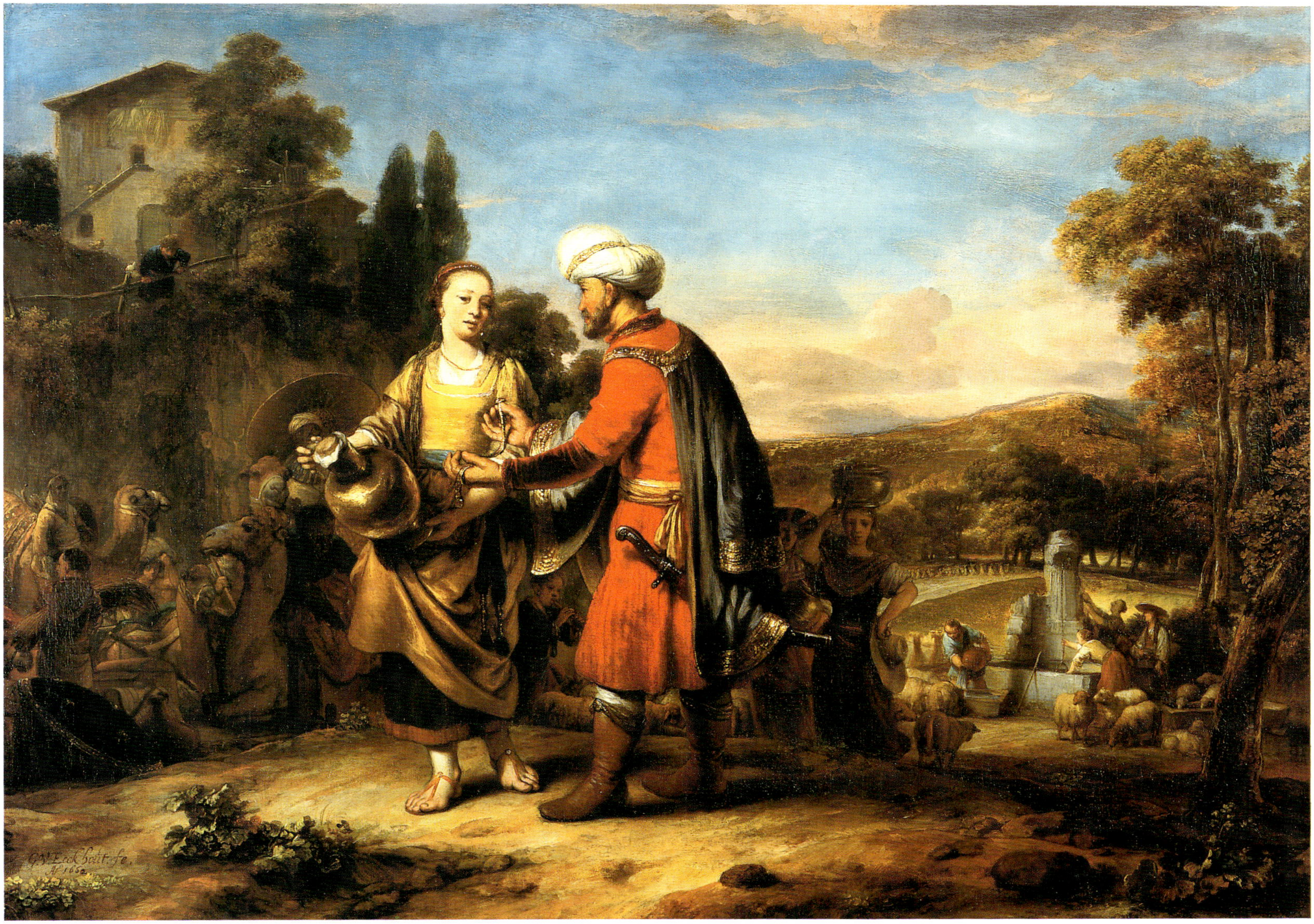

A painting that is closely related stylistically and compositionally to the present work and that is now at the National Gallery in London, dates to 1661 (fig. 53b).[2] It shows a slightly earlier moment, in which Eliezer – after having prayed for guidance, asking that whoever gave him and his convoy water would prove to be a woman eligible to marry Isaac – realizes that Rebecca is Isaac's future wife (Genesis 24:15–18). The Utrecht painting shows the subsequent presentation of the bridal gifts: Eliezer 'took a golden earring of half a shekel weight, and two bracelets for her hands of ten shekels weight of gold' (Genesis 24:22). In contrast to van den Eeckhout's 1663 painting of the same subject, at the Museum der bildenden Künste, Leipzig, in which work one clearly sees two bracelets,[3] the present painting shows neither the earring nor the bracelets.[4] Instead Eliezer presents Rebecca with a golden headdress in the form of a headband. This variation has its basis in the artist's use of the authorized Dutch translation of the Bible *(Staatenbijbel)*, published in 1637. There, Genesis 24:22 speaks of *voorhoofdsiersel* and *armringen* (headband and bracelets).

The reasons for the numerous representations of the encounter between Eliezer and Rebecca in Dutch painting of the seventeenth century are manifold. On the one hand the biblical text provided artists with the opportunity to combine a variety of human figures in exotic costumes, as well as animals and many narrative details, in a landscape setting. Working in this way met the theoretical ideal of *copia e varietà* (copiousness and variety), an ideal that theorists like Leon Battista Alberti, Leonardo da Vinci and Karel van Mander had demanded of history painters. A good painting, according to these writers, should include richness and variety of colours, as well as male and female figures of all ages, a diversity of human poses and movements, and animals of all kinds. By following these criteria and by applying the idea of copiousness and variety to the arcadian setting, van den Eeckhout turns the biblical story into a pastoral painting, a type of picture that became increasingly fashionable among the *nouveaux riches* burghers of Amsterdam and other Dutch cities.[5]

Rembrandt had treated the subject of Rebecca in several drawings (Benesch 491, 503, 566, 988). At some point during the second half of the 1630s he may even have discussed an aspect of the subject with his pupils, one of whom was van den Eeckhout. This is suggested by Rembrandt's inscription on a drawing of *Rebecca's Departure* now in the Staatsgalerie Stuttgart (Benesch 147). In his comment, Rembrandt demands for the scene a larger number of figures to witness the departure of the *hoge bruijt* (noble bride). The character of this inscription is didactic and admonishing and can possibly be understood as a reaction to an unsuccessful work by one of the master's students.

Rembrandt's term 'noble bride' indicates that the interpretation of Rebecca as a model wife presented another reason for her popularity as a subject. She plays an important role in the marriage iconography of the sixteenth and seventeenth centuries. Her behaviour towards Eliezer, whom she later – in obedience to God's will – follows to a foreign land in order to marry Isaac, was considered a symbol of her virtue. Numerous medals and engravings that were commissioned to commemorate marriages display scenes from Rebecca's life.[6]

However, it needs to be pointed out that van den Eeckhout chose an episode that had provoked criticism on the part of some Protestant theologians. Rebecca's acceptance of pieces of jewellery as her bridal gift was used, for instance, by John Calvin, in his commentary on the Book of Genesis *(Commentaries on the First Book of Moses)*, for an attack against haughtiness, luxury and the desire for splendour: 'But it may be asked, Whether God approves ornaments of this kind, which pertain not so much to neatness as to pomp? Not only must moderation, but even abstinence, be cultivated as far as possible'. Calvin warns explicitly against 'women who desire to shine in gold, [and] seek in Rebecca a pretext for their corruption ... they are deceived who imagine that the examples of the saints can sanction them in opposition to the common law of God'.[7]

Whether it was van den Eeckhout's intention to present his figure of Rebecca as a warning against luxury and the desire for splendour remains doubtful. However, some contemporaries of the artist may have been aware of inherent ambiguities in interpreting this biblical subject.

VM

1 Dirkse & Kootte 1995, p. 8. For a discussion of the influence of Lastman's painting in Hamburg on Rembrandt and his circle, see C. Tümpel, in Amsterdam 1991, pp. 67–8, repr.; N. van der Kamp, in Amsterdam / Jerusalem / Münster 1991–94, pp. 30, 74, pl. 2.

2 Sumowski, *Gemälde*, vol. II, 1985, no. 431. A signed painting of the same subject is at the Národní Galerie in Prague (Sumowski, *Gemälde*, vol. II, 1985, no. 477).

3 Sumowski, *Gemälde*, vol. II, 1985, no. 439.

4 Cf. Dirkse & Kootte 1995, p. 4.

5 For pastoral painting in the United Provinces, see Kettering 1983; Utrecht / Frankfurt / Luxembourg 1993.

6 For the figure of Rebecca in the context of marriage iconography in the sixteenth and seventeenth centuries, see De Jongh 1986, pp. 107–9, 319–21.

7 Calvin 1554, vol. II, p. 21.

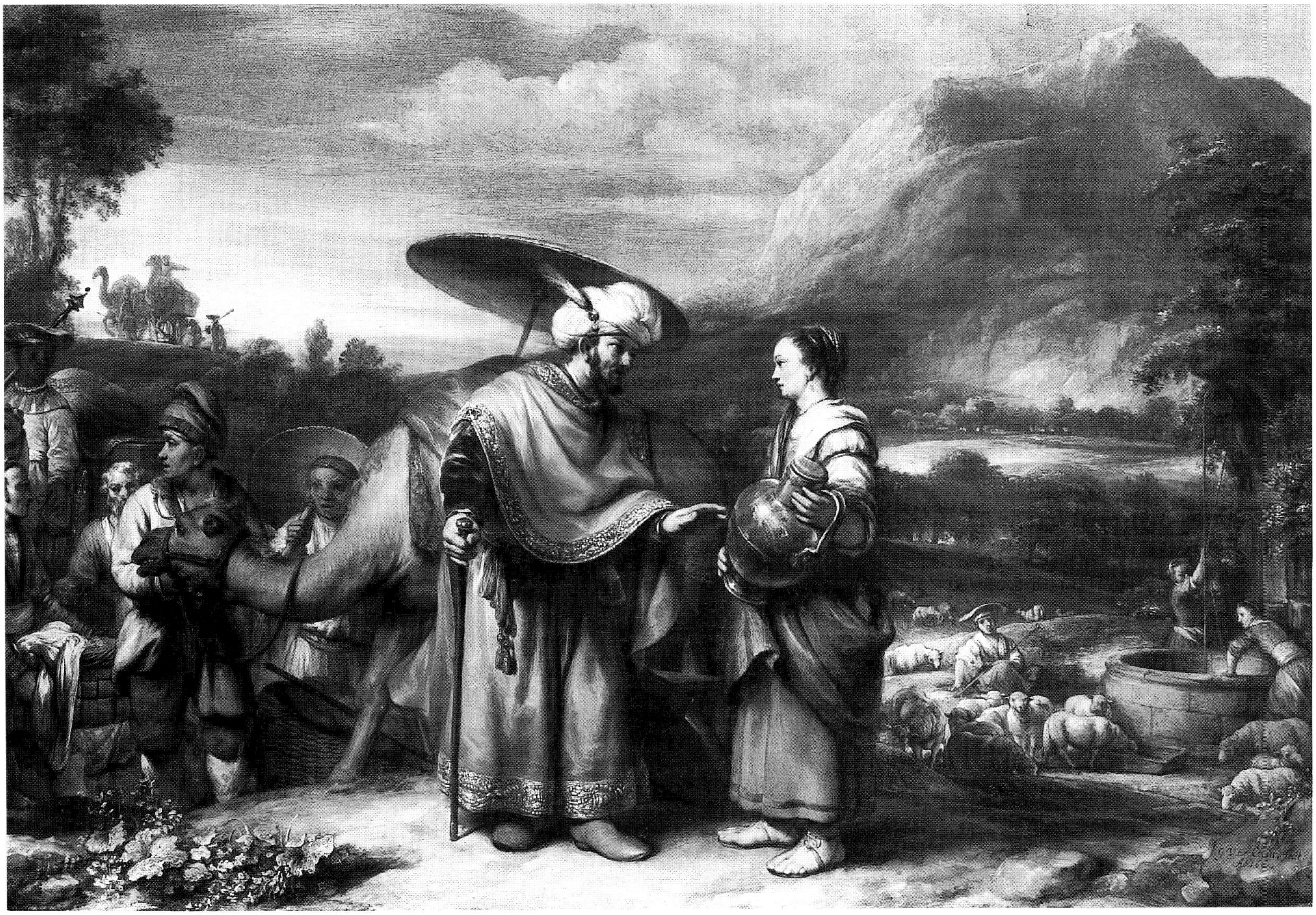

FIG. 53b
Gerbrand van den Eeckhout
Rebecca and Eliezer at the Well
Signed and dated 1661
Canvas
75.0 x 107.5 cm
The Trustees of the National Gallery, London

54

Gerbrand van den Eeckhout
Jacob's Dream

Signed and dated lower right
G. V. Eeckhout. / fecit. / A° 1669 / 12 M / 31
Canvas
128.0 x 104.0 cm
Staatliche Kunstsammlungen Dresden, Gemäldegalerie Alte Meister

PROVENANCE: Sale, Edward Habich, Kassel (Lempertz and Schall/Heberle), 9–10 May 1892, lot 42.

LITERATURE: Sumowski, *Gemälde*, vol. II, 1985, p. 741, no. 469; McTavish 1984, p. 30, under cat. no. 20.

Genesis, chapter 28, relates that Jacob, after having cheated his brother Esau out of his birthright, followed his father Isaac's order to go to his uncle Laban in Padan-aram (Syria) in order to find a wife for himself. On his way 'he lighted upon a certain place, and tarried there all night, because the sun was set; and he took of the stones of that place, and put them for his pillows, and lay down in that place to sleep'. In his dream he sees 'a ladder set up on the earth, and the top of it reached to heaven: and behold the angels of God ascending and descending on it' (Genesis 28:11–15). From the top of the ladder God spoke to Jacob and promised the land where Jacob was to his descendants, the Israelites. When Jacob woke he built a pillar from stones and poured oil on it, calling the place Beth-El (the House of God).

The present painting is one of three existing versions of this subject by van den Eeckhout. The earliest of these works is dated 1642 and is today at the Muzeum Narodowe in Warsaw (fig. 54a).[1] The latest version, dated 1672, belongs to the collection of Drs Alfred and Isabel Bader in Milwaukee (cat. no. 55).

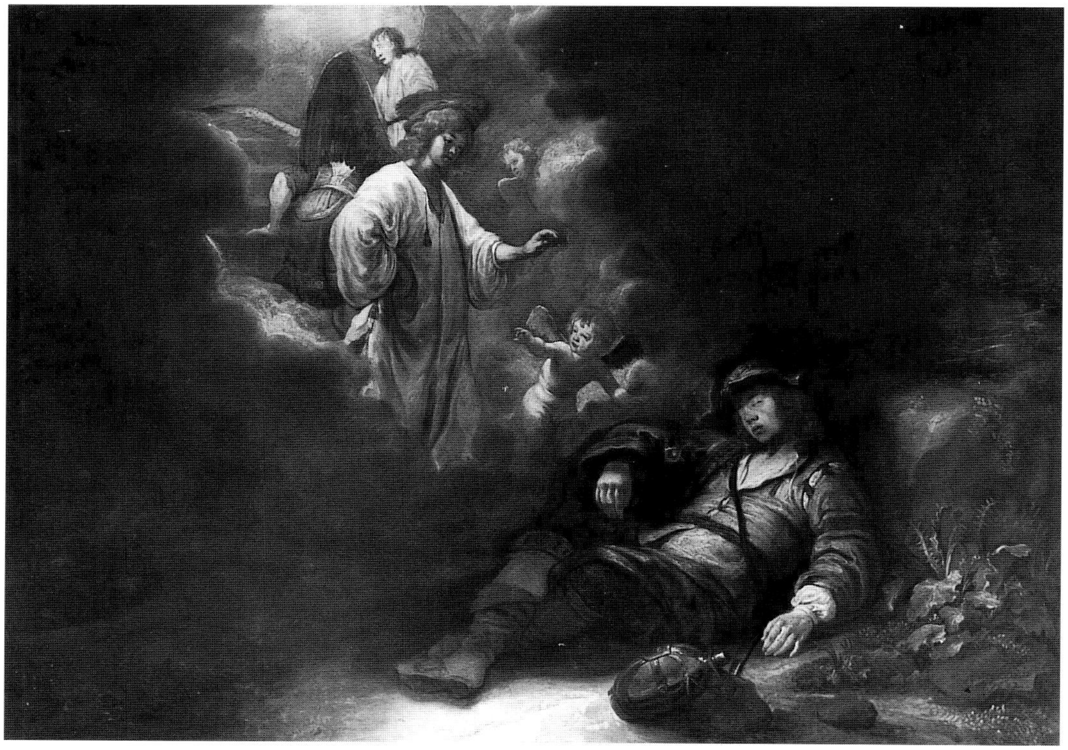

FIG. 54a
Gerbrand van den Eeckhout
Jacob's Dream
Signed and dated 1642
Canvas
76.0 x 116.0 cm
Muzeum Narodowe, Warsaw

This painting shows a more clearly structured spatial setting than does the version in the Bader collection. The present work is divided into the foreground, dominated by the figure of the sleeping Jacob, the middle ground with the figures of the angels, and the distant background to the right, where we see a campfire beneath a crescent moon. According to Sumowski, the motif of the group of shepherds by a fire may have been modelled after Hendrik Goudt's engraving after Adam Elsheimer's painting *The Flight into Egypt* (Alte Pinakothek, Munich). It is further conceivable that Rembrandt's *Rest on the Flight into Egypt*, signed and dated 1647 (National Gallery of Ireland, Dublin) (Bredius 576), a work that is also based on Goudt's print, may have served as a source for the motif of the campfire in van den Eeckhout's painting.

As in the 1672 version the artist has eliminated the 'ladder set up on the earth, and the top of it reached to heaven' (Genesis 28:12), replacing it with clouds suggesting a stairway. The figure of Jacob, leaning against a rock and supporting his head with his left hand, seems to be older than the corresponding figure in the Bader painting. The two versions differ further in their approach to the visionary character of the biblical account. In the Dresden picture the leading angel is approaching Jacob silently, almost as though anxious not to disturb his sleep. The pointing hand, a motif referring to the biblical account according to which God appears at the top of the ladder in order to promise land to Jacob's descendants, is missing. The formal stance of the angel and the deliberate placement of this figure in the centre of the composition emphasize the solemn and hieratic nature of the scene. In the Bader painting, by contrast, the angel is depicted in a more animated way and placed closer to the viewer, thus lending the relationship between the figures a more intimate character.

The Dresden painting is probably the most precisely dated of all of van den Eeckhout's works. Although many of his other paintings are signed and dated, this one includes the year followed by what is very likely the month and day of its completion: *A° 1669 / 12 M / 31* may well refer to the last day of the twelfth month of the year 1669. So far no convincing explanation for this unusual inscription can be provided, and for the time being it must be left open as to whether the date refers to an important event in the life of the artist or in the life of an unknown patron for the painting.

VM

1 Sumowski, *Gemälde*, vol. II, 1985, no. 395.

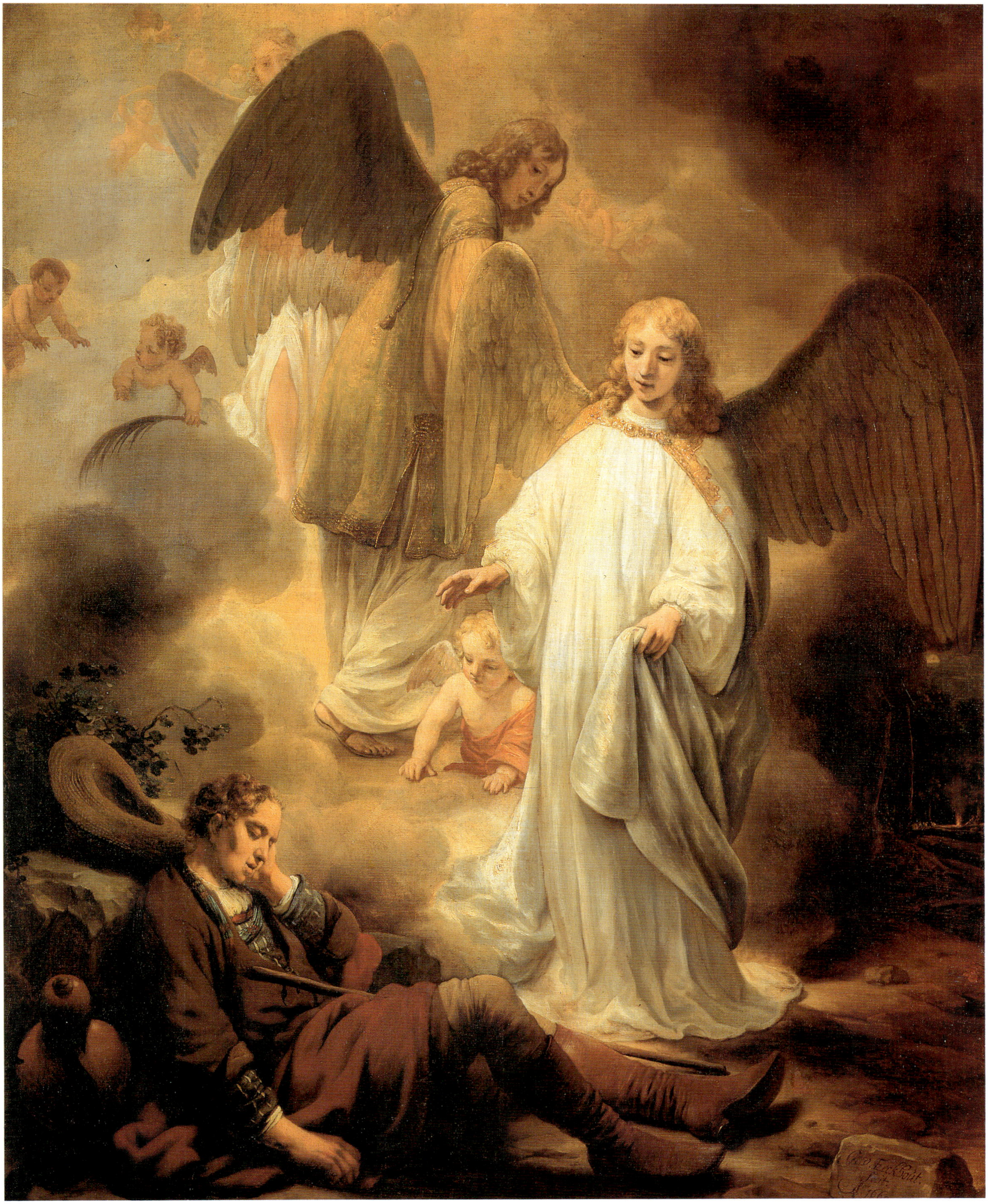

55

Gerbrand van den Eeckhout

Jacob's Dream

Signed and dated lower right
G. V. Eeckhout / A 1672
Canvas
121.3 x 102.8 cm
Drs Isabel and Alfred Bader

PROVENANCE: Sale, J. Turner et al. (anon. section), London (Sotheby's), 6 May 1953, lot 150 (as 1652); sale, London (Christie's), 11 March 1955, lot 170 (as 1652); Dr E. I. Schapiro, London; sale, An American Corporation et al. (section Dr E. I. Schapiro), London (Christie's), 13 July 1979, lot 10, repr. (as 1652).

LITERATURE: Sumowski, *Gemälde*, vol. II, 1985, pp. 722, 743, no. 481 (as dated 1672); McTavish 1984, p. 30, cat. no. 20 (as dated 1672).

The subject of this painting is the story of Jacob's vision of angels ascending to and descending from heaven, as described in Genesis 28:11–15 (see commentary to cat. no. 54).

Gerbrand van den Eeckhout treated this subject on several occasions, in paintings and drawings. The earliest painted version, today at the Muzeum Narodowe in Warsaw, is dated 1642 (fig. 54a).[1] Another version, dated 1669, can be found at the Dresden Gemäldegalerie (cat. no. 54). The picture from the Bader collection, whose date had been identified as 1652 until a recent cleaning, is actually dated 1672 and is thus van den Eeckhout's latest surviving painted version of the subject.

In all three paintings the artist dispenses with the motif of the ladder mentioned in the biblical text and replaces it with clouds reaching down to the ground. The lighting of the semi-dark surroundings in the present work is in keeping with the textual source, which indicates that the sun had already set. Jacob is lying in the foreground, almost parallel to the picture plane. His head is slumped back and turned to the viewer. His slouch hat has almost fallen off, now encircling his head in a manner reminiscent of a halo. Jacob's legs are nearly outstretched, his calabash, a walking-stick and his bag are lying close to his feet. Jacob's pose and the motif of the hat that has slipped off his head while he sleeps probably derive from an etching probably of 1602 by Jan Pynas, in which they appear in reverse (fig. 55a).[2]

The angel standing beside Jacob has raised his right hand as if to protect the sleeping man, and points with his left hand upward towards heaven. The figure shares great similarities with Ferdinand Bol's angel in his *Jacob's Dream* at the Dresden Gemäldegalerie (cat. no. 44). Comparing the latter with Rembrandt's etching *The Raising of Lazarus* (B.72) of 1642 (fig. 100a), Albert Blankert dates Bol's version also to *c.*1642, a *terminus post quem* (see commentary to cat. no. 44). As has been mentioned above, van den Eeckhout's earliest version of *Jacob's Dream* dates to 1642 as well. Between *c.*1640 and 1644 one may detect a close connection between Bol and van den Eeckhout with regard to their choice of subject matter and their Rembrandtesque painting style. Although both painters had been working as independent masters since around 1641, Rembrandt's influence remained noticeable in their work. However, at the same time van den Eeckhout was also employing distinct pre-Rembrandtist elements that went back to Rembrandt's teacher Pieter Lastman (1583–1633). Blankert assumes that Rembrandt may have given his two pupils the task of depicting the encounter between a biblical figure and an angel. They executed the subject 'with that combination of collaboration and competition which is so characteristic of apprenticeship'.[3]

For the painting in the Bader collection, van den Eeckhout made a preparatory red chalk drawing, today in the Staatliches Museum in Schwerin (fig. 55b).[4] Despite slight variations there can be no doubt about the close connection between the painting and the drawing. In 1984 McTavish made a detailed comparison of the two works and correctly observed that underneath the wings of the second angel in the background of the painting there is an earlier figure, with horizontally oriented wings, which is now visible through the top paint layer.[5] This original version corresponds closely to the angel in the background in the Schwerin drawing. For stylistic reasons the drawing must be dated to the 1650s. Van den Eeckhout referred back to it in his painting of 1672, in which the figure of the angel in the foreground – although less elegant and supernatural than its model – follows the angel in Ferdinand Bol's Dresden picture.

VM

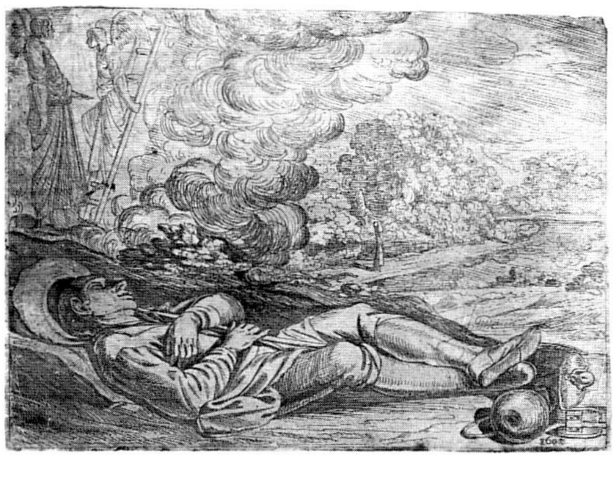

FIG. 55a
Jan Pynas 1583/84–1631
Jacob's Dream
Dated 160[2?]
Etching
15.2 x 20.5 cm
Rijksprentenkabinet, Rijksmuseum, Amsterdam

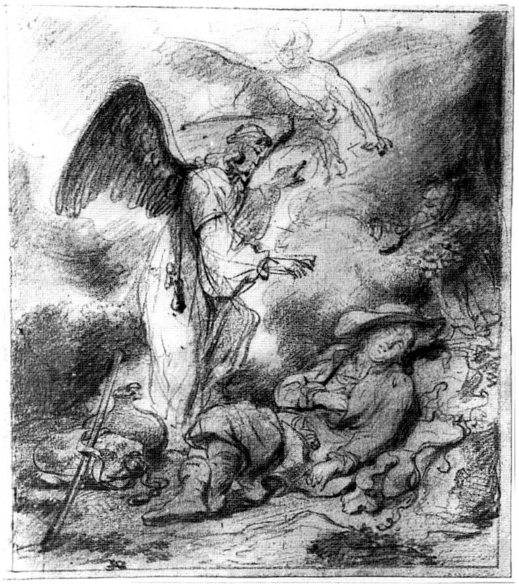

FIG. 55b
Gerbrand van den Eeckhout
Jacob's Dream
Chalk
26.1 x 20.0 cm
Staatliches Museum Schwerin

1 Sumowski, *Gemälde*, vol. II, 1985, no. 395. This is the only version van den Eeckhout painted in a horizontal format.
2 Hollstein 15; for Jan Pynas's etching and the pictorial tradition associated with Jacob's Dream in Dutch seventeenth-century prints, see P. van der Coelen, in Amsterdam 1996–97, p. 86, cat. no. 15.
3 Blankert 1982, p. 30. For Bol's *Jacob's Dream* in Dresden, see pp. 91–2, no. 5.
4 Sumowski, *Drawings*, vol. 3, 1980, p. 1346, no. 618. An alternate preparatory drawing for the same subject is at the Albertina in Vienna (Sumowski, *Drawings*, vol. 3, 1980, p. 1348, no. 619). A third drawing of *Jacob's Dream* is in the Victoria and Albert Museum, London (Sumowski, *Drawings*, vol. 3, 1980, p. 1538, no. 713[x]). The horizontal format and the figure of Jacob in this last-mentioned work seem to be related to the Warsaw painting dated 1642. The style, however, does not connect with that of van den Eeckhout's drawings of the early 1640s.
5 McTavish 1984, p. 30, cat. no. 20.

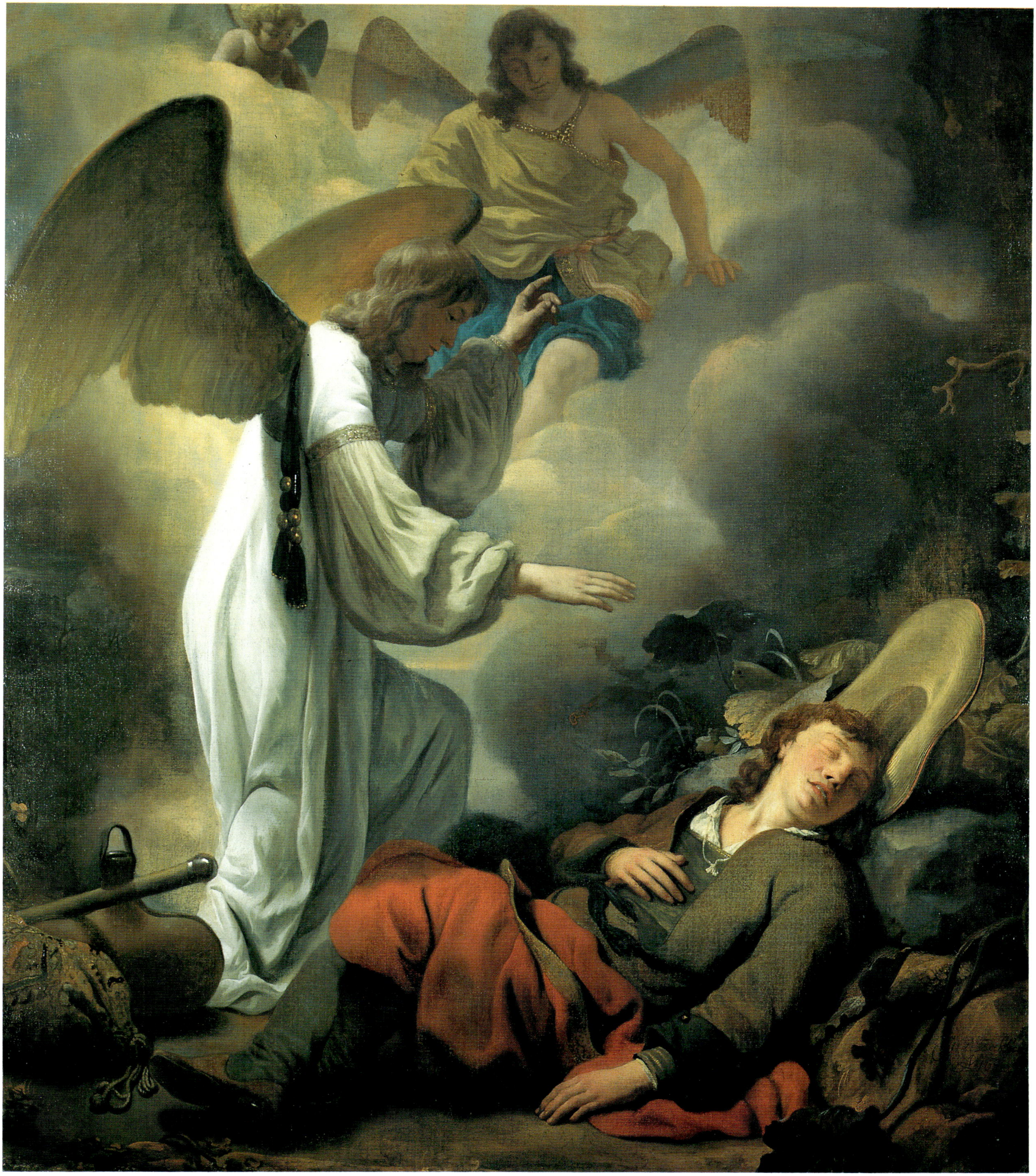

56

Gerbrand van den Eeckhout

The Twelve-Year-Old Christ Disputing with the Doctors

*c.*1670–72

Canvas
67.0 x 89.0 cm
Collection Netherlands Institute for Cultural Heritage, Rijswijk, Amsterdam (on loan to the Schilderijengalerij Prins Willem V, The Hague)

PROVENANCE: (Probably) Sale, Hendrik van der Vugt, Amsterdam, 27 April 1745, lot 86 ('Een stuk door G. van den Eekhout, daar Christus leert in den Tempel'; dimensions given as 'br. 2 v. 9 en drie vierde d., h. 2 v. 3 d.'), to Quinkert; sale, Viscount Fielding, London (Christie's), 1 July 1938, lot 43, repr., to Koetser for 250 gns; with dealer D. Katz, Dieren; Reichskanzlei, Berlin, 1940; Rijksdienst Beeldende Kunst, The Hague (now Netherlands Institute for Cultural Heritage); on loan to Schilderijengalerij Prins Willem V, The Hague.

LITERATURE: Sumowski, *Gemälde*, vol. II, 1985, p. 743, no. 478; P. Huys Janssen, in The Hague 1992, pp. 130–3, cat. no. 10.

The event shown in this painting is related by the evangelist Luke in his Gospel (2:41–52). Having attended the Pesach Feast in Jerusalem with his parents, the twelve-year-old Christ does not return home. We see the moment when, after a three-day search, Mary and Joseph find him in the Temple disputing with the doctors: 'And it came to pass, that after three days they found him in the temple, sitting in the midst of the doctors, both hearing them, and asking them questions. And all that heard him were astonished at his understanding and answers' (Luke 2:46–47). In the painting, Mary and Joseph are visible in the extreme left background.

It is quite likely that van den Eeckhout derived the setting for the scene from the model of a Jewish *sjoel* – a place for study attached to a synagogue. The wooden partition with the bench on which Christ is seated is a characteristic piece of furniture for this type of interior.[1]

Van den Eeckhout dealt with this subject on at least two occasions. One painting, dated 1662, went to Munich (Alte Pinakothek) in 1806 as part of the collection of the Palatinate Elector Johann Wilhelm (1658–1717) (fig. 56a).[2] In his life of the artist of 1719, Arnold Houbraken, van den Eeckhout's first biographer, praises a painting representing 'Christus, zittende in den Tempel, onder de Hebreeuse leeraren' (Christ, seated in the Temple, among the Hebrew doctors).[3] Houbraken claims to have seen the painting himself and commends the realistic expressions – based on accurate physiognomic detail – of the agitated, disputing doctors, as well as the closeness to Rembrandt. It is at least feasible that Houbraken is referring to the present painting, as by 1718 the Munich version had already left the Netherlands, being in the possession of the Elector Johann Wilhelm in Düsseldorf at the time of his death in 1717.[4] However, one cannot be sure, since Houbraken's vague description of the subject matter in the picture he saw might just as well refer to the related theme of Christ Teaching in the Synagogue at Nazareth (Luke 4:16–21). Van den Eeckhout's painting of 1658 at the National Gallery of Ireland in Dublin is an example of his treatment of this theme.[5]

The story of the twelve-year-old Christ among the doctors was a popular theme in the work of seventeenth-century artists. Among the artists of the United Provinces, the Utrecht Caravaggisti Dirck van Baburen (*c.*1595–1624) and Matthias Stom (*c.*1600–*c.*1649) particularly favoured the subject and rendered it several times.[6] Rembrandt, who repeatedly dealt with the theme of angels or Christ acting as intermediaries in bringing God's word to

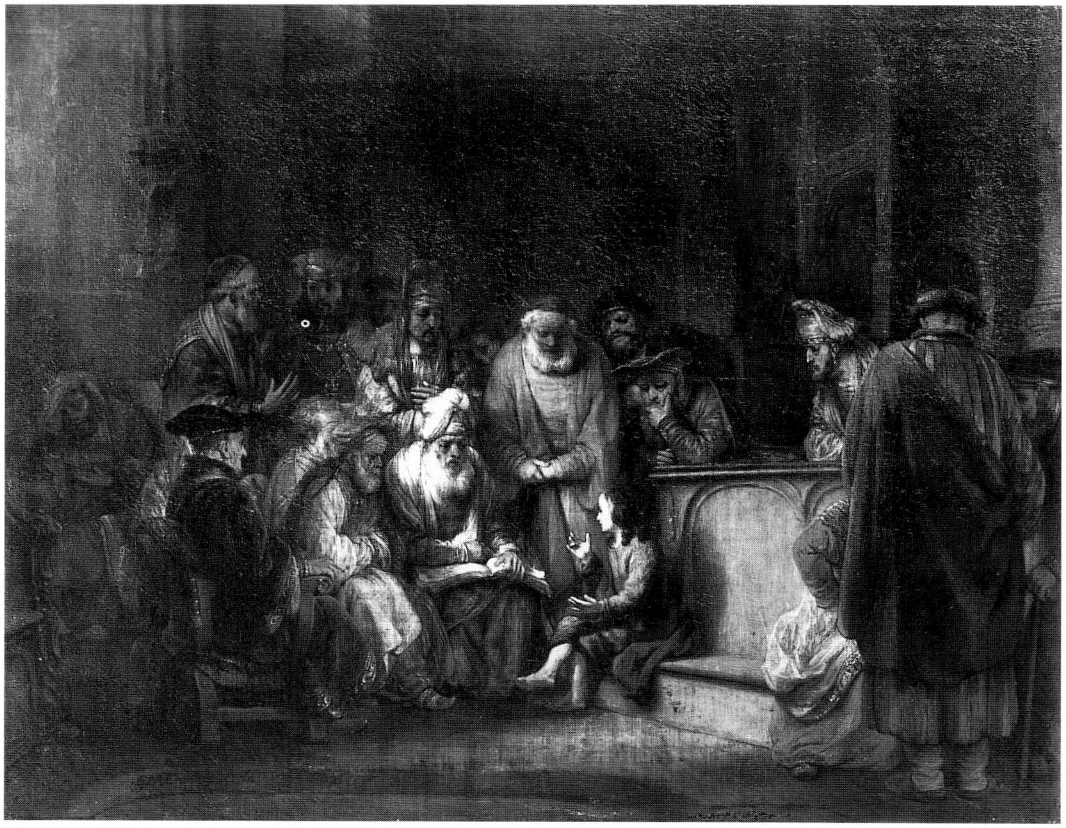

FIG. 56a
Gerbrand van den Eeckhout
The Twelve-Year-Old Christ Disputing with the Doctors
Signed and dated 1662
Canvas
68.0 x 83.0 cm
Alte Pinakothek, Munich

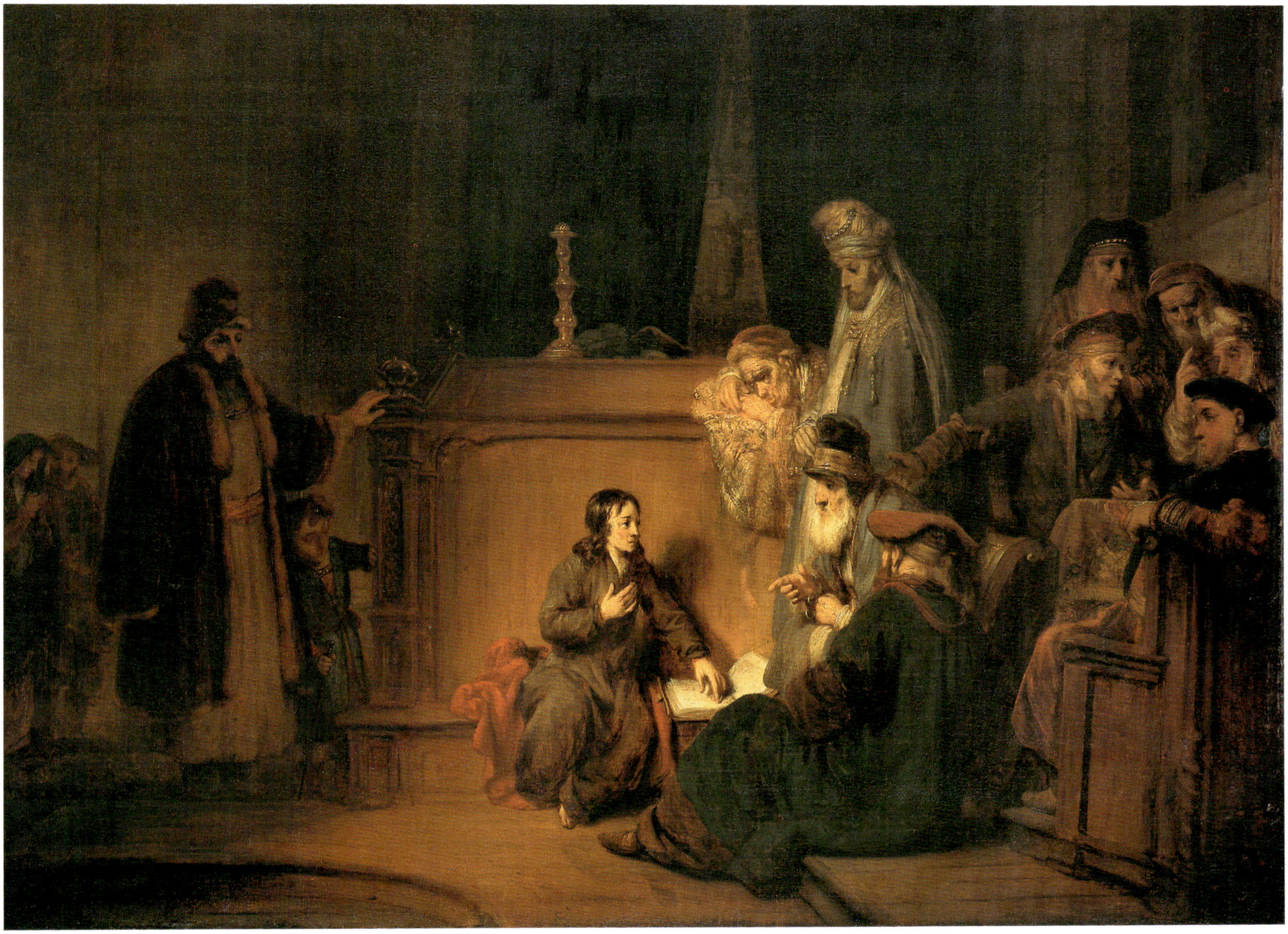

humankind, created three etchings of Christ with the doctors (B.66, 1630; B.65, 1652; B.64, 1654 (fig. 119a)). For the latter two etchings he chose a horizontal format, as van den Eeckhout did in his paintings. However, Rembrandt excluded Mary and Joseph and concentrated on the tightly crowded groups of scribes surrounding Christ. Hence it seems that van den Eeckhout merely drew thematic inspiration from his former teacher's work.

The reasons for the popularity of the scene depicted, which represents one of the very few events from Christ's youth told in the Bible, were certainly manifold and extended well beyond pictorial tradition. According to Catholic interpretations the loss and finding of the Christ Child in the Temple belong, respectively, to the so-called Seven Sorrows and the Seven Joys of the Virgin Mary. In Protestant theology and art this aspect is of course of lesser significance. Consequently, the reaction of Mary and Joseph upon the finding of the boy is secondary in the present painting, and in many examples they become merely small figures in the background or are even eliminated. Instead the emphasis is on the moment when Christ is interpreting the prophetic writings that refer to the overcoming of the Old Law. Van den Eeckhout's Christ is pointing emphatically to a text passage in an open book at his side. In Protestant theology the careful study of Scripture, as a necessary condition for biblical exegesis, becomes fundamentally important. This emphasis on the study and interpretation of the ancient texts goes back to Luther's principle of *sola scriptura* (Scripture alone). This principle determined the exclusive and binding authority of the canonical biblical text, without any additions from legend, as the foundation of Protestant belief. In the context of the Reformed Church, of which van den Eeckhout was a member, the representation of the twelve-year-old Christ in the Temple could be understood as an illustration of the central importance of the study of the biblical text, not only for the clergy but also for the laity.

As correctly noted by Sumowski, the colour scheme, the disposition of space, and the figure types in the present work point to a date of execution in the early 1670s.[7]

VM

1 Nystad 1975, passim.

2 Sumowski, *Gemälde*, vol. II, 1985, p. 734, no. 436.

3 Houbraken 1719–21, vol. II, 1719, p. 100.

4 The first catalogue of the collection in Düsseldorf was published in 1719 by the court painter and curator of the collection, Gerhard Joseph Karsch. The catalogue was reprinted in Van Gool 1750–51, vol. II, pp. 531–67 (for Gerbrand van den Eeckhout's painting, see esp. p. 531). The Munich painting can be found in Pigage 1778, no. 315, pl. XXIV. I would like to thank Paul Broekhoff, Amsterdam, for having checked Pigage's edition for me.

5 Sumowski, *Gemälde*, vol. II, 1985, p. 721, no. 428. For the iconography of the subject matter, see V. Manuth, in Berlin / Amsterdam / London 1991–92a, p. 348, cat. no. 71, repr.

6 For examples by these two artists, see Utrecht / Braunschweig 1986–87a, cat. nos 34, 76, 77, reprs.

7 Sumowski, *Gemälde*, vol. II, 1985, p. 743, no. 478.

Detail of cat. no. 56

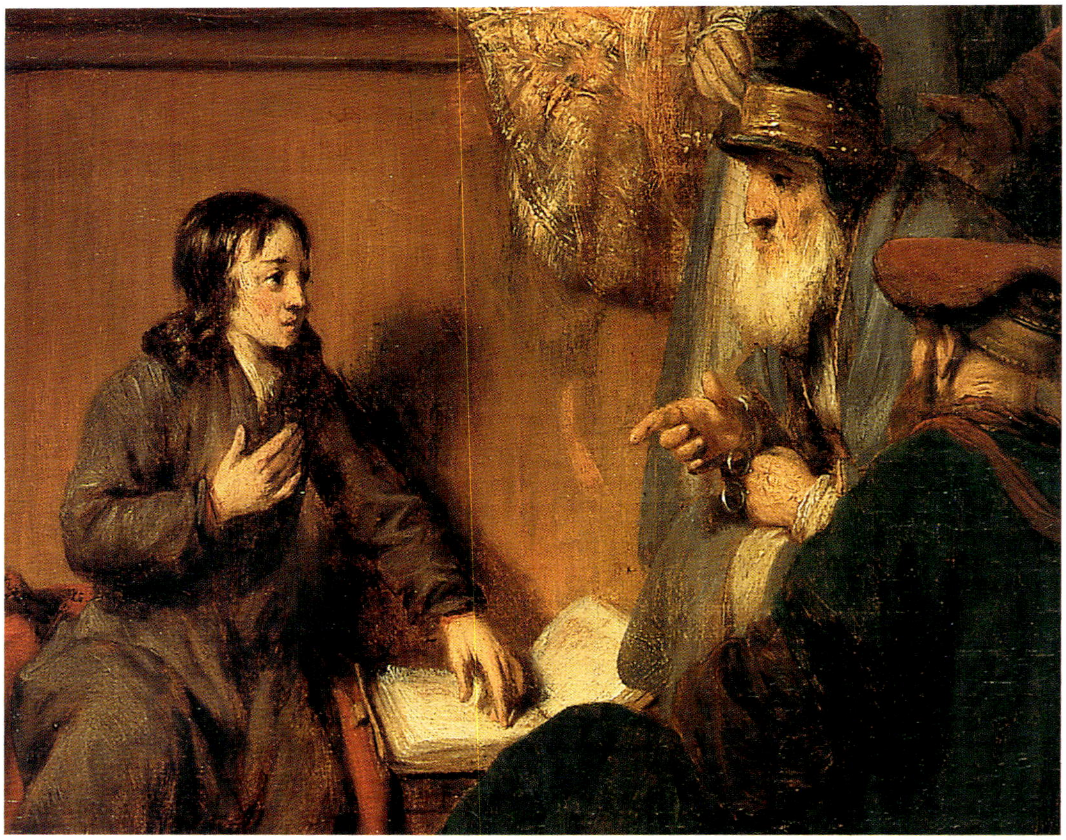

Carel Fabritius (1622–1654)

Baptized on 27 February 1622, in Midden-Beemster (thirty kilometres north of Amsterdam), Carel was the son of Pieter Carelsz, who worked as a teacher and sexton. In addition to his educational duties and obligations to the church, Carel's father was also granted a licence to serve as an official painter *(schildersampt)*. None of the father's works have been identified but three of his sons became painters – Carel, Barend (cat. nos 58, 59) and Johannes. The sons probably learned the rudiments of the profession from their father. However, both Carel and Barend seem also to have initially trained to be carpenters (their surname, Fabritius, derives from the Latin for carpenter or craftsman: *faber)*. In September 1641, 'Carel Pietersz Fabricius' married Heltge van Hasselt (who died two years later), and the couple moved soon thereafter to Amsterdam. Carel's presence in Rembrandt's workshop is confirmed by Samuel van Hoogstraten, whose *Inleyding* (1678) refers to Fabritius as a *medeleerling* (fellow pupil).

Carel's surviving work and the inventory of his wife's estate, drawn up in 1643, suggest that he painted portraits and *tronies* in Rembrandt's style. Following Heltge's death, he returned to Beemster, but his art suggests that he remained in contact with Rembrandt and his studio. In 1650 he was documented in Delft, where he married the widow Agatha van Pruysen. Two years later he became a member of the St Luke's Guild, paying the membership fee in two instalments. Financial burdens descended on him: he owed 728 guilders – a considerable sum – to a creditor in 1653. Nonetheless, Hoogstraten suggested that he received commissions for *trompe l'oeil* room decorations and perspectives. Fabritius's surviving paintings (for example, his *View of Delft* (National Gallery, London)) suggest that he may have also painted peep-shows, or perspective boxes. Carel died as a result of the explosion of the powder storage facility in Delft on 12 October 1654 – a cataclysmic disaster that destroyed one quarter of the city, and allegedly most of Fabritius's works.

Although Carel's development and contribution to the history of art are only partially understood, owing to his limited surviving oeuvre, he appears to have developed from a painter in the tenebrous Rembrandtesque manner to a pioneer of the Delft School – a group of painters, among whom Johannes Vermeer and Pieter de Hooch were the most famous, who developed a painting style with a lightened tonality and an interest in perspective and naturalistic effects.

LITERATURE: Van Hoogstraten 1678; Brown 1981; Sumowski, *Gemälde*, vol. III, 1987, pp. 979–97.

PCS

For Carel Fabritius's presumed self-portraits, see cat. no. 57 and fig. 57a.

57
Carel Fabritius
A Young Man in a Fur Cap and Cuirass (Self-Portrait?)

Signed and dated lower right *c. fabritius. / 1654*
Canvas
70.5 x 61.5 cm
The Trustees of the National Gallery, London

PROVENANCE: (Possibly) Catharina Scharckens (widow of Cornelis Smout), Amsterdam [7 December 1654 inventory: 'Het conterfeitsel van Carel Fabritsius']; Mr Marneffe, Bruges; acquired from Marneffe by George Rimington, Tynefield, Penrith, *c.*1824, for 400 frs; by descent to T.A. Brewerton, Manchester; his sale, London, 12 December 1924, lot 135; purchased for the National Gallery out of the Claude Phillips Fund.

LITERATURE: Sumowski 1968, pp. 278–83; C. Brown, in London 1976, p. 43, cat. no. 41; Brown 1981, pp. 44–7, 126; Sumowski, *Gemälde*, vol. II, 1985, p. 987, no. 609; C. Brown, in MacLaren / Brown 1991, vol. I, pp. 139–40, no. 4042.

Although there is no documented portrait of Carel Fabritius, this painting has often been assumed to be a self-portrait. Most authors agree that the sitter with dark features and full mouth is the same man portrayed in Carel Fabritius's bust-length portrait in Rotterdam, which is also assumed to be a self-portrait (fig. 57a).[1] Some viewers also speculate that Barend Fabritius's *Portrait of a Man in Fanciful Costume* in Munich depicts the same person (fig. 58a).[2] C. Brown notes that the directness of the sitter's gaze, the pose and the costume in both the London and the Rotterdam paintings support the presumption that they are self-portraits by Carel.[3]

In the Rotterdam painting, a young man with long flowing hair, open collar and work clothes is shown before a wall of crumbling masonry, while in the London painting he appears wearing a steel cuirass and fur cap and silhouetted against a cloudswept sky. The figures share an intensity of expression and a broodingly romantic countenance. As Brown observed, the present work recalls a self-portrait type that Rembrandt favoured in the late 1620s and 1630s when he painted himself several times in bust- and half-length, wearing a gorget or breastplate as, for example, in a self-portrait at the Mauritshuis, The Hague (Bredius 6) (fig. 57b).[4] Govaert Flinck and Jan Lievens also portrayed Rembrandt wearing a gorget in the 1630s[5] and armour became a popular

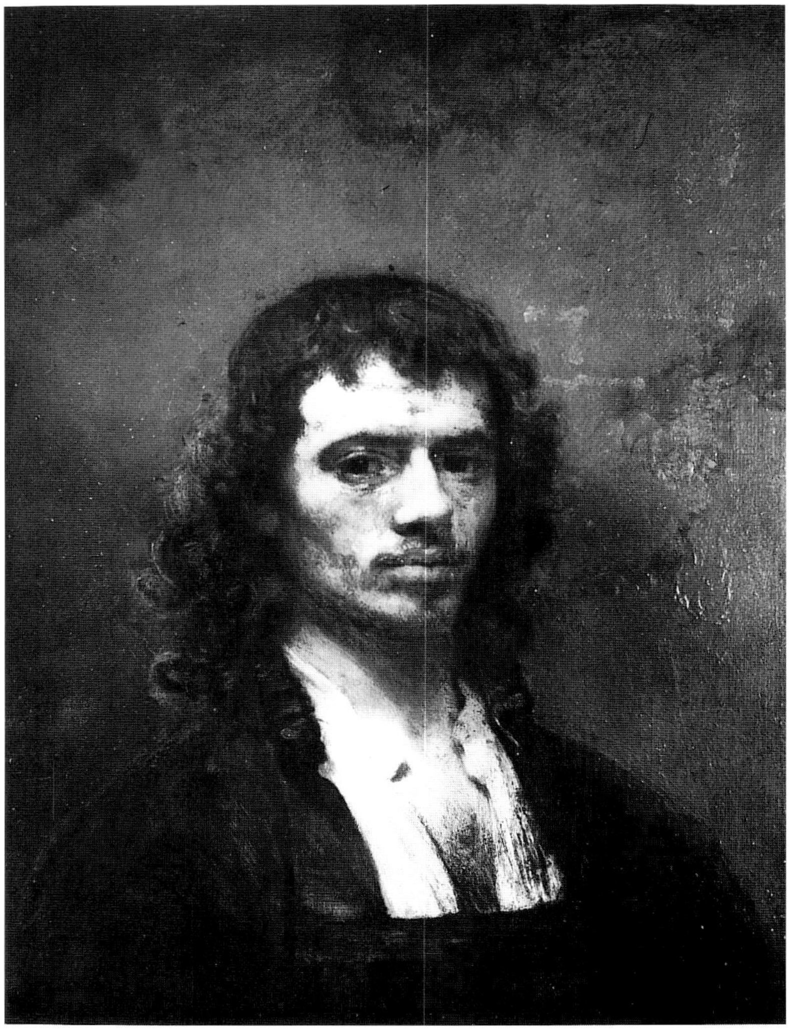

FIG. 57a
Carel Fabritius
Portrait of a Man (Self-Portrait?)
Signed
Panel
65.0 x 49.0 cm
Museum Boijmans Van Beuningen, Rotterdam

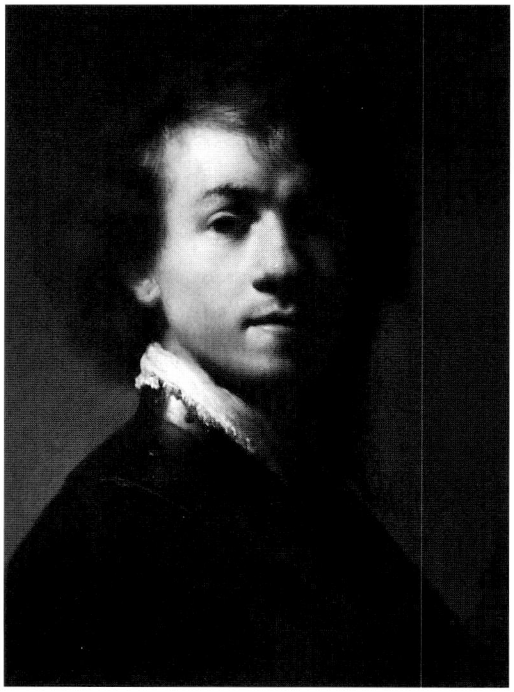

FIG. 57b
Rembrandt
Self-Portrait in Armour
Panel
37.5 x 29.0 cm
Mauritshuis, The Hague
Photograph: © Mauritshuis, The Hague, inv. no. 148

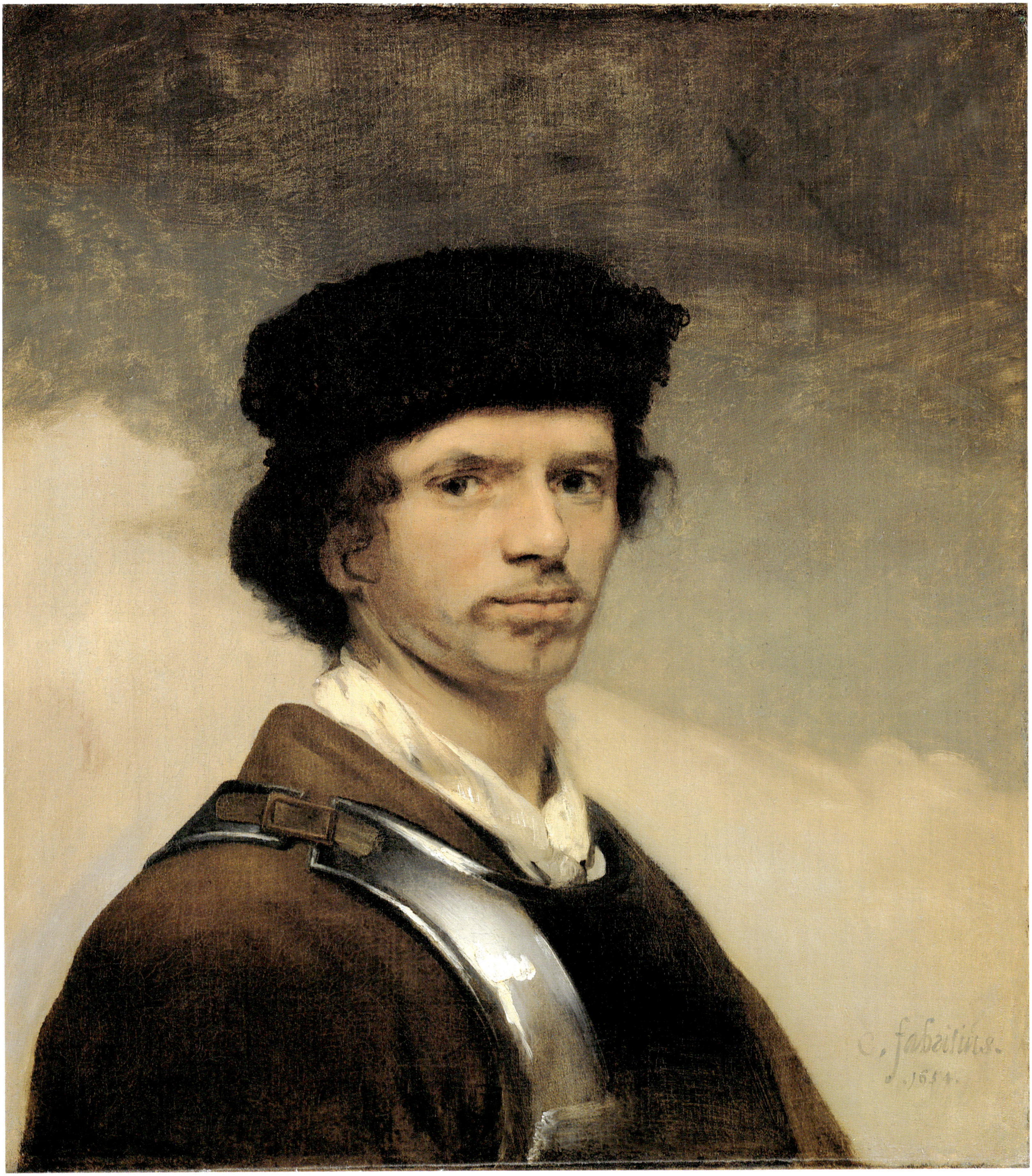
C. fabritius.
1654.

accoutrement for portraits and *tronies* among many Rembrandt School artists, including Gerrit Dou, Paulus Lesire, Lievens, Johan Ulrich Mayr and Jacques des Rousseaux.[6] Ferdinand Bol also portrayed himself in armour in an etching dated 1648.[7] Rembrandt's followers were just as likely to use such props for portraits of sitters other than themselves, or for anonymous subjects, as for self-portraits. Thus the cuirass Fabritius employs here certainly nods to his teacher's influence but is not proof that the artist was looking in the mirror.

The sitter's fur cap may call to mind headgear worn by Rembrandt's sitters in the 1630s, including in the *Portrait of Nicolaes Ruts* of 1631 (Frick Collection, New York) (Bredius 145) (p. 70, fig. 2) and the so-called *Portrait of a Polish Nobleman* of 1637 (National Gallery of Art, Washington DC) (Bredius 211).

While in the London portrait's pose and costume Fabritius clearly acknowledges traditions inaugurated by his teacher, the cloud-filled background was an innovation in Dutch art. Anthony van Dyck's earlier *Self-Portrait with a Sunflower* of 1633 had partly silhouetted the figure of the artist against a bright cloud-filled sky to underscore the heliotropic flower's emblematic message of Fidelity (fig. 57c; cf. cat. no. 47); however, in the present work the sky with rising clouds has no obvious symbolic function apart from its effect in monumentalizing the sitter and implying that he lives a vigorous life outdoors. Yet in the steadfast traditions of Dutch half-length portraits, this was a novelty or, if you will, at least a breath of fresh air.

Sumowski published a portrait of a woman (Niedersächsisches Landesmuseum, Hannover) that he claimed was the pendant to the present work.[8] It depicts the sitter bust-length and in profile, wearing a feather beret and pearls, and it bears the signature *fabritius* and the date 1654. Brown rightly rejected both the notion of the two works' companionship and the Hannover painting's attribution to Carel.[9]

PCS

1 Sumowski, *Gemälde*, vol. II, 1985, p. 985, no. 603.
2 Brown 1981, p. 123, no. 4.
3 Brown 1981, pp. 38–9, 44–5; C. Brown, in MacLaren / Brown 1991, vol. 1, p. 139.
4 C. Brown, in MacLaren / Brown 1991, vol. 1, p. 139; see also Bredius / Gerson 1969, nos 20 (Uffizi, Florence), 22 (dated 1634, Gemäldegalerie, Kassel).
5 Sumowski, *Gemälde*, vol. II, 1985, no. 658 (dated 1638, formerly A. van Weezenbeck collection, Lausanne); vol. III, 1987, no. 1260 (Daan Cevat, St Peter Port).
6 Sumowski, *Gemälde*, vol. I, 1983, nos 254, 259; vol. III, 1987, nos 1147, 1256, 1450; vol. IV, 1990, no. 1675b.
7 Hollstein 12, repr.
8 Sumowski 1968, pp. 278–83; Sumowski, *Gemälde*, vol. II, 1985, p. 987, no. 608.
9 Brown 1981, p. 136, no. R21; C. Brown, in MacLaren / Brown 1991, pp. 139–40, note 7 (reporting on his personal examination of the Hannover picture in 1987).

FIG. 57C
Anthony van Dyck
Flemish, 1599–1641
Self-Portrait with a Sunflower 1633
Canvas
60.0 x 73.0 cm
Collection of the Duke of Westminster, Eaton Hall, Cheshire

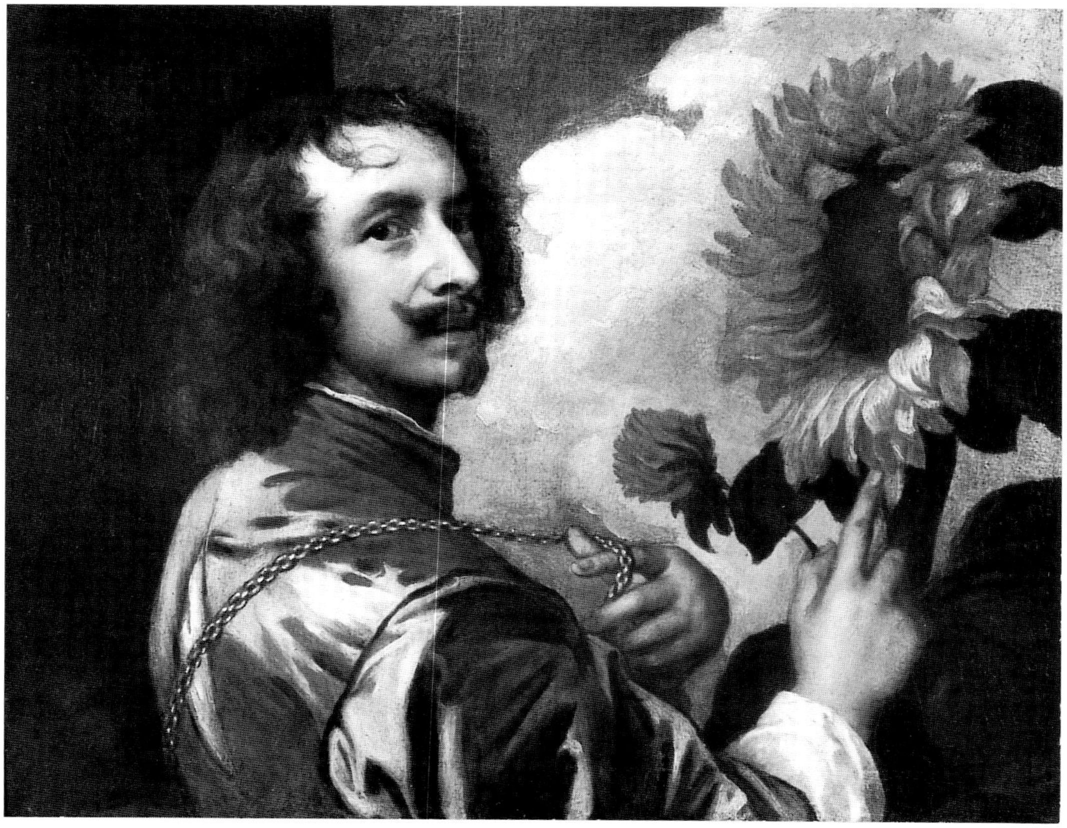

Barend Fabritius (1624–1673)

The younger brother of Carel (cat. no. 57), Barend Fabritius, like his sibling, worked as a carpenter before becoming a painter. Both took the name Fabritius from their trade (*faber* in Latin is a craftsman). The family had originally come from Ghent. The two artists' father was a schoolteacher and sexton, as well as a painter. While Carel went to Amsterdam to study with Rembrandt, Barend is assumed to have remained in Midden-Beemster. Barend signed a document in Amsterdam in 1643 and was living there in 1647 and in 1652, the year he returned to Midden-Beemster and married Catherina Mussers from Delft. Their union may have been facilitated by the fact that Carel was then living in Delft. However, Barend himself has never been proven to have lived in Delft; indeed the births of his sons in Midden-Beemster in 1653 and 1655 suggest that he only visited the important artistic centre of Delft. In 1656 he completed a family portrait of Leiden's leading architect, Willem van der Helm (Rijksmuseum, Amsterdam), and the following year rented a house in Leiden. In 1658 Barend also became a master of the St Luke's Guild in Leiden but the register's entry of October of that year reported that he had left the city. He was recorded in Midden-Beemster in 1665–66 and later resided in Amsterdam, until his death in 1673. He was survived by six children.

Barend primarily painted historical (biblical) subjects, allegories and portraits. His earliest dated work, a *Self-Portrait* signed and dated 1650 (Städelsches Kunstinstitut, Frankfurt), shows the influence of his brother Carel. Although his reputation was often overshadowed by that of his famous brother, Barend was a talented artist in his own right who requires no apology either for his Rembrandtesque manner or for the varied and imaginative paintings that he produced.

LITERATURE: Pont 1958; Sumowski, *Gemälde*, vol. II, 1985, pp. 910–78.

PCS

For a presumed self-portrait of Barend Fabritius, see fig. 58a.

58

Barend Fabritius

Portrait of a Man (Self-Portrait?) **as a Shepherd**

*c.*1655

Signed upper left *B. Fabritius*
Canvas
79.0 x 64.2 cm
Gemäldegalerie der Akademie der bildenden Künste in Wien, Vienna

PROVENANCE: Graf Anton Lamberg-Sprinzenstein; bequeathed by him to the Akademie in 1821.

LITERATURE: Schmidt-Degener 1912, p. 191; Eigenberger 1927, vol. 1, p. 128, vol. 2, no. 128; Benesch 1928, p. 65; Pont 1958, pp. 116–17, no. 34; G. Jansen, in Amsterdam / Groningen 1983, pp. 148–9, cat. no. 29; Sumowski, *Gemälde*, vol. II, 1985, p. 923, no. 586; Trnek 1992, pp. 131–5, no. 46.

Although little is known for certain about Barend Fabritius's life, the development of his early career is assumed, mostly on the basis of the style of his paintings, to have followed that of his elder brother, Carel, whose presence in Rembrandt's studio is documented in 1641 and who was active in Delft between 1650 and 1654. As a number of observers have remarked, the present work recalls Rembrandt's many self-portraits in its dramatic half-length conception, while its lightened tonality and suggestion of open sky in the background recall Carel's portraits from his Delft period, notably his *A Young Man in a Fur Cap and Cuirass (Self-Portrait?)*, which is signed and dated 1654 (cat. no. 57). The latter, like the present painting, is usually assumed to be a self-portrait because the sitter's pointed regard seems to attest to the artist's studied consideration of his own image in a mirror.

F. Schmidt-Degener was the first to identify Barend as the sitter in the present painting.[1] However, there is no certain self-portrait by either Carel or Barend. A bust-length portrait of a man at the Museum Boijmans Van Beuningen in Rotterdam (fig. 57a) is usually assumed to depict the former, and several other works have been discussed as possible self-portraits by Barend, notably the *Portrait of a Man in Fanciful Costume* in Munich (fig. 58a) and the *Portrait of a Man in a Broad-Brimmed Hat* (Städelsches Kunstinstitut, Frankfurt).[2] The physiognomic similarities between these figures are sufficiently pronounced for us to speak of a 'family' resemblance (indeed the man in the Munich portrait has been identified by turns as either Barend or Carel). Moreover, while the more 'square-shaped' visage of the sitter in the present image and his Munich *doppelgänger* (merely an illusion created by the high-collared costumes?) has been contrasted with the 'triangular-shaped' head in Carel's two presumed self-portraits,[3] one ought to consider whether they might not all depict the same person.

The shepherd's staff and oak leaf wreath worn by the sitter in the Vienna painting link the image to the tradition of arcadian subjects that found expression in both art and literature.[4] These themes were first popularized in Dutch art by the Caravaggisti and later widely adopted as portrait conventions. In Rembrandt's circle, Jacob Backer, Gerbrand van den Eeckhout and Govaert Flinck (especially in his *Portrait of Rembrandt as a Shepherd* at the Rijksmuseum, Amsterdam (fig. 58b), and in its presumed pendant, *Saskia as a Shepherdess*, dated 1636, at the Herzog Anton Ulrich-Museum, Braunschweig)[5] all portrayed sitters in pastoral dress. The low point of view that enhances the sitter's expression of *hauteur* in the present work also serves to remind us that aristocrats and nobles often had themselves portrayed in pastoral dress. Gerrit and Willem van Honthorst, as well as other court painters, made a number of portraits of this kind.

Although undated, the present painting is usually dated to the late 1650s or *c.*1660.[6] R. Trnek has rightly observed that this work undoubtedly followed closely upon Carel's painting in London dated 1654 (cat. no. 57).[7]

PCS

1 Schmidt-Degener 1912, p. 191.
2 Sumowski, *Gemälde*, vol. II, 1985, nos 584, 598.
3 Sumowski, *Gemälde*, vol. II, 1985, p. 922, under no. 584.
4 Kettering 1983.
5 Sumowski, *Gemälde*, vol. II, 1985, nos 655, 656.
6 Eigenberger 1927, vol. 1, p. 128, and Benesch 1928, p. 66, both date this work to 'around 1660'; Pont 1958, pp. 116–17, no. 34, suggested *c.*1658; Sumowski, *Gemälde*, vol. II, 1985, p. 923, no. 586, bracketed it on stylistic grounds between 1656 and 1660; while G. Jansen, in Amsterdam / Groningen 1983, p. 148, cat. no. 29, regarded 1660 as 'most likely' because of the resemblance to the *Portrait of a Man in a Broad-Brimmed Hat*, dated 1660 (Sumowski, vol. II, no. 598).
7 Trnek 1992, p. 134, no. 46.

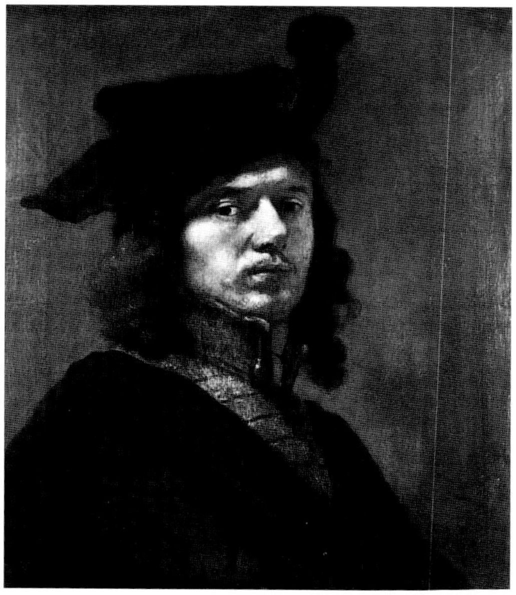

FIG. 58a
Barend Fabritius
Portrait of a Man in Fanciful Costume
Canvas
62.5 x 51.0 cm
Alte Pinakothek, Munich

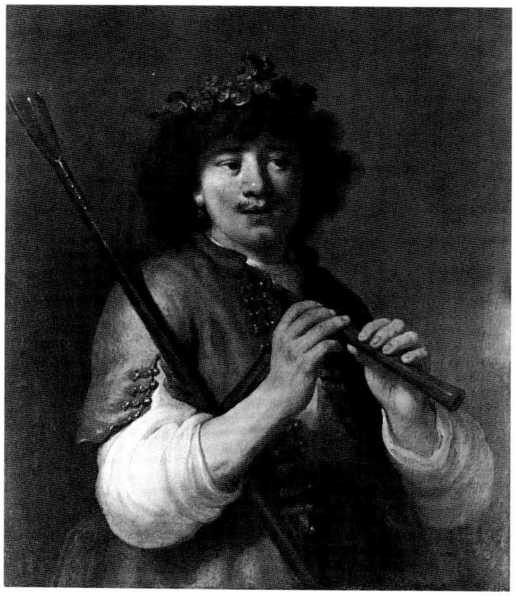

FIG. 58b
Govaert Flinck
Portrait of Rembrandt as a Shepherd
Signed
Canvas
74.5 x 64.0 cm
Rijksmuseum, Amsterdam

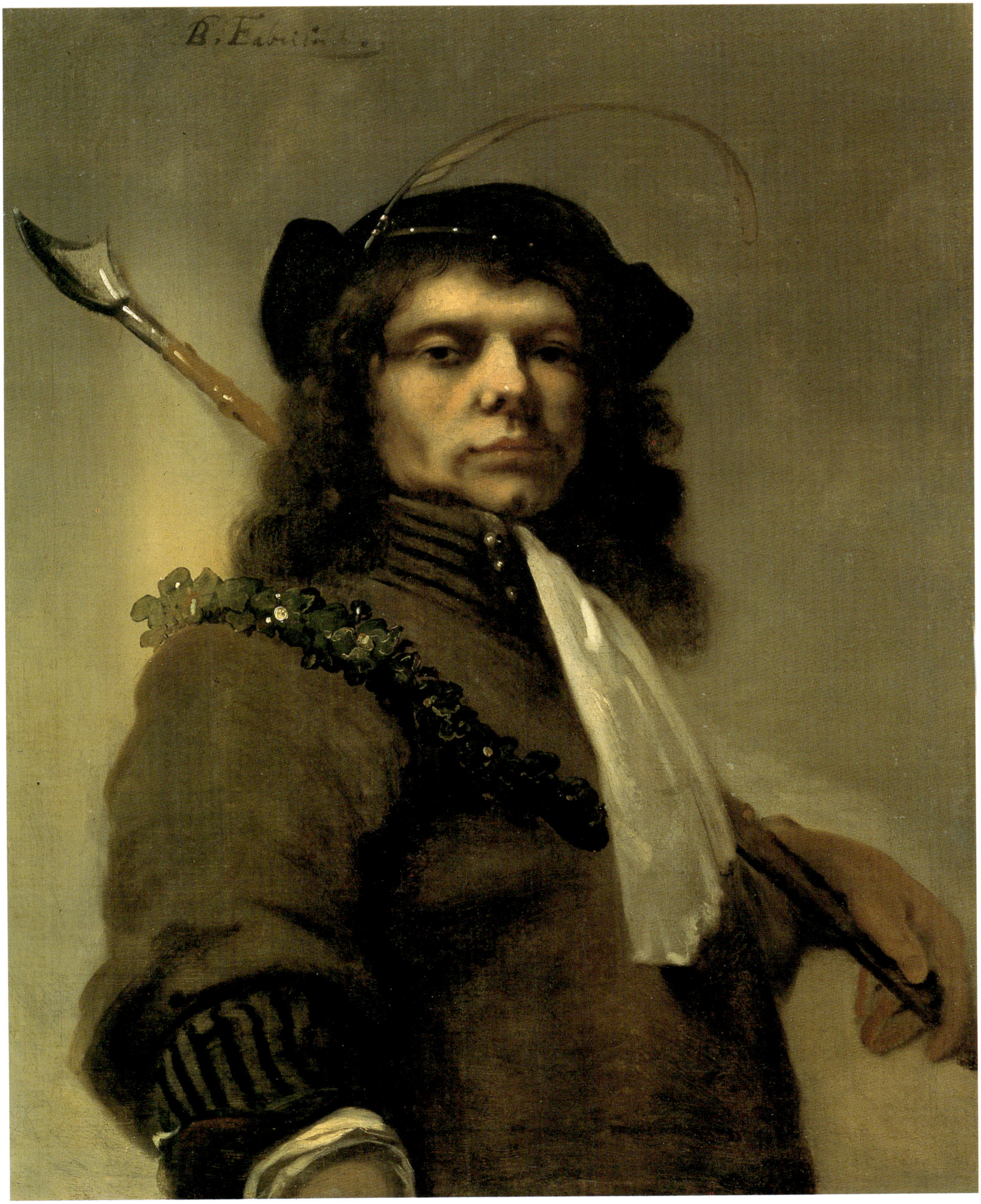
B. Fabritius

59

Barend Fabritius

The Evangelist Matthew

Signed and dated lower left *B. Fabritius. 1656*
Canvas
76.9 x 63.9 cm
The Montreal Museum of Fine Arts Collection
Gift of Mr. and Mrs. Michal Hornstein in honour of Frederik J. Duparc

PROVENANCE: Sale, London (Christie's), 29 June 1928, lot 51 (as 'Moses Writing the Pentateuch'); Dr C. J. K. van Aalst and N. J. van Aalst, Hoevelaken; sale, Amsterdam (Mak van Waay), 28 September 1966, lot 33; Daan Cevat; Mr and Mrs Michal Hornstein, Montreal.

LITERATURE: Von Moltke 1939, pp. xiii, 128; Sumowski 1959, p. 290; Sumowski, *Gemälde*, vol. II, 1985, p. 922, no. 583.

When this painting was sold in London at Christie's in 1928, its subject was incorrectly described as Moses writing the Pentateuch, the first five books of the Bible known as the Books of Moses. By the time the painting had entered the van Aalst collection, where it was catalogued by von Moltke (1939), its correct subject had been identified: the evangelist Matthew with the angel providing his divine inspiration. The author of the monograph on Barend Fabritius, D. Pont (1958), hypothesized that the painting might have formed part of a series of the Four Evangelists.[1] Series of this type had been produced earlier in Italy (for example, by Guido Reni) as well as in the Netherlands (by Frans Hals (fig. 22b), Hendrick ter Brugghen and Jan Lievens). However, the other three hypothetical paintings by Barend that would complete the series have not been identified.

In a review of Pont's book, Sumowski noted the present work's close resemblance in conception to Rembrandt's painting dated five years later, *The Evangelist Matthew* of 1661 (cat. no. 22).[2] Rembrandt's painting is also a half-length composition with the bearded evangelist seated behind a desk and holding a quill over an open book or manuscript. The angel in both cases stands close by the saint's ear, placing a hand lightly on his shoulder. As discussed in relation to the Rembrandt picture, Barend's angel has wings, a white robe and a halo, while Rembrandt foregoes any such obvious celestial attributes.

Sumowski rightly questioned that Barend would have been the initiator of the present composition, speculating that it was first developed in a lost Rembrandt drawing, although the two artists could just as readily have consulted another common source of inspiration. Sumowski later pointed out that the *Matthew* of 1656 is the earliest dated example of Barend's half-length historical figures or *tronies* in fantasy costumes, which mark a change from his more Rembrandtesque earlier manner to a more personal style.[3] Sumowski traced the inspiration for this picture's style to Carel Fabritius's so-called self-portrait at the National Gallery, London (cat. no. 57), which also employs a light, cloud-filled background like that which appears here at the upper left, and a colourful, painterly palette.

Sumowski was perhaps too critical of the present work's drawing, modelling, and mastery of technique, notably the placing of transparent forms on top of one another. With his emphatic use of colour accents, Barend sometimes introduces unexpectedly dramatic, unmodulated tonal contrasts, which have probably become more pronounced with time. The Montreal painting is rightly praised for its psychological insight: Matthew's hooded gaze, wrinkled brow and poised quill suggest the concentration of one who is conveying information rather than conceiving it himself. He seems to pause in the attitude of rapt concentration, intent upon providing the perfect conduit for the author's inspired words. Rembrandt's *Matthew*, on the other hand, scratches his beard as in thought, suggesting quite a different approach theologically to the transmission of God's word – at once more interpretative and creative.

PCS

1 Pont 1958, p. 112, no. 22.
2 Sumowski 1959, p. 20.
3 Sumowski, *Gemälde*, vol. II, 1985, p. 922, no. 583.

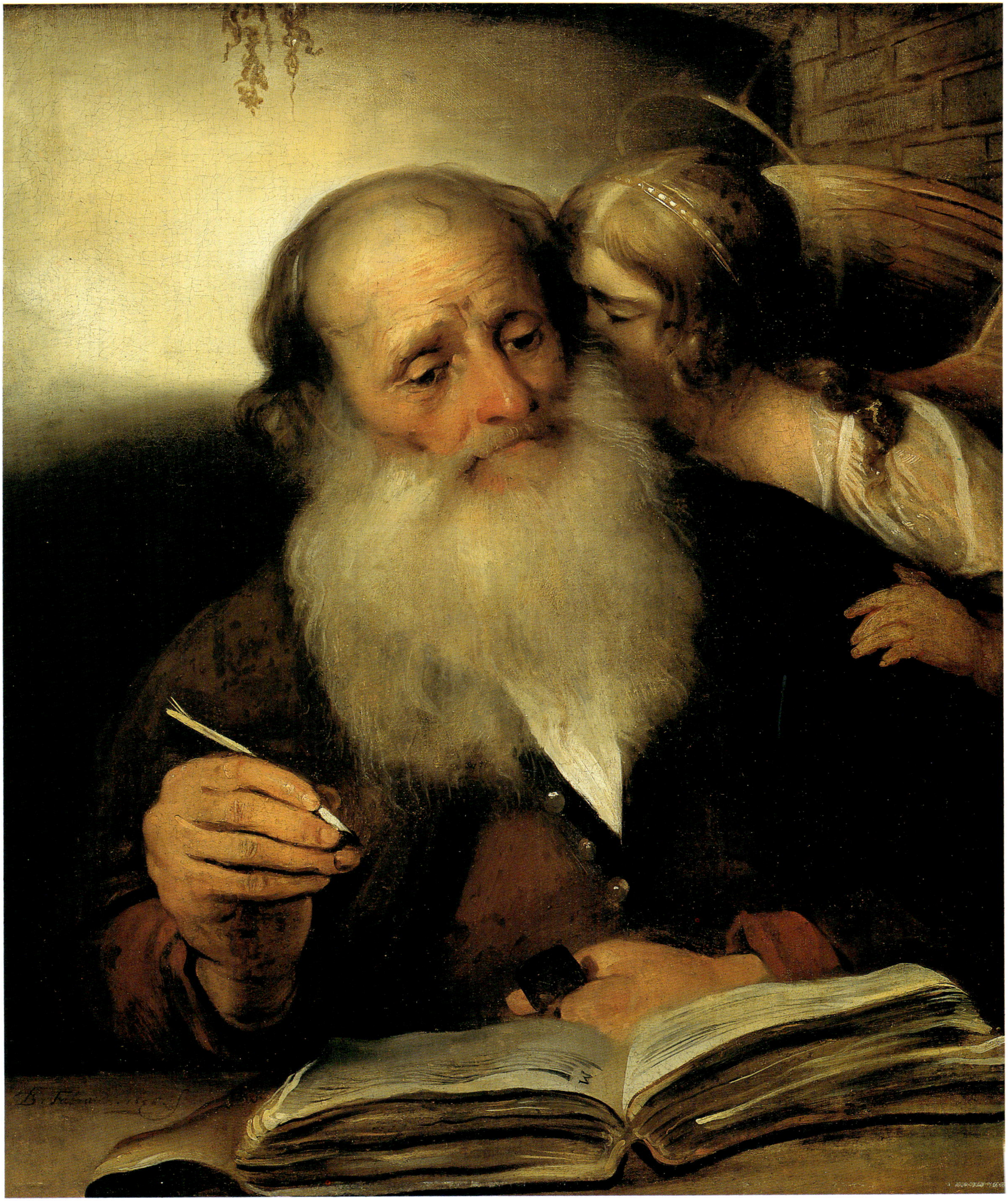

Christoph Paudiss (*c.*1625/30–1666)

Little is known of Paudiss's life; indeed the date of his birth in Hamburg has only been approximated broadly. However, Sandrart (1675) asserts that he was an accomplished 'Hamburgensis' student of Rembrandt, one of the aspiring artists from Lower Saxony. His period of study with the master probably occurred in the mid-1640s, after which he travelled widely, seeking and often finding noble patronage, although his service as a true court painter was probably only intermittent. The peripatetic Paudiss travelled to Hungary, worked at the court in Stuttgart (*c.*1656–57), and served Prince Johann Georg II in Dresden (1659–60), Archduke Leopold Wilhelm in Vienna (1660–62) and the archbishop in Salzburg (1662). For the last four years of his life he served Archbishop Sigismund von Bayern in Freising.

A varied painter, Paudiss produced history paintings, allegories, genre scenes, *tronies*, portraits, animal paintings, and still lifes. His earliest known dated painting, *Lot and His Daughters* (Szépmüvészeti Múzeum, Budapest), is from 1649.

LITERATURE: Sandrart 1675, p. 349; Peltzer 1937–38, p. 251ff; Sumowski, *Gemälde*, vol. IV, 1990, pp. 2313–60.
PCS

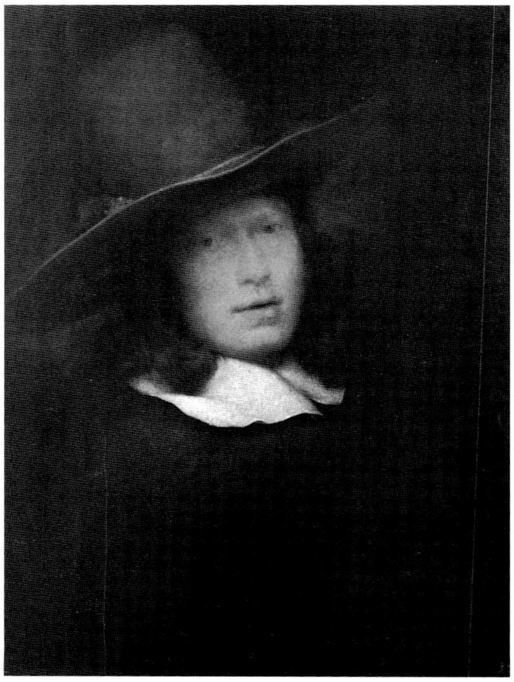

Christoph Paudiss
Presumed Self-Portrait
Canvas
75.5 x 60.0 cm
Sächsische Landes-, Staats- und Universitätsbibliothek Dresden
From a reproduction

60

Christoph Paudiss

Still Life with Herring and Onions

Signed and dated lower right under edge of table *Christofher Paudiss / 1660*
Panel
87.5 x 73.0 cm
Museum Boijmans Van Beuningen, Rotterdam

PROVENANCE: Prince Nicolas Esterhazy, Vienna; Samuel Graf von Festetics, Vienna; his sale, Vienna, 11 April 1859, lot 22; Joseph Daniël Böhm, Vienna; Friedrich J. Gsell, Vienna; his sale, Vienna, 14 March 1872, lot 217, to Miller; Eugen Miller von Aichholz, Vienna; Stephan von Auspitz, Vienna; acquired from von Auspitz, via the dealer Bachstitz, The Hague, by D. G. van Beuningen, 1932; acquired by the Museum with the Van Beuningen Collection in 1958.

LITERATURE: Sumowski, *Gemälde*, vol. IV, 1990, p. 2324, no. 1586; J. Giltaij & G. Jansen, in Rotterdam 1988, pp. 64–5, cat. no. 19.

According to Joachim von Sandrart, Christoph Paudiss was a 'first-rate disciple' *(ein trefflicher Discipel)* of Rembrandt;[1] he is assumed to have come to Amsterdam from northern Germany, probably Hamburg. The period of his study with the master is often thought to have begun as early as 1642, though it may have started somewhat later (Sumowski suggests *c.*1645),[2] and was surely concluded by 1649, when Paudiss signed and dated his first painting *(Lot and His Daughters*, Szépmüvészeti Múzeum, Budapest).[3] He subsequently lived a peripatetic life, working for noble patrons in Stuttgart (*c.*1656–58), Dresden (1659–60), Vienna (1660–62), Salzburg (1662) and Freising (1662–66), but he never abandoned the Rembrandtesque manner he had developed in the 1640s.

In addition to history paintings, portraits, genre scenes and animal paintings, Paudiss executed a series of kitchen still lifes between 1658 and 1661, most featuring utensils, crockery and ironware, smoking supplies and foodstuffs.[4] While Rembrandt himself did not make a speciality of still-life painting (although he painted a *Slaughtered Ox* (Louvre, Paris) (Bredius 457) and *Dead Peacocks* (Rijksmuseum, Amsterdam) (Bredius 456)), the blond tonality, 'monochromatic' palette, and contrasts of light and shade in Paudiss's still-life works have been repeatedly likened in style to the master's manner. A favourite motif figuring centrally in all of these designs was a string of onions suspended from a nail in the plaster wall.

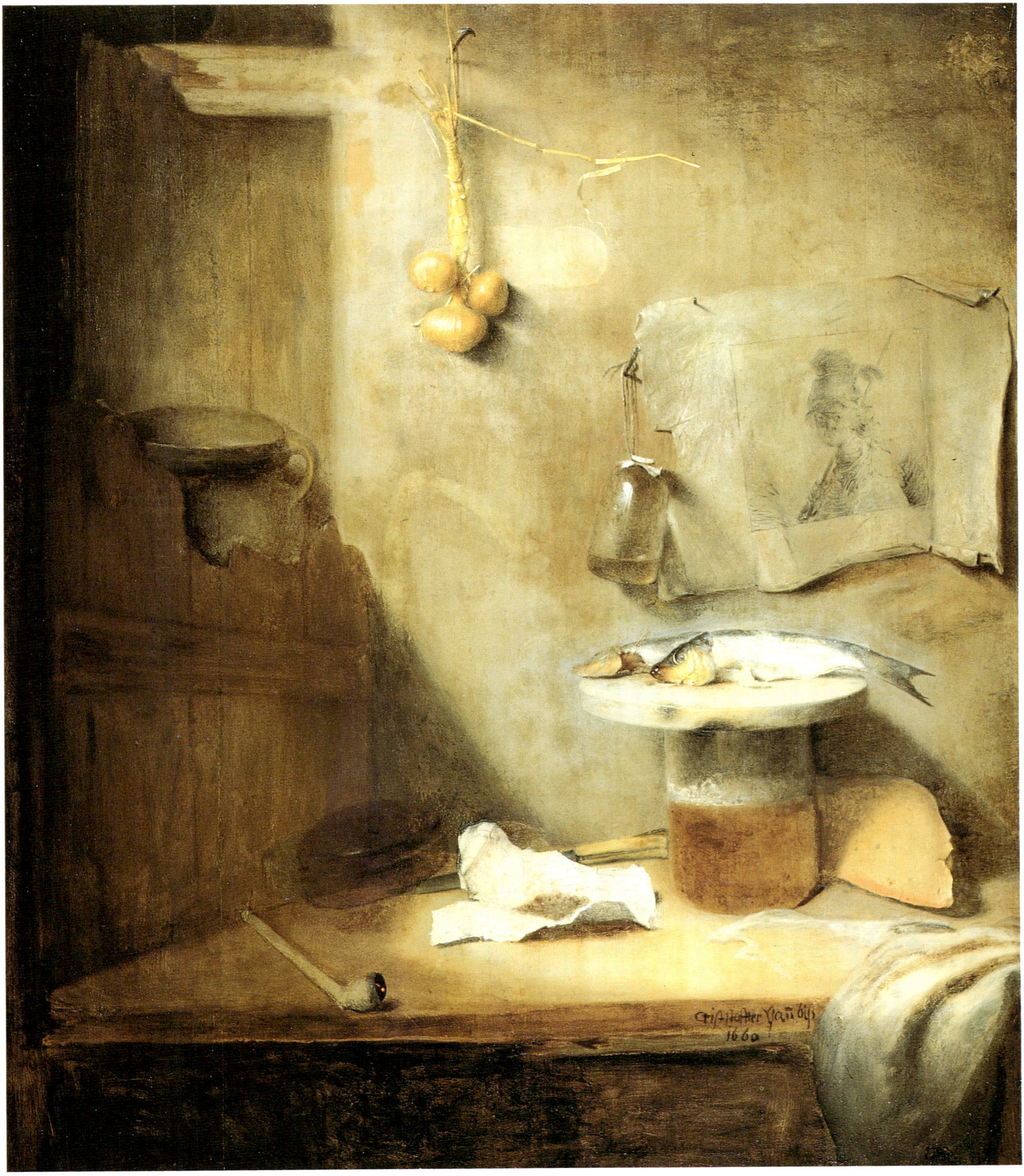

In an upright composition similar to the Rotterdam picture and also dated 1660, at the Hermitage, St Petersburg, crumpled sheet music appears among the unassuming objects of the larder (fig. 60a),[5] while the present painting includes a drawing or print of an exotic soldier, tacked to the back wall. J. Giltaij and G. Jansen noted the image's resemblance to several etchings by Rembrandt and posited that it was a 'homage to his teacher'.[6] Attesting to the painting's popularity are the several copies listed by A. Pigler[7] and by Sumowski.[8]

PCS

1 Sandrart 1675, p. 349.
2 Sumowski, *Gemälde*, vol. IV, 1990, p. 2313.
3 Sumowski, *Gemälde*, vol. IV, 1990, p. 2317, no. 1552.
4 Sumowski, *Gemälde*, vol. IV, 1990, nos 1584–1587.
5 Sumowski, *Gemälde*, vol. IV, 1990, p. 2324, no. 1585.
6 J. Giltaij & G. Jansen, in Rotterdam 1988, p. 64, cat. no. 19, referring to B. 20, 23, 98, 138, 152, 287, 288.
7 Pigler 1968, vol. 1, p. 531, no. 3827.
8 Sumowski, *Gemälde*, vol. IV, 1990, p. 2324, no. 1586.

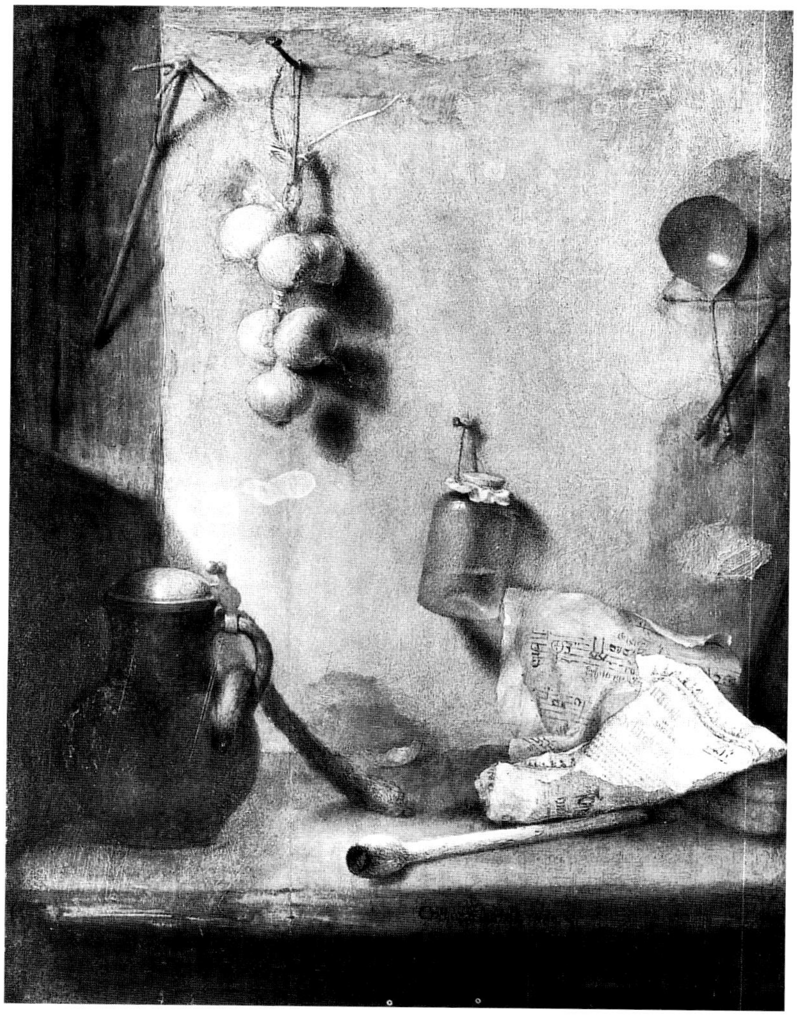

FIG. 60a
Christoph Paudiss
Kitchen Still Life with Sheet Music, Smoking Supplies and Onions
Signed and dated 1660
Panel transferred to canvas
62.0 x 46.5 cm
Hermitage, St Petersburg

Samuel van Hoogstraten (1627–1678)

Born in Dordrecht in August 1627, Samuel van Hoogstraten first studied with his father, after whose death in 1640 the family moved to The Hague. Around 1642 Samuel was sent to Amsterdam to study with Rembrandt. His fellow pupils included Abraham Furnerius (1628–1654), Constantijn Daniël van Renesse and Carel Fabritius (cat. no. 57). By April 1648 he was back in Dordrecht and was inducted into the Mennonite Brotherhood *(Doopsgezinde Broederschap)* but soon fell out with them after being accused by two fellow members of having been seen running around with a sword. After additional problems with the authorities, he departed for Vienna (1651), Rome (1652) and Regensburg (1653).

Houbraken reports that Hoogstraten presented three pieces to Ferdinand III in Vienna in August 1651 (see commentary to cat. no. 62), and won favour for his illusionistic painting style. In Rome he joined the Bentvuegels and took the nickname 'Batavier'. He lived there with the Dutch naturalist and still-life painter Otto Marseus van Schrieck (1619–1678). Hoogstraten retained his ties with Italy even after returning to Dordrecht in 1654, through his membership in the Society of Romanists. In his native city he became one of the *Muntmeesters*, or Masters of the Mint (his group portrait of them is preserved at the Dordrechts Museum), married Sara Balen, and joined the Reformed Church. Between 1662 and 1667, he lived in London, came in contact with the Royal Society and was patronized by Thomas Povey, for whom he painted two perspective pieces. He also painted large perspective views of palaces, *trompes l'oeil* and portraits during these years. He witnessed the outbreak of the Plague and the Great Fire of London in 1666 and composed a poem on these events.

During this period, England and the United Provinces renewed hostilities. In January 1668, Hoogstraten was back in Holland, where he joined the artists' society in The Hague known as Pictura. He returned to his native Dordrecht in the same year and bought a house on the Steegoversloot for 2000 florins. He soon rose to be Provost of the Mint.

An accomplished poet, Hoogstraten illustrated his own *Schoone Rosaliin* (published in 1650) with etchings and two years later an anthology of his verses appeared entitled *Goude schalmeij*. During his last years in Holland he composed his *Inleyding tot de hooge schoole der schilderkonst* (1678) and made the designs for the prints illustrating *Beschrijvinge der stad Dordrecht* (Description of Dordrecht) (1677), by his wife's uncle, Matthys Balen. He was buried in Dordrecht on 19 October 1678. Among his pupils were Godfried Schalcken, Arent de Gelder (cat. nos 69–72), Cornelis van der Meulen and Arnold Houbraken.

Hoogstraten had varied talents, being an accomplished author, playwright and poet as well as an artist. His painted oeuvre was also wide-ranging. His early history paintings and portraits recall Rembrandt, while the *trompe l'oeil* still lifes he developed in Vienna departed from the style of his master and established his originality. Today his best known subjects are his perspective boxes (most notably the large one at the National Gallery, London) and perspectives, although Houbraken claims he also painted landscapes, marines, animals and flowers. His later manner became less naturalistic and more classically refined and generalized.

LITERATURE: Houbraken 1718–21, vol. II, 1719, pp. 155–70; Sumowski, *Gemälde*, vol. II, 1985, pp. 1286–386; Dordrecht 1992–93, pp. 188–209; Roscam Abbing 1993; Brusati 1995.

PCS

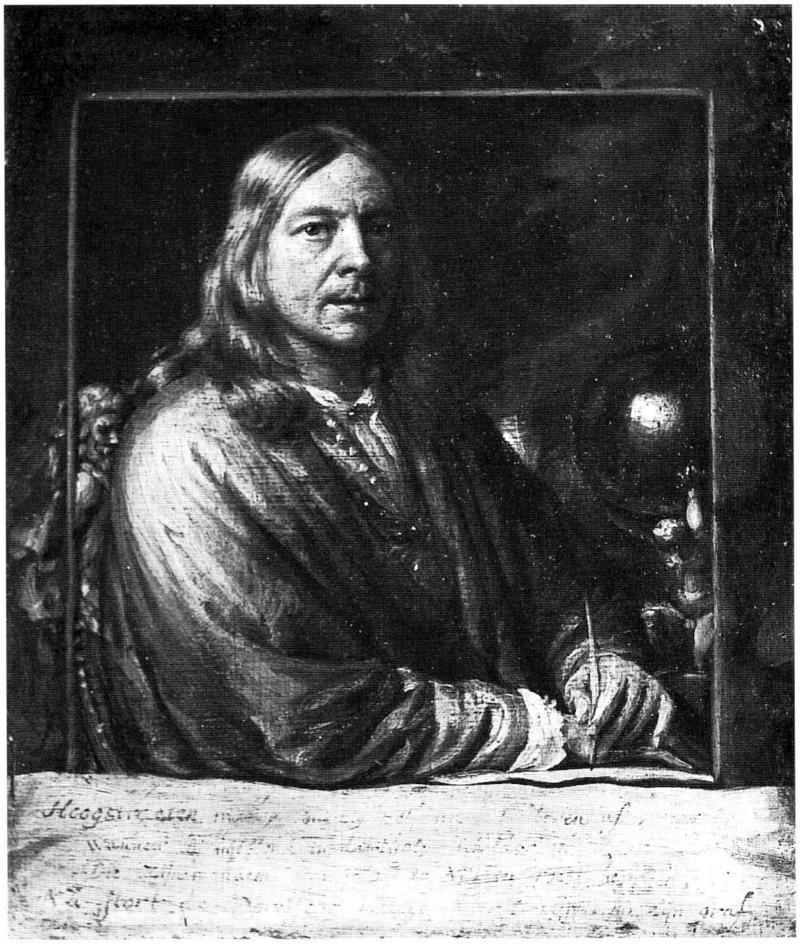

Samuel van Hoogstraten
Self-Portrait
Signed and dated 1677
Panel
20.0 x 16.4 cm
Dordrechts Museum, Dordrecht
(for a print after this painting, see p. 64, fig. 8)

61
Samuel van Hoogstraten
Adoration of the Shepherds

Signed lower right *S v Hoogstraten. / 1647*
Canvas
57.5 x 71.0 cm
Dordrechts Museum, Dordrecht

PROVENANCE: Sale, Paris (Drouot), 17 June 1980, lot 37, repr.; with dealer S. Nystad, The Hague.

LITERATURE: De Groot 1980, pp. 82–4; Sumowski, *Drawings*, vol. 5, 1981, p. 2526; Sumowski, *Gemälde*, vol. II, 1985, p. 1292, no. 823; C. Brusati, in Dordrecht 1992–93, pp. 190–2, cat. no. 43; Roscam Abbing 1993, p. 104; Brusati 1995, p. 33, no. 44.

Hoogstraten was Rembrandt's pupil in Amsterdam at the same time as Carel Fabritius (cat. no. 57), probably in 1642–43. As Sumowski pointed out,[1] this relatively early work by the artist seems to be inspired by Rembrandt's two related paintings of the same subject (Luke 2:16), dated the previous year: the work in Munich (Bredius 574) (fig. 61a), part of a series on the Life of Christ painted for the stadholder, and that at the National Gallery, London (Bredius 575). Although Hoogstraten converted the upright design to a horizontal format, he paraphrased aspects of Rembrandt's compositions and imitated his technique and tenebrous palette. As J. M. de Groot observed,[2] the pupil may also have recalled his master's *Holy Family with Angels* of 1645 (Hermitage, St Petersburg) (Bredius 570) in details like the angels hovering overhead and the fire at the right. C. Brusati in the Dordrecht exhibition catalogue of 1992–93[3] regarded the varied lighting effects in the present work as possibly anticipating Hoogstraten's later writings, specifically his chapter 'Van de graeden van schaduwen en lichten' in his *Inleyding tot de hooge schoole der schilderkonst.*[4]

Sumowski first observed that a series of four drawings by Hoogstraten (notably that in the Kunsthalle, Hamburg, and that in the Metropolitan Museum of Art, New York) seem to document the process by which Hoogstraten absorbed and transformed Rembrandt's precedents.[5] Although none of the drawings can properly be called a preparatory study for this painting, they attest to a thorough exploration of the expressive possibilities of the theme, a practice that seems to have been central to Rembrandt's teaching methods. C. Brusati has described these drawings evocatively as 'dress rehearsals' and has related them to Hoogstraten's description of the practice of drawing *uyt den geest* (literally: 'from the mind'), by which he meant drawing from the mind's store of images of things seen and mirrored in the imagination.[6]

Biblical and history paintings are not as common in Hoogstraten's oeuvre as portraits, genre scenes, perspectives and *trompe l'oeil* still lifes (cat. no. 62), but he returned to the Adoration theme in a later painting now in an English private collection.[7] De Groot observed that Hoogstraten's conception of the theme was unusual for including women among the adoring visitors to the stable, although there are precedents in the art of other Dutch history painters, such as Pieter de Grebber.[8]

PCS

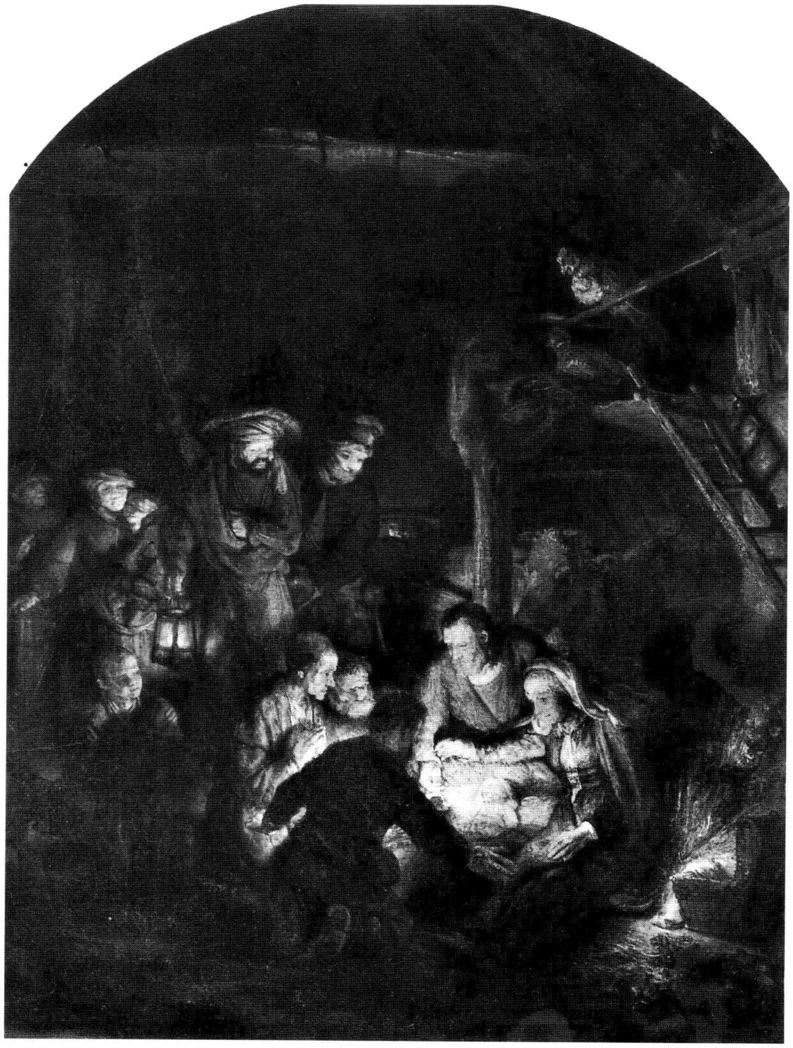

FIG. 61a
Rembrandt
Adoration of the Shepherds
Signed and dated 1646
Canvas
97.0 x 71.0 cm
Alte Pinakothek, Munich

1 Sumowski, *Gemälde*, vol. II, 1985, p. 1292, no. 823.
2 De Groot 1980, p. 83.
3 C. Brusati, in Dordrecht 1992–93, p. 192, note 2.
4 Van Hoogstraten 1678, pp. 259–64.
5 Sumowski, *Drawings*, vol. 5, 1981, pp. 2456, 2526–31, nos 1102, 1135–1137; see also Brusati 1995, figs 20, 21.
6 Brusati 1995, p. 54.
7 Sumowski, *Gemälde*, vol. V, 1990, no. 2093.
8 De Groot 1980, p. 84.

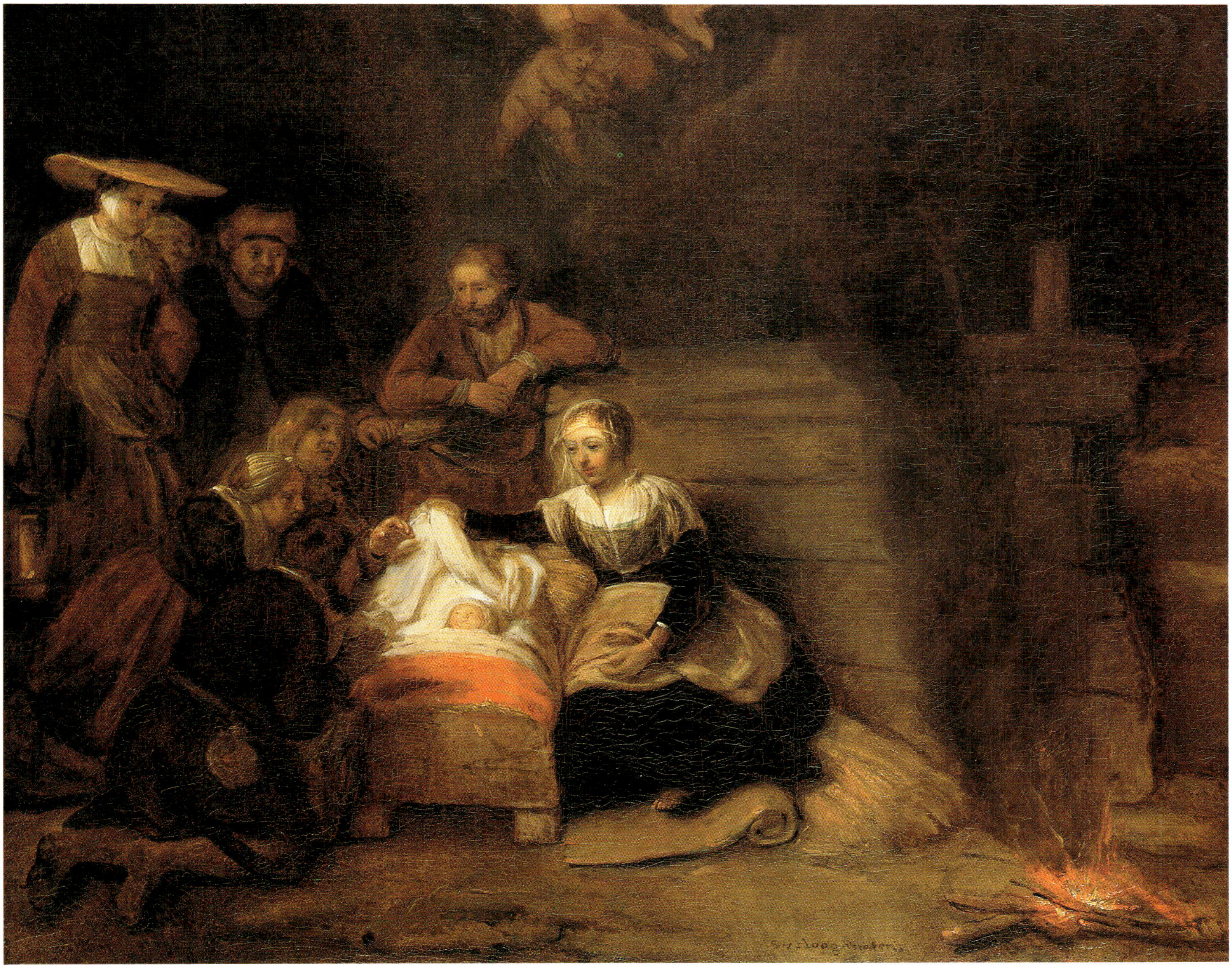

62

Samuel van Hoogstraten
Still Life on a Cupboard Door

Signed and dated on letter *Empfangen / Den 1[2] Feber / 1655 von / S. v. Hoogstrate / Wie[n]*; and monogrammed on hand-towel *SH* [or *SK*]
Canvas
92.3 x 72.2 cm
Gemäldegalerie der Akademie der bildenden Künste in Wien, Vienna

PROVENANCE: Fürsten Prosper von Sinzendorf; his sale, Vienna, 17 March 1823, lot 185; Jäger collection; Friedrich J. Gsell, Vienna; his sale, Vienna, 14 March 1872, lot 461, to Dr Schmidt; Joseph von Lippmann-Lissingen, Vienna and Paris (d. 1900); Eugenie von Lippmann-Lissingen; by descent to her son, Wolfgang von Wurzbach-Tannenberg; presented by him in 1957.

LITERATURE: Blankert 1975, pp. 26–30; E. de Jongh, in Auckland 1982, p. 145; Sumowski, *Gemälde*, vol. II, 1985, p. 1301, no. 884; Brusati 1990–91, pp. 180–2; Trnek 1992, pp. 235–41, no. 80; C. Brusati, in Dordrecht 1992–93, p. 203; Roscam Abbing 1993, p. 48, no. 38, p. 116; Brusati 1995, pp. 58, 62, 69, 152–3, 155–9, 161–2, 303, note 18, no. 79.

Although many of Rembrandt's pupils departed from his favoured themes and styles when they left his studio, few became devoted still life painters. An exception is Hoogstraten, who became a pioneering painter of *trompe l'oeil* still lifes. Notwithstanding the fact that in his own writing on art he lent support to the prevailing theory that history painting was the noblest pursuit, his own career was advanced by his illusionistic paintings of lesser subjects. According to his own pupil Arnold Houbraken, Hoogstraten travelled from his native Dordrecht to Vienna and there had an audience with the Holy Roman Emperor, Ferdinand III, on 6 August 1651.[1] Although the artist presented three paintings including a nobleman's portrait and a biblical scene of Christ Crowned with Thorns, it was his illusionistic still life (also commonly known as a *bedriegertje*, or deception piece, in the seventeenth century) which most impressed the emperor, who is quoted as exclaiming: 'Dit ist der eerste Maler die mir betrogen heeft' (This is the first painter who has ever deceived me). In recognition, he presented Hoogstraten with a golden courtier's chain with portrait medal (an example of which is reproduced by Roscam Abbing).[2] Although we do not know which, if any, of Hoogstraten's surviving still lifes caught the emperor's eye, the work in question probably resembled the Akademie's painting, which though painted just before he left Vienna is Hoogstraten's earliest surviving dated example. R. Trnek takes pains to point out that while the date inscribed on the paper stuck in the tidy attached to the cupboard has often been misread as 1654 it is certainly 1655 and was already deciphered correctly (as was the date 12 February) in the Fürsten Prosper von Sinzendorf sale catalogue of 1823.[3] Albert Blankert identified the painting as the first *trompe l'oeil* because it achieves its compelling effect of illusionism by representing relatively flat objects in a very shallow composition, thus minimizing the need for pictorial relief.[4]

The simple objects of the daily toilette hung from the cupboard door include a white hand-towel, a brush with bright red handle before a mirror, and below, inserted into the pockets of a tooled leather tidy, a comb, a paper receipt addressed to the artist, presumably for services rendered, and, dangling below this, a sponge. Just visible behind the towel is Hoogstraten's medal from the emperor. Thus the painting is not merely an exercise in depicting commonplace objects as faithfully as possible but is also a form of self-portraiture and self-promotion. C. Brusati has described it as a 'self reflexive image', which simultaneously flatters the patron while advertising the painter's craft.[5]

In another *trompe l'oeil* still life of a letter-rack, the work signed by Hoogstraten and dated 1664 that was recently acquired by the Dordrechts Museum, the medal and chain recur,[6] as they do in still another letter-rack painting, executed in 1669 or soon thereafter, at the Staatliche Kunsthalle, Karlsruhe (fig. 62a).[7] There, as in Hoogstraten's equally self-promoting still life in E. Winkler's collection, Hong Kong,[8] the imperial medal is supplemented with a letter inscribed with verses written by the Viennese poet Johan Wilhelm von Stubenberg (1619–1663), praising Hoogstraten in time-honoured fashion by comparing his artistic powers to those of the legendary Greek painter Zeuxis.[9]

Hoogstraten was not alone in finding royal favour through his illusionistic still lifes: the Flemish artist Cornelis Norbertus Gijsbrechts was employed by Frederick III and Christian V of Denmark as a court painter in Copenhagen in 1670–72.

Notwithstanding the fact that he described still-life painters as the 'common footsoldiers' in the army of art, in a chapter devoted in his *Inleyding* (1678) to the most deceptively true colouring *(kolorereren)*,[10] Hoogstraten encouraged his students to paint *trompe l'oeil* still lifes. No doubt reflecting on the turning-point in his own career, he specifically recommends painting a shallow composition, such as wood panelling with knotted grain, and then adding a few common objects *(gemeene dingen)* such as combs or letters, which should be as skilfully painted as possible from life, in order to deceive princely admirers.

PCS

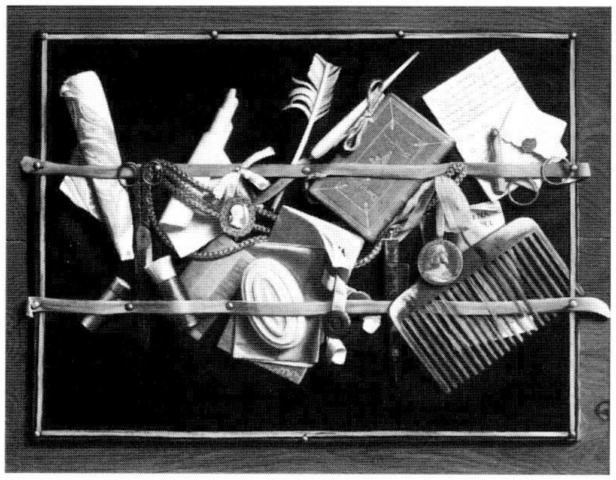

FIG. 62a
Samuel van Hoogstraten
Still Life of a Letter-Rack
Monogrammed
Canvas
63.0 x 79.0 cm
Staatliche Kunsthalle, Karlsruhe

1 Houbraken 1753, vol. II, pp. 158–9.
2 Roscam Abbing 1993, p. 43, fig. 11.
3 Trnek 1992, p. 239, note 17.
4 Blankert 1975, pp. 26–30.
5 Brusati 1995, p. 69.
6 C. Brusati, in Dordrecht 1992–93, pp. 203–5, cat. no. 47, repr.; Brusati 1995, no. 81, fig. 56, pl. VI.
7 Sumowski, *Gemälde*, vol. II, 1985, p. 1302, no. 885; Brusati 1995, no. 83.
8 Sumowski, *Gemälde*, vol. II, 1985, no. 881; Brusati 1995, no. 82.
9 For an extensive analysis of Hoogstraten's still lifes as self-portraits, see Brusati 1990–91, pp. 168–82; Brusati 1995, pp. 138–68.
10 Van Hoogstraten 1678, pp. 217–18.

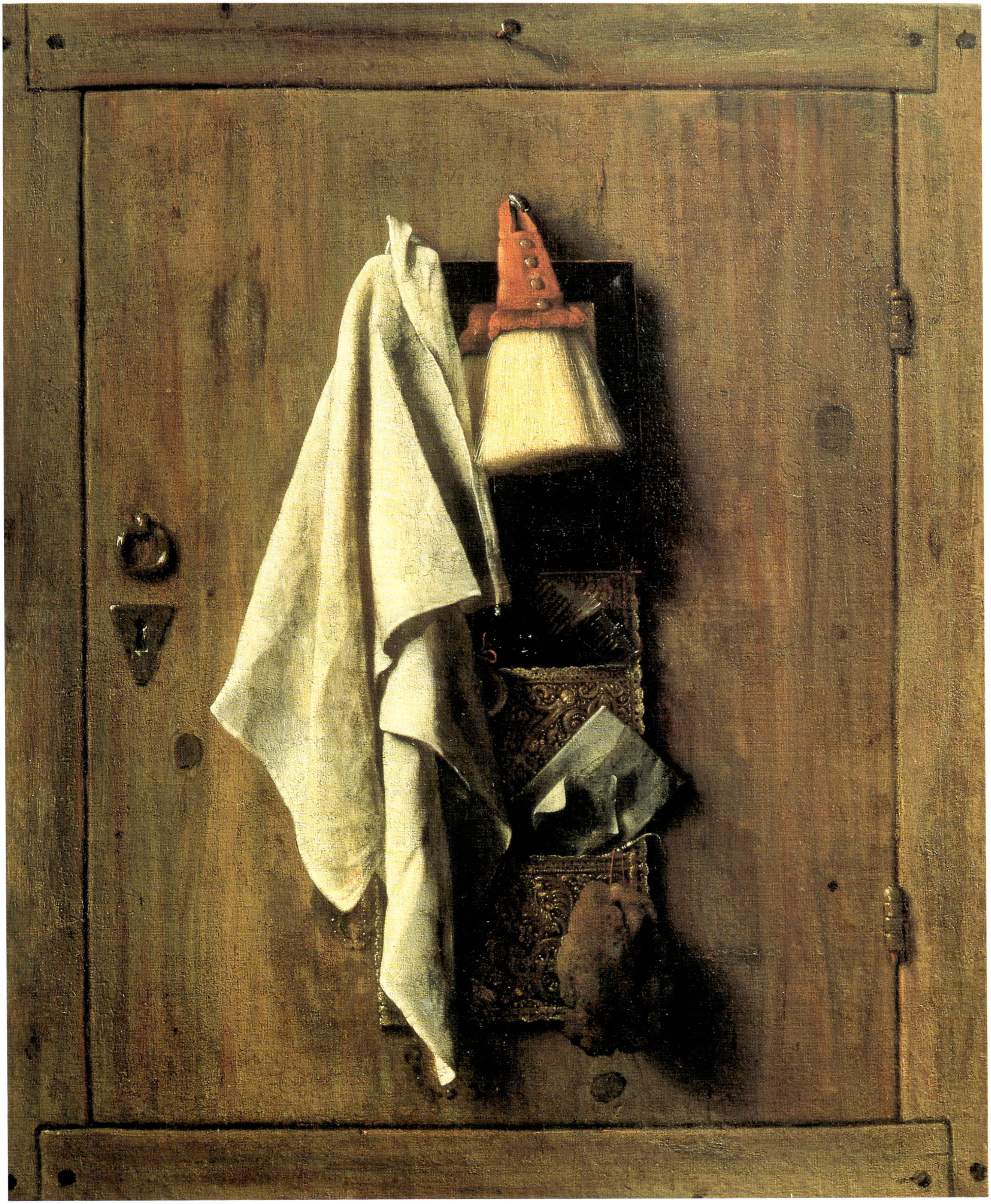

Willem Drost (active *c.*1650–after 1680)

The dates of this artist's birth and death are unknown. An etching by Drost (reproduced here) generally held to be a self-portrait is dated 1652, and dated works are known from 1653 to 1663. Houbraken mentions Drost's training under Rembrandt, a stay in Rome (which can be bracketed chronologically by portraits of native Dutch sitters, dated 1654 and 1663) with Jan van der Meer, and a friendship initiated in Munich and continued in Venice with Johan Carel Loth, called Carlotto. The latter collaborated with Drost on a series of the Evangelists, known to be in the collection of Giorgio Bergonzi in Vienna in 1709. One of the artist's greatest paintings is *Bathsheba with David's Letter*, dated 1654 (Louvre, Paris). In 1685 Grand Duke Cosimo III de' Medici purchased a self-portrait by Drost, perhaps painted in Venice around 1660, a work now preserved in the Uffizi. On 23 December 1680, Drost is recorded as a witness to the inventory of the collection of Jan van Spijckoort in Rotterdam.

Drost painted biblical scenes, allegorical figures and portraits. The timeframe for his period of study with Rembrandt is not certain, although it probably occurred in the late 1640s or early 1650s. The parameters of his oeuvre have been much debated in recent years, in part because some of the major paintings traditionally assigned to Rembrandt's production in the 1650s have now been reassigned by some authorities to Drost (for example, the so-called *Polish Rider* in the Frick Collection, New York (p. 50, fig. 24)). Moreover, Drost has recently become an artist who commands exceptionally high prices (fig. 63a). After his move to Italy he adopted a style closer to that of Loth and Venetian artists.

LITERATURE: Sumowski, *Gemälde*, vol. I, 1983, pp. 608–51; Bruyn 1984, pp. 153–8.

PCS

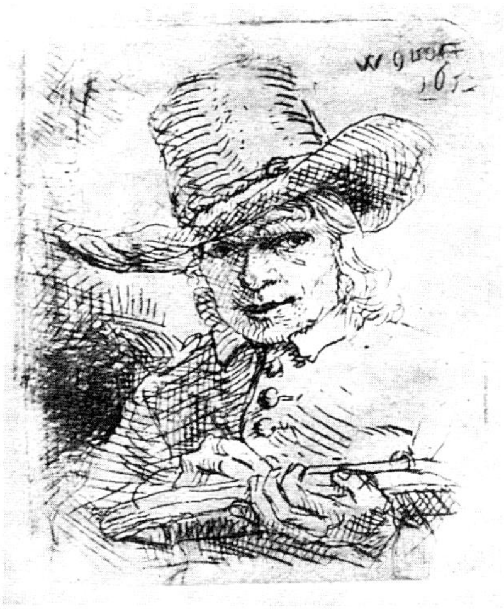

Willem Drost
Self-Portrait
Signed and dated 1652
Etching
6.4 x 5.2 cm
From a reproduction at the RKD

63

Willem Drost

Bearded Man in a Broad-Brimmed Hat

*c.*1654

Signed centre right *W. Drost*
Canvas
64.5 x 56.5 cm
National Gallery of Ireland, Dublin

PROVENANCE: Purchased by Joseph Strutt of Derby, between 1820 and 1821; by descent to Howard Galton of Hadzor, by 1854; by descent to Hubert Galton; his sale, London (Christie's), 22 June 1889, lot 26 (as Gerbrand van den Eeckhout); acquired for the National Gallery of Ireland for 96 guineas.

LITERATURE: (Probably) Derby 1827, no. 163 (as 'Rembrandt, *Head of a Jewish Rabbi*'); Waagen 1854, vol. III, p. 221 (as Gerbrand van den Eeckhout); Manchester 1857, cat. no. 676 (as Gerbrand van den Eeckhout); Potterton 1982, p. 104; Sumowski, *Gemälde*, vol. I, 1983, p. 615, no. 328; Potterton 1986, pp. 35–6, no. 107; B. P. Kennedy, in Chicago / Boston / San Francisco / New York 1992, p. 48, cat. no. 9.

This painting is probably identical with the so-called 'Head of a Rabbi' attributed to Rembrandt in the 1827 catalogue of Joseph Strutt of Derby's collection.[1] The present work was subsequently attributed to Gerbrand van den Eeckhout by G. Waagen in 1854,[2] was lent as by van den Eeckhout to the *Manchester Art Treasures* exhibition in 1857, and was sold under that name in 1889. The painting was reassigned to Willem Drost only in 1982, when the artist's signature reemerged during cleaning.[3] Sumowski observed that Drost used the same model in his *Man in Armour (Mars)* (Gemäldegalerie, Kassel), *Man in a Red Cap* (Gemäldegalerie, Dresden), and *Seated Man Wearing a Feathered Beret*, dated 1654 (formerly Rothschild Collection) (fig. 63a).[4] Sumowski's dating of *c.*1654 for Dublin's painting is acceptable based on the work's resemblance to the last-mentioned painting, which was recently sold in New York (Sotheby's, 30 January 1997, lot 23).

Sumowski also related the present picture to the *Portrait of a Young Woman in a Feathered Hat* (canvas, 67.4 x 58.3 cm) at the Cincinnati Art Museum, which according to him was first reattributed to Willem Drost by J. Nieuwstraten of the RKD.[5] The implication, though unstated by Sumowski, that the two comparably scaled works might be pendants was tacitly entertained by H. Potterton (1986). The putative pair would,

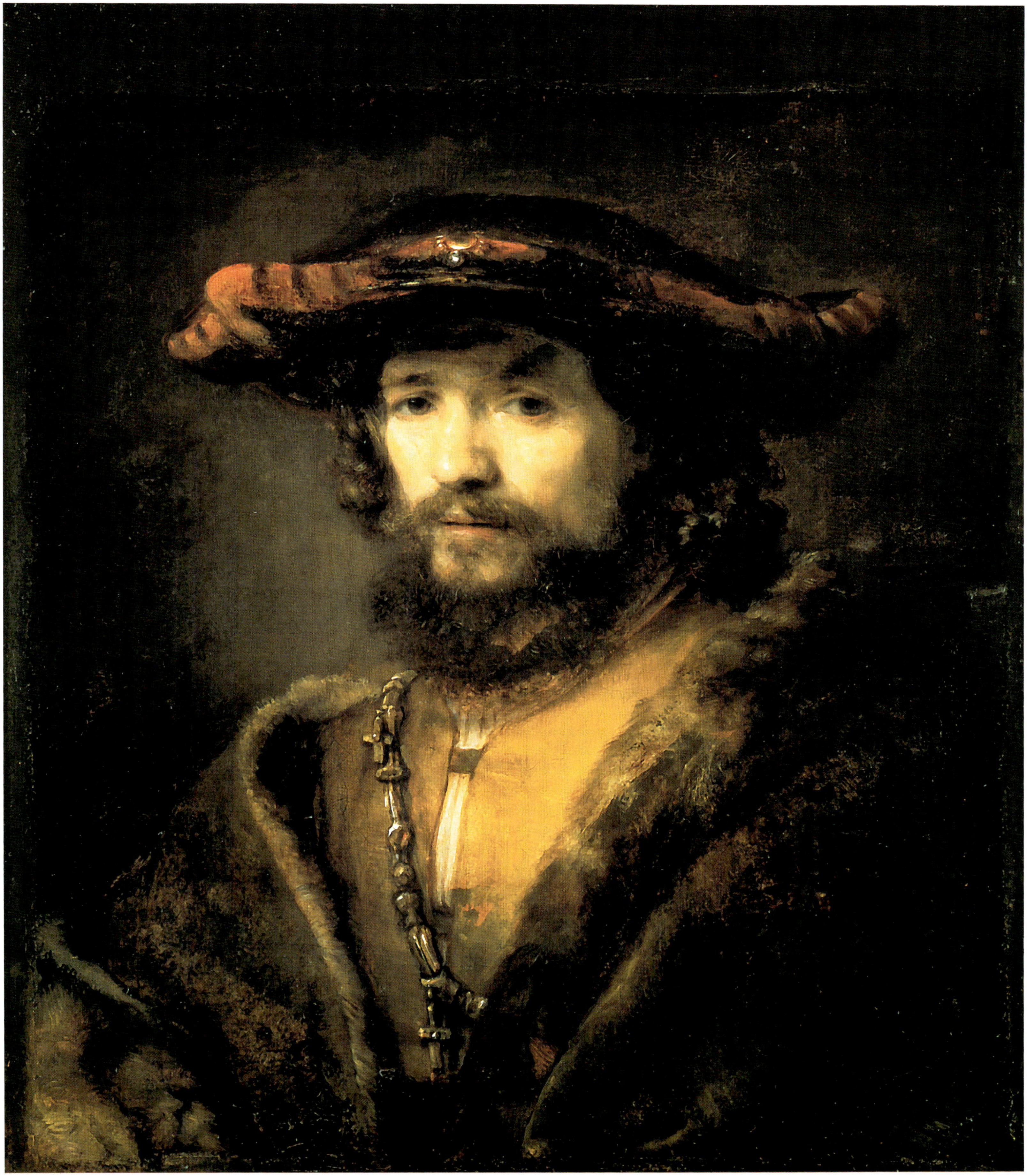

however, reverse the traditional sinister/dexter orientation of companion pieces; moreover, their relationship is complicated by the fact that their respective paint films have very different factures. While the Cincinnati painting's surface has suffered as a result of relining, the Dublin picture exhibits all of Drost's delicate mastery of Rembrandt's painterly style. Drost is especially effective in using flecked accents of highlighted colour over broader passages of tone, and has an admirably sure palette. While many of the lesser Rembrandt followers often turn muddy in their efforts to imitate the master's tenebrist manner, Drost's colours are consistently sure and true.

Potterton observed that the man's costume in the present work, with broad-brimmed beret, fur-trimmed coat and courtier's chain, recalls the outfit worn by Rembrandt in his *Self-Portrait at the Age of 34* at the National Gallery, London (cat. no. 13).[6] Scarcely the daily dress of the seventeenth century, this exotic attire was part of the artist's studio props.

PCS

1 Derby 1827, no. 163, as 'Rembrandt, *Head of a Jewish Rabbi*'.

2 Waagen 1854, vol. III, p. 221.

3 Potterton 1982, pp. 104, 107, notes 6–10; Potterton 1986, p. 36, no. 107.

4 Sumowski, *Gemälde*, vol. I, 1983, p. 615, no. 328 (referring to nos 321, 329, 331).

5 See also Scott 1987, pp. 51–4, no. 17 (as Willem Drost).

6 Potterton 1986, p. 36, no. 107.

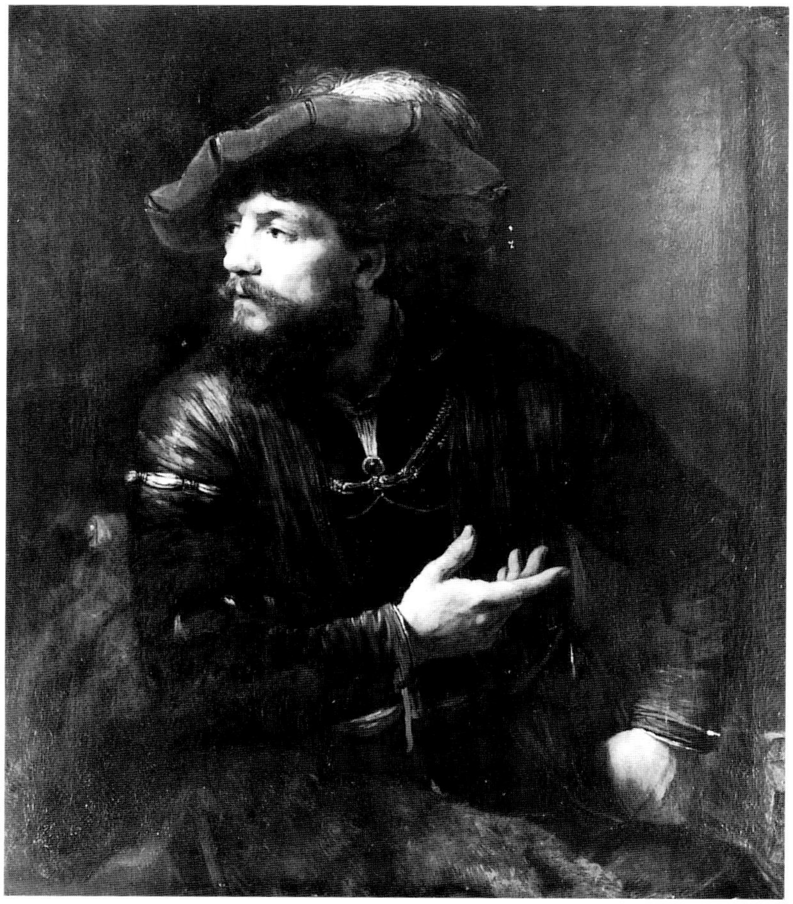

FIG. 63a
Willem Drost
Seated Man Wearing a Feathered Beret
Signed and dated 1654
Canvas
104.0 x 92.0 cm
Sale, New York (Sotheby's), 30 January 1997; present whereabouts unknown

Nicolaes Maes (1634–1693)

Born in Dordrecht in January 1634, Nicolaes Maes learned to draw, according to Houbraken, from an 'ordinary master' before going to Amsterdam to study painting with Rembrandt. Maes's arrival in Amsterdam and the duration of his stay in Rembrandt's workshop are not documented, but must date to between 1646 (the year in which Maes was twelve years old, the age at which an apprentice's training customarily began) and 1653. By December 1653 the nineteen-year-old artist had returned to Dordrecht, where he married in January 1654. The banns describe him as a painter by profession, and, since only qualified masters were permitted by guild regulations to sign their own work, the existence of a picture signed and dated 1653, *Abraham Dismissing Hagar and Ishmael* (Metropolitan Museum of Art, New York), is evidence of his independent status.

Documents in Dordrecht archives confirm Maes's continuous residence in his native town from December 1653 until December 1673. All of his subject paintings – five of biblical themes, one allegory, one still life and approximately forty genre scenes – date from the period *c.*1653 to *c.*1660.

Although indebted to Rembrandt's example, the early religious works, such as the *Sacrifice of Isaac* (cat. no. 64) and the *Adoration of the Shepherds* (cat. no. 66), exhibit a precocious originality in their interpretation of the Bible and of iconographic tradition. During the period 1654 to 1658, Maes also ranked among the most innovative Dutch genre painters. In pictures of spinners, lacemakers, kitchen maids, and mothers with children, he adapted Rembrandt's brush-work and poetic use of light and shade to domestic subjects, investing with an atmosphere of probity and studious concentration these scenes of women absorbed in household tasks. His most original genre paintings are the gently satirical domestic scenes featuring an eavesdropper who exposes the moral shortcomings of another member of the household (cat. no. 65).

In 1655, while at the summit of his productivity as a genre painter, Maes embarked on a long and successful career as a portraitist. During the second half of the 1650s, his output of subject pictures gradually diminished, as the number of portraits he executed steadily increased. From about 1660 until his death in 1693, he devoted himself exclusively to portraiture.

While early collectors of Maes's subject pictures remain unidentified, the known sitters in his portraits – including Jacob de Witt, father of Grand Pensionary Johan de Witt, the political leader of the United Provinces, and the great industrialist Jacob Trip (cat. no. 67) – attest that in this field Maes enjoyed from the outset the patronage of Dordrecht's patriciate and mercantile élite.

On 10 December 1673 Maes and his family moved to Amsterdam, where their presence is confirmed by a document of 20 January 1674. By 1673 the artists who had commanded the top Amsterdam portrait commissions for a generation – Rembrandt, Govaert Flinck (cat. no. 43), Jacob Backer, Bartholomeus van der Helst and Abraham van den Tempel – had all died. Maes must have realized that the field was open to an ambitious and capable portrait painter, and he moved quickly to establish his practice in the great metropolis. If he indeed anticipated a lively demand for his services in Amsterdam, his prediction was an astute one. Houbraken later recalled that 'so much work came his way that it was deemed a favour if one person was granted the opportunity to sit for his portrait before another, and so it remained for the rest of his life'.

Hundreds of surviving portraits from the 1670s and 1680s corroborate Houbraken's report. The majority are pendants in one of two favourite formats: a smaller rectangular canvas with a half-length figure within a painted oval; or a larger canvas with a three-quarter-length figure, usually shown leaning against a fountain, rock or column. In both types, the setting is often a garden or terrace before a sunset sky. Several group portraits of children or families depict the sitters full length, in landscape settings, and Maes executed one corporate group, *Six Governors of the Amsterdam Surgeons' Guild* of *c.*1680–81 (Amsterdam Historical Museum).

A self-portrait by Maes at the age of twenty-three or twenty-four is visible as a reflection in a mirror in the painting known as *The Naughty Drummer*, of *c.*1656–57, in the Fundación Colección Thyssen-Bornemisza, Madrid. A later, more conventional, self-portrait, datable to about 1685 and showing the artist before his easel, is at the Dordrechts Museum.

Maes was buried in the Oude Kerk, Amsterdam, on 24 December 1693.

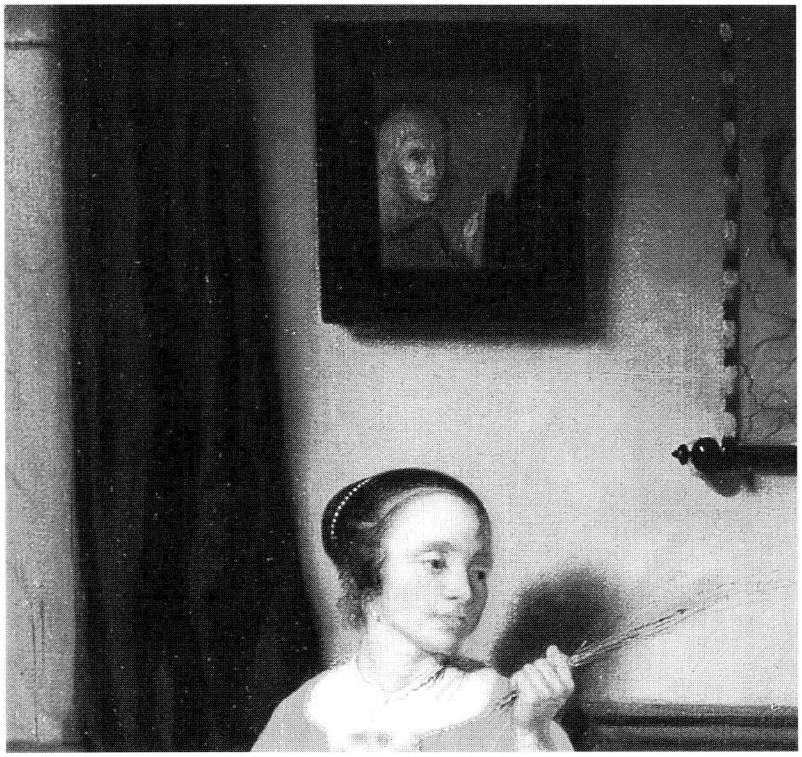

Nicolaes Maes
The Naughty Drummer *c.*1656–57
(detail showing self-portrait in mirror)
Canvas
Fundación Colección Thyssen-Bornemisza, Madrid
From a reproduction

LITERATURE: Houbraken 1718–21, vol. II, 1719, pp. 273–4, 276; Sumowski, *Drawings*, vol. 8, 1984, pp. 3951–4489; Robinson 1987; Sumowski, *Gemälde*, vol. III, 1987, pp. 1951–2174; Bruyn 1988; Robinson 1989; Robinson 1993; Robinson 1996.

WWR

64
Nicolaes Maes
The Sacrifice of Isaac
*c.*1653–54

Canvas
113.0 x 91.5 cm
Private collection, USA

PROVENANCE: [For earlier provenance, see Sumowski, *Gemälde*, vol. III, 1987, p. 2007, no. 1316]; private collection, USA, since 1991.

LITERATURE: Sumowski, *Gemälde*, vol. III, 1987, p. 2007, no. 1316 (with earlier literature); Bruyn 1988, p. 331; Robinson 1989, pp. 147, 148, 150, 153; P. C. Sutton, in The Hague / San Francisco 1990–91, pp. 111–12; C. Tümpel, in Amsterdam / Jerusalem 1991–92, pp. 31, 74; M. Wieseman, in Dordrecht 1992–93, pp. 25, 228, 231–2, cat. no. 58, 233; Sumowski, *Gemälde*, vol. VI, 1995, p. 3627; Robinson 1996, pp. 107–8, 113, 120–1, 155–9, 238–9, checklist no. A-2.

Although neither signed nor dated, the *Sacrifice of Isaac* is securely attributable to Nicolaes Maes and datable to *c.*1653–54 on the evidence of its unmistakable technical and chromatic similarities to the artist's earliest known painting, the 1653 *Abraham Dismissing Hagar and Ishmael* at the Metropolitan Museum of Art, New York.[1] Maes's authorship of the *Sacrifice of Isaac* is further attested by the five preliminary studies for the picture that have come down to us. Long before the painting itself came to light in 1981, these studies had been recognized as characteristic drawings by his hand.

The *Sacrifice of Isaac* is Maes's only painting with potential violence as its theme. While Rembrandt's 1635 picture of this subject (Hermitage, St Petersburg) (Bredius 498) and the workshop variant (Alte Pinakothek, Munich) must have served as his point of departure,[2] Maes's composition is distinguished by its original invention and taut drama. Stretched harshly over the firewood and an adjacent rock, the pale, forcefully illuminated figure of Isaac stands out from the brown tones in surrounding areas of the composition. The viewer's attention is drawn to his tender, creamily painted flesh, and his awkward pose enhances our awareness of his vulnerability. In contrast to his helplessly prostrate son, a resolute Abraham gathers himself into a coil of potentially explosive force, determined to execute unflinchingly the dreadful task God has demanded of him.

In Rembrandt's 1635 painting and in most of the numerous imitations it inspired, the angel either grasps Abraham's arm or swoops urgently down upon him. Depicting an angel who does not intervene physically to halt the slaughter, Maes adhered to the literal sense of the text 'And the angel of the Lord called unto him out of heaven' (Genesis 22:11). To be sure, Maes was not the only Dutch painter to show the angel at some distance from Abraham, and some artists omitted the physical presence of the angel altogether, showing Abraham looking heavenward in response to the invisible messenger's voice.[3]

As prescribed in the biblical text, the event takes place on a remote mountain. About halfway up the left edge of the canvas one can make out

FIG. 64a
Nicolaes Maes
The Sacrifice of Isaac
Pen and ink
13.5 x 10.9 cm
Musée du Louvre, Département des Arts Graphiques, Paris

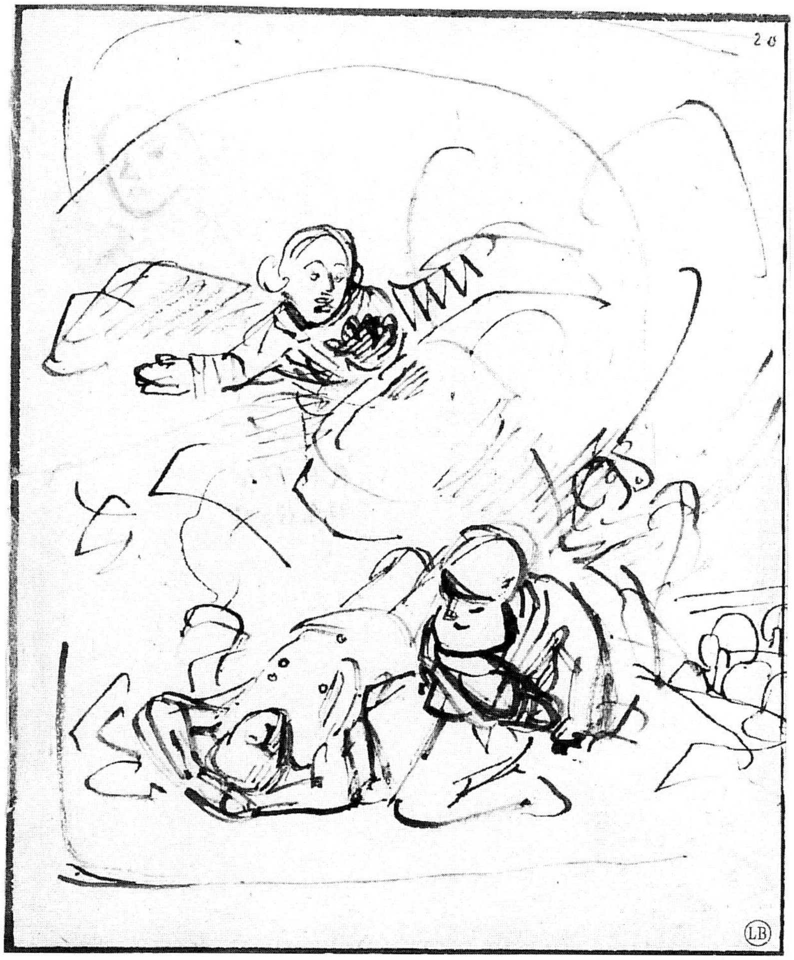

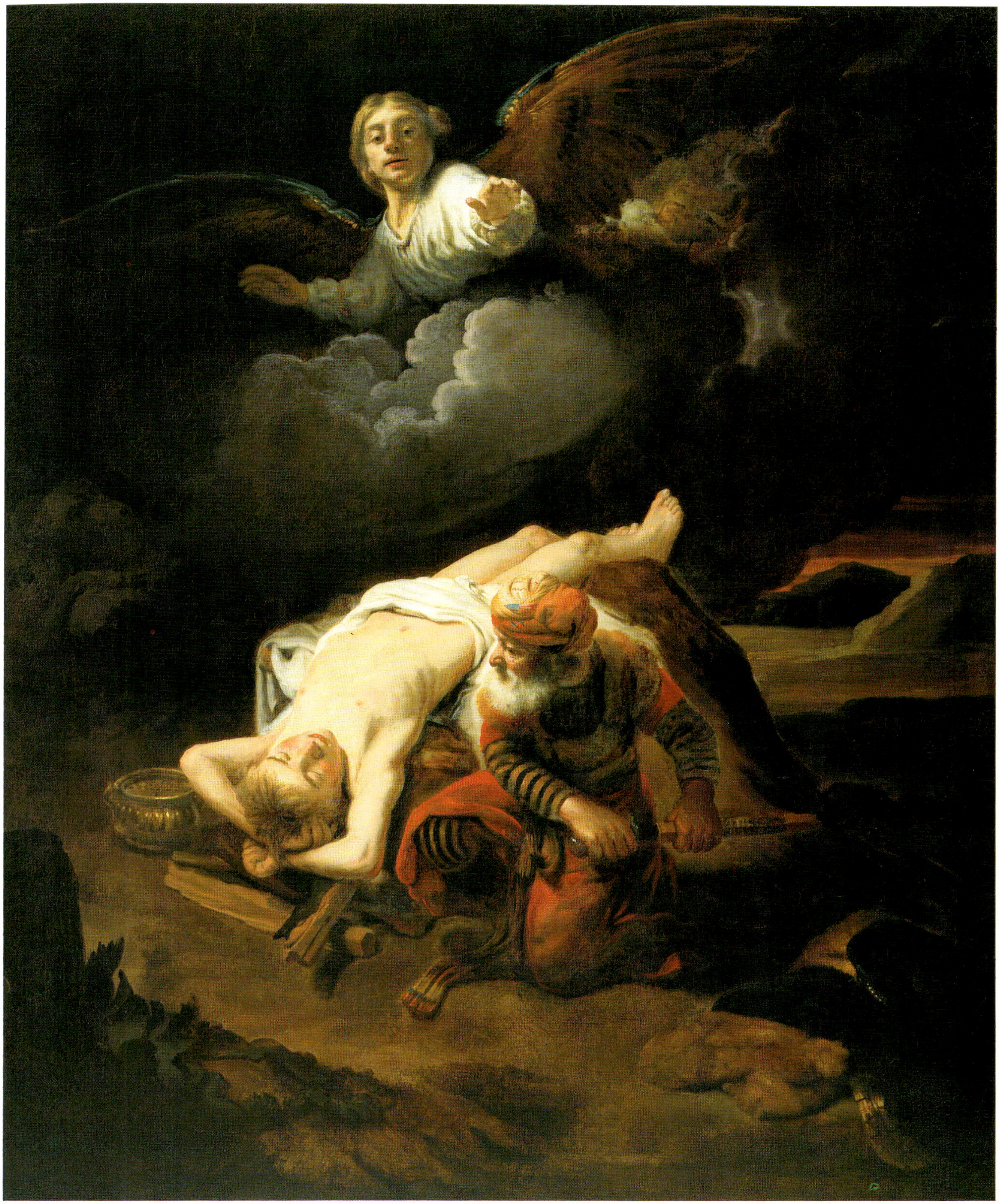

the head and forequarters of the 'ram caught in a thicket by his horns' that God provided for Abraham to offer in sacrifice in place of his son.

The five preliminary studies for the *Sacrifice of Isaac*, the largest number to have survived for one of Maes's pictures, constitute an invaluable record of his use of drawings in the design of a painting. A tiny pen sketch in a private collection, showing only the group of Abraham and Isaac and the head of the angel, evidently marks the genesis of the work,[4] while a composition study in the Louvre probably represents the next stage in its development (fig. 64a).[5] Corrections to the Louvre sheet attest to Maes's struggle with the figure of Abraham. In addition, Maes saw that the patriarch's low crouch and determined reach jeopardized his balance, and rectified the unsteady pose in a separate study now in a private collection.[6] One other detail of the Louvre sketch did not find its way onto the canvas. The ass that accompanied Abraham's party to the mountain appears in the drawing just over the patriarch's shoulder, but no trace of the animal can be found in the painting. On the verso of the Louvre composition, Maes jotted down an alternative idea for the angel's face and left hand.[7] Although hardly more than a scribble, this summary notation introduces the restrained countenance and a hint of the magisterial reserve that will characterize the angel in the finished work. Finally, an elaborate study from a live model represents Isaac in the pose determined in the preliminary designs, although he now reclines on the pile of firewood (fig. 64b),[8] which was not represented in the Louvre sketch, and his figure consequently occupies a higher position than it did in that drawing.

Maes made one major alteration when he executed the figure of Isaac on the canvas. In the life study, he posed the model with his legs bent at the knees, the attitude established in the earlier sketches, while in the painting Isaac extends his legs, his body thus forming a continuous, brightly illuminated diagonal, which unifies the design and serves as the visual and emotional centre of the work.

WWR

1 In an earlier article on this picture (Robinson 1984, p. 540), I presented circumstantial evidence suggesting it might have been executed as late as 1658, but I now agree with Sumowski (*Gemälde*, vol. III, 1987, p. 2007, no. 1316) that the painting's close resemblance to *Abraham Dismissing Hagar and Ishmael* supports a date of *c.*1653–54. For *Abraham Dismissing Hagar and Ishmael*, see Sumowski, *Gemälde*, vol. III, 1987, p. 2006, no. 1315.

2 For Rembrandt's St Petersburg picture and the workshop variant in Munich, see P. van Thiel, in Berlin / Amsterdam / London 1991–92a, pp. 181–3, cat. no. 21, reprs; see also commentary to our cat. no. 74.

3 See DIAL 71 C28.3–4 for examples. C. Tümpel, in Amsterdam / Jerusalem 1991–92, pp. 157–61, surveys the variant types of compositions of Abraham's Sacrifice, particularly in the Rembrandt circle.

4 Sumowski, *Drawings*, vol. 8, 1984, pp. 3972–3, no. 1765c.

5 Sumowski, *Drawings*, vol. 8, 1984, p. 3968, no. 1765a.

6 Sumowski, *Drawings*, vol. 8, 1984, p. 3976, no. 1767 verso.

7 Robinson 1984, p. 543, fig. 5; Sumowski, *Drawings*, vol. 8, 1984, p. 3968, no. 1765a verso.

8 Sumowski, *Drawings*, vol. 8, 1984, p. 3970, no. 1765b.

FIG. 64b
Nicolaes Maes
Reclining Male Nude
Chalk and pen and ink and brush
17.7 x 22.9 cm
The Board of Trustees of the Victoria & Albert Museum, London
V&A Picture Library

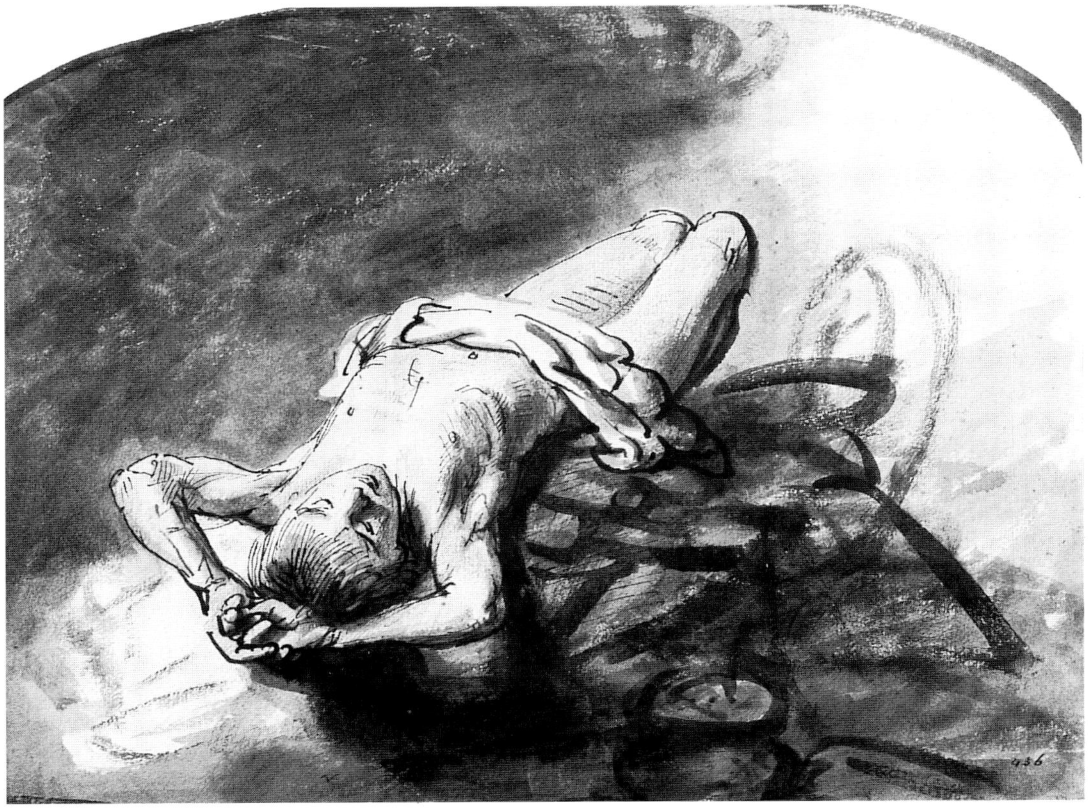

65
Nicolaes Maes
Lovers, with a Young Woman Listening

Signed and dated lower centre *N. MAES. F A° 1657*
Canvas
92.5 x 122.0 cm
Collection Netherlands Institute for Cultural Heritage, Rijswijk, Amsterdam (on loan to the Dordrechts Museum, Dordrecht)

PROVENANCE: For provenance, see Sumowski, *Gemälde*, vol. III, 1987, p. 2023, no. 1370.

LITERATURE: W. Robinson, in Philadelphia / Berlin / London 1984, pp. 242–3, cat. no. 67; Sumowski, *Gemälde*, vol. III, 1987, p. 2023, no. 1370; Robinson 1987, pp. 299–301; Smith 1990, pp. 160, 163; Smith 1990a, pp. 80–1; M. Wieseman, in Dordrecht 1992–93, pp. 240–2, cat. no. 62; Robinson 1996, pp. 203, 204, 209, 213, 214, 244, checklist no. A-15.

Lovers, with a Young Woman Listening is the latest work in a group of six paintings by Maes that feature an interior with an eavesdropper who exposes the peccadilloes of another member of the household. Dated or datable to between 1655 and 1657, the six eavesdropper pictures and the closely related *Idle Servant* of 1655 (fig. 65a) and *Woman Picking the Pocket of a Sleeping Man* (Penrhyn Castle, Bangor) employ gentle satire and an ingenious narrative structure to ridicule the vices of sloth, lust or anger.[1] In these works the eavesdropper or other principal figure smiles engagingly at the viewer, directing our attention to a shrewish housewife who scolds her husband, a drunken man asleep at a table, a kitchen maid napping on the job, or a servant entangled in the embrace of a lover. Maes's narrative gifts, his innovative approach to the representation of interior space, and his talent for inventing expressive poses and gestures and for portraying facial expressions that eloquently convey delicate shades of emotion are nowhere more evident than in these eight works.

All eight paintings carry an explicit didactic meaning. In the *Idle Servant*, Maes represented the sleeping kitchen maid in an attitude his contemporaries associated with the deadly sin of sloth.[2] The consequences of her negligence are laid out in detail: dirty dishes litter the floor, and a cat makes off with the plucked fowl intended for dinner. Some seventeenth-century viewers may have read the image of the cat stealing the meat as a metaphor for seduction and drawn the conclusion that, in her idleness, the servant's thoughts may dwell on love.[3] Like an actor who steps outside a dramatic situation to address the audience directly, the housewife invites us to inspect the evidence of her kitchen maid's indolence. Her smile expresses ridicule and mockery, and the same comic mode is employed to underscore the shortcomings of shrews, slatterns, and swillpots in the other paintings in the group.

A picture of *c.*1650 by the Leiden genre specialist Isaack Koedyck (1617/18–1668) provided the source for both the subject and the compositional scheme of Maes's eavesdropper scenes. Koedyck's lost original is known through

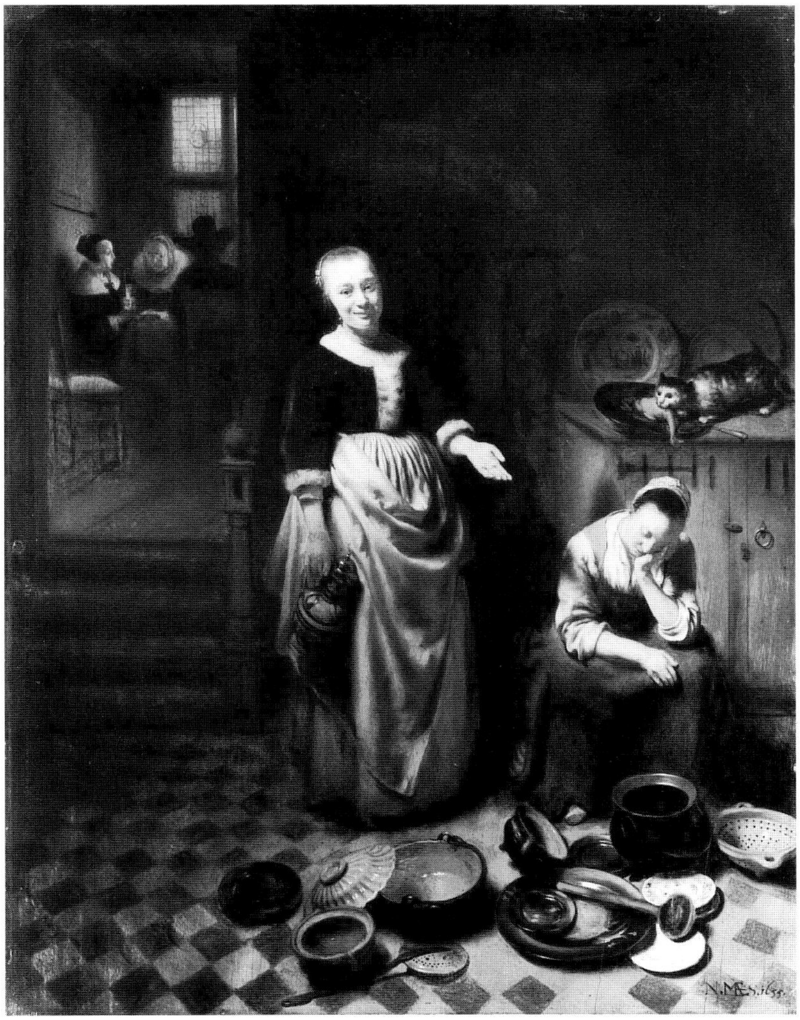

FIG. 65a
Nicolaes Maes
The Idle Servant
Signed and dated 1655
Panel
70.0 x 53.3 cm
The Trustees of the National Gallery, London

a watercolour copy by Willem Joseph Laquy, which carries the inscription *Coedijk pinx* (fig. 65b).[4] One of the earliest of Maes's eavesdropper pictures, *A Young Woman with Two Men in a Cellar, with a Young Woman Listening* of 1655 (fig. 65c),[5] follows Koedyck's composition closely.

The amorous escapades discovered by the eavesdroppers in the cellars and back rooms of the interiors depicted by Maes and Koedyck are illicit, lustful liaisons that would certainly have affronted the moral sensibilities of seventeenth-century viewers. In Koedyck's lost painting the scullery maid has deserted her post in the kitchen and has gone down to the cellar with a man who fondles her beneath her skirt. In case the viewer failed to grasp the didactic message of the work, Koedyck introduced a visual allusion to a popular saying. A dog takes advantage of the servant's negligence and eats from an overturned pot. The image of a dog with its head in an untended pot had figured in the proverbial lore of the Netherlands since the middle of the sixteenth century and is featured in the illustrated proverb collection *Spiegel van den ouden en nieuwen tyt* (Mirror of Olden and Modern Times), first published in 1632, by the prolific and popular Dutch author Jacob Cats.[6] The illustration in Cats's book shows a housewife punishing a kitchen maid because she has left a pot untended. As in Koedyck's lost painting, a dog has seized the opportunity and eaten the stew. In his commentary on the image, Cats explains the practical lesson of the proverb, namely, that anything desirable, if left untended, will lure a predator. Just as the unguarded stew attracts a hungry dog, an open purse will bring a thief or, more relevant to the paintings under discussion, a promiscuous woman will lure a seducer. Even a prudent and clever householder, Cats writes, cannot prevent a lascivious maidservant from having lovers.[7]

Maes's painting of 1657 seen here also features a questionable liaison: a very well dressed man, whose sword and cloak rest on a chair in the foreground, romances the scullery maid. Like her colleague in the *Idle Servant*, she has neglected her duties in the kitchen, allowing the cat to snatch the fowl intended for the guests upstairs. As in the *Idle Servant*, the predatory cat, a visual metaphor analogous to Koedyck's opportunistic dog, may connote a seducer.

The unlikely interior seen in this painting is less a reflection of actual domestic architecture than the product of Maes's ambition to create a complicated spatial effect and a setting appropriate to his narrative. The symmetrical composition, the elaborately contrived recession of the architecture, and the glimpses into adjacent rooms mark the climax of Maes's efforts in rendering interior space.

WWR

1 Sumowski, *Gemälde*, vol. III, 1987, nos 1344, 1349, 1352–1355, 1357, 1370. Robinson 1987, pp. 283–313, attempts to interpret the group.

2 Amsterdam 1976, pp. 145–6, cat. no. 33; C. Brown, in MacLaren / Brown 1991, vol. I, pp. 241–2, no. 207; Sumowski, *Gemälde*, vol. III, 1987, no. 1352.

3 Amsterdam 1976, pp. 145–6, cat. no. 33. Brown cites a proverb from Johan de Brune's *Banket-werk van goede gedagten* (Banquet of Good Thoughts), 1660: 'Een Keuckenmeyt moet d'eene ooghe, naer de panne, en d'ander, naer de Katte hebben' (C. Brown, in MacLaren / Brown 1991, vol. I, p. 241, no. 207).

4 For Koedyck's lost picture, see Bille 1961, vol. II, p. 11. Peter Sutton was the first to call attention to Koedyck's painting as a source for Maes's compositions (Sutton 1980, p. 62, note 34). Koedyck's work probably dates from around 1650, prior to his departure for Batavia, where he is recorded in August 1651. For Koedyck's biography, see C. von Bogendorf-Rupprath, in Philadelphia / Berlin / London 1984, p. 228.

5 Sumowski, *Gemälde*, vol. III, 1987, no. 1349.

6 Cats 1632, p. 104, no. XXXIV. The motto reads: 'Een open pot, of open kuyl, / Daer in steeckt licht een hond sijn muyl' (An open pot or open kettle / A dog will easily stick his snout in it). The dog in the pot figures in a print of *c.*1558 by Frans Hogenberg that illustrates some forty Netherlandish proverbs (Gibson 1977, fig. 43).

7 Cats 1632, p. 104, no. XXXIV.

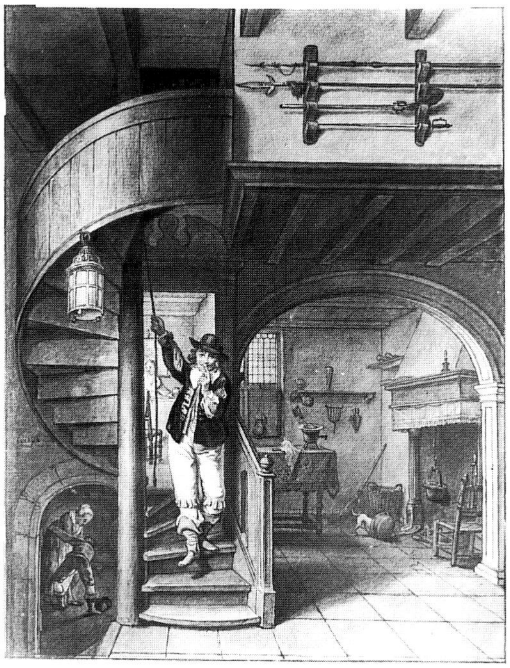

FIG. 65b
Willem Joseph Laquy (1738–1798), after Isaack Koedyck
Eavesdropper
Watercolour
26.0 x 19.5 cm
Amsterdam Historical Museum

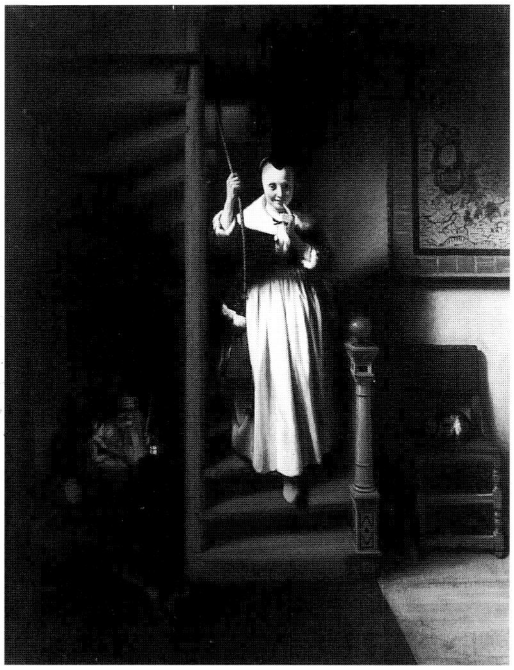

FIG. 65c
Nicolaes Maes
A Young Woman with Two Men in a Cellar, with a Young Woman Listening
Signed and dated 1655
Panel
74.9 x 60.3 cm
The Royal Collection © Her Majesty the Queen

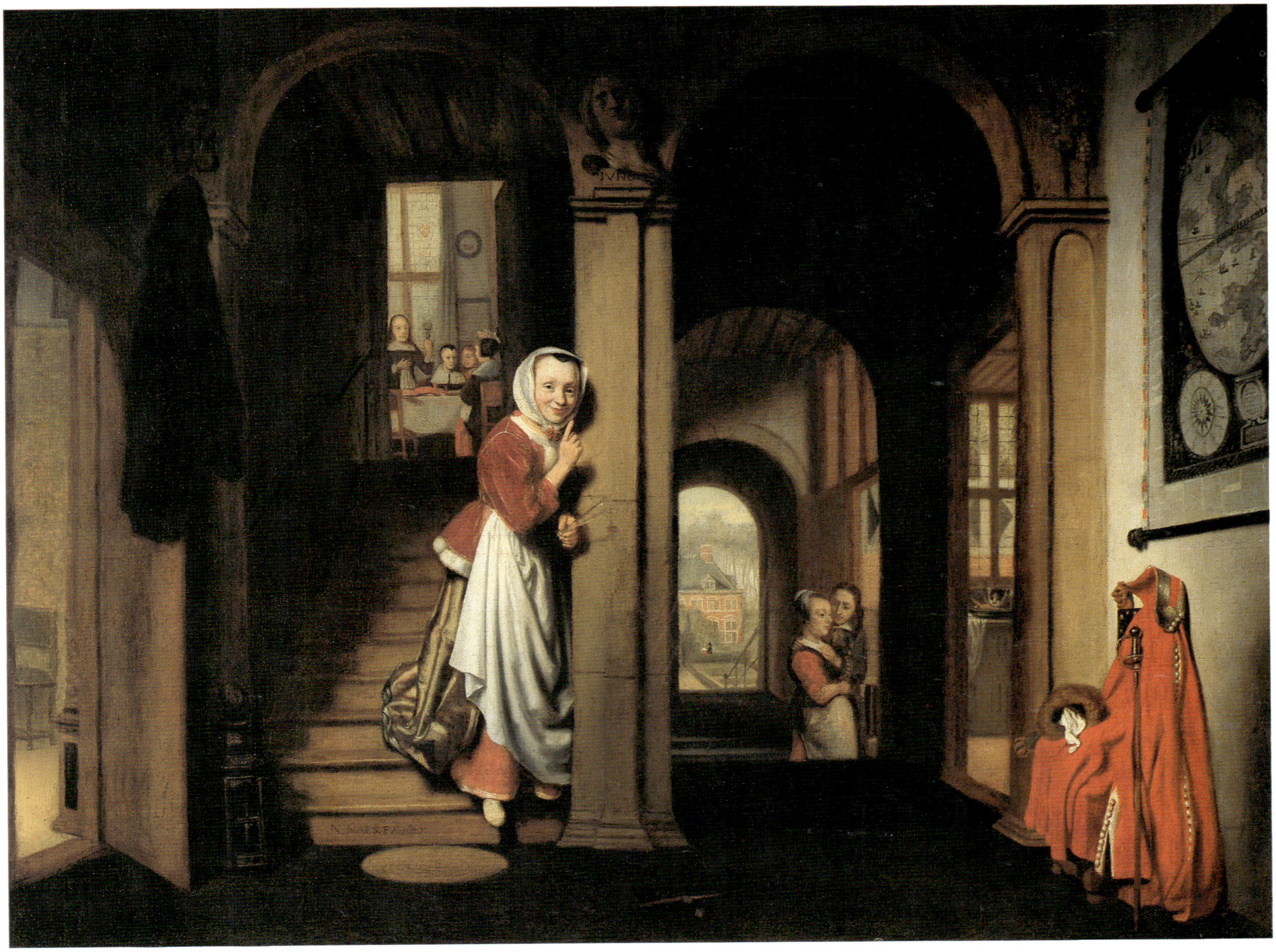

66

Nicolaes Maes

The Adoration of the Shepherds

Signed and dated centre left *N. MAES. 1658*
Panel
59.4 x 87.0 cm
The Montreal Museum of Fine Arts Collection
Purchase, Horsley and Annie Townsend Bequest

PROVENANCE: For provenance, see Sumowski, *Gemälde*, vol. III, 1987, p. 2007, no. 1318.

LITERATURE: Sumowski, *Gemälde*, vol. III, 1987, p. 2007, no. 1318 (with earlier literature); Robinson 1996, pp. 159–62, 239–40, checklist no. A-4.

The Sacrifice of Isaac (cat. no. 64) and the Montreal *Adoration of the Shepherds* are two of only five biblical paintings by Maes that have come down to us. The others are *Christ Blessing Little Children* (National Gallery, London), *Abraham Dismissing Hagar and Ishmael*, 1653 (Metropolitan Museum of Art, New York), and *The Adoration of the Shepherds* (J. Paul Getty Museum, Malibu).[1] The Montreal *Adoration* of 1658 is the latest of these to bear a date.

In his catalogue of the 1789 sale of pictures from the collection of L. B. Coclers, the French dealer and connoisseur Jean-Baptiste-Pierre Le Brun likened Maes's *Adoration* to the best performances of the acknowledged virtuosi of chiaroscuro and candlelight effects:

> This superb painting is of the greatest truth in its various effects of light; Rembran[d]t, Schalcken & Dietricy produced nothing more beautiful of this kind. The works of this master are very rare & this one is worthy of the finest cabinet in Europe.[2]

The eighteenth-century German painter Christian Wilhelm Ernst Dietrich, known as Dietricy, must have agreed with Le Brun's high opinion of the picture: he produced two paintings (fig. 66a) and an etching based closely on Maes's composition.[3] The present work is the only known painting in which Maes experimented with pronounced effects of artificial illumination, and this preoccupation helps account for its *retardataire*, Rembrandtesque character in the context of his more progressive works of the later 1650s, such as *Lovers, with a Young Woman Listening* (cat. no. 65) and other genre pictures.[4]

The Montreal *Adoration* offers an instructive example of Maes's adaptation of pictorial models,

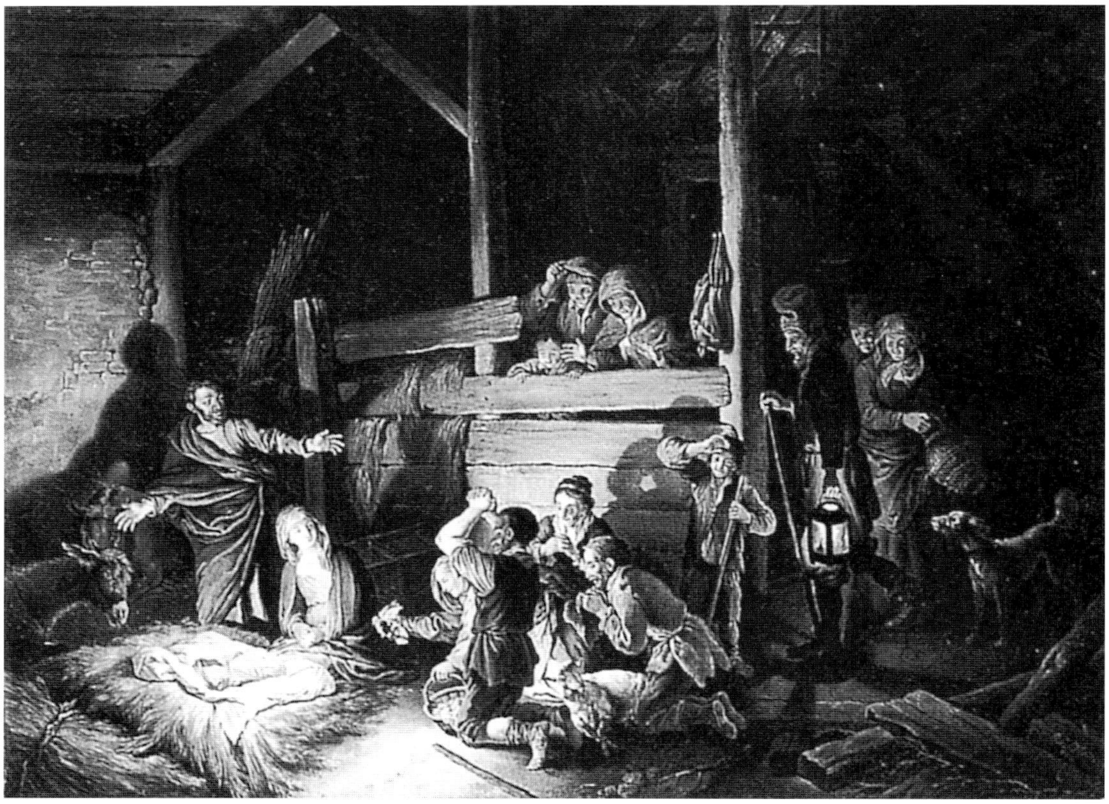

FIG. 66a
Christian Wilhelm Ernst Dietrich
German, 1712–1774
The Adoration of the Shepherds
Signed and dated 176[?]
Canvas
54.9 x 73.0 cm
The Metropolitan Museum of Art, New York

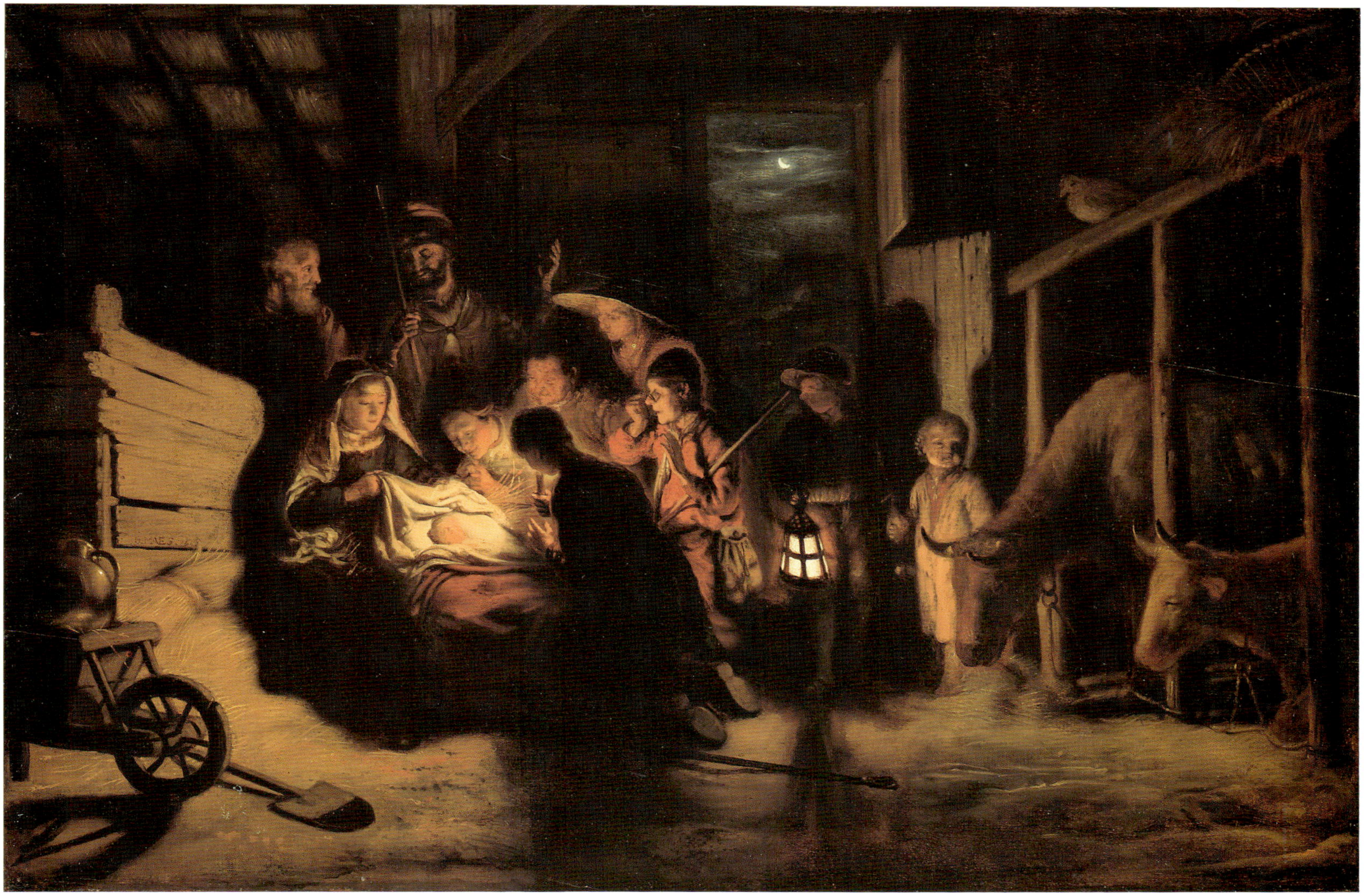

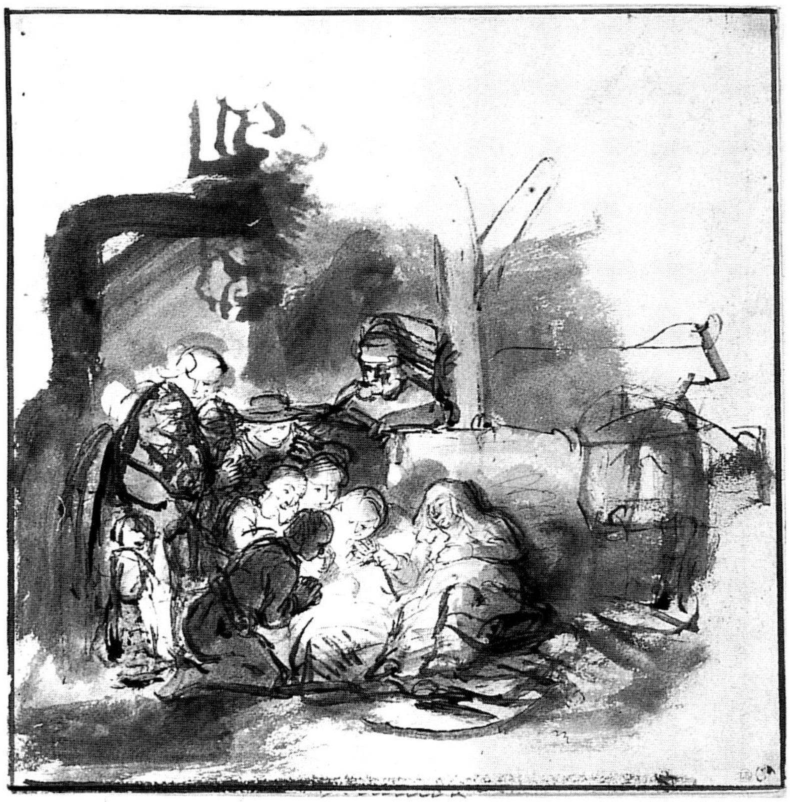

FIG. 66b
Nicolaes Maes
The Adoration of the Shepherds
Chalk and pen and ink and brush, with gouache
21.5 x 20.4 cm
Musée Bonnat, Bayonne

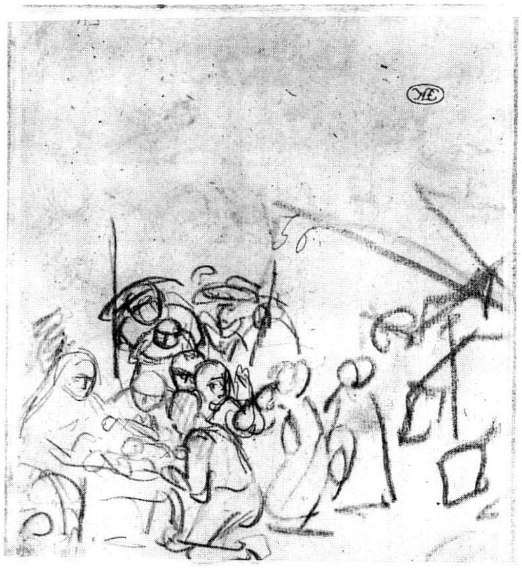

FIG. 66c
Nicolaes Maes
The Adoration of the Shepherds
Chalk
15.8 x 13.6 cm
Museum Boijmans Van Beuningen, Rotterdam

attesting that, even in the case of such a Rembrandtesque painting as this one, he drew inspiration from works by older Rembrandt pupils as well as from those by the master himself.

Rembrandt's *Adoration* of 1646 at the Alte Pinakothek, Munich (Bredius 574) (fig. 61a), is often cited as the model for Maes's composition,[5] but his immediate point of departure must have been a painting of 1647 by Samuel van Hoogstraten, which, although clearly inspired by Rembrandt's Munich picture, is horizontal in format and departs from its model in other significant details (cat. no. 61). In Maes's first compositional project for the *Adoration* (fig. 66b),[6] the shepherds enter from the left, as in Hoogstraten's painting, and the relative positions of the Virgin and Joseph, and particularly Joseph's pose, also recall the poses of the corresponding figures in Hoogstraten's work. While the placement of the Virgin and Child against the rustic boards of a stall also derives from Hoogstraten's composition, the Y-shaped structural support and the thatch and ribs of the roof are taken from a painting of 1646 at the National Gallery, London,[7] a work that is a variant, in reverse, of Rembrandt's Munich *Adoration.*

A red chalk sketch in Rotterdam marks the next stage in the development of the design (fig. 66c).[8] Here, the shepherds enter from the right, as in the London picture and in Maes's finished painting. Despite the summary character of the study, one can recognize several of the figures in the places and poses they will retain in the Montreal work. On the verso of the sheet reproduced as fig. 66b, Maes sketched two cursory red chalk studies of the shepherdess in the wide-brimmed hat.[9] As in the Rotterdam sketch, this figure holds a child, but there she is shown frontally, while here she is seen in profile. This profile view more nearly resembles the figure in the painting, where, however, she no longer holds the child and the angle of her hat brim is different. This figure derives from a similar shepherdess in the London *Adoration.* There, she appears in profile and carries a child, but she does not wear a large hat.

WWR

1 Sumowski, *Gemälde*, vol. III, 1987, pp. 2005–7, nos 1312, 1315, 1317.

2 Sale cat., L. B. Coclers sale, Le Brun, Paris, 9 February 1789, lot 114.T: 'Ce superbe Tableau est de la plus grande vérité dans ses différents effets de lumière; Rembrant, Skaken & Dietricy, n'ont rien produit de plus beau en ce genre. Les ouvrages de ce Maître sont forts rares, & celui-ci est digne du plus beau Cabinet de l'Europe'.

3 For the paintings, see Gerson 1973, p. 213, pl. 44, figs 184–186.

4 Sumowski, *Gemälde*, vol. III, 1987, p. 1953, stresses the retrospective character of the Montreal *Adoration.* Executed after the progressive genre paintings of the mid-1650s, the picture is indebted to models of the 1640s, reminding Sumowski of the mentality of Hendrick Goltzius's *Meisterstiche.* In his view, the Montreal painting, like those engravings, is a virtuoso exercise in the spirit of Rembrandt's art, while the J. Paul Getty Museum *Adoration* (Sumowski, *Gemälde*, vol. III, 1987, no. 1317) has a similar basis in Dürer's work.

5 Schatborn 1970, p. 13, repr.; Sumowski, *Drawings*, vol. 8, 1984, p. 3966, under no. 1765; Sumowski, *Gemälde*, vol. III, 1987, pp. 1953, 2007, no. 1318.

6 Sumowski, *Drawings*, vol. 8, 1984, pp. 4166–7, no. 1861^{x}.

7 C. Brown, in MacLaren / Brown 1991, vol. 1, pp. 331–2, no. 47; vol. 2, pl. 281. Most scholars attribute the London picture to Rembrandt himself, although some assign it to the master's workshop, and some have even suggested that it is by Maes, an attribution rightly dismissed by Brown. See also Tümpel 1993, pp. 246, 250, 423, no. A7 (as Rembrandt workshop).

8 Sumowski, *Drawings*, vol. 8, 1984, pp. 3966–7, no. 1765; Giltaij 1988a, pp. 223–4, no. 113 (verso).

9 Sumowski, *Drawings*, vol. 8, 1984, p. 4535, fig. 107.

67
Nicolaes Maes
Jacob Trip
*c.*1659–60

Canvas
88.0 x 68.0 cm
Szépmüvészeti Múzeum, Budapest

68
Nicolaes Maes
Margaretha de Geer
*c.*1659–60

Canvas
88.0 x 68.0 cm
Szépmüvészeti Múzeum, Budapest

PROVENANCE: For provenance, see Sumowski, *Gemälde*, vol. III, 1987, p. 2028, nos 1396, 1397.

LITERATURE: Sumowski, *Gemälde*, vol. III, 1987, p. 2028, nos 1396, 1397 (with earlier literature); Németh & Van Leeuwen 1992; J. Loughman, in Dordrecht 1992–93, pp. 246–9, cat. nos 64, 65; I. Ember, in Bad Homburg / Wuppertal 1995, p. 80, cat. no. 23; Németh 1996; Robinson 1996, pp. 27–9, 260, checklist nos A-72, A-73.

Between 1657 and 1669 Maes painted a series of eight portraits and replicas depicting the Dordrecht merchant Jacob Trip (*c.*1576–1661) and his wife Margaretha de Geer (1583–1672), one of the most extensive commissions of the artist's career. As far as we know, his earliest Trip portrait is the frontal half-length of Jacob dated 1657, now in the Burrell Collection, Glasgow.[1] The Budapest pendants are neither signed nor dated, but were probably executed in 1659 or 1660. They depict Jacob and Margaretha seated, three-quarter length, each of their figures filling most of the picture surface. Replicas of the Budapest pair, with the sitters set somewhat deeper in the pictorial space, were formerly in the collection of Baron van Wassenaer van Katwijk at Kasteel Nederhemert in Gelderland, where they were destroyed during World War II.[2] Also lost at Kasteel Nederhemert was a portrait by Maes of Margaretha de Geer seated beside a table covered with a red cloth, beneath voluminous folds of red drapery (fig. 68a). It was inscribed *Aet 81* and dated 1665, a date four years after Jacob Trip's death.[3] As Németh and van Leeuwen have ingeniously proposed, this lost painting of Margaretha of 1665 was almost certainly the pendant to Maes's portrait of Jacob Trip at the Mauritshuis, The Hague, which is inscribed *AE' 84* (aged 84) and thus records Trip's appearance in 1659 or 1660 (fig. 67a).[4] Although the date on the Mauritshuis picture is illegible, its technique, colour and design support Németh and van Leeuwen's hypothesis that it is a posthumous portrait of Jacob, based on the Budapest version and executed in 1665 as the pendant to the ex-Nederhemert portrait of Margaretha. Unfortunately, the dimensions of the Nederhemert work are unrecorded, so we cannot confirm that the two pictures were identical in size. Finally, there is another portrait of Margaretha, of the same type, but slightly different in design from the others. Recently acquired by the Dordrechts Museum, Dordrecht, it is dated 1669, and thus depicts the sitter at the age of eighty-five.[5]

The Trip family ranked among the great merchants and industrialists of the seventeenth century. The iron business begun by Elias Trip established the foundation of the family fortune. Elias's stake in the iron trade led the Trips into the manufacture of and commerce in weaponry, their success enhanced by marriage connections to the de Geer clan, renowned armaments dealers who extracted their own raw materials from Swedish copper mines. In addition to his interest in the family iron and armaments businesses, Jacob Trip had dealings in Dordrecht in cloth, wood, charcoal, foodstuffs and lime, and he operated a profitable saltworks across the river in Zwijndrecht.[6]

In 1660, about the time Maes executed the Budapest paintings – and perhaps the replicas formerly at Nederhemert – Louis and Hendrick Trip, sons of Jacob and Margaretha, laid the cornerstone of the Trippenhuis, their palatial Amsterdam residence. The construction of the Trippenhuis coincided with Hendrick Trip's giving a program of commissions for family portraits to Ferdinand Bol and to Rembrandt (cat. no. 23).[7] At the same time, Louis Trip may have ordered portraits of himself and his wife from Bartholomeus van der Helst, and pendants of his parents, in the same large format, from Maes. In any case, Louis Trip eventually owned portraits of himself and his wife by van der Helst as well as one of the sets of Maes's pendants, because in a will of 1683 he bequeathed to his granddaughter 'the largest portrait of the deceased himself and his late wife painted by Van der Helst' and '[the portraits] of the deceased's parents in the same format painted by Maes'.[8]

WWR

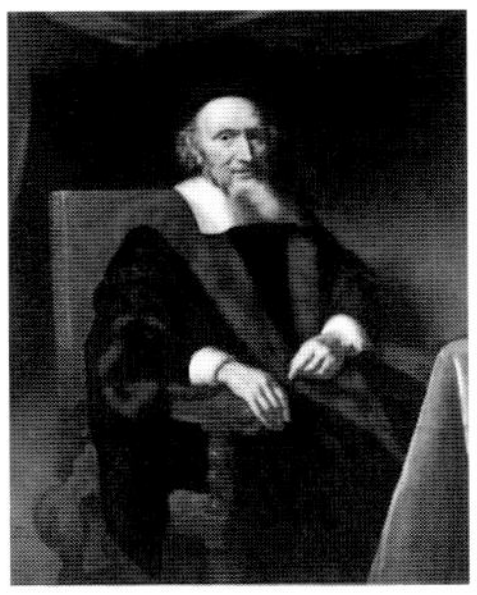

FIG. 67a
Nicolaes Maes
Jacob Trip
Signed and dated 16[...]
Canvas
126.0 x 100.5 cm
Mauritshuis, The Hague
Photograph:
© Mauritshuis,
The Hague, inv. no. 90

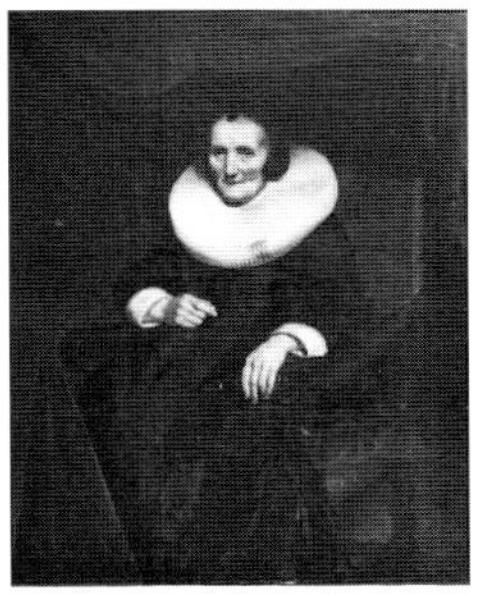

FIG. 68a
Nicolaes Maes
Margaretha de Geer
Signed and dated 1665
Canvas
Dimensions unrecorded
Formerly Baron van Wassenaer van Katwijk collection, Kasteel Nederhemert, Gelderland

1 Sumowski, *Gemälde*, vol. III, 1987, p. 2028, under no. 1396 (listed as at Barbizon House); Robinson 1993, pp. 104–5, fig. 4; Robinson 1996, pp. 27, 255, checklist no. A-52.
2 Vermeulen 1932, pp. 118–19, nos 9, 10, figs 111, 112; Sumowski, *Gemälde*, vol. III, 1987, p. 2028, under nos 1396, 1397; Robinson 1996, pp. 27–9, 260–1, checklist nos A-72a, A-73a.
3 Vermeulen 1932, p. 120, no. 11, fig. 113; Sumowski, *Gemälde*, vol. III, 1987, p. 2028, under no. 1397; Németh & Van Leeuwen 1992, p. 9, fig. 8.
4 For the Mauritshuis portrait of Jacob Trip, see Sumowski, *Gemälde*, vol. III, 1987, p. 2028, under no. 1396; Németh & Van Leeuwen 1992, p. 9; Németh 1996, pp. 79–83.
5 Bode 1914, no. 14; Hofstede de Groot 1908–27, vol. VI, pp. 574, 590, nos 429, 516; Valentiner 1924, p. 66, pl. 61; Sumowski, *Gemälde*, vol. III, 1987, p. 2028, under no. 1397. The picture was purchased by the Dordrechts Museum at a sale in Cologne (Kunsthaus Lempertz), 24 May 1997, lot 1068, repr.
6 Dudok van Heel 1979, pp. 14–15; J. Loughman, in Dordrecht 1992–93, p. 246, cat. nos 64, 65.
7 Dudok van Heel 1979, pp. 14–25.
8 'Het grootste conterfeytsel van hem heer testateur en zijn overleeden huysvrouw, geschildert door Van der Helst', and 'nog het conterfeytsel van sijn heer testateurs vader en moeder van gelijcke groote geschildert door Maes' (Dudok van Heel 1979, pp. 22, 26). Dudok van Heel 1979, p. 26, identifies the Budapest pair as the pendants by Maes cited in Louis Trip's will, but the will may of course refer to the Nederhemert replicas of the Budapest pair, or even to the Mauritshuis/ Nederhemert pair – although the latter pair was executed in the mid-1660s, not *c.*1660. Van der Helst's portraits of Louis Trip and his wife have not been identified.

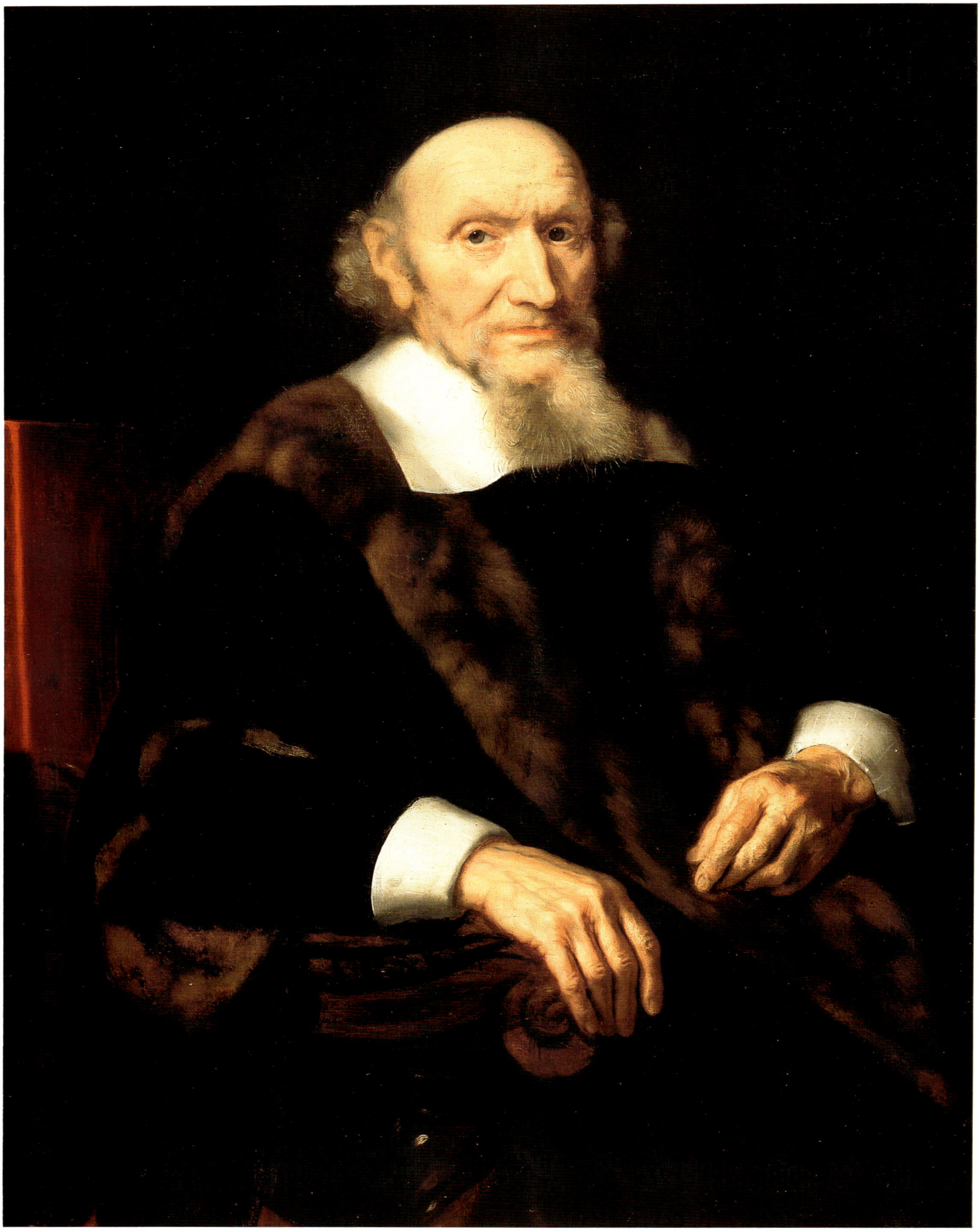

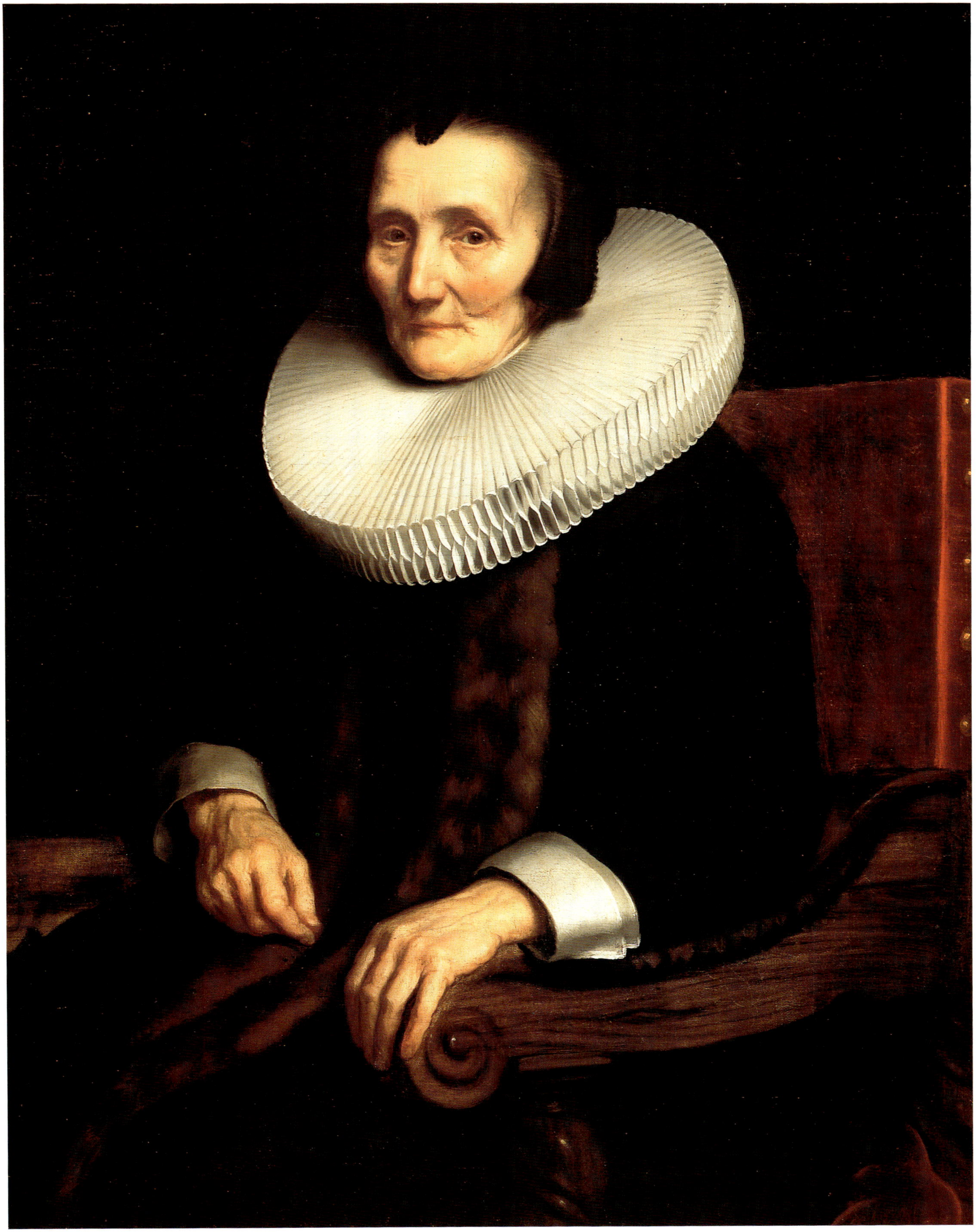

Arent de Gelder (1645–1727)

Baptized in November 1645, Arent (though often incorrectly referred to as Aert) de Gelder came from an affluent Dordrecht family with long ties to the Dutch West India Company. According to Houbraken, de Gelder first studied with Samuel van Hoogstraten (cat. nos 61, 62) before travelling to Amsterdam around 1660 for a two-year period of instruction with Rembrandt. Houbraken characterized de Gelder as following Rembrandt's manner more closely than did any of his pupils ('dat geen van alle hem zoo na gekomen is in die wijze van schilderen'). Returning to his native Dordrecht, he immersed himself in the social and artistic life of the city, serving together with Nicolaes Maes (cat. nos 64–68) and Godfried Schalcken in the civic guard. He was standard-bearer and later lieutenant and captain in the company 'Groot Hoofd'. De Gelder worked in Dordrecht with the Hague painter Augustin Terwesten (1649–1711) and the woodcarver Hendrick Noteman, whose portrait he painted (Dordrechts Museum). He also seems to have been close friends with Jacob Maelaert (1649–1727), a printseller who had studied with Maes.

To judge from the large number of his works that, according to his inventory, remained in his possession at his death, de Gelder in later years seems not to have painted much for patrons or the open market. However, documents and several extant portraits indicate that he worked for some of the members of the important regent class, such as Ernestus van Beveren, Lord of West-Yesselmonde and de Lindt (1685, Rijksmuseum, Amsterdam); he also portrayed the brothers Johan and Willem Abrahamsz de Witt, and Johan van der Burch and his wife (1702, Dordrechts Museum). When he was around seventy-seven years old, in *c.*1722, he also painted the family portrait of the famous Leiden professor and physician Hermanus Boerhaave with his wife and daughter (fig. 72a). De Gelder's family inheritance enabled him to work well into the eighteenth century in a painterly manner that was by then considered out-of-date. De Gelder remained a bachelor all his life and died in August 1727 in Dordrecht; his inventory was completed the following month. It is recorded in full by von Moltke (1994).

Primarily a history painter, as we have seen de Gelder also painted a few portraits. Inspired by Rembrandt's last manner, he developed his own highly personal style, which combined daring brushwork – often applied wet-into-wet – textured veils of paint, and a richly saturated palette.

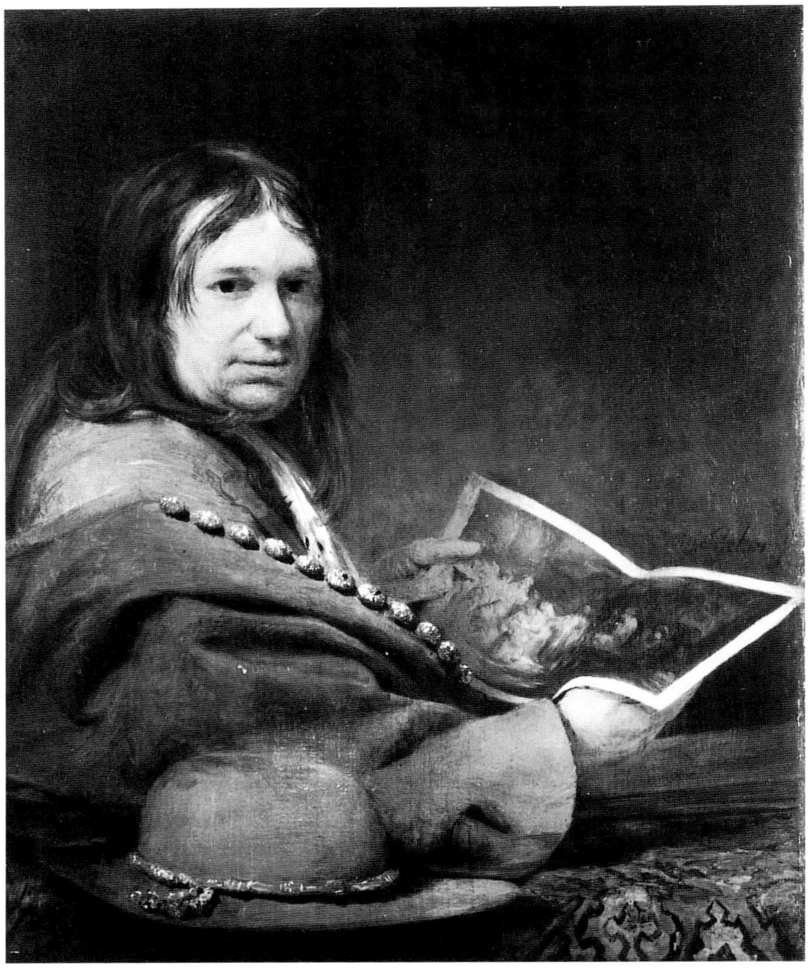

Arent de Gelder
Probable Self-Portrait, Holding Rembrandt's Hundred Guilder Print (cf. cat. no. 111)
Signed
Canvas
79.0 x 64.0 cm
Hermitage, St Petersburg

LITERATURE: Houbraken 1718–21, vol. III, 1721, pp. 206–9; Lilienfeld 1914; Sumowski, *Gemälde*, vol. II, 1985, pp. 1154–277; Von Moltke 1994, pp. 200–4.

PCS

69
Arent de Gelder
King Ahasuerus Condemning Haman
*c.*1680

Signed upper right *A. de Gelder f.*
Canvas
80.5 x 96.5 cm
National Gallery of Victoria, Melbourne;
Felton Bequest 1934

PROVENANCE: Said to have come from a private collection, Paris; with dealer Douwes, Amsterdam, 1934; Felton Bequest 1934.

LITERATURE: Sumowski, *Gemälde*, vol. II, 1985, p. 1161, no. 727; Von Moltke 1994, pp. 35, 75, no. 31; J. Boonen, in Amsterdam / Jerusalem / Münster 1991–94, p. 109; Hoff 1995, pp. 131–2.

King Ahasuerus (Xerxes) of Persia married the beautiful Esther, unaware that she was Jewish. Having discovered that the minister Haman was planning to massacre the Jews, Esther's uncle Mordecai asked her to intercede with the king. Risking her own life in requesting an audience that was forbidden, Esther dressed in her finest robes and went before Ahasuerus to plead for her people. The king spared the Jews and condemned Haman, the moment depicted here; Haman was subsequently to be hanged from the gallows that he had prepared for Mordecai (Esther 6:19, 7:1–3).

Although Esther had long been regarded as prefiguring the Virgin in her role as intercessor, the story of Esther grew in popularity in the seventeenth century, featuring prominently in literature, plays and history paintings. In their struggle for independence from Spain and for religious freedom, the Dutch identified with the Book of Esther's tales of the persecution and triumph of the Jews. Theatrical performances even likened the evil Haman to the hated Duke of Alba, and the good Mordecai to William of Orange, the country's founder. Among Rembrandt's pupils and followers, Arent de Gelder was especially fascinated by the Esther story, repeatedly depicting its episodes in a highly original series of paintings dating from 1680 to 1687. Although D. Lettieri hypothesized that de Gelder planned a cycle,[1] the differing formats and dimensions of the canvases make the theory unlikely.

Representations of the story of Esther multiplied following the appearance of Philips Galle's print series of 1564 after designs by Maarten van Heemskerck. The Pre-Rembrandtists, Pieter Lastman and Jan Tengnagel, painted Esther themes (for example, the *Wrath of Ahasuerus*, attributed to Tengnagel (formerly de Hoogh Collection, de Bilt, Utrecht)),[2] and Jan Lievens executed the large and ambitious *Feast of Esther*, long attributed to Rembrandt (North Carolina

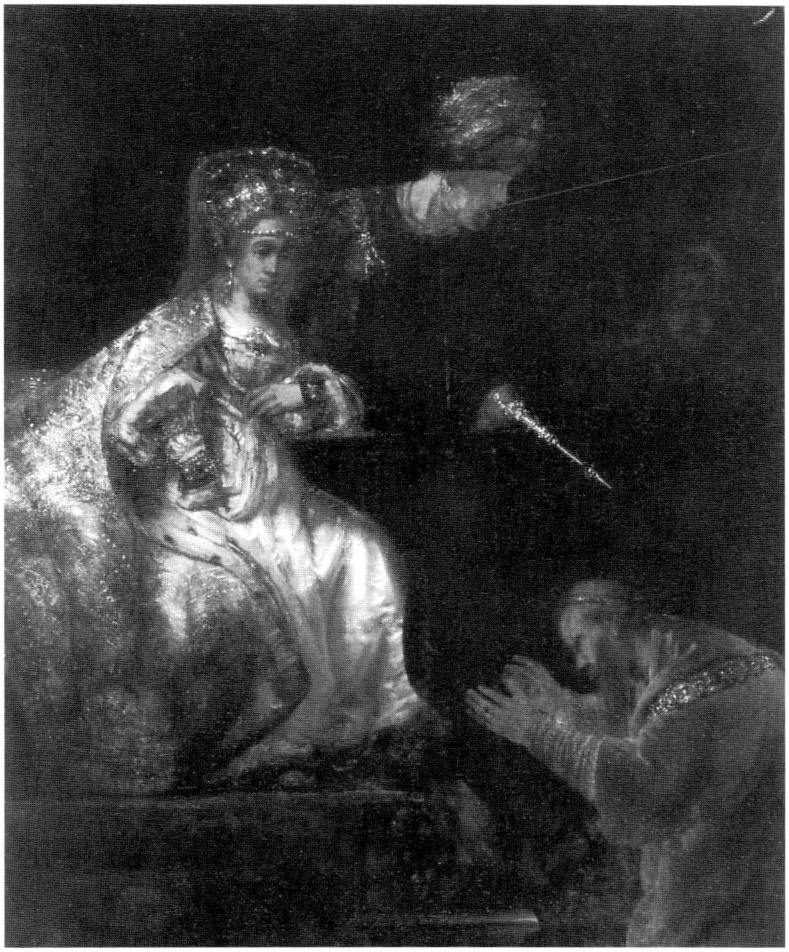

FIG. 69a
School of Rembrandt
Haman Begging for Mercy
Canvas
235.0 x 190.0 cm
National Museum of Art, Bucharest
From a reproduction

Museum of Art, Raleigh). Rembrandt's own *Haman and Ahasuerus at the Feast of Esther* (Pushkin Museum, Moscow) (Bredius 530) would undoubtedly have been known to his pupil de Gelder, since the latter painted the same subject, employing a similar composition (Musée de Picardie, Amiens).[3] De Gelder may also have known the Rembrandt School painting *Haman Begging for Mercy*, which depicts the king condemning his wicked minister from on high with a long pointed sceptre as Haman sinks to his knees (fig. 69a).[4]

In the present work de Gelder greatly enhanced the drama by compressing and concentrating the action around the three figures assembled at the banquet table. The looming figure of the Persian king, now gripping a dagger instead of the symbolic sceptre, turns menacingly towards the cowering Haman. As J. Boonen observed,[5] de Gelder also depicted Ahasuerus seated at the banquet table, holding a dagger and condemning Haman, in a painting at the Barber Institute of Fine Arts, Birmingham.[6] Boonen also referred to the *King Ahasuerus Presenting Mordecai with His Ring* (Statens Museum for Kunst, Copenhagen), a three-figured, horizontal composition that complements the present design.[7] Haman's terrified gesture in the Melbourne painting, where he covers his face with his hands, may recall the biblical passage (Esther 7:8): 'As the word went out of the king's mouth, they covered Haman's face'. J. W. von Moltke correctly observed that this is one of de Gelder's most accomplished works in terms of composition and expressiveness.[8] We also may appreciate the artist's remarkably innovative palette and brushwork in rendering the different textures and surfaces; for example, in the figures' exotically layered and beturbaned clothing, the glint of the tazza and the rapier, or the spongy peel of several of the artist's beloved oranges. As other writers have observed, before the arrival of Goya more than a century later there was scarcely an artist who rivalled de Gelder's daring brushwork.

PCS

1 Lettieri 1980, pp. 69–86.
2 Bauch 1960, fig. 81.
3 Von Moltke 1994, pp. 74–5, no. 30, pl. XVI; Sumowski, *Gemälde*, vol. II, 1985, no. 731.
4 Bredius / Gerson 1969, no. 522. The *Corpus* (vol. III, 1989, pp. 493–5, no. B9) suggests that this painting originated in Rembrandt's studio around 1635, being completely reworked there around 1660–65).
5 J. Boonen, in Münster 1991, p. 109.
6 Von Moltke 1994, pp. 72–3, no. 26, pl. 26; Sumowski, *Gemälde*, vol. II, 1985, no. 739.
7 Von Moltke 1994, p. 76, no. 33, pl. XVIII; Sumowski, *Gemälde*, vol. II, 1985, no. 742.
8 Von Moltke 1994, p. 35.

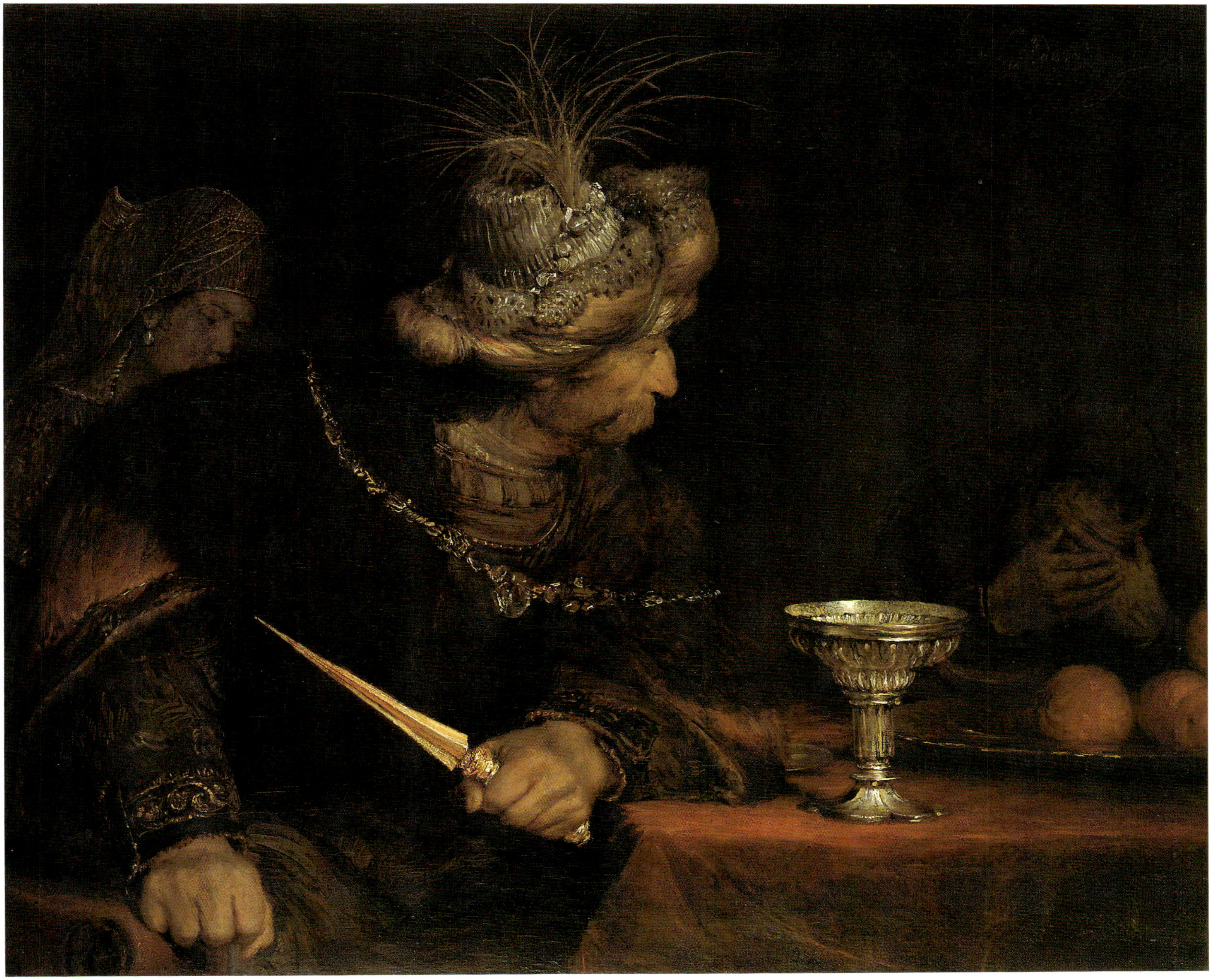

70
Arent de Gelder
Edna Blessing Tobias and Sarah
*c.*1700?

Signed upper right *A De Gelder f.*
Canvas
88.0 x 112.0 cm
Collection Netherlands Institute for Cultural Heritage, Rijswijk, Amsterdam (on loan to the Museum Catharijneconvent, Utrecht)

PROVENANCE: (Possibly) Sale, A. de Lange, Amsterdam, 12 December 1803, lot 36, to Josi for 99 fl.; Lady Florence Pelham-Clinton-Hope; with dealer J. Goudstikker, Amsterdam, 1929; with dealer Douwes, Amsterdam; with dealer D. Katz, Dieren, 1939; sale [Goudstikker et al.], Berlin, 12 March 1941, lot 42, repr.; Rijksdienst Beeldende Kunst, The Hague (now Netherlands Institute for Cultural Heritage); on loan to Museum Catharijneconvent, Utrecht.

LITERATURE: Van Fossen 1969, p. 249, no. 39; G. Jansen, in Amsterdam / Groningen 1983, pp. 168–9, cat. no. 39; Sumowski, *Gemälde*, vol. II, 1985, p. 1169, no. 762; Schwartz 1986, pp. 58–9, cat. no. 24; Schillemans 1989, pp. 51–3, no. 9; Rijksdienst Beeldende Kunst 1992, p. 104, no. 784; Sluiter 1992, p. 13, no. 10; J. Boonen, in Amsterdam / Jerusalem / Münster 1991–94, p. 296, cat. no. 63; Von Moltke 1994, pp. 43, 81–2, no. 45.

FIG. 70a
Arent de Gelder
Tobias in the House of Raguel
Signed
Canvas, 113.0 x 154.0 cm
Otto Naumann Ltd., New York

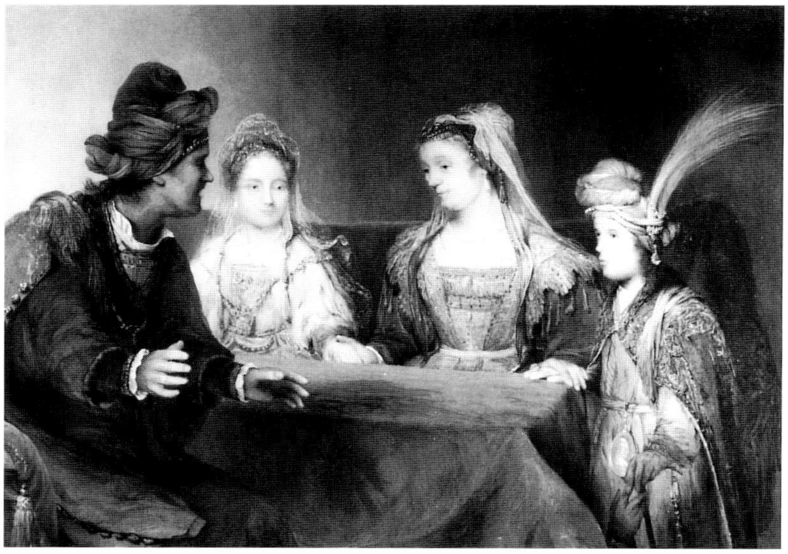

The subject of this painting has been much discussed. When a picture that was probably the present work was catalogued for auction in Amsterdam in 1803 it was described as 'A Fortune teller who looks into a young man's hand. Beside him stands a young woman who looks on thoughtfully'. In his dissertation on de Gelder, D. van Fossen described the scene as 'Hanna [Edna in the Septuagint, or Greek translation of the Hebrew Bible], the wife of Raguel, giving Tobias and Sarah her blessing', citing Tobit 7:15 from the Roman Catholic Vulgate as the source.[1] However, as Sumowski and G. Jansen both pointed out, it is Raguel rather than his wife who according to the text blesses their daughter and son-in-law.[2] Sumowski further proposed that the scene depicts Anna blessing her son, Tobias, and daughter-in-law, Sarah, after their return to Nineveh (Tobit 11:18). However, C. Tümpel points out that the iconography for that subject is very different. He proposes that the key to the subject of the present work resides in the fact that de Gelder consulted the Dutch *Statenbijbel* (published in 1637) rather than the Vulgate.[3] There Raguel's blessing of the young couple is followed by a short speech by Edna to Tobias, at the end of which she entrusts her daughter Sarah to him (Tobit 10:13).

Support for de Gelder's consulting the *Statenbijbel* is provided by the fact that he seems to have referred to it on other occasions; for example, like Rembrandt before him, de Gelder in his painting in Rotterdam apparently followed the specific text from the *Statenbijbel* in depicting Abraham visited by two angels and Jehovah himself rather than by three angels only, as is customary in the pictorial iconography.[4]

Although the Dutch Reformed Church, of which de Gelder was a member, was sceptical of the Apocrypha, it recognized these texts, including the Book of Tobit, but added a commentary to the *Statenbijbel* disclaiming their veracity. It is noteworthy, as J. W. von Moltke has observed, that de Gelder's three paintings of scenes from the Book of Tobit do not depict the most popular themes of Tobias's journey with the angel: his catching of the fish, the healing of his father's blindness, or the exorcism on his wedding night. Instead they take up less common themes related to Tobias's marriage to Sarah: *Tobias in the House of Raguel* (fig. 70a); the *Marriage Contract of Tobias and Sarah* (fig. 70b); and the present subject.[5]

De Gelder seems to have been especially drawn to subjects depicting the sealing of covenants, rituals of sanctification, and the composition of legal documents (his brother was a legal scholar). Nothing if not an independent spirit, he was a revolutionary not only in advancing painterly techniques but also in his personal taste in subject matter, which seems to have expressed his personal belief in the enduring value of the law and the social value of rites.

PCS

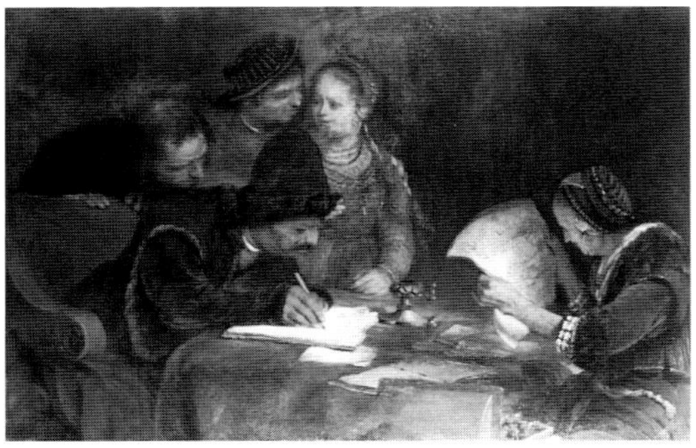

FIG. 70b
Arent de Gelder
The Marriage Contract of Tobias and Sarah
Canvas
94.5 x 143.0 cm
Royal Pavilion, Art Gallery & Museums, Brighton and Hove

1 Van Fossen 1969, p. 249, no. 39.
2 Sumowski, *Gemälde*, vol. II, 1985, p. 1169, no. 762; G. Jansen, in Amsterdam / Groningen 1983, pp. 168–9, cat. no. 39 (as 'The Blessing of Tobias and Sarah?').
3 Reported by Von Moltke 1994, p. 43.
4 Von Moltke 1994, pp. 27, 60, no. 1; Sumowski, *Gemälde*, vol. II, 1985, no. 759.
5 Von Moltke 1994, p. 43, nos 43–45; see also Sumowski, *Gemälde*, vol. II, 1985, p. 1163, no. 733 *(Marriage Contract of Tobias and Sarah).*

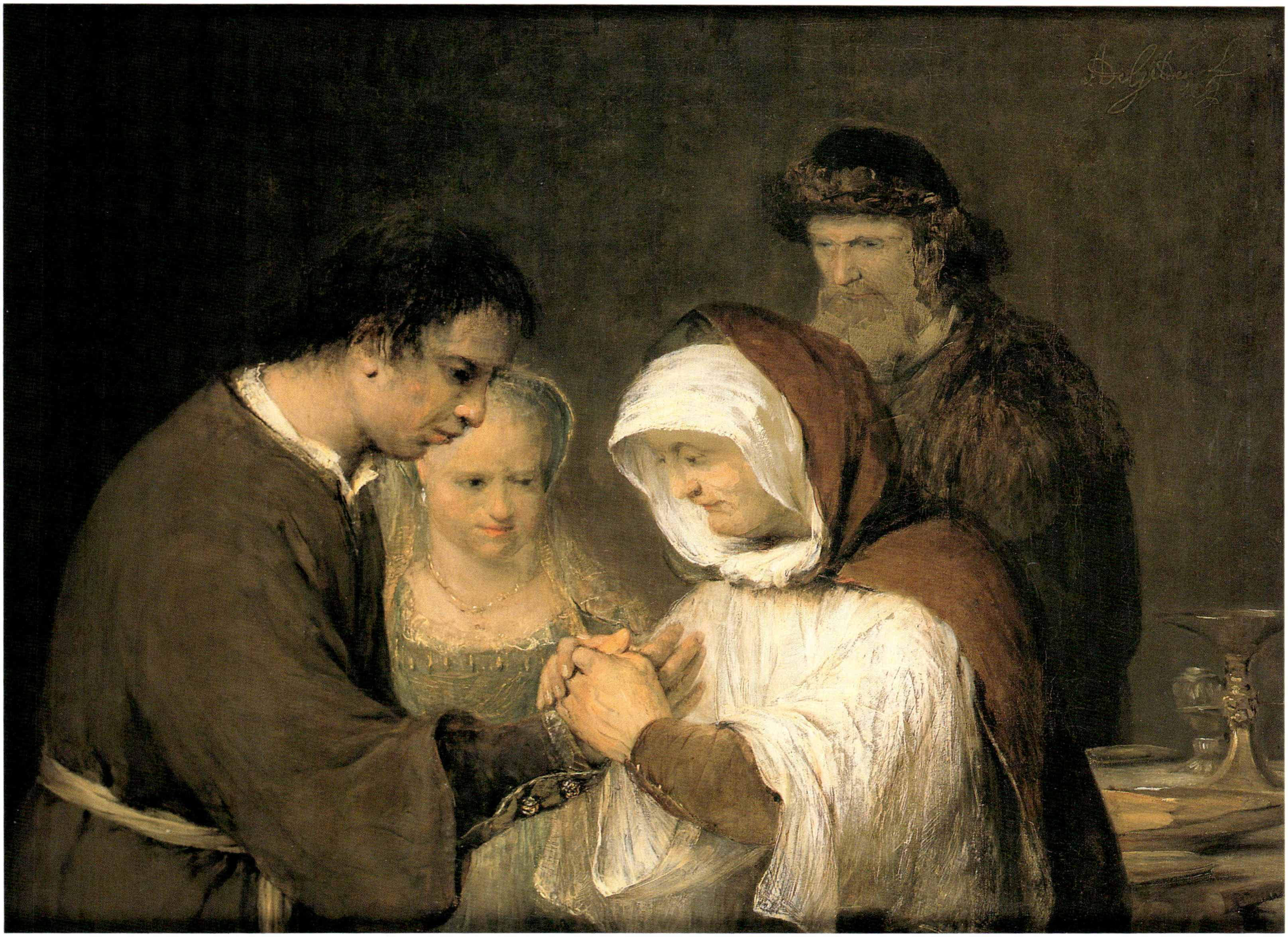

71
Arent de Gelder
Homer Dictating to Scribes
*c.*1700–10

Signed upper left *A. [de] Geld[er] f.*
Canvas
101.0 x 127.5 cm
Ernest Wadsworth Longfellow Fund
Museum of Fine Arts, Boston

PROVENANCE: Sale, widow of Pieter Steyn et al., The Hague (Rietmulder), 7–8 October 1783, lot 65 (dimensions given as 'hoog 38, breed 48 duim'); sale, Amsterdam (Van der Schley), 23–24 May 1798, lot 67 (39 x 50 duim), to Berkenbosch for 26 fl.; Maréchal Soult, Paris; his sale, Paris (George ... Laneuville), 19–22 May 1852, lot 150 (as 'Ecole de Rembrandt', 99 x 124 cm), to Bonnefonds; Beaumont Collection, Paris; acquired in 1939.

LITERATURE: Lilienfeld 1914, pp. 188–9, nos 147–148; Cunningham 1939, pp. 189–90; Wilmington 1951, cat. no. 12; De Vries, Tóth-Ubbens & Froentjes 1978, p. 174; Sumowski, *Gemälde*, vol. II, 1985, p. 1168, no. 760; J. Bruyn, in Berlin / Amsterdam / London 1991–92a, p. 86; Frankfurt 1993, pp. 196–7, cat. no. 31; Von Moltke 1994, pp. 45, 95, no. 76; Giltaij 1997, p. 65.

When this painting was in the collection of Maréchal Soult in Paris it was only attributed to the School of Rembrandt and was described thus: 'an old village schoolmaster, with white beard, seated in a large armchair and leaning on his cane, watches over his students as they write'.[1] As late as 1985 it was still catalogued at the Museum of Fine Arts, Boston, as a schoolmaster. The attribution to de Gelder, confirmed by the remnants of a signature still visible today, had been restored by C. Lilienfeld as early as 1914 and supported by C. Cunningham in 1939 when the work was acquired by Boston.[2] H. Gerson was the first to correctly identify the subject as blind Homer dictating to his scribes, linking the painting to Rembrandt's fragmentary *Homer* now in the Mauritshuis, The Hague (Bredius 483) (fig. 71a), as well as to the preparatory drawing for the latter, from Stockholm (cat. no. 97).[3]

De Gelder reverses Rembrandt's composition but clearly takes over Homer's hand gesture, staff and general appearance, as well as aspects of his costume. As Ben Broos has pointed out, the features of Rembrandt's Homer were probably inspired by a copy of an antique portrait bust, which may have been in his own collection,[4] although de Gelder's Homer is more gaunt and individualized. Before Rembrandt's painting was damaged and cut down it was described in the 1678 inventory of the family of the Sicilian collector Don Antonio Ruffo (1610–1678), who commissioned the work, as depicting 'Homer seated, instructing two pupils half length' and it measured approximately 206.4 x 154.8 cm.[5] The Stockholm drawing includes only one scribe but probably adumbrates Rembrandt's early thoughts on the design. Although two youths are mentioned as visible in de Gelder's painting when it is described in the catalogue of its earliest known sale (widow of Pieter Steyn, The Hague, 7–8 October 1783, lot 65), and even Gerson (1968) noticed only two,[6] de Gelder actually includes a battery of four scribes fervently recording the poet's words. As J. W. von Moltke has observed, the heavy wooden armchair in which Homer sits in de Gelder's painting recurs in other works by the artist, including the so-called *Dr Faust* (Goethe-Museum, Frankfurt) and a *Portrait of a Young Man* (Niedersächsisches Landesmuseum, Hannover).[7]

De Gelder's painting has been dated variously, but probably was executed around the first decade of the eighteenth century.[8] Thus it was in all likelihood painted a full forty years after de Gelder probably saw Rembrandt's painting (fig. 71a), possibly only in an incomplete state in the studio. Don Antonio Ruffo also owned Rembrandt's *Aristotle Contemplating the Bust of Homer* (Metropolitan Museum of Art, New York) (Bredius 478) (p. 27, fig. 8) and an 'Alexander the Great' (usually, though uncertainly, identified with Rembrandt's *Man in Armour* at the Glasgow Art Gallery and Museum (cat. no. 15), or with the *Pallas Athena*(?), possibly by Rembrandt, at the Museu Calouste Gulbenkian, Lisbon (fig. 15b)). Apparently conceived as part of a series of half-lengths by various artists, the *Homer* is mentioned in a document of July 1661 and in another of 1662, which states that it was returned from Messina to Amsterdam in 1662 to be completed. Today it bears the remnants of a signature and date *(andt f 1663)*, suggesting that it was finished the following year. It was finally returned to the Sicilian patron in late 1664.[9] Rembrandt had probably already been thinking about a Homer theme as much as ten years earlier, since he had executed a drawing, dated 1652, of *Homer Reciting Verses* (Six Collection, Amsterdam) (Benesch 913) (p. 327, fig. 9), a work dedicated to his friend Jan Six in the latter's *album amicorum*, the *Pandora*.[10] In an article on Rembrandt and Homer, F. Schmidt-Degener called attention to the fact that the Italian painter Pierfrancesco Mola also seems to have been influenced by Rembrandt's *Homer* (specifically, in his painting at the Galleria Nazionale, Rome), an interesting and relatively rare case of an Italian contemporary's response to Rembrandt.[11]

PCS

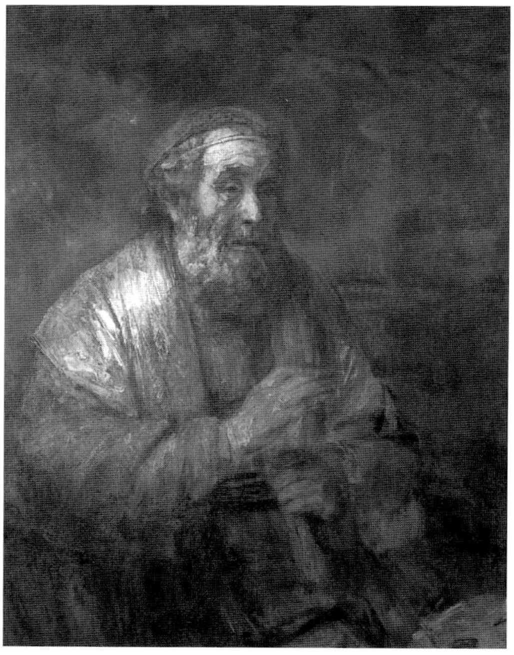

FIG. 71a
Rembrandt
Homer
Signed and dated 1663
Canvas (fragment)
107.0 x 82.0 cm
Mauritshuis, The Hague
Photograph: © Mauritshuis, The Hague, inv. no. 584

1 Sale cat., Maréchal Soult sale, Paris (George ... Laneuville), 19–22 May 1852, lot 150: 'Ecole de Rembrandt, Le Maître d'école. Un vieux magisteur de village, à barbe blanche, assis dans un grand fauteuil et appuyé sur sa canne, surveille des enfants occupés à ecrire'.
2 Lilienfeld 1914, pp. 188–9, nos 147–148; Cunningham 1939, pp. 189–90.
3 Gerson 1968, p. 139.
4 Broos 1987, p. 305 (see also commentary to our cat. no. 97).
5 Giltaij 1997, p. 61, Appendix A, VIII, no. 23.
6 Gerson 1968, p. 139.
7 Von Moltke 1994, pp. 44, 94–5, 104, nos 75, 94, pls 75, XL; Sumowski, *Gemälde*, vol. II, 1985, nos 778, 812.
8 Cunningham 1939, p. 189 (as *c.*1710); Sumowski, *Gemälde*, vol. II, 1985, p. 1168, no. 760 (as about 1700); Von Moltke 1994, p. 95, no. 76 (as about 1700/10).
9 De Vries, Tóth-Ubbens & Froentjes 1978, pp. 174–8; and see esp. Giltaij 1997, pp. 57–66.
10 Benesch 1973, vol. V, no. 913, fig. 1190.
11 Schmidt-Degener 1915, pp. 15–24; for Mola's painting, see Cocke 1972, pp. 55–6, no. 43, fig. 138; for discussion, see Giltaij 1997, pp. 65–6.

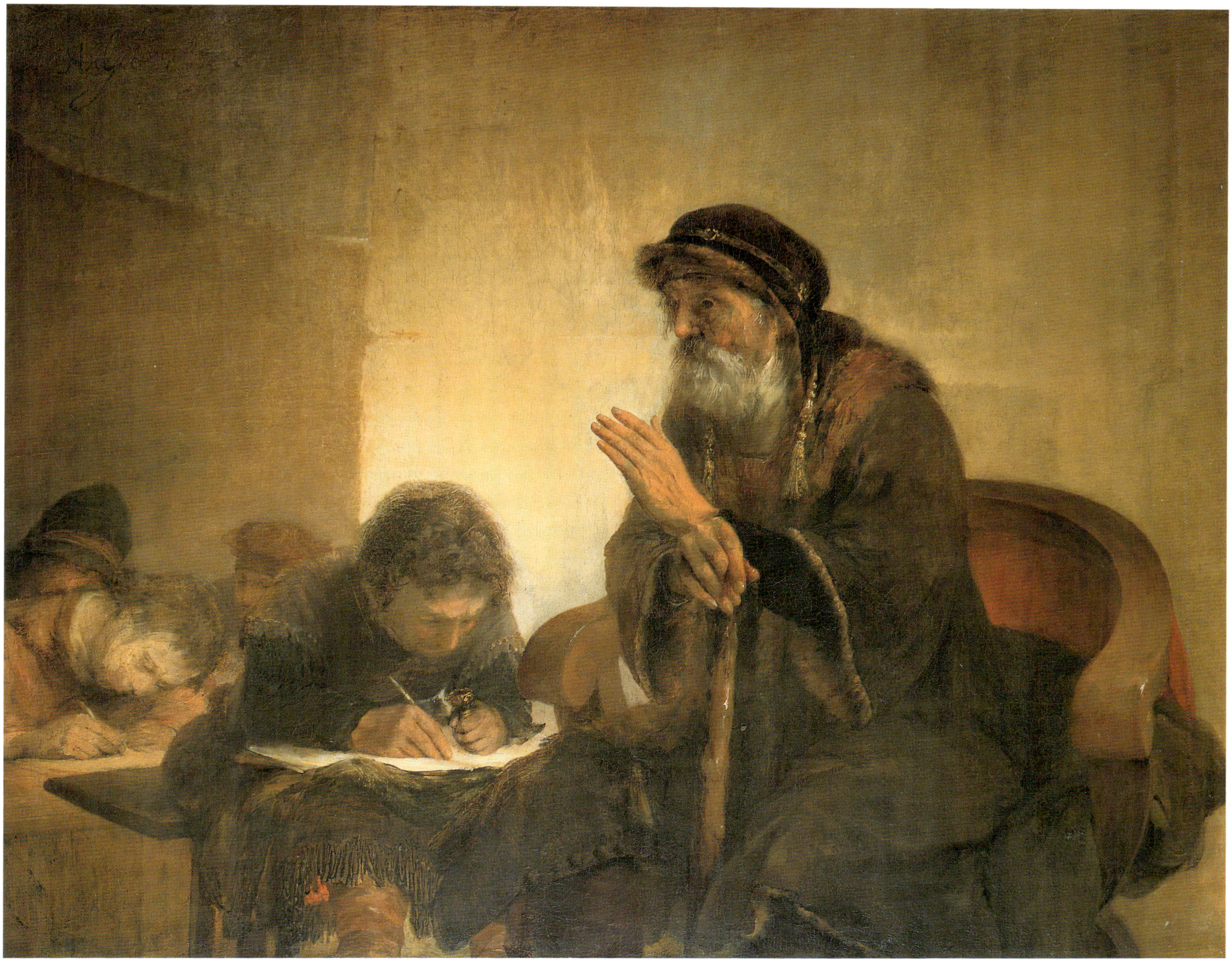

72
Arent de Gelder
Portrait of a Family
*c.*1720

Signed upper right *A de Gelder f*
Canvas
107.0 x 63.0 cm
Musée du Louvre, Département des Peintures, Paris
© Photo RMN

PROVENANCE: With Galerie Van Diemen & Co., Berlin and Amsterdam, until 1926; purchased from Galerie Van Diemen in 1926.

LITERATURE: Brière-Misme 1927, p. 87; Van Fossen 1969, p. 275, no. 86; Sumowski, *Gemälde*, vol. II, 1985, p. 1180, no. 816; Foucart 1988–89, pp. 102–3, cat. no. 103; Von Moltke 1994, pp. 49, 108, no. 102.

Although not consistently reliable as a biographer, J. C. Weyerman wrote his account of de Gelder only two years after his death, and in it claimed that the artist produced hundreds of portraits.[1] Today nearly twenty half-length single-figure and pendant portraits by de Gelder's hand have survived. They range in date across most of his career, or at least from *c.*1680 onwards. His three group portraits of families (de Gelder himself remained a bachelor throughout his life) all seem to date from the last years of his career. When it was first purchased by the Louvre, the present painting was dated by C. Brière-Misme on stylistic grounds 'to about 1700',[2] while D. van Fossen in his dissertation on the artist made minor adjustments, proposing a date 'shortly after 1702'.[3] K. Lilienfeld, who wrote the first monograph on the artist in 1914, was the first to note the painting's resemblance to the *Family Portrait of Hermanus Boerhaave, His Wife and Daughter* of *c.*1722 (fig. 72a). Lilienfeld's manuscript annotation was published only in 1988–89 by J. Foucart when the picture was exhibited in the latter's show in Paris.[4] Sumowski (1985)[5] and J. W. von Moltke (1994)[6] concurred in dating the Louvre's painting to '*c.*1720' and 'around 1720/22' respectively. The Rijksmuseum's half-length portrait of the famous physician from Leiden University and his wife and daughter is probably correctly dated *c.*1722, on the basis not only of the apparent ages of the sitters (Boerhaave (1668–1738) was twenty-three years de Gelder's junior), but also of a plausible date on the back of de Gelder's single-figure portrait of Boerhaave preserved in the Mauritshuis, The Hague.[7]

In its free execution, 'rococo' palette of heightened colours, and sympathetic conception of family affection, the painting in Amsterdam (fig. 72a) most resembles the present work (we may compare also the *Portrait of a Couple* (sometimes identified as Boerhaave and his wife) sold at Parke-Bernet, New York, 16 June 1977, lot 77).[8]

Just as the portrait of the Boerhaave family owes a debt to Rembrandt's *Family Portrait* at the Herzog Anton Ulrich-Museum, Braunschweig (Bredius 417), the design of the present work (probably marginally cropped at the left), with the figures situated before a window or archway behind a parapet or balcony wall, traces its ancestry to Rembrandt and his school. However, the colour scheme (veils of pale blue, ochre and white) announces the new century.

In this remarkable group portrait we admire not only the artist's precocious palette and idiosyncratic technique but also his refusal to flatter or idealize his sitters – a stylistic decision that naturally won him the abiding scorn of Arnold Houbraken and later classicist art theorists. Nonetheless, de Gelder, like Rembrandt before him, had a gift for plumbing human emotions – here notably tenderness.

PCS

1 Weyerman 1729–69, vol. III, 1729, p. 42.
2 Brière-Misme 1927, p. 87.
3 Van Fossen 1969, p. 275, no. 86.
4 Foucart 1988–89, pp. 102–3.
5 Sumowski, *Gemälde*, vol. II, 1985, p. 1180, no. 816.
6 Von Moltke 1994, p. 108, no. 102.
7 Von Moltke 1994, pp. 100–1, no. 85, pl. 85.
8 Von Moltke 1994, pp. 107–8, no. 101, pl. 101; Sumowski, *Gemälde*, vol. II, 1985, no. 815.

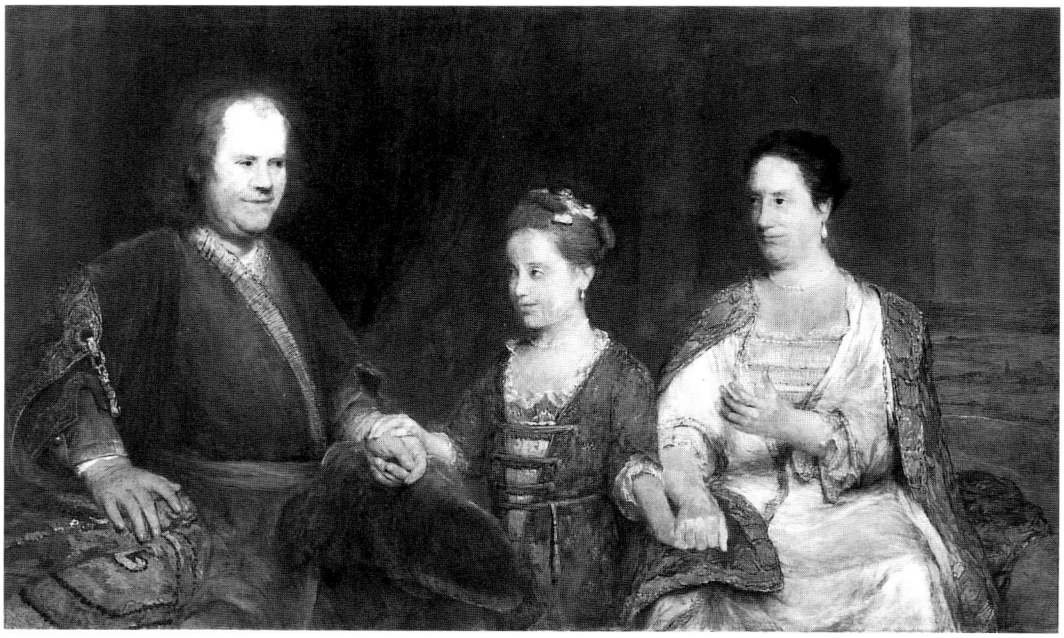

FIG. 72a
Arent de Gelder
Family Portrait of Hermanus Boerhaave, His Wife and Daughter *c.*1722
Canvas
104.5 x 173.0 cm
Rijksmuseum, Amsterdam

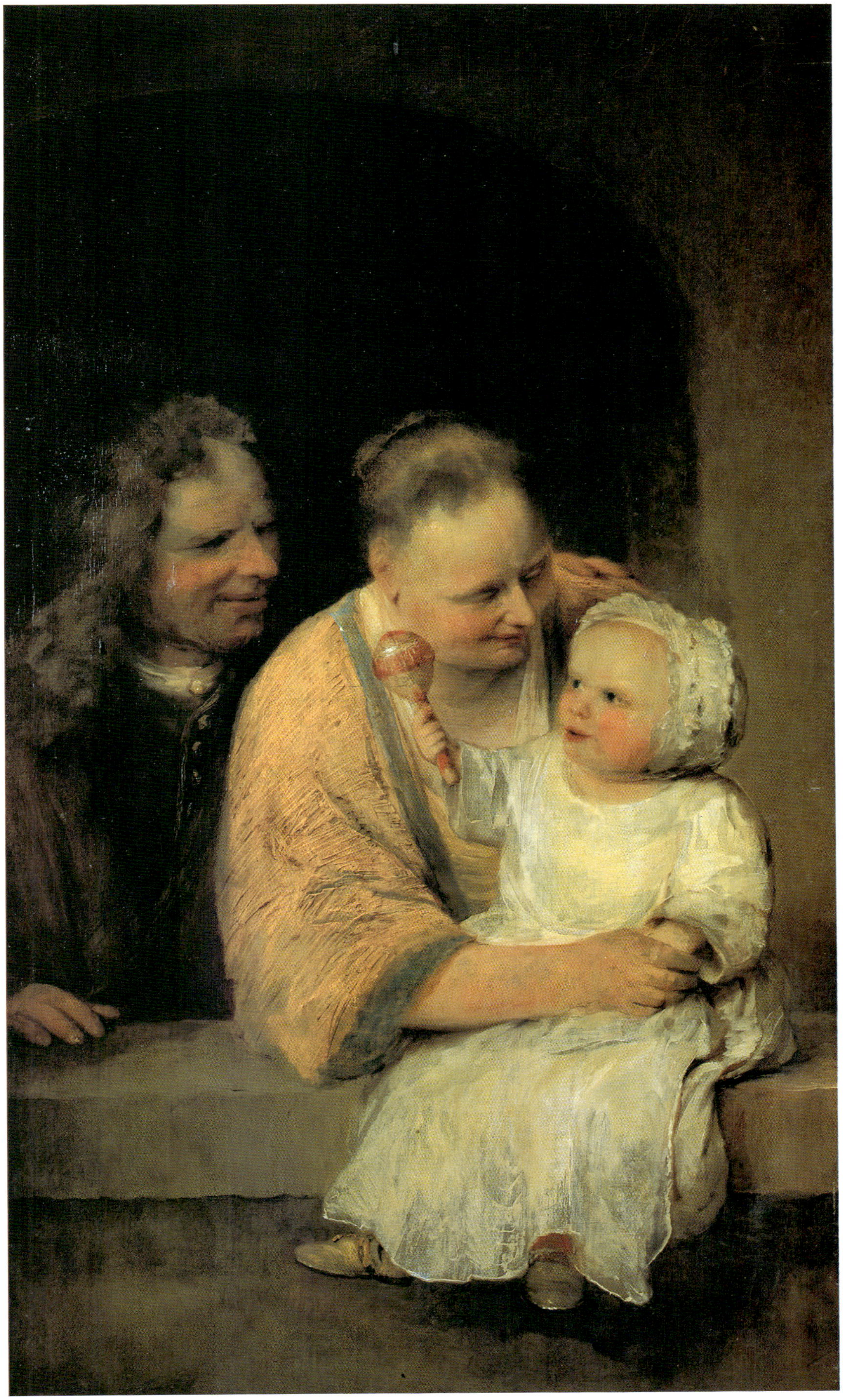

'Mr Rembrandt's Own Hand'

BEN BROOS

In his authoritative *Schilder-Boeck* (Painter's Book) of 1604, the theoretician and biographer Karel van Mander (1548–1606) remarks that 'the noble art of drawing may be seen as the father of painting'.[1] Inevitably, his theory is not always borne out in practice. Some of the great Dutch artists, among them Frans Hals, Jan Steen and Johannes Vermeer, left no drawn oeuvre for posterity, as far as we know, but there were others who indeed worked according to van Mander's ideal. There is no doubt, for instance, that 'the father of painting' played an important role in Rembrandt's oeuvre. His prodigious output and the very nature of his work seem to reflect an irrepressible need to record all that he saw or thought.

A passion for art on paper

Rembrandt elevated the art of drawing to great heights, making it a vital part of his artistic legacy. Art on paper appears to have been one of the very foundations of his life. From the beginning of his career, he made drawings with a pen or brush, in graphite or coloured chalk, on thick paper or thin, on parchment, on so-called Japanese paper or on whatever he happened to have at hand, including even the sheets of a cashbook (cat. no. 98). He also produced etchings on paper, regarding them as drawings of a kind which he was able to reproduce and therefore turn to commercial advantage.

Rembrandt's fascination with prints and sketches from the past undoubtedly inspired his own love of drawing, and he was happy to part with large sums of money to acquire drawings and prints by earlier artists, some of which works he subsequently sold. He was renowned far and wide – and looked upon with awe – for his love of collecting. Barely ten years after his death, his pupil Samuel van Hoogstraten wrote that Rembrandt's 'passion for art on paper' had induced him to pay exorbitant prices for prints by artists he admired, one of whom was Lucas van Leyden (1494–1533).[2]

Rembrandt's extravagant love of old graphic art was legendary. Even in Italy it was said that he collected prints 'per mettere in credito la professione' – for the glory of the profession.[3] He himself once said that he never felt the need to visit Italy, and that he found sufficient opportunity at home to study the art of southern Europe. By this he presumably meant thanks to the availability of etchings and engravings. It seems that his own collection of drawings and prints was a way of bringing the world to his doorstep.

Genuine or fake?

Precisely what it was that was valued in drawings in the late sixteenth and early seventeenth centuries was expressed by a contemporary collector with a particular interest in Rembrandt. In 1710 the German lawyer Zacharias Conrad von Uffenbach went to see the collection of Nicolaes Flinck (1645–1723) in Rotterdam. Appraising the work he had seen, he concluded that Nicolaes, like his father – Rembrandt's pupil Govaert Flinck – had a gift for 'art on paper'.

Nicolaes Flinck told his German visitor that he had started out collecting prints, but had gradually acquired an interest in drawings as well. There were certain risks involved, he confessed, as it was difficult to distinguish between authentic sheets and fakes, and fraud *(Betrug)* was by no means uncommon. Yet in spite of this he preferred drawings to graphic work, because 'a drawing captures the painter's initial impression', whereas the complicated process of producing prints often made them appear contrived.[4] Flinck's viewpoint, together with that expressed by van Mander in 1604, may be seen as indicative of the context within which Rembrandt's drawings were made.

It was at least partly due to Rembrandt's achievements in this field that later generations learned to appreciate the uniqueness of drawings – which over time became coveted possessions. Apart from artists themselves, there were relatively few collectors in the Dutch Republic of the seventeenth century. But it seems that dubious practices became rife as soon as the numbers of collectors increased, as Flinck's exchanges with von Uffenbach in any event imply. Not only works by pupils or followers,

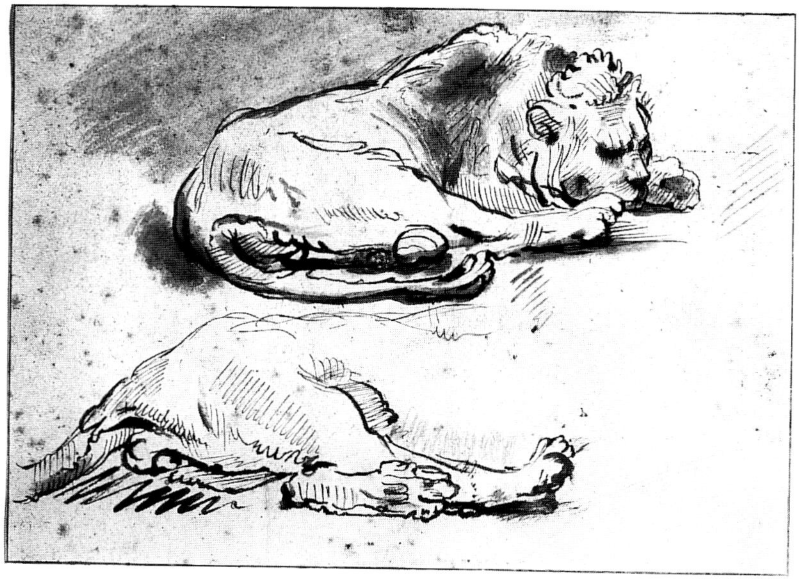

FIG. 1
Manner of Rembrandt
Two Studies of a Recumbent Lion early 18th century(?)
Pen and ink and brush
15.0 x 20.1 cm
Rijksprentenkabinet, Rijksmuseum, Amsterdam

but outright fakes, were soon being passed off as drawings by the great masters themselves.

The so-called 'lion drawings' are a good example. In 1722 the Amsterdam collector Jan Pietersz Zomer owned an album containing '19 [pictures of] lions, from life', all of which were attributed to Rembrandt.[5] In 1729 Bernard Picart made prints after eighteen of these(?) sheets, enabling us today to judge the quality of the works. In retrospect it transpires that many sheets in the album were mistaken for originals. There were drawings by pupils and even copies after their drawings, among other third-rate work (fig. 1).[6] Even today, only a few drawings of lions can be firmly attributed to Rembrandt (cat. no. 87).

Drawings were also sometimes treated in ways that spoiled their original features. They were mounted, cropped or cut out, and defaced with borders, signatures, inscriptions and collectors' marks. Some were even embellished with figures or washes to produce a more 'finished' effect. Dirck Dalens, for instance, altered the drawings from Jacob van Ruisdael's estate in order to prepare them for sale, and Cornelis Dusart 'enhanced' his inheritance of sketches by Adriaen and Isack van Ostade to suit his personal taste. In the eighteenth century in particular, carefully worked up sheets were valued more highly than relatively spontaneous sketches.[7]

In the nineteenth century, a heavily retouched 'Rembrandt' drawing fetched huge sums of money on several occasions because it was taken to be a masterpiece of the highest standard (fig. 2). On the basis of an old inscription, the sheet was long thought to represent the hunting lodge of the counts of Holland in The Hague, and it was firmly believed that only an artist of Rembrandt's stature could have drawn its hallowed portals. Before the erroneous inscription was added, the sheet had been worked up to appeal to the taste of the day, and the original design was almost completely obscured by generous applications of watercolour and opaque paint.[8] In this sorry state the drawing was copied, engraved, and reproduced in various publications on the history of The Hague. Not until the beginning of this century was the piece recognized as a mystification. What it showed was not, after all, a site in The Hague, but the principal facade of the Handboogdoelen in Amsterdam, the headquarters of the Archers' Civic Guard. The attribution to Rembrandt was widely contested, with the result that the drawing was undermined not only as a historical document but also as a work of art.[9]

Inscriptions on drawings, or additions of any kind, should generally be treated with suspicion (cat. no. 83). Rembrandt himself rarely signed his sheets and seldom added borders to his drawings. He signed a drawing only if he was intending to sell it or if he considered it a complete and self-contained work of art. It seems that his 'initial impressions' served primarily as study material for himself or his pupils, and they were therefore not generally for sale. For that purpose he made prints.

Drawings by the thousand

The drawings referred to above may be assumed with reasonable certainty to have come from Rembrandt's collection. The history of Rembrandt's own collection of art on paper has been a dramatic one. In 1656 an inventory was drawn up of all the goods in his house in the Jodenbreestraat (the present-day Museum het Rembrandthuis; p. 26, fig. 6). Burdensome mortgage repayments, financial speculations and a passion for collecting had presumably contributed to his declining fortunes.

Rembrandt's most treasured possessions were undoubtedly the albums in the first-floor room that he referred to as his 'art cabinet'.

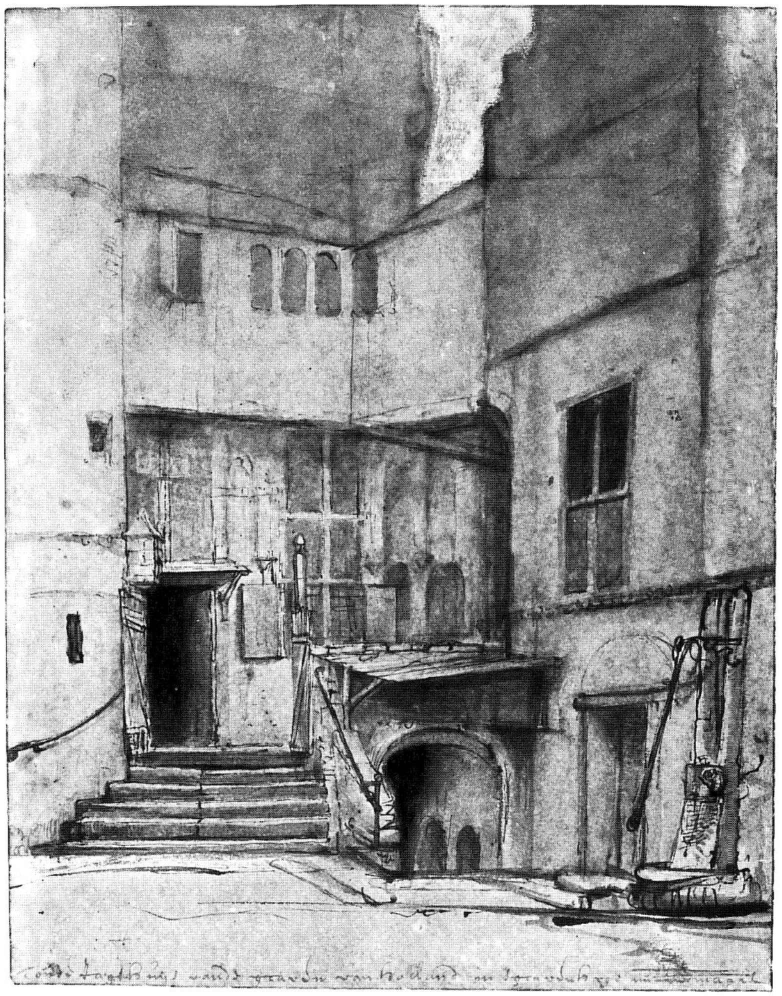

FIG. 2
Rembrandt(?) and others
Facade of the Headquarters of the Handboogdoelen (Archers' Civic Guard) in Amsterdam c.1650? and later
Pen and ink and brush, with later additions of watercolour and gouache
27.1 x 20.4 cm
Amsterdam Historical Museum

His collection of works on paper was stored in no fewer than ninety portfolios, most of them carefully organized. He kept his own oeuvre of drawings and prints in a series of separate files, together with large, bound volumes and small sketchbooks. There were individual files for male and female nudes, sketches after examples from antiquity, landscapes from life, imaginary views, animal studies, figure sketches and so forth. A book bound in black leather was reserved especially for 'Rembran[d]t's best sketches'.[10] In 1656, according to a later estimate, Rembrandt had well over a thousand, and possibly several thousand, drawings by his own hand.[11] As we have seen, they were intended first and foremost as study material for his personal use and for use by his pupils. Few collectors owned drawings by him before 1658 and certainly none had complete art books.

It is impossible even to estimate the size of his collection of drawings and prints by other artists. Of a total of ninety portfolios, there were at least seventy portfolios of graphic art, some for copperplate etchings,

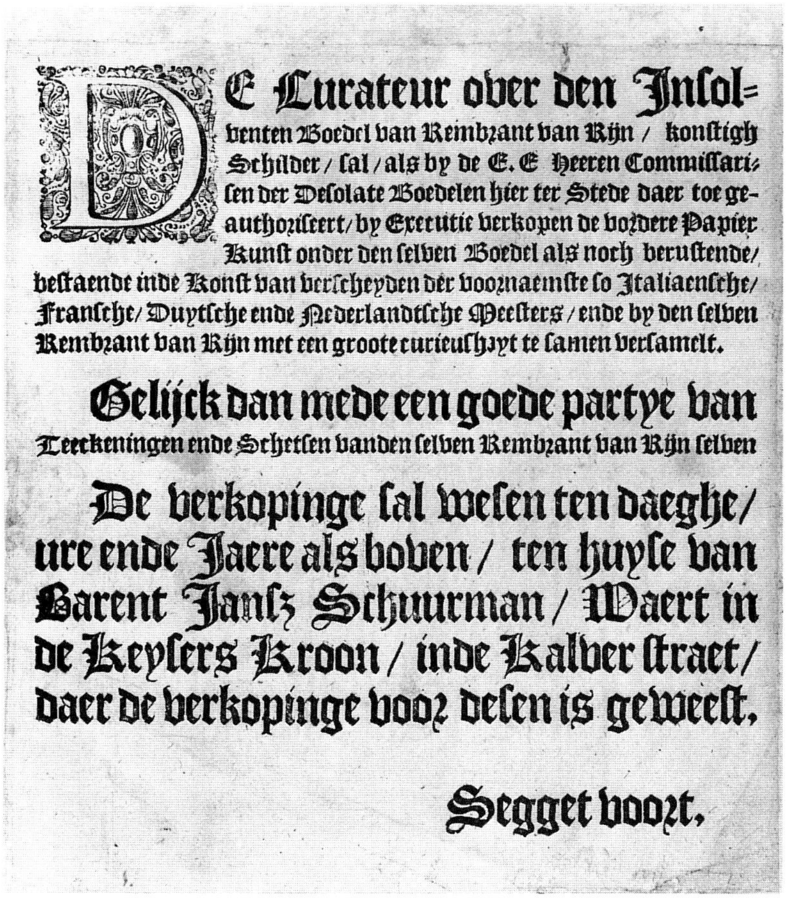
De Curateur over den Insol-
venten Boedel van Rembrant van Rijn / konstigh
Schilder / sal / als by de E. E Heeren Commissari-
sen der Desolate Boedelen hier ter Stede daer toe ge-
authoriseert / by Executie verkopen de vordere Papier
Kunst onder den selven Boedel als noch berustende /
bestaende inde Konst van verscheyden der voornaemste so Italiaensche /
Fransche / Duytsche ende Nederlandtsche Meesters / ende by den selven
Rembrant van Rijn met een groote curieusheyt te samen versamelt.

Gelijck dan mede een goede partye van
Teeckeningen ende Schetsen vanden selven Rembrant van Rijn selven

De verkopinge sal wesen ten daeghe /
ure ende Jaere als boven / ten huyse van
Barent Jansz Schuurman / Waert in
de Keysers Kroon / inde Kalver straet /
daer de verkopinge voor desen is geweest.

Segget voort.

FIG. 3
Advertisement for the sale of Rembrandt's 'art on paper', 1658.

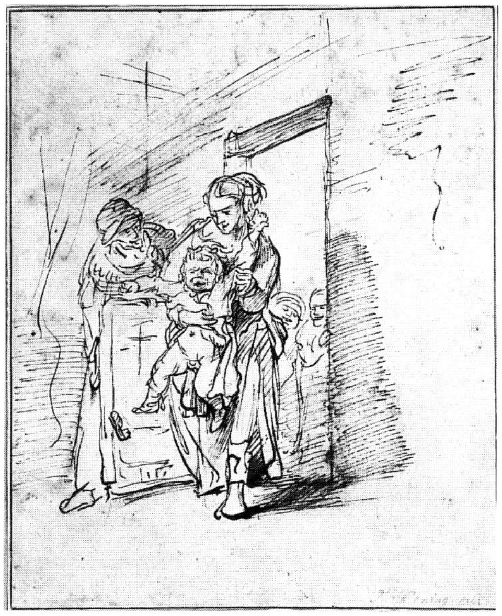

FIG. 4
Jan Boursse (1622–1671), after Rembrandt
'The Naughty Child' c.1670
Pen and ink, 20.9 x 17.0 cm
Hamburger Kunsthalle, Hamburg
Copyright Elke Walford, Hamburg

others for woodcuts, and separate files for work by Dutch, Italian and German masters. Rembrandt believed he had managed to obtain the entire print oeuvres of both Maarten van Heemskerck and Titian. He also possessed a book of Indian miniatures, which he used as examples for some of his own drawings (cat. no. 93). Another file contained erotic prints by early Italian masters. What Rembrandt had ultimately built up was nothing short of a museum of art on paper.

On 20 December 1658 his cherished collection was finally put up for auction. An advertising poster announcing the event described it as a sale of 'works of art by various prominent Italian, French, German, and Netherlandish masters, which the said Rembran[d]t van Rijn has assembled by his great curiosity'. The sale also included 'a large number of drawings and sketches by the said Rembran[d]t van Rijn' (fig. 3).[12] The auction was a complete fiasco. A godsend for collectors, it was disastrous for Rembrandt: the entire collection fetched a total of 470 guilders. In better times he himself had paid several hundred guilders for a single Lucas van Leyden. A year after the sale, Rembrandt's collection of 'art on paper, curiosa, antiques, medallions, seashells and corals' was valued at no less than 11,000 guilders.[13] Those who profited most, either directly or indirectly, were, as we shall see, a few collectors.

Collectors

Soon after the sale of his collection, Rembrandt's 'signature' appeared, in a variety of forms, on many of the sheets that were in the hands not only of well-meaning collectors but also of unscrupulous dealers. One anonymous collector, for instance, placed cryptic-looking marks on the front of all his sheets and inscribed either the front or the back with the 'signature' *Rembrant van Ryn*. The collector had a preference for landscapes and biblical scenes, and presumably bought a number of them *en bloc* when Rembrandt's drawings were auctioned in 1658. Although the inscriptions on his sheets are demonstrably fake, the mere fact that they date from so long ago – from a time when 'signatures' were often added to 'improve' original works – argues in favour of the drawings' authenticity.[14]

Experts are still grappling with the problem of deciding whether these drawings are autograph. In 1906 Cornelis Hofstede de Groot doubted that it would ever be possible to achieve a complete *'consensus eruditorum'* on what constitutes Rembrandt's drawn oeuvre.[15] Even in 1992, Martin Royalton-Kisch, of the Department of Prints and Drawings at the British Museum, admitted that it was as difficult as ever to reach a *'consensus omnium* (or *eruditorum*)'.[16] Since then, a concentrated effort has been made to develop reliable methods by which to establish whether drawings attributed to Rembrandt are indeed authentic. Photography has made it possible to compare different styles, while the discovery of a related etching (cat. no. 84) or painting (cat. nos 77, 80) has sometimes provided an important clue. It has also become more common to analyse watermarks and paper as a means of ascertaining the age of a sheet. An early provenance, dating back to the seventeenth century, is another significant factor in appraising the status of a drawing.

Some of the landscapes belonging to the 'cryptic-mark collector' were subsequently bought by Nicolaes Flinck, who was in the habit of stamping a decorative *F* on his drawings. In 1723 the 2nd Duke of Devonshire acquired a large batch of these initialled Rembrandt landscapes from Flinck, and these remained at Chatsworth for more than two hundred years. Today, these drawings bearing the cryptic collector's marks and Flinck's distinctive *F* are highly prized, thanks to these almost watertight guarantees, in which Rembrandt himself had no part. The eighteenth-century inscriptions or marks of the collectors Jan Pietersz Zomer (cat. nos 83, 91), Valerius Röver, Johan Goll van Franckenstein and Cornelis Ploos van Amstel (cat. no. 75) are also well known, and highly sought after, but are no absolute guarantee of authenticity.

Besides Flinck, there were several other seventeenth-century collectors who owned large groups of drawings that are attributed to Rembrandt and that probably once belonged to him – a fact that in itself would vouch for their authenticity. At first, these drawings seem to have been of interest to artists rather than investors. In 1671, for example, Jan Boursse, the brother of the painter Esaias Boursse, was the proud owner of two large albums containing 'drawings and prints ... by Rembran[d]t van Rijn' at different stages of completion.[17] Only one extant drawing, *'The Naughty Child'* (Kupferstichkabinett, Berlin) (Benesch 401) can be identified as having come from Boursse's album, thanks to the existence of a copy by Boursse himself (fig. 4).

No more than twenty years after the auction of Rembrandt's 'art on paper', a former pupil, Lambert Doomer (1624–1700), was in possession of four books and a portfolio of the master's drawings and etchings. Among Doomer's surviving works are a few copies he made after Rembrandt's examples; the existence of these copies guarantees the drawings' authenticity.[18] In 1680 the marine painter Jan van de Cappelle (1626–1679) had more than five hundred drawings by Rembrandt, arranged in five portfolios, one of which contained '135 drawings of the lives of women and children, by Rembran[d]t' (cat. no. 75). Such a select group of works could only have come from Rembrandt's own collection.[19]

From the title of the album alone we can conclude that Rembrandt must have rendered a great many domestic scenes, but today we can only speculate as to which sheets came from this portfolio. On the other hand, we know precisely which drawings from his collection Mathys Pool (1676–1740) copied in etchings around 1700. These were a series of twelve biblical scenes and figure studies, some of which have survived to this day (fig. 94b). Pool's copies are evidence that these unsigned sheets belong to the hard core of authentic drawings. They were published as 'Impressions on copperplate after original drawings and sketches by Rembrandt'. Like Flinck, Pool valued these drawings for the fact that they were an expression of the artist's '[initial] impression'.[20]

Vitality

Both the advertising poster for the sale of Rembrandt's collection, and the title of Mathys Pool's series of prints, refer to 'drawings and sketches' by Rembrandt, and it may be that these terms were indeed used to distinguish between polished sheets and comparatively rough drafts. Rembrandt himself preferred making direct, evocative sketches, but his work cannot be classified quite so simply. He made many different kinds of drawings – nudes and studies of other sitters, figures from life and imaginary figures, initial ideas for scenes as well as more complex compositions, landscapes, studies for portraits, copies of works by others, and a far larger group more difficult to categorize.

This diversity of subject matter was matched by a range of materials and a bewildering variety of styles. Yet it is the immediacy and vitality of the 'initial impression' that distinguishes a good Rembrandt drawing. The difference between the master's experienced hand and the work of a novice is perhaps most clearly evident from a correction Rembrandt made to a piece by Constantijn Daniël van Renesse (fig. 5). With just a few bold lines he transformed van Renesse's *Annunciation* into a more monumental and eloquent piece. He would sometimes add a few words of advice on the sheets handed in by his pupils. 'This needs more figures', he wrote under a pupil's drawing of *Rebecca's Departure*, *c.*1637 (Staatsgalerie Stuttgart),[21] while a drawing of the *Flight into Egypt*, *c.*1642, by the young Samuel van Hoogstraten (Kupferstichkabinett, Dresden) was returned with a note to the effect that all the proportions were wrong.[22] Rembrandt evidently had firm ideas about what constituted a good drawing.

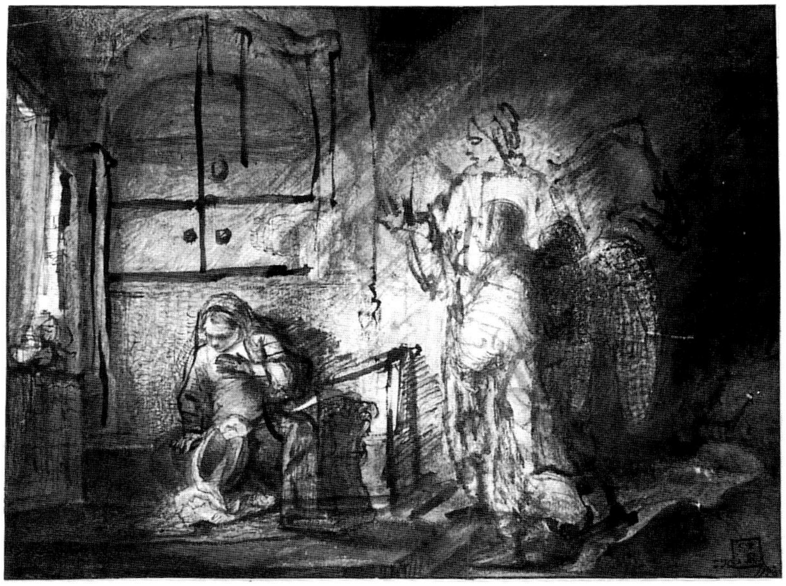

FIG. 5
Constantijn Daniël van Renesse (1626–1680), with corrections by Rembrandt
The Annunciation *c.*1650–52
Pen and ink and brush
17.3 x 23.1 cm
Staatliche Museen zu Berlin, Kupferstichkabinett

He imposed his style on the fledgling artists who came to work in his studio. They were taught to use old prints to study the proportions and movements of figures and to analyse compositions. They would also work together drawing from nude models. An interesting scene by an unidentified pupil shows the group at work (fig. 6).[23] The results of one of these sessions can be seen in two versions of a seated nude woman, one by Rembrandt (cat. no. 98), the other by a pupil (fig. 98a). In this case the master's hand is easy to distinguish from his pupil's, and even the wash in Rembrandt's drawing is superior.

In the centre foreground of the picture of the artists in Rembrandt's studio we see a few older men among the younger pupils. They would presumably have been amateur painters or former pupils, who attended these classes solely for their pleasure. It transpires from contemporary sources that even experienced artists would work together drawing nudes. This gives us an idea of the importance Rembrandt's circle attached to 'the father of painting'. The plaster casts we know about from the description of Rembrandt's 'art cabinet' from 1656 can also be seen on a ledge above the reclining model in the drawing. The picture gives an impression of Rembrandt's 'famous academy', as the studio was known, not just in the Republic but far further afield.[24] Many of his pupils were later to become productive and extremely competent draughtsmen, among them Ferdinand Bol (cat. nos 44–48), Gerbrand van den Eeckhout (cat. nos 53–56), Govaert Flinck (cat. nos 41–43), Samuel van

Hoogstraten (cat. nos 61–62), Philips Koninck and Nicolaes Maes (cat. nos 64–68).[25]

Drawing sessions were also held beyond the confines of the 'academy' walls. Samuel van Hoogstraten once portrayed a lion 'from life' (fig. 87a), possibly with Rembrandt seated beside him (see commentary to cat. no. 87). Similar motifs in landscapes rendered in different styles likewise suggest that Rembrandt went on drawing expeditions in the countryside in the company of other artists. For instance, an etching he made in about 1645 shows an acquaintance of his seated near a farm with his sketchbook (B.219) (fig. 7), while his pupils Ferdinand Bol and Gerbrand van den Eeckhout, in *c.*1640–45 and *c.*1661–63 respectively, drew panoramic scenes (Fondation Custodia, Paris; Kupferstichkabinett, Berlin) from almost exactly the same spot as his own *View of Haarlem* (cat. no. 90).[26] Philips Koninck's annotation on a sheet with a *View of Trompenburg*, *c.*1650 (Louvre, Paris) (Benesch 1220), expresses his appreciation for exercises of this kind: 'This drawing shows the outer Amstel, beautifully drawn by Mr Rembrandt's own hand. p. ko[ning]'. Even if Koninck was mistaken, as some believe, the inscription nevertheless reflects his esteem for the master.[27]

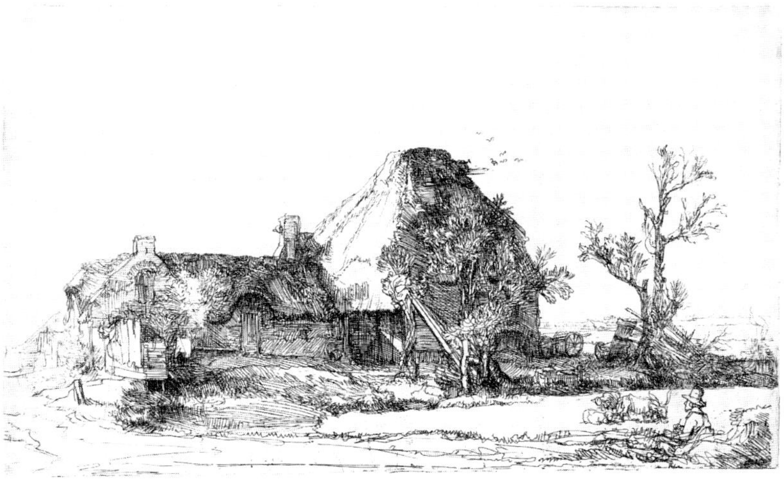

FIG. 7
Rembrandt
Farm with an Artist Drawing Nearby *c.*1645
Etching
12.9 x 20.9 cm
Rijksprentenkabinet, Rijksmuseum, Amsterdam

An intimate view

Koninck would have recognized 'Mr Rembrandt's' hand without any difficulty, whereas for us this poses one of the thorniest problems of all. It is mainly the superb technique and the range of expressive forms that catch one's eye in Rembrandt's work. His strong individuality emerges, for instance, from his drawn and written comments on the work of a pupil (fig. 5). But in a sense he also gave drawing lessons to some of the great masters of the past. He corrected his own teacher Pieter Lastman (1583–1633), for example, in a red chalk copy of his *Susanna and the Elders* (cat. no. 77). Rembrandt felt he could improve on the rather vague expression and gestures that Susanna has in Lastman's painting, and therefore portrayed her with her right hand protectively in her lap, and her left hand moving towards her breast. These changes have the effect of emphasizing the young woman's embarrassment.

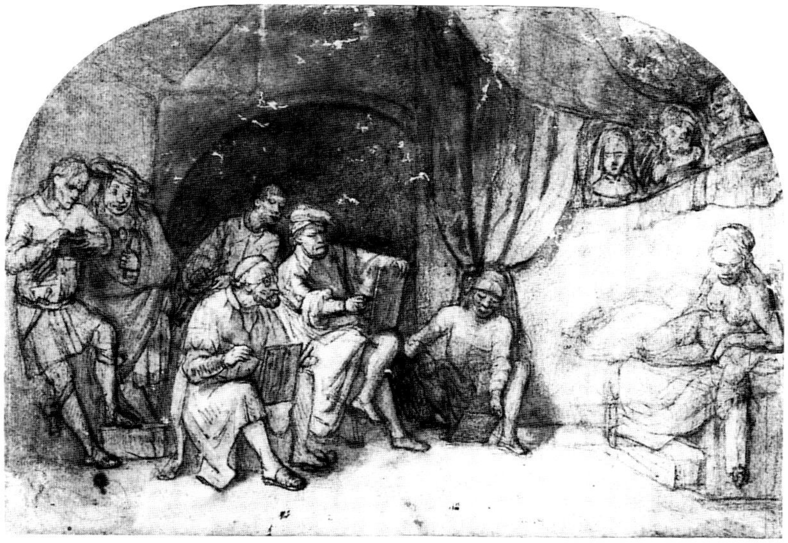

FIG. 6
Pupil of Rembrandt
Rembrandt's Studio with Artists Drawing *c.*1650–55
Pen and ink and brush
18.0 x 26.6 cm
Hessisches Landesmuseum, Darmstadt

In 1635 Rembrandt made three drawings after Leonardo's famous fresco *The Last Supper*, which he would have known from a print in his collection. One of these drawings, in red chalk, bears an autograph signature and would therefore have been regarded by Rembrandt as a completed work in its own right (Benesch 443) (fig. 8). This sheet was apparently made in two stages. It is clear from the figures of Christ and the apostles that Rembrandt first started drawing a carefully detailed scene, using a piece of fine chalk. But he evidently changed his mind. Irritated, perhaps, by the meticulous symmetry of the composition, he made radical changes in broad, bold strokes and drew Christ in front of a canopy which is deliberately set at an oblique angle behind the table. He sketched a few lines suggesting an aureole around Christ's head, thereby isolating him more effectively than in Leonardo's version. Finally, a few impulsive strokes convey the emotions of the apostles. The recoiling traitor Judas clutching his purse, to the left of Christ, is strongly accentuated, as is the dark-haired Matthew leaping up in anger on the right.

A composition by Raphael also came in for criticism when Rembrandt drew a variant on the Italian master's celebrated *Parnassus* fresco in 1652 (Benesch 913) (fig. 9), as part of the *Pandora*, the *album amicorum* of Rembrandt's friend Jan Six. He apparently felt that Raphael had not exploited the picture's anecdotal potential to the full. His own version gives far greater prominence to the blind Homer, who stands in the centre of the picture. He is leaning on a stick, with his hand raised as if he were reciting his verse. Gone is the pitiful upward gaze we see in Raphael's version. Homer has risen from a large chair and stands before his audience. A man leans over the backrest and listens to him attentively, and a scribe seated on a slope gazes at the poet with deep concentration and records his hexameters. The vitality of these human details appealed to Rembrandt.

Other good examples of Rembrandt's corrections are his copies after Indian miniatures (cat. no. 93). He changed the stylized poses that

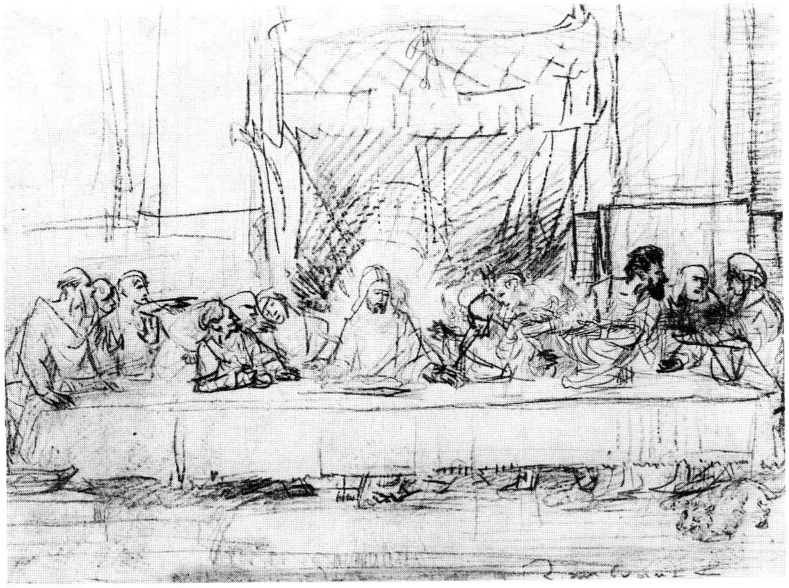

FIG. 8
Rembrandt, after Leonardo da Vinci
The Last Supper c.1635
Signed
Chalk
36.5 x 47.5 cm
The Metropolitan Museum of Art, New York

distinguish these oriental pictures, to form more natural shapes. He simply altered the positions of the feet, and applied washes to achieve a subtle three-dimensional effect and light in and around the figures. Yet, at the same time, he managed to retain the oriental character of his examples.

Comparisons of this kind provide an effective way of demonstrating Rembrandt's skill with the pen and with chalk. But his gift for expression is no less evident in his spontaneous drawings from life. His most poignant drawings, perhaps, are his portraits of his first wife, Saskia van Uylenburgh, and of a young woman who is most probably Hendrickje Stoffels. Both works are rendered in media he rarely used. He drew the *Portrait of Saskia* (Benesch 427) (fig. 10) in silverpoint on prepared vellum, and added a caption that makes the sketch more intimate and private: 'This is a portrait of my wife at the age of 21, on the third day of our marriage, 8 June 1633'. Some twenty years later he made the *Portrait of a Sleeping Woman* (Benesch 1103) (fig. 11), a work that has been published no less frequently and is therefore as widely known. The woman is believed to be the thirty-year-old Hendrickje Stoffels, whom a document from 1661 describes as 'the wife of the painter Mr Rembran[d]t van Reyn'.[28] The drawing is exceptional in that it is rendered solely with a brush, which Rembrandt normally used only to apply a wash.

Bob Haak once formulated what it is that makes Rembrandt's drawings so extraordinary, and it is perhaps impossible to do so more succinctly: 'The greatness of Rembrandt as draftsman lies in the combination of a number of qualities and certainly also in his determination to look anew at each subject and each situation in and of itself. He never repeated himself or lapsed into affectation. Unlike his paintings and his etchings, his drawings were hardly ever for display or sale. Therefore they give the most intimate view of his artistic mastery'.[29]

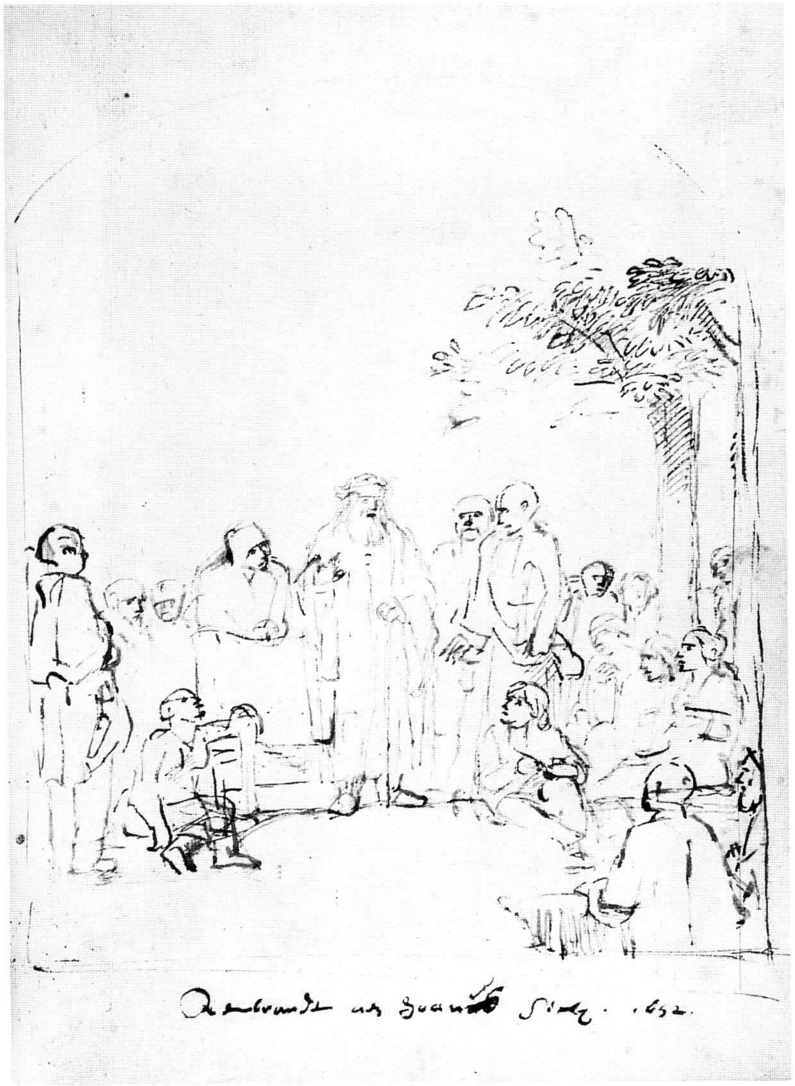

FIG. 9
Rembrandt
Homer Reciting Verses
Signed and dated *Rembrandt aen Joanus Sicx. 1652*
Pen and ink
25.5 x 18.0 cm
Six Collection, Amsterdam

Rembrandt three centuries later

By 1710, Nicolaes Flinck was complaining about counterfeit sheets, and in 1729 Bernard Picart was reproducing drawings in totally different styles as the work of a single artist. Rembrandt's tireless experimentation has sown a great deal of confusion among later admirers of his work. Although the thousands of drawings from his own collection were initially clustered together in portfolios, even these have been dismantled in the course of the years. The only collection to remain intact for any length of time was the group in the Chatsworth Settlement. Two centuries after Rembrandt's death, almost every opportunity to compare his sheets had been exhausted. Now, after the passage of more than three hundred years, new possibilities have been opened up.

Over the years, drawings by Rembrandt other than those reproduced

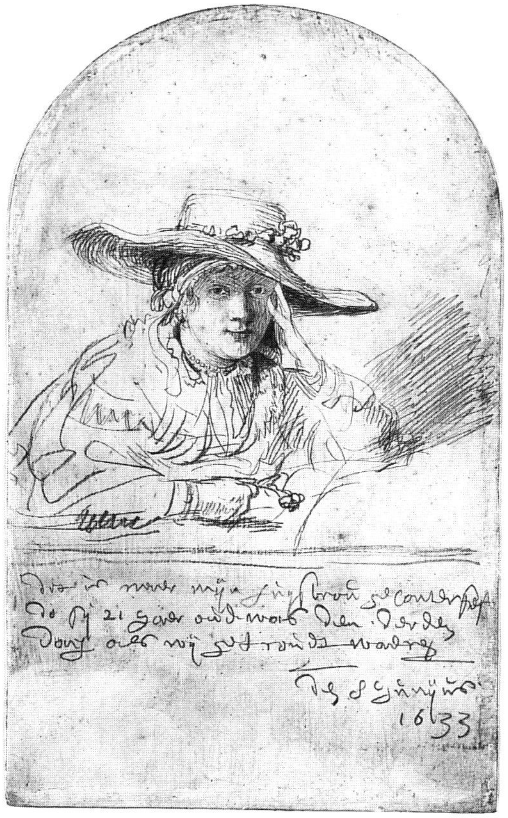

FIG. 10
Rembrandt
Portrait of Saskia
Dated 1633
Silverpoint on vellum
18.5 x 10.7 cm
Staatliche Museen zu Berlin, Kupferstichkabinett

by Pool and Picart occasionally appeared in print. Arnold Houbraken (1660–1719), for instance, published *Christ Vanishing at Emmaus*, a work presumably after a now lost original. But this did little to help the reader form a judgement about Rembrandt's skill as a draughtsman. Houbraken's comments on Rembrandt's ability to achieve a lifelike quality in his work aroused the impression that he knew more of the master's sheets: 'Anger, hatred, sadness, joy, and so forth, are captured to such realistic effect that the meaning is clear in every penstroke'.[30] Houbraken nevertheless complains about the price asked for one of Rembrandt's three copies after Leonardo's *Last Supper* (Kupferstich-kabinett, Berlin) (Benesch 445): it was 'valued at more than 20 ducatons' and that 'for a mere pen sketch on paper'.[31] Hence in Houbraken's estimation it was not so much the expressive force of a picture that counted, but the amount of labour that went into it.

The earliest catalogues of Rembrandt's drawings were not illustrated, so readers had to rely on the author's judgement. Carel Vosmaer in 1877 was the first to make systematic notes about the sheets he knew from museum collections and descriptions in auction catalogues.[32] The most important facsimile edition of a selection of drawings was the four-part publication by Friedrich Lippmann, Cornelis Hofstede de Groot et al. The first two series (1888–92, 1900–01) had reproductions in phototype, while the third and fourth series (1903–06, 1910–11) proudly announced that their pictures were 'reproduced in the colours of the originals'. These books contained a total of 550 sheets, which the public could now see for themselves.[33]

The text-only catalogue published by the same Hofstede de Groot in 1906 attributed some 1,600 drawings to Rembrandt.[34] Wilhelm R. Valentiner was apparently hoping to produce an even more comprehensive work, but his catalogues of 1925 and 1934 failed to achieve what he envisaged.[35] The most complete register, Otto Benesch's six-volume catalogue published in 1954–57, contained descriptions and illustrations of approximately 1,400 sheets. One of the most criticized works of its kind, it is also probably the most frequently consulted standard publication on Rembrandt's drawings.[36] The revised edition, which appeared in 1973, has an addendum with dozens more sheets.[37]

Werner Sumowski has been the most vociferous critic of the catalogues by Hofstede de Groot, Valentiner and Benesch.[38] Following the 1956 celebrations marking the 350th anniversary of Rembrandt's birth, Sumowski published a deluge of articles, based on thorough stylistic research, that advanced his views on the problems of attribution. Today many drawings, once attributed to Rembrandt, are catalogued in

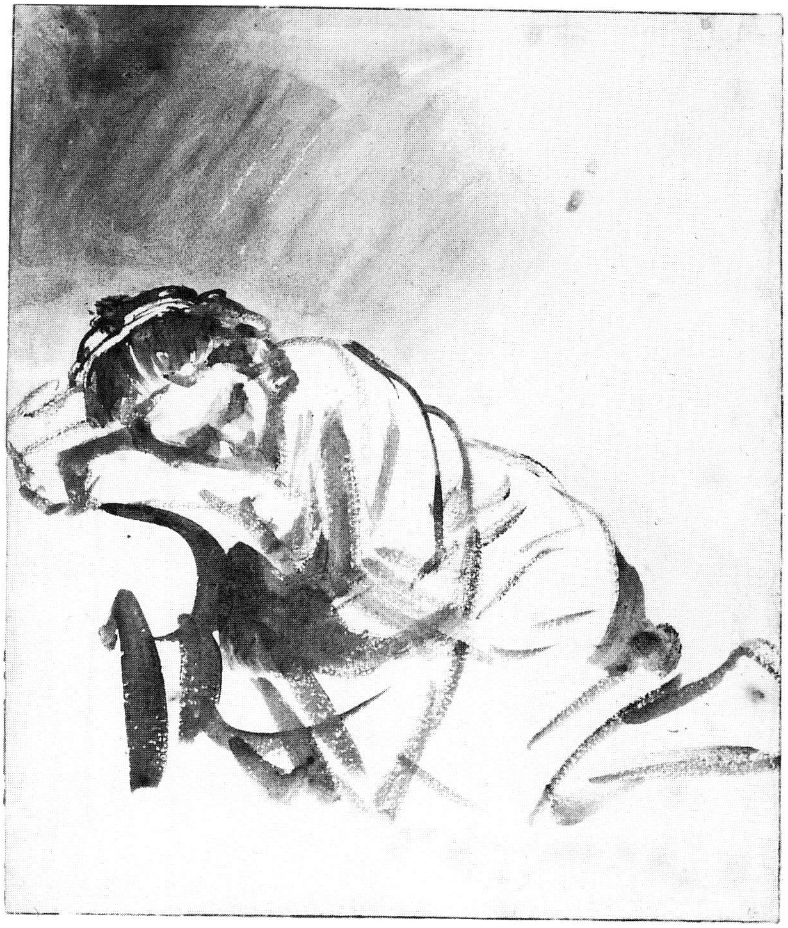

FIG. 11
Rembrandt
Portrait of a Sleeping Woman c.1655
Brush and ink
24.6 x 20.3 cm
Copyright © The British Museum, London

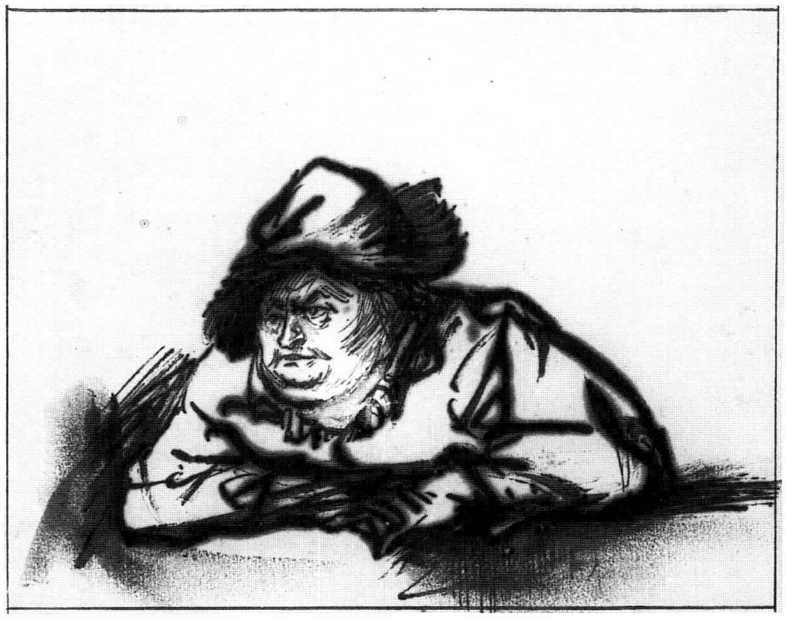

FIG. 12
Rembrandt
Portrait of the Actor Willem Bartolsz Ruyter
*c.*1638
Pen and ink and brush
13.9 x 14.7 cm
Rijksprentenkabinet, Rijksmuseum, Amsterdam

Sumowski's nine-volume series entitled *Drawings of the Rembrandt School* (1979–1985).[39] The author distinguishes three categories: a core of 'authentic' drawings, a less certain group of 'substantiated' drawings and a twilight zone of 'attributed' drawings. His main criterion, like that of Benesch, is style.

Yet this method has its shortcomings as well. Art historical research has taken great strides forward during the past few decades. As we have already seen, today's scholars are paying closer attention to inscriptions, signatures and collectors' marks. They also have a keener eye for types of paper and watermarks, and take more account of old descriptions, listings and prices in auction catalogues and other literature. Until recently, these valuable pointers were largely ignored by all but a few pioneers. Frits Lugt (1884–1970) stands out among them. The fruits of the endeavours of today's scholars can be seen in several recent collection catalogues, such as those published by museums in Amsterdam, Rotterdam and London.[40] The result has been the elimination of numerous attributions to Rembrandt that Benesch presented as more or less definitive. The drawings shown in this catalogue represent a selection of some of the finest autograph works, which have received the greatest measure of *'consensus eruditorum'.*

Very rarely does an unknown sheet come to light. In 1996 the Rijksmuseum bought a *Portrait of the Actor Willem Bartolsz Ruyter* (fig. 12), which came as a pleasant surprise to scholars: it was found to be perfectly consistent with the drawings in Rembrandt's accepted oeuvre.[41] It is reassuring in a sense to realize that our understanding of his technique, style and subjects has finally developed to a point where experts will apparently have little difficulty in recognizing 'Mr Rembrandt's own hand'.

1 Van Mander 1604, fol. 8a: 'Den Vader van t'schilderen mach men nommen/ Teyckenen/ oft de Teycken-const verheven'.
2 Van Hoogstraten 1678, p. 212.
3 Baldinucci 1686, p. 80; see also Broos 1981–82, p. 257.
4 Von Uffenbach 1753–55, vol. III, p. 317.
5 Dudok van Heel 1977, p. 106: '19 Leeuwen, na 't leven'.
6 Schatborn 1982, pp. 25–8.
7 Broos 1989, pp. 34–55.
8 Broos 1981, pp. 65–71.
9 Schatborn 1982a, p. 255, argues that Rembrandt had no hand in the work.
10 Broos 1995, p. 73: 'de beste schetsen van Rembran[d]t'.
11 Haak 1976, p. 10.
12 Strauss & Van der Meulen 1979, pp. 429–30, no. 1658/29: 'bestaende inde Konst van verscheyden der voornaemste so Italiaensche/ Fransche/ Duytsche ende Nederlandtsche Meesters/ ende by den selven Rembran[d]t van Rijn met een groote curieusheyt te samen versamelt. Gelijck dan mede een goede partye van Teeckeningen ende Schetsen vanden selven Rembran[d]t van Rijn selven'.
13 Strauss & Van der Meulen 1979, p. 444, no. 1659/14: 'de papiere konsten, rariteyten, antiquiteyten, medalien ende seegewassen'.
14 Schatborn 1982, pp. 17–21.
15 Hofstede de Groot 1906, p. VIII.
16 Royalton-Kisch 1992, p. 20.
17 Schatborn 1982, pp. 8–9: 'teyckeningen ende printen ... gedaen door Rembran[d]t van Rijn'.
18 Schatborn 1982, pp. 9–10.
19 Schatborn 1982, pp. 10–12.
20 Schatborn 1982, pp. 13–14.
21 Strauss & Van der Meulen 1979, p. 592, fig. 1.
22 Broos 1981–82, p. 258, fig. 10.
23 Amsterdam 1984–85, p. 18, cat. no. 7.
24 Baldinucci 1681–1728, vol. VI, p. 511; see also Broos 1981–82, p. 252.
25 Sumowski, *Drawings*, vols 1, 1979; 3, 1980; 4, 1981; 5, 1981; 6, 1982; 8, 1984.
26 Amsterdam 1984–85, pp. 46–7, cat. nos 33–4, figs 33, 34.
27 Broos 1981, pp. 150–1, no. 41; Schatborn 1990, p. 34: 'dees Tekeningh vertoont de buiten amstel kant / soo braaf getekent door heer rembran[d]ts Eijgen hant / p. ko'.
28 Strauss & Van der Meulen 1979, p. 491, no. 1661/12: 'huysvrouw van Sr. Rembran[d]t van Reyn, fijnschilder'.
29 Haak 1976a, p. 30.
30 Houbraken 1718–21, vol. I, 1718, p. 270: 'Toren, haat, droefheid, blydschap, en zoo voort, alles staat zoo natuurlyk afgebeeld dat men uit de pentrekken lezen kan wat elk zeggen wil'.
31 Houbraken 1718–21, vol. I, 1718, p. 270: 'meer als twintig Ducatons waard geschat word, schoon het maar een enkele schets met de pen op papier is'.
32 Vosmaer 1877, pp. 486–566.
33 Lippmann et al. 1888–1911.
34 Hofstede de Groot 1906.
35 Valentiner 1925–34.
36 Benesch 1954–57.
37 Benesch 1973.
38 Broos 1984, p. 163.
39 Sumowski, *Drawings*; see also Royalton-Kisch 1992, pp. 17–20.
40 Schatborn 1985; Giltaij 1988; Royalton-Kisch 1992.
41 Schatborn & De Winkel 1996.

73
Old Man with a Book
*c.*1628

Chalk and brush and ink on tinted paper
29.5 x 21.0 cm
Staatliche Museen zu Berlin, Kupferstichkabinett

LITERATURE: Benesch 1973, vol. I, p. 5, no. 7.

Rembrandt's drawing in red and black chalk on primed pale yellow paper shows a seated man, viewed from the back, holding a large book – undoubtedly an old Bible – with leather binding and clasps. The man gazes pensively before him. This sheet was a preparatory study for the repoussoir figure in *Two Old Men Disputing* (cat. no. 3), a painting that was discovered only in 1934 and is now at the National Gallery of Victoria.

In 1641 Jacques de Gheyn III described that work as 'a painting done by Rembrandt wherein two little old men are seated and disputing, one with a large book on his lap, while sunlight comes in'.[1] His observation about the sun is certainly apt, for the unusual lighting, which reveals the influence of the Utrecht Caravaggisti, is one of the most striking features of the painting. The drawing was clearly an exercise in rendering a figure facing a source of light and therefore covered in shadows of varying depth.

The figure in the Melbourne painting who marks a passage in the book with his finger can be seen in reverse in a second red chalk drawing, in which his flowing beard and his sword identify him as the apostle Paul (Benesch 15) (fig. 73a). Rembrandt used this study for his etching of *The Apostle Paul Lost in Thought* from around 1629 (B.149). The elderly man here is the same model we see, either as the apostle or in various other guises, in many of his drawings, etchings and paintings.[2]

The figure of the old man in the Berlin drawing has undergone some subtle changes in the painting. He is barefoot, for instance, as an apostle would be. A more significant difference, however, is that he is shown with a shorter beard, similar to that with which St Peter is normally portrayed. The figure in the painting may therefore be taken to represent Peter (for another view, see commentary to cat. no. 3).

BB

1 Bredius 1915, pp. 126–8.

2 Benesch 1973, vol. I, p. 7, no. 15, refers to Benesch 16, 18–20, 37–41, 56 (drawings); B. 260, 262, 309, 312, 315, 325 (etchings); and Bredius 602, 604, 605, 607 (paintings).

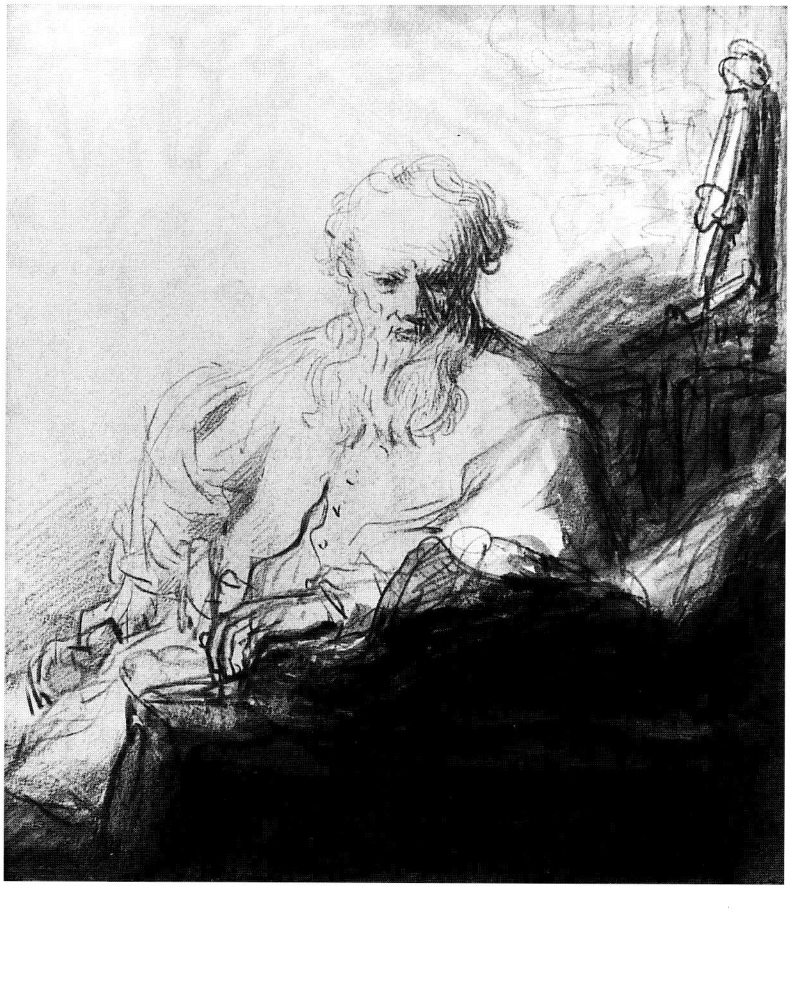

FIG. 73a
Rembrandt
The Apostle Paul *c.*1629
Chalk and brush and ink
23.6 x 20.1 cm
Musée du Louvre, Département des Arts Graphiques, Paris

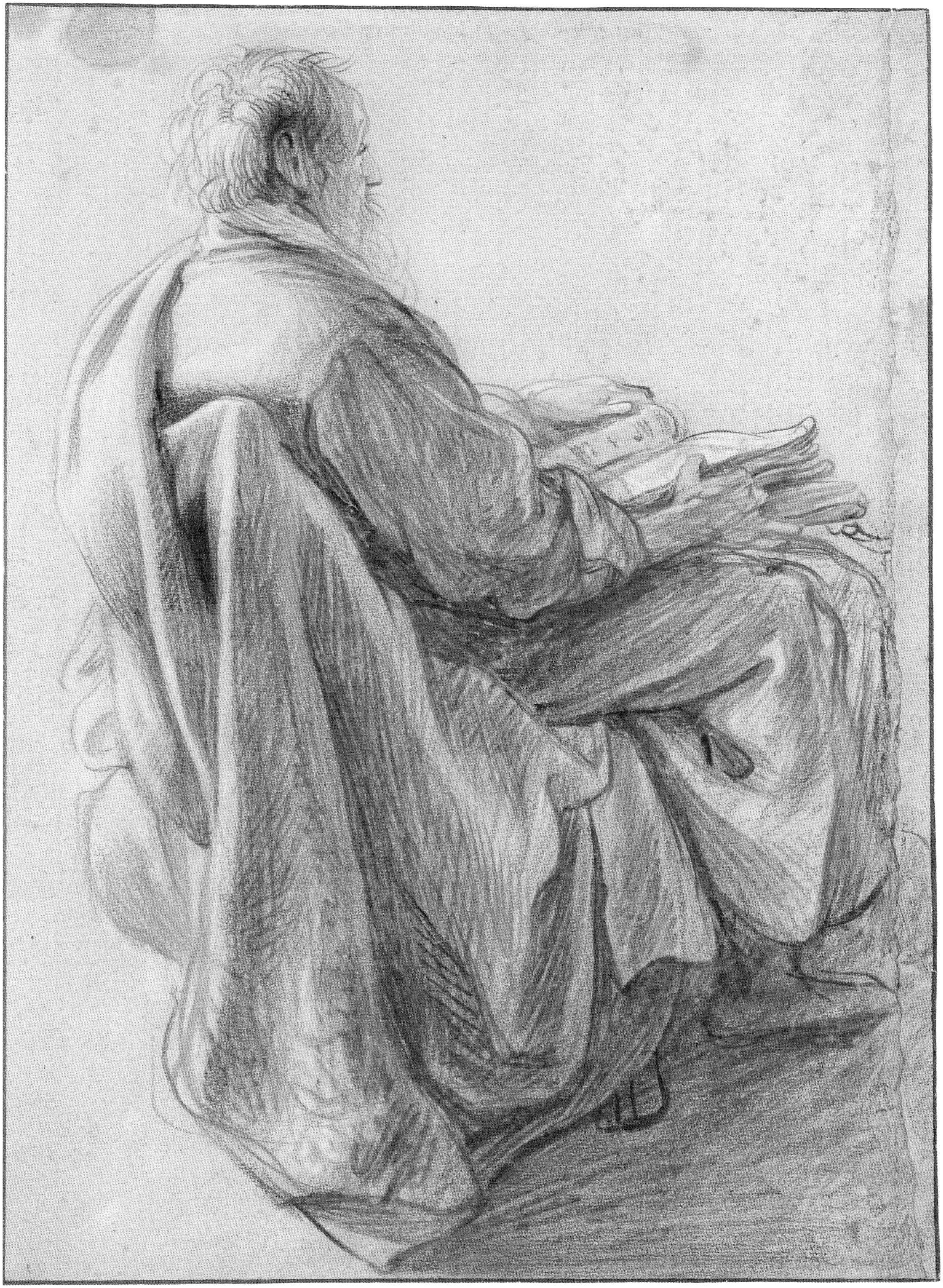

74
Abraham's Sacrifice
*c.*1634

Signed lower left *Rembrandt*
Chalk and brush and ink
19.5 x 14.7 cm
Trustees of the British Museum, London

LITERATURE: Benesch 1973, vol. I, p. 28, no. 90; Royalton-Kisch 1992, pp. 56–8, cat. no. 13.

Thursday, 16 January 1992 was a momentous occasion for Rembrandt specialists. Two painted versions of *Abraham's Sacrifice*, one from Munich and the other from St Petersburg, were brought together at the Rijksmuseum in Amsterdam. Experts took advantage of the opportunity to compare this drawing of Abraham, from the British Museum, with the two paintings of the same composition. The unanimous conclusion, it seemed, was that the painting from the Hermitage, signed *Rembrandt. f. 1635.* (Bredius 498) (fig. 74a), was of a higher standard and that no more than the head of the aged Abraham in the Alte Pinakothek version could have been executed by Rembrandt. The inscription on this canvas of *c.*1635–36, 'Rembrandt. altered. And painted over. 1636', is ambiguous but may be taken to mean that one of Rembrandt's pupils changed the master's original conception of the composition in accordance with Rembrandt's own instructions.

The drawing must have served as an aid in this process, as the main difference in the Munich version is the position of the angel. The angel was originally approaching from the left, as in a painting Rembrandt had seen by his own teacher Pieter Lastman (Museum het Rembrandthuis, Amsterdam). In another picture by Lastman, the angel is advancing directly from the centre background (fig. 74b), and this is how Rembrandt drew the figure. He had studied not only Lastman, but a scene by Rubens as well, which is known from an etching by Andreas Stock. In particular, the all-but-naked figure of Isaac is based on Rubens's work. Rembrandt was of course also familiar with the biblical narrative.[1] According to the Old Testament, God commanded Abraham to make a burnt offering of his son Isaac. Abraham built an altar and was about to slay his son with a knife when an angel appeared and spoke to him: 'Abraham, Abraham ... Lay not thine hand upon the lad, neither do thou any thing unto him: for now I know that thou fearest God' (Genesis 22:11–12).

In the drawing, the angel's iron grip on Abraham's wrist, the frozen gesture and the knife falling to the ground are testimony to the power of Rembrandt's imagination and the depth of his compassion. This haunting image, like Isaac's head forced back and held down by his father's hand, goes beyond anything Rembrandt would have found either in his examples or in the Bible.

This expressive drawing was also a study to find the appropriate lighting for the dramatic event. Rendered in red and black chalk with grey washes, it recalls a drawing, made by means of the same technique, of *Christ and the Apostles* (Teylers Museum, Haarlem) (Benesch 89), from 1634.[2] *Abraham's Sacrifice* could well have been made in the same year, and therefore before the two paintings of 1635–36. In any event, the drawing is not a copy of the composition in St Petersburg, as has been suggested. This is apparent in the handling of Isaac's left leg and the falling knife, as well as in the treatment of the angel. Rembrandt's pupil copied the angel's gesture, in the picture now in Munich, but was less successful in his attempt to represent the foreshortened figure.

BB

1 For the importance of the biblical text in relation to the illustration of the episode, see Angel 1642, pp. 48–9, and Broos 1972, pp. 139–43, repr.
2 Royalton-Kisch 1992, p. 57.

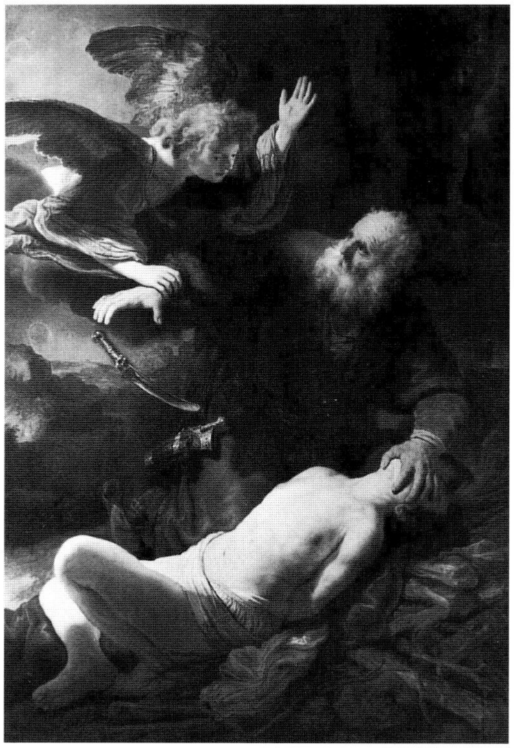

FIG. 74a
Rembrandt
Abraham's Sacrifice
Signed and dated 1635
Canvas
193.5 x 132.8 cm
Hermitage, St Petersburg

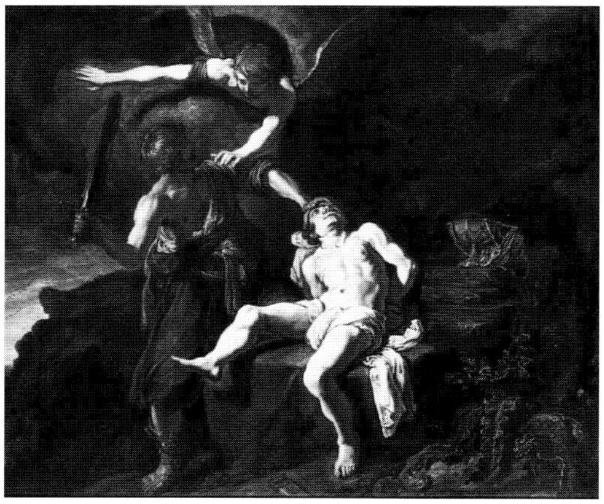

FIG. 74b
Pieter Lastman 1583–1633
Abraham's Sacrifice
Signed and dated 1616
Panel
36.0 x 42.0 cm
Musée du Louvre, Paris

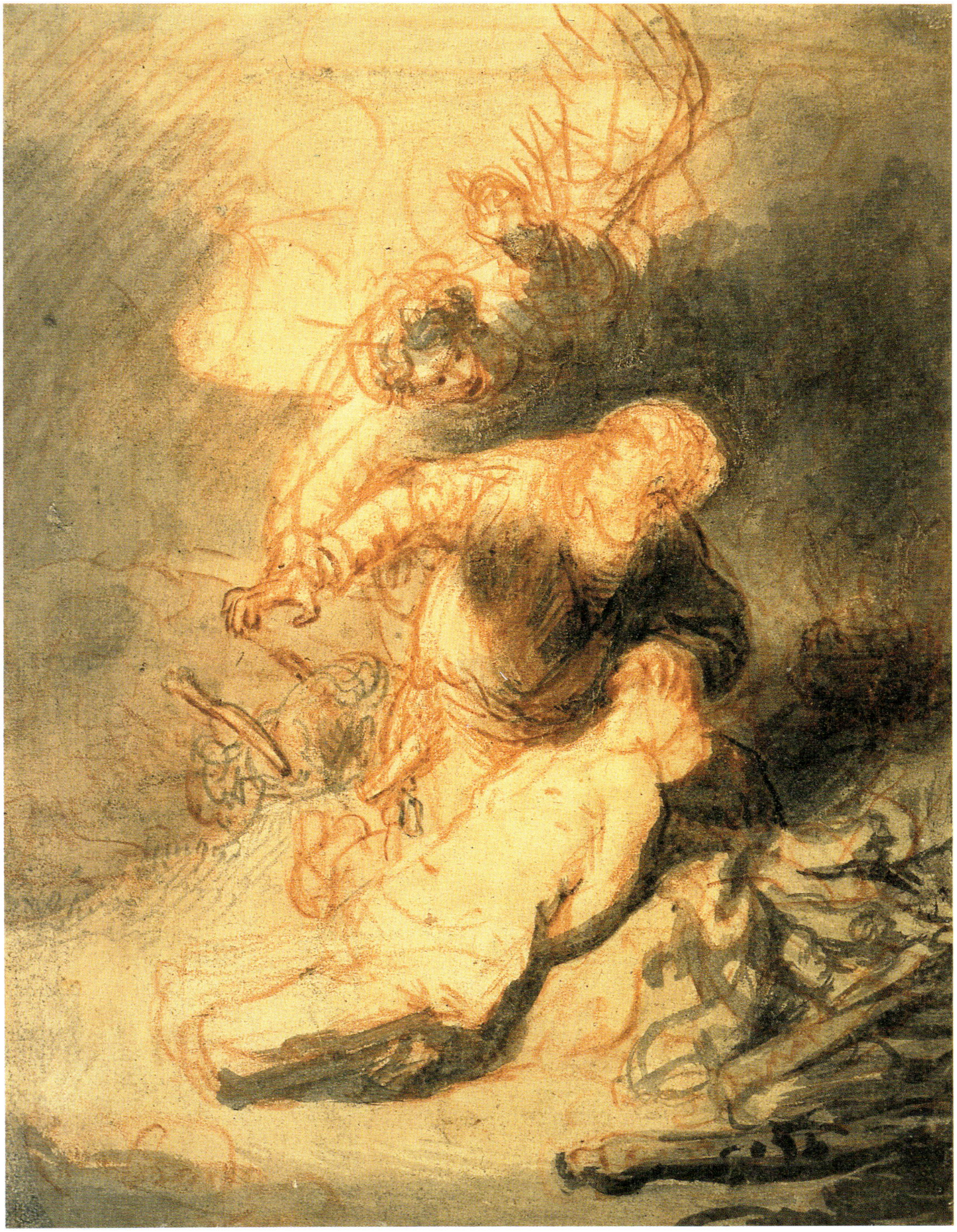

75
Figure Studies of Three Women
*c.*1635

Pen and ink
20.9 x 13.7 cm
Verso: *Young Man in a Turban and a Woman Asleep c.*1635
Inscriptions by Cornelis Ploos van Amstel
Pen and ink
National Gallery of Victoria, Melbourne;
Felton Bequest 1936

LITERATURE: Benesch 1973, vol. II, pp. 57–8, no. 194; Gregory & Zdanowicz 1988, pp. 116–17.

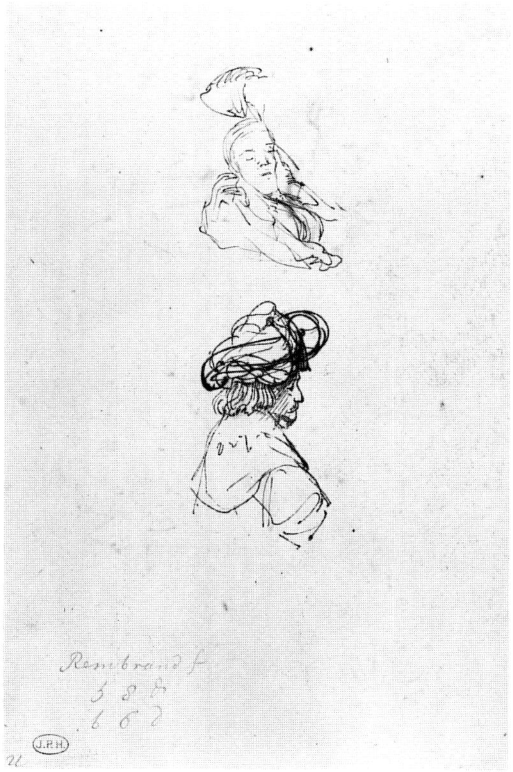

FIG. 75a
Rembrandt
Young Man in a Turban and a Woman Asleep
*c.*1635
National Gallery of Victoria, Melbourne
(cat. no. 75 verso)

The lifelike quality of many of Rembrandt's sketches of women and children has given rise to speculation that the models were members of his own family. As far as the children are concerned this could have been the case only in a few instances. This sheet carries two sketches of a seated woman with her hands folded in her lap, and a drawing of a mother or nurse standing with an infant in her arms. On the reverse we see a man in a turban, and a quick sketch of a woman asleep (fig. 75a). The woman may have been Rembrandt's first wife, Saskia van Uylenburgh, whom he often drew from life (cat. no. 82). The back of the sheet is also inscribed in the handwriting of Cornelis Ploos van Amstel (1726–1798), whose collection was sold in 1800.[1] The location of Ploos's annotations indicates that apparently he preferred the 'front' of the sheet with the three drawings of women, although the sketches on the back are in fact by no means inferior.

It has been suggested that some of Rembrandt's studies of small children – toddlers crawling on the floor, sitting in a high chair or leaning on their mother's arm – may have been portrayals of his first son, Rumbartus. According to I. H. van Eeghen, however, this would have been impossible in the majority of cases, as Rumbartus was christened at the Oude Kerk in Amsterdam on 15 December 1635 and was buried at the Zuiderkerk two months later to the day.[2] He could therefore have been portrayed only as an infant, as in a drawing in Rotterdam (Museum Boijmans Van Beuningen) (Benesch 360). The child in our picture could also be Rumbartus, although the woman bears little resemblance to his mother Saskia.

All the older children in Rembrandt's drawings must therefore have been the offspring of friends, relatives or acquaintances, or else sketches from his imagination. Rembrandt himself may have regarded these kinds of drawings as genre scenes rather than portraits. A batch of drawings in the possession of the marine painter Jan van de Cappelle after the sale of Rembrandt's collection were indeed described as such. An inventory of van de Cappelle's property compiled in 1680 included a portfolio containing '135 drawings of the lives of women and children, by Rembran[d]t'.[3] Van de Cappelle owned no fewer than five hundred sheets by Rembrandt, which he presumably bought at the sale of the master's collection in 1658.

This study sheet from the mid-1630s is similar in some respects to a model sheet of *Studies of Men's Heads and Three Women with Children* (cat. no. 79), which dates from the same period.[4] This is especially true of the figures on the right.

BB

1 Laurentius et al. 1980, p. 357, note that Ploos had numerous drawings by Rembrandt, including several figure studies done with the pen. Benesch 1973, vol. II, p. 58, no. 194, writes that the present sheet is 'Inscribed by a later hand: Rembrandt f. and several numbers (indications of prices?)'. The 'numbers', however, are the measurements of the sheet: 'h[oogte] 8 d[uim]' en 'b[reedte] 6 d[uim]' (*hoogte* = height, *duim* = inches, *breedte* = width).

2 Van Eeghen 1956a, p. 144.

3 Schatborn 1982, pp. 10–12; Hofstede de Groot 1906a, p. 412, no. 17.

4 Benesch 1973, vol. II, p. 57, no. 194, dates the Melbourne drawing 'about 1632', which is probably too early.

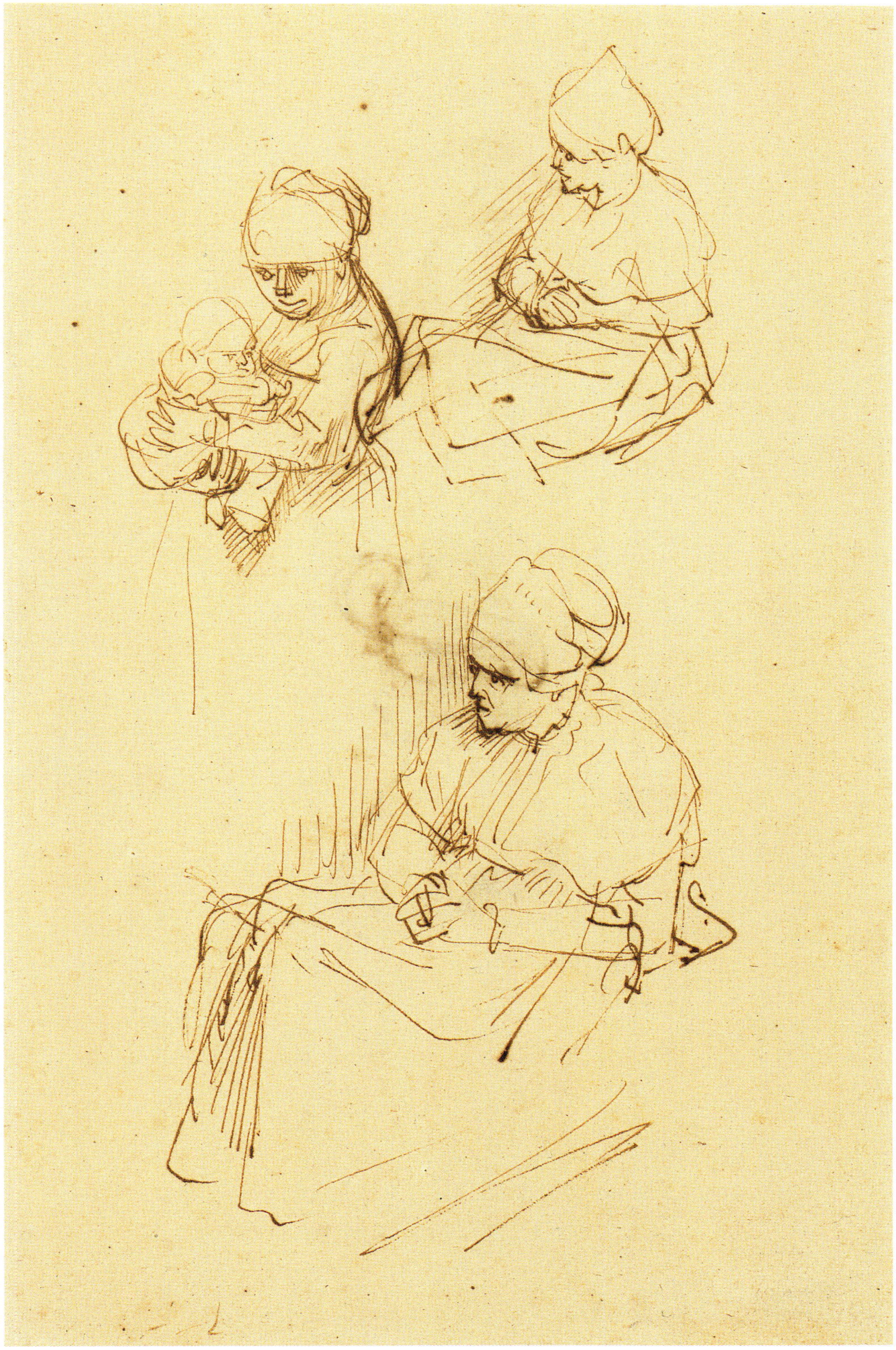

76
Pantalone
*c.*1635

Pen and ink
18.3 x 13.0 cm
Lower left: collector's mark of J. C. Robinson
Collection Groninger Museum, Groningen

LITERATURE: Benesch 1973, vol. II, pp. 75–6, no. 295; Bolten 1967, pp. 90–1, no. 56.

In the second half of the 1630s Rembrandt made several drawings of actors who were evidently quite happy to pose in their exotic costumes after a show. In 1638 Joost van den Vondel's *Gijsbreght van Aemstel* was staged to mark the opening of a new theatre in Amsterdam. Rembrandt attended some of the rehearsals to make sketches of the play. In 1996, the Rijksprentenkabinet of the Rijksmuseum, Amsterdam, acquired a fascinating portrait of Willem Bartolsz Ruyter, the actor who played the bishop Gozewijn in *Gijsbreght* in 1638 (p. 329, fig. 12).[1]

The man with the grin in the drawing shown here is a farcical character from the *commedia dell'arte*, a form of improvised theatre with stereotype comic figures. He is the lecherous Dottore, or Pantalone, whom Rembrandt immortalized in three works on paper of *c.*1635, the two others being in the Kunsthalle, Hamburg (Benesch 296), and the Städelsches Kunstinstitut, Frankfurt (Benesch 297) (fig. 76a). The actor in the present work is smiling broadly and seems to be posing for the artist, but his lifelike appearance belies the fact that the drawing was presumably not made from life. Instead, it recalls an etching of Pantalone – which Rembrandt would certainly have seen – by Jacques Callot (fig. 76b), one of his series of three *commedia dell'arte* characters. The two others Callot portrayed were the boastful young lover Capitano, and Scapino the wily rogue.

Rembrandt has copied Pantalone's dandyish pose from Callot: his bow, his leg extended forward, one hand on his heart and the other behind his back, lifting his coat so he does not trip over the hem. But the actor has neither the mask nor the pointed beard he would typically have worn in Italy. On the other hand, he has some extraordinary objects dangling from his waistband: two balls and a long, cylindrical sheath in which he may have kept a flute. Their phallic implications would be hard to ignore.[2] Rembrandt must have seen these attributes in reality on some occasion, as they do not appear in Callot's print. In any event he depicted them as a stock part of the costumes he depicted in at least four further drawings he made of actors, charlatans and other such figures (fig. 76a).[3] He obviously enjoyed this brand of bawdy humour, which seems rather unsophisticated today.

BB

1 Albach 1979, pp. 16–19.
2 Rob Ehrenstein has mentioned to the author that he also thinks it feasible that these objects were meant as phallic symbols.
3 See also, for example, Albach 1979, figs 5, 7, 9, 10, 12.

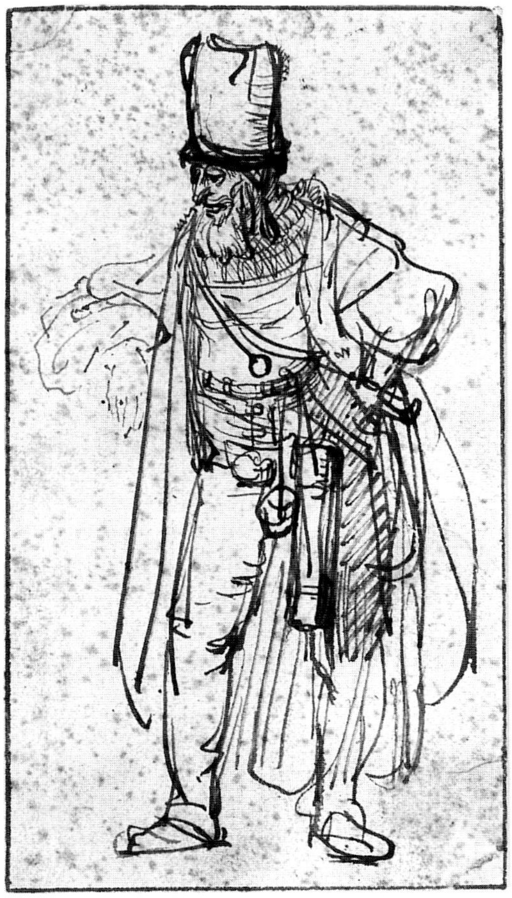

FIG. 76a
Rembrandt
Pantalone *c.*1635
Pen and ink
16.2 x 8.8 cm
Städelsches Kunstinstitut, Frankfurt

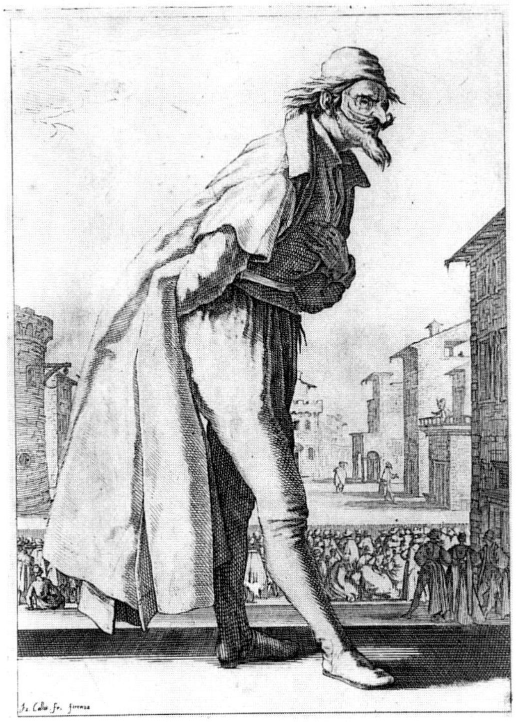

FIG. 76b
Jacques Callot French, 1592–1635
Pantalone *c.*1618–19
Signed *Ja. Callot. fe. firenza*
Etching
21.6 x 14.7 cm
Teylers Museum, Haarlem

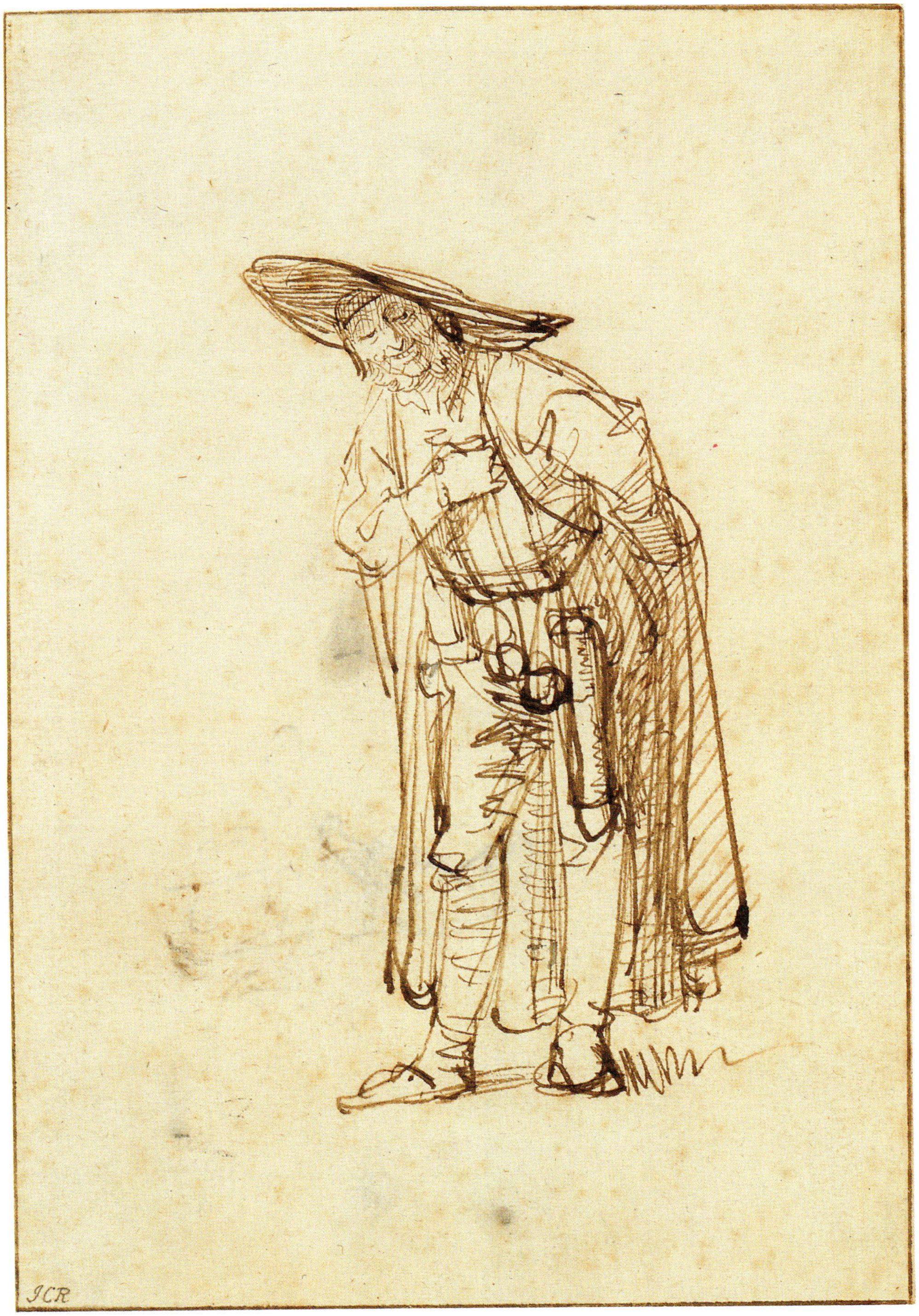
JCR

77

Susanna and the Elders

*c.*1635

Signed lower right *Rf*
Chalk
23.5 x 36.4 cm
Staatliche Museen zu Berlin, Kupferstichkabinett

LITERATURE: Benesch 1973, vol. II, pp. 106–7, no. 448.

Following the death of his teacher Pieter Lastman in 1633, Rembrandt made a few drawings after his paintings, apparently as a kind of *'in memoriam'*. Lastman's colourful history pieces with their small figures fascinated Rembrandt all his life. He used them as examples when teaching his own pupils, and drew inspiration from them himself.[1]

In 1636 he painted a picture of *Susanna* (cat. no. 10), illustrating a poignant scene from the Bible. The example on which he based this work is a painting of *Susanna and the Elders* (fig. 77a) by Lastman. The red chalk drawing shown here, which Rembrandt made after Lastman's painting in about 1635, is not merely a copy, for it is also a critical commentary on his teacher's work. Rembrandt apparently felt that the figures' actions in Lastman's picture were too tame for such an erotically charged scene from the Bible. He first made a fairly accurate copy of the beautiful garden with a sphinx fountain and with peacocks in the tree, although his lines are rough and sketch-like. But he obviously gave a great deal of thought to the figures in the scene. The elder on the right is standing more erect in the drawing, and he is beckoning or perhaps even making an obscene gesture to the naked girl. His companion leans over Susanna with brazen effrontery, and with his right hand points to a spot in the distance where he hopes to lure her.

The main changes Rembrandt made, however, were designed to alter the young woman's pose. Critical of the vague gesture of her right hand in Lastman's picture, he drew her right arm close to her body, with her hand protectively in her lap. Her left hand is moving towards her breast. These changes heighten Susanna's air of embarrassment. Moreover, they are consistent with an ancient pictorial tradition.

Susanna's improved pose is worked out in more detail in the painting referred to above, where we see what Rembrandt's corrections were intended to achieve. What he wanted to emphasize was Susanna's shame at her nakedness. Her gestures recall those of the *Venus pudica* ('the Capitoline Venus'), a sculpture from classical antiquity that has come to personify decorum (fig. 77b). Rembrandt's Susanna is likewise a 'Venus of Modesty'. Rembrandt embroidered on his work from 1636 in a version he finally completed in 1647. This picture captures with even greater force Susanna's timidity and her abhorrence of the old men (Gemäldegalerie, Berlin) (Bredius 516) (p. 20, fig. 3);[2] cf. cat. no. 80.

BB

1 Broos 1975–76, pp. 199–210.
2 Broos 1993, pp. 264–5.

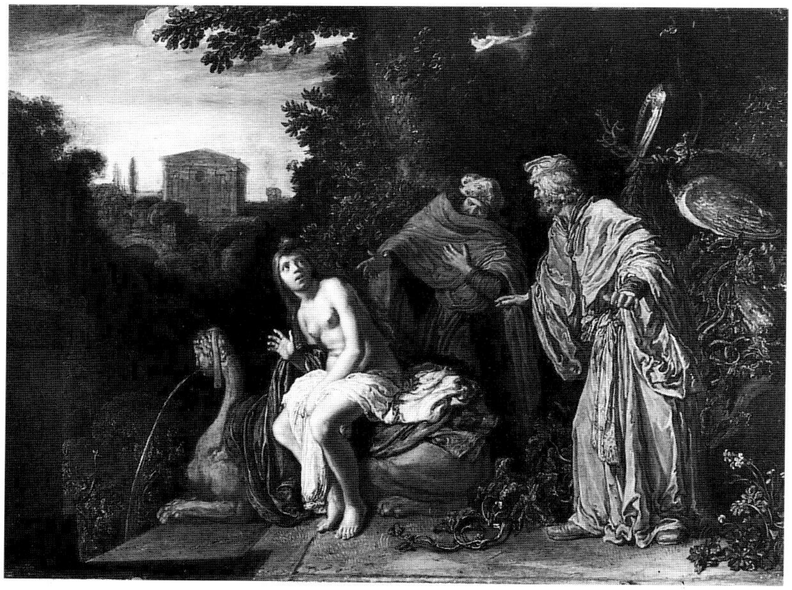

FIG. 77a
Pieter Lastman 1583–1633
Susanna and the Elders
Signed and dated 1614
Panel
42.0 x 58.0 cm
Staatliche Museen zu Berlin, Gemäldegalerie

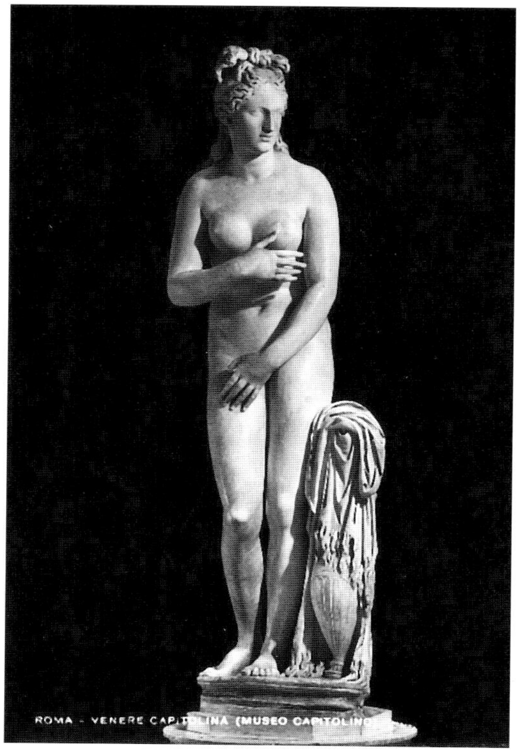

FIG. 77b
Roman (copy after Greek original, 4th century BC)
Venus pudica
Marble
Museo Capitolino, Rome
From a postcard

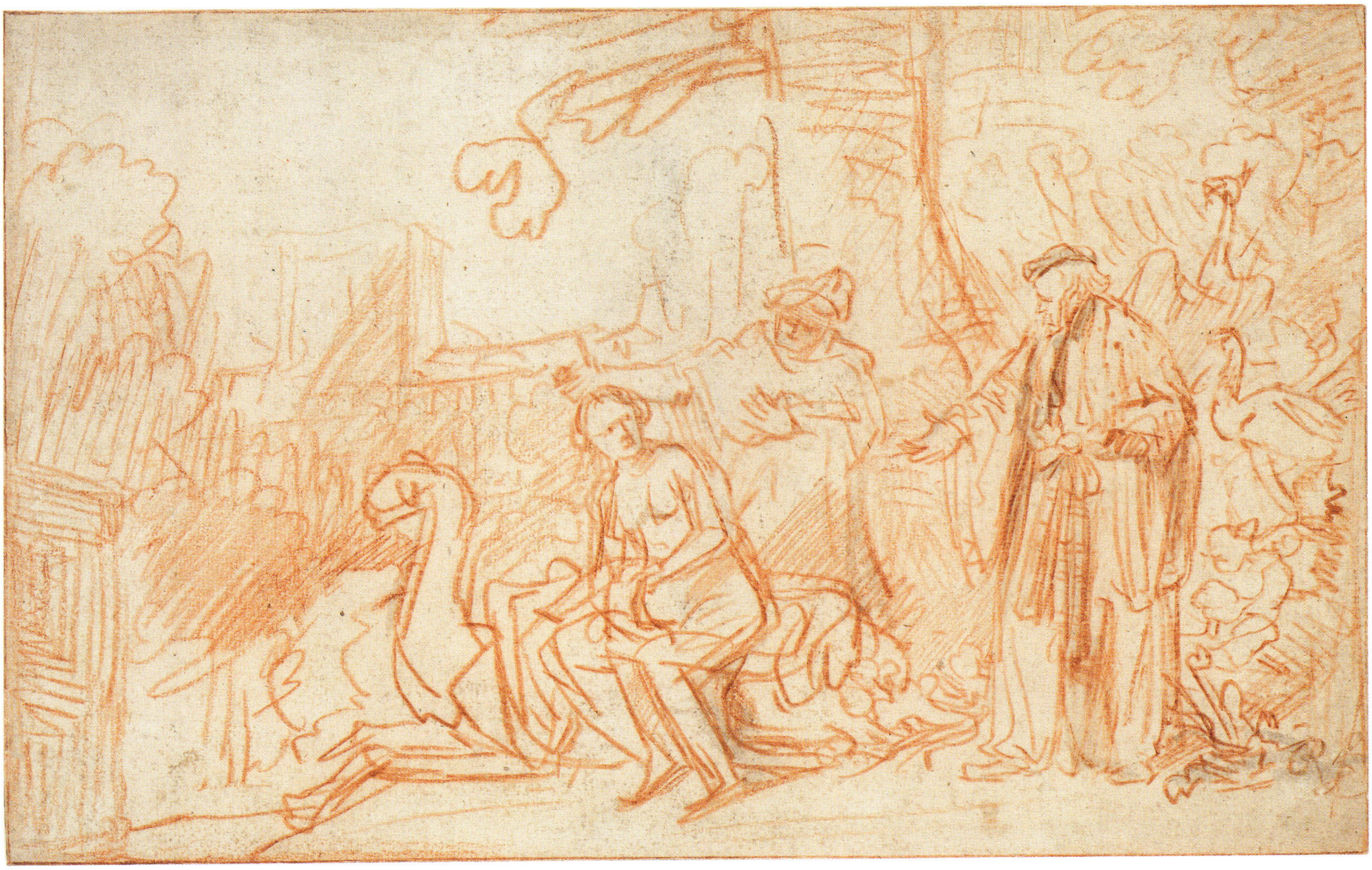

78

Venus and Mars in Vulcan's Net

*c.*1635

Pen and ink
21.1 x 28.9 cm
Amsterdam Historical Museum; legacy C. J. Fodor

LITERATURE: Benesch 1973, vol. III, p. 149, no. 540; Broos 1981, pp. 31–5, no. 3.

This drawing has all the eloquence of a good cartoon: it is humorous, familiar and entertaining. The figure of Vulcan on the left, his face contorted and his neck bulging with rage, is the focal point of the composition. Even without knowing the details of the story, one is struck by the contrast with the group of grinning figures in the centre. Rembrandt has illustrated an episode from the amorous adventures of the gods of antiquity. These mildly erotic scenes were popular in the 1630s.

Homer (*Odyssey* VII. 266–367) and Ovid (*Metamorphoses* IV. 171–89) relate the story of Vulcan's ill-fated marriage. Thanks to his prodigious wealth, the lame, ugly blacksmith was able to wed the beautiful Venus. Venus, however, fell in love with Mars and betrayed her husband. Upon discovering her infidelity, Vulcan forged a bronze net, light as gossamer, which he secretly fixed to Venus's bed. He thus managed to capture her lying naked in Mars's embrace. He summoned the gods to witness the couple's adultery, but their response was largely unsympathetic. Indeed, Mercury's remark – 'Oh, for the same opportunity!' – met with gales of laughter. Jupiter alone was not amused, for his son-in-law, the cuckold Vulcan, demanded the return of his dowry.

Rembrandt has exploited the anecdotal potential of the narrative to the full. Venus and Mars are sitting at the left, enmeshed in the net held by the outraged Vulcan, who is recognizable by the anvil under his arm and by his deformed left leg, which is slightly shorter than the right leg. Cupid, with a quiver of arrows, peers down from behind a cloud hovering above Vulcan's head. Some of the gods are huddled together in the centre, barely able to contain their mirth. Hercules can be identified by his club and by the lionskin he wears on his head. The two figures at the back could be Mercury and Apollo. Jupiter, wearing a sullen expression, is in the middle of the group. He is ensconced on his throne, with his symbol, the eagle, and with a bolt of lightning in his right hand. Juno and her attribute, the peacock, are at the far right. The protectress of marriage, Juno observes the spectacle with disapproval.

Rembrandt attended the university-preparatory Latin School in Leiden before embarking on his vocation as an artist. Although he may have read Homer and Ovid, the present work is more likely to have been inspired by a non-literary source. In essence, his representation of the assembled gods is based on a fresco by Raphael in the Villa Farnesina in Rome. Several prints were made after the fresco, with these taking certain liberties in respect of the original composition. The poses of Jupiter and Juno in the present drawing, and the setting of the scene in the clouds, have similarities in Caraglio's print after Raphael, which was probably in Rembrandt's collection (B.54) (fig. 78a). Raphael's scenes clearly appealed to Rembrandt, who would have seen his teacher Pieter Lastman's interpretations of them in his small history paintings.[1] It therefore stands to reason that the old works of graphic art he bought at auctions in Amsterdam in 1637 and 1638 included 'prints by [read: *after*] Raphael'.[2] These were what he saw as classical examples.

In a sense, the vision Rembrandt expresses in this drawing is also a commentary on Raphael's picture. The poses are less formal and stylized than in the older representation. Vulcan, for instance, has the appearance of a fisherman hauling in his catch, while Jupiter looks more like a seasoned sea captain with whiskers than a Greek deity.

The sheet most probably dates from the mid-1630s or shortly afterwards. In 163(5?) Rembrandt painted another satirical romantic scene from classical antiquity, *Diana, Actaeon and Callisto* (Fürsten zu Salm-Salm, Anholt) (Bredius 472) (fig. 29b), the theme of which, like that of the Amsterdam drawing, is the meting out of retribution for licentious behaviour. In this picture the revelation of Callisto's pregnancy has prompted the same strong emotions that Rembrandt so obviously loved to portray.

BB

1 Broos 1975–76, pp. 199–228.

2 Strauss & Van der Meulen 1979, p. 141, no. 1637/2; p. 150, no. 1638/2: 'printen van Rafel'.

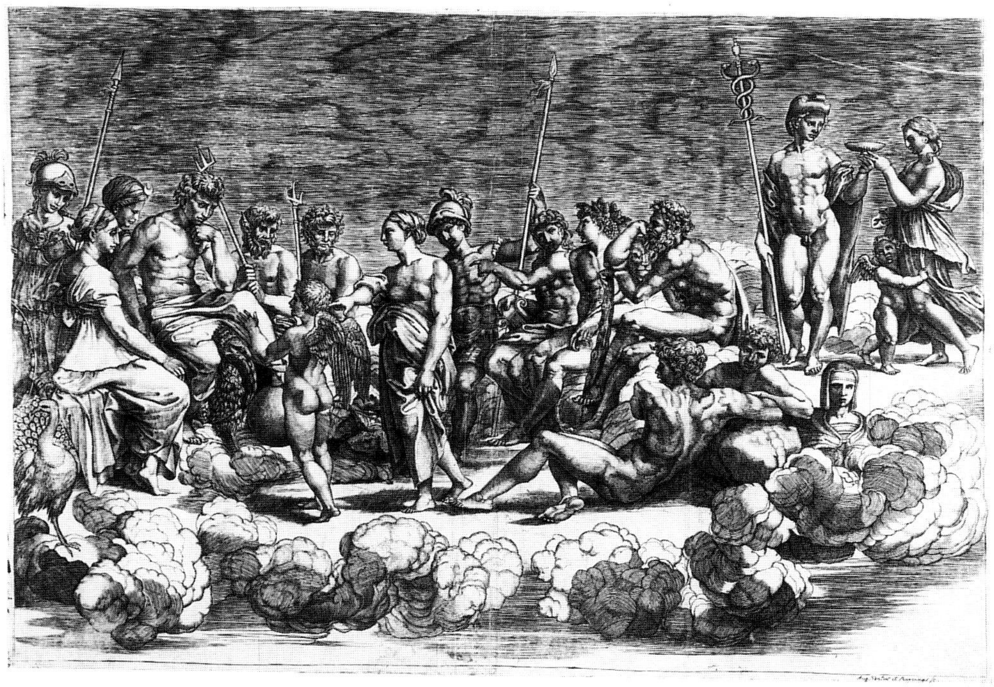

FIG. 78a
Gian Jacopo Caraglio (Italian, *c.*1500–1557), after Raphael
The Gods on Mount Olympus *c.*1525–30
Engraving
36.1 x 54.0 cm
Copyright © The British Museum, London

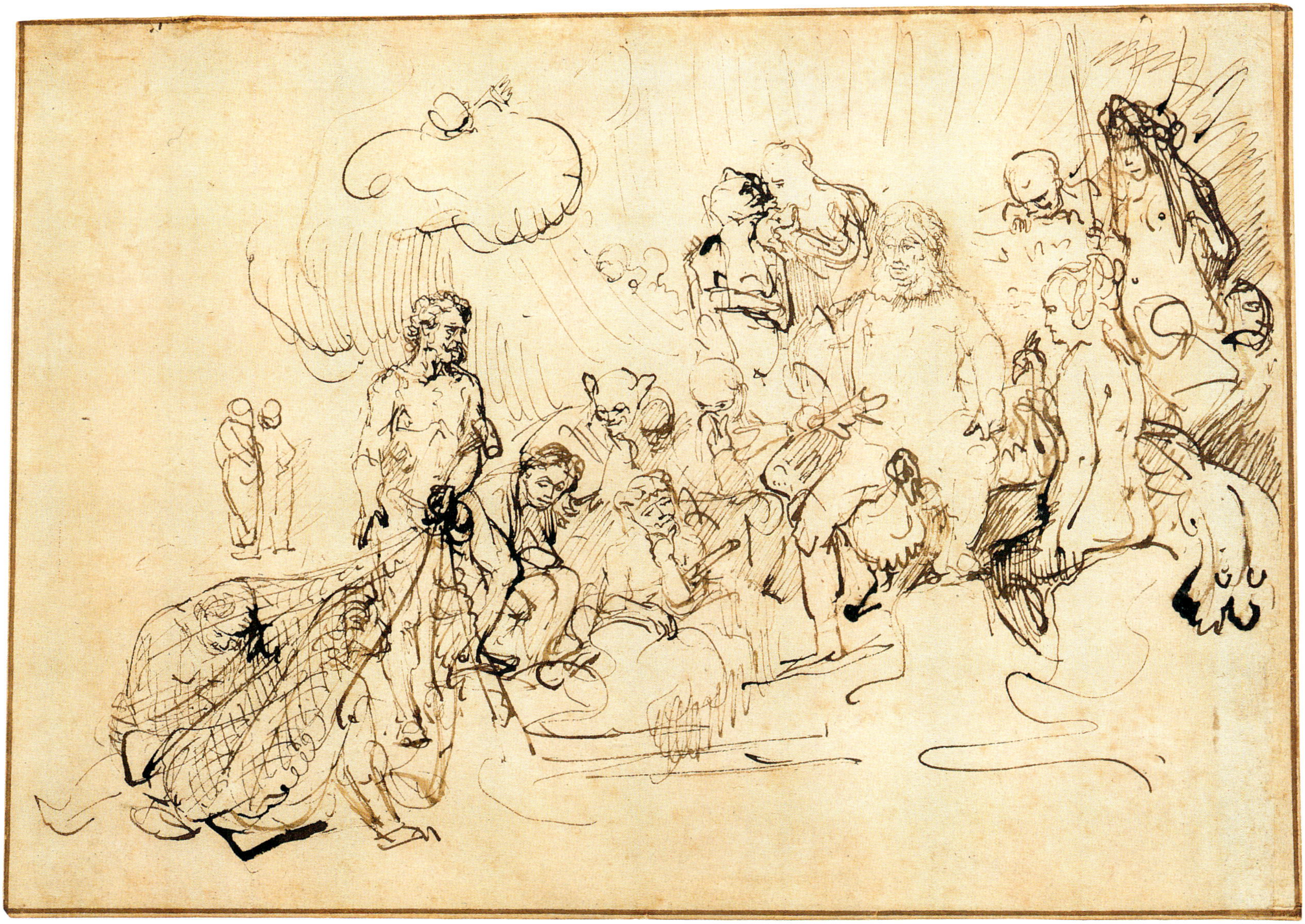

79

Studies of Men's Heads and Three Women with Children

*c.*1635–36

Pen and ink and brush
22.0 x 23.3 cm
The Trustees of the Barber Institute of Fine Arts, the University of Birmingham

LITERATURE: Benesch 1973, vol. II, pp. 83–4, no. 340.

From the Middle Ages it was common practice for model books to be used in painters' studios, by the master himself and of course by his pupils. Books of this kind contained sketches of a variety of subjects and served as *aides-mémoire:* they included figure studies, animals, flowers and landscapes. Centuries later, these collections of loose sheets were etched and engraved and thus made available to a wider public. One example is Abraham Bloemaert's *Artis Apellae liber*, which was published by his son in about 1650.[1] Like Bloemaert, Rembrandt was not only a prolific draughtsman but also a diligent teacher, ever willing to produce drawings of his own as examples for his pupils.

A portfolio listed in an inventory of the estate of the marine painter Jan van de Cappelle (1626–1679) in 1680, containing '135 drawings of the lives of women and children, by Rembran[d]t' (cat. no. 75), may also have been a drawing book of sorts from Rembrandt's studio. Dealers and collectors have dismantled these books over the years, so that none have survived intact. Loose sketchbook sheets carrying more than one representation were also generally cut to form separate works. The numerous studies on small-format paper that are now attributed to Rembrandt suggest that there must originally have been many more model sheets like the present example. This unimpaired study sheet with six men's heads and three women with children is a true rarity.

The sheet shown here is dominated by a man with a large, round face, who is wearing a fur coat and a plumed beret. The fine, detailed penstrokes defining his podgy features stand out sharply compared to the wide brushstrokes used for his torso and hat. His left hand marks the centre of the page, and eight figures form a circle around him. On the left are two sketches of a young man in a beret; one shows him in profile, and the other glancing over his shoulder. He bears a certain resemblance to the head of a man in an etching Rembrandt made in 1635 after an example by Jan Lievens (B.289) (fig. 79a). In the upper left section of the present sheet are two sketches of an oriental man in a turban, and on the right three drawings of a mother or wetnurse with a child. It seems that the infant has just been suckled and is now fast asleep. At the bottom of the sheet we see a red chalk sketch of a young man in a fur-trimmed hat, leaning on a table. The same medium has been used for corrections to the arm of the corpulent man in the centre.

Rembrandt made etchings, too, that combine studies from life with unrelated, picturesque subjects. One, dated 1636, contains several portraits of his wife Saskia van Uylenburgh as well as an elderly man in a turban (B.365). The model sheet discussed here was made around the same time.[2]

BB

1 Bolten 1979, pp. 26–9.
2 P. Schatborn, in Berlin / Amsterdam / London 1991–92d, p. 44, cat. no. 8.

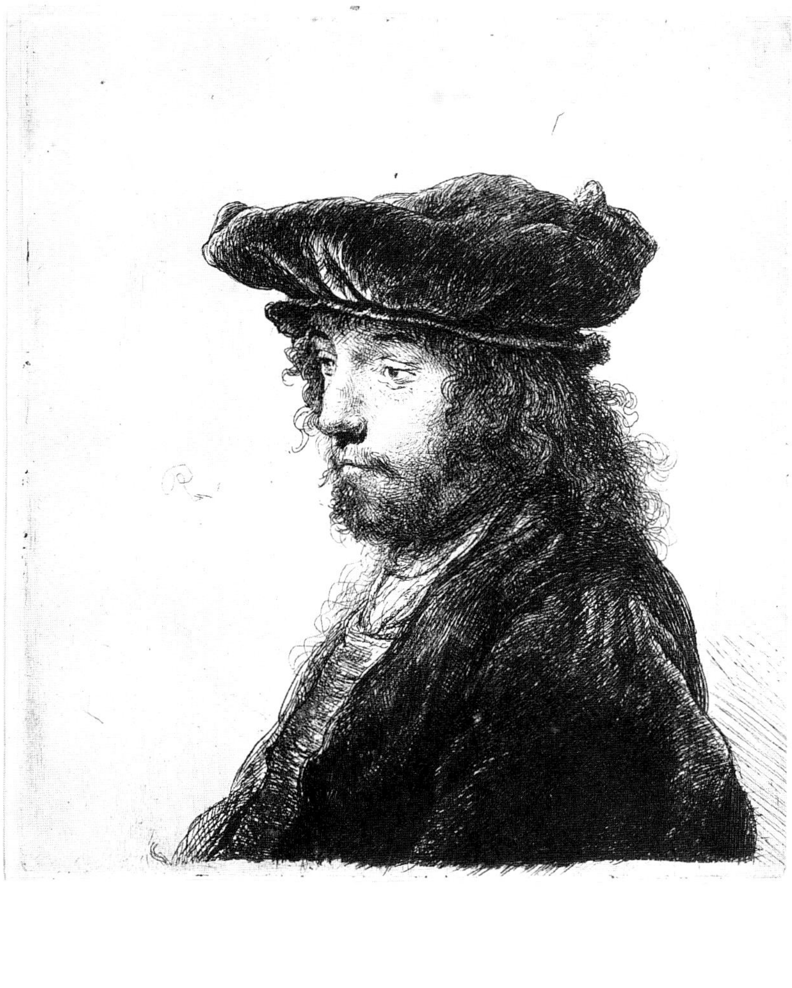

FIG. 79a
Rembrandt, after Jan Lievens
The Fourth Oriental Head 1635
Etching
15.7 x 13.7 cm
Rijksprentenkabinet, Rijksmuseum, Amsterdam

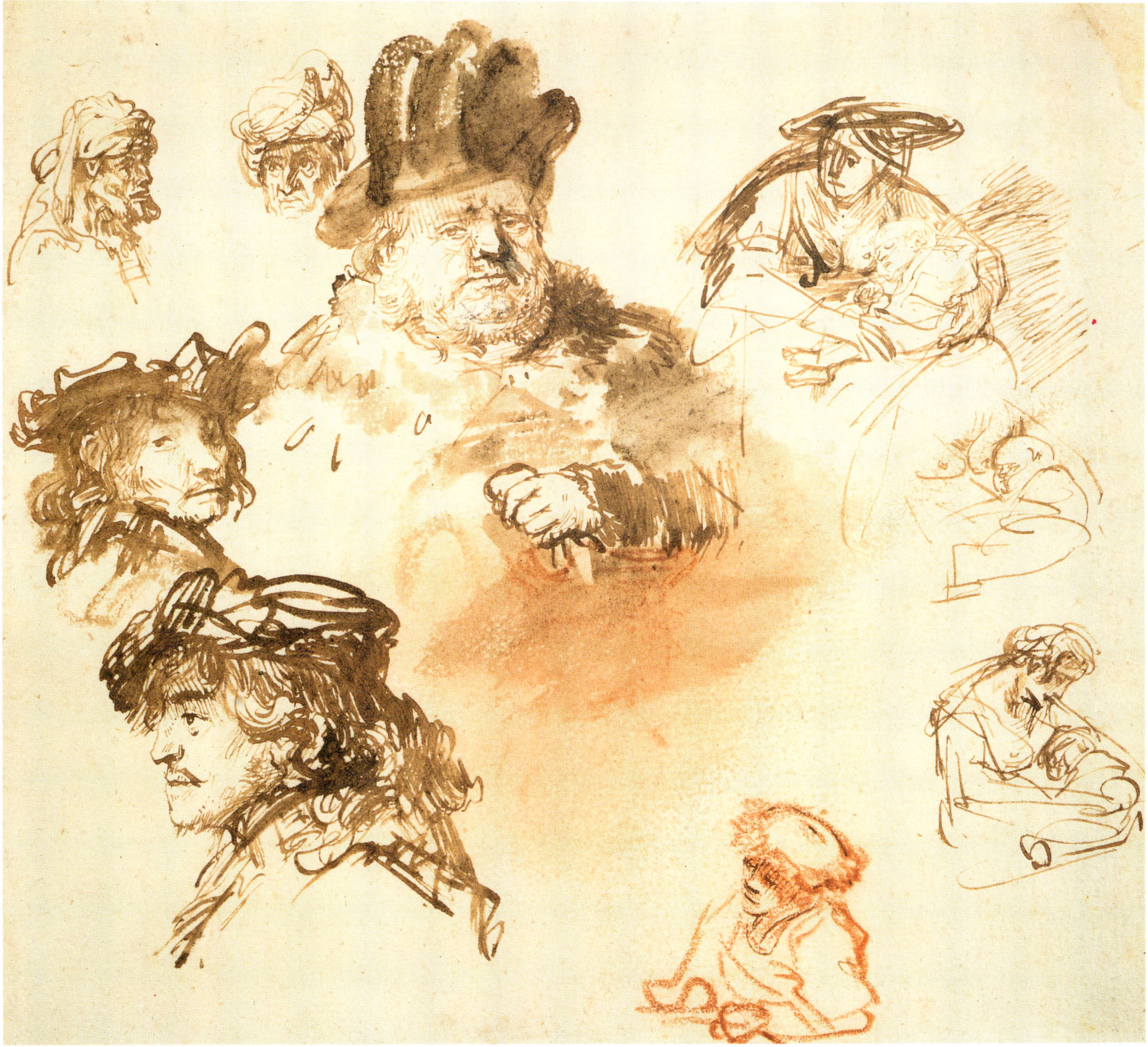

80

An Elder
*c.*1638

Inscribed upper left (apocryphal) *Rembrandt f. 1656*
Pen and ink on tinted paper
17.3 x 13.5 cm
National Gallery of Victoria, Melbourne;
Felton Bequest 1936

LITERATURE: Benesch 1973, vol. I, p. 45, no. 157; Gregory & Zdanowicz 1988, p. 117.

The theme of Susanna and the Elders preoccupied Rembrandt in his drawings and paintings throughout the 1630s and 1640s. In about 1635 he made a drawing after his teacher Pieter Lastman's painting of this subject from 1614, distilling from it a composition of his own (cat. no. 77). In 1636 he made a painting of the Susanna subject. Its central image is the naked Susanna being spied upon by two elders from the shelter of a thicket (cat. no. 10). Shortly afterwards Rembrandt designed a picture that shows the elders brazenly confronting the girl. The original scheme of this painting, which was completed only in 1647 (Gemäldegalerie, Berlin) (Bredius 516) (p. 20, fig. 3), is known from X-ray photographs and from a copy by one of Rembrandt's pupils, most probably Barend Fabritius (fig. 80a).[1] In this version Susanna is about to enter the water when one of the elders reaches out to clasp her left breast.

The lewd gesture appears to have struck the wrong chord. Rembrandt drew the man again and subsequently rendered the contour of Susanna's back in a single stroke running through the elder's left hand. He finally decided not to show the hand actually touching the woman's body but to depict it simply clutching her robe. Hence the present drawing was made only after Rembrandt had established that Susanna would be portrayed leaning forward. The rock on which she has laid her robe is suggested by a diagonal penstroke at the lower right. The right hand with the upturned thumb was also moved slightly higher in the drawing than in the initial version of the Berlin picture so that there could be no doubt at all that the gesture was meant to be obscene. In this sheet Rembrandt was primarily interested in seeing how far forward he could place the elder's right leg. In the final painted version we see his foot just behind Susanna's draped robe.

This study, in which an initial sketch of a turban(?) can also be seen, at the upper left, was executed in gallnut ink on yellow prepared paper, which the ink has corroded in parts. Rembrandt used the same technique in drawings that have been related to etchings and paintings from 1638 and 1639.[2] This suggests that the present drawing was made in or around 1638.

A drawing with some similarities to this work came to light for the first time on 9 October 1996, when the printroom of the Rijksmuseum in Amsterdam announced the purchase of a hitherto totally unknown drawing, the *Portrait of the Actor Willem Bartolsz Ruyter* (p. 329, fig. 12). This sheet is also executed in gallnut ink, in a similar style and on tinted paper.[3] It is likewise believed to have been made around 1638, the year in which the actor Willem Ruyter gave his last performances to packed theatres in Amsterdam. Ruyter died in 1639.

BB

1 Sumowski, *Drawings*, vol. 4, 1981, pp. 1792–3, no. 823x.
2 P. Schatborn, in Berlin / Amsterdam / London 1991–92d, p. 92, note 11.
3 *NRC Handelsblad*, 9 October 1996, p. 9; Schatborn & De Winkel 1996.

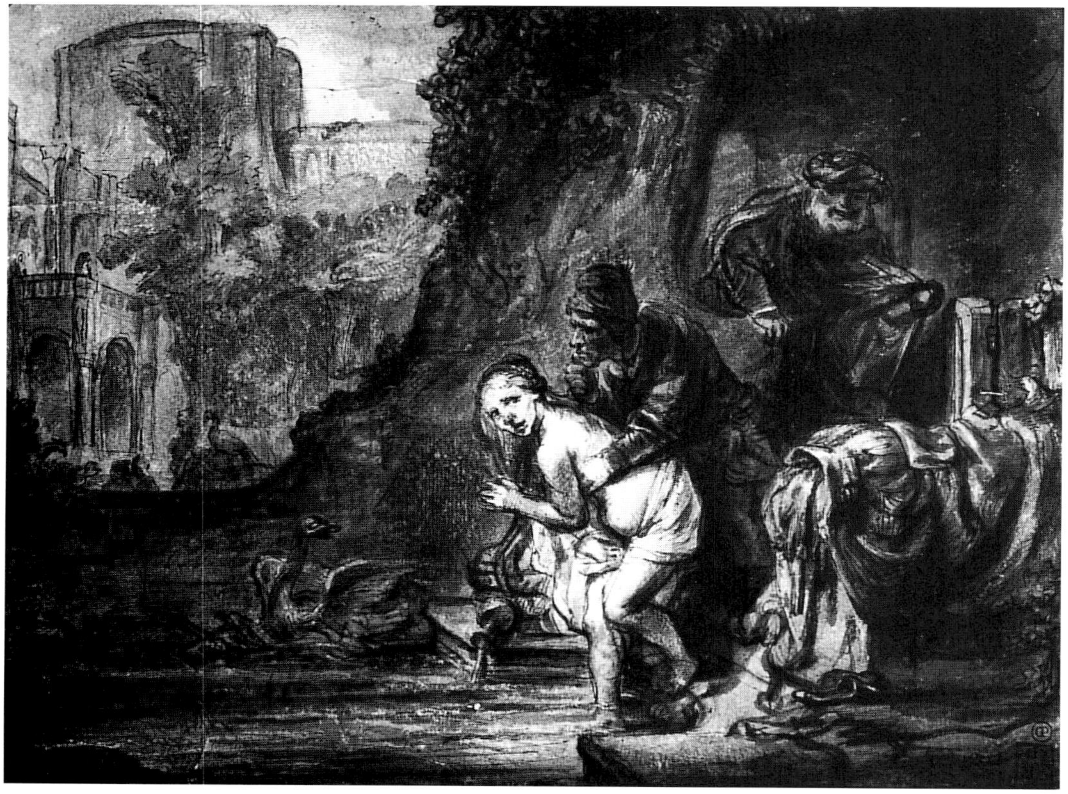

FIG. 80a
Barend Fabritius, after Rembrandt
Susanna and the Elders *c.*1638
Pen and ink and brush
17.8 x 23.8 cm
Szépmüvészeti Múzeum, Budapest

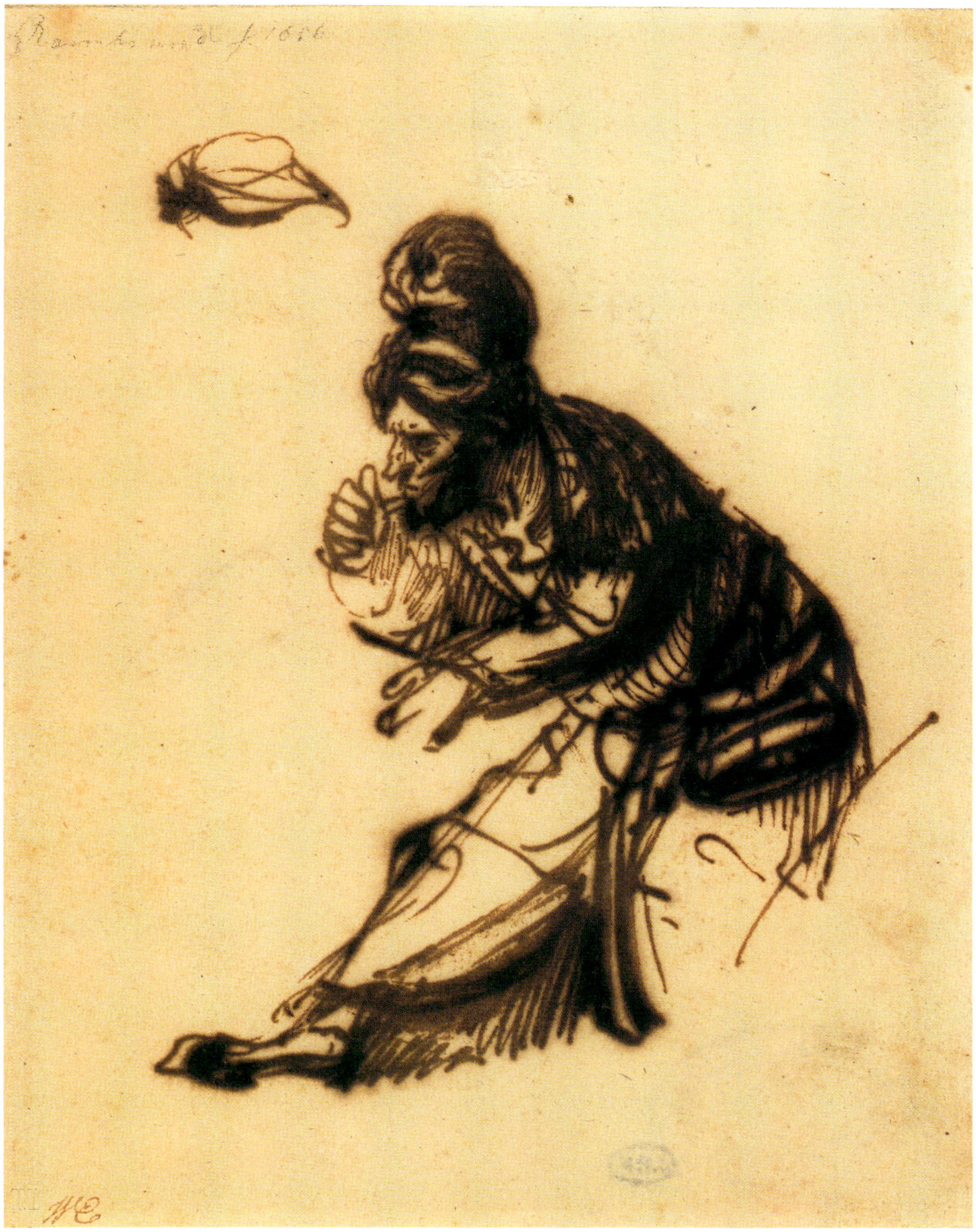

81

Horseman in a Pageant
*c.*1638

Pen and ink and brush, with chalk
21.0 x 16.4 cm
Lower left and lower right: collector's mark of Jonathan Richardson Sr
Trustees of the British Museum, London

LITERATURE: Benesch 1973, vol. II, p. 89, no. 367; Royalton-Kisch 1992, p. 73, cat. no. 22.

Rembrandt made four drawings of a pageant, two showing black musicians on foot (private collection) (Benesch 366) and on horseback (British Museum, London) (Benesch 365), and two that show a horseman in a tall hat (Benesch 367, 368). One of the latter works depicts this horseman frontally and shows him in the company of another rider (Benesch 368) (fig. 81a). He makes a rather comical impression in his strange hat, with his large moustache and goatee. The other drawing, that seen here, shows him from the rear. He is less droll in this version, although the old-fashioned ruff in combination with the type of hat generally worn by charlatans still looks fairly odd. The horse is merely hinted at in both pieces. It is interesting that out of a whole procession of people and animals this one particular man was fixed so firmly in Rembrandt's memory that he could portray him with absolute accuracy some time after the event.

The four drawings are rendered in the same style and technique: they have been executed in pen and brown ink, with a brush being used for the washes and subsequently red chalk for some of the hatching, white opaque paint for a few highlights, and yellow oil paint to colour small details of the costumes. They remained together for many years as part of the large collection brought together by Jonathan Richardson Sr. I. Q. van Regteren Altena suggested that they may have been made during the festivities held to celebrate the marriage of Wolfert van Brederode and Louise Christine van Solms in The Hague in February 1638.[1] The bride was the sister of Amalia van Solms, who was married to the stadholder Frederik Hendrik. Given that Rembrandt was no stranger to The Hague, this hypothesis is certainly plausible. In 1632, for instance, he painted the *Portrait of Maurits Huygens* (Kunsthalle, Hamburg) (Bredius 161) (fig. 8i) and its pendant, the *Portrait of Jacques de Gheyn III* (cat. no. 8), most likely during a visit to The Hague. In January 1639 he wrote a letter to the court, saying that he had spent several years working on a series of scenes of the Passion (Bredius 548, 550, 557, 560, 561, 574), which the stadholder had commissioned, and that he had now completed two pictures.[2]

BB

1 Van Regteren Altena 1952, pp. 59–63.
2 Gerson 1961, pp. 34–8. Cf. our pp. 24, 25.

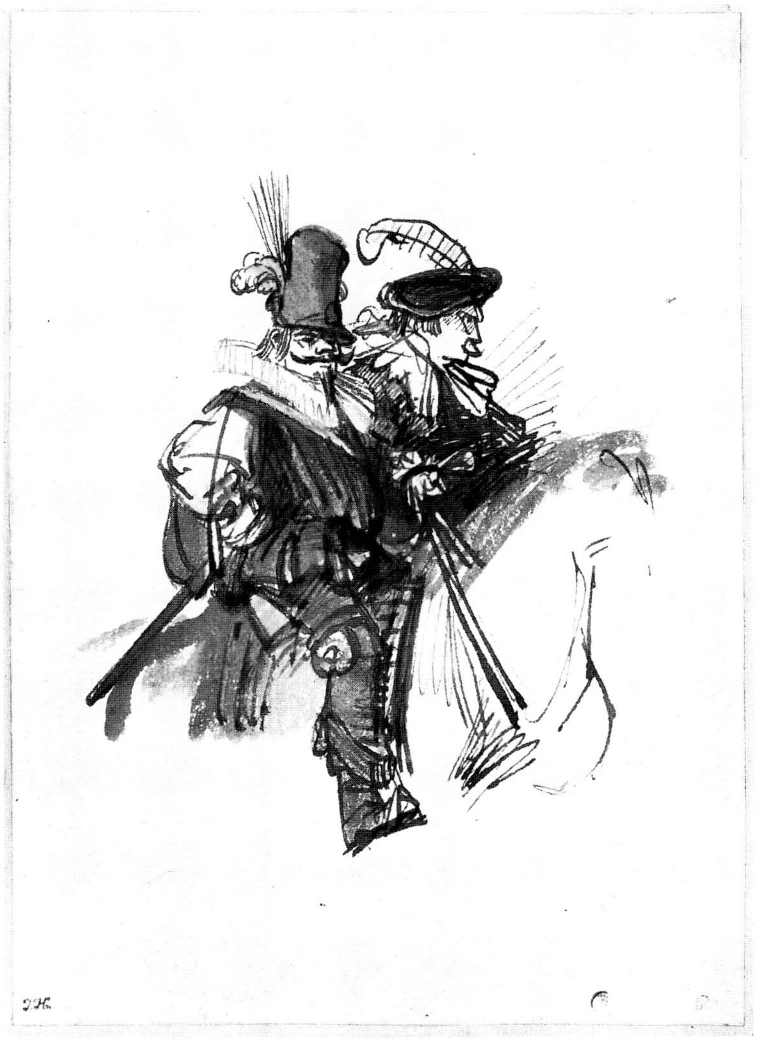

FIG. 81a
Rembrandt
Horsemen in a Pageant *c.*1638
Pen and ink and brush, with chalk
21.2 x 15.3 cm
The Pierpont Morgan Library, New York, I, 201

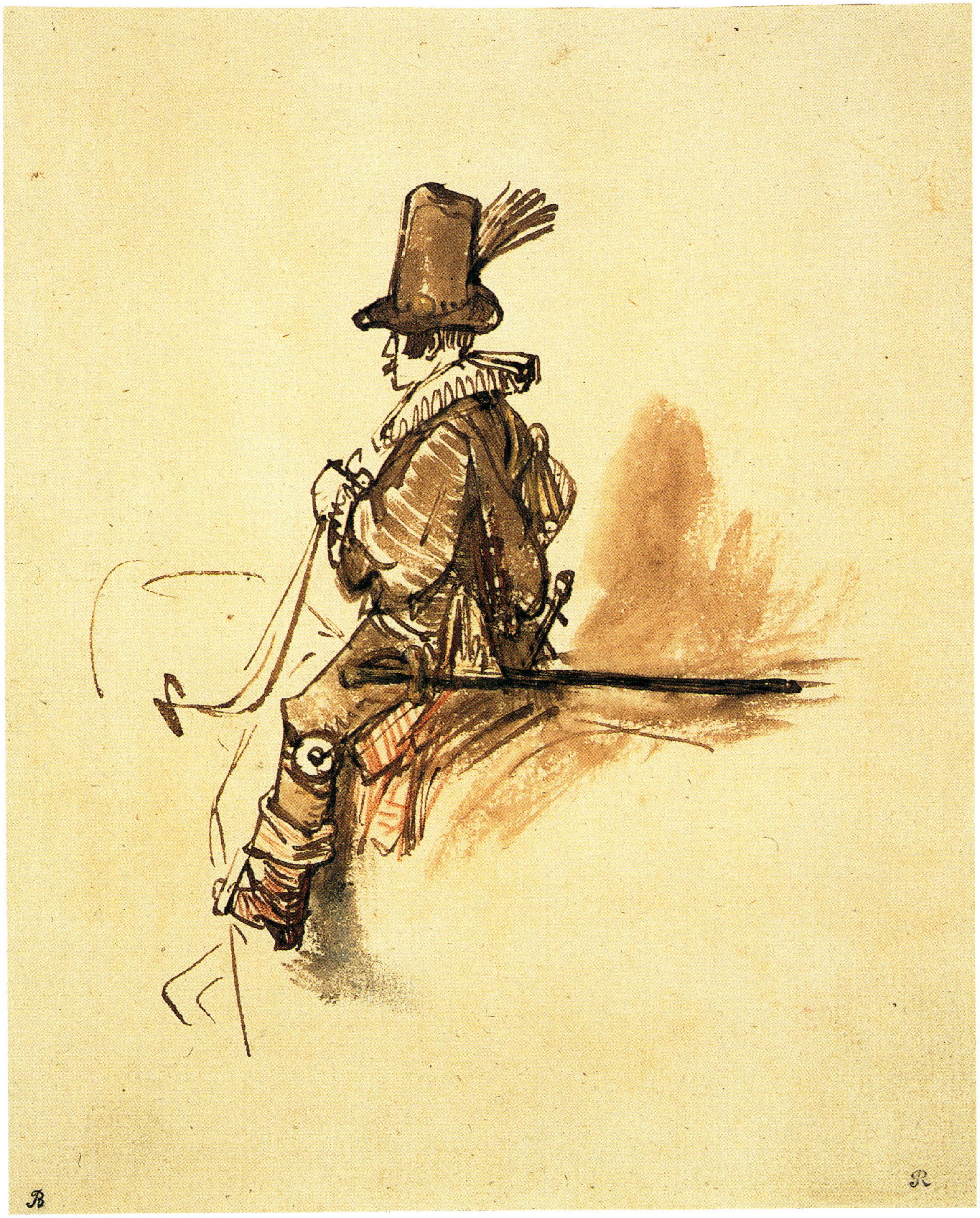

82

Saskia in Bed

1642

Inscribed lower right *Rembrant.*
Pen and ink and brush
13.7 x 20.3 cm
The Visitors of the Ashmolean Museum, Oxford

LITERATURE: Benesch 1973, vol. II, p. 72, no. 281A.

In this drawing Rembrandt has portrayed his wife asleep in bed, possibly during a pregnancy or when she was sick. This thumbnail sketch was obviously rendered from life, as we can see from Saskia's closed eyes and serene expression. Rembrandt drew these details with a fine-tipped pen, and used a brush to represent the wide contours of the pillow, the coverlet and the shadowy bedstead. The sheet was made two hundred years before the invention of photography, and few artists indeed would have been able to capture an image with such eloquence.

Rembrandt's first wife was one of his favourite models. He painted Saskia as Flora, for instance, in 1634 (Hermitage, St Petersburg) (Bredius 102), and *c.*1635 (National Gallery, London) (Bredius 103), and she is the subject of his most poignant drawn portrait, a silverpoint dating from 1633 ('This is a portrait of my wife')[1] (p. 328, fig. 10). She also appears in many of his etched study sheets and portraits (B. 342, 347, 365, 367, 368, 369). Rembrandt married Saskia van Uylenburgh on 22 June 1634. Their first son, Rumbartus, who was christened on 15 December 1635, lived for only a few weeks. During his son's brief life Rembrandt drew Rumbartus together with his mother (Museum Boijmans Van Beuningen, Rotterdam) (Benesch 360).

This is the earliest drawing of Saskia asleep. She brought four children into the world within the space of six years. Cornelia – named after Rembrandt's mother – was baptized on 22 July 1638, but she, too, died within a few weeks. A second daughter, also called Cornelia, was born in 1640 but survived for only a fortnight. The fourth child was a son, Titus, who was baptized on 22 September 1641. Six months later, 'ailing in bed', Saskia summoned a notary to draw up her will.[2] She was suffering from tuberculosis and died on 14 June 1642, not yet thirty years old.[3] This was also the year in which Rembrandt completed his famous masterpiece *The Night Watch* (Rijksmuseum, Amsterdam) (Bredius 410) (p. 26, fig. 7).

The drawing discussed here dates from one of Saskia's periods of confinement to her sickbed. It is most closely related to a sheet of studies of elderly men and women, etched at random over the page (B.369) (fig. 82a). In the middle of this page are two spontaneous sketches of a woman – undoubtedly Saskia – in bed. Given that her position in bed was reversed in the printing process, it may be assumed that the etching, too, was probably drawn from life. The uniqueness of this study sheet is underscored by the fact that only a single state was produced. It is generally believed to have been made in the spring of 1642, shortly after Titus's birth and in the last stage of Saskia's illness.[4] The related drawing probably dates from around the same time.[5]

BB

1 'Dit is naer mijn huijsvrou geconterfeijt'.
2 Strauss & Van der Meulen 1979, pp. 223–5, no. 1642/2.
3 Bijtelaar 1953, pp. 50–2.
4 Amsterdam 1987–88, p. 33, cat. no. 19.
5 Benesch 1973, vol. II, p. 72, no. 281A, dates it 'about 1635'.

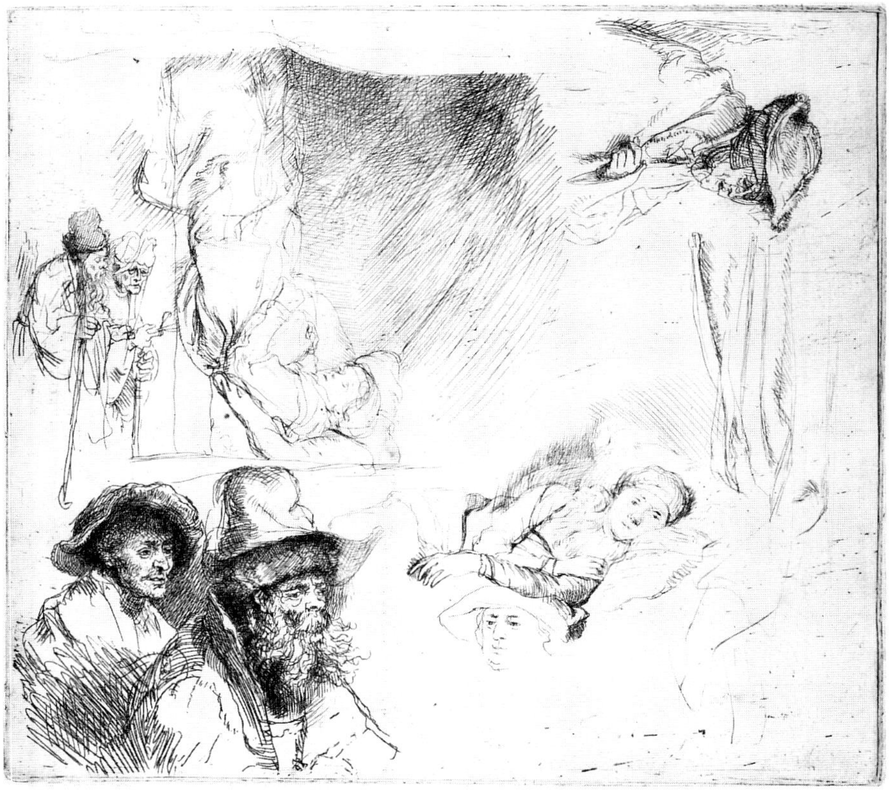

FIG. 82a
Rembrandt
Sheet with Studies, Including Saskia in Bed
1642
Etching
13.6 x 15.1 cm
Rijksprentenkabinet, Rijksmuseum, Amsterdam

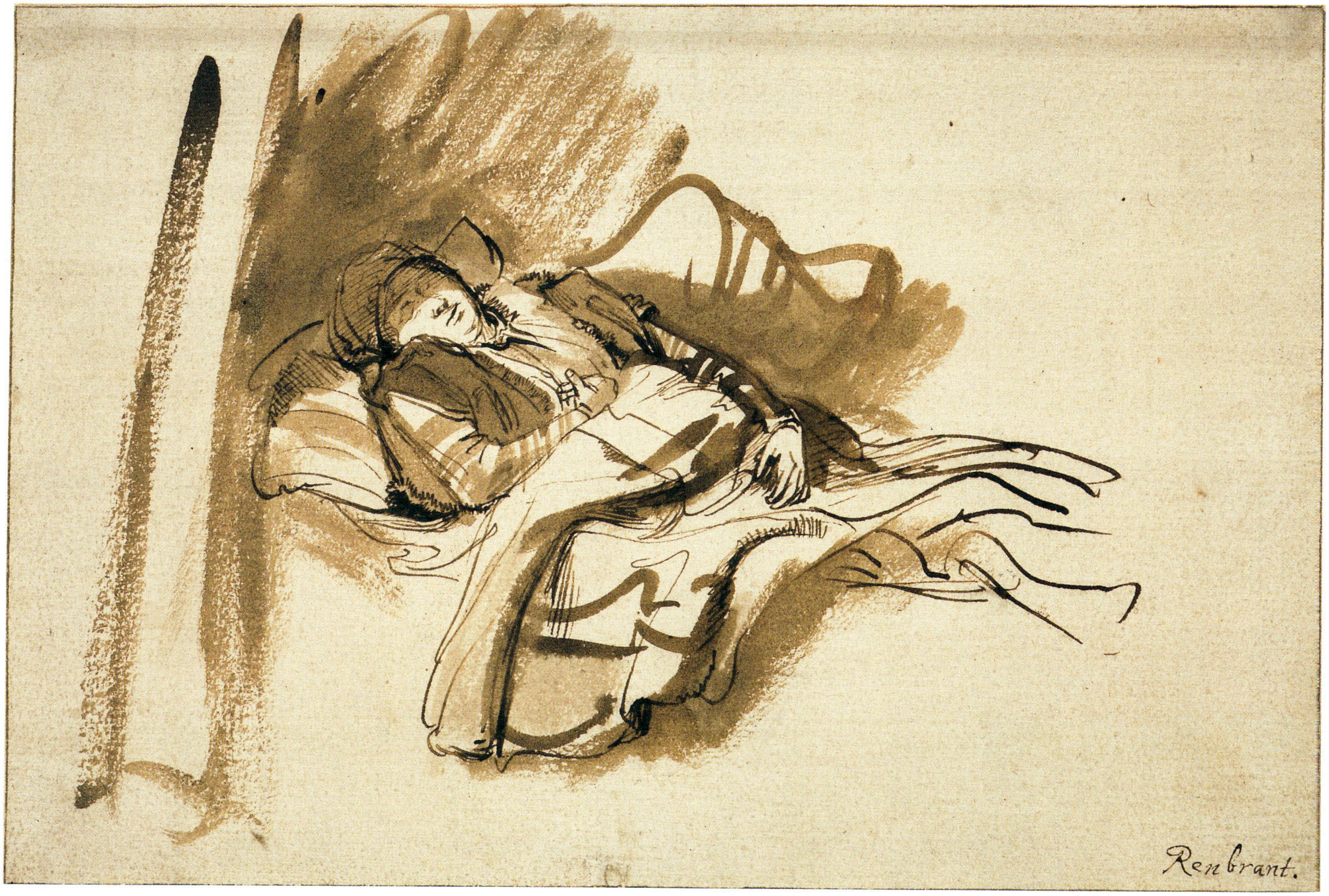
Renbrant.

83
Winter Scene
*c.*1646–48

Inscribed lower right (apocryphal – hand of Lambert ten Kate) *Rembrand*
Pen and ink and brush
10.4 x 18.0 cm
Lower right: collector's mark of Jan Pietersz Zomer
Rijksprentenkabinet, Rijksmuseum, Amsterdam

LITERATURE: Benesch 1973, vol. IV, p. 215, no. 837; Schatborn 1985, p. 70, no. 31.

Farmhouses and barns stand in a desolate white landscape. The only movement comes from a man lowering the sail of a flat-bottomed vessel on the right. It is clearly the depths of winter: the trees are bare and the world lies under a mantle of snow. Rembrandt drew the jetty in the foreground and the boat in the ice in rough, broad penstrokes, in contrast to the farmhouses and the trees in the background, which he rendered with a pen and brush in fine lines and in a wide range of browns and greys. The result is an incomparably subtle picture with sharply defined shapes etched against a pale, hazy background.

Rembrandt's only oil painting of a winter's day dates from 1646 (Bredius 452) (fig. 83a). He also made a few drawings, including those in the Fogg Art Museum, Cambridge, Massachusetts (Benesch 845), and in the Chatsworth Settlement (Benesch 846), and an etching (B.228) in about 1645, with bare trees evoking the mood of winter. The Amsterdam drawing probably dates from around the same time, in the late 1640s.[1]

At the beginning of the eighteenth century, parts of the sheet in and around the boat were worked up with grey washes, presumably to temper the effect of starkness that Rembrandt had tried to achieve. These changes may have been introduced by one of the later owners of the work, who left his mark on the sheet in other ways as well. At the lower right the 'signature' *Rembrand* can be seen in the handwriting of Lambert ten Kate (1674–1731), whose collection was sold in Amsterdam in 1732. Apocryphal inscriptions have been added to many more of Rembrandt's drawings. On this sheet the initials *I.P.Z.* have also been stamped in the lower right-hand corner. This was the mark of Jan Pietersz Zomer (1641–1724), one of the leading collectors of drawings in the early eighteenth century. A number of his sheets were subsequently acquired by ten Kate.

In around 1722 Zomer compiled a catalogue of his collection, which refers to a series by Rembrandt (in 'a small rectangular book' assembled by Zomer) as '60 landscapes in the vicinity of Amsterdam, beautifully drawn from life'.[2] Of course it is no longer possible to establish whether the drawings indeed represented scenes that existed in reality. The winter scene in Kassel is also said to have been painted outdoors, although in those days, some two centuries before oil paints became available in tubes, this would have been impracticable from a technical point of view.

Haak observes that the painting in Kassel and other similar winter scenes are consistent with a typically Dutch tradition, which evolved from anecdotal pictures, such as those by Hendrik Avercamp that show crowds of people enjoying a day on the ice, to the pure winter landscapes of Jacob van Ruisdael.[3] From this point of view, the drawing discussed here and the panel from Kassel are most closely related to Esaias van den Velde's painting of a *Winter Landscape* (fig. 83b) from more than twenty years earlier.[4] Rembrandt managed to capture the starkness of the winter landscape simply by dispensing with superfluous details. In the Kassel painting, for instance, the bare expanse of ice and the rime-frosted figures evoke the crispness of a bitterly cold day.

BB

1 Schatborn 1985, p. 70, no. 31.
2 Schatborn 1981, p. 21: 'Een kleinder boek over dwars ... 60 stuks Landschapjes, buiten Amsterdam, konstig na't leven'.
3 Haak 1968, p. 199.
4 Broos 1987, pp. 371–3.

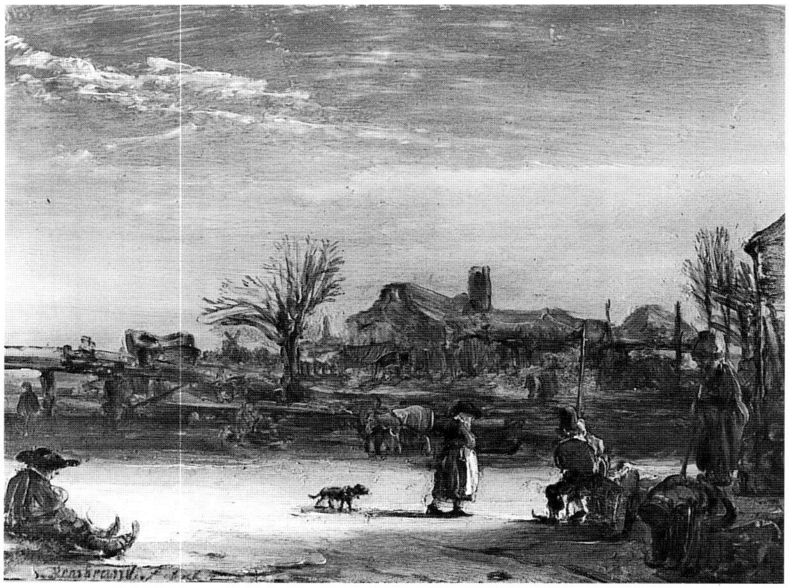

FIG. 83a
Rembrandt
Winter Landscape
Signed and dated 1646
Panel
17.0 x 23.0 cm
Gemäldegalerie, Kassel

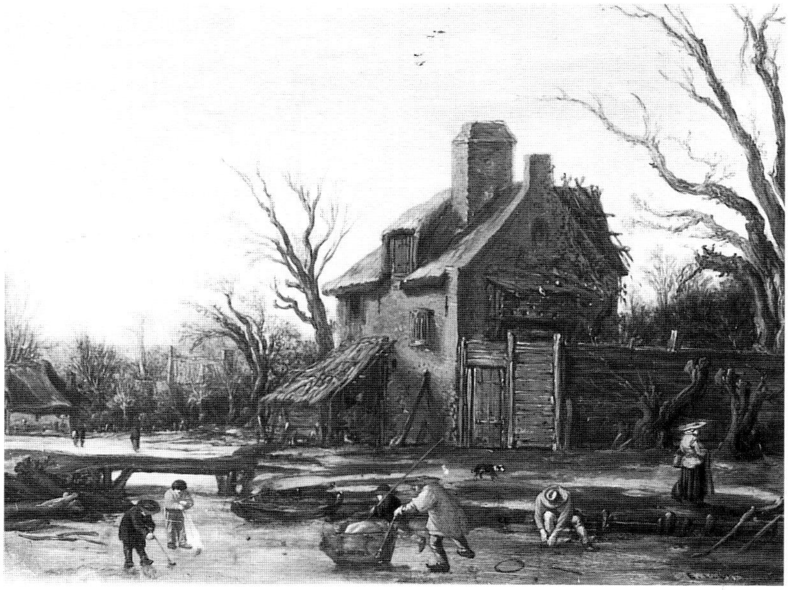

FIG. 83b
Esaias van den Velde 1587–1630
Winter Landscape
Signed and dated 1624
Panel
26.0 x 32.0 cm
Mauritshuis, The Hague
Photograph: © Mauritshuis, The Hague, inv. no. 673

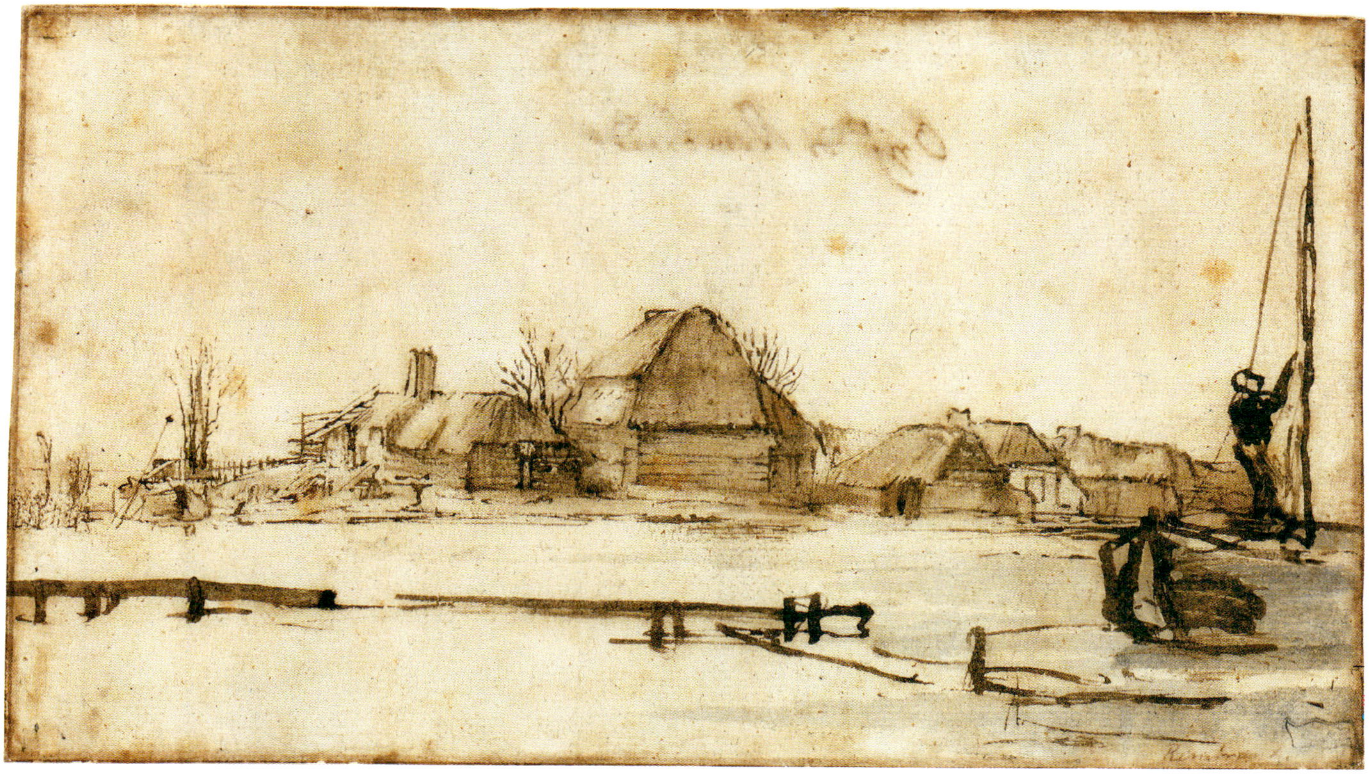

84
A Beggar's Family
*c.*1647–48

Inscribed lower right (apocryphal) *Rembrandt*
Chalk
13.1 x 9.6 cm
Verso: *Study for a Portrait Etching of Jan Six*
*c.*1647–48
Chalk
Amsterdam Historical Museum; legacy C. J. Fodor

LITERATURE: Benesch 1973, vol. IV, p. 196, no. 749; Broos 1981, pp. 55–9, no. 13.

In 1648 Rembrandt made an etching showing a family of paupers (cat. no. 110A). Simplicity and poverty are recurrent themes in his drawings and etchings from the 1630s onwards. There was a longstanding tradition in the northern and southern Netherlands of portraying genre subjects, the most famous exponent being Pieter Bruegel the Elder, the artist whom Karel van Mander referred to as 'droll Pieter'. Rembrandt, too, often emerged as a master of wit and realism. The black chalk drawing shown here, which was made as a preparatory sketch for the etching, is an almost stenographic impression of a street scene. We see the same group of figures as in the etching, a group comprising what appear to be an aged, blind father with his daughter and grandchildren, one of whom is no more than an infant. Like the man in the etching, the father is wearing a wide-brimmed hat over a kerchief wrapped around his head; the young woman wears a thick cap tucked firmly over her ears. She has a basket slung over her left arm, with which she is also supporting the baby. The small boy in front of them has his back to us. He is standing in the light, while subtle hatching in his mother's dress defines her place in the background. Rembrandt was initially intending to depict another child between mother and son, as we see from the few lines indicating its position, but he must have changed his mind and decided not to include this figure in the etching. In making the drawing he also seems to have made the old man's stick slightly longer than it was originally, so that it forms the axis of the composition. The image is worked up in the etching to include shading and small details, and we now see that the group's attention is focused on a man leaning over the lower half of his door, giving alms to the paupers.

On the back of the sheet is a bust portrait in black chalk of a man leaning on one elbow (fig. 84a). This was a quick, first draft for the etched portrait Rembrandt made of Jan Six in 1647 (B.285) (fig. 28b). We can trace every step Rembrandt took in producing the print, since several preliminary studies have survived, as have the four states of the etching and even the copperplate itself. This sketch, however, was identified as the first of the series of studies only at the beginning of this century.[1]

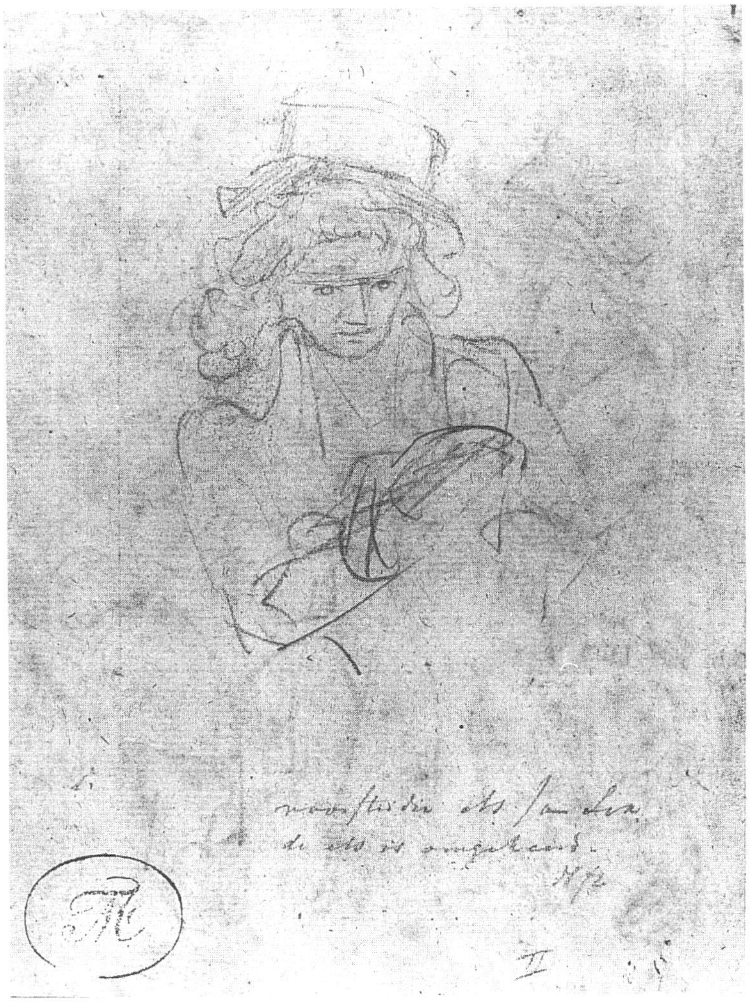

FIG. 84a
Rembrandt
Study for a Portrait Etching of Jan Six
*c.*1647–48
(cat. no. 84 verso)

Jan Six (1618–1700), the scion of a long line of merchants, was almost thirty years old in 1647. A collector and man of letters, he also wrote poetry and plays, including the tragedy *Medea*, the original copy of which was illustrated by his friend Rembrandt in 1648. The relationship between Six and Rembrandt found its finest expression in the brilliant *Portrait of Jan Six* from 1654 (Bredius 276), which has remained in the collection of the Six family in Amsterdam up to this day.

The dates 1647 and 1648, which appear on the etched portrait of Jan Six and on the etching of the paupers respectively, would likewise apply to the preliminary studies for the two works. These studies give an excellent impression of Rembrandt's drawing style in those years. Rembrandt is said to have abandoned black chalk as a medium later in his career, but this was apparently not the case.[2] Finally, it is revealing, perhaps, that on one and the same sheet Rembrandt portrayed the lowliest and most humble of human beings as lovingly as he depicted his friend Jan Six, one of the wealthiest young men in Amsterdam.

BB

1 Six 1908, p. 56; Broos 1981, p. 57, no. 13.
2 Hofstede de Groot 1906, p. 280, no. 1223.

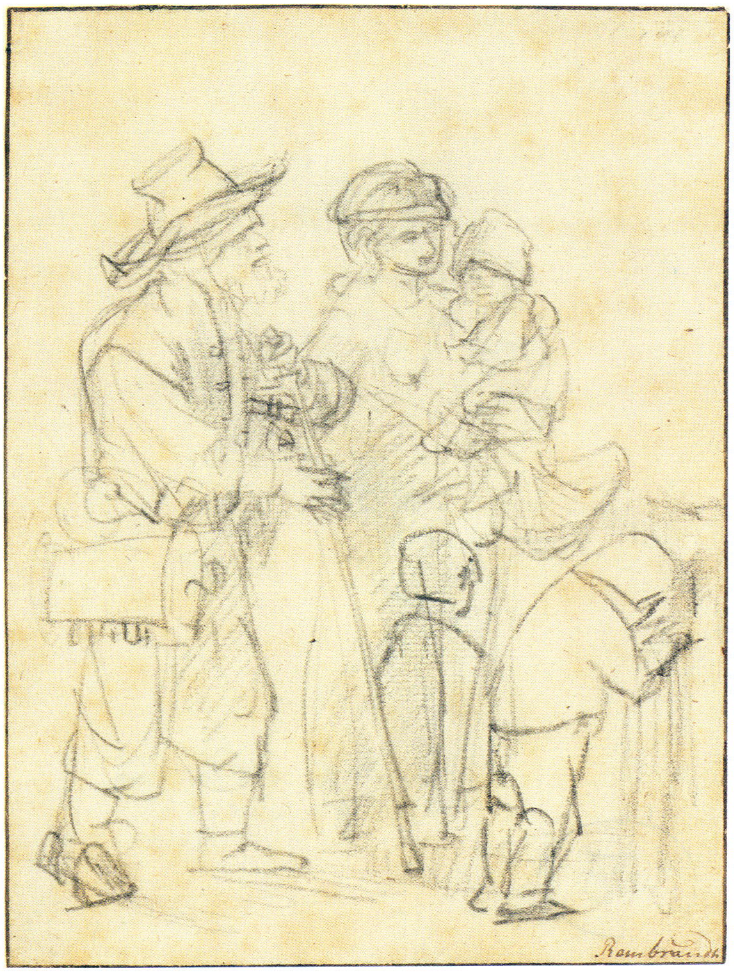
Rembrandt

85

Self-Portrait

*c.*1648–50

Inscriptions pasted to mount
Pen and ink
20.3 x 13.4 cm
Museum het Rembrandthuis, Amsterdam

LITERATURE: Benesch 1973, vol. V, p. 313, no. 1171; Filedt Kok 1972, p. 19, no. I.

Benesch described this fascinating drawing as 'one of the most magnificent and human documents of artistic self-revelation'.[1] But statements of this kind are stirring rather than illuminating. The drawing shows Rembrandt in a hat, as he portrayed himself in an etching in 1648 (B.22) (fig. 85a). His pose, hands on hips, recalls the *Self-Portrait* in Vienna from 1652 (Bredius 42) (fig. 85b). This drawn portrait may have been made in the intervening years. Here we see Rembrandt in a straight, narrow-brimmed hat and a loose overcoat with wide sleeves gathered in at the cuffs. He wears the same outfit in the etching. The figure's initial striding movement was altered, by a few penstrokes on the right leg, to create a stationary pose – and a considerably more monumental effect. The characterization of the broad face – the frown, the pursed lips, and details such as the tufts of hair around the ears – suggests that the drawing was made around the same time as the etching, in 1648 or a short time later, perhaps around 1650.

The upper of the two inscriptions pasted to the mount is in old-fashioned, probably seventeenth-century, handwriting, and was in any event not put there by the artist. The text reads: 'Self-portrait drawn by Rembran[d]t van Rhijn in the clothes he wore in his studio'.[2] Both the note and the drawing were cut out – presumably from separate sheets – and pasted onto a thick cardboard mount. The owner then drew a neat border around the drawing, and another encompassing the inscription as well. A French translation on a separate piece of paper was later pasted to the mount. It reads as follows: *Rembrandt avec l'habit dans lequel il avoit accoutumé de peindre.* The handwriting was identified in 1967 as that of the collector and connoisseur Pierre-Jean Mariette (1694–1774).[3] In 1741 Mariette compiled the catalogue for the sale of Pierre Crozat's collection, to which the present drawing then belonged, and he may have added the French translation at that time. It transpires from the catalogue that Crozat had acquired a large number of Rembrandt drawings from the French diplomat and art critic Roger de Piles, who collected drawings in the Netherlands in 1693. De Piles claimed to be an expert on Rembrandt on the basis of 'le grand nombre de ses desseins que j'ai dans mes mains' (the large number of his drawings that I own).[4] As far as this piece is concerned, he accepted the word of a Dutch dealer that the sheet he was buying was autograph. The drawing was proudly described in a separate entry in the Crozat catalogue, where it was published together with a pendant: 'Son portrait & celui de sa Mere, faits par lui-même' (His own portrait & that of his mother, by his own hand).[5] The latter was dismissed as apocryphal many years ago.

BB

1 Benesch 1973, vol. V, p. 313, no. 1171.
2 'getekent door Rembrant van Rhijn naer sijn selver sooals hij in sijn schilderkamer gekleet was'.
3 Mahon 1967, pp. 63–4.
4 Frerichs 1970, pp. 42–3.
5 Schatborn 1982, p. 41.

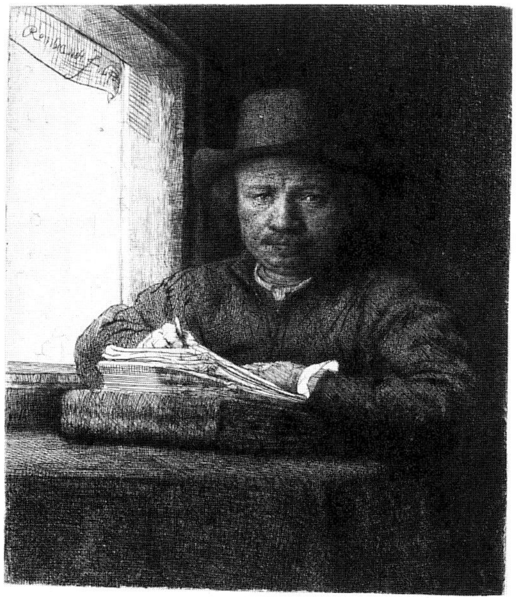

FIG. 85a
Rembrandt
Self-Portrait
Signed and dated 1648
Etching
16.0 x 13.0 cm
Rijksprentenkabinet, Rijksmuseum, Amsterdam

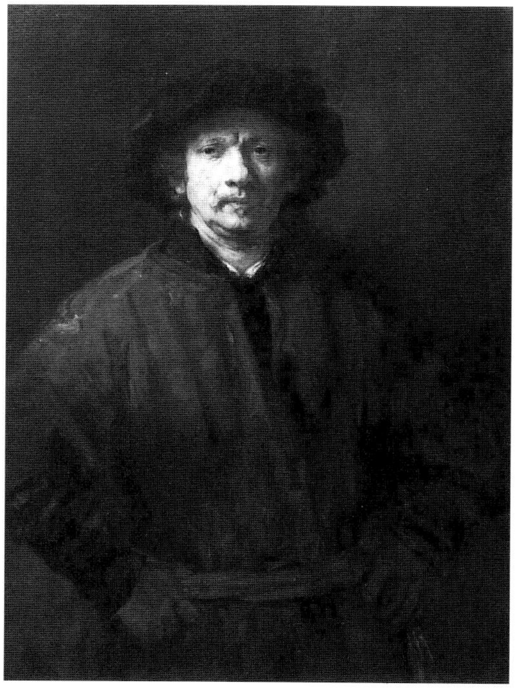

FIG. 85b
Rembrandt
Self-Portrait
Signed and dated 1652
Canvas
112.0 x 81.5 cm
Kunsthistorisches Museum, Vienna

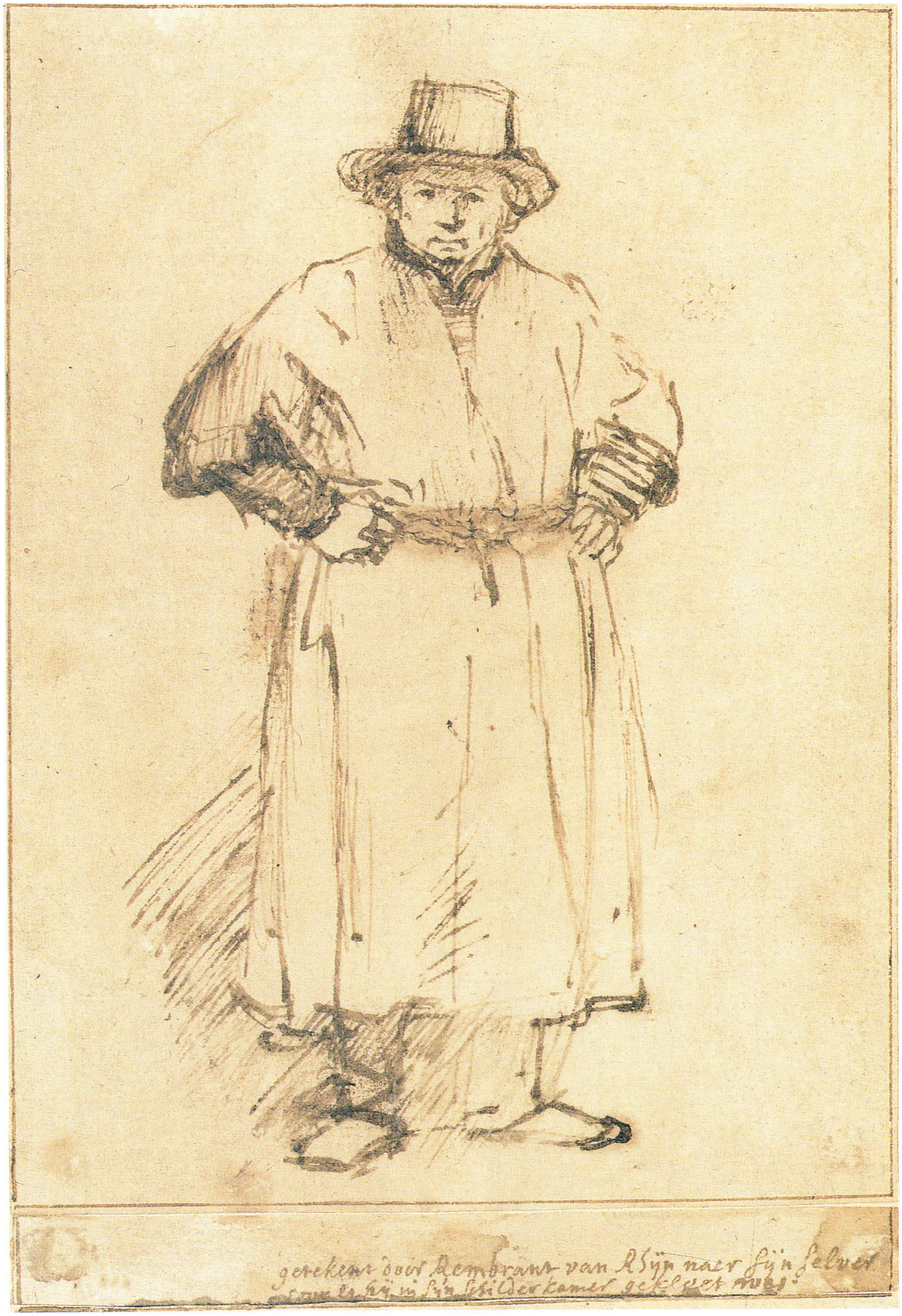
getekent door Rembrant van Rijn naer sijn selven

86

Daniel in the Lions' Den

*c.*1649

Pen and ink and brush
22.2 x 18.4 cm
Rijksprentenkabinet, Rijksmuseum, Amsterdam

LITERATURE: Benesch 1973, vol. V, p. 249, no. 887; Schatborn 1985, p. 56, no. 24.

As a young Israelite, Daniel was summoned to the Babylonian court, where he soon rose to a powerful position. Jealous of his influence, the governors accused him of praying to his own God, thus violating an edict that required the Medes and Persians to worship the king. Daniel's punishment was to be cast into the lions' den. Rembrandt has depicted the moment at which Nebuchadnezzar, weary after a sleepless night, opens the den and finds Daniel still alive. The vaulting of the cave is suggested by a few broad lines drawn with a reed pen. The astonished king peers into the depths from an opening at the top. Daniel has fallen to his knees, saying: 'O king, live for ever. My God hath sent his angel, and hath shut the lions' mouths, that they have not hurt me' (Daniel 6:21–22).

Rembrandt's rendering of the biblical text is not entirely literal, for a lion at the back of the cave, on the right-hand side of the picture, is snarling fiercely and exposing its savage teeth. This detail may have been copied from an engraving by Willem de Leeuw after a painting by Peter Paul Rubens (fig. 86a).[1] The lion standing behind Daniel with its head on his shoulder also appears to have been inspired by this print. Nevertheless, Rembrandt had seen lions in real life, as we know from several studies he made in the 1640s and 1650s (cat. no. 87). Two etchings of *St Jerome Reading in an Italian Landscape* also give an impression of how Rembrandt himself saw the 'king of the beasts'. In the earlier of the two, from 1634 (B.100), the lion looks like a longhaired dog with a feline head – suggesting that Rembrandt could not himself have seen a lion by this date – while the undated version, which was made about twenty years later (cat. no. 116) is a more lifelike representation.

This drawing was rendered quickly and spontaneously with the reed pen. Rembrandt evidently relied on more than one visual source. The dungeon, with its huge rounded arches and an entrance at the top, seems to have been based on that in an etching of *c.*1581 by Johan Sadeler the Elder.[2]

A similar, early composition by Constantijn Daniël van Renesse (fig. 86b) may be of relevance in dating this sheet. A pupil of Rembrandt's, van Renesse added an inscription on the back of his drawing saying that he had shown it to the master on 1 October 1649 (he finished it in 1652). He succeeded reasonably well in copying the kneeling figure of Daniel from Rembrandt's drawing, but had far more difficulty depicting the lions. The fact that he based his work on Rembrandt's example means that the latter must have been made in or before 1649.

BB

1 Hollstein 3; Schatborn 1985, p. 56, fig. 24c.
2 Hollstein 125; Schatborn 1985, p. 56, fig. 24b.

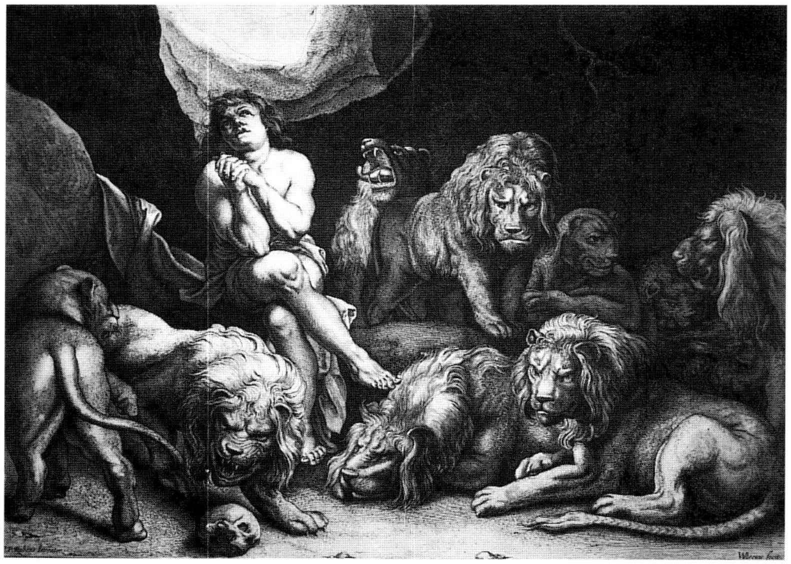

FIG. 86a
Willem de Leeuw (*c.*1603–*c.*1665), after Peter Paul Rubens
Daniel in the Lions' Den
Signed
Engraving
37.5 x 50.0 cm
Teylers Museum, Haarlem

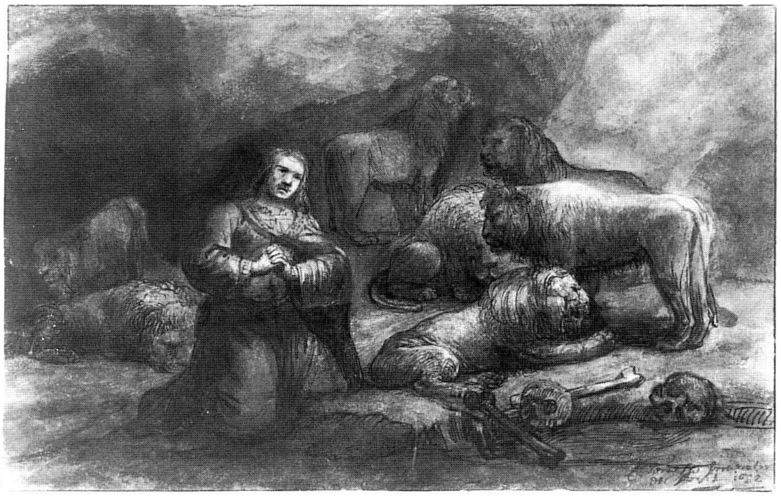

FIG. 86b
Constantijn Daniël van Renesse
1626–1680
Daniel in the Lions' Den
Signed and dated *CARenesse inventor et fecit 1652*
Pen and ink and brush
20.6 x 32.0 cm
Museum Boijmans Van Beuningen, Rotterdam
(see also p. 211, fig. 18)

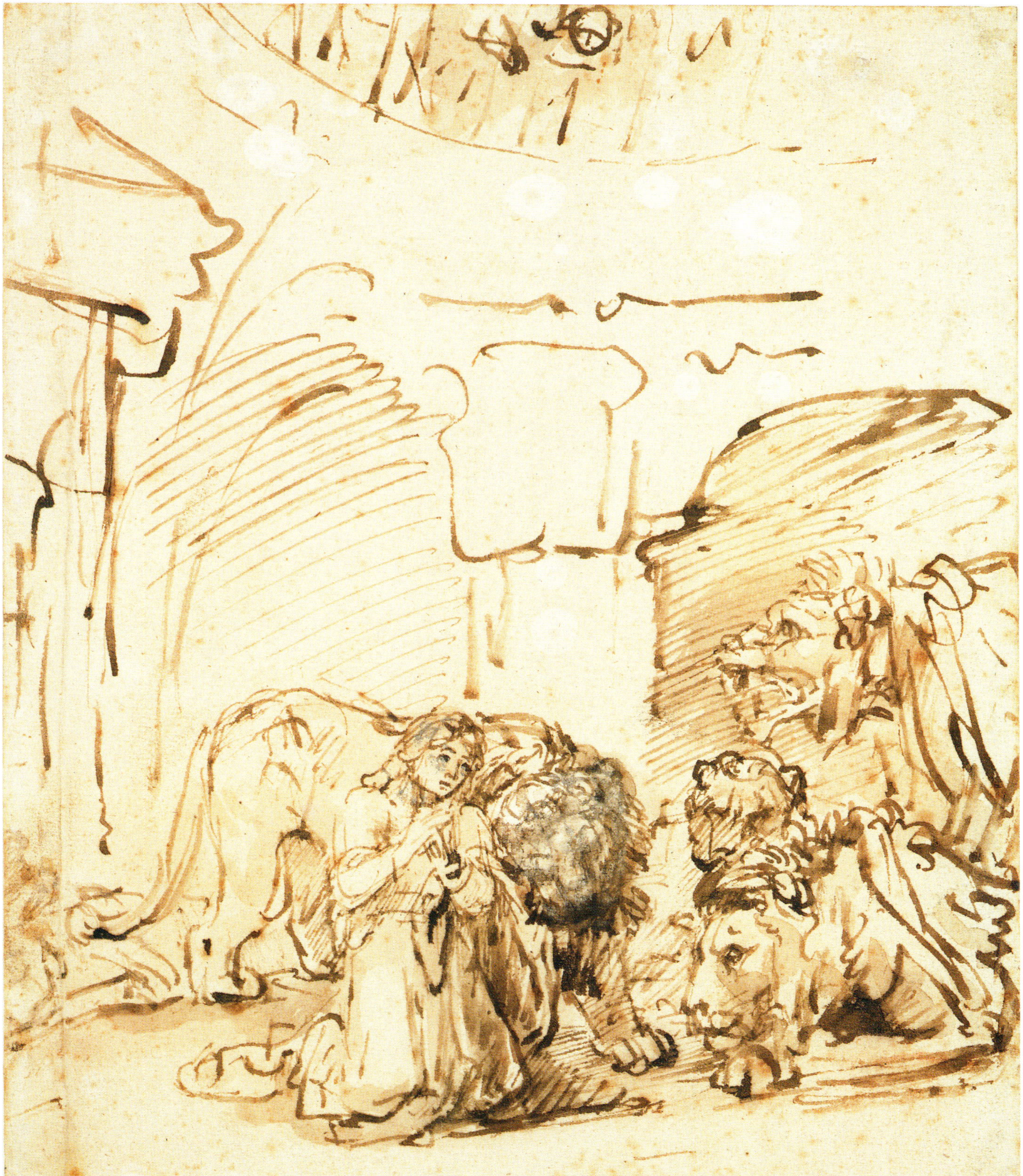

87

Recumbent Lion

*c.*1650

Pen and ink and brush
14.0 x 20.3 cm
Lower left and lower right: collector's marks of Sir Thomas Lawrence, William Esdaile, E. Wauters and Baron D. Vivant-Denon
Museum Boijmans Van Beuningen, Rotterdam

LITERATURE: Benesch 1973, vol. V, p. 330, no. 1211; Giltaij 1988, pp. 82–3, no. 23.

Rembrandt sketched a camel 'from life' in 1633 (formerly Kunsthalle, Bremen) (Benesch 453) and an Indian elephant four years later (Graphische Sammlung Albertina, Vienna) (Benesch 457). These exotic animals were occasionally put on display for the Amsterdam public, and Rembrandt would of course go to see them. During the 1640s and 1650s, he made a series of drawings, with a pen and brush and in some cases chalk, of lions he must have seen in a travelling menagerie or at the zoo. Of all the extraordinary animals he saw, the 'king of the beasts' apparently fascinated him most.

The large cat on this sheet from about 1650 is dozing contentedly with its eyes closed and its paws stretched out before it. Rembrandt used a pen to sketch in the rough mane, and a brush to render – with the greatest subtlety – the sleek fur and muscular frame. The animal is a Berber lion from the Atlas Mountains in northern Africa. This species has a square-shaped head, a mane extending to the belly, and a relatively solid build.[1] Rembrandt had not seen a lion before 1634, for the animal in the etching he made of St Jerome that year has the appearance of a long-haired dog with a feline face (B.100). He must have based the etching on an older print, probably one by Albrecht Altdorfer of *c.*1510–20 (B.57).[2] But by the time he made his drawing of *Daniel in the Lions' Den* in about 1649 (cat. no. 86) there can be no doubt that he had seen a lion in the flesh.

The numerous copies and imitations of Rembrandt's lion drawings attest to the popularity they must have enjoyed. According to the 1656 inventory of his collection of 'art on paper', Rembrandt kept a separate file for drawings of 'animals from life', which he and his pupils evidently used as study material.[3] There are, for instance, two relatively faithful copies after the present drawing (Louvre, Paris; Staatliche Graphische Sammlung, Munich), both of which may have been studio work.[4] It is also possible that Rembrandt and some of his pupils or former pupils visited a menagerie together to sketch. A drawing of a *Recumbent Lion* attributed to Samuel van Hoogstraten (fig. 87a) may have been made on such an occasion, as it is an attempt to imitate the style or form of a genuine Rembrandt.[5]

The lion drawings by Rembrandt and his pupils eventually came into the possession of the Amsterdam art broker Jan Pietersz Zomer, whose catalogue from around 1722 lists a book containing at least sixty figure studies by Rembrandt and '19 lions, from life'. In 1729 Bernard Picart published prints of eighteen of these(?) drawings in his *Recueil de Lions* (fig. 87b), which also included prints after works by followers of Rembrandt. On this occasion, the Rotterdam drawing was indented for etching.[6] Today, a few lion drawings at most are considered to be by Rembrandt's own hand, this sheet being one of the finest.

BB

1 Schatborn 1977, pp. 24–31.
2 Münz 1952, vol. 2, p. 111, no. 245, fig.
3 Strauss & Van der Meulen 1979, p. 375, no. 249.
4 Giltaij 1988, p. 82, note 9.
5 Broos 1981, pp. 147–9, no. 40.
6 Schatborn 1982, pp. 21–8.

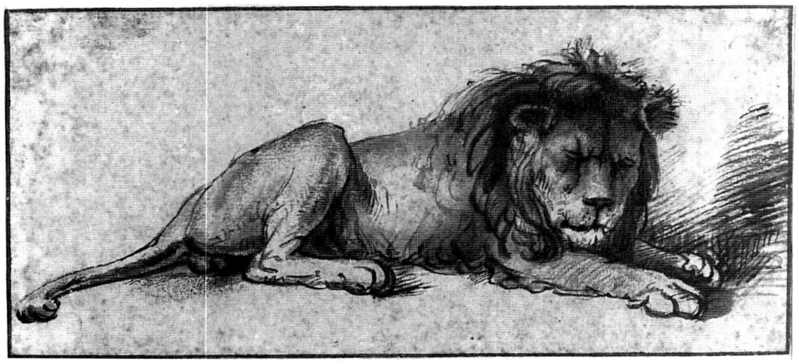

FIG. 87a
Samuel van Hoogstraten
*Recumbent Lion c.*1650
Pen and ink and brush
9.3 x 20.0 cm
Amsterdam Historical Museum

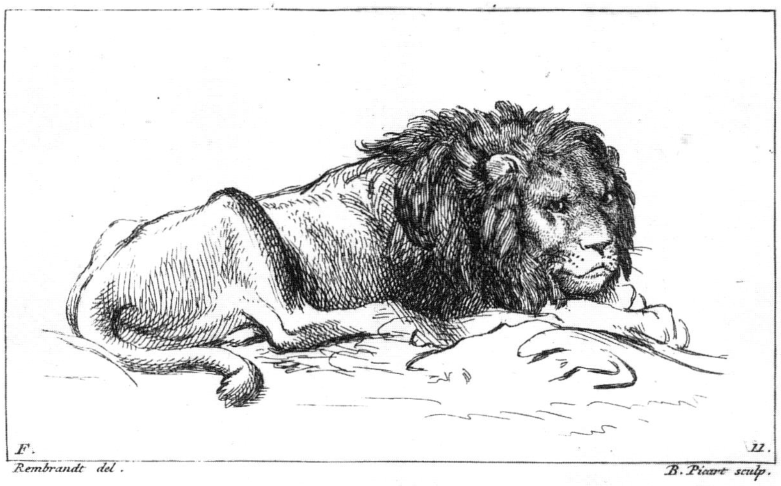

FIG. 87b
Bernard Picart (1673–1733), after Rembrandt
Recumbent Lion 1729
Inscribed *Rembrandt del. B. Picart sculp.*
Etching
7.0 x 11.0 cm
Rijksprentenkabinet, Rijksmuseum, Amsterdam

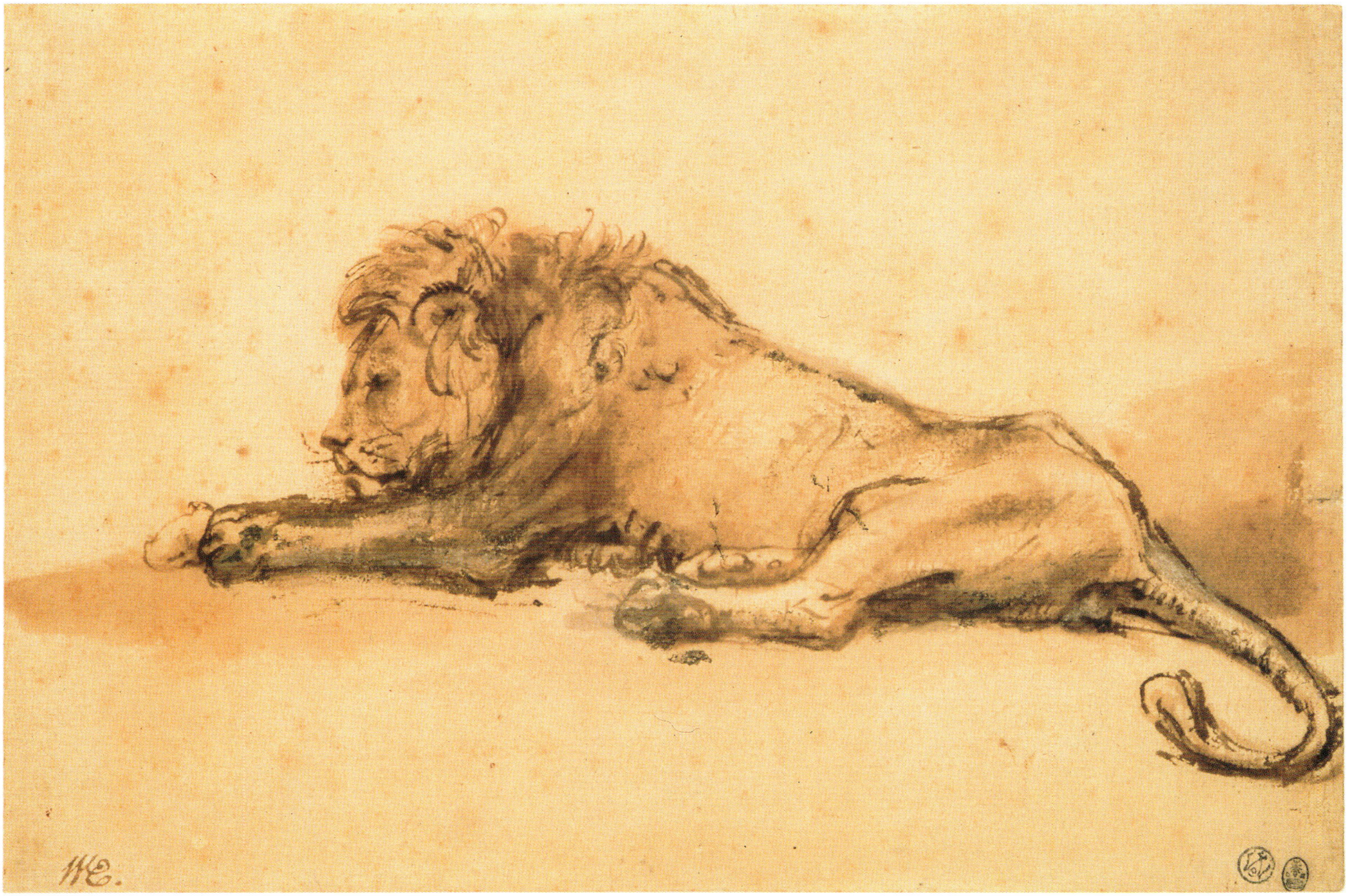

88
Christ Healing a Leper
*c.*1650–52

Pen and ink and brush
14.7 x 17.7 cm
Lower right: collector's mark of J. P. van Suchtelen
Rijksprentenkabinet, Rijksmuseum, Amsterdam

LITERATURE: Benesch 1973, vol. V, p. 280, no. 1026; Schatborn 1985, p. 94, no. 43.

One of Rembrandt's most famous etchings, dating from *c.*1643–49, is known as the *Hundred Guilder Print* (cat. no. 111). It owes this title to the fact that Rembrandt himself is said to have paid the sum of 100 guilders for a rare impression of the print. An illustration of the popular subject of Christ's healing of the sick, the picture in fact combines a series of successive events from chapter 19 of the Gospel of Matthew. The New Testament contains several accounts of the healing of a multitude of believers. Rembrandt portrayed Christ's miracles on numerous occasions, although it is not always clear which particular texts he had in mind.

In this drawing, Christ is healing a man in the presence of no more than a small group of followers, an indication that the scene indeed alludes to a specific passage from the Bible. According to Schatborn, it represents the first cleansing after the Sermon on the Mount, when a leper fell at Christ's feet: 'And Jesus put forth his hand, and touched him, saying, I will; be thou clean' (Matthew 8:3).[1] The Gospel of Luke, however, also tells of the ten lepers near Jerusalem, one of whom turned back when he saw he had been healed: 'And [he] fell down on his face at his feet, giving him thanks: and he was a Samaritan' (Luke 17:16).

Rembrandt drew a second picture of one of these episodes, likewise in the early 1650s (Kupferstichkabinett, Berlin) (Benesch 900). Here too he made a rough pen sketch of the figures, and used brisk, wide hatching to indicate the darker areas. In spite of his summary treatment of the subject, however, Rembrandt paid close attention to the details in both drawings. In the Amsterdam sheet, for instance, he appears to have been dissatisfied with his portrayal of Christ, who was originally holding the leper's hand. He covered this section with a layer of white paint and decided to depict Christ with his hand on the kneeling man's head. An old (seventeenth-century?) copy after this drawing (Louvre, Paris) shows only the amended version. In an etching that Mathys Pool made after the drawing in about 1700 we again see only the hand on the man's head (B.68) (fig. 88a). But Rembrandt's retouchings were not impervious to the ravages of time. The white paint has since disappeared, and the correction can now be seen quite distinctly.

We can see from the drawing that Pool pressed through the contours in the sheet when making his etching. His print is one of a series of copies entitled 'Impressions on copperplate after original drawings and sketches by Rembrandt'. These originals presumably remained together after Rembrandt's collection was sold in 1658, and came into Pool's possession later. The authenticity of the sheets in this group – mainly episodes from the Bible – has never been questioned.[2]

BB

1 Schatborn 1985, p. 94, no. 43.
2 Schatborn 1982, pp. 13–14.

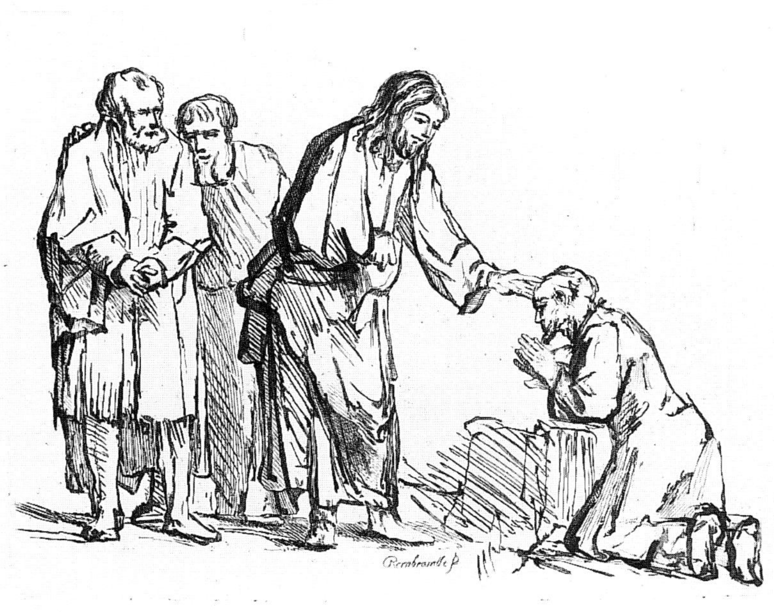

FIG. 88a
Mathys Pool (1676–1740), after Rembrandt
Christ Healing a Leper *c.*1700
Etching
13.0 x 17.0 cm
Rijksprentenkabinet, Rijksmuseum, Amsterdam

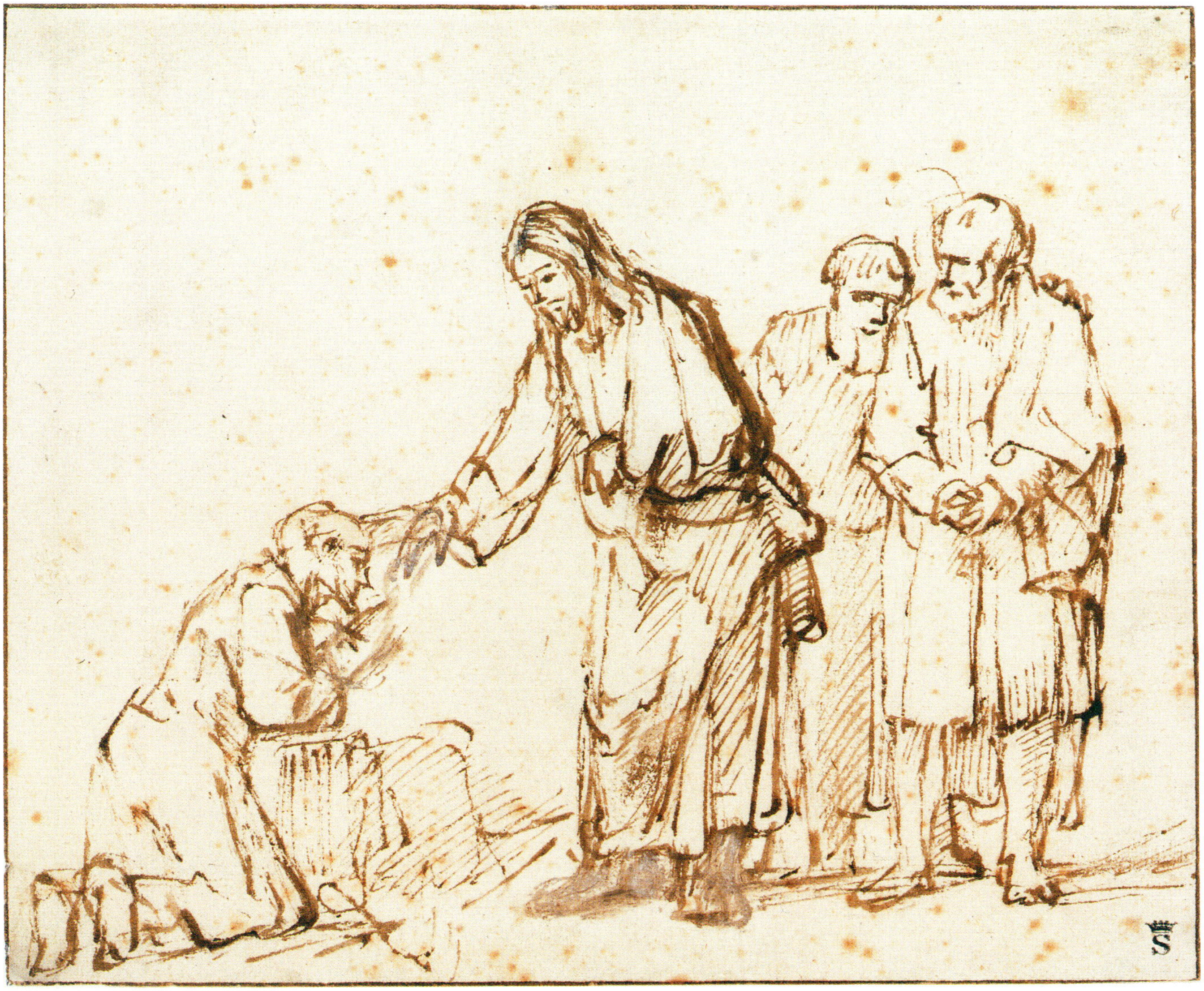

89

Elisha and the Miracle of the Floating Axe

*c.*1650–52

Pen and ink and brush
14.5 x 19.7 cm
Museum Bredius, The Hague

LITERATURE: Benesch 1973, vol. V, p. 258, no. 932; Blankert 1978, p. 160, no. T 7.

Rembrandt evidently had a penchant for tales from the Bible and other sources that had never been illustrated before. A famous example is his painting of *Samson's Riddle to the Wedding Guests*, 1638 (Gemäldegalerie, Dresden) (Bredius 507), a work commended in his own day as a well-conceived history piece.[1] His interest in relatively obscure themes was undoubtedly kindled by the work of his teacher Pieter Lastman, whose example and guidance continued to inspire him.[2] Subjects relating to Elisha are common in the oeuvres of Lastman and his followers, but none of them represented Elisha and the Miracle of the Floating Axe.[3] Like the depiction of Samson's wedding feast, the present work is the only picture of its kind.

Rembrandt made his drawing of this extraordinary story in the early 1650s. His economical style of drawing and brisk, parallel hatching are comparable to his rendering of *Christ Healing a Leper* (cat. no. 88). He also corrected a detail in both sheets, applying white gouache – which has now largely disappeared – to the right arm of the prostrate man in the present work.

Solomon's kingdom was divided into two nations after his death, with Israel in the north and Judah in the south. The Books of Kings, which cover this period, abound with tales of pious soothsayers, wise counsellors and men with supernatural powers. The episodes most popular with artists were those that featured the prophets Elijah and Elisha. Elisha was especially renowned for his miraculous deeds, which included curing the Syrian commander Naaman and restoring to life the son of a Shunamite woman (see commentary to cat. no. 30). In the narrative represented here, Elisha and his followers were building a dwelling near the River Jordan. 'But as one was felling a beam, the axe-head fell into the water: and he cried, and said, Alas, master! for it was borrowed. And the man of God said, Where fell it? And he shewed him the place. And he cut down a stick, and cast it in thither; and the iron did swim. Therefore said he, Take it up to thee. And he put out his hand, and took it' (2 Kings 6:5–7). The stick itself cannot be seen in the drawing. Elisha is dipping a rod into the water while his companion reaches out to retrieve the axe-head. Rembrandt may have found it difficult to visualize the scene, as the Bible describes the event in fairly cryptic terms.

BB

1 Angel 1642, pp. 47–8.
2 Broos 1975–76, pp. 199–228.
3 Amsterdam / Jerusalem 1991–92, pp. 161–6.

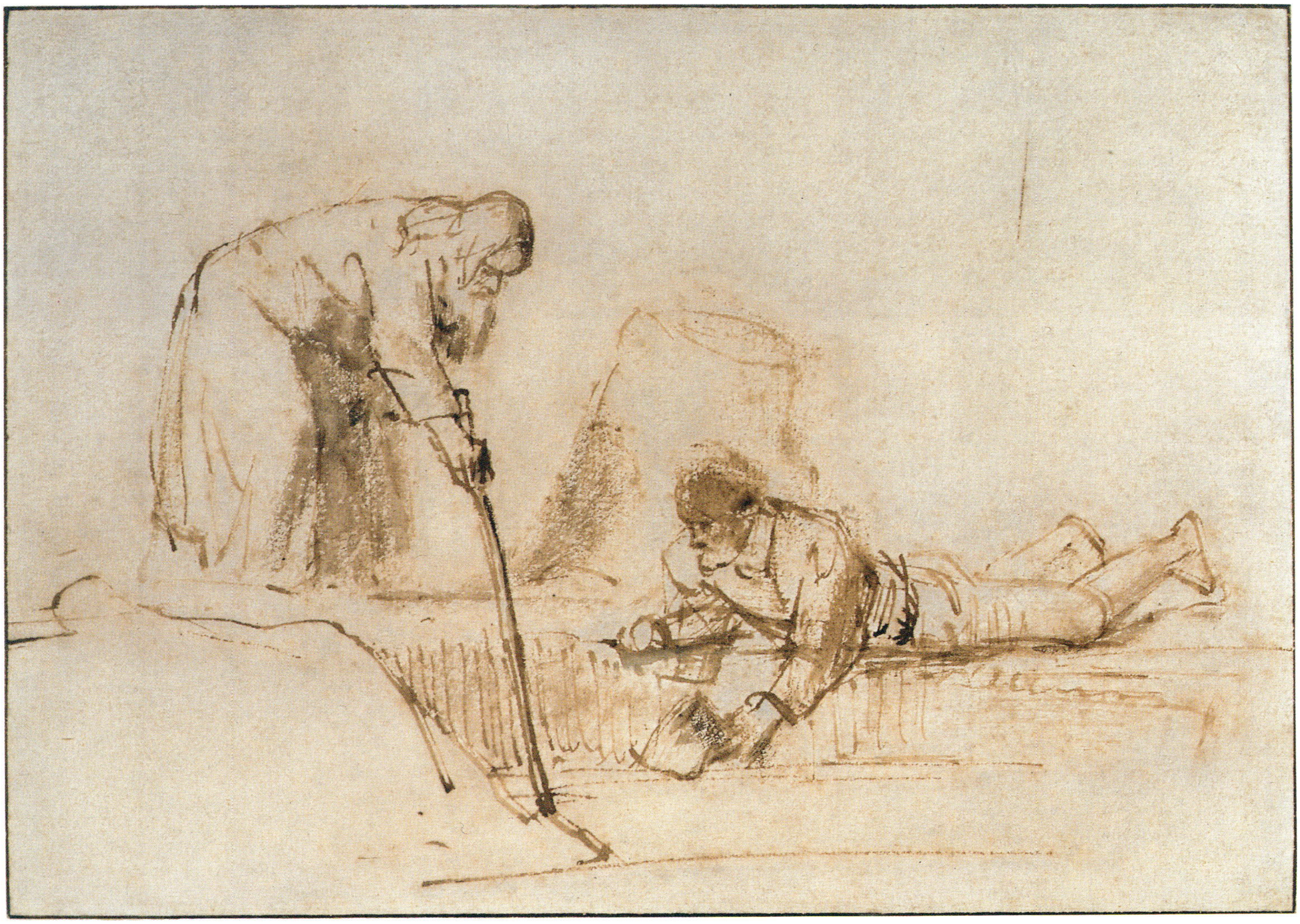

90
View of Haarlem
*c.*1651

Pen and ink and brush
8.9 x 15.2 cm
Lower left: collector's marks of Sir Thomas Lawrence and William Esdaile
Museum Boijmans Van Beuningen, Rotterdam

LITERATURE: Benesch 1973, vol. VI, p. 344, no. 1259; Giltaij 1988, pp. 78–9, no. 21.

Viewed from the dunes, Haarlem was a picturesque sight, dominated by the majestic body of the St Bavokerk with its distinctive central spire protruding above the rooftops. Rembrandt has drawn a panoramic view of the town, with the bleaching fields unfurling at his feet. He may have had in mind Karel van Mander's lyrical ode to Haarlem:

In my youth I journeyed, roamed and sailed
And trod almost every path,
In regions and domains with the finest of towns ...
Yet no place in Holland did I behold
So fair as Haarlem and her pleasant surrounds.[1]

A woodcut from around 1595 is probably the oldest representation of the city (fig. 90a). Rembrandt would presumably have drawn this prospect from life. The St Bavokerk forms a landmark in the centre of the sheet, with the tower of the Bakenesserkerk to its left. Near it we see the roof of the St Janskerk and, further to the right, the squat tower of the Klockhuis. The tower of the Nieuwe Kerk rises up in the distance to the right of St Bavo's, and a few windmills dot the banks of the town. The small church of Bloemendaal stands to the left of the Bakenesserkerk, while a country estate nestles in the landscape on the far left, halfway to the town. Rembrandt must have been standing on the 'kopje [small hill] of Bloemendaal', looking out towards Haarlem.

The skyline of Haarlem has inspired numerous draughtsmen and painters. It is revealing, for instance, that an inventory from as early as 1669 lists a 'Haerlempje van Ruysdael' – a small picture of Haarlem by Ruisdael – as something perfectly commonplace.[2] Scenes of the bleaching fields with Haarlem in the background became part of Jacob van Ruisdael's standard repertoire from 1670 on, and the theme was subsequently developed by painters such as Jan van Kessel and Jan Vermeer van Haarlem.[3]

In 1651 Rembrandt made a signed etching with the profile of Haarlem in the left background (cat. no. 113). The print has long been known as '*The Goldweigher's Field*', as the property slightly to the right of centre was thought to be that of the Amsterdam tax collector Johannes Wtenbogaert, whom in 1639 Rembrandt portrayed as the goldweigher (B.281)(fig. 8f). However, the same estate, which can be seen near the edge of the sheet in the drawing, has since been identified as Saxenburg, the home Christoffel Thijsz moved into in 1638.[4] In 1639 Thijsz and his brother-in-law sold Rembrandt the house in the Jodenbreestraat – the present-day Museum het Rembrandthuis – in which he spent twenty years of his life. In 1651 Rembrandt was still struggling to pay off his mortgage. He may have made the etching that year as a gift for Thijsz, in a bid to placate his creditors.[5] Ultimately, however, the repayments on his home were, *inter alia*, the cause of his financial ruin.

The scene in the drawing appears to have been rendered from a slightly higher vantage point than that in the etching, and from a little more to the right. It was therefore not intended specifically as a study for the print, although it was inspired during the same visit to Haarlem and its surrounding areas. Rembrandt may have drawn a second view that was preparatory to the etching (and that would therefore have been in reverse). It is possible, too, that the etching was not meant to be a topographically accurate representation, but an attempt to capture the atmosphere of the open countryside around Haarlem, as seen from the top of the dunes.

BB

1 Rutgers van der Loeff 1911, p. 19. One of the most celebrated paeans to Haarlem is Claes Jansz Visscher's series of prints entitled *Plaisante Plaetsen*, *c.*1611 (see Bakker 1993, pp. 109–11).
2 Bredius 1915–22, vol. II, p. 425, no. 87.
3 Broos 1987, pp. 330–7.
4 Van Regteren Altena 1954, p. 9.
5 Strauss & Van der Meulen 1979, p. 159, no. 1639/1; p. 295, no. 1653/1.

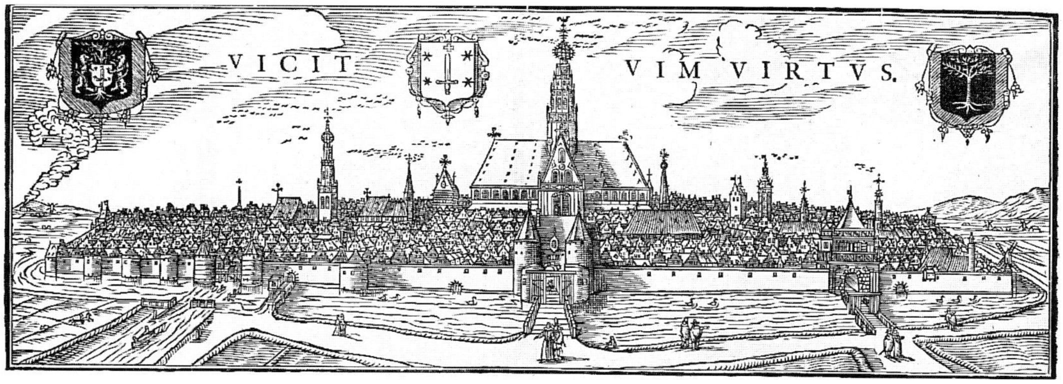

FIG. 90a
Dutch 16th century
View of the City of Haarlem
*c.*1595
Woodcut
12.0 x 33.5 cm
Municipal Archives, Haarlem

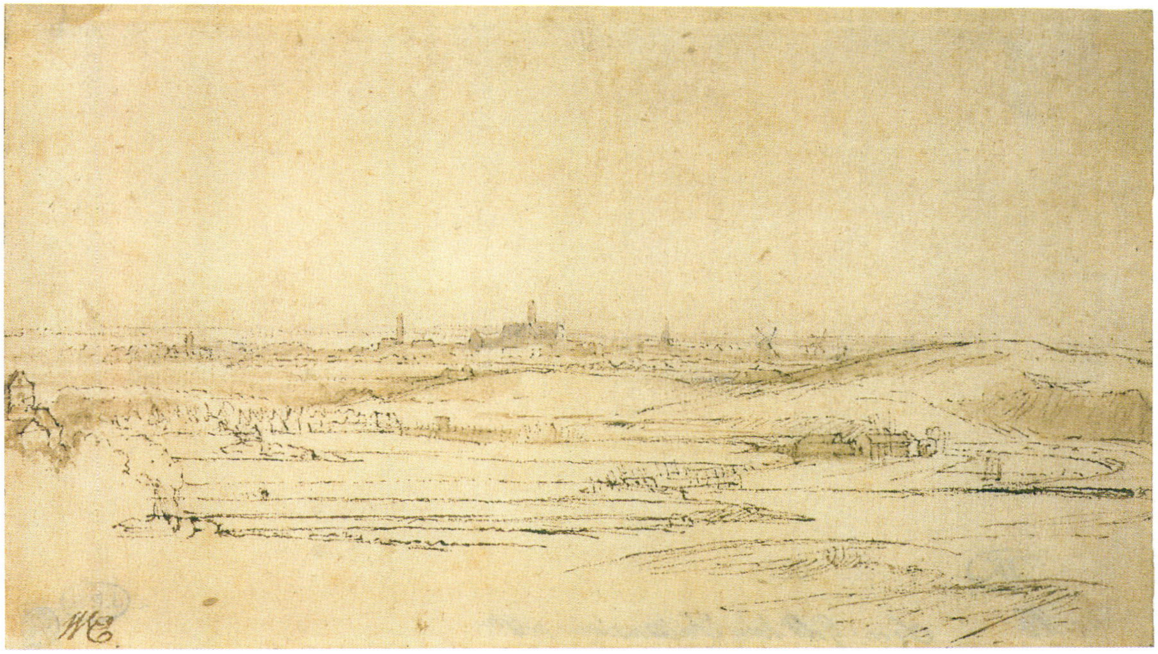

91
Farm with a Watermill
*c.*1651–52

Pen and ink and brush
16.0 x 24.0 cm
Lower left: collector's mark of Jan Pietersz Zomer
Collection Groninger Museum, Groningen

LITERATURE: Benesch 1973, vol. VI, pp. 342–3, no. 1247; Bolten 1967, pp. 99–100, no. 68.

This drawing of a landscape once belonged to Jan Pietersz Zomer (1641–1724), a broker in paintings with a large art collection of his own. Shortly before his death in 1724, his etchings and drawings were published in a catalogue. He himself kept his drawings in so-called art books, one of which albums he described as 'A small rectangular book, no. 41, bound in horn, containing 60 landscapes in the vicinity of Amsterdam, beautifully drawn from life by Rembrandt, 16 or 17 history pieces, and the same number of figures'.[1]

This *Farm with a Watermill* was undoubtedly one of those '60 landscapes', as the initials 'I.P.Z.' are embossed in the stamp of the collector Zomer. A number of landscapes from Zomer's collection are views of Diemen, Houtewaal and Sloten, all of which are indeed villages 'in the vicinity of Amsterdam'.[2] The drawing described here is of a farm with a small watermill, seen slightly left of centre on the sheet. In Rembrandt's day, mills of this kind were a common sight in the eastern part of the Netherlands but rare in the polders around Amsterdam. The undulating landscape also points to a location in the Gelderland region, which Rembrandt is known to have visited.

Benesch has identified a large group of stylistically related landscapes, which must have been made around 1650 and which culminated in an etching in 1652 of a *Clump of Trees with a Vista* (cat. no. 114).[3] The etching is similar in style to a drawing of *c.*1650–51 in Vienna (Graphische Sammlung Albertina) (Benesch 1246), which likewise shows a farmhouse surrounded by trees and has a relatively bare foreground and a wide expanse of sky. This sheet also belonged to Jan Pietersz Zomer, and it is possible that the two drawings remained together from the time of the sale of Rembrandt's 'art on paper' in 1658 until the auction of 1724.

BB

1 Dudok van Heel 1977, pp. 105–6: 'Een kleinder boek over dwars No. 41. met een hoorne band, daar in leggen 60 stuks Landschapjes, buiten Amsterdam, konstig na't leven, [die] door Rembrant zyn getekent, en 16 á 17 Historien, als Beeldjes dito'.

2 Schatborn 1982, pp. 21–3.

3 Benesch 1973, vol. VI, p. 342, no. 1246.

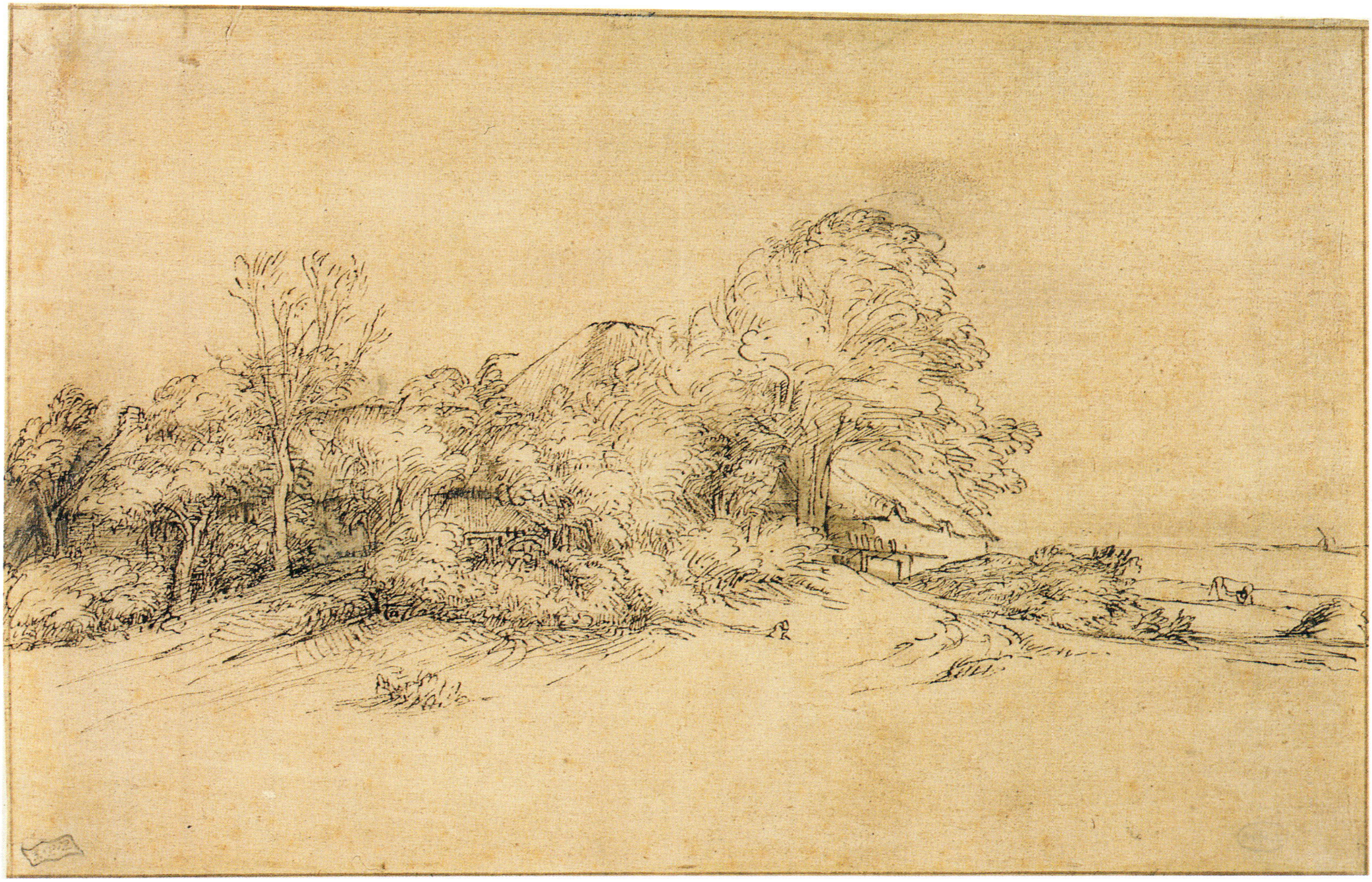

92
Joseph Sold by His Brothers
*c.*1651–52

Pen and ink and brush
15.8 x 20.5 cm
Staatliche Museen zu Berlin, Kupferstichkabinett

LITERATURE: Benesch 1973, vol. V, p. 246, no. 876.

Joseph was Jacob's favourite son and therefore the envy of his half-brothers. In *c.*1633 Rembrandt made an etching of the heart-rending scene where one of the brothers shows Jacob the bloodstained coat of his youngest son, leaving him to conclude that Joseph has been devoured by wild beasts (B.38) (fig. 92a). The Old Testament describes the events leading up to this drama. The brothers, who had planned to slay Joseph, eventually concluded that there was no advantage in killing him. Instead they sold him to passing merchants, who took him to Egypt (Genesis 37:28). Here, while he was in captivity, the wife of his master, Potiphar, tried to seduce him (see commentary to cat. no. 16). Later in life Joseph rose to a high position under the Pharaoh, thanks to his gift for prophecy. Joseph's adventures were extremely popular with Rembrandt's teacher Pieter Lastman and with his school.

This picture by Rembrandt shows Joseph's brothers receiving money from a Midianite in a turban, portrayed as a wealthy merchant. The men holding shepherds' staffs are the brothers – the Bible describes them as keepers of sheep. In their representations of this episode, Lastman and his followers also depicted the merchants' caravan as well as the brothers' flocks, but Rembrandt has chosen to concentrate on the actors themselves.[1]

The episode unfolds in two scenes. On the left we see the main figures from the biblical tale. Joseph has turned to one of his brothers, imploring his mercy. Joseph looks rather young for his years, since the Bible states explicitly that he was seventeen at the time (Genesis 37:2). Another brother standing behind him casts a furtive glance in his direction, as though ashamed of what he sees before him.

It has been speculated that Rembrandt's drawing may have been inspired by a picture Bible from 1659,[2] but this is probably incorrect, as the style of the work suggests a dating in the early 1650s. During this period Rembrandt made numerous illustrations of both Old and New Testament scenes, one being the related drawing of *Tobias and the Angel Taking Leave of Raguel* (Benesch 871) (fig. 92b).[3]

BB

1 Amsterdam / Jerusalem / Münster 1991–94, pp. 41–4.
2 Tümpel 1970, cat. no. 15.
3 Schatborn 1985, pp. 90–1, no. 41.

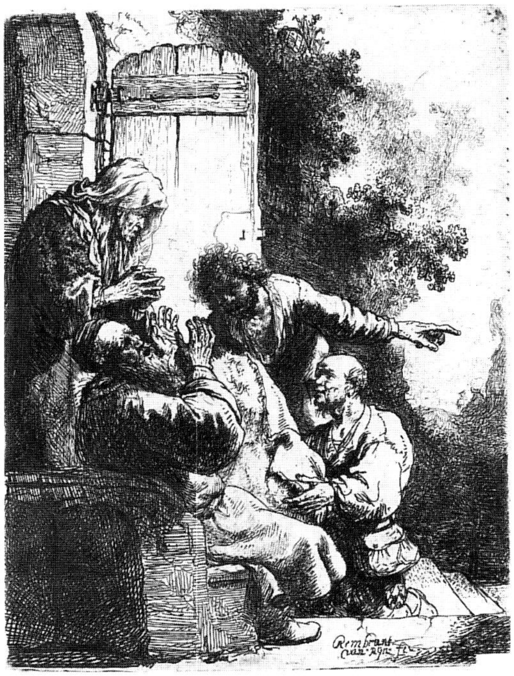

FIG. 92a
Rembrandt
Joseph's Robe Is Shown to Jacob *c.*1633
Signed
Etching
10.7 x 8.0 cm
Rijksprentenkabinet, Rijksmuseum, Amsterdam

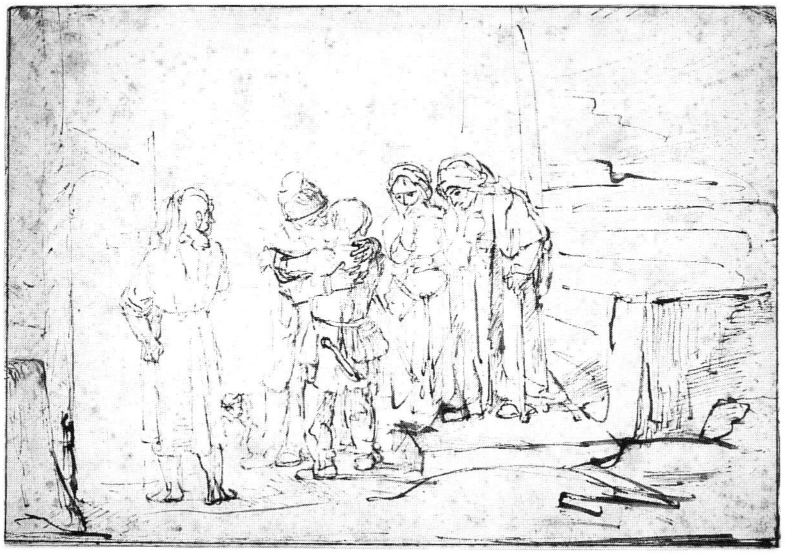

FIG. 92b
Rembrandt
Tobias and the Angel Taking Leave of Raguel
*c.*1650
Pen and ink and brush
19.4 x 27.3 cm
Rijksprentenkabinet, Rijksmuseum, Amsterdam

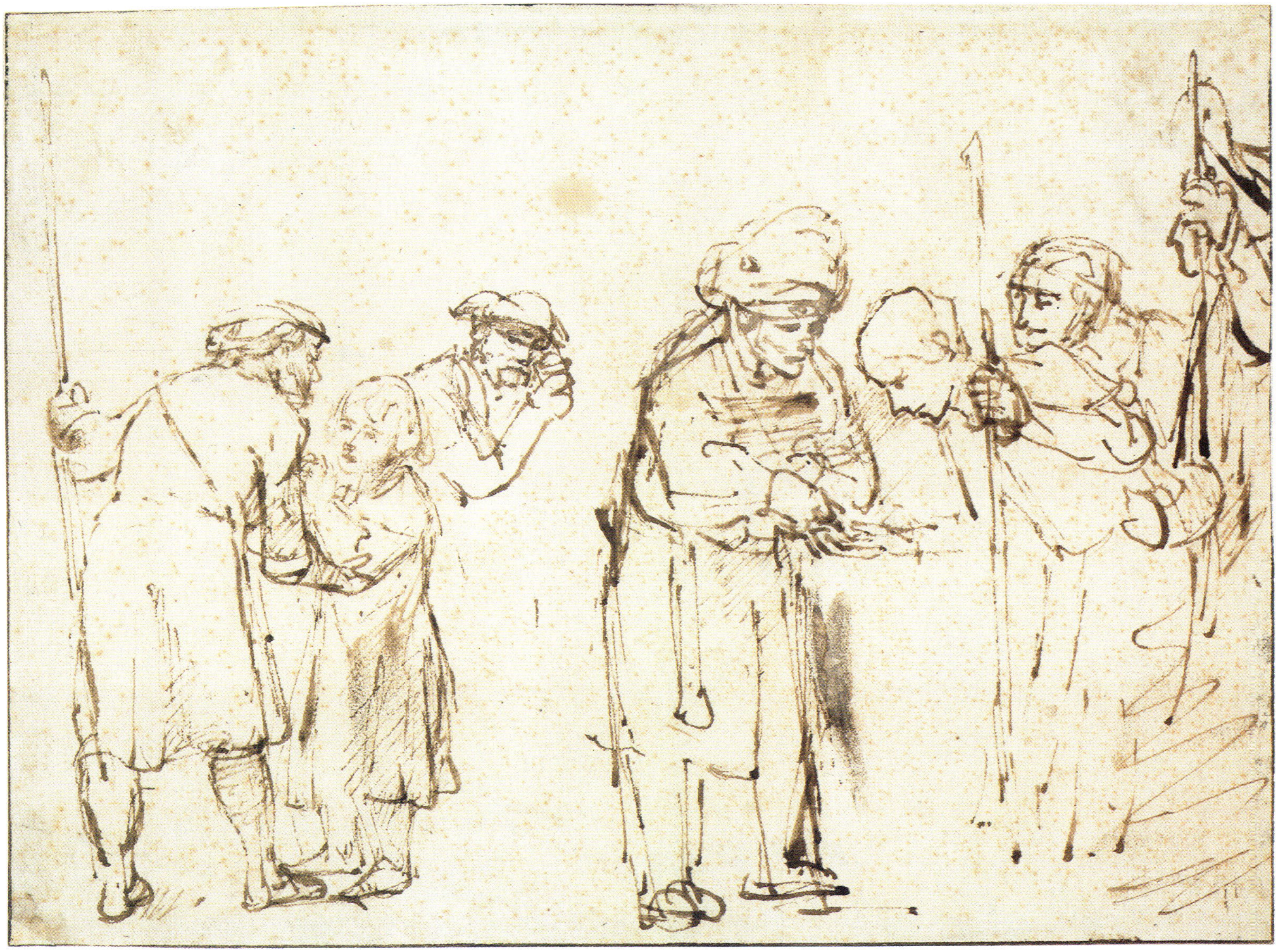

93

Shah Jahan as a Horseman

*c.*1656–58

Pen and ink and brush, with chalk
20.5 x 17.7 cm
Trustees of the British Museum, London

LITERATURE: Benesch 1973, vol. V, p. 325, no. 1205; Royalton-Kisch 1992, pp. 151–2, cat. no. 67.

In 1656 an inventory was drawn up of the art collection in Rembrandt's home in the Jodenbreestraat in Amsterdam. Among his most precious art books was an anthology of 'curious miniature drawings of different types of costume'. These were presumably the extraordinary Mogul miniatures on which Rembrandt based dozens of drawings. From the point of view of their subject matter, these drawings, many of them on so-called Japanese paper, form a unique ensemble in the master's oeuvre. They are all pictures of figures and appear to have been made mainly as costume studies (Benesch 1193) (fig. 93a). Yet few of their typically oriental elements – the intricately bound turbans, for instance – are to be seen in Rembrandt's later work. Moreover, only a single etching, a depiction of *Abraham and the Three Angels*, 1656 (B.29), may have been inspired by one of these Mogul miniatures (see, however, commentary to cat. no. 16). The print is dated 1656, giving some indication as to when the series of drawings was made. They probably date from no later than 1658, the year in which the miniatures were sold together with the rest of Rembrandt's collection.

The remarkable thing about these drawings is that Rembrandt managed to breathe new life into stylized oriental representations simply by altering the position of a limb, adding shadow and rendering more natural proportions. Some of the examples he used came from a single anthology. In 1762 Empress Maria Theresa of Austria had the 'treasure room' at Schloss Schönbrunn decorated with collages of Indian miniatures set in rococo frames. About 260 original sheets were cut for this purpose and pasted onto wooden panels. At least ten of the miniatures that survived as a result have since been identified as pictures that inspired Rembrandt's work.[1]

The drawing discussed here was probably based on two different miniatures. The black-bearded horseman is clearly recognizable as Shah Jahan, ruler of India, whom Rembrandt also depicted in his copy of the miniature with the shoes drawn twice (fig. 93a). This copy was a fairly accurate representation of a sheet now at Schönbrunn. The steed, on the other hand, was inspired by a miniature of an Indian prince on horseback (fig. 93b). Rembrandt has moved away from stylization, as he did in most of these pictures, in this case by restoring the animal's reduced head and exaggerated haunches to more natural proportions. The horse no longer seems to be hovering, but is posed in a levade, with its hind legs planted firmly on the ground and its forefeet in the air. Skilful hatching and washes lend depth to the picture. Rembrandt has copied the horse's grooming and tackle down to the tiniest details. Its mane, for instance, has been braided into small, tight knots, alternating with long plaits tied at the ends. The bridle and harness are exactly the same as in the miniature in terms of the striped girth and backband, the fall of the reins, and the bit. Identical, too, are the square shabrack, the oval, flower-patterned rolls, and the high saddle with the elegantly curved pommel.

The anonymous eastern miniaturists who provided Rembrandt with his examples were also his contemporaries. They were artists of the Mogul School, working at the court of the mighty Shah Jahan. It was during the emperor's reign in India, from 1628 to 1658, that the Taj Mahal was built. A man who exulted in splendour, Shah Jahan was a patron with discerning taste, who engaged artists from both East and West. At the same time, the United East India Company, which monopolized maritime trade in the region extending from the Cape of Good Hope to Japan, exposed the West to the cultural and spiritual heritage of the Orient. Rembrandt had a lifelong passion for exotic and decorative objects, and it found expression in his collection of curiosa.[2]

BB

1 Strzygowski 1923; Broos 1980, pp. 210–18.
2 Broos 1995, pp. 66–74.

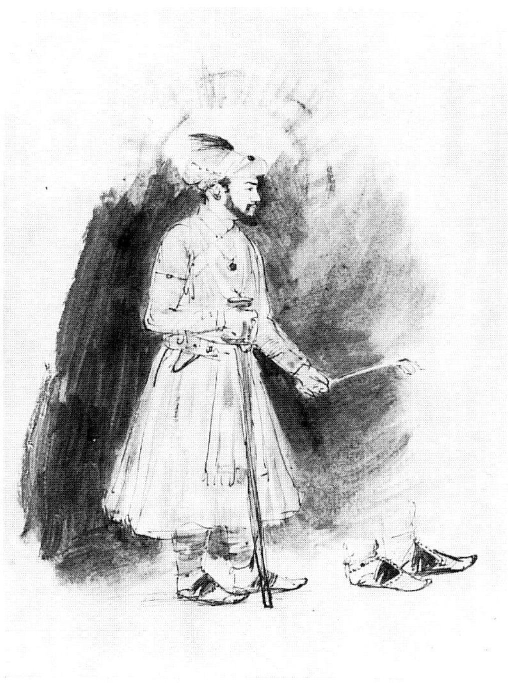

FIG. 93a
Rembrandt
Shah Jahan and a Study of Indian Footwear
*c.*1656–58
Pen and ink and brush
22.5 x 17.1 cm
© The Cleveland Museum of Art, Cleveland, 1997
Leonard C. Hanna, Jr., Fund, 1978.38

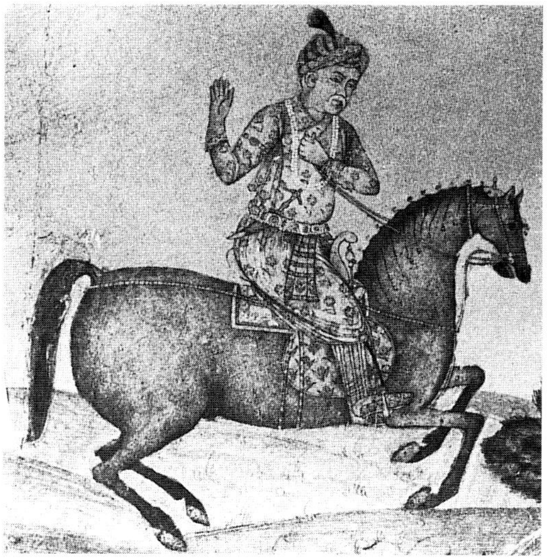

FIG. 93b
Indian 17th century
Indian Prince on Horseback
*c.*1650
Gouache (fragment)
Schloss Schönbrunn, Vienna

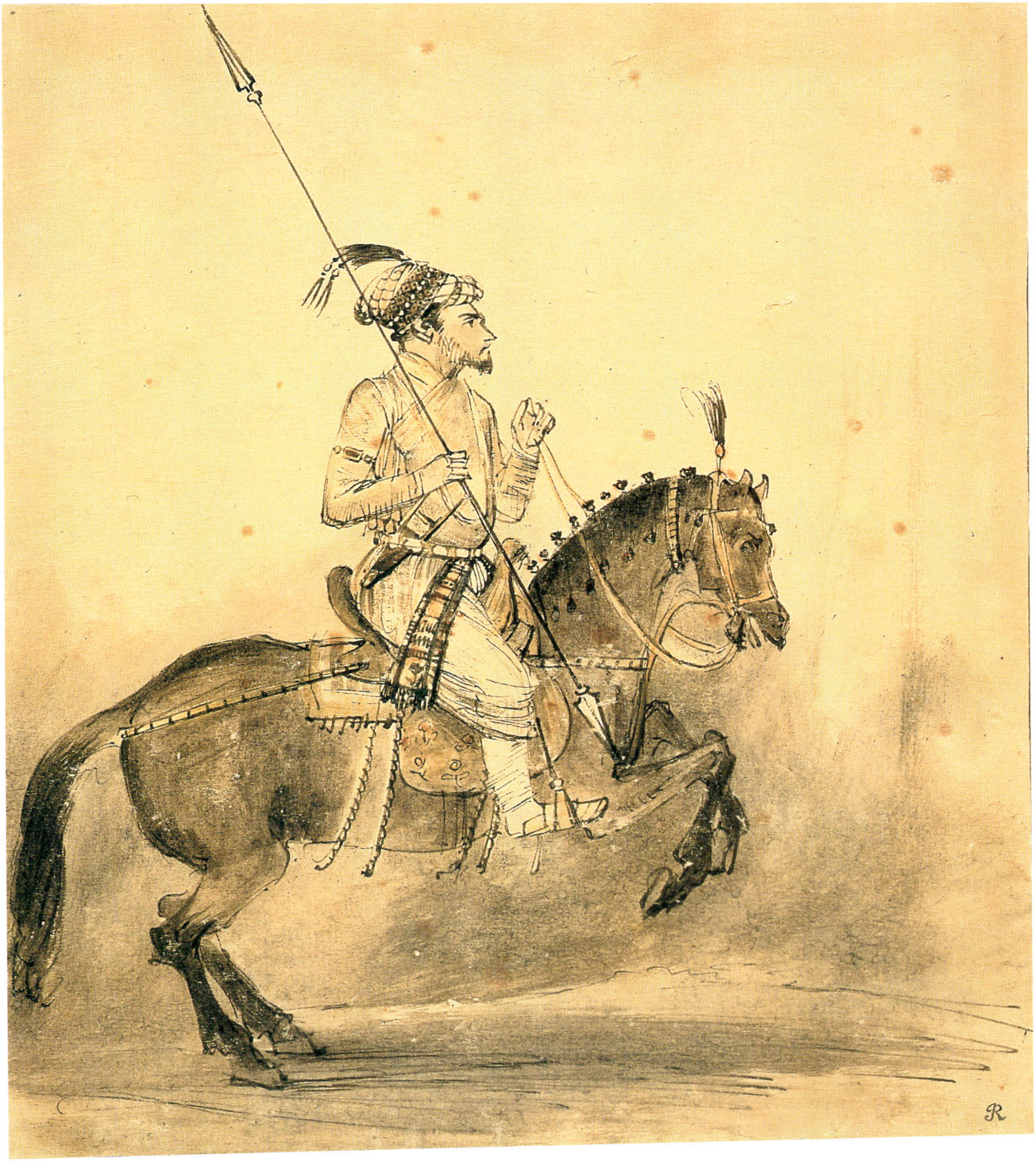
R

94
Saul with the Witch of Endor
*c.*1657

Pen and ink
15.6 x 23.5 cm
Museum Bredius, The Hague

LITERATURE: Benesch 1973, vol. V, p. 280, no. 1028; Blankert 1978, pp. 159–60, no. T 6.

Not surprisingly, the scene shown in this drawing was once described as a *'corps de garde'* or guardroom, with soldiers whiling away their time.[1] The figure in the helmet on the left is indeed characterized as a warrior. Yet Rembrandt had a biblical scene in mind, namely the episode of Saul with the witch of Endor. Several pupils of his also tackled the story of Saul, but most of them illustrated the passage in which Satan appears to Saul in the guise of the dead Samuel and foretells his imminent death and the victory of the Philistine army.[2]

Rembrandt, however, has depicted the passage that follows in in the Bible, wherein the witch of Endor emerges as a model of hospitality. Noticing that Saul was too frightened to touch his food, she slaughtered a fat calf and baked unleavened bread. 'And she brought it before Saul, and before his servants; and they did eat' (1 Samuel, 28:24–25). Rembrandt made another drawing of this fairly unremarkable incident (Benesch 911) (fig. 94a). This sheet and several others illustrating episodes from the Bible were etched by Mathys Pool around 1700 (fig. 94b).[3] The entire group almost certainly came from Rembrandt's own collection. The drawing in The Hague has been executed in the same technique as the other works in the group: the composition has been drawn with a reed pen, and then rubbed with a finger in parts. This work is by no means an imitation of the autograph sheet in Frankfurt, but a variant of that composition. If, as has been suggested, the present drawing was not in fact made by Rembrandt himself, the artist must have been a highly talented pupil with a strong mind of his own.

BB

1 Blankert 1978, pp. 159– 60, no. T 6.
2 Amsterdam / Jerusalem / Münster 1991–94, pp. 90, 102, note 11.
3 Schatborn 1982, p. 14, no. B77.

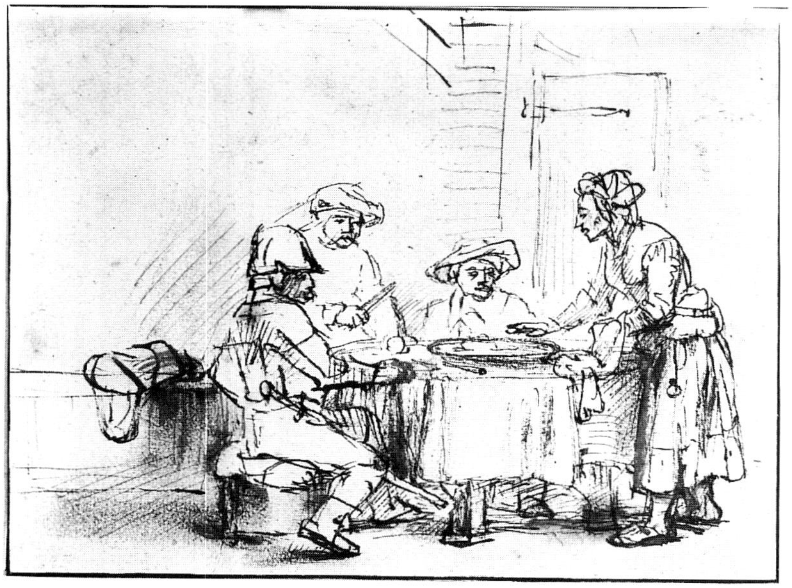

FIG. 94a
Rembrandt
Saul with the Witch of Endor
*c.*1655
Pen and ink
13.1 x 17.3 cm
Städelsches Kunstinstitut, Frankfurt

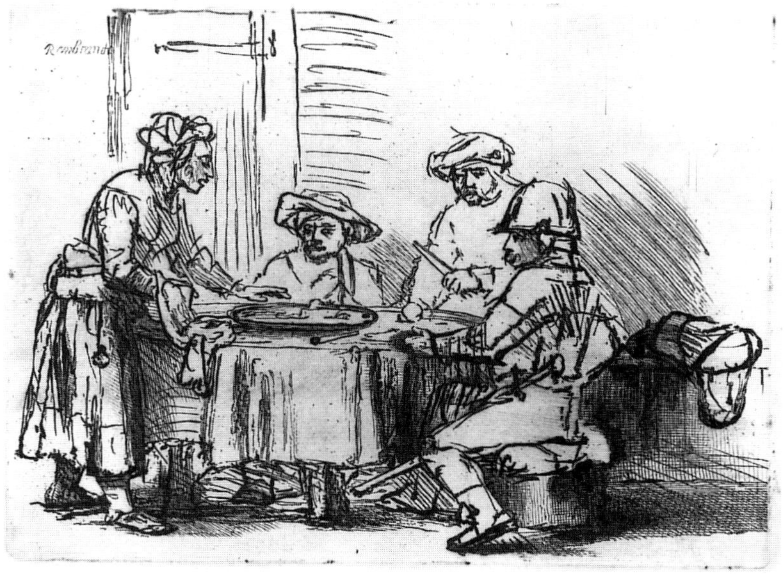

FIG. 94b
Mathys Pool (1676–1740), after Rembrandt
Saul with the Witch of Endor *c.*1700
Etching
11.4 x 15.2 cm
Rijksprentenkabinet, Rijksmuseum, Amsterdam

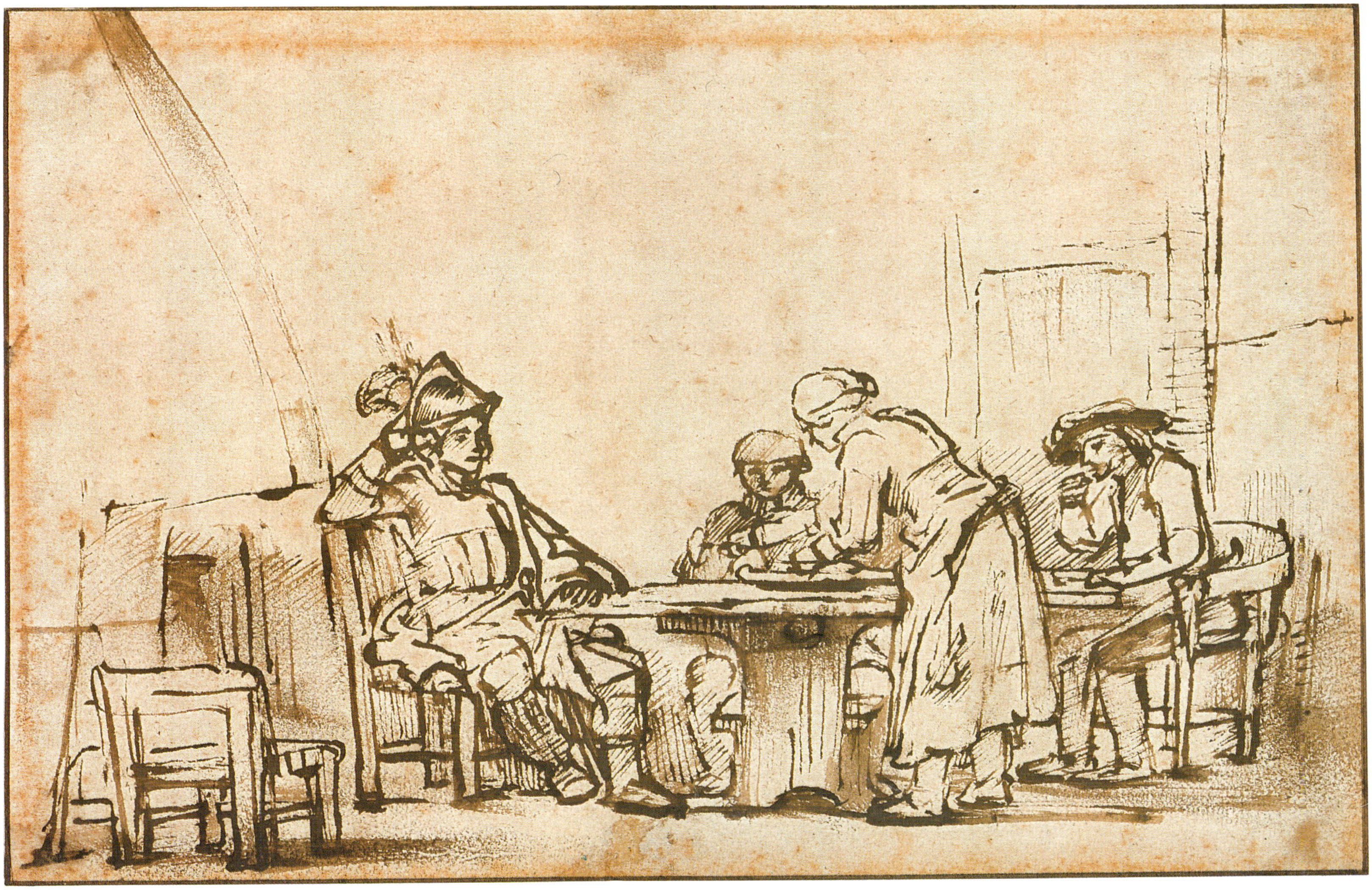

95

Hendrickje Stoffels Leaning at a Window

*c.*1657

Inscribed lower left by Frederik Sparre *1884*; lower centre by Pierre-Jean Mariette *257*
Pen and ink and brush
16.5 x 12.5 cm
Nationalmuseum, Stockholm

LITERATURE: Benesch 1973, vol. V, p. 299, no. 1102.

In the mid-1650s a young woman posed for some of Rembrandt's drawings and paintings, one example being the famous panel *A Woman Bathing* (Bredius 437) (p. 37, fig. 8). She is generally thought to have been Hendrickje Stoffels, the woman Rembrandt regarded as his 'wife', although the couple were not officially married. In fairly quick succession, Rembrandt made two reed pen drawings (Benesch 1101, 1102) of the same woman leaning at a window and apparently dozing (fig. 95a). His manner of portrayal in both the painting and the drawings is almost identical: brilliantly fluent, broad and confident.

The two drawings have the unusual distinction of having always remained together. In the late seventeenth century they belonged to the French collector Roger de Piles, who was also a distinguished art historian, and subsequently to Pierre Crozat, whose collection was auctioned in 1741. The Swedish ambassador to Paris, Carl Gustav Tessin, bought both works at the sale, together with about a hundred other drawings attributed to Rembrandt. In 1750 the Swedish Crown Prince acquired Tessin's collection. The dealer and collector Pierre-Jean Mariette (1694–1774), who wrote the catalogue for Crozat's sale, inscribed the number *257* at the lower centre of the present sheet, and it was probably he who thought to make the piece more 'presentable' by cropping all four sides and drawing a framing-line around the composition.

After the death of his first wife, Saskia van Uylenburgh, in 1642, Rembrandt had a brief romantic relationship with Geertje Dircx, his son Titus's nurse, before becoming involved with his second great love, Hendrickje Stoffels. On 15 June 1649 Stoffels witnessed a notarial contract concerning Dircx, and was described on this occasion as a 'spinster, aged 23'.[1] Rembrandt was almost twice her age at the time.

The provisions of Saskia's will prevented Rembrandt from marrying Hendrickje without forfeiting much of his property and money. Even so, his fortunes declined over the years and finally reached a point where he was forced to declare himself bankrupt. He lost many of his possessions, including his luxurious residence, which is today the Museum het Rembrandthuis (p. 26, fig. 6). In 1658 the family, consisting of Rembrandt, Hendrickje, Titus, and Rembrandt and Hendrickje's daughter Cornelia (b. 1654), moved to a less prestigious address.

In 1660 Hendrickje and Titus took control of Rembrandt's business affairs and made him a non-active partner. This meant that he could continue to paint, but the rest was left to them. He had a role as adviser, for which he received board and lodging in return.[2] The arrangement must have come as a great relief. In the years following this difficult period, he was almost as active as he had formerly been during his successful early years in Amsterdam. Rembrandt outlived both Hendrickje and Titus: Hendrickje was buried on 24 July 1663 and Titus on 7 September 1668.

BB

1 Strauss & Van der Meulen 1979, pp. 268–9, no. 1649/4.
2 Strauss & Van der Meulen 1979, pp. 462–3, no. 1660/20.

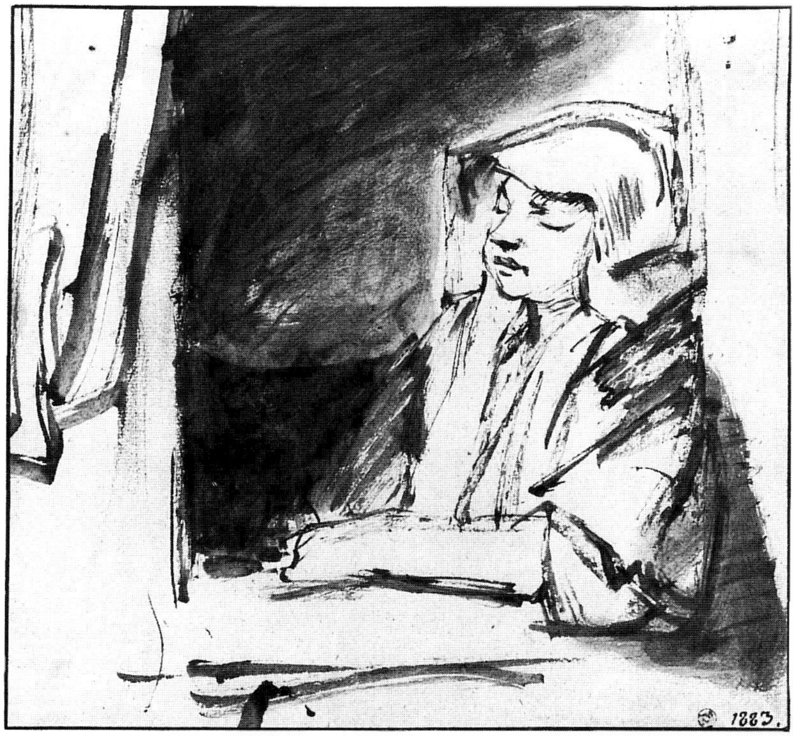

FIG. 95a
Rembrandt
Hendrickje Stoffels Leaning at a Window
*c.*1657
Pen and ink and brush
16.2 x 17.4 cm
Nationalmuseum, Stockholm
Photograph: Nationalmuseum, SKM, Stockholm

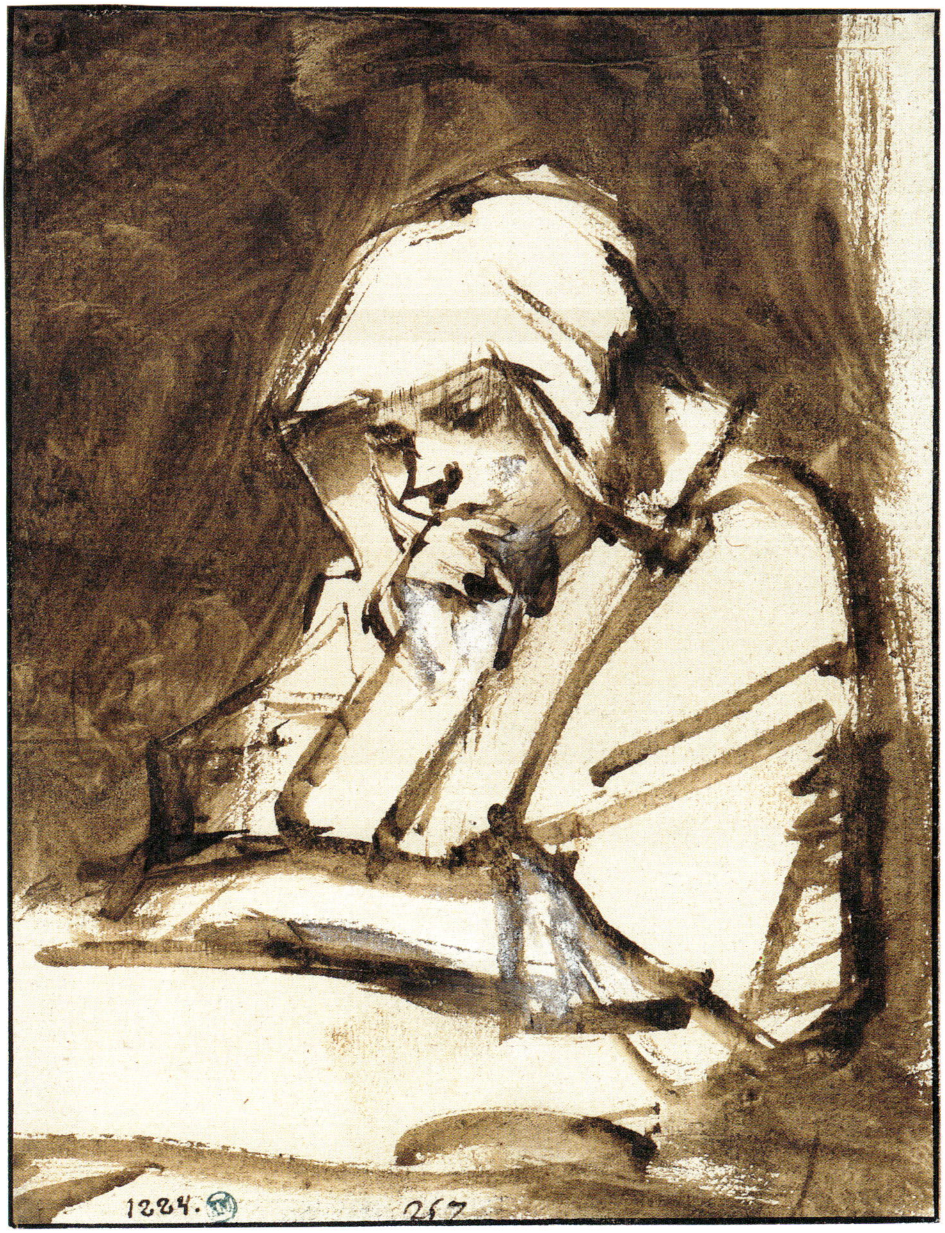
1284.

96
Rembrandt's Studio with a Nude Model (Hendrickje?)
*c.*1658

Pen and ink and brush
20.5 x 19.0 cm
Lower right: collector's marks of E. V. Uterson and Chambers Hall
The Visitors of the Ashmolean Museum, Oxford

LITERATURE: Benesch 1973, vol. V, pp. 310–11, no. 1161.

We know what Rembrandt looked like in his painter's smock in the early 1650s, thanks to a drawn self-portrait (cat. no. 85). The sheet bears the old inscription *sooals hij in sijn schilderkamer gekleet was* (in the clothes he wore in his studio). Rembrandt also drew an evocative picture of this 'studio' in his home on the Jodenbreestraat – now the Museum het Rembrandthuis – using numerous subtle washes to capture the fall of light to superb effect. In this drawing, Rembrandt gives us a glimpse of his world. On the left we see a painting on an easel, and slightly further back, tossed onto a stool, is the smock he is wearing in the *Self-Portrait*. A female model, nude from the waist up and brightly illuminated, is seated on the right. Part of the fireplace can be seen behind her. Rembrandt achieved the lighting he wanted by draping a white cloth over the ceiling to serve as a reflector, and by closing the shutters covering the lower half of the windows so that the sunshine poured in from above in a concentrated mass.

The table at the window has a raised section, rather like that of a writing-desk, on which Rembrandt used to produce his works on paper. The same piece of furniture can be seen in an etched *Self-Portrait* from 1648 (fig. 85a). To the right in the drawing is a cradle with a folded coverlet. It may have been Cornelia's, Rembrandt's third daughter with this name, who was christened on 30 October 1654. Her mother was Hendrickje Stoffels, to whom Rembrandt referred as his wife ('huysvrouw'), although the couple were never officially married. Hendrickje moved into Rembrandt's home in 1649, when she was twenty-three and he around twice her age, and formed a close friendship with his son Titus. On 23 July 1654, when she was almost due to give birth to Cornelia, Hendrickje was summonsed before the council of the Reformed Church and reprimanded for having 'prostituted herself to the painter Rembran[d]t'.[1]

The seated model in this picture may be Hendrickje.[2] She is also believed to have posed for *A Woman Bathing* (Bredius 437) (fig. 96a), one of Rembrandt's most intriguing paintings from the mid-1650s. Rembrandt was on the verge of bankruptcy at the time, and in this connection an inventory of his estate was drawn up in July 1656. He lost not only his art collection as a result but also his house on the Jodenbreestraat, which he probably portrayed for the last time in this drawing.

BB

1 Strauss & Van der Meulen 1979, p. 320, no. 1654/15: 'met Rembrant de schilder Hoererije heeft gepleecht'.
2 Schatborn 1981, p. 56.

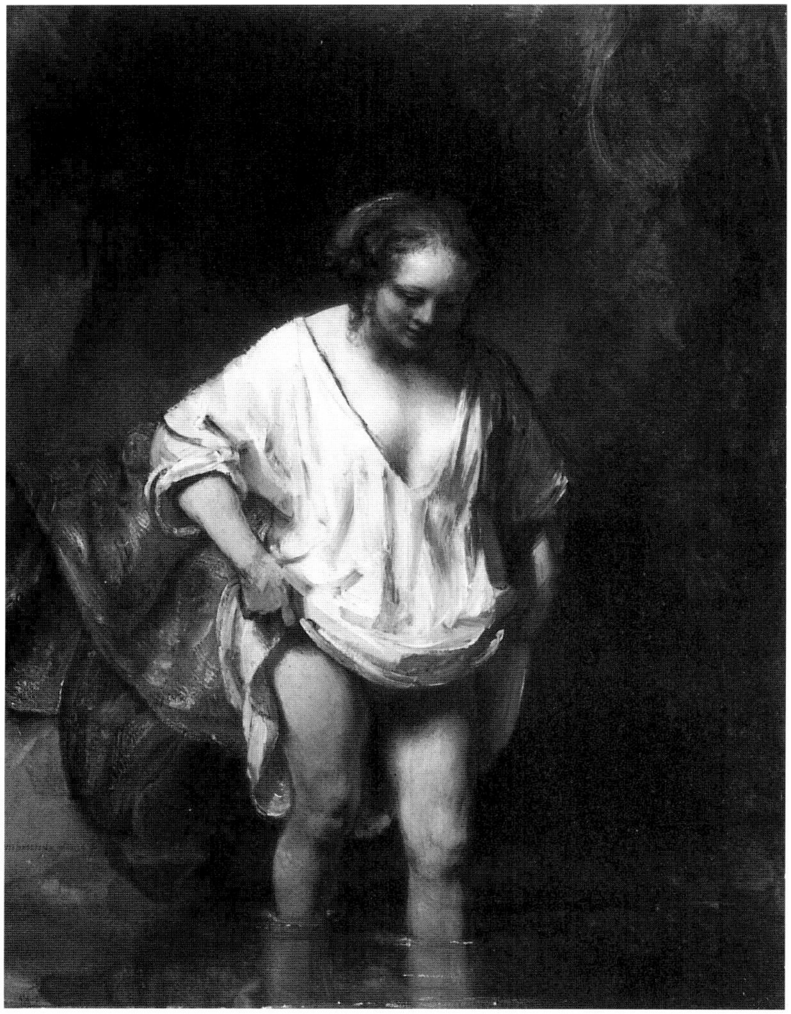

FIG. 96a
Rembrandt
A Woman Bathing
Signed and dated 1654
Panel
61.8 x 47.0 cm
The Trustees of the National Gallery, London
(for colour reproduction, see p. 37, fig. 8)

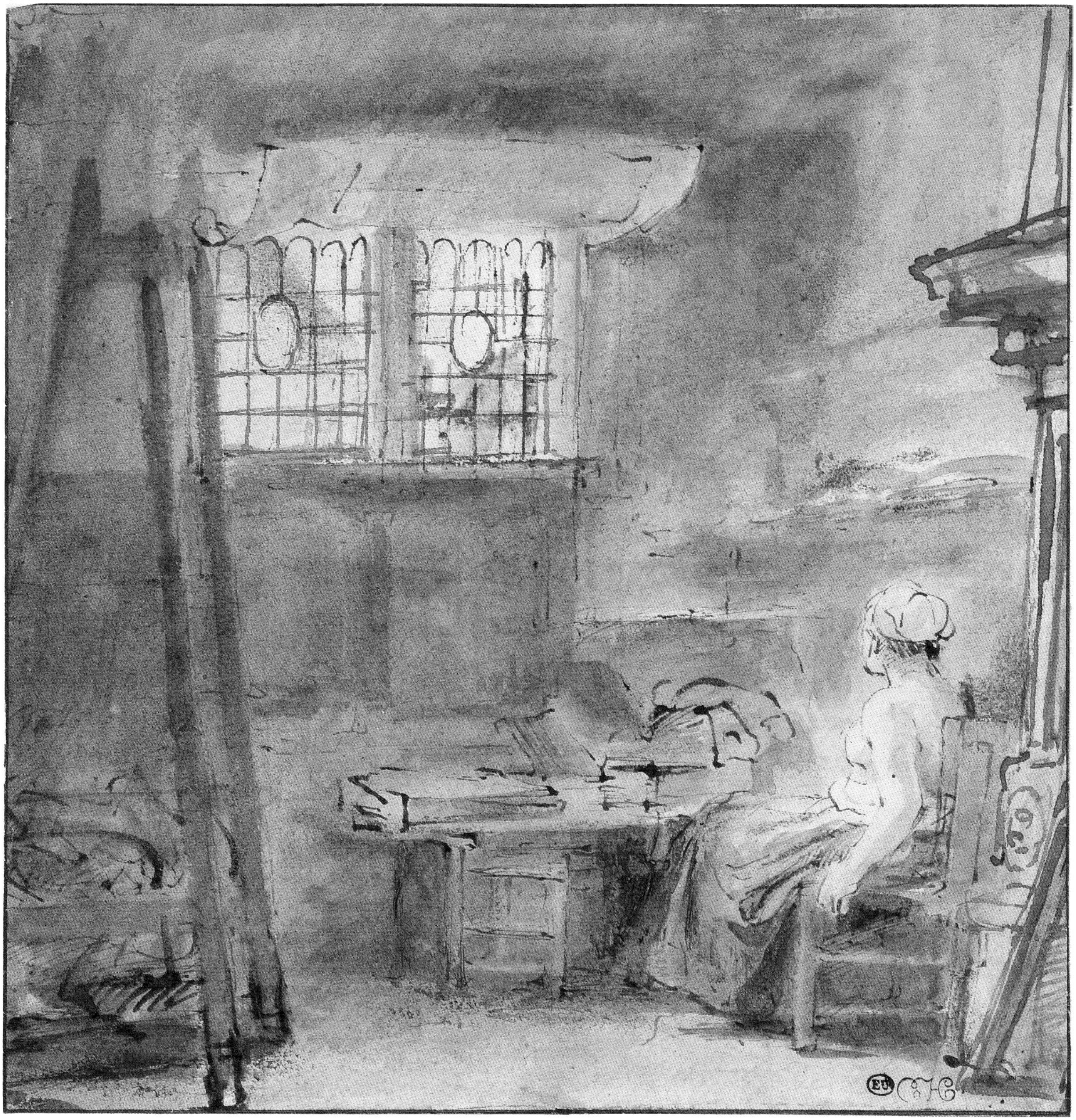

97
Homer Dictating to a Scribe
*c.*1660

Pen and ink and brush
14.9 x 16.8 cm
Nationalmuseum, Stockholm

LITERATURE: Benesch 1973, vol. V, p. 292, no. 1066.

This drawing is not only tangible evidence of Rembrandt's formidable mastery of the reed pen and the brush, but it is also a unique document. It forms a link in a series of works of art that owe their existence to a remarkable patron in faraway Sicily, Don Antonio Ruffo (1610/11–1678). In about 1652 this nobleman from Messina placed an order with Rembrandt, requesting a painting of a philosopher. This was the first of several commissions. G. J. Hoogewerff revealed the details of this fascinating story in 1917 (see also commentary to cat. no. 15).[1]

Rembrandt had long been specializing in half-length figures, in which he combined head studies and historical references. In 1653 he made for Ruffo the now famous picture of *Aristotle Contemplating the Bust of Homer* (The Metropolitan Museum of Art, New York) (p. 27, fig. 8). The bust of the Greek poet in this historical portrait was based on a copy of a sculpture from the Hellenistic period, one of the objects on display in Rembrandt's art cabinet, or *Kunst Caemer* (fig. 97a). The collection also included other statues of sages, poets and Roman emperors.[2]

Rembrandt sent the *Aristotle* to Ruffo together with a sketch on prepared canvas of a scene featuring Homer as the protagonist. This was the first draft of the painting that is now at the Mauritshuis, The Hague (Bredius 483) (fig. 97b). The canvas was later damaged by fire and all that remains is the principal subject – the blind Homer beating time as he recites his verses. The Stockholm drawing gives us some idea of what the original painted composition would have looked like. Rembrandt must have been profoundly moved by the poet's blindness. His portrayal of him is as poignant as that of his own, likewise disabled, father in a drawing he made in 1630, shortly before his father's death (Ashmolean Museum, Oxford) (Benesch 56).

At the lower right in the painting we see a piece of paper and two fingers clasping a pen; this was presumably the hand of the scribe recording Homer's poems. According to a 1678 inventory of Ruffo's collection, there were originally two disciples in the painting, either writing or listening. This implies that the scene may have extended further than the design sketch would suggest. The complete composition is thought to have been similar to a painting by Rembrandt's pupil Arent de Gelder from about 1700 (cat. no. 71). De Gelder was evidently deeply impressed by the painting he had seen the master working on some forty years earlier.

What is compelling about Rembrandt's drawing is that the scribe is gazing at the poet, watching his lips as he speaks, whereas de Gelder shows him absorbed in his own work. This makes it all the more intriguing to consider what the original composition was like. But as the situation stands, the sightless poet in the painting is a figure of monumental stature, matched by that in the drawing from Stockholm.

BB

1 Hoogewerff 1917, pp. 119–48; Broos 1993, pp. 269–78.
2 Strauss & Van der Meulen 1979, pp. 363–5, no. 1656/12.

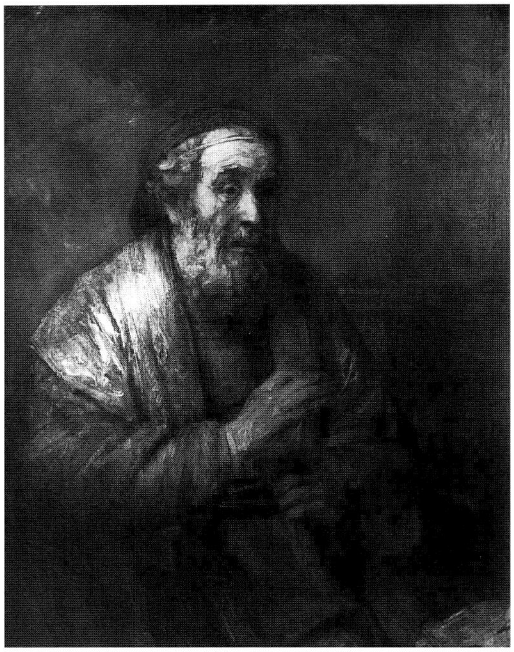

FIG. 97b
Rembrandt
Homer
Signed and dated 1663
Canvas (fragment)
107.0 x 82.0 cm
Mauritshuis, The Hague
Photograph: © Mauritshuis, The Hague, inv. no. 584

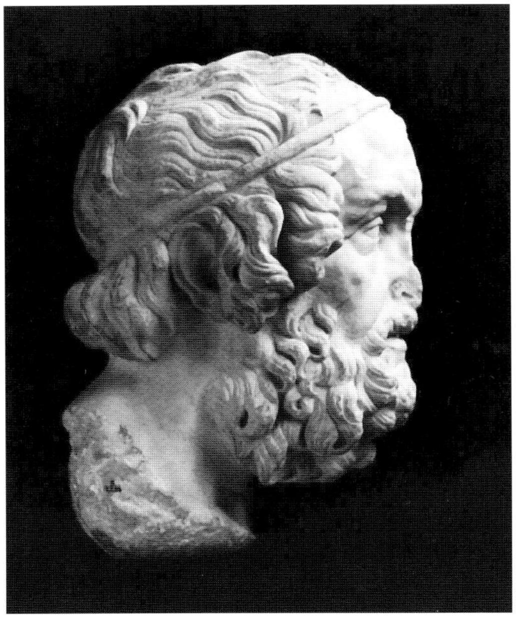

FIG. 97a
Copy after late Hellenistic original *c.*150 BC
Portrait of Homer
Marble
41.0 cm (height)
Henry Lillie Pierce Fund
Courtesy, Museum of Fine Arts, Boston

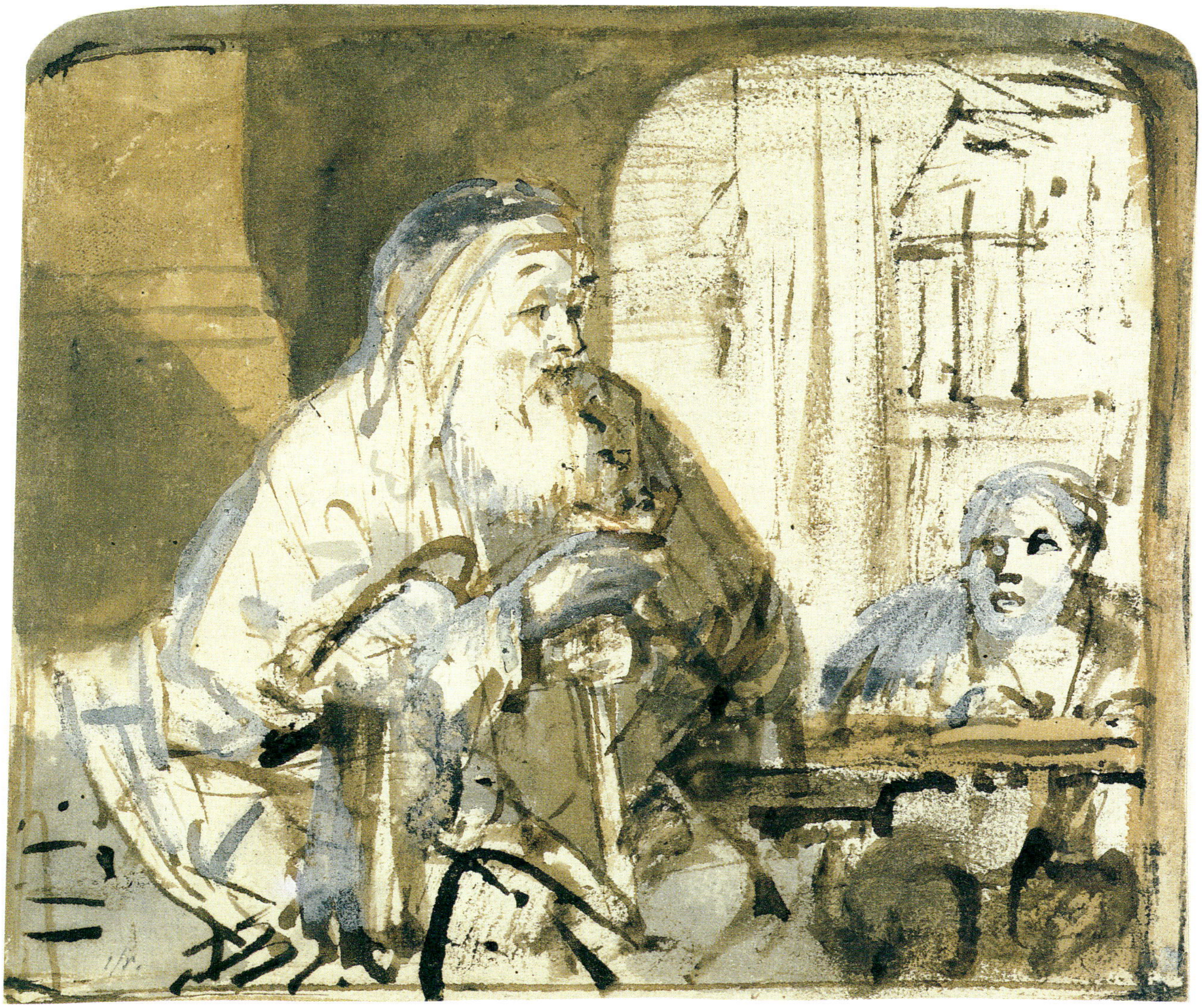

98
Seated Nude
*c.*1661

Pen and ink and brush
29.2 x 17.5 cm
Rijksprentenkabinet, Rijksmuseum, Amsterdam

LITERATURE: Benesch 1973, vol. V, p. 307, no. 1142; Schatborn 1985, p. 120, no. 55.

Rembrandt often sketched in the company of his pupils. With them he would work outdoors rendering animals (cat. no. 87) and landscapes, or in the studio portraying a nude model (cat. no. 96). Here Rembrandt has drawn a nude woman seated on a stool before a warm stove. A pupil of his, possibly Johannes Raven (1634–1662), must have been sitting to his right, working on a view of the model slightly more in profile (British Museum, London) (fig. 98a).[1] The pupil has applied a dense, dark wash to mark the contours in his piece, whereas Rembrandt's are not only far more subtle, but are also rendered in a variety of shades to suggest the room and the fall of light. Moreover, his superb treatment of the woman's hair and cap betray a skill that the pupil could never match.

The date assigned until now to the present drawing was established on the basis of a number of Rembrandt's etchings from 1658, one being a *Woman Sitting Half-Dressed beside a Stove* (cat. no. 121). This closely related scene was coveted by collectors, who dubbed it 'the woman at the stove, with and without the white cap',[2] referring to the numerous states of the etching that were in circulation at the time. Rembrandt's pupil Samuel van Hoogstraten may have had this etching in mind when he advised aspiring artists to practise sketching nudes from life.[3] A document of that same year, 1658, states that a certain Catharina Jans had 'posed stark naked' and that various artists, including Rembrandt's former pupils Ferdinand Bol and Govaert Flinck, had made drawings and paintings of her.[4] Hence we know that even accomplished masters continued to observe this academic practice. Rembrandt himself is the best example.

The sheet discussed here was probably made even later than 1658. Rembrandt drew the sketch on the same lined cashbook paper that he used *c.*1661–62 for the *Portrait of Jacob van Loon* (Rijksprentenkabinet, Rijksmuseum, Amsterdam) (Benesch 1179) and the *Portrait of Volckert Jansz* (Museum Boijmans Van Beuningen, Rotterdam) (Benesch 1180), both of which were studies for *The Syndics* (Rijksmuseum, Amsterdam) (p. 29, fig. 10). This famous painting is dated 1662 and, given that the two drawings referred to here and the *Seated Nude* are in a surprisingly similar shade of ink, all three must have been produced in the same period. Hence, in spite of the *Seated Nude*'s resemblance to the etching referred to above, the only feasible conclusion is that the drawing was made a few years after 1658, probably in the early 1660s. In fact the date can most likely be narrowed down to 1661, the year in which Rembrandt made his etching of a *Woman with an Arrow* (B.202) (fig. 98b).[5]

BB

1 Royalton-Kisch 1992, pp. 215–18, cat. no. 107.
2 Weyerman 1729–69, vol. II, p. 41: 'het Vrouwtje by de Kachel met en zonder 't wit mutsje'.
3 Van Hoogstraten 1678, p. 294: 'wanneer gy nae de Teycken-schoolen of Academien gaet, om mans – of vrouwe-naekten nae't leven in de warme stooven te teykenen'.
4 Bredius 1915–22, vol. IV, p. 1255: 'moeder naeckt als model geseten heeft, en dat sy getuygen daernaer geteeckent en geschilderd hebben'.
5 Schatborn 1983, p. 458, dates the present drawing *c.*1658. In 1985, Schatborn gave the date as 1661 (Schatborn 1985, p. 120, no. 55).

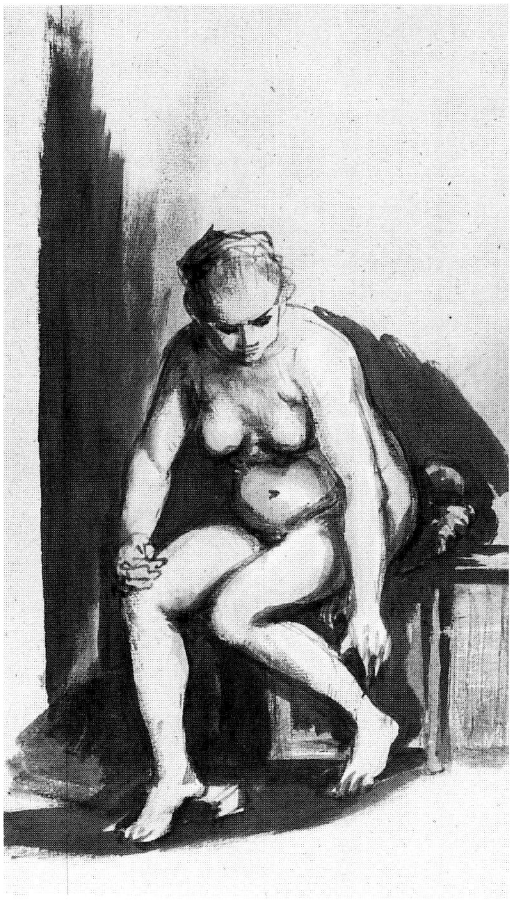

FIG. 98a
Pupil of Rembrandt (Johannes Raven?)
*Seated Nude c.*1661
Pen and ink and brush
28.6 x 16.2 cm
Copyright © The British Museum, London

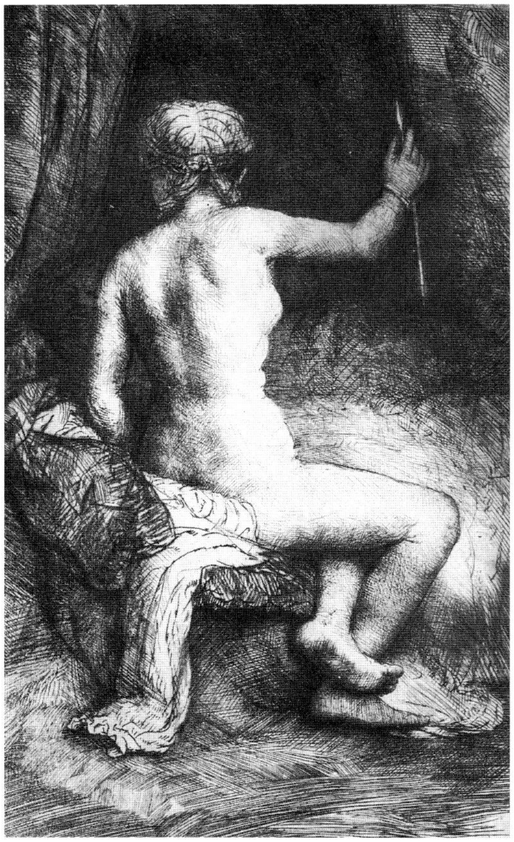

FIG. 98b
Rembrandt
Woman with an Arrow
Signed and dated 1661
Etching
20.5 x 12.3 cm
Rijksprentenkabinet, Rijksmuseum, Amsterdam

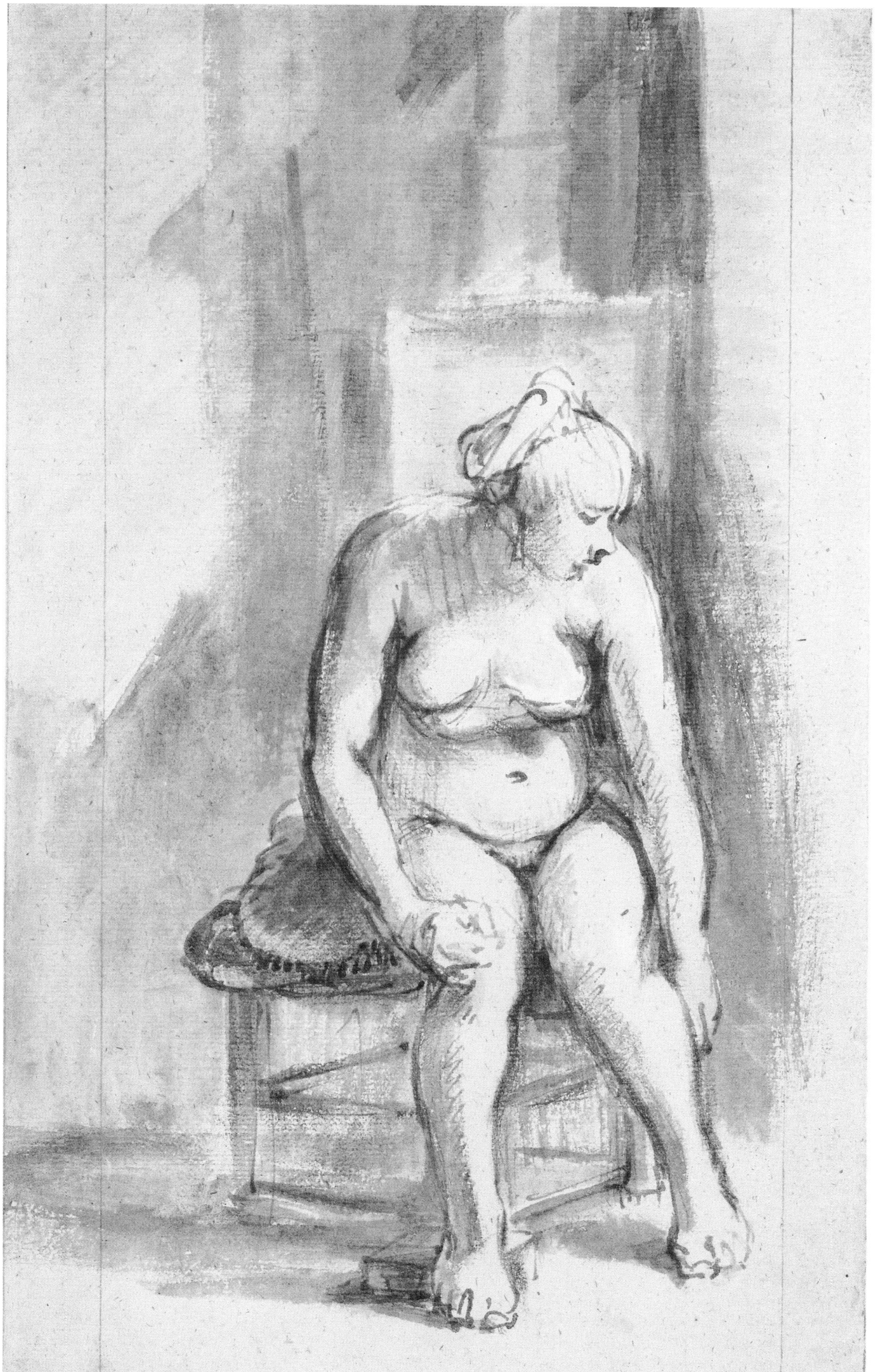

Rembrandt as an Etcher

CHRISTOPHER WHITE

Within his own lifetime, Rembrandt's etchings were acknowledged throughout Europe as an individual contribution to art, and were more consistently admired and collected than his paintings.[1] Baldinucci, writing little more than twenty years after the artist's death, claimed that 'in his peculiar way of engraving Rembrandt was much more esteemed by the professors of art than in painting'.[2] Prints, due to their reproductive nature and ease of dissemination, are much more potent in publicizing the name and work of an artist than either his paintings or his drawings can be, as Dürer was the first to discover. Thus Rembrandt, following the example of his near-contemporary Rubens – who built up an active business in reproductive engravings after his compositions – was able to establish a similar reputation during his own lifetime.

In England, where Rembrandt was, apart from one or two pictures in the royal collection, virtually unknown as a painter, in 1662 the diarist and collector John Evelyn was writing of 'The incomparable Reinbrand, whose etchings and gravings are of a particular spirit'.[3] In Italy, two of the foremost artists of the day paid their respects in different ways. Whereas Giovanni Battista Castiglione both copied and was influenced by Rembrandt's etchings,[4] Guercino, in a 1660 letter to a Sicilian patron of both himself and Rembrandt, wrote: 'I have seen divers of his printed works which have appeared in these parts which are very fine, engraved in good taste and in a good manner ... I frankly deem him to be a great virtuoso'.[5] In France there were already during the artist's lifetime two assiduous collectors of his etchings, Pierre Mariette and Michel de Marolles. The latter published in 1666 a catalogue of his print collection, which includes no fewer than 224 impressions of etchings by Rembrandt.[6] At home in the Netherlands his prints were collected and commented upon, and on at least one occasion were used as a stake in a bet about tulips at the height of tulipomania. They were highly admired and collected in a fashion that continues to this day. Whatever Rembrandt's critical fortune as a painter, there has hardly been a period when his prints were not appreciated.

Rembrandt began etching very early in his career, when he was still living in Leiden. Thereafter he continued without pause until about 1660, after which only one plate, a portrait commission, is recorded. Exactly why he should have abandoned etching almost entirely during the last nine years of his career remains unexplained. A testimony made a few years after his death that he 'had some polished plates ... in his hands, on which to make a Passion' might, if it referred to the last decade of Rembrandt's life, suggest that he had further work in mind.[7] And despite his forced move from his home in the Breestraat, Rembrandt had not lost interest in past work; his daughter-in-law, who lived with him and died only a few days after him, left 'three books full of all the most precious prints which Rembrandt van Rijn made in his life'.[8] Moreover, two months after the artist's death, his Sicilian admirer, Antonio Ruffo, noted the arrival of 189 prints by Rembrandt from Amsterdam, which makes it seem likely that he had retained possession of most of his copperplates.[9]

How many prints Rembrandt produced remains a matter for debate, although the subject has occasioned far less controversy than in the case of his paintings. One principal reason is that there are many more indisputable signatures, often accompanied by dates, in his etched oeuvre. (Scholars trying to determine the authenticity of Rembrandt's paintings might, with advantage, take more note than they do of this solid body of documented works.) The earliest catalogues of Rembrandt's etchings, compiled by Edmé Gersaint in Paris in 1751 and by Adam Bartsch in Vienna in 1797, accepted no fewer than 341 and 375 subjects respectively. Today the generally accepted oeuvre has been reduced to under 300, largely owing to the recognition of works more correctly attributable to pupils. Nevertheless, some disputed cases remain.

In combining the practice of painting and printmaking, Rembrandt was following a distinguished tradition going back to the fifteenth century, when artists of the calibre of Andrea Mantegna and Albrecht Dürer were active as *peintres-graveurs*, as Bartsch described such dual activity in his great catalogue of prints. In the sixteenth century the Emilian painter Francesco Parmigianino produced a group of etchings which, with their freedom and spirit, contained much of the quality of pen drawings. In Rembrandt's home town of Leiden, the painter Lucas van Leyden was creating prints imbued with a psychological insight that Rembrandt himself was to develop so memorably. In his own century he was influenced by such *peintres-graveurs* as Annibale Carracci in Italy and, above all, at least in a taste for experiment and originality, by the Dutch artist Hercules Segers. These and many other artists had created a substantial body of prints, to which Rembrandt, even during his last years, turned for guidance and inspiration. And his own personal collection contained substantial numbers of prints by both Italian and northern artists from the fifteenth century onwards. As his work demonstrates, he never hesitated to turn to the past, whether, for example, he was adapting a particular motif from Dürer, Raphael or Titian; learning from the engraving technique of Mantegna; or submitting to the stylistic influence of Titian and his Venetian contemporaries. From this assimilation of shared experience, Rembrandt created his own entirely personal language, which is as recognizable in his prints as in his drawings and paintings.

Subject matter

In a country noted for specialization, Rembrandt stands out from most other Dutch artists by illustrating at one time or another nearly all the accepted categories of subject matter. His repertoire covers religious and mythological subjects, portraiture, genre, landscape and the nude. But pride of place must be given to biblical subjects, which include many of his largest and most important plates and which represent nearly a quarter of his etched oeuvre.

Trained by Pieter Lastman, a successful and influential painter who had worked in Italy, Rembrandt was immediately attracted by dramatic and picturesque subjects taken from the Bible. Following Lastman's example he developed a range of lively expressions and dramatic gestures that enabled him to convey the different reactions of the protagonists in the stories he was illustrating. In the large etching of the *Raising of Lazarus* (cat. no. 100), Rembrandt has evolved a composition with very expressive figures who, in their varied reactions, reveal the essence of the events taking place. This eloquent and extroverted style of presenting his subjects reached a peak during the mid-1630s, nowhere more so than in the *Angel Appearing to the Shepherds* (B.44) (figs 1, 2). The miraculous event is conveyed by the highly dramatic effects of physical fear wrought on the shepherds and their animals by the apparition, in a blaze of heavenly light, of the angel and accompanying host.

By around 1640 Rembrandt's taste was changing. Eschewing the spectacular and miraculous, he gradually adopted a less dramatic style, more in harmony with his preference for stories involving the psychological interaction between a small number of protagonists. Despite a large gathering of people, the focal point of the *Death of the Virgin* (cat. no. 104), dated 1639, centres on the intimate and moving scene around the bedside, as the Virgin is comforted during her dying moments. But around the same time the artist had probably begun work on the *Hundred Guilder Print* (cat. no. 111) in which, exceptionally, he illustrates several different incidents from Christ's ministry, combining the various participants into a coherent group around the central figure of Christ. The image's variation in style and technique, the legacy of a lengthy period of creation, is brilliantly unified by the play of light and shadow, ranging from the highlight picking out the Pharisees on the left, to the penumbra from which the sick and infirm emerge on the right. The statuesque figure of Christ, the catalyst of the subject, is linked in masterly fashion to those around him, both by his placing and by the patina of shadow playing over his figure. Each incident – the rich young man, the mother and child, and the sick woman, whose faith inspires her belief in Christ's power to heal her – can be read individually; but, eventually, everything leads back to the all-powerful and controlling figure of Christ himself.

Within a few years the iconographical virtuosity of the *Hundred Guilder Print* was exchanged for greater simplicity both in subject and in composition, as can be seen in the *Entombment* (cat. nos 117A, 117B) and *Christ Appearing to the Apostles* (cat. no. 119). Both works convey an aura of inner concentration and spirituality. Rembrandt's sensitive depiction of human emotion is shrewdly varied to portray the underlying thoughts

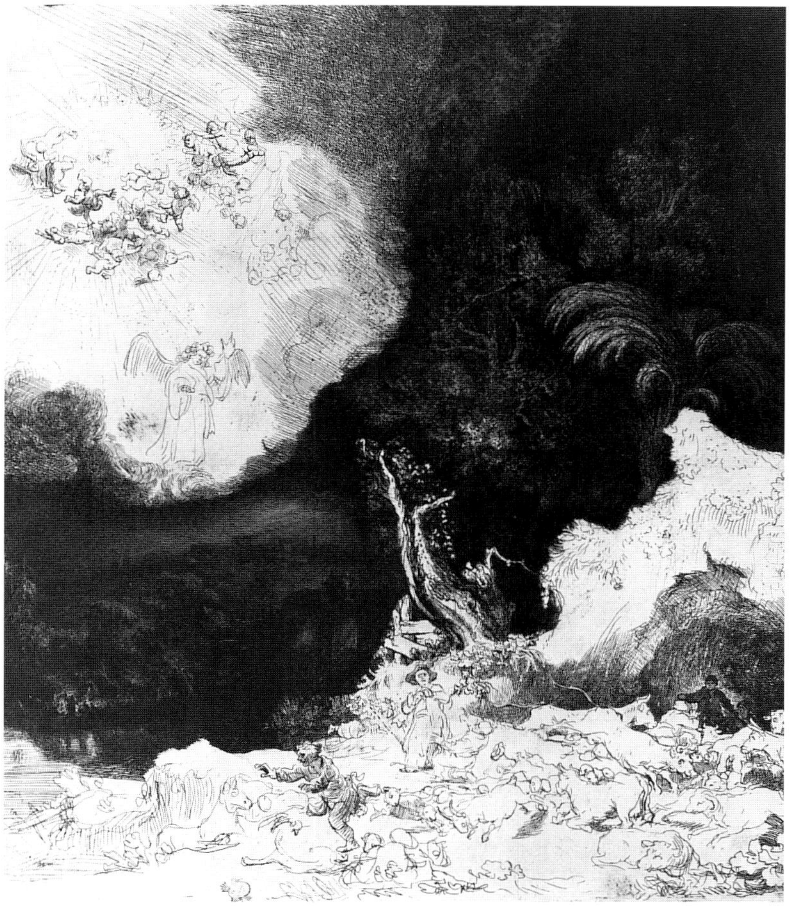

FIG. 1
Rembrandt
The Angel Appearing to the Shepherds 1634
Etching, burin and drypoint (first state)
26.2 x 21.8 cm
Copyright © The British Museum, London

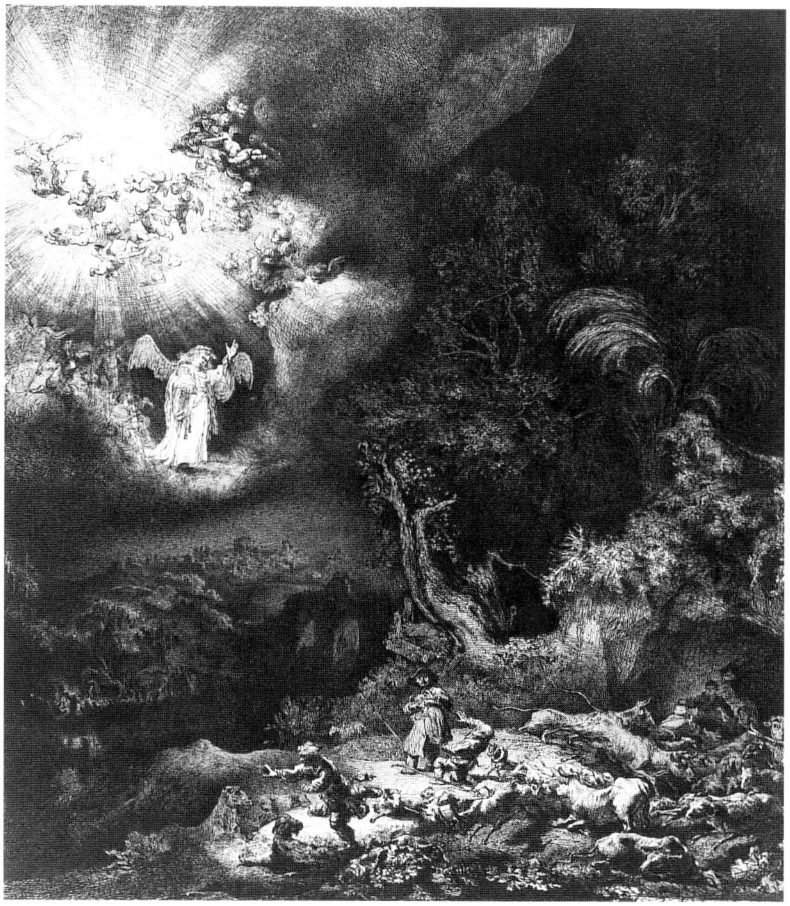

FIG. 2
Rembrandt
The Angel Appearing to the Shepherds
Signed and dated 1634
Etching, burin and drypoint (third state)
26.2 x 21.8 cm
Copyright © The British Museum, London

of each participant. And in delineating the facial features he uses a greater economy of line. Previously he had worked in strong contrasts, but now, gaining in intensity as a result, he tends to confine himself to a more restricted range of light. With subtle modulations, this usually emanates from the principal subject. The representation of light, whether nocturnal and mysterious as in the *Entombment*, or miraculous and radiant as in *Christ Appearing to the Apostles*, imparts individuality and originality to each subject depicted.

In the design of his compositions of the 1650s Rembrandt favoured simpler patterns, balancing horizontal accents against vertical. His figures acquired a greater scale and monumentality within their setting. The background, whether architectural or landscape, is brought forward in direct relationship with the figures, playing an essential role in establishing the overall design. This is nowhere more overpoweringly evident than in *Christ Presented to the People* (cat. no. 118), located in an imposing architectural setting that appears to be an inner courtyard.[10] The various levels allow the introduction, without crowding, of a variety of participants and human reactions. Above all the simple starkness of the architecture, with its sense of claustrophobia, movingly conveys Christ's spiritual isolation.

The *Three Crosses* (cat. nos 115A, 115B), in its two fundamentally different stages, representing two different works of art illustrating different moments in the same story,[11] must be regarded as the climax of Rembrandt's career as a printmaker. His extraordinary technical virtuosity in handling the drypoint (see below) – whether in delineating the figures in simple, block-like forms, recalling reed pen drawings of these years, or in building up areas of richly dark shadow, paralleled in the tonality of his late paintings – matches the tragic intensity of the interpretation of the subject. The strongly defined but limited space of the first stage, which allows a range of different figures to be included, gives way in the final state to a virtually two-dimensional pattern, in which the figure of Christ on the Cross is revealed in the prevailing gloom. It has the characteristics of a personal vision.

Turning to portraiture, from the outset of his career Rembrandt understood that the precise depiction of the human face would provide the foundation for representing humanity in one role or another. The conveying of thoughts and emotions was among the artist's primary means in realizing the essence of his subject, whether his work illustrated a story or portrayed a person or everyday situation. As a result many of Rembrandt's first paintings, drawings and etchings were confined to a study of the human head, for which the artist frequently used himself as a convenient model. In etching, these studies tended to be very small in scale. However, once established in Amsterdam as a successful portraitist, Rembrandt worked on a larger scale, producing several etched portraits as well as such indeterminate works as the so-called *Great Jewish Bride* (B.340) (cat. no. 101). He began with a beautiful rendering of the plump female face set off by the long tresses of hair (fig. 3), and then by stages built up the final portrayal with its balance of differently bitten areas of the plate.

Rembrandt continued to portray himself, and in his *Self-Portrait Leaning on a Stone Sill* (cat. no. 103) he achieves a profound understanding of expression by a very precise recording of his features. The pose, contrasting full face with body in profile, with its debt to both Raphael and Titian, aids the presentation of a sternly questioning appearance. This reflects Rembrandt's preoccupation with revealing the 'commotions of the mind'. His ability to suggest a reading of the sitter's thoughts is even more powerfully suggested in his portrait of *Ephraim Bonus, Jewish Physician* (cat. no. 109), of eight years later. Light and shadow flicker over the surface of the face in small areas of varying intensity, rendered by a beautifully controlled web of cross-hatching. The subtlest gradations are applied to the area around the eyes, which convey a mood of introspection and withdrawal. This psychological interpretation is made all the more evident when the portrait is compared with that made by Jan Lievens of the same sitter (fig. 109b).

Portraiture, whether in paint or etching, remained a staple activity throughout Rembrandt's life, and some of his finest prints during the 1650s fall within this category. The engraved or etched portrait was much in demand and Rembrandt received a number of commissions. Whereas in his painted portraits he tended to concentrate on the sitter, with the minimum of background detail, in his etchings Rembrandt often depicts not only the sitters but their setting, so that we read something of their occupation as well as their character. One of the most outstanding of his late portraits is that of *Arnold Tholinx, Inspector* (cat. no. 120), a member of the medical profession, which had provided the artist with such faithful patronage. Seated before a table with open books, medicinal bottles behind him, the subject looks up from his reading. His searching gaze, directed at the spectator, is enhanced by the beautiful play of reflected light falling on the upper part of the face beneath the wide brim of his hat. The portrait successfully combines a sense of timelessness with a relaxed, natural pose.

Unlike the *graveurs* of many other contemporary engraved or etched portraits who made little attempt to vary the pose from one sitter to another, Rembrandt invariably placed his sitters in different positions, varying both the lighting and the viewpoint. Each sitter, we are made to feel, was allowed to adopt a pose that would reveal his or her personality. In his late portraits Rembrandt reached a perfect blend between the psychological interpretation of the sitters and the ambience in which they existed.

Rembrandt's interest in the natural world extended beyond that surrounding his sitters. In his early years, when he was building up a repertoire of human forms and behaviour, he frequently drew or etched scenes taken from everyday life. What in his earlier years were essentially sketches became much less frequent later on, when a genre subject was more likely to be developed into a finished composition, such as the so-called *Beggars Receiving Alms at the Door of a House* (cat. no. 110). Some of the occupations and activities he recorded formed part of an accepted artistic tradition, and it has rightly been observed recently that the old man holds a hurdy-gurdy, and that therefore this print should be seen within the tradition of representations of the hurdy-gurdy player, an itinerant musician, albeit characteristically reinterpreted by Rembrandt.[12]

A more unusual study of a *Shell* (cat. no. 112) shows one of Rembrandt's rare incursions into the subject of still life and represents his only etching of such a subject. Possibly inspired by the etchings of shells made by Wenceslaus Hollar a few years earlier, it may well have been studied from a specimen in Rembrandt's own shell collection, recorded in the inventory of his possessions made in 1656.

The study of the nude was a fundamental part of an artist's training. Although following this tradition, Rembrandt was unusual inasmuch as after an initial study of the nude in etching and drawing he returned to the theme in the same media at two later periods of his career. Moreover, while other artists tended to regard such work as an academic exercise, Rembrandt, at least in etching, almost invariably worked up his study into a composition, whether he introduced a specific subject or not. (The theme of *Jupiter and Antiope*, which he illustrated in etching at both the beginning and the end of his etching career (cat. no. 122), was essentially a representation of the nude.)

His first etched representations of the female nude, notably the *Naked Woman Seated on a Mound* (cat. no. 99), have, since the classicizing art criticism of the later seventeenth century, been regarded as provocatively unconventional due to the unadorned realism of the models.[13] In his return to the theme of the nude in the mid-1640s, Rembrandt, at least in etching, confined himself to studies of young male models (cat. no. 108), possibly with some illustrated manual in mind.

The most original and most extensive of his nude studies were produced at the very end of his etching career. As well as a number of drawings, he made six fully worked-up prints, which represent an entirely personal exploration of female form suffused by light and shadow, far removed from conventional academic studies. Only one, as already mentioned, was devoted to a specific subject. The others showed the female model in various poses within some form of setting of a richly tonal pattern. Of the group, the *Woman Sitting Half-Dressed beside a Stove* (cat. no. 121), with its large stove and flue dominating the right of the composition, has the most specific setting, suggestive of the artist's studio.

Like Rembrandt's study of the nude, although in a different pattern, his preoccupation with Dutch landscape did not extend over the whole of his career. Several drawings and paintings were executed in the 1630s, but it was only from around 1640 that Rembrandt turned his attention, in both etching and drawing, to an exploration of the scenery in and around Amsterdam. Although he incorporated recognizable details of the landscape, his intention, unlike that of many of his contemporaries, was not topographical. Actual views and motifs were modified to suit his own artistic purpose.

His first intensive study of landscape dates from the time when his art was changing from the extrovert baroque style of the 1630s to a calmer, more classical style that evolved during the 1640s. The problem of simplifying the multiplicity of the forms of the landscape must have seemed relevant to his more general artistic purpose. In the first group of etchings, produced between 1640 and 1645, Rembrandt was attracted by several different types of subject. A favoured theme, seen in the large oblong plate of the *Landscape with a Cottage and Haybarn* of 1641 (cat. no. 105), is the ubiquitous farmhouse surrounded by trees. In this etching the composition is extended on either side of the principal motif by extensive but unrelated views. These views, which are recollections of the city of Amsterdam on the left, and of a house on the river Amstel on the right, demonstrate the artist's use of his studies from nature. The motif of the farm building was already an accepted subject found in the work of earlier Dutch printmakers, such as Jacques de Gheyn II; but, as in his treatment of traditional genre themes, Rembrandt reinterprets it in his own manner. In the *Omval* (cat. no. 107), of 1645, the foreground subject – the boscage on the left – and in the distance the view of a site on the river Amstel, are brought into closer, more immediate relationship. At the same time the delineation of the details of the river scenery has become freer and more open.

There is remarkably little repetition in Rembrandt's landscape subjects. The *Three Trees* (cat. no. 106), of 1643, ranks as his most pictorial landscape carried out in etching. It is unusual, both in its technique (see below) and in the grandeur of its conception of nature. The combination of a wide open view looking towards Amsterdam in the distance and a close-up study of trees on the bank on the right is unified by the vivid depiction of the elements, unique in Rembrandt's etched oeuvre. Instead of the usual peaceful scene, rain clouds contending with the sun's rays produce an effect of impending storm. It is essentially a landscape of mood, recalling the painting of the *Landscape with a Stone Bridge* (cat. no. 11), executed a few years earlier.

When in 1650, after a brief respite, Rembrandt returned to making landscape prints, he essentially studied the same range of subjects, but conceived them in a more measured and monumental style, in which the effects of light playing over the landscape increasingly became a dominant factor. The *Goldweigher's Field* (cat. no. 113), of 1651, based on an actual view of the dunes outside Haarlem, offers the most subtle and complex representation of spatial recession – starting in the foreground and leading without break into the distance – in which the accents of the drypoint burr (see below) played a crucial role. Drypoint employed on its own gives the *Clump of Trees with a Vista* (cat. no. 114), of 1652, a sense of spontaneity and scale, as the artist combines a dominant foreground motif of a barn largely hidden in a wood with a very summary distant view of fields.

But after two years of renewed study of the landscape around him Rembrandt must have concluded that he had gone as far as either he could or he wanted to go. His interest was now attracted to the landscape forms of the Venetian High Renaissance, which he absorbed by making copies or reworkings of drawings by Titian and Domenico Campagnola. In his last depiction of St Jerome, *St Jerome Reading in an Italian Landscape* (cat. no. 116), of about 1654, Rembrandt, unlike in his earlier representations, came to treat the saint more as a 'figure in a landscape' than as an isolated image of a holy man. And for the hilly landscape surmounted by a farmhouse, the serenity of which mirrors the calmness of the saint's thoughts, he unquestionably turned to the example of Venetian landscape.[14]

Technique

Whether painting, drawing or etching, Rembrandt developed a superb mastery of each, which increasingly allowed him to express his subjects with the most appropriate technical means. Moreover, although a general unity of style is apparent in his painting, drawing or etching at any one moment, Rembrandt, with his instinctive feeling for the different qualities of each medium, sometimes gives one a certain emphasis not found in the other two. Occasionally he also reserves one subject or one pictorial form of representation to one medium, rather than exploring it in all three. There is a continuously shifting relationship between his painting, drawing and etching that extends his powers of expression in a manner found in few other great artists.

Of the three intaglio processes – engraving, drypoint and etching – the last is the most incalculable, although the most suitable and attractive to the painter, as Rembrandt proved. Although etching, with its prepared surface or ground, allowed greater freedom and ease (the artist held the etching needle like a pen, drawing only into the ground rather than into the plate itself, as in engraving), the subsequent immersion of the plate in acid to bite the exposed lines required a different kind of experience. The calculation, involving both the strength and the nature of different acids and the length of immersion, was crucial to the final result. As even Rembrandt found, after one or two notable failures in the earlier part of his career, there remained an element of chance that, experience notwithstanding, could produce some unexpected and unwanted results.

In his earlier work, after one or two experiments in prints that emulate the qualities of a drawing, Rembrandt decided that his etching style, seen in such early prints as the *Raising of Lazarus* (cat. no. 100), should emulate the finish of a monochrome painting. A fine mesh of hatching of different densities was required to build up the contrasts of light and shadow that Rembrandt, clearly influenced by the Dutch

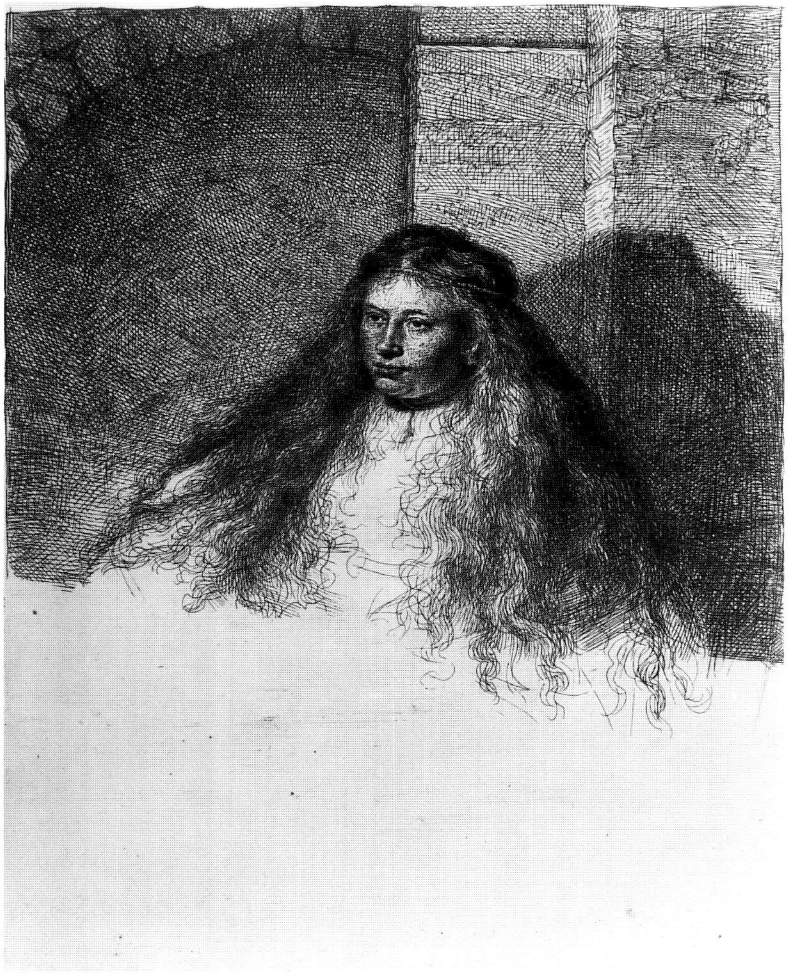

FIG. 3
Rembrandt
The Great Jewish Bride 1635
Etching with some drypoint and burin (first state)
21.9 x 16.8 cm
Copyright © The British Museum, London

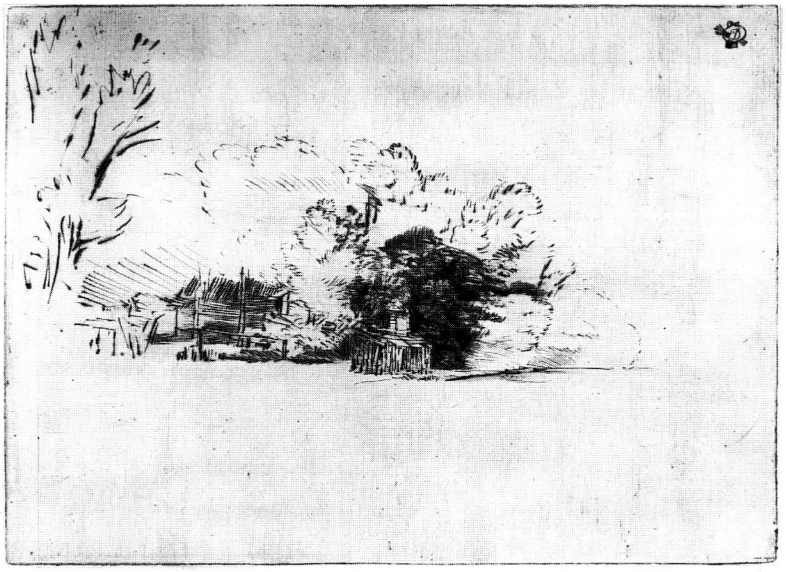

FIG. 4
Rembrandt
Clump of Trees with a Vista 1652
Drypoint (first state)
15.6 x 21.1 cm
Copyright © The British Museum, London

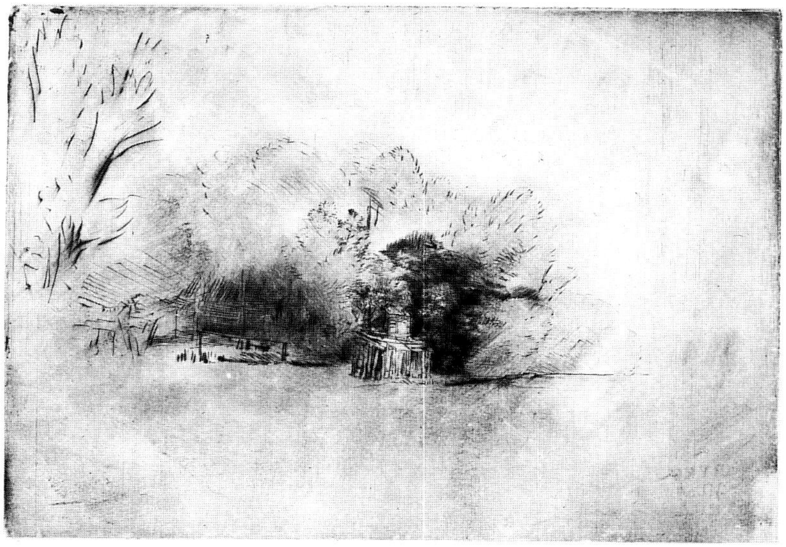

FIG. 5
Rembrandt
Clump of Trees with a Vista 1652
Drypoint, printed with surface tone (first state)
15.6 x 21.1 cm
Rijksprentenkabinet, Rijksmuseum, Amsterdam

followers of Caravaggio, favoured at this time. Both considerable skill and time were required to create the varied degrees of dark by submitting the plate to more than one immersion in the acid. To achieve the desired variety of tone, the artist had to undertake the laborious process of 'stopping-out' the areas that needed no further biting, before putting the plate back into the acid. Initially Rembrandt was not always successful in biting his plates and there are several plates that, for one reason or another, were abandoned before completion.

As a means of understanding how Rembrandt worked, we are fortunate that, throughout his career, he was in the habit of taking an impression from his plate as work proceeded, so that it becomes possible to watch him developing, refining and sometimes substantially changing his initial work on the plate. (Each stage in the process is known as a state.) In his own time Rembrandt was unique in revealing so much of the creative process. More often than not, the different states record work in progress, allowing him to take stock. In his earlier prints this practice can be seen, for example, in the *Angel Appearing to the Shepherds*, one of the darkest and most heavily etched plates in his oeuvre. In the first state (fig. 1) he worked up the intensely dark background landscape first, leaving the completion of the lighter areas in the sky and foreground until a later stage (fig. 2). (His procedure of working from dark background to lighter foreground, seen here, parallels his usual method of painting.) But in some instances what may have been intended as the finished work was, on inspection, subsequently changed by submitting the plate to one or more reworkings.

Rembrandt must have concluded that he was striving to realize more pictorial qualities than the medium of etching could easily provide, and during the second half of the 1630s he gave up seeking the high finish of such large prints as the *Raising of Lazarus* and the *Angel Appearing to the Shepherds*, which required more than one biting, in favour of smaller, less heavily worked plates, such as the *Return of the Prodigal Son* (cat. no. 102A), which could be realized in a single stage. A few years after he made this print Rembrandt began a fundamental change to his technique. Over a basic 'lay-in' of the composition in etching he then worked in drypoint, a process that was to play an increasingly important role in his work over the next two decades. (He had already used it occasionally for minor

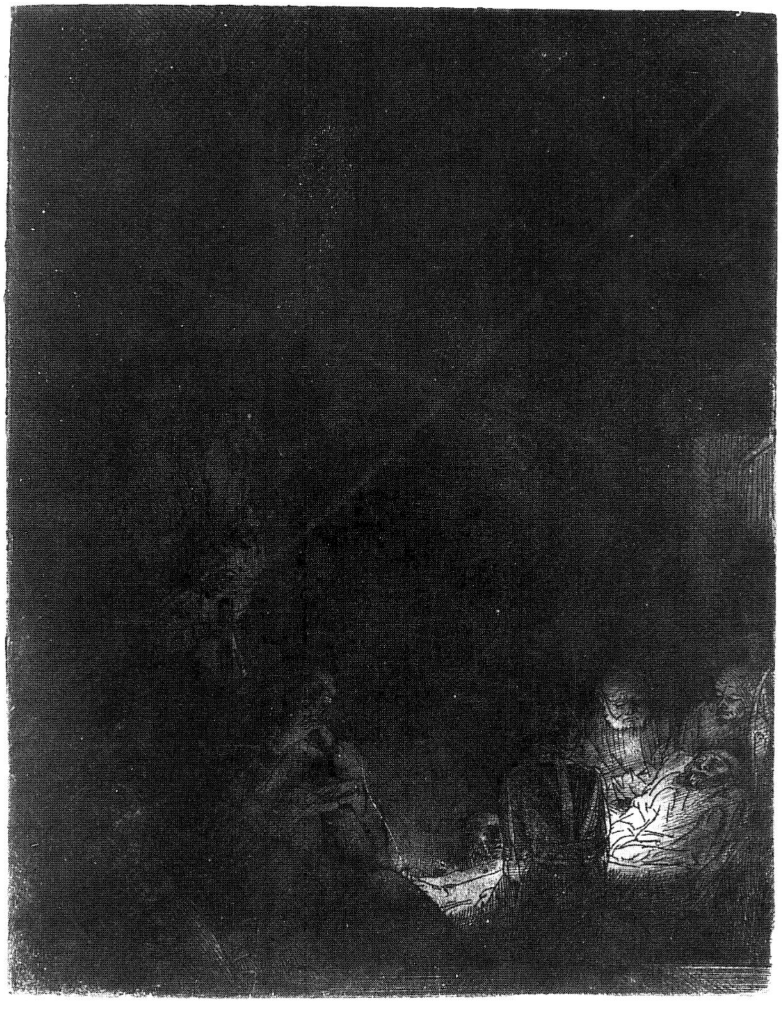

FIG. 6
Rembrandt
*The Entombment c.*1654
Etching, drypoint and burin (fourth state)
21.1 x 16.1 cm
Copyright © The British Museum, London

FIG. 7
Rembrandt
*The Entombment c.*1654
Etching, drypoint and burin, printed with surface tone on Japanese paper (second state)
21.1 x 16.1 cm
Copyright © The British Museum, London

retouching.) Drypoint – in which, as in engraving, the artist drew directly into the copper without the necessity of biting the plate – gave the artist greater freedom and more immediate control over his plate. (The drypoint needle was controlled like a pen, unlike in engraving, which required the burin to be held in the palm of the hand.) Drypoint also provided an increased range of tone deriving from the furrows of copper, known as burr, thrown up on either side of the line by the needle, which printed a rich velvety black, and which sometimes, in order to balance the tonal accents, had to be reduced by the artist. (Its major disadvantage was the faster wear of both the incised lines and the burr.) The combination of etching and drypoint can be seen very clearly in the *Death of the Virgin* (cat. no. 104) of 1639. The composition was predominantly etched, but in a much freer, more open style than Rembrandt had used for earlier large plates. One important compositional detail, the chair on the right-hand side, did not have sufficient darkness to establish its position in the foreground, and it was therefore much strengthened in drypoint.

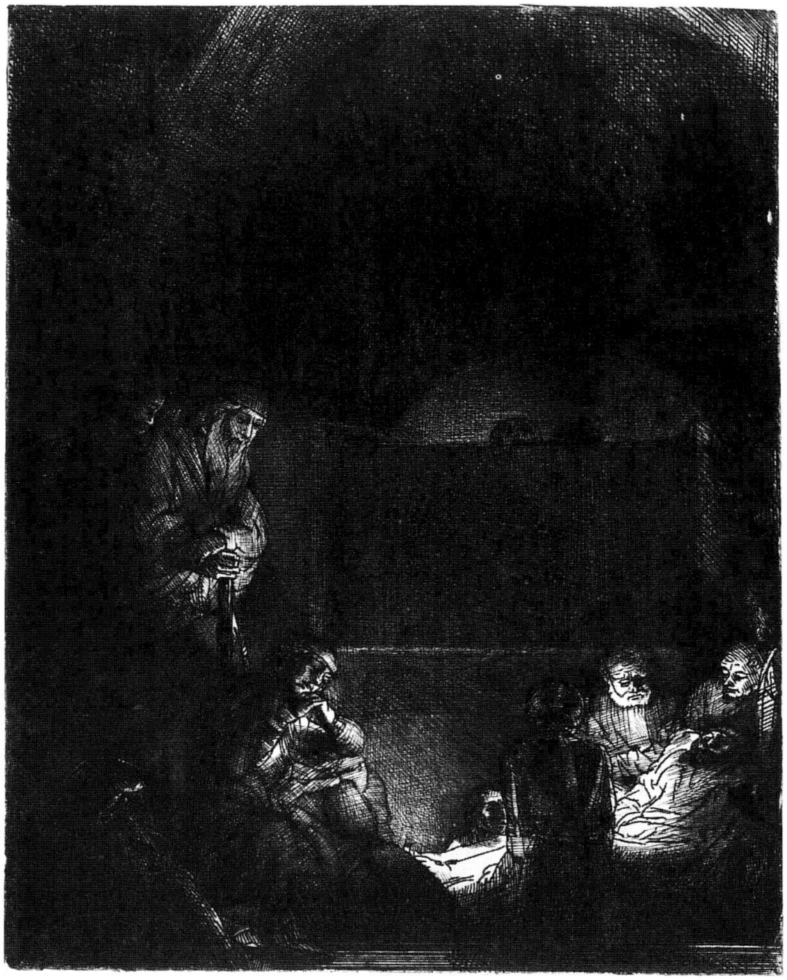

FIG. 8
Rembrandt
*The Entombment c.*1654
Etching, drypoint and burin, printed with surface tone (third state)
21.1 x 16.1 cm
Copyright © The British Museum, London
(our cat. no. 117B)

In the matter of technique what became the most challenging work is also Rembrandt's most famous print, the *Hundred Guilder Print* (cat. no. 111). It is generally concluded that the wide range of both technical and stylistic features indicate that he must have worked on the plate for much of the 1640s. In the end the artist managed to realize a print of great subtlety and complexity, by adding darker and lighter accents over a basic grey tone achieved by very fine hatching. (The plate is a well-integrated combination of etching, drypoint and engraving.) With three basic tones, Rembrandt was able to produce a far greater range than before, enabling him to depict the varied incidents and emotions illustrated within one very ambitious composition. The final result matches the richness and depth of tone that is characteristic of the mezzotint, a technique discovered in 1642 but not used by Rembrandt. (The chiaroscuro of his prints was particularly praised by such seventeenth-century writers as Baldinucci – 'a deep chiaroscuro of great vigour'[15] – and by Roger de Piles.)

The *Hundred Guilder Print* is unquestionably a watershed in the artist's career. Eventual triumph gave him a freedom to operate in the future without the struggle that can be detected from a close examination of that plate. Such works as the *St Jerome Reading in an Italian Landscape* (cat. no. 116) and the *Arnold Tholinx, Inspector* (cat. no. 120), both executed in the mid-1650s, exemplify the procedure he was to use regularly during the last decade of his printmaking. After establishing the composition in openly etched lines, probably obtained by a single biting of the plate, the artist employed the drypoint needle, and also – in the case of the portrait – the burin, to enrich and where necessary modify his subject.

Rembrandt increasingly sought variety in his prints. To what extent a plate was worked up depended on the subject in hand, as the contrast between the lightly etched *Christ Appearing to the Apostles* (cat. no. 119) and the deeply bitten plate of the *Woman Sitting Half-Dressed beside a Stove* (cat. no. 121) makes very evident.[16] Each print posed its own pictorial problem and demanded its own technical solution.

The qualities of drypoint came to appeal so strongly to Rembrandt during the 1650s that in a few plates, such as the *Clump of Trees with a Vista* (cat. no. 114), the *Three Crosses* (cat. nos 115A, 115B) and *Christ Presented to the People* (cat. no. 118), he worked exclusively in that technique. Although only to be fully appreciated in the earliest impressions, before the inevitable wear of the burr, they have a technical virtuosity that gives them a unique position in the history of printmaking, and they represent some of his most outstanding creations.

Rembrandt consistently tried to extend the possibilities of printmaking, experimenting with nearly every technical feature available to him. On two occasions in the mid-1640s he used a 'sulphur tone', which produced a similar effect to that of an aquatint (a medium that was invented in the 1650s), as can be seen in the *Three Trees* (cat. no. 106).[17]

Two other variations on conventional printmaking practice were more frequently used by Rembrandt. By the mid-1640s, when he was enlarging the tonal range of his prints with a generous use of drypoint, he started to print on papers other than the usual handmade white paper used by European printmakers. A handful of impressions are printed on a cheap, rough paper, grey in colour with small flecks in it, known as oatmeal paper. Richer and more exotic was the artist's relatively rare use of vellum, the colour and absorbency of which produced an unusual appearance in heavily worked plates. Far more often Rembrandt would employ a whole range of oriental papers, varying in colour and weight from a thick yellow paper (see cat. no. 111) to a thin ivory-white paper (see cat. no. 117A), which were imported into Holland from the Dutch East Indies. Certain plates in which light and softness of tone were paramount would be printed largely on oriental papers, whereas in other instances Rembrandt would vary the printing, so that there are impressions of the same plate on different papers.

In the second half of his printmaking career, Rembrandt employed another method of increasing the range of tone: instead of clean-wiping the plate so that only the bitten or incised lines printed, he left ink on the surface of the plate, which produced an area of dark tone when printed. This form of selective inking could be varied from impression to impression and, in many examples of this practice, so different was one from another, he was virtually producing monotypes. It can be seen very clearly in two impressions of the first state of the *Clump of Trees with a Vista* (B.222), one of which is clean-wiped (fig. 4), while the other has an area of tone left on the plate. The later darkened state of the *Entombment* (B.86) (cat. no. 117B) has been further darkened by the surface tone left on the plate. Impressions of the later darkened state of the subject, compared with a clean-wiped impression (fig. 6), show how Rembrandt varied such effects from impression to impression (figs 7, 8).

In his use of the various processes Rembrandt was a highly inventive craftsman, developing each one to the limit of its potential. In his later years he became very selective in matching technique and degree of finish to the subject in hand, so that each impression could become an individual work of art.[18] But for all his immense skill, Rembrandt did not employ technique for its own sake. As in drawing and painting, technique provided the means to express the subject in hand.

There is still much we do not know about Rembrandt's practice as an etcher. Little evidence survives to indicate how he distributed his prints. It appears that he largely kept his plates and presumably controlled the printing. In general Rembrandt probably worked consecutively on a plate. But sometimes, as in the case of the *Hundred Guilder Print*, he worked intermittently over a long timespan. In the case of other works, such as the *Three Crosses*, there appears to be a time gap between the early and later stages. Less fundamentally, Rembrandt may well have returned to earlier plates and made small alterations before reprinting. There is no evidence concerning the number of impressions printed, but given the variation in technique this must have varied considerably. An etched plate could offer more good-quality impressions than one worked in drypoint. Moreover, since Rembrandt's plates were often reworked after his death, it is difficult to be certain which stage in their history represents the artist's final work. The recent appearance on the art market of no fewer than seventy-eight of Rembrandt's copperplates (see commentary to cat. no. 102B) has led to an exemplary study that has increased our information and understanding considerably.[19]

Questions still arise as to whether Rembrandt, in working up certain plates, collaborated with an assistant, either by sharing the execution of the plate or by the master providing the assistant with a model in painting or drawing. Recently the role of the Leiden printmaker Johannes van Vliet, as a collaborator of Rembrandt in the latter's early years as a printmaker, has been fruitfully re-examined.[20]

But potentially the most important new research arises from the campaign, now well underway, to identify and date the watermarks on impressions of Rembrandt's etchings. This research will include prints in as many of the public collections throughout the world as possible. As part of this project, the impressions of Rembrandt's etchings in the National Gallery of Victoria have been similarly examined during preparation for the present exhibition. This international research has already yielded much new information and will throw increasing light on the artist's actual practice.[21]

1 For an overview of the subject of Rembrandt's etchings, see, for example, Münz 1952, vol. 1, pp. 1–61; White 1969; Bevers 1991–92.

2 Baldinucci 1686, p. 79.

3 Evelyn 1662, p. 81.

4 In 1972 Ray Lewis of California owned an undescribed trial proof of Castiglione's *Dream of St Joseph* (B.10), which on the verso contained pen and ink copies after two etchings by Rembrandt (B.263, B.287).

5 Guercino to Don Antonio Ruffo in Messina, 13 June 1660 (Ricci 1918, p. 11ff).

6 Marolles 1666, p. 54; Marolles's collection was purchased for Louis XIV and now forms part of the Bibliothèque Nationale, Paris. Mariette was accustomed to write his name and the date of acquisition on the back of the impression; the earliest recorded was in 1652.

7 Bredius 1909, p. 111ff.

8 Hofstede de Groot 1906a, p. 310.

9 For a history of the plates, see Hinterding 1995.

10 For a discussion of the architectural setting, see Carroll 1981, pp. 588–605.

11 This interpretation has been challenged by Carroll (Carroll 1981, p. 608, note 109).

12 Hellerstedt 1981.

13 However, recently it has been claimed that Rembrandt's nudes would have been regarded as being in the same tradition as those of Rubens and Jordaens in Flanders, echoing those of Michelangelo and the Venetian High Renaissance. See, *inter alia*, Reznicek 1977, pp. 91–9; for another view, see pp. 34–6 in the present catalogue.

14 Curiously, the print was described by both Gersaint and Bartsch as being done in the manner of Dürer.

15 Baldinucci / Manni 1767, p. 169.

16 For an interpretation of 'finish', see Dickey 1986.

17 Campbell 1980 first observed that Rembrandt initially used the plate for a discarded 'Death of the Virgin', the remains of which can be seen beneath the clouds at the upper left.

18 It is a tribute to Rembrandt's different states, differently inked impressions and the different papers on which they were printed that such variations were appreciated almost immediately by collectors, who often sought to own more than one impression of each subject. Moreover, they were aware of the rarity and beauty of individual impressions. Roger de Piles writes of 'a number of proofs taken on half-tint paper, especially China paper ... impressions of which are sought by connoisseurs' (Piles 1699, p. 434). For a study of seventeenth-century print collecting, see Robinson 1981, pp. xxvii–xlviii.

19 Hinterding 1995.

20 Royalton-Kisch 1984; Amsterdam 1996.

21 See, for example, Ash & Fletcher 1990; Laurentius et al. 1992; Hinterding 1996; Laurentius 1996.

99
Naked Woman Seated on a Mound
*c.*1631

According to White & Boon, signed very faintly in the plate upper left *RHL* (not discernible in this impression)
Etching
17.7 x 16.0 cm
Watermark: Countermark NA; variant a; probably belonging to paper with the Strasbourg Bend l.a. watermark
Rijksprentenkabinet, Rijksmuseum, Amsterdam

LITERATURE: White & Boon B.198 I (first of two states); Hind 42; Münz 258; Biörklund BB.31-4. See also White 1969, vol. 1, pp. 172–3; B. Welzel, in Berlin / Amsterdam / London 1991–92b, pp. 182–4, [etching] cat. no. 6.

Rembrandt's earliest etchings are chiefly scenes from the New Testament, portraits (including those of himself), and depictions of beggars. The nude does not appear until the early 1630s, some four years after he began to etch. However, when it does appear, it is used not only in a narrative context, but as a fully fledged, independent genre. Drawing from the nude was an essential part of academic training and Rembrandt worked on it throughout his career, initially as a student and later as a master drawing alongside his own students (cat. nos 96, 98).

Naked Woman Seated on a Mound dates from about 1631, from around the time when Rembrandt moved from Leiden to Amsterdam, and it belongs to the earliest of three groups of nudes in his etched oeuvre, the others dating from the mid-1640s (cat. no. 108), and the late 1650s (cat. nos 121, 122). The other two nudes from 1631 portray classical subjects, but this etching contains no attributes that might associate it with a literary source. A woman sits with her legs facing right, her torso twisted to the front, her left arm propped on a ledge behind her. The lightly sketched foliage and the rocky ground on which she is seated indicate an outdoor setting, but they are too schematically rendered to be convincing from the point of view of naturalism. Instead, they serve to heighten the realism of the figure and, simultaneously, to enhance the sense that this is a model lifted from the context of the studio into an imagined one on the page. The light that falls from the right sharply illuminates the texture and bulk of her corpulent body.

This etching has a counterpart in another that Rembrandt made at the same time, *Diana at the Bath* (B.201) (fig. 99a), whose dimensions are identical and whose pose is similar, but reversed. There, the woodland setting, the water and the quiver all serve to identify the figure as the goddess Diana, yet her body is portrayed with few concessions to her divine status, but with a realism approaching her earthly sister's. Diana's head was copied in an etching by Rembrandt's friend, the painter Jan Lievens (Hollstein 91), but it was the *Naked Woman Seated on a Mound* that made the greater impact. The second state was copied in reverse in an etching (Parthey / Pennington 603), dated 1635, by the Bohemian artist Wenceslaus Hollar (1607–1677) (p. 36, fig. 6). This explicit admiration of Rembrandt's contemporaries contrasts with later assessments of his portrayals of the nude. In 1681, with the ascendancy of classicizing taste, Rembrandt's countryman, the critic Andries Pels, rudely commented:

> He chose no Greek Venus as his model
> But rather a washerwoman or a treader of peat from the barn
> And called this whim 'imitation of nature'
> Everything else was idle ornament. Flabby breasts
> Ill-shaped hands, nay, the traces of the lacings
> of the corsets on the stomach, of the garters on the legs
> Must be visible if nature was to get her due.
> This is *his* nature which would stand no rules.
> No principle of proportion in the human body.[1]

This impression is the rare first state of the etching, before the addition of shading to parts of the woman's body and the background, and, at the same time, the burnishing out of some of the darker shadows on her body. The countermark, which has not been conclusively identified, but which probably belongs to a Strasbourg Bend watermark, is similar to that found in other early prints and indicates a very early printing, probably around 1631.[2]

IZ

1 White 1969, p. 172.
2 I am grateful to Erik Hinterding for information on the watermark.

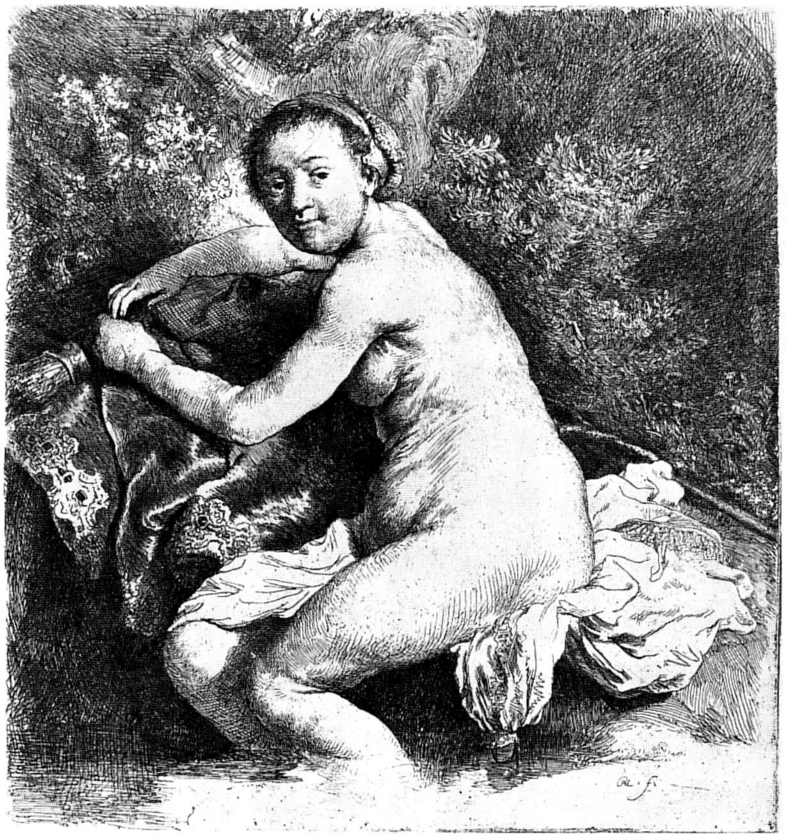

FIG. 99a
Rembrandt
Diana at the Bath *c.*1631
Etching
17.8 x 15.9 cm
Rijksprentenkabinet, Rijksmuseum, Amsterdam

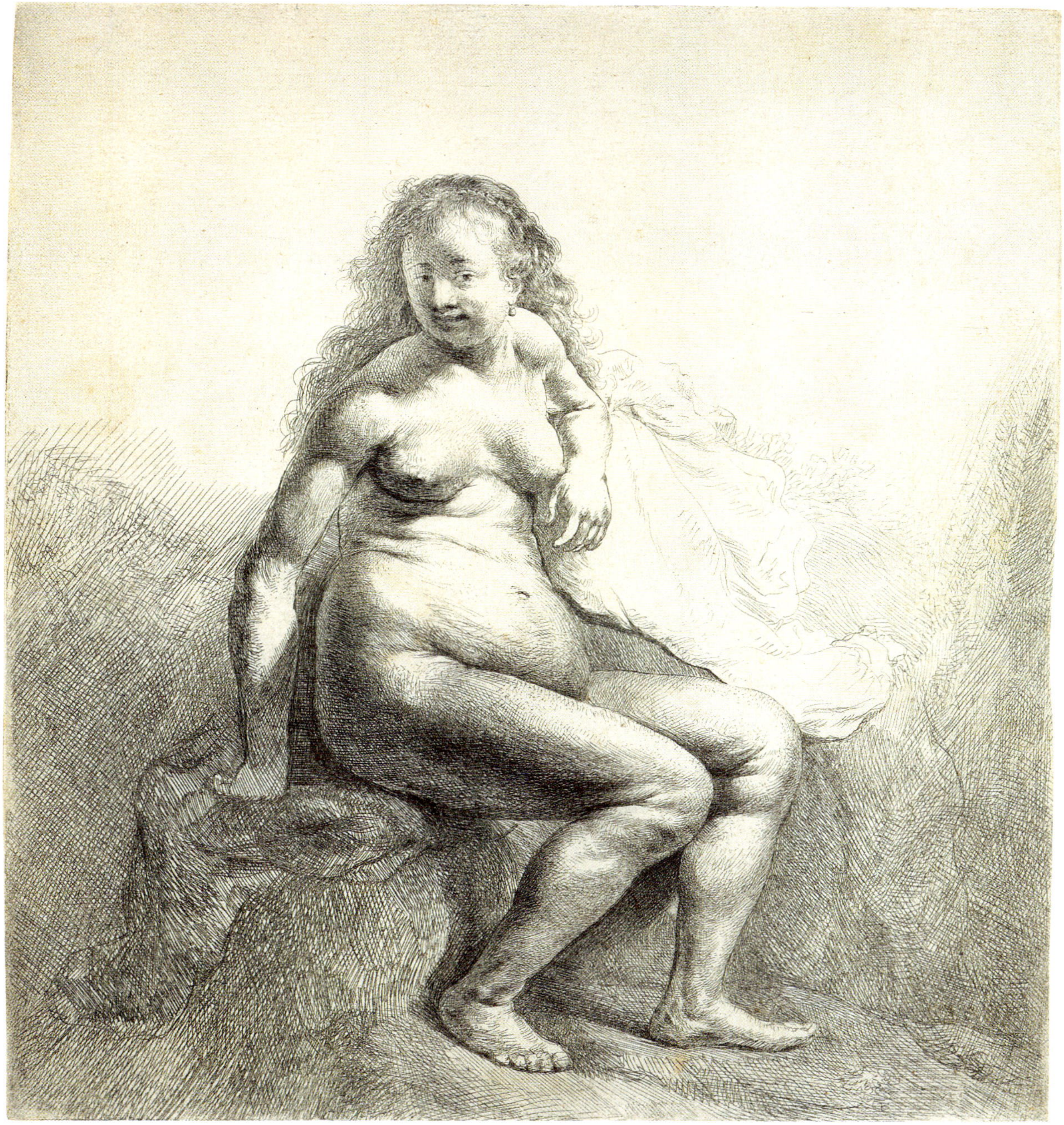

100

The Raising of Lazarus: The Larger Plate
c.1632

Signed in the plate at centre *RHL* (in monogram) *v. Ryn f.*
Etching and burin
36.6 x 25.8 cm (arched)
Watermark: Arms of Berne(?)
Trustees of the British Museum, London

LITERATURE: White & Boon B.73 V (fifth of ten states); Hind 96; Münz 192; Biörklund BB.32-4. See also White 1969, vol. 1, pp. 29–33; B. Welzel, in Berlin / Amsterdam /London 1991–92b, pp. 185–7, [etching] cat. no. 7; Royalton-Kisch 1992, cat. nos 6a, 15; *Corpus*, vol. I, 1982, pp. 293–308, no. A30.

Distinguished by its ambitious size, high finish and baroque drama, the *Raising of Lazarus* marks a major breakthrough in Rembrandt's early etchings. It is his most important religious etching from the early 1630s, and its large dimensions and etched frame declare his intention to imbue his prints with the presence and impact of his history paintings. It is also the immediate precursor of a series of large reproductive etchings that were inspired by the practice of Rubens and his workshop.

The story of Lazarus, the brother of Mary Magdalene and Martha, occurs in John 11:1–44. Christ was called to heal the sick Lazarus but by the time he arrived Lazarus had been dead for four days. Accompanied by a crowd of disciples and other people, Christ asked for the stone of the burial cave to be shifted and, after beseeching his Father, 'he cried out with a loud voice, Lazarus, come forth. And he that was dead came forth, bound in hand and foot with graveclothes and his face was bound about with a napkin' (John 11:43–44). The event as Rembrandt portrays it carries all the emotional drama of that moment: Christ's commanding presence and gesture, the startled multitude, Mary Magdalene behind the tomb, clutching the napkin with arms outstretched in astonishment, and her sister Martha bent forward amazed in the lower right corner. Miraculous light illuminates the scene and also reveals armour and exotic headgear hanging on the walls of the cave – the dead man's belongings.[1] Rembrandt's treatment of light here is informed by the dramatic modelling in light and shade that characterized the manner of the Utrecht Caravaggisti. His later etching of the subject (B.72) is conceived in quite a different manner, and in a mood that is altogether more subdued (fig. 100a).

The genesis of the composition is complex due to the great number of state changes – greater than for any other of Rembrandt's prints – and also because of its complicated relationship to his own painted and drawn versions of the subject, as well as to the versions painted and etched by his closest colleague at that time, Jan Lievens (see commentary to cat. no. 37). Both artists worked on the subject concurrently, apparently in a spirit of friendly rivalry, but the exact sequence in which the works were produced has never been conclusively established. Rembrandt's painting (fig. 37b) underwent many changes during its creation, presumably throughout 1630–31, and the etching, which reflects an early 'state' of the painting (recorded through X-ray photography), may thus have been started earlier than is usually assumed.[2] However, the form of the signature that appears here was used only in 1632, and the arched format – unique in Rembrandt's prints – is shared by the arched compositions used for the series of paintings of the Passion commissioned by Frederik Hendrik, which Rembrandt worked on for several years from around 1631. For details of the design of the etching Rembrandt drew on earlier representations of apostles preaching, and perhaps also on other portrayals of the subject;[3] however, the placement of the figure of Christ and its scale in relation to the composition overall is entirely original and arresting in its impact.

The fifth state represented here involved changing the pose of Martha, from a fearful figure shown backing away into the lower right corner to one who moves forward in Lazarus's direction. This change, which was first tried out in black chalk on a trial proof of the third state of the etching,[4] completes the circle of dramatis personae around the waking man, while also opening the pictorial space so as to admit the viewer as participant in the drama. In the later states, changes were made to two of the figures – the man with outstretched arms behind the tomb was given a hat (sixth state), and the man to his right a turban (seventh state) – and shading was subsequently added to various areas of the plate. Hind thought that Johannes van Vliet's hand may have been responsible for the later states of the print, while Münz considered the *Lazarus* to be the first of Rembrandt's large etchings to have been completed by students. Six engraved copies of it are recorded and the copperplate itself has survived, albeit considerably reworked by later hands; it is in an American private collection. This impression is printed on paper with what looks like the Arms of Berne watermark;[5] that is, a paper imported from Switzerland, as were many of the papers used in Rembrandt's early prints.

IZ

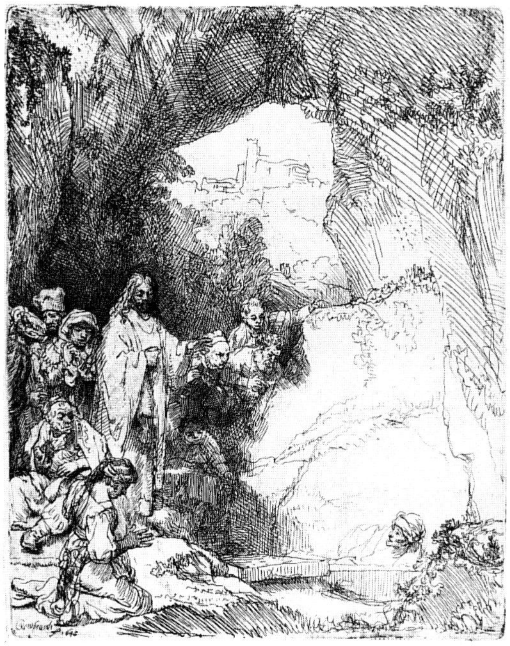

FIG. 100a
Rembrandt
The Raising of Lazarus: Small Plate
Signed and dated 1642
Etching
15.0 x 11.4 cm
National Gallery of Victoria, Melbourne; purchased 1891

1 According to the *Golden Legend*, Lazarus had been a knight or a soldier, and this explains the military equipment; see Tümpel 1993, p. 396, no. 42, who acknowledges the source of this information in H. Guratzsch, 'Die Auferweckung des Lazarus in der niederländischen Kunst von 1400–1700', in *Ars Neerlandica*, vol. 2, Part 1f, Kortrijk, 1980, pp. 215–21.
2 *Corpus*, vol. I, 1982, p. 304, no. A30.
3 *Corpus*, vol. I, 1982, pp. 305–6, no. A30; B. Welzel, in Berlin / Amsterdam / London 1991–92b, p. 186, [etching] cat. no. 7.
4 Royalton-Kisch 1992, pp. 38–9, cat. no. 6a.
5 I am grateful to Martin Royalton-Kisch for supplying this information.

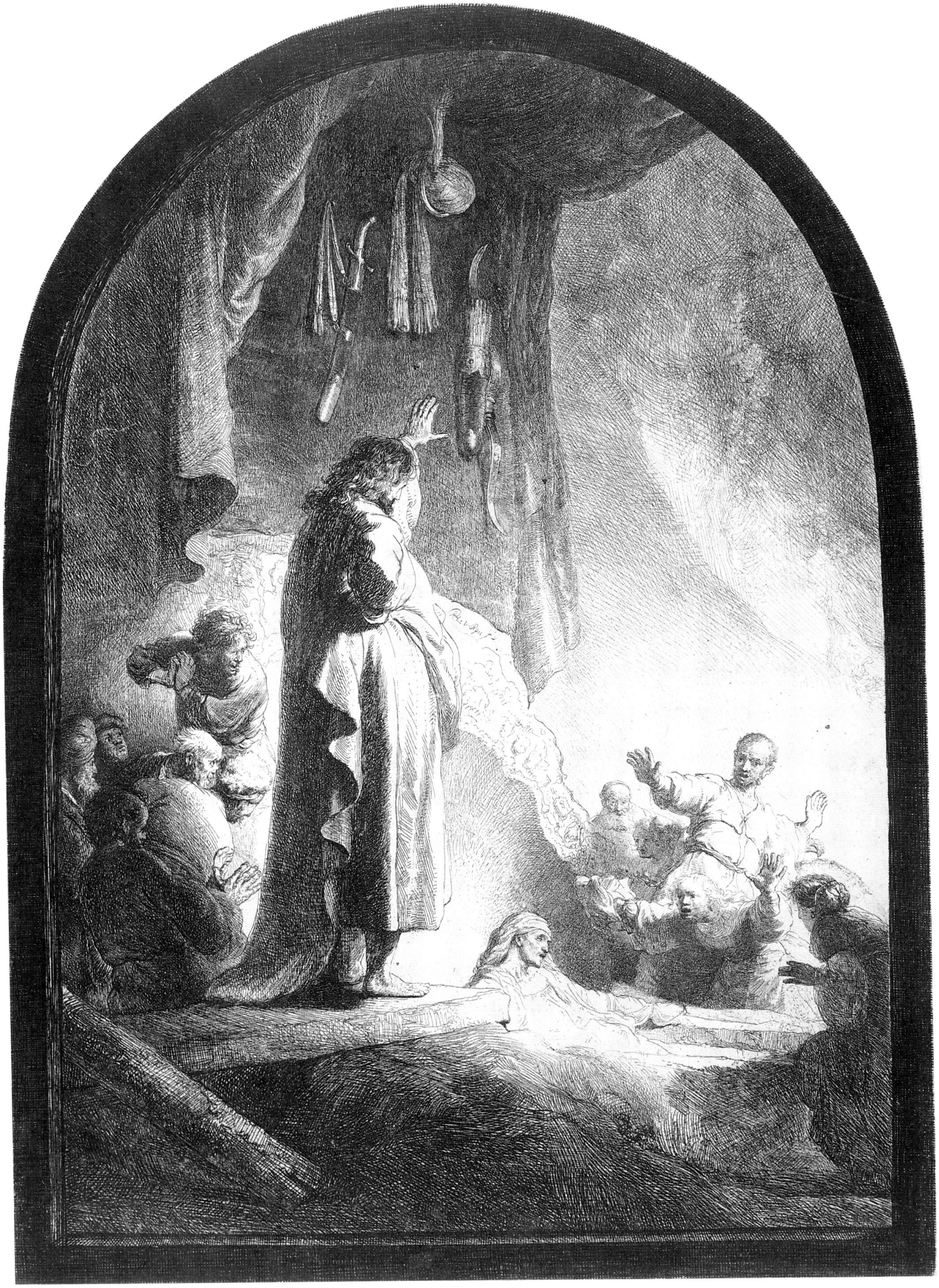

101

The Great Jewish Bride

Signed and dated in the plate lower left *R 1635* (in reverse)
Etching with some drypoint and burin, printed on Western laid paper
21.9 x 16.8 cm
The Visitors of the Ashmolean Museum, Oxford

LITERATURE: White & Boon B.340 V (fifth of five states); Hind 127; Münz 90; Biörklund BB.35-C. See also Benesch 1954–57, vol. II, no. 292; White 1969, vol. 1, pp. 114–16.

The title of this etching is a traditional one, based on an eighteenth-century identification of the subject as the daughter of the Jewish physician Ephraim Bonus (Bueno) (see cat. no. 109). In fact the woman bears a general resemblance to Rembrandt's wife, Saskia van Uylenburgh, to whom he was betrothed in 1633 and whom he married in the following year. From 1633, her physiognomy provided him with a model of a female type that came to dominate his portrayal of women. In painting he depicted her in different guises: as Esther, Flora, Sophonisba or Minerva; in etchings she appears in various forms: dressed in finery (B.347), as St Catherine (B.342) or as the subject of one of his distinctive sketches observed from life and etched into the copperplate (B.367) (fig. 101a).

This portrayal shows the woman in rich costume, seated in an armchair before a table or shelf laden with books. She holds a scroll, and her expression is composed, even steadfast. The architectural background enhances the monumentality of the composition. This etching was preceded by a masterly pen and ink study (Benesch 292) (fig. 101b), showing the figure full-length (but in reverse), with wash applied to indicate the disposition of light and shade. The woman's facial features are generalized, but derive from Saskia's type, and the drawing looks as though it might have been made from the imagination, rather than from life.[1]

No definitive identification of the subject in the etching has been made, though a number of interpretations have been offered: that the woman is a figure from the stage; Minerva; Esther holding the decree on her people; a Jewish bride holding the marriage contract, her hair ritualistically let down; or a sibyl.[2]

The etching is known in five states, the first of them with only the upper half of the print completed. The lower part was added in the third state, after the background had received further shading. The date was added at this stage. Hind considered only the first state to be worthy of Rembrandt, while Münz believed that even there he could detect a pupil's hand. During the first half of the 1630s, Rembrandt was certainly involved in making reproductive etchings after his own designs, and Johannes van Vliet's name has been put forward as a principal collaborator.[3] However, the consensus of opinion now gives the present plate entirely to Rembrandt.

Three etched copies after the print are recorded, including one of considerably smaller dimensions that was previously thought to be by Rembrandt (B.341) but is now attributed to Ferdinand Bol (Hollstein 21).

This fine impression of the final state is printed on European paper; however, since the sheet is stuck down it has not been possible to examine it for watermark evidence.

IZ

1 White 1969, p. 115.
2 For the relevant literature, see White & Boon, B.340; White 1969, p. 114.
3 Royalton-Kisch 1984; Amsterdam 1996.

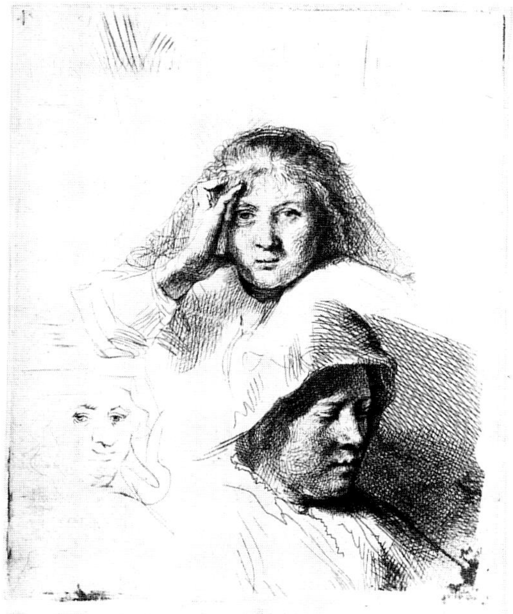

FIG. 101a
Rembrandt
Three Heads of Women, One Lightly Etched
*c.*1637
Etching (third state)
12.6 x 10.1 cm
National Gallery of Victoria, Melbourne; Everard Studley Miller Bequest 1962

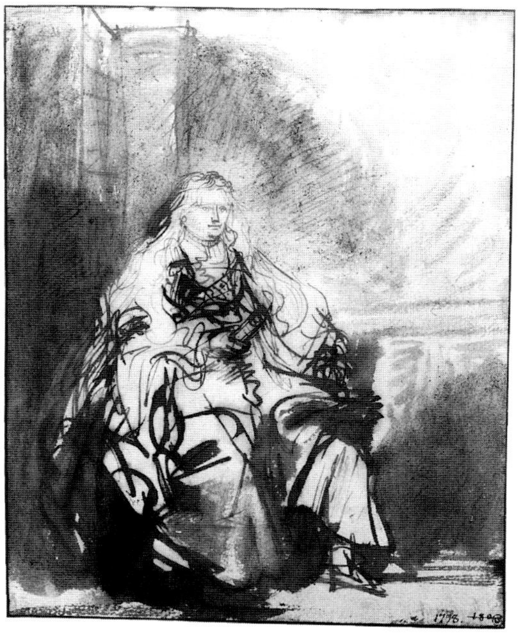

FIG. 101b
Rembrandt
Study for *The Great Jewish Bride*
*c.*1635
Pen and ink and brush
23.2 x 18.2 cm
Nationalmuseum, Stockholm
Photograph: Nationalmuseum, SKM, Stockholm

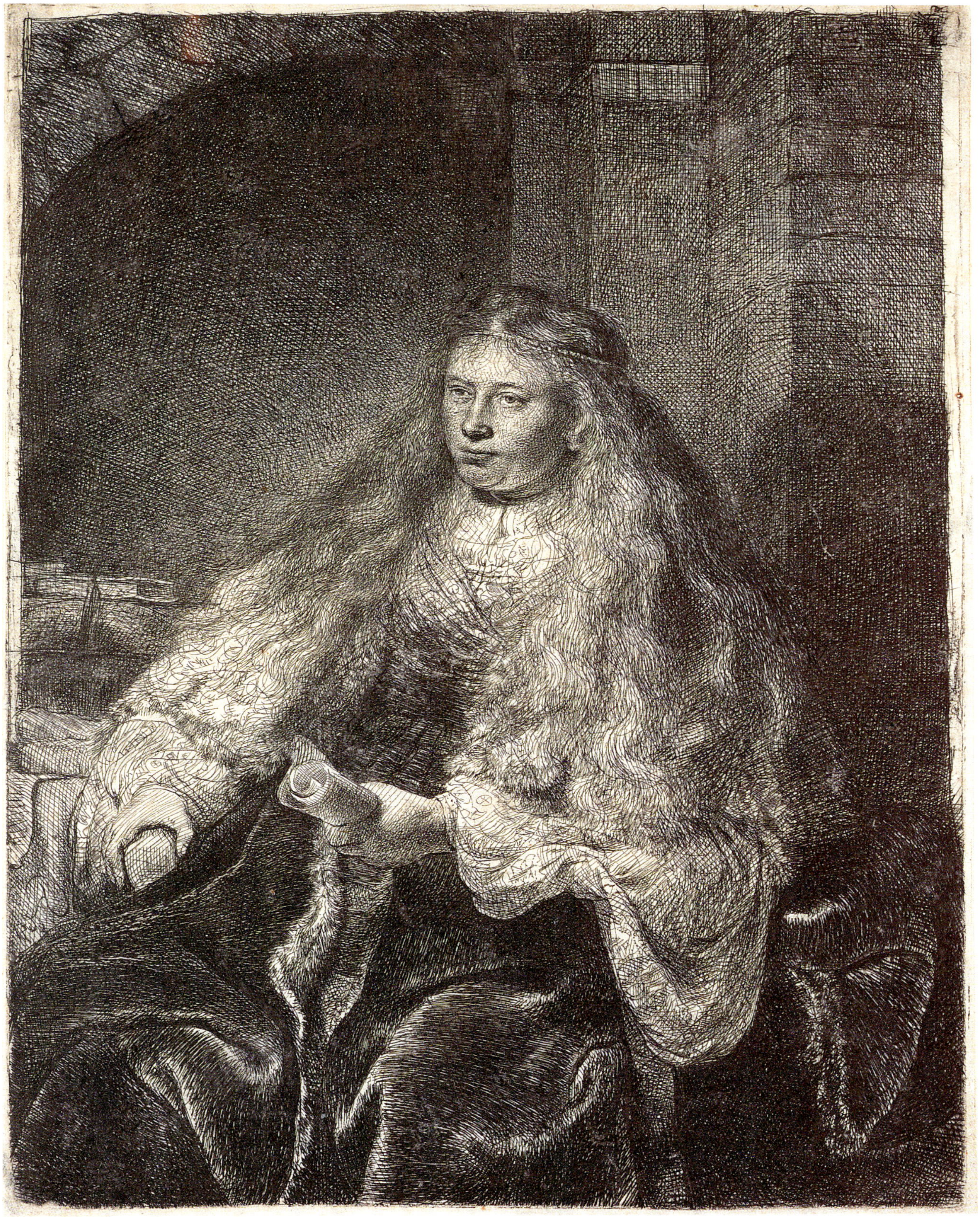

102A
The Return of the Prodigal Son

Signed and dated in the plate lower centre *Rembrandt f 1636*
Etching, printed on Western laid paper
15.6 x 13.6 cm
Museum het Rembrandthuis, Amsterdam

LITERATURE: White & Boon B.91 (only state); Hind 147; Münz 207; Biörklund BB.36-D. See also White 1969, vol. 1, pp. 40–1; Halewood 1982, pp. 52–63; Chapman 1990, pp. 117–18.

102B
Copperplate for The Return of the Prodigal Son

Signed and dated lower centre *Rembrandt f 1636* (in reverse)
Etched copperplate; verso engraved
15.9 x 13.9 x 1.3 cm; weight 242 g
Verso: geometrical figure illustrating the squaring of the circle
Museum het Rembrandthuis, Amsterdam

LITERATURE: Coppier 1917, p. 130; Boone 1980; Filedt Kok 1994; Hinterding 1995, pp. 9, 48.

The story of the Prodigal Son is told in Luke 15:11–32 as a parable of God's unconditional forgiveness to those who repent their sins. The younger of two sons asked his father to advance him his inheritance, which he proceeded to squander in riotous living. Having spent his money, he was reduced to eating with the swine. Filled with remorse, he eventually returned home to seek his father's forgiveness. On seeing him approach from afar, the father rushed out to greet him and ordered a calf to be killed for the celebratory meal. He calmed the resentment of his elder son by saying that it was right to celebrate: 'for this thy brother was dead, and is alive again; and was lost, and is found' (Luke 15:32).

The parable has a rich and varied visual tradition reaching back to the thirteenth century.[1] As a dramatic narrative, it was also given theatrical form, which persisted in seventeenth-century Holland.[2] Dürer's famous engraving (B.28), and the serialized narratives of his followers, popularized the subject in the sixteenth century; but it was the Dutch mannerist artist Maarten van Heemskerck (Hollstein 50) (fig. 102a) who provided Rembrandt with the immediate inspiration for his etching of 1636. There are many points of similarity between the two prints, from the general architectural setting to the basic arrangement of the principal figure group and the killing of the fatted calf in the distance, and extending even to such specific small details as the father's buttoned upper sleeve. However, Rembrandt's version shows the figures in a larger space and portrays a later moment in the story, beyond the extreme remorse reflected in the prodigal's face in Heemskerck's woodcut, to the emotional embrace of reconciliation.

The parable of the Prodigal Son was a perfect illustration of a key article of Protestant theology: that salvation could be attained through faith alone. And it was not only the scene of compassion that artists were drawn to illustrate; many of them found the opportunity of portraying the bawdy aspects of the story irresistible. In the same year that Rembrandt made this etching he also represented this other aspect of the story in a painted double portrait of himself and his wife, Saskia, as the prodigal and his companion in the very midst of high living (Bredius 30) (Gemäldegalerie, Dresden). He returned to the subject in the mid-1660s with the large canvas depicting the prodigal's return (Bredius 598) (Hermitage, St Petersburg), a work that was probably finished with the assistance of his workshop; it is his most internalized and moving depiction of the theme.

This etching is one of only four prints that Rembrandt made in 1636, and the only biblical subject among them. The other three prints include what has long been held to be a portrait of Menasseh ben Israel (B.269), a small self-portrait with Saskia (B.19) (p. 45, fig. 16), and a sheet of etched sketches showing Saskia's face (B.365), all of them etched in a looser, more open and relaxed manner than in earlier works and using a more varied array of strokes. As befits the seriousness of biblical illustration, the 1636 *Return of the Prodigal Son* is more formal and carefully delineated; however, it too shows a move towards a freer approach to the etching medium. Two engraved copies after this print are recorded.

The copperplate is one of eighty-one of Rembrandt's plates that have survived, and the only one that was recycled after earlier use. It is lightly reworked in various areas including the top and front of the lowest step and to its right.[3] The verso, with its engraved geometrical illustration (fig. 102b), was used by Ferdinand van Aertsz in 1598 for an engraving. Engraved copperplates were highly prized in the seventeenth century, since they represented a potential source of revenue from reprinting, so long as demand for the subject continued.[4] In 1637 Rembrandt himself sold one of his copperplates (B.30) and, soon afterwards, its new owner took legal action to prevent him from selling any of the impressions from it that he had retained.[5] The surviving plates are mostly those that passed through the hands of the Amsterdam publisher and dealer Clement de Jonghe (1624/25–1677), and thence through Pieter de Haan to French collectors Claude-Henri Watelet (1718–1786), Basan (1723–1797), Auguste Jean (d. 1820) and Auguste Bernard, a somewhat mysterious figure.[6] They resurfaced in the early twentieth century and were acquired by the Parisian dealer Alvin-Beaumont, who eventually sold them to an American, Robert Lee Humber (d. 1970). As recently as 1993 Humber's estate dispersed the plates by sale through Artemis (London) and B. M. Light (Santa Barbara, California) to institutions and private individuals (see cat. no. 110B for another of the plates).

IZ

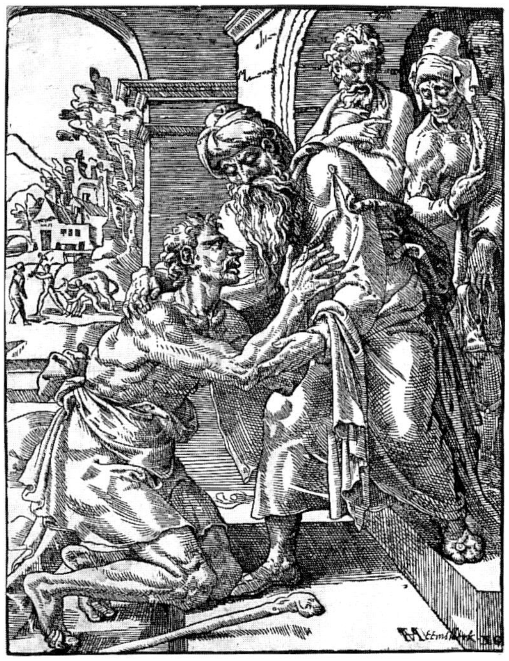

FIG. 102a
Maarten van Heemskerck 1498–1574
The Return of the Prodigal Son
Woodcut, 24.5 x 18.5 cm
Rijksprentenkabinet, Rijksmuseum, Amsterdam

1 For a survey of the theme, including references to earlier literature, see D'Oench 1995–96.

2 A modern-day version of the story, W. D. Hooft's play, *Heden-daeghsche Verlooren Soon*, was first performed in Amsterdam in 1630; see Chapman 1990, p. 117.

3 This description of the reworking is taken directly from Hinterding 1995, p. 91. The account of the provenance that follows is a précis of Hinterding's account of the history of the copperplates. See also Filedt Kok 1994.

4 Hinterding 1995, p. 9.

5 Strauss & Van der Meulen 1979, pp. 145–6, no. 1637/7.

6 Hinterding 1995, p. 33, note 139.

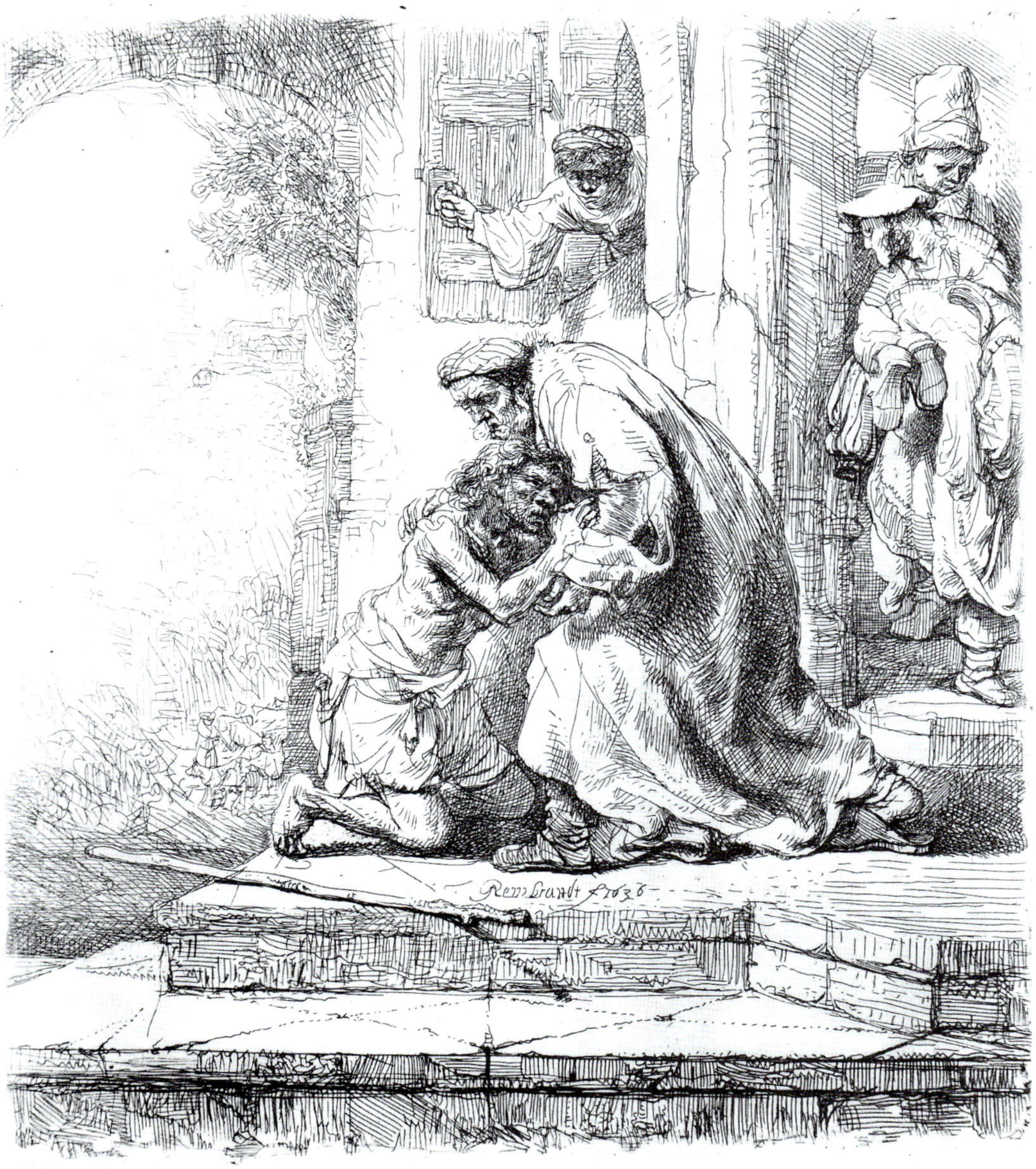

Cat. no. 102A

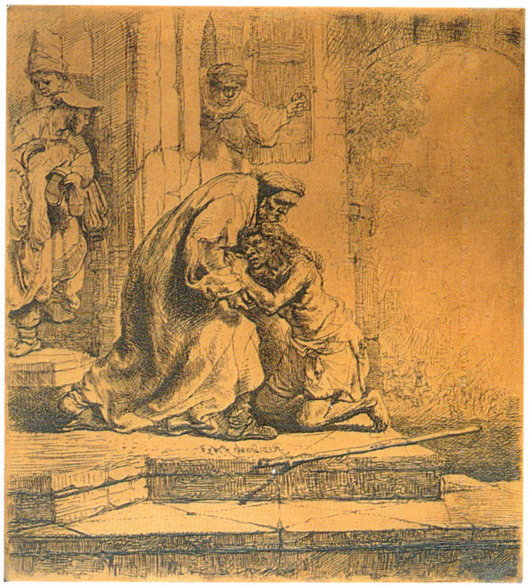

Cat. no. 102B

FIG. 102b
Verso of Rembrandt's copperplate for *The Return of the Prodigal Son* (with a geometrical illustration of the squaring of the circle, engraved by Ferdinand van Aertsz in 1598).

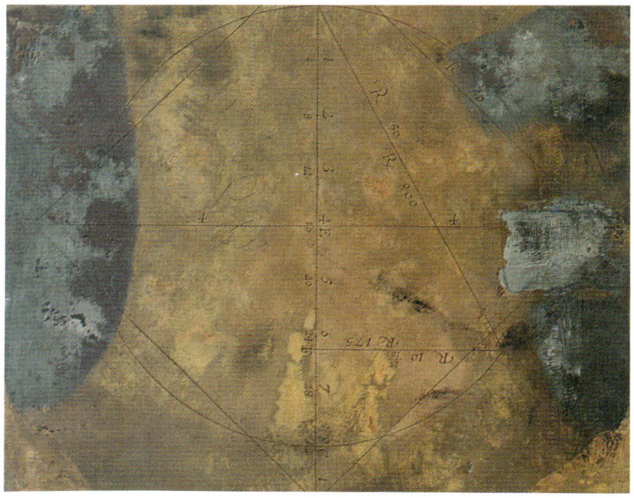

103
Self-Portrait Leaning on a Stone Sill

Signed and dated in the plate upper left
Rembrandt f 1639
Etching touched with black chalk
20.5 x 16.4 cm
Watermark: Strasbourg Lily with initials HP; variant A.b.
National Gallery of Victoria, Melbourne; purchased 1891

LITERATURE: White & Boon B.21 I (first of two states); Hind 168; Münz 24; Biörklund BB.39-E. See also White 1969, vol. 1, pp. 120–2; Gregory & Zdanowicz 1988, p. 119, no. 10; B. Welzel, in Berlin / Amsterdam / London 1991–92b, pp. 200–2, [etching] cat. no. 13; Zdanowicz 1993.

Self-portraits appear in Rembrandt's art from his earliest years, initially in the guise of characters inserted into history paintings and, soon afterwards, in an unprecedented series of paintings and etchings.[1] By the late 1630s he had made no fewer than twenty-five portrait etchings alone. Individually, the exaggerated expressions of many of these early portrayals appear extreme and impetuous; cumulatively, they reveal a deeply thoughtful, curious, reflective and individual nature capable of encompassing a wide variety of moods, emotions and personae.

In this 1639 self-portrait Rembrandt portrays himself from the reserved distance that his serious demeanour would seem to require. He is not dressed in contemporary attire, but in a rich, if indeterminate, costume that suggests earlier times. The pose itself is also based on earlier models: two sixteenth-century Italian paintings – Raphael's portrait of Baldassare Castiglione, the author of *Il cortegiano* (The Courtier) (fig. 13c), and Titian's so-called *Ariosto*, another famous Renaissance writer (fig. 13b). Both paintings were in private collections in Amsterdam in 1639. Rembrandt made a sketch of the Raphael portrait (fig. 13d) when it was sold (by an Amsterdam collector) at auction in April 1639 to the diplomat and collector Alphonso Lopez, Cardinal Richelieu's representative in Amsterdam. Lopez is also presumed to have owned the Titian painting.

In his 1639 etched portrait, Rembrandt portrayed himself in a pose that synthesized the poses in both earlier paintings. He adjusted his torso to a strict profile and placed his face at a sharper angle to the body so as to show himself looking directly at the viewer as he leans with formal composure against the stone sill. Unlike that of Titian's Ariosto, who is fenced off from the observer by a parapet, Rembrandt's voluminous sleeve hangs over the sill, thereby impinging upon the space in front.

This is Rembrandt's second etched self-portrait conceived in emulation of previous masters. The first – *Self-Portrait in a Soft Hat and Embroidered Cloak*, 1631 (B.7) (fig. 103a) – was cast in the manner of Rubens, but strained too hard for effect in terms of both representation and technique. Eight years later, Rembrandt had no need to make an effort in order to command the respect that was due to him for so successfully taking up the challenge of the masters of the past. And, as is clear from his demeanour and dress, his success at this time was not confined to the artistic challenges that he set himself. Rembrandt was also successful in wordly terms, for by 1639 he had become Amsterdam's most fashionable portrait painter.

Made with reference to other celebrated models, this self-portrait itself became a model, first for a painted version that Rembrandt made in the following year (1640) (cat. no. 13) and next as a format used by his students, including Ferdinand Bol (figs 45b, 45c) and Govaert Flinck. There are, moreover, ten engraved copies of it made by later artists.

This impression is one of six surviving impressions of the first state that were drawn over by Rembrandt with black chalk, as he deliberated on how much more detail was needed to finish the image. In the end, he decided upon only a small adjustment: the completion of the hatband. However, clear traces of the soft chalk may be seen here on the masonry, the baluster at right, the beret and the gloved hand. The impression is an early one and it retains the crisp, linear delicacy of even the wispiest hair, as well as the silvery tonal modulation of the rich garment. Like other impressions of the first state, it is printed on paper with the Strasbourg Lily watermark that Rembrandt seems to have reserved for this print alone.[2]

IZ

1 The chief study of Rembrandt's self-portraits is Chapman 1990.

2 I am grateful to Erik Hinterding for information on the watermark. His identification is based on beta-radiographs made at the National Gallery of Victoria by Lyndsay Knowles and Cobus van Breda.

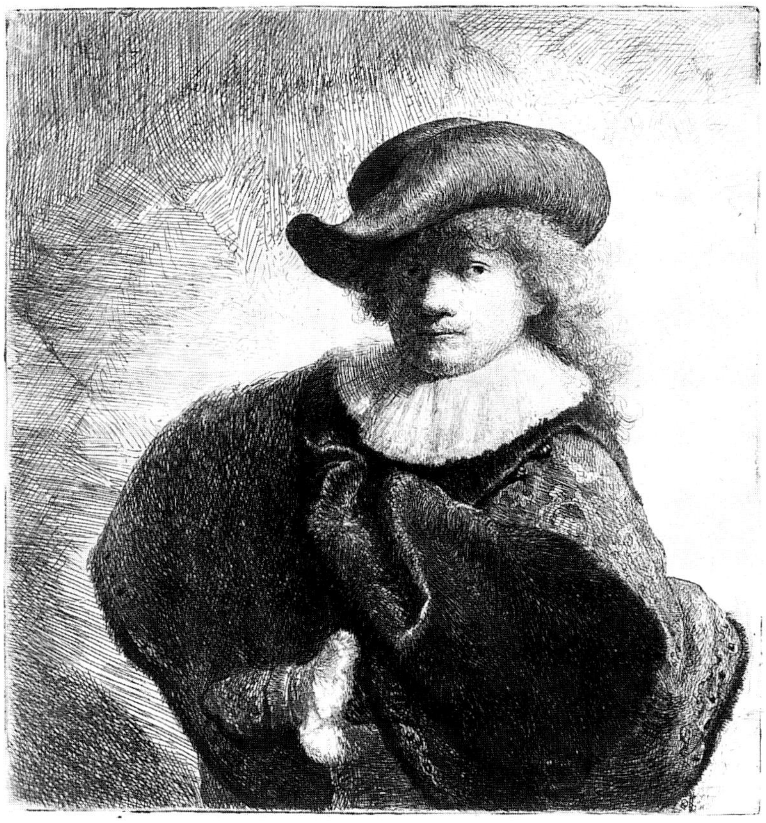

FIG. 103a
Rembrandt
Self-Portrait in a Soft Hat and Embroidered Cloak
Monogrammed and dated 1631
Etching (eighth state)
14.8 x 13.0 cm
Rijksprentenkabinet, Rijksmuseum, Amsterdam

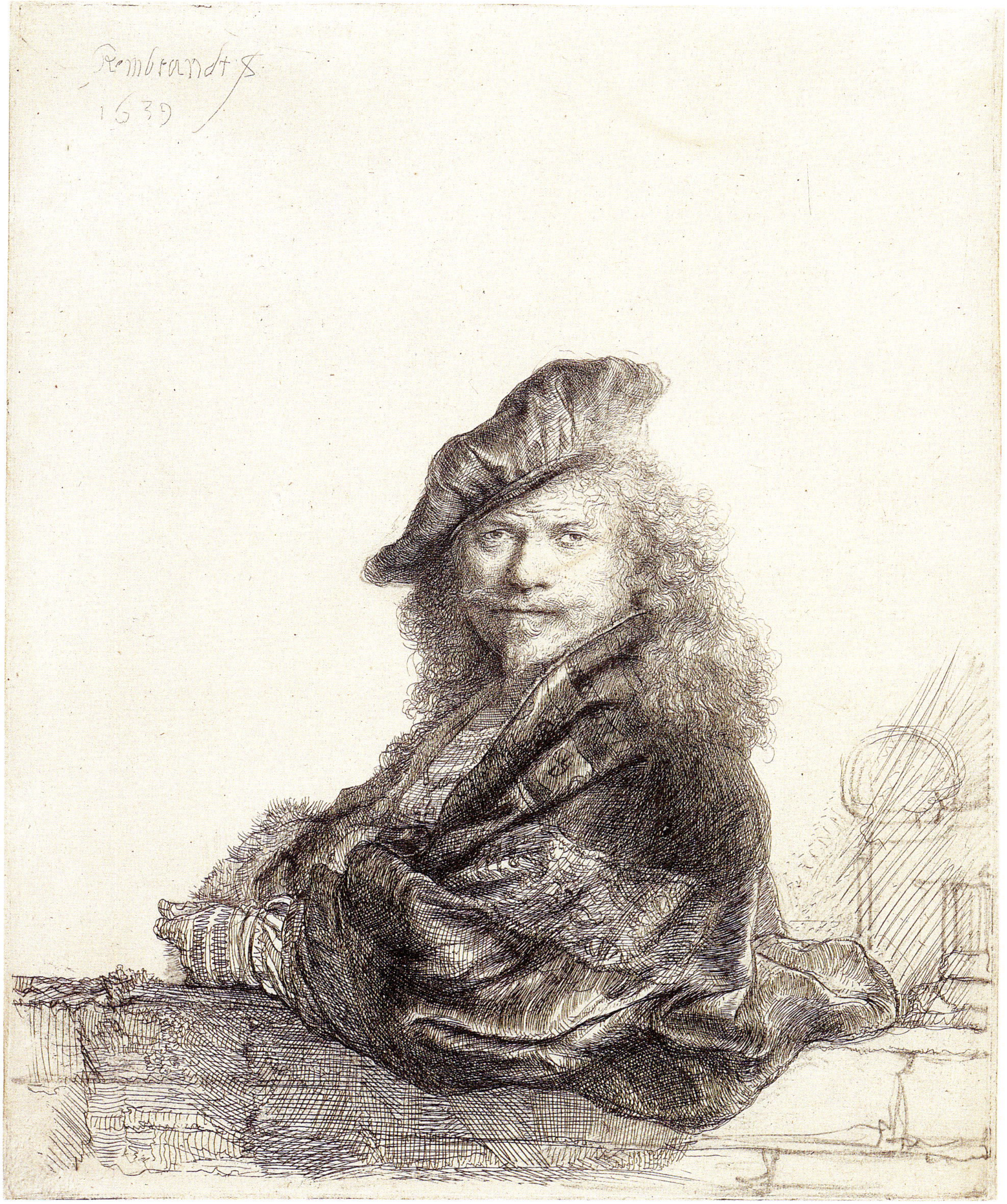
Rembrandt f.
1639

104

The Death of the Virgin

Signed and dated in the plate lower left
Rembrandt f. 1639.
Etching and drypoint
40.8 x 31.4 cm (with wide margins)
Watermark: Strasbourg Bend
Lent by the Syndics of The Fitzwilliam Museum, Cambridge

LITERATURE: White & Boon B.99 II (second of three states); Hind 161; Münz 208; Biörklund BB.39-A. See also White 1969, vol. 1, pp. 43–6; B. Welzel, in Berlin / Amsterdam / London 1991–92b, pp. 203–5, [etching] cat. no. 14.

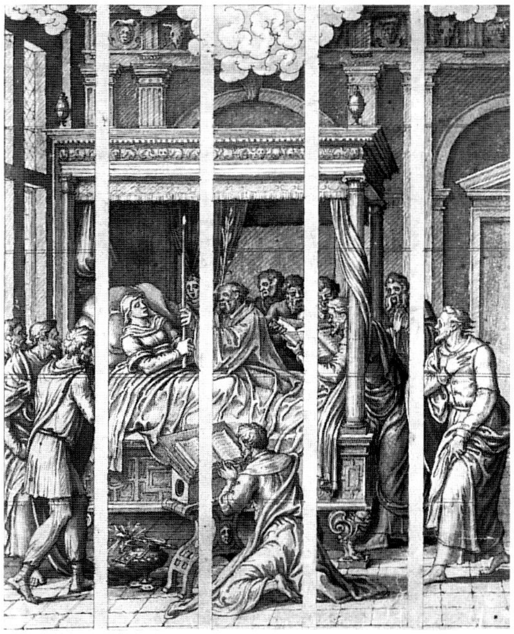

FIG. 104a
Dirck Crabeth d. 1574
The Death of the Virgin (design for a stained-glass window)
Pen and ink and brush
29.8 x 23.1 cm
Rijksprentenkabinet, Rijksmuseum, Amsterdam

The Death of the Virgin is not described in the New Testament but is known from apocryphal writings, chiefly Jacobus de Voragine's *Golden Legend.* According to that text, the angel who came to tell the Virgin of her imminent death acceded to her request to see the apostles before she died by causing them to be miraculously transported to her deathbed from the various places in which they were preaching.

The subject's visual traditions – always of the greatest significance for Rembrandt – provided him with important reference points for his own portrayal. Dürer's woodcut from the *Life of the Virgin* (B.93) and, perhaps, the engraving by Martin Schongauer that inspired it (Lehrs 16), suggested the general setting, as well as models for the physiognomies of specific characters. Closer to home was Dirck Crabeth's stained-glass window at Amsterdam's Oude Kerk, with the bed shown from the side and the kneeling figure reading from the Bible in front (fig. 104a). This figure, which also features prominently in Jacques Callot's etching (Lieure 1367), and is interpreted as a personification of the Church[1] or as an indication of the time-honoured sanctity of the event,[2] was shifted by Rembrandt towards the left corner, closer to the dying woman. The attendant crowd was not restricted to the apostles, according to tradition, but, as in Pieter Bruegel's depiction (Hollstein 116), includes women, young acolytes and a high priest – the whole of distressed humanity.

The theatrical majesty of the portrayal is underlined by the raised position of the bed, the enormous space, and the curtain at the right; however, the dying woman, the doctor who examines her pulse, and the array of emotions expressed by the mourners add a dimension of realism. While some of the figures, such as St John with his outstretched arms and the woman with clasped hands, assume traditional poses of sorrow, others – especially the dying Virgin – appear to be observed from life. The figure of Mary resembles Rembrandt's sketches of his wife, Saskia, when she was ill or confined to bed. In 1638 Saskia had given birth to their second child, a daughter, who, like their first-born son, died within weeks. Saskia herself died of tuberculosis in 1642. Rembrandt included a depiction of her in bed in a sheet of etched sketches done in the early 1640s (B.369) and portrayed her in various drawings (see cat. no. 82 and fig. 82a).

This etching, which was made in the same year as the *Self-Portrait Leaning on a Stone Sill* (cat. no. 103), is pictorially and technically more daring. It is one of Rembrandt's largest plates and bold in the extent to which he has admitted large areas of extremely sketchy drawing. The sketchiness in the upper half of the plate perfectly conveys the incorporeality of the divine realm, the miraculous movement of heavenly bodies in billowing clouds and, of course, the divine light. Rembrandt had earlier begun another version of the subject when he outlined part of the angel's wings on a plate that he later reused for the *Three Trees* (cat. no. 106) without completely burnishing away this detail.[3] The present print is notable for being the first of Rembrandt's etchings in which drypoint was used extensively, not just as emphasis but in a primary way, to describe entire objects, such as the chair in the lower right corner, and to provide the deepest accents of darkness.

In view of the fundamental criticism that was levelled by Protestantism against the excessive devotion to the Virgin traditionally practised in the Roman Church, this subject must be seen as typically Catholic. However, whether Rembrandt was commissioned to do it, or whether he intended the etching for the Catholic market generally, is unknown. His commissioned portraits alone confirm that he had clients from all the Christian denominations,[4] and his own lack of religious orthodoxy is well known.

This is a crisp and cleanly wiped impression of the second state, after the chair in the right corner was heavily shaded with drypoint, but before the addition of further shading to the foremost bedpost, in the third and final state. It is printed on paper with the Strasbourg Bend watermark. Five engraved copies after the etching are recorded.

IZ

1 White 1969, pp. 45–6.
2 B. Welzel, in Berlin / Amsterdam / London 1991–92b, p. 204, [etching] cat. no. 14.
3 Campbell 1980.
4 Manuth 1993–94, p. 236; see also Tümpel 1993, pp. 129–31.

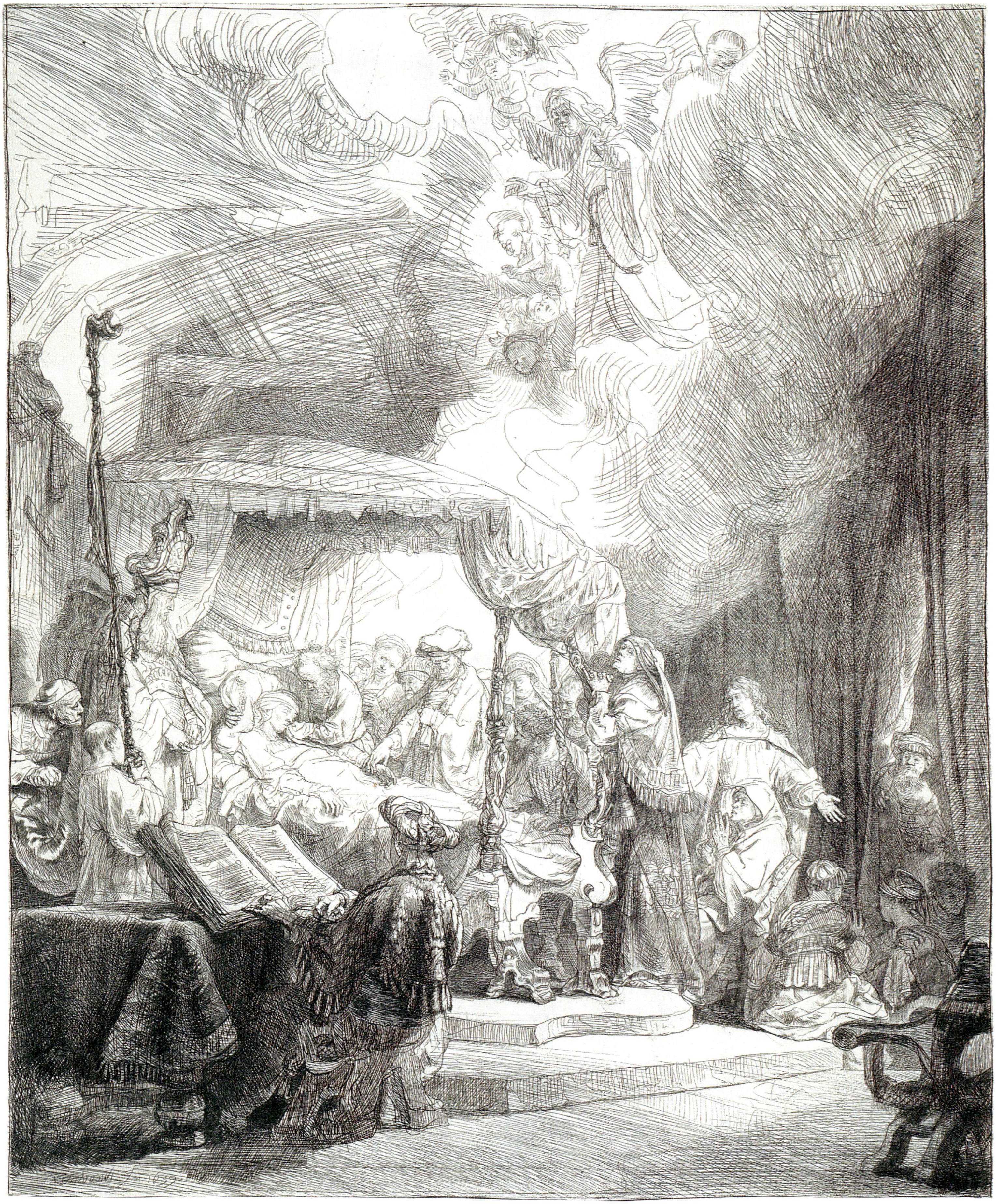

105

Landscape with a Cottage and Haybarn: Oblong Plate

Signed and dated in the plate lower right
Rembrandt f 1641
Etching and drypoint, printed on Western laid paper
12.9 x 32.1 cm
The Visitors of the Ashmolean Museum, Oxford

LITERATURE: White & Boon B.225 (only state); Hind 177; Münz 147; Biörklund BB.41-A.
See also White 1969, vol. 1, pp. 197–8; C. Schneider, in Washington 1990, pp. 83–4, cat. no. 6.

Rembrandt's twenty-six landscape etchings were made in two groups, essentially in the decade extending from the early 1640s to the early 1650s. The first group is clustered in the first half of the 1640s, the second in the early 1650s. The etchings differ from his few painted landscapes largely in their naturalistic focus and in their greater variety of type and format. Though landscapes make up a large proportion of his drawn oeuvre (see cat. nos 83, 90, 91), only one drawing (Benesch C.41) has been identified as a direct preparatory study for an etching (*Cottage with a White Paling* (B.232)). This paucity of preparatory drawings suggests what the prints themselves bear out: that, although they are based on careful and systematic observation, Rembrandt's landscape etchings are equally the result of his ceaseless artistic explorations.

Landscape with a Cottage and Haybarn is one of the earliest of Rembrandt's etched landscapes and belongs to a group of five he made in 1641. Its chief motif is a farmhouse, whose thatched roof is covered with mossy peat. A haybarn attached at the left is being used as temporary summer storage for a wagon. The cottage stands in prominent isolation against a low horizon, its ramshackle appearance signalling another of the features common to Rembrandt's art – his predilection for the picturesque.[1] The skyline at the far left is usually identified as Amsterdam, with the spires of the city's main churches reversed. The building rising from the trees in the middle distance on the right is thought to be the manor house of Kostverloren, which Rembrandt sketched on several occasions. It was built in the early 1500s, burnt down in 1650 and was demolished in 1657.[2] In reality, the relative positions of Kostverloren and Amsterdam were different and it has been suggested that their rearrangement here may have more than aesthetic purpose.[3]

Since it was first suggested by Gersaint in the mid-eighteenth century, this etching is usually considered to have a pair, *Landscape with a Cottage and Large Tree* (B.226) (fig. 105a), which is identical in size and dates from the same year. Both views continue a Dutch tradition of representing humble farm dwellings whose precedents may be found in the graphic work of Jacques de Gheyn II (1565–1629) and in the etchings of Jan van de Velde (1593–1641).

This is a fine early impression printed on European paper; however, since the sheet is stuck down it has not been possible to examine it for watermark evidence. Five engraved copies after this print are recorded.

IZ

1 C. Schneider, in Washington 1990, p. 16.
2 Cambridge 1993–94, cat. no. 7.
3 Stone-Ferrier 1992, p. 406, argues that the treatment stems from a deliberate decision to contrast rural tradition with encroaching modernity, thereby showing the isolation of the countryside from the city.

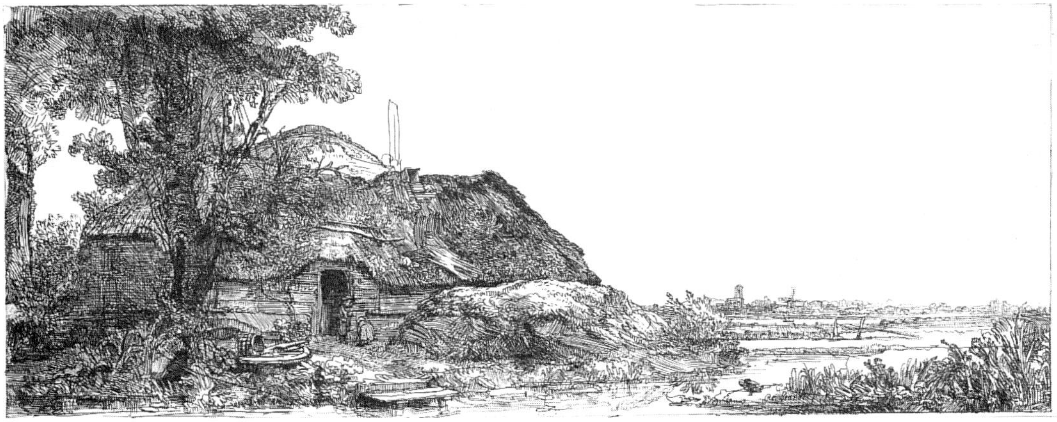

FIG. 105a
Rembrandt
Landscape with a Cottage and Large Tree
Signed and dated 1641
Etching
12.7 x 32.0 cm
Rijksprentenkabinet, Rijksmuseum, Amsterdam

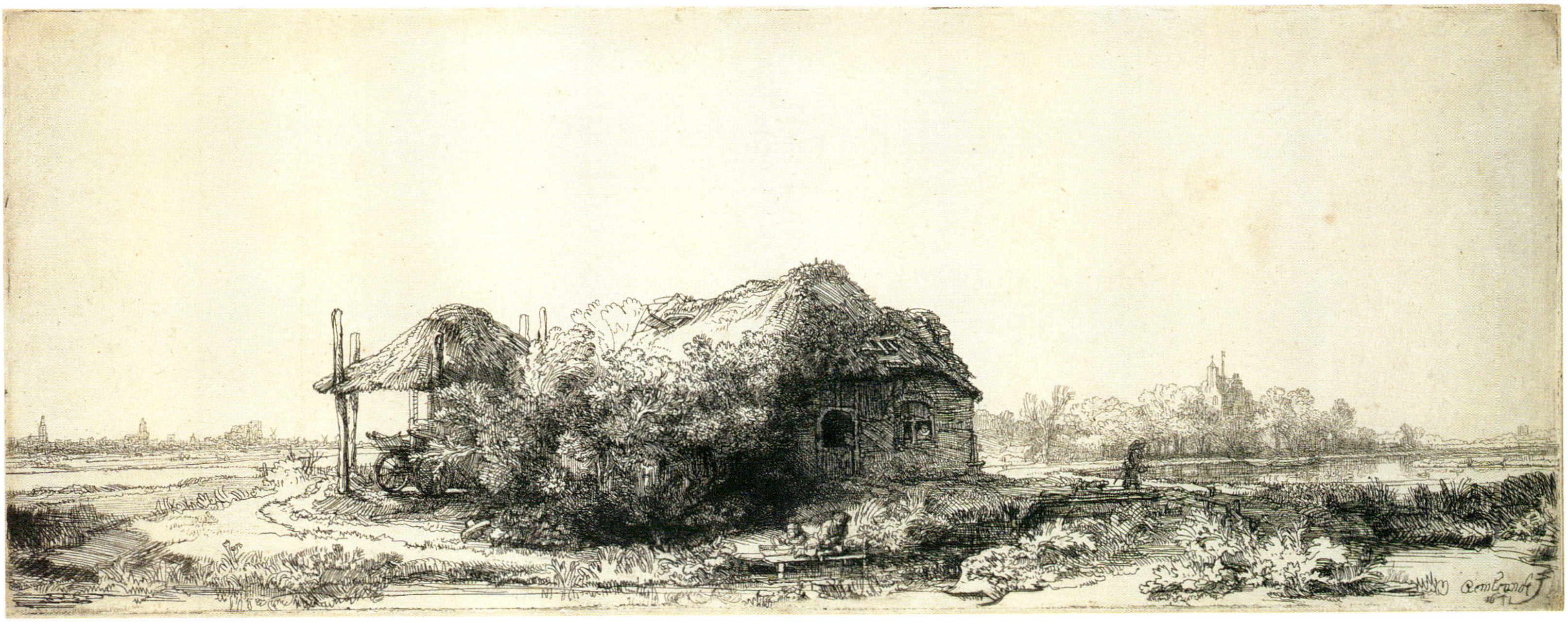

106
The Three Trees

Signed and dated in the plate lower right *Rembrandt f. 1643* (barely discernible)
Etching, drypoint and burin with some sulphur tint etching
21.3 x 28.0 cm
Watermark: Foolscap with five-pointed collar; variant A.a.a.
National Gallery of Victoria, Melbourne; purchased 1891

LITERATURE: White & Boon B.212 (only state); Hind 205; Münz 152; Biörklund BB.43-B. See also White 1969, vol. 1, pp. 198–200; Gregory & Zdanowicz 1988, pp. 103, 144, no. 97; C. Schneider, in Washington 1990, pp. 240–2, cat. no. 75; H. Bevers, in Berlin / Amsterdam / London 1991–92b, pp. 218–20, [etching] cat. no. 19; Cambridge 1993–94, cat. no. 13.

The grandest and most heroic of Rembrandt's etched landscapes, the *Three Trees* is also the most pictorial, idealized and highly finished. It is closer in conception to his paintings (cat. no. 11) than are any other of the landscape prints. Exceptional for showing nature in the midst of change,[1] it combines sweeping and dramatic views of land and sky, together with a great range of intriguing details that reveal themselves slowly.

Dominating the scene are the trees, silhouetted against the sky, starkly illuminated by the light of a passing storm, their heroic survival carrying moral overtones that connect the motif to the tree's role as emblem of persistence and, more specifically, to the three crosses of Calvary.[2] The view is thought to represent the countryside looking from the Diemerdyck, east of Amsterdam, whose skyline is seen at the left. A fisherman and his wife are occupied in the lower left corner, while hidden in the scrub at right – more difficult to make out in the shadows – are two lovers, a common feature of pastoral landscapes. Beside them in the thicket, and barely visible in this impression, is a goat, an animal traditionally associated with unfettered eroticism. On the right horizon, beside the traveller's wagon, is the tiny figure of an artist, seated on the ground, drawing. What is unusual here is not so much his presence as the direction in which he faces, away from the spectacularly lit view that spreads out before the onlooker. This detail has been understood as a small but significant reminder of the importance of the artist's inner faculties – his imagination and intellect[3] – in the creation of art, including a genre such as landscape that is fundamentally based on an observation of the natural world.

The massive cloud formation at left betrays evidence of having started out as an angel's wing, during a first attempt at a scene representing the Death of the Virgin (see commentary to cat. no. 104). The diagonal striations in the corner, here presumably depicting sheets of passing rain, were scored directly into the plate with drypoint, but with the burr kept under control; it is the first instance of Rembrandt's extensive use of drypoint in his landscapes. All aspects of this etching are characterized by a highly wrought finish, including the manipulation of sulphur tint, a form of grainy tonal etching. Its depth of tone is carefully graded, through burnishing in the area of the fields in the left middle distance, thereby enhancing the sense of receding space while also suggesting the quickly shifting illumination of stormy weather.

The *Three Trees* is one of Rembrandt's best known and most frequently copied landscapes, of which there are as many as eight engraved copies listed. The foolscap watermark in this impression is found in most other good impressions that constitute the first edition of this print.[4]

IZ

1 Stone-Ferrier 1983–84, pp. 169–72, cat. no. 46.
2 Brown 1986, p. 226, cat. no. 112. Brown also suggests that the lowering sky is intended to suggest the passage from Matthew 27:45 referring to the darkness that falls over the land during the Crucifixion. For a general discussion of the representational accuracy, and the significance, of clouds in Dutch seventeenth-century landscapes, with passing references to Rembrandt, see Walsh 1991.
3 C. Schneider, in Washington 1990, pp. 218–20, cat. no. 75.
4 I am grateful to Erik Hinterding for information on the watermark. His identification is based on beta-radiographs made at the National Gallery of Victoria by Lyndsay Knowles and Cobus van Breda.

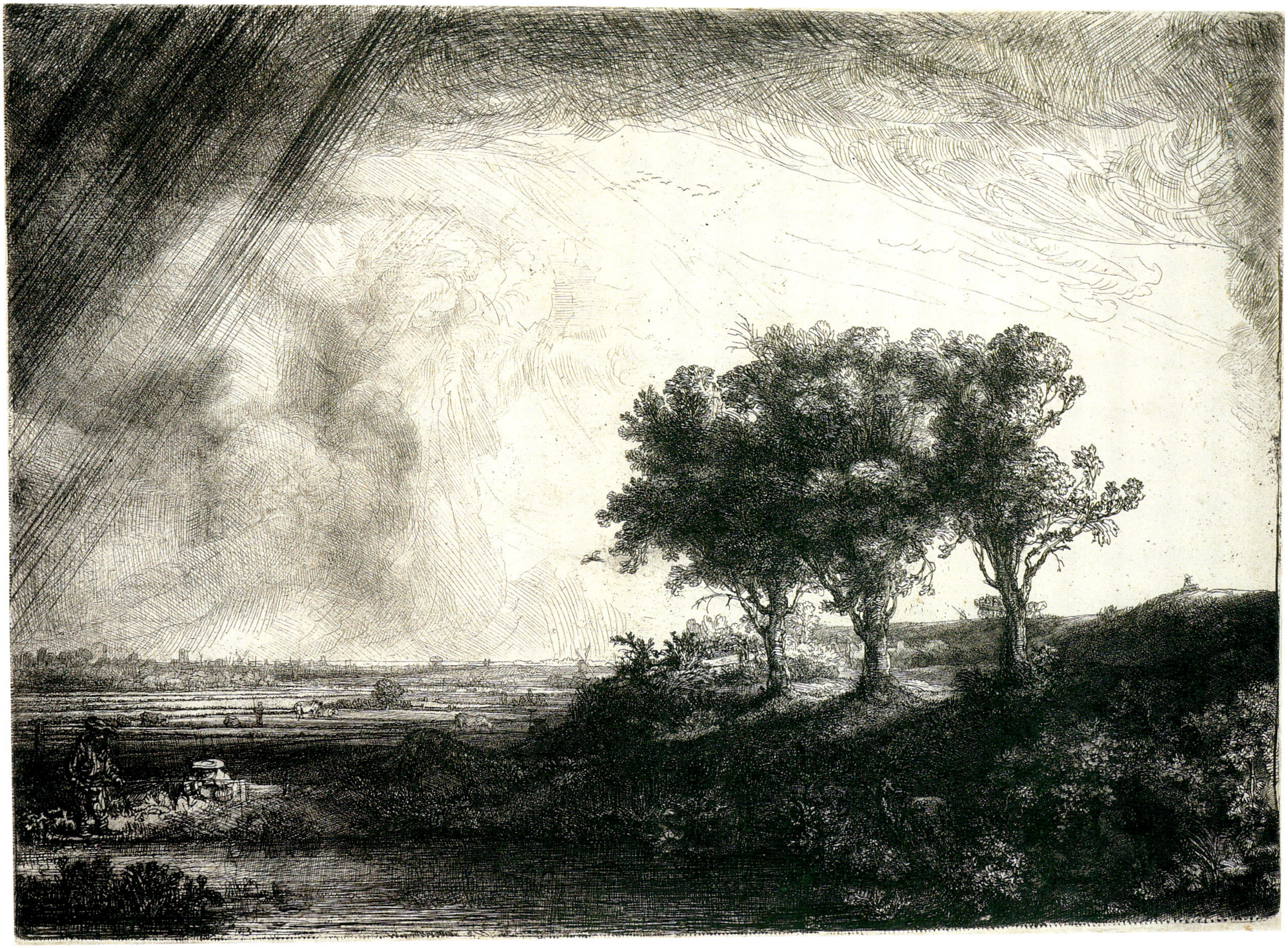

107
The Omval

Signed and dated in the plate lower right
Rembrandt 1645
Etching and drypoint with some sulphur tint etching
18.6 x 22.7 cm
Watermark: Countermark WK´; variant A.a. (countermark to Strasbourg Lily, variant E2.a.)
National Gallery of Victoria, Melbourne; purchased 1958

LITERATURE: White & Boon B.209 II (second of two states); Hind 210; Münz 155; Biörklund BB.45-B. See also White 1969, vol. 1, pp. 203–5; Gregory & Zdanowicz 1988, p. 145, no. 98; C. Schneider, in Washington 1990, pp. 196–9, cat. no. 54; Cambridge 1993–94, cat. no. 14.

The Omval is a spit of land that lies at the junction of the Amstel River and the Ringvaart canal south-east of Amsterdam. This was not far from where Rembrandt lived and he had made drawings of the landscape in the vicinity on several occasions.[1] In this etching he has created a scene with a distinctly bifurcated focus. To the right is the view across the Amstel, with the two mills and a cluster of buildings, all recognizable from Rembrandt's drawings (though reversed). In the left foreground, secluded within bushes that grow around a gnarled tree, is a pair of lovers, the man crowning his partner with a leafy garland. Facing away from them, and hence emphasizing their separateness, stands a man who looks towards the opposite bank, his upright figure creating a formal link between both shores.

The two halves of the print are etched in contrasting manners, in part to suggest the difference between close-up and distant views: the light-flooded view at right is sketched in an open and direct way, while that on the left is worked with a dense array of graphic marks. Here, for the first time, Rembrandt made particularly free use of drypoint to heighten the darkest areas; however, in the first state of the print he was not yet able to control the burr's capacity to produce intensely dark tone. This resulted in a somewhat blotchy left half of the image. He therefore reduced the burr in the second and final state.

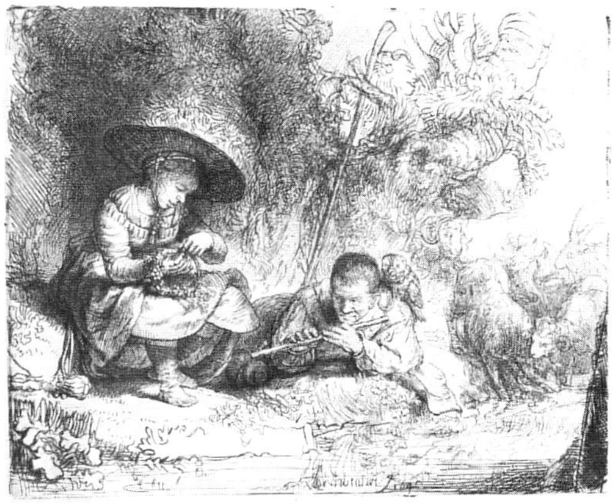

FIG. 107b
Rembrandt
The Flute Player
Signed and dated 1642
Etching
11.6 x 14.3 cm
Rijksprentenkabinet, Rijksmuseum, Amsterdam

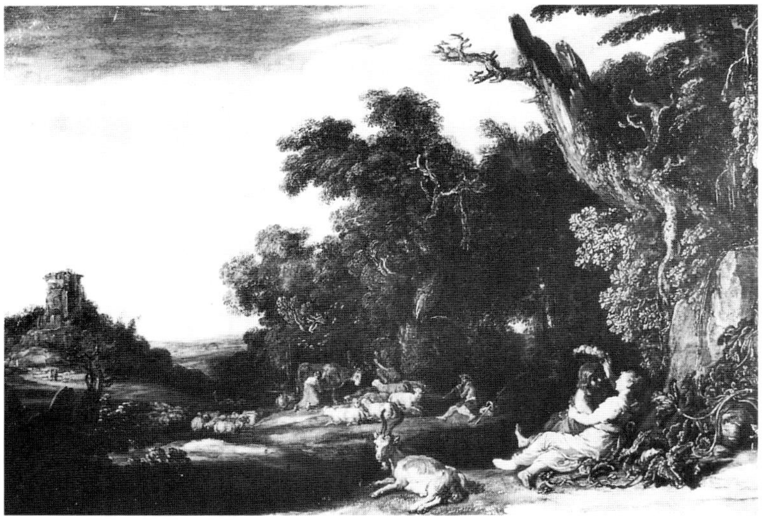

FIG. 107a
Pieter Lastman 1583–1633
*Pastoral Scene c.*1615–20
Panel
38.5 x 54.0 cm
Private collection, Amsterdam

Nonetheless, the composite view that Rembrandt has created eloquently evokes the dichotomy between the private and the public spheres, between the inner world of private feelings (at left) and the outer world of activity (at right), a contrast that he was much concerned with in his portraiture.[2]

The pair of lovers amidst trees is one of the stock motifs of the pastoral landscape that Rembrandt's master, Pieter Lastman, had employed on one occasion in a painting of a rural arcadia (fig. 107a). The *Omval*, with its echo of Lastman's blasted tree – but with the lovers hiding, rather than disporting themselves in the open – also fits into this pictorial tradition with its strong roots in literature.[3] Rembrandt had worked in the pastoral mode from the time of his earliest depictions of Saskia as Flora. But in the years immediately following her death in 1642, pastoral motifs recur in a cluster of etchings, mostly landscapes, sometimes with explicitly erotic overtones as in the *Flute Player* (B.188) (fig. 107b).[4] By placing the amorous couple in the contemporary, recognizable setting of the Omval, Rembrandt has brought the pastoral landscape up to date.[5]

This light, silvery impression is of the second state of the print with the width of the man's hat, and the drypoint accents, reduced. The very few surviving impressions of the first state indicate that the second state was made early in the plate's history, in 1645. This impression has few traces of drypoint burr, and a faint film of ink evenly covers the entire plate. The watermark, which probably belongs to a French paper, confirms what the muted quality of the impression indicates: namely, that it does not belong to the first edition, but was reprinted by Rembrandt around 1652–53, at a time when he was working on his second group of landscapes.[6] One engraved copy after this etching is recorded.

IZ

1 For example, Benesch 1954–57, vol. VI, nos 1321, 1322, figs 1555, 1557; see also Lugt 1915, ch. III.
2 Smith 1990, esp. pp. 158–60, 165.
3 Freedberg 1980, pp. 11–18; Kettering 1983.
4 Kettering 1983, pp. 95–9.
5 C. Schneider, in Washington 1990, p. 198, cat. no. 54.
6 I am grateful to Erik Hinterding for information on the dating of the states and on the watermark. His identification is based on beta-radiographs made at the National Gallery of Victoria by Lyndsay Knowles and Cobus van Breda. See also Stone-Ferrier 1992, p. 414.

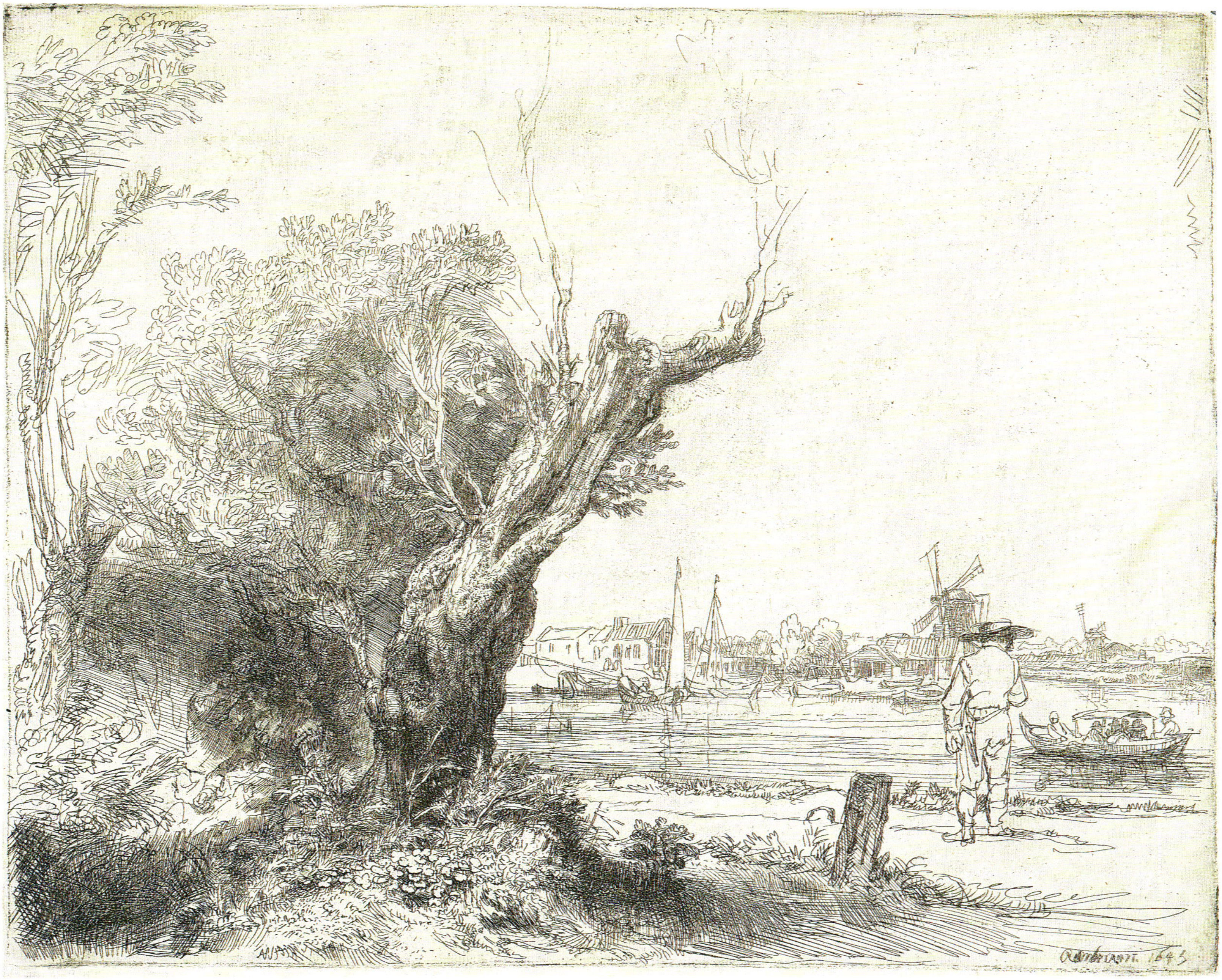

108
Nude Man Seated before a Curtain

Signed and dated in the plate lower left
Rembrandt. f. 1646
Etching, printed on Western laid paper
16.7 x 9.7 cm
National Gallery of Victoria, Melbourne;
Felton Bequest 1973

LITERATURE: White & Boon B.193 I (first of two states); Hind 220; Münz 135; Biörklund BB.46-B. See also White 1969, vol. 1, pp. 178–80; Stone-Ferrier 1983–84, pp. 45–7; Gregory & Zdanowicz 1988, p. 147, no. 103; H. Bevers, in Berlin / Amsterdam / London 1991–92b, pp. 224–6.

This etching is one of three nude subjects that Rembrandt depicted in 1646, all of them portraying the same young male models posing in the studio. The present work belongs to the second of three groups of nude etchings in Rembrandt's oeuvre which, unlike the other two, focuses on the male rather than on the female nude. Here the model sits in a relaxed position on a chair placed on a low podium, facing the front, his arms dropped with hands clasped, his head slightly tilted. The curtain that acts as a backdrop is summarily portrayed, principally in order that its folds can provide the deep shadows to give the white-skinned body focus and to set it clearly in relief. To both sides, the background merges into the informal, sketchy hatching that is associated with drawing, and was a manner of etching that Rembrandt pioneered.

Like the other two nude etchings from 1646 (B.194, B.196), this is executed in a clear, linear style, with minimal resort to tonal effects. Its diagrammatic clarity would have been an essential requirement if, as has been suggested, Rembrandt intended it for pedagogical purposes and as part of a wider plan to compile a drawing manual, comparable to those in contemporary use, and which he would have known.[1] Indeed, one of the associated etchings depicts an apparently unconnected scene, behind two male nudes, that shows a mother teaching her little child to walk (B.194) (fig. 108a). This has been interpreted as a reference, by visual analogy, to the importance of artistic instruction, constant practice, and the need to observe life not only in the confines of the studio but in the world outside it.[2]

The differences between the first and the final states of this etching are minor. However, it is interesting to note that although at this stage Rembrandt had access to oriental papers, he used them far less frequently for his male nudes than for his female subjects; only one impression of the *Nude Man Seated before a Curtain* printed on Chinese paper is listed by White and Boon. This is probably largely because these prints are not pictorially conceived – their purpose being descriptive rather than suggestive – and therefore required clarity above all else. However, they are far from being stiffly formal academies.

A group of drawings from male models, formerly attributed to Rembrandt but now considered to be the work of pupils, show the same model in attitudes very close to those portrayed in Rembrandt's etchings. They may well have been done at the same sessions as those at which Rembrandt made his drawings directly onto the etching plate.[3] One engraved copy after this print is recorded.

IZ

1 H. Bevers, in Berlin / Amsterdam / London 1991–92b, p. 224, [etching] cat. no. 21.
2 Emmens 1968, p. 154ff; Stone-Ferrier 1983–84, pp. 45–6, cat. no. 2.
3 H. Bevers, in Berlin / Amsterdam / London 1991–92b, p. 224, [etching] cat. no. 21.

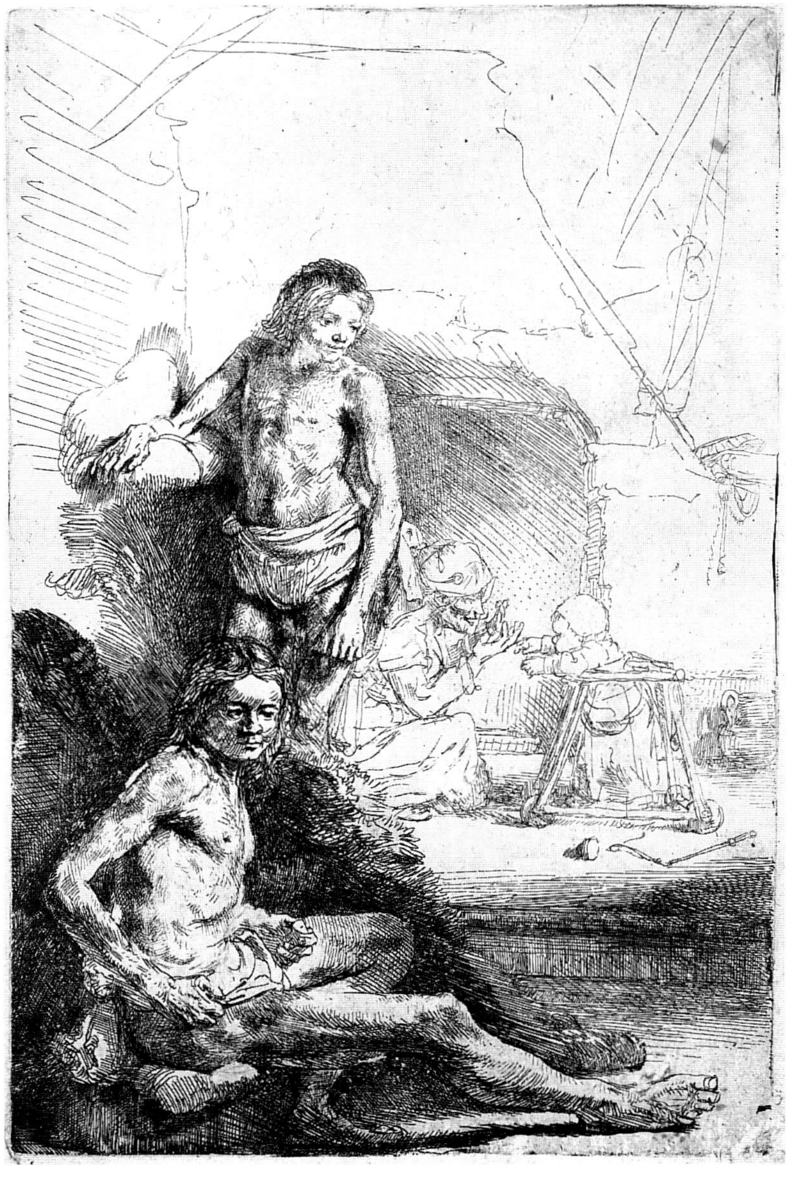

FIG. 108a
Rembrandt
Nude Man Seated and Another Standing, with a Woman and Baby Lightly Etched in the Background
c.1646
Etching (first state)
19.4 x 12.8 cm
Rijksprentenkabinet, Rijksmuseum, Amsterdam

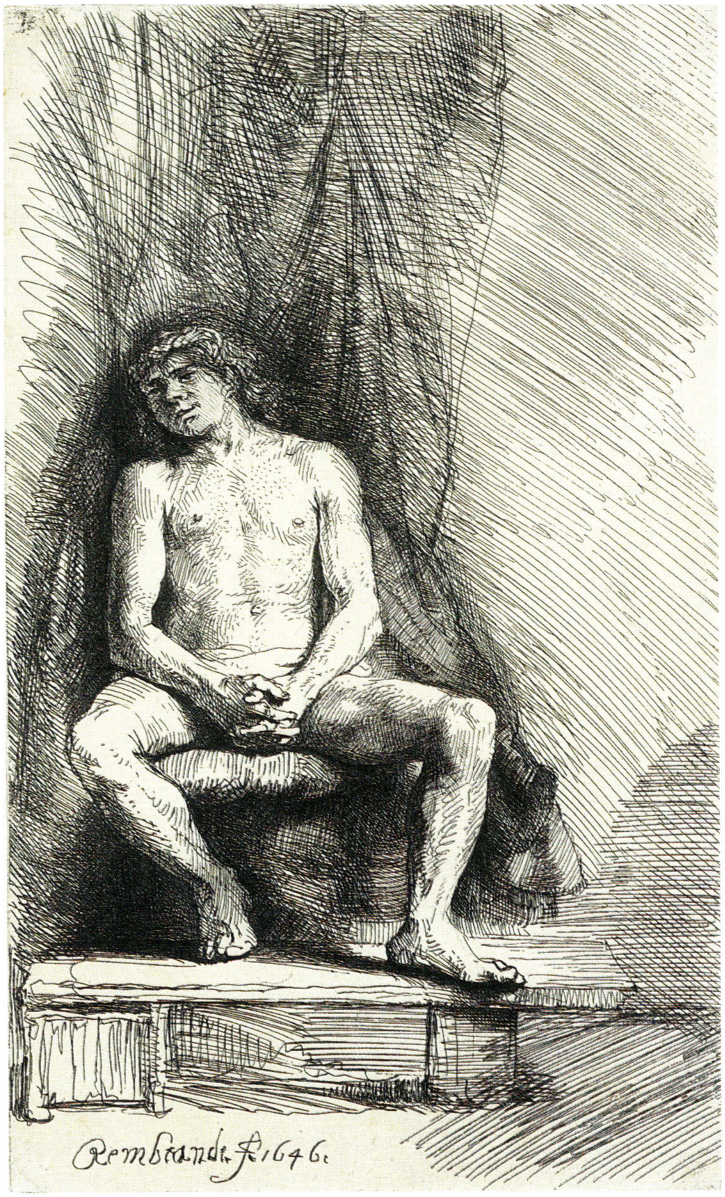
Rembrandt. f. 1646.

109

Ephraim Bonus, Jewish Physician

Signed and dated in the plate lower right
Rembrandt f. 1647 (barely discernible)
Etching, drypoint and burin
24.2 x 17.7 cm
Watermark: Basilisk with initials RP;
variant A'.a.a.
National Gallery of Victoria, Melbourne;
Everard Studley Miller Bequest 1959

LITERATURE: White & Boon B.278 II (second of two states); Hind 226; Münz 69; Biörklund BB.47-A. See also White 1969, vol. 1, pp. 128–9; Gregory & Zdanowicz 1988, p. 123, no. 31.

Portraiture, necessarily based on external appearance, was low in the hierarchy of artistic subject matter in Rembrandt's time, when history painting was held in greatest esteem. However, portraiture was in great demand with the growing class of people able to afford it, and it could be an extremely lucrative practice for an artist. Rembrandt's interest in the human face – both general types, and the faces of individuals – is apparent from the very beginning of his career.

The subject of this portrait, Ephraim Bonus (or Bueno) (1599–1665), was a distinguished physician and a respected member of Amsterdam's community of Portuguese Jews (see commentary to cat. no. 25). Rembrandt probably met him through the rabbinical scholar Menasseh ben Israel, who had been responsible for establishing the first Jewish printing press in Holland and whose portrait Rembrandt is thought to have etched in 1636 (B.269). Bonus was a supporter of Menasseh's press and published his own religious writings there.[1]

He is depicted in three-quarter length, descending a staircase, his arm resting on the balustrade.[2] Unlike in most of Rembrandt's etched portraits, which contain details alluding to the sitter's occupation (cf. cat. no. 120), there is nothing here to indicate Bonus's profession; rather, he is portrayed simply as one of Amsterdam's well-to-do citizens. This is the only etching in Rembrandt's oeuvre that was preceded by a preparatory oil sketch, made on a small wood panel (Bredius 252) (fig. 109a). The oil sketch depicts the subject from closer quarters and shows him looking directly at the viewer. Rembrandt was able to perfectly translate the tonal qualities of the sketch into their pictorial equivalents in etching. Here, a dense web of cross-hatching is modulated so as to describe the plain architectural background and to suggest an introspective mood of half-light that is enhanced by Bonus's enigmatic, somewhat melancholy, facial expression as he gazes into the distance. Deeper shadows are achieved through added work with drypoint and the burin. While we see virtually the whole figure of the man in a spacious interior, we are subtly directed towards his face, especially the eyes that look out from beneath his hat's dipping rim, cleverly accented by a sliver of white.

In its tonal conception this portrait is similar to another that Rembrandt etched in 1647, the celebrated portrait of Jan Six (B.285) (fig. 28b).[3] The degree to which Rembrandt was able to suggest the inner life of his subjects may be seen by a comparison with another portrait of Bonus, engraved by Rembrandt's old colleague Jan Lievens (B.56) (fig. 109b).

This impression is of the second state of this etching. It differs from the first principally in the removal of drypoint burr from the subject's ring, so that it is changed from a dense and distracting black to a white detail, which is better integrated with the hand. The impression is printed on a Swiss paper made in the vicinity of Basel by the Heuslers, an established family of papermakers famous for the quality of their product. The Heusler watermark is often found in early impressions of the second state of this portrait.[4] One engraved copy of this etching is recorded.

IZ

1 These biographical details are based on Schwartz 1985, p. 259, and Tümpel 1993, pp. 143–4.
2 Smith 1990, p. 160, describes Bonus as 'pausing on the doorstep', about to cross the threshold of his home and enter the public world outside.
3 Smith 1990, p. 160, describes the portraits of Bonus and Six in terms of directly related opposites, the former representing the move into the public sphere, the latter as a withdrawal into privacy.
4 I am grateful to Erik Hinterding for information on the watermark. His identification is based on beta-radiographs made at the National Gallery of Victoria by Lyndsay Knowles and Cobus van Breda.

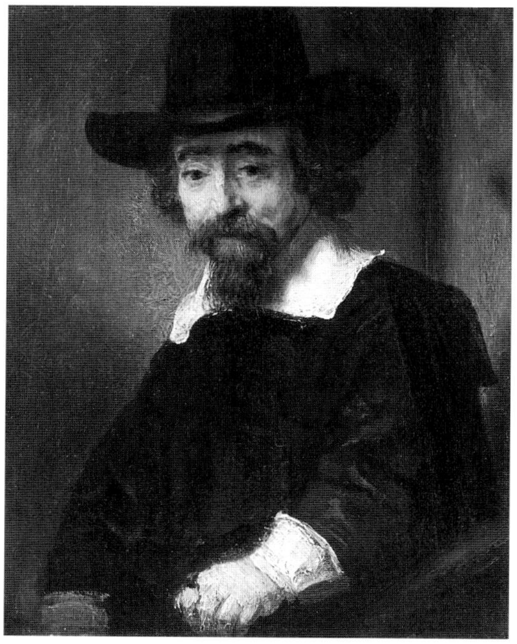

FIG. 109a
Rembrandt
Portrait of Ephraim Bonus c.1647
Panel
19.5 x 15.7 cm
Rijksmuseum, Amsterdam
(see also p. 76, fig. 10)

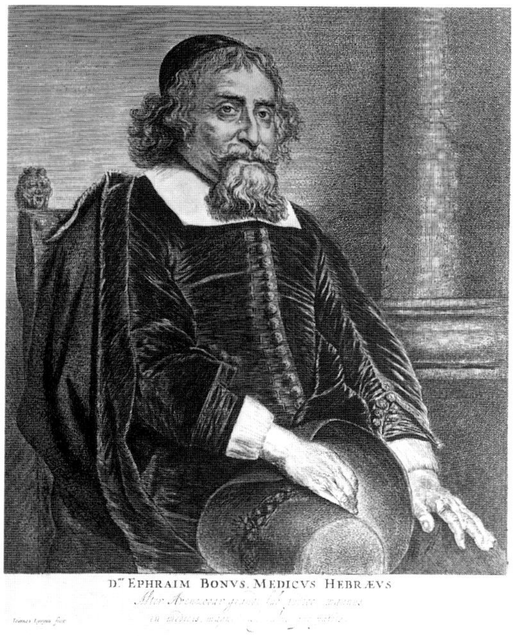

FIG. 109b
Jan Lievens
Ephraim Bonus
Etching
33.3 x 26.1 cm
Museum Boijmans Van Beuningen, Rotterdam

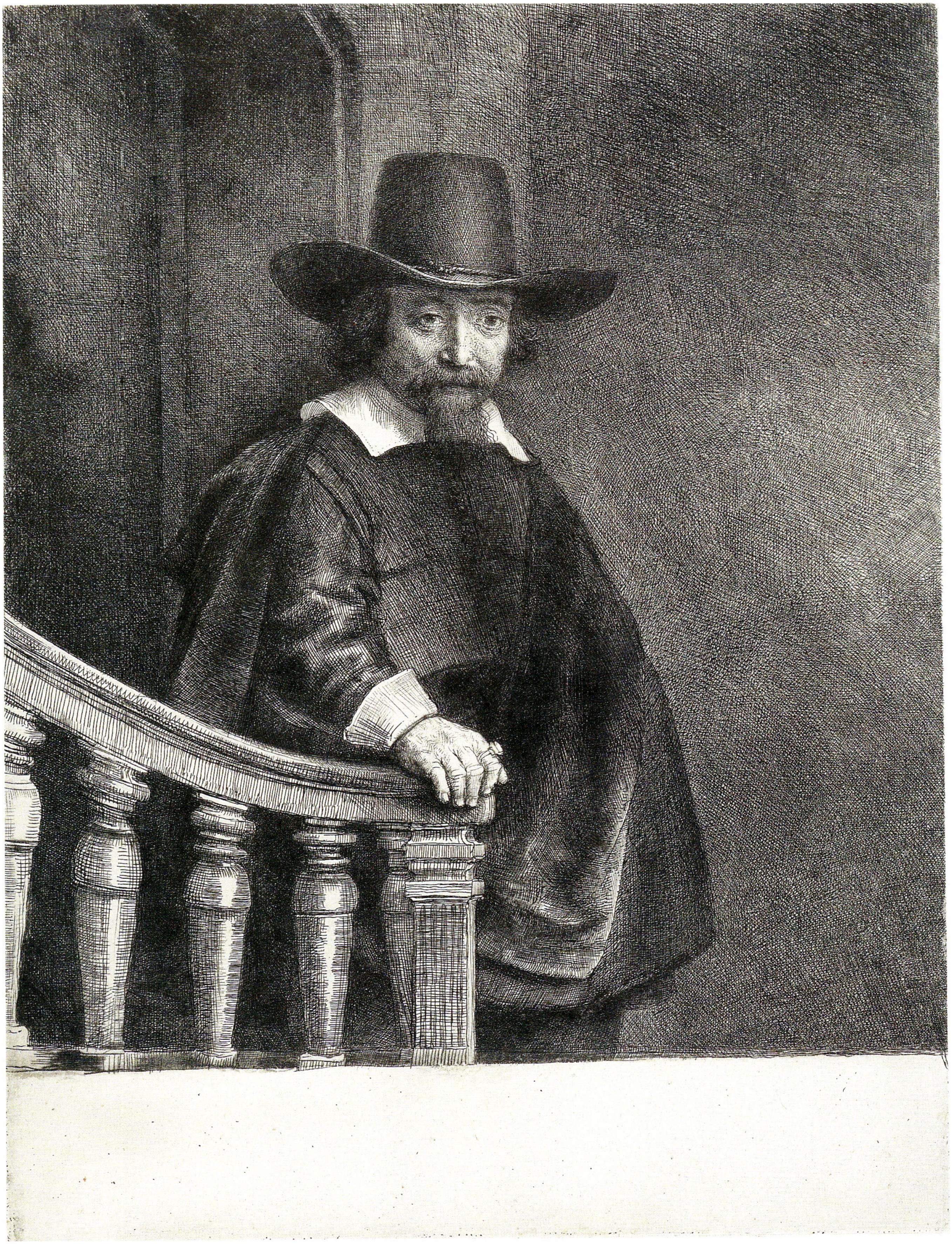

110A

The Hurdy-Gurdy Player and His Family Receiving Alms

Signed and dated in the plate lower right *Rembrandt f. 1648.*
Etching, drypoint and burin, printed on Western laid paper
16.5 x 12.9 cm
National Gallery of Victoria, Melbourne; purchased 1891

LITERATURE: White & Boon B.176 II (second of three states); Hind 233; Münz 271; Biörklund BB.48-C. See also White 1969, vol. 1, pp. 167–9; Hellerstedt 1981; Stone-Ferrier 1983–84, pp. 81–3, cat. no. 16; Stratton 1986; Gregory & Zdanowicz 1988, p. 151, no. 120; H. Bevers, in Berlin / Amsterdam / London 1991–92b, pp. 239–41, [etching] cat. no. 26; Zdanowicz 1993; G. Luijten, in Amsterdam 1997a, pp. 276–80, cat. no. 56.

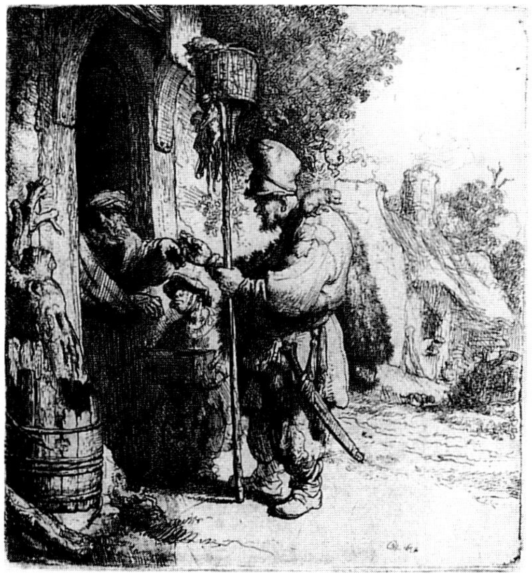

FIG. 110a
Rembrandt
The Rat Catcher
Monogrammed and dated 1632
Etching
14.0 x 12.5 cm
From a reproduction

110B

Copperplate for The Hurdy-Gurdy Player and His Family Receiving Alms

Copperplate worked in etching, drypoint and burin
15.9 x 13.9 x 0.13 cm [Hinterding 1995: 16.8 x 13.1 x 1.22 cm]; weight 186 g
Private collection, New York

LITERATURE: Coppier 1917, pp. 130–1; Hinterding 1995, p. 52.

The depiction of scenes from everyday life – or genre, as the subject matter came to be called in the nineteenth century – is an important theme in the pictorial traditions of northern Europe, especially in printmaking.[1] Lucas van Leyden (1494–1533), the greatest Dutch engraver of the sixteenth century, engraved an important group of such subjects, including the *Beggars* (also known as *Uilenspiegel*) (B.159), which was rare even by the mid-seventeenth century, and which Rembrandt purchased in 1642 for the large sum of 178 guilders.[2] Closer in time were the reproductive engravings after Pieter Bruegel the Elder's designs for genre compositions. Rembrandt's own depictions of beggars occur from the first years of his printmaking activity. The earliest generally portray single figures and, typologically and technically, are greatly indebted to the etchings of his older contemporary Jacques Callot (1592–1635), whose prints Rembrandt also collected.

The present example, traditionally known as 'Beggars Receiving Alms at the Door of a House',[3] is the latest, most mature and monumental depiction of the subject in Rembrandt's art, in which are synthesized the traditional representations of hurdy-gurdy players, beggars seeking alms, and acts of mercy.[4] An earlier etching, portraying a rat catcher collecting the dead vermin from a householder, shows a basically similar composition (B.121) (fig. 110a). The hurdy-gurdy player, often seen as a figure of fun, if not derision, in early seventeenth-century portrayals such as those of David Vinckboons, is here shown compassionately. He appears to be blind, and he stands behind a young woman, perhaps his daughter, and a younger boy. The right part of the composition is blank, casting the central cluster of figures into sharper prominence.

The half door and a stone gutter separate the two social ranks: the needy family and the wealthy burgher doing his Christian duty. There is no rhetorical flourish in the gesture of hands as the alms are exchanged, but a clear and simple eloquence. The tonal modelling of the figures and the wonderfully subtle rendering of shadows are reminiscent of the pictorial qualities of the *Hundred Guilder Print*, which Rembrandt was working on at the same time and which he probably completed in the following year (cat. no. 111). The biblical message of Christian charity towards the poor implicit in the *Hundred Guilder Print* is also present here. An acutely observed and speedily rendered chalk drawing of a beggar's family (cat. no. 84), dated *c.*1647–48, is considered to be a study, in the general sense, for the etching.

This is a superb impression of the second state, before the addition of cross-hatching to the half door; it is printed on European paper that lacks a watermark. The drypoint burr is rich throughout, but darkest in the area of the almsgiver's extended arm that serves to emphasize the focus on the act of charity. Seven engraved copies after this print are recorded, including two contemporary ones.

This copperplate is one of eighty-one of Rembrandt's etched plates that have survived, though not without being reworked at a much later date. For a concise account of the plates' history see cat. nos 102A and 102B. The light (posthumous) reworking in this plate may be observed in the shadows of the doorpost, the almsgiver, the area of the woman's bust, and elsewhere. All of the corners were originally square, but the lower left one was subsequently rounded and it is now much thinner and more uneven than the rest of the plate.[5]

IZ

1 For the most recent survey of the subject in Dutch prints, see Amsterdam 1997a.
2 Strauss & Van der Meulen 1979, p. 232, no. 1642/10.
3 Kahren Jones Hellerstedt first identified the subject as including a hurdy-gurdy player (Hellerstedt 1981).
4 G. Luijten, in Amsterdam 1997a, pp. 276–80, no. 56.
5 This description of the copperplate is taken directly from Erik Hinterding's account (Hinterding 1995, p. 52).

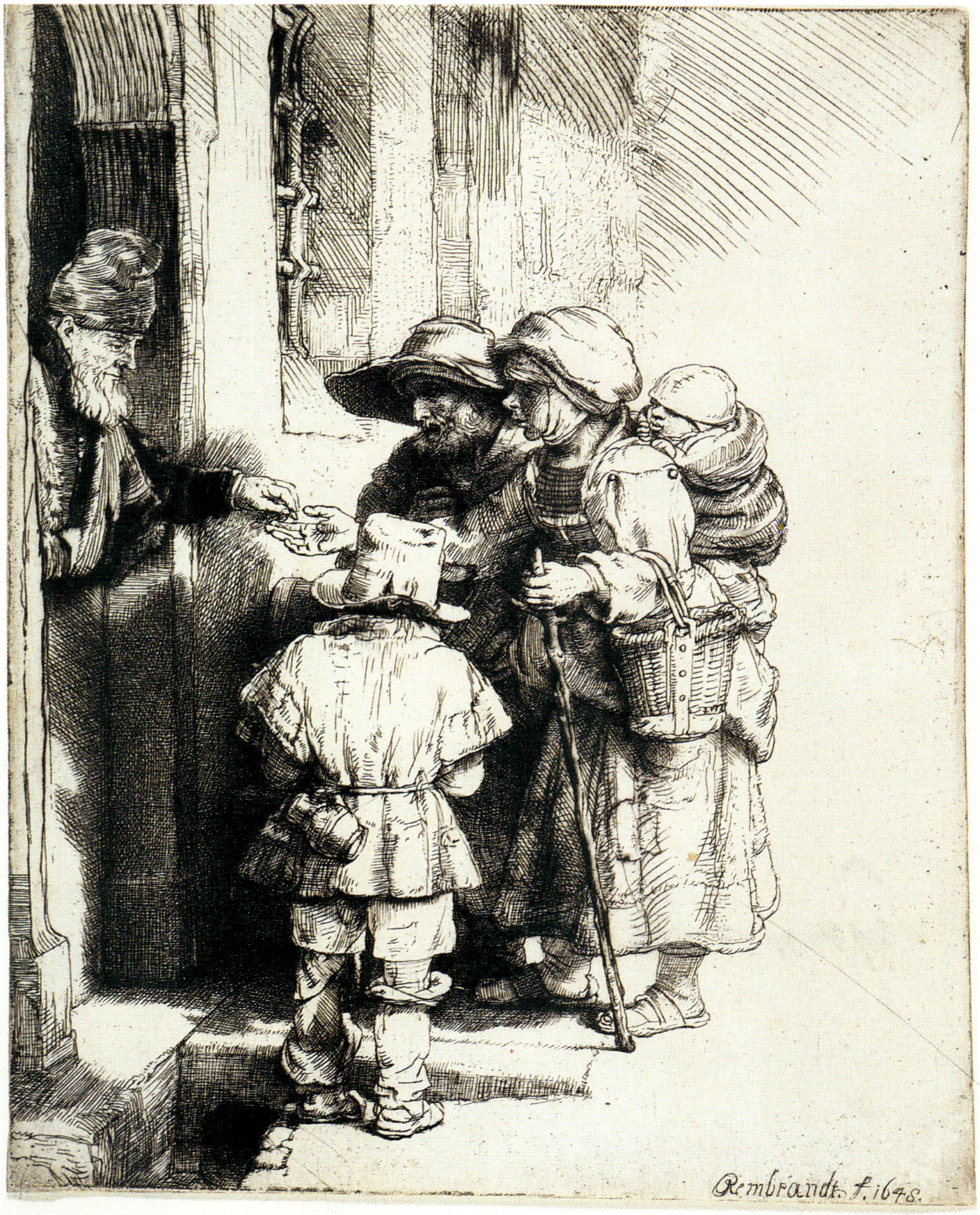

Cat. no. 110A

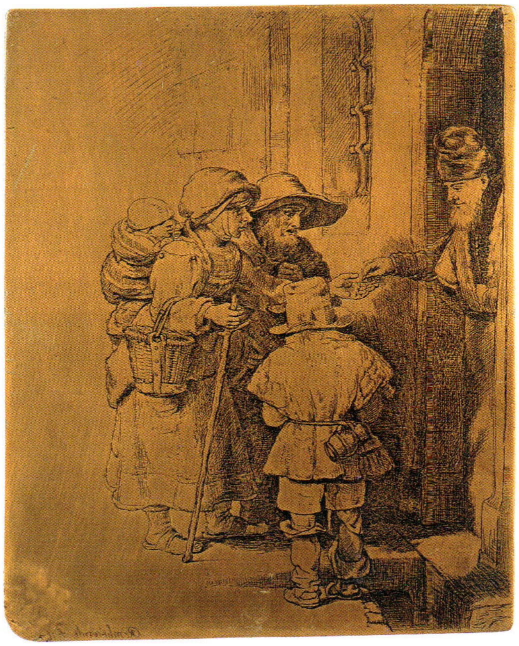

Cat. no. 110B

111

The Hundred Guilder Print
finished *c.*1649

Etching, drypoint and burin, printed on thick yellowish oriental (probably Japanese) paper
28.1 x 39.4 cm
National Gallery of Victoria, Melbourne; purchased 1891

LITERATURE: White & Boon B.74 II (second of two states); Hind 236; Münz 217 (1642/5); Biörklund BB.49-1. See also White 1969, vol. I, pp. 55–65; White 1969a, pp. 9–10, I, nos 1–8; Gregory & Zdanowicz 1988, p. 135, no. 74; B. Welzel, in Berlin / Amsterdam / London 1991–92b, pp. 242–4, [etching] cat. no. 27; Tümpel 1993, pp. 255–9; Zdanowicz 1993.

The *Hundred Guilder Print* is one of Rembrandt's best known, most popular and most ambitious compositions and also one of his key religious subjects. Its given name originated in the eighteenth century and refers to the considerable price that is said to have been fetched by an impression in Rembrandt's day.[1] The etching illustrates no single incident of Christ's ministry but rather synthesizes, in an entirely original way,[2] a sequence of events recounted in the nineteenth chapter of St Matthew's gospel. Here, following Matthew, Rembrandt portrays Christ healing the multitudes that followed him, responding to questions posed by the Pharisees (shown disputing among themselves at the left centre), rebuking Peter, and welcoming and blessing the little children. The young man who asked how he could attain salvation and was instructed to give his possessions to the poor is seated at left, his hand to his face as he ponders the words he has just heard. Among the crowd of sick and lame that pours in from the right is a camel, a reference to Christ's saying that it is easier for a camel to pass through the eye of the needle than it is for a rich man to enter heaven.

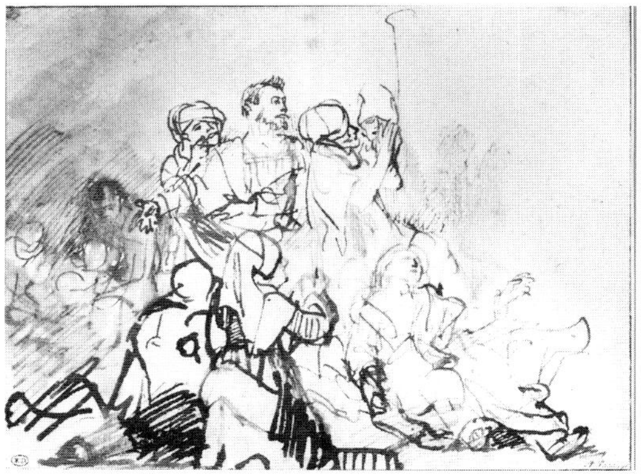

FIG. 111a
Rembrandt
Study (in reverse) for a Group of the Sick in The Hundred Guilder Print *c.*1639–40
Pen and ink and brush
14.4 x 18.5 cm
Staatliche Museen zu Berlin, Kupferstichkabinett

A poem by Rembrandt's contemporary H. F. Waterloos, which is inscribed on the verso of an impression of this print in the Bibliothèque Nationale, Paris, records an interpretation of the subject dating from Rembrandt's time:

And so Rembrandt drew from life, with his etching tool,
The Son of God in a world of sorrow,
Showing how, sixteen centuries ago,
He gave the sign of His miracles.
Here Jesus' hand helps the sick. And to the children
(Mark of Divinity!) He gives His blessing, and punishes those that hinder them.
Yet (oh!) the young man wails. And the scribes sneer
At the faith in Holiness that crowns Christ's Divinity.[3]

Paintings and engravings of the apostles performing acts of mercy have been cited as precedents for the composition. Within Rembrandt's oeuvre the grisaille of *St John the Baptist Preaching* (Bredius 555) (p. 67, fig. 12),[4] itself based on a painting by Rembrandt's teacher Pieter Lastman, might have provided the occasion for a first rehearsal of the idea, although *Christ and the Woman Taken in Adultery* of 1644 (Bredius 566) (National Gallery, London)[5] is closer to it in spirit.

The print is worked in a rich combination of etching, drypoint and, in places, the direct use of burin, and it has survived in just two states, with only minor differences of tonal adjustment between them. However, it does show clear evidence of a number of alterations that Rembrandt made at various stages of the design, though none make substantial changes to the composition as a whole. Among these are traces that show that the figure of Christ was originally smaller, and that his gesture was more exclusively directed to the figure of the mother and child who approach him from the left. The crowd of about forty people is arranged in groups that are linked not only through gesture, expression, and pose but also by the compassionate presence of Christ, who commands by virtue of his moral force rather than through action. Unifying all is the radiance of divine light.

Despite this unifying element, various parts of the composition show marked differences in the manner of etching, reflecting the print's long genesis. The Pharisees at the left are drawn in the loose, open manner seen in Rembrandt's prints of the late 1630s (cat. no. 104), while the extraordinarily rich and subtle modelling of other forms in light and shadow shows the supreme mastery of chiaroscuro that Rembrandt had attained by the late 1640s. Several preparatory drawings have survived, dated, on the basis of the print, from the late 1630s to the late 1640s. A study for the group of the sick immediately to Christ's right is important among these (Benesch 188) (fig. 111a).

The setting in which the event takes place is not entirely spatially coherent, as the ambiguous dark area extending in a tall, dome-like shape above Christ demonstrates. This does not function as an architectural detail, such as an applied arch, nor as a recessive space, but rather as a pictorial emphasis. Instead of being distracting, this lack of spatial realism heightens the conceptual aspects of the image, underlining the sense that this is a summation of Christian belief based on the gospels, a characterization of Christ.[6] Not surprisingly, Rembrandt's composition was appropriated by artists as early as the seventeenth century to illustrate other parts of the New Testament.[7]

If the *Hundred Guilder Print* can be said to have had an unusually long genesis, it had an even longer life. The copperplate itself survived intact until the late eighteenth century when it was acquired by Captain William Baillie, who 'retouched, and returned [it] to its original condition'.[8] Baillie reprinted the whole plate before cutting it into sections and, in a final attempt to prolong its existence, reprinted its dismembered remains.

Like most impressions of the *Hundred Guilder Print*, the one included here is printed on thick oriental paper, probably of Japanese origin; its yellowish hue casts the scene in a mellow golden light that is in keeping with the spirit of the subject. Three engraved copies after the print are recorded, as well as a set of copies made of the cut-up plate.

IZ

1 For a summary of the various explanations of the title's origins, see White 1969, pp. 55–6, note 29.
2 Tümpel 1993, p. 255.
3 B. Welzel, in Berlin / Amsterdam / London 1991–92b, p. 242, [etching] cat. no. 27, cites this translation and includes a transcription of the original Dutch verses.
4 This richly detailed composition might have been intended in preparation for an independent etching, which was never made (*Corpus*, vol. III, 1989, pp. 70–88, esp. pp. 79, 82, no. A106).
5 Tümpel 1993, p. 399, no. 63.
6 See note 2 above.
7 Münz 1952, vol. 2, p. 102.
8 Stogdon 1996, p. 56; see also Hinterding 1995, pp. 25–6.

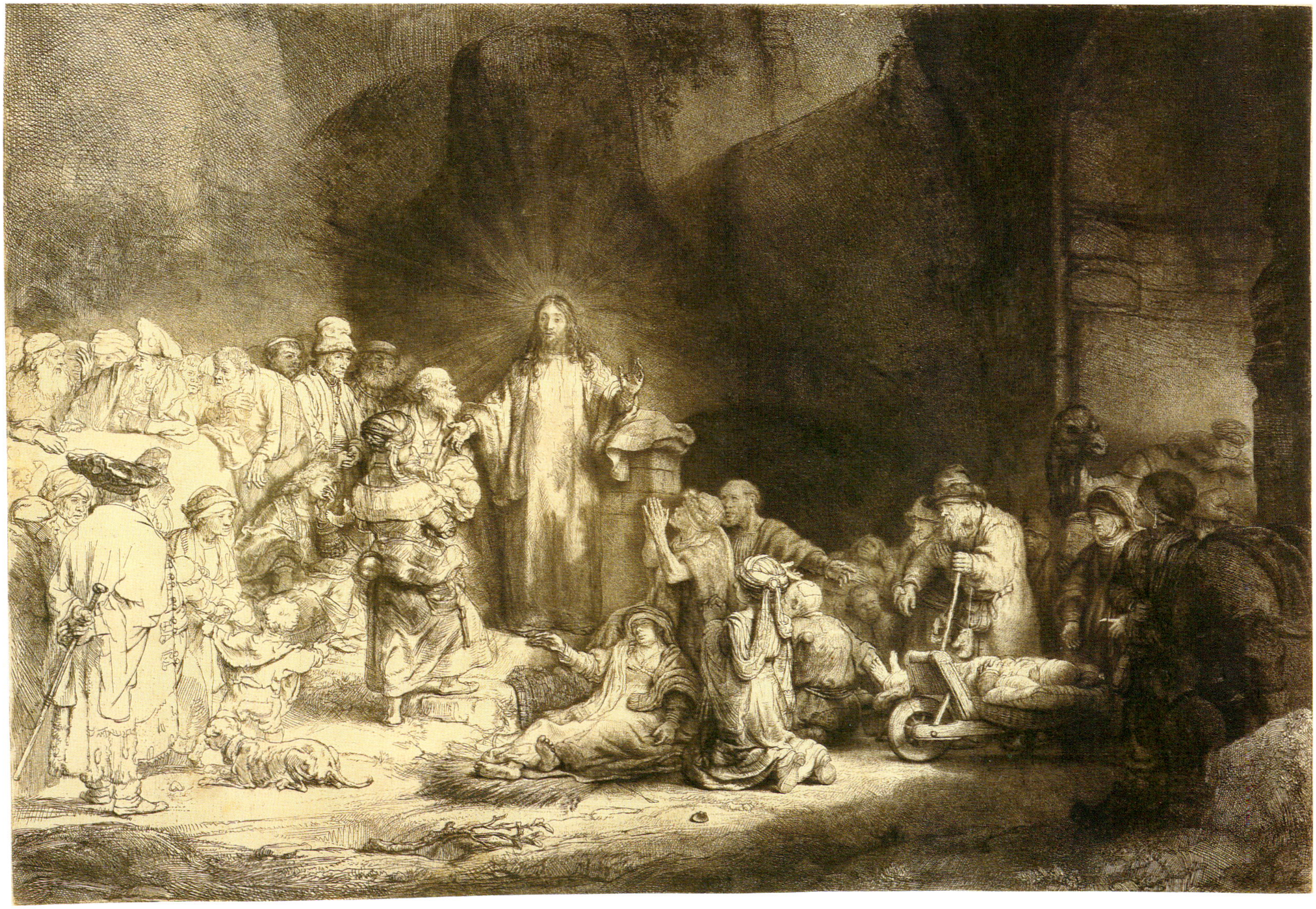

112
The Shell (*Conus marmoreus*)

Signed and dated in the plate lower left
Rembrandt f. 1650.
Etching, drypoint and burin
9.6 x 13.3 cm
Watermark: Foolscap with five-pointed collar; variant K.a.b.
National Gallery of Victoria, Melbourne; Felton Bequest 1973

LITERATURE: White & Boon B.159 II (second of three states); Hind 248; Münz 274; Biörklund BB.50-E. See also White 1969, vol. 1, p. 169; White 1969a, p. 12, IV, nos 22–24; Gregory & Zdanowicz 1988, p. 152, no. 123; Hoff 1975; H. Bevers, in Berlin / Amsterdam / London 1991–92b, pp. 248–50, [etching] cat. no. 29.

The *Shell* is Rembrandt's only still-life etching and one of the very few still lifes in his entire oeuvre. Made in the early 1650s, it shares the tonal concerns apparent in many of his etchings of this period. It depicts, in reverse, but probably according to the natural size of the specimen, the species *Conus marmoreus* L., a shell of Indian-Pacific origin[1] that may well have been included in Rembrandt's collection. Like earlier collections, those of the seventeenth century included not only works of art, but also works of nature, and Rembrandt's was no exception. The collection's detailed inventory, made in 1656, lists a 'great quantity of shells, coral branches ... and many other curios' stored on a shelf in the artist's *Kunst Caemer* (Art Chamber).[2]

Brought to Holland by the Dutch trading companies, shells became such popular collectors' items that, by the early seventeenth century, they were singled out for ridicule as emblems of pointless expenditure, akin to the mania for collecting tulips. In a famous emblem book of 1614, Roemer Visscher's *Sinnepoppen*, the picture of shells was accompanied by the motto 'It's sickening what a fool will spend his money on'.[3] In still-life paintings, shells appeared as symbols of mortality (the shell without the living creature), as well as of the beauty and wondrous inventiveness of nature that can rival art. Yet there is nothing in Rembrandt's depiction to suggest a dimension of symbolic meaning.

The print, which is densely worked with drypoint and burin over etching, exists in three states. The first, of which very few impressions survive, shows the specimen casting a shadow onto the flat surface on which it sits, but the background is blank and the space indeterminate (fig. 112a). In this state the print is comparable to Wenceslaus Hollar's etching of another species of conus, *Conus imperialis* L. (Parthey / Pennington 2195) (fig. 112b). Hollar's shell is portrayed totally abstracted from space, like a scientific specimen, against a blank sheet, while Rembrandt's shell, even in its unfinished state, is conceived as an object of individual experience, in real space.[4] In the second state Rembrandt took further steps to situate his shell within the chiaroscuro of the natural world by adding a dark background and making clear that the specimen sits on a table or shelf, perhaps like the shelf on which it was stored in his own art chamber. In the third and final state the highlights of the shell's spire were lightened in order to clarify its coiled shape and to emphasize the effect of the diagonal recession of the object in dark space.

This is a fine impression, probably from the first edition of the second state. It is printed on paper with the foolscap watermark that indicates a date around 1650–51. This watermark, possibly of French origin, is found in other impressions of this print as well as in a large number of other etchings.[5] Two engraved copies after Rembrandt's design are recorded.

IZ

1 Hoff 1975, p. 16.
2 Strauss & Van der Meulen 1979, p. 367, no. 1656/12 (no. 179).
3 Ackley 1981, p. 91, cat. no. 54.
4 Hoff 1975, p. 18.
5 I am grateful to Erik Hinterding for information on the watermark. His identification is based on beta-radiographs made at the National Gallery of Victoria by Lyndsay Knowles and Cobus van Breda.

FIG. 112a
Rembrandt
The Shell (Conus marmoreus)
Signed and dated 1650
Etching, burin and drypoint (first state)
9.7 x 13.2 cm
Rijksprentenkabinet, Rijksmuseum, Amsterdam

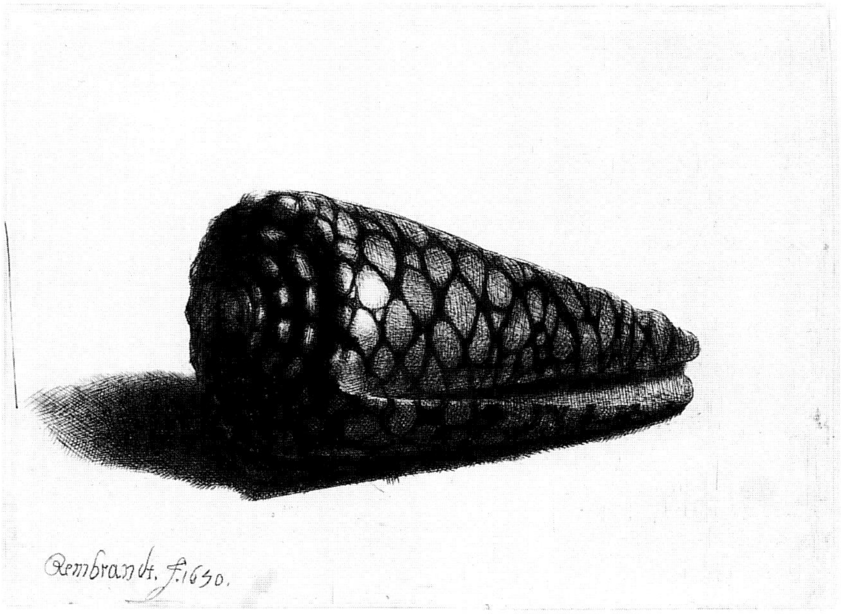

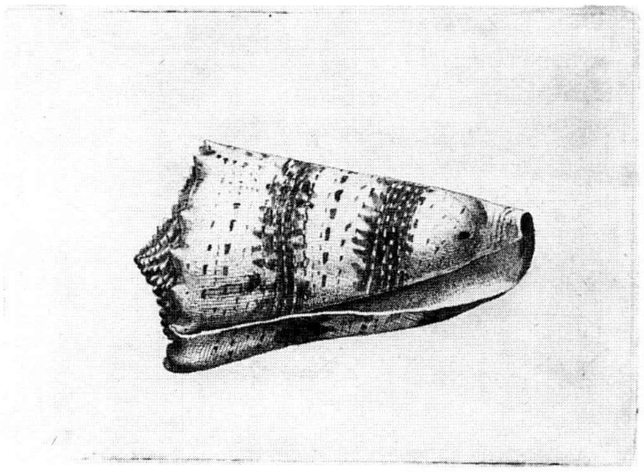

FIG. 112b
Wenceslaus Hollar 1607–1677
Conus imperialis L.
Etching
9.8 x 13.6 cm
Rijksprentenkabinet, Rijksmuseum, Amsterdam

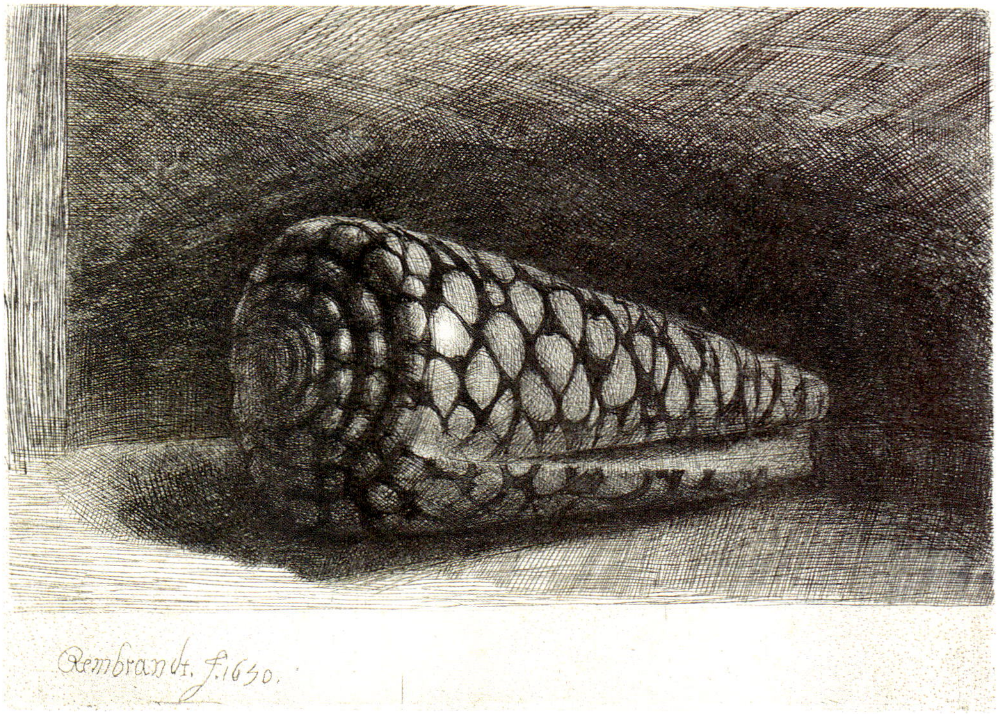
Rembrandt. f.1650.

113
'The Goldweigher's Field'

Signed and dated in the plate lower right
Rembrandt 1651
Etching and drypoint
12.1 x 32.1 cm
Watermark: Strasbourg Lily with initials 4WR; variant A.e.
National Gallery of Victoria, Melbourne; purchased 1891

LITERATURE: White & Boon B.234 (only state); Hind 249; Münz 167; Biörklund BB.51-A. See also White 1969, vol. 1, pp. 213–15; Gregory & Zdanowicz 1988, p. 146, no. 102; C. Schneider, in Washington 1990, pp. 260–1, cat. no. 84; H. Bevers, in Berlin / Amsterdam / London 1991–92b, pp. 245–7, [etching] cat. no. 28; Zdanowicz 1993; Cambridge 1993–94, cat. no. 30.

'The Goldweigher's Field' is Rembrandt's most expansive panorama, and belongs to the second of his two groups of etched landscapes made in the early 1650s. The title is a misnomer originating in the eighteenth century, based on a false identification of the location as the property of Johannes Wtenbogaert, Receiver General, whose portrait – known as *The Goldweigher* (B.281) – Rembrandt had etched in 1639 (fig. 8f). In fact the print represents a view towards Haarlem from the dunes outside the city, encompassing the village of Bloemendaal with its conspicuous church tower on the right, and Saxenburg, the country property of Christoffel Thijsz, in the middle left. In 1639 Rembrandt had purchased his house on the Jodenbreestraat from Thijsz, to whom he still owed money in 1651. Haarlem's skyline, dominated by its medieval Grote Kerk, appears on the far left horizon. Across the composition are the bleaching fields for the town's commercially important textile industry.[1]

The orientation of the view has been reversed in printing, and the six counterproofs that survive suggest that Rembrandt took pains to make the relative positions of the chief features correct. The very fact of reversal indicates that the view was drawn on the plate in the right direction, and could therefore conceivably have been made in the field. However, this is impossible to prove. A drawing of the scene, probably done on the spot, but from a higher point and a position slightly more to the right, shows the true orientation and might have been used as a reference for this print (cat. no. 90).

Although Rembrandt had used drypoint in his earlier landscapes, such as the *Omval* (cat. no. 107), he had never before wielded it so fluently, nor integrated it so well with etching, as in '*The Goldweigher's Field*'. He employs it in a primary way – but with a breathtaking economy – to structure the composition, to evocatively describe the details of the landscape, and to suggest atmosphere and space. Over a basic etched underlay of crossing shallow diagonals, the drypoint accents define the undulating flow of the fields as they recede towards the expansive horizon. The white of the paper is not relegated to a neutral function but plays a principal role in shaping the landscape in enveloping light.

Early in the seventeenth century the countryside around Haarlem inspired Hendrick Goltzius to produce sensitive drawings of panoramas made in the area (fig. 113a). These were the first of their kind in Holland and must count among the important precursors of Rembrandt's *'Goldweigher's Field'*.[2] However, of greater immediate impact were the etchings of another Haarlem artist, Hercules Segers. Rembrandt shared Segers's experimental approach to printmaking and owned a number of his etchings as well as one of his copperplates, which he boldly reworked (the *Flight into Egypt* altered from *Tobias and the Angel* (B.56)). Segers's *View of Amersfoort* (fig. 113b), or a comparable work, must have provided Rembrandt with a model for his own panoramic view of the environs of Haarlem.[3]

This is a very fine impression, with strong accents of burr and a very light film of ink tone covering the entire plate. The prominent vertical scratch at the left of the plate, visible in the earliest impressions, has here been carefully erased, presumably because it was thought to be disfiguring. The watermark, which occurs in other fine impressions of this print, probably indicates a French paper. This paper was used in what is likely to have been the first edition printed on Western paper. Other, later impressions are found printed on Paschal Lamb paper and these have reduced burr.[4]

IZ

1 For the exceptional nature of this landscape and its relationship to other views of Haarlem's bleaching fields, see Stone-Ferrier 1985, pp. 146–56.
2 Reznicek 1986, pp. 57–62.
3 Haverkamp Begemann 1973, p. 56, no. 30.
4 I am grateful to Erik Hinterding for information on the watermark. His identification is based on beta-radiographs made at the National Gallery of Victoria by Lyndsay Knowles and Cobus van Breda.

FIG. 113a
Hendrick Goltzius 1558–1617
Dune Landscape near Haarlem
Monogrammed and dated 1603
Pen and ink
8.7 x 15.3cm
Museum Boijmans Van Beuningen, Rotterdam

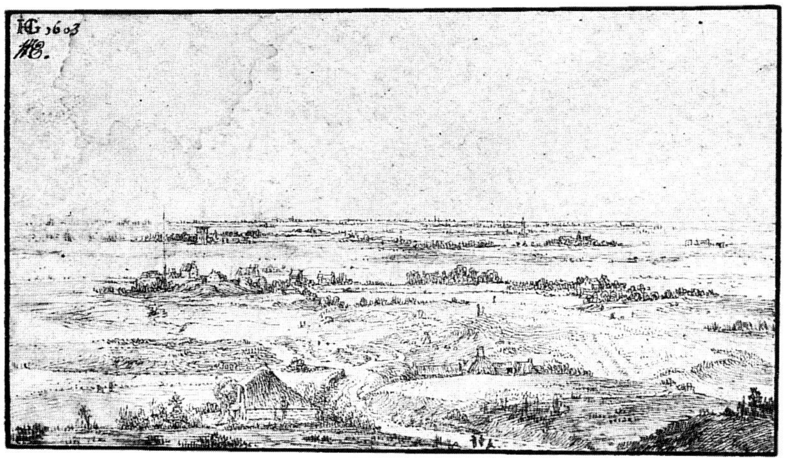

FIG. 113b
Hercules Segers *c.*1589/90–*c.*1638
View of Amersfoort
Etching and drypoint, printed in blue on greenish-blue prepared paper
8.6 x 30.1 cm
Rijksprentenkabinet, Rijksmuseum, Amsterdam

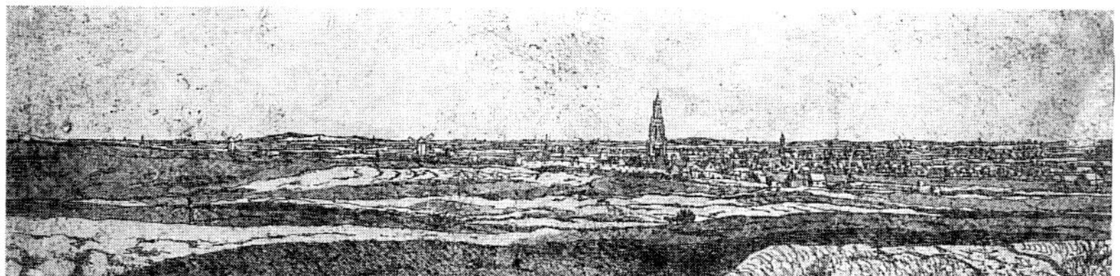

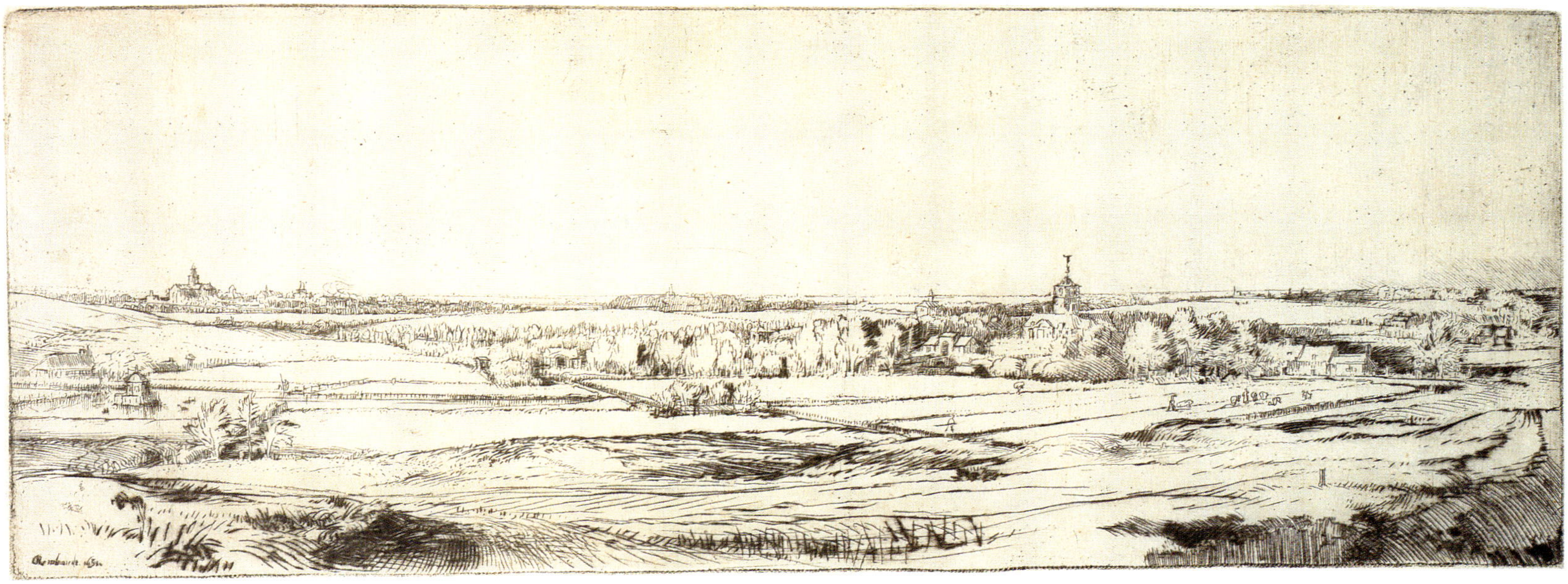

114
Clump of Trees with a Vista

Signed and dated in the plate lower right
Rembrandt f 1652
Drypoint, printed with plate tone
12.3 x 21.1 cm
Watermark: Paschal Lamb (undescribed variant)
Lent by the Syndics of The Fitzwilliam Museum, Cambridge

LITERATURE: White & Boon B.222 II (second of two states); Hind 263; Münz 169; Biörklund BB.52-D. See also White 1969, vol. 1, pp. 215–17; White 1969a, IX, p. 17, nos 48–53; C. Schneider, in Washington 1990, pp. 132–4, cat. no. 27; Cambridge 1993–94, cat. no. 39.

This is one of Rembrandt's last printed landscapes and one of only two that he executed entirely in drypoint. It was made a year after *'The Goldweigher's Field'* (cat. no. 113), in which he had been able to blend drypoint with etching so successfully. Here all the descriptive possibilities inherent in the blurred line and depth of tone that characterize the medium are exploited with complete mastery. Used in this way, drypoint often carries with it a sense of immediacy or spontaneity that can be startling. Unlike etching, in which the ink-bearing grooves are eroded chemically, drypoint is an entirely manual technique (see p. 387–8). It relies on the raised, ink-bearing burr for its specific effects, and, since this burr wears down rather quickly from each passage of the plate through the press, a plate worked in drypoint yields a very much smaller number of truly fresh impressions than an etched plate is capable of producing.[1]

The sense of spontaneity is particularly apparent in the first state of the print, which is thought to have been made in front of the subject, possibly somewhere along the Amstel River (fig. 114a). The first state has all the characteristics of a summary, impressionistic sketch, whose focus is the small building surrounded by trees, their shapes barely suggested. In the second state, presumably elaborated in the studio, the bottom edge of the plate was trimmed, and the trees were augmented into a sizeable copse and delineated with considerable detail.

Several drawings are related to this print though none shows the motif from precisely the same angle. The closest is a reed pen drawing in the Fitzwilliam Museum (Benesch 1274) (fig. 114b). This drawing may even have been made after the first state, in order to resolve ideas for the second and final state. The subject was also drawn from different vantage points by Rembrandt's pupils and is seen in a sheet by Jacob Koninck, which is finished in far greater detail than any of the master's depictions.[2] A painting previously attributed to Rembrandt, but now considered to have been painted in his manner in the late seventeenth or early eighteenth century, depicts the same subject in reverse.[3] Two modern engraved copies of this drypoint are recorded.

The richness and freshness of the saturated burr in this impression of the second state indicates that it is very early. A watermark with the Paschal Lamb motif would seem to indicate a Catholic origin for the paper, but its source has not yet been identified. Other very early impressions of this landscape, printed on Paschal Lamb paper, are known, and these constitute what is most probably the first edition.[4]

IZ

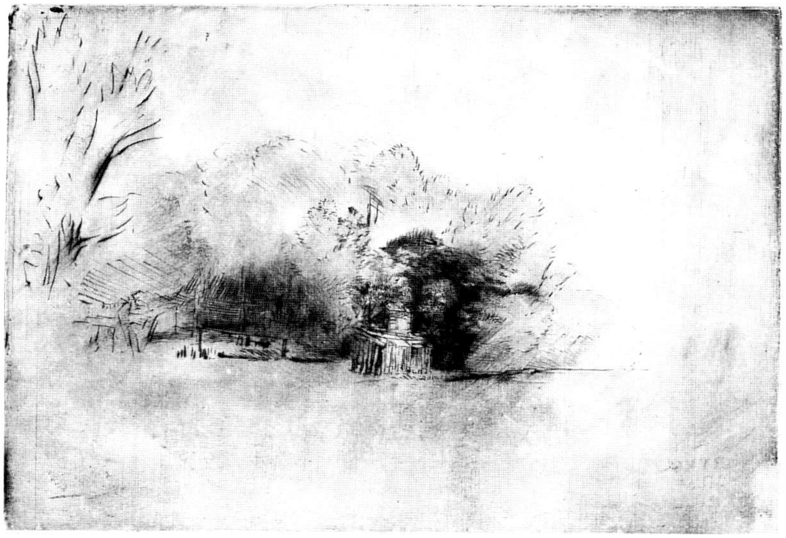

FIG. 114a
Rembrandt
Clump of Trees with a Vista 1652
Drypoint, printed with surface tone (first state)
15.6 x 21.1 cm
Rijksprentenkabinet, Rijksmuseum, Amsterdam
(See also p. 386, fig. 5)

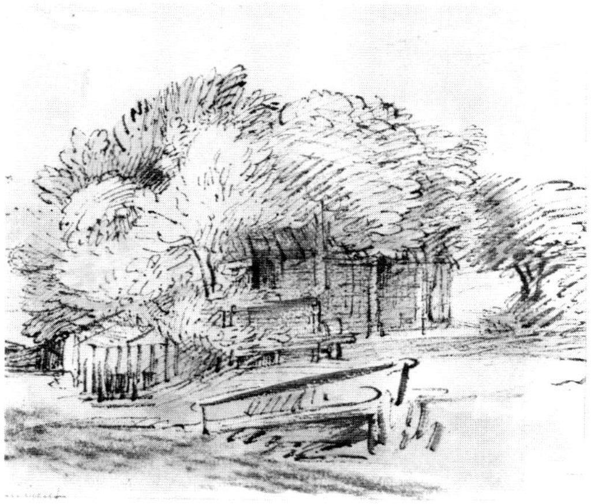

FIG. 114b
Rembrandt
Farmhouse beneath Trees with Footbridge
Pen and ink and brush, with chalk
15.7 x 18.1 cm
Fitzwilliam Museum, Cambridge

1 Erik Hinterding, referring to Morse 1966, suggests that, because seventeenth-century copperplates were cold hammered, they were harder than the rolled copperplates now in use, and therefore produced a more resilient burr, which probably resulted in the printing of as many as fifty good impressions, rather than the fifteen to twenty that has been assumed (Hinterding 1995, p. 10, note 14).
2 C. Schneider, in Washington 1990, pp. 130–1, repr. For other drawings of the same subject, see Washington 1990, pp. 128–31.
3 Schneider 1990, pp. 222–4, no. R11. The painting, *Evening Landscape with Cottage*, was formerly at the Montreal Museum of Fine Arts (its present whereabouts are unknown).
4 I am grateful to Erik Hinterding for information on paper with this watermark.

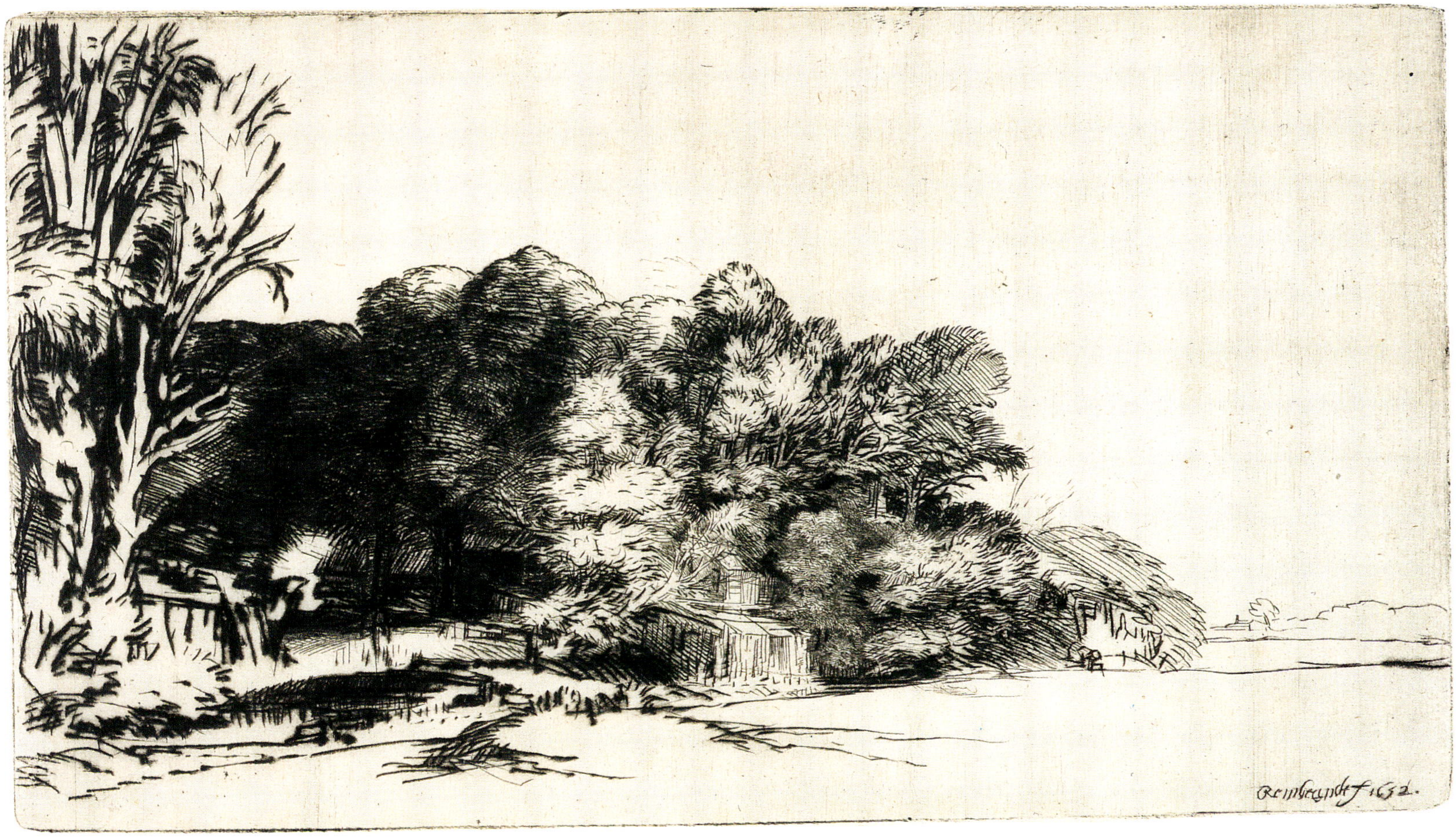
Rembrandt f 1652.

115A

Christ Crucified between the Two Thieves: 'The Three Crosses'

Signed and dated (only in this state) in the plate lower centre *Rembrandt. f. 1653*
Drypoint and burin, printed with plate tone on oriental (probably Japanese) paper, the highlights cleanly wiped
38.5 x 45.4 cm
Lent by the Syndics of The Fitzwilliam Museum, Cambridge

LITERATURE: White & Boon B.78 III (third of five states); Hind 270; Münz 223; Biörklund BB.53-A. See also White 1969, vol. 1, pp 75–9; White 1969a, pp. 18–19, X, nos 54–64; Carroll 1981, pp. 605–10; H. Bevers, in Berlin / Amsterdam / London 1991–92b, pp. 264–8, [etching] cat. no. 35.

115B

Christ Crucified between the Two Thieves: 'The Three Crosses' after 1653

Drypoint and burin, printed with surface tone, the wiping of the ink carefully manipulated on the plate
38.6 x 45.3 cm
Watermark: Strasbourg Bend; variant D'a.b.
National Gallery of Victoria, Melbourne; Felton Bequest 1949

LITERATURE: White & Boon B.78 IV (fourth of five states); Hind 270; Münz 223; Biörklund BB.53-A. See also White 1969, vol. 1, pp. 99–103; Gregory & Zdanowicz 1988, p. 137, no. 79.

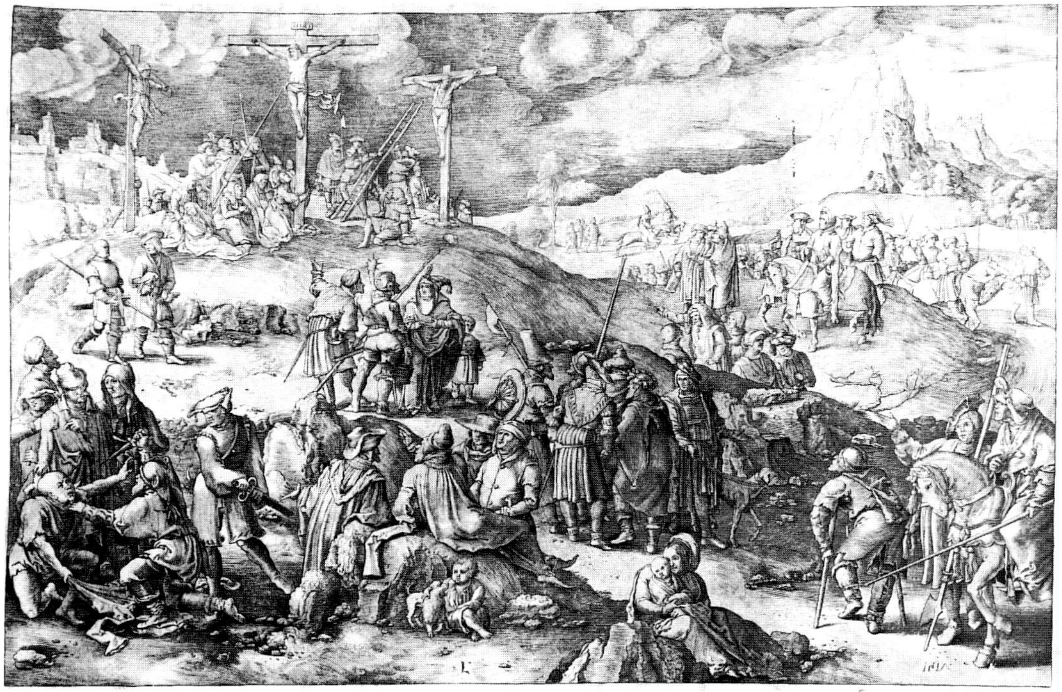

FIG. 115a
Lucas van Leyden 1494–1533
Golgotha
Monogrammed and dated 1517
Engraving
28.6 x 41.2 cm
Rijksprentenkabinet, Rijksmuseum, Amsterdam

The *Three Crosses* is Rembrandt's grandest and most powerful print. Large in format, and masterly in concept and execution, it exists in two versions. The transformation from the early representation (cat. no. 115A) to the later one (cat. no. 115B) bears witness to an artistic decision of great originality that is unprecedented in the history of printmaking.

By the early 1650s, drypoint had assumed such an important role for Rembrandt that he decided to use it in an entirely independent way, not combined with other intaglio techniques. His first pure drypoints were landscapes that appear so fresh and spontaneous as to convey the impression that they were done outdoors in front of the subject (cat. no. 114). Somewhat earlier, in the *Hundred Guilder Print* (cat. no. 111) and in the *Portrait of Jan Six* (B.285) (fig. 28b), both dating from the late 1640s, he demonstrated his ability to use the drypoint needle with the utmost delicacy and subtlety as though it were, above all, a means of attaining seamless tone. Finally, in his two late, large religious prints – the *Three Crosses* and the *Ecce Homo* (cat. no. 118), which may have been intended as pendants – he exploited those qualities of drypoint that are able to convey powerful drama.

The third state of the *Three Crosses* (cat. no. 115A) differs in tonal and psychological focus, rather than in discrete details, from the preceding two. It represents the final form of the earlier version of the subject, which depicts the moments following Christ's death and the sudden conversion of the Centurion, who has dismounted from his horse and fallen to his knees. The Gospel of Luke (23:44–48) is usually cited as the scriptural source. Rembrandt gives us a visionary interpretation of the scene that combines sudden spiritual revelation with death, destruction and overwhelming grief. Light descends from a point above the central Cross, slashing the darkness as it falls in a cone, illuminating the ground as well as the two thieves crucified on either side. People flee or fall to the ground. To the right John, the beloved apostle, raises his hands to his head in a gesture of despair, while the Virgin has collapsed and is being assisted by her female attendants.

The Passion of Christ had always been an important subject for printmakers, who frequently depicted it in the form of extensive, formal narrative series, with the Crucifixion itself as the culminating point, though the series sometimes also extended to the Resurrection. Lucas van Leyden engraved several of these cycles, and his large-format *Golgotha* of 1517 (B.74) (fig. 115a), which depicts the Crucifixion within a wide landscape crowded with figures, represents a type that was important in Netherlandish art during

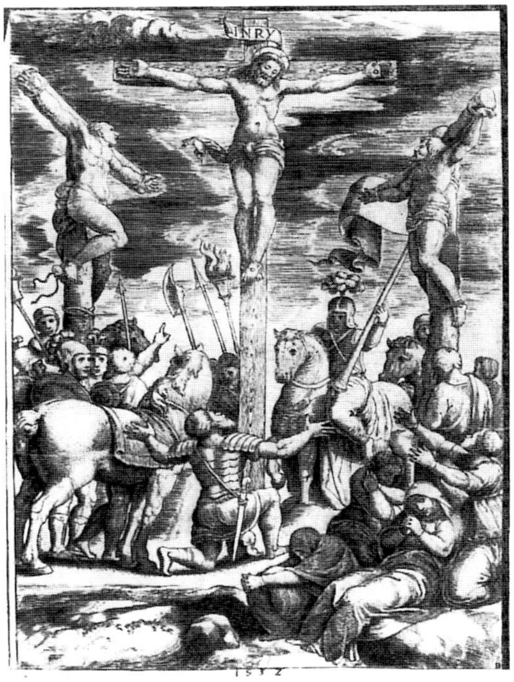

FIG. 115b
Master of the Die
The Conversion of the Centurion
Dated 1532
Engraving
21.6 x 15.5 cm
From a reproduction

the fifteenth and sixteenth centuries – but one that had become uncommon by the seventeenth.[1] This engraving may have provided Rembrandt with a starting point for his own depiction, which is so different from his other versions.[2] However, Lucas's engraving lacks the confronting and deep emotional engagement that is fundamental to Rembrandt's portrayal. The motif of the Centurion is even more directly dependent on an earlier source: a print by an Italian engraver called the Master of the Die (B.3) (fig. 115b).[3] Here, too, Rembrandt invests the motif with an inner drama lacking in his model.

Most surviving impressions of this state seem to have been printed on European paper but each one differs according to the way it has been inked.[4] The impression included here (cat. no. 115A) is on oriental paper and it has been printed with plate tone, but with the highlights cleanly wiped.

Some time after having finished the third state, which he dated 1653, Rembrandt decided to create another version of the subject. Instead of using a new plate he chose to reuse the existing one. In order to prepare it for his new idea he first had to obliterate what had already been done, by burnishing out the existing design and polishing back the copperplate as far as he was able; he then reingraved it with his new design, a process that has been described as one of the most inspired defacements in the history of art.[5] In the fourth state of the *Three Crosses* (cat. no. 115B) Rembrandt suppressed all traces of the redemptive aspects of the subject, turning instead to the darkest parts of the narrative – Christ's feeling of complete abandonment and his agonized death throes when darkness fell over all the earth, and the veil of the Temple was rent. The three crosses maintain their original positions, dividing the composition into four parts, but most other details have changed; this is not an elaboration of the earlier subject, but a very different interpretation of the same theme. In place of the Centurion's horse at the left of the central Cross, Rembrandt introduced a horseman with a distinctive tall hat who holds a lance; he is clearly based on Pisanello's medallion of Gian Francesco Gonzaga (fig. 115c). Further to the left is a rearing horse, adapted from an engraving of one of the Capitoline horsemen.[6]

Due to its compositional grandeur, the simplicity of its component parts, and its style of delineation, the fourth state of the *Three Crosses* has usually been dated to the 1660s. The summary and angular delineation of the helmeted soldier holding a sword, to the left of Christ – a quality of line that results in part from the natural resistance of the drypoint tool when it is scored deeply into the copper – is also comparable with Rembrandt's late drawings executed with the reed pen, while the commander's headgear is repeated in the painting of Claudius Civilis, made *c.*1661–62 (Bredius 482) (p. 0, fig. 9).

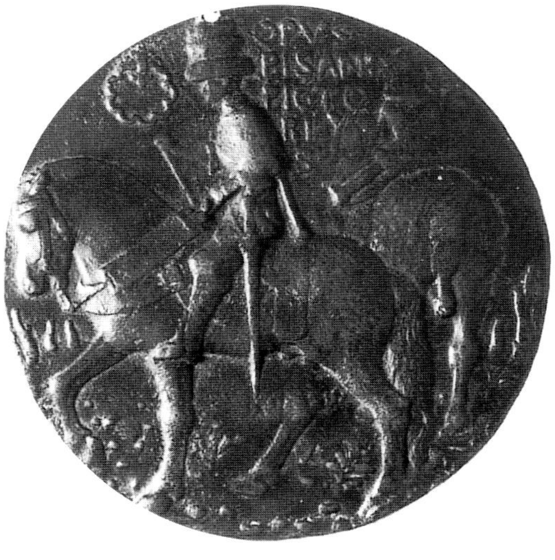

FIG. 115c
Antonio Pisano, called Pisanello
Italian, before 1395–1455
Medal of Gian Francesco Gonzaga
From a reproduction

Melbourne's impression of the fourth state is superb and is richly inked, with the imprint of sharp burr clearly visible in many areas. The verso also bears the deep imprint of the drypoint burr and parts of the composition have been transferred to the back through the seepage of oily ink. However, what is particularly interesting about this sheet is that its physical characteristics seem to indicate that it came from the very ream of paper that was used for an impression of *St Jerome Reading in an Italian Landscape* (cat. no. 116).[7] Since the St Jerome impression dates from around 1653 – the year in which the third state of the *Three Crosses* was completed – interesting questions are raised about Rembrandt's workshop practice as far as his prints are concerned, and they might, perhaps, throw new light on the dating of the fourth state.

A fifth state of this print carries the inscription of the publisher, Frans Carlese, who is otherwise unknown. Three engraved copies after this print have been recorded, one each of the first, third and fourth states.

IZ

1 H. Bevers, in Berlin / Amsterdam / London 1991–92b, p. 264, [etching] cat. no. 35.
2 *Christ on the Cross*, 1631 (Bredius / Gerson 1969, no. 543A; *Corpus*, vol. I, 1982, no. A35) is Rembrandt's only painting of this subject though of course there are also a number of paintings depicting other aspects of the Passion. The prints are *Christ Crucified between the Two Thieves: An Oval Plate*, *c.*1641 (B.79); *The Crucifixion*, *c.*1635 (B.80).
3 For the *Conversion of the Centurion* (B.3), after a drawing in the manner of Raphael, see *The Illustrated Bartsch*, vol. 29, 1982, p. 160.
4 White 1969, p. 79.
5 White 1969, p. 99.
6 Münz 1952, vol. 1, fig. 70.
7 This observation, which raises a number of questions, was made by Erik Hinterding, who based it on beta-radiographs made at the National Gallery of Victoria by Lyndsay Knowles and Cobus van Breda, and on the documentation of the sheet's physical characteristics.

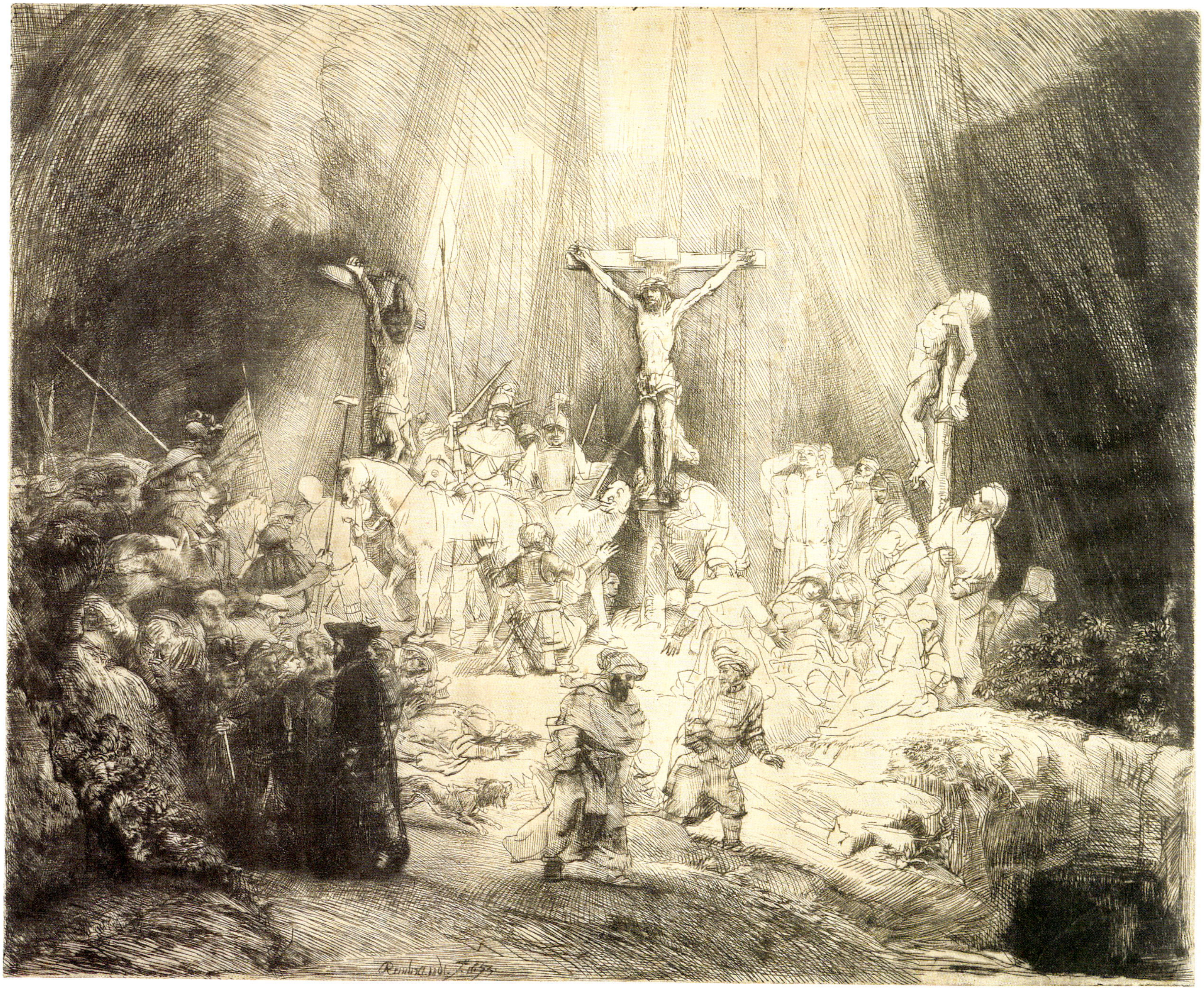

Cat. no. 115A

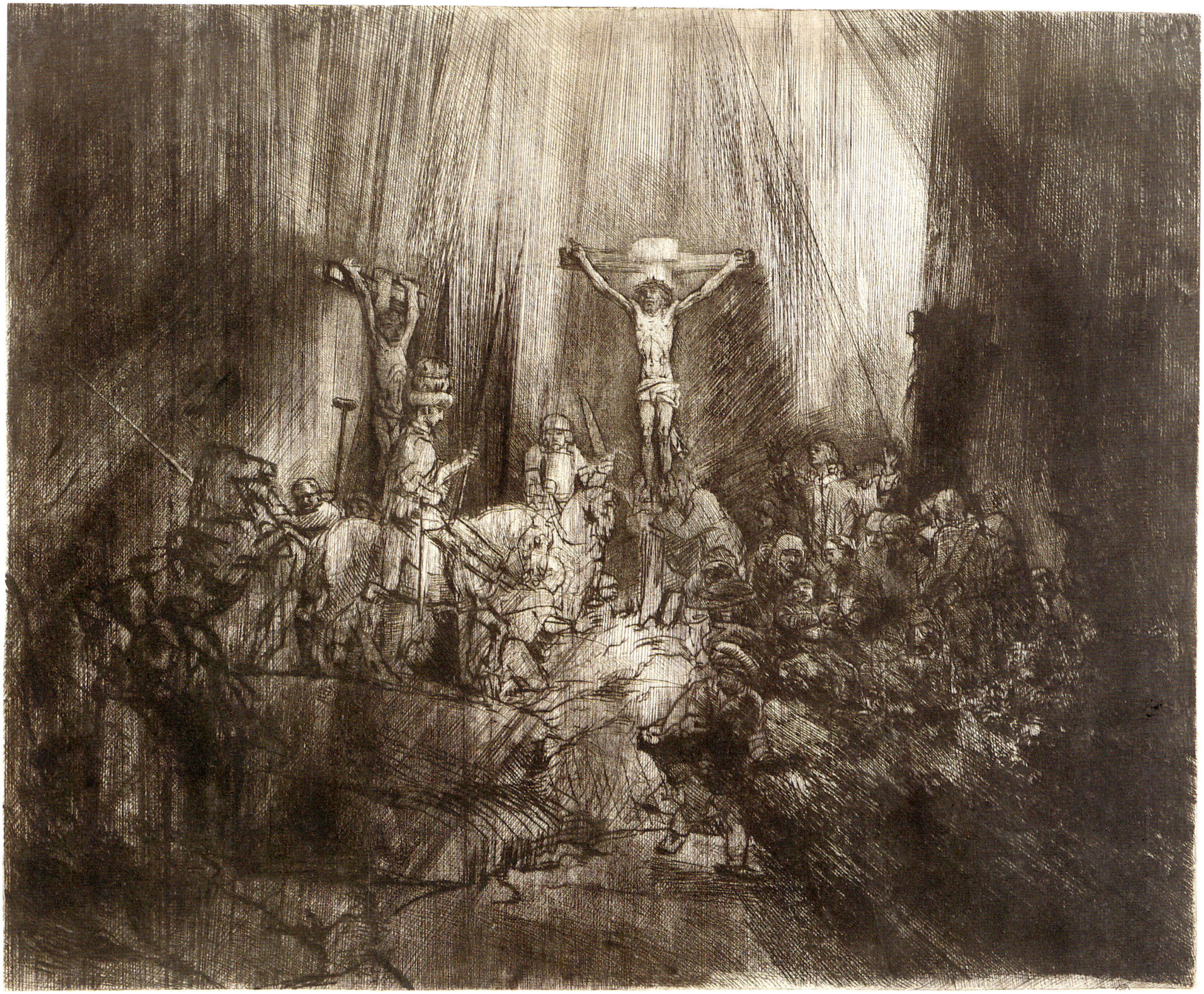

Cat. no. 115B

116

St Jerome Reading in an Italian Landscape

*c.*1653–54

Etching, drypoint and burin, with some sulphur tint etching
26.0 x 21.1 cm
Watermark: Strasbourg Bend; variant D'a.a.
National Gallery of Victoria, Melbourne;
Felton Bequest 1976

LITERATURE: White & Boon B.104 II (second of two states); Hind 267 (1653); Münz 249 (1651–52); Biörklund BB.53-3. See also White 1969, vol. 1, pp. 220–2; Gregory & Zdanowicz 1988, p. 143, no. 94; C. Schneider, in Washington 1990, pp. 166–70, cat. nos 42, 43 (1650–52); H. Bevers, in Berlin / Amsterdam / London 1991–92b, pp. 254–5, [etching] cat. no. 31; Cambridge 1993–94, cat. no. 49.

Renowned for his vast learning, especially his knowledge of the classics, St Jerome (*c.*341–420) was commissioned by Pope Damasus I (366–384) to translate the Bible from Greek and Hebrew sources into Latin; this translation became authorized by the Church of Rome as the Vulgate. Jerome spent several years living as a hermit in the desert wilderness and is known for his asceticism, which earned him the censure of the early Protestant Reformers.[1] A favourite of the Renaissance humanists for his learning, he was the subject of numerous portrayals in art from the fifteenth century onwards. Dürer's three engravings (B.59–61) (fig. 2b)and his painting of the scholar meditating on the vanity of earthly things (Museu Nacional de Arte Antiga) are the most famous portrayals of the saint in northern art before Rembrandt's time. Among Jerome's main attributes are the cardinal's hat and the lion that became his companion after he had taken a thorn from its paw. To these was added the flowering ancient tree stump that might symbolize the regenerative powers of Christian contemplation and the flowering of wisdom in old age.[2] In seventeenth-century Catholic Europe the preferred attribute for depictions of the saint was the trumpet of the Last Judgement.[3]

Images of St Jerome span Rembrandt's entire career as a printmaker, beginning with the large, early *St Jerome Kneeling*, *c.*1629 (B.106), which portrays him penitent in the wilderness, and concluding with this, his last depiction of the saint, as scholar in an Italian landscape. It is a mature amalgamation of several of the distinctive features of Rembrandt's art: his interest in a humanized landscape, his considered appropriation of foreign artistic traditions, and the application of his keen observation of human behaviour to traditional subject matter.

St Jerome sits on a rocky outcrop beside a leafy, truncated tree, absorbed in reading, wearing not the cardinal's distinctive hat but a sun-hat to shield his eyes from the light; one of his sandals has been casually cast off.[4] The lion standing guard to protect him from intruders confirms the saint's identity, while the small bird that perches on the tree stump may be a reminiscence of the dove as Holy Spirit, through which Jerome heard the word of God.[5] The landscape in the right distance is distinctly Venetian in flavour, and reflects Rembrandt's study of northern Italian drawings and prints, especially those of Titian's circle. Giulio Campagnola's engraving of St Jerome (Hind 7) has been cited as a source,[6] as has Cornelis Cort's engraving after Bruegel (Bastelaer 7). One of the drawings that Rembrandt owned was a landscape traditionally attributed to Domenico Campagnola, which he reworked, covering the original delicate pen and ink lines with the broad strokes of a reed pen (fig. 116a).

This etching is one of the few for which a summary preparatory drawing, also done with a reed pen, has survived (Benesch 886) (fig. 116b). It shows how inventively Rembrandt approached his work: while the drawing indicates that he initially thought of placing the foreground in shade, he reconsidered the idea as he worked on the copperplate and, by leaving this area blank, was able to suggest that it is flooded in light. He varied the degree of detail and technical finish throughout the plate, yet left no doubt that what remains is a finished composition.[7]

In this impression of the second state of the etching (after a minor change was made, widening the struts of the bridge), the burr remains strong but is not so abundantly saturated with ink as in the earliest impressions of the first and second states. The watermark, which is French, confirms that this is an early impression, which comes from the first edition that was printed on European paper. Moreover, close examination of the paper's physical characteristics suggests that this sheet came from the same ream as the sheet on which Melbourne's impression of the fourth state of the *Three Crosses* was printed (cat. no. 115B).[8]

IZ

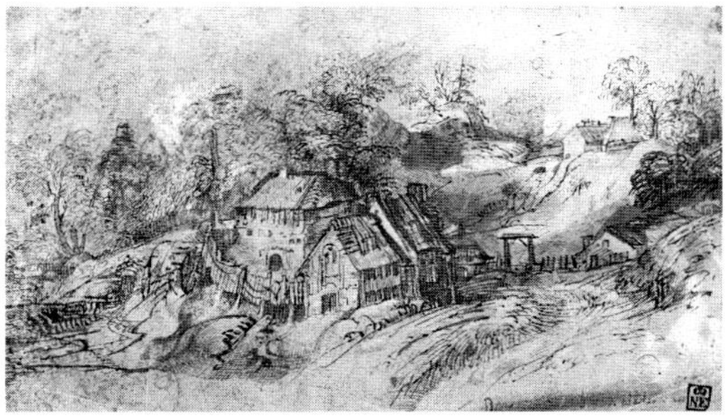

FIG. 116a
Attributed to Domenico Campagnola (Italian, 1500–1564) and Rembrandt
Mountainous Landscape with Houses and Watermill
reworked *c.*1648–52
Pen and ink and brush
15.9 x 27.7 cm
Szépmüvészeti Múzeum, Budapest

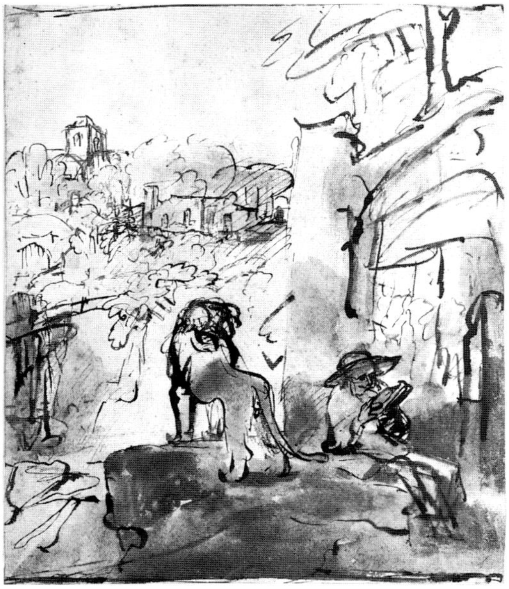

FIG. 116b
Rembrandt
St Jerome Reading in a Landscape
Pen and ink and brush
26.0 x 20.4 cm
Hamburger Kunsthalle, Hamburg
Copyright Elke Walford, Hamburg

1 Rice 1985, ch. 6, esp. pp. 138–43.
2 Kuretsky 1974; Dickey 1986, p. 256.
3 Rice 1985, p. 172.
4 H. Bevers, in Berlin / Amsterdam / London 1991–92b, p. 254, note 1, quotes C. Wiebel, *Askese und Endlichkeitsdemut in den italienischen Renaissance: Ikonologische Studien zum Bild des heiligen Hieronymus*, Weinheim, 1988, and offers the reminder that the removed shoes have a symbolic meaning in traditional iconography, indicating a preparedness to meet God.
5 Rice 1985, p. 189.
6 H. Bevers, in Berlin / Amsterdam / London 1991–92b, p. 254, [etching] cat. no. 31.
7 This was not thought to be the case by Gersaint and Bartsch, who both considered the plate to be unfinished.
8 I am grateful to Erik Hinterding for information on the watermark. His identification is based on beta-radiographs made at the National Gallery of Victoria by Lyndsay Knowles and Cobus van Breda and their documentation of the sheet's physical characteristics.

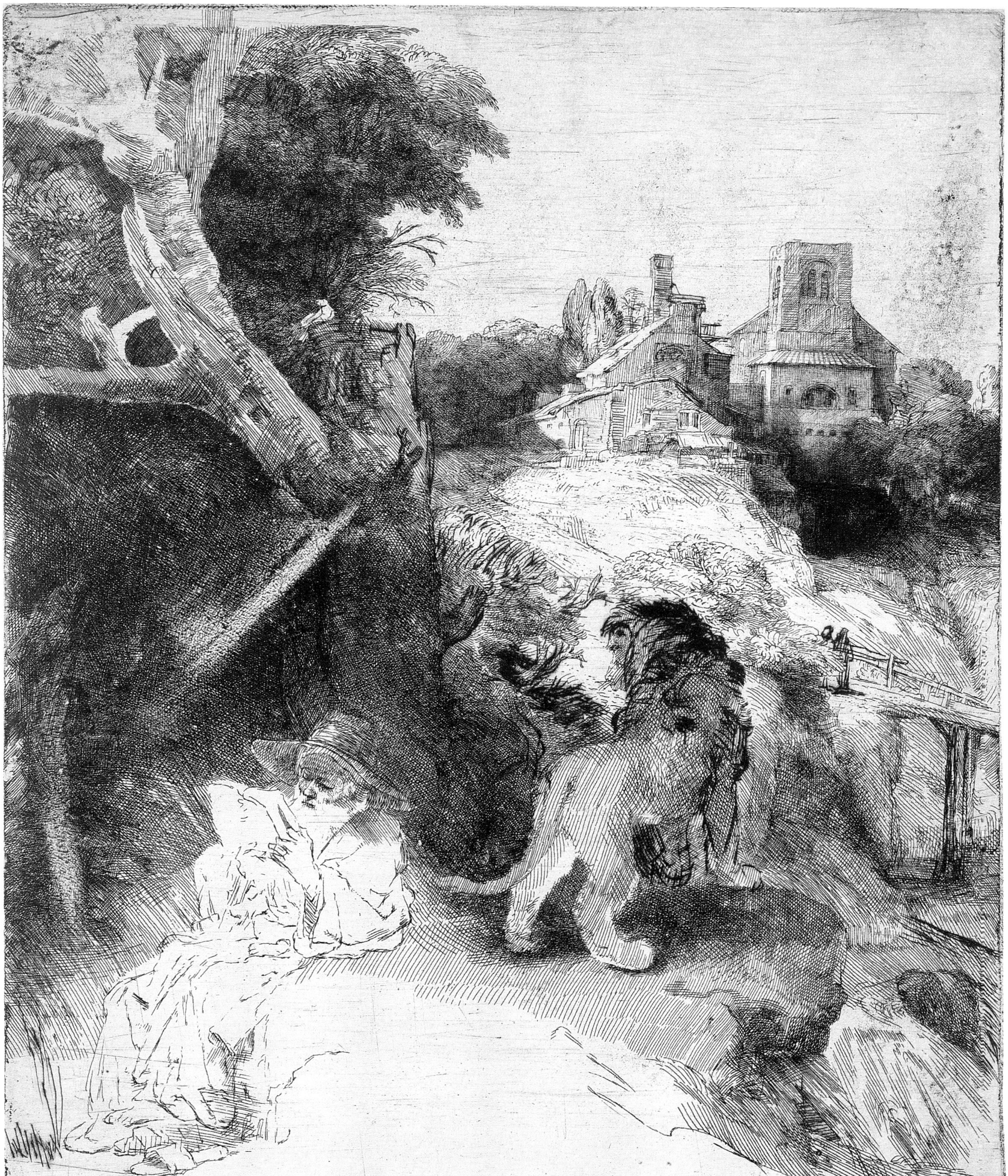

117A
The Entombment
*c.*1654

Etching touched with drypoint, printed on oriental (probably Chinese) paper
20.9 x 16.1 cm
The Board of Trustees of the Victoria & Albert Museum, London

LITERATURE: White & Boon B.86 I (first of four states); Hind 281; Münz 241 (1658/59); Biörklund BB.54-2. See also Boston / New York 1969–70, pp. 123–4, cat. nos 78–86; White 1969, vol. 1, pp. 81–4; White 1969a, nos 75–82; Scallen 1997.

117B
The Entombment
*c.*1654

Etching, drypoint and burin, printed with surface tone on yellowish oriental (probably Japanese) paper
21.1 x 16.1 cm
Trustees of the British Museum, London

LITERATURE: White & Boon B.86 III (third of four states).

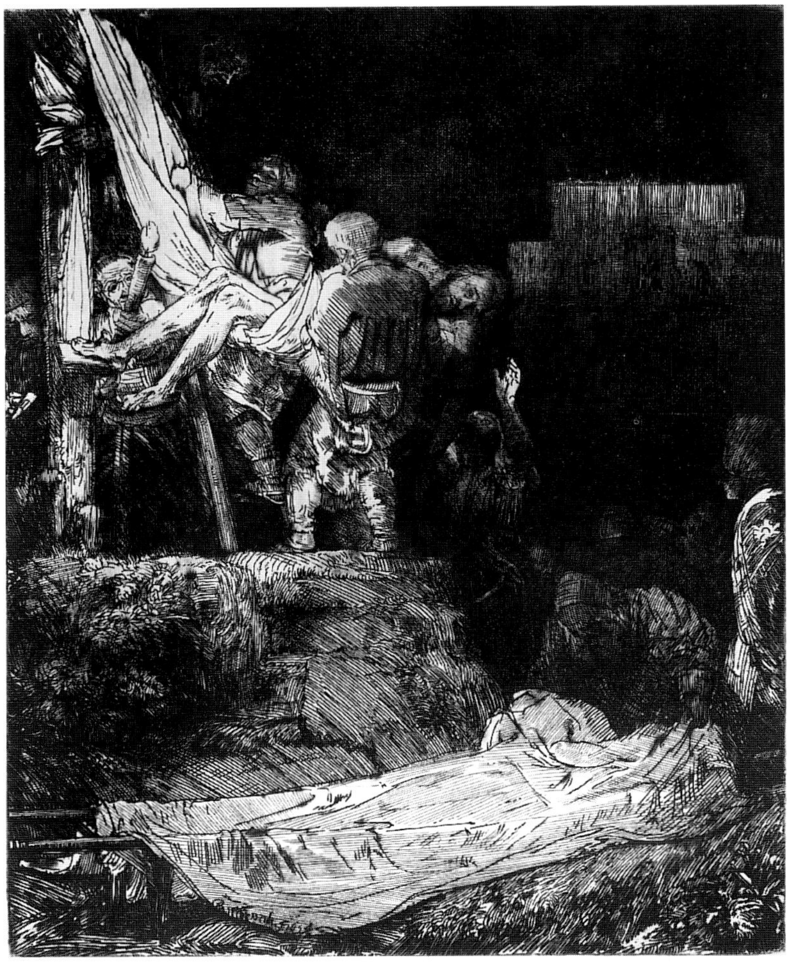

FIG. 117a
Rembrandt
The Descent from the Cross by Torchlight
Signed and dated 1654
Etching and drypoint
21.0 x 16.1 cm
Rijksprentenkabinet, Rijksmuseum, Amsterdam

Although this etching is not inscribed in the plate it is usually grouped with three others, two of them dated 1654.[1] All four share the same vertical format and three of them deal with events following the Crucifixion – a subject Rembrandt had etched in the previous year (cat. nos 115A, 115B). All of these etchings employ a widely spaced mesh of regular hatching, at least in their initial states.

The account of the burial of Christ is substantially the same in all four gospels. After the Crucifixion, Joseph of Arimathea, a disciple of Jesus, received Pilate's permission to remove Christ's body from the Cross (B.83) (fig. 117a) and bury it in a rock-hewn sepulchre. The burial was carried out at night and witnessed by Nicodemus (John 19), Mary Magdalene and another Mary (Matthew 27, Mark 15), and the women of Galilee (Luke 23). The Virgin is not mentioned in Scripture, but, as chief mourner, she is traditionally represented at the scene. The first state of the etching clearly depicts the details of the event, which takes place within a tall arched vault bisected by a stone ledge on which sit two skulls. The mourners are grouped in an inverted arc in the lower part of the composition. Along the very bottom, bathed in light, is the body of the dead Christ, which is being lowered into the tomb. At his feet is his grieving mother sitting in a pose not entirely dissimilar from that which she assumes in Rembrandt's small etching of 1654, where she is shown lovingly cradling her infant son in her arms (B.62). That print, inspired by Andrea Mantegna's engraving of the Virgin and Child (B.8), points to a formative influence that underlies Rembrandt's etching style around the mid-1650s: Mantegna's disciplined engraved hatching, as well as his formal drawing style, which Rembrandt adapted with complete fluency to etching.[2] The restraint inherent in this method enabled him to create in the first state of the *Entombment* an atmosphere of poignant stillness, while simultaneously evoking a sense of the emotional intensity of his subject.[3]

The idea for the setting, and for such details as the skulls, derives from a drawing by Polidoro da Caravaggio (*c.*1499–*c.*1543), which Rembrandt copied (Benesch 1208) (fig. 117b). However, in his etching he adapted Polidoro's graceful and elegiac horizontal composition, changing the format into a dramatic vertical and suffusing the subject with deeply felt sorrow. The glowing light that emanates from the area of the tomb is achieved with the simplest of means, which seem to transform blank paper into the very source of light.

Having completed a perfectly coherent and moving rendering of the subject, Rembrandt nonetheless was impelled to transform it into a literal night scene (cat. no. 117B). Using the drypoint needle and burin he progressively added a dense mesh of shading, and clarified the architectural definition, until the print reached its final form in the fourth state. All of the dark states of this etching, from the second state forward, are notable for the enormous variety of ways in which they were inked, to such an extent that it is hard to speak of an edition. Rather, each individual impression has been treated as if it were a monotype, a unique impression. The present third state includes substantial amounts of surface tone, especially noticeable in the lightly etched areas (such as the Virgin's features and those of the bearded man standing behind her); the lightest highlight is reserved for a small area on Christ's body.

The procedures used in making this etching not only demonstrate Rembrandt's experimental attitude to printmaking, they also illustrate what has been described as the underlying feature in the development of Dutch printmaking during the seventeenth century: the search for printed tone, especially the quest for dark tonalities, that was to culminate in the invention of mezzotint.[4] Some impressions of the last state of this print were so heavily inked that Rembrandt actually painted in white highlights over the finished print. Both impressions of the *Entombment* included here are printed on oriental paper, which Rembrandt first began using in the second half of the 1640s. Not surprisingly for a print that survives in so many variant impressions, there are no engraved copies of it recorded.

IZ

1 The three etchings are *The Presentation in the Temple* (B.50) (fig. 2d); *The Descent from the Cross by Torchlight*, 1654 (B.83) (fig. 117a); and *Christ at Emmaus: The Larger Plate*, 1654 (B.87).

2 Rembrandt's interest in Mantegna is witnessed not only in specific motifs that he borrowed, but in the copies he made after Mantegna's drawings, at least one of which copies has survived: *The Calumny of Apelles* (Benesch 1207) (British Museum, London); see also Royalton-Kisch 1992, pp. 123–5, cat. no. 53. The 1656 inventory of Rembrandt's art collection lists a 'precious book of Andrea Mantegna', the contents of which are unknown (Strauss & Van der Meulen 1979, p. 369, no. 1656/12 (no. 200)).

3 Münz 1952, vol. 1, p. 39.

4 Ackley 1981, pp. xix–xxvi. Mezzotint is a purely tonal form of engraving, in which the copperplate is pitted with a spiked rocking tool so as to create a surface covered with burr. If the plate were inked and printed at this stage it would print a solid black. Light tones are created by burnishing down the burr, since the smaller the burr the less ink it holds and, consequently, the lighter it prints. Mezzotint is fundamentally unlike etching, since the artist has to work from dark to light.

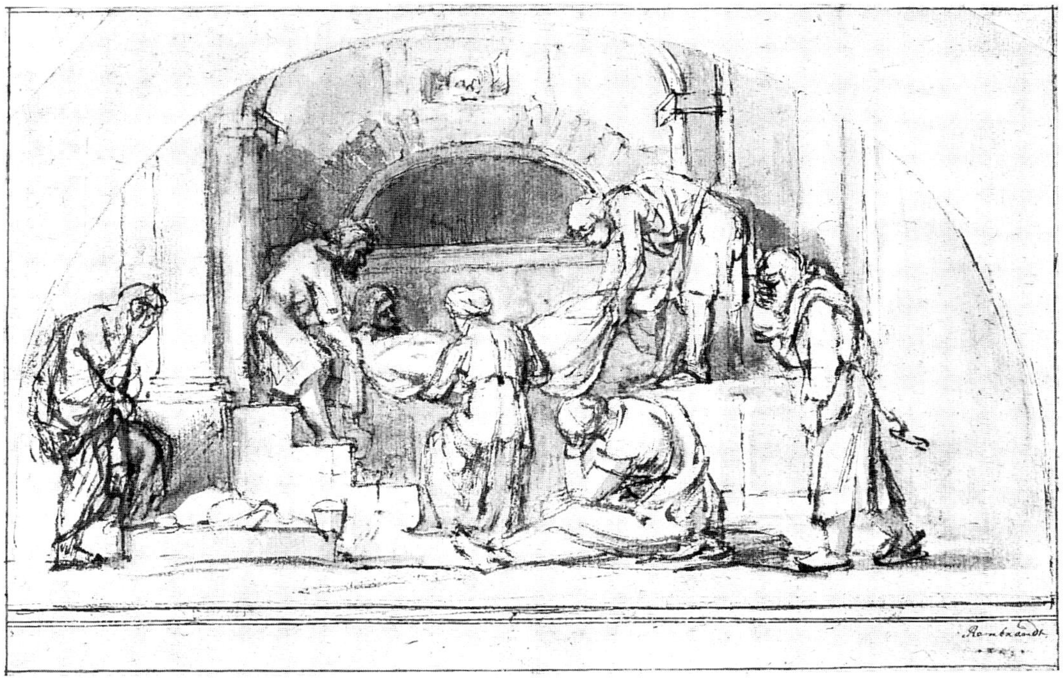

FIG. 117b
Rembrandt, after Polidoro da Caravaggio
The Entombment of Christ
Pen and ink and brush, with white bodycolour
18.0 x 28.3 cm
Teylers Museum, Haarlem

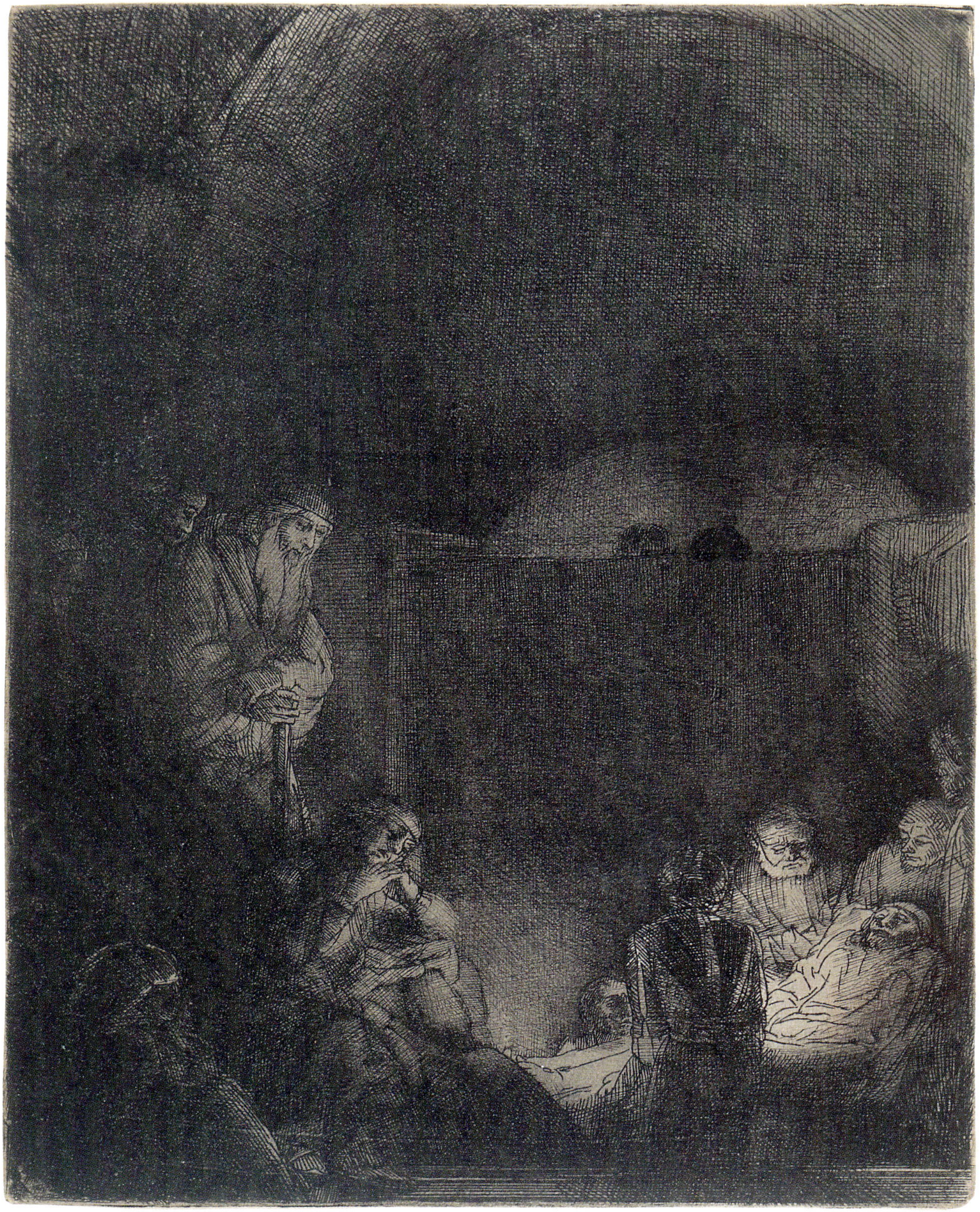

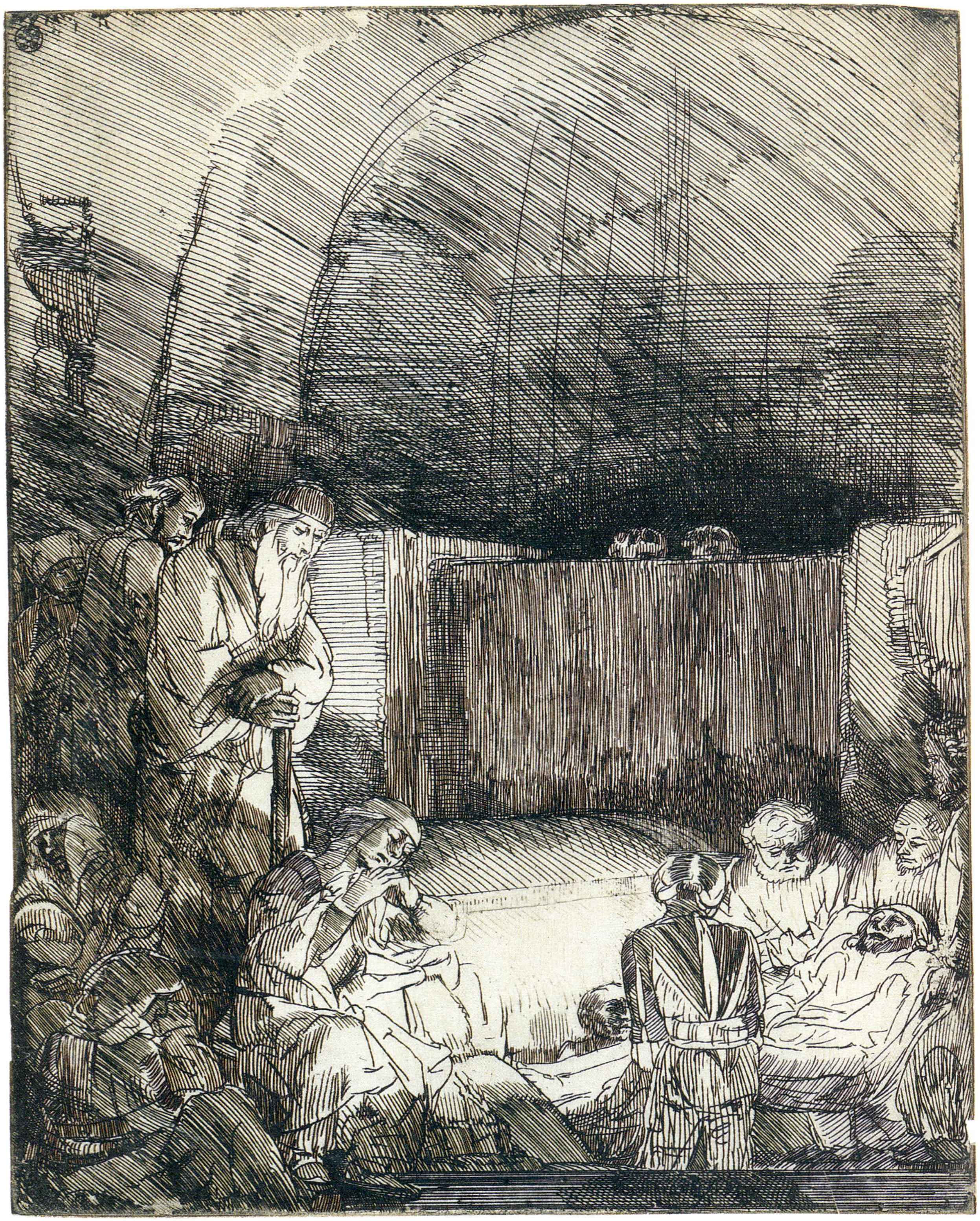

118

Christ Presented to the People (Ecce Homo): Oblong Plate
*c.*1655

Signed and dated in the plate from seventh state onwards *Rembrandt f 1655.*
Drypoint, printed with ink tone on oriental (probably Japanese) paper
38.7 x 45.4 cm
Rijksprentenkabinet, Rijksmuseum, Amsterdam

LITERATURE: White & Boon B.76 III (third of eight states); Hind 271; Münz 235; Biörklund BB.55-A. See also Boston / New York 1969–70, pp. 101–11, cat. nos 64–69; White 1969, vol. 1, pp. 87–92; White 1969a, pp. 23–4, XV, nos 88–95; Winternitz 1969; Van de Waal 1974a; *Bulletin van het Rijksmuseum*, vol. 23, no. 3, 1975, pp. 178–9; Carroll 1981, esp. pp. 588–605; B. Welzel, in Berlin / Amsterdam / London 1991–92b, pp. 274–7, [etching] cat. no. 38.

Ecce Homo – Behold the Man – were the words addressed by Pontius Pilate to the people as he presented Jesus to them for sentencing.[1] The subject first appears in Rembrandt's oeuvre in 1634 when he painted a grisaille (Bredius 546) (National Gallery, London) in preparation for a large etching, executed with the assistance of Johannes van Vliet (B.77) (fig. 118a). The etching's baroque composition, demonstrative display of gestures and emotions, and depiction of Christ in devotional guise, crowned with thorns, bear the hallmarks of an early work, quite different in conception from the monumental grandeur of the late drypoint.

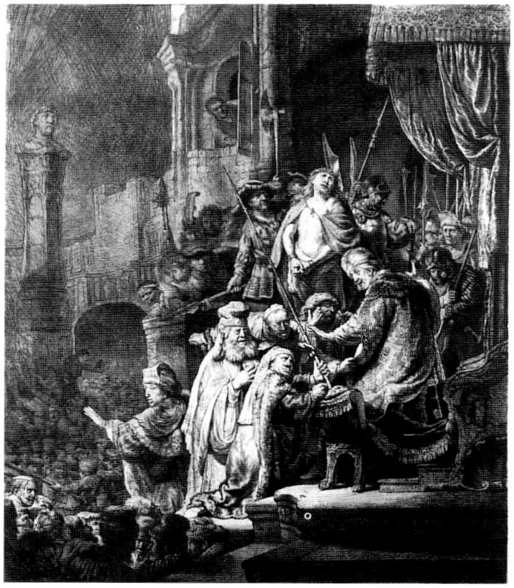

FIG. 118a
Rembrandt
Christ before Pilate: Large Plate 1636
Etching
54.9 x 44.7 cm
Rijksprentenkabinet, Rijksmuseum, Amsterdam

For his 1655 drypoint, Rembrandt referred to a number of earlier representations of the theme, notably Lucas van Leyden's engraving of 1510, from which he borrowed the general idea of the outdoor setting. Nicolaes de Bruyn (1571–1656), who engraved two versions of the subject in 1604 and 1618 (Hollstein 75, 78–89), and Jacques Callot (Lieure 285) provided two more precedents.

The event depicted in the *Ecce Homo* takes place on a raised podium in front of an impressive civic building, adorned with two sculpted figures representing Justice, at the upper left, and Fortitude[2] (instead of the traditional Prudence) on the right. Pontius Pilate, turbaned and holding his rod of office, gestures to Christ as he presents him to the people. Christ stands beside Pilate, bareheaded, barefooted and shackled. Behind them, centrally placed, is Barabbas, whose life will be spared in place of Christ's, and whose appearance in the scene is rare in art.[3] Below them stand an animated crowd comprising men, women and children of all ages. They are clothed in a combination of the fanciful, vaguely orientalizing, costumes in which Rembrandt frequently depicted his biblical figures so as to suggest distant times, but some also appear to wear contemporary dress. As in the *Hundred Guilder Print* (cat. no. 111) the narrative is condensed in the most economical and effective manner: for example, at the far left of the group of Pilate's attendants on the podium are a scribe taking notes of the proceedings and a young man holding a jug and a dish, in which Pilate later will wash his hands.

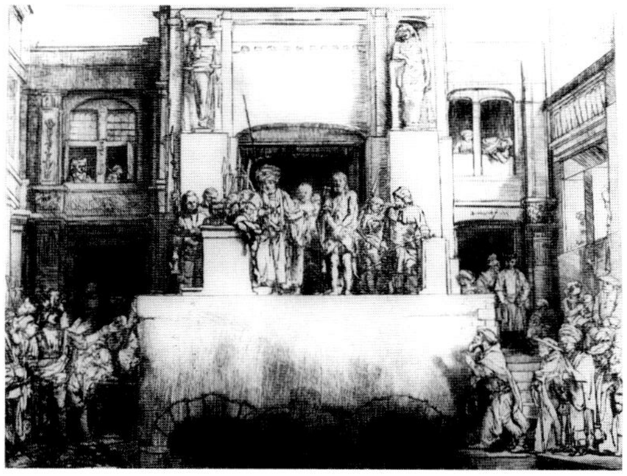

FIG. 118b
Rembrandt
Christ Presented to the People (Ecce Homo): Oblong Plate
Signed and dated 1655
Drypoint (eighth state)
35.8 x 45.4 cm
Copyright © The British Museum, London

Departing from his usual practice of providing biblical pictures with architectural settings denoting earlier times and cultures, Rembrandt chose instead to depict a building designed in the contemporary Dutch style of civic architecture, its classicizing features bearing a marked resemblance to the new Amsterdam Town Hall, which was opened in 1655, the very year in which this print was made. In this way he gave the biblical subject a direct contemporary relevance.

By compressing the space in the design, giving it such a confronting aspect, and unambiguously indicating that the action extends beyond each edge of the picture, Rembrandt forcefully engages the viewer as a participant in the moral drama. The severe symmetry of the composition[4] is based on a structure of strong horizontals and verticals, with all details of the design defined in drypoint, by means of the somewhat blocky shapes that are characteristic of Rembrandt's late style. The result is grave and monumental. We are not being asked to empathize – as we are inevitably drawn to do in the *Three Crosses* (cat. nos 115A, 115B) – but to pass judgement.

This print exists in eight states during which Rembrandt made alterations to the plate. The first three involved minor modifications, but in the fourth state he decided to trim the copperplate by cutting a strip 2.5 cm wide from the top edge. This further compressed the pictorial space and enabled the plate more readily to be printed on a standard-size sheet, instead of one enlarged by the addition of another strip to the top edge, as is the case in some impressions. However, the major changes to the image occurred only from the sixth state onwards. In the sixth state Rembrandt burnished away the crowd below the podium, thereby further shifting the weight of responsibility for the judgement from the historical crowd (the ancient Jews) to the onlooker (the viewer of Rembrandt's age, and all subsequent beholders). Next, in place of the crowd, he added two arches leading to dark, subterranean cells below the podium, separated by a sculpted relief of an ancient-looking bearded man. This figure was removed in the final, eighth state of the print (fig. 118b). The most crucial of these changes was the removal of the crowd, whose absence from the later states of the print emphasizes a point present from the very beginning: it is *we*, the beholders of the scene, not just the crowd of ancient Jews, who condemn Christ to be crucified.[5]

IZ

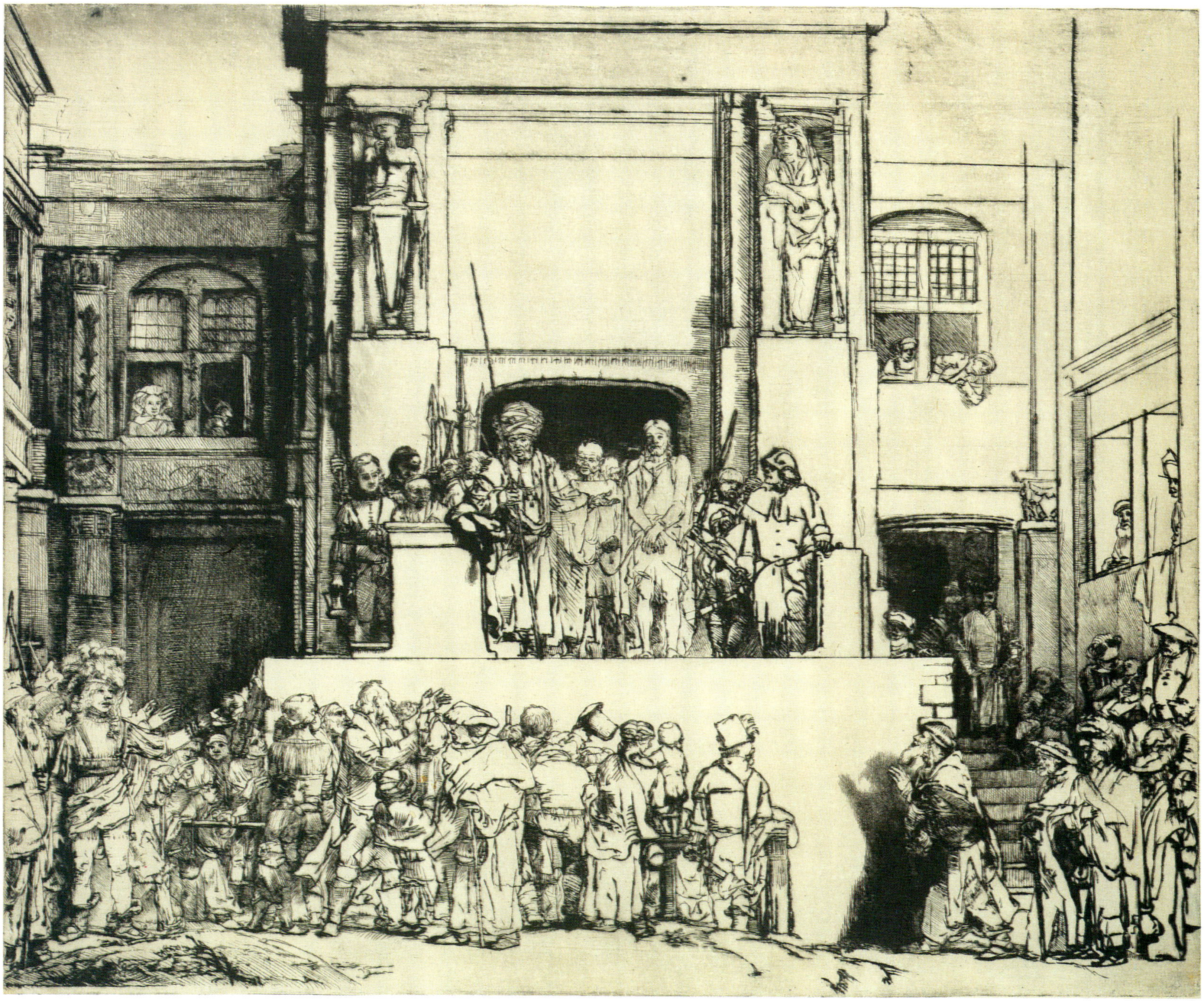

1 Matthew 27:11–25, Mark 15:1–15, Luke 23:1–25, John 18:28–40.
2 Van de Waal 1974, pp. 186–7, identifies this figure as Omphale, Queen of Lydia, who managed to subdue Hercules and usurp his masculine attributes, thereby becoming a symbol of order perverted, or the world turned upside-down.
3 Winternitz 1969, pp. 179–80; Van de Waal 1974, pp. 182–3.
4 'Pedantic symmetry' in Winternitz's apt words (Winternitz 1969, p. 177).
5 Winternitz 1969, pp. 189–90.

119

Christ Appearing to the Apostles

Signed and dated in the plate lower centre
Rembrandt f. 1656
Etching, printed on oriental (probably Japanese) paper
16.3 x 20.7 cm
National Gallery of Art, Washington, Rosenwald Collection 1950.1.114

LITERATURE: White & Boon B.89 (only state); Hind 237 (1650); Münz 220 (1650); Biörklund BB.56-A. See also White 1969, vol. 1, pp. 94–6; Ackley 1977; Ackley 1981, pp. 244–5, cat. no. 168.

Following his death and resurrection, Christ appeared twice to the assembled apostles. Thomas, who was absent on the first occasion, refused to believe, his incredulity vanishing only with the second miraculous appearance when he was told to touch Christ's wounds. Although the subject of this etching has sometimes been interpreted as the latter event, it is now generally identified with the first occasion,[1] which is described in Luke 24:36–40:

> And as they thus spake, Jesus himself stood in the midst of them, and saith unto them, 'Peace be unto you'. But they were terrified and affrightened, and supposed that they had seen a spirit. And he said unto them, 'Why are ye troubled? and why do thoughts arise in your hearts? Behold my hands and my feet, that it is I myself: handle me, and see; for a spirit hath not flesh and bones, as ye see me have'. And when he had thus spoken, he shewed them his hands and his feet.[2]

During the 1650s, the decade to which his most sustained series of nocturnal prints belongs, Rembrandt also created etchings that were conceived in light tonalities. In these prints (which include the 1654 etchings depicting the childhood and boyhood of Christ) he created his own graphic vocabulary, fusing lessons learned from his observation of fifteenth-century Italian engravings with those learned from the Baroque etchers such as Federico Barocci (*c.*1535–1612) and Simone Cantarini (1612–1648).[3] Italian etchers were more concerned with portraying their subjects modelled in light than in shadow. To this end they used open outline and broadly spaced, regular hatching, as well as stippling and broken contours, all of which best suggested forms enveloped in light. Among Rembrandt's prints there is no better example of this manner of etching than *Christ Appearing to the Apostles*, in which physical shapes are made to dissolve and the atmosphere is splintered by the power and radiance of divine light. The suddenness of Christ's miraculous arrival seems to displace the air on either side of him. He appears to hover as he points to his wounds, while the disciples – not eleven, but at least fifteen in number – reel from the blinding force of the apparition, two of them falling to their knees.

Like the *Supper at Emmaus* (B. 87, 88) the Incredulity of Thomas and other scenes of miraculous revelation, the subject of the present etching was one that had special appeal for the Dutch Catholic community. While officially Catholicism was suppressed in Holland, in fact the Catholic Church was allowed to remain clandestinely active, and Catholic patrons, including priests, would often commission paintings of post-Resurrection themes.[4]

Stylistically and technically this etching is comparable to the smaller plate from 1654, *Christ Seated Disputing with the Doctors* (B.64) (fig. 119a), for which the copperplate has survived. The present work is etched with a broad and deep line, very different from the fine lines of many of Rembrandt's early etchings, indicating that a strong acid was probably used.[5] This would have speeded up the etching process and, in the case of *Christ Appearing to the Apostles*, which exists in a single state only, contributed to the instantaneity of the moment represented. Since Rembrandt's prints have been appreciated above all for their subtle chiaroscuro, such radical ways of portraying the light of divine revelation as witnessed here have not generally been appreciated.[6] It is therefore not surprising that there are no engraved copies of this print recorded.

IZ

1 For a persuasively argued account supporting this identification, see White 1969, pp. 94–5.
2 See also John 20:19–24.
3 Münz 1952, vol. 1, pp. 40–2; Ackley 1977.
4 Van Eck 1993–94.
5 Morse 1966, pp. 103–4.
6 Hinterding 1995, pp. 22–3.

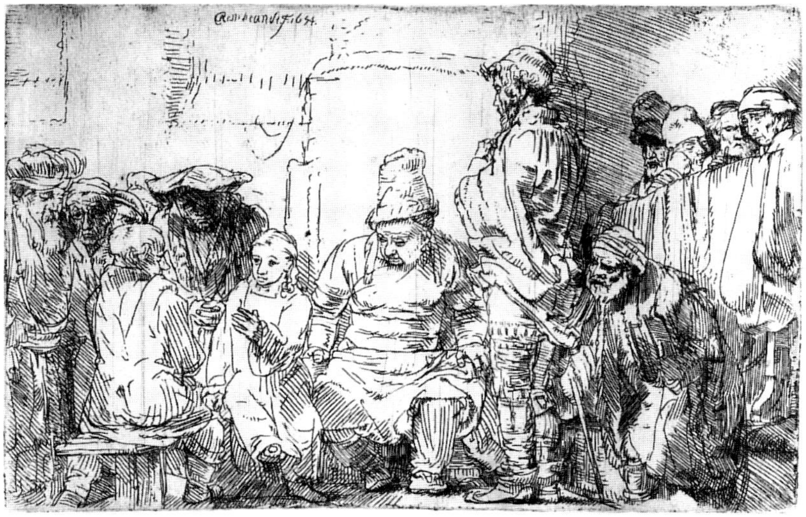

FIG. 119a
Rembrandt
Christ Seated Disputing with the Doctors
Signed and dated 1654
Etching
9.5 x 14.4 cm
Rijksprentenkabinet, Rijksmuseum, Amsterdam

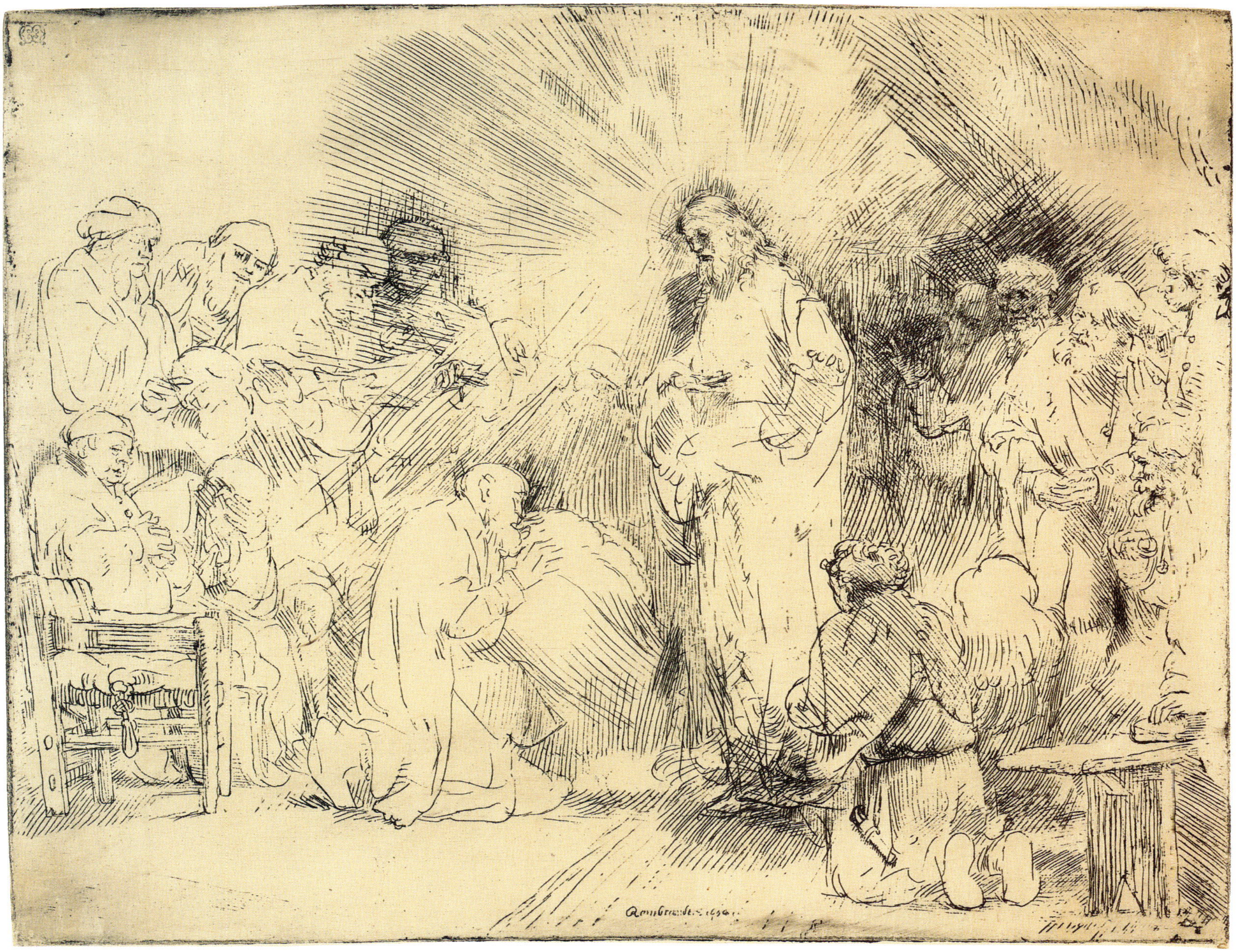

120

Arnold Tholinx, Inspector
*c.*1656

Etching, drypoint and burin, printed with a veil of ink tone
Inscribed in pen and ink in lower margin (in a later hand) *Tolinc*
19.7 x 14.8 cm
Watermark: Foolscap with five-pointed collar; variant G.b.
Rijksprentenkabinet, Rijksmuseum, Amsterdam

LITERATURE: White & Boon B.284 II (second of two states); Hind 289 (1656); Münz 73 (1655/56); Biörklund BB.56-2. See also White 1969, vol. 1, pp. 141–3.

Made at around the time Rembrandt finally succumbed to bankruptcy, this portrait is one of a series that he etched in the 1650s, beginning with the portrait of Clement de Jonghe, 1651 (B.272). Most of these works portray the subject in three-quarter length and seated, a reflection of the lessons Rembrandt imbibed from Venetian art.[1] These late etched portraits have a simple grandeur and a penetrating, if ultimately unfathomable, psychological presence: each sitter retains his mysterious individuality.

The portrait of Tholinx is another reminder of Rembrandt's longstanding links with Amsterdam's medical community, which were initiated by the commission to paint the *Anatomy Lesson of Nicolaes Tulp* (Bredius 403) (Mauritshuis, The Hague) (p. 24, fig. 3) in 1632, not long after Rembrandt arrived in Amsterdam. Dr Arnold Tholinx (1607–1679) had married Tulp's daughter, Catharina, in 1648. He was inspector of medical colleges in Amsterdam from 1643 until 1653, when he was succeeded by Dr Joan Deyman, whose anatomy lesson Rembrandt painted in 1656 (Bredius 414) (Rijksmuseum, Amsterdam).

In 1656 Rembrandt also painted a bust-length portrait of Tholinx set against a neutral background (Bredius 281) (fig. 120a). The etched portrait, on the other hand, shows Tholinx in three-quarter length, seated behind a table in a study, with the generalized attributes of learning and science: the great open tome, and bottles with tubes nearby. Holding a pair of spectacles he looks at the viewer with a steady gaze, his eyes and most of his face in shadow. His expression is grave. Rich drypoint is used to model the figure and enhance the shadows, but not to create the darkened atmosphere that is found in Rembrandt's other etched portraits of the late 1650s.

This is an extremely rare etching that survives in only four impressions in the first state; the second state has added shading in areas of the face and the breast. It seems never to have been reprinted. Only three watermarked impressions have so far been found, two of them bearing the foolscap watermark that occurs in this impression and in one other impression of the second state (Bibliothèque Nationale, Paris). The fine quality of these impressions suggests that they were very early, and printed in around 1656. The source of foolscap paper is difficult to identify, but it might have come from France.[2] This portrait has been greatly admired, as the six engraved copies of it testify.

IZ

1 For an account of Rembrandt's assimilation of Venetian portrait conventions during the 1650s and 1660s, see Chapman 1990, pp. 92–4.

2 I am grateful to Erik Hinterding for information regarding the watermark and the dating of this impression.

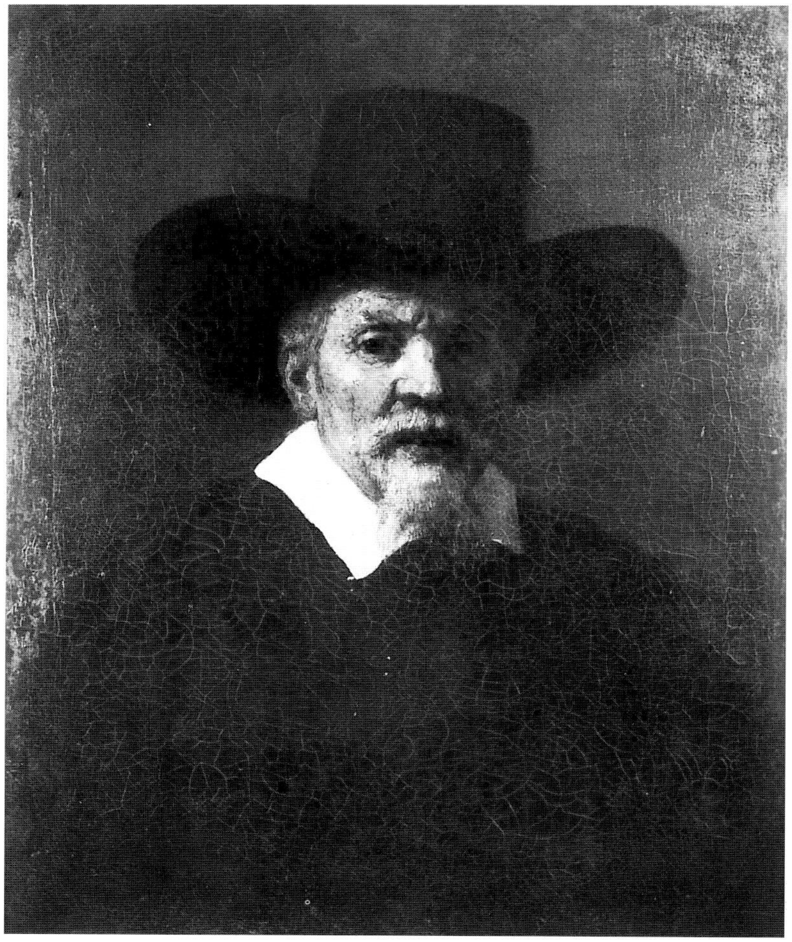

FIG. 120a
Rembrandt
Arnold (Arnout) Tholinx, Inspector
Signed and dated 1656
Canvas
76.0 x 63.0 cm
Musée Jacquemart-André, Paris

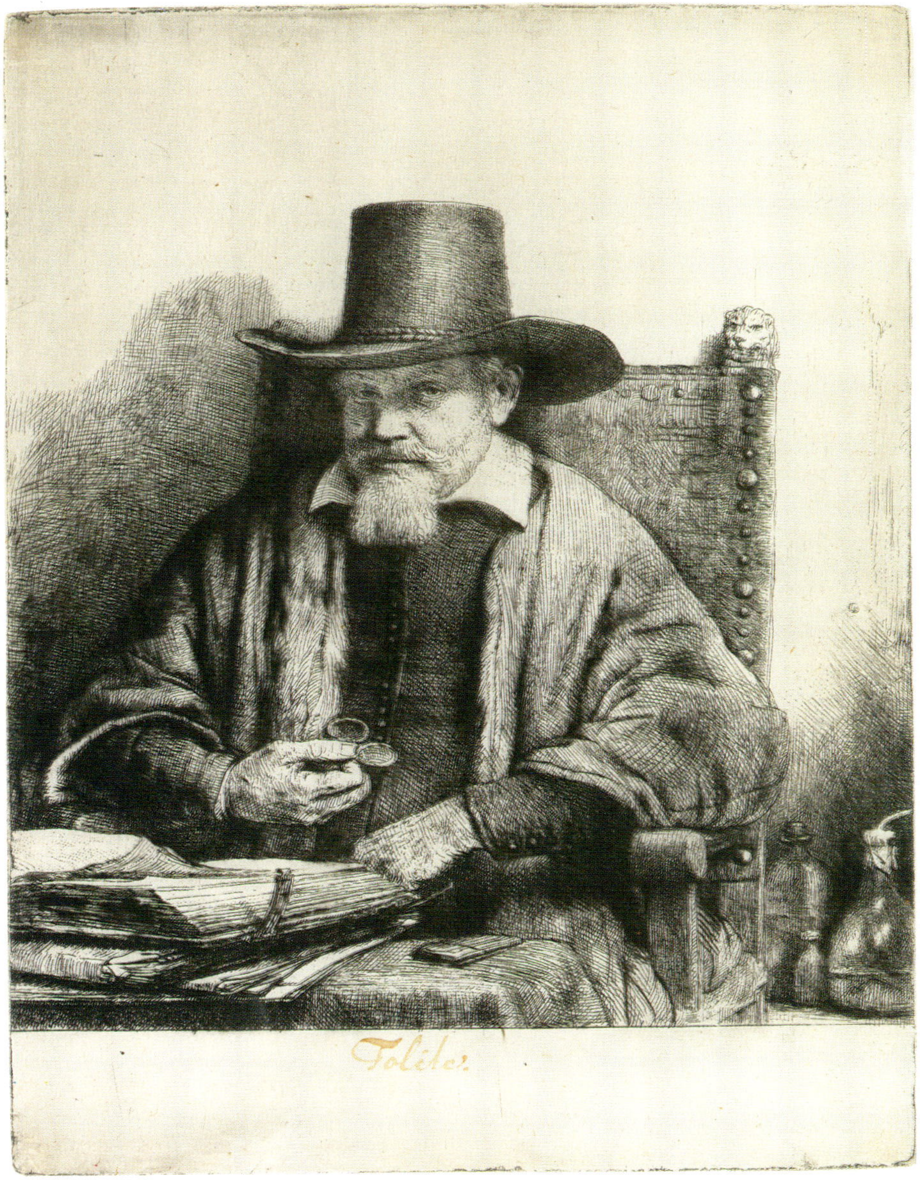

121

Woman Sitting Half-Dressed beside a Stove

Signed and dated in the plate upper right *Rembrandt f. 1658*
Etching, drypoint and burin, printed with plate tone on thick oriental (probably Japanese) vellum-like paper
22.8 x 18.4 cm
Lent by the Syndics of The Fitzwilliam Museum, Cambridge

LITERATURE: White & Boon B.197 III (third of seven states); Hind 296; Münz 141; Biörklund BB.58-B. See also White 1969, vol. 1, pp. 181–2; White 1969a, p. 30, XXII, nos 129–35; Cambridge 1996–97, cat. no. 33.

The last period of intense focus on the nude in Rembrandt's graphic work occurs in the late 1650s and may be said to have been inaugurated earlier in the decade by his painting of *Bathsheba Reading David's Letter* of 1654 (Bredius 521) (Louvre, Paris). In 1658 he etched no fewer than four female nudes, including the present example. All of them portray single figures, either in dark interiors or outdoors in deep shadow. They contain no evidence to identify them with mythological or biblical subjects. Unlike Rembrandt's first two large etched nudes of *c.*1631 (see cat. no. 99), who look directly at the viewer, the women in the later works look away, or are portrayed from behind. This gives them the appearance of existing in a more private sphere than their earlier counterparts, and also serves to draw attention to the more simplified volumes of their bodies – indeed, of the entire compositions.

Of the four etched nudes from 1658, the *Woman Sitting Half-Dressed beside a Stove* is the only one who is not fully naked. She is seated, facing right, on a chair, wearing a voluminous skirt that reveals the position of her legs, with her undergarments rolled down at the waist; her left foot rests on a patten. Her torso and the position of her arms bear a marked resemblance (in reverse) to the pose of Bathsheba in the 1654 painting, but her face is rendered in stricter profile. The room in which the woman is seated is uncluttered and, as is typical of many of Rembrandt's mature works, its sparse, architectural features are designed as much to frame the main subject as to define particular space. The niche at the left frames the woman's head and torso against an arch of richly modulated darkness. The stove in the right background is decorated with elaborate relief ornamentation, including a medallion that shows a woman (possibly the Magdalene) kneeling in prayer at the foot of the Cross. This detail is clear only in cleanly wiped impressions such as this one.

Rembrandt took this print through as many as seven different states: he perfected the modelling of the body by adding extra shading, 'tuned' the shadows in the skirt and the background to a darker pitch, added – in the fifth state – a damper key to the stove, and finally, in the seventh state, removed the white cap worn by the model. The last change caused the figure of the woman to be better integrated in her setting, while also emphasizing her luminous torso. As with all the nude etchings of 1658, Rembrandt frequently printed this one on oriental papers, thereby enhancing the sensuality that characterizes his female nudes. He also experimented with inking and wiping. In some proofs of this print the manipulation of ink film on the surface of the plate creates pictorial effects of deepest shadow, in which the body glows in darkness. One engraved copy after this etching is recorded.

IZ

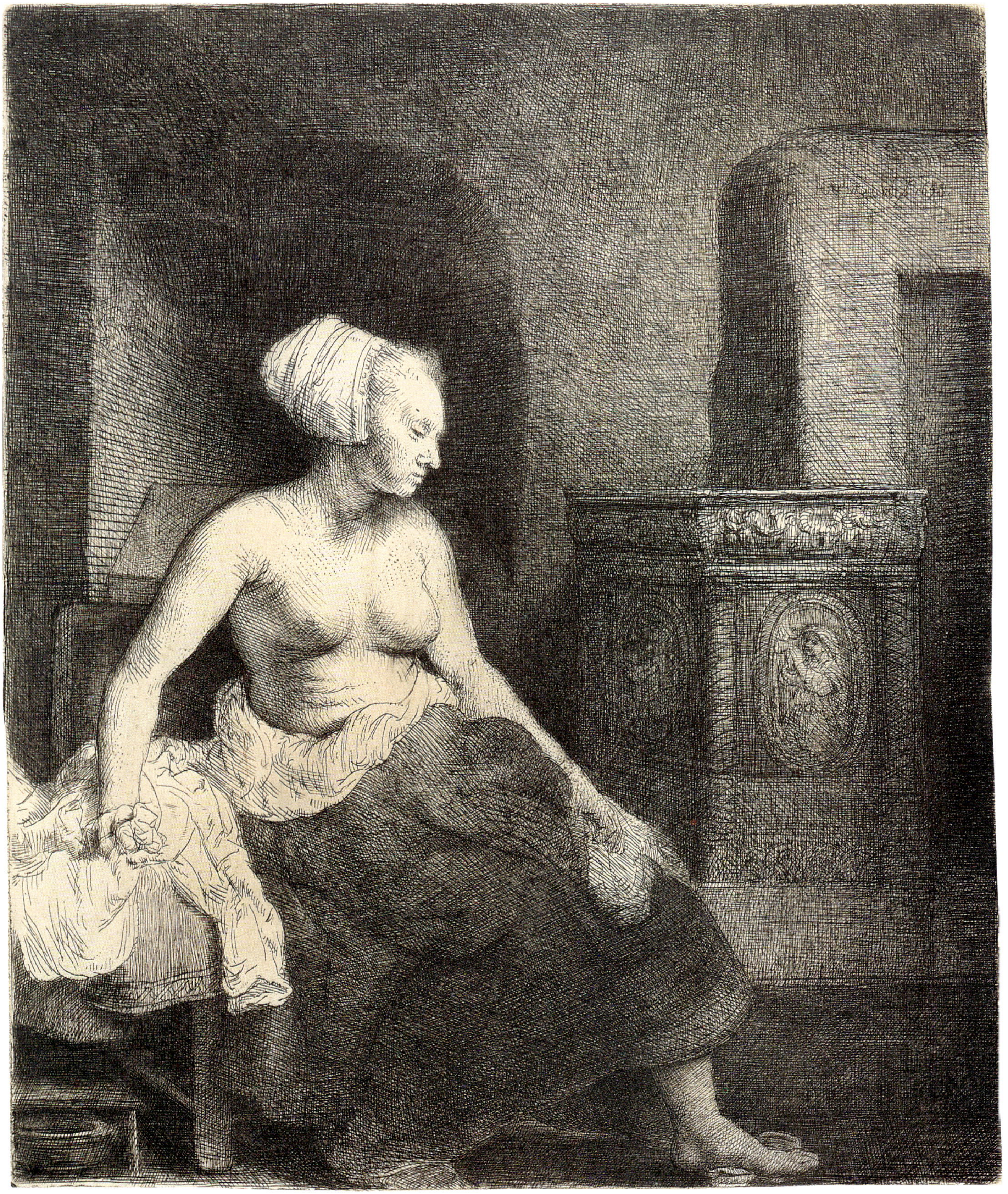

122

Jupiter and Antiope: The Larger Plate

Signed and dated in the plate lower centre
Rembrandt f. 1659
Etching, drypoint and burin, printed on Western laid paper
13.8 x 20.5 cm
The Visitors of the Ashmolean Museum, Oxford

LITERATURE: White & Boon B.203 I (first of two states, the additions to the second state not by Rembrandt); Hind 302; Münz 143; Biörklund BB.59-B. See also White 1969, vol. 1, pp. 184–6; B. Welzel, in Berlin / Amsterdam / London 1991–92b, pp. 281–3, [etching] cat. no. 40.

The story of Antiope is related in several classical texts including Homer (*Odyssey* XI. 260) and Ovid (*Metamorphoses* VI. 110–11). Together with Europa, Danaë, Diana and Ganymede – all subjects painted by Rembrandt (figs 29a, 29b and fig. 3, p. 35) – she was one of the loves of Jupiter. The principal source of the myth is a play by Euripides, of which only fragments survive. Although the literary sources are scant, the subject itself has a rich, if controversial, pictorial tradition in the sixteenth and seventeenth centuries.[1] The title of Rembrandt's etching reflects this iconographic uncertainty, since the subject's identification in the earliest inventories was with Venus and Satyr, the title accepted by Gersaint, who published the first catalogue of Rembrandt's etchings in 1751. The etching's present title probably also dates from the eighteenth century, when an engraved inscription was added, identifying the male figure as Jupiter.

Jupiter's appearance at Antiope's side in the guise of a satyr is a detail that comes from Ovid, the single most important source of classical subjects for Renaissance and Baroque artists. Rembrandt portrays Jupiter not with the exaggeratedly pointed features often given satyrs, but as an ordinary, older man. Crowned with a wreath of leaves, he creeps up on Antiope, who reclines on pillows, abandoned and unaware, in deepest sleep. As he stoops to remove her covering, one of his horns catches the curtain, allowing light to illuminate the back of his head and his shoulders. Antiope's pose is based on that of Venus in Annibale Carracci's engraving of *Venus and a Satyr* (B.17) (fig. 122a), but in reverse.[2] However, Rembrandt departs from his model by changing the position of Antiope's arms, which he shows lifted over her head, her left arm raised in an attitude reminiscent of that found in paintings of Venus by Correggio[3] and Titian.[4] Rembrandt also brings the scene forward – not least by cutting the left arm at the margin – thereby engaging the viewer as a witness to the event depicted. It is a scene of ambiguous intimacy in which the main elements of Annibale's design are retained but the composition is distilled to its essentials through the elimination of the distant landscape, the curtain and the figure of Cupid.

This was Rembrandt's second (and last) depiction of the subject, his first being the smaller version etched in *c.*1631 (B.204) (fig. 122b). That was a more impersonal portrayal, in which Jupiter's shadowy presence functioned as a cipher of his intentions; here, their carnality is made explicit. The 1659 Antiope is altogether more monumental, Italianate and idealized, while retaining startling details of naturalistic observation, in particular Antiope's mouth open in sleep and (probably, as a deliberate visual *double entendre*) Jupiter's right horn catching the curtain. Rembrandt's interest here was in a subtler form of chiaroscuro that evokes intimate space and models the sensuous physicality of Antiope's body. Now, completely at ease with the etching medium, Rembrandt uses the whole repertoire of intaglio techniques with absolute fluency, outlining forms with straight etching and burin, using stippling to suggest half-tones, deepening shadows with cross-hatching and enhancing them and suggesting texture with drypoint. He also frequently experimented with printing the plate on various oriental papers whose receptiveness to inks was capable of producing impressions of great sensual richness.

The four etchings of female nudes that Rembrandt made in the previous year (1658), were all exercises in rendering deep chiaroscuro (see cat. no. 121). They reflect his interest in the composition, colour, forms and texture of Italian – specifically Venetian – art, an interest that is so apparent in his work of the 1650s. Yet none of the etchings of 1658 carry literary allusions as here. In his last etched works, Rembrandt again turned to history subjects – on this occasion from classical mythology, rather than the Bible – as a context that best enabled him to combine observation from nature, psychological insight, and the classical learning expected of a painter of histories. Rembrandt made only two other etchings after completing *Jupiter and Antiope*: another nude in 1661 (B.202) (fig. 98b) and lastly, in 1665, a commissioned portrait (B.264).

IZ

1 For a concise account of this iconographic controversy, see Wethey 1975, pp. 53–6.
2 Bohlin 1979, no. 17.
3 *Venus, Cupid and a Satyr*, Louvre, Paris (Gould 1976, pp. 238–9).
4 *Jupiter and Antiope (Pardo Venus)*, Louvre, Paris (Wethey 1975, vol. III, pp. 53–6, 161–2, no. 21).

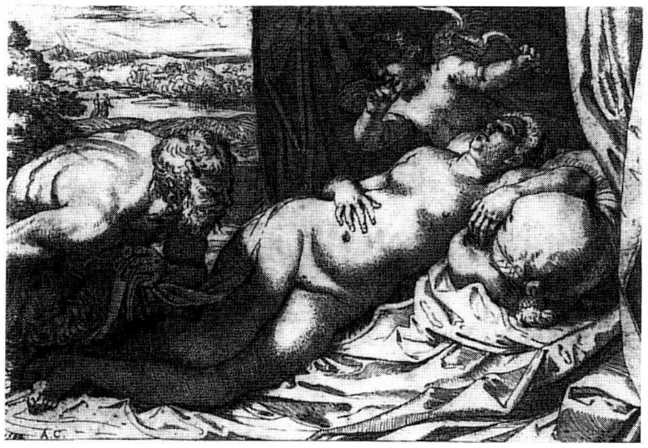

FIG. 122a
Annibale Carracci
Italian, 1560–1609
Venus and a Satyr
Monogrammed and dated 1592
Etching and engraving
15.6 x 22.7 cm
From a reproduction

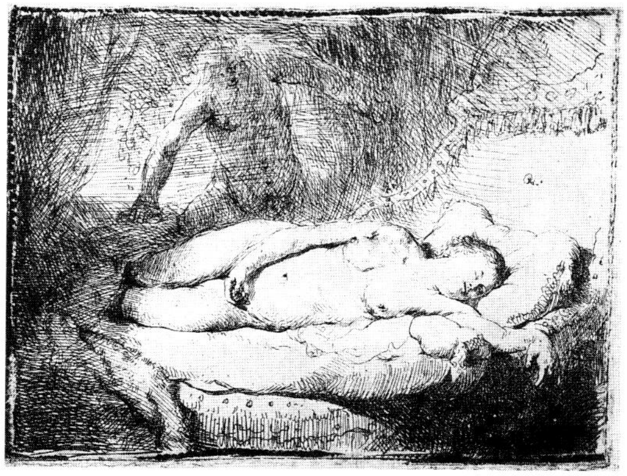

FIG 122b
Rembrandt
Jupiter and Antiope: The Smaller Plate
*c.*1631
Etching (first state)
8.4 x 11.4 cm
From a reproduction

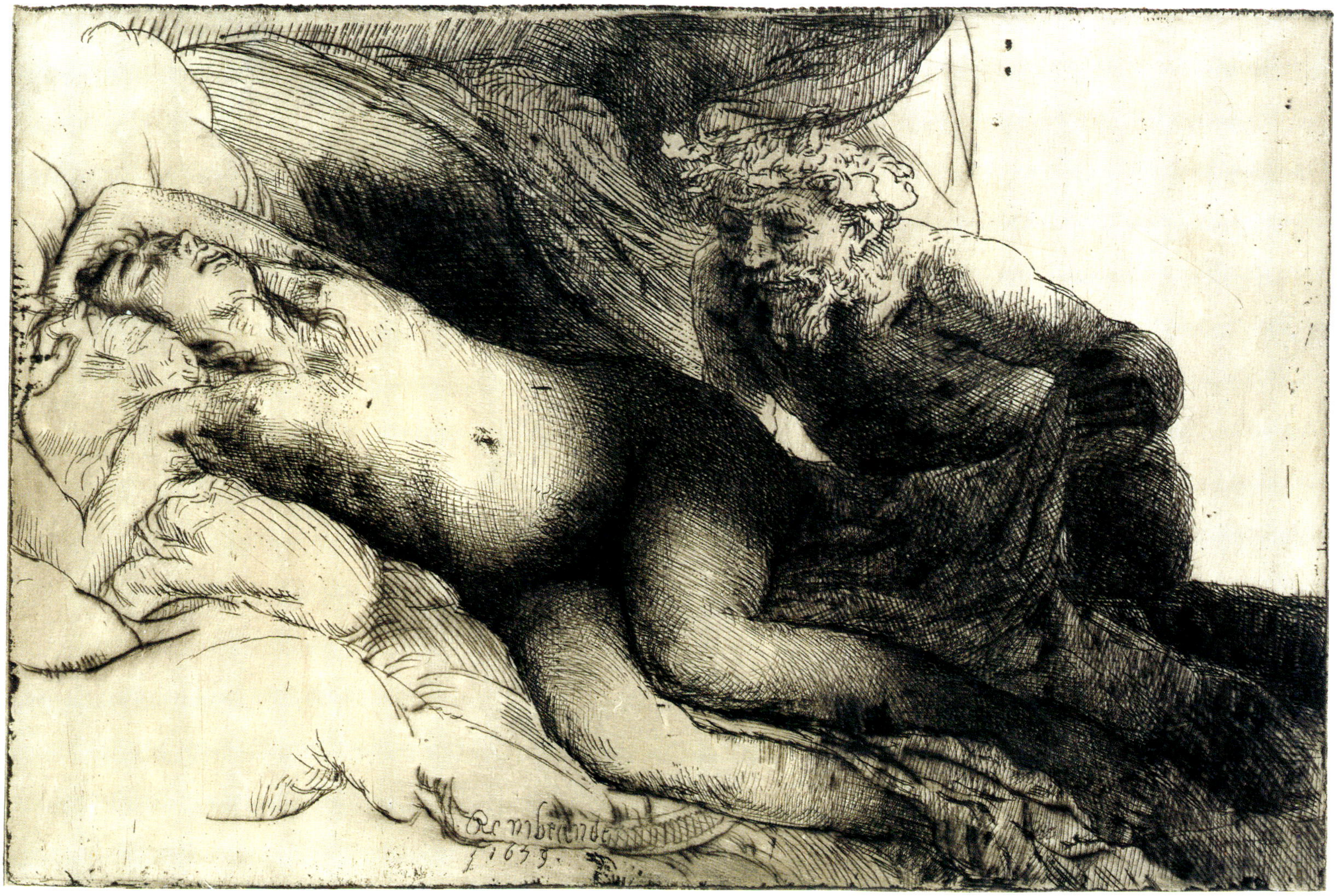

Bibliographic and Other Abbreviations

A Brief Note to the Reader

To enhance the readability of this catalogue, each essay and entry has been treated as a self-contained narrative. For this reason, certain details, and occasionally an illustration, are repeated in various places.

The literature accompanying the catalogue entries is not intended to be complete. It is provided only as a guide to the principal sources available with respect to the individual works.

Provenance data has not been provided for works on paper.

General Abbreviations

DIAL	Decimal Index of the Art of the Low Countries
diss.	dissertation
GAA	Gemeentearchief [Municipal Archives], Amsterdam
GAL	Gemeentearchief [Municipal Archives], Leiden
GAU	Gemeentelijke Archiefdienst [Municipal Archives], Utrecht
inv. no.	inventory number
NAA	Notarial Archives, Municipal Archives, Amsterdam
RKD	Rijksbureau voor Kunsthistorische Documentatie [Netherlands Institute for Art History], The Hague

Bibliographic Abbreviations

Ackley 1977
C. S. Ackley, 'Rembrandt's "Christ Appearing to the Apostles"', *The Print Collector's Newsletter*, vol. VIII, no. 1, March–April 1977, pp. 6–7.

Ackley 1981
C. S. Ackley, *Printmaking in the Age of Rembrandt* (exh. cat.), Museum of Fine Arts, Boston, 1981. See also ROBINSON 1981.

Adams 1985
A. Jensen Adams, The Paintings of Thomas de Keyser (1596/7–1667): A Study of Portraiture in Seventeenth-Century Amsterdam, PhD diss., 4 vols, Harvard University, Cambridge, Massachusetts, 1985.

Adams 1988
A. Jensen Adams, with E. Haverkamp-Begemann, *Dutch and Flemish Paintings from New York Private Collections* (exh. cat.), National Academy of Design, New York, 1988.

Adelson et al. 1996
C. J. Adelson et al., *Timken Museum of Art: European Works of Art, American Paintings, and Russian Icons in the Putnam Foundation Collection*, San Diego, 1996.

Albach 1972
B. Albach, 'Een tekening van het Amsterdamse toneel in 1638', *Kroniek van het Rembrandthuis*, vol. 26, 1972, pp. 111–25.

Albach 1979
B. Albach, 'Rembrandt en het toneel', *Kroniek van het Rembrandthuis*, vol. 31, no. 2, 1979, pp. 2–32.

Allgemeines Künstler-Lexikon
Allgemeines Künstler-Lexikon: Die bildenden Künstler aller Zeiten und Völker, 15 vols to date, Leipzig / Munich, 1983–.

Alpers 1988
S. Alpers, *Rembrandt's Enterprise: The Studio and the Market*, London, 1988.

Ambulator 1774
The Ambulator; or, The Stranger's Companion in a Tour round London; within the Circuit of Twenty-Five Miles: Describing Whatever Is Remarkable, either for Grandeur, Elegancy, Use, or Curiosity; and Comprehending Catalogues of the Pictures by Eminent Artists, London, 1774.

Ambulator 1792
Ambulator; or, A Pocket Companion in a Tour round London; within the Circuit of Five Miles, 4th edn, London, 1792.

Amsterdam 1976
E. de Jongh et al., *Tot lering en vermaak: Betekenissen van Hollandse genrevoorstellingen uit de zeventiende eeuw* (exh. cat.), Rijksmuseum, Amsterdam, 1976.

Amsterdam 1984–85
Bij Rembrandt in de leer / Rembrandt as Teacher (exh. cat.), Museum het Rembrandthuis, Amsterdam, 1984.

Amsterdam 1986–87
R. E. O. Ekkart & E. Ornstein-van Slooten, *Oog in oog met de modellen van Rembrandts portret-etsen / Face to Face with the Sitters for Rembrandt's Etched Portraits* (exh. cat.), Museum het Rembrandthuis, Amsterdam, 1986. See also EKKART 1986–87.

Amsterdam 1987–88
S. A. C. Dudok van Heel, P. Schatborn & E. Ornstein-van Slooten, *Dossier Rembrandt: Documenten, tekeningen en prenten / The Rembrandt Papers: Documents, Drawings and Prints* (exh. cat.), Museum het Rembrandthuis, Amsterdam, 1987.

Amsterdam 1989
De Hollandse fijnschilders: Van Gerard Dou tot Adriaen van der Werff (exh. cat.), Rijksmuseum, Amsterdam, 1989.

Amsterdam 1991
A. Tümpel & P. Schatborn, *Pieter Lastman: Leermeester van Rembrandt / The Man Who Taught Rembrandt* (exh. cat.), Museum het Rembrandthuis, Amsterdam, 1991.

Amsterdam 1996
C. Schuckman, M. Royalton-Kisch & E. Hinterding, *Rembrandt & van Vliet: A Collaboration on Copper* (exh. cat.), Museum het Rembrandthuis, Amsterdam, 1996. See also HINTERDING 1996.

Amsterdam 1996–97
P. van der Coelen et al., *Patriarchs, Angels and Prophets: The Old Testament in Netherlandish Printmaking from Lucas van Leyden to Rembrandt* (exh. cat.), Museum het Rembrandthuis, Amsterdam, 1996.

Amsterdam 1997
E. de Jongh & G. Luijten, *Spiegel van alledag: Nederlandse genreprenten 1550–1700* (exh. cat.), Rijksmuseum, Amsterdam, 1997. See also AMSTERDAM 1997a.

Amsterdam 1997a
E. de Jongh & G. Luijten, *Mirror of Everyday Life: Genreprints in the Netherlands 1550–1700* (exh. cat.), trans. M. Hoyle, Rijksmuseum, Amsterdam, 1997. See also AMSTERDAM 1997.

Amsterdam / Boston / Philadelphia 1987–88
P. C. Sutton et al., *Masters of 17th-Century Dutch Landscape Painting* (exh. cat.), Rijksmuseum, Amsterdam, Museum of Fine Arts, Boston, Philadelphia Museum of Art, 1987.

Amsterdam / Groningen 1983
A. Blankert, B. Broos, E. van de Wetering, G. Jansen & W. van de Watering, *The Impact of a Genius: Rembrandt, His Pupils and Followers in the Seventeenth Century* (exh. cat.), trans. I. Rike, Waterman Gallery, Amsterdam, Groninger Museum, Groningen, 1983. See also BROOS 1983, VAN DE WETERING 1983.

Amsterdam / Jerusalem 1991–92
C. Tümpel et al., *Het Oude Testament in de schilderkunst van de Gouden Eeuw* (exh. cat.), Joods Historisch Museum, Amsterdam, Israel Museum, Jerusalem, 1991. See also AMSTERDAM / JERUSALEM / MÜNSTER 1991–94.

Amsterdam / Jerusalem / Münster 1991–94
C. Tümpel (ed.), *Im Lichte Rembrandts: Das Alte Testament im Goldenen Zeitalter der niederländischen Kunst* (exh. cat.), Joods Historisch Museum, Amsterdam, Israel Museum, Jerusalem, Westfälisches Landesmuseum für Kunst und Kulturgeschichte, Münster, 1994. See also AMSTERDAM / JERUSALEM 1991–92 [of which the 1994 catalogue is the expanded edition], and VAN DE KAMP 1991–94, TÜMPEL 1991–94, VAN VOOLEN 1991–94.

Amsterdam / Rotterdam 1956
Rembrandt tentoonstelling ter herdenking van de geboorte van Rembrandt op 15 juli 1606: Schilderijen (exh. cat.), Rijksmuseum, Amsterdam; Museum Boymans, Rotterdam, 1956.

Angel 1642
P. Angel, *Lof der schilder-konst*, Leiden, 1642.

Ash & Fletcher 1990
N. Ash & S. Fletcher, 'Watermarks in Rembrandt's Landscape Etchings', in WASHINGTON 1990, pp. 263–81.

Auckland 1982
E. de Jongh et al., *Still-Life in the Age of Rembrandt* (exh. cat.), Auckland City Art Gallery, 1982.

B. (+ no.)
See BARTSCH 1803–21

Baarsen 1996
R. Baarsen, 'Herman Doomer, Ebony Worker in Amsterdam', *Burlington Magazine*, vol. CXXXVIII, no. 1124, November 1996, pp. 739–49.

Bad Homburg / Wuppertal 1995
I. Ember & M. Chiarini, *Rembrandt, Rubens, Van Dyck … : Italiensehnsucht nordischer Barockmaler – Meisterwerke aus dem Museum der Bildenden Künste, Budapest* (exh. cat.), Sinclair-Haus, Bad Homburg, Von der Heyt-Museum, Wuppertal, 1995.

Baer 1990
R. Baer, The Paintings of Gerrit Dou, PhD diss., Institute of Fine Arts, New York University, 1990.

Bailey 1990
A. Bailey, 'A Young Man on Horseback', *New Yorker*, 5 March 1990, pp. 45–77.

Bailey 1994
A. Bailey, *Responses to Rembrandt*, New York, 1994.

Baker & Henry 1995
C. Baker & T. Henry, *The National Gallery: Complete Illustrated Catalogue*, London, 1995.

Bakker 1993
B. Bakker, 'Levenspelgrimage of vrome wandeling? Claes Janszoon Visscher en zijn serie *Plaisante Plaetsen*', *Oud Holland*, vol. 107, no. 1, 1993, pp. 97–115.

Baldinucci 1681–1728
F. Baldinucci, *Notizie de' professori del disegno da Cimabue in qua, per le quali si dimostra come, e per chi le bell'arti di pittura, scultura, e architettura lasciata la rozzezza delle maniere greca, e gotica, si siano in questi secoli ridotte all'antica loro perfezione*, 6 vols, Florence, 1681–1728.

Baldinucci 1686
F. Baldinucci, *Cominciamento, e progresso dell'arte dell' intagliare in rame, colle vite di molti de' più eccellenti maestri della stessa professione*, Florence, 1686. See also BALDINUCCI / MANNI 1767.

Baldinucci / Manni 1767
F. Baldinucci, *Cominciamento, e progresso dell'arte dell' intagliare in rame, colle vite di molti de' più eccellenti maestri della stessa professione*, 2nd edn, with annotations by D. M. Manni, Florence, 1767. See also BALDINUCCI 1686.

Baligand 1978–79
F. Baligand, 'Peinture hollandaise, Musée de la Chartreuse, Douai', *Mémoires de la Société d'Agriculture, Sciences et Arts de Douai*, 5th series, vol. 7, 1978–79, pp. 35–8.

Bartsch 1797
A. Bartsch, *Catalogue raisonné de toutes les estampes qui forment l'oeuvre de Rembrandt et ceux de ses principaux imitateurs*, 2 vols, Vienna, 1797. See also BARTSCH 1803–21, ILLUSTRATED BARTSCH.

Bartsch 1803–21
A. Bartsch, *Le Peintre graveur*, 21 vols, Vienna, 1803–21. See also BARTSCH 1797, ILLUSTRATED BARTSCH.

Basel 1984
Tobias Stimmer (1539–1584) (exh. cat.), Kunstmuseum Basel, 1984.

Basel 1987
P. ten Doesschate-Chu, E. Hüttinger, R. Baumstark & M. Roethlisberger, *Im Lichte Hollands: Holländische Malerei des 17. Jahrhunderts aus den Sammlungen des Fürsten von Liechtenstein und aus Schweizer Besitz* (exh. cat.), Kunstmuseum Basel, 1987.

Bastelaer
R. van Bastelaer, *Les Estampes de Peter Bruegel l'Ancien*, Brussels, 1908.

Bauch 1960
K. Bauch, *Der frühe Rembrandt und seine Zeit: Studien zur geschichtlichen Bedeutung seines Frühstils*, Berlin, 1960.

Bauch 1966
K. Bauch, *Rembrandt: Gemälde*, Berlin, 1966.

Benesch (+ no.)
See BENESCH 1973

Benesch 1924–25
O. Benesch, 'Rembrandts "Falkenjäger"', *Wiener Jahrbuch für Kunstgeschichte*, vol. 3, 1924–25, pp. 115–18.

Benesch 1928
O. Benesch, 'Zu Barent Fabritius', *Belvedere*, vol. 12, March 1928, pp. 65–6.

Benesch 1935
O. Benesch, *Rembrandt: Werk und Forschung*, Vienna, 1935.

Benesch 1954–57
O. Benesch, *The Drawings of Rembrandt*, 6 vols, London, 1954–57. See also BENESCH 1973.

Benesch 1956
O. Benesch, 'Wordly and Religious Portraits in Rembrandt's Late Art', *Art Quarterly*, vol. XIX, no. 4, Winter 1956, pp. 335–55.

Benesch 1973
O. Benesch, *The Drawings of Rembrandt*, 6 vols, 2nd edn, rev. E. Benesch, London, 1973. See also BENESCH 1954–57.

Berlin / Amsterdam / London 1991–92a
C. Brown, J. Kelch & P. van Thiel, *Rembrandt: The Master and His Workshop – Paintings* (exh. cat.), trans. E. Clegg, M. Hoyle & P. Vincent, Gemäldegalerie Staatliche Museen Preußischer Kulturbesitz, Altes Museum, Berlin, Rijksmuseum, Amsterdam, National Gallery, London, 1991. See also BERLIN / AMSTERDAM / LONDON 1991–92c, and DUDOK VAN HEEL 1991–92a, VAN DE WETERING 1991–92a.

Berlin / Amsterdam / London 1991–92b
H. Bevers, P. Schatborn & B. Welzel, *Rembrandt: The Master and His Workshop – Drawings and Etchings* (exh. cat.), trans. E. Clegg, F. Healy, J. Meijer & P. Vincent, Kupferstichkabinett, Berlin, Rijksmuseum, Amsterdam, National Gallery, London, 1991. See also BERLIN / AMSTERDAM / LONDON 1991–92d, and BEVERS 1991–92.

Berlin / Amsterdam / London 1991–92c
C. Brown, J. Kelch & P. van Thiel, *Rembrandt: De meester en zijn werkplaats – schilderijen* (exh. cat.), Gemäldegalerie Staatliche Museen Preußischer Kulturbesitz, Altes Museum, Berlin, Rijksmuseum, Amsterdam, National Gallery, London, 1991. See also BERLIN / AMSTERDAM / LONDON 1991–92a, and BOOMGAARD & SCHELLER 1991–92, BRUYN 1991–92, VAN DEURSEN 1991–92, DUDOK VAN HEEL 1991–92, VAN DE WETERING 1991–92c.

Berlin / Amsterdam / London 1991–92d
H. Bevers, P. Schatborn & B. Welzel, *Rembrandt: De meester en zijn werkplaats – tekeningen en etsen* (exh. cat.), Kupferstichkabinett, Berlin, Rijksmuseum, Amsterdam, National Gallery, London, 1991. See also BERLIN / AMSTERDAM / LONDON 1991–92b.

Bevers 1991–92
H. Bevers, 'Rembrandt as an Etcher', in BERLIN / AMSTERDAM / LONDON 1991–92b, pp. 160–9.

Van Biema 1906
E. van Biema, 'Nalezing van de stadsrekeningen van Amsterdam van af het jaar 1531. IV', *Oud-Holland*, vol. 26, 1906, pp. 109–28.

Bijtelaar 1953
B. Bijtelaar, 'Het graf van Saskia', *Amstelodamum*, vol. 40, 1953, pp. 50–2.

Bille 1961
C. Bille, *De tempel der kunst of het cabinet van den Heer Braamcamp*, 2 vols, Amsterdam, 1961.

Biörklund
G. Biörklund, with O. H. Barnard, *Rembrandt's Etchings: True and False – A Summary Catalogue*, Stockholm, 1955.

Blankert 1967
A. Blankert, 'Heraclitus en Democritus, in het bijzonder in de Nederlandse kunst van de 17e eeuw', *Nederlands Kunsthistorisch Jaarboek*, vol. 18, 1967, pp. 31–124.

Blankert 1973
A. Blankert, 'Rembrandt, Zeuxis and Ideal Beauty', in BRUYN ET AL. 1973, pp. 32–9.

Blankert 1975
A. Blankert, *Johannes Vermeer van Delft 1632–1675*, Utrecht, 1975. See also BLANKERT 1978a.

Blankert 1975a
A. Blankert, *Kunst als regeringszaak in Amsterdam in de 17e eeuw: Rondom schilderijen van Ferdinand Bol* [with English summary] (exh. cat.), Koninklijk Paleis, Amsterdam, 1975.

Blankert 1975–79
A. Blankert, with R. Ruurs, *Amsterdams Historisch Museum: Schilderijen daterend van voor 1800 – Voorlopige catalogus*, Amsterdam, 1975–79.

Blankert 1976
A. Blankert, *Ferdinand Bol (1616–1680), een leerling van Rembrandt* (diss.), Utrecht, 1976.

Blankert 1978
A. Blankert, *Museum Bredius: Catalogus van de schilderijen en tekeningen*, The Hague, 1978. See also BLANKERT 1991.

Blankert 1978a
A. Blankert, *Vermeer of Delft: Complete Edition of the Paintings*, Oxford, 1978. See also BLANKERT 1975.

Blankert 1982
A. Blankert, *Ferdinand Bol (1616–1680), Rembrandt's Pupil*, Monographs on Dutch & Flemish Painting, vol. II, 2nd edn, trans. I. Rike, Doornspijk, 1982. See also BLANKERT 1976.

Blankert 1986–87
A. Blankert, 'Caravaggio en Noord-Nederland', in UTRECHT / BRAUNSCHWEIG 1986–87, pp. 17–41.

Blankert 1986–87a
A. Blankert, 'Caravaggio und die nördlichen Niederlande', in UTRECHT / BRAUNSCHWEIG 1986–87a, pp. 17–41.

Blankert 1991
A. Blankert, *Museum Bredius: Catalogus van de schilderijen en tekeningen*, rev. edn, Zwolle, 1991. See also BLANKERT 1978.

Blankert 1992
A. Blankert, 'Ferdinand Bol in een Utrechts burgerpaleis', *Kunstschrift*, vol. 36, no. 6, 1992, pp. 22–7.

Blankert 1992–93
A. Blankert, 'Rembrandt, hans elever och hans skola / Rembrandt, His Pupils and His Studio', in STOCKHOLM 1992–93, pp. 41–70.

Blankert 1993
A. Blankert, 'Rembrandt and His Followers: Notes on Connoisseurship – Its Potential and Pitfalls', in CAVALLI-BJÖRKMAN 1993, pp. 77–97.

Blankert & Van Velzen 1986–87
A. Blankert & T. van Velzen, 'Some Observations on Bredius the Connoisseur', in *Dutch Masterworks from the Bredius Museum: A Connoisseur's Collection* (exh. cat.), National Academy of Design, New York, and 6 other venues, 1986, pp. 8–12.

Blechinger 1980
E. Blechinger, *Residenzgalerie mit Sammlung Czernin und Sammlung Schönborn-Buchheim*, Salzburg, 1980.

Bock & Rosenberg 1930
E. Bock & J. Rosenberg, *Die niederländischen Meister: Beschreibendes Verzeichnis sämtlicher Zeichnungen*, 2 vols, Berlin, 1930.

Bode 1883
W. Bode, *Studien zur Geschichte der holländischen Malerei*, Braunschweig, 1883.

Bode 1891
W. Bode, 'Das Bildniss von Rembrandt's Bruder Adriaen Harmensz van Rijn im Mauritshuis', *Oud-Holland*, vol. 9, 1891, pp. 1–6.

Bode 1907
W. Bode, *Rembrandt und seine Zeitgenossen: Charakterbilder der grossen Meister der holländischen und vlämischen Malerschule im siebzehnten Jahrhundert*, 2nd edn, Leipzig, 1907 (1st edn, 1906).

Bode 1914
W. Bode (ed.), *Die Gemäldesammlung Marcus Kappel in Berlin*, Berlin, 1914.

Bode 1917
W. Bode, 'Ein Studienkopf aus Rembrandts Spätzeit im Berliner Schloss, und seine Beziehung zu den slawischen Pilger- und Mönchsbildnissen des Meisters aus dem Jahre 1661', *Jahrbuch der Preussischen Kunstsammlungen*, vol. 38, 1917, pp. 107–11.

Bode & Hofstede de Groot 1897–1905
W. Bode & C. Hofstede de Groot, *Rembrandt: Beschreibendes Verzeichnis seiner Gemälde mit den heliographischen Nachbildungen, Geschichte seines Lebens und seiner Kunst*, 8 vols, Paris, 1897–1905. See also BODE & HOFSTEDE DE GROOT 1897–1906.

Bode & Hofstede de Groot 1897–1906
W. Bode & C. Hofstede de Groot, *The Complete Work of Rembrandt: History, Description, and Heliographic Reproduction of All the Master's Pictures, with a Study of His Life and His Art*, 8 vols, trans. F. Simmonds, Paris, 1897–1906. See also BODE & HOFSTEDE DE GROOT 1897–1905.

Bohlin 1979
D. DeGrazia Bohlin, *Prints and Related Drawings by the Carracci Family: A Catalogue Raisonné*, Washington DC, 1979.

Bok 1994
M. J. Bok, *Vraag en aanbod op de Nederlandse kunstmarkt 1580–1700* (diss.), Utrecht, 1994.

Bol 1982
L. J. Bol, *Holländische Maler des 17. Jahrhunderts nahe den grossen Meistern: Landschaften und Stilleben*, 2nd edn, Munich, 1982.

Bolten 1967
J. Bolten, *Dutch Drawings from the Collection of Dr C. Hofstede de Groot: An Introduction and Critical Catalogue*, Utrecht, 1967.

Bolten 1979
J. Bolten, *Het noord- en zuidnederlandse tekenboek, 1600–1750* (diss.), Ter Aar, 1979.

Boomgaard & Scheller 1991–92
J. Boomgaard & R. W. Scheller, 'In wankel evenwicht: De Rembrandt-waardering in vogelvlucht', in BERLIN / AMSTERDAM / LONDON 1991–92c, pp. 106–23.

Boone 1980
P. R. Boone, 'The Geometrical Engraving at [*sic*] Rembrandt's Plate for The Return of the Prodigal Son', *Museologia*, vol. XI, no. 15, 1980, pp. 25–31.

Boston 1992
P. C. Sutton et al., *Prized Possessions: European Paintings from Private Collections of Friends of the Museum of Fine Arts, Boston* (exh. cat.), Museum of Fine Arts, Boston, 1992.

Boston / New York 1969–70
Rembrandt: Experimental Etcher (exh. cat.), Museum of Fine Arts, Boston, Pierpont Morgan Library, New York, 1969.

Van Brabant 1967
J. van Brabant, *Sint Bavo: Edelman, boeteling en monnik*, Wilrijk, 1967.

Braunschweig 1979
R. Klessmann, J. Bialostocki, R. E. O. Ekkart & S. Jacob, *Jan Lievens: Ein Maler im Schatten Rembrandts* (exh. cat.), Herzog Anton Ulrich-Museum, Braunschweig, 1979.

Braunschweig 1983
R. Klessmann et al., *Die holländischen Gemälde* (exh. cat.), Herzog Anton Ulrich-Museum, Braunschweig, 1983.

Braunschweig 1993–94
Bilder vom alten Menschen in der niederländischen und deutschen Kunst 1550–1750 (exh. cat.), Herzog Anton Ulrich-Museum, Braunschweig, 1993.

Brayley 1808
E. W. Brayley, *The Beauties of England and Wales; or, Original Delineations, Topographical, Historical, and Descriptive, of Each County, Embellished with Engravings*, vol. VII, London, 1808.

Brederode 1622
G. A. Brederode, *Groot lied-boeck, naar de oorspronkelijke uitgave van 1622 ...* (1622), ed. A. A. van Rijnbach, Rotterdam, 1966.

Bredius (+ no.)
See BREDIUS 1935 or BREDIUS 1937. See also BREDIUS / GERSON 1969.

Bredius 1889
A. Bredius, 'Kunstkritiek der XVIIe eeuw', *Oud-Holland*, vol. 7, 1889, pp. 41–4.

Bredius 1890
A. Bredius, 'Het schildersregister van Jan Sysmus, stads-doctor van Amsterdam', *Oud-Holland*, vol. 8, 1890, pp. 1–17, 217–34, 297–313.

Bredius 1892
A. Bredius, 'De schilder Johannes van de Cappelle', *Oud-Holland*, vol. 10, 1892, pp. 26–40.

Bredius 1894
A. Bredius, 'Het schildersregister van Jan Sysmus, stads-doctor van Amsterdam', *Oud-Holland*, vol. 12, 1894, pp. 160–71.

Bredius 1895
A. Bredius, 'Het schildersregister van Jan Sysmus, stads-doctor van Amsterdam', *Oud-Holland*, vol. 13, 1895, pp. 112–20.

Bredius 1899
A. Bredius, 'De Rembrandt tentoonstelling in Londen', *De Amsterdammer*, nos 1126–9, 22–29 January, 5–12 February 1899.

Bredius 1899a
A. Bredius, 'Nieuwe Rembrandtiana', *Oud-Holland*, vol. 17, 1899, pp. 1–5.

Bredius 1907
A. Bredius, *De Leidsche tentoonstelling in MCMVI ter herdenking en eere van het derde eeuwfeest van Rembrandt's geboortedag XV juli MDCVI*, Haarlem, 1907.

Bredius 1909
A. Bredius, 'Rembrandt als plaatsnijder', *Oud-Holland*, vol. 27, 1909, pp. 111–14.

Bredius 1912*
A. Bredius, 'Did Rembrandt Paint the Portrait of Elizabeth Bas?', *Burlington Magazine*, vol. XX, no. 108, March 1912, pp. 330–41.
* Referred to in text as Bredius 1911

Bredius 1915
A. Bredius, 'Rembrandtiana', *Oud-Holland*, vol. 33, 1915, pp. 126–8.

Bredius 1915–22
A. Bredius (ed.), *Künstler-Inventare: Urkunden zur Geschichte der holländischen Kunst des XVIten, XVIIten, und XVIIIten Jahrhunderts*, 8 vols, The Hague, 1915–22.

Bredius 1921
A. Bredius, 'Wiedergefundene Gemälde Rembrandts', *Zeitschrift für bildende Kunst*, vol. LVI, 1921, pp. 146–52.

Bredius 1924
A. Bredius, 'Some Early Rembrandts', *Burlington Magazine*, vol. XLV, no. 259, October 1924, p. 159.

Bredius 1935
A. Bredius, *Rembrandt: Gemälde*, Vienna, 1935.
or
A. Bredius, *Rembrandt: Schilderijen*, Utrecht, 1935.
See also BREDIUS 1937, BREDIUS / GERSON 1969.

Bredius 1937
A. Bredius, *The Paintings of Rembrandt*, trans. J. Byam Shaw, Vienna, 1937. See also BREDIUS 1935, BREDIUS / GERSON 1969.

Bredius & De Roever 1890
A. Bredius & N. de Roever, 'Rembrandt: Nieuwe bijdragen tot zijne levensgeschiedenis. III', *Oud-Holland*, vol. 8, 1890, pp. 173–86.

Bredius / Gerson 1969
A. Bredius, *Rembrandt: The Complete Edition of the Paintings*, 3rd edn, rev. H. Gerson, London, 1969. See also BREDIUS 1935, BREDIUS 1937.

Brejon de Lavergnée, Foucart & Reynaud 1979
A. Brejon de Lavergnée, J. Foucart & N. Reynaud, *Catalogue sommaire illustré des peintures du Musée du Louvre*, vol. I, Paris, 1979.

Brière-Misme 1927
C. Brière-Misme, 'Le Portrait de famille de Arent de Gelder', *Bulletin des musées: Musée du Louvre*, vol. 5, 15 March 1927, pp. 87–8.

Broos 1972
B. Broos, 'Rembrandt. Verandert. En overgeschildert', *Kroniek van het Rembrandthuis*, vol. 26, 1972, pp. 137–52.

Broos 1975–76
B. P. J. Broos, 'Rembrandt and Lastman's *Coriolanus*: The History Piece in 17th-Century Theory and Practice', *Simiolus*, vol. 8, no. 4, 1975–76, pp. 199–228.

Broos 1977
B. P. J. Broos, *Index to the Formal Sources of Rembrandt's Art*, Maarssen, 1977.

Broos 1980
B. P. J. Broos, 'Rembrandts Indische Miniaturen', *Spiegel Historiael*, vol. 15, 1980, pp. 210–18.

Broos 1981
B. Broos, *Rembrandt en tekenaars uit zijn omgeving*, Oude tekeningen in het bezit van de Gemeentemusea van Amsterdam waaronder de collectie Fodor, vol. III, Amsterdam, 1981.

Broos 1981–82
B. P. J. Broos, '[review of STRAUSS & VAN DER MEULEN 1979]', *Simiolus*, vol. 12, no. 4, 1981–82, pp. 245–62.

Broos 1983
B. Broos, 'Fame Shared Is Fame Doubled', in AMSTERDAM / GRONINGEN 1983, pp. 35–58.

Broos 1984
B. P. J. Broos, '[review of SUMOWSKI, DRAWINGS, vols 1–4]', *Oud Holland*, vol. 98, no. 3, 1984, pp. 162–86.

Broos 1987
B. Broos, *Meesterwerken in het Mauritshuis*, The Hague, 1987.

Broos 1989
B. Broos, 'Improving and Finishing Old Master Drawings: An Art in Itself', *Hoogsteder-Naumann Mercury*, no. 8, 1989, pp. 34–55.

Broos 1991
B. Broos, 'Het mysterie van de Poolse ruiter', *Vrij Nederland*, 7 December 1991, pp. 52–6.

Broos 1993
B. Broos, *Liefde, list en lijden: Historiestukken in het Mauritshuis*, Ghent, 1993.

Broos 1995
B. Broos, 'Rembrandts schatkamer', *Tableau*, vol. 18, 1995, pp. 66–74.

Broun 1987
F. Broun, Sir Joshua Reynolds' Collection of Paintings, PhD diss., Princeton University, Princeton, New Jersey, 1987.

Brown 1980
C. Brown, *Second Sight: Titian,* Portrait of a Man, *and Rembrandt,* Self-Portrait at the Age of 34 (exh. cat.), National Gallery, London, 1980.

Brown 1981
C. Brown, *Carel Fabritius: Complete Edition with a Catalogue Raisonné*, Oxford, 1981.

Brown 1986
C. Brown, *Dutch Landscape: The Early Years – Haarlem and Amsterdam 1590–1650* (exh. cat.), National Gallery, London, 1986. See also REZNICEK 1986.

Brown & Roy 1992
C. Brown & A. Roy, 'Rembrandt's "Alexander the Great"', *Burlington Magazine*, vol. CXXXIV, no. 1070, May 1992, pp. 285–97.

Brugmans 1930
H. Brugmans, *Geschiedenis van Amsterdam van den oorsprong af tot heden*, 8 vols, Amsterdam, 1930.

Brusati 1990–91
C. Brusati, 'Stilled Lives: Self-Portraiture and Self-Reflection in Seventeenth-Century Netherlandish Still-Life Painting', *Simiolus*, vol. 20, nos 2–3, 1990–91, pp. 168–82.

Brusati 1995
C. Brusati, *Artifice and Illusion: The Art and Writing of Samuel van Hoogstraten*, Chicago, 1995.

Bruyn 1951
J. Bruyn, 'David Bailly, "fort bon peintre en pourtraicts et en vie coye"', *Oud-Holland*, vol. 66, no. 3, 1951, pp. 148–64.

Bruyn 1970–71
J. Bruyn, 'Rembrandt and the Italian Baroque', *Simiolus*, vol. 4, no. 1, 1970–71, pp. 28–48.

Bruyn 1982
J. Bruyn, 'The Documentary Value of Early Graphic Reproductions', in CORPUS, vol. I, 1982, pp. 35–51.

Bruyn 1984
J. Bruyn, '[review of SUMOWSKI, GEMÄLDE, vol. I]', *Oud Holland*, vol. 98, no. 3, 1984, pp. 146–62.

Bruyn 1986
J. Bruyn, 'Patrons and Early Owners', in CORPUS, vol. II, 1986, pp. 91–8.

Bruyn 1987
J. Bruyn, 'Ikonographische Bemerkungen zur *tronie*', in *Hendrick ter Brugghen und die Nachfolger Caravaggios in Holland*, ed. R. Klessmann, Braunschweig, 1987, pp. 67–76.

Bruyn 1988
J. Bruyn, '[review of SUMOWSKI, GEMÄLDE, vol. III]', *Oud Holland*, vol. 102, no. 4, 1988, pp. 322–33.

Bruyn 1989
J. Bruyn, 'Studio Practice and Studio Production', in CORPUS, vol. III, 1989, pp. 12–50.

Bruyn 1990
J. Bruyn, 'An Unknown Assistant in Rembrandt's Workshop in the Early 1660s', *Burlington Magazine*, vol. CXXXII, no. 1051, October 1990, pp. 715–18.

Bruyn 1991–92
J. Bruyn, 'Rembrandts werkplaats: Functie en produktie', in BERLIN / AMSTERDAM / LONDON 1991–92c, pp. 68–89.

Bruyn 1996
J. Bruyn, '[review of SUMOWSKI, GEMÄLDE, vol. VI]', *Oud Holland*, vol. 110, nos 3–4, 1996, pp. 165–73.

Bruyn & Van de Wetering 1986
J. Bruyn & E. van de Wetering, 'Stylistic Features of the 1630s: The Portraits', in CORPUS, vol. II, 1986, pp. 3–13.

Bruyn et al. 1973
J. Bruyn, J. A. Emmens, E. de Jongh & D. P. Snoep (eds), *Album Amicorum J. G. van Gelder*, The Hague, 1973. See also BLANKERT 1973, JUDSON 1973.

Bruyn et al. 1993
J. Bruyn, B. Haak, S. H. Levie & P. J. J. van Thiel, 'The Rembrandt Research Project' [letter], *Burlington Magazine*, vol. CXXXV, no. 1081, April 1993, p. 279.

De Bruyn Kops 1965
C. J. de Bruyn Kops, 'Vergeten zelfportretten van Govert Flinck en Bartholomeus van der Helst', *Bulletin van het Rijksmuseum*, vol. 13, no. 1, 1965, pp. 20–9.

Budick 1988
S. Budick, 'Rembrandt's *Jeremiah*', *Journal of the Warburg and Courtauld Institutes*, vol. LI, 1988, pp. 260–4.

Buijnsters-Smets 1995
L. Buijnsters-Smets, *Jan Massijs: Een Antwerps schilder uit de zestiende eeuw*, Zwolle, 1995.

Bürger 1858–60
W. Bürger [E. J. T. Thoré], *Musées de la Hollande*, 2 vols, Paris, 1858–60.

Calvin 1554
J. Calvin, *Commentaries on the First Book of Moses Called Genesis* (1554), trans. J. King, Grand Rapids, Michigan, 1948.

Cambridge 1993–94
C. Hartley, *Rembrandt Landscape Prints in the Collection of the Fitzwilliam Museum* (exh. handlist), Fitzwilliam Museum, Cambridge, 1993.

Cambridge 1996–97
C. Hartley, *Rembrandt and the Nude* (exh. handlist), Fitzwilliam Museum, Cambridge, 1996.

Campbell 1980
C. Campbell, 'Rembrandts etsen *Het sterfbed van Maria* en *De drie bomen*', *Kroniek van het Rembrandthuis*, vol. 32, no. 2, 1980, pp. 2–33.

Campbell 1990
L. Campbell, *Renaissance Portraits: European Portrait Painting in the 14th, 15th and 16th Centuries*, New Haven, Connecticut, 1990.

Carroll 1981
M. Deutsch Carroll, 'Rembrandt as Meditational Printmaker', *Art Bulletin*, vol. LXIII, no. 4, December 1981, pp. 585–610.

Castiglione 1528
B. Castiglione, *Il libro del cortegiano* (1528), trans. A. Haakman, Amsterdam, 1981.

Cats 1632
J. Cats, *Spiegel van den ouden en nieuwen tyt*, The Hague, 1632.

Cavalli-Björkman 1993
G. Cavalli-Björkman (ed.), *Rembrandt and His Pupils: Papers Given at a Symposium in Nationalmuseum Stockholm, 2–3 October 1992*, Stockholm, 1993. See also BLANKERT 1993, ROBINSON 1993, SLUIJTER 1993a.

Chapman 1990
H. P. Chapman, *Rembrandt's Self-Portraits: A Study in Seventeenth-Century Identity*, Princeton, New Jersey, 1990.

Chicago 1969
E. Haverkamp Begemann et al., *Rembrandt after Three Hundred Years* (exh. cat.), The Art Institute of Chicago, 1969. See also HAVERKAMP BEGEMANN 1969.

Chicago / San Francisco / Boston / New York 1992–93*
R. Keaveney et al., *Master European Paintings from the National Gallery of Ireland: Mantegna to Goya* (exh. cat.), Art Institute of Chicago, The Fine Arts Museums of San Francisco, Museum of Fine Arts, Boston, IBM Gallery of Science and Art, New York, 1992.
*Referred to in text as Chicago/San Francisco/Boston/New York 1992

Cocke 1972
R. Cocke, *Pier Francesco Mola*, Oxford Studies in the History of Art and Architecture, Oxford, 1972.

Collection catalogue, Comte de Vence, 1759
Catalogue des tableaux du cabinet de monsieur le Comte de Vence, Paris, 1759.

Collection catalogue, Comte de Vence, 1761
R. Remy, *Catalogue raisonné des tableaux, desseins, originaux et estampes, du feu M. le Comte de Vence*, Paris, 1761.

Coppier 1917
A.-C. Coppier, *Les Eaux-Fortes de Rembrandt*, Paris, 1917.

Corpus
J. Bruyn, B. Haak, S. H. Levie, P. J. J. van Thiel, E. van de Wetering, *A Corpus of Rembrandt Paintings*, Stichting Foundation Rembrandt Research Project, 3 vols to date, trans. D. Cook-Radmore, The Hague / Dordrecht / Boston / London, 1982–. See also BRUYN 1982, BRUYN 1986, BRUYN 1989, BRUYN & VAN DE WETERING 1986, VAN DE WETERING 1986.

Cunningham 1939
C. C. Cunningham, 'Four Paintings of the Rembrandt School at Boston', *Art in America*, vol. 27, 1939, pp. 185–90.

Dacier 1911
E. Dacier, *Catalogues de ventes et livrets de salons illustrés par Gabriel de Saint-Aubin*, vol. V, *Catalogue de la vente Louis-Michel Vanloo (1772)*, Paris, 1911.

Davies 1993
A. Davies, *16th and 17th Century Dutch and Flemish Paintings in the Springfield Museum of Fine Arts*, Springfield, Massachusetts, 1993.

Delacroix / Joubin 1950
A. Joubin (ed.), *Journal d'Eugène Delacroix*, 3 vols, 2nd edn, Paris, 1950.

Derby 1827
A Catalogue of Paintings, Drawings etc. in the Collection of Joseph Strutt, Derby, Derby, 1827.

Van Deursen 1991–92
A. T. van Deursen, 'Rembrandt en zijn tijd: Het leven van een Amsterdamse burgerman', in BERLIN / AMSTERDAM / LONDON 1991–92c, pp. 40–9.

Dezallier d'Argenville 1745–52
J. A. Dezallier d'Argenville, *Abrégé de la vie des plus fameux peintres, avec leurs portraits gravés en taille-douce, les indications de leurs principaux ouvrages, quelques réflexions sur leurs caractères, et la manière de connoître des desseins et les tableaux des grands maîtres*, 3 vols, Paris, 1745–52.

Dickey 1986
S. S. Dickey, '"Judicious Negligence": Rembrandt Transforms an Emblematic Convention', *Art Bulletin*, vol. LXVIII, no. 2, June 1986, pp. 253–62.

Dickey 1994
S. S. Dickey, Prints, Portraits and Patronage in Rembrandt's Work around 1640, PhD diss., New York University, New York, 1994.

Dickey 1995
S. S. Dickey, '"Met een wenende ziel ... doch droge ogen": Women Holding Handkerchiefs in Seventeenth-Century Dutch Portraits', *Nederlands Kunsthistorisch Jaarboek*, vol. 46, 1995, pp. 333–67.

Dirkse & Kootte 1995
P. P. W. M. Dirkse & T. G. Kootte, '"De ontmoeting van Eliëzer en Rebekka" van Gerbrand van den Eeckhout', *Catharijnebrief*, no. 52, December 1995, pp. 3–8.

Dodsley 1761
R. & J. Dodsley, *London and Its Environs Described: Containing an Account of Whatever Is Most Remarkable for Grandeur, Elegance, Curiosity or Use, in the City and in the Country Twenty Miles round It. Comprehending Also Whatever Is Most Material in the History and Antiquities of This Great Metropolis*, London, 1761.

D'Oench 1995–96
E. G. D'Oench, *Prodigal Son Narratives 1480–1980* (exh. cat.), Yale University Art Gallery, New Haven, Connecticut, Davison Art Center, Wesleyan University, Middletown, Connecticut, Sterling and Francine Clark Institute, Williamstown, Massachusetts, 1995.

Dordrecht 1992–93
De zichtbaere werelt: Schilderkunst uit de Gouden Eeuw in Hollands oudste stad (exh. cat.), Dordrechts Museum, 1992.

Dudok van Heel 1977
S. A. C. Dudok van Heel, 'Jan Pietersz Zomer (1641–1724): Makelaar in schilderijen (1690–1724)', *Amstelodamum*, vol. 69, 1977, pp. 89–106.

Dudok van Heel 1979
S. A. C. Dudok van Heel, 'Het maecenaat Trip: Opdrachten aan Ferdinand Bol en Rembrandt van Rijn', *Kroniek van het Rembrandthuis*, vol. 31, no. 1, 1979, pp. 14–26.

Dudok van Heel 1982
S. A. C. Dudok van Heel, 'Het "schilderhuis" van Govert Flinck en de kunsthandel van Uylenburgh aan de Lauriergracht te Amsterdam', *Jaarboek Amstelodamum*, vol. 74, 1982, pp. 70–90.

Dudok van Heel 1991–92a
S. A. C. Dudok van Heel, 'Rembrandt van Rijn (1606–1669): A Changing Portrait of the Artist', in BERLIN / AMSTERDAM / LONDON 1991–92a, pp. 50–67.

Dudok van Heel 1991–92c
S. A. C. Dudok van Heel, 'Rembrandt van Rijn (1606–1669): Een veranderend schildersportret', in BERLIN / AMSTERDAM / LONDON 1991–92c, pp. 50–67.

Dudok van Heel 1993
S. A. C. Dudok van Heel, 'Rembrandt en Menasseh ben Israel', *Kroniek van het Rembrandthuis*, vol. 45, no. 1, 1993, pp. 22–9.

Dutuit 1885
E. Dutuit, *Tableaux et dessins de Rembrandt: Catalogue historique et descriptif* (suppl. to *L'Oeuvre complet de Rembrandt*), Paris, 1885.

Duverger 1965
E. Duverger, 'Een betwist schilderij van Paulus Bril bij een Gents kanunnik', *Belgisch Tijdschrift voor Oudheidkunde en Kunstgeschiedenis*, vol. 35, 1965, pp. 191–200.

Van Eck 1993–94
X. van Eck, 'From Doubt to Conviction: Clandestine Catholic Churches as Patrons of Dutch Caravaggesque Painting', *Simiolus*, vol. 22, no. 4, 1993–94, pp. 217–34.

Edinburgh 1950
Rembrandt (exh. cat.), National Gallery of Scotland, Edinburgh, 1950.

Van Eeghen 1956
I. H. van Eeghen, 'De Familie De la Tombe en Rembrandt', *Oud Holland*, vol. 71, 1956, pp. 43–9.

Van Eeghen 1956a
I. H. van Eeghen, 'De kinderen van Rembrandt en Saskia', *Amstelodamum*, vol. 43, 1956, pp. 144–6.

Van Eeghen 1983
I. H. van Eeghen, 'De familie Trip en het Trippenhuis', in *Het Trippenhuis te Amsterdam*, eds R. Meischke & H. E. Reeser, Amsterdam, 1983, pp. 27–125.

Eigenberger 1927
R. Eigenberger, *Der Gemäldegalerie der Akademie der bildenden Künste in Wien*, 2 vols, Vienna, 1927.

Ekkart 1986–87
R. Ekkart, introduction to AMSTERDAM 1986–87, pp. 4–12.

Elsum 1700
J. Elsum, *Epigrams upon the Paintings of the Most Eminent Masters, Ancient and Modern, with Reflexions upon the Several Schools of Painting*, London, 1700.

Emmens 1964
J. A. Emmens, *Rembrandt en de regels van de kunst* (diss.), Utrecht, 1964. See also EMMENS 1968, EMMENS 1979.

Emmens 1968
J. A. Emmens, *Rembrandt en de regels van de kunst* [with English summary], Utrechtse kunsthistorische studiën, vol. 10, Utrecht, 1968. See also EMMENS 1964, EMMENS 1979.

Emmens 1979
J. A. Emmens, *Rembrandt en de regels van de kunst* [with English summary], rev. edn, Amsterdam, 1979. See also EMMENS 1964, EMMENS 1968.

Evelyn 1662
J. Evelyn, *Sculptura; or, The History and Art of Chalcography and Engraving in Copper ...* , London, 1662.

Eyffinger 1987
A. Eyffinger, 'De politieke component van het humanistendrama', *De zeventiende eeuw*, vol. 3, no. 7, 1987, pp. 24–38.

Filedt Kok 1972
J. P. Filedt Kok, *Rembrandt Etchings and Drawings in the Rembrandt House: A Catalogue*, Amsterdam, 1972.

Filedt Kok 1994
J. P. Filedt Kok, 'Het belang van de terugkeer van een aantal van Rembrandts etsplaten naar Nederland', *Kroniek van het Rembrandthuis*, vol. 46, no. 1, 1994, pp. 2–19.

Fokkens 1662
M. Fokkens, *Beschrijvinge der wijdt vermaarde Koop-Stadt Amstelredam*, Amsterdam, 1662.

Van Fossen 1969
D. R. van Fossen, The Paintings of Aert de Gelder, PhD diss., Harvard University, Cambridge, Massachusetts, 1969.

Foucart 1982
J. Foucart, *Les Peintures de Rembrandt au Louvre*, Paris, 1982.

Foucart 1988–89
J. Foucart, *Peintres rembranesques au Louvre* (exh. cat.), Musée du Louvre, Paris, 1988.

Frankfurt 1993
S. Schulze et al., *Leselust: Niederländische Malerei von Rembrandt bis Vermeer* (exh. cat.), Schirn Kunsthalle, Frankfurt, 1993.

Franz 1969
H. G. Franz, *Niederländische Landschafts-malerei im Zeitalter des Manierismus*, Graz, 1969.

Fredericksen 1972
B. B. Fredericksen, *Catalogue of the Paintings in the J. Paul Getty Museum*, Malibu, 1972.

Freedberg 1980
D. Freedberg, *Dutch Landscape Prints of the Seventeenth Century*, British Museum Prints and Drawings Series, London, 1980.

Frerichs 1970
L. C. J. Frerichs, 'Nieuw licht op een oud opschrift', *Kroniek van het Rembrandthuis*, vol. 24, 1970, pp. 35–44.

Gaehtgens 1987
B. Gaehtgens, *Adriaen van der Werff 1659–1722*, Munich, 1987.

Gantner 1959
J. Gantner, 'Rembrandts "Falkenier" in Göteborg: Ein letztes Echo aus dem "Abendmahl" des Leonardo', in *Festschrift Karl M. Swoboda zum 28. Januar 1959*, Vienna, 1959, pp. 97–102.

Gantner 1964
J. Gantner, *Rembrandt und die Verwandlung klassischer Formen*, Bern, 1964.

Van Gelder 1935
J. G. van Gelder, 'Rembrandt's philosophen in den kunsthandel D. A. Hoogendijk & Co., Amsterdam', *Elsevier's Geïllustreerd Maandschrift*, vol. 89, no. 45, 1935, pp. 65–6.

Van Gelder 1963
J. G. van Gelder, 'Jeremia, treurende over de verwoesting van Jeruzalem', *Openbaar Kunstbezit*, vol. 7, 1963.

Gersaint 1751
C. E. Gersaint, *Catalogue raisonné de toutes les pièces qui forment l'oeuvre de Rembrandt*, Paris, 1751.

Gerson 1942
H. Gerson, *Ausbreitung und Nachwirkung der holländischen Malerei des 17. Jahrhunderts*, Haarlem, 1942.

Gerson 1961
H. Gerson, *Seven Letters by Rembrandt*, The Hague, 1961.

Gerson 1968
H. Gerson, *Rembrandt Paintings*, trans. H. Norden, London, 1968.

Gerson 1973
H. Gerson, 'Zur Nachwirkung von Rembrandts Kunst', in VON SIMSON & KELCH 1973, pp. 207–20.

Gherardini 1878
G. Gherardini, *Vocabolario della lingua italiana*, vol. VI, Milan, 1878.

Gibson 1977
W. Gibson, *Bruegel*, New York, 1977.

Gibson-Wood 1982
C. J. Gibson-Wood, *Studies in the Theory of Connoisseurship from Vasari to Morelli*, London, 1982.

Van Gils 1936
J. B. F. van Gils, 'Hippocrates op bezoek bij Democritus', *Bijdragen tot de Geschiedenis der Geneeskunde*, vol. 16, 1936, p. 115.

Giltaij 1988
J. Giltaij, *De tekeningen van Rembrandt en zijn school in het Museum Boymans-van Beuningen*, Rotterdam, 1988. See also GILTAIJ 1988a.

Giltaij 1988a
J. Giltaij, *The Drawings by Rembrandt and His School in the Museum Boymans-van Beuningen*, trans. P. Wardle, Rotterdam, 1988. See also GILTAIJ 1988.

Giltaij 1997
J. Giltaij, *Ruffo en Rembrandt, over een Siciliaanse verzamelaar in de zeventiende eeuw die drie schilderijen bij Rembrandt bestelde* (diss.), Amsterdam, 1997.

Goeree 1670
W. Goeree, *Inleydingh tot de praktijck der algemeene schilderkonst*, Middelburg, 1670.

Goldscheider 1960
L. Goldscheider, *Rembrandt: Paintings, Drawings and Etchings*, London, 1960.

Gombrich 1984
E. H. Gombrich, 'Raphael: A Quincentennial Address', *Art History*, vol. 7, no. 2, 1984, pp. 164–75.

Gonnet 1920
C. J. Gonnet, 'Rembrandt en Geertje Dircx', *Oud-Holland*, vol. 38, 1920, pp. 80–2.

Van Gool 1750–51
J. van Gool, *De nieuwe schouburg der Nederlantsche kunstschilders en schilderessen: Waer in de levens- en kunstbedryven der tans levende en reets overleedene schilders, die van Houbraken, noch eenig ander schryver, zyn aengeteekend, verhaelt worden*, 2 vols, The Hague, 1750–51.

Gould 1976
C. Gould, *The Paintings of Correggio*, London, 1976.

Gregory & Zdanowicz 1988
J. Gregory & I. Zdanowicz, *Rembrandt in the Collections of the National Gallery of Victoria*, The Robert Raynor Publications in Prints and Drawings, no. 2, Melbourne, 1988.

Grimm 1991
C. Grimm, *Rembrandt selbst: Eine Neubewertung seiner Porträtkunst*, Stuttgart, 1991.

De Groot 1980
J. M. de Groot, 'Aanbidding van het Kind, Samuel van Hoogstraten, 1627–1678', *Vereniging Rembrandt, Verslag over 1980*, 1980, pp. 82–4.

Gudlaugsson 1948–49
S. J. Gudlaugsson, 'De datering van de schilderijen van Gerard ter Borch', *Nederlands Kunsthistorisch Jaarboek*, vol. 2, 1948–49, pp. 235–67.

Van Guldener 1947
H. T. van Guldener, *Het Jozefverhaal bij Rembrandt en zijn school* (diss.), Utrecht, 1947.

Guratzsch 1975
H. Guratzsch, 'Die Untersicht als ein Gestaltungsmittel in Rembrandts Frühwerk', *Oud Holland*, vol. 89, no. 4, 1975, pp. 243–65.

Guratzsch 1976
H. Guratzsch, Die Auferweckung des Lazarus in der niederländischen Kunst von 1400–1700 (diss.), Munich, 1976. See also GURATZSCH 1980.

Guratzsch 1980
H. Guratzsch, *Die Auferweckung des Lazarus in der niederländischen Kunst von 1400 bis 1700: Ikonographie und Ikonologie*, Ars Neerlandica, vol. 2, Kortrijk, 1980. See also GURATZSCH 1976.

Haak 1968
B. Haak, *Rembrandt: Zijn leven, zijn werk, zijn tijd*, Amsterdam, [1968]. See also HAAK 1969.

Haak 1969
B. Haak, *Rembrandt: His Life, His Work, His Time*, trans. E. Willems-Treeman, New York, 1969. See also HAAK 1968.

Haak 1976
B. Haak, *Rembrandt tekeningen*, Amsterdam, 1976. See also HAAK 1976a.

Haak 1976a
B. Haak, *Rembrandt Drawings*, trans. E. Willems-Treeman, London, 1976. See also HAAK 1976.

Haarlem 1986
See DE JONGH 1986

The Hague 1992
P. Huys Janssen & W. Sumowski, *The Hoogsteder Exhibition of Rembrandt's Academy* (exh. cat.), trans. R. Koenig et al., Hoogsteder & Hoogsteder, The Hague, 1992.

The Hague / San Francisco 1990–91
B. Broos et al., *Great Dutch Paintings from America* (exh. cat.), Mauritshuis, The Hague, The Fine Arts Museums of San Francisco, 1990. See also THE HAGUE / SAN FRANCISCO 1990–91a.

The Hague / San Francisco 1990–91a
B. Broos et al., *Hollandse meesters uit Amerika* (exh. cat.), Mauritshuis, The Hague, The Fine Arts Museums of San Francisco, 1990. See also THE HAGUE / SAN FRANCISCO 1990–91.

Halewood 1982
W. H. Halewood, *Six Subjects of Reformation Art: A Preface to Rembrandt*, Toronto, 1982.

Van Hall 1963
H. van Hall, *Portretten van Nederlandse beeldende kunstenaars: Repertorium*, Amsterdam, 1963.

Hamann 1936
R. Hamann, 'Hagars Abschied bei Rembrandt und im Rembrandt-Kreise', *Marburger Jahrbuch für Kunstwissenschaft*, vols 8–9, 1936, pp. 471–578.

Hanover / Wellesley / Providence / Storrs 1969
Dutch Drawings from the Abrams Collection: Selections from the Collection of Dutch Drawings of Maida & George Abrams (exh. cat.), Hopkins Center Art Galleries, Dartmouth College, Hanover, New Hampshire, Jewett Arts Center, Wellesley College Museum, Wellesley, Massachusetts, Museum of Art, Rhode Island School of Design, Providence, Rhode Island, Museum of Art, University of Connecticut, Storrs, Connecticut, 1969.

Haverkamp Begemann 1969
E. Haverkamp Begemann, 'Rembrandt as a Teacher', in CHICAGO 1969, pp. 21–30.

Haverkamp Begemann 1973
E. Haverkamp Begemann, *Hercules Segers: The Complete Etchings*, Amsterdam, 1973.

Haverkamp-Begemann 1988
E. Haverkamp-Begemann, with C. Logan, *Creative Copies: Interpretative Drawings from Michelangelo to Picasso* (exh. cat.), The Drawing Center, New York, 1988.

Haverkamp-Begemann 1990
E. Haverkamp-Begemann, in *An Important Painting by Rembrandt from a Private Collection* (sale cat.), Christie's, New York, 1990, pp. 10–28.

Haverkamp-Begemann 1992–93*
E. Haverkamp-Begemann, 'Rembrandts Simeon och Jesusbarnet / Simeon and the Christ Child', in STOCKHOLM 1992–93, pp. 31–40.
*Referred to in text as Haverkamp-Begemann 1993.

Haverkamp Begemann 1995
E. Haverkamp Begemann, 'Presumed Portrait of Rembrandt's Father', in *Inaugural Exhibition of Old Master Paintings* (exh. cat.), Otto Naumann Ltd., New York, 1995.

Haverkamp Begemann & Logan 1970
E. Haverkamp Begemann & A.-M. S. Logan, *European Drawings and Watercolors in the Yale University Art Gallery 1500–1900*, 2 vols, New Haven, Connecticut, 1970.

Hellerstedt 1981
K. Jones Hellerstedt, 'A Traditional Motif in Rembrandt's Etchings: The Hurdy-Gurdy Player', *Oud Holland*, vol. 95, no. 1, 1981, pp. 16–30.

Hind
A. M. Hind, *A Catalogue of Rembrandt's Etchings: Chronologically Arranged and Completely Illustrated*, 2 vols, 2nd edn, London, 1923.

Hinterding 1993–94
E. Hinterding, 'The History of Rembrandt's Copperplates, with a Catalogue of Those That Survive', *Simiolus*, vol. 22, no. 4, 1993–94, pp. 253–315. See also HINTERDING 1995.

Hinterding 1995
E. Hinterding, *The History of Rembrandt's Copperplates, with a Catalogue of Those That Survive*, Zwolle, 1995. See also HINTERDING 1993–94.

Hinterding 1996
E. Hinterding, 'Rembrandt and van Vliet: The Watermarks', in AMSTERDAM 1996, pp. 24–37.

Hoet 1752
G. Hoet, *Catalogus of naamlyst van schilderyen, met derselver pryzen, zedert een langen reeks van jaaren zoo in Holland als op andere plaatzen in het openbaar verkogt*, 2 vols, The Hague, 1752. See also HOET / TERWESTEN 1770.

Hoet / Terwesten 1770
P. Terwesten, *Catalogus of naamlyst van schilderyen, met derselver pryzen, zedert een langen reeks van jaaren zoo in Holland als op andere plaatzen in het openbaar verkogt* (vol. III of HOET 1752), The Hague, 1770. See also HOET 1752.

Hoff 1975
U. Hoff, 'Rembrandt's Shell – *Conus marmoreus* L.', *Art Bulletin of Victoria*, 1975, pp. 16–19.

Hoff 1995
U. Hoff, *European Paintings before 1800 in the National Gallery of Victoria*, 4th edn, Melbourne, 1995.

Hofstede de Groot 1894
C. Hofstede de Groot, 'Entlehnungen Rembrandts', *Jahrbuch der Königlich Preussischer Kunstsammlungen*, vol. 15, 1894, pp. 175–81.

Hofstede de Groot 1899
C. Hofstede de Groot, 'Die Rembrandt-Ausstellungen zu Amsterdam (September–Oktober 1898) und zu London (Januar–März 1899)', *Repertorium für Kunstwissenschaft*, vol. 22, 1899, pp. 159–64.

Hofstede de Groot 1906
C. Hofstede de Groot, *Die Handzeichnungen Rembrandts: Versuch eines beschreibenden und kritischen Katalogs*, Haarlem, 1906.

Hofstede de Groot 1906a
C. Hofstede de Groot, *Die Urkunden über Rembrandt (1575–1721)*, The Hague, 1906.

Hofstede de Groot 1907–28
C. Hofstede de Groot, *Beschreibendes und kritisches Verzeichnis der Werke des hervorragendsten holländischen Maler des XVII. Jahrhunderts, nach dem Muster von John Smith's Catalogue raisonné*, 10 vols, Esslingen, 1907–28. See also HOFSTEDE DE GROOT 1908–27.

Hofstede de Groot 1908–27
C. Hofstede de Groot, *A Catalogue Raisonné of the Works of the Most Eminent Dutch Painters of the Seventeenth Century, Based on the Work of John Smith*, 8 vols, trans. E. G. Hawke, London, 1908–27. See also HOFSTEDE DE GROOT 1907–28.

Hofstede de Groot 1915
C. Hofstede de Groot, 'Rembrandts onderwijs aan zijne leerlingen', in *Feest-bundel Dr. Abraham Bredius, aangeboden den achttienden april 1915*, Amsterdam, 1915, pp. 79–94.

Hofstede de Groot 1922
C. Hofstede de Groot, *Die holländische Kritik der jetztigen Rembrandt-Forschung und neuest wiedergefundene Rembrandtbilder*, Stuttgart, 1922.

Hofstede de Groot 1928
C. Hofstede de Groot, 'De portretten van het echtpaar Jacob Trip en Margaretha de Geer door de Cuyp's, N. Maes en Rembrandt', *Oud-Holland*, vol. 45, 1928, pp. 255–64.

Hollander 1975
A. Hollander, *Seeing through Clothes*, New York, 1975.

Hollstein
F. W. H. Hollstein et al., *Dutch and Flemish Etchings, Engravings and Woodcuts, ca.1450–1700*, 46 vols to date, Amsterdam / Roosendaal / Rotterdam, 1949–.

Hoogewerff 1917
G. J. Hoogewerff, 'Rembrandt en een Italiaansche maecenas', *Oud-Holland*, vol. 35, 1917, pp. 129–48.

Hoogewerff 1919
G. J. Hoogewerff, *De twee reizen van Cosimo de' Medici, Prins van Toscane, door de Nederlanden (1667–1669): Journalen en documenten*, Amsterdam, 1919.

Hoogewerff & Van Regteren Altena 1928
G. J. Hoogewerff & J. Q. van Regteren Altena (eds), *Arnoldus Buchelius, 'Res pictoriae': Aanteekeningen over kunstenaars en kunstwerken voorkomende in zijn diarium, res pictoriae, notae quotidianae en descriptio urbis ultrajectinae (1583–1639)*, Quellenstudien zur holländischen Kunstgeschichte, vol. XV, The Hague, 1928.

Van Hoogstraten 1678
S. van Hoogstraten, *De Inleyding tot de hooge schoole der schilderkonst anders de zichtbaere werelt*, Rotterdam, 1678.

De Hoop Scheffer 1972
D. de Hoop Scheffer, 'Nogmaals de inventarislijst van Clement de Jonghe', *Kroniek van het Rembrandthuis*, vol. 26, 1972, pp. 126–34.

De Hoop Scheffer & Boon 1971
D. de Hoop Scheffer & K. G. Boon, 'De inventaris-lijst van Clement de Jonghe en Rembrandts etsplaten', *Kroniek van het Rembrandthuis*, vol. 25, 1971, pp. 1–17.

Houbraken 1718–21
A. Houbraken, *De groote schouburgh der Nederlantsche konstschilders en schilderessen: Waar van 'er vele met hunne beeltenissen ten tooneel verschynen, en hun levensgedrag en konstwerken beschreven worden, zynde een vervolg op het Schilderboek van K. van Mander*, 3 vols, Amsterdam, 1718–21. See also HOUBRAKEN 1753.

Houbraken 1753
A. Houbraken, *De groote schouburgh der Nederlantsche konstschilders en schilderessen ...*, 3 vols, 2nd edn, The Hague, 1753. See also HOUBRAKEN 1718–21.

Hugenholtz 1977
F. W. N. Hugenholtz, *Floris V: Vermoord en getekend*, Nieuwkoop, 1977.

Huygens 1876–88
C. Huygens, *Journaal van Constantijn Huygens, den zoon*, Werken Historisch Genootschap (new series), nos 23, 25, 32, 46, 4 vols, Utrecht, 1876–88.

Huygens / Heesakkers 1987
C. Huygens, *Mijn jeugd*, trans. C. L. Heesakkers, Amsterdam, 1987.

Huygens / Kan 1946
C. Huygens, *De jeugd van Constantijn Huygens door hemzelf beschreven*, trans. A. H. Kan, Rotterdam, 1946. See also HUYGENS / KAN 1971.

Huygens / Kan 1971
C. Huygens, *De jeugd van Constantijn Huygens door hemzelf beschreven*, rev. edn, trans. A. H. Kan, Rotterdam, 1971. See also HUYGENS / KAN 1946.

Huyskens 1992
W. Huyskens, *De vrije vogelvlugt: Kunst en valkerij – motief, portret, gedicht*, Zutphen, 1992.

Illustrated Bartsch
W. L. Strauss et al. (eds), *The Illustrated Bartsch*, New York, 1978–. See also BARTSCH 1797, BARTSCH 1803–21.

Immerzeel 1855
J. Immerzeel, Jr, *De levens en werken der Hollandsche en Vlaamsche kunstschilders, beeldhouwers, graveurs en bouwmeesters van het begin der vijftiende eeuw tot heden* (1855 [1st edn 1842–43]), Amsterdam, 1974 (3 vols in 1).

Jerusalem 1965
Inaugural Exhibition (exh. cat.), Israel Museum, Jerusalem, 1965.

De Jongh 1969
E. de Jongh, '"The Spur of Wit": Rembrandt's Response to an Italian Challenge', *Delta*, vol. 12, no. 2, Summer 1969, pp. 49–67.

De Jongh 1986
E. de Jongh, *Portretten van echt en trouw: Huwelijk en gezin in de Nederlandse kunst van de zeventiende eeuw* (exh. cat.), Frans Halsmuseum, Haarlem, 1986.

De Jongh 1991
E. de Jongh, 'Oude portretten, hun zwijgzaamheid en mededeelzaamheid', in *Koninklijke Nederlandse Akademie van Wetenschappen: Verslag van de verenigde vergadering van de beide Afdelingen der Akademie, op maandag 8 april 1991*, Amsterdam, 1991, pp. 15–44.

Judson 1973
J. R. Judson, 'Rembrandt and Jacob de Gheyn II', in BRUYN ET AL. 1973, pp. 207–10.

Kahr 1973
M. Kahr, 'Rembrandt and Delilah', *Art Bulletin*, vol. LV, no. 2, June 1973, pp. 240–59.

Van de Kamp 1991–94
N. van de Kamp, 'Genesis, de oergeschiedenis en de verhalen van de aartsvaders', in AMSTERDAM / JERUSALEM / MÜNSTER 1991–94, pp. 14–53.

Kaufmann 1973
H. Kaufmann, 'Anmerkungen zu Rembrandts Potipharbildern', in VON SIMSON & KELCH 1973, pp. 50–7.

Kelch 1986
J. Kelch, *Bilder im Blickpunkt: Der Mann mit dem Goldhelm*, Berlin, 1986.

Kellenbenz 1958
H. Kellenbenz, *Sephardim an der unteren Elbe: Ihre wirtschaftliche und politische Bedeutung vom Ende des 16. bis zum Beginn des 18. Jahrhunderts*, Wiesbaden, 1958.

Keller 1979
U. Keller, 'Knechtschaft und Freiheit: Ein neutestamentliches Thema bei Rembrandt', *Jahrbuch der Hamburger Kunstsammlungen*, vol. XXIV, 1979, pp. 77–112.

Kettering 1983
A. McNeil Kettering, *The Dutch Arcadia: Pastoral Art and Its Audience in the Golden Age*, Montclair, New Jersey, 1983.

Kielich 1997
M. Kielich, 'Het laatste olifantje is Christus', *NRC Handelsblad*, 18 February 1997, p. 24.

Klein 1965
P. W. Klein, *De Trippen in de 17de eeuw: Een studie over het ondernemersgedrag op de Hollandse stapelmarkt*, Assen, 1965.

Klemm 1980
C. Klemm, 'Trophaën', in *Stilleben in Europa* (exh. cat.), eds G. Langemeyer et al., Westfälisches Landesmuseum für Kunst und Kulturgeschichte, Münster, Staatliche Kunsthalle, Baden-Baden, 1980, pp. 244–51.

Klemm 1986
C. Klemm, *Joachim von Sandrart: Kunst-Werke und Lebens-Lauf*, Berlin, 1986.

Klibansky, Panofsky & Saxl 1964
R. Klibansky, E. Panofsky & F. Saxl, *Saturn and Melancholy: Studies in the History of Natural Philosophy, Religion and Art*, London, 1964.

Knuttel 1914
W. P. C. Knuttel, *Nieuw Nederlandsch biografisch woordenboek*, vol. 3, Leiden, 1914.

Kobayashi-Sato 1994
Y. Kobayashi-Sato, 'The Portrait and the *Tronie* as Seen in the Art of Rembrandt', in E. de Jongh et al., *Faces of the Golden Age: Seventeenth-Century Dutch Portraits* (exh. cat.), Yamaguchi Kenritsu Bijutsukan, Yamaguchi, and 3 other venues, 1994, pp. 11–17.

Kolloff 1854
E. Kolloff, *Rembrandts Leben und Werke, nach neuen Actenstücken und Gesichtspunkten geschildert* (1854), ed. C. Tümpel, Hamburg, 1971.

Kraaijpoel & Van Wijnen 1996
D. Kraaijpoel & H. van Wijnen, *Han van Meegeren 1889–1947 en zijn meesterwerk van Vermeer*, Zwolle, 1996.

Kramm 1857–64
C. Kramm, *De levens en werken der Hollandsche en Vlaamsche kunstschilders, beeldhouwers, graveurs en bouwmeesters, van den vroegsten tot op onzen tijd* (1857–64), Amsterdam, 1974 (4 vols in 2).

Kuretsky 1974
S. Donahue Kuretsky, 'Rembrandt's Tree Stump: An Iconographic Attribute of St. Jerome', *Art Bulletin*, vol. LVI, no. 4, December 1974, pp. 571–80.

Lairesse 1707
G. de Lairesse, *Het groot schilderboek*, Amsterdam, 1707.

Landsberger 1946
F. Landsberger, *Rembrandt, the Jews and the Bible*, trans. F. Gerson, Philadelphia, 1946. See also LANDSBERGER 1962.

Landsberger 1962
F. Landsberger, *Rembrandt, the Jews and the Bible*, Philadelphia, 1962. See also LANDSBERGER 1946.

Langedijk 1992
K. Langedijk, *Die Selbstbildnisse der holländischen und flämischen Künstler in der Galleria degli Autoritratti*, Florence, 1992.

Laurentius 1996
T. Laurentius, *Etchings by Rembrandt: Reflections of the Golden Age – An Investigation into the Paper Used by Rembrandt*, Amsterdam, 1996.

Laurentius et al. 1980
T. Laurentius, J. Niemeijer & J. G. Ploos van Amstel, *Cornelis Ploos van Amstel, 1726–1798: Kunstverzamelaar en prentuitgever*, Assen, 1980.

Laurentius et al. 1992
T. Laurentius, H. van Hugten, E. Hinterding & J. P. Filedt Kok, 'Het Amsterdamse onderzoek naar Rembrandts papier: Radiographie van de watermerken in de etsen van Rembrandt', *Bulletin van het Rijksmuseum*, vol. 40, 1992, pp. 353–84.

Lavallée 1804–15
J. Lavallée, *Galerie du Musée Napoléon*, 11 vols, Paris, 1804–15.

Le Brun 1849
P. Le Brun, 'Recueuil [*sic*] des essaies des merveilles de la peinture' (1635), in *Original Treatises on the Arts of Painting*, vol. II, ed. M. P. Merrifield, London, 1849, pp. 767–841.

Lee 1967
R. W. Lee, *Ut pictura poesis: The Humanistic Theory of Painting*, New York, 1967.

Lehrs
M. Lehrs, *Geschichte und kritischer Katalog des deutschen, niederländischen und französischen Kupferstichs im XV. Jahrhundert* (1908–34), 9 vols, Liechtenstein, 1969.

Leiden 1976–77
'Geschildert tot Leyden Anno 1626' (exh. cat.), Stedelijk Museum de Lakenhal, Leiden, 1976.

Leiden 1988
Leidse fijnschilders: Van Gerrit Dou tot Frans van Mieris de jonge, 1630–1760 (exh. cat.), Stedelijk Museum de Lakenhal, Leiden, 1988.

Leiden 1991–92
C. Vogelaar, P. J. M. de Baar, I. W. L. Moerman, E. van de Wetering, R. E. O. Ekkart & P. Schatborn, *Rembrandt & Lievens in Leiden: 'een jong en edel schildersduo'* [with English summary] (exh. cat.), Stedelijk Museum de Lakenhal, Leiden, 1991.

Leja 1996
J. Leja, 'Rembrandt's "Woman Bathing in a Stream"', *Simiolus*, vol. 24, no. 4, 1996, pp. 320–7.

Lettieri 1980
D. Lettieri, 'Text, Narrative and Tradition: Scenes from *Esther* by Aert de Gelder', *The J. Paul Getty Museum Journal*, vol. 8, 1980, pp. 69–86.

Leupe 1856
P. A. Leupe, 'Rijklof van Goens, gouverneur-generaal van Nederlandsch-Indië, 1678–1681', *Berigten van het Historisch Genootschap te Utrecht*, 1856, pp. 28–48.

Lieure
J. Lieure, *Jacques Callot*, 3 vols, Paris, 1924–29.

Lilienfeld 1914
K. Lilienfeld, *Arent de Gelder: Sein Leben und seine Kunst*, Quellenstudien zur Holländischen Kunstgeschichte, vol. IV, The Hague, 1914.

Lindner 1909
P. Lindner, *Professbuch der Benediktiner-Abtei Weingarten*, Munich, 1909.

Lippmann et al. 1888–1911
F. Lippmann et al. (eds), *Original Drawings by Rembrandt Harmensz. van Ryn, Reproduced in Phototype*, 1st, 2nd, 3rd & 4th series, 10 vols, London / Berlin / Leipzig, 1888–1911.

Lloyd Williams 1992
J. Lloyd Williams, *Dutch Art and Scotland: A Reflection of Taste* (exh. cat.), National Gallery of Scotland, Edinburgh, 1992.

London 1821
[*Catalogue of exhibition at the British Institution*], London, 1821.

London 1845
Catalogue of Pictures by Italian, Spanish, Flemish, Dutch, French and English Masters, with Which the Proprietors Have Favoured the Institution (exh. cat.), British Institution, London, 1845.

London 1876
Winter Exhibition: Works by the Old Masters, and by Deceased Masters of the British School (exh. cat.), Royal Academy, London, 1876.

London 1899
Winter Exhibition: Works by Rembrandt (exh. cat.), Royal Academy, London, 1899.

London 1938
Catalogue of the Exhibition of 17th Century Art in Europe (exh. cat.), Royal Academy, London, 1938.

London 1952–53
Dutch Pictures 1450–1750 (exh. cat.), Royal Academy, London, 1952.

London 1976
Art in Seventeenth-Century Holland (exh. cat.), National Gallery, London, 1976.

London 1988–89
D. Bomford, C. Brown, A. Roy et al., *Art in the Making: Rembrandt* (exh. cat.), National Gallery, London, 1988.

Los Angeles 1947
Loan Exhibition of Paintings by Frans Hals & Rembrandt (exh. cat.), Los Angeles County Museum, 1947.

Los Angeles 1991–92
Masterpieces in Focus: Rembrandt's 'The Raising of Lazarus' (exh. cat.), Los Angeles County Museum of Art, 1991.

Lugt 1915
F. Lugt, *Wandelingen met Rembrandt in en om Amsterdam*, 2nd edn, Amsterdam, 1915.

Lunsingh Scheurleer, Fock & Van Dissel 1986–92
T. H. Lunsingh Scheurleer, C. W. Fock & A. J. van Dissel, *Het Rapenburg: Geschiedenis van een Leidse gracht*, 7 vols, Leiden, 1986–92.

MacLaren 1960
N. MacLaren, *The Dutch School*, National Gallery Catalogues, London, 1960.

MacLaren / Brown 1991
N. MacLaren, *The Dutch School 1600–1900*, National Gallery Catalogues, 2 vols, 2nd edn, rev. C. Brown, London, 1991.

McTavish 1984
D. McTavish, *Pictures from the Age of Rembrandt* (exh. cat.), Agnes Etherington Art Centre, Queen's University, Kingston, Ontario, 1984.

Mahon 1967
D. Mahon, *I disegni del Guercino della collezione Mahon*, Bologna, 1967.

Mâle 1932
E. Mâle, *L'Art religieux après le Concile de Trente*, Paris, 1932.

Manchester 1857
Catalogue of the Art Treasures of the United Kingdom, Collected at Manchester in 1857 (exh. cat.), Museum of Ornamental Art, Manchester, 1857.

Manchester 1957
Art Treasures Centenary: European Old Masters (exh. cat.), City Art Gallery, Manchester, 1957.

Mancini 1956–57
G. Mancini, *Considerazioni sulla pittura* (*c.*1620), 2 vols, ed. A. Marucchi, Rome, 1956–57.

Van Mander 1604
C. van Mander, *Het Schilder-Boeck ...* , Haarlem, 1604.

Van Mander / Miedema 1994–96
K. van Mander, *The Lives of the Illustrious Netherlandish and German Painters* (1604), 3 vols, ed. H. Miedema, trans. D. Cook-Radmore, C. Ford, M. Hoyle & J. Pennial-Boer, Doornspijk, 1994–96.

Manke 1963
I. Manke, *Emanuel de Witte 1617–1692*, Amsterdam, 1963.

Manuth 1987
V. Manuth, Ikonographische Studien zu den Historien des Alten Testaments bei Rembrandt und seiner frühen Amsterdamer Schule. Mit einem kritischen Katalog der biblischen Gemälde des Amsterdamer Malers Jan Victors, diss., Freie Universität Berlin, 1987.

Manuth 1993–94
V. Manuth, 'Denomination and Iconography: The Choice of Subject Matter in the Biblical Painting of the Rembrandt Circle', *Simiolus*, vol. 22, no. 4, 1993–94, pp. 235–52.

Marolles 1666
M. de Marolles, *Catalogue de livres, d'estampes et de figures en taille-douce, avec un dénombrement des pièces qui y font contenues*, Paris, 1666.

Martin 1901
W. Martin, *Het leven en de werken van Gerrit Dou, beschouwd in verband met het schildersleven van zijn tijd*, Leiden, 1901.

Martin 1911
W. Martin, *Het leven en de werken van Gerrit Dou*, Leipzig, 1911.

Martin 1913
W. Martin, *Gerard Dou*, Klassiker der Kunst in Gesamtausgaben, Stuttgart, 1913.

Martyn 1766
[T. Martyn?], *The English Connoisseur; Containing an Account of Whatever Is Curious in Painting, Sculpture, &c. in the Palaces and Seats of the Nobility and Principal Gentry of England, Both in Town and Country*, London, 1766.

Van der Meer Mohr 1996
J. van der Meer Mohr, 'Eerherstel voor Abraham Bredius?' [with English summary], *Tableau*, vol. 19, 1996, pp. 39–45.

Michel 1893
E. Michel, *Rembrandt: Sa vie, son oeuvre et son temps*, Paris, 1893.

Miedema 1973
H. Miedema, *Karel van Mander: 'Den grondt der edel vry schilder-const'*, 2 vols, Utrecht, 1973.

Miedema 1981
H. Miedema, *Kunst, kunstenaar en kunstwerk bij Karel van Mander: Een analyse van zijn levensbeschrijvingen*, Alphen aan den Rijn, 1981.

Miles 1961
H. Miles, *Dutch and Flemish, Netherlandish and German Paintings*, Glasgow Art Gallery and Museum, 2 vols, Glasgow, 1961.

Miller 1985
D. Miller, Jan Victors (1619–76), PhD diss., 2 vols, University of Delaware, Newark, Delaware, 1985.

Miller 1992
D. Miller, 'The Word of Calvin in the Art of Jan Victors', *Konsthistorisk Tidskrift*, vol. 61, 1992, pp. 99–105.

Von Moltke 1939
J. W. von Moltke, *Dutch and Flemish Old Masters in the Collection of Dr. C. J. K. van Aalst*, Verona, 1939.

Von Moltke 1965
J. W. von Moltke, *Govaert Flinck 1615–1660*, Painters of the Past, Amsterdam, 1965.

Von Moltke 1994
J. W. von Moltke, *Arent de Gelder, Dordrecht 1645–1727*, Doornspijk, 1994.

Monconys 1667
B. de Monconys, *Iournal des voyages*, Paris, 1667.

Morse 1966
P. Morse, 'Rembrandt's Etching Technique: An Example', *United States National Museum Bulletin 250: Contributions from The Museum of History and Technology*, 1966, pp. 95–107.

Müller Hofstede 1968
J. Müller Hofstede, 'Zur Kopfstudie im Werk von Rubens', *Wallraf-Richartz-Jahrbuch*, vol. XXX, 1968, pp. 223–52.

Münz (+ no.)
See MÜNZ 1952

Münz 1948
L. Münz, 'A Newly Discovered Late Rembrandt', *Burlington Magazine*, vol. XC, no. 540, March 1948, p. 64.

Münz 1952
L. Münz, *Rembrandt's Etchings*, 2 vols, trans. N. MacLaren, London, 1952.

Münz 1953
L. Münz, 'Rembrandts Bild von Mutter und Vater', *Jahrbuch der kunsthistorischen Sammlungen in Wien*, vol. 50, 1953, pp. 141–90.

Németh 1996
I. Németh, 'De portretten van Jacob Trip en Margaretha de Geer door Nicolaes Maes in Boedapest', *Oud Holland*, vol. 110, no. 2, 1996, pp. 79–84.

Németh & Van Leeuwen 1992
I. Németh & R. van Leeuwen, 'Onthullingen over onze Jacob Trip', *Mauritshuis Nieuwsbrief*, vol. 5, nos 3–4, 1992, pp. 8–9.

New Haven 1983
C. White, D. Alexander & E. D'Oench, *Rembrandt in Eighteenth Century England* (exh. cat.), Yale Center for British Art and British Studies, New Haven, Connecticut, 1983.

New York 1909
The Hudson-Fulton Celebration (exh. cat.), 2 vols, Metropolitan Museum of Art, New York, 1909.

New York 1995–96
H. von Sonnenburg, W. Liedtke, C. Logan, N. M. Orenstein & S. S. Dickey, *Rembrandt / Not Rembrandt in The Metropolitan Museum of Art: Aspects of Connoisseurship* (exh. cat.), 2 vols, Metropolitan Museum of Art, New York, 1995.

Nicolson / Vertova 1989
B. Nicolson, *Caravaggism in Europe*, 2nd edn, rev. L. Vertova, Turin, 1989.

NRC 1927
'Titus lacht ... De veiling van een Rembrandt', *Nieuwe Rotterdamsche Courant*, 21 February 1927.

Nystad 1975
S. Nystad, 'Joseph and Mary Find Their Son among the Doctors', *Burlington Magazine*, vol. CXVII, no. 864, March 1975, pp. 140–7.

Orlers 1641
J. J. Orlers, *Beschrijvinge der Stadt Leyden*, 2nd edn, Leiden, 1641.

Van Os 1991
H. van Os, *I Hate Rembrandt*, Amsterdam, 1991.

Panofsky 1934
E. Panofsky, 'Jan van Eyck's *Arnolfini* Portrait', *Burlington Magazine*, vol. LXIV, no. 372, March 1934, pp. 117–27.

Panofsky 1973
E. Panofsky, 'Rembrandt und das Judentum', *Jahrbuch der Hamburger Kunstsammlungen*, vol. XVIII, 1973, pp. 75–108.

Paris 1970–71
J. Foucart et al., *Le Siècle de Rembrandt: Tableaux hollandais des collections publiques françaises* (exh. cat.), Musée du Petit Palais, Paris, 1970.

Parthey / Pennington
R. Pennington, *A Descriptive Catalogue of the Etched Work of Wenceslaus Hollar 1607–1677*, Cambridge, 1982.

De Pauw-de Veen 1969
L. de Pauw-de Veen, *De begrippen 'schilder', 'schilderij' en 'schilderen' in de zeventiende eeuw*, Brussels, 1969.

Pels 1681
A. Pels, *Gebruik en misbruik des tooneels* Amsterdam, 1681.

Peltzer 1937–38
R. A. Peltzer, 'Christoph Paudiss und seine Tätigkeit in Freising', *Münchner Jahrbuch der bildenden Kunst*, new series, vol. 12, 1937–38, pp. 251–80.

Perk 1900
M. A. Perk, *Schetsen en beelden*, Haarlem, 1900.

Perlove 1995
S. Perlove, '*Templum Christianum*: Rembrandt's *Jeremiah Lamenting the Destruction of Jerusalem* (1630)', *Gazette des Beaux-Arts*, vol. CXXVI, November 1995, pp. 159–70.

Philadelphia / Berlin / London 1984
Masters of Seventeenth-Century Dutch Genre Painting (exh. cat.), Philadelphia Museum of Art, Gemäldegalerie, Staatliche Museen Preussischer Kulturbesitz, Berlin, Royal Academy of Arts, London, 1984.

Pigage 1778
N. de Pigage, *La Galerie électorale de Düsseldorff ou catalogue raisonné et figuré de ses tableaux*, Basle, 1778.

Pigler 1968
A. Pigler (ed.), *Katalog der Galerie Alter Meister*, Museum der bildenden Künste / Szépmüvészeti Múzeum, Budapest, 2 vols, Tübingen, 1968.

Piles 1699
R. de Piles, *Abrégé de la vie des peintres avec des réflexions sur leurs ouvrages, et un traité du peintre parfait, de la connoissance des desseins & de l'utilité des estampes*, Paris, 1699.

Pont 1958
D. Pont, *Barent Fabritius 1624–1673*, Utrecht, 1958.

Popper-Voskuil 1973
N. Popper-Voskuil, 'Self-Portraiture and *Vanitas* Still-Life Painting in 17th-Century Holland in Reference to David Bailly's *Vanitas* Oeuvre', *Pantheon*, vol. 31, 1973, pp. 58–74.

Potterton 1982
H. Potterton, 'Recently-Cleaned Dutch Pictures in the National Gallery of Ireland', *Apollo*, vol. CXV, no. 240, February 1982, pp. 104–7.

Potterton 1986
H. Potterton, *Dutch Seventeenth and Eighteenth Century Paintings in the National Gallery of Ireland: A Complete Catalogue*, Dublin, 1986.

Puype 1981
J. P. Puype, *Blanke wapens: Nederlandse slag- en steekwapens sinds 1600*, Laken, 1981.

Raleigh 1956
Rembrandt and His Pupils (exh. cat.), North Carolina Museum of Art, Raleigh, North Carolina, 1956.

Raupp 1980
H.-J. Raupp, 'Zur Bedeutung von Thema und Symbol für die holländische Landschaftsmalerei des 17. Jahrhunderts', *Jahrbuch der Staatlichen Kunstsammlungen in Baden-Württemberg*, vol. 17, 1980, pp. 85–110.

Raupp 1984
H.-J. Raupp, *Untersuchungen zu Künstlerbildnis und Künstlerdarstellung in den Niederlanden im 17. Jahrhundert*, Hildesheim, 1984.

Réau 1955–59
L. Réau, *Iconographie de l'art chrétien*, 6 vols, Paris, 1955–59.

Van Regteren Altena 1936
J. Q. van Regteren Altena, *The Drawings of Jacques de Gheyn: An Introduction to Their Study with a Biography of the Artist and a Survey of His Paintings* (diss.), trans. D. Kuenen, Amsterdam, 1936.

Van Regteren Altena 1952
I. Q. van Regteren Altena, 'Retouches aan ons Rembrandt-beeld IV: De Eendracht van het Land 2', *Oud-Holland*, vol. 67, 1952, pp. 59–67.

Van Regteren Altena 1954
I. Q. van Regteren Altena, 'Retouches aan ons Rembrandt-beeld II: Het Landschap van den Goudweger', *Oud-Holland*, vol. 69, 1954, pp. 1–17.

Van Regteren Altena 1983
I. Q. van Regteren Altena, *Jacques de Gheyn: Three Generations*, 3 vols, trans. M. Charles, The Hague, 1983.

Reynolds 1801
J. Reynolds, *The Works of Sir Joshua Reynolds, Knight, Late President of the Royal Academy*, 3 vols, rev. edn, London, 1801.

Reznicek 1977
E. K. J. Reznicek, 'Opmerkingen bij Rembrandt', *Oud Holland*, vol. 91, nos 1–2, 1977, pp. 75–107.

Reznicek 1986
E. K. J. Reznicek, 'Hendrick Goltzius and His Conception of Landscape', in BROWN 1986, pp. 57–62.

Ricci 1918
C. Ricci, *Rembrandt in Italia*, Milan, 1918.

Rice 1985
E. F. Rice, Jr, *Saint Jerome in the Renaissance*, Baltimore, 1985.

Van Rijckevorsel 1932
J. L. A. A. M. van Rijckevorsel, *Rembrandt en de traditie*, Rotterdam, 1932.

Rijksdienst Beeldende Kunst 1992
Rijksdienst Beeldende Kunst, *Old Master Paintings: An Illustrated Summary Catalogue*, trans. S. der Pols-Harris, Zwolle, 1992.

Robb 1978
D. Robb, Jr, 'Rembrandt's *Portrait of a Young Jew*', *Apollo*, vol. CVII, no. 191, January 1978, pp. 44–7.

Robinson 1981
W. Robinson, '"This Passion for Prints": Collecting and Connoisseurship in Northern Europe during the Seventeenth Century', in ACKLEY 1981, pp. xxvii–xlviii.

Robinson 1984
W. Robinson, '"The Sacrifice of Isaac": An Unpublished Painting by Nicolaes Maes', *Burlington Magazine*, vol. CXXVI, no. 978, September 1984, pp. 540–4.

Robinson 1987
W. W. Robinson, 'The *Eavesdroppers* and Related Paintings by Nicolaes Maes', in *Holländische Genremalerei im 17. Jahrhundert: Symposium Berlin 1984*, *Jahrbuch Preußischer Kulturbesitz*, special vol. 4, eds H. Bock & T. W. Gaehtgens, Berlin, 1987, pp. 283–313.

Robinson 1989
W. W. Robinson, 'Nicolaes Maes as a Draughtsman', *Master Drawings*, vol. 27, no. 2, Summer 1989, pp. 146–62.

Robinson 1993
W. W. Robinson, 'Nicolaes Maes: Some Observations on His Early Portraits', in CAVALLI-BJÖRKMAN 1993, pp. 98–118.

Robinson 1996
W. W. Robinson, The Early Works of Nicolaes Maes, 1653–1661, PhD diss., Harvard University, Cambridge, Massachusetts, 1996.

Roethlisberger 1993
M. Roethlisberger, with M. J. Bok, *Abraham Bloemaert and His Sons: Paintings and Prints*, 2 vols, Doornspijk, 1993.

Rogge 1868
H. C. Rogge, *Brieven en onuitgegeven stukken van Johannes Wttenbogaert, verzameld en met aantekeningen uitgegeven door H. C. Rogge*, 2 vols, Utrecht, 1868.

Roh 1948
F. Roh, *Der verkannte Künstler: Studien zur Geschichte und Theorie des kulturellen Missverstehens*, Munich, 1948.

Roscam Abbing 1993
M. Roscam Abbing, with P. Thissen, *De schilder en schrijver Samuel van Hoogstraten, 1627–1678: Eigentijdse bronnen en oeuvre van gesigneerde schilderijen*, Leiden, 1993.

Roscam Abbing 1994
M. Roscam Abbing, 'Houbrakens onbeholpen kritiek op de Rembrandt-ets "De Zondeval" (B.28)', *Kroniek van het Rembrandthuis*, vol. 46, no. 2, 1994, pp. 14–23.

Rosenberg 1948
J. Rosenberg, *Rembrandt*, 2 vols, Cambridge, Massachusetts, 1948.

Rosenberg 1959
J. Rosenberg, '[review of BENESCH 1954–57]', *Art Bulletin*, vol. XLI, no. 1, March 1959, pp. 108–19.

Rosenberg 1964
J. Rosenberg, *Rembrandt: Life & Work*, rev. edn, London, 1964.

Rotterdam 1988
Een gloeiend palet: Schilderijen van Rembrandt en zijn school / A Glowing Palette: Paintings of Rembrandt and His School (exh. cat.), Museum Boymans-van Beuningen, Rotterdam, 1988.

Roy 1972
R. Roy, Studien zu Gerbrand van den Eeckhout, diss., Universität Wien, Vienna, 1972.

Royalton-Kisch 1984
M. Royalton-Kisch, 'Over Rembrandt en van Vliet', *Kroniek van het Rembrandthuis*, vol. 36, nos 1–2, 1984, pp. 3–23.

Royalton-Kisch 1991
M. Royalton-Kisch, 'Rembrandt's Drawing of *The Entombment of Christ* over *The Raising of Lazarus*', *Master Drawings*, vol. 29, no. 3, 1991, pp. 263–83.

Royalton-Kisch 1992
M. Royalton-Kisch, *Drawings by Rembrandt and His Circle in the British Museum* (exh. cat.), British Museum, London, 1992.

Ruffo 1916
V. Ruffo, 'Galleria Ruffo nel secolo XVII in Messina con lettere di pittori ed altri documenti inediti', *Bollettino d'Arte*, vol. X, 1916.

Ruffo 1919
V. Ruffo, 'La Galleria Ruffo (appendice)', *Bollettino d'Arte*, vol. XIII, 1919, pp. 3–16.

Rutgers van der Loeff 1911
J. D. Rutgers van der Loeff, *Drie lofdichten op Haarlem: Het middelnederlandsch gedicht van Dirck Mathijszen en Karel van Mander's Twee Beelden van Haarlem*, Haarlem, 1911.

Sandrart 1675
A. R. Peltzer (ed.), *Joachim von Sandrarts Academie der Bau-, Bild-, und Mahlerey-Künste von 1675: Leben der berühmten Maler, Bildhauer und Baumeister* (1675), Munich, 1925.

Savelsberg 1992
W. H. Savelsberg, *Die Darstellung des H. Franziskus von Assisi in der flämischen Malerei und Graphik des späten 16. und 17. Jahrhunderts*, Istituto Storico dei Cappuccini, Iconographia Franciscana, no. 6, Rome, 1992.

Saxl 1923–24
F. Saxl, 'Rembrandt und Italien', *Oud-Holland*, vol. 41, 1923–24, pp. 145–60.

Scallen 1997
C. B. Scallen, 'Rembrandt's Nocturne Prints', *On Paper*, vol. 1, no. 3, January–February 1997, pp. 13–17.

Schatborn 1970
P. Schatborn, 'A Work of Touching Simplicity', *M: A Quarterly Review of the Montreal Museum of Fine Arts*, vol. 2, no. 3, December 1970, pp. 12–15.

Schatborn 1977
P. Schatborn, 'Beesten nae't leven', *Kroniek van het Rembrandthuis*, vol. 29, no. 2, 1977, pp. 3–31.

Schatborn 1981
P. Schatborn, *Figuurstudies: Nederlandse tekeningen uit de 17de eeuw*, The Hague, 1981.

Schatborn 1982
P. Schatborn, 'Van Rembrandt tot Crozat: Vroege verzamelingen met tekeningen van Rembrandt', *Nederlands Kunsthistorisch Jaarboek*, vol. 32, 1982, pp. 1–53.

Schatborn 1982a
P. Schatborn, '[review of BROOS 1981]', *Oud Holland*, vol. 96, no. 4, 1982, pp. 251–8.

Schatborn 1983
P. Schatborn, 'Rembrandt: From Drawings to Prints and Paintings', *Apollo*, vol. CXVII, no. 256, June 1983, pp. 452–60.

Schatborn 1985
P. Schatborn, *Tekeningen van Rembrandt, zijn onbekende leerlingen en navolgers*, Catalogus van de Nederlandsche tekeningen in het Rijksprentenkabinet, vol. IV, The Hague, 1985.

Schatborn 1986
P. Schatborn, '[review of CORPUS, vol. I]', *Oud Holland*, vol. 100, no. 1, 1986, pp. 55–63.

Schatborn 1990
P. Schatborn, 'Met Rembrandt naar buiten', *Kroniek van het Rembrandthuis*, vol. 42, nos 1–2, 1990, pp. 31–9.

Schatborn 1997
P. Schatborn, 'Tekeningen van de gebroeders Jan en Jacob Pynas. II: Jacob Pynas', *Bulletin van het Rijksmuseum*, vol. 45, no. 1, 1997, pp. 3–25.

Schatborn & De Winkel 1996
P. Schatborn & M. de Winkel, 'Rembrandts portret van de acteur Willem Ruyter', *Bulletin van het Rijksmuseum*, vol. 44, no. 4, 1996, pp. 382–93.

Scheller 1969
R. W. Scheller, 'Rembrandt en de encyclopedische kunstkamer' [with English summary], *Oud Holland*, vol. 84, nos 2–3, 1969, pp. 81–147.

Scheltema 1853
P. Scheltema, *Rembrand: Redevoering over het leven en de verdiensten van Rembrand van Rijn, met eene menigte geschiedkundige bijlagen meerendeels uit echte bronnen geput*, Amsterdam, 1853.

Schillemans 1987
R. Schillemans, 'Gabriel Bucelinus and "The Names of the Most Distinguished European Painters"', *Hoogsteder-Naumann Mercury*, no. 6, 1987, pp. 25–37.

Schillemans 1989
R. Schillemans, *Bijbelschilderkunst rond Rembrandt*, Utrecht, 1989.

Schillemans 1991
R. Schillemans, '"Rimprant, nostrae aetatis miraculum" (Rembrandt, het wonder van onze tijd)', *Kroniek van het Rembrandthuis*, vol. 43, no. 1, 1991, pp. 17–20.

Schmid 1945
H. A. Schmid, *Hans Holbein der Jüngere: Sein Aufstieg zur Meisterschaft und sein englischer Stil*, Basel, 1945.

Schmidt-Degener 1912
F. Schmidt-Degener, 'Het geboortejaar van Carel Fabritius', *Oud-Holland*, vol. 30, 1912, pp. 189–91.

Schmidt-Degener 1915
F. Schmidt-Degener, 'Rembrandt en Homerus', in *Feest-bundel Dr. Abraham Bredius, aangeboden den achttienden april 1915*, Amsterdam, 1915, pp. 15–24.

Schnackenburg 1996
B. Schnackenburg, *Staatliche Museen Kassel, Gemäldegalerie Alte Meister, Gesamtkatalog*, 2 vols, Mainz, 1996.

Schnapper 1994
A. Schnapper, *Curieux du Grand Siècle*, Paris, 1994.

Schneider 1932
H. Schneider, *Jan Lievens: Sein Leben und seine Werke*, Haarlem, 1932. See also SCHNEIDER / EKKART 1973.

Schneider 1990
C. P. Schneider, *Rembrandt's Landscapes*, New Haven, Connecticut, 1990.

Schneider / Ekkart 1973
H. Schneider, *Jan Lievens: Sein Leben und seine Werke* (1932), with suppl. by R. E. O. Ekkart, Amsterdam, 1973. See also SCHNEIDER 1932.

Scholten 1995
F. Scholten, *Gebeeldhouwde portretten* (exh. cat.), Rijksmuseum, Amsterdam, 1995.

Schriftlicher Nachlass
H. Rupprich (ed.), *Dürers Schriftlicher Nachlass*, 3 vols, Berlin, 1956–69.

Schwartz 1984
G. Schwartz, *Rembrandt: Zijn leven, zijn schilderijen*, Maarssen, 1984. See also SCHWARTZ 1985.

Schwartz 1985
G. Schwartz, *Rembrandt: His Life, His Paintings*, Harmondsworth, Middlesex, 1985. See also SCHWARTZ 1984.

Schwartz 1986
G. Schwartz, *The Dutch World of Painting* (exh. cat.), Vancouver Art Gallery, 1986.

Schwartz 1989
F. Schwartz, '"The Motions of the Countenance": Rembrandt's Early Portraits and the *Tronie*', *Res: Anthropology and Aesthetics*, nos 17–18, Spring–Autumn 1989, pp. 89–116.

Scott 1987
M. A. Scott, *Dutch, Flemish and German Paintings in the Cincinnati Art Museum*, Cincinnati, 1987.

Silberfeld 1972
K. Silberfeld, 'Examination and Treatment of Rembrandt's "Titus, the Artist's Son"', *Baltimore Museum of Art Annual*, vol. IV, part II, 1972, pp. 41–9.

Von Simson & Kelch 1973
O. von Simson & J. Kelch (eds), *Neue Beiträge zur Rembrandt-Forschung: Rembrandt Kongress, Berlin, 1969*, Berlin, 1973. See also GERSON 1973, KAUFMANN 1973.

Six 1908
J. Six, 'Rembrandt's verbeelding van de etsen van Jan Six en Abraham Francen', *Onze Kunst*, vol. 14, no. 7, 1908, pp. 53–65.

Six 1925
J. Six, 'La famosa Accademia di Eeulenborg', *Jaarboek der Koninklijke Akademie van Wetenschappen*, 1925–26, pp. 229–41.

Slatkes 1992
L. J. Slatkes, *Rembrandt: Catalogo completo dei dipinti*, Archivi di arte antica e moderna, Florence, 1992.

Slive 1953
S. Slive, *Rembrandt and His Critics 1630–1730*, The Hague, 1953.

Slive 1965
S. Slive, 'An Unpublished *Head of Christ* by Rembrandt', *Art Bulletin*, vol. XLVII, no. 4, December 1965, pp. 406–17.

Slive 1970–74
S. Slive, *Frans Hals*, 3 vols, National Gallery of Art: Kress Foundation Studies in the History of European Art, no. 4, London, 1970–74.

Slive 1980
S. Slive, in *Armand Hammer Collection: Five Centuries of Masterpieces*, ed. J. Walker, New York, 1980, pp. 46–9.

Slive 1988
S. Slive, '[review of AMSTERDAM / BOSTON / PHILADELPHIA 1987–88]', *Burlington Magazine*, vol. CXXX, no. 1022, May 1988, pp. 395–8.

Sluijter 1993
E. J. Sluijter, *De lof der schilderkunst: Over schilderijen van Gerrit Dou (1613–1675) en een traktaat van Philips Angel uit 1642*, Hilversum, 1993.

Sluijter 1993a
E. J. Sluijter, 'Rembrandt's Early Paintings of the Female Nude: Andromeda and Susanna', in CAVALLI-BJÖRKMAN 1993, pp. 31–54.

Sluiter 1992
G. Sluiter, '"Een loffelijke daad": De vergeten tentoonstellingen van Aert de Gelder in 1929–1930', *Kunstlicht*, vol. 13, 1992, pp. 12–19.

Smith 1829–42
J. Smith, *A Catalogue Raisonné of the Works of the Most Eminent Dutch, Flemish and French Painters ...* , 9 vols (incl. 1842 suppl.), London, 1829–42.

Smith 1990
D. R. Smith, 'Carel Fabritius and Portraiture in Delft', *Art History*, vol. 13, no. 2, June 1990, pp. 151–74.

Smith 1990a
D. Smith, 'Rhetoric and Prose in Dutch Portraiture', *Dutch Crossing*, vol. 41, 1990, pp. 72–109.

Stechow 1966
W. Stechow, *Dutch Landscape Painting of the Seventeenth Century*, New York, 1966.

Steengracht van Oost-Capelle 1826–30
J. Steengracht van Oost-Capelle, *De voornaamste schilderijen van het Koninklijk Kabinet te 's-Gravenhage*, The Hague, 1826–30.

Sterk 1974
J. J. B. M. M. Sterk, 'Johannes de Witt Stevenszoon', *Jaarboek Oud Utrecht*, 1974, pp. 108–62.

Van der Stighelen 1991
K. van der Stighelen, 'Burgers en hun portretten', in *Stad in Vlaanderen: Cultuur en Maatschappij 1477–1787* (exh. cat.), ed. J. van der Stock, Galerij van het Gemeentekrediet te Brussel, Brussels, 1991, pp. 141–56.

Stockholm 1992–93
Rembrandt och hans tid: Människan i centrum / Rembrandt and His Age: Focus on Man (exh. cat.), Nationalmuseum, Stockholm, 1992. See also BLANKERT 1992–93, HAVERKAMP-BEGEMANN 1992–93.

Stogdon 1996
N. Stogdon, 'Captain Baillie and "The Hundred Guilder Print"', *Print Quarterly*, vol. XIII, no. 1, 1996, pp. 53–7.

Stone-Ferrier 1983–84
L. A. Stone-Ferrier, *Dutch Prints of Daily Life: Mirrors of Life or Masks of Morals?* (exh. cat.), Spencer Museum of Art, University of Kansas, Lawrence, Kansas, Yale University Art Gallery, New Haven, Connecticut, Huntington Gallery, University of Texas at Austin, 1983.

Stone-Ferrier 1985
L. Stone-Ferrier, *Images of Textiles: The Weave of Seventeenth-Century Dutch Art and Society*, Ann Arbor, Michigan, 1985.

Stone-Ferrier 1992
L. Stone-Ferrier, 'Rembrandt's Landscape Etchings: Defying Modernity's Encroachment', *Art History*, vol. 15, no. 4, December 1992, pp. 403–33.

Straat 1928
H. L. Straat, 'Lambert Jacobsz.: Schilder', *De Vrije Fries: Tijdschrift Friesch Genootschap van Geschied-, Oudheid- en Taalkunde*, vol. 82, 1928, pp. 53–76.

Stratton 1986
S. Stratton, 'Rembrandt's Beggars: Satire & Sympathy', *The Print Collector's Newsletter*, vol. XVII, no. 3, July–August 1986, pp. 78–82.

Strauss & Van der Meulen 1979
W. L. Strauss & M. van der Meulen, *The Rembrandt Documents*, New York, 1979.

Strzygowski 1923
J. Strzygowski, *Die indischen Miniaturen im Schlosse Schönbrunn*, Vienna, 1923.

Stump 1976
T. J. Stump, *Mit Stift und Zirkel: Gabriel Bucelinus 1599–1681 als Zeichner und Kartograph, Architekt und Kunstfreund*, Sigmaringen, 1976.

Sumowski, Drawings
W. Sumowski, *Drawings of the Rembrandt School*, 10 vols, trans. W. L. Strauss, New York, 1979–92.

Sumowski, Gemälde
W. Sumowski, *Gemälde der Rembrandt-Schüler*, 6 vols, Landau/Pfalz, 1983–95 [vol. I, 1983; vol. II, 1985; vol. III, 1987; vol. IV, 1990; vol. V, 1990; vol. VI, 1995].

Sumowski 1959
W. Sumowski, '[review of PONT 1958]', *Kunstchronik*, vol. 12, no. 10, October 1959, pp. 287–94.

Sumowski 1962
W. Sumowski, 'Gerbrand van den Eeckhout als Zeichner', *Oud Holland*, vol. 77, no. 1, 1962, pp. 11–39.

Sumowski 1968
W. Sumowski, 'Zu einem Gemälde von Carel Fabritius', *Pantheon*, vol. 26, 1968, pp. 278–83.

Sutton 1980
P. C. Sutton, *Pieter de Hooch: Complete Edition*, Oxford, 1980.

Sutton 1986
P. C. Sutton, *A Guide to Dutch Art in America*, Washington DC, 1986.

Sweeny 1972
B. Sweeny, *Catalogue of Flemish and Dutch Paintings: John G. Johnson Collection*, Philadelphia, 1972.

Taylor 1992
P. Taylor, 'The Concept of *Houding* in Dutch Art Theory', *Journal of the Warburg and Courtauld Institutes*, vol. LV, 1992, pp. 210–32.

Van Thiel 1971
P. J. J. van Thiel, 'De aanbidding der koningen en ander vroeg werk van Hendrick ter Brugghen', *Bulletin van het Rijksmuseum*, vol. 19, no. 3, 1971, pp. 91–116.

Van Thiel et al. 1976
P. J. J. van Thiel, C. J. de Bruyn Kops, J. Cleveringa, W. Kloek, A. Vels Heijn, *All the Paintings of the Rijksmuseum in Amsterdam: A Completely Illustrated Catalogue*, trans. M. Buikstra-de Boer & G. Schwartz, Amsterdam, 1976.

Tommaseo & Bellini 1865–79
N. Tommaseo & B. Bellini, *Dizionario della lingua italiana*, 4 vols, Turin, 1865–79.

Trnek 1992
R. Trnek, *Die holländischen Gemälde des 17. Jahrhunderts in der Gemäldegalerie der Akademie der bildenden Künste in Wien*, Vienna, 1992.

Tümpel 1968
C. Tümpel, Studien zur Ikonographie der Historien Rembrandts (diss.), Hamburg, 1968. See also TÜMPEL 1969.

Tümpel 1969
C. Tümpel, 'Studien zur Ikonographie der Historien Rembrandts: Deutung und Interpretation der Bildinhalte', *Nederlands Kunsthistorisch Jaarboek*, vol. 20, 1969, pp. 107–98. See also TÜMPEL 1968.

Tümpel 1970
C. Tümpel, with A. Tümpel, *Rembrandt legt die Bibel aus: Zeichnungen und Radierungen aus dem Kupferstichkabinett der Staatlichen Museen Preussischer Kulturbesitz* (exh. cat.), Kupferstichkabinett, Berlin, 1970.

Tümpel 1971
C. Tümpel, 'Ikonographische Beiträge zu Rembrandt: Zur Deutung und Interpretation einzelner Werke. II', *Jahrbuch der Hamburger Kunstsammlungen*, vol. XVI, 1971, pp. 20–38.

Tümpel 1984
C. Tümpel, 'Die Rezeption der jüdischen Altertümer des Flavius Josephus in den holländischen Historiendarstellungen des 16. und 17. Jahrhunderts', in *Wort und Bild in den niederländischen Kunst und Literatur des 16. und 17. Jahrhunderts*, eds H. Vekeman & J. Müller Hofstede, Erftstadt, 1984, pp. 173–204. See also TÜMPEL 1991–94.

Tümpel 1986
C. Tümpel, *Rembrandt*, Antwerp, 1986. See also TÜMPEL 1993.

Tümpel 1986a
C. Tümpel, with A. Tümpel, *Rembrandt: Mythos und Methode*, Königstein im Taunus, 1986.

Tümpel 1991–94
C. Tümpel, 'Die Rezeption der jüdischen Altertümer von Flavius Josephus in den holländischen Historien-darstellungen des 16. und 17. Jahrhunderts', in AMSTERDAM / JERUSALEM / MÜNSTER 1991–94, pp. 194–206. See also TÜMPEL 1984.

Tümpel 1993
C. Tümpel, *Rembrandt: All Paintings in Colour*, 2nd edn, trans. E. Jephcott et al., Antwerp, 1993. See also TÜMPEL 1986.

Tzeutschler Lurie 1969
A. Tzeutschler Lurie, 'Gerard van Honthorst: Samson and Delilah', *Bulletin of The Cleveland Museum of Art*, vol. LVI, no. 9, November 1969, pp. 332–44.

Von Uffenbach 1753–55
Z. C. von Uffenbach, *Merkwürdigen Reisen durch Niedersachsen Holland und Engelland*, 3 vols, Frankfurt, 1753–55.

Utrecht / Braunschweig 1986–87
A. Blankert & L. J. Slatkes, et al., *Nieuw licht op de Gouden Eeuw: Hendrick ter Brugghen en tijdgenoten* (exh. cat.), Centraal Museum, Utrecht, Herzog Anton Ulrich-Museum, Braunschweig, 1986. See also UTRECHT / BRAUNSCHWEIG 1986–87a, and BLANKERT 1986–87.

Utrecht / Braunschweig 1986–87a
A. Blankert & L. J. Slatkes, et al., *Holländische Malerei im neuem Licht: Hendrick ter Brugghen und seine Zeitgenossen* (exh. cat.), Centraal Museum, Utrecht, Herzog Anton Ulrich-Museum, Braunschweig, 1986. See also UTRECHT / BRAUNSCHWEIG 1986–87, and BLANKERT 1986–87a.

Utrecht / Frankfurt / Luxembourg 1993–94
P. van den Brink et al., *Het gedroomde land: Pastorale schilderkunst in de Gouden Eeuw* (exh. cat.), Centraal Museum, Utrecht, Schirn Kunsthalle, Frankfurt, Musée National d'Histoire et d'Art, Luxembourg, 1993.

Valentiner 1908
W. R. Valentiner, *Rembrandt: Des Meisters Gemälde*, Klassiker der Kunst in Gesamtausgaben, Stuttgart, 1908.

Valentiner 1920
W. R. Valentiner, 'Die vier Evangelisten Rembrandts', *Kunstchronik und Kunstmarkt* (new series), vol. 32, no. 12, 1920, pp. 219–22.

Valentiner 1921
W. R. Valentiner, *Rembrandt: Wiedergefundene Gemälde*, Klassiker der Kunst in Gesamtausgaben, Stuttgart, 1921.

Valentiner 1924
W. R. Valentiner, *Nicolaes Maes*, Klassiker der Kunst in Gesamtausgaben, Stuttgart, 1924.

Valentiner 1924–35
W. R. Valentiner, *Rembrandt: Des Meisters Handzeichnungen*, Klassiker der Kunst in Gesamtausgaben, 2 vols, Stuttgart, 1924–35.

Valentiner 1948
W. R. Valentiner, 'Rembrandt's Conception of Historical Portraiture', *Art Quarterly*, vol. XI, no. 2, Spring 1948, pp. 117–35.

Valentiner 1956
W. R. Valentiner, 'The Rembrandt Exhibitions in Holland, 1956', *Art Quarterly*, vol. XIX, no. 4, Winter 1956, pp. 390–404.

Vasari 1550
G. Vasari, *Le vite de' piu eccellenti architetti, pittori et scultori italiani, da Cimabue insino a' tempi nostri*, 3 vols in 2, Florence, 1550. See also VASARI 1568, VASARI 1906, VASARI 1963.

Vasari 1568
G. Vasari, *Le vite de' piu eccellenti pittori, scultori e architettori*, 3 vols, 2nd edn, Florence, 1568. See also VASARI 1550, VASARI 1906, VASARI 1963.

Vasari 1906
G. Vasari, *Le vite de' più eccellenti pittori, scultori ed architettori* (1550; 1906 edn), in Vasari's *Opere*, ed. G. Milanesi, Florence, 1981. See also VASARI 1550, VASARI 1568, VASARI 1963.

Vasari 1963
G. Vasari, *The Lives of the Painters, Sculptors and Architects* (1550), 4 vols, London, 1963. See also VASARI 1550, VASARI 1568, VASARI 1906.

Verkaik 1995
J. W. Verkaik, *De moord op graaf Floris V*, Hilversum, 1995.

Vermeulen 1932
F. A. J. Vermeulen, *De Nederlandsche monumenten van geschiedenis en kunst: De monumenten van geschiedenis en kunst in de provincie Gelderland*, vol. I, The Hague, 1932.

Verslag Dordrecht 1889
Jaarlijks verslag over den toestand van het Dordrechts museum, van 1 mei 1886 tot 30 april 1887, Dordrecht, 1889.

Veth 1906
J. Veth, *Rembrandt's leven en kunst*, Amsterdam, 1906.

Vis 1965
D. Vis, *Rembrandt en Geertje Dircx*, Haarlem, 1965.

Vlieghe 1972–73
H. Vlieghe, *Saints*, Corpus Rubenianum Ludwig Burchard, part VIII, 2 vols, trans. P. S. Falla, London, 1972.

Van den Vondel 1640
J. van den Vondel, *Joseph in Egypten* (1640), eds G. C. Dupuis & D. F. Kouwenhoven, Gorinchem, 1962.

Van Voolen 1991–94
E. van Voolen, 'Juden in Amsterdam Rembrandts', in AMSTERDAM / JERUSALEM / MÜNSTER 1991–94, pp. 207–18.

Voragine
G. Ryan & H. Ripperberger (eds & trans.), *The Golden Legend of Jacobus de Voragine*, New York, 1969.

Vosmaer 1877
C. Vosmaer, *Rembrandt: Sa vie et ses oeuvres*, 2nd edn, The Hague, 1877.

De Vries 1989
L. de Vries, 'Tronies and Other Single Figured Netherlandish Paintings', *Leids Kunsthistorisch Jaarboek*, vol. VIII, 1989, pp. 185–215.

De Vries, Tóth-Ubbens & Froentjes 1978
A. B. de Vries, M. Tóth-Ubbens & W. Froentjes, *Rembrandt in the Mauritshuis: An Interdisciplinary Study*, trans. J. Brockway, Alphen aan den Rijn, 1978.

Waagen 1854
G. Waagen, *Treasures of Art in Great Britain: Being an Account of the Chief Collections of Paintings, Drawings, Sculptures, Illuminated MSS., &c &c* (1854), 4 vols (incl. 1857 suppl.), London, 1970.

Van de Waal 1952
H. van de Waal, *Drie eeuwen vaderlandsche geschied-uitbeelding 1500–1800: Een iconologische studie*, 2 vols, The Hague, 1952.

Van de Waal 1958
H. van de Waal, 'Rembrandt van Rijn: Landschap met stenen brug', *Openbaar Kunstbezit*, vol. 2, 1958, pp. 26a–b.

Van de Waal 1974
H. van de Waal, *Steps Towards Rembrandt: Collected Articles 1937–1972*, ed. R. H. Fuchs, trans. P. Wardle & A. Griffiths, Amsterdam, 1974.

Van der Waals 1988
J. van der Waals, *De prentschat van Michiel Hinloopen: Een reconstructie van de eerste openbare papierkunstverzameling in Nederland* (exh. cat.), The Hague, 1988.

Walsh 1991
J. Walsh, 'Skies and Reality in Dutch Landscape', in *Art in History / History in Art: Studies in Seventeenth-Century Dutch Culture*, Issues & Debates, vol. 1, eds D. Freedberg & J. de Vries, Santa Monica, California, 1991, pp. 94–117.

Warnke 1986
M. Warnke, 'Zur Herkunft und zur Deutung der "Lobpreisung Simeons" von Rembrandt in der Kunsthalle', *Idea*, vol. 5, 1986, pp. 35–45.

Washington 1990
C. P. Schneider, B. Bakker, N. Ash & S. Fletcher, *Rembrandt's Landscapes: Drawings and Prints* (exh. cat.), National Gallery of Art, Washington DC, 1990. See also ASH & FLETCHER 1990.

Washington / Detroit / Amsterdam 1980–81
A. Blankert et al., *Gods, Saints & Heroes: Dutch Painting in the Age of Rembrandt* (exh. cat.), National Gallery of Art, Washington DC, Detroit Institute of Arts, Rijksmuseum, Amsterdam, 1980. See also WASHINGTON / DETROIT / AMSTERDAM 1980–81a.

Washington / Detroit / Amsterdam 1980–81a
A. Blankert et al., *God en de goden: Verhalen uit de bijbelse en klassieke oudheid door Rembrandt en zijn tijdgenoten* (exh. cat.), National Gallery of Art, Washington DC, Detroit Institute of Arts, Rijksmuseum, Amsterdam, 1980. See also WASHINGTON / DETROIT / AMSTERDAM 1980–81.

Weisner 1964
U. Weisner, 'Die Gemälde des Moyses van Uyttenbroeck', *Oud Holland*, vol. 79, no. 4, 1964, pp. 189–228.

Welcker 1940
A. Welcker, 'Schildersportretten I: Govaert Flinck – Tevens een bijdrage tot het probleem van Rembrandt's veronderstelde reis naar Engeland in 1640', *Oud-Holland*, vol. 57, 1940, pp. 115–22.

Van de Wetering 1983
E. van de Wetering, 'Isaac Jouderville, a Pupil of Rembrandt', in AMSTERDAM / GRONINGEN 1983, pp. 59–69.

Van de Wetering 1986
E. van de Wetering, 'Problems of Apprenticeship and Studio Collaboration', in CORPUS, vol. II, 1986, pp. 45–90.

Van de Wetering 1991–92a
E. van de Wetering, 'Rembrandt's Manner: Technique in the Service of Illusion', in BERLIN / AMSTERDAM / LONDON 1991–92a, pp. 12–39. See also VAN DE WETERING 1991–92c.

Van de Wetering 1991–92c
E. van de Wetering, 'Rembrandts schilderwijze: Techniek in dienst van illusie', in BERLIN / AMSTERDAM / LONDON 1991–92c, pp. 12–39. See also VAN DE WETERING 1991–92a.

Van de Wetering 1993
E. van de Wetering, 'The Rembrandt Research Project' [letter], *Burlington Magazine*, vol. CXXXV, no. 1088, November 1993, pp. 764–5.

Van de Wetering 1995
E. van de Wetering, 'De schilder', in *Gestalten van de Gouden Eeuw*, eds H. M. Beliën, A. T. van Deursen & G. J. van Setten, Amsterdam, 1995, pp. 219–39.

Van de Wetering 1995a
E. van de Wetering, 'Rembrandt's *Satire on Art Criticism* Reconsidered', in *Shop Talk: Studies in Honor of Seymour Slive, Presented on His Seventy-Fifth Birthday*, eds C. P. Schneider, W. W. Robinson & A. I. Davies, Cambridge, Massachusetts, 1995, pp. 264–70.

Van de Wetering 1997
E. van de Wetering, *Rembrandt: The Painter at Work*, Amsterdam, 1997.

Wethey 1975
H. E. Wethey, *The Paintings of Titian: Complete Edition*, 3 vols, London, 1975.

Weyerman 1729–69
J. C. Weyerman, *De levens-beschryvingen der Nederlandsche konst-schilders en konst-schilderessen, met een uytbreiding over de schilder-konst der ouden; verrykt met de konterfeytsels der voornaamste konst-schilders en konst-schilderessen, cierlyk in koper gesneden door J. Houbraken*, 4 vols, The Hague, 1729–69.

Wheelock 1995
A. K. Wheelock, Jr, *Dutch Paintings of the Seventeenth Century*, The Collections of the National Gallery of Art, Systematic Catalogue, Washington DC, 1995.

White 1969
C. White, *Rembrandt as an Etcher: A Study of the Artist at Work*, 2 vols, London, 1969.

White 1969a
C. White, *The Late Etchings of Rembrandt: A Study in the Development of a Print* (exh. cat.), British Museum, London, 1969.

White 1982
C. White, *The Dutch Pictures in the Collection of Her Majesty the Queen*, Cambridge, 1982.

White 1994
C. White, '[review of TÜMPEL 1993]', *Burlington Magazine*, vol. CXXXVI, no. 1100, November 1994, p. 767.

White & Boon
C. White & K. G. Boon, *Hollstein's Dutch and Flemish Etchings, Engravings and Woodcuts*, vols XVIII–XIX, Amsterdam, 1969.

Wijnman 1959
H. F. Wijnman, 'Rembrandt als huisgenoot van Hendrick Uylenburgh te Amsterdam (1631–1635): Was Rembrandt doopsgezind of libertijn?', in *Uit de kring van Rembrandt en Vondel: Verzamelde studies over hun leven en omgeving*, Amsterdam, 1959, pp. 1–18.

Wijnman 1964
H. F. Wijnman, in C. White, *Rembrandt*, The Hague, 1964, p. 151, note 40.

Wildenstein 1957
G. Wildenstein, 'Inventaire de Madame Regnard, 1653', *Gazette des Beaux-Arts*, vol. XLIX, 1957, pp. 219–22.

Wilmington 1951
Paintings by Dutch Masters of the Seventeenth Century (exh. cat.), Delaware Art Center, Wilmington, 1951.

De Winkel 1995
M. de Winkel, '"Eene der deftigste dragten": The Iconography of the Tabbaard and the Sense of Tradition in Dutch Seventeenth-Century Portraiture', *Nederlands Kunsthistorisch Jaarboek*, vol. 46, 1995, pp. 145–67.

Winternitz 1969
E. Winternitz, 'Rembrandt's "Christ Presented to the People" – 1655: A Meditation on Justice and Collective Guilt', *Oud Holland*, vol. 84, nos 2–3, 1969, pp. 177–98.

Wischnitzer 1957
R. Wischnitzer, 'Rembrandt, Callot, and Tobias Stimmer', *Art Bulletin*, vol. XXXIX, no. 3, September 1957, pp. 224–30.

WNT
Het Woordenboek der Nederlandsche taal, 25 vols to date, The Hague, 1882–.

Worp 1897
J. A. Worp, 'Fragment eener autobiographie van Constantijn Huygens', *Bijdragen en mededeelingen van het Historisch Genootschap (gevestigd te Utrecht)*, vol. 18, 1897, pp. 1–121.

Worp 1911–17
J. A. Worp, *De briefwisseling van Constantijn Huygens (1608–1687)*, 6 vols, The Hague, 1911–17.

Von Wurzbach 1886
A. von Wurzbach, *Rembrandt-Galerie: Eine Auswahl von hundert Gemälden Rembrandts*, Stuttgart, 1886.

Von Wurzbach 1906–11
A. von Wurzbach, *Niederländisches Künstler-Lexikon*, 3 vols, Vienna, 1906–11.

Wustmann 1906
R. Wustmann, 'Die Joseph-geschichte bei Vondel und Rembrandt', *Kunstchronik* (new series), vol. 18, no. 6, 23 November 1906, pp. 81–4.

Yokohama / Fukuoka / Kyoto 1986–87
C. Brown, E. Haverkamp-Begemann & C. White, *Rembrandt and the Bible* (exh. cat.), Sogo Museum of Art, Yokohama, Fukuoka Art Museum, Fukuoka, National Museum of Modern Art, Kyoto, 1986.

Zdanowicz 1993
I. Zdanowicz, 'Prints of Fortune: Hubert Herkomer's 1891–92 Etching Purchases for the National Gallery of Victoria', *Art Bulletin of Victoria*, no. 33, 1993, pp. 1–17.